$$I = Prt \tag{6-1}$$

$$S = P(1 + rt) \tag{6-2}$$

$$\text{Proceeds (price)} = \frac{S}{1 + rt} \tag{7-1}$$

$$i = \frac{j}{m} \tag{8-1}$$

$$S = P(1 + i)^n \tag{8-2}$$

$$S = P(1 + i_1)(1 + i_2)(1 + i_3) \cdots (1 + i_n) \tag{8-2a}$$

$$n = m \times \text{(Number of years in the term)} \tag{8-3}$$

$$i = \sqrt[n]{\frac{S}{P}} - 1 = \left(\frac{S}{P}\right)^{1/n} - 1 \tag{9-1}$$

$$n = \frac{\ln(S/P)}{\ln(1 + i)} \tag{9-2}$$

$$f = (1 + i)^m - 1 \tag{9-3}$$

$$S_n = R\left[\frac{(1 + p)^n - 1}{p}\right] \tag{10-1}$$

$$p = (1 + i)^c - 1 \tag{10-2}$$

$$c = \frac{\text{Number of compoundings per year}}{\text{Number of payments per year}} \tag{10-3}$$

$$A_n = R\left[\frac{1 - (1 + p)^{-n}}{p}\right] \tag{10-4}$$

$$S_n(\text{due}) = S_n \times (1 + p) = R\left[\frac{(1 + p)^n - 1}{p}\right] \times (1 + p) \tag{11-1}$$

$$A_n(\text{due}) = A_n \times (1 + p) = R\left[\frac{1 - (1 + p)^{-n}}{p}\right] \times (1 + p) \tag{11-2}$$

$$A = \frac{R}{p} \tag{13-1}$$

$$A(\text{due}) = A(1 + p) = \frac{R}{p}(1 + p) \tag{13-2}$$

$$A_n(\text{def}) = R\left[\frac{1 - (1 + p)^{-n}}{p(1 + p)^d}\right] \tag{13-3}$$

$$S_n(\text{def}) = S_n \tag{13-4}$$

$$\text{Bond price} = Fb\left[\frac{1 - (1 + p)^{-n}}{p}\right] + F(1 + p)^{-n} \tag{15-1}$$

BUSINESS MATHEMATICS
IN CANADA

Second Edition

BUSINESS MATHEMATICS
IN CANADA

F. Ernest Jerome

Malaspina University-College

Represented in Canada by

McGraw-Hill Ryerson Limited

IRWIN

Toronto • Chicago • New York • Auckland • Bogotá • Caracas • Lisbon • London
Madrid • Mexico City • Milan • New Delhi • San Juan • Singapore • Sydney • Tokyo

BUSINESS MATHEMATICS IN CANADA

This book is printed on acid-free paper.

2 3 4 5 6 7 8 9 0 VH/VH 9 0 9 8 7

ISBN 0-256-18673-1

Senior sponsoring editor: *Evelyn Veitch*
Marketing manager: *Gary Bennett*
Project supervisor: *Susan Trentacosti*
Production supervisor: *Dina L. Genovese*
Art director: *Keith McPherson*
Cover designer: *Cindy Crampton*
Cover photographer: *Chicago Photographic Company*
Prepress buyer: *Jon Christopher*
Compositor: *Carlisle Communications, Ltd.*
Typeface: *9½/12 Helvetica*
Printer: *Von Hoffmann Press, Inc.*

Library of Congress Catalog card number 96-60971

http://www.mhcollege.com

To Seth and David

"Time is the fourth dimension of the space-time continuum."

Albert Einstein, Special Theory of Relativity, *1905*

"Time in Euclidean space-time is imaginary and indistinguishable from directions in space."

Stephen Hawking, A Brief History of Time, *1988*

"Time is money"

Many anonymous business managers, frequently

Preface

Most business administration programs in Canadian colleges include an introductory course in business mathematics or mathematics of finance. *Business Mathematics in Canada* is designed for use in such courses. The text's primary objective is to develop the student's understanding of the mathematics needed to succeed in such fields as accounting, finance, management, marketing, and business information systems.

The overall approach is to identify and build upon unifying and integrative concepts. For example, several topics in the mathematics of finance involve the concept of *economic equivalence* between alternative payment streams. The *Valuation Principle* underlies the discounting of promissory notes; the calculation of loan balances; and the pricing of Treasury bills, annuities, mortgages, bonds, and preferred shares. Students are encouraged to work with a few fundamental formulas rather than to search an expanded set containing equivalent formulas for the "ready-made" version for a particular case.

It is intended that the text be adaptable to either a one- or a two-semester course in business mathematics. Chapter and section headings preceded by an asterisk (*) may be omitted with no loss of continuity nor lack of preparation for later topics. It is also intended that the text be suitable for courses that emphasize either an algebraic approach or a preprogrammed financial calculator approach to compound interest problems. Instructions are given in the use of the basic financial functions on five of the most popular financial calculator models: Sharp EL-733A, Sharp EL 735, Texas Instruments BA 35, Texas Instruments BA II PLUS, and Hewlett-Packard 10B. Both algebraic and financial calculator solutions are presented for most example problems involving compound interest.

KEY FEATURES

Business Mathematics in Canada incorporates several features to enhance the learning and retention of mathematical concepts and their applications in business.

CLEAR EXPLANATIONS Each topic is presented in a clear, easy-to-read style. The reading grade-level of the expository material averages 10.8 (according to both the Flesch-Kincaid and the Bormuth criteria, measures widely used in North America). The discussion of each topic is followed by one or more full-solution example problems. Each example problem has a heading that indicates the nature of the problem or application.

MANY CANADIAN APPLICATIONS The book contains a wider range of applications of mathematics in business and finance than other texts. These include but are not limited to currency conversion, Treasury bills, Canada Savings Bonds, reverse mortgages, and student loans.

WIDE SELECTION OF PROBLEMS Each section of a chapter is followed by an exercise set designed to apply and reinforce the new material. The text contains 2400 problems, of which two-thirds are "word" problems. Considerable effort has been made to make the problems instructive, practical, realistic, and interesting.

PROBLEM RATINGS Problems are rated according to three degrees of difficulty. Problems preceded by a single bullet (•) are more difficult than problems without a bullet. The double bullet (••) problems are the most challenging.

TIPS AND TRAPS Boxed elements inserted at appropriate points in the text draw the student's attention to simplifications, pitfalls, short-cuts, or common errors.

"POINT OF INTEREST" VIGNETTES Each chapter contains a segment illustrating an application or misapplication of mathematics in business or personal finance.

GRAPHS AND DIAGRAMS This text presents more graphs and diagrams with the expository material than other texts. Transparency masters are available for most of these graphics.

FINANCIAL CALCULATOR COMPATIBILITY Any basic financial calculator model may be used with this text. Specific instructions are provided for five popular models in cases where it may not be apparent how to adapt generic instructions to a particular model.

CASH-FLOW SIGN CONVENTION All popular financial calculators[1] (as well as the financial functions in most spreadsheet software) employ a cash-flow sign convention. In a feature unique among currently available textbooks, we explain and faithfully use the cash-flow sign convention of finance. This results in significant advantages.

- The range of problems that may be solved is broadened.
- Solutions are frequently more efficient. For example, some solutions that would otherwise require two steps may be completed in a single step.
- In this text, unlike other texts, there is no need to give artificial or seemingly arbitrary instructions: (1) to ignore a negative sign when it appears with a calculated dollar amount in the financial calculator's display, and (2) to enter a dollar amount as a negative value in some circumstances.
- Students are better prepared: (1) to use the financial functions available in spreadsheet software, and (2) to undertake a subsequent course in finance.

PRACTICAL MATH REVIEW Review topics in the first three chapters are integrated with practical applications. The review also incorporates the sort of "messy" coefficients and numbers that will be encountered in later chapters (and in real life). Instructions are provided on the number of (significant) figures required in intermediate steps to ensure the desired degree of accuracy in the final result.

---

[1]The Texas Instruments BA 35 uses a nonstandard sign convention. Its single digression from the standard sign convention is pointed out at the appropriate point in the text.

THOROUGH, UP-TO-DATE COVERAGE The broad scope of this text allows an instructor to select the topics and applications most relevant to a particular course. The student can refer to other topics in later years as they are encountered in subsequent courses, in business, or in private borrowing and investing. The thorough coverage of demand loans and mortgage loans reflects their importance in business financing and personal borrowing. Several topics are, at the time of publishing, unique to this text. Examples include Canada Savings Bonds, reverse mortgages, and student loans.

In the expository material, example problems, and exercise problems, every effort has been made to reflect current practices in Canadian business and personal finance. Real financial instruments and real economic data are frequently used. Tables, examples, and problems usually employ recent data.

END-OF-CHAPTER ELEMENTS Each chapter concludes with a set of review problems, a self-test exercise, a summary of notation, key formulas, and a glossary of terms.

INSIDE-COVER SUMMARIES For easy reference, the key formulas are summarized on the inside front cover. Frequently used algebraic symbols are listed on the inside back cover. A tear-out card listing the more complicated formulas is included in the back of the book for use in test situations (where a "cheat sheet" is permitted) or for posting at the student's workstation.

CHANGES TO THE FIRST EDITION

For those familiar with the first edition, the following list summarizes the major changes appearing in the second edition.

EASIER READING LEVEL A conscious effort has been made to shorten long sentences and use simple language. As already stated, the average reading grade-level of the explanatory material is now 10.8 (according to American standards).

MORE PROBLEMS Approximately 150 new problems have been added at the lowest of the three degrees of difficulty. Another 70 problems of medium difficulty are new. Some of the "double-bullet" problems have been dropped or simplified.

REVISION OF PERCENT, PERCENT CHANGE, AND RATE OF RETURN ON INVESTMENT The topics formerly covered in Sections 1.5, 1.6, and 3.3 have been completely rewritten.

NEW SUPPLEMENTS The **Student's Solutions Manual** containing solutions to odd-numbered problems is now available. Spreadsheet templates are available on diskette for problems suited to a spreadsheet solution. A spreadsheet icon appears in the text's margin adjacent to such problems. Also available to instructors is the **Problems Diskette** (in either Word or Wordperfect versions) containing all the problems in the text. Instructors may "copy," "paste," and "edit" problems from the diskette to compose tests or problem sets. (In our 1995 survey, 24 of 33 respondents indicated a preference for this type of resource instead of a multiple-choice test bank.)

ANNUITY COVERAGE RESTRUCTURED The first edition took the usual approach of presenting four categories of annuities in the sequence: ordinary simple annuities, simple annuities due, ordinary general annuities, and general annuities due. This approach results in repetitive coverage of the calculation of the five variables (present value, future value, payment size, number of payments, and interest rate), as discussion of one type of annuity is closed before moving on to the next category. A further disadvantage of the segregation of the four categories is that students do not develop the habit, as an intentional first step in solving annuity problems, of identifying the type of annuity involved. Instead, the type is predetermined by the chapter at hand!

In this second edition, the future value and present value of *ordinary* annuities are initially developed in Chapter 10 in terms of the interest rate per payment interval (symbol p for payment interval). Then two possibilities are considered: (1) $p = i$ (ordinary *simple* annuities) and (2) $p \neq i$ (ordinary *general* annuities).[2] In Chapter 11, the future value and present value of annuities *due* become a modest "stretch" of the Chapter 10 ideas. Then in Chapter 12, the calculation of payment size, number of payments, and interest rate is addressed for *all* annuities. Students thereby become accustomed to distinguishing among the types of annuities.

INSTRUCTIONS FOR VARIOUS MODELS OF FINANCIAL CALCULATORS The appendix to Chapter 8 provides instructions in the use of the basic financial functions on five of the most popular financial calculator models: Sharp EL-733A, Sharp EL 735, Texas Instruments BA 35, Texas Instruments BA II PLUS, and Hewlett-Packard 10B. A student may readily adapt any of these models to the generic instructions in the text.

CONTRIBUTION MARGIN EMPHASIZED IN COST-VOLUME-PROFIT ANALYSIS In keeping with business practice, the contribution margin approach to CVP and break-even analysis has been given "top billing." The revenue function/cost function and graphical approaches have been "downsized."

REDUCED USE OF THE "ANGLE" NOTATION At the request of some users and reviewers, the angle notation has been eliminated from most of the text; it is now used only in Section 15.6 and Chapter 16.

NEW MODEL FOR SOLVING MARKUP/MARKDOWN PROBLEMS The new model presents the components of the regular selling price in a table format that helps students identify both additive and proportional relationships.

NEW "POINT OF INTEREST" VIGNETTES Five new vignettes appear in the second edition.

CASE STUDIES Six case studies appear in the **Instructor's Manual.**

OTHER ADDITIONS AND DELETIONS Figures 8.4, 11.3, 14.3, and 14.4 are new in the second edition. A discussion of Canada Savings Bonds has been added to Section 8.4 as another application of compound interest. Coverage of logarithms, graphical

---

[2]This approach also has the desirable outcome that students naturally view p, not i, as the fundamental interest rate variable for annuities. The use of the symbol p instead of f for the interest rate per payment interval avoids the possibility (which exists in the first edition and most other texts) of confusing students by the use of f for *both* the interest rate per payment interval *and* the effective (annual) rate of interest.

solution of two linear equations, algebraic determination of the interest rate for annuities, and consumer credit has been reduced or eliminated. A few other topics have been relegated to appendixes.

SUPPLEMENTS

The **Student's Solutions Manual** presents full solutions to the odd-numbered problems whose answers are given at the back of the text. The **Instructor's Solutions Manual** contains solutions to all problems, transparency masters, and six case studies that may be reproduced for classroom use. Also available to instructors are the Problems Diskette (in *Word* and *WordPerfect* versions) and the Spreadsheet Template Diskette (in *Excel* or *Lotus* versions). The **Problems Diskette** contains all problems appearing in the text. Instructors can use their word processors to "copy" and "paste" their favourite problems when creating tests and problem sets. Then the numerical values used or the "flavour" of a problem may be easily changed. The **Spreadsheet Templates Diskette** contains formatted templates for solving problems flagged in the text by a spreadsheet icon in the margin.

ACKNOWLEDGEMENTS

I must again thank the individuals named in the first edition for their contributions to its considerable success. Comments and suggestions from users of the first edition have been helpful in making further improvements. I am especially indebted to the following dedicated educators who carefully critiqued the first edition or the draft manuscript for the second edition. Their insights and suggestions are embodied in many of the changes appearing in this revision.

Margaret Beresford	Kwantlen University College
Michael Conte	Durham College
Millard Evans	Grant MacEwan Community College
Ed Fox	Niagara College
Rick Knowles	Mohawk College
Veronica Legg	Kingstec Campus—Nova Scotia Community College
Colleen Quinn	Seneca College
Stanley A. Shaw	Humber College

The following individuals and organisations provided technical information needed to make *Business Mathematics in Canada* reflect current business practices and applications.

David Adamo	Scotia McLeod Inc.
Barry Bain	BC Ministry of Housing and Consumer Services
Mike Barcham	Meyers Holland Motors Ltd.
Richard Bowes	Alberta Law Reform Institute
Zane Brown	Industry Canada
Michael Burford	Toronto Dominion Bank
Karlissa Castro	

David Chilton	Financial Awareness Corporation
Elaine Ellingham	Campbell Resources Inc.
Brian Frost	Royal Bank of Canada
Dick Gilpen	Canadian Imperial Bank of Commerce
Shaun Hurley	Canada Trust
Investment Funds Institute of Canada	
Troy Lanigan	Canadian Taxpayers Federation
David Long	Scotia McLeod Inc.
Renée Moir	Toronto Dominion Bank
David Morris	BC Ministry of the Attorney General
Val Nickerson	Royal Bank of Canada
Society of Actuaries	
Mary Anne Waldron	Faculty of Law, University of Victoria
Ted Waugh	
Bob Wilson	Canada Trust

It has been a pleasure to work with the talented staff at Irwin/McGraw-Hill Ryerson Limited. My sponsoring editor (and unofficial psychotherapist), Evelyn Veitch, has all the "right stuff" to keep the project on course and the author on an even keel. I also want to acknowledge the contributions of Denise McGuinness, Susan Trentacosti (project supervisor), Keith McPherson (art director), Dina Genovese (production supervisor), Jon Christopher, and the composition staff at Carlisle Communications Ltd.

When in "author mode," I fail to give my family the attention they deserve (except when their help is needed to piece and paste manuscript or to proofread galley pages). Their forbearance, understanding, and support are deeply appreciated.

F. Ernest Jerome

To the Student

"Why are textbook prices so high?"

This is, by far, the most frequently asked question heard in the publishing industry. There are many factors that influence the price of your new textbook. Here are just a few:

- **The Cost of Instructor Support Materials:** Your instructor may be making use of teaching supplements, many of which are provided by the publisher. Teaching supplements include videos, colour transparencies, instructor's manuals, software, computerized testing materials, and more. These supplements are designed as part of a learning package to enhance your educational experience.

- **Developmental Costs:** These are costs associated with the extensive development of your textbook. Expenses include permissions fees, manuscript review costs, artwork, typesetting, printing and binding costs, and more.

- **Author Royalties:** Authors are paid based on a percentage of new book sales and **do not** receive royalties on the sale of a used book. They are also deprived of their rightful royalties when their books are illegally photocopied.

- **Marketing Costs:** Instructors need to be made aware of new textbooks. Marketing costs include academic conventions, remuneration of the publisher's representatives, promotional advertising pieces, and the provision of instructor's examination copies.

- **Book Store Markups:** In order to stay in business, your local book store must cover its costs. A textbook is a commodity, just like any other item your bookstore may sell, and bookstores are the most effective way to get the textbook from the publisher to you.

- **Publisher Profits:** In order to continue to supply students with quality textbooks, publishers must make a profit to stay in business. Like the authors, publishers **do not** receive any compensation from the sale of a used book or the illegal photocopying of their textbooks.

We at Irwin/McGraw-Hill Ryerson Limited hope you will find this information useful and that it addresses some of your concerns. We also thank you for your purchase of this new textbook. If you have any questions that we can answer, please write to us at:

McGraw-Hill Ryerson Limited
College Division
300 Water Street
Whitby, Ontario
L1N 9B6

List of Figures

List of Tables

Brief Contents

Contents

(Chapters or sections preceded by an asterisk * may be omitted without loss of continuity.)

CHAPTER TEN

Ordinary Annuities: Future Value and Present Value   *371*

CHAPTER ELEVEN

Annuities Due: Future Value and Present Value   *411*

CHAPTER TWELVE

Annuities: Payment Size, Term, and Interest Rate   *433*

1

REVIEW AND APPLICATIONS OF BASIC MATHEMATICS

CHAPTER OUTLINE

LEARNING OBJECTIVES

After completing this chapter, you will be able to:

• Perform arithmetic operations in their proper order

• Convert fractions to their percent and decimal equivalents

• Maintain a sufficient number of digits in intermediate calculations to obtain an answer accurate to the desired number of significant figures

• Solve for any one of percent rate, portion, or base, given the other two quantities

• Calculate the gross earnings of salaried, hourly wage, or commission employees paid at weekly, biweekly, semimonthly, or monthly intervals

• Calculate the weighted average of a set of values based on their relative importance or frequency of occurrence

INTRODUCTION

Most routine calculations in business are now performed using electronic devices: point-of-sale terminals, computers, and programmable calculators. These devices have eliminated most of the toil of manual computations from the workplace. When the correct input data are provided, there is a virtual certainty of obtaining the correct output. Consequently, modern data processing technology enables people with weak mathematical skills to perform clerical duties effectively. Nevertheless, mathematics remains a fundamental skill needed for success in many careers to which college business students aspire. Consider the following in support of this statement.

- A customer may ask you for an explanation or interpretation of the calculated results. To satisfy the customer, you must understand the concepts involved and the nature of the calculations performed by the computer.
- If you supply incorrect input to a calculation, the output will be incorrect. In "technospeak" this natural consequence is described as "garbage in, garbage out!" The embarrassment and cost caused by input errors can often be avoided by considering the "reasonableness" of the calculated results. In some cases, the use of common sense may be sufficient—for example, an item's price after a discount cannot be greater than the original price. In other cases, mathematical intuition and approximation techniques provide insights about the reasonableness of computed values. The more you study and practice mathematics, the better your ability to determine reasonableness becomes.
- A client's particular situation may require special treatment or analysis. You must determine whether the standard approach can be customized to handle it. If not, an alternative method—perhaps manual—must be found.
- The potential of many sophisticated software applications now used in business is limited primarily by the mathematical abilities of the user. Good examples are spreadsheet programs such as Excel, Lotus 1-2-3, and Quattro Pro. Powerful customized worksheets may be created by programming mathematical formulas into appropriate worksheet locations or "cells." These formulas may be as complex as the user's mathematical skills and ingenuity can conceive.

Chapter 1 provides a review of basic arithmetic procedures and computations. These skills are then employed in the calculation of percentages, employee wages and salaries, and weighted averages.

1.1 ORDER OF OPERATIONS

In evaluating an expression such as

$$5 + 3^2 \times 2 - 4 \div 6$$

there is potential for confusion about the sequence of mathematical steps. Do we just perform the indicated operations in a strict left-to-right sequence, or is some other order intended? To remove any possible confusion, mathematicians have agreed on the use of brackets and a set of rules for determining the intended order of operations. The rules for the sequence of mathematical operations are:

1. Perform operations within brackets (in the order of steps 2, 3, and 4 below).
2. Evaluate the powers.[1]
3. Perform multiplication and division in order from left to right.
4. Perform addition and subtraction.

■ EXAMPLE 1.1A   EXERCISES ILLUSTRATING THE ORDER OF MATHEMATICAL OPERATIONS

a. $30 - 6 \div 3 + 5 = 30 - 2 + 5$
$= 33$

Do division before subtraction and addition.

b. $(30 - 6) \div 3 + 5 = 24 \div 3 + 5$
$= 8 + 5$
$= 13$

Do operation within brackets first; then do division before addition.

c. $\dfrac{30 - 6}{3 + 5} = \dfrac{24}{8}$
$= 3$

Brackets are implied in the numerator and the denominator.

d. $72 \div (3 \times 2) - 6 = 72 \div 6 - 6$
$= 12 - 6$
$= 6$

Do operation within brackets first; then do division before subtraction.

e. $72 \div (3 \times 2^2) - 6 = 72 \div (3 \times 4) - 6$
$= 72 \div 12 - 6$
$= 6 - 6$
$= 0$

Do operations within brackets (the power before the multiplication); then do division before subtraction.

f. $72 \div (3 \times 2)^2 - 6 = 72 \div 6^2 - 6$
$= 72 \div 36 - 6$
$= 2 - 6$
$= -4$

Do operation within brackets first, then the power, then division, then subtraction.

g. $4(2 - 5) - 4(5 - 2) = 4(-3) - 4(3)$
$= -12 - 12$
$= -24$

Do operations within brackets first, then multiplication, then subtraction.   ■

EXERCISE 1.1

Answers to the odd-numbered problems are at the end of the book.
Evaluate each of the following.

1. $20 - 4 \times 2 - 8$
2. $18 \div 3 + 6 \times 2$
3. $(20 - 4) \times 2 - 8$
4. $18 \div (3 + 6) \times 2$
5. $20 - (4 \times 2 - 8)$
6. $(18 \div 3 + 6) \times 2$
7. $54 - 36 \div 4 + 2^2$
8. $(5 + 3)^2 - 3^2 \div 9 + 3$
9. $(54 - 36) \div (4 + 2)^2$
10. $5 + (3^2 - 3)^2 \div (9 + 3)$
11. $\dfrac{8^2 - 4^2}{(4 - 2)^3}$
12. $\dfrac{(8 - 4)^2}{4 - 2^3}$
13. $3(6 + 4)^2 - 5(17 - 20)^2$
14. $(4 \times 3 - 2)^2 \div (4 - 3 \times 2^2)$
15. $[(20 + 8 \times 5) - 7 \times (-3)] \div 9$
16. $5[19 + (5^2 - 16)^2]^2$

---

[1] A power is a quantity such as 3^2 or 5^3, which are shorthand methods for representing 3×3 and $5 \times 5 \times 5$, respectively. Section 2.2 presents a more complete review of powers and exponents.

1.2 FRACTIONS

DEFINITIONS

In a **proper fraction**, the numerator is smaller than the denominator. An **improper fraction** has a numerator that is greater than or equal to the denominator. A **mixed number** contains a whole number plus a fraction. **Equivalent fractions** are fractions that are equal in value. An equivalent fraction may be created by multiplying both the numerator and the denominator of a given fraction by the same number.

■ **EXAMPLE 1.2A** *EXAMPLES OF TYPES OF FRACTIONS*

a. $\frac{6}{13}$ is a proper fraction.

b. $\frac{17}{13}$ is an improper fraction.

c. $2\frac{4}{13}$ is a mixed number.

d. $\frac{5}{13}, \frac{10}{26}, \frac{15}{39},$ and $\frac{20}{52}$ are equivalent fractions. Note that the second, third, and fourth fractions may be obtained by multiplying both the numerator and the denominator of the first fraction by 2, 3, and 4 respectively. ■

■ **EXAMPLE 1.2B** *CALCULATING AN EQUIVALENT FRACTION*

Find the missing numbers that make the following three fractions equivalent.

$$\frac{?}{300} = \frac{7}{12} = \frac{56}{?}$$

☑ **SOLUTION**

To generate a fraction equivalent to $\frac{7}{12}$, both the numerator and the denominator must be multiplied by the same number. In the first case, 12 must be multiplied by $\frac{300}{12} = 25$ to give the new denominator of 300. The numerator, 7, must also be multiplied by 25. The equivalent fraction is

$$\frac{7 \times 25}{12 \times 25} = \frac{175}{300}$$

The numerator of the second equivalent fraction is obtained by multiplying 7 by 8. Hence, the denominator is 12 × 8 = 96. In summary,

$$\frac{175}{300} = \frac{7}{12} = \frac{56}{96}$$ ■

DECIMAL AND PERCENT EQUIVALENTS

In calculations involving the addition or subtraction of fractions, it is often convenient to first convert each fraction to its *decimal equivalent* value. This is accomplished simply by dividing the numerator by the denominator.

A fraction may be viewed as a comparison of the quantity in the numerator with the quantity in the denominator. In such a comparison, we are better able to grasp the relative size when a "standard" size of 100 is used for the denominator. For example,

$$\frac{496}{640} = 0.775 = \frac{77.5}{100}$$

Hence, 496 compared to 640 is equivalent to 77.5 compared to 100. However, the relative size of the numerator and denominator is more apparent in the second comparison. The numerator of the equivalent fraction having a denominator of 100 is the *percent equivalent* of the fraction. In the present example, 77.5% is the percent equivalent of $\frac{496}{640}$. As a practical procedure, we usually determine a fraction's percent equivalent by first calculating its decimal equivalent, and then shifting the decimal point *two places to the right*.

■ **EXAMPLE 1.2c**   *FINDING THE DECIMAL AND PERCENT EQUIVALENTS OF FRACTIONS AND MIXED NUMBERS*

Convert each of the following fractions and mixed numbers to their decimal equivalent and percent equivalent values.

a. $\frac{2}{5} = 0.4 = 40\%$ *b.* $\frac{5}{2} = 2.5 = 250\%$

c. $2\frac{3}{4} = 2.75 = 275\%$ *d.* $\frac{5}{8} = 0.625 = 62.5\%$

e. $1\frac{3}{16} = 1.1875 = 118.75\%$ *f.* $\frac{3}{1500} = 0.002 = 0.2\%$ ■

ROUNDING OF DECIMAL AND PERCENT EQUIVALENTS

The decimal and percent equivalents of a fraction will often contain as many digits or figures as we wish to calculate. Such a number is called a *nonterminating decimal*. Sometimes a nonterminating decimal may contain an endlessly repeating digit or group of digits. This particular type of nonterminating decimal is described as a *repeating decimal*. A shorthand notation used for repeating decimals places a horizontal bar over the first occurrence of the repeating digit or group of digits. For example,

$$\frac{2}{9} = 0.222222 \ldots = 0.\overline{2} \quad and \quad 2\frac{4}{11} = 2.36363636 \ldots = 2.\overline{36}$$

When an intermediate result in a multistep calculation is a nonterminating decimal, we prefer to write down no more digits than necessary. If, however, too few digits are retained, subsequent calculations based on the rounded number will be of limited precision. Such imprecisions often become magnified in successive calculations in a multistep problem. The following general rule will be sufficient for determining how many digits to keep in the vast majority of our calculations.

> **Significant Figure Rule:** At each step in a series of calculations, keep one more figure than the number of figures required in the final result.

Suppose, for example, that the final answer to a problem is expected to be in the order of a few hundred dollars. If we want the answer to be accurate to the cent, the answer must have five-figure accuracy. The Significant Figure Rule directs us to keep a minimum of six figures at each stage of the calculation.

The digits that are to be counted in applying this rule are the significant figures or digits. **Significant figures** are all the digits except zeros serving only to position the decimal point. For example, 0.005 has only one significant figure. The zeros in this case are needed only to position the decimal point two place values before the 5 digit. The fact that 0.005 has only one significant figure is more apparent if it is converted to its percent equivalent, 0.5%. However, the value 1.005 and its percent equivalent 100.5% have four significant figures. In this case the two zeros are not required solely to position the decimal point.

Trap

Note that the Significant Figure Rule is based on the number of figures rather than the number of decimal places. A corresponding rule stated in terms of the number of decimal places *cannot* be relied upon to give the desired precision.

Once the desired number of significant figures is established, a numerical result is rounded by dropping the extra digits and possibly changing the last retained digit according to the following rules.

Rules for Rounding Decimals:
1. If the first digit dropped is 5 or greater, increase the last retained digit by 1.
2. If the first digit dropped is less than 5, leave the last retained digit unchanged.

Tip

The memory register(s) in your calculator should be used whenever possible to store intermediate results. This will save time and eliminate the possibility of keystroke errors upon data reentry. It also virtually eliminates the introduction of rounding errors since most calculators internally retain two or three figures more than are shown in the display.

■ **EXAMPLE 1.2D**   *FRACTIONS HAVING REPEATING DECIMAL EQUIVALENTS*

Convert each of the following fractions to its decimal equivalent value expressed in the repeating decimal notation.

a. $\frac{2}{3} = 0.6666\ldots = 0.\overline{6}$

b. $\frac{14}{9} = 1.5555\ldots = 1.\overline{5}$

c. $6\frac{1}{12} = 6.08333\ldots = 6.08\overline{3}$

d. $3\frac{2}{11} = 3.181818\ldots = 3.\overline{18}$

e. $5\frac{2}{27} = 5.074074\ldots = 5.\overline{074}$

f. $\frac{5}{7} = 0.714285714285\ldots = 0.\overline{714285}$

■

■ **EXAMPLE 1.2E**   *CALCULATING AND ROUNDING THE DECIMAL EQUIVALENTS OF FRACTIONS*

Convert each of the following fractions and mixed numbers to its decimal equivalent value rounded to four significant figures.

a. $\frac{2}{3} = 0.6667$

b. $6\frac{1}{12} = 6.083$

c. $\frac{173}{11} = 15.73$

d. $\frac{2}{1071} = 0.001867$

e. $\frac{17,816}{3} = 5939$

■

■ **EXAMPLE 1.2F**   **OBTAINING THE ANSWER FOR A MULTISTEP CALCULATION TO A SPECIFIED ACCURACY**

Evaluate

$$\$140\left(1 + 0.11 \times \frac{113}{365}\right) + \$74\left(1 + 0.09 \times \frac{276}{365}\right)$$

a. Accurate to the nearest dollar

b. Accurate to the nearest cent

✓ SOLUTION

To determine the number of significant figures that must be maintained at each step in the calculations, first roughly estimate the answer. For the purpose of this kind of estimation, it is sufficient to determine whether the answer is in the order of a few dollars, tens of dollars, or hundreds of dollars—an "error" of 20% or 30% is quite acceptable. In this example we first note that the values of the expressions inside both sets of brackets are slightly larger than 1. After multiplication by the respective dollar amounts, the first cluster will be about $150 and the second cluster about $80. Therefore, the answer will be in the neighbourhood of $200 to $250.

a. For the answer to be accurate to the nearest dollar, three-figure precision is required. The Significant Figure Rule calls for the retention of four digits in intermediate results.

$$\$140\left(1 + 0.11 \times \frac{113}{365}\right) + \$74\left(1 + 0.09 \times \frac{276}{365}\right)$$
$$= \$140(1 + 0.11 \times 0.3096) + \$74(1 + 0.09 \times 0.7562)$$
$$= \$140(1.034) + \$74(1.068)$$
$$= \$144.8 + \$79.03$$
$$= \$223.83$$
$$= \$224 \qquad \text{to the nearest dollar}$$

b. Two additional figures must be retained. Keep six digits in intermediate results in order to achieve five-figure accuracy in the answer.

$$\$140\left(1 + 0.11 \times \frac{113}{365}\right) + \$74\left(1 + 0.09 \times \frac{276}{365}\right)$$
$$= \$140(1 + 0.11 \times 0.309589) + \$74(1 + 0.09 \times 0.756164)$$
$$= \$140(1.03405) + \$74(1.06805)$$
$$= \$144.767 + \$79.0357$$
$$= \$223.80 \qquad \text{to the nearest cent}$$

Note: It is possible, through the use of the memory register, to obtain this answer without manually reentering any intermediate results in the calculator. If your solution is to be evaluated, you should present enough intermediate results to reveal the steps in your solution.

■

Point of Interest[2]

Small Rounding Errors Can Make a Big Difference

On January 1, 1982, the Vancouver Stock Exchange (VSE) launched its first share price index. A share price index is intended to measure the overall level of the prices of shares traded on the exchange. The percent change in the value of the index from one date to another date is indicative of the average percent change in share prices during the period. Taking advantage of its computer system, the VSE introduced the innovative procedure of recalculating the index whenever a change occurred in the price of any stock included in the index.[3] This resulted in the index being recalculated an average of 2800 times per day!

The index declined during most of 1982. Increasing concern about the validity of the index developed in early 1983 when the index rose only modestly in the face of strong gold prices and generally rising share prices. The index then resumed a steady decline, from 930 at the beginning of February 1983 to 530 by the end of October 1983. High-powered consultants were brought in from the Toronto Stock Exchange (TSE), the University of British Columbia, and Wilshire Associates in Santa Monica, California, to review the strange behaviour of the VSE index.

The error causing the problem turned out to be embarrassingly simple. The practice had been to calculate the index to six significant figures. The computer had been programmed, however, to truncate rather than to round the answer at the sixth signifi-

cant figure. Truncation simply drops the extra digits; unlike rounding, it does not increase the last retained digit by 1 if the first digit dropped is 5 or greater. For example, an index value of 832.43982 was truncated to 832.439 instead of being rounded to 832.440. (Incidentally, virtually all handheld calculators automatically round rather than truncate answers at the last digit in the display.)

Truncation will always leave a smaller value than the original number; rounding gives a smaller value half the time and a larger value half the time. In a long series of multiplications and additions, repeated truncations will bias the results downward, whereas the random upward and downward variations from repeated roundings will tend to offset one another.

The downward truncation bias on the VSE index accumulated to serious proportions because the calculation of the index was repeated 2000 to 3000 times on each trading day for almost 2 years. After the problem was identified in October 1983, the VSE spent 3 weeks recalculating the index through the hundreds of thousands of trades that had taken place during the previous 22 months. Investors awakened on Monday morning, November 28, 1983, to discover that, to correct the accumulated computational error, the VSE index had been revised upward to 1124, more than double its Friday closing value of 537. All share prices would have had to rise by 109% to generate an equivalent increase in the index!

[2]Points of Interest are inserted throughout the text to bring attention to special situations illustrating the use and abuse of mathematics in the realms of business and personal finance. It is not expected that you comprehend all the subtleties involved. Rather, the purpose of presenting the Points of Interest is to leave you with impressions—that mathematics is important and relevant, and that mathematics can be abused and misused to the disadvantage of the unwary and unknowing. Two impressions may be gained form this particular Point of Interest. One is that the experts did all the complicated things correctly, but "messed up" at a rather elementary level by failing to follow the simple rules for rounding numbers! The other is that the error went undiscovered for a surprisingly long time—over a year and a half—while it increasingly distorted a stock market index followed by thousands of investors!

[3]The formula used to calculate the value of the index after a change in the price of a company's stock was

$$I_2 = I_1 \left[1 + \frac{1}{N}\left(\frac{P_2 - P_1}{P_1}\right) \right]$$

where I_2 = the new value of the index, I_1 = the previously calculated value of the index, N = the number of companies whose shares were included in the index, P_2 = the price of the company's shares in the current transaction, and P_1 = the price of the same company's shares in the previous transaction. There were about 1400 companies in the index in 1982.

EVALUATING COMPLEX FRACTIONS

A **complex fraction** is a fraction containing one or more other fractions in its numerator or denominator. In simplifying complex fractions, particular attention should be paid to the correct order of mathematical operations as discussed in Section 1.1.

■ EXAMPLE 1.2G *EVALUATING COMPLEX FRACTIONS*

Evaluate the following complex fractions accurate to the cent.

a.
$$\frac{\$1265\left(1 + 0.115 \times \frac{87}{365}\right)}{1 + 0.125 \times \frac{43}{365}}$$

The quantity in brackets and the denominator are each slightly larger than 1. The answer is likely to be between $1000 and $2000.

$$= \frac{\$1265(1 + 0.02741096)}{1 + 0.01472603}$$

For six-figure accuracy (to the cent) in the answer, keep seven figures in intermediate results. Both 0.02741096 and 1.027411 contain seven significant figures.

$$= \frac{\$1265(1.027411)}{1.014726}$$

$$= \frac{\$1299.675}{1.014726}$$

$$= \$1280.81$$

b.
$$\frac{\$425\left(1 + \frac{0.10}{12}\right)^3}{\left(1 + \frac{0.09}{12}\right)^2}$$

The answer is likely to be in the $400 to $500 range. Therefore, we need five-figure accuracy. Maintain six figures in intermediate results.

$$= \frac{\$425(1.00833)^3}{1.00750^2}$$

$$= \frac{\$425 \times 1.02520}{1.01506}$$

$$= \$429.25$$

EXERCISE 1.2

Answers to the odd-numbered problems are at the end of the book.

Convert each of the following fractions and mixed numbers to its decimal equivalent and percent equivalent values.

1. $\frac{7}{8}$
2. $\frac{65}{104}$
3. $\frac{47}{20}$
4. $-\frac{9}{16}$

5. $\frac{-35}{25}$
6. $1\frac{7}{25}$
7. $\frac{25}{1000}$
8. $\frac{1000}{25}$

9. $2\frac{2}{100}$
10. $-1\frac{11}{32}$
11. $\frac{37.5}{50}$
12. $\frac{22.5}{-12}$

Convert each of the following fractions and mixed numbers to its decimal equivalent and percent equivalent values expressed in the repeating decimal notation.

13. $\frac{5}{6}$
14. $-\frac{8}{3}$
15. $7\frac{7}{9}$
16. $1\frac{1}{11}$

17. $\frac{10}{9}$
18. $\frac{-4}{900}$
19. $-\frac{7}{270}$
20. $\frac{37}{27}$

Round each of the following to four significant figures.

21. 11.3845 22. 9.6455 23. 0.5545454 24. 1000.49

25. 1.0023456 26. 0.030405 27. 40.09515 28. 0.0090909

Convert each of the following fractions and mixed numbers to its decimal equivalent and percent equivalent values rounded to five significant figures.

29. $\dfrac{1}{6}$ 30. $\dfrac{7}{6}$ 31. $\dfrac{1}{60}$ 32. $2\dfrac{5}{9}$

33. $\dfrac{250}{365}$ 34. $\dfrac{15}{365}$ 35. $\dfrac{0.11}{12}$ 36. $\dfrac{0.095}{12}$

Evaluate each of the following accurate to the cent.

37. $\$92\left(1 + 0.095 \times \dfrac{112}{365}\right)$

38. $\$100\left(1 + 0.11 \times \dfrac{5}{12}\right)$

39. $\$454.76\left(1 - 0.105 \times \dfrac{11}{12}\right)$

40. $\dfrac{\$790.84}{1 + 0.13 \times \frac{311}{365}}$

41. $\dfrac{\$3490}{1 + 0.125 \times \frac{91}{365}}$

42. $\dfrac{\$10{,}000}{1 - 0.10 \times \frac{182}{365}}$

43. $\$650\left(1 + \dfrac{0.105}{2}\right)^2$

44. $\$950.75\left(1 - \dfrac{0.095}{4}\right)^2$

45. $\dfrac{\$15{,}400}{\left(1 + \frac{0.13}{12}\right)^6}$

46. $\dfrac{\$550}{\left(1 + \frac{0.115}{2}\right)^4}$

47. $\dfrac{\$6600\left(1 + 0.085 \times \frac{153}{365}\right)}{1 + 0.125 \times \frac{82}{365}}$

48. $\dfrac{\$780\left(1 + \frac{0.0825}{2}\right)^5}{\left(1 + \frac{0.10}{12}\right)^8}$

49. $\$1000\left[\dfrac{\left(1 + \frac{0.09}{12}\right)^7 - 1}{\frac{0.09}{12}}\right]$

50. $\dfrac{\$350}{\frac{0.0975}{12}}\left[1 - \dfrac{1}{\left(1 + \frac{0.0975}{12}\right)^5}\right]$

51. $\dfrac{\$9500}{\dfrac{\left(1 + \frac{0.075}{4}\right)^5 - 1}{\frac{0.075}{4}}}$

52. $\$45\left[\dfrac{1 - \dfrac{1}{\left(1 + \frac{0.0837}{2}\right)^4}}{\frac{0.0837}{2}}\right] + \dfrac{\$1000}{\left(1 + \frac{0.0837}{2}\right)^4}$

1.3 THE BASIC PERCENTAGE PROBLEM

There are many situations in which we wish to compare a portion or part of a quantity to the whole amount. One measure of the relative size is the fraction

$$\frac{\text{Portion}}{\text{Base}}$$

where the term *Base* is used to represent the whole or entire amount. The fraction is called the *Rate* and its percent equivalent is called the *Percent Rate*. That is,

$$\text{Rate} = \frac{\text{Portion}}{\text{Base}} \qquad \text{and} \qquad \%\text{Rate} = \frac{\text{Portion}}{\text{Base}} \times 100\%$$

where *%Rate* is used as an abbreviation for *Percent Rate*. Although we have presented this relation for a case where the *Portion* is a part of the *Base*, it can be used in a more general way to compare one quantity—the *Portion*—to some other standard or benchmark—the *Base*. In these cases the *Portion* may be larger than the *Base*. Then the *Rate* will be greater than 1 and the *%Rate* will be more than 100%.

Multiplying both sides of each equation by the *Base* allows us to express the *Portion* in terms of the *Base* and the *Rate* or *%Rate*.

The Basic Percentage Formula

$$\text{Portion} = \text{Rate} \times \text{Base}$$
$$\text{Portion} = \frac{\%\text{Rate}}{100\%} \times \text{Base}$$

(1–1)

Tip

The key to solving percentage problems is to distinguish between the *Base* and the *Portion*. The *Base* is always the standard or benchmark *to* which the *Portion* is being compared. In the wording of problems, the quantity preceded by "of" is almost always the *Base*.

Trap

When a *%Rate* is less than 1%, students sometimes forget to move the decimal two places to the left to obtain the decimal equivalent *Rate*. For example, be clear on the distinction between 0.25% and 25%. The former is just ¼ of 1%; the latter is 25 *times* 1%. Their decimal equivalents are 0.0025 and 0.25, respectively. In terms of equivalent fractions, 0.25% equals ¹⁄₄₀₀, while 25% equals ¼.

■ **EXAMPLE 1.3A** *USING THE BASIC PERCENTAGE FORMULA*

 a. What is 40¼% of $140.25?
 b. How much is 0.08$\overline{3}$% of $5000?
 c. What percentage is 7.38 kg of 4.39 kg?
 d. 250% of what amount is $10?

☑ **SOLUTION**

 a. We are asked to calculate a part (*Portion*) of a given whole (*Base*). Formula (1–1) may be used in its existing form.

$$\text{Portion} = \frac{\%\text{Rate}}{100\%} \times \text{Base} = \frac{40.25\%}{100\%} \times \$140.25 = \$56.45$$

 Therefore, $56.45 is 40.25% of $140.25.

 b. Again the *%Rate* and *Base* are given.

$$\text{Portion} = \frac{0.08\overline{3}\%}{100\%} \times \$5000 = 0.0008\overline{3} \times \$5000 = \$4.17$$

 $4.17 is 0.08$\overline{3}$% of $5000.

 c. We are given both the *Portion* and the *Base* for a comparison. Here 7.38 kg is being compared to the reference amount (*Base*) of 4.39 kg. The answer will be greater than 100%, since the *Portion* is larger than the *Base*.

Rearranging formula (1−1) to isolate *%Rate*, we obtain

$$\%Rate = \frac{Portion}{Base} \times 100\% = \frac{7.38 \text{ kg}}{4.39 \text{ kg}} \times 100\% = 168.1\%$$

Thus, 7.38 kg is 168.1% of 4.39 kg.

d. Now the unknown is the amount to which the $10 is being compared. Therefore, the unknown is the *Base*. Solving formula (1−1) for the *Base* gives

$$Base = \frac{100\%}{\%Rate} \times Portion = \frac{100\%}{250\%} \times \$10 = 0.4 \times \$10 = \$4.00$$

250% of $4.00 is $10.00. ■

■ EXAMPLE 1.3B   *A WORD PROBLEM REQUIRING THE BASIC PERCENTAGE FORMULA*

A battery manufacturer encloses a 50-cent rebate coupon in a package of four AAA batteries retailing for $4.29. What percent rebate does the coupon represent?

✔ SOLUTION

In effect, the question is asking for the rebate to be compared, in percentage terms, to the retail price. Therefore, the retail price is the *Base*.

$$\%Rate = \frac{Portion}{Base} \times 100\% = \frac{\$0.50}{\$4.29} \times 100\% = 11.7\%$$

The manufacturer's percent rebate on the batteries is 11.7%. ■

Tip

When calculating a *Rate* or *%Rate,* the *Portion* and the *Base* must be expressed in terms of the *same* units.

EXERCISE 1.3

Answers to the odd-numbered problems are at the end of the book.

Calculate dollar amounts accurate to the cent and percent amounts to three significant figures.

1. Calculate 1.75% of $350?

2. Calculate 6.$\overline{6}$% of $666.66?

3. What percent is $1.50 of $11.50?

4. What percent is 88¢ of $44?

5. $45 is 60% of what amount?

6. $69 is 30% of what amount?

7. What is 233.3% of $75?

8. What is 0.075% of $1650?

9. $134 is what percent of $67?

10. $1.34 is what percent of $655?

11. 150% of $60 is what amount?

12. 0.58$\overline{3}$% of $1500 is what amount?

13. 7½% of what amount is $1.46?

14. 12¾% of what amount is $27.50?

15. What percent of $950 is $590?

16. What percent of $590 is $950?

17. 95% of what amount is $100?

18. 8⅓% of what amount is $10?

19. 30 m is what percent of 3 km?

20. 500 g is what percent of 2.8 kg?

21. How much is ½% of $10?

22. 0.75% of $100 is what amount?

23. $180 is 120% of what amount?

24. $559.35 is 113% of what amount?

25. 130½% of $455 is what amount?

26. 0.0505% of $50,000 is what amount?

27. $281.25 is 225% of what amount?

28. 350% of what amount is $1000?

29. $10 is 0.5% of what amount?

30. $1.25 is ¾% of what amount?

31. A sales manager received a bonus of $7980 on the year's sales of $532,000. What was the bonus as a percent of sales and as a percent of her base salary of $45,000?

32. 113 of Freightway Trucks' employees belong to the Teamsters' Union; the remaining 31 employees are not union members. What percent of employees are in the union?

33. In a basketball game, the Langara College Falcons scored 54.$\overline{54}$% of 33 shots from the 2-point zone, 46.$\overline{6}$% of 15 attempts from the 3-point distance, and 79.3% of 29 foul shots (1 point each). How many points did the Falcons score?

34. Marilyn's net or take-home pay is 65% of her gross salary. If her take-home pay for May was $2000, what was her gross salary for the month?

35. Actual expenses of $169,400 for the most recent fiscal quarter were 110% of budgeted expenses. What were the forecast expenses?

36. The 6½% commission on the sale of a house was $13,975. What was the selling price of the property?

37. A property sold for 250% of what the vendors originally paid for it. What was that original price if the recent selling price was $210,000?

38. The fixed annual dividend on a company's preferred share is 8% of the share's original issue price (par value). If the annual dividend is $3.50, what is the par value of a share?

39. An individual's annual Registered Retired Savings Plan (RRSP) contribution limit for 1996 and subsequent years is the lesser of $13,500 or 18% of the previous year's earned income. At what level of earned income will $13,500 be the maximum contribution?

40. Stan is a real estate salesperson. He receives 60% of the 6% commission that the real estate agency charges on sales. If his income for the past year was $75,000, what was his dollar volume of sales for the year?

•41. A stockbroker is paid 45% of the commission her firm charges her clients. If she personally received $134.55 on a $11,500 transaction, what is the commission rate?

•42. A mortality rate indicates the fraction of individuals in a population who are expected to die in the next year. If the mortality rate among 35-year-old males is 0.34%, what is the expected number of deaths per year among a province's total of 50,000 such males? If 35-year-old males constitute 0.83% of the overall population in a city of 1.45 million, how many deaths of such males are expected in that city in a year?

*1.4 PAYROLL

An employee's remuneration may be based on an hourly wage, a salary, or a rate of commission. In some cases, earnings are based on a combination of a commission with a wage or a salary. This section will deal only with the calculation of *gross earnings*—the amount earned in a period before any deductions.[4]

SALARIES

Where employment tends to be predictable and steady, an employee typically receives a salary quoted in terms of a biweekly, a monthly, or an annual amount. A monthly salary is usually paid on a monthly or semimonthly basis.[5] An annual salary may be paid at monthly, semimonthly, biweekly, or weekly intervals. For monthly and semi-monthly pay periods, the gross earnings per pay are calculated by dividing the annual salary by 12 and 24, respectively.

A complication arises when an annual salary is paid at weekly or biweekly intervals. It occurs because a year does not contain exactly 52 weeks or 26 fortnights. A 365-day year contains 52 weeks *plus 1 day*. A leap year is 2 days longer than 52 weeks. Therefore, every fifth or sixth year will have 53 Fridays, the customary payday for weekly and biweekly payrolls.

The most commonly used approach is for the employer to divide the annual salary by the actual number of paydays falling in the calendar year. That is,

$$\text{Periodic gross pay} = \frac{\text{Annual salary}}{\text{Number of paydays in the year}}$$

With no change in annual salary, weekly gross earnings will then drop by about 2% in going from a 52-pay year to a 53-pay year. This can be difficult to explain to employees. Some additional complexities arise for employees who work for just a portion of a year.[6]

---

[4]Employers are required by law to withhold income tax and the employee's share of Canada Pension Plan contributions and employment insurance premiums. By agreement with its employees or their union, an employer may also deduct and remit various insurance premiums, union dues, and pension plan contributions.

[5]Provincial employment standards usually provide that, if requested by the employees, monthly salaries be paid no less frequently than semimonthly. Some employers satisfy the requirement by providing a midmonth advance of approximately half the monthly take-home pay.

[6]To avoid these complexities, a few employers use another approach. The periodic gross pay is obtained by dividing the annual salary by the *average* number of pay periods in a year. Since every fourth year is a leap year, the average length of a year is 365.25 days. This average length contains

$$\frac{365.25 \text{ days}}{14 \text{ days}} = 26.0893 \text{ biweekly pay periods}$$

or

$$\frac{365.25 \text{ days}}{7 \text{ days}} = 52.1786 \text{ weekly pay periods}$$

Assuming that an employee's base salary remains the same, this method results in no change to the periodic gross pay when a year contains an extra payroll date.

■ EXAMPLE 1.4A   *CALCULATING BIWEEKLY AND WEEKLY PAYMENTS FROM ANNUAL SALARIES*

An employee's annual salary is $45,000. Determine the gross earnings each payday in a year that has:

a. 26 biweekly paydays

b. 27 biweekly paydays

c. 52 weekly paydays

d. 53 weekly paydays

☑ SOLUTION

a. Biweekly gross pay $= \dfrac{\text{Annual salary}}{\text{Number of paydays in the year}} = \dfrac{\$45,000}{26} = \$1730.77$

b. Biweekly gross pay = $45,000 ÷ 27 = $1666.67

c. Weekly gross pay = $45,000 ÷ 52 = $865.38

d. Weekly gross pay = $45,000 ÷ 53 = $849.06   ■

HOURLY WAGES

In jobs where the amount of work available is irregular or unpredictable, or where overtime is a common occurrence, employees are typically paid an hourly wage. Usually, a collective agreement between the employer and employees sets the number of hours per day (typically 7½ or 8) and hours per week (typically 37½ or 40) beyond which higher overtime rates apply. If no such agreement exists, federal or provincial employment standards apply.[7] The most common overtime rate, 1.5 times the regular hourly rate, is usually referred to as "time and a half."

Each province recognizes certain general holidays (often called "statutory" holidays, or "stat" holidays). New Year's Day, Good Friday, Canada Day, Labour Day, Thanksgiving Day, Christmas, and Boxing Day tend to be common to all provinces. Employees receive their normal pay for a statutory holiday *not* worked. If an employee is required to work on a stat holiday, she must be paid *at least* 1.5 times her regular wage rate. This is *in addition to* her regular wages for the day.

Gross earnings for a pay period are obtained by adding overtime and "stat" holiday pay to the regular pay. That is,

> Regular hourly rate × Regular hours
> + Overtime hourly rate × Overtime hours
> + Stat holiday hourly rate × Stat holiday hours worked
> = Gross earnings

When counting an employee's hours, remember the following points:

- Among "regular hours," always include the usual length of a working day for a statutory holiday falling in the pay period.
- If an employee works on a stat holiday, count the hours actually worked as "statutory holiday hours worked." Do not include them in "overtime hours" even if the employee exceeds the limit on regular hours for the pay period.

---

[7]For example, the Canada Labour Code applies to any "work, undertaking, or business that is within the legislative authority of Parliament." Several specific areas of application are listed in the code.

Sometimes wages in production and manufacturing jobs are structured to create an incentive for higher productivity. A *piecework rate* is based on the unit of production, such as $1 per garment sewn, or $2 per typed page, or $15 per ton of output.

$$\text{Piecework earnings} = \text{Number of units produced} \times \text{Piecework rate}$$

■ EXAMPLE 1.4B   CALCULATING THE GROSS EARNINGS OF AN HOURLY PAID EMPLOYEE

Steve is paid $18.30 an hour for his work on an assembly line. The regular workweek is 37.5 hours (five 7.5-hour shifts). In the most recent biweekly pay period (midnight Friday to midnight of the second following Friday), he worked full shifts from Monday to Friday of both weeks. The first Monday of the pay period was a statutory holiday. In addition, he worked 6 hours on the first Saturday. Overtime is paid at 1½ times the regular rate and statutory holiday time at "double time." What will be Steve's gross pay for the period?

☑ SOLUTION

Steve should be credited with 7.5 regular hours for the statutory holiday whether he works it or not. In addition to regular pay for the stat holiday, he will be paid twice his hourly rate for work on the holiday. The *actual* hours worked on the stat holiday do not figure into the calculation of overtime. As illustrated in the following table, it is the 7.5 *regular* hours attributed to the holiday that cause Steve to exceed the 37.5-hour limit by 6 hours in the first week.

Week 1	Sat.	Mon.	Tue.	Wed.	Thur.	Fri.	Total
Regular hours	6	7.5	7.5	7.5	7.5	1.5	37.5
Overtime hours						6	6
"Stat" holiday hours		7.5					7.5
Week 2	Sat.	Mon.	Tue.	Wed.	Thur.	Fri.	Total
Regular hours		7.5	7.5	7.5	7.5	7.5	37.5
Overtime hours							
"Stat" holiday hours							

$$
\begin{aligned}
\text{Gross pay} &= \text{Regular rate} \times \text{Regular hours} + 1.5 \times \text{Regular rate} \times \text{Overtime hours} \\
&\quad + 2 \times \text{Regular rate} \times \text{Statutory holiday hours} \\
&= (\$18.30 \times 2 \times 37.5) + (1.5 \times \$18.30 \times 6) + (2 \times \$18.30 \times 7.5) \\
&= \$1372.50 + \$164.70 + \$274.50 \\
&= \$1811.70
\end{aligned}
$$

Steve's gross pay will be $1811.70.   ■

■ EXAMPLE 1.4C   CALCULATING GROSS EARNINGS INCLUDING A PIECEWORK WAGE

An orchardist pays apple pickers $5.50 per hour plus $3.00 for each 100 kg of apples picked during an 8-hour shift. If a worker picks, on average, 180 kg of apples per hour for a 40-hour workweek, what will be the gross earnings for the week?

☑ SOLUTION

$$\begin{aligned}\text{Gross} \atop \text{earnings} &= \left(\text{Hourly} \atop \text{rate} \times \text{Number} \atop \text{of hours}\right) + \left(\text{Piecework} \atop \text{rate} \times \text{Number} \atop \text{of units}\right) \\ &= (\$5.50 \times 40) + \$3.00 \left(\frac{180}{100} \times 40\right) \\ &= \$220 + \$216 \\ &= \$436 \end{aligned}$$

The worker's gross earnings for the week will be \$436.   ∎

COMMISSIONS

The most common incentive in sales positions is to base at least a portion of the salesperson's remuneration on sales volume. A person whose entire earnings are calculated as a percent of sales is working on *straight commission*. A salesperson who receives a basic fixed salary in addition to a commission on sales is working on a *salary plus commission* basis. Sometimes the commission is paid only on sales exceeding a minimum level called the *quota*.

   Because some overhead costs are fixed, an employer's cost per unit of sales will usually decline with increasing sales volume. Consequently, the profit per unit of sales will usually increase as the monthly sales volume increases. Some employers pass on a portion of the increased profit to their sales personnel and, at the same time, create a stronger incentive to further increase sales by offering a graduated commission. A *graduated commission* structure employs a pattern of progressively larger commission rates for higher levels of sales.

■ EXAMPLE 1.4D   *CACULATING GROSS EARNINGS BASED ON A SALARY PLUS COMMISSION*

James manages a men's clothing store for a national chain. His monthly remuneration has three components: a \$1500 base salary, plus 2% of the amount by which the store's total sales volume for the month exceeds \$20,000, plus 8% of the amount by which his personal sales exceed \$2000. Calculate his gross compensation for a month in which his sales totaled \$4950 and other staff had sales amounting to \$54,630.

☑ SOLUTION

Base salary	\$1500.00
Commission on total store volume:	
0.02(\$54,630 + \$4950 − \$20,000)	791.60
Commission on personal sales:	
0.08(\$4950 − \$2000)	236.00
Total compensation	\$2527.60

James's gross earnings for the month are \$2527.60.   ∎

■ EXAMPLE 1.4E   *CALCULATING GROSS EARNINGS BASED ON A GRADUATED COMMISSION*

Tanya sells mutual funds for Pacific Financial Services Ltd. The "load" or commission charged on mutual fund sales averages 7%. Tanya works on a graduated commission structure in which she receives 40% of the gross commission on the first \$50,000 worth of mutual funds sold in a month, and 60% of the gross commission on additional sales. What will her earnings be for a month in which she sells $90,000 worth of mutual funds?

✓ SOLUTION

Commission on first $50,000:	
0.40 × 0.07 × $50,000	$1400
Commission on next $40,000:	
0.60 × 0.07 × $40,000	1680
Total earnings	$3080

Tanya will earn $3080 from the sale of $90,000 worth of mutual funds in one month.

∎

EXERCISE 1.4

Answers to the odd-numbered problems are at the end of the book.

1. Patricia's annual salary of $29,400 is paid weekly. Her regular workweek is 35 hours. What hourly rate would she be paid for overtime at time and a half during a year containing:

   a. 52 paydays?   b. 53 paydays?

2. Lucille receives an annual salary of $37,500 based on a 37.5-hour workweek.

   a. What is Lucille's hourly rate of pay in a year with 26 pays?

   b. What would be her gross earnings for a pay period in which she worked 9 hours of overtime at 1½ times the regular rate of pay?

3. Morris is paid an annual salary of $38,600 based on a 35-hour workweek.

   a. What is his equivalent hourly wage in a year having 27 biweekly paydays?

   b. What would be his total remuneration for a 2-week period in that year if he worked 10.5 hours of overtime at double time?

4. Ross's compensation is to be changed from an hourly rate of $15.75 for a 40-hour week to a salary paid semimonthly. What should he be paid semimonthly in order for his annual earnings to remain the same? Assume there are exactly 52 weeks in a year.

5. Allison's regular hourly rate of pay is $17.70. She is paid time and a half for all work on weekends and for any time over 7.5 hours on weekdays. Calculate her gross earnings for a week in which she works 4.5, 7.5, 8.5, 6, 6, and 9 hours on Saturday to Friday, respectively.

6. Sam is paid $24.50 per hour as a power plant engineer. He is paid 1½ times the regular rate for all time exceeding 8 hours in a day or 40 hours in a week. Statutory holidays worked are paid at double time. What were his gross earnings for a week in which he clocked 8, 9.5, 8, 8, 10, 0, and 8 hours on Saturday to Friday, respectively, where Monday was a statutory holiday?

7. Mary sews for a clothing manufacturer. She is paid $6.25 per hour plus a piece rate that depends on the type of garment in production. The current production run is men's trousers, for which she is paid $2.25 for each unit exceeding her quota of 20 trousers in an 8-hour shift. What will be her total pay for a regular workweek in which her output on successive days was 24, 26, 27, 28, and 30 trousers?

8. Herb packs fish in 500-g cans on a processing line. He is paid $8.25 per hour plus $0.18 per kilogram for production in excess of 500 kg in a 7.5-hour shift. How much will he earn per day if he packs 250 cans per hour?

9. A shoe store salesman is paid the greater of $450 per week or 11% of sales.
   a. What will be his earnings for a week in which sales are $4236?
   b. At what volume of sales per week will he start to earn more from the commission-based compensation?

10. Sharon is a manufacturer's representative selling office furniture directly to businesses. She receives a monthly salary of $2000 plus a 2.2% commission on sales exceeding her quota of $150,000 per month.
    a. What are her earnings for a month in which she has $227,000 in sales?
    b. If her average monthly sales are $235,000, what straight commission rate would generate the same average monthly earnings as her current basis of remuneration?

11. Julio is paid on a graduated commission scale of 5% on the first $20,000 of sales in a month, 7.5% on the next $20,000, and 10% on all additional sales.
    a. What will he be paid for a month in which his sales are $54,880?
    b. What fixed commission rate would result in the same earnings for the month?

12. Karen works in a retail computer store. She receives a weekly base salary of $300 plus a commission of 3% of sales exceeding her quota of $20,000 per week. What were her sales for a week in which she earned $630.38?

13. Jason's gross pay for August was $3296.97 on sales totalling $151,342. If his base salary is $1500 per month, what is his rate of commission on sales exceeding his monthly quota of $100,000?

14. Tom sells mutual funds on a graduated commission structure. He receives 3.3% on the first $50,000 of sales in a month, 4.4% on the next $50,000, and 5.5% on all further sales. What will be his gross earnings for a month in which he sells $140,000 worth of mutual funds?

•15. Daniella's gross monthly earnings are based on commission rates of 4% of the first $40,000 of sales, 5% of the next $50,000, and 6% of all additional sales for the month. What was her sales total for a month in which she was paid $5350?

•16. Trevor earns a base monthly salary of $2000 plus a commission of 3% on sales exceeding his monthly quota of $25,000. He receives a further 3% bonus on sales in excess of $50,000. What must his sales be in order to gross $4000 per month?

*1.5 SIMPLE AND WEIGHTED AVERAGES

The type of average initially encountered in basic mathematics is called the *simple average*. To calculate the simple average, the values for all the items are added together and then divided by the number of items. We use this averaging procedure in cases where each item has the *same* importance or each value occurs the *same* number of times.

$$\text{Simple average} = \frac{\text{Sum of the values}}{\text{Total number of items}}$$

In cases where the values being averaged have *differing* relative importance, or where some values occur more often than others, a weighted average should be computed. A *weighted average* is obtained by a three-step procedure:

1. Each value is multiplied by a number representing the relative importance of the value or the number of times that it occurs. These multipliers are called *weighting factors.*
2. The products from step 1 are added.
3. The sum from step 2 is divided by the sum of the weighting factors.

The following word equation incorporates all three steps.

$$\text{Weighted average} = \frac{\text{Sum of (Weighting factors} \times \text{Values)}}{\text{Sum of weighting factors}}$$

■ EXAMPLE 1.5A   CALCULATION OF SIMPLE AND WEIGHTED AVERAGES

Northern Transport has 86 drivers earning $15.90 per hour, 14 clerical staff members earning $12.35 per hour, and 8 mechanics earning $24.67 per hour.

a. What is the simple average of the three hourly rates?
b. Calculate the weighted-average hourly rate earned by the three categories of employees.

☑ SOLUTION

a. Simple average $= \dfrac{\$15.90 + \$12.35 + \$24.67}{3} = \$17.64$

b. For determining the weighted average hourly rate paid by the firm, each hourly rate should be assigned a weighting factor reflecting the relative importance of that rate. The greater the number of employees receiving a particular wage rate, the more importance should be given to that rate. It is natural, then, to use the number of employees receiving an hourly rate as the weighting factor.

$$\begin{aligned}
\text{Weighted average} &= \frac{(86 \times \$15.90) + (14 \times \$12.35) + (8 \times \$24.67)}{86 + 14 + 8} \\
&= \frac{\$1367.40 + \$172.90 + \$197.36}{108} \\
&= \$16.09
\end{aligned}$$

The weighted average is less than the simple average because a high proportion of the employees earn the lowest hourly rate.   ■

APPLICATIONS OF WEIGHTED AVERAGE   There are many examples of the use of weighted averages in business. Accountants sometimes place a value on a firm's inventory at the end of a fiscal period by calculating a weighted average of the costs to the firm of the goods in inventory.

In business and economics, the *consumer price index* (CPI) is used as a measure of retail price levels. The CPI is based on a weighted average of the prices of over 400 goods and services commonly purchased by consumers. The weighting factors are intended to be representative of the proportion of consumer expenditures made on each item. For example, a 10% increase in apartment rental rates has a bigger financial impact on consumers than a 10% increase in the price of haircuts. Therefore, the apartment rental rate has a much larger weighting factor in the index than the price of a haircut.

Other applications of weighted averages are presented in the following examples and in the exercise at the end of this section.

■ **EXAMPLE 1.5B**   *CALCULATING A (WEIGHTED) GRADE POINT AVERAGE*

Most colleges compute a grade point average (GPA) as the overall measure of a student's academic achievement. To compute the GPA, each letter grade is first converted to a grade point value. Each course's grade point value is then weighted by the number of credits the course carries.

The table on the left gives City College's scale for converting letter grades to grade point values. The table on the right presents Louise's courses and grades. Calculate her GPA.

Letter grade	Grade point value
A	4.0
A–	3.7
B+	3.3
B	3.0
B–	2.7
C+	2.3
C	2.0
C–	1.7
D	1.0

Course	Credits	Grade
English 100	3	B+
Math 100	4	B
Business 100	2	A
Economics 120	3	B–
Accounting 100	4	C+
Marketing 140	2	A–
Computing 110	3	C
Total	21	

✓ **SOLUTION**

$$GPA = \frac{(3 \times 3.3) + (4 \times 3.0) + (2 \times 4.0) + (3 \times 2.7) + (4 \times 2.3) + (2 \times 3.7) + (3 \times 2.0)}{21}$$

$$= \frac{60.6}{21}$$

$$= 2.89$$

Louise's grade point average is 2.89.   ■

■ **EXAMPLE 1.5C**   *CALCULATING THE WEIGHTED-AVERAGE RATE OF RETURN FOR AN INVESTMENT PORTFOLIO*

One year ago, Mrs. Boyd allocated her savings among four mutual funds as follows: 20% to a bond fund, 15% to a money market fund, 40% to an equity fund, and 25% to a balanced fund. During the past year, the individual funds had returns of 8%, 12%, –2%, and 6%, respectively. What is the overall rate of return on her portfolio?

✓ **SOLUTION**

A simple average of the four rates of return is not the appropriate calculation because Mrs. Boyd has differing proportions of her money in each of the four funds. Each rate of return should be weighted by the fraction of her investment earning the respective rate of return. The denominator in the weighted average calculation will be 1 since the sum of the parts gives the whole.

$$\begin{aligned} \text{Average return} &= (0.2 \times 8\%) + (0.15 \times 12\%) + [0.4 \times (-2\%)] + (0.25 \times 6\%) \\ &= 1.6\% + 1.8\% - 0.8\% + 1.5\% \\ &= 4.1\% \end{aligned}$$

The value of Mrs. Boyd's portfolio went up 4.1% during the past year. ∎

■ **EXAMPLE 1.5D** **CALCULATING THE WEIGHTED AVERAGE OF A VARYING INVESTMENT IN A BUSINESS**

As of January 1, Alan had already invested $63,000 in his business. On February 1 he invested another $5000. Alan withdrew $12,000 on June 1 and injected $3000 on November 1. What was his average cumulative investment in the business during the year? (Assume that all months have the same length.)

☑ **SOLUTION**

A common error made in this type of problem is to attempt, in some way, to average the amounts that are contributed to or withdrawn from the business. We should instead average the cumulative balance of the invested funds. The amounts contributed and withdrawn from time to time are used only to revise the cumulative investment.

Period	Cumulative investment	Number of months
Jan. 1–Jan. 31	$63,000	1
Feb. 1–May 31	$63,000 + $5000 = $68,000	4
June 1–Oct. 31	$68,000 − $12,000 = $56,000	5
Nov. 1–Dec. 31	$56,000 + $3000 = $59,000	2

A weighted-average investment should be calculated since the various balances are invested for differing lengths of time. Each investment balance should be weighted by the number of months for which the balance lasted.

$$\begin{aligned} \text{Average investment} &= \frac{(1 \times \$63,000) + (4 \times \$68,000) + (5 \times \$56,000) + (2 \times \$59,000)}{12} \\ &= \$61,083 \end{aligned}$$

Alan's average monthly investment in the business was $61,083. ∎

EXERCISE 1.5

Answers to the odd-numbered problems are at the end of the book.

1. A survey of 254 randomly chosen residences in a city revealed that 4 had four television sets, 22 had three sets, 83 had two sets, 140 had one set, and 5 had no TV set at all. Based on the survey, what would you estimate to be the average number of TV sets per household?

2. An investor accumulated 1800 shares of Corel Corporation over a period of several months. She bought 1000 shares at $15.63, 500 shares at $19.00, and 300 shares at $21.75. What was her average cost per share? (*Note:* Investors who purchase shares in the same company at more than one price must eventually do this calculation. Tax rules

require that the capital gain or loss on the sale of any of the shares be calculated using the weighted-average price paid for all the shares rather than the particular price paid for the shares actually sold.)

3. A hockey goalie's "goals against average" (GAA) is the average number of goals scored against him per (complete) game. In his first 20 games in goal, O. U. Sieve had one shutout, two 1-goal games, three 2-goal games, four 3-goal games, seven 4-goal games, two 6-goal games, and one 10-goal disaster. Calculate his GAA.

4. Serge's graduated commission scale pays him 3% on his first $30,000 of sales, 4% on the next $20,000, and 6% on all additional sales in a month. What will be his average commission rate on sales for a month totalling:

   a. $60,000?   b. $100,000?

5. The Royal Bank offers an "add-on option" on fixed-rate mortgages. The option allows the customer to borrow additional funds partway through the term of the mortgage. The interest rate charged on the combined mortgage debt becomes the weighted average of the old rate on the former balance and the current competitive rate on new mortgage financing. Suppose Herschel and Julie have a mortgage balance of $37,500 at 9½% when they borrowed another $20,000 at 8%. What interest rate will they be charged by the Royal Bank on the new balance?

6. Margot's grades and course credits in her first semester at college are listed below.

Grade	C+	B–	B+	C–	B	C
Credits	5	3	4	2	3	4

Using the conversion table in Example 1.5b, calculate her grade point average for the semester.

7. The distribution of scores obtained by 30 students on a quiz graded on a scale of 1 to 10 is shown below.

Score	10	9	8	7	6	5	4	3	2	1
Number of students	2	6	9	7	3	2	0	1	0	0

What was the average score on the test?

8. Sam's transcript shows the following academic record for four semesters of part-time college studies. Calculate his cumulative GPA at the end of his fourth semester.

Semester	Credits	GPA
1	6	3.5
2	9	3.0
3	12	2.75
4	7.5	3.2

9. The "age" of an account receivable is the length of time that it has been outstanding. At the end of October, a firm has $12,570 in receivables that are 30 days old, $6850 in receivables that are 60 days old, and $1325 in receivables that are 90 days old. What is the average age of its accounts receivable?

24   Chapter 1

10. One year ago, Dan allocated the funds in his portfolio among five securities in the proportions listed in the following table. The rate of return on each security for the year is
given in the third column of the table.

Security	Proportion invested	Rate of return for the year
Company A shares	15%	14%
Province B bonds	20	10
Company C shares	10	−13
Units in fund D	35	12
Company E shares	20	27

Calculate the rate of return for the entire portfolio.

11. One of the methods permitted by Generally Accepted Accounting Principles for reporting
the value of a firm's inventory is *weighted-average inventory pricing*. The Boswell Corporation began its fiscal year with an inventory of 156 units valued at $10.55 per unit.
During the year, it made the purchases listed in the following table.

Date	Units purchased	Unit cost
February 10	300	$10.86
June 3	1000	10.47
August 23	500	10.97

At end of the year, 239 units remained in inventory. Determine:

a. The weighted-average cost of the units purchased during the year.

b. The weighted-average cost of the beginning inventory and all units purchased during
the year.

c. The value of the ending inventory based on the weighted-average cost calculated in b.

12. Suppose a group of consumers spends 30% of its disposable income on food, 20% on
clothing, and 50% on rent. If over the course of a year the price of food rose 10%, the
price of clothing dropped 5%, and rent rose 15%, what was the average price increase
experienced by these consumers?

13. The gross profit margin on the sale of an item is the percentage of the selling price
remaining after the wholesale cost of the item has been paid. A restaurant owner has set
prices so that the gross profit margin is 67% on appetizers, 45% on entrees, 70% on
desserts, and 50% on beverages. If the breakdown of total sales' revenue is 10% from
appetizers, 50% from entrees, 25% from beverages, and 15% from desserts, what is the
average gross profit margin?

•14. The balance on Nucorp's revolving loan began the month at $35,000. On the eighth of
the month another $10,000 was borrowed. Nucorp was able to repay $20,000 on the
25th of the 31-day month. What was the average balance on the loan during the month?
(Use each day's closing balance as the loan balance for the day.)

•15. A seasonal manufacturing operation began the calendar year with 14 employees. It
added 7 on April 1, 8 on May 1, and 11 more on June 1. Six were laid off on September
1, and another 14 were let go on October 1. What was the average number of employees on the payroll during the calendar year? (Assume that each month has the same
length.)

•16. Marcel must temporarily invest some extra funds in his retail business every fall to purchase inventory in preparation for the Christmas season. On September 1 he already

had a total of $57,000 invested in his business. On October 1 he invested another $15,000, and on November 1 he injected $27,000. He was able to withdraw $23,000 on February 1, $13,000 on March 1, and $6000 on May 1. What was the average investment in the business during the period from September 1 to August 31? (Assume that each month has the same length.)

*APPENDIX: TAXES

A **tax rate** is the fraction of a price or taxable amount that is payable as tax. A tax rate is usually quoted as the percent equivalent. The tax payable is then calculated using the formula

$$\text{Tax payable} = \text{Tax rate} \times \text{Taxable amount}$$

where the tax rate must be substituted in its decimal equivalent form.

GOODS AND SERVICES TAX (GST)

WHITHER THE GST?   At this text's publication deadline in the summer of 1996, the future form of the federal Goods and Services Tax (GST) was unclear. Right from its inception in 1991, the GST was a widely despised tax. Consumers disliked paying an additional 7% for most goods, but they particularly hated paying the tax on services. (Services had always been and continued to remain exempt from provincial sales taxes.) Businesses resented the complexity of the GST and the time spent complying with it. The GST and provincial sales tax systems had different rules, separate paperwork, and independent bureaucracies.

Most consumers and businesses agreed that the patchwork of provincial sales taxes along with the GST was very inefficient and costly for businesses and governments to administer. Most also agreed in principle with the notion of "harmonization" of the GST and provincial sales taxes. Harmonization means one tax, one base of taxable goods and services, common paperwork, one filing and tax remittance by a business, and one bureaucracy to administer it. While the theory is good, many voters do not trust federal and provincial politicians to achieve harmonization with a "tax-neutral" outcome—that is, with no increase in the overall consumption tax burden. Of particular concern is broadening the tax base for the provincial component of a harmonized tax to include services. Provincial governments are figuratively all "over the map" with respect to negotiating harmonization.[8] The GST is so loathed by many voters that some provincial politicians fear being tainted by any action that might be construed as an endorsement of the GST.

A memorandum of understanding between the federal government and the provincial governments of Nova Scotia, New Brunswick, and Newfoundland was announced in late April 1996. It set out the main elements of the *proposed* harmonized sales tax.

• A single tax rate of 15% across all three provinces starting April 1, 1997. (The existing provincial sales taxes were 12% in Newfoundland, 11% in Nova Scotia, and 11% in New Brunswick.)

---

[8]In 1991, Quebec adopted the GST tax base as the base for its provincial sales tax. However, the two tax regimes were otherwise kept separate and autonomous.

- The same tax base as for the current GST. (This effectively broadened the base for the provincial component of the tax.)
- "Tax-included pricing." (The sticker price is to be the final price *including* the 15% tax. Previously the sticker price on consumer goods did not, in most provinces, include GST or provincial sales tax.)
- Administration of the tax by the federal government.

The proposed harmonization remained to be approved by each of the three provincial governments.

As of the summer of 1996, the governments of Ontario, Alberta, and British Columbia were strongly opposed to harmonization. It appeared that many Canadians would continue to endure the GST in close to its original form for a few more years. Therefore, this section remains in the second edition but is consigned to an appendix.

OPERATION OF THE GST   The federal Goods and Services Tax (GST) is charged at the rate of 7% on the vast majority of goods and services.

$$GST = 0.07 \times Selling\ price\ of\ the\ good\ or\ service$$

The tax is paid by the purchaser to the seller of the good or service. Many goods are bought and sold several times as they move through successive stages of manufacturing and then through the merchandising chain. In every transaction, the purchaser pays the GST on the transfer price to the seller. Consequently, any particular business pays the GST on the goods and services that it purchases, and the same business collects the GST on the goods and services that it sells. When the business files its GST return, it remits only the difference between the tax collected from sales and the tax paid on purchases. If, in a reporting period, the tax paid on purchases exceeds the tax collected from sales, the difference will be refunded to the business. Two effects of this tax system are:

- The *net* GST a business pays ends up being 7% of the *value added* to the goods and services that it sells. This happens because the business is credited with the GST it pays on its inputs.
- Ultimately, the *full* GST burden is passed on to the final retail consumers, who are not eligible for GST credits.

■ **EXAMPLE 1AA**   *CALCULATION OF THE GST PAYABLE BY A BUSINESS*

Ace Appliance Repair files GST returns quarterly. During the first quarter of the year, Ace billed its customers $17,650 for labour and $4960 for parts, and then added on the GST. In the same period, Ace paid $3250 to suppliers for parts, $1800 for rent, $673 for utilities, $594 for truck repairs, and the GST on these goods and services.

a. What GST must be remitted by Ace or refunded by the government for the first quarter?

b. Repeat part *a* for the case where Ace also bought a new truck for $24,000 on the last day of the quarter.

☑ **SOLUTION**

a. GST collected = 0.07($17,650 + $4960) = $1582.70
   GST paid = 0.07($3250 + $1800 + $673 + $594) = $442.19
   GST remittance payable = $1582.70 − $442.19 = $1140.51

b. GST paid on truck purchase = 0.07 × $24,000 = $1680
   GST refund receivable = $1680.00 − Answer in part *a*
                      = $1680.00 − $1140.51
                      = $539.49   ∎

PROVINCIAL SALES TAX (PST)

Subject to the implementation of the previously mentioned harmonized tax, all provinces except Alberta charge a sales tax at the *retail* level. This tax typically applies to a somewhat narrower range of goods and to a much more restricted range of services than the GST. The various provincial sales tax (PST) rates[9] are presented in Table 1.1. In Ontario and the western provinces, the tax rate is applied to the retail price.

PST = Sales tax rate × Retail price
(in Ontario and the western provinces)

In Quebec and Prince Edward Island, the PST is calculated on the combination of the retail price *plus* the GST. The consumer then pays a tax on a tax—provincial sales tax is paid on the GST!

PST = Sales tax rate × (Retail price + GST)
(in Quebec and the eastern provinces)

TABLE   1.1

Provincial Sales Tax Rates (as of July 1, 1996)

Province	Tax rate
Alberta	0%
British Columbia	7
Manitoba	7
Ontario	8
Prince Edward Island	10
Quebec	8
Saskatchewan	9

∎ **EXAMPLE 1AB**   *CALCULATING THE PST*

Calculate the PST on a $100 item in (*a*) Ontario and (*b*) Quebec.

☑ **SOLUTION**

a. PST = 0.08 × $100 = $8.00

b. In Quebec the PST is based on the list price plus GST.

GST = 0.07 × $100 = $7.00
PST = 0.08 × ($100 + GST)
    = 0.08 × $107
    = $8.56   ∎

---

[9]Rates are not given for the three Maritime Provinces that proposed in 1996 to harmonize their provincial sales taxes with the GST.

PROPERTY TAX

Real estate property tax rates are set by provincial and municipal governments, and by other agencies (such as school boards) authorized by the provincial government to levy property taxes. Property tax rates in most provinces are quoted as a mill rate. Whereas a percent tax rate specifies, in effect, the amount of tax per $100 of taxable value, a **mill rate** represents the amount of tax per $1000 of taxable value. For example, a mill rate of 13.732 means a tax of $13.732 per $1000 of taxable value. The percent equivalent of a mill rate is therefore one-tenth of the mill rate. The decimal equivalent of a mill rate may be obtained by moving the decimal point *three places to the left*.

The annual tax on a property is calculated by applying the mill rate to the assessed or taxable value of the property.

$$\text{Property tax} = \frac{\text{Mill rate}}{1000} \times \text{Assessed value of the property}$$

■ EXAMPLE 1AC   CALCULATING THE PROPERTY TAX ON A RESIDENTIAL PROPERTY

A homeowner's tax notice lists the following mill rates for various local services and capital developments. If the assessed value of the property is $164,500, calculate each tax levy and the current year's total property taxes.

Tax rate	Mill rate
Schools	6.7496
General city	7.8137
Water	0.8023
Sewer and sanitation	0.7468

☑ SOLUTION

$$\text{School tax levy} = \frac{\text{Schools mill rate}}{1000} \times \text{Assessed value}$$
$$= \frac{6.7496}{1000} \times \$164,500$$
$$= \$1110.31$$

Similarly

$$\text{General city levy} = \frac{7.8137}{1000} \times \$164,500 = \$1285.35$$
$$\text{Water levy} = \frac{0.8023}{1000} \times \$164,500 = \$131.98$$
$$\text{Sewer levy} = \frac{0.7468}{1000} \times \$164,500 = \$122.85$$
$$\text{Total property taxes} = \$1110.31 + \$1285.35 + \$131.98 + \$122.85$$
$$= \$2650.49$$

■

EXERCISE 1A

Answers to the odd-numbered problems are at the end of the book.

1. Johnston Distributing, Inc., files quarterly GST returns. The purchases on which it paid the GST and the sales on which it collected the GST for the last four quarters were as follows:

Quarter	Purchases	Sales
1	$596,476	$ 751,841
2	967,679	627,374
3	823,268	1,231,916
4	829,804	994,622

   Calculate the GST remittance or refund due for each quarter.

2. Sawchuk's Home and Garden Center files monthly GST returns. The purchases on which it paid the GST and the sales on which it collected the GST for the last four months were as follows:

Month	Purchases	Sales
March	$135,650	$ 57,890
April	213,425	205,170
May	176,730	313,245
June	153,715	268,590

   Calculate the GST remittance or refund due for each month.

3. Calculate the price, including both GST and PST, that an individual will pay for a car sold for $21,900 in:

   a. Alberta   *b.* Ontario   *c.* Quebec

4. How much more will a consumer pay for an item listed at $1000 (pretax) in Quebec than in British Columbia?

•5. In its most recent operating quarter, Robertson's Footwear had sales of $87,940. All sales are subject to GST, but $28,637 of the total represented PST-exempt sales. Calculate the PST that must be remitted if Robertson's is located in:

   a. Saskatchewan   *b.* Prince Edward Island

•6. Prepare a table showing the single tax rate for each province that is equivalent to the combined effect of the GST and PST on retail purchases. (Hint: Find the aftertax price of a $100 item in each province.)

7. What will be the taxes on a property assessed at $227,000 if the mill rate is 16.8629?

8. *a.* What is the percent equivalent of 0.1 mill?

   b. If the mill rate increases by 0.1 mill, what will be the dollar increase in property taxes on a $200,000 home?

9. The assessment on a farm consists of $143,000 for the house and $467,000 for the land and buildings. A mill rate of 15.0294 applies to residences, and a rate of 4.6423 applies to agricultural land and buildings. What are the total property taxes payable on the farm?

10. The assessment on a property increased from $185,000 last year to $198,000 in the current year. Last year's mill rate was 15.6324.

   a. What will be the change in the property tax from last year if the new mill rate is set at 15.2193?

   b. What would the new mill rate have to be for the dollar amount of the property taxes to be unchanged?

•11. The school board in a municipality will require an extra $2,430,000 for its operating budget next year. The current mill rate for the school tax component of property taxes is 7.1253.

   a. If the total of the assessed values of properties in the municipality remains at the current figure of $6.78 billion, at what value must next year's school mill rate be set?

   b. If the total of all assessed values rises by 5% over this year's aggregate assessment, at what value must next year's school mill rate be set?

•12. The total assessed value of property in Brockton has risen by $97 million from last year's figure of $1.563 billion. The mill rate last year for city services was 9.4181. If the city's budget has increased by $750,000, what mill rate should it set for the current year?

REVIEW PROBLEMS

Answers to the odd-numbered review problems are at the end of the book.

1. Evaluate each of the following:

    a. $(2^3 - 3)^2 - 20 \div (2 + 2^3)$

    b. $4(2 \times 3^2 - 2^3)^2 \div (10 - 4 \times 5)$

    c. $\$213.85\left(1 - 0.095 \times \dfrac{5}{12}\right)$

    d. $\dfrac{\$2315}{1 + 0.0825 \times \frac{77}{365}}$

    e. $\$325.75\left(1 + \dfrac{0.105}{4}\right)^2$

    f. $\dfrac{\$710}{\left(1 + \frac{0.0925}{2}\right)^3}$

    g. $\$885.75\left(1 + 0.0775 \times \dfrac{231}{365}\right) - \dfrac{\$476.50}{1 + 0.0775 \times \frac{49}{365}}$

    h. $\$859\left(1 + \dfrac{0.0825}{12}\right)^3 + \dfrac{\$682}{\left(1 + \frac{0.0825}{12}\right)^2}$

2. What percent of $6.39 is $16.39?

3. 80% of what amount is $100?

4. ¾% of what amount is $1.00?

5. Six in. is what percent of 2 yds.?

6. The actual profit of $23,400 for the most recent fiscal quarter was 90% of the forecast profit. What was the forecast profit?

7. Luther is paid an annual salary of $56,600 based on a 37½-hour workweek.

    a. What is his equivalent hourly wage in a year having 26 biweekly paydays?

    b. What would be his total remuneration for a 2-week period of that year if he worked 4.5 hours of overtime at time and a half?

8. Sonja is paid $32.50 per hour as a veterinarian. She is paid 1½ times the regular rate for all time exceeding 7½ hours in a day or 37½ hours per week. Work on a statutory holiday is paid at double time. What were her gross earnings for a week in which she worked 6, 0, 3, 7½, 9, 7½, and 8 hours on Saturday to Friday, respectively, and the Monday was a statutory holiday?

9. Lauren's gross pay for July was $3188.35 on net sales totaling $88,630. If her base salary is $1000 per month, what is her rate of commission on sales exceeding her monthly quota of $40,000?

10. One year ago Helga allocated the funds in her portfolio among five securities in the amounts listed in the following table. The rate of return on each security for the year is given in the third column of the table.

Security	Amount invested	Rate of return for the year
Company U shares	$ 5000	30%
Province V bonds	20,000	-3
Company W shares	8000	-15
Units in fund X	25,000	13
Company Y shares	4500	45

Calculate the rate of return for the entire portfolio.

11. The fiscal year for Pine Valley Skiing Ltd., the owner of a downhill skiing facility, ends on June 30. The company began the recently completed fiscal year with its summer maintenance crew of 7. It took on 6 more employees on September 1, hired another 18 on November 1, and added 23 more on December 1. Eleven employees were laid off on March 1, 20 were let go on April 1, and another 16 left on May 1, leaving only the permanent maintenance personnel. What was the average number of employees per month working for Pine Valley during the fiscal year? (Assume that each month has the same length.)

SELF-TEST EXERCISE

Answers to the self-test problems are at the end of the book.

1. Evaluate each of the following:

   a. $96 - (6 - 4^2) \times 7 - 2$

   b. $81 \div (5^2 - 16) - 4(2^3 - 13)$

   c. $\dfrac{\$827.69}{1 + 0.125 \times \frac{273}{365}} + \$531.49\left(1 + 0.125 \times \dfrac{41}{365}\right)$

   d. $\$550.45\left(1 + 0.0875 \times \dfrac{195}{365}\right) - \dfrac{\$376.29}{1 + 0.0875 \times \frac{99}{365}}$

   e. $\$1137\left(1 + \dfrac{0.0975}{12}\right)^2 + \dfrac{\$2643}{\left(1 + \frac{0.0975}{12}\right)^3}$

2. 167.5% of what amount is $100?

3. Through a mechanism (on Canadian Individual Tax Returns) known as the "Old Age Security clawback," an individual receiving Old Age Security (OAS) benefits must repay an increasing proportion of these benefits to the federal government as the individual's net income rises beyond a certain threshold. If the OAS clawback is 15% of net income exceeding $54,000, at what amount of net income must a taxpayer repay all $4500 of OAS benefits received in the year?

4. Jason earns an annual salary of $61,000 as an executive with a provincial utility. He is paid biweekly based on 26 pay periods in the year. During a strike, he worked 33 hours more than the regular 75 hours for a 2-week pay period. What was his gross pay for that period if the company agreed to pay 1.5 times his equivalent hourly rate for overtime?

5. Marion receives a monthly base salary of $1000. On the first $10,000 of sales above her monthly quota of $20,000, she is paid a commission of 8%. On any additional sales, the commission rate is 10%. What were her gross earnings for the month of August, in which she had sales amounting to $38,670?

6. Ms. Yong invested $16,800 in a Canadian equity mutual fund, $25,600 in a U.S. equity mutual fund, and $31,000 in a global fund that holds a variety of foreign securities. If in the subsequent 6 months, the value of the units in the Canadian fund dropped by 4.3%, the U.S. fund declined by 1.1%, and the global fund rose by 8.2%, what was the overall rate of return on Ms. Yong's mutual fund portfolio for the 6-month holding period?

•7. Anthony began the year with $96,400 already invested in his Snow 'n Ice retail store. He withdrew $14,200 on March 1 and another $21,800 on April 1. On August 1, he invested $23,700, and on November 1 he contributed another $19,300. What was his average cumulative investment during the year? (Assume that each month has the same length.)

SUMMARY OF NOTATION AND KEY FORMULAS

> **Significant Figure Rule:** At each step in a series of calculations, keep one more figure than the number of figures required in the final result.

> **Rules for Rounding Decimals:**
> 1. If the first digit dropped is 5 or greater, increase the last retained digit by 1.
> 2. If the first digit dropped is less than 5, leave the last retained digit unchanged.

$$\text{Portion} = \text{Rate} \times \text{Base} = \frac{\%\text{Rate}}{100\%} \times \text{Base} \tag{1–1}$$

$$\text{Simple average} = \frac{\text{Sum of the values}}{\text{Total number of items}}$$

$$\text{Weighted average} = \frac{\text{Sum of (Weighting factors} \times \text{Values)}}{\text{Sum of weighting factors}}$$

GLOSSARY OF TERMS

Complex fraction   A fraction containing one or more other fractions in its numerator or denominator.

Equivalent fractions   Fractions that have the same value.

Improper fraction   A fraction whose numerator is larger than or equal to the denominator.

Mill rate   The amount of property tax per $1000 of taxable value.

Mixed number   A number consisting of a whole number plus a fraction.

Proper fraction   A fraction whose numerator is less than the denominator.

Significant figures   All of the digits except zeros serving only to position the decimal point.

Tax rate   The fraction of a price or taxable amount that is payable as tax.

2

REVIEW OF ALGEBRA

LEARNING OBJECTIVES

After completing this chapter, you will be able to:

- Simplify algebraic expressions
- Apply the rules of exponents to the simplification and evaluation of powers
- Solve linear equations in one variable
- Solve "word problems" that lead to a linear equation in one unknown
- Given any two of the three quantities percent change, final value, and initial value, calculate the third quantity

- Given an investment's initial and final values and income for a holding period, calculate its income yield, percent capital gain, and rate of return on investment
- Determine the overall effect of compounding a series of percent changes or rates of return on investment

INTRODUCTION

It is often helpful to express the mathematical relationship between two or more quantities in terms of letters or symbols representing the quantities. The nature of their interdependence is then more readily visualized and understood. Such an algebraic formulation makes it easier to handle a wide range of applications. Knowledge of the algebraic relationship among the relevant variables is required to program calculators, use spreadsheet software, or use computers to process data.

The chapter begins by reviewing basic terminology, techniques for simplifying algebraic expressions, exponents, and the procedure for solving a linear equation in one unknown. To prepare for more difficult problems, a general approach for solving word problems is then presented. The topics "percent change," "rate on investment," and "compounding percent changes" provide practice in applying these skills and in problem-solving.

2.1 OPERATIONS WITH ALGEBRAIC EXPRESSIONS

DEFINITIONS

We will use a simple example to illustrate some of the basic terms used in algebra. Suppose that you work in the payroll department of a large retail store. Every month you must calculate each employee's gross earnings. The sales staff are paid a base salary of $1000 per month plus a commission of 4% of sales. The gross earnings of a salesperson in a month are calculated using the formula:

$$\$1000 + 0.04 \times \text{Sales for the month}$$

The only quantity that varies from one salesperson to another, and from one month to another, is the amount of each individual's sales. Sales for the month is therefore the mathematical *variable* in this calculation. In algebra we use a letter or symbol to represent a mathematical variable. Using s to represent the sales for 1 month, we can write the following algebraic expression for the gross monthly earnings:

$$\$1000 + 0.04s$$

An **algebraic expression** is a statement of the mathematical operations to be carried out on a combination of numbers and variables. To obtain any salesperson's gross earnings, we substitute that person's sales for the month as the value for s. The expression tells us to first multiply the sales by 0.04 and then add $1000.

The components of an algebraic expression that are separated by addition or subtraction signs are called **terms.** This particular expression has two terms: $1000 and 0.04$s$. An expression containing only one term is called a **monomial. A binomial** expression has two terms, and a **trinomial** has three terms. The name **polynomial** may be used for any expression with more than one term.

Each term in an expression consists of one or more **factors** separated by multiplication or division signs. (Multiplication may be implied by writing factors side by side with no multiplication symbol between them.) The numerical factor in a term is called the **numerical coefficient,** and the combination of the variable factors in a term is called the **literal coefficient** of the term. The first term in our sample binomial contains only one factor, $1000. The second term contains two factors: the numerical coefficient 0.04 and the literal coefficient s.

■ EXAMPLE 2.1A   *IDENTIFYING THE TERMS, FACTORS, AND COEFFICIENTS IN A POLYNOMIAL*[1]

$3x^2 + xy - 6y^2$ is a trinomial.

Term	Factors	Numerical coefficient	Literal coefficient
$3x^2$	3, x, x	3	x^2
xy	x, y	1	xy
$-6y^2$	6, y, y	-6	y^2

■

ADDITION AND SUBTRACTION

Sometimes an algebraic expression may be simplified by adding or subtracting certain terms before any values are substituted for the variables. Terms with the same *literal* coefficients are called **like terms.** Only like terms may be directly added or subtracted. Addition or subtraction of like terms is performed by adding or subtracting their numerical coefficients while keeping their common literal coefficient. For example, $2xy + 3xy = 5xy$. Adding or subtracting like terms is often referred to as *collecting* or *combining* like terms because only one term will remain with each differing literal coefficient.

■ EXAMPLE 2.1B   *SIMPLIFYING ALGEBRAIC EXPRESSIONS BY COMBINING LIKE TERMS*

a. $3a - 4b - 7a + 9b$

$= 3a - 7a - 4b + 9b$

$= (3 - 7)a + (-4 + 9)b$

$= -4a + 5b$

$3a$ and $-7a$ are like terms; $-4b$ and $9b$ are like terms. Combine the numerical coefficients of like terms.

b. $0.2x + 5x^2 + \dfrac{x}{4} - x + 3$

$= 5x^2 + (0.2 + 0.25 - 1)x + 3$

$= 5x^2 - 0.55x + 3$

Convert numerical coefficients to their decimal equivalents; then combine like terms.

c. $\dfrac{2x}{1.25} - \dfrac{4}{5} - 1\dfrac{3}{4}x$

$= 1.6x - 0.8 - 1.75x$

$= -0.15x - 0.8$

Convert numerical coefficients to their decimal equivalents; then combine like terms.

d. $\dfrac{3x}{1.0164} + 1.049x - x$

$= 2.95159x + 1.049x - x$

$= (2.95159 + 1.049 - 1)x$

$= 3.0006x$

Evaluate the numerical coefficients.

Combine like terms.

e. $x\left(1 + 0.12 \times \dfrac{241}{365}\right) + \dfrac{2x}{1 + 0.12 \times \frac{81}{365}}$

$= 1.07923x + \dfrac{2x}{1.02663}$

$= (1.07923 + 1.94812)x$

$= 3.02735x$

Evaluate the numerical coefficients.

Combine like terms.

■

---

[1]Exponents and powers will be discussed in Section 2.2. For now, it is sufficient to recall that a^2 means $a \times a$, a^3 means $a \times a \times a$, and so on.

MULTIPLICATION AND DIVISION

MULTIPLICATION   The product of a monomial and a polynomial is obtained by multiplying *each term* of the polynomial by the monomial. To obtain the product of two polynomials, multiply *each term* of one polynomial by *each term* of the other polynomial. The product of any pair of terms, one from each polynomial, will simply be the product of their numerical coefficients multiplied by the product of their literal coefficients. After all possible pairs of terms are multiplied, like terms should be collected.

■ **EXAMPLE 2.1c**   *MULTIPLICATION OF ALGEBRAIC EXPRESSIONS*

Expand each of the following expressions by carrying out the indicated multiplication.

a. $-x(2x^2 - 3x - 1)$
   $= -2x^3 + 3x^2 + x$ Each term in the trinomial is multiplied by $(-x)$.

b. $3m(4m - 6n + 2)$
   $= 3m(4m) + 3m(-6n) + 3m(2)$ Each term in the trinomial is multiplied by the monomial.
   $= 12m^2 - 18mn + 6m$ Within each term, the literal and numerical coefficients are separately multiplied.

c. $(7a - 2b)(3b - 2a)$
   $= 7a(3b - 2a) - 2b(3b - 2a)$ Each term of the first binomial is multiplied by the second binomial.
   $= 21ab - 14a^2 - 6b^2 + 4ab$ Multiplication in each case is carried out as in part *b*.
   $= 25ab - 14a^2 - 6b^2$ Combine like terms.

d. $(x - 2)(2x^2 - 3x - 4)$
   $= x(2x^2 - 3x - 4) - 2(2x^2 - 3x - 4)$ Each term of the binomial is multiplied by the trinomial.
   $= 2x^3 - 3x^2 - 4x - 4x^2 + 6x + 8$
   $= 2x^3 - 7x^2 + 2x + 8$ Combine like terms.   ■

DIVISION   To divide a polynomial by a monomial, *each term* of the polynomial must be divided by the monomial. The quotient for each division is the quotient of the numerical coefficients multiplied by the quotient of the literal coefficients.

Although you will encounter a few situations in this book where a monomial or polynomial is divided by a polynomial, you will not be required to perform the division algebraically. Division will take place only after numerical values are substituted for the variables involved.

Trap

When "cancelling" a common factor, remember that *every term* in the numerator and *every term* in the denominator must be divided by that common factor. A common error in dividing a polynomial by a monomial is to cancel one of the factors in the monomial (denominator) with the same factor in only one of the terms in the numerator. The common factor must be cancelled in *every* term in the numerator.

Tip

If you are in doubt about the legitimacy of an algebraic manipulation you have performed, often you can check it as follows. Substitute a numerical value for the variable in both the original expression and in the expression obtained from your questionable manipulation. If the resulting values are equal, it is highly probable that your manipulation was legal. For example, suppose that you attempt the simplification

$$\frac{4x + 2}{2} \rightarrow 2x + 2$$

where you have divided the 2 in the denominator into only the numerical coefficient of x. (This common error was brought to your attention in the preceding Trap.) If you pick an arbitrary value to substitute for x, say $x = 3$, the value of the original expression is

$$\frac{(12 + 2)}{2} = 7$$

but the value of the derived expression is $6 + 2 = 8$. Since the values differ, the simplification was either illegal or incorrectly carried out.

■ **EXAMPLE 2.1D**   *DIVISION BY A MONOMIAL*

Simplify each of the following expressions.

a. $\dfrac{36x^2y}{60xy^2}$

$= \dfrac{3(12)(x)(x)y}{5(12)(x)(y)y}$ Identify factors in the numerator and denominator.

$= \dfrac{3x}{5y}$ Cancel factors that appear in both the numerator and the denominator.

b. $\dfrac{48a^2 - 32ab}{8a}$

$= \dfrac{48a^2}{8a} - \dfrac{32ab}{8a}$ Divide each term in the numerator by the denominator.

$= 6a - 4b$ Cancel factors that appear in both the numerator and the denominator.

c. $\dfrac{225(1 + i)^4}{75(1 + i)^2}$

$= \dfrac{3(75)(1 + i)^2(1 + i)^2}{75(1 + i)^2}$ Identify and cancel factors that are common to both the numerator and the denominator.

$= 3(1 + i)^2$ ■

SUBSTITUTION

Substitution means assigning a numerical value to each of the algebraic symbols in an expression. The expression is then evaluated by carrying out all of the indicated operations. Referring back to our earlier example of the algebraic expression for the gross monthly earnings of the sales staff in the retail store, we can calculate any salesperson's earnings by substituting his or her actual sales figure for s in the expression

$$\$1000 + 0.04s$$

■ EXAMPLE 2.1E   *EVALUATING ALGEBRAIC EXPRESSIONS AFTER SUBSTITUTING NUMERICAL VALUES FOR THE VARIABLES*

Evaluate each of the following expressions for the given values of the variables.

a. $8p - 9q$ for $p = 2.5$, $q = -6$

b. $3x^2 - 7x - 4$ for $x = -3$

c. $P(1 + rt)$ for $P = \$100$, $r = 0.09$, $t = \dfrac{7}{12}$

d. $(1 + i)^m - 1$ for $i = 0.05$, $m = 2$

e. $\dfrac{S}{(1+i)^n}$ for $S = \$1240$, $i = 0.025$, $n = 4$

f. $R\left[\dfrac{(1+i)^n - 1}{i}\right]$ for $R = \$2000$, $i = 0.0225$, $n = 3$

✔ SOLUTION

a. $8p - 9q = 8(2.5) - 9(-6)$ Replace p by 2.5 and q by –6.

$\quad = 20 + 54$

$\quad = 74$

b. $3x^2 - 7x - 4 = 3(-3)^2 - 7(-3) - 4$

$\quad = 3(9) + 21 - 4$

$\quad = 27 + 17$

$\quad = 44$

c. $P(1 + rt) = \$100\left(1 + 0.09 \times \dfrac{7}{12}\right)$

$\quad = \$100(1 + 0.0525)$

$\quad = \$105.25$

d. $(1 + i)^m - 1 = (1 + 0.05)^2 - 1$

$\quad = 1.05^2 - 1$

$\quad = 1.1025 - 1$

$\quad = 0.1025$

e. $\dfrac{S}{(1 + i)^n} = \dfrac{\$1240}{(1 + 0.025)^4}$

$\quad = \dfrac{\$1240}{1.025^4}$

$\quad = \dfrac{\$1240}{1.103813}$

$\quad = \$1123.38$

f. $R\left[\dfrac{(1 + i)^n - 1}{i}\right] = \$2000\left[\dfrac{(1 + 0.0225)^3 - 1}{0.0225}\right]$

$\quad = \$2000\left(\dfrac{1.0225^3 - 1}{0.0225}\right)$

$\quad = \$2000\left(\dfrac{1.0690301 - 1}{0.0225}\right)$

$\quad = \$2000(3.068006)$

$\quad = \$6136.01$ ■

EXERCISE 2.1

Answers to the odd-numbered problems are at the end of the book.

Simplify each of the following and collect the like terms.

1. $(-p) + (-3p) + (4p)$
2. $(5s - 2t) - (2s - 4t)$

3. $4x^2y + (-3x^2y) - (-5x^2y)$
4. $1 - (7e^2 - 5 + 3e - e^3)$

5. $(6x^2 - 3xy + 4y^2) - (8y^2 - 10xy - x^2)$

6. $(7m^3 - m - 6m^2 + 10) - (5m^3 - 9 + 3m - 2m^2)$

7. $2(7x - 3y) - 3(2x - 3y)$
8. $4(a^2 - 3a - 4) - 2(5a^2 - a - 6)$

9. $15x - [4 - 2(5x - 6)]$
10. $6a - [3a - 2(2b - a)]$

•11. $\dfrac{2x + 9}{4} - 1.2(x - 1)$
•12. $\dfrac{x}{2} - x^2 + \dfrac{4}{5} - 0.2x^2 - \dfrac{4}{5}x + \dfrac{1}{2}$

•13. $\dfrac{8x}{0.5} + \dfrac{5.5x}{11} + 0.5(4.6x - 17)$
•14. $\dfrac{2x}{1.045} - \dfrac{2.016x}{3} + \dfrac{x}{2}$

•15. $\dfrac{P}{1 + 0.095 \times \frac{5}{12}} + 2P\left(1 + 0.095 \times \dfrac{171}{365}\right)$
•16. $y\left(1 - 0.125 \times \dfrac{213}{365}\right) + \dfrac{2y}{1 + 0.125 \times \frac{88}{365}}$

•17. $k(1 + 0.04)^2 + \dfrac{2k}{(1 + 0.04)^2}$
•18. $\dfrac{h}{(1 + 0.055)^2} - 3h(1 + 0.055)^3$

Perform the multiplication or division indicated in each of the following expressions and collect the like terms.

19. $4a(3ab - 5a + 6b)$
20. $9k(4 - 8k + 7k^2)$

21. $-5xy(2x^2 - xy - 3y^2)$
22. $-(p^2 - 4pq - 5p)\left(\dfrac{2q}{p}\right)$

23. $(4r - 3t)(2t + 5r)$
24. $(3p^2 - 5p)(-4p + 2)$

25. $3(a - 2)(4a + 1) - 5(2a + 3)(a - 7)$
26. $5(2x - y)(y + 3x) - 6x(x - 5y)$

27. $\dfrac{18x^2}{3x}$
28. $\dfrac{6a^2b}{-2ab^2}$

29. $\dfrac{x^2y - xy^2}{xy}$
30. $\dfrac{-4x + 10x^2 - 6x^3}{-0.5x}$

31. $\dfrac{12x^3 - 24x^2 + 36x}{48x}$
32. $\dfrac{32a^2b - 8ab + 14ab^2}{2ab}$

33. $\dfrac{4a^2b^3 - 6a^3b^2}{2ab^2}$
34. $\dfrac{120(1 + i)^2 + 180(1 + i)^3}{360(1 + i)}$

Evaluate each of the following expressions for the given values of the variables. In problems 39 to 43 and 45 to 50, calculate the result accurate to the cent.

35. $3d^2 - 4d + 15$ for $d = 2.5$

36. $15g - 9h + 3$ for $g = 14$, $h = 15$

37. $7x(4y - 8)$ for $x = 3.2$, $y = 1.5$

38. $I \div Pr$ for $P = \$500$, $I = \$13.75$, $r = 0.11$

39. $\dfrac{I}{rt}$ for $r = 0.095$, $I = \$23.21$, $t = \dfrac{283}{365}$

40. $\dfrac{N}{1 - d}$ for $N = \$89.10$, $d = 0.10$

•41. $L(1 - d_1)(1 - d_2)(1 - d_3)$ for $L = \$490$, $d_1 = 0.125$, $d_2 = 0.15$, $d_3 = 0.05$

42. $P(1 + rt)$ for $P = \$770$, $r = 0.013$, $t = \dfrac{223}{365}$

43. $\dfrac{S}{1 + rt}$ for $S = \$2500$, $r = 0.085$, $t = \dfrac{123}{365}$

44. $(1 + i)^m - 1$ for $i = 0.0225$, $m = 4$

45. $P(1 + i)^n$ for $P = \$1280$, $i = 0.025$, $n = 3$

46. $\dfrac{S}{(1 + i)^n}$ for $S = \$850$, $i = 0.0075$, $n = 6$

•47. $R\left[\dfrac{(1+i)^n-1}{i}\right]$ for $R = \$550$, $i = 0.085$, $n = 3$

•48. $R\left[\dfrac{(1+f)^n-1}{f}\right](1 + f)$ for $R = \$910$, $f = 0.1038129$, $n = 4$

•49. $\dfrac{R}{i}\left[1 - \dfrac{1}{(1+i)^n}\right]$ for $R = \$630$, $i = 0.115$, $n = 2$

•50. $P(1 + rt_1) + \dfrac{S}{1+rt_2}$ for $P = \$470$, $S = \$390$, $r = 0.075$, $t_1 = \dfrac{104}{365}$, $t_2 = \dfrac{73}{365}$

2.2 RULES AND PROPERTIES OF EXPONENTS

The use of exponents allows us to write algebraic expressions containing repeated factors in a more concise form. If n is a positive integer, then a^n is defined by

$$a^n = a \times a \times a \times \cdots \times a \quad \text{to } n \text{ factors}$$

In this notation, a is called the **base,** n is called the **exponent,** and a^n is read as "a raised to the power n" or "a raised to the exponent n." The value obtained for a^n is referred to as "the n th power of a" or sometimes just as "the **power.**" That is,

$$\boxed{\text{Power} = \text{Base}^{\text{Exponent}}}$$

We will use powers extensively in compound interest calculations in the mathematics of finance.

■ EXAMPLE 2.2A   *EVALUATING POWERS WITH POSITIVE INTEGRAL EXPONENTS*

a. $3^4 = 3 \times 3 \times 3 \times 3 = 81$

The base is 3, the exponent is 4, and the power is 81. The fourth power of 3 is 81.

b. $(0.1)^4 = 0.1 \times 0.1 \times 0.1 \times 0.1 = 0.0001$

c. $\left(\dfrac{3}{4}\right)^3 = \left(\dfrac{3}{4}\right)\left(\dfrac{3}{4}\right)\left(\dfrac{3}{4}\right) = \dfrac{3 \times 3 \times 3}{4 \times 4 \times 4} = \dfrac{27}{64}$
$= (0.75)(0.75)(0.75) = 0.421875$

d. $(1.035)^3 = 1.035 \times 1.035 \times 1.035 = 1.108718$

e. $(-2)^3 = (-2)(-2)(-2) = -8$

An odd power of a negative base is negative.

f. $(-0.9)^4 = (-0.9)(-0.9)(-0.9)(-0.9) = 0.6561$

An even power of a negative base is positive. ∎

RULES OF EXPONENTS A few mathematical operations involving powers occur so frequently that it is convenient to have a set of rules that provide shortcuts. The derivation of the following rules of exponents is straightforward and may be found in any introductory algebra text.

Rules of Exponents:

1. $a^m \times a^n = a^{m+n}$ 2. $\dfrac{a^m}{a^n} = a^{m-n}$

3. $(a^m)^n = a^{m \times n}$ 4. $(ab)^n = a^n b^n$

5. $\left(\dfrac{a}{b}\right)^n = \dfrac{a^n}{b^n}$

Trap

Note the following inequalities in order to avoid some frequently made errors.

$$(a + b)^n \neq a^n + b^n \qquad a^n - a^m \neq a^{n-m}$$

$$(a - b)^n \neq a^n - b^n \qquad a^n + a^m \neq a^{n+m}$$

■ **EXAMPLE 2.2B** *USING THE RULES OF EXPONENTS TO SIMPLIFY ALGEBRAIC EXPRESSIONS*

Simplify the following expressions.

a. $3^2 \times 3^3 = 3^{2+3} = 3^5 = 243$ Rule 1

b. $y^5 \times y^4 = y^{5+4} = y^9$ Rule 1

c. $(1 + i)^6 \times (1 + i)^{11} = (1 + i)^{6+11} = (1 + i)^{17}$ Rule 1

d. $\dfrac{1.01^8}{1.01^5} = 1.01^{8-5} = 1.01^3 = 1.030301$ Rule 2

e. $\dfrac{(1 + i)^{20}}{(1 + i)^8} = (1 + i)^{20-8} = (1 + i)^{12}$ Rule 2

f. $\dfrac{x^5 \times x^{14}}{x^9} = x^{5+14-9} = x^{10}$ Rules 1 and 2

g. $(k^4)^5 = k^{4 \times 5} = k^{20}$ Rule 3

h. $(3^2)^4 = 3^{2 \times 4} = 3^8 = 6561$ Rule 3

i. $\dfrac{(p^4 \times p^2)^3}{\left(\dfrac{p^8}{p^5}\right)^2} = \dfrac{(p^6)^3}{(p^3)^2}$ Rule 1

    Rule 2

$\qquad = \dfrac{p^{18}}{p^6}$ Rule 3

    Rule 3

$\qquad = p^{12}$ Rule 2

j. $(5q)^3 = 5^3 q^3 = 125q^3$ ⟶ Rule 4

k. $\left(\dfrac{0.5}{x}\right)^2 = \dfrac{0.5^2}{x^2} = \dfrac{0.25}{x^2}$ ⟶ Rule 5

l. $\left(\dfrac{3x^6 y^3}{x^2 z^3}\right)^2 = \left(\dfrac{3x^4 y^3}{z^3}\right)^2$ ⟶ Rule 2

$= \dfrac{3^2 x^{4\times 2} y^{3\times 2}}{z^{3\times 2}}$ ⟶ Rules 4 and 5

$= \dfrac{9x^8 y^6}{z^6}$

m. $\left(\dfrac{b^5 - b^3}{b^2}\right)^2 = \left(\dfrac{b^5}{b^2} - \dfrac{b^3}{b^2}\right)^2$

$= (b^3 - b)^2$ ⟶ Rule 2

No further simplification is possible using the rules of exponents. ■

ZERO, NEGATIVE, AND FRACTIONAL EXPONENTS Zero, negative, and fractional exponents must be given specific meanings in order to be consistent with the definition of a^n and the first three rules of exponents. The justifications for the following interpretations are presented in the appendix to this chapter.

Zero, Negative, and Fractional Exponents:

$$a^0 = 1 \qquad a^{-n} = \dfrac{1}{a^n} \qquad a^{1/n} = \sqrt[n]{a}$$

$$a^{m/n} = (\sqrt[n]{a})^m = \sqrt[n]{a^m}$$

Tip

Powers for negative and fractional exponents may be obtained using the $\boxed{y^x}$ function on electronic calculators.

For a fractional exponent, first calculate the decimal equivalent of the fraction and save it in the calculator's memory. Then perform the usual steps for calculating a power but with the single change that, when you would normally enter the exponent manually, recall it from the memory.

To enter a negative exponent, enter the exponent without a sign and then press the "sign change" key, $\boxed{+/-}$.

■ EXAMPLE 2.2c   EVALUATING POWERS FOR ZERO, NEGATIVE, AND FRACTIONAL EXPONENTS

Simplify or evaluate the following.

a. $7.132^0 = 1$

b. $(0.001)^0 = 1$

c. $(0.001)^{-1} = \dfrac{1}{0.001} = 1000$

d. $(1 + i)^{-n} = \dfrac{1}{(1 + i)^n}$

e. $\left(\dfrac{x}{y}\right)^{-2} = \dfrac{1}{\left(\dfrac{x}{y}\right)^2} = \dfrac{1}{\dfrac{x^2}{y^2}} = \dfrac{y^2}{x^2} = \left(\dfrac{y}{x}\right)^2$

f. $\left(-\dfrac{4}{5}\right)^{-2} = \left(-\dfrac{5}{4}\right)^2 = (-1.25)^2 = 1.5625$

g. $(1.0125)^{-5} = \left(\dfrac{1}{1.0125}\right)^5 = (0.987654)^5 = 0.93978$

h. $(1.0125)^{1/5} = \sqrt[5]{1.0125} = (1.0125)^{0.2} = 1.00249$

i. $\left(\dfrac{3}{2}\right)^{3/2} = 1.5^{3/2} = \sqrt{1.5^3} = \sqrt{3.375} = 1.8371$
$= 1.5^{1.5} = 1.8371$

j. $\$175(1 + 0.05)^{3.5} = \$175(1.18621) = \$207.59$

k. $\$321(1 + 0.025)^{-8} = \$321(0.8207465) = \$263.46$

l. $\dfrac{(1 + 0.0075)^{59.65} - 1}{0.0075} = \dfrac{1.5615918 - 1}{0.0075} = 74.87891$

m. $\dfrac{1 - (1.025)^{-30}}{0.025} = \dfrac{1 - 0.4767426}{0.025} = 20.93029$

EXERCISE 2.2

Answers to the odd-numbered problems are at the end of the book.
Simplify each of the following.

1. $a^2 \times a^3$
2. $(x^6)(x^{-4})$
3. $b^{10} \div b^6$
4. $h^7 \div h^{-4}$
5. $(1 + i)^4 \times (1 + i)^9$
6. $(1 + i) \times (1 + i)^n$
7. $(x^4)^7$
8. $(y^3)^3$
9. $(t^6)^{1/3}$
10. $(n^{0.5})^8$
11. $\dfrac{(x^5)(x^6)}{x^9}$
12. $\dfrac{(x^5)^6}{x^9}$
13. $[2(1 + i)]^2$
14. $\left(\dfrac{1 + i}{3i}\right)^3$
•15. $\dfrac{4r^5t^6}{(2r^2t)^3}$
•16. $\dfrac{(-r^3)(2r)^4}{(2r^{-2})^2}$
•17. $\left(\dfrac{3a^3b^2}{a - b}\right)^4$
•18. $\left(\dfrac{3}{2x^2}\right)^2\left(\dfrac{6x^3}{5^2}\right)\left(-\dfrac{x}{5}\right)^{-1}$
•19. $\dfrac{(-2y)^3(x^4)^{-2}}{(x^{-2})^2(4y)^2}$
•20. $\dfrac{[(x^{1/3})(x^{2/3})x]^{3/2}}{(8x^3)^{2/3}}$

Evaluate each of the following expressions to six significant figures.

21. $8^{4/3}$
22. $-27^{2/3}$
23. $7^{3/2}$
24. $5^{-3/4}$
25. $(0.001)^{-2}$
26. $0.893^{-1/2}$
27. $(1.0085)^5(1.0085)^3$
28. $(1.005)^3(1.005)^{-6}$

29. $\sqrt[3]{1.03}$

30. $\sqrt[6]{1.05}$

•31. $(4^4)(3^{-3})\left(-\dfrac{3}{4}\right)^3$

•32. $\left[\left(-\dfrac{3}{4}\right)^2\right]^{-2}$

•33. $\left(\dfrac{2}{3}\right)^3\left(-\dfrac{3}{2}\right)^2\left(-\dfrac{3}{2}\right)^{-3}$

•34. $\left(-\dfrac{2}{3}\right)^3 \div \left(\dfrac{3}{2}\right)^{-2}$

35. $\dfrac{1.03^{16} - 1}{0.03}$

36. $\dfrac{(1.008\overline{3})^{30} - 1}{0.008\overline{3}}$

•37. $\dfrac{1 - 1.0225^{-20}}{0.0225}$

•38. $\dfrac{1 - (1.00\overline{6})^{-32}}{0.00\overline{6}}$

39. $(1 + 0.0275)^{1/3}$

40. $(1 + 0.055)^{1/6} - 1$

2.3 SOLVING A LINEAR EQUATION

DEFINITIONS An **equation** is a statement of the equality of two algebraic expressions. A large majority of the applications and problems encountered in this book will result in an equation containing a single variable or unknown. The discussion in this chapter is confined to equations with one variable; Chapter 5 will include a category of equations having two variables.

If the variable is raised only to the first power, the equation is said to be **linear.** If the variable appears with an exponent other than 1, or it appears as part of a mathematical function, the equation is **nonlinear.**

A particular numerical value for the variable that makes the two sides of the equation equal is a **root** or solution of the equation. A linear equation in one variable has only one root; a nonlinear equation may have more than one root. The process of determining the root or roots of the equation is called *solving the equation.*

■ EXAMPLE 2.3A   EXAMPLES OF LINEAR AND NONLINEAR EQUATIONS

a. $3x - 7 = 5 - 9x$ is a linear equation.

b. $x^2 - x = 12$ is a nonlinear equation because of the x^2 term.

c. $\$150(1 + i)^4 = \$219.62$ is a nonlinear equation because of the presence of terms in i^4, i^3, and i^2 when $(1 + i)^4$ is expanded.

d. $2^x = 32$ is nonlinear in x because x is an exponent.   ■

SOLVING LINEAR EQUATIONS IN ONE VARIABLE   The solution procedure involves a series of three steps:

1. Separate like terms, leaving terms containing the variable on one side of the equation and the remaining terms on the other side of the equation.
2. Combine the like terms on each side of the equation.
3. Obtain the root by dividing both sides of the equation by the numerical coefficient of the variable.

Tip

An important principle to keep in mind while manipulating an equation is that both sides of the equation must be treated in exactly the same way in order to preserve the equality.

To obey the preceding tip, the same terms must be added to or subtracted from both sides in the first step.[2] Both sides must be multiplied or divided by the same quantity in the third step. Once the root has been calculated, its accuracy can be verified by substituting its value in the original equation. The root is correct (and is said to *satisfy* the equation) if the numerical values of both sides of the equation are equal.

■ EXAMPLE 2.3B   *SOLVING LINEAR EQUATIONS IN ONE VARIABLE*

Solve the following equations and verify the solutions.

a.

$$8x - 11 = 5x + 4$$

$8x - 11 - 5x = 5x + 4 - 5x$	Subtract $5x$ from both sides to have terms in x on the left side.
$3x - 11 = 4$	
$3x - 11 + 11 = 4 + 11$	Add 11 to both sides to have numerical terms on the right side.
$3x = 15$	
$\dfrac{3x}{3} = \dfrac{15}{3}$	Divide both sides by the numerical coefficient of x.
$x = 5$	

Verification:

Left-hand side (LHS) $= 8x - 11$ Right-hand side (RHS) $= 5x + 4$
$\qquad\qquad\qquad\qquad\quad = 8(5) - 11$ $\qquad\qquad\qquad\qquad\qquad\quad = 5(5) + 4$
$\qquad\qquad\qquad\qquad\quad = 29$ $\qquad\qquad\qquad\qquad\qquad\quad\ = 29$

Since LHS $=$ RHS, $x = 5$ is the root or solution.

b.

$0.5x - 0.75 + 7x = 3x + 1.5$	
$0.5x + 7x - 3x = 1.5 + 0.75$	Transpose $3x$ to the LHS and -0.75 to the RHS, and change their signs.
$4.5x = 2.25$	
$x = \dfrac{2.25}{4.5}$	Divide both sides by the numerical coefficient of x.
$= 0.5$	

Verification:

LHS $= 0.5(0.5) - 0.75 + 7(0.5) = 0.25 - 0.75 + 3.5 = 3.0$
RHS $= 3(0.5) + 1.5 = 1.5 + 1.5 = 3.0$
Since LHS $=$ RHS, $x = 0.5$ is the solution.

c.
$$\frac{x}{1 + 0.11 \times \frac{75}{365}} + 2x\left(1 + 0.11 \times \frac{92}{365}\right) = \$1150.96$$

This is a linear equation, but the numerical coefficients of x are now "messy." The basic procedure for solving the equation is the same as for parts *a* and *b*, except for a preliminary step: the numerical coefficient in each term should first be reduced to its decimal equivalent value.

---

[2]Adding a term to or subtracting a term from both sides of the equation is equivalent to the more efficient procedure of transferring or "transposing" a term from one side to the other with a change of sign.

$$\frac{x}{1.0226027} + 2x\,(1.0277260) = \$1150.96$$

$$0.9778969x + 2.0554521x = \$1150.96$$

$$3.0333489x = \$1150.96$$

$$x = \frac{\$1150.96}{3.0333489}$$

$$= \$379.44$$

Verification:

$$\text{LHS} = \frac{\$379.44}{1 + 0.11 \times \frac{75}{365}} + 2(\$379.44)\left(1 + 0.11 \times \frac{92}{365}\right)$$

$$= \frac{\$379.44}{1.0226027} + 2(\$379.44)(1.0277260)$$

$$= \$371.05 + \$779.92$$

$$= \$1150.97$$

$$= \text{RHS}$$

The \$0.01 difference between the LHS and the RHS arises from rounding the solution $x = \$379.4354$ to the nearest cent and then using the rounded value for the verification. ∎

EXERCISE 2.3

Answers to the odd-numbered problems are at the end of the book.

Solve the following equations. The solutions to problems 13 to 18 should be accurate to six figures.

1. $10a + 10 = 12 + 9a$

2. $29 - 4y = 2y - 7$

3. $0.5(x - 3) = 20$

4. $\frac{1}{3}(x - 2) = 4$

5. $y = 192 + 0.04y$

6. $x - 0.025x = 341.25$

7. $12x - 4(2x - 1) = 6(x + 1) - 3$

8. $3y - 4 = 3(y + 6) - 2(y + 3)$

9. $8 - 0.5(x + 3) = 0.25(x - 1)$

10. $5(2 - c) = 10(2c - 4) - 6(3c + 1)$

11. $3.1t + 145 = 10 + 7.6t$

12. $1.25y - 20.5 = 0.5y - 11.5$

•13. $\dfrac{x}{1.1^2} + 2x(1.1)^3 = \$1000$

•14. $\dfrac{3x}{1.025^6} + x(1.025)^8 = \$2641.35$

•15. $\dfrac{2x}{1.03^7} + x + x(1.03^{10}) = \$1000 + \dfrac{\$2000}{1.03^4}$

•16. $x(1.05)^3 + \$1000 + \dfrac{x}{1.05^7} = \dfrac{\$5000}{1.05^2}$

•17. $x\left(1 + 0.095 \times \dfrac{84}{365}\right) + \dfrac{2x}{1 + 0.095 \times \frac{106}{365}} = \$1160.20$

•18. $\dfrac{x}{1 + 0.115 \times \frac{78}{365}} + 3x\left(1 + 0.115 \times \dfrac{121}{365}\right) = 1000\left(1 + 0.115 \times \dfrac{43}{365}\right)$

2.4 SOLVING WORD PROBLEMS

In the preceding section, we reviewed the procedure for solving a *given* linear equation in one unknown. With practice, solving a given equation can become a mechanical procedure that follows a fairly routine series of steps. But *practical* applications of mathematics rarely arise in this way. Instead, a situation is presented to us in a more informal descriptive manner. We must deduce mathematical relationships from the given information and from our broader knowledge of general concepts and principles.

It is a large step to progress from just solving a *given* equation to *creating* an equation from a word problem *and then* solving it. The second stage is usually the easier and more routine part of solving a word problem. The first stage—the construction of an algebraic equation from the given information—cannot be reduced to a simple prescription or recipe. We can, however, outline a general procedure for solving word problems.

A GENERAL APPROACH TO SOLVING PROBLEMS

If you are having difficulty with a problem, systematically work through the following five steps:

Step 1: Read the entire problem to gain a sense of the topic involved and what is being asked. For example, you might find that the problem involves a loan repayment and that you are asked to find the size of the monthly payment.

Step 2: On a second reading, *extract and label the given data. Identify the unknown quantity and specify its symbol. Draw and label a diagram if appropriate.* There are standard symbols for many quantities. These should be used to label numerical values as they are extracted. Otherwise, use one or two words to identify each numerical value. Specify the symbol being used to represent the unknown. Diagrams are particularly useful in problems involving multiple payments over a period of time.

Step 3: Identify the principle, concept, or idea that can be used to construct a word equation. This may be a fundamental principle of broad application, or it may be a unique relationship stated or implied in the problem itself. It provides a basis for writing a word equation tailored to the particular problem. An example of a word equation is

$$\text{Profit} = \text{Revenues} - \text{Expenses}$$

Step 4: Convert the word equation to an algebraic equation and substitute the values identified in step 2. Replace the words and phrases in the word equation with algebraic expressions or numerical values. All too often, students begin their solution at this stage and attempt to immediately write the algebraic equation, bypassing steps 2 and 3. Their thinking is often muddled because they have not first clearly identified the idea or concept that is to be expressed in mathematical form. Mistakes are frequently made in trying to do too many steps at once. In all but the simplest of problems, you are strongly urged to consciously use this five-step procedure.

Step 5: Solve the equation and write a concluding statement that directly responds to the question asked.

Steps for Solving Word Problems:

1. Read the entire problem.
2. Extract and label the data. Identify the unknown quantity and specify its symbol. Draw and label a diagram if appropriate.
3. Identify the principle, concept, or idea that can be used to construct a word equation relating the given data to the unknown quantity.
4. Convert the word equation to an algebraic equation and substitute the values identified in step 2.
5. Solve the equation.

Trap

Some common tendencies on the part of students attempting a multiple-step word problem are:

* To write down too little when summarizing and organizing the given data, drawing diagrams, and presenting the solution.
* To try to mentally juggle too much information (since too little is written down in an organized manner).
* To try to mentally visualize all the steps to the solution before starting to develop the solution on paper.
* To attempt to solve the problem in a mighty leap instead of a series of smaller steps.

The result is frequently a blank worksheet and the feeling, "I just can't seem to get started on this problem!" It often turns out that a student has difficulty "getting started" because he or she is trying to get "half finished" by accomplishing too much in the initial step.

Trap

Being able to "follow" problem solutions presented in this text and in your classes does not necessarily mean that you understand the concepts and techniques adequately. A substantially deeper understanding is required to *create* a solution than to *follow* the steps in someone else's solution. The keys to gaining a higher level of comprehension are to:

* Keep current with assigned readings and problems.
* Make a serious attempt to solve many problems on your own.

Remember that you can learn more from a problem with which you have difficulty than from a problem you do correctly on the first attempt. The "sticking points" identify gaps in your understanding and flaws in your reasoning. Use the resources available to you—your instructor, the campus math tutorial centre, your textbook, your classmates, and so on—to remedy them.

The following examples illustrate the steps in solving a word problem.

■ EXAMPLE 2.4A

A retailer reduced his prices by 15% for a fall sale. What was the original price of an item on sale at $123.25?

☑ SOLUTION

Step 1: Read the problem. (This step is assumed hereafter.)

Step 2: Extract and label the data. Identify the unknown and define its symbol.

Discount rate = 15%   Sale price = $123.25
Let *P* represent the original price.

Step 3: Identify the idea that connects the data with the unknown. Write the word equation.

Sale price = Regular price − Price reduction
= Regular price − (Discount rate × Regular price)

Step 4: Convert the word equation to an algebraic equation.

$$\$123.25 = P - 0.15P$$

Step 5: Solve the equation.

$$\$123.25 = 0.85P$$
$$P = \frac{\$123.25}{0.85} = \$145.00$$

The original price of the item was $145.00   ■

■ EXAMPLE 2.4B

A manufacturing plant has in its inventory 1800 type A gaskets and 2560 type B gaskets, with a combined value of $12,234. If a type A gasket costs 50 cents less than three times the cost of a type B gasket, what is the unit cost of each type of gasket?

☑ SOLUTION

Step 2: Number of type A = 1800   Number of type B = 2560
Total value = $12,234
Cost of type A = 3(Cost of type B) − 50 cents
Let *b* represent the cost, in dollars, of a type B gasket.

Step 3: Total cost = (Quantity of A × Cost of A) + (Quantity of B × Cost of B)

Step 4: $12,234 = 1800(3b − $0.50) + 2560b

Step 5: $12,234 = 5400b − $900 + 2560b
$13,134 = 7960b
$$b = \frac{\$13,134}{7960} = \$1.65$$

The cost of a type B gasket is $1.65, and the cost of a type A gasket is 3($1.65) − $0.50 = $4.45.   ■

■ EXAMPLE 2.4C

Tom, Dick, and Harry formed a business partnership. Whenever additional capital is required, their agreement requires Dick to contribute 50% more than Tom, and Harry to contribute three-fifths as much as Dick. If an injection of $5000 is required, how much should each one contribute?

☑ SOLUTION

All three partners' contributions are initially unknown. However, if any one partner's contribution is known, the other two can be calculated using the relative sizes provided. Therefore, the solution may be set up in terms of a single variable.

Step 2: Dick = 1.5(Tom), Harry = ⅗(Dick)
Capital required = $5000
With interrelated quantities such as these, the quantity chosen as the solution variable should be the one in terms of which the others can most easily be expressed. Since Harry's contribution is in terms of Dick's, and Dick's contribution is in terms of Tom's, Tom's contribution should be the variable. Let T = the amount of Tom's contribution.

Step 3: Sum of the three contributions = $5000

Step 4: $T + 1.5T + ⅗(\text{Dick's contribution}) = \$5000$
$$T + 1.5T + ⅗(1.5T) = \$5000$$

Step 5: $T + 1.5T + 0.9T = \$5000$
$$3.4T = \$5000$$
$$T = \frac{\$5000}{3.4} = \$1470.59$$

Tom should contribute $1470.59, Dick should contribute 1.5($1470.59) = $2205.88, and Harry should contribute ⅗($2205.88) = $1323.53. ∎

EXERCISE 2.4

Answers to the odd-numbered problems are at the end of the book.

1. The current consumer price index of 134.4 represents an increase of one-fourteenth of the value of the index 1 year ago. What was the index 1 year ago?

2. The retail price of a pair of skis is $295.20. This includes a markup of four-fifths of the wholesale cost. What is the wholesale cost?

3. The price tags in Annie's Flower Shop include the 7% Goods and Services Tax (GST). How much GST will she report for a plant sold at $39.95?

4. A stockbroker's commission on a transaction is 2.5% of the first $5000 of the value of the transaction and 1.5% of the remainder. What was the amount of a transaction that generated a total commission of $227?

5. A caterer has the following price structure for banquets. The first 20 meals are charged the basic price per meal. The next 20 meals are discounted by $2 each and all additional meals are each reduced by $3. If the total cost for 73 meals comes to $810, what is the basic price per meal?

•6. A firm received a bill from its accountant for $1655, representing a total of 41 "billable" hours of the Certified General Accountant (CGA) and her accounting technician for conducting the firm's audit. If the CGA charges her time at $60 per hour and the technician's time at $25 per hour, how many hours did each work on the audit?

•7. For developing a roll of 36-exposure film, Green's One-Hour Photos charges $2 less than 1½ times the $9.50 charge for developing a 24-exposure roll. The total charge on a batch of 24 rolls came to $288.50. How many rolls of each type were developed?

•8. A $12,000 performance bonus is to be divided between two store managers. The manager of store A is to receive $1500 less than twice the bonus paid to the manager of store B. How much should each manager be paid?

•9. Joan and Sue have agreed to form a partnership. For the original capital investment of $34,000, Sue agrees to contribute $2000 more than three-fifths of Joan's investment. How much will each invest in the partnership?

•10. The annual net income of the S&R partnership is to be distributed so that Sven receives $10,000 less than 140% of Robert's share. If the past year's net income was $88,880, what amount should have been allocated to each?

•11. It takes 20 minutes of machine time to manufacture product X and 30 minutes of machine time to manufacture product Y. If the machine operated 47 hours last week to produce a combined total of 120 units of the two products, how many units of Y were manufactured?

•12. The tickets for a hockey game cost $9.50 for the red section and $12.75 for the blue section. If 4460 tickets were sold for a total of $46,725, how many seats were sold in each section?

••13. Mr. Parker structured his will so that each of his four children will receive half as much from the proceeds of his estate as his wife, and each of 13 grandchildren will receive one-third as much as each child. After his death, $759,000 remains after expenses and taxes for distribution among his heirs. How much will each child and grandchild receive?

••14. To coordinate production in a three-stage manufacturing process, stage B must be assigned 60% more workers than stage A. Stage C requires three-quarters as many workers as stage B. How should the foreman allocate 114 workers among the three stages?

••15. Fred has centralized the purchasing and record-keeping functions for his three pharmacies in a single office. The annual costs of the office are allocated to the three stores. The Hillside store is charged $1000 less than twice the charge to the Barnett store. The Westside store is charged $2000 more than the Hillside store. What is the charge to the Westside store if the cost of operating the central office for a year is $27,600?

••16. The "dump" from a parking meter contained 36 fewer dimes than twice the number of quarters, and 17 more loonies than half the number of dimes. If the total amount was $123, how many coins were in the meter?

••17. José works in a toy manufacturing plant. The wooden toy he fabricates requires three steps: cutting, assembly, and painting. Assembly takes 2 minutes longer than half the cutting time, and painting requires half a minute longer than half the assembly time. How long does each step require if José made 72 units in 42 hours of work?

2.5 PERCENT CHANGE

When a quantity changes over a period of time, it is common to compare the change to the initial value. This is usually done by calculating the change as a *percentage* of the initial value. That is,

$$\text{Percent change} = \frac{\text{Final value} - \text{Initial value}}{\text{Initial value}} \times 100\%$$

We can write a more compact formula if we define the following symbols:

$$V_i = \text{Initial (or beginning or original or old) value}$$
$$V_f = \text{Final (or ending or new) value}$$
$$\%c = \text{Percent change}$$

Then

Percent Change

$$\%c = \frac{V_f - V_i}{V_i} \times 100\%$$

(2–1)

> **Tip**
>
> The order of the final value and initial value in the numerator is important: it determines the sign of the percent change. If a quantity decreases in size, its percent change will be negative.

To illustrate a point on language, consider the example of a company whose sales declined from $4 million in year 1 to $3 million in year 2. The percent change in sales is

$$\frac{\text{Year 2 sales} - \text{Year 1 sales}}{\text{Year 1 sales}} \times 100\% = \frac{\$3 \text{ million} - \$4 \text{ million}}{\$4 \text{ million}} \times 100\%$$

$$= \frac{-1}{4} \times 100\%$$

$$= -25\%$$

We can say either "the sales changed by –25%" or "the sales decreased by 25%" from year 1 to year 2. The direction of the change may be indicated either by an algebraic sign or by a descriptive word such as rose, fell, increased, or decreased. However, it would be redundant and confusing to say that "the sales decreased by –25%."

■ EXAMPLE 2.5A   CALCULATING THE PERCENT CHANGE

The share price of Klondike Resources rose from $2 on January 1, 1995, to $4 on December 31, 1995. It fell back to $2 by December 31, 1996. Calculate the percent change in share price for each of the years 1995 and 1996, and for the entire 2-year period.

✓ SOLUTION

$$\%c \text{ in } 1995 = \frac{\text{Dec. 31, 1995, price} - \text{Jan. 1, 1995, price}}{\text{Jan. 1, 1995, price}} \times 100\%$$

$$= \frac{\$4 - \$2}{\$2} \times 100\%$$

$$= 100\%$$

Similarly,

$$\%c \text{ in } 1996 = \frac{\$2 - \$4}{\$4} \times 100\% = -50\%$$

$$\text{Overall } \%c = \frac{\$2 - \$2}{\$2} \times 100\% = 0\%$$

The share price increased by 100% in 1995 and then decreased by 50% in 1996. For the entire two-year period, there was no net price change.   ■

> **Trap**
>
> As the preceding example demonstrates, the net percent change for a series of intervals cannot be obtained simply by adding the individual percent changes in successive intervals. The reason is that the base for the percent change calculation is different in each interval.

Note that when a quantity doubles, the percent change is 100%. If it triples, the percent change is 200%, and so on.

■ **EXAMPLE 2.5B** *CALCULATING THE PERCENT CHANGE IN A PERCENTAGE*

A chartered bank is raising the interest rate on its Visa card from 14% to 16%. What will be the percent increase in the interest charges on a given balance?

✓ SOLUTION

The interest charges will increase proportionately with the rise in the interest rate. The interest rate change must be calculated in relative terms [using formula (2−1)], not in absolute terms (16% − 14% = 2%). Therefore, the percent change in interest charges will be

$$\%c = \frac{V_f - V_i}{V_i} \times 100\% = \frac{16\% - 14\%}{14\%} \times 100\% = \frac{2}{14} \times 100\% = 14.29\% \quad ■$$

CALCULATING V_i OR V_f WHEN %c IS KNOWN Sometimes the percent change and either the initial value or the final value are known. To calculate the remaining unknown, formula (2−1) should be rearranged to isolate the unknown variable. After multiplying both sides by $\frac{V_i}{100\%}$, we obtain

$$\left(\frac{\%c}{100\%}\right)V_i = V_f - V_i$$

Note that $\frac{\%c}{100\%}$ is just the decimal equivalent of %c. Substituting

$$c = \text{the decimal equivalent of } \%c$$

and transposing V_i to the left side give

$$V_i + cV_i = V_f$$

Therefore, if c and V_i are known, V_f may be calculated using

$$V_f = V_i (1 + c) \qquad (2-1a)$$

Dividing both sides by (1 + c) gives the version of formula (2−1) appropriate for calculating V_i when c and V_f are known.

$$V_i = \frac{V_f}{1 + c} \qquad (2-1b)$$

Keep in mind that the three formulas designated (2−1), (2−1a), and (2−1b) are just three versions of the *same* mathematical relationship. Given any one of them, the other two may be derived merely by rearranging the given equation.[3]

> **Tip**
> Whenever the percent change represents a decrease, a negative value must be substituted in formulas (2−1a) and (2−1b) for c, the decimal equivalent of the percent change.

■ **EXAMPLE 2.5C** *CALCULATING V_i GIVEN V_f AND %c*

What amount when increased by 230% equals $495?

---

[3]Where equivalent versions of the same formula are mentioned, only one of them will be emphasized in a formula box. This prevents an unnecessary and potentially confusing proliferation of formulas. It also encourages us to understand a fundamental relationship well enough to be able to adapt it to a wide range of applications.

☑ SOLUTION

We are given $\%c = 230\%$ and $V_f = \$495$. Note that the decimal equivalent of $\%c$ is $c = 2.3$. Two solutions are presented. The first is based on a version of formula (2−1). The second is a more intuitive algebraic approach working from first principles.

Method 1: Substituting in formula (2−1*b*).

$$\text{Initial amount, } V_i = \frac{V_f}{1 + c} = \frac{\$495}{1 + 2.3} = \$150$$

Method 2: Formulating and solving an algebraic equation.

Let x represent the initial amount. Express in mathematics the fact that the initial amount (x) increased by 230% (add $2.3x$) equals $495. That is,

$$x + 2.3x = \$495$$
$$3.3x = \$495$$
$$x = \frac{\$495}{3.3} = \$150$$

Therefore, $150 increased by 230% equals $495.   ∎

■ EXAMPLE 2.5D   *CALCULATING V_f GIVEN V_i AND $\%c$*

How much is $9550 decreased by 0.75%?

☑ SOLUTION

The initial amount is $9550, and we need to calculate the final amount after a decrease of 0.75% ($c = -0.0075$). As in the previous example, two solutions are presented.

Method 1: Substituting in formula (2−1*a*).

Final amount, $V_f = V_i (1 + c) = \$9550[1 + (-0.0075)] = \$9550(0.9925) = \$9478.38$

Method 2: Formulating and solving an algebraic equation.

Let x represent the final amount. The initial amount ($9550) decreased by 0.75% of the initial amount (subtract $0.0075 \times \$9550$) equals the final amount (x). That is,

$$\$9550 - 0.0075 \times \$9550 = x$$
$$x = \$9550 - \$71.625 = \$9478.38$$

$9550 decreased by 0.75% is $9478.38.   ∎

■ EXAMPLE 2.5E   *CALCULATING V_i GIVEN V_f AND $\%c$*

For the fiscal year just completed, a company had sales of $157,500. This represents a 5% increase over the prior year. What were the sales in the prior year?[4]

☑ SOLUTION

We are given the "final" sales and need to calculate the "initial" sales.

---

[4]It is tempting but incorrect to reason that the prior year's sales must be 100% − 5% = 95% of $157,500 (which is $149,625). The 5% increase in sales means that

Most recent year's sales = 105% of (Prior year's sales)

rather than

Prior year's sales = 95% of (Most recent year's sales)

Method 1: Substituting in formula (2−1*b*).

$$\text{Prior year's sales, } V_i = \frac{V_f}{1 + c} = \frac{\$157{,}500}{1 + 0.05} = \$150{,}000$$

Method 2: Formulating and solving an algebraic equation.
Let *x* represent the prior year's sales. The most recent year's sales ($157,500) represent the prior year's sales (*x*) plus a 5% increase (0.05*x*). That is,

$$\$157{,}500 = x + 0.05x = 1.05x$$

Then

$$x = \frac{\$157{,}500}{1.05} = \$150{,}000$$

The sales in the prior year totalled $150,000.   ■

EXERCISE 2.5

Answers to the odd-numbered problems are at the end of the book.
Calculate the missing value for problems 1 through 12.

Calculate dollar amounts in problems 1 to 37 accurate to the cent, and percent amounts throughout accurate to three significant figures.

Problem	Initial value	Final value	Percent change
1	$95	$100	?
2	$100	$95	?
3	35 kg	135 kg	?
4	135 kg	35 kg	?
5	0.11	0.13	?
6	0.095	0.085	?
7	$134.39	?	−12
8	112 g	?	112
9	26.3 cm	?	300
10	0.043	?	−30
11	?	$75	200
12	?	$75	−50

13. $100 is what percent more than $90?

14. $100 is what percent less than $110?

15. What amount when increased by 25% equals $100?

16. What sum of money when increased by 7% equals $52.43?

17. $75 is 75% more than what amount?

18. How much is $56 increased by 65%?

19. $754.30 is what percent less than $759.00?

20. 77,787 is what percent more than 77,400?

21. How much is $75 increased by 75%?

22. $100 is 10% less than what number?

23. What amount when reduced by 20% equals $100?

24. What amount when reduced by 25% equals $50?

25. What amount after a reduction of 16.$\overline{6}$% equals $549?

26. How much is $900 decreased by 90%?

27. How much is $102 decreased by 2%?

28. How much is $102 decreased by 100%?

29. $750 is what percent more than $250?

30. $250 is what percent less than $750?

31. How much is $10,000 increased by ¾%?

32. How much is $1045 decreased by 0.5%?

33. What amount when increased by 150% equals $575?

34. What amount after being increased by 210% equals $465?

35. How much is $150 increased by 150%?

36. How much is $10 increased by 900%?

37. The total cost of a coat, including GST and provincial sales tax totalling 15% of the ticket price, was $148.35. What was the ticket price of the coat?

38. The population of Lotustown increased by 24% over the last 5 years. If the current population is 109,500, what was the population 5 years ago?

39. Becker Tools sold 32,400 hammers at an average price of $7.55 in 1996 and 27,450 hammers at an average price of $7.75 in 1997. What was the percent change from 1996 to 1997 in:

    a. The number of hammers sold?

    b. The average selling price?

    c. The revenue from the sale of hammers?

40. An investor purchased shares of Digger Resources at a price of $0.55 per share. One year later, the shares traded at $1.55, but they fell back to $0.75 by the end of the second year after the date of purchase. Calculate the percent change in the share price:

    a. In the first year

    b. In the second year

    c. Over both years

41. The current quarter's sales of 599 units represent a 6% increase over the previous quarter. How many units were sold in the previous quarter?

42. In a 35%-off sale, the reduced price of a dress was $122.85. What was the regular price of the dress?

43. The price of the common shares of Campbell Mines fell by $1 in 1995 and by the same amount in 1996. If the share price was $4 at the end of 1995, what was the percent change in share price each year?

44. A wholesaler sells to retailers at a 27% discount from the suggested retail price. What is the suggested retail price of an item that costs the retailer $100?

45. The revenues of Petrocorp in the most recent quarter were $4.360 million, which represents an 18% increase over revenues for the same quarter in the previous year. What is the dollar amount of the year-to-year increase in revenues?

46. A commission salesperson's rate of commission increased from 7% to 8% of net sales. What will be the percent increase in commission income if the volume of sales is unchanged?

47. A chartered bank dropped the interest rate it charges on consumer loans from 10.5% to 9.75%. What is the percent reduction in the dollar amount of interest on these loans?

48. During the past 15 years the price of milk has increased by 280%. If the price is now $1.30 per litre, what is the dollar amount of the price increase per litre?

49. The price of the shares of Nadir Explorations Ltd. fell by 76% in the past year, to the current price of $0.45 per share. In dollars and cents, how much did the price of each share drop in the past year?

50. A piece of machinery has depreciated by 55% of its original purchase price during the past 4 years, to the current value of $24,300. What is the dollar amount of the total depreciation during the last 4 years?

•51. The owner listed a property for 140% more than she paid for it 12 years ago. After receiving no offers during the first 3 months of market exposure, she dropped the list price by 10%, to $172,800. What was the original price that the owner paid for the property?

•52. A car dealer normally lists new cars at 22% above cost. A demonstrator model was sold for $17,568 after a 10% reduction from the list price. What amount did the dealer pay for this car?

2.6 APPLICATION: RATE OF RETURN ON INVESTMENT

In general, the financial benefit or *return* from an investment during a holding period has two components.

- The investor may receive some cash from the investment without selling any portion of the investment. This is the **income** component. Examples are interest from savings accounts, bonds, or loans receivable; dividends from common and preferred shares; and rent from real estate.

- The market value of the investment itself may increase or decrease over time. This is the *capital* component. An increase in market value is called a **capital gain.** That is,

    Capital gain = End-of-period value − Beginning-of-period value

    If the value of an investment declines during the holding period, the capital gain will be negative, indicating a **capital loss.**

The **total return** from an investment during a holding period is the sum of the income and capital gain components.

    Total return (on investment) = Income + Capital gain

The following symbols enable us to express the two preceding word equations algebraically:

V_i = Value of the investment at the beginning of the period (initial value)
V_f = Value of the investment at the end of the period (final value)
Y = Income
G = Capital gain
ROI = Total return (on investment)

In terms of these symbols, we have

$$G = V_f - V_i$$
$$ROI = Y + G$$
$$= Y + V_f - V_i$$

The usual measure of the performance of an investment during a period is the **rate of return on investment**—the total return expressed as a percentage of the investment's value at the start of the period. Stated mathematically,

$$\text{Rate of return on investment} = \frac{\text{Total return on investment}}{\text{Beginning-of-period value}} \times 100\%$$

That is,

$$\%ROI = \frac{ROI}{V_i} \times 100\%$$

The %ROI has an income component and a capital gain component. These two components are more evident if we substitute $ROI = Y + G$ in the definition of %ROI.

$$\%ROI = \frac{Y + G}{V_i} \times 100\%$$

$$= \frac{Y}{V_i} \times 100\% + \frac{G}{V_i} \times 100\%$$

The first term on the right-hand side is defined as the income yield, %Y. That is, the **income yield** is the income for the period expressed as a percentage of the initial value of the investment. The second term is the **percent capital gain,** %G. It is the capital gain expressed as a percentage of the initial investment. In terms of these new symbols, we can rewrite the preceding equation for the rate of return on investment as

Rate of Total Return

$$\%ROI = \%Y + \%G \tag{2–2}$$

where

$$\%Y = \frac{Y}{V_i} \times 100\% \qquad \text{and} \qquad \%G = \frac{G}{V_i} \times 100\%$$

The rate of total return may therefore be viewed as the sum of two components—the income yield and the percent capital gain. Note that the rate of total return will be negative if the magnitude of a capital loss exceeds the income yield. The investor's wealth will be reduced if an investment produces a negative %ROI.

Trap

Life in the world of finance is made a little confusing by two common practices.

- The term "yield" is generally understood to mean "annual yield." In other words, a 1-year holding period is usually assumed.

- Specific names are frequently used for certain types of income yield. For example, shareholders refer to a stock's "dividend yield" while bond investors speak of a bond's "current yield."

Also be aware that terms are often used with less precision in everyday life than in academic textbooks. Those "in the know" understand the meanings of potentially ambiguous terms from the context and prevailing practice. For example, when the holding period of an investment is less than 1 year, a quoted rate of return might refer to a return calculated from formula (2–2). On the other hand, it might be an equivalent annualized rate of return calculated using the method described in Appendix 9A. When in doubt, ask for clarification of ambiguous terms.

■ EXAMPLE 2.6A CALCULATING INVESTMENT RETURNS WHEN THERE IS A CAPITAL LOSS

Richard purchased 1000 shares of Canadian Petroleum Ltd. on February 17 at $14.50 per share. On March 31 and June 30 dividends of $0.25 per share were paid. On the following September 1, the shares were trading on the stock market at $13.25. For the February 17 to September 1 holding period, what was Richard's:

a. Income yield (dividend yield)?

b. Percent capital gain?

c. Rate of return on investment?

d. Total return (in dollars)?

☑ SOLUTION

The calculation of percent rates in parts a, b, and c may be done in terms of one share or in terms of all 1000 shares. Since all 1000 shares are identical, the income yield, percent capital gain, and rate of return on a single share will be the same as on any number of the shares. However, the dollar amount of the total return (part d) depends on the actual number of shares owned.

a. The income per share is two dividends of $0.25 each.

$$\text{Income yield, } \%Y = \frac{Y}{V_i} \times 100\% = \frac{2(\$0.25)}{\$14.50} \times 100\% = 3.448\%$$

b.
$$\text{Percent capital gain, } \%G = \frac{V_f - V_i}{V_i} \times 100\%$$
$$= \frac{\$13.25 - \$14.50}{\$14.50} \times 100\%$$
$$= -8.621\%$$

That is, Richard has a capital loss[5] of 8.62% up to September 1.

c.
$$\text{Rate of return on investment, } \%ROI = \%Y + \%G$$
$$= 3.448\% - 8.621\%$$
$$= -5.173\%$$

d.
$$\text{Total return} = \text{Rate of return on investment} \times \text{Initial investment}$$
$$= -0.05173 \times 1000 (\$14.50)$$
$$= -\$750.09$$

The negative total return means that, up to September 1, Richard has *lost* $750.09 on the investment (inclusive of dividends received).

The total return could also have been obtained by simply adding the total dividend income to the total capital gain. That is,

$$\text{Total return} = 1000(\$0.50) + 1000(\$13.25 - \$14.50)$$
$$= \$500.00 + 1000(-\$1.25)$$
$$= -\$750.00$$

The $0.09 difference between the two answers arises from rounding the rate of return on investment to four figures. Consequently, we can be assured of only three-figure accuracy in the total return. Therefore, the last reliable figure in $750.09 is in the dollar position. ■

---

[5]Since Richard still owns the shares, the capital loss is sometimes described in everyday language as a "paper" loss. The proper terminology in finance and accounting is "unrealized capital loss." When an investment is actually sold for less than the initial investment, it becomes a "realized capital loss." A capital gain may similarly be described as "unrealized" or "realized."

■ **EXAMPLE 2.6B**   *CALCULATING INVESTMENT RETURNS WHEN THERE ARE EXPENSES*

One year ago, Pierre purchased a rental house for $129,000. During the year, he has collected $825 per month in rent but paid out $1563 for property taxes and a total of $1149 for maintenance and other expenses. The current appraised value of the property is $135,000. What is Pierre's:

a. Income yield?

b. Percent capital gain?

c. Rate of return on investment?

d. Total return?

☑ **SOLUTION**

When there are expenses associated with an income-earning investment, the net income (after expenses) should be used in calculating the income yield.

a. Net income for the year, $Y = 12(\$825) - \$1563 - \$1149 = \$7188$

Income yield, $\%Y = \dfrac{\$7188}{\$129,000} \times 100\% = 5.572\%$

b. Percent capital gain, $\%G = \dfrac{\$135,000 - \$129,000}{\$129,000} \times 100\% = 4.651\%$

c. Rate of return on investment, $\%ROI = 5.572\% + 4.651\% = 10.223\%$

d. Total return, $ROI = Y + G = \$7188 + \$6000 = \$13,188$ ■

■ **EXAMPLE 2.6C**   *CALCULATING V_f GIVEN V_i, Y, AND $\%ROI$*

An investor is prepared to buy common shares of Eagle Brewing Ltd. at the current share price of $11.50 if he can expect at least a 15% rate of total return over the next year. Assuming that the company repeats its $0.40 per share dividend of the past year, what will the share price have to be 1 year from now for the minimum return objective to be achieved?

☑ **SOLUTION**

The mathematical relationships developed in this section were set up to calculate $\%Y$, $\%G$, and $\%ROI$. For this example and similar problems, you will need to rearrange one or more of the basic relationships to solve for an unknown quantity on the right-hand side.

We are given $V_i = \$11.50$, $\%ROI = 15\%$, and $Y = \$0.40$. We want to determine what V_f must be one year from now to make $\%ROI = 15\%$. The $\%G$ must make up the difference between $\%ROI = 15\%$ and the expected $\%Y$. Thus,

$$\%G = \%ROI - \%Y = 15\% - \dfrac{\$0.40}{\$11.50} \times 100\% = 15\% - 3.478\% = 11.522\%$$

Since the share price must increase by 11.522% from $V_i = \$11.50$, we can use version (2−1a) of the percent change formula to solve for V_f. Substituting the decimal equivalent of $\%G$ for c,

$$V_f = V_i (1+c) = \$11.50(1 + 0.11522) = \$12.83$$

The share price must be at $12.83 1 year from now for the investor to achieve the minimum desired rate of total return (15%).   ■

EXERCISE 2.6

Answers to the odd-numbered problems are at the end of the book.

Calculate the missing quantities in problems 1 through 16. Calculate yields and rates of return to 0.01%. Calculate dollar amounts correct to the cent.

Problem	Initial value	Income	Final value	Income yield	Percent cap. gain	Rate of return on investment
1	$ 100	$ 10	$ 110	?	?	?
2	100	10	90	?	?	?
3	90	10	86	?	?	?
4	135	0	151	?	?	?
5	1367	141	1141	?	?	?
6	879	280	1539	?	?	?
7	2500	200	0	?	?	?
8	1380	250	2875	?	?	?
•9	2000	?	2200	5%	?	?
•10	4300	?	3950	?	?	−5%
•11	3730	250	?	?	?	5%
•12	1800	50	?	?	150%	?
•13	?	?	1800	?	−40%	−30%
•14	?	100	?	5%	15%	?
•15	1600	?	?	8%	?	0%
••16	?	150	2700	?	?	80%

17. Jack bought 10 Government of Canada bonds in a new series issued at $1000 each. Each bond pays $47.50 interest 6 months after issue and every 6 months thereafter. One year later Jack sold the bonds for $1034 each. For the entire year, what was his:

    a. Income yield (interest yield)?

    b. Percent capital gain?

    c. Total return (in dollars)?

    d. Rate of return on investment?

18. Bernice purchased 15 bonds from her broker for $1025 each. These bonds each pay semiannual interest of $42.50. Over the next 1½ years, the price of the bonds declined to $980 because of rising interest rates. Over the entire 18-month period, what was her:

    a. Percent capital gain?

    b. Total return (in dollars)?

    c. Rate of return on investment?

19. Jeff purchased some Mitel $2.00 preferred shares on the Toronto Stock Exchange (TSE) for $13.50. The shares pay a quarterly dividend of $0.50. Nine months later the shares were trading at $15.25. What was Jeff's rate of return on investment for the 9-month period?

20. Lily bought 200 shares in Maritime Trust Co. at $29.37 just before it paid a dividend of $0.60 per share. Rumours of loan losses sent the shares tumbling to $24.50 only 3 months after she purchased them. For these 3 months, what was her:

    a. Percent capital gain?

    b. Rate of return on investment?

•21. Mr. Furlan purchased an older home for $75,000 and spent another $15,000 on repairs and renovations soon after the purchase date. Two months after the purchase, he rented the house for $700 per month net of all expenses except property taxes, which came to $1550 for the year.

a. If he "flips" the property one year after purchase for $110,000, what will be his rate of return on investment for the year? Treat the initial repairs and renovations as part of the original investment.

b. What is his rate of return on investment if a 6% real estate commission on the sale of the house is deducted from the sale proceeds?

•22. Mrs. Wilson bought a duplex a year ago for $160,000, using $40,000 of her own money and $120,000 borrowed from the bank on a mortgage loan. She collected monthly rents of $575 and $550 from the two units, net of all expenses except property taxes of $2173 and interest on the mortgage, which for the year was $10,127. If the property has increased in value to $170,000, what is the rate of return, net of expenses, on her personal investment of $40,000 for the year?

•23. One year ago, Morgan invested $5000 to purchase 400 units of a mutual fund. He has just noted in the *Financial Post* that the fund's rate of return on investment for the year was 22% and that the current price of a unit is $13.75. What amount did the fund distribute as income per unit during the year?

•24. Lori can buy Government of Canada bonds paying $50 interest every 6 months for $1090. What market price of the bonds 1 year from now would produce a rate of return on investment of 12%?

•25. As a consequence of rising interest rates, Union Gas bonds have produced a capital loss of 8% and a rate of return on investment of 1% for the past year. If the bonds pay interest of $52.50 every 6 months, what is their current price?

••26. The *Globe and Mail* Report on Business reports that the shares of Compact Computers have produced a return on investment of 55% in the last year. The shares paid a dividend of $0.72 per share in the past year, and they currently trade at $37.50. What was the price of the shares one year ago?

••27. Ed can buy a duplex for $230,000. He would borrow 60% of the funds and pay interest charges totalling $12,400 on the mortgage during the next year. Repairs and maintenance would average $300 per month, and annual property taxes would be $2400. If property values increase 6% in the next year, what monthly rental income would the property have to generate for Ed to earn a 15% rate of return on his equity?

2.7 APPLICATION: COMPOUNDING PERCENT CHANGES AND RATES OF RETURN

When percent changes are given for each of a series of consecutive time periods, the percent change for any period is understood to apply to the amount at the end of the *preceding* period. For example, suppose sales in 1995 and 1996 increased by 10% and 12%, respectively, from 1994 sales of $100,000. Obviously, we use 1994 sales as the base for calculating the 10% increase in 1995.

1995 sales, $V_f = V_i (1 + c) =$ 1994 sales $(1 + c) = \$100,000(1.1) = \$110,000$

But the base for applying the 12% increase in 1996 is understood to be 1995 sales, not 1994 sales. That is,

1996 sales, $V_f = V_i (1 + c) =$ 1995 sales $(1 + c) = \$110,000(1.12) = \$123,200$

When we adjust the base for the next period to the cumulative amount that exists after the preceding period, we are **compounding** the percent changes. The effect of compounding is that each percent change builds on all previous changes as well as on the original amount. In the present example, the 1996 sales increase of $13,200 results from both a 12% increase to the original 1994 sales of $100,000 ($12,000) and a 12% increase to the 1995 increase of $10,000 ($1200).

Rates of return on an investment for a series of periods may be viewed as percent changes in the value of the investment in successive periods. They too are calculated and quoted with the understanding that they are to be compounded.

One approach to the mathematics of compounding is to work through the calculations period by period as we just did in calculating the 1996 sales figure. But if only the combined or cumulative result of a series of percent changes is desired, there is a more efficient method. To derive a formula for this approach, let

c_1 = the decimal equivalent of the percent change in period 1
c_2 = the decimal equivalent of the percent change in period 2

.

.

.

c_n = the decimal equivalent of the percent change in period n

Amount after one period, $V_{f1} = V_i (1 + c_1)$

This amount now becomes the beginning amount or base for the second period, so that

Amount after two periods, $V_{f2} = V_{f1}(1+c_2) = V_i (1+c_1)(1+c_2)$

Similarly,

Amount after three periods, $V_{f3} = V_{f2}(1+c_3) = V_i (1+c_1)(1+c_2)(1+c_3)$

The pattern for subsequent periods is now apparent and we can anticipate the formula for the final amount, V_{fn}, after all n periods.

Compounding Percent Changes

$$V_{fn} = V_i (1 + c_1)(1 + c_2)(1 + c_3)\cdots(1 + c_n)$$ (2–3)

Tip

When the percent changes in some of the periods are the same, the $(1 + c)$ factors for those periods may be combined in a power. For example, if the percent change or rate of return for any three periods is 8%, their $(1 + c)$ factors may be combined as $(1.03)^3$. (The factors so combined need not be from consecutive periods.) Some further efficiency is gained in the computation by using a calculator's $\boxed{y^x}$ function to calculate the power.

Trap

The cumulative effect of n compounded changes $c_1, c_2, c_3, \cdots c_n$ is not the same as a single change of $c_1 + c_2 + c_3 + \cdots + c_n$. For example, two (compounded) 10% increases produce a larger final value than a single 20% increase.

When a quantity decreases in a period, the percent change is negative. The corresponding negative decimal equivalent must be substituted for c. You may prefer the following version of formula (2–3) for handling cases involving decreases. Let

d_t = the *magnitude* of the decrease or discount in period number t

For any period in which there is a decrease, we can replace $(1 + c)$ by $(1 - d)$. A modified version of formula (2–3) might look like

$$V_{fn} = V_i\,(1+c_1)(1-d_2)(1-d_3)(1+c_4) \cdots (1+c_{n-1})(1-d_n)$$

where there are increases in periods 1, 4, ..., $n - 1$ and decreases in periods 2, 3, ..., n. In this formulation, strictly positive values are substituted for all c's and d's. Decreases are handled by the negative signs preceding the d's.

■ EXAMPLE 2.7A   CALCULATING A CUMULATIVE PERCENT CHANGE AND THE ABSOLUTE AMOUNT OF ONE OF THE CHANGES

Prices in the British Columbia roe herring fishery are highly volatile. The percent changes in four consecutive years were 40%, –25%, 20%, and –20%. If the price at the beginning of the first year was $1100 per tonne,

a. What was the cumulative percent change in price over the 4-year period?

b. What was the dollar amount of the price change in the third year?

☑ SOLUTION

a. *Method 1:* Calculate the final price and then the overall percent change. We will use the version of formula (2–3) with c replaced by $-d$ in any year in which the price decreases. The price at the end of the 4-year period was

$$\begin{aligned}
V_{f4} &= V_i\,(1+c_1)(1-d_2)(1+c_3)(1-d_4) \\
&= \$1100(1+0.4)(1-0.25)(1+0.2)(1-0.2) \\
&= \$1100(1.4)(0.75)(1.2)(0.8) \\
&= \$1108.80 \text{ per tonne}
\end{aligned}$$

Using formula (2–1) to calculate the overall percent change,

$$\%c = \frac{V_{f4} - V_i}{V_i} \times 100\% = \frac{\$1108.80 - \$1100}{\$1100} \times 100\% = 0.80\%$$

Method 2: Calculate the single equivalent rate of change. Part a can, in fact, be answered without knowledge of V_i. If we do not substitute the value for V_i in formula (2–3), we obtain

$$\begin{aligned}
V_{f4} &= V_i\,(1+c_1)(1-d_2)(1+c_3)(1-d_4) \\
&= V_i\,(1+0.4)(1-0.25)(1+0.2)(1-0.2) \\
&= V_i\,(1.4)(0.75)(1.2)(0.8) \\
&= V_i\,(1.008) \\
&= V_i\,(1+0.008)
\end{aligned}$$

The amount by which the coefficient of V_i differs from 1 is the decimal equivalent of the overall percent change. Thus $c = 0.008$ and $\%c = 0.8\%$. That is, the cumulative percent change over the 4-year period was 0.8%.

b. The dollar amount of the price change in the third year was

(Price in year 2) × (Decimal equivalent change for year 3)
$$= V_i\,(1+c_1)(1-d_2) \times c_3$$
$$= \$1100(1+0.4)(1-0.25) \times 0.2$$
$$= \$231 \text{ per tonne}$$

The price increased by $231 per tonne in year 3. ∎

■ EXAMPLE 2.7B   *CALCULATING ONE OF A SERIES OF PERCENT CHANGES*

Teri invested in a stock that doubled in the first year and rose another 50% in the second year. Now at the end of the third year, Teri is surprised to discover that the stock's price is up only 80% from her purchase price. By what percentage did the stock's price change in the third year?

☑ SOLUTION

The compounding of the three annual percent changes must produce an 80% increase. Hence,

$$V_f = V_i\,(1+c) = V_i\,(1+0.8)$$

But in terms of the annual percent changes,

$$V_f = V_i\,(1+c_1)(1+c_2)(1+c_3)$$
$$= V_i\,(1+1.00)(1+0.50)(1+c_3)$$
$$= V_i\,(3.00)(1+c_3)$$

For the same final value in both cases, we require

$$V_i\,(3)(1+c_3) = V_i\,(1.8)$$
$$1+c_3 = \frac{1.8}{3} = 0.60$$
$$c_3 = 0.60 - 1 = -0.40$$

The stock's price declined 40% in year 3. ∎

■ EXAMPLE 2.7C   *EVALUATING THE MEDIUM-TERM PERFORMANCE OF A MUTUAL FUND*

The following table lists the annual rates of return on investment from the Investors Canadian Equity Fund for 1989 to 1993 inclusive. Comparable figures are also given for the Toronto Stock Exchange (TSE) Total Return Index.[6] Calculate the percent differential by which the fund outperformed or underperformed the TSE index over the 5-year period.

Fund name	1989 return	1990 return	1991 return	1992 return	1993 return
Investors Canadian Equity Fund	15.4%	−7.7%	14.6%	6.5%	31.2%
TSE Total Return Index	21.4	−14.8	12.0	−1.4	32.6

[6]The TSE Total Return Index measures the performance of a portfolio of the common shares of the 300 largest Canadian companies trading on the Toronto Stock Exchange. The index is often used as a benchmark for evaluating the performance of other portfolios of Canadian stocks.

☑ SOLUTION

For the Investors Canadian Equity Fund,

$$
\begin{aligned}
V_{f5} &= V_i\,(1+c_1)(1+c_2)(1+c_3)(1+c_4)(1+c_5) \\
&= V_i\,(1+0.154)(1-0.077)(1+0.146)(1+0.065)(1+0.312) \\
&= V_i\,(1.7056)
\end{aligned}
$$

For the TSE Total Return Index,

$$
\begin{aligned}
V_{f5} &= V_i\,(1+c_1)(1+c_2)(1+c_3)(1+c_4)(1+c_5) \\
&= V_i\,(1+0.214)(1-0.148)(1+0.120)(1-0.014)(1+0.326) \\
&= V_i\,(1.5146)
\end{aligned}
$$

The coefficients of V_i indicate that the Investors Fund increased 70.56% in value, while the benchmark TSE Total Return Index was up just 51.46% for the five-year period. Therefore, the Investors Fund outperformed the TSE index by 70.56% − 51.46% = 19.10%.   ∎

Point of Interest

The Ups and Downs of Percent Returns on Investment

When positive and negative rates of return are compounded, the outcome can be surprising. As a rather extreme example, suppose an investment had a 100% gain in one year and a 50% loss in the next year. We might be tempted to estimate the overall two-year gain as 100% − 50% = 50%. On more careful thought, we note that the investment doubled in the first year and then "halved" in the second year. Consequently, the value of the investment was back at its initial value—the actual two-year return was 0%!

Consider other examples of the asymmetrical effects of compounding positive and negative percent returns.

- A 50% gain one year can be wiped out by a 33.3% loss in the next year.

- To offset a 50% loss in one period requires a 100% gain in the next period.

- To recover from a 25% loss, you would need a 33.3% gain.

- *Two* consecutive gains of 61.8% can be wiped out by a *single* 61.8% loss.

Any of the preceding cases can be verified using formula (2–3). The general conclusion we can draw is that the negative impact of a given percent loss (on the final value of an investment) is more significant than the positive impact of the same magnitude of percent gain. A 50% loss will erase a 100% gain but a 50% gain can be wiped out by a loss of only 33.3%.[7]

These asymmetries are most pronounced for large magnitudes of gains and losses. While the sizes of gains and losses used in the preceding examples would be very unusual in most areas of investing, they are not unrealistic for investments in emerging market mutual funds, speculative stocks such as those trading on the Vancouver Stock Exchange, and investments in derivative securities (such as "options" and "futures"). For example, the average rate of return on emerging market mutual funds available from Canadian mutual fund managers in the years 1993, 1994, and 1995 was 70.3%, −10.6%, and −10.0%, respectively.

(*continued*)

---

[7]These examples also demonstrate that the *arithmetic* average of a series of rates of return on investment can give a very misleading indication of the overall long-term performance of an investment. Using the example of a 100% gain followed by a 50% loss in the second year, the average annual rate of return was [100% + (−50%)]/2 = 25%. But the overall rate of return for the two-year holding period was 0%! In this case the average annual return is worse than useless—it is misleading. In Chapter 9, you will learn how to calculate the equivalent annual rate of return that would produce the same overall growth as a series of unequal rates of return.

(*concluded*)

The overall three-year gain was only 37% (whereas the sum of the three returns is almost 50%.)

Knowledgeable investors should not make the mistake of adding the rates of return for successive intervals in order to obtain the rate of return for the entire holding period. However, this type of error was unwittingly impounded in the formula used by the Vancouver Stock Exchange (VSE) from January 1982 until December 1986 to calculate its stock price index.

When it created the index, the VSE introduced the innovative approach of recalculating the index after *every* transaction involving a stock that was included in the index. The formula used to calculate the value of the index was

$$I_2 = I_1 \left[1 + \frac{1}{N}\left(\frac{P_2 - P_1}{P_1}\right) \right]$$

where

P_2 = the price of the company's shares in the current transaction,
P_1 = the price of the same company's shares in the previous transaction,
N = the number of companies whose shares are included in the index,
I_1 = the previously calculated value of the index, and
I_2 = the new value of the index.

To illustrate the bias that the formula placed on the index, consider the following scenario. Suppose there are $N = 100$ companies and the index stands at $I_1 = 1000$. In two successive transactions, the price of the shares of *one* of the companies first rises from $1.00 to $1.25 and then falls back to $1.00 in the second transaction. In the meantime, the prices of shares in the other 99 companies did not change. Therefore, there are no net stock price changes as a result of the two transactions—all stocks are at the same prices as before the transactions when the index stood at 1000. By any logic, the index should be back at 1000 after the

two transactions. Let us calculate the index after each transaction.

For the first transaction, $P_2 = \$1.25$ and $P_1 = \$1.00$. The stock price index after this transaction is

$$I_2 = 1000 \left[1 + \frac{1}{100}\left(\frac{\$1.25 - \$1.00}{\$1.00}\right) \right]$$
$$= 1002.50$$

For the second transaction, $I_1 = 1002.50$, $P_2 = \$1.00$, and $P_1 = \$1.25$. The index after the transaction is

$$I_2 = 1002.50 \left[1 + \frac{1}{100}\left(\frac{\$1.00 - \$1.25}{\$1.25}\right) \right]$$
$$= 1002.50 \, (1 - 0.0020)$$
$$= 1000.495$$

Hence, the index is *higher* after the two transactions! This ought to mean that stocks have a higher *average* price than when the index was at 1000. But they clearly have the same average price if all that happens is a "round-trip" price excursion by one of the stocks in the index.

In another scenario where a stock's price first drops and then returns to its original price, the index would again end at a *higher* level after the two transactions. Any "round-trip" price excursion, whether "up-then-down" or "down-then-up," pushes this index higher. Consequently, the index had a "built-in" *upward* bias that caused it to rise too much when a share's price increased and decline too little when a share's price dropped.

A 1987 study[8] estimated that the cumulative effect of the bias over the years 1982 to 1986 was to make the index almost twice as high as it should have been at the end of the period. To this day, there has been no indication that the VSE was ever aware of the problem. (Note that this index bias flaw is an entirely different matter than the truncation problem discussed in the Point of Interest in Chapter 1.) The VSE changed to a different index formula at the beginning of 1987 for entirely unrelated reasons.

[8]F. E. Jerome, "The Suitability of the Vancouver Stock Exchange Index as a Performance Standard for Equally Weighted Stock Portfolios," *MBA Thesis* (Faculty of Commerce, University of British Columbia, 1987).

EXERCISE 2.7

Answers to the odd-numbered problems are at the end of the book.

1. A union agreed to a collective agreement providing for wage increases of 5%, 3%, and 1% in successive years of a 3-year contract. What wage will an employee earning $15 per hour at the beginning be making at the end of the term of the contract?

2. Inflation rates as determined from the consumer price index (CPI) were 4.8%, 5.6%, 1.5%, 1.8%, and 0.3% for the years 1990 to 1994, respectively. What would a basket of goods, representative of the CPI and costing $1000 at the beginning of 1990, cost at the end of 1994?

3. Inflation rates as determined by the CPI were 10.2%, 12.4%, 10.9%, 5.7%, and 4.4% for the years 1980 to 1984, respectively. What would a wage of $10 per hour at the beginning of 1980 have had to become by the end of 1984 in order to keep pace with the CPI?

4. The value of assets under the management of Canadian mutual funds increased by 6.2%, 100.3%, 34.8%, 70.4%, and 11.1% in successive years from 1990 to 1994, respectively.

   a. What was the overall percent change in mutual fund assets during the five years?

   b. If Canadian mutual fund assets totalled $67.3 billion at the end of 1992, what was the total at the end of 1994?

5. The price of Bionex Inc. shares rose by 25% in each of 2 successive years. If they began the 2-year period at $12 per share, what was the percent increase in price over the entire 2 years?

6. The price of Biomed Corp. shares also began the same 2-year period at $12 but fell 25% in each of the years. What was their overall percent decline in price?

7. What rate of return in the second year of an investment will wipe out a 50% gain in the first year?

8. What rate of return in the second year of an investment will nullify a 25% return on investment in the first year?

9. What rate of return in the second year of an investment is required to break even after a 50% loss in the first year?

10. What rate of return in the second year of an investment is required to break even after a rate of return on investment of –20% in the first year?

11. After 2 consecutive years of 10% rates of return, what rate of return in the third year will produce a cumulative gain of 30%?

12. After two consecutive years of 10% losses, what rate of return in the third year will produce a cumulative loss of 30%?

13. Annual sales of microcomputers increased by 35%, 40%, 30%, and 25% in 4 consecutive years. What was the cumulative percent increase in microcomputer sales over the 4 years?

14. A car manufacturer announced a 3-year "downsizing" program whereby the number of employees will be reduced by 10%, 6%, and 5% in years 1, 2, and 3, respectively. How many of the current 6750 positions will be eliminated over the next 3 years?

15. A provincial government presented a budget that projects (compound) annual cuts in the provincial deficit of 20%, 40%, and 60%.

   a. What will the deficit be after the third year if it starts the first year at $1 billion?

   b. What is the dollar amount of the projected decrease in the third year?

16. The price of newsprint rose in four steps from $400 per tonne in January 1994 to $740 per tonne in September 1995. If the first three increases were 10%, 22%, and 18%, what was the fourth increase:

    a. in percent?   b. in dollars?

17. Calculate and compare the cumulative percent increase for the following two cases:

    a. 10 years of constant 10% annual increases.

    b. 5 years of 20% increases and five years of 0% increases.

    Note that in both cases the average of the annual increases is 10%.

18. Victor cannot find the original record of his purchase 4 years ago of units of the Phillips, Hager and North U.S. Equity fund. The current statement from the fund shows that the total current value of the units is $47,567. From a mutual fund database, Victor found that the rates of return on investment in the fund for years 1 to 4 have been 15.4%, 24.3%, 32.1%, and −3.3%, respectively.

    a. What was Victor's original investment in the fund?

    b. What was the dollar increase in the value of the fund in year 3?

19. A major automobile manufacturer recently announced that it will make cuts of 9%, 7%, and 5% to its current work force of 18,750 over the next 3 years. If the cuts proceed as indicated:

    a. How many employees will the company have at the end of the 3 years?

    b. How many employees will be cut in the second year?

20. A town in a rural area of Saskatchewan reported population declines of 4.5%, 6.7%, and 10.5% for the three successive 5-year periods 1979 to 1983, 1984 to 1988, and 1989 to 1993. If the population at the end of 1993 was 7450:

    a. How many lived in the town at the beginning of 1979?

    b. What was the population loss in each of the 5-year periods?

•21. The number of jobs in the British Columbia forest industry fell by 22% from the beginning of 1990 to the end of 1992. If the decline was 5.3% in 1990 and 10.4% in 1991, what was the percent decrease in 1992?

•22. The index used to measure the overall performance of the Japanese stock market is the Nikkei Stock Average. On three successive days—March 31, April 1, and April 2, 1992— the average fell 1.64%, 3.95%, and 1.59%, to close at 18,286.

    a. What was the Nikkei average at the opening of the market on March 31?

    b. How many points did it lose on April 1?

23. In three successive years the price of the common shares of Abysmal Resources Ltd. fell 35%, 55%, and 80%, ending the third year at 75 cents.

    a. What was the share price at the beginning of the 3-year skid?

    b. How much (in dollars and cents) did the share price drop in the third year?

The following table lists the rates of return on investment for each of 5 years on each of 5 well-known Canadian equity mutual funds. Comparable figures are also given for the TSE Total Return Index. For each fund, calculate:

- The percent increase (over the entire 5 years) in the value of an investment made at the beginning of 1990.
- The percentage differential by which the fund outperformed or underperformed the TSE Index over the 5-year period.

Problem	Fund name	1990 return	1991 return	1992 return	1993 return	1994 return
24.	Altamira Equity	−1.8%	34.5%	30.2%	46.6%	1.7%
25.	AGF Canadian Equity	−20.0	9.2	2.6	30.4	−8.4
26.	Industrial Growth	−15.0	2.3	−4.8	46.9	−1.4
27.	Royfund Equity	−14.7	1.7	2.8	31.8	−0.4
28.	Trimark Canadian	−12.1	20.2	6.6	37.8	2.5
	TSE Total Return Index	−14.8	12.0	−1.4	32.6	−0.2

29. In most circumstances, the Ontario Securities Act requires a publicly traded company to provide shareholders with a 5-year performance summary in the annual report. The summary must show what a $100 investment in the company's common shares at the *beginning* of the most recent 5 fiscal years would have been worth at the end of *each* fiscal year. For the same years, the company must also show for comparison the value of $100 growing at the same rate as the TSE Total Return Index.

The following table presents the annual rate of return on investment for common shares of Campbell Resources Inc. and the TSE Total Return Index for 1990 to 1994. The quoted rates of return assume that any dividends paid were reinvested in more shares of the same security. Complete the table by calculating the value at each year's end of $100 invested at the beginning of 1990.

	1990 return	1991 return	1992 return	1993 return	1994 return
Campbell Resources shares	−52.2%	8.2%	−20.5%	232.1%	−11.8%
Value of $100 investment	?	?	?	?	?
TSE Total Return Index	−14.8%	12.0%	−1.4%	32.6%	−0.2%
Value of $100 investment	?	?	?	?	?

APPENDIX: INTERPRETATION OF NEGATIVE AND FRACTIONAL EXPONENTS

INTERPRETATION OF a^0

Clearly,

$$\frac{a^n}{a^n} = 1$$

But rule 2 gives

$$\frac{a^n}{a^n} = a^{n-n} = a^0$$

Therefore, we must interpret $a^0 = 1$

INTERPRETATION OF a^{-n}

Using the previous result that

$$a^0 = 1$$

we can write

$$\frac{a^0}{a^n} = \frac{1}{a^n}$$

But rule 2 gives

$$\frac{a^0}{a^n} = a^{0-n} = a^{-n}$$

For consistency, we must define

$$a^{-n} = \frac{1}{a^n}$$

INTERPRETATION OF $a^{1/n}$

Rule 1 gives

$$a^{1/2} \times a^{1/2} = a^{1/2+1/2} = a^1 = a$$

Similarly,

$$a^{1/3} \times a^{1/3} \times a^{1/3} = a^{1/3+1/3+1/3} = a^1 = a$$

However, we already know that

$$\sqrt{a} \times \sqrt{a} = a$$

and that

$$\sqrt[3]{a} \times \sqrt[3]{a} \times \sqrt[3]{a} = a$$

Therefore, consistency requires that

$$a^{1/2} = \sqrt{a}$$

and that

$$a^{1/3} = \sqrt[3]{a}$$

Generalizing from these particular results, we can conclude that

$$a^{1/n} = \sqrt[n]{a}$$

INTERPRETATION OF $a^{m/n}$

Building on rule 3 and the interpretation of $a^{1/n}$, we can write

$$a^{m/n} = (a^{1/n})^m = (\sqrt[n]{a})^m$$

and also

$$a^{m/n} = (a^m)^{1/n} = \sqrt[n]{a^m}$$

These results for the interpretation of zero, negative, and fractional exponents are summarized below.

Zero, Negative, and Fractional Exponents:

$$a^0 = 1 \qquad a^{-n} = \frac{1}{a^n} \qquad a^{1/n} = \sqrt[n]{a}$$

$$a^{m/n} = (\sqrt[n]{a})^m = \sqrt[n]{a^m}$$

REVIEW PROBLEMS

Answers to the odd-numbered review problems are at the end of the book.

•1. Simplify and collect the like terms.

a. $\dfrac{9y - 7}{3} - 2.3(y - 2)$ b. $P\left(1 + 0.095 \times \dfrac{135}{365}\right) + \dfrac{2P}{1 + 0.095 \times \frac{75}{365}}$

2. Multiply and collect the like terms:

$$4(3a + 2b)(2b - a) - 5a(2a - b)$$

3. Evaluate each of the following expressions for the given values of the variables. The answer should be accurate to the cent.

a. $L(1 - d_1)(1 - d_2)(1 - d_3)$ for $L = \$340$, $d_1 = 0.15$, $d_2 = 0.08$, $d_3 = 0.05$

b. $\dfrac{R}{i}\left[1 - \dfrac{1}{(1+i)^n}\right]$ for $R = \$575$, $i = 0.085$, $n = 3$

•4. Simplify:

$$\left(-\frac{2x^2}{3}\right)^{-2}\left(\frac{5^2}{6x^3}\right)\left(-\frac{15}{x^5}\right)^{-1}$$

5. Evaluate the following expressions to six significant figures.

a. $\dfrac{(1.00\overline{6})^{240} - 1}{0.00\overline{6}}$ b. $(1 + 0.025)^{1/3} - 1$

•6. Solve the following equations for x to five-figure accuracy and verify the solution.

a. $\dfrac{x}{1.08^3} + \dfrac{x}{2}(1.08)^4 = \$850$

b. $2x\left(1 + 0.085 \times \dfrac{77}{365}\right) + \dfrac{x}{1 + 0.085 \times \frac{132}{365}} = \$1565.70$

7. Solve each of the following:

a. What amount is 17.5% more than $29.43?

b. What amount reduced by 80% leaves $100?

c. What amount reduced by 15% equals $100?

d. What is $47.50 increased by 320%?

e. What amount when decreased by 62% equals $213.56?

f. What amount when increased by 125% equals $787.50?

g. What amount is 30% less than $300?

8. Yellowknife Mining sold 34,300 oz of gold in 1992 at an average price of $320 per ounce. Production was down to 23,750 oz in 1993 because of a strike of the miners, but the average price obtained was $360 per ounce. What was the percent change from 1992 to 1993 in:

a. The amount of gold produced?

b. The average selling price per ounce?

c. The revenue from the sale of gold?

9. Two years ago the shares of Diamond Strike Resources traded at a price of $3.40 per share. One year later the shares were at $11.50, but then they declined in value by 35% during the subsequent year. Calculate:

a. The percent change in the share price during the first year.

b. The current share price.

10. Barry recently sold some stock after holding it for 2 years. The stock rose 150% in price during the first year but fell 40% in the second year. At what price did he buy the stock if he sold it for $24 per share?

11. Christos bought 15 Government of Canada bonds in a new series issued at $1000 each. Each bond pays $40 interest 6 months after issue and every 6 months thereafter. One year later he sold the bonds for $980 each. For the entire year what was his:

    a. Interest yield?

    b. Percent capital gain?

    c. Total return in dollars?

    d. Rate of return on investment?

12. From the end of 1990 to the end of 1995, the number of cellular phones doubled. If during the first 4 years, the year-to-year increases were 18%, 17%, 14%, and 13%, what was the percent change in the last year?

13. A company's annual report states that the prices of its common shares had changes of 23%, 10%, –15%, and 5% during the past 4 fiscal years. If the shares were trading at $30.50 just after the 5% increase in the most recently completed year,

    a. What was the price of the shares at the beginning of the 4-year period?

    b. How much (in dollars and cents) did the price decline in the third year?

•14. The profits from a partnership are to be distributed so that Grace receives 20% more than Marie, and Mary Anne receives five-eighths as much as Grace. How much should each receive from a total distribution of $36,000?

•15. Rory invested a total of $7800 in shares of ABC Ltd. and XYZ Inc. One year later the investment was worth $9310, after the shares of ABC had increased in value by 15% and the shares of XYZ were up 25%. How much did Rory invest in each company?

••16. Phillips Furniture allocates its overhead costs among three departments. Appliances is charged $4000 less than 150% of the amount charged to Upholstered Furniture. Wood Furniture is allocated $5000 more than three-quarters of the amount charged to Appliances. How should overhead costs of $36,440 be allocated among the three departments?

SELF-TEST EXERCISE

Answers to the self-test problems are at the end of the book.

1. Perform the indicated multiplication and division, and combine the like terms.

    a. $6(4y - 3)(2 - 3y) - 3(5 - y)(1 + 4y)$

    • b. $\dfrac{5b - 4}{4} - \dfrac{25 - b}{1.25} + \dfrac{7}{8}b$

    • c. $\dfrac{x}{1 + 0.085 \times \frac{63}{365}} + 2x\left(1 + 0.085 \times \dfrac{151}{365}\right)$

    d. $\dfrac{96nm^2 - 72n^2m^2}{48n^2m}$

•2. Evaluate:

$$P(1 + i)^n + \dfrac{S}{1 + rt}$$

accurate to the cent for $P = \$2500$, $i = 0.1025$, $n = 2$, $S = \$1500$, $r = 0.09$, and $t = \dfrac{93}{365}$.

3. Simplify:

   a. $\dfrac{(-3x^2)^3(2x^{-2})}{6x^5}$

   • b. $\dfrac{(-2a^3)^{-2}(4b^4)^{3/2}}{(-2b^3)(0.5a)^3}$

4. Evaluate the following expressions to six significant figures.

   a. $(1.0075)^{24}$

   b. $(1.05)^{1/6} - 1$

   c. $\dfrac{(1 + 0.0075)^{36} - 1}{0.0075}$

   d. $\dfrac{1 - (1 + 0.045)^{-12}}{0.045}$

•5. Solve the following equations for x to five-figure accuracy.

   a. $\dfrac{2x}{1 + 0.13 \times \frac{92}{365}} + x\left(1 + 0.13 \times \dfrac{59}{365}\right) = \$831$

   b. $3x(1.03^5) + \dfrac{x}{1.03^3} + x = \dfrac{\$2500}{1.03^2}$

6. Albion Distributors' revenues and expenses for the fiscal year just completed were $2,347,000 and $2,189,000, respectively.

   a. If in the current year revenues rise by 10% but expense increases are held to 5%, what will be the percent increase in operating profit?

   b. If, instead, revenues decline by 10% and expenses are reduced by 5%, what will be the percent change in operating profit?

•7. Marsha and Steve bought a small house 2 years ago for $95,000, using $45,000 of personal savings and a $50,000 mortgage loan. They rented the house for $500 per month for the first year and, after a 2-month vacancy, found new tenants who paid $525 per month. Both rental rates are net of all expenses except property taxes and mortgage interest. Property taxes were $1456 in the first year and $1515 in the second year. Mortgage interest totalled $5453 in the first year and $5387 in the second. What is the rate of return on their $45,000 investment for the entire 2-year holding period if they now sell the house for $112,000 less a selling commission of 5.5%?

8. Three years ago, General Avionics announced plans to triple its annual R&D spending over the next 4 years. If R&D spending was increased by 25%, 30%, and 35% in the first 3 years, what minimum percent increase is required in the fourth year to reach the target?

•9. One thousand shares of Gonzo Software were purchased at $6.50 per share. The share price rose 110% in the first year after purchase, dropped 55% in the second year, and then dropped another 55% in the third year.

   a. What was the percent change in the price of the shares over the entire 3-year period?

   b. How much (in dollars and cents) did the share price drop in the second year?

10. The annual net income of the Todd Bros. partnership is distributed so that Ken receives $15,000 more than 80% of Hugh's share. How should a net income of $98,430 be divided between the partners?

SUMMARY OF NOTATION AND KEY FORMULAS

V_i = Initial (or beginning or original or old) value
V_f = Final (or ending or new) value
%c = Percent change
c = Decimal equivalent of the percent change

In the context of investments,

V_i = Value of the investment at the beginning of the holding period
V_f = Value of the investment at the end of the holding period
Y = Income
%Y = Income yield
G = Capital gain
%G = Percent capital gain
ROI = Total return (in dollars)
%ROI = Rate of return on investment

For compound percent changes,

V_{ft} = Final value at the end of period t
c_t = Decimal equivalent of the percent change in period t
d_t = Decimal equivalent of the percent decrease in period t

Formula (2–1) $\%c = \dfrac{V_f - V_i}{V_i} \times 100\%$

Finding the percent change in a quantity.

Formula (2–2) $\%ROI = \%Y + \%G$ where

Finding the rate of return on an investment

$\%Y = \dfrac{Y}{V_i} \times 100\%$ and $\%G = \dfrac{G}{V_i} \times 100\%$

Formula (2–3) $V_{fn} = V_i (1 + c_1)(1 + c_2)(1 + c_3) \cdots (1 + c_n)$

Finding the final value after a series of compound percent changes

---

Rules of Exponents:

1. $a^m \times a^n = a^{m+n}$ 2. $\dfrac{a^m}{a^n} = a^{m-n}$

3. $(a^m)^n = a^{m \times n}$ 4. $(ab)^n = a^n b^n$

5. $\left(\dfrac{a}{b}\right)^n = \dfrac{a^n}{b^n}$

Zero, Negative, and Fractional Exponents:

$a^0 = 1$ $a^{-n} = \dfrac{1}{a^n}$ $a^{1/n} = \sqrt[n]{a}$

$a^{m/n} = (\sqrt[n]{a})^m = \sqrt[n]{a^m}$

Steps for Solving Word Problems:

1. Read the entire problem.
2. Extract and label the data. Identify the unknown quantity and specify its symbol. Draw and label a diagram if appropriate.
3. Identify the principle, concept, or idea that can be used to construct a word equation relating the given data to the unknown quantity.

4. Convert the word equation to an algebraic equation and substitute the values identified in step 2.
5. Solve the equation.

GLOSSARY OF TERMS

Algebraic expression   A statement of the mathematical operations to be carried out on a combination of numbers and variables.

Base   In the context of powers, the quantity that is multiplied by itself in a power. In the context of percent change, the initial amount to which a percent change is applied.

Binomial   An expression containing two terms.

Capital gain   The amount by which the end-of-period value of an investment exceeds its beginning-of-period value.

Capital loss   The amount by which the beginning-of-period value of an investment exceeds its end-of-period value.

Compounding   Applying each successive percent change to the cumulative amount after the preceding percent change.

Equation   A statement of the equality of two algebraic expressions.

Exponent   The number of times that the base is multiplied by itself in a power.

Factors   The components of a term that are separated by multiplication or division signs; the components of a product or quotient.

Income   Revenue earned from an investment without selling any portion of the investment.

Income yield   An investment's income (during a holding period), expressed as a percentage of the amount invested at the beginning of the period.

Like terms   Terms having the same literal coefficient.

Linear equation   An equation in which the variable is raised only to the first power.

Literal coefficient   The nonnumerical factor in a term.

Monomial   An expression containing only one term.

Nonlinear equation   An equation in which the variable appears with an exponent other than 1, or appears as part of a mathematical function.

Numerical coefficient   The numerical factor in a term.

Percent capital gain   An investment's capital gain (during a holding period), expressed as a percentage of the amount invested at the beginning of the period.

Polynomial   An expression containing more than one term.

Power   A mathematical operation indicating the multiplication of a quantity (the base) by itself a certain number (the exponent) of times.

Rate of return on an investment   The investment's combined income and capital gain during a holding period, expressed as a percentage of the amount invested.

Root (of an equation)   A particular numerical value for the variable that makes the two sides of the equation equal.

Substitution   Assigning a numerical value to each of the algebraic symbols for the variables in an expression.

Terms   The components of an algebraic expression that are separated by addition or subtraction signs.

Total return   The sum of the income and capital gain from an investment during a holding period.

Trinomial   An expression containing three terms.

3

RATIOS AND PROPORTIONS

LEARNING OBJECTIVES

After completing this chapter, you will be able to:

- Set up and manipulate ratios
- Set up and solve proportions
- Use proportions to allocate or prorate an amount on a proportionate basis
- Use quoted exchange rates to convert funds between currencies
- Calculate the percent appreciation or depreciation of one currency relative to another, given the beginning and ending exchange rates
- Interpret and use index numbers

INTRODUCTION

Raw business data often take on greater meaning when comparisons are made between related quantities. For example, a firm's profit for a year is an important figure in itself. However, profit in relation to invested capital, to total sales, and to the prior year's profit provide useful insights into the firm's profitability, efficiency, and earnings growth. Ratios are widely used to make such comparisons. In accounting and finance, one of the main techniques used for the detailed analysis and interpretation of a firm's financial statements is known as *ratio analysis.* It is based on the premise that the relative sizes of various balance sheet and income statement figures provide key indicators of the financial strengths and weaknesses of a firm.

Ratios and proportions also arise in situations where resources, costs, profits, and other amounts must be allocated on a pro rata or proportionate basis. There are many quantities in economics and finance that are ratios in disguise. The chapter concludes with discussions of two such quantities—currency exchange rates and index numbers.

3.1 RATIOS

A **ratio** is a comparison, by division, of the relative sizes of two or more quantities. Suppose that, in 1 month, a store sells $2000 worth of product X and $1500 worth of product Y. The ratio of the sales of product X to the sales of product Y may be expressed in any of the following ways:

- Using a colon, as in "2000 : 1500" which is read "2000 to 1500."
- As a common fraction, $\frac{2000}{1500}$.
- As the decimal equivalent of the common fraction, $1.3\overline{3}$.
- As the percent equivalent of the common fraction, $133\frac{1}{3}\%$.

In the first two of these forms, the numbers appearing in the ratio are called the **terms[1] of the ratio.** Each of the terms in a ratio may be multiplied or divided by the same number to give an **equivalent ratio.** For example, both terms in the preceding ratio may be divided by 100 to give the equivalent ratio 20 : 15 or $\frac{20}{15}$. It is customary to express a ratio in its *lowest terms,* that is, as the equivalent ratio having the smallest integral values for the terms. For the example of the sales of products X and Y, the lowest terms for the ratio are 4 : 3 or $\frac{4}{3}$.

■ EXAMPLE 3.1A   *EXPRESSING A RATIO IN EQUIVALENT FORMS*

a. A hospital ward has 10 nurses caring for 60 patients. The ratio of nurses to patients can be expressed as:

10 : 60	Using the colon notation
1 : 6	Using the colon notation with the lowest terms
$\frac{1}{6}$	As a common fraction
$0.1\overline{6}$	As a decimal equivalent
$16.\overline{6}\%$	As a percent equivalent

---

[1]It is unfortunate that the word *term* has two quite different usages in basic algebra. In Chapter 2, *term* referred to a component of an algebraic expression separated from the rest of the expression by addition or subtraction signs. In this chapter, *term* refers to a component set apart by division in a ratio. The meaning of *term* must be inferred from the context in which it is used.

b. A survey of cars in a parking lot indicated that two-fifths of the cars were North American brands and one-third were Japanese brands. The ratio of North American to Japanese cars was:

$\frac{2}{5} : \frac{1}{3}$ Ratio with given terms in the colon notation

6 : 5   As an equivalent ratio obtained by multiplying both terms by 5 and by 3 to clear the terms of fractions

$\frac{6}{5}$ As a common fraction

1.2   As a decimal equivalent

120%   As a percent equivalent

c. The costs of manufacturing an item are \$150 for materials and \$225 for labour. The ratio of labour to materials costs is:

225 : 150   Ratio with the given terms in the colon notation

9 : 6   Equivalent ratio (each term divided by 25)

3 : 2   Equivalent ratio with lowest terms (after division by 3)

d. A municipal development bylaw requires that a shopping centre provide four parking spots for each 100 sq m of developed retail area. The ratio of parking spots to retail area is:

4 : 100   Ratio with the given terms in the colon notation

1 : 25   Equivalent ratio with lowest terms (after division by 4)

Even though the two values in a ratio can have differing units (parking spaces and square metres in this case), the units are often omitted when they are generally known from the context. In this case, one parking space is required for each 25 sq m of retail area.

Continued Ratios   The relative sizes of three or more quantities may be expressed as a continued ratio. A **continued ratio** is composed of three or more terms, usually written in the colon notation. If, in the earlier example, the store sold \$2500 worth of product Z in the same month, the (continued) ratio of the sales of products X, Y, and Z would be

$$2000 : 1500 : 2500 \qquad \text{or} \qquad 4 : 3 : 5$$

Reducing a Ratio to Its Lowest Terms   The terms in the original statement of a ratio may be integers, decimal numbers, or fractions. The procedure in each case for reducing the ratio to its lowest terms is summarized below. Example 3.1b presents an example of each case.

- *The terms of the ratio are all integers.* Divide every term in the ratio by factors that are common to all terms.

- *The terms of the ratio are decimal numbers.* Shift the decimal point in every term to the right by the same number of positions until all the terms are integers. Then reduce the ratio to its lowest terms, as in the previous case.

- *The terms of the ratio are fractions.* First convert one of the fractions to an integer by multiplying every term of the ratio by this term's denominator. Repeat this process on other terms until the ratio contains only integers. Then reduce the ratio to its lowest terms, as in the first case.

■ **EXAMPLE 3.1B** *REDUCING A RATIO TO ITS LOWEST TERMS*

Reduce the following ratios to their lowest terms.

a. $105 : 63 : 84$ b. $1.2 : 1.68 : 0.72$ c. $\dfrac{3}{8} : \dfrac{5}{6} : \dfrac{1}{3}$

✓ **SOLUTION**

a. $105 : 63 : 84$
   $= 35 : 21 : 28$ Each term divided by 3
   $= \ \ 5 : 3 : 4$ Each term divided by 7

b. $1.2 : 1.68 : 0.72$
   $= 120 : 168 : 72$ Decimal point moved two positions to the right
   $= \ \ 30 : 42 : 18$ Each term divided by 4
   $= \ \ \ \ 5 : 7 : 3$ Each term divided by 6

c. $\dfrac{3}{8} : \dfrac{5}{6} : \dfrac{1}{3}$

   $= \dfrac{9}{8} : \dfrac{5}{2} : 1$ Each term multiplied by 3

   $= \dfrac{9}{4} : 5 : 2$ Each term multiplied by 2

   $= 9 : 20 : 8$ Each term multiplied by 4   ■

CONVERTING A RATIO TO AN EQUIVALENT RATIO WHOSE SMALLEST TERM IS 1

There is a general preference for a ratio to be expressed in its lowest terms if these terms are relatively small integers. But the ratio

$$179 : 97 : 29$$

is already in its lowest terms and still contains rather large integers. In this situation, many people prefer to have the ratio expressed as the equivalent ratio whose *smallest* term has the value 1. In the present example, we would divide all terms by the value of the smallest term, giving

$$\dfrac{179}{29} : \dfrac{97}{29} : \dfrac{29}{29} \qquad \text{or} \qquad 6.17 : 3.34 : 1$$

where the terms have been rounded to three significant figures. The relative size of the terms is more readily seen in the latter version of the ratio.

■ **EXAMPLE 3.1C** *DETERMINING THE EQUIVALENT RATIO HAVING 1 AS THE SMALLEST TERM*

Convert each of the following ratios to the equivalent ratio having 1 as the smallest term.

a. $117 : 79 : 167$ b. $1.05 : 8.1 : 2.2$ c. $\dfrac{18}{19} : 1\frac{13}{14}$

✓ **SOLUTION**

a. $117 : 79 : 167$
   $= \dfrac{117}{79} : \dfrac{79}{79} : \dfrac{167}{79}$ Each term is divided by the smallest term, 79.
   $= 1.48 : 1 : 2.11$

b. $1.05 : 8.1 : 2.2$

$\quad = \dfrac{1.05}{1.05} : \dfrac{8.1}{1.05} : \dfrac{2.2}{1.05}$ Each term is divided by the smallest term, 1.05.

$\quad = 1 : 7.71 : 2.10$

c. $\dfrac{18}{19} : 1\frac{13}{14}$

$\quad = 0.947 : 1.929$ Convert the fractions to decimal equivalent forms.

$\quad = 1 : 2.04$ Divide by the smaller term, 0.947.   ■

Point of Interest

Ratios That Affect Your Eligibility for a Mortgage Loan

Lenders consider many factors in the loan approval process. There are qualitative factors such as the applicant's credit history, education and training, and stability of employment. Even if favourable ratings are received on these attributes, the applicant must also satisfy some additional quantitative measures before the loan can be approved. These measures take the form of ratios that provide an indication to the lender of the risk of default and the borrower's ability to repay the loan.

Suppose that Marge and Homer Sampson are applying to a bank for a $100,000 mortgage loan to be used to purchase a home priced at $140,000. Since the property will provide the security for the loan, the bank wants assurance that the value of the property will exceed the balance owing on the loan at a later date, should the Sampsons be unable to make the payments on the loan. The bank therefore calculates the

$$\begin{array}{c}\text{Loan to}\\\text{value}\\\text{ratio}\end{array} = \dfrac{\begin{array}{c}\text{The principal amount}\\\text{of the loan}\end{array}}{\begin{array}{c}\text{The lending value}\\\text{of the property}\end{array}} \times 100\%$$

The lending value is a conservative estimate of the value of the property. Banks often use the lesser of the purchase price and the value placed on the property by an independent appraiser. If the home that the Sampsons are buying is appraised at $135,000, the

$$\begin{array}{c}\text{Loan to}\\\text{value}\\\text{ratio}\end{array} = \dfrac{\$100,000}{\$135,000} \times 100\% = 74.1\%$$

The maximum loan to value ratio for loans granted by federally chartered financial institutions is set at 75%, unless the mortgage is insured. If mortgage default insurance is obtained—the Canadian Mortgage and Housing Corporation is the most common source—a maximum loan to value ratio of 90% is permitted. The Sampsons are barely under the maximum loan to value ratio for uninsured mortgages.

Lenders also want assurance that the borrowers have enough income to be able to meet all the expenditures associated with home ownership, and still have enough left over to enjoy a reasonable lifestyle. Therefore lenders calculate the gross debt service (GDS) ratio defined as

$$\begin{array}{c}\text{GDS}\\\text{ratio}\end{array} = \dfrac{\begin{array}{c}\text{Monthly payments for}\\\text{mortgage loan, property}\\\text{taxes, and heat}\end{array}}{\text{Gross monthly income}} \times 100\%$$

The GDS ratio represents the percentage of a borrower's gross income consumed by the major fixed expenditures associated with home ownership. Some lenders do not include heating costs in the numerator; other lenders include both heating costs and half of condominium common area fees, if applicable. The maximum GDS ratio is set by each lending institution and is usually in the 30% to 33% range. In order to include a second person's full income in the denominator, both individuals must be registered on the title of the property.

A mortgage lender is also concerned that a borrower be able to handle any other fixed financial commitments such as car payments, personal loan payments, and credit card payments. The lender wants to prevent

(continued)

(*concluded*)

a scenario in which, for example, a borrower misses a mortgage payment in order to make a car payment. Therefore the lender calculates the total debt service (TDS) ratio defined as

$$\frac{\text{TDS}}{\text{ratio}} = \frac{\begin{array}{c}\text{Total monthly payments}\\ \text{on mortgage, other}\\ \text{debt, taxes, and heat}\end{array}}{\text{Gross monthly income}} \times 100\%$$

There is considerable variation among lenders in determining the monthly credit card charges that are included in the numerator. Some use the loan applicant's actual monthly payment. Other lenders use 5% of the debit balance while still others take 5% of the maximum line of credit. Other obligations such as lease payments, alimony, and child support payments may be included in the numerator. The maximum TDS ratio is usually set in the 40% to 42% range. This means that lenders do not want the financial obligations that are included in the numerator to exceed this fraction of the borrower's gross income.

Remember that the loan to value ratio establishes the upper limit on the mortgage loan. Applicants can qualify for this maximum loan (or any smaller loan) only if they are also below the specified maxima for the GDS and TDS ratios. Lenders are relatively inflexible with respect to exceeding their institution's maxima for these ratios. Factors that might allow some relaxation are: a high net worth of the borrower, additional liquid collateral security, substantial RRSP/mutual fund/GIC business with the lender, or a low loan to value ratio.

EXERCISE 3.1

Answers to the odd-numbered problems are at the end of the book.

Express each of the following ratios in its lowest terms.

1. 12 : 64
2. 56 : 21
3. 45 : 15 : 30
4. 26 : 130 : 65
5. 0.08 : 0.12
6. 2.5 : 3.5 : 3
7. 0.84 : 1.4 : 1.96
8. 11.7 : 7.8 : 3.9
9. 0.24 : 0.39 : 0.15
10. 0.091 : 0.021 : 0.042
11. $\frac{1}{8} : \frac{3}{4}$
12. $\frac{4}{3} : \frac{3}{2}$
13. $\frac{3}{5} : \frac{6}{7}$
14. $\frac{11}{3} : \frac{11}{7}$
15. $1\frac{1}{4} : 1\frac{2}{3}$
16. $2\frac{1}{2} : \frac{5}{8}$
17. $4\frac{1}{8} : 2\frac{1}{5}$
18. $\frac{2}{3} : \frac{3}{4} : \frac{5}{6}$
19. $\frac{1}{15} : \frac{1}{5} : \frac{1}{10}$
20. $10\frac{1}{2} : 7 : 4\frac{1}{5}$

Express each of the following ratios as an equivalent ratio whose smallest term is 1.

21. 7.6 : 3
22. 1.41 : 8.22
23. 0.177 : 0.81
24. 0.0131 : 0.0086
25. $\frac{3}{7} : \frac{19}{17}$
26. $4\frac{3}{13} : \frac{27}{17}$
27. 77 : 23 : 41
28. 11 : 38 : 27

29. $3.5 : 5.4 : 8$

30. $0.47 : 0.15 : 0.26$

31. $\dfrac{5}{8} : \dfrac{17}{11} : \dfrac{6}{7}$

32. $5\frac{1}{2} : 3\frac{3}{4} : 8\frac{1}{3}$

Set up a ratio for each of the following problems. If the ratio cannot be reduced to an equivalent ratio in terms of small integers, then express it as a ratio of decimal equivalents with the smallest term set at 1.

33. During the last 3 months, Mako Distributing made 25% of its sales in region A, 35% in region B, and 40% in region C. What is the ratio of the sales in region A to the sales in region B to the sales in region C?

34. Don, Bob, and Ron Maloney's partnership interests in Maloney Bros. Contracting are in the ratio of their capital contributions of $78,000, $52,000, and $65,000, respectively. What is the ratio of Bob's to Ron's to Don's partnership interest?

35. Victoria Developments has obtained $3.6 million of total capital from three sources. Preferred shareholders contributed $550,000 (preferred equity), common shareholders contributed $1.2 million (common equity), and the remainder was borrowed (debt). What is the firm's ratio of debt to preferred equity to common equity?

36. The cost to manufacture a fibreglass boat consists of $2240 for materials, $3165 for direct labour, and $1325 for overhead. Express the three cost components as a ratio.

37. A provincial government budget forecasts expenditures of $1.04 billion on education, $910 million on health services, and $650 million on social services. Express the three budget items as a ratio.

3.2 PROPORTIONS

In Section 3.1 we illustrated the concept of a ratio using an example where the sales in a month of products X, Y, and Z equaled $2000, $1500, and $2500, respectively. We will extend the same example to illustrate proportions. The mathematical notation employed to concisely express the word statement

the ratio of the sales of X to the sales of Y is 4 : 3

is

Sales of X : Sales of Y $= 4 : 3$

If the variable x is used to represent a month's sales of product X and the variable y is used to represent a month's sales of product Y, a still more compact mathematical statement is

$$x : y = 4 : 3$$

This equation is an example of a proportion. In general, a **proportion** is a statement of the equality of two ratios. The language used to express or read this proportion is

"x is to y as 4 is to 3"

If mathematical operations are to be carried out on a proportion, each ratio is first converted to an equivalent fraction. In the current example, we can rewrite the proportion as the equation

$$\frac{x}{y} = \frac{4}{3}$$

The two ratios in this proportion contain two terms each—a total of four terms. If three of these four terms are known, the fourth may be calculated. As an example, suppose that the sales of product X in the next month are forecast to be $1800. What will be the sales of product Y next month if the sales of the two products maintain the same ratio? The answer to this question is found by substituting $x = \$1800$ in the equation and solving for y:

$$\frac{\$1800}{y} = \frac{4}{3}$$

In order to solve for y, first clear the equation of fractions by multiplying both sides of the equation by both denominators. This gives

$$\frac{\$1800}{y} \times 3y = \frac{4}{3} \times 3y$$

After simplifying each side, we obtain

$$\$1800 \times 3 = 4y$$

Tip

We could have immediately obtained the preceding equation from

$$\frac{\$1800}{y} = \frac{4}{3}$$

by using a shortcut known as *cross-multiplication.* This involves multiplying the numerator on each side by the denominator from the other side, as indicated below.

$$\frac{\$1800}{y} \diagtimes \frac{4}{3}$$

Solving for y,

$$y = \frac{\$1800 \times 3}{4} = \$1350$$

The projected sales of product Y for the next month are $1350.

■ EXAMPLE 3.2A   *SOLVING A PROPORTION*

Solve each of the following proportions.

a. $3 : 5 = 9 : x$

$\dfrac{3}{5} = \dfrac{9}{x}$ The colons have been replaced by division operations.

$5x\left(\dfrac{3}{5}\right) = 5x\left(\dfrac{9}{x}\right)$ Multiply both sides by both denominators.

$3x = 45$ Cross-multiplication at the second line would give this equation directly.

$x = \dfrac{45}{3} = 15$

b. $2.5 : y = 4 : 7$

$\dfrac{2.5}{y} = \dfrac{4}{7}$ Convert to fractional form.

$2.5(7) = 4y$ Cross-multiply.

$y = \dfrac{17.5}{4} = 4.375$

■

A PROPORTION COMPOSED OF CONTINUED RATIOS   The proportion expressing the relative sales of products X, Y, and Z for the given month is

$$\text{Sales of X : Sales of Y : Sales of Z} = 4 : 3 : 5$$

or

$$x : y : z = 4 : 3 : 5$$

where *x, y,* and *z* represent the monthly sales of products X, Y, and Z, respectively. This proportion is read

$$\text{"}x \text{ is to } y \text{ is to } z, \text{ as 4 is to 3 is to 5"}$$

A proportion whose ratios possess three terms implies two equations. In the present case we can write

$$\frac{x}{y} = \frac{4}{3} \qquad \text{and} \qquad \frac{y}{z} = \frac{3}{5}$$

Having two equations[2] allows us to solve problems where two of the six terms are unknown. Example 3.2b provides an illustration.

■ EXAMPLE 3.2B   *SOLVING A PROPORTION CONTAINING CONTINUED RATIOS*

Solve the following proportion for *x* and *y*.

$$2 : 5 : 3 = 7 : x : y$$

☑ SOLUTION

Based on the given proportion, we can write the following two equations.

$$\frac{2}{5} = \frac{7}{x} \qquad \text{and} \qquad \frac{5}{3} = \frac{x}{y}$$

After cross-multiplication, these equations become

$$2x = 35 \qquad \text{and} \qquad 5y = 3x$$

The first equation can immediately be solved for *x:*

$$x = \frac{35}{2} = 17.5$$

Then *y* may be obtained from the second equation after substituting *x* = 17.5:

$$5y = 3(17.5) = 52.5$$
$$y = \frac{52.5}{5} = 10.5$$

■

_____

[2]The proportion also implies a third equation,

$$\frac{x}{z} = \frac{4}{5}$$

but it does not contain any information beyond that already included in the other two equations. This third equation can, in fact, be derived from the other two. After multiplying the left side of one equation by the left side of the second, and similarly multiplying the right sides together, we obtain the equation

$$\frac{x}{y} \times \frac{y}{z} = \frac{4}{3} \times \frac{3}{5} \qquad \text{which, after simplification, gives} \qquad \frac{x}{z} = \frac{4}{5}$$

Since the proportion implies only two independent equations, we need to know the numerical value of one of the three variables, *x, y,* and *z,* in order to be able to solve for the other two.

■ **EXAMPLE 3.2c** S*OLVING A* W*ORD* P*ROBLEM* T*HAT* I*NVOLVES A* P*ROPORTION*

Betty and Lois have already invested $8960 and $6880, respectively, in their partnership. If Betty invests another $5000, what amount should Lois contribute to maintain their investments in the original ratio?

◪ **SOLUTION**

Let Lois's additional investment be represented by *x*. In the colon notation, the proportion may be written

$$x : \$5000 = \$6880 : \$8960$$

Writing the ratios as fractions,

$$\frac{x}{\$5000} = \frac{\$6880}{\$8960}$$

Therefore,

$$x = \frac{\$6880}{\$8960} \times \$5000 = \$3839.29$$

Lois should contribute $3839.29 to maintain the same ratio of investment in the partnership.   ■

■ **EXAMPLE 3.2d** S*OLVING A* P*ROBLEM* I*NVOLVING A* C*ONTINUED* P*ROPORTION*

A 560-bed hospital operates with 232 registered nurses and 185 other support staff. The hospital is about to open a new 86-bed wing. Assuming the same proportionate staffing levels, how many more nurses and support staff will need to be hired?

◪ **SOLUTION**

Let *n* represent the number of additional nurses and *s* the number of additional staff. *n* and *s* must satisfy the proportion

$$560 : 232 : 185 = 86 : n : s$$

Therefore,

$$\frac{560}{86} = \frac{232}{n} \quad \text{and} \quad \frac{560}{86} = \frac{185}{s}$$

$$560n = 86 \times 232 \qquad\qquad 560s = 86 \times 185$$

$$n = \frac{86 \times 232}{560} \qquad\qquad s = \frac{86 \times 185}{560}$$

$$= 35.6 \qquad\qquad\qquad = 28.4$$

Rounding the calculated values to the nearest integer, the hospital should hire 36 nurses and 28 support staff for the new wing.   ■

■ **EXAMPLE 3.2e** S*OLVING A* C*ONTINUED* P*ROPORTION* W*HERE THE* T*ERMS OF A* R*ATIO*
                       A*RE* F*RACTIONS*

The profit of the BGK partnership is to be divided among Barry, Guiseppe, and Karla in the ratio $\frac{1}{2} : \frac{1}{4} : \frac{1}{3}$, respectively. How much should each partner receive from a profit of $14,560 in the most recent quarter?

☑ SOLUTION

> **Trap**
>
> Do not interpret the given ratio to mean that Barry is to receive one-half of the profit, Guiseppe one-quarter, and Karla one-third. There is no reason that the three fractions should add to equal 1. Simply view the fractional terms as you would the terms in a ratio such as $5 : 7 : 4$—three numbers that establish the relative sizes of the three partners' shares of the profit.

Let the partners' initials represent their respective shares of the profit. Then

$$B : G : K = \frac{1}{2} : \frac{1}{4} : \frac{1}{3} = 6 : 3 : 4$$

where the ratio has been converted to its lowest terms by multiplying every term by 12. Now we can take the approach of breaking the profit into 13 parts (the sum of the terms). Barry should receive 6 of the 13 parts, Guiseppe should receive 3, and Karla should receive 4. That is,

$$\text{Barry should receive } \frac{6}{13} \times \$14{,}560 = \$6720$$

$$\text{Guiseppe should receive } \frac{3}{13} \times \$14{,}560 = \$3360$$

$$\text{Karla should receive } \frac{4}{13} = \$14{,}560 = \$4480 \qquad ■$$

■ EXAMPLE 3.2F   *SOLVING A PROBLEM INVOLVING SUCCESSIVE PARTITIONING OF A WHOLE*

Getty Oil and Gas had a 47% interest in an oil well. Paliser Energy owns a 29% interest in the same well. If Getty sells five-eighths of its interest for $470,000, what value does the transaction imply for Paliser's interest?

☑ SOLUTION

The following diagram helps to organize the data and show the composition of the ownership of the oil well.

Let G represent the value of Getty's interest before the sale. Hence,

$$\frac{5}{8}G = \$470{,}000$$

and

$$G = \frac{8}{5} \times \$470{,}000 = \$752{,}000$$

If P represents the value of Paliser's interest, then

$$P : G = 29 : 47$$

and

$$\frac{P}{G} = \frac{29}{47}$$

Therefore,

$$P = \frac{29}{47} \times G = \frac{29}{47} \times \$752{,}000 = \$464{,}000$$

Assuming that each ownership interest has a market value proportional to the size of the interest, the transaction implies a value of $464,000 for Paliser's interest. ∎

EXERCISE 3.2

Answers to the odd-numbered problems are at the end of the book.

Solve the following proportions for the unknown quantities.

1. $9 : 7 = 54 : b$

2. $17 : q = 119 : 91$

3. $88 : 17 = a : 45$

4. $d : 13.2 = 16 : 31$

5. $1.89 : 0.31 = 175 : k$

6. $1.56 : h = 56.2 : 31.7$

7. $0.043 : y = 550 : 198$

8. $0.057 : 0.149 = z : 0.05$

9. $m : \dfrac{3}{4} = \dfrac{1}{2} : \dfrac{9}{8}$

10. $\dfrac{10}{3} : \dfrac{12}{7} = \dfrac{5}{18} : r$

•11. $6 : 7 : 5 = n : 105 : m$

•12. $3 : 4 : 13 = x : y : 6.5$

•13. $625 : f : 500 = g : 3 : 4$

•14. $a : 58 : 132 = 38 : 27 : b$

•15. $0.69 : 1.17 : 0.4 = r : s : 6.5$

•16. $8500 : x : y = \dfrac{1}{3} : \dfrac{1}{4} : \dfrac{5}{12}$

Solve the following problems using proportions.

17. Mr. Borelli has just received notice that the current year's property tax on his home, which has an assessed value of $210,000, is $2376. What will be the property taxes on his neighbour's house, assessed at $235,000, if the taxes are in the same ratio as the assessed values?

18. The West Essex School Board employs 348 teachers for the 7412 students registered in the district's schools in the current year. The enrollment forecast for next year is 7780 students. Assuming the same student-teacher ratio for the next year, how many additional teaching positions must the board fill?

19. An electrical generator will run for 1 hour and 30 minutes on 4 l of gasoline. For how many hours was the generator operated since it was last refueled, if 29.5 l is required to fill the fuel tank today?

20. Connie's neighbour sold 14.5 hectares of raw land for $128,000. If Connie were to sell her 23.25-hectare parcel at a proportionate price, what amount would she receive?

21. Based on past experience, a manufacturing process requires 2.3 hours of direct labour for each $87 worth of raw materials processed. If the company is planning to consume $39,150 worth of raw materials, what total amount should it budget for labour at $18.25 per hour?

22. Mr. Bartlett's will specified that, upon liquidation of any asset, the proceeds be divided among his wife, his son, and his sister in the ratio of $7 : 5 : 3$.

    a. If the son received $9500 from the sale of securities, what amounts did his mother and aunt receive?

b. What amount would the sister receive from the sale of the deceased's boat for $27,000?

23. An international equity mutual fund includes American stocks, Japanese stocks, German stocks, and British stocks in the ratio 27 : 19 : 14 : 11, respectively. If its current holdings of German stocks are valued at $US238 million, what are the values of its holdings in the securities of the other three countries?

24. Last year, the U.S. sales of Ford, General Motors, and Chrysler, respectively, were in the ratio 92 : 121 : 35. GM has just announced sales of $10.8 billion for the first half of the current fiscal year. If the three companies have maintained the same market share as they had last year, what were the first-half sales of Ford and Chrysler?

•25. A punch recipe calls for fruit juice, ginger ale, and vodka to be mixed in the ratio $\frac{3}{2} : \frac{3}{5} : \frac{1}{4}$. How much fruit juice and ginger ale should be mixed with a 0.75-litre bottle of vodka?

26. Larry, Curley, and Moe formed a partnership. The partnership agreement requires them to provide capital when and as required by the partnership in the ratio of 1 : 1.35 : 0.85.

   a. If the total required initial investment was $102,400, how much did each contribute?

   b. One year later, Moe's share of another injection of capital was $6528. What was Curley's share?

27. A business consultant is analysing the cost structure of two firms in the same retail business. On sales of $3.66 million, Thriftys had wholesale costs of $2.15 million and overhead expenses of $1.13 million. If Economart had the same proportionate costs on its sales of $5.03 million, what would its wholesale costs and overhead expenses have been?

28. A province's Ministry of Social Services has found that the number of people receiving social assistance and the province's expenditures on social assistance tend to be proportional to the rate of unemployment. Last August when the provincial unemployment rate was 11.6%, the province provided benefits to 89,300 individuals at a cost of $53.7 million. What are the expected number of claimants and the total cost next August if the forecast unemployment rate is 10.3%?

•29. The Ministry of Education reported that the average school district in the province has 13,450 students in "K to 12" programs, an annual budget of $66.3 million, and 635 full-time-equivalent teachers. The Middleton School District (MSD), with an annual budget of $52.1 million and 498 teachers, serves 10,320 students. What adjustments would have to be made to MSD's budget and staffing to have them in the same proportion to enrollment as the provincial average?

•30. Shirley had a three-sevenths interest in a partnership. She sold three-fifths of her interest for $27,000.

   a. What is the implied value of Shirley's remaining partnership interest?

   b. What is the implied value of the entire partnership?

•31. Regal Resources owns a 58% interest in a mineral claim. Yukon Explorations owns the remainder. If Regal sells one-fifth of its interest for $1.2 million, what is the implied value of Yukon's interest?

•32. The statistics for a professional accounting program indicate that five-sevenths of those who enter the program complete level 1. Two-ninths of level 1 completers do not finish level 2. If 587 students completed level 2 last year, how many (including this group of 587) began level 1?

•33. Executive Fashions sold four-sevenths of its inventory at cost in a bankruptcy sale. The remainder was sold to liquidators for $6700, representing 45% of its cost.

   a. What was the original cost of the inventory that was sold to the liquidators?

   b. What were the proceeds from the bankruptcy sale?

3.3 PERCENTAGES AS RATIOS

The French word for the number 100 is *cent,* and in English *percent* is used to mean "per 100." Any percent figure can be quickly converted to the equivalent ratio based on 100. For example, 27% means the ratio 27 : 100.

Formula (1−1) in the form

$$\text{Rate} = \frac{\text{Portion}}{\text{Base}}$$

suggests an interpretation that *Rate* is the ratio of the *Portion* to the *Base.* Similarly, formula (2−2), for percent change,

$$\%c = \frac{V_f - V_i}{V_i} \times 100\%$$

suggests the view of %c as the ratio of the change in value to the initial value.

Percent change problems of the sort encountered in Section 2.5 may also be solved by setting up a proportion; the choice is a matter of preference. For illustration and comparison, Examples 2.5c, 2.5d, and 2.5e will be repeated here as Examples 3.3a, 3.3b, and 3.3c, respectively.

■ **EXAMPLE 3.3A**   *CALCULATING V_i GIVEN V_f AND %C*

What amount when increased by 230% equals $495?

☑ **SOLUTION**

The following table helps to organize the data and set up a proportion. Columns are provided for entering amounts in terms of both dollars and percent. In this example, we are given the change in percent (230%) and the final amount in dollars ($495). We also deduce that the 230% change is added to an initial value of 100%, giving a final value of 330%.

	$	%
Initial value	?	100
+ Change	+ ?	+230
= Final value	495	330

The table may now be used to set up a proportion to solve for either of the unknown dollar amounts. The key point is that any two figures in the $ column have the same ratio as the corresponding figures in the % column. For example,

$$\frac{\text{Initial value (\$)}}{\text{Final value (\$)}} = \frac{\text{Initial value (\%)}}{\text{Final value (\%)}}$$

Hence,

$$\frac{\text{Initial value (\$)}}{\$495} = \frac{100\%}{330\%}$$

and

$$\text{Initial value} = \frac{10}{33} \times \$495 = \$150$$

We conclude that $150 increased by 230% equals $495.   ■

■ **EXAMPLE 3.3B**   *CALCULATING V_f GIVEN V_i AND %C*

How much is $9550 decreased by $\frac{3}{4}$%?

☑ SOLUTION

Again construct the table as shown below. The proportion for calculating the final value is

	$	%
Initial value	9550	100.00
+ Change	+ ?	−0.75
= Final value	?	99.25

$$\frac{\$9550}{\text{Final value}} = \frac{100\%}{99.25\%}$$

Therefore,

$$\text{Final value} = \frac{99.25}{100} \times \$9550 = \$9478.38$$

In summary, $9550 decreased by $\frac{3}{4}\%$ is $9478.38.   ■

■ EXAMPLE 3.3C   CALCULATING V_i GIVEN V_f AND %C

For the fiscal year just completed, a company had sales of $157,500. This represents a 5% increase over the prior year. What were the sales in the prior year?

☑ SOLUTION

Enter the known values in the customary table. Then,

	$	%
Initial value	?	100
+ Change	+ ?	+ 5
= Final value	157,500	105

$$\frac{\text{Initial value}}{\$157,500} = \frac{100\%}{105\%}$$

$$\text{Initial value} = \frac{100}{105} \times \$157,500 = \$150,000$$

The sales in the prior year were $150,000.   ■

EXERCISE 3.3

Use problems in Exercise 2.5 to practise the technique presented in this section.

3.4 APPLICATION: PRORATION

There are many instances in business where an amount of money must be divided among two or more people, departments, cost centres, time periods, or other units. **Proration** is a procedure in which an amount is allocated on a proportionate basis. Some examples are:

- Upon cancellation of insurance coverage, the premium refunded is usually the prorated amount based on the unexpired portion of the period of coverage.
- The allocation of a partnership's profits is usually prorated, based on each partner's equity investment in the partnership.
- For accounting purposes, overhead costs in a business are often prorated among departments, divisions, branches, or other cost centres. The basis chosen for the pro rata allocation is usually the one that best reflects the relative benefit each derives from the expenditure. The proration might be based on unit or dollar sales volume, number of employees, or floor area occupied.
- The lease agreements for commercial space in malls and shopping centres often require that common area costs, such as property taxes, janitorial services,

landscape maintenance, and snow removal, be allocated among the tenants. These common area costs are typically prorated on the basis of the floor area leased.

■ **EXAMPLE 3.4A** *PRORATING A REFUND BASED ON THE UNUSED TIME PERIOD*

Franco paid $1058 for his automobile insurance coverage for the period July 1 to June 30. He sold his car and cancelled the insurance on March 8. The insurer's procedure is to calculate a refund prorated to the exact number of days remaining in the period of coverage. (March 8 is not included in the refundable days.) A $20 service charge is then deducted. What refund will Franco receive?

☑ **SOLUTION**

The basis for calculating the refund (before the service charge) is:

$$\frac{\text{Refund}}{\text{Annual premium}} = \frac{\text{Number of remaining days of coverage}}{365 \text{ days}}$$

The "unused" days in the July 1 to June 30 period are the 23 days remaining in March plus all of April, May, and June. (See the appendix to Chapter 6 for a method of determining the number of days in each month.) Hence,

$$\frac{\text{Refund}}{\$1058} = \frac{23 + 30 + 31 + 30}{365}$$

$$\text{Refund} = \frac{114 \times \$1058}{365}$$

$$= \$330.44$$

After deduction of the service charge, the net refund will be $310.44. ■

■ **EXAMPLE 3.4B** *ALLOCATING PROFITS BASED ON THE AMOUNT INVESTED BY EACH OWNER*

The partnership of Mr. X, Mr. Y, and Ms. Z has agreed to distribute profits in the same proportion as their respective capital investments in the partnership. How will the recent period's profit of $28,780 be allocated if Mr. X's capital account shows a balance of $34,000, Mr. Y's shows $49,000, and Ms. Z's shows $54,500?

☑ **SOLUTION**

The ratio of a partner's share of the profit to the total profit will equal the ratio of that partner's capital investment to the total investment.

$$\text{Total investment} = \$34,000 + \$49,000 + \$54,500 = \$137,500$$

$$\frac{\text{Mr. X's share}}{\text{Total profit}} = \frac{\text{Mr. X's investment}}{\text{Total investment}}$$

$$\frac{\text{Mr. X's share}}{\$28,780} = \frac{\$34,000}{\$137,500}$$

$$\text{Mr. X's share} = \frac{\$34,000}{\$137,500} \times \$28,780 = \$7116.51$$

Similarly,

$$\text{Mr. Y's share} = \frac{\$49,000}{\$137,500} \times \$28,780 = \$10,256.15$$

Either of two approaches may now be employed to calculate Ms. Z's share. The longer approach has the advantage of providing a means of checking the answers. In it we calculate Ms. Z's share in the same manner as the other two shares:

$$\text{Ms. Z's share} = \frac{\$54,500}{\$137,500} \times \$28,780 = \$11,407.35$$

The allocations can be checked by verifying that their total is $28,780:

$$\$7116.51 + \$10,256.15 + \$11,407.35 = \$28,780.01$$

The shorter method for calculating Ms. Z's share is to calculate the balance left from the $28,780 after Mr. X's and Mr. Y's shares have been paid out:

$$\text{Ms. Z's share} = \$28,780.00 - \$7116.51 - \$10,256.15$$
$$= \$11,407.34$$

However, we do not have a means of checking the calculations since, in effect, we have forced Ms. Z's share to be the balance of the $28,780 (whether Mr. X's and Mr. Y's shares were correctly calculated or not). ∎

■ EXAMPLE 3.4c   ALLOCATING A FIRM'S OVERHEAD COSTS

The Quebec plant of a manufacturing company produced 10,000 units of a product during the last fiscal quarter using 5000 hours of direct labour. In the same period, the Ontario plant produced 20,000 units using 9000 hours of direct labour. How will overhead costs of $49,000 for the period be allocated between the two plants if the allocation is based on:

a. Direct labour hours?

b. Units of output?

☑ SOLUTION

a.
$$\frac{\text{Quebec's share}}{\text{Total overhead}} = \frac{\text{Quebec's labour hours}}{\text{Total labour hours}}$$

$$\text{Quebec's share} = \frac{5000}{14,000} \times \$49,000 = \$17,500$$

Similarly,

$$\text{Ontario's share} = \frac{9000}{14,000} \times \$49,000 = \$31,500$$

b.
$$\frac{\text{Quebec's share}}{\text{Total overhead}} = \frac{\text{Quebec's output}}{\text{Total output}}$$

$$\text{Quebec's share} = \frac{10,000}{30,000} \times \$49,000 = \$16,333$$

Similarly,

$$\text{Ontario's share} = \frac{20,000}{30,000} \times \$49,000 = \$32,667$$ ∎

■ EXAMPLE 3.4d   MAINTAINING PROPORTIONATE OWNERSHIP IN A BUYOUT

The ownership interests of the four partners in a marina are 20% for Mr. P, 30% for Mr. Q, 15% for Mr. R, and 35% for Mr. S. The partners have agreed on an arrangement to buy out Mr. P for $100,000. Mr. Q, Mr. R, and Mr. S are to split the 20% interest and contribute to the $100,000 price in proportions that will leave them with the same relative ownership interests as they now possess.

a. What will their ownership interests be after the sale?

b. How much should each partner contribute toward the $100,000 purchase price?

☑ SOLUTION

a. Before the sale, the ownership ratio for the three continuing partners is

$$Q : R : S = \frac{30}{100} : \frac{15}{100} : \frac{35}{100} = 30 : 15 : 35$$

After the sale, 100% ownership is to be allocated to Mr. Q, Mr. R, and Mr. S in the ratio 30 : 15 : 35. Since

$$30 + 15 + 35 = 80$$

we can allocate the 100% ownership in the required ratio by assigning

$$\frac{30}{80} \times 100\% = 37.5\% \qquad \text{to Mr. Q}$$

$$\frac{15}{80} \times 100\% = 18.75\% \qquad \text{to Mr. R}$$

$$\frac{35}{80} \times 100\% = 43.75\% \qquad \text{to Mr. S}$$

After the sale of Mr. P's interest in the marina, Mr. Q, Mr. R, and Mr. S will own 37.5%, 18.75%, and 43.75%, respectively, of the partnership.

b. The partners' allocation of the $100,000 purchase price should be in the same ratio as their ownership interests. Therefore,

Mr. Q should contribute 0.375 × $100,000 = $37,500.
Mr. R should contribute 0.1875 × $100,000 = $18,750.
Mr. S should contribute 0.4375 × $100,000 = $43,750.   ■

EXERCISE 3.4

Answers to the odd-numbered problems are at the end of the book.

1. A 3-year magazine subscription costing $136 may be cancelled at any time, and a prorated refund will be made for the remaining weekly issues. If Juanita cancels her subscription after receiving 17 issues in the second year, what refund should she get? Assume there are exactly 52 weeks in a year.

2. When real estate is sold, the year's property taxes are allocated to the vendor and the purchaser in proportion to the number of days that each party owns the property during the year. If the purchaser took possession of a property effective August 8 (of a 365-day year), how will the year's property taxes of $2849 be allocated to the vendor and purchaser?

3. On May 3, Mary Ann bought a 2-year membership in a fitness club for $495, on a special promotion. Cancellation is allowed at any time. A prorated refund will be paid based upon the number of days remaining in the membership period. If she cancelled the membership on the following September 9, what refund should she receive? (Count both May 3 and September 9 as days used.)

4. In some instances Revenue Canada allows an individual to deduct from income a portion of the annual operating expenses for a personally owned automobile that is used to earn employment income. If an individual qualifies for the deduction, the deductible portion is based on the ratio of the distance travelled on business to the total distance travelled in the year.

   Harold spent a total of $5674 during the last year on gas, oil, insurance, licence and registration fees, and repairs and maintenance for his automobile. From his travel log he has determined that 14,488 km were driven for business use and 8329 km were driven for personal use during the year. What automobile expense can he deduct from income?

5. An individual who operates a business primarily from his or her personal residence may deduct certain "office-in-home" expenses in the calculation of taxable income. The proportion of the annual costs of heat, insurance, electricity, property taxes, and mortgage interest that may be deducted must be determined on a basis that Revenue Canada finds "reasonable under the circumstances."

   Rose uses 2 of the 11 rooms in her home for a real estate appraisal business that she operates with one assistant. The combined area of the 2 rooms is 360 square feet, and the remainder of the house has an area of 1470 square feet. The total of the eligible expenses for the taxation year is $8756. What amount will be deductible if the expenses are prorated based on:

   a. The number of rooms used for the business?

   b. The floor area devoted to business use?

6. The leases in multiple-unit commercial developments commonly permit the landlord to allocate to the tenants various common area and general costs such as property taxes, janitorial services, security services, and snow removal. These costs are usually prorated on the basis of the floor area leased to each tenant. Granny's Chicken, Toys 'n Novelties, and Pine Tree Pharmacy are the three tenants in Pine Tree Square. They lease 172 square metres, 136 square metres, and 420 square metres, respectively. How should common costs totaling $9872 for the past year be allocated?

7. Three insurance companies agree to jointly insure a cargo ship for $38.6 million. If insurers A, B, and C allocate premiums received and accept the risk in the ratio 3 : 8 : 5, respectively:

   a. How will the annual premium of $900,000 be distributed?

   b. What is the maximum claim exposure of each insurer?

•8. Kevin, Lyle, and Marnie operate Food Country as a partnership. Their agreement provides that half the profit in each calendar quarter be distributed in proportion to each partner's investment in the partnership, and that the other half be distributed in proportion to the total number of hours that each partner works in the business. How should the most recent quarter's profit of $56,230 be allocated if their respective investments are $65,000, $43,000, and $14,500, and their hours of work for the quarter were 210, 365, and 632, respectively?

•9. The following table shows National Paper Products' capital investment in each of its three divisions, and the most recent year's gross sales for each division. The operating costs of the head office for the year were $839,000. These costs are allocated to

Division	Investment	Gross sales
Industrial products	$25,300,000	$21,200,000
Fine paper	17,250,000	8,350,000
Containers and packaging	11,900,000	7,450,000

the divisions before each division's profit is determined. How much should be allocated to each division if the costs are prorated on the basis of:

   a. The capital investment in each division?

   b. The sales of each division?

•10. Last year, Reliable Securities established a sales achievement bonus fund of $10,000 to be distributed at the year's end among its four-person mutual fund sales force. The distribution is to be made in the same proportion as the amounts by which each person's sales exceed the basic quota of $500,000. How much will each salesperson receive from the fund if the sales figures for the year were $910,000 for Mr. A, $755,000 for Ms. B, $460,000 for Mr. C, and $615,000 for Ms. D?

•11. Geological Consultants Ltd. is a private company with four shareholders—W, X, Y, and Z—owning 300, 500, 350, and 400 shares, respectively. X is retiring and has come to an agreement with the other three shareholders to sell his shares for $175,000. The agreement calls for the 500 shares to be purchased and allocated to W, Y, and Z in the same ratio as their present shareholdings. The shares are indivisible, and consequently the share allocation must be rounded to integer values.

   a. What implied value does the transaction place on the entire company?

   b. How many shares will W, Y, and Z each own after the buyout?

   c. What amount will each of the continuing shareholders contribute toward the $175,000 purchase price? Prorate the $175,000 on the basis of the allocation of the shares in part b.

••12. Canadian Can Co. operates a profit-sharing plan wherein half the annual profits are distributed to employees. By agreement, the amounts received by *individual* executives, supervisors, and production workers are to be in the ratio of 10 : 7 : 5, respectively. During the last fiscal year, there were 4 executives, 8 supervisors, and 45 production personnel. What profit-sharing amount will each executive, supervisor, and production worker receive if the year's profit was $265,000?

*3.5 APPLICATION: EXCHANGE RATES AND CURRENCY CONVERSION

If $1 Canadian equals $0.75 American, how much in Canadian funds is required to purchase $1 American? If your answer is $1.25 Canadian, you have made the common mistake of using the difference between the given currency equivalents, instead of their ratio, to answer the question.

The **exchange rate** between two currencies may be viewed as the ratio of equivalent amounts of the currencies. The ratio is usually reported with the second term adjusted to one unit of that currency. In the present case, where

$$\$1.00 \text{ Canadian} = \$0.75 \text{ American}$$

the exchange rate may be reported as

$$\frac{C\$1.00}{US\$0.75} = \frac{C\$1.3\overline{3}}{US\$1.00} = C\$1.3\overline{3} \text{ per US}\$1$$

The answer to the question posed at the beginning is now evident: $1.33 Canadian would be required to purchase $1.00 American.[3]

---

[3]Institutions that provide currency exchange services profit from that service by charging a markup. They pay less when they buy a currency than they charge when they sell that currency. In practice, then, one faces differing buy and sell rates in any foreign exchange transaction. In this brief introduction, we will assume that a foreign currency may be bought or sold at the same exchange rate.

The exchange rate between two currencies can be quoted in two ways, depending on the order of the currencies in the terms of the ratio. The preceding exchange rate may also be reported as

$$\frac{US\$0.75}{C\$1.00} = US\$0.75 \text{ per } C\$1$$

Each quotation represents the number of units of the first-mentioned currency that is equivalent to one unit of the second currency. Note that either exchange rate is the mathematical inverse or reciprocal of the other. That is, $\frac{1}{0.75} = 1.3\overline{3}$.

Most exchange rates are continuously changing in foreign exchange markets. Therefore quotations in the financial pages will be obsolete, to some degree, by the time you read them. A table of exchange rates will usually specify the time of day as well as the date when the rates were extracted. The *Financial Post* and the *Globe and Mail*'s Report on Business present exchange rates in two formats. The less commonly traded currencies are listed in a table similar to Table 3.1. Exchange rates are reported for over 40 currencies in terms of C$ per unit of foreign currency and US$ per unit of foreign currency. Only a sample of exchange rates is presented here.

TABLE 3.1

Foreign Exchange Rates (April 12, 1996)

Country	Currency	C$ per Unit	US$ per Unit
Australia	Dollar	0.93195	0.73722
Brazil	Real	1.3742	1.0131
Greece	Drachma	0.00560	0.00413
India	Rupee	0.03961	0.02920
Italy	Lira	0.000865	0.000638
Netherlands	Guilder	0.8074	0.5952
South Korea	Won	0.001733	0.001277
Taiwan	Dollar	0.0503	0.0371

The major currencies of international trade are presented in a currency cross rate table in the form shown in Table 3.2. The figure in any cell of the table is the number of units of the currency in the row heading per unit of the currency in the column heading. For example, from the top row we see that, on April 12, 1996, it required C$1.35645 to purchase US$1.00, C$0.90198 to purchase DM1.00, and so on. The obvious value 1.00000 has been omitted from the cells along the diagonal to avoid unnecessary clutter.

TABLE 3.2

Cross Currency Rates (April 12, 1996)

Currency	Per C$	Per US$	Per DM	Per ¥	Per £	Per Fr. fr.
Canadian dollar (C$)	•	1.35645	0.90198	0.01249	2.05407	0.26574
U.S. dollar (US$)	0.73722	•	0.66496	0.00921	1.51430	0.19591
German mark (DM)	1.10867	1.50385	•	0.01385	2.27728	0.29461
Japanese yen (¥)	80.06	108.60	72.21	•	164.45	21.27
British pound (£)	0.48684	0.66037	0.43912	0.00608	•	0.12937
French franc (Fr. fr.)	3.76313	5.10450	3.39429	0.04700	7.72974	•

The notation E(C1 : C2) will be used for the exchange rate specifying the number of units of currency, C1, equal to one unit of currency, C2. Although the E(C1 : C2) notation is not used in the financial press, the two columns on the right in Table 3.1 correspond to E(C$: foreign currency) and E(US$: foreign currency). In terms of the E(C1 : C2) notation, the exchange rate in any cell of Table 3.2 is

$$E(\text{row currency} : \text{column currency})$$

For example, E(C$: DM) = 0.90198. This means that C$0.90198 was equal to 1 German mark on April 12, 1996.

It was mentioned earlier in this section that the two alternative quotations for the exchange rate between a pair of currencies are mathematical reciprocals of each other. In terms of the E(C1 : C2) notation, this means that

Exchange Rate Inverse Relationship

$$E(C1 : C2) = \frac{1}{E(C2 : C1)}$$

This inverse relationship can be verified for any pair of currencies in Table 3.2. For example, in the top row we find E(C$: £) = 2.05407. In the first column, we find E(£ : C$) = 0.48684. Confirm that $\frac{1}{2.05407}$ = 0.48684.

■ EXAMPLE 3.5A   CONVERTING ONE CURRENCY TO ANOTHER

Using an exchange rate from Table 3.2, calculate the number of yen that C$650 will purchase.

◪ SOLUTION

Multiply C$650 by the number of yen that C$1 will purchase. The latter amount is given by the exchange rate E(¥ : C$).

$$
\begin{aligned}
C\$650 &= 650 \times E(¥ : C\$) \\
&= 650 \times ¥80.06 \\
&= ¥52,039
\end{aligned}
$$

■ EXAMPLE 3.5B   CONVERTING FROM ONE CURRENCY TO A SECOND, AND THEN FROM THE SECOND CURRENCY TO A THIRD

Show that the same number of yen as in Example 3.5a would be purchased if the C$650 were first converted to German marks and the German marks then converted to yen. (Assume that no charges are imposed by the institutions providing the currency exchange services.)

◪ SOLUTION

Converting the C$650 to German marks,

$$
\begin{aligned}
C\$650 &= 650 \times E(DM : C\$) \\
&= 650 \times DM1.10867 \\
&= DM720.6355
\end{aligned}
$$

Then converting the marks to yen, we obtain

$$DM720.6355 = 720.6355 \times E(¥ : DM)$$
$$= 720.6355 \times ¥72.21$$
$$= ¥52,037$$

The small discrepancy arises because $E(¥ : DM)$ is provided with only four significant figures. We need six figures in $E(¥ : DM)$ to ensure five-figure precision in the result.

■

■ **EXAMPLE 3.5c** *COMPARING PRICES QUOTED IN TWO CURRENCIES*

If gasoline sold for $0.609 per litre in Vancouver and $1.39 per gallon in Seattle on April 12, 1996, by what percentage (based on the Vancouver price) was gas cheaper in Seattle (1 U.S. gallon = 3.785 litres)?

☑ SOLUTION

The price in Canada of 3.785 litres (1 U.S. gallon) of gasoline was

$$3.785 \text{ litres} \times C\$0.609 \text{ per litre} = C\$2.305$$

Using the exchange rate from Table 3.2, the Canadian dollar equivalent of the Seattle price of US$1.39 per U.S. gallon was

$$1.39 \times E(C\$: US\$) = 1.39 \times C\$1.35645 = C\$1.885$$

A U.S. gallon of gasoline was C$2.305 − C$1.885 = C$0.420 cheaper in Seattle. The percent difference was

$$\frac{C\$0.420}{C\$2.305} \times 100\% = 18.2\%$$

Gasoline was 18.2% cheaper in Seattle.

■

APPRECIATION AND DEPRECIATION OF CURRENCIES Suppose that $E(US\$: C\$)$ changed from 0.75 to 0.76 over a period of 1 month. In other words, the exchange rate rose from US$0.75 per C$1.00 at the beginning of the month to US$0.76 per C$1.00 at the end of the month. Which currency strengthened (appreciated) relative to the other over the course of the month?

Since it required 1 more U.S. cent to purchase a Canadian dollar at the end of the month than at the beginning, the U.S. dollar weakened (depreciated) relative to the Canadian dollar. The flip side of the coin (so to speak) is that the Canadian dollar strengthened (appreciated) relative to the U.S. dollar. A Canadian dollar purchased 1 more U.S. cent at the end of the month than at the beginning of the month. The percent increase in the value of the C$ relative to the US$ was

$$\frac{V_f - V_i}{V_i} \times 100\% = \frac{0.76 - 0.75}{0.75} \times 100\% = 1.\overline{3}\%$$

Canadians importing goods from the United States or travelling in the United States would benefit from this $1.\overline{3}\%$ increase in the purchasing power of the "Canuck buck." Conversely, Americans importing goods priced in Canadian dollars or travelling in Canada would find Canadian prices converted to US$ about $1.\overline{3}\%$ higher.

While E(US\$: C\$) was rising from 0.75 to 0.76, E(C\$: US\$) was declining from 1.3333 to 1.3158. [Remember that E(C\$: US\$) is the reciprocal of E(US\$: C\$).] An appreciating C\$ caused E(US\$: C\$) to increase but E(C\$: US\$) to decrease.

> **Tip**
>
> When given the numerical change to an exchange rate, the line of reasoning for deciding which currency is appreciating can be tricky, particularly with unfamiliar currencies. The recommended approach is to view an exchange rate E(C1 : C2) as the amount of currency C1 required to purchase *one* unit of current C2.
>
> If E(C1 : C2) increases, then it requires more of C1 to purchase one unit of C2. Each unit of C1 is worth less. Therefore, C1 has *depreciated* relative to C2.
>
> If E(C1 : C2) decreases, then it requires less of C1 to purchase one unit of C2. Each unit of C1 is worth more. Therefore, C1 has *appreciated* relative to C2.

■ EXAMPLE 3.5D *INTERPRETING CHANGES IN EXCHANGE RATES*

If E(C\$: £) decreased from 2.081 to 2.043, which currency depreciated? What was the percent depreciation?

☑ SOLUTION

Less Canadian currency is needed to purchase £1.00 at the end than at the beginning. Therefore the C\$ appreciated and the £ depreciated. The percent depreciation is

$$\frac{2.081 - 2.043}{2.081} \times 100\% = 1.83\%$$

The £ depreciated by 1.83%.   ■

■ EXAMPLE 3.5E *CONSEQUENCES OF EXCHANGE RATE SHIFTS*

Many commodities produced by Canadian mining and forest product companies are priced in US\$ in international markets. A Canadian producer sells newsprint for US\$800 per tonne. What is the consequence for the C\$ revenue per tonne if E(C\$: US\$) drops from 1.348 to 1.325?

☑ SOLUTION

The Canadian producer will still be paid US\$800 per tonne. However, the US\$ revenues must be converted to C\$ to pay employee wages, taxes, and other goods and services sourced in Canada. The firm's income statement will be presented in terms of C\$. In general, the C\$ revenue per tonne is

$$US\$800 \times E(C\$: US\$)$$

The strengthening of the C\$ from C\$1.348 to C\$1.325 per US\$ means that, after conversion of revenues to C\$, the producer will receive

$$800 \times C\$1.325 = C\$1060 \text{ per tonne}$$

instead of

$$800 \times C\$1.348 = C\$1078.40 \text{ per tonne}$$

The appreciation of the C\$ results in the C\$ revenue per tonne falling by C\$18.40, a decline of 1.74%.   ■

EXERCISE 3.5

Answers to the odd-numbered problems are at the end of the book.

For problems 1 through 12, use the currency exchange rates in Table 3.2 to calculate the amount of the currency in the third column of the following table that is equivalent to the specified amount in the second column.

Problem	Specified amount	Equivalent amount
1.	US$1856	C$?
2.	£123.50	DM ?
3.	C$14,500	¥ ?
4.	¥3,225,000	£ ?
5.	DM3251	C$?
6.	£56,700	US$?
7.	¥756,000	C$?
8.	DM159,500	US$?
9.	C$94,350	£ ?
10.	DM37,650	¥ ?
11.	C$49,900	DM ?
12.	£8950	¥ ?

13. Calculate the exchange rates in the third column in the following table using the exchange rates given in the second column.

Part	Given exchange rate	Desired exchange rate
a.	E(French franc : C$) = 3.76313	E(C$: Ffr) = ?
b.	E(¥ : Australian $) = 85.90	E(A$: ¥) = ?
c.	E(Swiss franc : £) = 1.85729	E(£ : Sfr) = ?
d.	E(C$: Australian $) = 1.07302	E(A$: C$) = ?

If the necessary exchange rates are not given in the following problems, use the exchange rates in Table 3.2.

14. How much will it cost in Canadian dollars to purchase US$200 of currency at a bank that charges a 1.5% commission on the transaction?

15. Simon returns from a weekend in the United States with US$48 of currency. How much will he receive from the bank when he converts the currency back to Canadian dollars? (Assume that the bank charges a 1.5% commission on the transaction.)

16. How much will it cost (in Canadian funds) to purchase £2000 worth of traveller's cheques if the commission rate for this quantity of cheques is 0.5%?

17. Lois returned from a holiday in Britain with £350 of uncashed traveller's cheques. How much will she receive in Canadian funds if the bank charges a fee of 0.75% to convert the traveller's cheques to Canadian funds?

18. If Canadian auto workers earn an average of C$28 per hour and their American counterparts earn US$23 per hour, which country has a cost of labour advantage after adjusting for the currency exchange rate? What is the size of the advantage in C$?

19. If cheese costs $5.50 per pound in Canada and US$3.85 per pound in the United States, what is the saving in Canadian cents per pound if cheese is bought in the United States?

20. If E(£ : C$) increases by 0.054 from the value in Table 3.2, which currency has depreciated and by what percent?

21. If E(C$: ¥) decreases by 0.00054 from the value in Table 3.2, which currency has appreciated and by what percent?

•22. If the C$ weakens by 0.5% relative to the DM in Table 3.2, what will be the new values for E(DM : C$) and E(C$: DM)?

•23. If the C$ strengthens by 1.2% relative to the US$ in Table 3.2, what will be the new values for E(US$: C$) and E(C$: US$)?

•24. If the C$ appreciates (from the value in Table 3.2) by C$0.0017 relative to the £, what will be the new value of E(£ : C$)?

•25. If the C$ weakens (from the value in Table 3.2) by C$0.0033 relative to the US$, what will be the new value of E(US$: C$)?

•26. If the C$ strengthens by £0.0021 from the value in Table 3.2, what will be the new value of E(C$: £)?

•27. If the C$ weakens by DM 0.021 from the value in Table 3.2, what will be the new value of E(C$: DM)?

•28. If E(US$: C$) rises from 0.7543 to 0.7822, what will be the change in the C$ price to an importer of a US$1500 item?

•29. If E(¥ : C$) declines from 71.91 to 68.33, what will be the change in the C$ price to an importer of a ¥195,000 item?

•30. If E(£ : C$) rises from 0.5032 to 0.5338, what will be the change in the C$ revenue from a foreign contract fixed at £23,000?

•31. If E(US$: C$) declines from 0.7521 to 0.7388, what will be the change in the C$ price per ounce of gold which a Canadian gold mine sells at the international price of US$395 per ounce?

•32. Using the exchange rates in Table 3.2, show that you will receive as many German marks for C$1150 by first converting the dollars to pounds and then converting the pounds to German marks as you would by converting the dollars directly to German marks.

•33. Using the exchange rates in Table 3.2, show that you will receive as many pounds for US$2560 by first converting the dollars to yen and then converting the yen to pounds as you would by converting the dollars directly to pounds.

•34. A cross-border shopping trip reveals that milk sells for US$0.79 per quart versus C$1.27 per litre in Canada. Calculate the percent difference (using the Canadian price as the base) in the exchange rate–adjusted price of milk between Canada and the United States (1 U.S. quart = 0.94635 litres).

•35. If pork chops cost US$3.25 per pound in the United States and C$8.50 per kilogram in Canada, in which country are the chops more expensive (1 kg = 2.2 lb)? How much more expensive in US$ per pound?

*3.6 APPLICATION: INDEX NUMBERS

You cannot read far in the business section of a newspaper before encountering important index numbers such as the consumer price index (CPI) or the Toronto Stock Exchange 300 Composite Price Index (TSE 300 Index). An index number is commonly used in economics and finance as a measure of the overall level of prices in a group of related items. For example, the consumer price index is used to indicate the overall price level of goods and services typically consumed by an urban Canadian family.

The TSE 300 Index is used to measure the levels of the share prices of 300 large representative Canadian companies listed on the Toronto Stock Exchange.

We will use the Canadian consumer price index to illustrate the construction of an index. Statistics Canada maintains a list of about 500 consumer goods and services whose overall price level it wishes to track. For historical CPI data quoted during the years 1990 to 1996, Statistics Canada assigned a *base value*[4] of 100 to the price of this "basket" of goods and services on the *base date* in mid-1986.

The index value on any date is calculated so that it is in the same ratio to 100 as the price of the basket of goods and services on that date is to the price on the base date. That is,

$$\frac{CPI}{100} = \frac{\text{Price of list on selected date}}{\text{Price of list on base date}}$$

Therefore

$$CPI = \frac{\text{Price of list on selected date}}{\text{Price of list on base date}} \times 100$$

In January 1996 the CPI was at 134.3. This means that the list of nearly 500 consumer goods and services cost 34.3% more in January 1996 than in mid-1986.

We can generalize the preceding to any index number.

$$\text{Index number} = \frac{\text{Price or value on selected date}}{\text{Price or value on base date}} \times \text{Base value}$$

In the case of the TSE 300 Index, a base value of 1000 was assigned to the (weighted) average share price of the 300 representative companies during 1975. Hence

$$\text{TSE 300 Index} = \frac{\text{Average price of shares on selected date}}{\text{Average price of shares on base date}} \times 1000$$

At the end of December 1995 the TSE 300 Index stood at 4713. Therefore, the weighted average of the prices of the 300 companies' shares at the end of 1995 was 4.713 times the average price during 1975. In other words, the average share price had increased by 371% over the 20-year period.

■ EXAMPLE 3.6A *CALCULATING AN INDEX NUMBER*

Suppose that a portfolio consisting of the 300 companies making up the TSE 300 Index cost $168,400 in 1975, when the base value of the index was set at 1000. What will be the value quoted for the TSE 300 Index on a later date when the same portfolio has a value of $717,700?

✓ SOLUTION

$$\text{TSE 300 Index} = \frac{\text{Average price of shares on selected date}}{\text{Average price of shares on base date}} \times 1000$$

---

[4]The relative sizes of two quantities can be appreciated more readily if one of the quantities has a "nice" value such as 1, 10, 100, or 1000. For this reason, the base value is usually chosen as 100 or 1000. Most index numbers that are used in economics employ 100 as the base value. A base value of 100 has the further advantage that the index number on a selected date is numerically equal to the price on that date expressed as a percentage of the price on the base date. The most common base value used for stock market price indexes is 1000.

The average price of the TSE 300 shares will be in the same ratio as the values of the portfolio on the respective dates.

$$\text{TSE 300 Index} = \frac{\text{Value of portfolio on selected date}}{\text{Value of portfolio on base date}} \times 1000$$

$$= \frac{\$717,700}{\$168,400} \times 1000$$

$$= 4261.88$$

The index will stand at 4261.88 on the date when the portfolio is worth $717,700. ■

■ **EXAMPLE 3.6B** *CALCULATING THE RATE OF INFLATION AND AMOUNTS HAVING EQUIVALENT PURCHASING POWER, USING CPI DATA*

The consumer price index averaged 67.2 in 1980, 96.0 in 1985, and 119.5 in 1990 (using a base value of 100 for 1986).

a. What amount in 1980 had the same purchasing power as $1000 in 1985?

b. What was the total percentage inflation (i.e., increase in consumer price levels) from 1980 to 1990?

c. What would a person earning $25,000 in 1985 have to earn in 1990 in order to keep pace with inflation?

☑ **SOLUTION**

These questions may each be answered by constructing a proportion involving a ratio of the appropriate CPIs.

a. Amounts that have the same purchasing power are in the same ratio as the respective CPIs:

$$\frac{1980 \text{ amount}}{1985 \text{ amount}} = \frac{1980 \text{ CPI}}{1985 \text{ CPI}}$$

$$\frac{1980 \text{ amount}}{\$1000} = \frac{67.2}{96.0}$$

$$1980 \text{ amount} = 0.7000 \times \$1000 = \$700$$

b.

$$\frac{1990 \text{ price level}}{1980 \text{ price level}} = \frac{1990 \text{ CPI}}{1980 \text{ CPI}} = \frac{119.5}{67.2} = 1.778$$

1990 consumer prices were, on average, 1.778 times 1980 prices. The total inflation was therefore 77.8%.

c. To keep pace with inflation, salaries must be in the same ratio as the corresponding CPIs.

$$\frac{1990 \text{ salary}}{1985 \text{ salary}} = \frac{1990 \text{ CPI}}{1985 \text{ CPI}}$$

$$\frac{1990 \text{ salary}}{\$25,000} = \frac{119.5}{96.0}$$

$$1990 \text{ salary} = 1.24479 \times \$25,000$$

$$= \$31,120$$

A person earning $25,000 in 1985 would have to earn $31,120 in 1990 to have the same purchasing power. ■

Exercise 3.6

Answers to the odd-numbered problems are at the end of the book.

Calculate the missing quantities in problems 1 through 8 to four-figure accuracy.

Problem	Value on base date	Base value	Current value	Current index number
1.	$3278	100	$4961	?
2.	3278	1000	4961	?
3.	7532	100	?	119.5
4.	189.50	?	431.70	2278
5.	735	10	689	?
6.	8950.	100	?	89.50
7.	?	1000	7729.	2120
8.	451.10	?	398.60	441.8

9. If the "basket" of goods and services included in the consumer price index cost $21,350 in the base year, 1986, and cost $26,090 in December 1990, what was the CPI in December 1990? (The base level in 1986 was 100.)

10. A basket of goods and services representative of the CPI cost $2750 in July 1995 when the CPI stood at 133.3.

    a. What did the basket of goods cost 10 years earlier, when the CPI was at 96.0?

    b. What was the percent inflation experienced by consumers for the entire 10-year period?

11. The CPI ended 1991 at 126.7 and finished 1992 at 129.4. How much money was required at the end of 1992 in order to have the same purchasing power as $1000 at the end of 1991?

12. A college student wants to check whether tuition fee increases over the last 5 years have exceeded the general increase in the cost of living. Tuition increased from $115 per course to $155 per course, while the CPI rose from 119.5 to 134. What would be the current tuition per course if tuition had merely kept pace with inflation?

13. Statistics Canada calculates separate subindexes of the CPI for goods and for services. The goods index rose from 96.8 in 1985 to 127 in 1995. During the same period, the services index rose from 95.2 to 142.

    a. How much did $1000 worth of representative goods in 1985 cost in 1995?

    b. How much did $1000 worth of representative services in 1985 cost in 1995?

    c. Expressed as a percentage of 1985 prices, by how much did the increase in the price of services exceed the increase in the price of goods during the decade?

14. From the end of 1982 until the end of 1992, the TSE 300 Index rose from 1958 to 3350. If an investor had invested $50,000 in a portfolio of the shares of these 300 companies at the end of 1982, what would the value of those shares have been at the end of 1992? (This calculation considers only the price appreciation of the original shares. It does not include the portion of the growth in the portfolio's value resulting from the receipt and reinvestment of dividends.)

•15. Did the share prices in problem 14 increase more or less than prices experienced by consumers if the CPI rose from 86.1 at the end of 1982 to 129.4 at the end of 1992? Expressed as a percentage of 1982 price levels, how much more or less did the share prices increase than consumer prices?

16. Between the end of November 1987 and the end of November 1989, the Montreal Stock Exchange's market portfolio index rose from 1464.4 to 1999.8. If, at the end of November 1987, $30,000 had been invested in a portfolio containing the shares of the 25 companies in the index, what was the portfolio worth 2 years later?

17. The late 1970s and early 1980s were years of historically high rates of inflation in Canada. The CPI was at 70.8, 77.1, 84.5, 94.6, 105.4, and 114.1 at the beginning of 1978, 1979, 1980, 1981, 1982, and 1983, respectively. These price index numbers are quoted in terms of the 1981 base year having an average base value of 100.

   a. What amount was required at the beginning of 1983 in order to have the same purchasing power as $100 just 5 years earlier?

   b. What were the inflation rates for each of the years 1978 to 1982 inclusive?

*APPENDIX: LINKAGES AMONG EXCHANGE RATES

Suppose that we begin with 1000 units of currency C3 and put it through three successive currency conversions, as follows.

1000 units of C3
↓
Convert to currency C2 giving
$1000 \times E(C2 : C3)$ units of C2
↓
Convert to currency C1 giving
$1000 \times E(C2 : C3) \times E(C1 : C2)$ units of C1
↓
Convert back to original currency C3 giving
$1000 \times E(C2 : C3) \times E(C1 : C2) \times E(C3 : C1)$ units of C3

Note that we have formed a "closed loop," in the sense that we started with currency C3 and ended back in C3 after passing through two other currencies. If

$$E(C2 : C3) \times E(C1 : C2) \times E(C3 : C1) > 1$$

we would end up with a profit from moving money through the loop. Since this little gambit beats working for a living, we would do it again and again with more and more money—and so would thousands of others!

This movement of funds would create forces of supply and demand that would reduce the value of the currency being sold relative to the value of the currency being purchased. The flow of funds would continue and the exchange rates would adjust until the rates reach values at which no profit can be earned merely by converting currencies around a three-step closed path. When this equilibrium is reached, the exchange rates among the three currencies satisfy the equation

$$E(C2 : C3) \times E(C1 : C2) \times E(C3 : C1) = 1$$

A more easily remembered version of this equilibrium condition is

$$\boxed{E(C1 : C2) \times E(C2 : C3) \times E(C3 : C1) = 1}$$

Note how the currency pairs "rotate" through the three currencies.

If the original loop had produced a loss, that is,

$$E(C2 : C3) \times E(C1 : C2) \times E(C3 : C1) < 1$$

then reversing the direction of the money flow would produce a profit. The previous line of reasoning would lead us to the same equilibrium condition.

In practice, any set of three freely trading currencies will satisfy the equilibrium relation quite closely.[5] Consequently, if two of the exchange rates among any three currencies are known, the equilibrium condition permits the calculation of the third exchange rate.

We could generalize the preceding discussion by looking at a closed path involving 4, 5, . . . , n currencies. The same kind of equilibrium will tend to be reached among any number of freely trading currencies.

EXAMPLE 3A   *CONVERSION AROUND A CLOSED PATH OF THREE CURRENCIES*

Show that there was no profit or loss if an American converted $1000 to British pounds on April 12, 1996, then converted the pounds to German marks, and finally converted the German marks back to US dollars. Again assume that there are no transaction costs. (Use exchange rates from Table 3.2.)

SOLUTION

The solution may be developed in three steps corresponding to the two-step solution for Example 3.5*b.* A more efficient solution uses a chain of currency conversion factors.

$$US\$1000 \times E(\pounds : US\$) \times E(DM : \pounds) \times E(US\$: DM)$$

$$\underbrace{\text{converts}}_{US\$ \to \pounds} \quad \underbrace{\text{converts}}_{\pounds \to DM} \quad \underbrace{\text{converts}}_{DM \to US\$}$$

$$= US\$1000 \times 0.66037 \times 2.27728 \times 0.66496$$
$$= US\$1000 \times 1.00000$$
$$= US\$1000.00$$

Clearly, no profit or loss was realized in the "round trip" currency conversions. ∎

EXAMPLE 3B   *CALCULATING THE THIRD EXCHANGE RATE AMONG THREE CURRENCIES GIVEN THE OTHER TWO EXCHANGE RATES*

If E(US\$: C\$)=0.7632 and E(DM : C\$)=1.1251, determine the value for E(DM : US\$) at which no profits can be made by a series of exchange transactions among the three currencies.

SOLUTION

When the currencies are in equilibrium,

$$E(DM : US\$) \times E(US\$: C\$) \times E(C\$: DM) = 1.000$$

Hence,

$$E(DM : US\$) = \frac{1.000}{E(US\$: C\$) \times E(C\$: DM)}$$

We are given

$$E(US\$: C\$) = 0.7632 \quad \text{and} \quad E(DM : C\$) = 1.1251$$

Therefore,

$$E(C\$: DM) = \frac{1}{E(DM : C\$)} = \frac{1}{1.1251} = 0.88881$$

and

$$E(DM : US\$) = \frac{1.000}{0.7632 \times 0.88881} = 1.4742$$

In equilibrium, $E(DM : US\$) = 1.4742$.   ∎

EXERCISE 3A

1. If $E(A\$: Ffr)=0.2477$ and $E(Ffr : £) = 7.730$, what must $E(£ : A\$)$ be to preclude anyone from profiting through a series of conversions involving the three currencies?

2. If $E(DM : Sfr)=1.2261$ and $E(DM : C\$)=1.1091$, what must $E(C\$: Sfr)$ be to prevent anyone from profiting through a series of conversions involving the three currencies?

•3. Find a table in *The Financial Post* similar to Table 3.2, giving current foreign exchange rates. Using these exchange rates, present two examples of the condition for zero profit from a round-trip series of currency exchange transactions being satisfied. In other words, find two sets of three currencies that satisfy

$$E(C1 : C2) \times E(C2 : C3) \times E(C3 : C1) = 1$$

REVIEW PROBLEMS

Answers to the odd-numbered review problems are at the end of the book.

1. Express each of the following ratios in its lowest terms.

   a. $0.18 : 0.60 : 0.45$ b. $\frac{9}{8} : \frac{3}{4} : \frac{3}{2}$

   c. $\frac{1}{6} : \frac{1}{3} : \frac{1}{9}$ d. $6\frac{1}{4} : 5 : 8\frac{3}{4}$

2. Solve the following proportions for the unknown quantities.

   a. $t : 26 : 10 = 24 : 39 : s$

   b. $x : 3600 : y = \frac{4}{5} : \frac{2}{3} : \frac{7}{4}$

3. Mark, Ben, and Tanya own 4250, 2550, and 5950 shares, respectively, of MBT Inc. What is the ratio of their share holdings?

4. Coral paid a total of $4845, including a 2% brokerage commission, for 200 shares of Terra Corp.

   a. What dollar amount of commission did she pay on the transaction?

   b. What (before-commission) price per share did she pay for the stock?

5. The new University Hospital is scheduled to have 436 beds. The ratio of nurses to beds to nurses' aides for staffing the hospital is $4 : 9 : 2$. How many nurses and aides will need to be hired?

6. For the last 5 years the sales of departments D, E, and F have maintained a relatively stable ratio of $13 : 17 : 21$. Department E is forecasting sales of $478,000 for next year. Based on the past sales ratio, what sales would be expected for departments D and F?

7. Bart purchased 60% of a three-eighths interest in a ski chalet for $25,000. What was the implied value of the chalet?

8. Wendy, Simone, and Leif share the costs of their coffee fund in the ratio $\frac{3}{2} : \frac{2}{3} : \frac{5}{3}$. How will $50 be allocated among them?

9. How should common area costs totalling $28,575 be allocated among commercial tenants A, B, C, and D if the costs are prorated based on leased areas of 1260, 3800, 1550, and 2930 sq ft, respectively?

10. A bartenders' handbook recommends that one bottle of spirits be provided per 10 guests at a New Year's Eve party. Furthermore, the relative consumption of scotch, rye, and rum is in the ratio of $3 : 5 : 4$. How many bottles of each liquor should be stocked for a party expecting 480 guests?

11. A partnership agreement provides that half of the annual profit be distributed in proportion to each partner's investment in the partnership, and that the other half be distributed in proportion to the total number of hours that each partner worked in the business during the year. How should the most recent year's profit of $84,780 be allocated if the amounts invested by Huey, Dewey, and Louie are $70,000, $30,000, and $45,000, and their hours of work for the year were 425, 1680, and 1440, respectively?

12. Before Mr. and Mrs. Percival left for Great Britain, they purchased British pounds at an exchange rate of $E(C\$: £) = 2.053$. When they returned to Canada 8 weeks later they converted the £242 they had left over back to Canadian currency at the rate of $E(C\$: £) = 2.091$. How much did they gain or lose in Canadian dollars on the round-trip transaction involving the £242?

•13. $E(C2 : C1)$ is currently 0.05614. If C1 weakens by 1.5% relative to C2, what will be the new values for $E(C2 : C1)$ and $E(C1 : C2)$?

•14. If E(US$: C$) declines from 0.7543 to 0.7367, what will be the change in the C$ price to an importer of a US$2000 item?

15. The CPI based on a value of 100 on July 1, 1986, stood at 104.4, 108.6, 114.0, 119.5, 126.2, and 128.1 on the same date in 1987, 1988, 1989, 1990, 1991, and 1992, respectively.

   a. What was the inflation rate:
      i. Between July 1, 1990, and July 1, 1991?
      ii. Between July 1, 1991, and July 1, 1992?

   b. What amount was required in 1992 in order to have the same purchasing power as $100 just five years earlier?

SELF-TEST EXERCISE

Answers to the self-test problems are at the end of the book.

1. Solve the following proportions.

   a. $65 : 43 = 27.3 : x$

   b. $1410 : 2330 : 870 = a : 550 : b$

2. Milan, Stephen, and Fred started their partnership with a total investment of $135,000 contributed in the ratio of 3 : 4 : 2. If each partner contributes another $10,000, what will be the ratio of their total contributions?

3. A test-marketing of a newly released video in a representative Canadian city, with a population of 120,000, resulted in sales of 543 units in a 3-month period. If the video sells at the same rate in the rest of the country, where 21,000,000 Canadians have access to retail outlets, what 3-month sales may be forecast for the video?

4. A provincial government allocates 29% of its budget to education, 31% to health care, and 21% to social services. If the dollar amount budgeted for education is $3.17 billion, how much is budgeted for health care and for social services?

5. The total cost, including the 7% Goods and Services (GST) tax, for a business lunch was $23.22. What was the dollar amount of the GST?

6. A profit-sharing bonus was divided among four employees—Ms. L, Mr. M, Ms. N, and Mr. P—in the ratio of 1.5 : 1 : 0.75 : 0.5, respectively. If Ms. N received $2000, how much did each of the others receive?

7. Mr. Nolan's will specifies that the proceeds from his estate be divided among his wife, son, and stepson in the ratio of $\frac{7}{5} : 1 : \frac{5}{7}$, respectively. How much will each receive from the distribution of his $331,000 estate?

8. If E(C$: Italian lira) = 0.0009526, how many lira can be purchased with C$1500?

9. Three years ago, when the CPI was at 127.6, the members of a union were earning $22.25 per hour. Now, with the current CPI at 148.4, they are negotiating for a new hourly rate that will restore their former purchasing power. What hourly rate are they seeking?

•10. If E(¥ : C$) rises from 72.11 to 73.89, what will be the change in the C$ price to an importer of a ¥2,965,000 car?

•11. A steel company in Hamilton can purchase Alberta coal at C$39.50 per metric tonne (1000 kg) or Virginia coal at US$27.25 per tonne (2000 lb) (1 kg = 2.205 lb). How much cheaper in C$ per metric tonne is the less expensive source if E(US$: C$) = 0.7528?

SUMMARY OF NOTATION AND KEY FORMULAS

$E(C1 : C2) =$ Number of units of currency C1 equal to one unit of currency C2

$$E(C1 : C2) = \frac{1}{E(C2 : C1)}$$

The two alternatives for stating the exchange rate between two currencies are reciprocals

$$\text{Index number} = \frac{\left(\begin{array}{c}\text{Price or value on}\\\text{selected date}\end{array}\right)}{\left(\begin{array}{c}\text{Price or value on}\\\text{base date}\end{array}\right)} \times \text{Base value}$$

Calculating an index number

GLOSSARY OF TERMS

Continued ratio   A ratio containing three or more terms.

Equivalent ratio   A ratio obtained from another ratio by multiplying or dividing each term of the ratio by the same number.

Exchange rate   The ratio of equivalent amounts of two currencies.

Proportion   A statement of the equality of two ratios.

Proration   A procedure in which an amount is subdivided and allocated on a proportionate basis.

Ratio   A comparison, by division, of the relative sizes of two or more quantities.

Terms of a ratio   The numbers being compared in the ratio.

4 MATHEMATICS OF MERCHANDISING

LEARNING OBJECTIVES

After completing this chapter, you will be able to:

- Calculate the net price of an item after single or multiple trade discounts
- Calculate a single discount rate that is equivalent to a series of multiple discounts
- Apply the basic equation for discounting to other applications involving a fractional reduction from an initial amount
- Understand the notation for expressing the terms of payment on an invoice

- Calculate the amount of the cash discount for which a payment qualifies
- Solve merchandise pricing problems involving:
    Unit cost, unit overhead, and unit profit
    Markup and markdown

INTRODUCTION

Goods move from a manufacturer to the ultimate consumer through what is referred to as the *distribution chain* or *merchandising chain.* The longest distribution chain is illustrated in Figure 4.1. The goods are first sold by a *manufacturer* to a *distributor,* who handles a limited variety of products for a large geographic region. The distributor then resells the goods to a number of *wholesalers,* each of whom carries a broader range of products for resale to *retailers* within a smaller geographic area. The retailers sell mainly to the ultimate consumers of the goods. In many cases, one of the intermediate links may be absent. Large national retailers often have enough buying power to purchase directly from manufacturers.

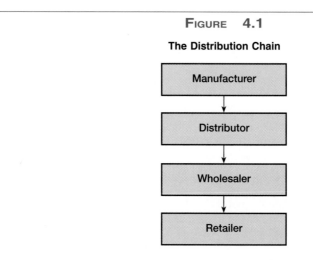

FIGURE   4.1

The Distribution Chain

Most transactions within the distribution chain from the manufacturer to the retailer are on credit terms. Price and discount structures are usually designed to encourage the customers at each stage to buy early, buy in quantity, and pay promptly. The first three sections of this chapter discuss common practices for the quotation and calculation of trade discounts and cash discounts.

When setting resale prices of goods, each link in the distribution chain must have accurate knowledge of its costs and its profit targets. The last three sections in the chapter present some of the terminology and calculations used in making pricing decisions.

4.1 TRADE DISCOUNTS

Suppliers of a product often attempt to influence its retail price by basing prices on a "suggested retail price," "suggested list price," or "recommended selling price." We will refer to this simply as the **list price.** The price that a distributor, a wholesaler, or a retailer pays for the product is then determined by deducting a certain percentage, called the **trade discount** (rate), from the list price. The resulting price is called the **net price.**

Trap

The term *trade discount* is the first example in this chapter of the use of the same term in business to mean either the percentage amount or the dollar amount of a given quantity. The intended meaning is sometimes obvious from the units quoted (% or $). To avoid confusion in other cases, we will use "*rate* of trade discount" or "trade discount *rate*" to refer to the trade discount measured as a percentage of the list price. The "*amount* of the trade discount" will refer to the trade discount measured in dollars. For example, if a trade discount *rate* of 35% applies to a $200 list price item, the *amount* of the trade discount is $70.

Distributors are normally offered larger trade discount rates than wholesalers, who, in turn, receive larger trade discount rates than retailers. Large retail chain stores and department stores may be offered larger trade discounts than small independent retailers because of their greater volume of purchases. Independent retailers often cooperate in "buying groups" to gain the benefits of volume buying and to increase their strength in negotiations with distributors and manufacturers.

Following a transaction between two levels of the merchandising chain, the seller usually issues an invoice to the buyer. A sample invoice is shown in Figure 4.2. An invoice presents details of the items purchased, their unit prices, the trade discounts granted, the terms of payment, and the total amount owed on the purchase. The treatment of multiple trade discounts, such as those granted on the soccer balls and pucks listed in Figure 4.2, will be presented in Section 4.2. The interpretation of the entry "terms: 2/10, n30" will be discussed in Section 4.3.

FIGURE   4.2

A Sample Sales Invoice

ATLANTIC ATHLETIC WHOLESALE LTD.
177 Main Avenue
Halifax, Nova Scotia B3M 1B4

Sold to:
  McGarrigle Sports   Date: July 17, 1997   Invoice No: 3498
  725 Kings Road   Terms: 2/10, n30   Via: Beatty Trucking
  Sydney, N.S. B1S 1C2

Quantity	Product number	Description	Unit list price	Trade discount	Amount
5	W-32	Universal Gymnasium	$1150	30%	$4025.00
150	S-4	Soccer balls	$38.00	25%, 15%	3633.75
1000	H-8a	Hockey pucks	$2.10	35%, 10%, 7%	1142.51

Invoice total:	$8,801.26
GST:	616.09
PST:	na
Shipping charges:	346.00
Total amount due:	$9,763.34

1.5% per month on overdue accounts

The following symbols will be used to derive a formula for calculating the net price after applying a trade discount rate to the list price.

L = List price
d = Rate of trade discount
N = Net price

The *amount* of the discount is the product, dL, of the discount rate and the list price. Since

$$\text{Net price} = \text{List price} - \text{Amount of discount}$$

then

$$N = L - dL = L(1 - d)$$

Net Price after a Trade Discount

$$\boxed{N = L(1 - d)} \qquad (4\text{–}1)$$

Note that the rate of trade discount is nothing more than a percent change to be applied to the list price, L. Taking this point of view, formula (2–1a) can be used to calculate the final or net price after the percent change. Substituting $V_i = L$ and $c = (-d)$ in

$$V_f = V_i(1 + c) \qquad (2\text{–}1a)$$

gives the final price, V_f, which in this context we call the net price, N. That is,

$$V_f = N = L[1 + (-d)] = L(1 - d)$$

This demonstrates that formula (4–1) is a special case of formula (2–1a) and therefore, of formula (2–1).

■ EXAMPLE 4.1A   CALCULATING THE DISCOUNT AMOUNT AND NET PRICE

A wholesaler lists an item at $117 less 20%. What is the amount of the discount and the net price to a retailer?

☑ SOLUTION

Given: L = $117, d = 0.20.

$$\text{Amount of discount} = dL = (0.20)(\$117) = \$23.40$$

$$\begin{aligned}\text{Net price} &= \text{List price} - \text{Amount of discount}\\ &= \$117 - \$23.40\\ &= \$93.60\end{aligned}$$ ■

■ EXAMPLE 4.1B   CALCULATING THE LIST PRICE

After a trade discount of 30%, a garage is able to purchase windshield wiper blades for a net price of $9.73. What is the list price of the blades?

☑ SOLUTION

Given: d = 0.30, N = $9.73.

If formula (4–1) is rearranged to isolate L, we obtain

$$L = \frac{N}{1 - d} = \frac{\$9.73}{1 - 0.30} = \frac{\$9.73}{0.7} = \$13.90$$

The list price of the blades is $13.90.   ■

■ EXAMPLE 4.1c *CALCULATING THE TRADE DISCOUNT RATE*

A clothing store is able to purchase men's leather coats at a net price of $173.40 after a discount of $115.60. What rate of trade discount was obtained?

☑ SOLUTION

Given: Net price = $173.40, Amount of discount = $115.60.

$$\text{List price} = \text{Net price} + \text{Amount of discount}$$
$$= \$173.40 + \$115.60$$
$$= \$289.00$$

$$d = \frac{\text{Amount of discount}}{\text{List price}}$$
$$= \frac{\$115.60}{\$289.00}$$
$$= 0.40$$

The trade discount rate is 40%.   ■

OTHER APPLICATIONS You may prefer to use $N = L(1 - d)$ instead of $V_f = V_i(1 + c)$ in other situations where an initial amount is reduced by a percentage. Such applications include the calculation of sales revenue net of commission, net income after income tax, security prices after a percentage loss in value, sale price after a percentage markdown, and budget amounts after a percentage cut. The following example and the subsequent exercise set present a variety of applications.

■ EXAMPLE 4.1d *USING THE DISCOUNT FORMULA TO CALCULATE INCOME RETAINED AFTER INCOME TAX*

Scott is in the lowest of the three main income tax brackets. In his province of residence, the combined federal and provincial income tax rate in his bracket is 25.9%. Scott will therefore pay an additional 25.9¢ of income tax on each additional dollar of income.

a. How much will Scott retain after tax if he earns an additional $100?

b. What additional amount must Scott earn to retain $100 of it after income tax?

c. When Scott's income reaches the point at which he enters the middle tax bracket, his tax rate on additional income will be 39.7%. Then what additional amount must he earn to retain $100 of it after tax?

☑ SOLUTION

a. We want to know the net amount remaining after $100 ($L$) is reduced by $d = 0.259$.

$$N = L(1 - d) = \$100(1 - 0.259) = \$74.10$$

Scott will retain $74.10 after deduction of income tax.

b. In this case $100 represents the net amount N after the fractional reduction d. The required additional earnings are

$$L = \frac{N}{1 - d} = \frac{\$100}{1 - 0.259} = \$134.95$$

Scott must earn $134.95 before tax to retain $100 after tax.

c.
$$L = \frac{N}{1 - d} = \frac{\$100}{1 - 0.397} = \$165.84$$

In the middle tax bracket, Scott must earn an additional $165.84 in order to net $100 after tax.   ■

EXERCISE 4.1

Answers to the odd-numbered problems are at the end of the book.

Calculate the missing values in problems 1 through 10.

Problem	List price ($)	Discount rate (%)	Discount amount ($)	Net price ($)
1.	249.00	$33\frac{1}{3}$	?	?
2.	995.00	$16\frac{2}{3}$	?	?
3.	127.98	?	?	106.65
4.	49.95	?	?	34.97
5.	?	35	612.50	?
6.	?	40	7.99	?
7.	?	?	12.33	15.07
8.	?	?	258.75	891.25
•9.	?	12.5	?	2849.00
•10.	?	$16\frac{2}{3}$	?	413.05

11. The distributor of Nikita power tools is offering a trade discount of 38% to hardware stores. What will be their cost to purchase a rotary saw listed at $135?

12. SuperSave stores can purchase Annapolis Gold apple juice for $11.50 per case less a trade discount of 30%. It can also obtain No-Name apple juice at a discount of 22% from the suggested retail price of $10.50 per case. Which juice will have the lower cost to SuperSave?

13. A 37.5% trade discount on a camera represents a discount of $111.57 from the suggested retail price. What is the net price to the buyer?

14. The net price of a product after a discount of 15% is $845.75. What is the (dollar) amount of the discount?

15. The net price on an item listed for $369 is $287.82. What trade discount rate is being given?

16. Green Thumb Nursery sells spreading junipers to the gardening departments of local grocery and building supply stores. The net price per tree is $27.06 after a trade discount of $22.14. What rate of trade discount is the nursery giving to retailers?

•17. Niagara Dairies gives convenience stores a discount of 24% on butter listed at $72.00 per case. What rate of discount will Silverwood Milk Products have to give on its list price of $74.50 per case to match Niagara's price to convenience stores?

18. A grocery store is offering an in-store special of 15% off the sticker price of all cheese. What will a customer pay for a pound of cheese listed at $5.23?

19. The net proceeds to the vendor of a house after payment of a 5.5% real estate commission was $160,555.50. At what price did the house sell?

20. A merchant pays a 3.5% fee to the Bank of Montreal on all MasterCard sales.

    a. What amount will she pay on sales of $17,564 for a month?

    b. What were her gross sales for a month in which the bank charged total fees of $732.88?

21. Cynthia and Byron sell mutual funds for Syndicated Investors. Purchasers of mutual funds from agents of Syndicated Investors pay a front-end commission of 5.5%. The commission is paid on the total amount placed with Syndicated Investors, not on just the net amount actually invested in mutual funds.

    a. Mr. and Mrs. Stevens placed $5500 through Cynthia. What (net) amount was actually invested in mutual funds after the commission was paid?

    b. If the net amount invested in mutual funds as a result of Byron's sale to Mrs. Stocker was $6426, what (dollar) amount of commission was paid on the sale?

22. a. Lauren's income tax rate on additional income is 42%. She has just received a wage increase of $1.25 per hour. What is her after-tax increase in hourly pay?

    b. Marvin's tax rate on additional income is 47%. How much extra must he earn to keep an additional $1000 after tax?

23. The evening news reports that the TSE 300 index dropped 1.3% on the day to close at 3561 points. How many points did the index fall on the day?

24. At its current price of $0.80 per share, the price of Golden Egg Resources stock is down 73% from its price one year ago. What was that price?

•25. Randy earns $26.50 an hour as a lineman for a provincial electric utility. He is offered the chance to work a substantial amount of overtime paid at 1.5 times his regular wage. He decides to work enough overtime to buy a new $2500 engine for his boat. If his tax rate on additional income is 41.5%, how many hours of overtime must he work to save $2500 of after-tax earnings?

•26. a. In a budget speech the federal government announced a $132 million cut in defense spending. This represents 11.4% of the previous year's defense budget. What is the new budgeted amount?

    b. The number of military personnel is to be reduced by 8.8% to 76,500. How many people are to be cut from the military?

4.2 TRADE DISCOUNT SERIES

A manufacturer may sell a product to more than one level of the distribution chain, or it may sell to a variety of customers who purchase vastly differing quantities of the product. In either of these circumstances some customers may be offered two or three discounts. For example, there may be three discounts—25%, 10%, and 7%—of which the 25% discount is given to retailers, both the 25% and 10% discounts are given to wholesalers, and distributors receive all three discounts.

Multiple discounts may also be used between two levels of the merchandising chain to give the vendor more flexibility to:

• Encourage large-volume ordering.

• Encourage early ordering of seasonal items.

- Offer special promotions and cooperative advertising.
- Compensate retailers who provide greater product servicing.

On the invoice in Figure 4.2, for example, the first listed discount is the regular discount that the wholesaler offers to retailers. The second discount offered on the soccer balls and hockey pucks might be for purchases exceeding a particular volume, such as 99 soccer balls and 999 pucks. The third discount on the pucks might be for purchases before August 1.

A set of multiple discounts is called a **discount series** or a *discount chain*. The industry practice is to compound the discounts rather than simply add them. Consequently, we can adapt formula (2–3) for a series of compound percent changes to create a formula for calculating the net price after all discounts. Since a discount represents a negative percent change, we begin with the version of formula (2–3) in which c's have been replaced by $(-d)$'s. Then each d represents the magnitude of the decimal equivalent value of a discount.

$$V_{fn} = V_i(1 - d_1)(1 - d_2) \cdots (1 - d_n) \qquad (2\text{–}3)$$

The list price, L, corresponds to the initial value, V_i, and the net price, N, corresponds to the final value, V_{fn}, after all n discounts. Hence,

Net Price after a Discount Series

$$\boxed{N = L(1 - d_1)(1 - d_2) \cdots (1 - d_n)} \qquad (4\text{–}2)$$

Although the formula allows for any number of discounts, more than three discounts in any merchandising transaction would be very unusual.[1]

> **Trap**
>
> The net price cannot be calculated by simply adding the multiple discounts and then using this total as an equivalent single discount d in formula (4–1).

■ EXAMPLE 4.2A   CALCULATING THE NET PRICE AFTER A DISCOUNT SERIES

WGW Manufacturing and Ace Clothing produce basic work shirts that are very similar in quality and popularity. Both manufacturers quote a list price of $29.90 for the shirt. WGW offers a regular trade discount of 25% plus an additional volume discount of 10% on orders of at least 1000 shirts. Ace offers a standard discount of 30% and a further 5% on orders exceeding 500 shirts. Which source will give the lower net price on an order for 1000 shirts?

☑ SOLUTION

A problem involving a discount series may be approached by repeatedly using formula (4–1) to apply each successive discount to the net price after the previous discount. Alternatively, formula (4–2) may be employed to apply all discounts in a single step. We will present both approaches for the solution to this problem.

---

[1] The use of multiple discounts in transactions in the merchandising chain has declined in recent years. Department stores, discount stores, franchise chains, and buying groups are increasingly bypassing "middlemen" and short-circuiting the traditional merchandising chain. They are primarily interested in the "bottom line" or net price; they do not care whether the best price happens to result from two discounts applied to a higher list price or from a single discount applied to a lower list price (or, for that matter, whether list prices and trade discounts are mentioned at all).

Using Formula (4−1):
For a shirt from WGW the net price after the regular trade discount is

$$N = L(1 - d) = \$29.90(1 - 0.25) = \$22.43$$

The net price after the additional 10% volume discount is

$$N = L(1 - d) = \$22.43(1 - 0.10) = \$20.18$$

For a shirt from Ace the net price after the standard 30% discount is

$$N = \$29.90(1 - 0.30) = \$20.93$$

After the additional 5% volume discount the net price is

$$N = \$20.93(1 - 0.05) = \$19.88$$

Therefore, Ace's net price is

$$\$20.18 - \$19.88 = \$0.30$$

lower per shirt.

Using Formula (4−2):
The net price of a shirt from WGW is

$$
\begin{aligned}
N &= L(1 - d_1)(1 - d_2) \\
&= \$29.90(1 - 0.25)(1 - 0.10) \\
&= \$29.90(0.75)(0.90) \\
&= \$20.18
\end{aligned}
$$

The net price from Ace Clothing is

$$
\begin{aligned}
N &= L(1 - d_1)(1 - d_2) \\
&= \$29.90(1 - 0.30)(1 - 0.05) \\
&= \$29.90(0.70)(0.95) \\
&= \$19.88
\end{aligned}
$$

Therefore, Ace's net price is 30 cents per shirt lower.

This example also demonstrates that the combined effect of multiple discounts cannot be determined by simply adding the discounts. For both manufacturers the sum of the discounts is 35%, but their combined effects differ from each other (and from a single discount of 35%). ∎

EQUIVALENT DISCOUNT RATE An **equivalent discount rate** is the single discount rate that would give the same net price as the discount series. Let

$$d_e = \text{Discount rate equivalent to the discount series } d_1, d_2, d_3$$

If d_e has the same effect as the discount series, then the net price calculated using d_e in formula (4−1) must equal the net price calculated using the discount series with formula (4−2). That is,

$$L(1 - d_e) = L(1 - d_1)(1 - d_2)(1 - d_3)$$

Dividing both sides by L gives

$$1 - d_e = (1 - d_1)(1 - d_2)(1 - d_3)$$

Therefore,

**Equivalent
Discount Rate**

$$d_e = 1 - (1 - d_1)(1 - d_2)(1 - d_3)$$

(4–3)

Note: The equivalent discount rate always turns out to be *smaller* than the sum of the three individual discounts.

■ EXAMPLE 4.2B CALCULATING AN EQUIVALENT DISCOUNT RATE

What single discount rate is equivalent to the discount series 20%, 8⅓%, 5%?

☑ SOLUTION

Using Direct Substitution in Formula (4–3):

$$
\begin{aligned}
d_e &= 1 - (1 - d_1)(1 - d_2)(1 - d_3) \\
&= 1 - (1 - 0.20)(1 - 0.08\overline{3})(1 - 0.05) \\
&= 1 - (0.80)(0.91\overline{6})(0.95) \\
&= 1 - 0.69\overline{6} \\
&= 0.30\overline{3}
\end{aligned}
$$

A single discount of 30.33% is equivalent to the three series discounts.

Using a More Intuitive Approach:
Suppose the discounts apply to an item with a list price of $100. The net price will be

$$
\begin{aligned}
N &= L(1 - d_1)(1 - d_2)(1 - d_3) \\
&= \$100(1 - 0.20)(1 - 0.08\overline{3})(1 - 0.05) \\
&= \$100(0.80)(0.91\overline{6})(0.95) \\
&= \$69.67
\end{aligned}
$$

The total amount of the discount is $30.33. The single equivalent discount rate is

$$d = \frac{\text{Discount amount}}{\text{List price}} = \frac{\$30.33}{\$100} = 0.3033 = 30.33\%$$ ■

■ EXAMPLE 4.2C CALCULATING ONE OF THE DISCOUNTS IN A DISCOUNT SERIES

The manufacturer of Sonee television sets gives its Canadian distributor discounts of 30%, 10%, and 5%. Hamaya produces a line of competing television sets. What third discount must it offer in addition to 25% and 12% to match Sonee's total trade discount?

☑ SOLUTION

Given: For Sonee, $d_1 = 0.30$, $d_2 = 0.10$, $d_3 = 0.05$. For Hamaya, $d_1 = 0.25$, $d_2 = 0.12$.

The solution is based on finding a third discount d_3 for Hamaya that will make the equivalent discount the same for both firms.

$$
\begin{aligned}
d_e \text{ (Sonee)} &= 1 - (1 - d_1)(1 - d_2)(1 - d_3) \\
&= 1 - (1 - 0.30)(1 - 0.10)(1 - 0.05) \\
&= 1 - (0.70)(0.90)(0.95) \\
&= 1 - 0.5985 \\
&= 0.4015
\end{aligned}
$$

This must also be the equivalent discount rate for Hamaya.

$$d_e \text{ (Hamaya)} = 1 - (1 - 0.25)(1 - 0.12)(1 - d_3)$$
$$0.4015 = 1 - (0.75)(0.88)(1 - d_3)$$
$$0.4015 - 1 = -0.66(1 - d_3)$$
$$0.5985 = 0.66(1 - d_3)$$
$$1 - d_3 = \frac{0.5985}{0.66} = 0.9068$$
$$d_3 = 1 - 0.9068 = 0.0932$$

Hamaya would need to offer a third discount of 9.32% to match Sonee's overall discount to its distributor. ∎

EXERCISE 4.2

Answers to the odd-numbered problems are at the end of the book.

Calculate the missing values in problems 1 through 10.

Problem	List price ($)	Series discounts (%)	Equivalent discount rate (%)	Net price ($)
1.	99.00	30, $16\frac{2}{3}$	?	?
2.	595.00	20, 12.5, $8\frac{1}{3}$	?	?
3.	?	25, 10, 7.5	?	93.03
4.	?	20, 10, $8\frac{1}{3}$	?	989.00
5.	366.00	?, 12.5, $8\frac{1}{3}$	$48\frac{2}{3}$	?
6.	39.95	20, ?, 5	33.4	?
7.	?	$33\frac{1}{3}$, ?, 5	44.27	769.12
8.	?	?, $16\frac{2}{3}$, 7.5	$38\frac{1}{3}$	122.10
9.	49.95	20, 15, ?	?	30.57
10.	1295.00	25, 7.5, ?	?	831.03

11. A manufacturer of snowmobiles sells through distributors in some regions of the country, through wholesalers in other regions, and directly to retailers in its home province. The manufacturer gives a 25% trade discount to retailers, an additional 10% discount to wholesalers, and a further 7.5% discount to distributors. What net price does the manufacturer receive from each buying level on a snowmobile listed at $5800?

12. A retailer is offered a regular discount of 25%, a further discount of 7.5% if she places an order exceeding $10,000 (at list prices), and another 5% discount for participating in a joint promotion with the distributor.

    a. If the retailer is eligible for all three discounts, what will be the net price of an order totalling $11,500?

    b. What is the dollar amount of the saving for the quantity discount (assuming that she does not participate in the joint promotion)?

    c. What is the dollar amount of the discount received for participating in the joint promotion?

13. An invoice shows a net price of $176.72 after discounts of 30%, 10%, and 2% have been deducted.

    a. What was the list price of the goods?

    b. What single discount would be equivalent to the discount series?

14. A wholesaler lists an item for $48.75 less 20%. What additional "special promotion" discount must be offered to retailers to get the net price down to $36.66?

15. The representative for an European ski manufacturer offers Snow 'n Surf Sporting Goods a regular discount of 25%, a volume discount of 10% for an order of at least 100 pairs of skis, and an early booking discount of 5% for orders placed before July 1.

   a. If Snow 'n Surf is eligible for all three discounts on skis listed at a suggested retail price of $445, what is the net price per pair of skis?

   b. Assuming that Snow 'n Surf qualifies for the volume discount, what is the dollar amount of the early-order discount per pair of skis?

   c. The net price after all three discounts on a less expensive model of skis is $205.20. What is the suggested retail price?

   d. What single trade discount rate would be equivalent to the three trade discounts?

16. In addition to the basic trade discount of 20%, an outboard motor manufacturer gives a boat dealer an additional discount of 12.5% for providing follow-up warranty service, and a 5% discount for cooperative advertising and boat show promotions.

   a. After the basic discount, what further price reduction (in dollars) does the 12.5% discount represent on a $1000 list price motor?

   b. After the first two discounts, what price reduction does the 5% discount give on the $1000 motor?

17. DRT Industries offers a series of three discounts on its products. The combined discounts result in a total discount of $58.15 from a list price of $160. If two of the discounts are 25% and 12½%, what is the third discount rate?

•18. Everest sells its mattresses for $480 less 25%. Posture-Perfect mattresses are listed at $440 less 20% and 5%. What second discount would Everest need to offer to match Posture-Perfect's net price?

•19. Javelin Manufacturing and Noremco produce similar, competitively priced product lines. They both want Interprovincial Distributing to handle their products. Noremco first offered discounts of 33⅓% and 10%. Javelin then offered discounts of 30% and 16⅔%. What third discount would Noremco need to add to match Javelin's combined discounts?

4.3 CASH DISCOUNTS AND TERMS OF PAYMENT

As mentioned previously, most transactions within the merchandising chain are on (trade) credit. When goods are sold on credit, the terms of payment must be clearly stated on the invoice to the buyer. The **terms of payment** include:

- The length of the credit period.
- The cash discount (rate) offered, if any.
- The length of the discount period.
- The date on which the credit and discount periods start.

The **credit period** or *net period* is the length of time for which credit is granted. Any balance owed on the invoice is due at the end of the credit period. The usual practice is to not charge interest for the credit period. However, the purchaser is normally liable for interest charges on overdue amounts.

Businesses granting trade credit will frequently offer customers a cash discount incentive[2] for prompt payment of the amount owed. A **cash discount** is a percentage

---

[2]It is generally advisable for the purchaser to take advantage of a cash discount since the discount normally represents a high equivalent annual rate of return on the early payment. The failure of a customer to take a cash discount therefore provides an early warning signal to the creditor that the customer may, at least temporarily, be in a weak financial condition.

deduction allowed for early payments applied to the net amount of the invoice. The time period within which a payment qualifies for the cash discount is called the **discount period.**

Shorthand notations have evolved for the concise disclosure of the payment terms on an invoice. For example, the terms of payment on the invoice in Figure 4.2 are specified as "2/10, n/30." This notation incorporates all four elements previously listed for the terms of payment. Three variations of the basic notation are used to identify the beginning of the credit and discount periods.

ORDINARY DATING OR INVOICE DATING

The credit period and the discount period both begin on the date of the invoice. Figure 4.3 illustrates how a particular example of ordinary dating—2/10, n/30 (read as "two ten, net thirty")—is interpreted. This notation means that a 2% cash discount is allowed on payments made within the 10-day discount period after the invoice date. Otherwise the net amount (after any trade discounts) is due by the end of the 30-day credit period.

FIGURE   **4.3**

Interpreting the Terms of Payment in Ordinary Dating

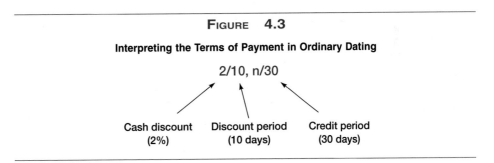

Figure 4.4 shows the time relationships among the invoice date, discount period, and credit period for the ordinary dating example 2/10, n/30. (This figure is most useful for later comparison with Figures 4.5 and 4.6, which illustrate the other two terms-of-payment notations.) Note that the day *following* the invoice date is the first day of the credit and discount periods. If you are uncertain about the number of days in any month, refer to Table 6.1 in Section 6.2.

FIGURE   **4.4**

Discount and Credit Periods for the Ordinary Dating Case 2/10, n/30

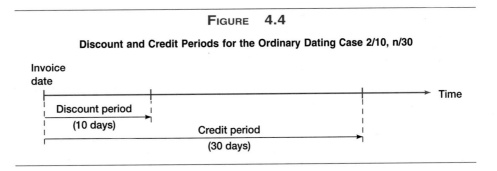

A variation of the ordinary dating notation is "2/10, 1/30, n/60," where a reduced cash discount of 1% is also offered on payments made any time from the eleventh to the thirtieth day after the invoice date.

The following are common practices with all three dating notations discussed in this section.

- If the last day of the discount period or the credit period falls on a non-business day, the period is extended to the next business day.
- If the net figure for the credit period is not stated, the credit period is understood to end 20 days *after* the end of the discount period.

Formula (4−1), $N = L(1 - d)$, may be used to calculate the amount required to settle an invoice if the cash discount is taken. The cash discount may be viewed as just one more discount to be applied *after* any trade discounts. Substitute the invoiced amount (after trade discounts) for L and the cash discount rate for d. The value calculated for N is the payment that will settle the invoice within the discount period.

■ EXAMPLE 4.3A   INVOICE SETTLEMENT WITH ORDINARY DATING

An invoice for $1079.80 with terms 2/10, n/30 is dated November 25 and received in the mail on November 27. What payment will settle the invoice if payment is made on:

a. December 1?

b. December 5?

c. December 7?

☑ SOLUTION

a., b. The discount period ends at the end of the tenth day after the invoice date. Payments made on or before December 5 are eligible for the 2% cash discount. The payment required to settle the invoice is:

$$N = L(1 - d)$$
$$= \$1079.80(1 - 0.02)$$
$$= \$1058.20$$

c. The full amount of the invoice must be paid after December 5. The payment required is $1079.80.   ■

END-OF-MONTH (EOM) DATING

In **end-of-month dating,** the discount and credit periods both begin at the end of the month in the invoice date. Figure 4.5 shows the time relationships among the invoice

---

FIGURE   4.5

Discount and Credit Periods for the EOM Dating Case 2/10, n/30, EOM

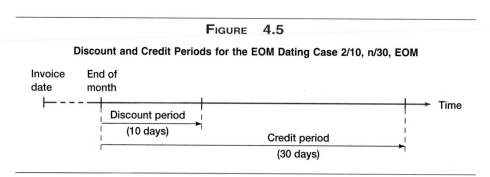

---

date, the end-of-month date, the discount period, and the credit period for the dating example 2/10, n/30, EOM. In this case the 2% cash discount may be taken within the 10 days *following* the last day of the month shown in the invoice date. If no credit period is explicitly stated, it is understood that the credit period ends 20 days after the discount period. Therefore, n/30 is implied in the notation 2/10, EOM.

End-of-month dating is sometimes called *proximo dating* based on the Latin phrase *proximo mense* meaning "in the next month." The notation "2/10, prox" means the same as "2/10, EOM."

■ EXAMPLE 4.3B   *INVOICE SETTLEMENT WITH EOM DATING*

An invoice for $650.48 with terms 1½ /10, EOM is dated November 25. What payment will settle the invoice on:

a. November 28?

b. December 6?

c. December 10?

d. December 11?

☑ SOLUTION

a., b., c. The discount period ends at the end of the tenth day after the month's end. Payments made on or before December 10 qualify for the 1½% cash discount. The payment required to settle the invoice is

$$N = L(1 - d)$$
$$= \$650.48(1 - 0.015)$$
$$= \$640.72$$

d. Payment of the full $650.48 is required.   ■

RECEIPT-OF-GOODS (ROG) DATING

When the goods being purchased are to be shipped over a long distance with an uncertain delivery date, **receipt-of-goods** (ROG) **dating** is often used. Payment terms quoted in the form "2/10, n/30, ROG" mean that the discount and credit periods start on the date of receipt of the goods. Figure 4.6 shows the time relationships among the invoice date, the date of receipt of the goods, the discount period, and the credit period for the ROG dating example 2/10, n/30, ROG.

FIGURE   4.6

Discount and Credit Periods for the ROG Dating Case 2/10, n/30, ROG

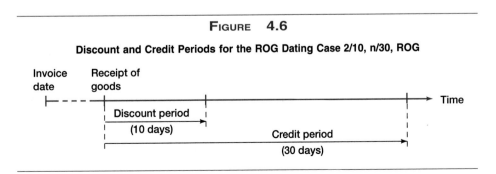

■ EXAMPLE 4.3c   ROG DATING

An invoice dated November 25 for $5340 with terms 1/15, ROG was received on December 1. The merchandise was shipped from Vancouver on December 15 and was received by the purchaser on January 8.

a. What is the last day of the discount period?

b. What is the last day of the credit period?

☑ SOLUTION

a. The discount period ends at the end of the fifteenth day after the date of receipt of the goods. January 23 is the last day of the discount period.

b. When a net period is not stated, the understanding is that the credit period ends 20 days after the end of the discount period. This makes February 12 the last day of the credit period. Any unpaid balance is due on that date.   ■

PARTIAL PAYMENTS

A **partial payment** is any payment smaller than the amount required to fully settle the invoice. Unless otherwise indicated on the invoice, partial payments made within the discount period are eligible for the cash discount *on the amount credited.* The basic discount formula (4–1), $N = L(1 - d)$, may be used to calculate the amount credited to the customer's account. The amount credited will, of course, be greater than the amount paid. In formula (4–1), L, the pre-discount amount, is larger than N, the post-discount amount. Therefore,

- L corresponds to the amount credited.
- N corresponds to the amount paid.
- d corresponds to the cash discount rate.

Consequently,

$$\text{Amount credited, } L = \frac{\text{Amount paid, } N}{1 - d}$$

Trap

A very common error is to calculate the cash discount allowed on a partial payment as $d \times$ payment. To understand why this is incorrect, recall how you calculate the cash discount when you pay an invoice in full. Suppose an invoiced amount of $1000 is eligible for a 2% cash discount. A payment of $980 will settle the account within the discount period because you will be allowed a $20 cash discount. Notice that the $20 discount is 2% of the $1000 credit ($L$), not 2% of the $980 paid ($N$). Similarly, if a partial payment of $500 ($N$) is made within the discount period, the cash discount will be 2% of the initially unknown amount credited (L), not 2% of $500 payment ($N$). The amount credited will be

$$L = \frac{N}{1 - d} = \frac{\$500}{1 - 0.02} = \$510.20$$

The cash discount allowed on the $500 payment is therefore

$$\$510.20 - \$500 = \$10.20$$

which is 2% of the amount credited ($510.20).

■ EXAMPLE 4.3D *PARTIAL PAYMENTS WITH EOM DATING*

Counter Culture Microbiological Labs received an invoice for $3000 dated October 20 with terms 2/10, EOM.

a. What amount must Counter Culture pay on November 10 to reduce the balance owed by $1000?

b. What will be the balance owed if Counter Culture pays $1000 on November 10?

☑ SOLUTION

a. November 10 is the last day of the discount period. Any partial payment within the discount period qualifies for the cash discount. Using the adaptation of formula (4−1),

$$\text{Amount paid, } N = \text{Amount credited, } L \times (1 - d)$$
$$= \$1000(1 - 0.02)$$
$$= \$980.00$$

b. This is an example of the situation you were cautioned about in the preceding Trap. The cash discount is not simply $d \times$ payment ($20 in this case). Instead, go back to the adaptation of formula (4−1):

$$\text{Amount paid} = \text{Amount credited} \times (1 - d)$$
$$\$1000 = \text{Amount credited} \times (1 - 0.02)$$
$$\text{Amount credited} = \frac{\$1000}{1 - 0.02} = \frac{\$1000}{0.98} = \$1020.41$$
$$\text{Balance owed} = \$3000 - \$1020.41 = \$1979.59$$

■ EXAMPLE 4.3E *PARTIAL PAYMENTS WITH ORDINARY DATING*

Roland Electric received an invoice for $3845 dated March 25 with terms 3/10, 1/20, n/60. Roland paid $1500 on April 4, $500 on April 12, and $500 on April 30. What balance was still owed after April 30?

☑ SOLUTION

The $1500 payment qualifies for the 3% discount, and the first $500 payment qualifies for the 1% discount. Since

$$\text{Amount credited} = \frac{\text{Amount paid}}{1 - d}$$

the total amount credited for the three payments is

$$\frac{\$1500}{1 - 0.03} + \frac{\$500}{1 - 0.01} + \$500 = \$1546.39 + \$505.05 + \$500$$
$$= \$2551.44$$
$$\text{Balance owed} = \$3845 - \$2551.44 = \$1293.56$$

EXERCISE 4.3

Answers to the odd-numbered problems are at the end of the book.

For problems 1 through 8, determine the payment required to settle the invoice on the indicated payment date.

Problem	Invoice amount	Credit terms	Invoice date	Date goods received	Payment date
1.	$2365.00	2/10, n/30	Sept 25	Sept 30	Oct 5
2.	2365.00	1½/15, n/45	Oct 25	Oct 30	Nov 10
3.	815.49	2/10, 1/20, n/60	June 27	June 15	July 7
4.	5445.00	3/10, 1½/20, n/60	March 23	April 3	April 13
5.	3765.25	1½/15, n/30, EOM	Dec 24	Jan 2	Jan 17
6.	775.50	2/10, EOM	Aug 4	July 30	Sept 5
7.	1450.61	2/10, ROG	May 23	May 28	June 8
8.	995.00	1½/15, n/60, ROG	Nov 19	Dec 2	Dec 16

Calculate the missing values in problems 9 through 16. Assume in each case that the payment is made within the discount period.

Problem	Invoice amount	Credit terms	Payment	Amount credited	Balance owed
9.	$2365.00	2/10, n/30	?	$1365.00	?
10.	2365.00	1½/10, EOM	?	1421.32	?
11.	815.49	2/10, n/45, ROG	$ 500	?	?
12.	5445.00	3/10, n/90	3000	?	?
13.	3765.25	1⅓/15, n/45	?	?	$2042.28
14.	775.50	1¼/15, n/60	?	?	293.98
15.	1450.61	?/15, n/60, ROG	500	?	943.00
16.	995.00	?/10, EOM	700	?	285.54

17. An invoice for $2678.50 dated April 15 has terms 1½/15, EOM.

　　a. When does the discount period end?

　　b. When does the credit period end?

　　c. What payment on April 30 will reduce the outstanding balance by $800?

　　d. If an additional payment of $800 is made on May 5, what will be the new balance?

　　e. What further payment on May 10 will reduce the outstanding balance to $800?

18. An invoice for $13,600 dated May 18 has terms 2/10, ROG. The goods were shipped on May 21 and received on May 28.

　　a. When does the discount period end?

　　b. When does the credit period end?

　　c. What payment on May 30 will reduce the outstanding balance by $5000?

　　d. If, instead of the payment in part c, $5000 is paid on May 30, what will be the balance owed?

　　e. Instead of the payment in part c or d, what payment on June 5 will reduce the outstanding balance to $5000?

19. What total amount must be paid on July 4 to settle invoices dated June 20 for $485, June 24 for $367, and June 30 for $722, all with terms 1½/10, n/30?

20. The Simcoe School Board has three invoices from Johnston Transport, all with terms 2/10, 1/20, n/60. Invoice 277, dated October 22, is for $14,200; invoice 327, dated

November 2, is for $8600; and invoice 341, dated November 3, is for $11,500. What total payment to Johnston on November 12 will settle all three invoices?

21. Burlingame Carpets received a cheque for $8000 on December 10 from Sorenson Flooring as partial payment of Burlingame's invoice 2319. The invoice, dated November 20, was for $14,772 with terms 2/10, 1/20, n/45, EOM.

    a. How much should Burlingame credit Sorenson's account?

    b. What is the balance still owed?

22. Ballard Jewellers received an invoice dated August 22 from Safeguard Security Systems for $2856.57 with terms 2½/10, 1/20, n/45. Ballard made payments of $900 on September 1, $850 on September 10, and $700 on September 30. What amount was still owed on October 1?

23. Peak Roofing sent Jensen Builders an invoice dated July 12 for $5400 with terms 3/10, 1½/20, n/45. Jensen made a payment of $2000 on July 20, and a second payment on August 1 that reduced the balance owed to $1000. What was the size of the second payment?

24. Lakeside Marine received an invoice from Osborne Boats dated March 26 with terms 1½/15, n/45, ROG for four 19-foot Barracuda boats at $23,500 each, less 20%, 5%. The boats arrived on April 27. Lakeside made a payment of $60,000 on the account on May 10. How much does Lakeside still owe?

•25. McAfee Furniture received an invoice dated September 14 from Palisade Industries with terms 2½/10, EOM for the following items: four Prestige bedroom suites at $3900 each, less 20%, 7%; six Oak Traditional dining room suites at $4880 each, less 25%, 5%. What amount paid on October 10 will cut the amount owed in half?

•26. On August 6, A&B Construction received a progress payment from one of its projects that will enable it to apply $10,000 to three outstanding invoices payable to A-1 Builders Supply. Invoice 535, dated July 16, is for $3228.56; invoice 598, dated July 24, is for $2945.31; and invoice 678, dated August 3, is for $6217.69. All invoices have terms 4/10, 2/20, n/60. If A&B makes a $10,000 payment to A-1 on August 6, what further payment on August 15 will settle the account? Note that A-1 applies payments to the oldest invoices first.

••27. Sutton Trucking made two equal payments, on June 25 and July 15, on an invoice for $6350 dated June 15 with terms 3/10, 1/30, n/60. The payments reduced the balance owed on the invoice to $1043.33. What was the amount of each payment?

••28. An invoice for $2956.60, dated February 2, has terms 2/15, 1/30, n/90. What three equal payments on February 17, March 2, and May 2 will settle the account?

4.4 MARKUP

A merchandising operation must set the selling price of an item far enough above its cost to cover a portion of the operating expenses (such as wages, rent, and utilities) and make an appropriate contribution to the operating profit. The amount added to the unit cost to arrive at the selling price is most commonly known as the **markup** or **margin.** (Other terms that may be encountered elsewhere are *gross margin, mark-on,* and *gross profit.*) Thus,

$$\text{Selling price} = \text{Unit cost} + \text{Markup}$$

As previously mentioned, the markup on an item covers its prorated share of the overall operating expenses, and contributes to the overall operating profit. In other words,

$$\text{Markup} = \text{Overhead expenses per unit} + \text{Operating profit[3] per unit}$$

In terms of the following symbols:

SP = Unit selling price of the goods
C = Unit cost of the goods
M = Amount of markup
OE = Overhead or operating expenses per unit
OP = Operating profit per unit

the algebraic counterparts of the two preceding word equations are

Selling Price

Markup

$$SP = C + M \qquad (4\text{–}4)$$
$$M = OE + OP \qquad (4\text{–}5)$$

Thus, the selling price can be viewed as having two components: the unit cost and the markup. The markup, in turn, is made up of the unit overhead expense and the unit operating profit.[4] If a retailer wishes to break even ($OP = 0$) on a clearance sale of old stock, then the clearance price need cover only the unit cost and the unit overhead expense. That is, $M = OE$ and $SP = C + OE$ in order to break even.

A pictorial representation of these relationships is presented in Figure 4.7, where the length of each horizontal bar represents the selling price. In the upper bar, the cost and markup components of the selling price are identified. In the lower bar, the markup is subdivided into the unit overhead expense and the unit operating profit.

FIGURE   **4.7**

Relationships among *SP, C, M, OE,* and *OP*

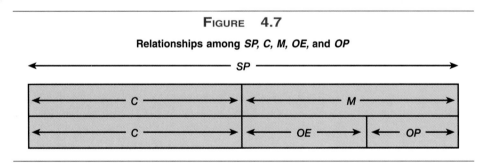

It is evident from the lower bar that

Selling Price

$$SP = C + OE + OP \qquad (4\text{–}6)$$

This result can also be obtained by substituting formula (4–5) into formula (4–4).

---

[3]We use the term *operating profit* because the quantity referred to here is essentially the "operating profit" encountered on an income statement in accounting, but expressed on a per-unit basis. Operating profit is profit that results from normal business operations; unusual revenues from the sale of capital assets or other nonrecurring events are not included.

[4]In applications of formulas (4–4), (4–5), and (4–6) in this chapter, we will assume that the operating expenses and operating profit per unit are constant over the range of sales being considered. In practice, economies of scale usually result in the operating expenses per unit decreasing at a slow rate as the sales volume rises.

Some retailers prefer to think of the markup on an item in relation to the selling price of the item. Most major department stores and national chain stores calculate the rate of markup as a percentage of the retail selling price. This makes the rate of markup correspond, on a per-unit basis, to the overall *gross profit margin*[5] calculated from an income statement.

Rate of Markup (Based on Selling Price)

$$\%M = \frac{M}{SP} \times 100\% \qquad (4\text{–}7)$$

Small independent retailers, wholesalers, and manufacturers frequently calculate the markup rate as a percentage of cost.[6]

Rate of Markup (Based on Cost)

$$\%M = \frac{M}{C} \times 100\% \qquad (4\text{–}8)$$

When pricing their merchandise, retailers tend to first decide upon the percentage markups for various categories of items. Then they calculate the corresponding dollar amounts of the markups and add them to the respective units costs to arrive at the selling prices.

Unfortunately, the same term "markup" is used in retailing for three different measures of markup. If a markup is quoted in dollars, then there is no confusion; it refers to $M = SP - C$. If a markup is quoted in percent, then a new employee of a store or an outsider may not know whether the markup has been calculated as a percentage of cost or of selling price. A particular retailer will consistently use only one method for calculating the rate of markup. Therefore experienced staff will have come to know which base is used for the markup calculation. However, new employees, bookkeepers, and so on should ask which method is used; the manager may not even know that there are two methods in general use.

To eliminate any possibility of confusion surrounding the meaning of "markup" in this text, we will use "amount of markup" and the symbol M to refer to the dollar amount of markup. "Rate of markup" and %M, each qualified as "based on cost" or "based on selling price," will be used when a percent markup is intended.

	$	%
OE		
+ OP	+	+
M		
+ C	+	+
SP	=	100

The table shown here is a very useful aid for setting up and solving problems with markup. Note that the first column impounds formulas (4–4), (4–5), and (4–6). Markup is the subtotal, OE plus OP. Selling price is the sum of M and C, which also makes it the sum of OE, OP, and C. Known dollar values of the components of SP may be entered in the centre column. The third column is for each component's percentage of SP. The first benefit of the table is in helping to organise the given information.

The main advantage to working with the table is that, in comparison to working directly with formulas (4–4), (4–5), and (4–6), we can more readily see *which* quantity can be calculated next *and how* it can be calculated. Not only does the table "build in" the additive relationships of formulas (4–4), (4–5), and (4–6), it also assists us in

[5]*Gross profit* is defined as net sales minus cost of goods sold. The *gross profit margin* is gross profit expressed as a percent of net sales.
[6]Firms that base the rate of markup on cost tend to use "margin" or "gross profit margin" for the rate of markup based on the selling price.

setting up proportions. The ratio of any two items from the $ column is equal to the ratio of the corresponding two items from the % column. The following examples will illustrate the utility of the table.

■ EXAMPLE 4.4A CALCULATING *M*, %*M*, AND *OP* GIVEN *C*, *SP*, AND %*OE*

Cal-Tire retails its regular tires at $80 each and its high-performance tires at $120 each. Cal-Tire obtains the tires from the factory for $55 and $85, respectively. Overhead expenses are 20% of the selling price. For each line of tires, determine:

a. The amount of markup.

b. The rate of markup based on cost.

c. The rate of markup based on selling price.

d. The profit per tire.

☑ SOLUTION

Enter the given information for each tire in its own table. Quantities to be determined are indicated by *a* for part *a, c* for part *c,* and so on.

Regular tire				High-performance tire		
	$	%			$	%
OE	$0.2SP$	$\overline{20}$		*OE*	$0.2SP$	$\overline{20}$
+*OP*	+ *d*	+		+*OP*	+ *d*	+
M	*a*	*c*		*M*	*a*	*c*
+ *C*	+ 55	+		+ *C*	+ 85	+
SP	80	100		*SP*	120	100

An inspection of the tables reveals that *M* may be calculated immediately using *M* + *C* = *SP.*

Regular Tire:

a. $M + \$55 = \$80$
$M = \$80 - \$55$
$= \$25$

b. $\%M(\text{on } C) = \frac{M}{C} \times 100\%$
$= \frac{\$25}{\$55} \times 100\%$
$= 45.45\%$

c. $\%M(\text{on } SP) = \frac{M}{SP} \times 100\%$
$= \frac{\$25}{\$80} \times 100\%$
$= 31.25\%$

High-Performance Tire:

$M + \$85 = \$120$
$M = \$120 - \$85$
$= \$35$

$\%M(\text{on } C) = \frac{M}{C} \times 100\%$
$= \frac{\$35}{\$85} \times 100\%$
$= 41.18\%$

$\%M(\text{on } SP) = \frac{M}{SP} \times 100\%$
$= \frac{\$35}{\$120} \times 100\%$
$= 29.17\%$

d. As values are calculated, they should be entered in the appropriate cells of the tables. After part *c,* the tables will appear as follows:

	Regular tire			High-performance tire	
	$	%		$	%
OE	$0.2\overline{2}SP$	$20\overline{}$	OE	$0.2\overline{2}SP$	$20\overline{}$
$+OP$	+	+	$+OP$	+	+
M	25	31.25	M	35	29.17
$+\ C$	+ 55	+	$+\ C$	+ 85	+
SP	80	100	SP	120	100

From the % column of the table on the left, it is evident that

$$OP = 31.25\% - 20\% = 11.25\% \text{ of } SP$$

Hence,

$$OP = 0.1125 \times \$80 = \$9.00 \text{ for the regular tire}$$

Similarly, for the high-performance tire,

$$OP = (0.2917 - 0.20) \times \$120 = \$11.00$$ ∎

EXAMPLE 4.4B CALCULATING M AND SP GIVEN C AND %M

The cost of a gas barbecue to a retailer is $245. If the retailer prices barbecues at a markup rate of 30% of the selling price, determine the amount of the markup and the selling price.

☑ SOLUTION

Tabulate the given information. The 70% "plug" for C in the % column is then apparent. The table at this stage is presented at the left. Do not expect to be able to determine a requested quantity directly. Instead, just start calculating whatever items you can until you obtain the one that answers the question. If we construct a proportion equating the $ and % values for the ratio $\dfrac{C}{SP}$, SP will be the only unknown. That is,

	$	%
OE	–	–
$+ OP$	+	+
M	$0.3SP$	30
$+\ C$	+ 245	+ 70
SP		100

$$\frac{\$245}{SP} = \frac{70}{100}$$

Hence

$$SP = \frac{100}{70} \times \$245 = \$350$$

Finally,

$$M = 0.3 \times SP = 0.3(\$350) = \$105$$

The selling price after a markup of $105 is $350. ∎

EXAMPLE 4.4C CALCULATING %M AND SP GIVEN %OE, %OP, AND C

A sporting goods store sets the selling price of baseball gloves to provide for overhead expenses of 25% of the selling price and profit of 20% of the selling price. Determine the selling price and the markup as a percentage of cost for a glove that costs the store $56.50.

☑ SOLUTION

Tabulate the given information. *OE* and *OP* may then be added in both columns to give the following contents for the table. It next becomes apparent that we can use the lower section of the middle column to create an equation containing *SP* as the only unknown. That is,

	$	%
OE	$0.25SP$	25
+ *OP*	$+0.20SP$	+20
M	$0.45SP$	45
+ *C*	+ 56.50	+
SP		100

$$0.45SP + \$56.50 = SP$$
$$0.55SP = \$56.50$$
$$SP = \frac{\$56.50}{0.55} = \$102.73$$

Then

$$\%M(\text{on } C) = \frac{M}{C} \times 100\% = \frac{0.45(\$102.73)}{\$56.50} \times 100\% = 81.8\%$$

The selling price of the glove is $102.73 after a markup of 81.8% of cost.   ■

THE CONNECTION BETWEEN THE NET PRICE, *N*, AND THE UNIT COST, *C*   In Sections 4.1 and 4.2, formulas (4−1) and (4−2) were used to calculate the net price, *N*, after one or more trade discounts. In this section we have been using *C* to represent an item's unit cost. In most cases that we will encounter, *N* calculated for one unit and *C* will be equal.

There are two common situations in which *N* will not be equal to *C*. Since *cash discounts* for prompt payment are credited toward *N*, any cash discounts taken on the purchase of an item will make *C* less than *N*. Any *shipping charges* included in the invoiced amount are added to the net price after trade discounts. Therefore, shipping charges on purchases to inventory will make *C* greater than *N*. Unless a cash discount or shipping charges apply in a problem, assume that the net price (per unit) after trade discounts will also be the unit cost.

EXERCISE 4.4

Answers to the odd-numbered problems are at the end of the book.

For problems 1 through 6, determine:

a. The amount of markup.

b. The amount of operating (overhead) expenses.

c. The operating profit or loss.

d. The rate of markup as a percentage of cost.

e. The rate of markup as a percentage of selling price.

Problem	Cost, *C*	Selling price, *SP*	Operating expenses, *OE*
1.	$30.00	$50.00	40% of cost
2.	64.00	96.00	25% of selling price
3.	55.65	79.50	30% of selling price
4.	17.50	29.75	50% of cost
5.	53.90	77.00	35% of selling price
6.	23.00	29.90	45% of cost

Calculate the missing values in problems 7 through 14.

Problem	Cost, C	Overhead, OE	Profit, OP	Markup, M	Selling price, SP	$\dfrac{M}{C}$	$\dfrac{M}{SP}$
7.	$152.50	?	$15.35	$ 47.45	?	?	?
8.	51.30	$ 18.65	?	?	$ 79.90	?	?
9.	?	308.00	?	435.00	1990.00	?	?
10.	?	?	2.45	?	19.90	?	50%
11.	?	11.25	3.75	?	?	?	38
12.	8.89	?	1.37	?	?	90%	?
•13.	6.60	3.15	?	?	?	?	40
•14.	?	?	0.14	?	0.95	150	?

15. Computer Warehouse buys a printer for $380 less trade discounts of 20% and 10%. If the operating expenses are $57 per printer:

   a. What should the selling price be to generate a profit of $33 per printer?

   b. What is the markup as a percentage of cost?

   c. What is the markup as a percentage of selling price?

   d. What would be the break-even selling price for an inventory clearance sale?

16. Young Damsels orders a line of jeans at a suggested retail price of $58 less trade discounts of 30% and 7%. The manager intends to sell the jeans at the suggested retail price. If overhead expenses are 25% of the selling price:

   a. What will be the unit operating profit?

   b. What is the markup as a percentage of cost?

   c. What is the markup as a percentage of selling price?

   d. What would be the break-even selling price for an inventory clearance sale?

17. The markup on a toaster selling at $54.95 is 45% of cost.

   a. What was the cost of the toaster to the retailer?

   b. What is the markup as a percentage of selling price?

18. Cuddly Pets purchased a litter of six puppies for $38.50 each. If the markup is 45% of the selling price:

   a. What is the selling price of each puppy?

   b. What is the markup as a percentage of cost?

•19. If the markup on lettuce in a grocery store is 60% of the selling price, what is the markup expressed as a percentage of cost?

•20. The markup on fresh peaches in a grocery store is 125% of cost because of the large losses from spoilage and bruising while the peaches are in storage and on display. What is the markup as a percentage of selling price?

21. The markup on a line of cosmetics is 85% of cost. If the markup on an eye shadow kit is $14:

   a. What is the retail selling price of the kit?

   b. What is the markup as a percentage of the selling price?

22. A hardware store marks up a line of electric power tools by 27% of the selling price. If the markup on a drill is $12.50:

   a. What is the cost of the drill to the store?

   b. What is the markup as a percentage of cost?

•23. No-Nonsense Liquidators bought 250 pairs of gum boots at $15 per pair. In the first month, 165 pairs sold at the regular price of $29.50 per pair. Another 43 pairs sold in the second month at a "one-third-off" sale price. The remaining boots, consisting primarily of odd sizes, were cleared out in the third month at $14.95. The store's overhead is 40% of cost.

   a. What was the break-even price on a pair of the boots?

   b. What was the average rate of markup as a percentage of cost?

   c. What was the total operating profit or loss on the sale of all of the boots?

•24. A florist buys potted poinsettias from a nursery at $15 each less 40% and 10%. The florist prices her stock to allow for overhead of 55% of cost and an operating profit of 20% of the selling price. At what price should she mark the poinsettias?

•25. Beaver Building Supply obtains 4- by 8-ft sheets of half-inch plywood from Macmillan Forest Products at $18 per sheet less 30% and 5%. The price is to be set to cover Beaver's overhead of 20% of the selling price and to provide an operating profit of 12% of the selling price. What should be the retail price per sheet?

4.5 MARKDOWN

A **markdown** is a reduction in the selling price of an item. Retailers use markdowns for many reasons: special "sale" events, reducing excess inventories, clearing out damaged or discontinued items, or just attracting additional customers to the store by marking down the prices of a few popular items. The term *markdown* is used in merchandising for both the dollar amount of the price reduction and the rate of markdown. The unit used for the markdown reveals whether the figure refers to the amount of markdown ($) or the rate of markdown (%). The **markdown rate** is consistently calculated as a percentage of the regular selling price. The word equations defining the two usages of markdown are

$$\text{Amount of markdown} = \text{Regular selling price} - \text{Reduced selling price}$$
$$\text{Rate of markdown} = \frac{\text{Amount of markdown}}{\text{Regular selling price}} \times 100\%$$

Using the symbols

D = Amount of markdown
RSP = Reduced selling price
$\%D$ = Rate of markdown

the algebraic forms of the two preceding word equations are

$$D = SP - RSP$$

Rate of Markdown

$$\%D = \frac{D}{SP} \times 100\% \qquad (4\text{–}9)$$

If the regular selling price and rate of markdown are given, the reduced selling price may be quickly calculated using the basic discounting formula (4–1), $N = L(1 - d)$, with the following interpretations placed on the variables:

L = Regular selling price, SP
d = Rate of markdown, $\%D$
N = Reduced selling price, RSP

The customised version of formula (4−1) becomes

$$RSP = SP(1 - \%D)$$

■ EXAMPLE 4.5A   CALCULATION OF RSP AND %D

Toby's Cycle Shop advertises a 20% markdown on an Alpine mountain bike regularly priced at $445. Cycle City's regular selling price for the same model of bike is $429.

a. What is the reduced price at Toby's?

b. What rate of markdown would Cycle City have to offer to match Toby's reduced price?

☑ SOLUTION

a. The reduced or marked-down price may be calculated using formula (4−1):

$$N = L(1 - d)$$
$$= \$445(1 - 0.20)$$
$$= \$356$$

The reduced price is $356.

b. In order to match Toby's reduced price, Cycle City must mark down its price by

$$D = SP - RSP$$
$$= \$429 - \$356$$
$$= \$73$$

The necessary rate of markdown is

$$\%D = \frac{D}{SP} \times 100\% = \frac{\$73}{\$429} \times 100\% = 17.0\%$$

A markdown of 17.0% will enable Cycle City to match Toby's reduced price. ■

■ EXAMPLE 4.5B   CALCULATING SP AND %D GIVEN C, %M(OF SP), AND RSP

An item costing $150 was marked up by 40% of the selling price. During the store's Tenth Anniversary Sale, the selling price was reduced to $175. What was the regular selling price, and what was the rate of markdown during the sale?

☑ SOLUTION

For the more difficult problems, a table similar to that used in the example problems in Section 4.4 is very helpful. In this problem, *OE* and *OP* are not involved but *D* and *RSP* must be included. The table at left has omitted *OE* + *OP* = *M* from the top of the first column but included *SP* − *D* = *RSP* at the bottom. All figures in the % column are still expressed as a percentage of *SP*. The information given in the statement of the problem has been entered in the table.

	$	%
M		40
+ *C*	+150	+
SP		100
− *D*	−	−
RSP	175	

In the % column, we can see that 60% is the "plug" in the addition. In other words, unit cost is 60% of selling price. After entering 60% for *C*, it becomes apparent that a proportion equating the $ and % values of the ratio $\frac{C}{SP}$ may be constructed to solve for SP. That is,

$$\frac{\$150}{SP} = \frac{60}{100}$$

Hence,

$$SP = \frac{100}{60} \times \$150 = \$250$$

After entering $SP = \$250$ in the middle column, we quickly see that D is the amount which when subtracted from $250 gives $175. Therefore, $D = \$75$ and

$$\%D = \frac{D}{SP} \times 100\% = \frac{\$75}{\$250} \times 100\% = 30\%$$

The regular selling price was $250 and the rate of markdown was 30%.   ■

EXERCISE 4.5

Answers to the odd-numbered problems are at the end of the book.

Calculate the missing values in problems 1 through 8.

Problem	Cost, C	$\frac{M}{C}$	$\frac{M}{SP}$	Selling price, SP	Markdown, D	$\frac{D}{SP}$	Reduced price, RSP
1.	$185.00	50%	?	?	$60	?	?
2.	58.50	?	?	$ 95.00	?	30%	?
3.	?	?	50%	49.98	?	50	?
4.	580.00	30	?	?	?	30	?
•5.	19.25	?	35	?	?	25	?
•6.	249.00	?	25	?	?	?	$249.00
•7.	?	75	?	395.00	?	40	?
•8.	?	40	?	?	?	20	100.00

9. Patti's Lingerie marked up an article from its $37.50 cost to $59.98.

   a. What is the rate of markup based on cost?

   b. What is the rate of markup based on selling price?

   c. What rate of markdown can be advertised if, at a later date, the price is reduced to the cost price for a clearance sale?

10. a. Merchant A operates on a markup of 45% of cost. If she later marks the price of a few items down to their cost price in order to attract additional customers to the store, what rate of markdown can she advertise?

    b. Merchant B operates on a markup of 45% of the selling price. If he later marks the price of a few items down to their cost price in order to attract additional customers to the store, what rate of markdown can he advertise?

11. The Ski Hut purchased Lampinen cross-country skis for $96.80 per pair and marked them up by 45% of the selling price. When the skis were discontinued, the Ski Hut marked down its remaining stock by 35%. What was the sale price after the markdown?

12. The sign on a rack of sport coats reads: "All prices marked down 30%!" What is the regular selling price of a coat marked at:

    a. $100?

    b. $196.49?

13. Merchants C and D sell the same article at $69.95 and $64.95, respectively. They both advertise that they will match the price offered by any other store on any product that they stock.

   a. What discount rate must C give to match D's price marked down by 20% during a sale?

   b. What discount rate must D give to match C's price marked down by 20% during a sale?

•14. A pharmacy marks up its springtime shipment of sunglasses to provide for overhead expenses of 40% of cost and a profit of 70% of cost. At the end of the summer, what rate of markdown can the pharmacy apply to the remaining inventory of sunglasses and still break even on sales at this level?

4.6 INTEGRATED APPLICATIONS

The problems in this section bring together elements from two or more sections of the chapter. Consequently, their solution usually requires a few steps and has a higher degree of difficulty.

   For more complex problems such as these, the use of an extended version of the tables introduced in the preceding two sections pays even greater dividends. In Figure 4.8, the new element included in the solution model is the calculation of the reduced operating profit, *ROP*, resulting from a markdown, *D*. Since the unit cost, *C*, and the overhead expenses per unit, *OE*, do not change when a retailer decides to drop the price below the regular selling price, then

$$ROP = RSP - C - OE$$

SP remains the base for all the percentages in the % column. Examples 4.6*a* and 4.6*b* demonstrate the use of this model in solving the more complex problems.

FIGURE   4.8

Table Model for Solutions

	$	%
OE		
+ *OP*	+ ____	+ ____
M		
+ *C*	+ ____	+ ____
SP	____	100
– *D*	– ____	– ____
RSP		
↘ *C*	–	–
– *OE*	– ____	– ____
ROP		

■ EXAMPLE 4.6A   *CALCULATING %M, %D, AND ROP GIVEN C, OE, SP, AND RSP*

Standard Appliances obtains Frigid-Air refrigerators for $1460 less 30% and 5%. Standard's overhead works out to 18% of the regular selling price of $1495. A scratched demonstrator unit from their floor display was cleared out for $1195.

   a. What is the regular markup as a percentage of cost?

   b. What is the rate of markdown?

c. What was the operating profit or loss on the demonstrator unit?

d. What markup, as a percentage of cost, was actually realized?

☑ SOLUTION

Standard Appliances's cost for one refrigerator was

$$C = N = L(1 - d_1)(1 - d_2)$$
$$= \$1460(1 - 0.30)(1 - 0.05)$$
$$= \$970.90$$

Now construct a table similar to the one in Figure 4.8. Enter all given values and the value calculated above for C. Parts b and c require us to calculate the quantities flagged by b and c in the table. Parts a and d require calculations using other unknown quantities in the table.

	$	%
OE	–	$\frac{}{18}$
+ OP	+	+
M		
+ C	+970.90	+
SP	1495.00	100
– D	–	– b
RSP	1195.00	
– C	–970.90	–
– OE	–	–
ROP	c	

a. The question is asking for %M (based on C). We can see in the middle column how to obtain M.

$$M + \$970.90 = \$1495.00$$

Therefore,

$$M = \$1495 - \$970.90 = \$524.10$$

and

$$\%M(\text{on } C) = \frac{M}{C} \times 100\% = \frac{\$524.10}{\$970.90} \times 100\% = 54.0\%$$

The regular markup is 54.0% of cost.

b. This part is asking for %D. In the middle column we observe that

$$\$1495.00 - D = \$1195.00$$

Isolating D on the left side of the equation gives

$$D = \$1495.00 - \$1195.00 = \$300.00$$

Hence

$$\%D = \frac{D}{SP} \times 100\% = \frac{\$300}{\$1495} \times 100\% = 20.1\%$$

The rate of markdown is 20.1%.

	$	%
OE		$\frac{}{18}$
+ OP	+	+
M	524.10	
+ C	+970.90	+
SP	1495.00	100
– D	–300.00	–20.1
RSP	1195.00	
– C	–970.90	–
– OE	–	–18
ROP		

c. The values determined as of the end of part b are included in the table. This part asks for the value of ROP. We need to fill in the value of OE in the lower part of the middle column before ROP can be calculated. In the % column, we are reminded that OE is 18% of SP. Therefore,

$$OE = 0.18 \times \$1495 = \$269.10$$

and

$$ROP = \$1195.00 - \$970.90 - \$269.10 = -\$45.00$$

The negative sign means that the store suffered a loss of $45.00 on the demonstrator unit.

d. The actual amount of markup at the reduced price was

$$M = OE + ROP = \$269.10 + (-\$45.00) = \$224.10$$

The rate of markup actually realized was

$$\%M = \frac{M}{C} \times 100\% = \frac{\$224.10}{\$970.90} \times 100\% = 23.1\% \text{ of cost}$$ ∎

SALES, SALES, AND MORE SALES!   Some merchants seem to almost always have a sale of some sort happening in their store. A few "SALE!" signs around the premises help to induce curious shoppers to investigate potential bargains. Once in the store, the shopper may make other purchases. Some retailers initially price certain lines of merchandise in order to provide "room" for a substantial planned markdown in a future sale event. Some merchandise may sell at the high "regular" price, but the merchant fully expects the bulk of the sales volume to occur at the reduced price.[7] In such cases the merchant may regard the ultimate marked-down price as the primary selling price that provides the "normal" unit operating profit.[8]

■ EXAMPLE 4.6B   CALCULATING *RSP* AND *SP* GIVEN *C, OE,* AND *ROP*

Fromme's Jewellers purchased sterling silver tea services for $960 each, less 35% and 15%. The "regular" selling price was set so that, in a "30% off" sale, overhead expenses represent 25% of the sale price and the operating profit is 15% of the sale price.

a. At what price will a tea service sell in a "30% off" sale?

b. What was the "regular" price before the markdown?

c. If the last set in inventory is cleared out at 50% off the regular price, what will the operating profit be on that set?

☑ SOLUTION

Fromme's cost of a silver tea service was

$$\begin{aligned} C = N &= L(1 - d_1)(1 - d_2) \\ &= \$960(1 - 0.35)(1 - 0.15) \\ &= \$530.40 \end{aligned}$$

Construct a table similar to Figure 4.8. Enter all given values and the value for *C*.

---

[7]Mattresses are an example of a product line for which the majority of sales occur at a significant markdown, for one reason or another, from the "regular" price. The following footnote appeared in a display advertisement placed in a Victoria newspaper by one of Vancouver Island's largest furniture stores: "The reference to our 'regular selling price' is to a price at which goods are regularly offered for sale in our store and is not a representation that this is the price at which most of a product is actually sold."

[8]Truth-in-advertising legislation is supposed to prohibit merchants from advertising sale prices or discounts if the merchandise has not had significant sales at the "regular" price, or the merchandise does not ordinarily sell at the "regular" price in the market area. However, authorities do not necessarily enforce the legislation and regulations. An investigation of retail jewellers in the United States by the NBC network's "Dateline" newsmagazine program found that a significant segment of retailers (including the jewellery departments of some well-known department store chains) followed a practice of setting very high "regular" prices but offering "sales" during all but 5 to 7 days in a month. The "sale" prices turned out to be competitive with the regular prices offered by retailers that did not take the "any-excuse-for-a-sale" approach to retailing.

	$	%
OE		
+ OP	+ ___	+ ___
M		
+ C	+530.40	+ ___
SP		100
− D	− ___	−30
RSP		70
− C	−530.40	−
− OE	−0.25RSP	−
ROP	0.15RSP	___

a. The question is asking for *RSP*. We note from the lower part of the middle column that

$$RSP - \$530.40 - 0.25(RSP) = 0.15(RSP)$$

Solving for *RSP*,

$$RSP - 0.40(RSP) = \$530.40$$

$$RSP = \frac{\$530.40}{0.60} = \$884.00$$

b. We now want to calculate *SP*. We can use the proportion

$$\frac{SP}{RSP} = \frac{SP}{\$884} = \frac{100}{70}$$

Then

$$SP = \frac{100}{70} \times \$884 = \$1262.86$$

The "regular" price of the tea service was $1262.86.

	$	%
SP	1262.86	100
− D	− ___	−50
RSP		50
− C	−530.40	−
− OE	−221.00	−
ROP		

c. This part presents a new scenario—a markdown of 50%. The question is requesting the *ROP* at this markdown. We should start a new table as shown. The upper rows are not needed. The dollar amount of *OE* does not change if a discount is offered or if %*D* is changed. Therefore, *OE* remains at

$$OE = 0.25(RSP \text{ in } b) = 0.25(\$884) = \$221.00$$

The "clear-out" price will be

$$RSP = 0.50(SP) = 0.50(\$1262.86) = \$631.43$$

As the middle column indicates,

$$ROP = \$631.43 - \$530.40 - \$221.00 = -\$119.97$$

Fromme's will lose $119.97 on the last set.   ■

Point of Interest

Misleading Price Representation

A few categories of consumer goods seem to be "on sale" so frequently or for so long that the consumer may wonder:

- When and where are the items ever sold at the "regular price"?

- Does any significant volume of sales take place at the "regular price"?

The federal Competition Act contains provisions relating to misleading advertising and deceptive marketing practices. The act is administered by the Bureau of Competition Policy, which is part of Consumer and Corporate Affairs Canada. Most provinces also administer legislation dealing with advertising and marketing practices.

Price representations usually fall under section 52(1)(d) of the Competition Act. In layperson's terms, the section states that

(continued)

(*concluded*)

any materially misleading representation as to the price at which a product is ordinarily sold is prohibited. The courts have interpreted the notion of an "ordinary selling price" to include words and phrases (such as "Compare to . . ." or "*x* % off") used to give the impression that the implied comparison price is the price at which the product is ordinarily sold.

Section 52(1)(d) explicitly states that the quoted or implied ordinary selling price should be one of the following:

- The price at which the product ordinarily sells in the market area.

- The advertiser's own regular selling price, clearly identified by such words as "our regular price."

The comparison price should be sufficiently recent to have relevance. The "ordinary selling price" implied or quoted for comparison should be one at which the product has had significant sales, not merely a price at which it was offered for sale. The volume needed in order to be regarded as significant depends on the product and the market. However, the volume should have been large enough to justify a consumer's believing that the markdown represented a genuine bargain or real savings. On the other hand, if the price of a product had been raised for a few weeks during which very few sales took place, then the merchant should not state or imply that the inflated price was the regular or ordinary selling price. Furthermore, the use of a "Manufacturer's Suggested Retail Price" or a "Suggested List Price" can constitute deceptive pricing if this price is not the product's ordinary selling price.

Enforcement of deceptive marketing practices under the Competition Act can be achieved through the laying of criminal charges. For example, the pricing practices of the window-blind industry came under scrutiny in 1987 as a consequence of numerous consumer complaints. Retailers were frequently advertising window blinds at up to 60% off the manufacturers' suggested retail prices. An investigation by the Marketing Practices Branch of the Bureau of Competition Policy revealed that the purported discounts and savings rarely related to the ordinary selling prices in the relevant markets.

In 1987 and 1988, the Marketing Practices Branch sent out information letters and presented seminars to manufacturers, distributors, and retailers in the window-blind industry in an effort to change the unacceptable pricing practices. A small number of firms persisted with deceptive pricing. Therefore, prosecutions were initiated.

Over a 3-year period, one-quarter of all convictions under section 52(1)(d) of the Competition Act were against firms in the window-blind business. In every case, the conviction was for advertising misleading regular price claims regarding the ordinary selling price in the relevant market.

EXERCISE 4.6

Answers to the odd-numbered problems are at the end of the book.
Calculate the missing values in problems 1 through 6.

Problem	Cost, C ($)	Overhead, OE	Markup, M	Regular price, SP ($)	Markdown %D	Sale price, RSP ($)	Reduced profit, ROP ($)
1.	115.70	20% of SP	35% of SP	?	25	?	?
2.	?	18% of SP	$33\frac{1}{3}$% of SP	147.00	$16\frac{2}{3}$	?	?
3.	37.25	? % of C	? % of C	59.60	?	41.72	−2.98
4.	?	70% of C	150% of C	19.80	?	?	2.38
5.	?	50% of C	50% of SP	?	$33\frac{1}{3}$	111.80	?
6.	420.00	? % of SP	? % of C	575.40	15	?	11.55

•7. Hi-Lites Inc. purchased a ceiling fixture for $480 less 40% and 25%, and marked it up 120% based on cost. For its Fifth Anniversary Sale, Hi-Lites offered the fixture at 40% off.

   a. What was the sale price?

   b. At the sale price, what was the rate of markup based on cost?

•8. Long Lake Nursery bought fertilizer in bulk in March at $18.60 less $33\frac{1}{3}$%, 12.5%, and 5% per 20-kg bag. The fertilizer is normally marked up by 55% of the selling price. The fertilizer was marked down 45% for an inventory reduction sale in late July.

   a. What was the sale price?

   b. What was the (reduced) rate of markup based on the sale price?

•9. Water Sports Ltd. pays $360 less 25% for a backyard aboveground pool kit. Overhead expenses are $16\frac{2}{3}$% of the regular selling price, and the operating profit is 15% of the selling price.

   a. What is the maximum rate of markdown the store can offer and still break even?

   b. What is the profit or loss per unit if Water Sports clears out its remaining stock at 20% off in a Hot August Bargains sale?

•10. A lawn mower retails for $349. The dealer's overhead is 25% of cost, and normal operating profit is $16\frac{2}{3}$% of cost.

   a. What is the largest amount of markdown that will allow the dealer to break even?

   b. What rate of markdown will price the lawn mower at cost?

•11. Rainbow Paints is discontinuing a line of paint that it purchased at $30 less 45% and 10% per 4-litre pail. The store's overhead is 50% of cost, and normal operating profit is 30% of cost. If the manager of the store is prepared to accept a loss of one-quarter of the overhead expenses, what discount rate can the store offer in order to clear out the paint?

•12. United Furniture buys reclining rocking chairs at $550 less 40% and 10%. The price is marked up to allow for overhead of 50% of cost and profit of 35% of cost. The unit on display in the store acquired a stain. What rate of discount from the regular price can the store offer if it is to recover only half of the unit overhead costs?

•13. Fashion Master purchased men's sweaters for $72 less 40% and 15%. The normal markup is 40% of the regular selling price, and overhead is 25% of the selling price. The sweaters were reduced to $45.90 for the store's Boxing Day Blowout.

   a. What was the rate of markdown for the sale?

   b. What was the profit or loss on each sweater at the sale price?

   c. At the sale price, what was the markup as a percentage of cost?

•14. Mr. Vacuum obtains vacuum cleaners for $360 less $33\frac{1}{3}$% and 15%. A demonstration unit regularly priced at $375 was sold for $225. The shop's overhead is 12% of the regular selling price.

   a. What was the markdown rate on the vacuum cleaner?

   b. What was the profit or loss on the sale of the demonstrator?

   c. What rate of markup based on cost was realized at the reduced price?

•15. A discount furniture store bought a waterbed at the wholesale price of $665. The "regular price" of the waterbed is set so that, in a "20% off" sale, the markup based on the sale price is 30%.

   a. What is the price of the waterbed in a "20% off" sale?

   b. What is the "regular price" of the waterbed?

•16. A jewellery store purchased a diamond ring for $2500 less 40% and 5%. The "regular price" of the ring is established so that, if it is sold in a "20% off" sale, overhead expenses amounting to 20% of the sale price and unit operating profit amounting to 12.5% of the sale price will be covered.

   a. What is the reduced price of the ring in a "20% off" sale?

   b. What is the "regular price" of the ring?

••17. Sonic Boom obtained a stereo system for $2400 less 30% and 15%. The system was originally priced so that, when sold in a "20% off" sale, the store's overhead and operating profit represent 25% and 15%, respectively, of the sale price. In a Midnight Madness Special, the system was sold at a "⅓-off" special price.

   a. What was the original "regular price"?

   b. What was the profit or loss at the special price?

••18. Furniture Warehouse bought upright freezers for $1800 less 33⅓% and 5%. The store's overhead works out to 30% of cost and its profit requirement to 16⅔% of cost. The freezers are initially priced so that the required amount of markup is realized when a freezer is sold at a "15% off" price.

   a. What is the initial rate of markup based on cost?

   b. During its Scratch-and-Save sale, customers qualify for an extra discount of either 5%, 7%, or 10%. This extra discount appears when the customer scratches a ticket at the time of a purchase. It is added to the basic 15% discount, making the combined discount 20%, 22%, or 25%, respectively. What is the store's profit or loss per freezer at each of these discounts?

REVIEW PROBLEMS

Answers to the odd-numbered review problems are at the end of the book.

1. A 28% trade discount on a VCR represents a discount of $136.92 from the suggested retail price. What is the net price to the buyer?

2. The net price of an item after a discount of 22% is $155.61. What is the (dollar) amount of the discount?

•3. Chicken Little Farms gives convenience stores a discount of 25% on eggs listed at $43.00 per case. What discount will Sunnyside Farms have to give on its list price of $44.50 per case to match Chicken Little's price to convenience stores?

4. The net proceeds to the vendor of a house after payment of a 4.5% real estate commission were $275,995. At what price did the house sell?

5. A merchant pays a 2.9% fee to the Royal Bank on all Visa sales.

   a. What amount will she pay on sales for a month of $28,476?

   b. What were her gross sales for a month in which the bank charged fees totalling $981.71?

•6. The evening news reports that the Vancouver Stock Exchange index dropped 0.9% on the day to close at 1098.6 points. How many points did the index fall?

•7. At its current price of $1.10 per share, the price of Apex Resources stock is down 78% from its price 1 year ago. What was that price?

8. An invoice shows a net price of $199.16 after discounts of 22%, 7%, and 5% are deducted.

   a. What was the list price of the goods?

   b. What single discount would be equivalent to the discount series?

9. Veitch Lighting offers a series of three discounts on a line of fixtures. The combined discounts result in a total discount of $77.85 from a list price of $249.50. If two of the discounts are 15% and 7½%, what is the third discount rate?

•10. Canadian Business Equipment (CBE) sells its filing cabinets to office supply stores for $420 less 30%. James Office Furniture lists similar filing cabinets at $390 less 20% and 10%. What second discount would CBE need to offer to match James's net price?

11. A uranium mining town reported population declines of 3.2%, 5.2%, and 4.7% for the three successive 5-year periods 1980–84, 1985–89, and 1990–94. If the population at the end of 1994 was 9320:

   a. How many lived in the town at the beginning of 1980?

   b. What was the population loss in each of the 5-year periods?

12. The number of jobs in the Canadian steel industry fell by 15% from the beginning of 1990 to the end of 1992. If the decline was 4.9% in 1990 and 6.6% in 1991, what was the percent decrease in 1992?

13. In 3 successive years the price of the common shares of Bedrock Resources Ltd. fell 40%, 60%, and 70%, ending the third year at 50 cents.

   a. What was the share price at the beginning of the 3-year skid?

   b. How much (in dollars and cents) did the share price drop in the second year?

14. An invoice for $12,600 dated March 17 has terms 2/10, ROG. The goods were shipped on March 20 and received on March 27.

    a. When does the discount period end?

    b. When does the credit period end?

    c. What payment on March 29 will reduce the outstanding balance by $6000?

    d. If, instead of the payment in part *c*, $6000 is paid on March 29, what will be the balance owed?

    e. Instead of the payment in part *c* or *d*, what payment on April 4 will reduce the outstanding balance to $6000?

15. What total amount must be paid on May 4 to settle invoices dated April 20 for $650, April 24 for $790, and April 30 for $465, all with terms 1½/10, n/30?

16. Omega Restaurant received an invoice dated July 22 from Industrial Kitchen Equipment for $3691, with terms 2/10, 1/20, n/45. Omega made payments of $1100 on August 1, $900 on August 10, and $800 on August 31. What amount was still owed on September 1?

•17. Homewood Appliances received an invoice dated April 15 from Kitchen-Aid Industries with terms 1½/10, EOM for the following:
    10 refrigerators at $1100 each less 20% and 10%
    15 electric ranges at $880 each less 25% and 5%
What amount paid on May 10 will cut the amount owed in half?

18. Nelson Hardware ordered a shipment of gas barbecues at a suggested retail price of $459 less trade discounts of 25% and 10%. The manager intends to sell the barbecues at the suggested retail price. If overhead expenses are 20% of the selling price:

    a. What will be the unit operating profit?

    b. What is the markup as a percentage of cost?

    c. What is the markup as a percentage of selling price?

    d. What would be the break-even selling price for an inventory clearance sale?

•19. If the markup on tomatoes in a grocery store is 55% of the selling price, what is the markup expressed as a percentage of cost?

•20. Sunrise Building Supply obtains 4- by 8-ft sheets of wallboard from Canadian Gypsum at $15 per sheet less 30% and 10%. The price is to be set to cover Sunrise's overhead of 20% of the selling price and to provide an operating profit of 18% of the selling price. What should be the retail price per sheet?

•21. Ski 'n Cycle purchased Elan 200 skis for $246 per pair and marked them up by 40% of the selling price. When this model was discontinued, the store marked down its remaining stock by 30%. What was the sale price after the markdown?

•22. A pharmacy marked up its sunscreen to provide for overhead expenses of 40% of cost and a profit of 45% of cost. At the end of the summer, what rate of markdown can the pharmacy apply to the remaining inventory of sunscreen and still break even on sales at the reduced price?

•23. A snowblower retails for $489. The dealer's overhead is 20% of cost, and normal operating profit is 16⅔% of cost.

    a. What is the largest amount of markdown that will allow the dealer to break even?

    b. What rate of markdown will price the snowblower at cost?

•24. Bateman's purchased men's overcoats for $275 less 30% and 10%. The normal markup is 35% of the regular selling price, and overhead is 20% of the selling price. The overcoats were reduced to $199 for a January clearance sale.

a. What was the rate of markdown for the sale?

b. What was the profit or loss on each overcoat at the sale price?

c. At the sale price, what was the markup as a percentage of cost?

•25. A discount furniture store bought a bedroom suite at the wholesale price of $1750. The "regular price" of the suite is set so that, in a "20% off" sale, the markup based on the sale price is 20%.

a. What is the price of the suite in a "20% off" sale?

b. What is the "regular price" of the suite?

SELF-TEST EXERCISE

Answers to the self-test problems are at the end of the book.

1. Specialty Builders Supply has two sources for the same power saw. Source A sells the saw at $196.00 less 20%, and source B offers it at $186.60 less 16⅔%. Which source is less expensive for the purchaser?

2. A trade discount of 22.5% from the suggested selling price for a line of personal computers translates to a $337.05 discount. What net price will a retailer pay?

3. Mr. and Mrs. Ogrodnik want to list their house at a price that will net them a minimum of $160,000 after a real estate commission of 5.5% of the selling price. Rounded to the nearest $100, what is the lowest offer they could accept on their home?

4. In addition to the regular trade discount of 25% and a volume purchase discount of 8⅓% from a major manufacturer, Appliance Warehouse is offered a further 5% discount for orders placed in January.

a. What is the net price after all three discounts on refrigerators listed at $1195?

b. What is the list price on an electric range whose net price works out to be $470.25?

c. What single discount is equivalent to the three trade discounts?

d. What dollar amount of savings does the extra discount for January orders represent on a $1000 list price item?

5. The buying group for some independent office supply retailers is offered discounts of 30% and 15% by the distributor of Accura calculators. The distributor of a similar line of Packard calculators quotes discounts of 25% and 16⅔%.

a. What third discount would Packard need to offer to match the combined trade discounts of Accura?

b. Alternatively, how much would Packard need to increase its second discount to match Accura's combined discount?

•6. In the most recent annual budget speech, the federal government presented a three-year timetable for phasing in cuts to the armed forces. The announced budget cuts in years 1, 2, and 3 are 8%, 11%, and 8%, respectively. If the dollar amount of the budgetary reduction in the first year is $850 million, what will be the amounts of the cuts in the second and third years?

7. Custom Kitchens received an invoice dated November 17 from Idea Cabinets Ltd. for $7260 with terms 3/15, 1½/30, n/60. If Custom Kitchens made a payment of $4000 on December 2, what further payment on December 16 will settle the account?

8. A payment of $500 on an invoice for $887 reduced the balance owed to $378.09. What cash discount rate was allowed on the $500 payment?

9. What is the cost of an item that sells for $87.49 if the markup is:

    a. 30% of cost?

    b. 30% of selling price?

10. Bosley's Pet Foods buys dog kibbles for $19.50 per bag less 40%. The store's overhead is 33⅓% of the selling price, and the desired profit is 10% of the selling price.

    a. At what price per bag should the dog food be sold?

    b. At this price, what is the markup as a percentage of cost?

    c. What is the break-even price?

•11. The Pro Shop at Sunny Lake Golf and Country Club prices its golf club sets to allow for overhead of 33⅓% of cost and profit of 20% of cost.

    a. What is the regular selling price as a percentage of cost?

    b. What discount rate can the Pro Shop offer to club members if it will accept half of the normal profit on member purchases?

•12. Central Ski and Cycle purchased 50 pairs of ski boots for $360 per pair less 33⅓% and 10%. The regular markup on the boots is 40% of the selling price, and the store's overhead is 22% of the selling price. During a January clearance sale, the price was reduced to $270 per pair.

    a. What was the rate of markdown for the sale?

    b. What was the profit or loss on each pair of boots at the sale price?

    c. At the sale price, what was the markup as a percentage of cost?

••13. A national department store's catalogue advertises a special saving of 40% off the regular individual item prices when a mattress and a box spring are purchased as a set. The store purchased the sets for $1200 each less 40% and 10%.

    a. What should be the regular total price of a mattress and box spring so that overhead expenses of 25% of the reduced price and profit of 12½% of the reduced price are covered by the reduced price?

    b. If the floor sample set became slightly soiled from customers lying on the mattress, what rate of markdown from the regular prices will permit the store to break even on that set?

SUMMARY OF NOTATION AND KEY FORMULAS

L = List price
d = Rate of trade discount (decimal equivalent)
N = Net price
d_e = Discount rate equivalent to the series discounts d_1, d_2, d_3

In the broader context of calculating the final amount after a percentage reduction to an initial amount:

L = Initial amount
d = Decimal equivalent of percentage reduction
N = Final amount after the reduction

The variables used in pricing and profit calculations are:

SP = Unit selling price of the goods
C = Unit cost of the goods

M = Amount of markup
$\%M$ = Rate of markup
OE = Overhead or operating expenses per unit
OP = Operating profit per unit
D = Amount of markdown
$\%D$ = Rate of markdown
RSP = Reduced selling price
ROP = Reduced operating profit per unit

Formula (4–1)	$N = L(1 - d)$	Finding the net amount or net price after applying a single rate of discount to the original amount or list price.
Formula (4–2)	$N = L(1 - d_1)(1 - d_2) \ldots (1 - d_n)$	Finding the net price after applying a discount series or discount chain.
Formula (4–3)	$d_e = 1 - (1 - d_1)(1 - d_2)(1 - d_3)$	Finding the single discount rate that is equivalent to a discount series.
Formula (4–4)	$SP = C + M$	The selling price is composed of the amount of markup and the unit cost.
Formula (4–5)	$M = OE + OP$	The amount of markup is composed of the unit operating expenses and the unit operating profit.
Formula (4–6)	$SP = C + OE + OP$	The selling price is composed of the cost plus operating expenses plus operating profit.
Formula (4–7)	$\%M = \dfrac{M}{SP} \times 100\%$	Finding the rate of markup as a percentage of selling price.
Formula (4–8)	$\%M = \dfrac{M}{C} \times 100\%$	Finding the rate of markup as a percentage of cost.
Formula (4–9)	$\%D = \dfrac{D}{SP} \times 100\%$	Finding the rate of markdown.

GLOSSARY OF TERMS

Cash discount A discount allowed for a payment within the discount period.

Credit period The time period given to a customer to pay an invoice.

Discount period The time period within which a payment qualifies for a cash discount.

Discount series Two or more discounts that are successively applied to the list price.

End-of-month (EOM) dating Terms of payment where the credit and discount periods start at the end of the month in the date of the invoice.

Equivalent discount rate The single discount rate that would produce the same effect as a given discount series.

List price The price quoted by a supplier of a product before any trade discounts.

Margin See *markup*.

Markdown (amount) The amount by which the price of an item is reduced.

Markdown rate The markdown expressed as a percentage of the regular price.

Markup (amount) The difference between the selling price and the cost of an item of merchandise.

Markup rate   The markup expressed as a percentage of either the selling price or the cost of the merchandise.

Net price   The price paid after the deduction of trade discounts.

Ordinary dating   Terms of payment where the credit and discount periods start on the date of the invoice.

Partial payment   Any payment that is smaller than the initial amount required to fully settle an invoice.

Receipt-of-goods (ROG) dating   Terms of payment where the credit and discount periods start on the date that the goods are received.

Terms of payment   The specifications on an invoice of the length of the credit period, any cash discount offered and the corresponding discount period, and the date on which the credit and discount periods start.

Trade discount   A discount granted by the supplier to a purchaser of goods for resale.

5

APPLICATIONS OF LINEAR EQUATIONS

LEARNING OBJECTIVES

After completing this chapter, you will be able to:

- Solve two linear equations in two variables by the algebraic elimination of one of the variables
- Solve problems that require setting up two linear equations in two variables
- Graph a linear equation in two variables

- Perform linear cost-volume-profit and break-even analysis employing:
    The contribution margin approach
    The algebraic approach of solving the cost and revenue functions
    A break-even chart

INTRODUCTION

A large number of quantitative problems encountered in business may be described or simulated by linear equations. These range from one- and two-variable problems of the kind included in this book to applications in production, transportation, scheduling, and distribution involving dozens of variables.[1]

As previously mentioned in Chapter 2, each variable in a *linear equation* appears with an exponent of +1. Also, there are no products or quotients of the variables. The procedure for solving linear equations in one variable was discussed in Chapter 2. In this chapter we progress to the next level of complexity: solving linear equations in two variables. Cost-volume-profit analysis is an important application of linear equations that will be studied in considerable detail.

5.1 SOLVING TWO EQUATIONS IN TWO UNKNOWNS

Recall from Section 2.3 that there is only one numerical value that satisfies a linear equation in one variable. That value is called the *solution* to the equation. In contrast, a linear equation in two variables has an *infinite* number of solutions. For example, the equation $y = x + 2$ has solutions $(x,y) = (0,2)$, $(1,3)$, $(2,4)$, and so on.

If, however, two variables must *simultaneously* satisfy two different linear equations, there is *only one solution to the pair of equations;* only one combination of values of the two variables will satisfy *both* equations.

ALGEBRAIC METHOD FOR SOLVING TWO EQUATIONS IN TWO UNKNOWNS The strategy in an algebraic method is to combine the two equations in some way that will eliminate one of the two variables, leaving a single linear equation in one variable. One technique will be illustrated using the following pair of equations. The equations are numbered for ease of reference.

$$2x - 3y = -6 \qquad ①$$
$$x + y = 2 \qquad ②$$

It is legitimate to add the respective sides of two equations or to subtract the respective sides of two equations. For example, if we add equations ① and ②, we obtain $3x - 2y = -4$. Equation ① minus equation ② gives $x - 4y = -8$. Although legal, neither the addition nor the subtraction operations has moved us closer to a solution in this case; we have only produced another equation containing two unknowns.

The insight that leads to a technique for solving the equations is that, if the numerical coefficient of x in equation ② had been 2, the subtraction ① − ② would have produced an equation without a term in x. Furthermore, we can achieve this outcome by multiplying both sides of equation ② by 2 before the subtraction. Then the equations to be subtracted are

$$
\begin{array}{rl}
① & 2x - 3y = -6 \\
② \times 2: & 2x + 2y = 4 \\
\hline
\text{Subtraction gives:} & \quad -5y = -10 \\
& y = \dfrac{-10}{-5} = 2
\end{array}
$$

---

[1]Linear programming is a sophisticated mathematical procedure employed in operations management to determine the optimal utilization of resources. The relationships and constraints involved are expressed in linear form.

The solution for the other variable may now be obtained by substituting the value of the known variable into either of the original equations. Substitution of $y = 2$ into equation ① gives

$$2x - 3(2) = -6$$
$$2x = -6 + 6$$
$$x = 0$$

The solution is $x = 0$, $y = 2$ or $(x,y) = (0,2)$. The solution may be checked by substituting the values into the equation that was not used in the preceding step. If we substitute $x = 0$ and $y = 2$ into the left side of equation ②, we obtain

$$x + y = 0 + 2 = 2$$

This equals the right-hand side (RHS) of equation ② and verifies that $(x,y) = (0,2)$ is the solution.

The two equations can be solved just as well by eliminating y instead of x. To eliminate y, multiply equation ② by 3, followed by *addition* of the existing equation ① and the new equation ②.

In general, it may be necessary to multiply *each* equation by a different number to set up the elimination of one variable. Suppose the objective is to eliminate x. The coefficients of x in both equations can always be made equal by:

1. Multiplying both sides of the first equation by the coefficient of x from the second equation, and

2. Multiplying the second equation by the coefficient of x from the original version of the first equation.

The terms in x may then be eliminated by adding the two new equations if the coefficients of x have opposite signs. If the coefficients have the same sign, subtract the equations to eliminate x. The following examples demonstrate the technique.

■ **EXAMPLE 5.1A** *SOLVING TWO EQUATIONS HAVING "NICE" COEFFICIENTS*

Solve the following pair of equations to three significant figures. Check the solution.

$$7x - 5y = 3 \quad ①$$
$$5x + 2y = 9 \quad ②$$

☑ **SOLUTION**

To eliminate y, first make the numerical coefficients of y the same in both equations:

$$① \times 2: \qquad 14x - 10y = 6$$
$$② \times -5: \qquad -25x - 10y = -45$$

Subtracting the second equation from the first eliminates the variable y:

$$14x - (-25x) = 6 - (-45)$$
$$39x = 51$$
$$x = \frac{51}{39} = 1.308$$

Substitute this value for x into equation ② and solve for y:

$$5(1.308) + 2y = 9$$
$$2y = 9 - 6.538$$
$$y = 1.231$$

To three significant figures, the solution is $x = 1.31$, $y = 1.23$.

Check:
Substitute $x = 1.308$ and $y = 1.231$ into equation ①:

$$\text{LHS of ①} = 7(1.308) - 5(1.231)$$
$$= 3.002$$
$$= \text{RHS of ① to three significant figures.} \quad\blacksquare$$

■ EXAMPLE 5.1B   *SOLVING TWO EQUATIONS HAVING "NASTY" COEFFICIENTS*

Solve the following pair of equations to three significant figures. Check the solution.

$$1.9a + 3.8b = 85.5 \quad ①$$
$$3.4a - 5.1b = -49.3 \quad ②$$

☑ SOLUTION

$$
\begin{array}{lrr}
① \times 3.4: & 6.46a + 12.92b = & 290.7 \\
② \times 1.9: & 6.46a - 9.69b = & -93.67 \\
\text{Subtract:} & 22.61b = & 384.27 \\
& b = & 17.00
\end{array}
$$

Substitute $b = 17.00$ into equation ①:

$$1.9a + 3.8(17.00) = 85.5$$
$$a = \frac{85.5 - 3.8(17.00)}{1.9}$$
$$= 11.00$$

The solution is $a = 11.0$, $b = 17.0$.

Check:
Substitute $a = 11.00$ and $b = 17.00$ into equation ②:

$$\text{LHS of ②} = 3.4(11.00) - 5.1(17.00)$$
$$= 37.40 - 86.70$$
$$= -49.30$$
$$= \text{RHS of ②} \quad\blacksquare$$

■ EXAMPLE 5.1C   *CREATING AND SOLVING TWO EQUATIONS FROM A WORD PROBLEM*

Whistling Mountain sells downhill skiing day passes at $29 and cross-country skiing passes at $8.50. If a day's total revenue from the sale of 760 passes was $17,366, how many of each type of pass were sold?

☑ SOLUTION

Let d and c represent the respective numbers of downhill and cross-country passes sold.[2]

$$d + c = 760 \quad ①$$

---

[2]The solution to this problem can also be developed in terms of a single variable, say d for the number of downhill passes sold. Then the number of cross-country passes sold is $760 - d$. In the present context of solving two equations in two variables, we are choosing the two-variable approach.

The total revenue from the sale of both types of passes was

$$29.0d + 8.5c = 17,366 \quad ②$$

$$① \times 8.5: \quad \underline{8.5d + 8.5c = 6,460}$$

$$\text{Subtract:} \quad 20.5d = 10,906$$

$$d = 532$$

Substitute $d = 532$ into equation ①:

$$c = 760 - 532 = 228$$

On this particular day, 532 downhill skiing passes and 228 cross-country skiing passes were sold:

Check:

Substitute $c = 228$ and $d = 532$ into equation ②:

$$\text{LHS of } ② = \$29(532) + \$8.50(228)$$
$$= \$15,428 + \$1938$$
$$= \$17,366$$
$$= \text{RHS of } ②$$

■

■ EXAMPLE 5.1D   *A WORD PROBLEM GIVING TWO EQUATIONS WITH LARGE COEFFICIENTS*

Westwood Orchard received $1921.95 for its first shipment of 1530 kg of Macintosh apples and 945 kg of Delicious apples to the processing plant. Its second shipment, consisting of 2485 kg of Macintosh and 2370 kg of Delicious, resulted in a payment of $3697.85. What was Westwood Orchard paid per kilogram for each variety of apple?

☑ SOLUTION

Shipment	Macintosh (kg)	Delicious (kg)	Total revenue ($)
1	1530	945	1921.95
2	2485	2370	3697.85

The details of each shipment are summarized in the table. Let M and D represent the price per kilogram that Westwood received for Macintosh and Delicious apples, respectively. The idea in words that provides the basis for constructing algebraic equations in terms of M and D is:

Revenue from Macintosh apples + Revenue from Delicious apples = Total revenue

Expressing this idea in algebraic terms for each shipment gives

$$1530M + 945D = \$1921.95 \quad ①$$
$$2485M + 2370D = \$3697.85 \quad ②$$

Since multiplication by the numerical coefficient of either M or D will result in large unwieldy numbers, divide each equation by its own coefficient of M. This will make the coefficient of M equal to 1 in both equations and permit the elimination of M by subtraction.

$$\begin{array}{rll}
\text{①} \div 1530: & M + 0.6176D = & \$1.2562 \\
\text{②} \div 2485: & M + 0.9537D = & \$1.4881 \\
\hline
\text{Subtract:} & -0.3361D = & -\$0.2319 \\
& D = \dfrac{\$0.2319}{0.3361} = & \$0.6900
\end{array}$$

Substitute $D = \$0.69$ into one of the modified equations to solve for M with the least amount of work:

$$M = \$1.2562 - 0.6176 \times \$0.69 = \$0.8301$$

Westwood Orchard receives 69 cents per kilogram for Delicious apples and 83 cents per kilogram for Macintosh apples.

Check:
Substitute $D = \$0.69$ and $M = \$0.83$ into equation ②:

$$\begin{aligned}
\text{LHS of ②} &= 2485(\$0.83) + 2370(\$0.69) \\
&= \$2062.55 + \$1635.30 \\
&= \$3697.85 \qquad \blacksquare
\end{aligned}$$

■ EXAMPLE 5.1E   *A MORE DIFFICULT WORD PROBLEM INVOLVING TWO UNKNOWNS*

An automotive supply store sells motor oil at \$3.20 per litre. In a 1-day special promotion, it offers 5 litres for the price of 4 litres. At the end of the day, the revenue from the sale of 1171 litres of oil was \$3052.80. How many litres were sold at the regular price and how many were sold at the special promotion price?

☑ SOLUTION

Let

$r =$ Number sold at the regular price
$s =$ Number sold at the special price

Then

$$r + s = 1171 \quad \text{①}$$

The tricky part is writing an equation that expresses the total revenue in terms of r and s. We can view the special offer as paying the regular price for 4 litres and getting the fifth litre for free. In effect, then, four-fifths of s are sold at the regular price. Hence,

$$3.20r + 3.20 \left(\frac{4}{5} s \right) = 3052.80$$

Dividing both sides by 3.20 gives

$$r + 0.8s = 954 \quad \text{②}$$

If equation ② is now subtracted from equation ①, the variable r will be eliminated.

$$\begin{aligned}
s - 0.8s &= 1171 - 954 \\
0.2s &= 217 \\
s &= \frac{217}{0.2} = 1085 \text{ litres}
\end{aligned}$$

Substitution of this value for s into equation ① gives

$$r + 1085 = 1171$$
$$r = 1171 - 1085$$
$$= 86 \text{ litres}$$

Therefore, the store sold 86 litres at the regular price and 1085 litres at the promotional price. ■

EXERCISE 5.1

Answers to the odd-numbered problems are at the end of the book.

Solve each of the following pairs of equations. Verify your solution in each case.

1. $x - y = 2$
   $3x + 4y = 20$

2. $y - 3x = 11$
   $5x + 30 = 4y$

3. $4a - 3b = -3$
   $5a - b = 10$

4. $7p - 3q = 23$
   $-2p - 3q = 5$

5. $y = 2x$
   $7x - y = 35$

6. $g - h = 17$
   $\frac{4}{3}g + \frac{3}{2}h = 0$

Solve each of the following pairs of equations to three significant figures. Verify your solution in each case.

7. $d = 3c - 500$
   $0.7c + 0.2d = 550$

8. $0.03x + 0.05y = 51$
   $0.8x - 0.7y = 140$

9. $2v + 6w = 1$
   $-9w + 10v = 18$

10. $2.5a + 2b = 11$
    $8a + 3.5b = 13$

11. $37x - 63y = 235$
    $18x + 26y = 468$

12. $68.9n - 38.5m = 57$
    $45.1n - 79.4m = -658$

13. $0.33e + 1.67f = 292$
    $1.2e + 0.61f = 377$

14. $318j - 451k = 7.22$
    $-249j + 193k = -18.79$

15. The annual dues for the Southern Pines Golf Club are $1070 for regular members and $428 for student members. If the total revenue from the dues of 583 members for the past year was $471,014, how many members did the club have in each category?

16. Product X requires 30 minutes of machining on a lathe, and product Y requires 45 minutes of machining. If the lathe was operated for 60.5 hours last week for machining a combined total of 93 units of products X and Y, how many units of each product were produced?

17. Marion bought 5 litres of milk and four dozen eggs for $13.97. Lonnie purchased 9 litres of milk and 3 dozen eggs for $16.83. What were the prices for a litre of milk and a dozen eggs?

18. Tiny-Tot School purchases the same amount of milk and orange juice each week. After price increases from $1.10 to $1.15 per litre of milk and from $0.98 to $1.14 per can of frozen orange juice, the weekly bill rose from $42.20 to $45.85. How many litres of milk and cans of orange juice are purchased every week?

•19. Marcel and Maurice agree to invest a total of $83,000 in the M&M Appliance Repair partnership. If the partnership agreement requires Marcel to invest $8000 less than four-thirds of Maurice's investment, how much should each partner invest?

•20. Morton Office Supplies sent First United Church an invoice in the amount of $113.30 for three boxes of large envelopes and seven boxes of small envelopes. If a box of large envelopes sells for 50 cents more than twice the price of a box of small envelopes, what is the price of a box of large envelopes?

•21. In the first week of July a beer and wine store sold 871 cases of beer and paid refunds on 637 cases of empty bottles, for a net revenue of $12,632.10. For the following week the net revenue was $13,331.70 from the sale of 932 cases and the return of 805 cases of empties. What refund did the store pay per case of empty bottles?

•22. As a fund-raiser, a local charity sold raffle tickets on a trip to Disney World at $2 each or 3 for $5. In all, 3884 tickets were sold for a total of $6925. How many people bought tickets at the 3-for-$5 discount?

•23. A convenience store sells canned soft drinks at $4.35 for a six-pack or 90 cents for a single can. If revenue from the sale of 225 cans of soft drinks on a weekend was $178.35, how many six-packs and how many single cans were sold?

•24. A partnership in a public accounting practice has 7 partners and 12 accounting technicians. Each partner draws the same salary, and each technician is paid the same salary. The partners calculate that if they give the technicians a raise of 8% and if they increase their own salaries by 5%, the gross annual salaries for all accounting personnel will rise from the current $1,086,000 to $1,156,500. What are the current annual salaries of a partner and an accounting technician?

•25. A manufacturing firm pays monthly salaries of $3400 to each production worker and $2800 to each assembly worker. As the economy drops into a recession, the firm decides to reduce its total monthly manufacturing payroll from $253,800 to $198,000 by laying off 20% of its production workers and 25% of its assembly workers. How many layoffs will there be from each of the assembly and production divisions?

5.2 COST-VOLUME-PROFIT AND BREAK-EVEN ANALYSIS

Cost-volume-profit analysis is a basic planning tool in business. It is a technique for estimating a firm's *operating profit* (or net income[3] before taxes) at any sales *volume* given the firm's *cost* structure. Cost-volume-profit (CVP) analysis helps managers answer questions such as, How will total costs, revenues, and operating profit be affected:

- If the firm sells 100 more units in the next operating period?
- If prices are raised 10% resulting in the sale of 150 fewer units each month?
- If the occupancy rate in a hotel is increased by 5%?
- If the acquisition of a new machine reduces unit manufacturing costs but increases fixed costs?

CVP analysis can be used to estimate the volume of sales required to generate a particular net income. A key component of CVP analysis is **break-even analysis** to determine the break-even point where a firm's net income will be zero. The **break-even point** is the volume of sales at which the business will "break even," that is, just manage to cover all costs but have zero operating profit.

DEFINITIONS AND ASSUMPTIONS

Basic cost-volume-profit analysis assumes that costs may be treated as either fixed or variable. A **fixed cost** is the same regardless of the volume of sales. Examples include rent, management salaries, some forms of depreciation expense, and property taxes. **Variable costs** grow in direct proportion to the volume of sales. In other words, if unit

---

[3]The terms *operating profit* and *net income* (before taxes) will be used interchangeably in this chapter to refer to:

Total revenue − Operating expenses (such as cost of goods sold and overhead expenses)

sales increase by 10%, total variable costs will increase by 10% (but total fixed costs will not change). Examples of variable costs include materials costs and direct labour costs in manufacturing, and the wholesale cost of goods in retailing. For *total* variable costs to grow in direct proportion to unit sales, *unit* variable costs must be the *same* for each and every unit sold.

The initial assumption that costs may be neatly classified as fixed or variable appears at first to be unrealistic—we can readily identify costs that are not strictly fixed or purely variable. Some costs, referred to as *semivariable costs,* rise as volume increases but not in a proportional way. These usually result from economies of scale realized as production or sales volume increases. The compensation of sales personnel by a salary plus commission is an example of a *mixed cost* that has fixed and variable cost components.

Our simplified approach[4] to cost-volume-profit analysis may still provide useful insights in situations where these other types of costs are significant. The fixed and variable components of a mixed cost should be assigned to the respective fixed or variable cost category. Semivariable costs may be approximated reasonably well by variable costs.

Other assumptions of CVP analysis are:

- The unit selling price remains the same regardless of sales volume. (The basic CVP analysis does not, therefore, accommodate volume discounts or price reductions during a sale or promotion.)
- Production volume equals sales volume. (Consequently, the business neither builds up nor runs down its inventory during the time frame of the analysis.)

In the following example, we describe a proposed business, analyze its costs, and begin to organize the given information in a form appropriate for CVP analysis. The notation needed at this point is:

SP = Selling price or revenue per unit
VC = Variable costs per unit
FC = Fixed costs

■ EXAMPLE 5.2A   *DETERMINING SP, VC, AND FC IN PREPARATION FOR CVP ANALYSIS*

Chuck is conducting a financial analysis for a neighbourhood pub that he is planning to open in a small shopping centre. The landlord is prepared to pay for the leasehold improvements, fixtures, and furniture, and to recover the extra investment through higher rent. The total rent will be $4300 per month.

Three full-time cooks, each earning $2200 per month, can cover the hours of operation. Six full-time-equivalent (FTE) waiters and waitresses will be sufficient to handle the expected 1500 to 3000 customers per month. They will receive the minimum wage, which works out to $1200/month/FTE. If the number of customers exceeds 3000 per month, three more FTE staff will be required. Chuck will manage the pub but does not need to draw a salary for several months.

---

[4]A more thorough analysis of costs and a more rigorous treatment of CVP relationships will be encountered in a course in managerial accounting. Such an analysis includes the handling of another category of costs, called *semifixed costs.* These are costs that rise abruptly at certain levels of production where a major change must be made to further increase production. For example, a new production line or an additional shift may have to be added. When semifixed costs are involved, a separate CVP analysis may be undertaken for each range of operations between abrupt changes in fixed costs. In our analysis, we assume that semifixed costs do not change over the relevant range of operations and therefore can be treated as fixed costs in this range.

Other monthly expenses are $150 for electricity, $200 for natural gas, $100 for telephone, $900 for janitorial service, $250 for the lease of a computer and cashier terminal, and $200 for licences and miscellaneous fixed expenses. The annual insurance premium is $1200.

Chuck's previous experience at another pub in the city indicates that, on average, each customer will buy 2.5 drinks at an average price of $3.60, and will also spend $6 on food. Drinks and food will be priced at three times the cost of the ingredients to the pub.

a. Classify the various costs as fixed or variable.

b. Determine values for

    SP, the revenue per customer
    VC, the variable costs per customer
    FC, the (monthly) fixed costs

if the number of customers is between 1500 and 3000 per month.

☑ SOLUTION

a. Fixed costs are those costs that remain the same, regardless of the number of customers per month. They include rent, salaries of the cooks, electricity, gas,[5] telephone, janitorial service, computer lease, licences and miscellaneous fixed expenses, and insurance. Over the range of 1500 to 3000 customers per month, the wages paid to the waiters and waitresses are also fixed costs.

Variable costs are costs that vary in direct proportion to the number of customers. In this example, the only variable costs are the expenditures by the pub on the ingredients for the drinks and food it serves.

b. Since each customer buys, on average, $6.00 worth of food and 2.5 drinks at $3.60 each,

$$SP = 2.5(\$3.60) + \$6.00 = \$15.00 \text{ per customer}$$

Since food and beverages are priced at three times the cost of ingredients,

$$VC = \frac{SP}{3} = \frac{\$15.00}{3} = \$5.00 \text{ per customer}$$

Monthly fixed costs are as follows:

Rent	$ 4300
Salaries of cooks	6600
Wages of waiters, etc.	7200
Electricity and gas	350
Telephone	100
Janitorial service	900
Computer lease	250
License and misc.	200
Insurance	100
Fixed costs (*FC*)	$20,000

---

[5]Arguably, electricity and gas are semivariable costs since more customers will mean more cooking, dishwashing, and so forth. However, the dependence on the number of customers is so weak that a fixed-cost assumption for these relatively small costs is reasonable.

Contribution Margin Approach to CVP Analysis

Most managers use this approach for CVP analysis. When variable costs were defined earlier in this section, it was pointed out that variable costs *per unit, VC*, are the *same* for every unit. If one more unit is sold, *total* variable costs will be increased by *VC*. If one less unit is sold, *total* variable costs will be reduced by *VC*. In either case, total fixed costs are still *FC*.

Since variable costs are incurred only as units are sold, managers conceptually allocate the first portion of the unit selling price to paying the unit variable cost. The remainder, *SP* − *VC*, is then available to pay the fixed costs, *FC*. After enough units have been sold to cover the fixed costs, the amount *SP* − *VC* from each *additional* unit sold goes entirely to operating profit.

The difference between the unit selling price and the unit variable cost is called the **contribution margin** (per unit). That is,

$$\text{Contribution margin} = SP - VC$$

The contribution margin should be thought of as the amount "contributed" or available from the sale of each unit toward payment of fixed costs and generating a profit. The contribution margin expressed as a percentage of the unit selling price is known as the **contribution rate.** If we let

CM = Contribution margin per unit
CR = Contribution rate

then

Contribution Margin

Contribution Rate

$$\boxed{\begin{aligned} CM &= SP - VC \\ CR &= \frac{CM}{SP} \times 100\% \end{aligned}}$$

(5–1)

A contribution rate of 53%, for example, means that 53 cents from each dollar of sales are available to pay fixed costs and generate an operating profit. (The other 47 cents represent the variable cost per dollar of sales.)

With each unit contributing *CM* toward the payment of fixed costs, *FC*, the number of units that must be sold to just break even is

$$\text{Unit sales at the break-even point} = \frac{FC}{CM}$$

Let

X = Total number of units sold in the period
NI = Net income (or operating profit) for the period

The total unit sales required to generate a net income, *NI*, after payment of fixed costs, *FC*, is

**Unit Sales for a
Target Net Income**

$$\boxed{X = \frac{FC + NI}{CM}}$$

(5–2)

Note that this formula gives the break-even sales volume as the special case where $NI = 0$.

To calculate the net income at any particular value of forecast unit sales, we need to rearrange formula (5–2) to solve for *NI,* giving

$$NI = (CM)X - FC \qquad\qquad (5\text{--}2a)$$

This equation puts into mathematics the intuitive idea that the net income is what remains after fixed costs are paid (deducted) from the total contribution margin.

■ EXAMPLE 5.2B   *CVP ANALYSIS USING THE CONTRIBUTION MARGIN APPROACH*

In Example 5.2A concerning the neighbourhood pub proposal, we found that

SP = $15.00 per customer
VC = $5.00 per customer
FC = $20,000 per month

for the range of 1500 to 3000 customers per month.

a. Calculate and interpret the unit contribution margin.

b. What is the break-even point in:
  (i) customers per month?   (ii) revenue per month?

c. What will be the monthly net income if there are:
  (i) 1600 customers per month?   (ii) 2300 customers per month?

d. How many customers per month are required for a net income of $5000 per month?

e. If the average revenue turns out to be only $13.50 per customer, how many customers per month will be needed to break even?

f. If the customer volume reaches 3000 per month, the owner/manager intends to start drawing a salary of $4000 per month and to hire three more waiters/waitresses at $1200 per month. With these additional costs and an average revenue of $15.00 per customer from 3000 customers per month, what would be the monthly net income?

☑ SOLUTION

a. The contribution margin per customer is:

$$CM = SP - VC = \$15.00 - \$5.00 = \$10.00$$

This means that, after covering unit variable costs (of $5.00), each customer contributes $10.00 toward the payment of fixed costs. Once the cumulative total of contribution margins reaches the fixed costs for the month ($20,000), each *additional* customer will contribute $10.00 to the net income (operating profit) for the month.

b. (i) With each customer contributing $10.00 toward fixed costs totalling $20,000, the break-even point is at

$$\frac{FC}{CM} = \frac{\$20,000}{\$10} = 2000 \text{ customers per month}$$

  (ii) Since each customer generates an average revenue of $15.00 per visit, the break-even revenue is 2000($15.00) = $30,000 per month.

c. In general, $NI = (CM)X - FC$

(i) If $X = 1600$ customers per month,

$$NI = (\$10.00)1600 - \$20,000 = -\$4000$$

That is, the pub will lose $4000 per month.

Note: A more intuitive approach to answering this part is to begin with the break-even volume of 2000 customers per month from part *a.* (i). For each customer short of 2000, the pub will lose $CM = \$10.00$. If the pub falls 400 customers short of the break-even point, it will lose $(\$10.00)400 = \$4000$.

(ii) If $X = 2300$ customers per month,

$$NI = (\$10.00)2300 - \$20,000 = \$3000$$

Note: We can arrive at the same figure by noting that each of the 300 customers beyond the break-even point contributes $10 to the net income. Hence the net income is $3000 per month.

d. Using formula (5–2),

$$X = \frac{FC + NI}{CM} = \frac{\$20,000 + \$5000}{\$10} = 2500 \text{ customers per month}$$

The pub requires 2500 customers per month to generate a net income of $5000 per month.

e. Recall from the information given in Example 5.2A that the variable costs are the food and drink ingredients, and that they amount to one-third of the selling prices. Under the new scenario, $SP = \$13.50$ and $VC = \$13.50/3 = \$4.50$. The fixed costs remain at $20,000. The contribution margin will be

$$CM = SP - VC = \$13.50 - \$4.5- = \$9.00$$

Now the break-even point is

$$\frac{FC}{CM} = \frac{\$20,000}{\$9} = 2223 \text{ customers per month}^6$$

f. In this scenario, SP and VC are at their original estimates but fixed costs are increased by $\$4000 + 3(\$1200) = \$7600$ to $27,600. In this case formula (5–2*a*) gives

$$NI = \$10.00(3000) - \$27,600 = \$2400$$

With 3000 customers per month and the increased payroll, the net income will be $2400 per month.   ∎

---

[6]The mathematical result of 2222.222 has been rounded *up* to 2223 for two reasons. The first is that the unit of sale (a customer) is indivisible. The reason for rounding up (instead of rounding down according to the usual mathematical rules for rounding) is a practical business argument. There is a greater imperative for a business to pay its expenses than to generate a profit. Failure to pay the bills breaks "the law"; failure to generate a profit only upsets the owners. A volume of 2222 customers per month will actually leave the pub

$$0.222 \times CM = 0.222 \times \$9 = \$2.00$$

short of being able to pay all the operating costs from operating revenues. An additional customer is needed to achieve this minimal financial goal (and produce an operating profit of $CM - \$2 = \$7$).

■ EXAMPLE 5.2c   *CVP ANALYSIS USING THE CONTRIBUTION MARGIN APPROACH*

A manufacturing company is studying the feasibility of producing a new product. A new production line could manufacture up to 800 units per month at a cost of $50 per unit. Fixed costs would be $22,400 per month. Variable selling and shipping costs are estimated to be $20 per unit. Market research indicates that a unit price of $110 would be competitive.

a. What is the break-even point as a percent of capacity?

b. What would be the net income at 90% of capacity?

c. What would unit sales have to be to attain a net income of $9000 per month?

d. In a serious recession, sales might fall to 55% of capacity. What would be the resulting net income?

e. What dollar amount of sales would result in a loss of $2000 per month?

f. In the highest cost scenario, fixed costs might be $25,000 per month, production costs might be $55 per unit, and selling and shipping costs might be $22 per unit. What would be the break-even point under these circumstances?

☑ SOLUTION

In the expected scenario, $SP = \$110$, $VC = \$50 + \$20 = \$70$, and $FC = \$22,400$. Hence,

$$CM = SP - VC = \$110 - \$70 = \$40$$

a. The break-even volume is

$$\frac{FC}{CM} = \frac{\$22,400}{\$40} = 560 \text{ units}$$

This represents

$$\frac{560}{800} \times 100\% = 70\% \text{ of capacity}$$

b. At 90% of capacity, production would be $0.9 \times 800 = 720$ units per month. This is $720 - 560 = 160$ units above the break-even point. The contribution margin from these units goes entirely to net income. Therefore,

$$NI = 160(\$40) = \$6400 \text{ per month}$$

Note: This answer can also be obtained by substitution in formula (5–2a).

c. For a net income of $9000 per month, the number of units sold in excess of the break-even point would have to be

$$\frac{NI}{CM} = \frac{\$9000}{\$40} = 225$$

Total unit sales would have to be $560 + 225 = 785$ per month.
Note: This answer can also be obtained by substitution in formula (5–2).

d. In the recession scenario, unit sales would be $0.55 \times 800 = 440$ per month. Then

$$NI = (CM)X - FC = (\$40)440 - \$22,400 = -\$4800$$

The company would lose $4800 per month in the recession.

e. Each unit that the company falls short of the break-even point will contribute a loss of CM = $40. For a loss of $2000 in a month, the company must fall

$$\frac{NI}{CM} = \frac{\$2000}{\$40} = 50 \text{ units}$$

short of the break-even point. Total unit sales would be 560 − 50 = 510 units per month. The dollar amount of sales would be 510($110) = $56,100 per month.

f. In the highest cost scenario, FC = $25,000 per month and VC = $77 per unit. Then

$$CM = \$110 - \$77 = \$33$$

and

$$\text{Break-even volume} = \frac{FC}{CM} = \frac{\$25,000}{\$33} = 757.6 \text{ units}$$

The break-even point in this scenario would be at 758 units per month (94.75% of capacity). ∎

■ EXAMPLE 5.2D   *CVP ANALYSIS WITH SALES VOLUME IN DOLLARS INSTEAD OF UNITS*

Last year Marconi Printing had total sales of $375,000 while operating at 75% of capacity. The total of its variable costs was $150,000. Fixed costs were $180,000.

a. What is Marconi's break-even point expressed:
   (i) In dollars of sales?   (ii) As a percent of capacity?

b. If the current prices and cost structure are the same as last year's, what net income can be expected from sales of $450,000 in the current year?

✓ SOLUTION

When no information is provided about the unit price and unit variable cost, cost-volume-profit analysis may still be undertaken. The further assumption required is that the firm sells a single product or, if more than one product, the product mix does not change from one period to the next.

Although we do not have sufficient information to calculate the unit contribution margin, we can calculate the total contribution margin and the contribution rate. That is,

$$
\begin{aligned}
CR &= \frac{\text{Total contribution margin}}{\text{Total sales}} \times 100\% \\
&= \frac{\text{Total sales} - \text{Total variable costs}}{\text{Total sales}} \times 100\% \\
&= \frac{\$375,000 - \$150,000}{\$375,000} \times 100\% \\
&= 60\%
\end{aligned}
$$

The most useful interpretation of this figure is that 60 cents from every dollar of sales is available to pay fixed costs. Once fixed costs are covered for the period, 60 cents of each additional dollar of sales "flow through to the bottom line" (that is, becomes net income or operating profit for the period).

a. (i) The break-even point will occur when

$$\text{Sales} \times CR = FC$$

That is,

$$\text{Sales} = \frac{FC}{CR} = \frac{\$180,000}{0.60} = \$300,000$$

(ii) If sales of \$375,000 represent 75% of capacity, then

$$\text{Full capacity} = \frac{\$375,000}{0.75} = \$500,000 \text{ of sales}$$

The break-even point of \$300,000 of sales represents

$$\frac{\$300,000}{\$500,000} \times 100\% = 60\% \text{ of capacity}$$

b. The new sales level of \$450,000 is \$150,000 beyond the break-even point. Since *CR* = 60%, then 60 cents of each dollar of sales beyond the break-even point becomes net income. Hence,

$$\text{Net income} = 0.60 \times \$150,000 = \$90,000$$

Sales of \$450,000 in the current year should produce a net income of \$90,000. ∎

■ EXAMPLE 5.2E   *USING THE CONTRIBUTION MARGIN APPROACH TO CVP ANALYSIS*

Alberta Oilseed Co. processes rapeseed to produce canola oil and rapeseed meal. The company can process up to 20,000 tonnes of rapeseed per year. The company pays growers \$80 per tonne, and each tonne yields \$200 worth of oil and meal. Variable processing costs are \$47 per tonne, and fixed processing costs are \$340,000 per year at all production levels. Administrative overhead is \$300,000 per year regardless of the volume of production. Marketing and transportation costs work out to \$23 per tonne processed.

a. Determine the break-even volume in terms of:
   (i) Tonnes of rapeseed processed per year.
   (ii) Percent capacity utilization.
   (iii) Dollar amount of product sales for the year.

b. In order to attain the net income of \$240,000 in a year,
   (i) How many tonnes of rapeseed must be processed and sold in the year?
   (ii) What dollar amount of oil and meal must be sold?

c. What is the maximum price that the company can pay per tonne of rapeseed and still break even on a volume of 16,000 tonnes per year?

☑ SOLUTION

From the given information,

$$\text{Full capacity} = 20,000 \text{ tonnes per year}$$
$$VC = \$80 + \$47 + \$23 = \$150 \text{ per tonne}$$
$$SP = \$200 \text{ per (input) tonne}$$
$$FC = \$340,000 + \$300,000 = \$640,000 \text{ per year}$$

Hence,
$$CM = SP - VC = \$200 - \$150 = \$50 \text{ per tonne}$$

a. (i) Break-even volume $= \dfrac{FC}{CM} = \dfrac{\$640,000}{\$50} = 12,800$ tonnes per year

   (ii) 12,800 tonnes per year represent $\dfrac{12,800}{20,000} \times 100\% = 64\%$ of capacity

  (iii) Sales revenue at the break-even point is $12,800(\$200) = \$2,560,000$

b. (i) Each tonne above the break-even point contributes $CM = \$50$ to the net income. A net income of \$240,000 will require the sale of

$$\dfrac{\$240,000}{\$50} = 4800 \text{ tonnes more than the break-even point}$$

Total sales must be $12,800 + 4800 = 17,600$ tonnes in the year.

  (ii) The sales revenue required to generate a net income of \$240,000 is

$$17,600(\$200) = \$3,520,000$$

c. In this scenario, SP and FC are unchanged but VC is higher, raising the break-even point from 12,800 tonnes to 16,000 tonnes. Since

$$\text{Break-even volume} = \dfrac{FC}{CM}$$

then

$$CM = \dfrac{FC}{\text{Break-even volume}} = \dfrac{\$640,000}{16,000} = \$40 \text{ per tonne}$$

This is \$10 per tonne less than the former *CM*. Therefore, at the same selling price as before, the *VC* per tonne is \$10 higher, representing the increase in the price paid to rapeseed growers. The maximum price that can be paid to growers and still break even at a volume of 16,000 tonnes is $\$80 + \$10 = \$90$ per tonne.

■

*REVENUE AND COST FUNCTION APPROACH TO CVP ANALYSIS

This approach is more mechanical and less intuitive than the contribution margin approach. The strategy is to substitute known values in a set of general equations and then solve the equations for the desired unknown. Two new variables need to be introduced.

    $TR = $ Total revenue (from the sale of X units)
    $TC = $ Total costs (for X units)

General equations for *TC* and *TR* are easily derived in terms of variables defined earlier in this section.

    $TR = $ Unit selling price $\times$ Number of units sold
       $= (SP)X$
    $TC = $ Total variable costs $+$ Fixed costs
       $= $ (Variable costs per unit $\times$ Number of units sold) $+$ Fixed costs
       $= (VC)X + FC$

The equation for *TR* is called the *revenue function* and the equation for *TC* is called the *cost function*.

The net income for a period is the total revenue minus the total costs. Hence,

$$NI = TR - TC$$
$$= (SP)X - [(VC)X + FC]$$
$$= (SP - VC)X - FC$$

In summary,

Revenue Function
Cost Function
Net Income

$$TR = (SP)X$$
$$TC = (VC)X + FC$$
$$NI = (SP - VC)X - FC$$

(5–3)

Note that the third equation in the set is the same as formula (5–2a) where $SP - VC$ is replaced by the contribution margin, CM. This is a key difference between the two approaches to CVP analysis. The approach in this part gives no particular attention to the interpretation and significance of the quantity $SP - VC$. The contribution margin approach provides a more intuitive and insightful analysis.

We can obtain the break-even volume in this approach by substituting $NI = 0$ in the third equation for the special case X = break-even volume. That is,

$$0 = (SP - VC)(\text{Break-even volume}) - FC$$

$$\text{Break-even volume} = \frac{FC}{SP - VC}$$

(5–3a)

Example problems 5.2B, 5.2C, and 5.2D will now be repeated as Examples 5.2F, 5.2G, and 5.2H, respectively, to demonstrate and contrast this second approach.

■ EXAMPLE 5.2F   *CVP ANALYSIS USING THE REVENUE AND COST FUNCTION APPROACH*

In Example 5.2a concerning the neighbourhood pub proposal, we found that

SP = $15.00 per customer
VC = $5.00 per customer
FC = $20,000 per month

for a range of 1500 to 3000 customers per month.

a. Part a in Example 5.2B dealt with the contribution margin, which is not applicable in the current approach.

b. What is the break-even point in:
(i) customers per month?   (ii) revenue per month?

c. What will be the monthly net income if there are:
(i) 1600 customers per month?   (ii) 2300 customers per month?

d. How many customers per month are required for a net income of $5000 per month?

e. If the average revenue turns out to be only $13.50 per customer, how many customers per month will be needed to break even?

f. If the customer volume reaches 3000 per month, the owner/manager intends to start drawing a salary of $4000 per month and to hire three more waiters or waitresses at $1200 per month. With these additional costs and an average revenue of $15.00 per customer from 3000 customers per month, what would be the monthly net income?

✓ Solution

Substituting the known quantities into formulas (5–3) gives

$$TR = (SP)X = \$15X$$
$$TC = (VC)X + FC = \$5X + \$20{,}000$$
$$NI = (SP - VC)X - FC = \$10X - \$20{,}000$$

b. (i) To calculate the break-even volume, solve for X when $NI = 0$ in the third equation.

$$\text{Break-even volume} = \frac{\$20{,}000}{\$10} = 2000 \text{ customers per month}$$

(ii) When $X = 2000$ customers per month,

$$TR = (\$15)2000 = \$30{,}000 \text{ per month}$$

c. (i) If $X = 1600$ customers per month,

$$NI = (\$10)1600 - \$20{,}000 = -\$4000$$

That is, the pub will lose $4000 per month.

(ii) If $X = 2300$ customers per month,

$$NI = (\$10)2300 - \$20{,}000 = \$3000$$

At 2300 customers per month, the net income will be $3000 per month.

d. Substituting $NI = \$5000$ in the third equation,

$$\$5000 = \$10X - \$20{,}000$$
$$X = \frac{\$20{,}000 + \$5000}{\$10} = 2500 \text{ customers per month}$$

The pub requires 2500 customers per month to generate a net income of $5000 per month.

e. Recall from the information given in Example 5.2A that the variable costs are the food and drink ingredients, and that they amount to one-third of the selling prices. Under the new scenario, $SP = \$13.50$ and $VC = \$13.50/3 = \$4.50$. The fixed costs remain at $20,000 per month. The net income equation becomes

$$NI = (\$13.50 - \$4.50)X - \$20{,}000 = \$9X - \$20{,}000$$

The break-even point where $NI = 0$ is at

$$X = \frac{\$20{,}000}{\$9} = 2223 \text{ customers per month}$$

f. In this scenario, SP and VC are at their original estimates but fixed costs are increased by $4000 + 3(\$1200) = \$7600$ to $27,600 per month. In this case, the third equation gives

$$NI = (\$10)3000 - \$27{,}600 = \$2400$$

With 3000 customers per month and the increased payroll, the net income will be $2400 per month.   ∎

■ EXAMPLE 5.2G   *CVP ANALYSIS USING THE REVENUE AND COST FUNCTION APPROACH*

A manufacturing company is studying the feasibility of producing a new product. A new production line could manufacture up to 800 units per month at a cost of $50 per unit. Fixed costs would be $22,400 per month. Variable selling and shipping costs are estimated to be $20 per unit. Market research indicates that a unit price of $110 would be competitive.

a. What is the break-even point as a percent of capacity?

b. What would be the net income at 90% of capacity?

c. What would unit sales have to be to attain a net income of $9000 per month?

d. In a serious recession sales might fall to 55% of capacity. What would be the resulting net income?

e. What dollar amount of sales would result in a loss of $2000 per month?

f. In the highest cost scenario, fixed costs might be $25,000, production costs might be $55 per unit, and selling and shipping costs might be $22 per unit. What would the break-even point be in these circumstances?

☑ SOLUTION

In the expected scenario, $SP = \$110$, $VC = \$50 + \$20 = \$70$, and $FC = \$22,400$. Hence,

$$TR = \$110X$$
$$TC = \$70X + \$22,400$$
$$NI = \$40X - \$22,400$$

a. Using formula (5–3a),

$$\text{Break-even volume} = \frac{FC}{SP - VC} = \frac{\$22,400}{\$110 - \$70} = 560 \text{ units}$$

This represents

$$\frac{560}{800} \times 100\% = 70\% \text{ of capacity}$$

b. At 90% of capacity, production would be $0.9 \times 800 = 720$ units per month. Using the third equation,

$$NI = \$40(720) - \$22,400 = \$6400 \text{ per month}$$

c. Setting $NI = \$9000$ in the third equation, we obtain

$$\$9000 = \$40X - \$22,400$$

Unit sales would have to be $X = \dfrac{\$9000 + \$22,400}{40} = 785$ per month.

d. In the recession scenario, unit sales would be $0.55 \times 800 = 440$ per month. Then

$$NI = (\$40)440 - \$22,400 = -\$4800$$

The company would lose $4800 per month in the recession.

e. Substituting $NI = -\$2000$ per month in the third equation,

$$-\$2000 = \$40X - \$22{,}400$$

$$X = \frac{-\$2000 + \$22{,}400}{\$40} = 510 \text{ units per month}$$

The dollar amount of sales would be

$$TR = (\$110)X = (\$110)510 = \$56{,}100$$

f. In the highest cost scenario, $FC = \$25{,}000$ and $VC = \$77$ per unit. Then

$$\text{Break-even volume} = \frac{FC}{SP - VC} = \frac{\$25{,}000}{\$110 - \$77} = 758 \text{ units}$$

The break-even point in this scenario would be at 758 units per month (94.75% of capacity). ∎

EXAMPLE 5.2H   *CVP ANALYSIS WITH SALES VOLUME IN DOLLARS INSTEAD OF UNITS*

Last year Marconi Printing had total sales of $375,000 while operating at 75% of capacity. The total of its variable costs was $150,000. Fixed costs were $180,000.

a. What is Marconi's break-even point expressed:
   (i) In dollars of sales?   (ii) As a percent of capacity?

b. If the current prices, cost structure, and product mix are the same as last year's, what net income can be expected from sales of $450,000 in the current year?

☑ SOLUTION

In this situation, we let $SP = \$1$ and then X represents the number of $1 units sold. The revenue function is simply

$$TR = \$1X$$

In the cost function, $TC = (VC)X + FC$, VC must be interpreted as the variable cost per $1 of sales. In the present case,

$$VC = \frac{\text{Total variable costs}}{\text{Total unit sales}} = \frac{\$150{,}000}{375{,}000} = \$0.40$$

Then

$$TC = \$0.40X + \$180{,}000$$

and

$$NI = (\$1.00 - \$0.40)X - \$180{,}000 = \$0.60X - \$180{,}000$$

a. (i) Setting $NI = 0$ in the net income equation, we obtain

$$\text{Break-even point} = \frac{\$180{,}000}{\$0.60} = 300{,}000 \text{ units}$$

Since each unit is deemed to sell at $1, Marconi will break even on sales of $300,000.
   (ii) If sales of $375,000 represents 75% of capacity, then

$$\text{Full capacity} = \frac{\$375{,}000}{0.75} = \$500{,}000 \text{ of sales}$$

The break-even point of $300,000 of sales represents

$$\frac{\$300,000}{\$500,000} \times 100\% = 60\% \text{ of capacity}$$

b. Substitute $X = 450,000$ in the net income equation.

$$NI = \$0.60(450,000) - \$180,000 = \$90,000$$

Sales of $450,000 in the current year should produce a net income of $90,000. ■

Point of Interest

Break-Even Analysis as Part of a Business Plan

The Royal Bank of Canada has published a series of booklets titled *Your Business Matters* to help entrepreneurs achieve their business goals. *Starting Out Right,* the first book in the series, emphasizes the importance of a thorough business plan.

> "Completing a business plan requires that you compile information on yourself and other principals, the industry you're in and its key success factors, the market and competition, the history of your business, types and sources of financing, and its future prospects."

Borrowing Money, the second book in the series, is aimed at entrepreneurs who are considering applying for a bank loan. It points out that:

> "When you apply for a small business loan, you'll be asked for a great deal of information, most of which should be

contained in one key document—your business plan. Not only does a plan show lenders that you have a firm grasp of your business, it's also your own road map for running and planning your enterprise on an ongoing basis."

However, the book laments that:

> "Fewer than one-half of small-business loan applicants approach their bank with a business plan in hand."

One of the key elements recommended for the financial section of the business plan is:

> ". . . a break-even calculation indicating your variable costs, your fixed costs, and what you will be charging for each unit of your product or service. Only by calculating the level of sales at which your revenues equal your expenses will you know at what point your business is likely to be profitable."

EXERCISE 5.2

Answers to the odd-numbered problems are at the end of the book.

1. A small manufacturing operation can produce up to 250 units per week of a product that it sells for $20 per unit. The variable cost per unit is $12, and the fixed cost per week is $1200.

   a. What is the contribution margin per unit?

   b. How many units must it sell per week to break even?

   c. Determine the firm's weekly profit or loss if it sells:
      (i) 120 units per week   (ii) 250 units per week

   d. At what level of sales will the net income be $400 per week?

2. Valley Peat Ltd. sells peat moss for $10 per bag. Variable costs are $7.50 per bag and annual fixed costs are $100,000.

   a. What are the contribution margin and the contribution ratio?

   b. How many bags of peat must be sold to break even?

   c. What will be the net income for a year in which 60,000 bags of peat are sold?

   d. How many bags must be sold for a net income of $60,000 in a year?

   e. What annual sales in terms of bags and in terms of dollars would produce a loss of $10,000?

   f. How much do the break-even unit sales and break-even revenue increase per $1000 increase in annual fixed costs?

3. Reflex Manufacturing Corp. manufactures borgels at a unit variable cost of $43. It sells them for $70 each. It can produce a maximum of 3200 borgels per month. Annual fixed costs total $648,000.

   a. What is the contribution margin per unit?

   b. What is the break-even volume?

   c. What is the monthly net income at a volume of 2500 borgels per month?

   d. What is the monthly net income if Reflex operates at 50% of capacity during a recession?

   e. At what percent utilization would the annual net income be $226,800?

   f. If fixed and variable costs remain the same, how much do the monthly break-even unit sales change for a $1 increase in the selling price?

4. Bentley Plastics Ltd. has annual fixed costs of $450,000, variable costs of $15 per unit, and a contribution rate of 40%.

   a. What annual revenue is required to break even?

   b. What annual unit sales are required to break even?

   c. What will be the annual net income at annual sales of:
      (i) 50,000 units?   (ii) $1,000,000?

   d. What minimum annual unit sales are required to limit the annual loss to $50,000?

   e. If the unit selling price and fixed costs remain the same, what are the changes in break-even unit sales and break-even revenue for a $1 increase in variable costs?

•5. Calculate the missing quantities:

Part	Sales ($)	Variable costs ($)	Contribution margin ($)	Fixed costs ($)	Net income ($)	Unit sales
a	400,000	?	20	100,000	60,000	?
b	?	60,000	10	?	12,500	4000
c	360,000	?	?	90,000	60,000	5000

•6. Calculate the missing quantities:

Part	Sales ($)	Variable costs ($)	Contribution rate (%)	Fixed costs ($)	Net income ($)
a	800,000	?	40	?	100,000
b	450,000	360,000	?	?	47,500
c	?	?	30	180,000	120,000

•7. A college ski club is planning a weekend package for its members. The members will each be charged $135. For a group of 15 or more, the club can purchase a 2-day down-hill pass and 2 nights' accommodation for $110 per person. A 36-passenger capacity bus can be chartered for $700.

   a. How many must sign up for the package for all costs to be covered?

   b. If the bus is filled, how much profit will the club make?

   c. If the student government agrees to cover any loss up to $200, what is the minimum number of participants required?

•8. Genifax reported the following information for September:

Sales	$180,000
Fixed manufacturing costs	22,000
Fixed marketing and overhead costs	14,000
Total variable costs	120,000
Unit price	9

   a. Determine the unit sales required to break even.

   b. What unit sales would generate a net income of $30,000?

   c. What unit sales would generate a profit of 20% of the sales dollars?

   d. What sales dollars are required to produce a profit of $20,000?

   e. If unit variable costs are reduced by 10% with no change in the fixed costs, what will the break-even point become?

•9. The social committee of a college's student government is planning the annual gradua-tion dinner and dance. The preferred band can be signed for $500 plus 10% of ticket revenues. A hall can be rented for $2200. Fire regulations limit the hall to 400 guests plus the band and caterers. A food caterer has quoted a price of $12 per person for the dinner.

   The committee thinks that the event will be a sellout if ticket prices are set at $23 per person. Some on the committee are in favour of less crowding at the dance and argue for a ticket price of $28. They estimate that 300 will attend at the higher price.

   a. Calculate the number of tickets that need to be sold at each price to break even.

   b. What will the profit be at the predicted sales at each ticket price?

•10. This problem is designed to illustrate how the relative proportions of fixed and variable costs affect a firm's net income when the sales volume changes.

   Two hypothetical firms, A and B, manufacture and sell the same product at the same price of $50. Firm A is highly mechanized with monthly fixed costs of $4000 and unit variable costs of $10. Firm B is labour-intensive and can readily lay off or take on more workers as production requirements warrant. B's monthly fixed costs are $1000, and its unit variable costs are $40.

   a. Calculate the break-even volume for both firms.

   b. At each firm's break-even point, calculate the proportion of the firm's total costs that are fixed and the proportion that are variable.

   c. For a 10% increase in sales above the break-even point, calculate the dollar increase in each firm's net income. Explain the differing results.

   d. For a 10% decrease in sales below the break-even point, calculate the dollar decrease in each firm's net income. Explain the differing results.

   e. What is each firm's net income at sales of 150 units per month and each firm's loss at sales of 50 units per month?

•11. In the year just ended, a small appliance manufacturer sold its griddle at the wholesale price of $37.50. The unit variable costs were $13.25, and the monthly fixed costs were $5600.

   a. If unit variable costs are expected to rise to $15.00 and fixed costs to $6000 per month for the next year, at what amount should the griddle be priced in order to have the same break-even volume as last year?

   b. What should the griddle's price be in order to have the same profit as last year on sales of 300 griddles per month in both years?

•12. Mickey's Restaurant had a net income last year of $40,000 after fixed costs of $130,000 and total variable costs of $80,000.

   a. What was the restaurant's break-even point in sales dollars?

   b. If fixed costs in the current year rise to $140,000 and variable costs remain at the same percentage of sales as for last year, what will be the break-even point?

   c. What sales in the current year will result in a profit of $50,000?

•13. A farmer is trying to decide whether to rent his neighbour's land to grow additional hay for sale to feedlots at $90 per delivered tonne. The land can be rented at $200 per hectare for the season. Cultivation and planting will cost $300 per hectare; spraying and fertilizer will cost $225 per hectare. It will cost $21 per tonne to cut, condition, and bale the hay, and $12 per tonne to transport it to the feedlots.

   a. How many tonnes per hectare must be produced to break even?

   b. How much is the break-even tonnage lowered if the selling price is $5 per tonne higher?

   c. What is the profit or loss at the $90 per tonne price if the crop yield is:
     (i) 15 tonnes per hectare?
     (ii) 10 tonnes per hectare?

•14. A sporting goods manufacturer lost $400,000 on sales of $3 million in a year during the last recession. The production lines operated at only 60% of capacity during the year. Variable costs represent one-third of the sales dollars.

   a. At what percent of capacity must the firm operate in order to break even?

   b. What would its net income be at 80% of capacity?

   c. What dollar sales would generate a net income of $700,000?

   d. How much does each additional dollar of sales increase the net income?

   e. How much does a $1 increase in fixed costs raise the break-even sales?

*5.3 INTRODUCTION TO GRAPHICAL TECHNIQUES

The relationship between two variables may be presented in a variety of ways. Three common methods are:

- A table listing pairs of values of the two variables.
- An algebraic equation involving the two variables.
- A graph depicting the relationship between the two variables.

   The graphical presentation is best for quickly giving an impression of the nature of the relationship between the two variables. It also allows a user to *quickly estimate* the value of one variable that corresponds to any selected value of the other variable.

The algebraic equation has the advantage of expressing the relationship with the greatest degree of precision. Graphical analysis is usually limited to three-figure precision. An algebraic equation is as precise as the numerical coefficients in it and the assumptions lying behind it.

GRAPHING A LINEAR EQUATION IN TWO UNKNOWNS

The notation used to indicate that a mathematical relationship exists between two variables is

$$y = f(x)$$

which is read "y is a function of x." A pair of numerical values of the variables, customarily written in the order (x,y), is said to *satisfy* the equation if the two sides of the equation are equal after substitution of the values into the equation.

A single pair of (x,y) values gives a point when plotted on graph paper. In the context of graphing, this pair of values is called the *coordinates* of the point. A graph of the equation $y = f(x)$ is a plot of all pairs of (x,y) values within a certain range that satisfy the equation. Conversely, if the x-coordinate and the y-coordinate of *any* point on a plotted curve are substituted into the corresponding algebraic equation, both sides of the equation will have the same numerical value.

In practice, we obtain the graph of an equation through the following steps:

1. Construct a *table of values* consisting of pairs of (x,y) values that satisfy the equation. Each pair is obtained by assigning a value to one variable and then solving the resulting equation in one unknown for the other variable.
2. Construct and label the x-axis and the y-axis to accommodate the range of values in the table.
3. Plot the points using the (x,y) pairs from the table of values as the (x,y) coordinates.
4. Connect the plotted points with a *smooth* curve.

■ EXAMPLE 5.3A   GRAPHING A LINEAR EQUATION IN TWO VARIABLES

Graph the equation $2x - 3y = -6$ over the range $x = -6$ to $x = 6$.

✓ SOLUTION

The first step listed above is to construct a table of values. To do this, assign a range of values to one of the variables and solve for the corresponding values of the other variable. Since the range over which the graph is to be plotted is specified in terms of x in this case, it is natural to assign a series of values to x covering the specified range. Since we will be repeatedly solving the equation for y, it will be a convenience if we rearrange the equation so that y is isolated on one side.

Transposing $2x$ to the right side and dividing both sides by -3, we obtain

$$y = \frac{2}{3}x + 2$$

Now substitute a few values for x over the range $x = -6$ to $x = 6$:

$$x = -6: \qquad y = \frac{2}{3}(-6) + 2 = -2$$

$$x = -3: \qquad y = \frac{2}{3}(-3) + 2 = 0$$

$$x = 0: \qquad y = \frac{2}{3}(0) + 2 = 2$$

$$x = 3: \qquad y = \frac{2}{3}(3) + 2 = 4$$

$$x = 6: \qquad y = \frac{2}{3}(6) + 2 = 6$$

The table of values summarizing these (x,y) pairs is:

x:	−6	−3	0	3	6	← Assigned x value
y:	−2	0	2	4	6	← Calculated y value

The next step is to draw axes, with the x-axis including the range from −6 to +6 and the y-axis encompassing the range from −2 to +6. The five points can then be plotted and a smooth curve drawn to connect the points.

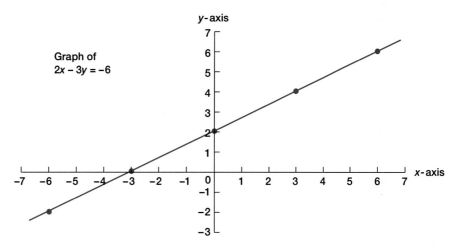

The most notable feature about the graph is that the plotted points fall on a straight line. This is a general outcome for linear equations in two variables and, of course, is the reason they are called *linear* equations. ∎

Tips

- To construct the graph of a *linear* equation, it is sufficient to have just two (x,y) pairs in the table of values.

- For the best precision in constructing the graph of a linear equation, the two points used should be near the ends of the range over which the graph is to be drawn.

- The easiest (x,y) pair to determine comes from assigning the value 0 to x.

- If x has a fractional coefficient, assign values to x that are a multiple of the coefficient's denominator. This makes the calculations easier and is likely to yield a "nicer" value to plot for y.

■ EXAMPLE 5.3B   *GRAPHING A LINEAR EQUATION IN TWO VARIABLES*

Graph the equation $3y - 150x = 24,000$ over the range $x = 0$ to $x = 200$.

☑ SOLUTION

$$3y = 150x + 24,000$$

Divide both sides by 3 to isolate y on the left side of the equation:

$$y = 50x + 8000$$

Construct a table of values[7] for the range of x:

$$x = 0: \qquad y = 50(0) + 8000 = 8000$$
$$x = 100: \qquad y = 50(100) + 8000 = 13,000$$
$$x = 200: \qquad y = 50(200) + 8000 = 18,000$$

x:	0	100	200
y:	8000	13,000	18,000

Construct and label the axes. Then plot the points.

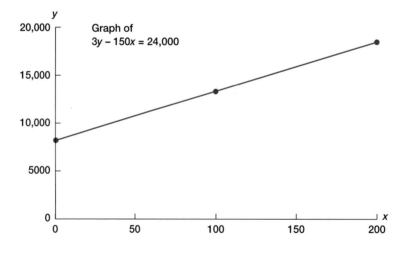

GRAPHICAL APPROACH TO COST-VOLUME-PROFIT ANALYSIS

This approach requires that both the cost function and the revenue function be plotted on the same graph as in Figure 5.1. Such a graph is called a **break-even chart** because the sales volume at which the business will break even is immediately apparent.

The intersection of the *TR* and *TC* lines is the only point at which total revenue equals total costs, and the firm breaks even. This intersection is therefore called the *break-even point*. The coordinates of the point give the sales volume and total revenue required for the firm to break even. At higher sales, the business will show a profit

---

[7]Although two points are sufficient to define the line, plotting a third point provides a check of the calculation. If the three points do not all fall on a straight line, then at least one mistake has been made in calculating the coordinates of the points or in plotting the points.

FIGURE 5.1

Break-Even Chart

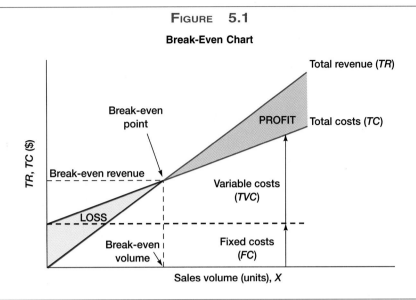

because the revenue line is above the total cost line. The profit equals the vertical separation of the lines. At any sales volume to the left of the break-even point, total costs exceed total revenue. The size of the loss is determined by the vertical separation of the two lines. At zero sales volume, there are no revenues or variable costs, but the business still incurs the fixed costs.

■ **EXAMPLE 5.3c** *GRAPHICAL CVP ANALYSIS OF THE BUSINESS DESCRIBED IN EXAMPLE 5.2A*

We will use the data presented in Example 5.2A for the neighbourhood pub proposal. There it was determined that $SP = \$15$, $VC = \$5$, and $FC = \$20,000$.

a. What are the revenue and cost functions for this business?

b. Construct a break-even chart for the range of 1500 to 3000 customers per month.

c. What is the break-even point in:
   (i) customers per month?   (ii) revenue per month?

d. What will the monthly net income be if there are:
   (i) 1600 customers per month?   (ii) 2300 customers per month?

e. How many customers per month are required for a net income of $5000 per month?

f. If the customer volume reaches 3000 per month, the owner/manager intends to start drawing a salary of $4000 per month and to hire three more waiters or waitresses at $1200 per month. With these additional costs and an average revenue of $15.00 per customer from 3000 customers per month, what would be the monthly net income?

Note: Parts *c, d, e,* and *f* were answered in Example 5.2B using the contribution margin approach and in Example 5.2F by solving the revenue and cost functions algebraically. The three sets of solutions to the identical questions may be used to compare the three approaches to CVP analysis.

☑ Solution

a. Using formulas (5–3), we obtain

Revenue function: $TR = (SP)X = \$15X$
Cost function: $TC = (VC)X + FC = \$5X + \$20,000$

b. Construct a table of values for both the revenue function and the cost function. The two end points of the range for X are good choices to plot.

X:	1500	3000
TR:	$22,500	$45,000
TC:	$27,500	$35,000

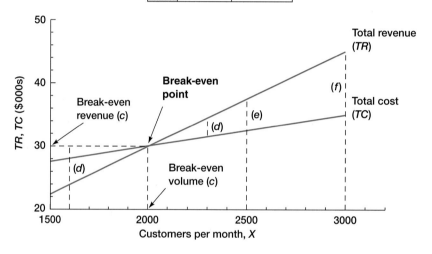

c. (i) At the break-even point, the pub requires 2000 customers per month.
   (ii) The revenue is then $30,000 per month.

d. (i) At $X = 1600$ customers per month, the TC line is $4000 above the TR line. The pub will lose $4000 per month if it has only 1600 customers per month.
   (ii) At $X = 2300$ customers per month, the TR line is $3000 above the TC line. The pub will have a profit of $3000 per month if it has 2300 customers per month.

e. The answer will be the value for X at which the TR line is $5000 above the TC line. This occurs at $X = 2500$ customers per month.[8]

f. At $X = 3000$ customers per month, the TR line is $10,000 above the TC line. That is, the profit is $10,000 per month. The additional cost of Chuck's salary and three more waiters would be $7600 per month. The pub would still have a profit of $2400 per month if these extra fixed costs were incurred at a volume of 3000 customers per month. ■

---

[8]The graphical approach to CVP analysis has the disadvantage of limited accuracy. The error in plotting or reading the coordinates of a point can be in the 2% to 4% range. The cumulative effects of limited precision in each of a few successive steps can easily lead to a 10% error in the answer to a question such as this one.

■ EXAMPLE 5.3D   *GRAPHICAL COST-VOLUME-PROFIT AND BREAK-EVEN ANALYSIS*

The board of directors of a Tier 2 Junior A hockey team is preparing financial projections for the next season's operations. The team rents the city's 4000-seat arena for the entire season for $100,000 plus 25% of revenue from ticket sales. The city operates the food concessions at the games and pays the team one-third of the gross revenue.

The team will pay $100,000 for uniforms and equipment, $100,000 for travel costs, $50,000 for the coach's salary, $50,000 for housing subsidies for team members not living at home, and $20,000 for insurance. The average ticket price will be $8, and past experience shows that each fan spends an average of $3 on food and beverages at the games.

Use a break-even chart to answer the following questions.

a. What must the aggregate attendance be for the 30 home games for the team to just cover all of its costs for the season?

b. What will the profit or loss be if the attendance averages 75% of capacity?

c. The team has $140,000 in a contingency fund to absorb losses. What season attendance would just wipe out this fund?

☑ SOLUTION

a. The total of the fixed costs is

$$FC = \$100,000 + \$100,000 + \$100,000 + \$50,000 + \$50,000 + \$20,000$$
$$= \$420,000$$

The unit variable cost is the 25% of the price of each ticket that the team must pay to the city as part of the rent.

$$VC = 0.25 \times \$8 = \$2$$

The cost function for the analysis is

$$TC = FC + (VC)X$$
$$= \$420,000 + \$2X$$

Each ticket sold generates revenue for the team of $8 from the admission price and $1 from the team's share (one-third) of the concession revenue ($3 per fan). The revenue function is

$$TR = (\$8 + \$1)X$$
$$= \$9X$$

The cost and revenue functions should be plotted for the range from $X = 0$ to $X = 120,000$, which is full capacity (30 × 4000) for the season.

X:	0	120,000
TR:	$420,000	$660,000
TC:	$0	$1,080,000

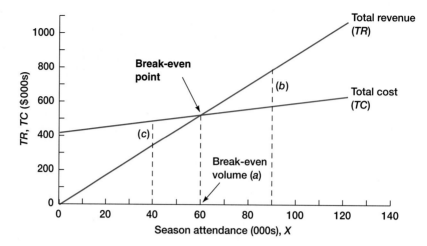

For the team to cover its costs, it must have the attendance figure at the break-even point. Therefore, the team will just cover all its expenses if the total season attendance is 60,000.

b. The season attendance at 75% of capacity is

$$0.75 \times 120{,}000 = 90{,}000$$

At an attendance of 90,000, the *TR* line is $210,000 above the *TC* line. The team will then have a profit of $210,000.

c. The answer will be the attendance at which the *TC* line is $140,000 above the *TR* line. This separation occurs at an attendance of 40,000. ■

EXERCISE 5.3

Answers to the odd-numbered problems are at the end of the book.

Graph each of the following equations.

1. $-2x + y = 0$ over the range $x = -3$ to $x = 6$
2. $-2x + y = 4$ over the range $x = -3$ to $x = 6$
3. $2x + y = 4$ over the range $x = -3$ to $x = 6$
4. $y = 4$ over the range $x = -3$ to $x = 6$
5. $3x - 4y + 12 = 0$ over the range $x = -8$ *to* $x = 12$
6. $y = 60x + 6000$ over the range $x = 0$ to $x = 50$
7. $y = 4.5x + 5000$ over the range $x = 0$ to $x = 6000$

The graphical approach to CVP analysis may be used to solve problems 1, 2, 3, 7, 8, and 13 in the Exercise at the end of Section 5.2.

REVIEW PROBLEMS

Answers to the odd-numbered review problems are at the back of the book.

1. Solve each of the following pairs of equations to three significant figures.

    a. $4a - 5b = 30$ b. $76x - 29y = 1050$
        $2a - 6b = 22$ $-13x - 63y = 250$

2. Deanna is paid a base salary plus commission. On sales of $27,000 and $35,500 in 2 successive months, her gross pay was $2815.00 and $3197.50, respectively. What are her base salary and commission rate (in percent)?

3. Nguyen fishes for red snapper and ling cod off the coast of British Columbia and delivers his catch each week to a fish buyer. On one delivery, he received $2454.20 for 370 kg of red snapper and 264 kg of ling cod. On another occasion he was paid $2124.70 for 304 kg of ling cod and 255 kg of red snapper. What price per kg was Nguyen paid for each type of fish?

•4. Durable Toys Inc. wants to calculate from recent production data the monthly fixed costs and unit variable costs on its Mountain Trike product line. In the most recent month, it produced 530 Trikes at a total cost of $24,190. In the previous month, it produced 365 Trikes at a total cost of $18,745. What are the fixed costs per month and the unit variable costs? *Hint:* Recall from Section 5.2 that

    Total costs = Fixed costs + (Unit variable costs) × (Number of units produced)

5. Calculate the missing quantities:

	Unit selling price	Variable cost per unit	Unit sales	Total contribution margin	Total fixed costs	Net income
a.	?	$10	150,000	$300,000	$220,000	?
b.	$25	?	180,000	900,000	800,000	?
c.	20	14	?	120,000	?	$12,000

6. The Armour Company had the following revenue and costs in the most recently completed fiscal year:

Total revenue	$10,000,000
Total fixed costs	$2,000,000
Total variable costs	$6,000,000
Total units produced and sold	1,000,000

    a. What is the contribution margin per unit?

    b. What is sales volume at the break-even point?

    c. How many units must be produced and sold for the company to have a net income of $1,000,000 for the year?

7. During an economic slowdown, an automobile plant lost $6,000,000 on the production and sale of 9000 cars. Total revenue for the year was $135,000,000. If the break-even volume for the plant is 10,000 cars per year, calculate:

    a. The contribution margin per car.

    b. The plant's total fixed costs for a year.

    c. The net income if unit sales for the year had been equal to the 5-year average of 12,000.

8. Fisher Publishing Inc. is doing a financial feasibility analysis for a new book. Editing and preproduction costs are estimated at $45,000. The printing costs are a flat $7000 for setup plus $8.00 per book. The author's royalty is 8% of the publisher's net price to bookstores. Advertising and promotion costs are budgeted at $8000.

   a. If the price to bookstores is set at $35, how many books must be sold to break even?

   b. In a highest cost scenario, fixed costs might be $5000 higher and the printing costs might be $9.00 per book. By how many books would the break-even volume be raised?

   c. The marketing department is forecasting sales of 4800 books at the $35 price. What will be the net income from the project at this volume of sales?

   d. The marketing department is also forecasting that, if the price is reduced by 10%, unit sales will be 15% higher. Which price should be selected? (Show calculations that support your recommendation.)

•9. Norwood Industries has annual fixed costs of $1.8 million and a contribution rate of 45%.

   a. What annual revenue is required to break even?

   b. What revenue would result in a loss of $100,000 in a year?

   c. What annual revenue would produce an operating profit of $300,000?

   d. It the firm raises all its selling prices by 10% but variable costs are unchanged, what will be the new contribution rate?

   e. Market research indicates that if prices are increased by 10%, total revenue will remain at the part c amount because the higher prices will be offset by reduced sales volume. Will the operating profit remain at $300,000? Present calculations to justify your answer.

•10. Cambridge Manufacturing is evaluating the introduction of a new product that would have a unit selling price of $100. The total annual fixed costs are estimated to be $200,000, and the unit variable costs are projected at $60. Forecast sales volume for the first year is 8000 units.

   a. What sales volume (in units) is required to break even?

   b. What volume is required to generate a net income of $100,000?

   c. What would be the net income at the forecast sales volume?

   d. At the forecast sales volume, what will be the change in the net income if fixed costs are:
      (i) 5% higher than expected?   (ii) 10% lower than expected?

   e. At the forecast sales volume, what will be the change in the net income if unit variable costs are:
      (i) 10% higher than expected?   (ii) 5% lower than expected?

   f. At the forecast sales volume, what will be the change in the net income if the unit selling price is:
      (i) 5% higher?   (ii) 10% lower?

   g. At the forecast sales volume, what will be the change in the net income if unit variable costs are 10% higher than expected and fixed costs are simultaneously 10% lower than expected?

SELF-TEST EXERCISE

Answers to the self-test problems are at the end of the book.

1. Solve the following equations.

$$3x + 5y = 11$$
$$2x - y = 16$$

2. During a 1-day special, a grocery store sells cucumbers at 49 cents each or four for the price of three. At the end of the day, the store's computer reports that revenue from the sale of 541 cucumbers was $209.23. How many cucumbers were sold on the four-for-three promotion?

•3. A hockey arena has 2500 seats in the preferred blue sections near centre ice and 4500 seats in the less desirable red sections. At regular season prices, a sellout would generate ticket revenue of $50,250 for a single game. Ticket prices are raised by 20% in the "reds" and 30% in the "blues" for the play-offs. Ticket revenue from a play-off sellout would be $62,400. What are the ticket prices for the play-offs?

•4. To raise funds for its community activities, a Lions' Club chapter is negotiating with International Carnivals to bring its midway rides and games to town for a 3-day opening. The event will be held on part of the parking lot of a local shopping centre, which is to receive 10% of the gross revenue. The Lions' Club members will sell the ride and game tickets at the site. International Carnivals requires either $15,000 plus 30% of revenue or $10,000 plus 50% of revenue. Contacts in other towns that have held the event indicate that customers spend an average of $10 per person on rides and games.

   a. What is the break-even attendance under each basis for remunerating International Carnivals?

   b. For each alternative, what will be the club's profit or loss if the attendance is:
      (i) 3000?   (ii) 2200?

   c. How would you briefly explain the advantages and disadvantages of the two alternatives to a club member?

•5. The monthly fixed costs of operating a 30-unit motel are $14,000. The price per unit per night for next year is set at $55. Costs arising from rentals on a per-unit per-day basis are $6 for maid service, $3 for supplies and laundry, and $3 for heat and utilities.

   a. Based on a 30-day month, at what average occupancy rate will the motel break even?

   b. What will the motel's net income be at an occupancy rate of:
      (i) 40%?   (ii) 30%?

   c. Should the owner reduce the price from $55 to $47 per unit per night if it will result in an increase in the average occupancy rate from 40% to 50%? Present calculations that justify your answer.

SUMMARY OF NOTATION AND KEY FORMULAS

The following notation was introduced for cost-volume-profit analysis:

SP = Selling price or revenue per unit
VC = Variable costs per unit
FC = Fixed costs
CM = Contribution margin per unit
CR = Contribution rate
X = Total number of units sold in the period
NI = Net income (or operating profit) for the period
TC = Total costs (for X units)
TR = Total revenue (from the sale of X units)

Formula (5–1) $CM = SP - VC$ Finding the contribution margin and the
$$CR = \frac{CM}{SP} \times 100\%$$ contribution rate

Formula (5–2) $X = \dfrac{FC + NI}{CM}$ Finding the unit sales required to produce a
                                                   specified net income

Formula (5–3) $TR = (SP)X$ Finding the total revenue, total costs, and net
$TC = (VC)X + FC$ income from the sale of X units
$NI = (SP - VC)X - FC$

GLOSSARY OF TERMS

Break-even analysis   A procedure for determining the level of sales at which a firm's net income is zero.

Break-even chart   A graph presenting both total costs and total revenue as a function of sales volume so that the break-even point may be determined.

Break-even point   The sales volume at which net income is zero; the intersection of the total cost and total revenue lines on a break-even chart.

Contribution margin   The amount by which the unit selling price exceeds the unit variable cost.

Contribution rate   The contribution margin expressed as a percentage of the unit selling price.

Cost-volume-profit analysis   A procedure for estimating a firm's *operating profit* (or net income before taxes) at any sales *volume* given the firm's *cost* structure.

Fixed costs   Costs that do not change with the volume of sales.

Variable costs   Costs that grow in direct proportion to the volume of output or sales.

6

SIMPLE INTEREST

LEARNING OBJECTIVES

After completing this chapter, you will be able to:

- Apply the formulas $I = Prt$ and $S = P(1 + rt)$ to cases of loans and investments at simple interest

- Define or explain the terms *maturity value, time value of money, equivalent value, future value, present value, equivalent payment streams, equation of value*

- Present details of the amount and timing of payments in a time diagram

- Calculate the equivalent value on any date of a specified payment or stream

- of payments, given the interest rate that money can earn

- Given all but one of the payments, calculate the remaining payment required to settle a loan

- Given the number and timing of a series of equal loan payments, calculate the size of the payments

- Calculate an unknown payment in a payment stream so that the stream will be equivalent to a given payment stream

INTRODUCTION

Every day, money is borrowed and loaned in tens of thousands of transactions amounting, in total, to hundreds of millions of dollars. **Interest** is the fee or rent that lenders charge to borrowers for the temporary use of the borrowed money. The amount borrowed is called the **principal.** The **rate of interest** is the percentage of the principal that will be charged for a specified period of time, normally 1 year.

Borrowing and lending are two sides of the same transaction. To the lender a loan represents an *investment* in a debt obligation. The interest charged provides income from the investment. In a retail purchase using a credit card, the customer borrows an amount equal to the purchase price (plus any added tax) from the credit card issuer. The card issuer makes an investment in the form of a loan to the customer. The rate of return on the investment is equal to the rate of interest charged to the customer.

The purchase of a 30-day term deposit at a bank is another example of a borrowing/lending or borrowing/investing transaction. The bank customer invests in a 30-day loan *to* the bank and agrees to receive interest at the rate posted in the bank's rate schedule for 30-day term deposits.

Since borrowing and lending are so central to our daily lives and our economic system, it is essential that every business student be able to perform and explain the computation of interest in borrowing/lending transactions.

6.1 BASIC CONCEPTS

The type of interest that is most commonly calculated on short-term loans (that is, loans for periods of up to 1 year) is simple interest. **Simple interest** is calculated and paid only when the principal is repaid. The following variables will be used in our mathematical treatment of simple interest:

$$P = \text{Principal amount of the loan or investment}$$
$$r = \text{Annual rate of simple interest}$$
$$t = \text{Time period (term), in years, of the loan or investment}$$
$$I = \text{Amount of interest paid or received}$$

In 1 year the amount of interest earned will be Pr. If Pr is earned in each of t years, the total interest earned will be

Simple Interest Formula

$$\boxed{I = Prt} \qquad\qquad (6\text{--}1)$$

Even though the simple interest method is used primarily for loans and investments whose term is less than 1 year, it is common practice to quote r as an annual rate.[1] If an annual rate is used in formula (6–1) for r, the value substituted for t must be the loan period expressed as a fraction of a year. As a general requirement, the values for r and t that are substituted into formula (6–1) must have the *same time units.* For example, if r is the simple interest rate for one month, t must be measured in months.

---

[1]Unless otherwise stated, assume that a given rate of simple interest is the annual rate. Sometimes the letters "pa," meaning "per annum," are written after a quoted interest rate as an explicit indicator that it is an annual rate.

> **Tip**
>
> In substituting the numerical value for an interest rate into *any* algebraic equation or formula, the *decimal* equivalent form of the interest rate must be used.

If any three of the four variables *I, P, r,* and *t* in formula (6−1) are known in a particular application, the formula may be easily manipulated to solve for the unknown variable. The three versions of formula (6−1) rearranged to solve for *P, r,* and *t* are

$$P = \frac{I}{rt}$$

$$r = \frac{I}{Pt}$$

$$t = \frac{I}{Pr}$$

> **Tip**
>
> Instead of trying to remember different versions of the same fundamental formula, you should learn how to quickly rearrange the fundamental formula to obtain the equivalent versions.

■ EXAMPLE 6.1A   *CALCULATION OF THE AMOUNT OF INTEREST*

What amount of interest will be charged on $6500 borrowed for 5 months at a simple interest rate of 11% per annum (abbreviated 11% pa)?

☑ SOLUTION

Given: $P = \$6500$, $t = \frac{5}{12}$ year, $r = 11\%$ pa
The amount of interest payable at the end of the loan period is

$$I = Prt = \$6500(0.11)\left(\frac{5}{12}\right) = \$297.92 \qquad ■$$

■ EXAMPLE 6.1B   *CALCULATION OF THE PRINCIPAL AMOUNT*

If a 3-month term deposit at a bank pays a simple interest rate of $8\frac{1}{2}\%$ pa, how much will have to be deposited to earn $100 of interest?

☑ SOLUTION

Given: $t = \frac{3}{12}$, $r = 8.5\%$ pa, $I = \$100$
Divide both sides of formula (6−1) by rt to isolate P:

$$P = \frac{I}{rt} = \frac{\$100}{(0.085)\left(\frac{3}{12}\right)} = \$4705.88$$

$4705.88 must be placed in the 3-month term deposit to earn $100 of interest.   ■

■ EXAMPLE 6.1C   *CALCULATION OF THE INTEREST RATE*

Interest of $429.48 was charged on a loan of $9500 for 7 months. What simple annual rate of interest was charged on the loan?

☑ SOLUTION

Given: I = \$429.48, P = \$9500, $t = \frac{7}{12}$
Rearrange formula (6−1) to isolate r:

$$r = \frac{I}{Pt} = \frac{\$429.48}{(\$9500)\frac{7}{12}} = \frac{\$429.48}{\$5541.66} = 0.0775 = 7.75\%$$

An interest rate of 7.75% pa was charged on the loan.   ■

■ EXAMPLE 6.1D   CALCULATION OF THE TIME PERIOD

The interest earned on a \$6000 term deposit was \$240. How many months was the term if the interest rate was 6% pa?

☑ SOLUTION

Given: P = \$6000, I = \$240, r = 6% pa
Rearrange formula (6−1) to solve for t:

$$t = \frac{I}{Pr} = \frac{\$240}{(\$6000)(0.06)} = 0.66667 \text{ year } = 8 \text{ months}$$

The duration of the term deposit was 8 months.   ■

■ EXAMPLE 6.1E   USING MONTHS AS THE UNIT OF TIME

The simple interest rate being charged on a \$5000 loan is three-quarters of 1% per month. If the principal and interest are to be paid in 9 months, how much interest will be charged?

☑ SOLUTION

Given: P = \$5000, loan term = 9 months, interest rate = 0.75% per month
We normally use formula (6−1) with r representing the annual rate of interest and t representing the term in years. However, we can substitute the monthly interest rate for r if the term t is measured in months. We will present both approaches.

Method 1: With time expressed in years,

$$t = \frac{9}{12} = 0.75 \text{ years} \quad \text{and} \quad r = 12(0.75\%) = 9\% \text{ pa}$$
$$I = Prt = \$5000 \times 0.09 \times 0.75 = \$337.50$$

Method 2: With time expressed in months,

$$t = 9 \text{ months} \quad \text{and} \quad r = 0.75\% \text{ per month}$$
$$I = Prt = \$5000 \times 0.0075 \times 9 = \$337.50$$

The interest that will be charged on the loan is \$337.50.   ■

EXERCISE 6.1

Answers to the odd-numbered problems are at the end of the book.

Calculate the missing values in problems 1 through 8.

Problem	Principal ($)	Rate	Time (months)	Interest ($)
1.	1500	9.5% pa	7	?
2.	?	$10\frac{1}{4}$% pa	11	328.85
3.	4850	$11\frac{1}{2}$% pa	?	371.83
4.	15,000	?% pa	5	546.88
5.	6800	7.7% pa	13	?
6.	25,000	1.1% per month	3	?
7.	9125	0.8% per month	?	511.00
8.	8900	?% per month	8	890.00

9. How much interest will be earned in 5 months on $5000 if the interest rate is 5.5% pa?

10. An invoice states that interest will be charged on overdue accounts at the rate of $1\frac{1}{2}$% per month. What will be the interest charges on a $3760 billing that is 3 months overdue?

11. The interest owed on a loan after 5 months was $292.50. If the simple interest rate charged on the loan was 0.9% per month, what was the amount borrowed?

12. How much must be placed in a 5-month term deposit earning 8.3% pa simple interest in order to earn $500 interest?

13. Carl has forgotten the rate of simple interest he earned on a 3-month term deposit at the Bank of Montreal. At the end of the 3-month period, he received interest of $214.65 on his $10,600 deposit. What annual rate of simple interest did his deposit earn?

14. Daniella paid interest charges of $169.05 on a $4830 invoice that was 2 months overdue. What monthly rate of simple interest was she charged?

15. Ken's calculations show that the total interest owed to Barbara on his $2700 loan is $315.90. If he pays simple interest at the rate of 0.9% per month, for how long did Ken borrow the money?

16. Trevor cashed in a 1-year term deposit after only 5 months had elapsed. In order to do so, he accepted an interest rate penalty—a reduction from the scheduled 7.5% per annum rate of simple interest. If he was paid $187.50 interest on the $10,000 term deposit, what reduction was made in the per-annum rate of simple interest?

•17. Evelyn put $10,000 in a 3-month term deposit at Canada Trust, earning a simple interest rate of 7.8% pa. After the 3 months, she invested the entire amount of the principal and interest from the first term deposit in a new 3-month term deposit earning the same rate of interest. How much interest did she earn on each term deposit? Why are the two interest amounts not equal?

••18. Randall has $5000 to invest for 6 months. The rates offered on 3-month and 6-month term deposits at his bank are 5.5% pa and 5.8% pa, respectively. He is trying to choose between the 6-month term deposit and two consecutive 3-month term deposits. What would the simple interest rate on 3-month term deposits have to be, 3 months from now, for Randall to end up in the same financial position with either alternative? Assume that he would place both the principal and the interest from the first 3-month term deposit in the second 3-month term deposit.

6.2 DETERMINING THE TIME PERIOD

Whenever possible, the time period t should be determined using the *exact* number of days involved. For example, if the only information provided is that a loan is made for 3 months, the best that can be done is to use $t = \frac{3}{12} = 0.25$ year. But if it is known that the 3-month loan was advanced on September 21, the exact number of days to the December 21 repayment date can be determined. *The current practice among Canadian financial institutions is to count the starting date* (September 21 in this case) *but not the ending date* (December 21).[2] The number of days in each month is listed in Table 6.1. The 3-month loan period from September 21 to December 21 includes 10 days in September (September 21 to 30 inclusive), 31 days in October, 30 days in November, and 20 days in December (December 1 to 20 inclusive), for a total of 91 days. The value that should then be used for t is 91/365 = 0.24932.

TABLE   6.1

The Number of Days in Each Month

Month	Days	Month	Days	Month	Days
January	31	May	31	September	30
February	28	June	30	October	31
March	31	July	31	November	30
April	30	August	31	December	31

Figure 6.8 in the appendix to this chapter presents a technique for determining which months have 31 days.

Leap years occur in years that are divisible by 4. Therefore, 1996, 2000, and 2004 are leap years, with February having 29 days. When a portion of a loan period falls within a leap year, there is no uniform practice across financial institutions for adjusting the length of the year in the denominator of t. The majority of them continue to use 365 days as the length of the year for calculating t, and the minority use 366 days. In this text we will follow the more common practice and always use 365 days in the denominator.[3] If a loan period includes February 29, that day should be counted in the numerator of t.

Another approach to calculating the number of days in a loan period is to use a table in which the days of the year are consecutively numbered. (See Table 6.2.) The use of the table is illustrated in Example 6.2A.

■ EXAMPLE 6.2A   CALCULATING AND USING THE EXACT NUMBER OF DAYS

a. Calculate the term for each of the following loans.

b. Calculate the interest due on the repayment date for each loan.

	Loan principal	Date advanced	Date repaid	Interest rate pa
(i)	$ 3000	March 31, 1997	September 4, 1997	$12\frac{3}{4}\%$
(ii)	$23,000	November 29, 1997	April 1, 1998	13.4%
(iii)	$14,600	January 11, 1996	June 4, 1996	$14\frac{1}{4}\%$

---

[2]There is a good business rationale for not counting *both* the start and the end dates. Consider that if you borrow money today and repay it at the same time tomorrow, you have had the use of the money for a time *interval* of just 1 day, not 2 days. Agreement on whether to count the first or the last day of the interval matters only in cases where the interest rate changes part way through the interval. An example later in the section will illustrate this point.

[3]The United States and some other countries compute simple interest based on a 360-day year in what they call the "ordinary interest method."

☑ SOLUTION

a. The term will be calculated by two methods:
Method 1: Counting the number of days of each partial and full month within the interval (using Table 6.1).
Method 2: Subtracting the serial number of the beginning date of the interval from the serial number of the ending date (using Table 6.2).

(i) *Method 1* (using Table 6.1):

Month	Days
March	1
April	30
May	31
June	30
July	31
August	31
September	3
Total	157

Method 2 (using Table 6.2):

Date	Day number
September 4, 1997	247
March 31, 1997	−90
	157

(ii) When the term of a loan spans a year-end, the calculation of the length of the term using Table 6.2 requires two steps. First calculate the number of days from the initial loan date to the end of the year. Then add the number of days until the repayment date in the following year.

Method 1:

Month	Days
November	2
December	31
January	31
February	28
March	31
April	0
Total	123

Method 2:

Date	Day number
December 31, 1997	365
November 29, 1997	−333
Subinterval (days)	32
April 1, 1998	+ 91
Term (days)	123

(iii) When the period includes February 29 of a leap year, the serial number for the *end date* in Table 6.2 must be increased by 1.

Method 1:

Month	Days
January	21
February	29
March	31
April	30
May	31
June	3
Total	145

Method 2:

Date	Day number
June 4 (general)	155
	+ 1
June 4, 1996	156
January 11, 1996	− 11
Time period	145

TABLE 6.2

The Serial Number of Each Day of the Year

Day of Month	Jan	Feb	Mar	Apr	May	Jun	Jul	Aug	Sep	Oct	Nov	Dec	Day of Month
1	1	32	60	91	121	152	182	213	244	274	305	335	1
2	2	33	61	92	122	153	183	214	245	275	306	336	2
3	3	34	62	93	123	154	184	215	246	276	307	337	3
4	4	35	63	94	124	155	185	216	247	277	308	338	4
5	5	36	64	95	125	156	186	217	248	278	309	339	5
6	6	37	65	96	126	157	187	218	249	279	310	340	6
7	7	38	66	97	127	158	188	219	250	280	311	341	7
8	8	39	67	98	128	159	189	220	251	281	312	342	8
9	9	40	68	99	129	160	190	221	252	282	313	343	9
10	10	41	69	100	130	161	191	222	253	283	314	344	10
11	11	42	70	101	131	162	192	223	254	284	315	345	11
12	12	43	71	102	132	163	193	224	255	285	316	346	12
13	13	44	72	103	133	164	194	225	256	286	317	347	13
14	14	45	73	104	134	165	195	226	257	287	318	348	14
15	15	46	74	105	135	166	196	227	258	288	319	349	15
16	16	47	75	106	136	167	197	228	259	289	320	350	16
17	17	48	76	107	137	168	198	229	260	290	321	351	17
18	18	49	77	108	138	169	199	230	261	291	322	352	18
19	19	50	78	109	139	170	200	231	262	292	323	353	19
20	20	51	79	110	140	171	201	232	263	293	324	354	20
21	21	52	80	111	141	172	202	233	264	294	325	355	21
22	22	53	81	112	142	173	203	234	265	295	326	356	22
23	23	54	82	113	143	174	204	235	266	296	327	357	23
24	24	55	83	114	144	175	205	236	267	297	328	358	24
25	25	56	84	115	145	176	206	237	268	298	329	359	25
26	26	57	85	116	146	177	207	238	269	299	330	360	26
27	27	58	86	117	147	178	208	239	270	300	331	361	27
28	28	59	87	118	148	179	209	240	271	301	332	362	28
29	29	*	88	119	149	180	210	241	272	302	333	363	29
30	30		89	120	150	181	211	242	273	303	334	364	30
31	31		90		151		212	243		304		365	31

Note: For leap years February 29 becomes day number 60 and the serial number for each subsequent day in the table must be increased by 1.

b. Each loan's term should be expressed as a fraction of a year when substituted in formula (6–1):

$$\text{(i)} \quad I = Prt = \$3000(0.1275)\left(\frac{157}{365}\right) = \$164.53$$

$$\text{(ii)} \quad I = Prt = \$23{,}000(0.134)\left(\frac{123}{365}\right) = \$1038.59$$

$$\text{(iii)} \quad I = Prt = \$14{,}600(0.1425)\left(\frac{145}{365}\right) = \$826.50 \quad \blacksquare$$

■ EXAMPLE 6.2B   *VARIABLE INTEREST RATES*

Winston borrowed $5000 on April 7. The interest rate was tied to the prime lending rate and consequently it changed whenever the prime lending rate changed. The interest rate was initially 10.5% pa. It increased to 11% pa effective May 23, and to 11.25% pa effective July 13. What amount was required to repay the loan on August 2?

☑ SOLUTION

The statement that the interest rate "changed to 11% pa effective May 23" means that interest is charged for May 23 (and subsequent days) at the new 11% rate. We need to break the overall loan period into intervals within which the interest rate is constant.

In the following table, the beginning and ending dates have been given for each interval with the practice of "counting the first date but not the last date" in mind. Consequently, May 23 is counted only once with the middle interval and July 13 is counted only with the third interval. This approach is consistent with a new interest rate taking effect on each of these dates.

Interval	Number of days	Interest rate	Interest
April 7 to May 23	24 + 22 = 46	10.50%	$ 66.16 ①
May 23 to July 13	9 + 30 + 12 = 51	11.00	76.85 ②
July 13 to August 2	19 + 1 = 20	11.25	30.82
Total			$173.83

① Interest = Prt = $5000(0.105)$\frac{46}{365}$ = $66.16
② Interest = Prt = $5000(0.11)$\frac{51}{365}$ = $76.85

Note that this circumstance of a variable interest rate is the case when it matters which end date of the overall loan period is counted. If we had counted August 2 instead of April 7, we would have had 45 days at the 10.5% interest rate and 21 days at the 11.25% rate.

The amount required to repay the loan on August 7 was $5000 + $173.83 = $5173.83. ∎

Point of Interest

Faster Collection Means Higher Profits

Suppose that a law office in another city is sending you a $100,000 cheque representing the proceeds from the sale of a property you owned in that city. Since it costs only $5 to have the cheque sent by registered mail instead of $20 to send it by courier, you instruct the lawyer to use registered mail. You thereby save $15 in disbursements charged by the lawyer. The cheque is mailed on Thursday and you receive it on Monday.

Suppose that you have an investment account at an investment dealer and you can purchase units of a no-load money market mutual fund yielding 5%. Then if you had instead chosen next-day delivery by courier and invested the $100,000 with the dealer on Friday, by Monday you would have earned 3 days' interest amounting to:

$$I = Prt$$
$$= \$100,000 \times 0.05 \times \frac{3}{365}$$
$$= \$41.10$$

In this case, sending the cheque by courier has a net advantage of $26.10 over the registered-mail alternative. However, most individuals do not have the arrangements in place to take advantage of such infrequent opportunities.

Many businesses selling on credit terms receive the bulk of their payments through
(continued)

(concluded)

the mail. Often steps may be taken that can knock 1, 2, or 3 days off the time interval between the customer's writing the cheque and the deposit's going into the firm's bank account. Businesses are also in a better position than individuals to effectively utilise extra cash for a few days. For example, many businesses have a demand operating loan—extra cash can be employed to pay down the loan for a few days. The business would then, in effect, earn a rate of return on the extra cash equal to the interest rate it is being charged on the operating loan.

If a large business receives payments of accounts receivable averaging $10,000 per day, shortening the average collection time by 1 day would result in the firm's average bank balance being $10,000 larger than before the change. The firm could then permanently reduce its borrowing requirements by $10,000, resulting in an annual interest saving of $800 if it is paying 8% on its debt. If an insurance company receiving premium payments of $100,000 per day reduced the average collection period by 1 day, the annual savings would be ten times as large. For a megacorporation like Exxon, with average daily sales of over $250 million, the numbers get truly interesting. Using a cost of capital of 8%, a 1-day reduction in the average collection period would result in an imputed saving of approximately

$$I = Prt$$
$$= \$250,000,000 \times 0.08 \times 1$$
$$= \$20,000,000$$

How, then, can a business reduce the time spent by cheques in the mail? Some large firms receiving payments from distant regions of the country will arrange to have lockboxes in a few large cities. Lockboxes are special post office boxes. Payments from customers in various regions are addressed to the closest lockbox. A local branch of the firm's bank picks up the payments from the lockbox and quickly processes them for credit to the firm's account. The combination of the reduced mailing time to the local lockbox and the prompt processing of payments by bank employees can reduce the overall collection and processing time by 2 or 3 days.

In cases such as life insurance premiums or cable TV service, where customers make equal regular payments, most firms avoid mail lag time by avoiding the mail. Preauthorized payments assure the firm of payment on the precise due date. In retail merchandising, the ultimate in reduction of the collection and processing period is achieved with the debit card. Point-of-sale terminals accepting debit cards immediately transfer funds from the customer's bank account to the retailer's bank account.

EXERCISE 6.2

Answers to the odd-numbered problems are at the end of the book.

Calculate the amount of interest owed on the repayment date in problems 1 through 6.

Problem	Loan principal ($)	Date advanced	Date repaid	Interest rate pa (%)
1.	3800	June 17, 1997	Oct. 1, 1997	$10\frac{3}{4}$
2.	7350	Nov. 30, 1997	Mar. 4, 1998	$7\frac{1}{2}$
3.	85,000	Dec. 1, 1996	May 30, 1997	9.9
4.	850	Jan. 7, 1996	July 1, 1996	14
5.	27,000	Oct. 16, 1995	Apr. 15, 1996	8.7
6.	14,400	May 21, 1996	July 19, 1997	$11\frac{1}{4}$

Calculate the missing values in problems 7 through 12.

Problem	Principal ($)	Start date	End date	Interest rate pa (%)	Interest ($)
7.	1000	Jan. 15, 1996	July 7, 1996	?	40.52
8.	?	Oct. 28, 1997	Apr. 14, 1998	$9\frac{1}{2}$	67.78
•9.	1000	?	Nov. 16, 1997	$7\frac{1}{4}$	50.05
•10.	1000	?	Mar. 13, 1999	11	49.42
•11.	1000	June 26, 1996	?	$10\frac{3}{4}$	63.91
•12.	1000	Apr. 18, 1997	?	7.7	32.28

13. On June 26 Laura put $2750 into a term deposit until September 3, when she needs the money for tuition, books, and other expenses to return to college. For term deposits in the 60–89-day range, her credit union pays an interest rate of $4\frac{1}{4}$% per annum. How much interest will she earn on the term deposit?

14. Raimo borrowed $750 from Chris on October 30 and agreed to repay the debt with simple interest at the rate of 12.3% pa on May 10. How much interest was owed on May 10? Assume that February has 28 days.

15. Joyce had $2146 in her daily interest savings account for the entire month of June. Her account was credited with interest of $9.70 on June 30 (for the exact number of days in June). What annual rate of simple interest did her balance earn?

16. Tony's chequing account was $329 overdrawn beginning on September 24. On October 9 he made a deposit that restored a credit balance. If he was charged overdraft interest of $2.50, what annual rate of simple interest was charged?

17. In addition to a $2163 refund of his income tax overpayment, Revenue Canada paid Roy $23.08 of interest on the overpayment. If the simple interest rate paid by Revenue Canada was $9\frac{1}{2}$% pa, how many days' interest were paid?

18. Megan was charged $124.83 interest on her bank loan for the period September 18 to October 18. If the rate of interest on her loan was 8.25% pa, what was the outstanding principal balance on the loan during the month?

•19. Bruce borrowed $6000 from Darryl on November 23. When Bruce repaid the loan, Darryl charged $203.22 interest. If the rate of simple interest on the loan was $10\frac{3}{4}$%, on what date did Bruce repay the loan? Assume that February has 28 days.

•20. Sharon's $9000 term deposit matured on March 16, 1996. Based on a simple interest rate of 7.5% pa, she received $221.92 in interest. On what date did she originally make the term deposit?

•21. Mario borrowed $6000 on March 1 at a variable rate of interest. The interest rate began at 7.5% pa, increased to 8% effective April 17, and then fell by 0.25% effective June 30. How much interest will be owed on the August 1 repayment date?

•22. Penny invested $4500 on October 28 at a floating rate of interest that initially stood at 6.3% pa. Effective December 2, the rate dropped by $\frac{1}{2}$%, and then it declined another $\frac{1}{4}$% effective February 27. What total amount of principal plus interest will Penny receive when the investment matures on March 15? Assume that the new year is a leap year.

•23. How much will be required on February 1 to pay off a $3000 loan advanced on the previous September 30 if the variable interest rate began the interval at 10.7% pa, rose to 11.2% effective November 2, and then dropped back to 11% effective January 1?

•24. The total accrued interest owed as of August 31 on a loan advanced the preceding June 3 was $169.66. If the variable interest rate started at $8\frac{3}{4}$% pa, rose to 9% effective July 1, and increased another $\frac{1}{2}$% effective July 31, what was the principal amount of the loan?

6.3 MATURITY VALUE OF A LOAN OR AN INVESTMENT

A loan or an investment that is made for a specific period of time is said to *mature* on the date of expiry of the period. The **maturity value** of a loan or investment is the total of the original principal plus the interest due on the maturity date.[4] Using the symbol S to represent the maturity value, we have

$$S = P + I$$

From formula (6–1),

$$I = Prt$$

Substituting the second equation into the first equation gives

$$S = P + Prt$$

Extracting the common factor P yields:

Maturity Value (Simple Interest)

$$\boxed{S = P(1 + rt)}$$ (6–2)

■ **EXAMPLE 6.3A**   *CALCULATING THE MATURITY VALUE*

Celia makes an investment by lending $1500 to Chuck for 8 months at an interest rate of $9\frac{1}{4}$% pa. What is the maturity value of the investment/loan?

☑ SOLUTION

This problem reminds us that, when an interest-bearing debt is created, the lender has made an interest-earning investment.

Given: $P = \$1500$, $t = \frac{8}{12}$, $r = 9.25\%$

The maturity value of the investment/loan is:

$$S = P(1 + rt)$$
$$= \$1500\left[1 + 0.0925\left(\frac{8}{12}\right)\right]$$
$$= \$1500(1.061667)$$
$$= \$1592.50$$

Note that this answer can be obtained just as easily by first calculating the interest due at maturity using $I = Prt$. Then simply add the principal to obtain the maturity value ($S = P + I$). The choice of method is a matter of personal preference.

The maturity value that Chuck must pay to Celia at the end of the 8 months is $1592.50. ■

■ **EXAMPLE 6.3B**   *CALCULATING THE PRINCIPAL*

What amount of money would have to be invested at $10\frac{3}{4}$% pa to grow to $10,000 after 91 days?

---

[4]Other terms used for the maturity value are *accumulated value* and *amount*. The use of *amount* with this specific meaning is avoided in this book because of potential confusion with the more common usage of *amount* in expressions such as "an amount of money" or "the amount of interest."

☑ SOLUTION

Given: $r = 10.75\%$, $S = \$10,000$, $t = 91/365$

Substitute the known values into formula (6−2) and then solve for P.

$$S = P(1 + rt)$$

$$\$10,000 = P\left[1 + 0.1075\left(\frac{91}{365}\right)\right]$$

$$= P(1.026801)$$

The value for P will be a few hundred dollars less than $10,000. To have P accurate to the cent (six figures), seven-figure accuracy should be maintained in intermediate steps. Solving for P,

$$P = \frac{\$10,000}{1.026801} = \$9738.98$$

The required investment is $9738.98   ∎

Tip

If any three of the four variables S, P, r, and t are known, formula (6−2) can be used to solve for the remaining variable. However, if r or t is the unknown, the manipulations required to solve for r or t are not trivial. It is usually simpler to first calculate $I = S - P$ and then to solve $I = Prt$ for r or t. The following example illustrates the latter approach.

■ EXAMPLE 6.3C   *CALCULATING THE INTEREST RATE*

Mrs. Falk has enough baking flour on hand to last another 4 weeks. However, her favourite brand is on special this week at $5.95 per bag instead of the regular price of $6.95 per bag. If she "invests" $5.95 today to avoid spending $6.95 in 4 weeks, what simple annual interest rate does she earn, in effect, on her "investment"?

☑ SOLUTION

This problem illustrates a return-on-investment approach to evaluating the savings available in sales, specials, markdowns, and other bargains. It is appropriate in cases where the item would otherwise be purchased at a higher price on a later date.

An equivalent question to that asked above is "What annual rate of return would an investment of $5.95 have to earn in order to grow to $6.95 four weeks from now?" To answer either question, we need to solve for r given $P = \$5.95$, $S = \$6.95$, and $t = \frac{28}{365}$. The amount of interest that must be earned is

$$I = S - P = \$6.95 - \$5.95 = \$1.00$$

The annual rate of simple interest required to earn this amount of interest is

$$r = \frac{I}{Pt} = \frac{\$1.00}{\$5.95 \times \frac{28}{365}} = 2.19 = 219\%$$

By taking advantage of the sale price, Mrs. Falk realizes a 219% annual rate of return during the 4-week period. In other words, if the rate of return for the 4-week period were to continue for an entire year, the rate of return on investment would be 219%.

Generally speaking, this analysis will reveal that early purchases at discounted prices represent good "investments." But remember that we are referring to purchases that you would otherwise make on a later date at the higher price. There is no saving if you buy an on-sale item that does not replace a planned purchase! ■

■ **EXAMPLE 6.3D**   *CALCULATING THE MATURITY VALUES OF MULTIPLE INVESTMENTS MADE ON DIFFERENT DATES*

What will be the combined maturity value on January 17 of $4000 invested on (the previous) September 28, $5000 invested on November 1, and $6000 invested on December 8 if:

a. All three investments earn 6% pa?

b. The three investments earn 7%, $6\frac{1}{2}$%, and 6%, respectively?

☑ **SOLUTION**

a. Since all three amounts earn the same rate of interest, we can break the overall interval into three subintervals in which the cumulative investment is $4000, $9000, and $15,000 respectively. Then the interest earned on the cumulative investment in each subinterval can be calculated and added.

Subinterval	Number of days	Cumulative Investment	Interest for subinterval
Sept. 28 to Nov. 1	3 + 31 = 34	$ 4000	$ 22.36 ①
Nov. 1 to Dec. 8	30 + 7 = 37	9000	54.74 ②
Dec. 8 to Jan. 17	24 + 16 = 40	15,000	98.63
Total			$175.73

① Interest = Prt = $4000(0.06)$\frac{34}{365}$ = $22.36

② Interest = Prt = $9000(0.06)$\frac{37}{365}$ = $54.74

Trap

Do not add interest to the principal at the end of a subinterval and treat that interest as part of the principal in the next subinterval. That would have the effect of interest from an earlier subinterval earning interest in a subsequent subinterval. This is a property of compound interest (Chapter 8) but not of simple interest.

The combined maturity value on January 17 will be

$$\$15,000 + \$175.73 = \$15,175.73$$

b. In this case the principal amounts cannot be combined as in part *a* because a different interest rate applies to each one. Instead, calculate the maturity value of each of the three investments and then add their maturity values.

Interval	Number of days	Rate of interest (%)	Principal	Interest
Sept. 28 to Jan. 17	3 + 31 + 30 + 31 + 16 = 111	7.0	$ 4000	$ 85.15 ①
Nov. 1 to Jan. 17	30 + 31 + 16 = 77	6.5	5000	68.56 ②
Dec. 8 to Jan. 17	24 + 16 = 40	6.0	6000	39.45
Total			$15,000	$193.16

① Interest = Prt = $4000(0.07)$\frac{111}{365}$ = $85.15

② Interest = Prt = $5000(0.065)$\frac{77}{365}$ = $68.56

The combined maturity value on January 17 will be

$$\$15,000 + \$193.16 = \$15,193.16$$

EXERCISE 6.3

Answers to the odd-numbered problems are at the end of the book.

Calculate the missing values in problems 1 through 14.

Problem	Principal ($)	Interest rate pa (%)	Time	Maturity value ($)
1.	2950.00	$13\frac{1}{2}$	7 months	?
2.	12,800.00	$11\frac{3}{4}$	237 days	?
3.	?	$10\frac{1}{2}$	23 days	785.16
4.	?	7.7	360 days	2291.01
5.	?	9.9	11 months	15,379.58
6.	?	$8\frac{1}{4}$	14 months	7348.25
7.	1750.00	?	5 months	1828.02
8.	2875.40	?	8 months	3000.00
9.	780.82	?	45 days	798.63
10.	680.00	?	300 days	730.30
11.	9625.63	7.8	? days	10,000.00
12.	3500.00	8.4	? days	3646.60
13.	7760.00	$6\frac{1}{4}$	? months	8083.33
14.	859.50	$10\frac{1}{4}$	? months	907.22

15. What will be the maturity value in 15 months of a $4500 loan at a simple interest rate of 11.9% pa?

16. Ian placed $17,000 in a 270-day term deposit earning $7\frac{1}{4}$% pa. How much will the bank pay Ian on the maturity date?

17. Sharon received the proceeds from an inheritance on March 25. She wants to set aside enough on March 26 so that she will have $20,000 available on October 1 to purchase a car when the new models are introduced. If the current interest rate on 181- to 270-day deposits is $6\frac{3}{4}$% pa, what amount should she place in the term deposit?

18. The bookkeeper for Durham's Garage is trying to allocate to principal and interest the payment that was made to settle a loan. The cheque stub has the note "$3701.56 for principal and 7 month's interest at 12.5% pa." What are the principal and interest components of the payment?

19. The annual membership fee at the Oak Meadows Golf Club is $1800 payable at the beginning of the year. A member may delay payment of half the annual membership fee for 5 months if she pays a surcharge of $60 with the second $900 payment. In effect, what annual rate of simple interest is the golf club charging on the $900 owed?

20. The snow tires that you are planning to buy next October 1 at the regular price of $107.50 each are advertised at $89.95 in a spring clearance special that will end on the preceding March 25. What annual rate of simple interest will you earn if you "invest" in the new snow tires at the sale price on March 25 instead of waiting until October 1 to buy them at the regular price?

21. A&B Appliances sells a washer-dryer combination for $1535 cash. C&D Appliances offers the same combination for $1595 with no payments and no interest for 6 months. Therefore, you can pay $1535 now or invest the $1535 for 6 months and then pay $1595. Above what annual rate of interest would the latter alternative be to your advantage?

22. How many days will it take $2500 to grow to $2614.47 at 8.75% pa?

•23. Karen borrowed $2000 at $10\frac{1}{4}$% pa on July 13. On what date would the amount owed first exceed $2100?

•24. On what date did a corporation borrow $350,000 at 7.5% from its bank if the debt was settled by a payment of $356,041 on February 28?

•25. Village Finance Co. advanced three loans to Kamiko—$2200 on June 23, $1800 on August 5, and $1300 on October 31. Simple interest at 14.5% pa was charged on all three loans, and all were repaid on December 31 when some bonds that she owned matured. What total amount was required to pay off the loans?

•26. The cash balance in Roger's account with his stockbroker earns interest on the daily balance at 4% per annum payable on June 30 and December 31. His cash balance on January 1 was $3347. As a result of the purchase or sale of securities from time to time, the balance changed to $8687 on March 4, to $2568 on May 24, and to $5923 on June 17. What interest was credited to Roger's account on June 30? The brokerage firm includes interest for both January 1 and June 30 in the June 30 payment. Assume that February had 28 days.

•27. Dominion Contracting invested surplus funds in term deposits all chosen to mature on April 1 when the firm intends to purchase a new grader. If $7400 was invested at 6.3% on the previous November 16, $6600 was invested at 5.9% on December 30, and $9200 was invested at 5.1% on February 8, what total amount will be available from the maturing term deposits on April 1 (of a leap year)?

6.4 THE TIME VALUE OF MONEY

> **Tip**
>
> The concepts that will be developed in Sections 6.4, 6.5, and 6.6 are very important. They are fundamental to many other topics and applications in later chapters. Extra work and effort invested at this stage to gain a thorough understanding of these concepts will pay substantial dividends later.

Suppose that someone is scheduled to pay $100 to you 1 year from now. What amount would you accept today instead of the scheduled payment? What amount would you accept 2 years from now instead of the scheduled payment? Let us answer these questions for the case where money can earn an interest rate of 10% per annum.

If a replacement payment is received today, it can earn interest for the next year. Therefore, you should be willing to accept less than $100 today as a substitute for the scheduled $100 payment. The amount you should be prepared to accept today is the principal amount that, invested for 1 year at 10% pa, will have a maturity value of $100. This principal is

$$P = \frac{S}{1 + rt} = \frac{\$100.00}{1 + 0.10 \times 1} = \$90.91$$

Consequently, 1 year from now, you will have $100 regardless of whether you receive the $100 payment as scheduled or you accept $90.91 today. Alternative payments that, with equal assurance, would enable you to have the same number of dollars at a future date, are **economically equivalent payments**. In the present example, we can say that $90.91 is the equivalent value today of $100 paid 1 year from now. In general, a scheduled payment's **equivalent value** on another date is the amount which, if paid on that date, would place the recipient in the same economic position.

If the interest rate remains at 10% pa, then $110 received 2 years from now is economically equivalent to $100 received 1 year from now. The extra $10 replaces the interest that the scheduled $100 payment could have earned during the subsequent year.

It follows that $90.91 paid today, $100 paid 1 year from now, and $110 paid in 2 years are all economically equivalent amounts. The further we go into the future, the larger the equivalent payment will become. But all these *nominally*[5] different amounts have the *same* economic value—the economic value that $90.91 has today.

The **time value of money** refers to the property that a larger dollar amount must be paid at a later date to have the same economic value as a smaller dollar amount paid at an earlier date. The property arises from the ability of money to earn interest.[6]

Tip

Because of the time value of money, payments that are made on *different* dates should be compared only after finding their economically equivalent values on the *same* date.

When a series of two or more payments are part of the same transaction, we are inclined to add the payments to obtain their combined effect. However, the addition of the nominal values of payments made on *different* dates implies that a dollar on one date has the same economic value as a dollar on any of the other dates. In short, the addition of the nominal values ignores the time value of money.

Trap

Payments made on different dates should not be added together to obtain their combined economic value. Instead, their individual equivalent values on the chosen date should first be calculated. Then their combined economic value is the sum of the equivalent values.

The longer the time over which the series of payments is made, the greater will be the error from ignoring the time value of money.[7]

We now need to develop formulas and techniques for calculating the amount, at any date we choose, that is economically equivalent to a scheduled payment or a series of scheduled payments.

---

[5] *Nominal* means "in name only" or "not real or effective." The effective economic value of the $100 payment is not $100 on any date other than the scheduled payment date.

[6] The expression "money is worth 10%" is sometimes used to indicate that money can earn a rate of interest of 10%.

[7] In the financial analysis commonly undertaken by a business to evaluate a potential long-term investment (Chapter 16), it is standard procedure to ignore timing differences among operating receipts and disbursements *within* each fiscal year. They are generally assumed to all occur at the year-end. However, the time value of money is taken into consideration when the net cash flows from each year of the investment's lifetime are combined to determine the overall economic benefit from the potential investment.

6.5 THE EQUIVALENT VALUE OF A SINGLE PAYMENT

TIME DIAGRAMS

The analysis of problems involving multiple payments is assisted by a time diagram. For more complex problems a time diagram is virtually essential. In its basic form a time diagram consists of a time axis or *time line* indicating the dollar amounts and the dates or timing of the payments. Figure 6.1 illustrates a time diagram for a case where payments of $1000, $500, and $1500 are scheduled for March 1, April 1, and December 1, respectively. The dates are indicated on one side of the time line, and the amounts of the corresponding payments are entered on the opposite side.

FIGURE   6.1

A Time Diagram

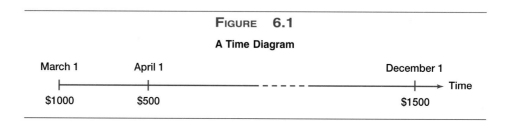

Some effort should be made to approximate the correct proportions of the time intervals between payments. If this would result in an inappropriate scale, then indicate a break in the time line by a dashed section (- - -). For the example presented in Figure 6.1, the actual time interval (8 months) between the second and third payments is much longer than the interval (1 month) between the first and the second payments. The dashed section indicates that some of the time line is missing. Thus, the *actual* relative size of the intervals differs from the *apparent* relative size in the diagram.

We frequently indicate on a time diagram that a payment's equivalent value at another date is to be calculated. This is done by drawing an arrow from the scheduled payment to the date at which we desire the equivalent value. In Figure 6.2 the equivalent value of the $1000 payment is to be determined for June 23 (111 days later). The equivalent value of the $500 payment is also to be calculated as of June 23 (160 days earlier). The date for which the equivalent values of the scheduled payments are calculated is called the **focal date**. The symbol E (with a subscript if more than one equivalent value is involved in a problem) is used to represent the equivalent value.

FIGURE   6.2

Indicating Equivalent Values on a Time Diagram

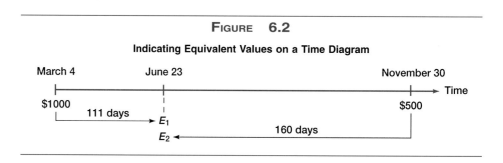

Future Value and Present Value

We now turn our attention to developing a formula for calculating a payment's equivalent value at any date. The **future value** of a payment is its equivalent value at a *later* date, allowing for the time value of money. In Section 6.3, we derived $S = P(1 + rt)$ for the maturity value S of a principal amount P borrowed or invested at a simple rate of interest r for a time period t. The maturity value includes both the original principal and the interest on the principal. A payment's economically equivalent value at a later date should likewise include both the originally scheduled payment and the interest it could earn between the scheduled date and the later date. Therefore, $S = P(1 + rt)$, *can also be used to calculate the future value S of a scheduled payment P a time interval t after the scheduled date, if money can earn a simple rate of interest r.*

The amount S calculated using $S = P(1 + rt)$ is economically equivalent to the earlier payment P. Consequently, you should be indifferent between the alternatives of receiving P as scheduled or receiving S at the later date. P may therefore be viewed as the equivalent value a time interval t before a scheduled payment S. The equivalent value, at an earlier date, of a scheduled payment is called its **present value**. *Formula (6–2), in the form $P = S/(1 + rt)$, is used to calculate the present value P of a scheduled payment S a time interval t before the scheduled date, if money can earn a simple rate of interest r.*

In summary, there are three areas of application of $S = P(1 + rt)$:

- Calculating the *maturity value* of a loan or investment.
- Calculating the *future value* of a scheduled payment.
- Calculating the *present value* of a scheduled payment.

Maturity Value or Future Value

Present Value

$$S = P(1 + rt)$$

$$P = \frac{S}{1 + rt}$$

(6–2)

Tip

A memory aid for selecting the proper version of formula (6–2) in calculating an equivalent value of a scheduled payment on another date is to:

- Calculate S when you want a *S*ubsequent equivalent value.
- Calculate P when you want a *P*rior equivalent value.

Tip

Note that the present-value formula may be written

$$P = S \times \left(\frac{1}{1 + rt}\right)$$

With calculators that do not allow the use of brackets, the most efficient procedure for evaluating the right side of this equation is to:

1. Calculate the denominator, $1 + rt$.
2. Press the reciprocal function key, $\boxed{1/x}$. The value of $1/(1 + rt)$ then appears in the calculator's display.
3. Multiply the number in the display by the value of S.

■ EXAMPLE 6.5A   *CALCULATING A FUTURE VALUE*

What is the equivalent value on September 15 of a $1000 payment on July 6, if money can earn 7% pa?

✓ SOLUTION

Since we want the equivalent value at a later date, we should calculate the future value on September 15 of the $1000.

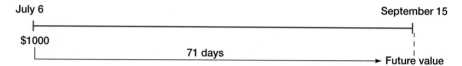

The number of days in the interval is

$$26 + 31 + 14 = 71$$

Substitute $P = \$1000$, $r = 7\%$, and $t = \frac{71}{365}$ into formula (6–2) to obtain the future value:

$$S = P(1 + rt)$$
$$= \$1000\left[1 + 0.07\left(\frac{71}{365}\right)\right]$$
$$= \$1013.62$$

$1000 on July 6 has the equivalent value of $1013.62 on the following September 15.

■

■ EXAMPLE 6.5B   *CALCULATING A PRESENT VALUE*

What is the equivalent value on March 12 of a $1000 payment on the following July 6 if money is worth 6.8% pa?

✓ SOLUTION

Since we want the equivalent value at an earlier date, we should calculate the present value on March 12 of the $1000.

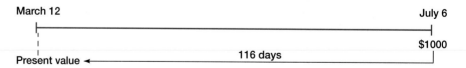

The number of days in the interval is

$$20 + 30 + 31 + 30 + 5 = 116$$

Substituting $S = \$1000$, $r = 6.8\%$, and $t = \frac{116}{365}$ into formula (6–2), we obtain

$$P = \frac{S}{1 + rt} = \frac{\$1000}{1 + 0.068\left(\frac{116}{365}\right)} = \$978.85$$

$1000 on July 6 has the equivalent value of $978.85 on the preceding March 12. ■

■ EXAMPLE 6.5C   *CALCULATING THE EQUIVALENT PAYMENT AT A LATER DATE*

Herb is supposed to pay $1500 to Ranjit on September 20. Herb wishes to delay payment until December 1.

a. What amount should Herb expect to pay on December 1 if Ranjit can earn 8.25% simple interest?

b. Show that Ranjit should not care whether he receives the scheduled payment or the delayed payment.

☑ SOLUTION

a. For single-payment problems, the time diagram will be omitted.
Herb is seeking a postponement of

$$11 + 31 + 30 = 72 \text{ days}$$

He should expect to pay an amount that is equivalent to $1500, 72 days later, allowing for an $8\frac{1}{4}$% pa time value of money. That is, he should expect to pay the future value of $1500, 72 days later.
Substituting $P = \$1500$, $t = \frac{72}{365}$, and $r = 8.25\%$ into formula (6−2), the future value is

$$S = P(1 + rt) = \$1500\left[1 + 0.0825\left(\frac{72}{365}\right)\right] = \$1524.41$$

Herb should expect to pay $1524.41 on December 1 instead of $1500 on September 20.

b. Suppose that Herb makes the $1500 payment as scheduled on September 20. Since Ranjit can earn an $8\frac{1}{4}$% rate of interest, by December 1 the $1500 will grow to

$$S = P(1 + rt) = \$1500\left[1 + 0.0825\left(\frac{72}{365}\right)\right] = \$1524.41$$

Ranjit should therefore be indifferent between receiving $1500 on September 20 or $1524.41 on December 1 because he will end up with $1524.41 on December 1 under either alternative.   ■

■ EXAMPLE 6.5D   *CALCULATING THE EQUIVALENT PAYMENT AT AN EARLIER DATE*

Tanis owes Lola $1000 payable on December 10. If money can earn $7\frac{1}{2}$% pa, what amount should Lola accept in settlement of the debt:

a. 30 days before the scheduled payment date?

b. 60 days before the scheduled payment date?

☑ SOLUTION

a. Lola should accept the amount that is equivalent to $1000, 30 days earlier, allowing for a $7\frac{1}{2}$% pa time value of money. This amount is the present value of the $1000 at a point 30 days earlier. Using formula (6−2),

$$P = \frac{S}{1 + rt} = \frac{\$1000}{1 + 0.075\left(\frac{30}{365}\right)} = \$993.87$$

Lola should accept $993.87, 30 days before the scheduled payment of $1000.

b. The present value of $1000, 60 days earlier is

$$P = \frac{\$1000}{1 + 0.075\left(\frac{60}{365}\right)} = \$987.82$$

Lola should accept $987.82, 60 days before the scheduled payment date.

This example also demonstrates that the further back one goes before the scheduled payment date, the smaller the equivalent payment will be. ■

GRAPH OF PRESENT VALUE AND FUTURE VALUE VERSUS TIME Figure 6.3 shows a $100 payment at its scheduled date on a time line. Expressions are indicated for its future value at a date that is a time interval t_1 later, and its present value at a date that is a time interval t_2 earlier.

FIGURE 6.3

Present and Future Values on a Time Diagram

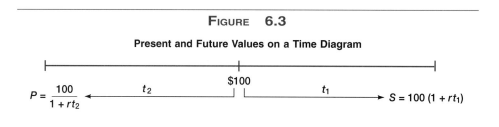

Figure 6.4 presents a graph of the present value and the future value of $100. Numerical values are indicated at 4-month intervals prior to and subsequent to the scheduled payment date (zero on the time axis). The simple interest rate used to construct the graph is 12% per annum. The future value increases in a straight-line pattern as the time after the scheduled payment date increases. The present value gets progressively smaller for longer time periods in advance of the scheduled payment. However, the rate of decrease is less than linear. This is evident from the widening gap between the present-value curve and the straight line extending backward from the future-value region (and ending at the $88.00 figure).

SUMMARY OF APPLICATIONS OF $S = P(1 + rt)$ The formula $S = P(1 + rt)$ presents the general mathematical relationship for a *prior* amount P to be economically equivalent to a *subsequent* amount S, allowing for the time value of money. It provides the mathematical tool for shifting money through time and finding the economically equivalent amount at another date. There are many applications of the formula. Some care is required in placing the proper interpretation on P and S, depending on the context. The following list summarizes several common circumstances in which this fundamental formula may be used.

1. Solve for S to obtain:

   - The maturity value of an amount P *borrowed* at an interest rate r for time t.
   - The maturity value of an amount P *invested* at an interest rate r for time t.
   - The future value of P: the amount that is equivalent to P a time period t later, allowing for interest at the rate r.

FIGURE 6.4

Graph of Present and Future Values of $100

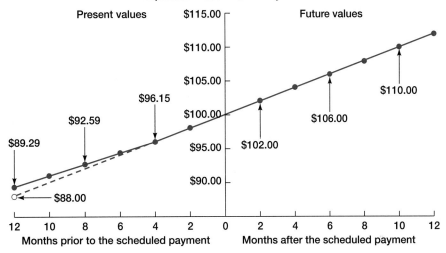

2. Solve for P to obtain:

  * The amount that would have to be invested now at an interest rate r in order to accumulate the amount S after time t.

  * The amount that, if paid now for an investment returning the amount S after time t, would provide a rate of return r on the amount invested.

  * The present value of S: the amount that is equivalent to S a time interval t earlier, allowing for interest at the rate r.

3. Solve for t to obtain:

  * The time required for an investment P earning interest at the rate r to grow to S.

  * The time period after which the amount S is owed on a loan P with interest charged at the rate r.

4. Solve for r to obtain:

  * The rate of return earned if an amount P is invested and then grows to a value S after time t.

  * The rate of interest charged on the principal P of a loan if the amount S is owed after time t.

  * The interest rate that money must earn in order for two payments, P and S, occurring time t apart, to be equivalent.

■ **EXAMPLE 6.5E** *COMPARING THE ECONOMIC VALUES OF ALTERNATIVE PAYMENTS*

Marcus can purchase an airplane ticket now on the airline's Early Bird Sale for $459, or he can wait and pay $479 in 3 months. If he can earn 9% pa on his money, which option should he choose?

☑ SOLUTION

Marcus should choose the price having the smaller economic value, recognizing the time value of money. To compare the economic values, first calculate the future value 3 months from now of the Early Bird price of $459. Then compare the future value with the regular price of $479. Select the option having the smaller value.

$$S = P(1 + rt) = \$459\left[1 + 0.09\left(\frac{3}{12}\right)\right] = \$469.33$$

Marcus should buy the ticket at the Early Bird price. However, his true saving is not $20 but $479.00 − $469.33 = $9.67.   ■

■ EXAMPLE 6.5F   FINDING THE INTEREST RATE THAT MAKES TWO PAYMENTS EQUIVALENT

Extending the problem in Example 6.5E, what rate of interest would Marcus have to earn in order to be indifferent between the two prices?

☑ SOLUTION

He will be indifferent between the two prices if $459 invested for 3 months will grow to $479. In other words, he will be indifferent if $459 can earn $479 − $459 = $20 interest in 3 months. The interest rate that would cause this to occur is

$$r = \frac{I}{Pt} = \frac{\$20}{\$459 \times \frac{3}{12}} = 0.174 = 17.4\%$$

If Marcus could earn a 17.4% rate of interest, he could invest the $459 for 3 months and it would mature at $479, providing exactly the right amount to buy the ticket. (If Marcus could earn more than 17.4% pa, it would be to his advantage to invest the $459 now and buy the ticket 3 months later.)   ■

■ EXAMPLE 6.5G   CALCULATING A PRIOR EQUIVALENT PAYMENT

A furniture store advertises a dining table and chairs for $1495 with nothing down, no payments, and no interest for 6 months. What cash price should the store be willing to accept if its money can earn:

a. 11% pa?

b. 13% pa?

☑ SOLUTION

The store faces the choice between the cash offer and $1495 to be received 6 months from now (if a customer takes the credit terms). The store should be willing to accept a cash amount that is today's equivalent of $1495. In other words, the store should accept the present value of $1495.

a. If money has a time value of 11% pa,

$$P = \frac{S}{1 + rt} = \frac{\$1495}{1 + 0.11\left(\frac{6}{12}\right)} = \frac{\$1495}{1.055} = \$1417.06$$

The store should accept a cash offer of $1417.06

b. If money has a time value of 13% pa,

$$P = \frac{\$1495}{1 + 0.13\left(\frac{6}{12}\right)} = \$1403.76$$

The store should accept $1403.76 cash.   ■

EXERCISE 6.5

Answers to the odd-numbered problems are at the end of the book.

Calculate the missing values in problems 1 through 10.

Problem	Scheduled payment ($)	Interest rate (%)	Equivalent payment ($)	
1.	560	$10\frac{3}{4}$	?	5 months earlier
2.	1215	$8\frac{1}{2}$	?	7 months later
3.	5230	9.25	?	174 days later
4.	1480	6.75	?	60 days earlier
5.	1975	?	1936.53	100 days earlier
6.	2370	?	2508.79	190 days later
7.	830	9.9	850.26	? days ?
8.	3500	$12\frac{1}{4}$	3362.69	? months ?
9.	4850	$8\frac{3}{4}$	4574.73	? days ?
10.	2740	$13\frac{1}{2}$	2785.60	? days ?

In problems 11 through 14 determine:
a. Whether the earlier or the later payment has the greater economic value at the given time value of money.
b. The time value of money at which the two payments would be equivalent.

Problem	Earlier payment ($)	Later payment ($)	Time Interval	Time value of money
11.	560	570	60 days	$10\frac{3}{4}$% pa
12.	1215	1280	11 months	$8\frac{1}{2}$% pa
13.	5230	5500	5 months	0.6% per month
14.	1480	1515	150 days	6.75% pa

15. What amount on September 24 is equivalent to $1000 on the following December 1 if money can earn 14% pa?

16. What amount on January 13 is equivalent to $1000 on the preceding August 12 if money can earn 9.5% pa?

17. Victor wishes to postpone for 90 days the payment of $450 that he owes to Roxanne. If money now earns 6.75% pa, what amount can he reasonably expect to pay at the later date?

18. Allan owes Value Furniture $1600, which is scheduled to be paid on August 15. Allan has surplus funds on June 15 and will settle the debt early if Value Furniture will make an adjustment reflecting the current short-term interest rate of 7.25%. What amount should be acceptable to both parties?

19. On September 10 Duncan Stereo and TV advertised that any TV set may be purchased with nothing down, no interest, and nothing to pay until next year (January 2). What cash price should Duncan accept on a TV set listed at $1195 if Duncan can use cash to pay off debt on which it pays a 13.5% rate of interest?

20. A $5000 payment is scheduled for 120 days from now. If money is worth 7.25% pa, calculate the payment's equivalent value at each of nine different dates—today and every 30 days for the next 240 days.

21. A $3000 payment is scheduled for 6 months from now. If money is worth 6.75% pa, calculate the payment's equivalent values at 2-month intervals beginning today and ending 1 year from now.

22. During its 50-50 Sale, Marpole Furniture will sell its merchandise for 50% down, with the balance payable in 6 months. No interest is charged for the first six months. What 100% cash price should Marpole accept on a $1845 chesterfield and chair set if Marpole can earn a return of 10.75% pa on its funds?

23. Jody received a $2000 college entrance scholarship. Nine months later Brian was awarded a $2100 academic proficiency scholarship for his outstanding grades in the first year of studies. Which scholarship had the greater economic value if money can earn 8.25% pa?

•24. Mr. and Mrs. Chan are considering two offers on a building lot that they own in a nearby town. One is for $49,000, consisting of $10,000 down and the balance to be paid in a lump payment in 8 months. The second is for $50,000, with $10,000 down and the balance to be paid in 1 year. Which offer has the greater economic value if money can earn 7.5% pa?

•25. What rate of return must money earn for Mr. and Mrs. Chan to be indifferent between the two offers in problem 24?

•26. What interest rate must money earn for a payment of $1389 on August 20 to be equivalent to a payment of $1348 on the previous March 29?

6.6 THE EQUIVALENT VALUE OF A PAYMENT STREAM

In the preceding section we learned how to calculate the equivalent value, on any date, of a scheduled payment. We will now use this knowledge to determine the equivalent value, on any date, of a scheduled payment stream. A **payment stream** refers to a series of two or more payments required by a single transaction or contract. The procedure is illustrated in the following example.

A payment stream consists of three payments, $1000, $2000, and $3000, scheduled for March 1, May 1, and December 1 of the same year. The objective is to calculate the equivalent value of the three payments on August 1 if money can earn a simple interest rate of 8% pa.

> **Tip**
>
> For problems involving multiple payments, it is *strongly recommended* that a time diagram be constructed. The given data can then be organized in a manner that makes time and payment relationships very clear. Often the solution concept and the steps required for the solution may be indicated on the diagram.

Figure 6.5 presents the given information in a time diagram. We can readily calculate the equivalent values,[8] E_1, E_2, and E_3, on August 1 for each of the individual payments using the present-value and future-value versions of formula (6–2). The equivalent value of the entire payment stream on the August 1 focal date is simply the sum, E_T, of the three equivalent values.

FIGURE   6.5

Time Diagram for the Equivalent Value of a Payment Stream

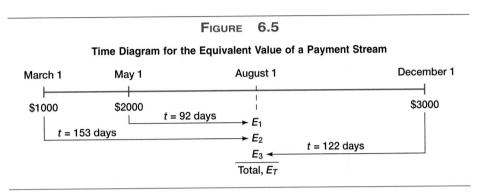

E_1 = Future value on August 1 of $2000

$\quad = \$2000\left(1 + 0.08 \times \dfrac{92}{365}\right)$

$\quad = \$2040.33$

E_2 = Future value on August 1 of $1000

$\quad = \$1000\left(1 + 0.08 \times \dfrac{153}{365}\right)$

$\quad = \$1033.53$

E_3 = Present value on August 1 of $3000

$\quad = \dfrac{\$3000}{\left(1 + 0.08 \times \frac{122}{365}\right)}$

$\quad = \$2921.87$

The equivalent value on August 1 of the payment stream is

$E_T = E_1 + E_2 + E_3$
$\quad = \$2040.33 + \$1033.53 + \$2921.87$
$\quad = \$5995.73$

The significance of this equivalent value is that a payment of $5995.73 on August 1 is economically equivalent to the three scheduled payments. The recipient will be in the *same economic position* whether she accepts $5995.73 on August 1 or she receives the three payments as scheduled.

■ **EXAMPLE 6.6A**   *CALCULATING A PAYMENT EQUIVALENT TO THREE SCHEDULED PAYMENTS*

A financial obligation was supposed to be settled by payments of $1000 on a date 2 months ago, $2000 today, and $3000 on a date 6 months from now. The creditor has agreed to accept a single equivalent payment 2 months from now instead of the scheduled payments. If money can earn 12% pa, what will be the size of the equivalent payment?

<hr />

[8]Equivalent values are also known as dated values.

☑ SOLUTION

Construct a time diagram indicating the scheduled payments and their equivalent values on the date of the replacement payment.

Note: In the absence of specific calendar dates, we will represent today as time 0 on the time axis. Dates prior to today will have negative labels. However, time *intervals* to be substituted for *t* in $S = P(1 + rt)$ will always be positive.

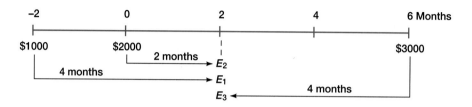

The size of the single replacement payment 2 months from now will be

$$E_1 + E_2 + E_3$$

where

$$E_1 = \text{Future value of \$1000}$$
$$= \$1000\left[1 + 0.12\left(\frac{4}{12}\right)\right]$$
$$= \$1040$$

$$E_2 = \text{Future value of \$2000}$$
$$= \$2000\left[1 + 0.12\left(\frac{2}{12}\right)\right]$$
$$= \$2040$$

$$E_3 = \text{Present value of \$3000}$$
$$= \frac{\$3000}{1 + 0.12\left(\frac{4}{12}\right)}$$
$$= \$2884.62$$

Then

$$E_1 + E_2 + E_3 = \$1040.00 + \$2040.00 + \$2884.62$$
$$= \$5964.62$$

The single equivalent payment 2 months from now is $5964.62.   ∎

■ EXAMPLE 6.6B   *CALCULATING A PAYMENT EQUIVALENT TO INTEREST-EARNING OBLIGATIONS*

Four months ago Darren borrowed $1000 from Sean and agreed to repay the loan in two payments to be made 5 and 10 months after the date of the agreement. Each payment is to consist of $500 of principal, and interest at the rate of 9% pa on that $500 from the date of the agreement. Today Darren is asking Sean to accept instead a single payment 3 months from now to settle the debt. What payment should Sean require if money can now earn 7% pa?

☑ SOLUTION

In this problem we do not initially know the dollar amounts of the scheduled payments because we do not know how much interest must be paid along with each $500 of principal. The first step, then, is to calculate the maturity value of each $500 payment on its scheduled payment date.

The maturity values are represented by S_1 and S_2 in the following time diagram.

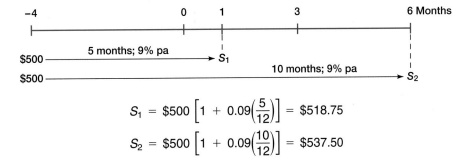

$$S_1 = \$500 \left[1 + 0.09\left(\frac{5}{12}\right)\right] = \$518.75$$

$$S_2 = \$500 \left[1 + 0.09\left(\frac{10}{12}\right)\right] = \$537.50$$

Now we can construct a time diagram presenting the scheduled payments and their equivalent values, E_1 and E_2, on the date of the replacement payment.

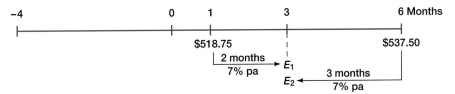

The *current* rate of interest, 7%, is used to calculate the equivalent values of the scheduled payments.

$$E_1 = \text{Future value of \$518.75 on a date 2 months later}$$
$$= \$518.75 \left[1 + 0.07\left(\frac{2}{12}\right)\right]$$
$$= \$524.80$$

$$E_2 = \text{Present value of \$537.50 on a date 3 months earlier}$$
$$= \frac{\$537.50}{1 + 0.07\left(\frac{3}{12}\right)}$$
$$= \$528.26$$

The single equivalent payment is

$$E_1 + E_2 = \$524.80 + \$528.26 = \$1053.06$$

Sean should require a payment of $1053.06 on a date 3 months from now. ■

■ EXAMPLE 6.6c   *COMPARING THE ECONOMIC VALUE OF TWO PAYMENT STREAMS*

Which of the following two payment streams has the greater economic value today if money can earn 6.5%: $500 in 2 months plus $500 in 5 months, or $600 in 3 months plus $400 in 4 months?

☑ SOLUTION

Construct a time line for each payment stream, indicating the scheduled payments and their equivalent values today. The stream with the larger total equivalent value today has the greater economic value.

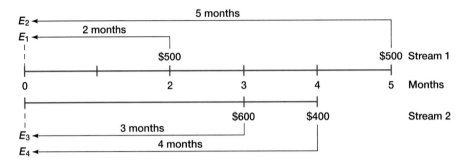

$$\text{Equivalent value of stream 1} = E_1 + E_2$$
$$= \frac{\$500}{1 + 0.065\left(\frac{2}{12}\right)} + \frac{\$500}{1 + 0.065\left(\frac{5}{12}\right)}$$
$$= \$494.641 + \$486.815$$
$$= \$981.46$$

$$\text{Equivalent value of stream 2} = E_3 + E_4$$
$$= \frac{\$600}{1 + 0.065\left(\frac{3}{12}\right)} + \frac{\$400}{1 + 0.065\left(\frac{4}{12}\right)}$$
$$= \$590.406 + \$391.517$$
$$= \$981.92$$

Even though the sum of the nominal payments in each stream is $1000, the second stream's economic value today is 46 cents greater than the first stream's value. This happens because, on average, the money in the second stream is received sooner (3.4 months for stream 2 versus 3.5 months for stream 1).   ■

EXERCISE 6.6

Answers to the odd-numbered problems are at the end of the book.

In problems 1 through 6, calculate the equivalent value of the scheduled payments if money can earn the rate of return specified in the last column. Assume that any payments due before today have been missed.

Problem	Scheduled payments	Equivalent value as of:	Interest rate (%)
1.	$500 6 months ago, $300 in 3 months	Today	$9\frac{1}{2}$
2.	$1000 today, $1500 in 5 months	2 months from now	$10\frac{1}{4}$
3.	$900 150 days ago, $1000 in 30 days	90 days from now	$7\frac{3}{4}$

4.	$2500 in 70 days, $4000 in 200 days	30 days from now	12
5.	$1000 60 days ago, $1500 in 10 days, $2000 in 150 days	Today	$8\frac{1}{2}$
6.	$1750 75 days ago, $1750 today, $1750 in 75 days	45 days from now	9.9

7. Payments of $850 and $1140 were scheduled to be paid 5 months ago and 4 months from now, respectively. If the first payment was not made, what payment 3 months from now would place the payee in the same financial position as the scheduled payments? Money can earn $8\frac{1}{4}$% pa.

8. For the scheduled payments in problem 7, determine the equivalent payment today.

9. Two payments of $2000 each are to be received 6 and 12 months from now. If money is worth 10% pa, what is the total equivalent value of the payments:

   a. Today?

   b. 6 months from today?

   c. Explain why the answer in part b is larger.

10. Two payments of $3000 each are due in 50 and 100 days. What is their combined economic value today if money can earn:

   a. 9% pa?

   b. 11% pa?

   c. Explain why the answer in part b is smaller.

11. If money earns 9.5% pa, calculate and compare the economic value today of the following payment streams:

   a. Payments of $900 and $1400 due 150 and 80 days ago, respectively.

   b. Payments of $800, $600, and $1000 due 30, 75, and 125 days from now, respectively.

12. What is the economic value today of each of the following payment streams if money is worth 7.5% pa? (Note that the two streams have the same total nominal value.)

   a. $1000, $3000, and $2000 due in 1, 3, and 5 months, respectively.

   b. Two $3000 payments due 2 and 4 months from now.

•13. Eight months ago, Louise agreed to pay Thelma $750 and $950 6 and 12 months, respectively, from the date of the agreement. With each payment Louise agreed to pay interest at the rate of 9.5% pa from the date of the agreement. Louise failed to make the first payment and now wishes to settle her obligations with a single payment 4 months from now. What payment should Thelma be willing to accept if money can earn 7.75%?

•14. Ninety days ago Stella signed an agreement with Ed requiring her to make three payments of $400 plus interest 90, 150, and 210 days, respectively, from the date of the agreement. Each payment was to include interest on the $400 principal at the rate of 13.5% from the date of the agreement. What payment should Ed accept 30 days from now if money is worth 8.5%?

•15. On November 14, 1997, Executive Fashions agreed to pay Thomson Distributing three installments of $6000 on January 14, March 14, and April 14, 1998, respectively, along with the accrued interest on each $6000 amount at 10% pa from the date of the agreement. After extraordinarily strong Christmas sales, the owner of Executive Fashions decided to propose a single payment on January 14 to settle the account in full. Thomson can effectively earn 11.5% pa on funds it receives by paying down its own short-term debt on which it pays an 11.5% rate of interest. What equivalent payment should Thomson Distributing be prepared to accept on January 14?

6.7 LOAN PRINCIPAL AS THE PRESENT VALUE OF LOAN PAYMENTS

In this section we will develop an important fundamental relationship between the principal amount of a loan and the payments required to pay off the loan. The relationship will be used several times in future chapters since it applies to all types of loans regardless of whether interest is calculated on a simple or compound interest basis.

We will use three loan repayment scenarios to infer a general relationship. Suppose $10,000 is borrowed at a simple interest rate of 10% pa. We will first calculate the payments required for each of three repayment arrangements. Then we will calculate the present value (at the date on which the loan was advanced) of the payments in each case. The three repayment arrangements are:

1. A single lump payment after 1 year.
2. Two payments after 6 and 12 months. Each payment is to consist of $5000 principal plus accrued interest on the respective $5000 since the date the loan was advanced.
3. Two payments after 137 days and 342 days. The first payment is composed of $2371 principal plus 137 days' interest on this portion of the principal. The second payment is to consist of the remaining $7629 of principal plus 342 days' interest on $7629.

The calculation of the payments for each of the loans is presented in the following table.

Loan	Payment 1	Payment 2
1.	$10,000(1 + 0.1 \times 1) = \$11,000$	na
2.	$5000\left(1 + 0.1 \times \frac{6}{12}\right) = \$5250$	$5000\left(1 + 0.1 \times \frac{12}{12}\right) = \$5500$
3.	$2731\left(1 + 0.1 \times \frac{137}{365}\right) = \$2833.51$	$7629\left(1 + 0.1 \times \frac{342}{365}\right) = \$8343.83$

Using the 10% interest rate on the loan as the time value of money, the present values of the payments in the three cases are:

1. $\text{Present value} = \dfrac{\$11{,}000}{1 + 0.1 \times 1} = \$10{,}000$

2. $\text{Present value} = \dfrac{\$5250}{1 + 0.1 \times \frac{6}{12}} + \dfrac{\$5500}{1 + 0.1 \times 1} = \$5000 + \$5000 = \$10{,}000$

3. $\text{Present value} = \dfrac{\$2833.51}{1 + 0.1 \times \frac{137}{365}} + \dfrac{\$8343.83}{1 + 0.1 \times \frac{342}{365}} = \$2731 + \$7629 = \$10{,}000$

In every case the present value of the payments is $10,000, the original principal amount of the loan. This is a general result regardless of the number of payments required to extinguish the loan.[9] The most common application of this fundamental principle is in the calculation of the size of one or more of the payments required to settle a loan.

> **Present Value of Loan Payments:** The sum of the present values of all of the payments required to pay off a loan equals the original principal of the loan. The interest rate used in the present-value calculation is the rate of interest charged on the loan.

The following examples illustrate two typical applications of this general principle.

■ EXAMPLE 6.7A   *CALCULATING THE SIZE OF THE FINAL LOAN PAYMENT*

A $5000 loan advanced on April 1 at $10\frac{1}{2}\%$ pa requires payments of $1800 on each of June 1 and August 1, and a final payment on October 1. What must the final payment be to satisfy the loan in full?

✓ SOLUTION

Let x represent the amount of the final payment. The payments and their equivalent (present) values, E_1, E_2, and E_3, are shown in the following time diagram.

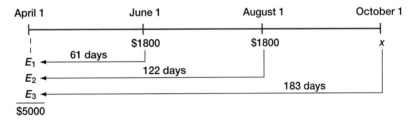

Since the original loan equals the present value of all of the payments, then

$$\$5000 = E_1 + E_2 + E_3$$

where

$$E_1 = \frac{\$1800}{1 + 0.105\left(\frac{61}{365}\right)} = \frac{\$1800}{1.0175479} = \$1768.96$$

$$E_2 = \frac{\$1800}{1 + 0.105\left(\frac{122}{365}\right)} = \frac{\$1800}{1.0350959} = \$1738.97$$

$$E_3 = \frac{x}{1 + 0.105\left(\frac{183}{365}\right)} = \frac{x}{1.0526438} = 0.9499889x$$

---

[9]Note that the $(1 + rt)$ divisor in the calculation of the present value of a payment simply reverses the corresponding $(1 + rt)$ multiplier in the prior calculation of the size of the payment. Consequently the present value of each payment equals the principal portion of the payment. When we come to loans based on *compound* interest, it will still be the case that the original principal equals the present value of all of the payments. However, the present value of an individual payment will *not* be equal to the principal portion of the payment.

Thus

$$\$5000 = \$1768.96 + \$1738.97 + 0.9499889x$$
$$\$1492.07 = 0.9499889x$$
$$x = \frac{\$1492.07}{0.9499889} = \$1570.62$$

The final payment on October 1 must be $1570.62.   ■

Trap

Do not attempt to solve the preceding problem by having each payment cover all accrued interest on the *entire* principal balance outstanding since the previous payment. For example, the first $1800 payment should not be used to pay the accrued interest on the entire $5000 principal balance outstanding during the first 61 days. The payment of interest on principal that is not repaid *at the same time* is a characteristic of *compound* interest (Chapter 8). The calculation of loan payments using the present-value method in this section has the effect of *paying interest on only the portion of the principal that is simultaneously repaid.* This is the defining characteristic of *simple* interest.

■ **EXAMPLE 6.7B**   *CALCULATING THE SIZE OF EQUAL LOAN PAYMENTS*

A $4000 loan made at 11.75% pa is to be repaid in three equal payments due 30, 90, and 150 days, respectively, after the date of the loan. Determine the size of the payments. (In loan repayment problems, the focal date is understood to be the date on which the original loan was advanced.)

☑ **SOLUTION**

Let the amount of each payment be represented by x. The payments and their equivalent (present) values are presented in the following time diagram.

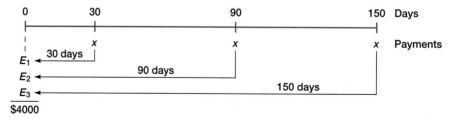

The original loan is equal to the present value of all of the payments:

$$\$4000 = E_1 + E_2 + E_3$$

where

$$E_1 = \frac{x}{1 + 0.1175\left(\frac{30}{365}\right)} = \frac{x}{1.0096575} = 0.9904348x$$

$$E_2 = \frac{x}{1 + 0.1175\left(\frac{90}{365}\right)} = \frac{x}{1.0289726} = 0.9718432x$$

$$E_3 = \frac{x}{1 + 0.1175\left(\frac{150}{365}\right)} = \frac{x}{1.0482877} = 0.9539366x$$

Thus,

$$\$4000 = 0.9904348x + 0.9718432x + 0.9539366x$$
$$= 2.916215x$$
$$x = \frac{\$4000}{2.916215} = \$1371.64$$

Each payment should be $1371.64.   ■

EXERCISE 6.7

Answers to the odd-numbered problems are at the end of the book.

For each of problems 1 through 4, the original $3000 loan was advanced on March 1. The loan is to be repaid by three payments whose dates (in the same year) are indicated in the column following the respective payment. Calculate the unknown payment in each case. Use the loan date as the focal date.

Problem	Payment ($)	Date	Payment ($)	Date	Payment ($)	Date	Interest rate (%)
•1.	1000	May 1	1000	June 1	?	July 1	11
•2.	1000	April 1	?	June 1	1000	August 1	$9\frac{1}{2}$
•3.	?	April 13	1100	May 27	1100	July 13	10.2
•4.	500	March 31	1000	June 15	?	August 31	$8\frac{1}{4}$

Calculate the size of the equal payments for problems 5 through 10. Use the loan date as the focal date.

Problem	Original loan ($)	Interest rate (%)	Number of payments	Dates of payments (after the date of the loan)
5.	1000	9	2	30 and 60 days
6.	3000	$10\frac{1}{4}$	2	50 and 150 days
•7.	2500	$8\frac{3}{4}$	3	2, 4, and 7 months
•8.	8000	$11\frac{1}{2}$	3	30, 90, and 150 days
•9.	5000	12	4	100, 150, 200, and 250 days
•10.	7500	9.9	4	2, 5, 9, and 12 months

•11. Payments of $2600, due 50 days ago, and $3100, due in 40 days, are to be replaced by $3000 today and another payment in 30 days. What must the second payment be if the payee is to end up in an equivalent financial position? Money now earns 8.25% pa. Use 30 days from now as the focal date.

•12. A loan of $10,000 is to be repaid by three payments of $2500 due in 2, 4, and 6 months, and a fourth payment due in 8 months. What should be the size of the fourth payment if an interest rate of 11% is charged on the loan? Use today as the focal date.

•13. A loan of $4000 at 13% pa is to be repaid by three equal payments due 4, 6, and 8 months after the date on which the money was advanced. Calculate the amount of each payment.

•14. Anthony borrowed $7500 on September 15 and agreed to repay the loan by three equal payments on the following November 10, December 30, and February 28. Calculate the payment size if the interest rate on the loan was $11\frac{3}{4}$% pa.

•15. Maurice borrowed $6000 from Heidi on April 23 and agreed to make payments of $2000 on June 1 and $2000 on August 1, and pay the balance on October 1. If simple interest at the rate of 10% pa was charged on the loan, what is the amount of the third payment?

*6.8 CRITERION FOR THE EQUIVALENCE OF TWO PAYMENT STREAMS

Sometimes a scheduled payment stream must be replaced by another payment stream that is economically equivalent, allowing for the time value of money. A common example is the rescheduling of debt obligations. Revised payments are calculated so that they are, in combination, equivalent to the originally scheduled payments. The concepts and techniques will be illustrated by an example.

Suppose that payments of $2000 and $1000 scheduled for March 1 and December 1, respectively, are to be replaced by two equal payments on May 1 and September 1 of the same year. The size of the two equal payments must be calculated so that the recipient will be placed in the same economic position by either payment stream. In other words, the alternative payment streams must be equivalent. Assume that money can earn 7% pa.

Figure 6.6 presents the given information on a time diagram. Separate time lines are used for the scheduled stream and the replacement stream. The equal but unknown replacement payments are each represented by x.

FIGURE   6.6

Partial Time Diagram for Equivalent Payment Streams

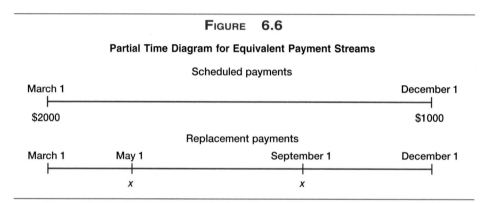

It was emphasized in Section 6.4 that two payments occurring on different dates may be compared only after their equivalent values on the *same* date have been determined. It follows that two payment streams should be compared only after each stream's equivalent value on the same focal date has been calculated.

> **Criterion for the Equivalence of Two Payment Streams:** Two payment streams are equivalent if the sum of the equivalent values of the payments in one stream equals the sum of the equivalent values of the payments in the other stream, all evaluated at the *same* focal date.

Tip

The final answer is weakly dependent on the choice of the focal date. Therefore, the focal date should be agreed upon by the two parties in the transaction. Problems in this chapter will specify the focal date to be used in the solution.

Tip

A natural choice for the focal date in a problem is the date of one of the unknown payments. Then the equivalent value of that payment on the focal date is just its nominal amount.

In Figure 6.7 May 1 has been chosen as the focal date, and the equivalent values on the focal date are indicated by E_1, E_2, and E_3. Since the first replacement payment falls on the focal date, its equivalent value equals its nominal value, x.

FIGURE   6.7

Completed Time Diagram for Equivalent Payment Streams

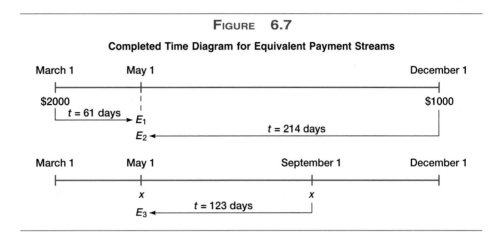

An equation expressing the economic equivalence of two payment streams at a particular focal date is called an **equation of value** or an *equation of equivalence*. The equation of value for the current problem is:

$$E_1 + E_2 = x + E_3$$

The equivalent values of the individual payments are calculated in the usual way.

$$E_1 = \text{Future value of \$2000 on May 1}$$
$$= \$2000 \left(1 + 0.07 \times \frac{61}{365}\right)$$
$$= \$2023.40$$

$$E_2 = \text{Present value of \$1000 on May 1}$$
$$= \frac{\$1000}{\left(1 + 0.07 \times \frac{214}{365}\right)}$$
$$= \$960.58$$

$$E_3 = \text{Present value of } x \text{ on May 1}$$
$$= \frac{x}{\left(1 + 0.07 \times \frac{123}{365}\right)}$$
$$= 0.976955x$$

Substituting these results into the equation of value, we obtain

$$\$2023.40 + \$960.58 = x + 0.976955x$$
$$\$2983.98 = 1.976955x$$
$$x = \$1509.38$$

We have determined that equal payments of $1509.38 on May 1 and September 1 are equivalent to the scheduled payments of $2000 on March 1 and $1000 on December 1.

■ **EXAMPLE 6.8A**   *SOLVING FOR REPLACEMENT PAYMENTS SO THAT TWO STREAMS WILL BE EQUIVALENT*

Two payments, $800 due 60 days ago and $500 due 30 days ago, are to be replaced by a payment 30 days from today and a second payment, twice as large, due 90 days from today. Calculate the replacement payments so that they are equivalent to the scheduled payments if money can earn 7.75% pa. Use 30 days from now as the focal date.

☑ **SOLUTION**

Let the replacement payments be represented by x and $2x$. Construct a time diagram indicating the scheduled payments, the replacement payments, and the equivalent values.

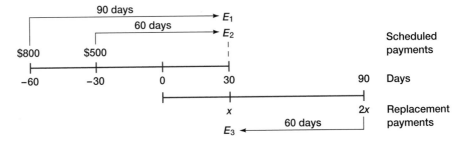

The equation of value (expressing the equivalence of the two payment streams) is

$$E_1 + E_2 = x + E_3$$

where

$$E_1 = \$800\left[1 + 0.0775\left(\frac{90}{365}\right)\right] = \$815.29$$

$$E_2 = \$500\left[1 + 0.0775\left(\frac{60}{365}\right)\right] = \$506.37$$

$$E_3 = \frac{2x}{1 + 0.0775\left(\frac{60}{365}\right)} = 1.974841x$$

Substitution in the equation of value gives

$$\$815.29 + \$506.37 = x + 1.974841x$$
$$\$1321.66 = 2.974841x$$
$$x = \frac{\$1321.66}{2.974841}$$
$$= \$444.28$$

The two equivalent payments are $444.28 in 30 days and $888.56 in 90 days.   ■

■ **EXAMPLE 6.8B**   *SOLVING FOR REPLACEMENT PAYMENTS SO THAT TWO STREAMS WILL BE EQUIVALENT*

The parties involved have agreed to replace payments of $2000 due 2 months ago and $1000 due 9 months from now by a payment of $500 today and two equal payments due in 4 months and 10 months. What should be the amount of each equal payment if the payee is to be placed in an equivalent financial position and money is worth 9% pa? Use 4 months from now as the focal date.

☑ SOLUTION

Let x represent each replacement payment. Construct the time diagram.

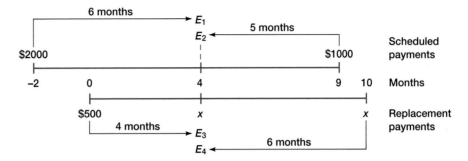

For the two streams to be economically equivalent, the sum of the equivalent values of one stream must equal the sum of the equivalent values of the second stream at the focal date (Criterion for Equivalence). This gives the equation of value:

$$E_1 + E_2 = x + E_3 + E_4$$

where

$$E_1 = \text{Future value of \$2000}$$
$$= \$2000\left[1 + 0.09\left(\frac{6}{12}\right)\right]$$
$$= \$2090.00$$

$$E_2 = \text{Present value of \$1000}$$
$$= \frac{\$1000}{1 + 0.09\left(\frac{5}{12}\right)}$$
$$= \$963.86$$

$$E_3 = \text{Future value of \$500}$$
$$= 500\left[1 + 0.09\left(\frac{4}{12}\right)\right]$$
$$= \$515.00$$

$$E_4 = \text{Present value of } x$$
$$= \frac{x}{1 + 0.09\left(\frac{6}{12}\right)}$$
$$= 0.9569378x$$

Substituting these amounts into the equation of value,

$$\$2090.00 + \$963.86 = x + \$515.00 + 0.9569378x$$
$$\$2538.86 = 1.9569378x$$
$$x = \frac{\$2538.86}{1.9569378}$$
$$= \$1297.36$$

Each of the two equal payments should be $1297.36.

EXERCISE 6.8

Answers to the odd-numbered problems are at the end of the book.

Calculate the replacement payments in problems 1 through 10 if money can earn the rate of return given in the last column. Assume that scheduled payments due before today have not been paid.

Problem	Scheduled payments	Replacement payments	Focal date	Interest rate (%)
•1.	$600 4 months ago, $900 in 11 months	$800 today, balance in 12 months	Today	$8\frac{1}{2}$
•2.	$1300 123 days ago, $600 in 75 days	$1000 in 75 days, balance in 150 days	Today	$11\frac{1}{4}$
•3.	$6700 2 months ago	Two equal payments due in 3 and 6 months	3 months from now	9.9
•4.	$5000 in 4 months	$1000 today and two equal payments due in 3 and 7 months	Today	$13\frac{3}{4}$
•5.	$3000 5 months ago, $3000 today	Three equal payments due today and in 2 and 4 months	Today	9
•6.	$1800 today, $2500 in 100 days	Three equal payments due in 50, 100, and 150 days	50 days from now	$10\frac{1}{2}$
•7.	$1500 in 6 months, $2500 in 9 months	A payment in 2 months and another, twice as large, in 5 months	2 months from now	$6\frac{3}{4}$
•8.	$850 80 days ago, $1200 in 160 days	A payment in 30 days, and another, half as large, in 100 days	30 days from now	14
••9.	$1000 plus 4 months' interest at 11% due today, $1200 plus 8 months' interest at 11% due in 4 months	Two equal payments due in 6 months and 1 year	Today	$8\frac{3}{4}$
••10.	$5000 plus 3 months' interest at 8% due 2 months ago, $3000 plus 10 months' interest at 8% due in 5 months	Three equal payments due today, 5 months from now, and 10 months from now	Today	$10\frac{1}{2}$

•11. Payments of $2600, due 50 days ago, and $3100, due in 40 days, are to be replaced by $3000 today and another payment in 30 days. What must the second payment be if the payee is to end up in an equivalent financial position? Money now earns $8\frac{1}{4}$%. Use 30 days from now as the focal date.

•12. Repeat Problem 11 using today as the focal date. (A comparison of the answers to these two problems demonstrates that the answer to an equivalent payment stream problem involving simple interest depends slightly on the placement of the focal date.)

•13. A payment of $5000 due today is to be replaced by 3 payments: $2000 in 3 months, $1500 in 5 months, and a third payment in 8 months. What must the third payment be to make the three payments economically equivalent to $5000 today, allowing for a 9.75% time value of money? Use today as the focal date.

•14. Repeat Problem 13 with the date of the third payment chosen as the focal date. (A comparison of the answers to these two problems demonstrates that the answer to an equivalent payment stream problem involving simple interest depends slightly on the placement of the focal date.)

•15. A payment of $7000 was supposed to be made on July 1. What three equal payments on May 24, August 13, and September 30 are equivalent to the scheduled payment if money can earn 13% pa? Choose August 13 as the focal date.

•16. Payments of $3500 due 3 months ago and $6100 due in 5 months are to be replaced by an equivalent payment stream consisting of a payment 1 month from now and a second payment, half as large, in 6 months. Calculate these payments if money can earn $8\frac{1}{4}$% pa. Use the date of the first unknown payment as the focal date.

•17. A contract was signed 7 months ago requiring the payment of $6500 plus interest at 9% 10 months later. What two equal payments made today and 4 months from now are equivalent to the scheduled payment if money is now worth 8.5%? Choose today as the focal date.

•18. On March 1 Heinz contracted to pay to Larry $12,000 plus interest at $13\frac{1}{2}$% pa on August 1. Larry later agreed to a rescheduling of the obligation allowing for a time value of money of 10%. Heinz is now to make one payment on July 1 and a second payment, twice as large, on November 1. Calculate the payments using July 1 as the focal date.

*APPENDIX: AN AID FOR DETERMINING THE NUMBER OF DAYS IN EACH MONTH

Figure 6.8 presents a method for determining which months have 31 days. The knuckles and the spaces between them are consecutively given the names of the months as shown in the figure. Then each knuckle corresponds to a month with 31 days and each space corresponds to a short month.

FIGURE   6.8

"Knuckle Months" Have 31 Days

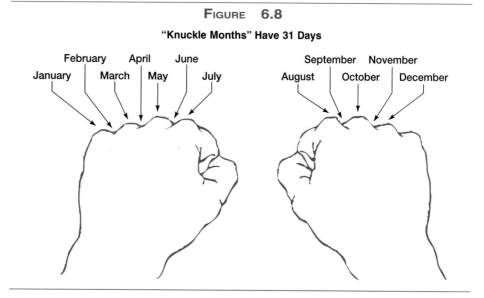

REVIEW PROBLEMS

Answers to the odd-numbered review problems are at the end of the book.

1. Peter has forgotten the rate of simple interest he earned on a 120-day term deposit at the Bank of Nova Scotia. At the end of the 120 days, he received interest of $327.95 on his $21,000 deposit. What rate of simple interest was his deposit earning?

•2. Evelyn put $15,000 into a 90-day term deposit at Montreal Trust paying a simple interest rate of 5.2% pa. When the term deposit matured, she invested the entire amount of the principal and interest from the first term deposit into a new 90-day term deposit earning the same rate of interest. What total amount of interest did she earn on both term deposits?

3. Mary borrowed $1750 from Jason on November 15, 1996, and agreed to repay the debt with simple interest at the rate of 7.4% pa on June 3, 1997. How much interest was owed on June 3?

•4. Bert borrowed $7500 from Delores on November 7, 1997. When Bert repaid the loan, Delores charged $190.02 interest. If the rate of simple interest on the loan was $6\frac{3}{4}$%, on what date did Bert repay the loan?

5. Jack received the proceeds from an inheritance on March 15. He wants to set aside, in a term deposit on March 16, an amount sufficient to provide a $45,000 down payment for the purchase of a home on November 1. If the current interest rate on 181-day to 270-day deposits is $5\frac{3}{4}$%, what amount should he place in the term deposit?

6. A rototiller that you are planning to buy next April 1 is advertised at $499.95 in a fall clearance special that will end on the preceding September 15. What annual rate of simple interest will you earn if you "invest" in the rototiller at the sale price on September 15 instead of waiting until the following April 1 to purchase it at the regular price of $579.00? (Assume that the intervening February has 28 days.)

7. What amount on January 23 is equivalent to $1000 on the preceding August 18 if money can earn $6\frac{1}{2}$% pa?

8. Mr. and Mrs. Parsons are considering two offers to purchase their summer cottage. One is for $100,000, consisting of $20,000 down and the balance to be paid in a lump payment in 1 year. The second is for $96,000, with $48,000 down and the balance to be paid in 6 months. Compare the current economic values of the two offers if money can earn:

   a. 6% pa

   b. 9% pa

9. Payments of $1000 and $7500 were originally scheduled to be paid 5 months ago and 4 months from now respectively. What payment 2 months from now would place the payee in an equivalent financial position if money can earn $6\frac{1}{4}$% pa?

10. If money earns 7.5% pa, calculate and compare the economic value today of the following payment streams:

   a. Payments of $1800 and $2800 due 150 and 90 days ago, respectively.

   b. Payments of $1600, $1200, and $2000 due 30, 75, and 120 days from now, respectively.

•11. Nine months ago Muriel agreed to pay Tanya $1200 and $800 on dates 6 and 12 months, respectively, from the date of the agreement. With each payment Muriel agreed to pay interest at the rate of $8\frac{1}{2}$% pa from the date of the agreement. Muriel now wishes to settle her obligations with a single payment 4 months from now. What payment should Tanya be willing to accept if money can earn $6\frac{3}{4}$%?

•12. Ninety days ago Wayne signed an agreement with Todd requiring Wayne to make three payments of $500 plus interest 90, 180, and 270 days, respectively, from the date of the agreement. Each payment was to include interest on the $500 principal at the rate of 8.5% from the date of the agreement. What single equivalent payment should Todd accept at a focal date 30 days from now if money is worth 6.9%?

13. A $9000 loan is to be repaid in three equal payments occurring 60, 180, and 300 days, respectively, after the date of the loan. Calculate the size of these payments if the interest rate on the loan is $7\frac{1}{4}$% pa. Use the loan date as the focal date.

14. Payments of $2000 due 50 days ago and $3000 due in 60 days are to be replaced by $3000 today and another payment in 40 days. What must the second payment be if the payee is to end up in an equivalent financial position? Money now earns $6\frac{1}{4}$%. Use 40 days from now as the focal date.

•15. A contract was signed 5 months ago requiring the payment of $6500 plus interest at 8% in 9 months. What two equal payments made today and 6 months from now are equivalent to the scheduled payment if money is now worth $7\frac{1}{4}$%? Choose today as the focal date.

•16. On April 15 Howard contracted to pay to Laura $7000 plus interest at $6\frac{1}{2}$% pa on August 1, and another $7000 plus interest at $6\frac{1}{2}$% pa on December 15. In each case the interest is calculated on $7000 from the date of the contract. Laura later agreed to a rescheduling of the payments allowing for a time value of money of 8% pa. Howard is now to make one payment on July 1 (preceding the first scheduled payment) and a second payment, twice as large, on the following January 1. Calculate the payments using July 1 as the focal date.

SELF-TEST EXERCISE

Answers to the self-test problems are at the end of the book.

1. If $3702.40 earned $212.45 interest from September 17, 1995, to March 11, 1996, what rate of interest was earned?

2. A loan of $3300 at $9\frac{1}{4}$% pa simple interest was made on March 27. On what date was it repaid if the interest cost was $137.99?

3. What amount invested at $9\frac{1}{2}$% on November 19, 1997, will have a maturity value of $10,000 on March 3, 1998?

4. Although Judy has enough laundry detergent on hand to last another 6 weeks, what simple annual rate of interest will she earn, in effect, by purchasing a box now at the special price of $7.95 instead of buying at the regular price of $8.95 in 6 weeks?

5. Sheldrick Contracting owes Western Equipment $60,000 payable on June 14. In late April Sheldrick has surplus cash and wants to settle its debt to Western Equipment if Western will agree to a fair reduction reflecting the current 7.6% interest rate that short-term funds can earn. What amount on April 29 should Sheldrick propose to pay to Western?

6. Peter and Reesa can book their Horizon Holiday package at the early-booking price of $3850, or wait 4 months and pay the full price of $3995.

   a. Which option should they select if money can earn 9.25% pa?

   b. At what interest rate would they be indifferent between the two prices?

7. Three payments—$1200 due 7 months ago, $900 due 2 months ago, and $1500 due in 1 month—are to be replaced by a single equivalent payment due in 3 months. What should the payment be if money is worth 9.9% pa? Use today as the focal date.

•8. A $10,000 loan was granted 6 months ago requiring repayment of the full principal plus interest at 13.5% pa 10 months from the date of the loan. The lender and borrower have subsequently agreed to a rescheduling of the debt's repayment to an equivalent stream of three payments allowing for a 9.5% time value of money. The rescheduled payments are $3000 today, a second payment due in 3 months, and a third payment, twice the size of the second, due in 7 months. Calculate the second and third payments using the second payment's date as the focal date.

9. Two payments of $5000 are to be received 4 and 8 months from now.

   a. What is the equivalent economic value of the two payments today if money can earn 9% pa?

   b. If the rate of interest that money can earn were 7% pa, what would be the payments' economic value today? Give an explanation for the greater economic value at the lower interest rate.

SUMMARY OF NOTATION AND KEY FORMULAS

P = Principal amount of a loan or investment
r = Annual rate of simple interest
t = Time period (term), in years, of the loan or investment
I = Amount of interest paid or received
S = Maturity value of a loan or investment

In the context of equivalent values,

P = Present value of a scheduled payment, S
S = Future value of a scheduled payment, P
r = Interest rate that money can earn (i.e., the time value of money)
t = Time interval between the scheduled payment and the equivalent payment
E = Equivalent value of a scheduled payment

Formula (6–1) $I = Prt$ Finding the amount of simple interest earned

Formula (6–2) $S = P(1 + rt)$ Finding the maturity value of the principal or the future value of a scheduled payment

---

Present Value of Loan Payments: The sum of the present values of all of the payments required to pay off a loan equals the original principal of the loan. The interest rate used in the present-value calculation is the rate of interest charged on the loan.

Criterion for the Equivalence of Two Payment Streams: Two payment streams are equivalent if the sum of the equivalent values of the payments in one stream equals the sum of the equivalent values of the payments in the other stream, all evaluated at the *same* focal date.

GLOSSARY OF TERMS

Economically equivalent payments   Alternative payments that will ultimately put the recipient in the same financial position.

Equation of value   An equation expressing the economic equivalence of two payment streams at a particular focal date.

Equivalent value An alternative amount on a different date that would place the recipient in the same financial position as the scheduled payment or stream of payments.

Focal date The date selected for the calculation of the equivalent values.

Future value A payment's equivalent value at a subsequent date, allowing for the time value of money.

Interest The fee or rent that lenders charge to borrowers for the temporary use of the borrowed money.

Maturity value The total of the original principal plus the interest due on the expiry or maturity date of a loan or investment.

Payment stream A series of two or more payments required by a single transaction or contract.

Present value A payment's equivalent value at a prior date, allowing for the time value of money.

Principal The original amount borrowed or invested.

Rate of interest The percentage of the principal that will be charged for a specified period of time, normally 1 year.

Simple interest Interest calculated using the formula $I = Prt$, and paid only when the principal is repaid.

Time value of money The property that a given *nominal* amount of money on a specified date has a different economic value at every other point in time.

7

APPLICATIONS OF SIMPLE INTEREST

LEARNING OBJECTIVES

After completing this chapter, you will be able to:

- Calculate the maturity value of an interest-bearing promissory note
- Discount promissory notes using the Simple Discount Method
- State the Valuation Principle and apply it to the calculation of the fair market value or price of a contract entitling its owner to specified future cash receipts
- Calculate the market price and rate of return for Treasury bills and commercial paper

- Calculate the interest paid on savings accounts, term deposits, and short-term guaranteed investment certificates
- Describe typical terms, conditions, and repayment arrangements for revolving (demand) loans and blended-payment (demand) loans
- Prepare a loan repayment schedule for revolving and blended-payment demand loans

Introduction

The simple-interest method for calculating interest is used in a variety of borrowing and investing situations in both personal and business finance. We begin by discussing promissory notes, which are used in some circumstances to formalize debt obligations. In the discussion of promissory notes, we encounter the need to determine the fair market value on a particular date of the future payment promised by the note. This naturally leads us to the Valuation Principle, a fundamental concept closely related to the notion of equivalent values presented in the previous chapter. The Valuation Principle is then applied to the pricing of two types of short-term investments: Treasury bills and commercial paper.

Savings accounts, term deposits, and guaranteed investment certificates are widely used by the general public for saving and investing. Their characteristics are described, and the procedures for calculating their interest earnings are presented. Finally, common arrangements for the payment of interest and principal on demand loans are discussed.

7.1 Promissory Notes

A simple type of contract called a *promissory note* is sometimes written to document a debt arising from a loan or a credit sale. The advantage of the promissory note to the lender/creditor is that it provides formal evidence that the debt rightfully exists. In the event of default in the payment of the debt, court action is more straightforward and has better chances of success if a promissory note supports the claim.

Concepts and Definitions

A **promissory note** is a written promise by one party to pay a certain sum of money to another party on a specific date, or on demand.

The required elements and the general rules of law that apply to promissory notes are set out in the federal Bills of Exchange Act.[1] The basic information required in a promissory note is illustrated in Figure 7.1. A *demand* promissory note, typical of the kind used by financial institutions in connection with demand loans, is shown in Figure 7.2. Several terms will be defined and standard practices explained with reference to Figure 7.1.

1. The **maker** of the note is the party (debtor) promising the payment.
2. The **payee** is the party (creditor) to whom the payment is to be made.
3. The **face value** is the principal amount of the debt.
4. The **issue date** is the date on which the note was written or "made" and the date from which interest, if any, is computed.
5. The **term** of the note is the nominal length of the loan period. (A *demand* note is payable at any time the payee chooses.)
6. The Bills of Exchange Act provides that, unless otherwise specified,[2] an extra *3 days of grace* are added at the end of a note's term to determine the note's **legal**

---

[1]The legal definition of a promissory note in the Bills of Exchange Act is as follows: "A *promissory note* is an unconditional promise in writing made by one person to another person, signed by the maker, engaging to pay, on demand or at a fixed or determinable future time, a sum certain in money to, or to the order of, a specified person or to bearer."

[2]To extinguish the normal 3 days of grace, "NO DAYS OF GRACE" should be marked on the note.

FIGURE   7.1

Term Promissory Note

PROMISSORY NOTE

(3)
$7200.00   Edmonton, Alberta   (4) November 30, 1997

(5) *Three months*   after date ___/___ promise to pay to the order of

(2) *Western Builders Supply Ltd.*

the sum of ___ *seventy-two hundred and* — — — — — — — — — — — *00* /100 Dollars

at ___ (8) *Royal Bank, Terminal Plaza Branch*

for value received, with interest at (7) ___ *12%* ___ per annum.

Due: (6) *March 3, 1998*   Signed: (1) *J. Anderson*

FIGURE   7.2

Demand Promissory Note

---

(3)
$5000.00   Hamilton, Ontario   (4) April 30, 1997

ON DEMAND after date for value received, ___/___ promise to pay to the order of

(2) *Acme Distributing Ltd.* at

(8) *the Royal Bank of Canada, Limeridge Mall Branch* the sum of

(3) *five thousand* — *00* /100 Dollars

(7) with interest thereon calculated and payable monthly at a rate equal to the Royal Bank of Canada's prime interest rate per annum in effect from time to time plus _2_ % per annum as well after as before maturity, default and judgement. At the date of this note, such prime interest rate is _8_ % per annum.

Prime interest rate is the annual rate of interest announced from time to time by the Royal Bank of Canada as a reference rate then in effect for determining interest rates on Canadian dollar commercial loans in Canada.

Signed: (1) *R. A. Matthews*

---

due date. The maker is not in default until after the legal due date. No days of grace are allowed in the case of demand notes.

7. If interest is to be charged on the face value, the rate must be specified on the note. This makes it an interest-bearing promissory note. The days of grace are included in the interest period for calculating the *maturity value* (face value plus interest) of the note on the legal due date.[3] For terms of 1 year or less, it is understood that the simple-interest method should be used. The maturity value

---

[3]The Bills of Exchange Act provides that, whenever the last day of grace falls on a Saturday, a Sunday, or a legal holiday, the next following business day becomes the last day of grace. Technically, any extra calendar days added as a consequence of this provision should be included in the interest period. We will ignore this fine point of law to avoid the extra complication. The dollar amount involved (in relation to the maturity value otherwise calculated) is not material.

may therefore be calculated using formula (6–2), $S = P(1 + rt)$. The maturity value of a non-interest-bearing note will just be its face value.

8. The note can specify the location at which the maker is to make the payment to the credit of the payee.

■ EXAMPLE 7.1A   DETERMINING THE LEGAL DUE DATE

Show how the due date of the promissory note in Figure 7.1 is obtained.

☑ SOLUTION

When the term of the note is specified in months, the end of the term is normally on the same numbered day in the expiry month as the date of issue. This particular instance is different, as there is no February 30. In such cases the last day of the expiry month is used as the end of the term. The legal due date is then 3 days later.

For the note in Figure 7.1, the term expires on February 28, 1998, and the legal due date is March 3, 1998.   ■

■ EXAMPLE 7.1B   CALCULATING AN INTEREST-BEARING NOTE'S MATURITY VALUE

What is the maturity value of the note in Figure 7.1?

☑ SOLUTION

Even though the term is specified in months, the interest is calculated to the exact number of days, including the 3 days of grace.

Month	Days of interest
November	1
December	31
January	31
February	28
March	2
	93

$$\text{Maturity value} = P(1 + rt)$$
$$= \$7200\left[1 + 0.12\left(\frac{93}{365}\right)\right]$$
$$= \$7420.14$$

The maturity value required to settle the note on March 3, 1998, is $7420.14.   ■

■ EXAMPLE 7.1C   LEGAL DUE DATE AND MATURITY VALUE OF AN INTEREST-BEARING NOTE

What would be the legal due date of the promissory note in Figure 7.1 if the term were 120 days instead of 3 months? What would be the maturity value of the note?

☑ SOLUTION

The legal due date will occur 123 days after the issue date.

Interval	Number of days of interest in the interval	Remaining days of interest in the term
Nov 30 to Dec 31	32	123 − 32 = 91
Jan 1 to Jan 31	31	91 − 31 = 60
Feb 1 to Feb 28	28	60 − 28 = 32
March 1 to Mar 31	31	32 − 31 = 1
April 1 to Apr 2	1 ①	0

① We have counted the first day (Nov 30) of the term but not the last day (Apr 2).

The legal due date falls on April 2, 1998.

$$\text{Maturity value} = \$7200\left[1 + 0.12\left(\frac{123}{365}\right)\right] = \$7491.16$$

The maturity value on the legal due date is $7491.16. ■

DISCOUNTING PROMISSORY NOTES—SIMPLE DISCOUNT METHOD[4]

Promissory notes are *negotiable*. This means that a payee can transfer ownership of a note by *endorsing* it—that is, by signing his or her name on the back of the note. The payee will do this if he or she sells the note to another party (the buyer) at any time before the note's legal due date. The maker is then obliged to pay the maturity value to the bearer/holder of the endorsed note on its due date.

The usual reason for selling a note is that the payee needs cash before the due date of the note. The price received for the note is often referred to as the **proceeds** of the note. The general case is presented in Figure 7.3. The face value P of an interest-bearing note earns interest at the rate r_1 (specified in the note) for the time period t_1 until the due date.[5] The selling price of the note is to be determined for a date of sale that is a time period t_2 prior to the due date. When counting the number of days in the time period between two dates, the common practice is to count the first date but not the second date.

FIGURE 7.3
Calculating the Proceeds of a Promissory Note

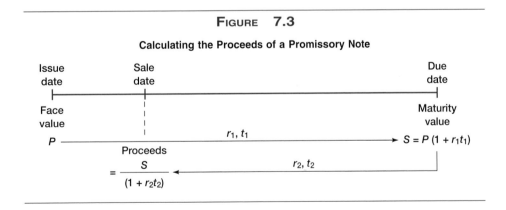

----
[4]Another rarely used method for discounting promissory notes, the bank discount method, is presented in Appendix 7A. The bank discount method is still included in the curriculum of some accounting courses.
[5]Even though prevailing interest rates may change during the term of a note, the maker of the note is obligated to pay interest at the rate contracted in the note.

A prospective buyer should be viewed as an investor who has a choice among many investment alternatives. By purchasing a promissory note, an investor acquires the right to receive the note's maturity value S on its due date. That maturity value will be

$$S = P(1 + r_1 t_1)$$

The basis for a "fair deal" for both the buyer and seller should be that the buyer receives a rate of return on the purchase price (proceeds) close to the rate of return that she can obtain from other, *similar* investments.[6] Suppose the buyer requires a rate of return equal to r_2. Then the appropriate purchase price is the amount that, earning interest at the rate r_2, would grow to S during the time period t_2. That is,

$$S = \text{Purchase price } (1 + r_2 t_2)$$

Solving for the purchase price (proceeds), we obtain

$$\text{Purchase price (proceeds)} = \frac{S}{(1 + r_2 t_2)}$$

But this is just the *present* value (of the maturity amount) at the date of sale, with the required rate of return used as the interest rate. The process of calculating the present value of the maturity amount is called **discounting** the note. The interest rate used in the discounting process is referred to as the **discount rate.** The difference between the note's maturity value and the proceeds is the **discount.**

In summary, the determination of the selling price or proceeds of a promissory note is a two-step calculation:

1. Calculate the maturity value on the due date using the interest rate *specified in the note.* If the note does not bear interest, its maturity value is just its face value.
2. Calculate the present value, on the date of sale, of the maturity amount using the discount rate agreed upon by the buyer and the seller.

Simple Discount Proceeds

$$\boxed{\text{Proceeds (price)} = \frac{S}{1 + rt}} \qquad (7\text{–}1)$$

The maturity value of a promissory note will also be discounted if the maker and payee agree that the maker will pay off the note before the due date. The appropriate discount rate to use for a "fair" settlement is the current short-term rate at which the payee can reinvest the proceeds.

■ EXAMPLE 7.1D CALCULATING THE PROCEEDS OF A NON-INTEREST-BEARING NOTE

A 150-day non-interest-bearing note for $2500 was made on June 15. The note was sold on August 21 at a price reflecting a discount rate of 12.5% pa. What were the proceeds of the note?

✓ SOLUTION

There are 153 days from the issue date until the legal due date. By August 21, $16 + 31 + 20 = 67$ of the days have passed and $153 - 67 = 86$ days remain.

---

[6]Competition among investors tends to cause investments with similar risk and maturity characteristics to have similar rates of return.

This information and the solution approach are presented in the following time diagram.

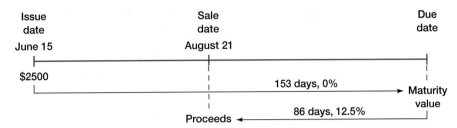

Since the face value does not earn interest, the maturity value will equal the face value of $2500.

The proceeds of the note will be the present value, 86 days earlier, of the maturity value discounted at the rate of 12.5% pa.

$$\text{Proceeds} = \frac{S}{1 + rt} = \frac{\$2500}{1 + 0.125\left(\frac{86}{365}\right)} = \$2428.48$$

Note: By paying this price, the extra

$$\$2500 - \$2428.48 = \$71.52$$

received on the note's legal due date provides a 12.5% rate of return for 86 days on the investment of $2428.48. To verify this, calculate

$$r = \frac{I}{Pt} = \frac{\$71.52}{\$2428.48\left(\frac{86}{365}\right)} = 0.125 = 12.5\%$$

∎

■ EXAMPLE 7.1E   *CALCULATING THE PROCEEDS OF AN INTEREST-BEARING NOTE*

A 4-month note for $1260 dated July 31 bears interest at the rate of 11.25% pa. If the maker wishes to pay off the note on September 15, what will be a fair settlement if money can now earn 9.5% pa?

☑ SOLUTION

The term of the note expires November 30. The legal due date is December 3, which is

$$1 + 31 + 30 + 31 + 30 + 2 = 125 \text{ days}$$

after the issue date. By September 15,

$$1 + 31 + 14 = 46 \text{ days}$$

have passed, leaving 79 days until the due date.

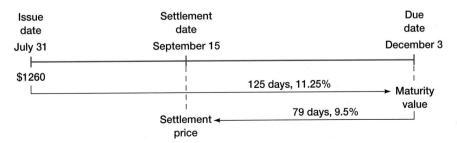

$$\text{Maturity value of note} = \$1260\left[1 + 0.1125\left(\frac{125}{365}\right)\right] = \$1308.54$$

The settlement price requires discounting the maturity value at the current short-term rate that money can earn.

$$\text{Settlement price} = \frac{\$1308.54}{1 + 0.095\left(\frac{79}{365}\right)} = \$1282.18$$

A fair settlement would be for the payee to accept $1282.18 on September 15. The reason it is a fair settlement is that, if the payee takes this amount and invests it for 79 days at 9.5%, the investment will grow to $1308.54 by December 3. This is exactly the same amount as the payee would receive if the note were paid as scheduled on December 3. The payee's financial position on December 3 will be the same under either alternative. ∎

■ EXAMPLE 7.1F   CALCULATING THE PROCEEDS OF AN INTEREST-BEARING NOTE

Old Country Antiques accepted a 6-month promissory note from a customer for the $2850 balance owed on the purchase of a dining room suite. The note was dated November 8, 1995, and charged interest at 13% pa. The store's proprietor sold the promissory note 38 days later to a finance company at a price that would yield the finance company 18% pa on its purchase price. What price did the finance company pay?

☑ SOLUTION

The note's legal due date was May 11, 1996 (May 8 + 3 days). The total number of days from the issue date until the due date was

$$23 + 31 + 31 + 29 + 31 + 30 + 10 = 185 \text{ days}$$

When the note was sold, $185 - 38 = 147$ days remained until the due date. The given information and the steps in the solution can be presented in a time diagram.

$$\text{Maturity value of note} = \$2850\left[1 + 0.13\left(\frac{185}{365}\right)\right] = \$3037.79$$

The price paid by the finance company was the present value, 147 days earlier, of the maturity value discounted at 18% pa.

$$\text{Price} = \frac{\$3037.79}{1 + 0.18\left(\frac{147}{365}\right)} = \$2832.46$$

The finance company paid $2832.46 for the promissory note. ∎

EXERCISE 7.1

Answers to the odd-numbered problems are at the end of the book.

Calculate the missing values for the promissory notes described in problems 1 through 22.

Problem	Issue date	Term	Legal due date
1.	May 19	120 days	?
2.	June 30	90 days	?
3.	July 6	? days	Oct 17
4.	Nov 14	? days	Jan 31
5.	?	4 months	Feb 28
6.	?	9 months	Oct 3
7.	?	180 days	Sept 2
8.	?	60 days	March 1 (leap year)

Problem	Issue date	Face value ($)	Term	Interest rate (%)	Maturity value ($)
9.	April 30	1000	4 months	9.50	?
10.	Feb 15	3300	60 days	8.75	?
11.	July 3	?	90 days	10.20	2667.57
12.	Aug 31	?	3 months	7.50	7644.86
13.	Jan 22	6200	120 days	?	6388.04
14.	Nov 5	4350	75 days	?	4445.28
15.	Dec 31	5200	? days	11.00	5275.22
16.	March 30	9400	? days	9.90	9560.62

Problem	Face value ($)	Issue date	Interest rate (%)	Term	Date of sale	Discount rate (%)	Proceeds ($)
17.	1000	March 30	0	50 days	April 8	10	?
18.	6000	May 17	0	3 months	June 17	9	?
19.	2700	Sept 4	10	182 days	Dec 14	12	?
20.	3500	Oct 25	10	120 days	Dec 14	8	?
21.	9000	July 28	8	91 days	Sept 1	?	9075.40
22.	4000	Nov 30	8	75 days	Jan 1	?	4015.25

23. Determine the legal due date for:

    a. A 5-month note dated September 29, 1997.

    b. A 150-day note issued September 29, 1997.

24. Determine the legal due date for:

    a. A 4-month note dated April 30, 1994.

    b. A 120-day note issued April 30, 1994.

25. Calculate the maturity value of a 120-day, $1000 face value note dated November 30, 1997, and earning interest at 10.75% pa.

26. Calculate the maturity value of a $1000 face value, 5-month note dated December 31, 1997, and bearing interest at 9.5% pa.

27. A 90-day non-interest-bearing note for $3300 is dated August 1. What would be a fair selling price of the note on September 1 if money can earn 7.75% pa?

28. A 6-month non-interest-bearing note issued on September 30, 1997, for $3300 was discounted at 11.25% on December 1. What were the proceeds of the note?

29. A 100-day $750 note with interest at 12.5% was written on July 15. The maker approaches the payee on August 10 to propose an early settlement. What amount should the payee be willing to accept on August 10 if short-term investments can earn 8.25% pa?

30. The payee on a 3-month $2700 note earning interest at 8% wishes to sell the note to raise some cash. What price should she be prepared to accept for the note (dated May 19) on June 5 in order to yield the purchaser an 11% rate of return?

31. A 6-month note dated June 30 for $2900 bears interest at 13.5%. Determine the proceeds of the note if it is discounted at 9.75% on September 1.

32. An investor is prepared to buy short-term promissory notes at a price that will provide him with a return on investment of 12%. What amount would he pay on August 9 for a 120-day note dated July 18 for $4100 with interest at 10.25% pa?

7.2 VALUATION PRINCIPLE

The discounting of a promissory note to determine its appropriate purchase/selling price is our first encounter with valuing an investment. *When we make an investment, in effect we purchase the right to receive some future cash payments.* For example, the purchase of a bond entitles the investor to receive specified regular interest payments and the full face value of the bond at its maturity date.

The crucial question facing investors is: What price should be paid today for the expected future cash receipts, in order to obtain an appropriate rate of return? Valuation of investments is central to the study of finance. In this section, we will develop the most commonly used mathematical technique for determining the appropriate price or *fair market value* of an investment.

Let us extend the reasoning employed in Section 7.1 for calculating the fair market value of a promissory note. In that case, the investor purchased the right to receive a single future payment. We showed that the appropriate price or value on the purchase date was the present value of the future payment, discounted at the required rate of return.

If another investment promises two separate payments on future dates, each payment can be treated in the same way as the single payment from a promissory note. Thus, the appropriate price to pay for this investment is the *sum* of the present values of both future cash flows, discounted at the *required* rate of return.

For investments offering several future cash flows, the basic idea still applies: Each cash flow should be discounted back to the purchase date using the required or market-based rate of return as the discount rate. These individual present values on the purchase date are then added to give the fair market value of the investment on that date. This procedure is embodied in the Valuation Principle, which will be frequently called upon to determine the price or fair market value of an investment.

Valuation Principle: The fair market value of an investment is the sum of the present values of the expected cash flows. The discount rate used in the present-value calculations should be the market-based rate of return required for this type of investment.

If the expected cash flows are received as forecast, the investor's actual rate of return on the amount invested will be precisely the discount rate used in the original price calculation. If the investment can be acquired at a price below the fair market value computed using the Valuation Principle, the investor can expect an actual rate of return exceeding the discount rate.

The Valuation Principle is an extension of the concept of the equivalent value of a payment stream (Section 6.6). The sum of the present values of the expected cash flows represents their combined equivalent value on the investment date. The time value of money in this context is the market-based required rate of return.

■ **EXAMPLE 7.2A** *VALUATION OF A NON-INTEREST-BEARING OBLIGATION*

An investment contract calls for a payment of $1000 5 months from now and another payment, 10 months from now, of $1500.

a. What price will an investor be prepared to pay for the investment today if the required rate of return is 12% pa?

b. Demonstrate that the investor will realize a 12% rate of return on the purchase price if the payments are received as expected.

✓ **SOLUTION**

a. According to the Valuation Principle,

$$\text{Price} = \text{Present value of } \$1000 + \text{Present value of } \$1500$$
$$= \frac{\$1000}{1 + 0.12\left(\frac{5}{12}\right)} + \frac{\$1500}{1 + 0.12\left(\frac{10}{12}\right)}$$
$$= \$952.38 + \$1363.64$$
$$= \$2316.02$$

An investor requiring a 12% rate of return should be willing to pay $2316.02 today for the contract.

b. Think of the $952.38 and $1363.64 components of the $2316.02 price as separately buying the future cash flows of $1000 and $1500, respectively.
   The sum of $952.38 invested for 5 months at 12% will grow to

$$S = P(1 + rt) = \$952.38\left[1 + 0.12\left(\frac{5}{12}\right)\right] = \$1000.00$$

Therefore, the $1000 payment received after 5 months returns the $952.38 investment along with 5 months' interest on $952.38 at 12%.
   Similarly, it can be shown that the $1500 payment received after 10 months returns the $1363.64 component of the initial investment plus 10 months' interest on $1363.64 at 12%.   ■

■ **EXAMPLE 7.2B** *VALUATION OF AN INTEREST-EARNING OBLIGATION*

On March 1 Murray signed a contract to pay Anton or his designate $2000 plus interest at 8% pa on June 1, and $3000 plus interest at 8% pa on September 1. Anton sold the contract on May 1 at a price that will yield the buyer a 10% rate of return. What was the price?

☑ SOLUTION

According to the Valuation Principle, the price was the present value on May 1 of the two scheduled payments discounted at 10% pa.

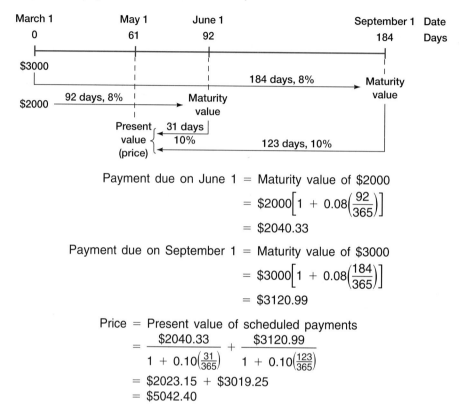

$$\text{Payment due on June 1} = \text{Maturity value of }\$2000$$
$$= \$2000\left[1 + 0.08\left(\frac{92}{365}\right)\right]$$
$$= \$2040.33$$

$$\text{Payment due on September 1} = \text{Maturity value of }\$3000$$
$$= \$3000\left[1 + 0.08\left(\frac{184}{365}\right)\right]$$
$$= \$3120.99$$

$$\text{Price} = \text{Present value of scheduled payments}$$
$$= \frac{\$2040.33}{1 + 0.10\left(\frac{31}{365}\right)} + \frac{\$3120.99}{1 + 0.10\left(\frac{123}{365}\right)}$$
$$= \$2023.15 + \$3019.25$$
$$= \$5042.40$$

The buyer paid $5042.40 for the contract.   ■

EXERCISE 7.2

Answers to the odd-numbered problems are at the end of the book.

1. An investment promises two payments of $500, on dates 3 and 6 months from today. If the required return on investment is 9% pa:
   a. What is the price of the investment today?
   b. What will its price be in 1 month if the required return remains at 9%?
   c. Give an explanation for the change in price as time passes.

2. An investment promises two payments of $1000, on dates 60 and 90 days from today. What price will an investor pay today:
   a. If her required return is 10% pa?
   b. If her required return is 11% pa?
   c. Give an explanation for the lower price at the higher required return.

3. Certificate A pays $1000 in 4 months and another $1000 in 8 months. Certificate B pays $1000 in 5 months and another $1000 in 9 months. If the current rate of return required

on this type of investment certificate is 5.75% pa, determine the current value of each of the certificates. Give an explanation for the lower price of B.

4. A contract requires payments of $1500, $2000, and $1000 in 100, 150, and 200 days, respectively, from today. What is the value of the contract today if the payments are discounted to yield a 10.5% pa rate of return?

5. An agreement stipulates payments of $4000, $2500, and $5000 in 3, 6, and 9 months, respectively, from today. What is the highest price an investor will offer today to purchase the agreement if he requires a minimum rate of return of 9.25% pa?

•6. An assignable loan contract executed 3 months ago requires two payments of $1800 plus interest at 10% pa on each $1800 from the date of the contract, to be paid 5 and 10 months after the contract date. The payee is offering to sell the contract to a finance company in order to raise cash. If the finance company requires a return of 15% pa, what price will it be prepared to pay today for the contract?

•7. Claude Scales, a commercial fisherman, bought a new navigation system for $10,000 from Coast Marine Electronics on March 20. He paid $2000 in cash and signed a conditional sales contract requiring a payment on July 1 of $3000 plus interest on the $3000 at 11% pa, and another payment on September 1 of $5000 plus interest at 11% pa from the date of the sale. The vendor immediately sold the contract to a finance company, which discounted the payments at its required return of 16% pa. What proceeds did Coast Marine receive from the sale of the contract?

7.3 TREASURY BILLS AND COMMERCIAL PAPER

Treasury bills are promissory notes issued by the federal government and most provincial governments to borrow money for short terms. Treasury bill (T-bill) denominations (face values) of $1000, $5000, $25,000, $100,000, and $1,000,000 are available. The government does not pay interest on the face value to a T-bill investor; it promises only to pay the full face value to the investor at maturity. In that sense Treasury bills are *non-interest-bearing notes.* Investors obtain a return on their investment by paying just the present value of the face value, consistent with the Valuation Principle. The difference between the face value and the discounted price will provide a rate of return on the purchase price equal to the discount rate employed in the present-value calculation.

A few billion dollars' worth of new 91-day, 182-day, and 364-day maturity[7] Government of Canada Treasury bills are sold every Tuesday by the Bank of Canada, acting as the agent for the federal government. The main buyers in this primary issue of T-bills are large financial institutions—mainly chartered banks and investment dealers.[8] The financial institutions that purchase the Treasury bills sell most of them to client investors—individuals, corporations, mutual funds, and so on.

---

[7]No days of grace are allowed on Treasury bills or on commercial paper.

[8]These financial institutions submit price bids just prior to each week's auction. The prices in the bids are calculated using the Valuation Principle. The institutions use their own required rate of return as the discount rate when determining the present value of the expected cash receipt (the face value). An institution arrives at its required rate of return based on the knowledge of the previous week's successful bids, the expected demand for T-bills from its clients, and informed opinions on the trend of short-term interest rates. If the bid is accepted, the discount rate used will become the rate of interest earned on the T-bill investment. The Bank of Canada accepts bids in the order of decreasing prices until the government's borrowing requirements for the week are met. Reserve bids submitted by the Bank of Canada itself serve to influence minimum prices (and maximum discount rates). The average rate of return on successful bids in each maturity category sets a very important benchmark rate of return for the financial markets. It represents the market-determined rate of return for an essentially riskfree investment having that maturity.

There is an active market for the sale/purchase of T-bills that are partway through their terms. On any day, the price at which a T-bill may be sold or bought is the present value of the face value, discounted at the *current* market-determined rate over the *time remaining* until maturity. Typical market rates for a few maturities are listed in the financial pages each day.

Some large corporations also borrow money for short periods by selling promissory notes, called **commercial paper,** through investment dealers. Common maturities are 30, 60, and 90 days. The minimum face value is usually $100,000. These notes are also non-interest-bearing and are priced at their discounted present value.[9]

■ **EXAMPLE 7.3A**   *VALUATION OF A T-BILL ON ITS ISSUE DATE*

Suppose the average rate of return or yield on 182-day Government of Canada Treasury bills sold at a Tuesday auction was 7.21% pa. At this yield, what price would be paid for a $25,000 face value T-bill?

☑ SOLUTION

Price = Present value of $25,000 discounted at 7.21% for 182 days

$$= \frac{\$25,000}{1 + 0.0721\left(\frac{182}{365}\right)}$$

$$= \$24,132.14$$

To yield 7.21%, $24,132.14 would be paid for the 182-day, $25,000 face value T-bill.

■

■ **EXAMPLE 7.3B**   *VALUATION OF A T-BILL*

The institutional purchaser of the T-bill in Example 7.3A might sell it to a client at a higher price that yields the client 7.01% pa. What profit would the institution make on the transaction?

☑ SOLUTION

$$\text{Selling price to client} = \frac{\$25,000}{1 + 0.0701\left(\frac{182}{365}\right)} = \$24,155.66$$

$$\begin{aligned}\text{Profit} &= \text{Price charged to client} - \text{Acquisition price} \\ &= \$24,155.66 - \$24,132.41 \\ &= \$23.25\end{aligned}$$

The institution's profit on the resale of the T-bill would be $23.25.

■

■ **EXAMPLE 7.3C**   *CALCULATION OF THE RATE OF RETURN ON A T-BILL SOLD BEFORE MATURITY*

Suppose the client who purchased the 182-day, $25,000 T-bill in Example 7.3B for $24,155.66 sold the T-bill after holding it for 73 days in order to invest the proceeds elsewhere.

---

[9]The required rate of return (discount rate) on commercial paper is usually 0.1% to 0.2% higher than that on Treasury bills. The higher rate of return is required because of the small risk that the corporation might not be able to pay the face value on the due date.

a. What price will she receive if the short-term rate for this maturity had risen to 7.58% pa by the date of sale?

b. What rate of return (per annum) did she realize while holding the T-bill?

☑ SOLUTION

a. Days remaining to maturity = 182 − 73 = 109

Selling price = Present value of $25,000 discounted at 7.58% for 109 days

$$= \frac{\$25,000}{1 + 0.0758\left(\frac{109}{365}\right)}$$

$$= \$24,446.62$$

The client sold the T-bill for $24,446.62.

b. We want the rate of return when $24,155.66 grows to $24,446.62 in 73 days. In effect, the initial investment of $24,155.66 earned interest amounting to

$$I = \$24,446.62 - \$24,155.66 = \$290.96$$

Formula (6–1) may now be used to obtain the corresponding rate of return.

$$r = \frac{I}{Pt} = \frac{\$290.96}{\$24,155.66\left(\frac{73}{365}\right)} = 0.06023 = 6.023\%$$

The client's rate of return *during the holding period* was only 6.023% pa. This is lower than the yield (7.01% in Example 7.3B) she would realize if she held the T-bill until its maturity. To enable the new purchaser to realize a rate of return (7.58% pa) greater than 7.01% pa during the remaining 109 days, the first investor must accept a yield lower than 7.01% pa for the first 73 days. ∎

■ EXAMPLE 7.3D *CALCULATION OF THE RATE OF RETURN ON COMMERCIAL PAPER*

Sixty-day commercial paper with face value $100,000 was issued by the Nova Corporation of Alberta for $98,940. What rate of return will be realized if the paper is held through to maturity?

☑ SOLUTION

In effect, the interest earned on an investment of $98,940 for 60 days is

$$\$100,000 - \$98,940 = \$1060$$

Using formula (6–1) rearranged to solve for *r*, we have

$$r = \frac{I}{Pt} = \frac{\$1060}{\$98,940\left(\frac{60}{365}\right)} = 0.06517 = 6.517\%$$

A 6.517% rate of return will be realized if the paper is held until it matures. ∎

EXERCISE 7.3

Answers to the odd-numbered problems are at the end of the book.

1. Calculate the price of a $25,000, 91-day Province of British Columbia Treasury bill on its issue date if the current market rate of return is 7.672% pa.

2. Calculate the price on its issue date of $100,000 face value, 90-day commercial paper issued by Northern Telecom Limited if the prevailing market rate of return is 8.560% pa.

3. A money market mutual fund purchased Montreal Trustco Inc. 90-day commercial paper with $1 million face value 28 days after its issue. What price was paid if the paper was discounted at 7.10% pa?

4. A $100,000, 91-day Province of Ontario Treasury bill was issued 37 days ago. What will it sell at today in order to yield the purchaser 8.12% pa?

5. Calculate (to the nearest dollar) and compare the issue date prices of $100,000 face value commercial paper investments with 30-, 60-, and 90-day maturities, all priced to yield 8% pa.

6. Calculate (to the nearest dollar) and compare the market values of a $100,000, 91-day Government of Canada Treasury bill on dates that are 91 days, 61 days, 31 days, and 1 day before maturity. Assume that the return required in the market stays constant at 7% pa over the lifetime of the T-bill.

7. A $100,000, 90-day commercial paper certificate issued by Noranda Inc. was sold on its issue date for $98,245. What rate of return (to four significant figures) will it yield to the buyer?

•8. A 182-day, $100,000 T-bill was initially issued at a price that would yield the buyer 6.2% pa. If the yield required by the market remains at 6.2%, how many days before its maturity date will the T-bill's market price first exceed $99,000?

•9. An investor purchased a 182-day, $25,000 Province of Alberta Treasury bill on its date of issue for $24,010 and sold it 60 days later for $24,425.

   a. What rate of return was implied in the original price?

   b. What rate of return did the market require on the sale date?

   c. What rate of return did the original investor actually realize during the 60-day holding period?

•10. A $100,000, 182-day Government of Canada Treasury bill was purchased on its date of issue to yield 8.5% pa.

   a. What price did the investor pay?

   b. Calculate the market value of the T-bill 85 days later if the rate of return then required by the market has:
   (i) Risen to 9%.   (ii) Remained at 8.5%.   (iii) Fallen to 8%.

   c. Calculate the rate of return actually realized by the investor if the T-bill is sold at each of the three prices calculated in part b.

*7.4 Savings Accounts, Term Deposits, and Short-Term GICs

Banks, trust companies, and credit unions use the simple-interest method for computing the interest that they pay to depositors and investors on a variety of savings accounts and short-term investment products. The most common arrangement for savings accounts is to *calculate* interest on each day's closing balance and to *pay* the interest at month's end. For some accounts there is a graduated scale of interest rates, with higher rates paid when the account's balance reaches certain higher levels. The interest rates are floating; they are adjusted to roughly follow the trend of short-term rates in the financial markets. A few savings and chequing accounts pay interest monthly or semiannually on the *minimum monthly* balance.

Deposit-taking financial institutions also offer two types of short-term investments paying a *fixed rate* of simple interest for the *fixed term* of the investment. *Term deposits* (sometimes called *certificates of deposit*) may be purchased with terms of 30 days to 1 year. Generally speaking, higher interest rates are paid for longer maturities and larger investments. The interest is paid on the maturity date. The investor can redeem or "cash in" the term deposit before maturity but will be penalized by receiving a significantly lower interest rate for the partial term.

The second type of short-term investment is the *Guaranteed Investment Certificate,* usually referred to as a GIC. A GIC is usually issued by a mortgage-lending subsidiary of a bank or trust company and is *unconditionally guaranteed* by the parent company. The Canada Deposit Insurance Corporation also guarantees up to $60,000 per investor. The main difference between term deposits and short-term GICs from an investor's point of view is that GICs are *nonredeemable:* the investor cannot cash in a GIC before its maturity date. Consequently, a GIC pays a higher rate of interest than a term deposit having the same principal and term because the financial institution is assured of the use of the funds for the full term.

■ **EXAMPLE 7.4A** *SAVINGS ACCOUNT INTEREST BASED ON A GRADUATED INTEREST RATE*

Mr. and Mrs. Hernandez have a Performance 55 bank account that pays a slightly higher rate to depositors age 55 or older. Interest is calculated on the daily closing balance and paid monthly as follows:

Portion of balance	Interest rate
From 0 to $1000.00	3.50%
From $1000.01 to $3000.00	3.75
Over $3000.00	4.50

On April 1 their balance was $1416.32. They withdrew $500 on April 9, deposited $1200 on April 15, and deposited another $1200 on April 29. Calculate the interest that they will be paid for the month of April.

☑ **SOLUTION**

The following table organizes the given information in preparation for the interest calculation:

Period	Number of days	Balance	Amount subject to a rate of: 3.5%	3.75%	4.50%
April 1–8	8	$1416.32	$1000.00	$ 416.32	—
April 9–14	6	916.32	916.32	—	—
April 15–28	14	2116.32	1000.00	1116.32	—
April 29–30	2	3316.32	1000.00	2000.00	$316.32

The interest earned for the period April 1 to 8 inclusive is

$$I(\text{April } 1\text{–}8) = P_1 r_1 t + P_2 r_2 t$$
$$= (P_1 r_1 + P_2 r_2)t$$
$$= [\$1000.00(0.035) + \$416.32(0.0375)]\left(\frac{8}{365}\right)$$
$$= (\$35.00 + \$15.61)(0.021918)$$
$$= \$1.109$$

Similarly,

$$I(\text{April } 9\text{–}14) = \$916.32(0.035)\left(\frac{6}{365}\right) = \$0.527$$

$$I(\text{April } 15\text{–}28) = [\$1000.00(0.035) + \$1116.32(0.0375)]\left(\frac{14}{365}\right)$$
$$= (\$35.00 + \$41.86)(0.038356)$$
$$= \$2.948$$

$$I(\text{April } 29\text{–}30) = [\$1000(0.035) + \$2000(0.0375) + \$316.32(0.045)]\left(\frac{2}{365}\right)$$
$$= (\$35.00 + \$75.00 + \$14.23)(0.005479)$$
$$= \$0.681$$

$$\text{Total interest for April} = \$1.109 + \$0.527 + \$2.948 + \$0.681 = \$5.27$$

Mr. and Mrs. Hernandez will earn $5.27 interest in April.   ■

■ EXAMPLE 7.4B   CALCULATION OF INTEREST ON A TERM DEPOSIT

A credit union pays an interest rate of 4.25% pa on term deposits of $5000 to $99,999 with terms of 30 to 179 days. If the term deposit is redeemed before maturity, the interest rate is reduced to 3%. Edith made a term deposit of $25,000 for 150 days.

a. How much will she be paid at the maturity date?

b. How much will she receive if she redeems the deposit after 95 days?

☑ SOLUTION

a. Maturity value, $S = P(1 + rt)$ Using formula (6–2)

$$= \$25,000\left[1 + 0.0425\left(\frac{150}{365}\right)\right]$$
$$= \$25,436.64$$

Edith will receive $25,436.64 on the maturity date of the term deposit.

b. She will receive the principal plus 95 days' interest at 3.0% pa.

$$\text{Redemption amount} = \$25,000\left[1 + 0.03\left(\frac{95}{365}\right)\right] = \$25,195.21$$

Upon early redemption after 95 days, Edith will be paid $25,195.21.   ■

EXERCISE 7.4

Answers to the odd-numbered problems are at the end of the book.

1. *a.* What will be the maturity value of $15,000 placed in a 120-day term deposit paying an interest rate of 5.25% pa?

    b. If on the maturity date the proceeds are "rolled over" into a 90-day term deposit paying 4.75% pa, what amount will the depositor receive when the second term deposit matures?

2. For amounts between $10,000 and $24,999, a credit union pays a rate of 5% pa on term deposits with maturities in the 91- to 120-day range. However, early redemption will result in a rate of 3.25% pa being applied. How much more interest will a 91-day, $20,000 term deposit earn if it is held until maturity than if it is redeemed after 80 days?

3. For 90- to 365-day GICs, the Toronto-Dominion Bank offered a rate of 6.000% on investments of $25,000 to $59,999 and a rate of 6.375% on investments of $60,000 to $99,999. How much more will an investor earn from a single $60,000, 270-day GIC than from two $30,000, 270-day GICs?

4. On the same date, a bank offered interest rates of 6.75% on a $10,000, 1-year GIC and 6.000% on a $10,000, 180- to 269-day GIC. How much more will an investor earn from the 1-year GIC than from consecutive 183-day and 182-day GICs? (Assume that interest rates on 180- to 269-day GICs are the same at the renewal date as they are today. Remember that interest earned from the first, 183-day GIC can be invested in the second, 182-day GIC.)

5. For investments of $5000 to $24,999, a bank quotes interest rates of 5.75% on 90-day GICs and 6.00% on 180-day GICs. How much more interest will an investor earn by placing $15,000 in a 180-day GIC than by purchasing two consecutive 90-day GICs? (Assume that interest rates do not change over the next 90 days. Remember that interest earned from the first 90-day GIC can be invested in the second 90-day GIC.)

•6. Suppose that the current rates on 90- and 180-day GICs are 6.25% and 6.50%, respectively. An investor is weighing the alternatives of purchasing a 180-day GIC versus purchasing a 90-day GIC and then reinvesting its maturity value in a second 90-day GIC. What would the interest rate on 90-day GICs have to be 90 days from now for the investor to end up in the same financial position with either alternative?

•7. Joan has savings of $12,000 on June 1. Since she may need some of the savings during the next 3 months, she is considering two options at her bank. An Investment Builder savings account earns a 4.00% rate of interest on the entire balance for balances between $10,000 and $24,999. The interest is calculated on the daily closing balance and paid on the first day of the following month. A redeemable 90- to 179-day term deposit of the same amount earns interest at the rate of 4.2%, paid at maturity. If the interest rate on the savings account does not change during the next 3 months and Joan does not withdraw any of the funds, how much more interest will she earn from the term deposit up to September 1? (Keep in mind that savings account interest paid on the first day of the month will itself subsequently earn interest.)

8. A savings account pays interest of 3.5% pa. Interest is calculated on the daily closing balance and paid at the close of business on the last day of the month. A depositor had a $2239 opening balance on September 1, deposited $734 on September 7 and $627 on September 21, and withdrew $300 on both September 10 and September 21. What interest will be credited to the account at the month's end?

•9. An Investment Savings account offered by a trust company pays a rate of 3.25% on the first $1000 of daily closing balance, 4% on the portion of the balance between $1000 and $3000, and 4.5% on any balance in excess of $3000. What interest will be paid for the month of April if the opening balance was $2439, $950 was deposited on April 10, and $500 was withdrawn on April 23?

10. The Moneybuilder account offered by a chartered bank calculates interest daily based on the daily closing balance as follows:

Interest rate (%)	Amount to which the rate applies
0.00	Balance when it is below $1000
3.25	Entire balance when it is between $1000 and $3000
4.00	Portion of balance above $3000

The balance at the beginning of March was $1678. On March 5, $700 was withdrawn. Then $2500 was deposited on March 15, and $900 was withdrawn on March 23. What interest will be credited to the account for the month of March?

•11. The Super Savings account offered by a trust company calculates interest daily based on the *lesser* of each day's opening or closing balance as follows:

Interest rate (%)	Amount to which the rate applies
3.00	Entire balance when it is between $0 and $2999.99
3.75	Entire balance when it is between $3000 and $4999.99
3.90	Entire balance when it is between $5000 and $9999.99
4.02	Entire balance when it is between $10,000 and $24,999.99
5.09	Entire balance when it is between $25,000 and $49,999.99
5.50	Entire balance when it is $50,000 or more

September's opening balance was $8572. The transactions in the account for the month were a $9500 deposit on September 6, a deposit of $8600 on September 14, and a withdrawal of $25,000 on September 23. What interest will be credited to the account at the end of September?

•12. On the same day, a bank advertised the following interest rates for investments of $5000 to $25,000 with 120- to 179-day maturities:
(i) 3.50% on fully redeemable term deposits.
(ii) 4.0% on term deposits that pay only 3.0% upon early redemption.
(iii) 5.75% on nonredeemable guaranteed investment certificates.
For a $20,000 investment with a 150-day term:

a. What is the dollar differential between alternatives (i) and (ii) if redemption does take place on day 120?

b. What is the dollar differential between alternatives (i) and (ii) if redemption does not occur?

c. What dollar amount of interest is sacrificed over the full 150-day term by maintaining full redemption privileges in alternative (i) versus no redemption privileges in alternative (iii)?

7.5 DEMAND LOANS

A high proportion of businesses obtain demand loans to meet short-term financing requirements. Many individuals obtain personal lines of credit which are set up on a demand basis.

COMMON TERMS AND CONDITIONS

The name **demand loan** derives from the fact that the lender is entitled to demand full repayment of the loan at any time without notice. This rarely happens if payments are made as agreed, unless the lender has reason to believe that the financial condition of the borrower is deteriorating. The borrower may repay any portion of the loan at any time without penalty.

The rate of interest charged on demand loans is usually variable—it is typically linked to the prime rate of interest in the banking system and quoted as "prime plus" some additional amount. A small business viewed by the lender as a moderate risk might be charged a rate of prime plus 2% or 3%. An interest rate that is tied to the prime rate is often described as a *floating rate* of interest since it rises and falls with the prime lending rate set by the chartered banks.

Interest on a demand loan is normally paid on the same day each month. It is calculated using the simple-interest method based on the daily closing loan balance and on the interest rate in effect each day.

Arrangements for repaying the loan principal are negotiated between the borrower and the lender. Acceptable terms will depend upon the purpose of the loan, the nature of the security given, and the seasonality of the business. The two most common demand loan arrangements are:

- A revolving or operating loan.
- A blended-payment loan.

Two other arrangements—the straight-line loan and the fixed-percentage-payment loan—are presented in Appendix 7B.

REVOLVING LOANS

Firms in seasonal lines of business have varying short-term financing requirements during the year. Their maximum requirement typically occurs when inventories are accumulated for the period of highest sales volume. The short-term financing is later paid down as sales from inventory generate cash receipts in excess of cash disbursements. Businesses usually obtain a revolving loan (or a revolving line of credit) to satisfy such a seasonal financing requirement. The principal amount of a **revolving loan** can fluctuate within a maximum credit limit.

Negotiations between the business and the lending institution establish the terms and conditions of the loan—the credit limit, the security required, the interest rate, and so on. Subject to the credit limit and a few general guidelines, draws (or advances) of principal and repayments of principal are at the discretion of the management of the business.

The business is required to have a current chequing account with the lending institution. Accrued interest is deducted from the borrower's account on the same day each month. Interest is calculated using the simple-interest method based on the daily closing loan balance and on the interest rate in effect each day.

■ **EXAMPLE 7.5A** *CALCULATION OF INTEREST ON A REVOLVING LOAN*

On March 20 Hank's Cycle Shop received an initial advance of $10,000 on its revolving demand loan. On the 15th of each month, interest is calculated (up to but not including the 15th) and deducted from Hank's current account. The floating rate of interest started at 9.75% and dropped to 9.5% on April 5. On April 19, another $10,000 was drawn on the line of credit. What interest was charged to the current account on April 15 and May 15?

☑ **SOLUTION**

The period between interest payment dates must be broken into intervals within which the balance on the loan and the interest rate are constant. In the following table, the dates bracketing each interval are quoted mindful of the convention of counting the first day but not the last.

Interval	Principal	Rate	Amount of interest
March 20–April 5	$10,000	9.75%	$10,000(0.0975)$\left(\frac{16}{365}\right)$ = $42.74
April 5–April 15	10,000	9.5	$10,000(0.095)$\left(\frac{10}{365}\right)$ = 26.03
			Interest charged on April 15: $68.77
April 15–April 19	10,000	9.5	$10,000(0.095)$\left(\frac{4}{365}\right)$ = $ 10.41
April 19–May 15	20,000	9.5	$20,000(0.095)$\left(\frac{26}{365}\right)$ = 135.34
			Interest charged on May 15: $145.75

The interest charged to the current account was $68.77 on April 15 and $145.75 on May 15. ■

REVOLVING LOAN REPAYMENT SCHEDULE   A **loan repayment schedule** is a table presenting a record of interest charges, loan payments, and outstanding balances. It enables the lender to systematically record the data needed to calculate the interest charges and to properly allocate payments to interest and principal. The schedule provides both a detailed record of past payments and the current status of the loan.

Figure 7.4 presents a format designed for revolving loans. A row is entered in the schedule when any of the following three events takes place:

- A payment of interest or principal is made.
- The interest rate changes.
- A principal amount is advanced.

FIGURE 7.4

Revolving Loan Repayment Schedule

(1)	(2)	(3)	(4)	(5)	(6)	(7)	(8)
Date	Number of days	Interest rate	Interest	Accrued interest	Interest charged to account	Principal repaid (advanced)	Balance

The columns in the table are used as follows. (Each item refers to the corresponding numbered column in Figure 7.4.)

(1) Record the date on which a payment is made, the interest rate changes, or an additional amount of principal is advanced to the borrower.

(2) Enter the number of days in the interval ending on the date in column (1). This is the number of days from (and including) the *previous* row's date to (but not including) the *current* row's date.

(3) Enter the interest rate that applies to the interval in column (2). On the date of a change in the interest rate, the entry will be the *old rate* since the days in column (2) refer to the period *up to but not including* the date in column (1).

(4) Enter the interest charge for the number of days in column (2) at the interest rate in column (3) on the balance from column (8) of the preceding line.

(5) Enter the cumulative total of unpaid or accrued interest as of the current date. This amount is the interest just calculated for column (4) plus any previously accrued but unpaid interest from the preceding line.

(6) If the date in the first column is an interest payment date, the accrued interest in column (5) is paid from the borrower's current account. Record the amount paid in column (6). Put a single stroke through the accrued interest in column (5) as a reminder that it should not be carried forward to the next period.

(7) This column is used both for loan advances and for payments applied against the principal. In loan repayment schedules, payments that reduce the principal balance are entered as positive numbers. Therefore, a loan advance is enclosed in parentheses to distinguish it from a loan payment.

(8) The new loan balance is the previous line's balance reduced by any principal repaid or increased by any principal advanced per the column (7) entry.

■ EXAMPLE 7.5B *REPAYMENT SCHEDULE: REVOLVING LOAN*

The Bank of Montreal approved a $50,000 line of credit on a demand basis to Tanya's Wardrobes to finance the store's inventory. Interest at the rate of prime plus 3% was calculated and charged to Tanya's current account at the bank on day 23 of each month. The initial advance was $25,000 on September 23, when the prime rate stood at 8.25%. There were further advances of $8000 on October 30 and $10,000 on November 15. Payments of $7000 and $14,000 were applied against the principal on December 15 and January 15, respectively. The prime rate rose to 8.75% effective December 5. What was the total interest paid on the loan for the period September 23 to January 23?

☑ SOLUTION

A large amount of information is given in the statement of the problem. The best way to organise the data is to construct a repayment schedule using the model in Figure 7.4. In the date column, list in chronological order all the dates on which a transaction or an event affecting the loan occurs. These will be the dates of advances, payments of principal or interest, and interest rate changes. Next enter the information that is given for each transaction or event. At this point the schedule will have the following entries.

Date	Number of days	Interest rate	Interest	Accrued interest	Interest charged to account	Principal repaid (advanced)	Balance
Sept 23	—	—	—	—	—	($25,000)	$25,000
Oct 23		11.25%					
Oct 30		11.25				(8000)	
Nov 15		11.25				(10,000)	
Nov 23		11.25					
Dec 5		11.25					
Dec 15		11.75				7000	
Dec 23		11.75					
Jan 15		11.75				14,000	
Jan 23		11.75					

Note that 11.25% has been entered on the December 5 line. Although the interest rate changes to 11.75% effective December 5, the "Number of days" column will contain the figure for the number of days from (and including) November 23 to (but not including) December 5. These 13 days are still charged interest at the 11.25% rate. The 11.75% rate will first apply to the December 5–December 15 period, which is handled on the December 15 line.

The "Number of days" column may be completed next. Then the calculations can proceed row by row to obtain the full schedule. The circled numbers (①, ②, etc.) in the following schedule refer to the sample calculations listed below the schedule.

Date	Number of days	Interest rate	Interest	Accrued interest	Interest charged to account	Principal repaid (advanced)	Balance
Sept 23	—	—	—	—	—	($25,000)	$25,000
Oct 23	30	11.25%	$231.16①	$231.16	$ 231.16		25,000
Oct 30	7	11.25	53.94	53.94		(8000)	33,000
Nov 15	16	11.25	162.74②	216.68③		(10,000)	43,000
Nov 23	8	11.25	106.03④	322.71⑤	322.71		43,000
Dec 5	12	11.25	159.04	159.04			43,000
Dec 15	10	11.75	138.42	297.46		7000	36,000
Dec 23	8	11.75	92.71	390.17	390.17		36,000
Jan 15	23	11.75	266.55	266.55		14,000	22,000
Jan 23	8	11.75	56.66	323.21	323.21		22,000

Total: $1267.25

①$I = Prt = \$25,000(0.1125)\left(\frac{30}{365}\right) = \$231.16$

②$I = \$33,000(0.1125)\left(\frac{16}{365}\right) = \$162.74$

③Accrued interest = $\$53.94 + \$162.74 = \$216.68$

④$I = \$43,000(0.1125)\left(\frac{8}{365}\right) = \$106.03$

⑤Accrued interest = $\$216.68 + \$106.03 = \$322.71$

The total interest paid on the loan to January 23 was $1267.25. ■

BLENDED-PAYMENT LOANS

An arrangement for regular payments requiring *equal* payments of *combined* principal and interest is called a **blended-payment loan.** The interest component of each payment is the interest that has accrued on the outstanding principal balance since the preceding regular payment. As the balance remaining on the loan declines, each successive payment consists of a smaller interest component and a larger principal component. If the interest rate is variable, the date on which the loan will be fully repaid cannot be predicted with certainty. A rise in the interest rate will make the interest components of subsequent payments larger and the principal components correspondingly smaller. More time may then be required to pay off the loan.

BLENDED-PAYMENT LOAN REPAYMENT SCHEDULE Two modifications to the schedule in Figure 7.4 make it better suited to blended-payment loans. The changes are reflected in Figure 7.5. On loan payment dates, the amount of the regular blended payment is entered in column (6). The principal portion of the payment is then entered in column (7). The principal portion is simply the payment in column (6) minus the accrued interest in column (5). The new loan balance entered in column (8) is the previous balance minus the principal portion of the payment.

FIGURE   7.5

Blended-Payment Loan Repayment Schedule

(1) Date	(2) Number of days	(3) Interest rate	(4) Interest	(5) Accrued interest	(6) Payment made	(7) Principal portion	(8) Balance

■ **EXAMPLE 7.5c**   *REPAYMENT SCHEDULE: BLENDED-PAYMENT LOAN*

Bailey & Co. borrowed $4000 at prime plus 1½% from their bank on May 29 to purchase a new computer. The variable-rate demand loan specified blended monthly payments of $800 on the first day of each month beginning July 1. The prime rate was at 7.25% on May 29 and increased to 7.5% effective August 4. Construct a full repayment schedule showing details of the allocation of each payment to interest and principal.

☑ SOLUTION

Begin a schedule modelled on Figure 7.5 by entering, in chronological order, the dates of payments and of interest rate changes. Information known about these events can also be entered. At this point, the schedule will have the following entries and you are ready to begin the calculations.

Date	Number of days	Interest rate	Interest	Accrued interest	Payment made	Principal portion	Balance
May 29	—	8.75%	—	—	—	—	$4000.00
July 1		8.75			$800		
Aug 1		8.75			800		
Aug 4		8.75					
Sept 1		9.00			800		
Oct 1		9.00			800		
Nov 1		9.00			800		
Dec 1		9.00					

The calculations then proceed row by row to construct the schedule. The circled numbers (①, ②, etc.) in the following schedule refer to the sample calculations listed below the schedule.

Date	Number of days	Interest rate	Interest	Accrued interest	Payment made	Principal portion	Balance
May 29	—	8.75%	—	—	—	—	$4000.00
July 1	33	8.75	$31.64 ①	$31.64	$800.00	$768.36 ②	3231.64 ③
Aug 1	31	8.75	24.02	24.02	800.00	775.98	2455.66
Aug 4	3	8.75	1.77	1.77			
Sept 1	28	9.00	16.95	18.72	800.00	781.28	1674.38
Oct 1	30	9.00	12.39	12.39	800.00	787.61	886.77
Nov 1	31	9.00	6.78	6.78	800.00	793.22	93.55
Dec 1	30	9.00	0.69	0.69	94.24 ④	93.55	0

① $I = Prt = \$4000(0.0875)\left(\dfrac{33}{365}\right) = \$31.64$

② Principal portion = $800 − $31.64 = $768.36

③ Balance = $4000 − $768.36 = $3231.64

④ Payment = $93.55 + $0.69 = $94.24

The interest portion of any payment is the accrued interest figure on the same line as the payment. (A stroke is drawn through an accrued interest figure when the interest is paid, as a reminder not to carry the interest forward into the next period.) ■

Point of Interest

Not Taking Enough Interest

Canada Trust offers a revolving line of credit on a demand basis called PowerLine. The floating interest rate that is charged on the loan depends on whether the loan is secured or unsecured. On fully secured loans the rate of interest is usually the prime rate. On unsecured loans over $2500 a premium of 2.25% to 2.75% over prime is typically charged.

The reverse side of the monthly statement received by the borrower quotes the interest rate applicable to the period covered by the current statement, and the rate that will apply on the next statement. For example, when the prime rate was at 6% the monthly statement indicated that, for fully secured accounts, "Interest is calculated at an annual rate of 6.00% (0.01643% per day)."

In a particular instance the interest charged on a $15,000 loan at 6% for 31 days was $76.39. Now that we know how to calculate interest on a demand loan, we can check this figure using formula (6–1):

$$I = Prt$$
$$= \$15,000 \times 0.06 \times \frac{31}{365}$$
$$= \$76.44$$

Our calculation indicates that Canada Trust should have charged $0.05 more interest. How can the discrepancy be explained? If we use the daily interest rate specified by Canada Trust, we obtain

$$I = Prt = \$15,000 \times 0.0001643 \times 31$$
$$= \$76.3995$$

where the result has not yet been rounded to the nearest cent. Therefore, we can obtain Canada Trust's interest charge of $76.39 if we use its quoted daily interest rate of 0.01643% *and truncate rather than round* the answer at the cent position. Truncating a number at a certain position simply means deleting all digits occurring beyond that position; unlike rounding, it does not increase the last retained digit by 1 if the first digit dropped is 5 or greater.

There must also be a discrepancy between the daily interest rate used by Canada Trust and the daily interest rate effectively employed by our own calculation. The daily interest rate corresponding to an annual rate of 6% is

$$\frac{6\%}{365} = 0.0164384\%$$

to six significant figures. It is now apparent that Canada Trust *truncates* the daily interest rate at the fourth significant figure before using it in the calculation of interest charges. Consequently, we can expect inaccuracy in the fourth figure of the computed interest charges. The imprecision will be to the benefit of the borrower because the truncated daily interest rate will always be smaller than the daily rate expressed to five or six significant figures. Therefore, Canada Trust is forgoing interest earnings to which it is entitled. With the interest rate at 6% per annum, it is forgoing interest at the rate of 0.0000084% per day.

Over all interest rates at 0.25% intervals between 6% and 11%, the average truncation error works out to 0.0000053% per day. This may seem to be a minuscule amount, but let us make a crude estimate of the dollar amount that it might represent for a whole year on Canada Trust's entire portfolio of demand loans.

Canada Trust's financial statements for the year ended December 31, 1995, show consumer and collateral loans totalling about $7.5 billion and nonmortgage loans to corporations amounting to $0.75 billion. If we assume that the monthly interest charges on all these loans are calculated in the same way as on PowerLine loans (using a daily interest rate truncated at four significant figures), the expected truncation error in the year's interest charges is

$$I = Prt$$
= Total loans × Truncation error in the daily rate × 365 days
$$= \$8,250,000,000 \times 0.000000053 \times 365$$
$$\doteq \$160,000$$

(continued)

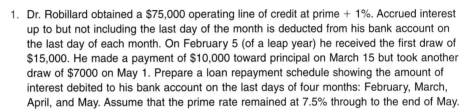

(concluded)

This magnitude of additional interest revenue would be realized annually by Canada Trust if six-figure accuracy were retained in the daily interest rates. Another few thousand dollars could be gained every year by *rounding* instead of *truncating* the dollar amount of interest at the penny.

EXERCISE 7.5

Answers to the odd-numbered problems are at the end of the book.

Some problems in this and later Exercises have spreadsheet icons in the left margin. Formatted spreadsheet templates are available for these problems on the diskette enclosed with the Student Solutions Manual.

REVOLVING DEMAND LOANS

1. Dr. Robillard obtained a $75,000 operating line of credit at prime + 1%. Accrued interest up to but not including the last day of the month is deducted from his bank account on the last day of each month. On February 5 (of a leap year) he received the first draw of $15,000. He made a payment of $10,000 toward principal on March 15 but took another draw of $7000 on May 1. Prepare a loan repayment schedule showing the amount of interest debited to his bank account on the last days of four months: February, March, April, and May. Assume that the prime rate remained at 7.5% through to the end of May.

2. Mr. Michaluk has a $50,000 personal (revolving) line of credit with the Canadian Imperial Bank of Commerce (CIBC). The loan is on a demand basis at a floating rate of prime plus 1.5%. Interest up to but not including the 15th of the month is deducted from his chequing account at the CIBC on the 15th of each month. The principal balance on September 15 was $23,465.72. Show the loan repayment schedule for the September 15–January 15 period, during which he made principal payments of $2000 on each of September 30 and November 14 but took a $2500 advance of principal on December 16. The prime rate of interest remained at 8.25% for the entire 4-month period.

3. McKenzie Wood Products negotiated a $200,000 revolving line of credit with the Bank of Montreal at prime plus 2%. On the 20th of each month, interest is calculated (up to but not including the 20th) and debited to the company's current account. If the initial draw of $25,000 on July 3 was followed by a further advance of $30,000 on July 29, how much interest was charged on July 20 and August 20? The prime rate was at 8% on July 3 and fell to 7.75% on August 5.

•4. On the June 12 interest payment date, the outstanding balance on Delta Nurseries' revolving loan was $65,000. The floating interest rate on the loan stood at 9.25% on June 12 but rose to 9.5% on July 3 and to 10% on July 29. If Delta made principal payments of $10,000 on June 30 and July 31, what were the interest charges to its current account on July 12 and August 12? Present a repayment schedule supporting the calculations.

•5. The Bank of Nova Scotia approved a $75,000 line of credit for Curved Comfort Furniture on the security of its accounts receivable. Curved Comfort drew down $30,000 on October 7, $15,000 on November 24, and $20,000 on December 23. The bank debited interest at the rate of prime plus 1.5% from the business's current account on the 15th of each month. The prime rate was 10.25% on October 7 and dropped by 0.25% on December 17. Present a loan repayment schedule showing details of transactions up to and including January 15.

•6. Shoreline Yachts has a $1 million line of credit with the Royal Bank secured by its inventory of sailboats. Interest is charged at the floating (naturally!) rate of prime plus 2% on the 10th of each month. On February 10 (of a non-leap year) the loan balance stood at $770,000 and the prime rate at 9.5%. Shoreline took an additional $100,000 on March 1.

Spring sales enabled Shoreline to make payments of $125,000 and $150,000 against the principal on March 30 and April 28. The prime rate rose by 0.5% on April 8. What total amount of interest was Shoreline charged for the period from February 10 to May 10? Present a repayment schedule showing how this interest figure was determined.

 •7.   Hercules Sports obtained a $60,000 operating line of credit on March 26. Interest charges at the rate of prime plus 2.5% were deducted from its current account on the 18th of each month. Hercules took an initial draw of $30,000 on March 31, when the prime rate was 8.25%. Further advances of $10,000 and $15,000 were taken on April 28 and June 1. Payments of $5000 and $10,000 were applied against the principal on June 18 and July 3. The prime rate rose to 8.5% effective May 14. Present a repayment schedule showing details of transactions up to and including July 18.

BLENDED-PAYMENT DEMAND LOANS

 8.   A $5000 demand loan was advanced on June 3. Blended monthly payments of $1000 were required on the first day of each month beginning July 1. Prepare the full repayment schedule for the loan. Assume that the interest rate remained at 12.5% for the life of the loan.

 •9.   Giovando, Lindstrom & Co. obtained a $6000 demand loan at prime plus 1.5% on April 1 to purchase new office furniture. The company agreed to blended monthly payments of $1000 on the first of each month beginning May 1. Calculate the total interest charges over the life of the loan if the prime rate started at 9.75% on April 1, decreased to 9.5% effective June 7, and returned to 9.75% on August 27.

 •10.   Dwayne borrowed $3500 from his credit union on a demand loan on July 20 to purchase a motorcycle. The terms of the loan require blended monthly payments of $700 on the first day of each month beginning September 1. The floating rate on the loan is prime plus 3%. The prime rate started at 8.25% but rose 0.5% on August 19 and another 0.25% effective November 2. Prepare a loan repayment schedule presenting the amount of each payment and the allocation of each payment to interest and principal.

 •11.   Beth borrowed $2500 on demand from Canada Trust on February 23 for a Registered Retirement Savings Plan (RRSP) contribution. Because she used the loan proceeds to purchase Canada Trust's mutual funds for her RRSP, she received a special interest rate of prime plus 0.5%. Beth was required to make blended monthly payments of $500 on the 15th of each month beginning April 15. The prime rate was initially 8.5%, but it jumped to 9% effective June 15 and increased another 0.25% on July 31. (It was not a leap year.) Construct a repayment schedule showing the amount of each payment and the allocation of each payment to interest and principal.

 •12.   Dr. Chan obtained a $15,000 demand loan at prime plus 1.5% on September 13 from the Toronto-Dominion Bank to purchase a new dental X-ray machine. Blended payments of $700 will be deducted from the dentist's current account on the 20th of each month, beginning October 20. The prime rate was 9.5% at the outset, dropped to 9.25% on the subsequent November 26, and rose to 9.75% on January 29. Prepare a loan repayment schedule showing the details of the first five payments.

*APPENDIX 7A: BANK DISCOUNT METHOD OF DISCOUNTING PROMISSORY NOTES

In recent years, the bank discount method for discounting promissory notes has been in declining use by financial institutions in Canada.[10] It is more commonly employed in

---

[10]The main reason for presenting the bank discount method here is that some accounting textbooks and courses still treat this method as though it is a common procedure for discounting notes receivable.

the United States, particularly to determine the market value of Treasury bills and corporate commercial paper.

Although it is now difficult to find instances of its use by Canadian banks, the name originates from a past practice used by banks to discount promissory notes. The effect of the bank discount calculation is to deliver the quoted rate of return *on the maturity value* of the note rather than on the price paid for the note.

To illustrate the difference between the simple discount and bank discount methods, consider a promissory note maturing in 1 year with a maturity value of $1000. Using a 10% discount rate, the proceeds today based on the simple discount method would be

$$\frac{\$1000}{1 + 0.1(1)} = \$909.09$$

When the maturity value of $1000 is received 1 year later, the $90.91 received in excess of the $909.09 purchase price provides a return of 10% on the amount invested.

The bank discount approach is to require the 10% rate of return on the $1000 maturity value rather than on the amount that will be paid for the note. A 10% rate of return on $1000 for 1 year translates into a $100 return. The buyer must therefore pay only $900 for the note. The actual rate of return on the amount invested will be

$$r = \frac{I}{Pt} = \frac{\$100}{\$900(1)} = 0.111 = 11.1\%$$

The bank discount method always produces a larger true rate of return than the nominal rate used in the calculation of the proceeds.

The following symbols will be used to derive a general formula for the proceeds of a note using the bank discount method:

S = Maturity value of the note
d = Rate of bank discount
t = Time remaining until the maturity of the note
P_b = Bank discount proceeds of the note

If the buyer of the note requires a rate of return d on the maturity value S for the time t, then the amount of the discount will have to be

$$\text{Maturity value} \times \text{Rate} \times \text{Time} = Sdt$$

The maturity value of the note must, therefore, exceed the price paid by Sdt. Hence,

$$S - P_b = Sdt$$

Solving for P_b,

$$P_b = S - Sdt = S(1 - dt)$$

Bank Discount Proceeds

$$\boxed{P_b = S(1 - dt)} \qquad (7\text{--}2)$$

In summary, the calculation of the proceeds from the sale of a note using the bank discount method involves two steps similar to those used in the simple discount method. The two steps and the formulas involved are depicted in Figure 7.6. The maturity value of the note is calculated first. Then the maturity value is discounted to the date of sale to calculate the proceeds. The difference between the two methods of discounting a promissory note arises in the second step. Formula (7–2) is used for the bank discount proceeds, whereas formula (7–1) is used for the simple discount proceeds.

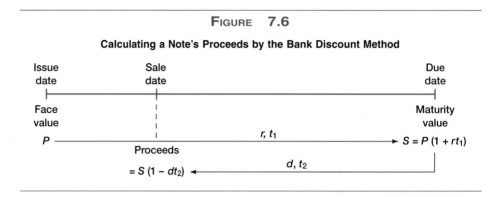

FIGURE   7.6

Calculating a Note's Proceeds by the Bank Discount Method

■ **EXAMPLE 7A**   *COMPARISON OF BANK DISCOUNT AND SIMPLE DISCOUNT PROCEEDS*

A 100-day note for $2350 dated December 17 bears interest at the rate of 10% pa. Calculate the proceeds of the note if it is discounted on January 24 at 12% pa:

a. Using the bank discount method.

b. Using the simple discount method.

c. What discount rate using the simple discount method would result in the same proceeds as in part *a?*

✓ SOLUTION

The note is discounted on January 24, 38 days after the date of issue. Sixty-five days (100 + 3 − 38) remain until the due date.

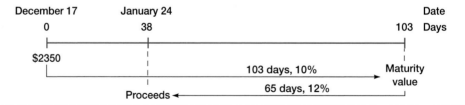

The calculation of the maturity value is not affected by the discount method used in the subsequent step.

$$\text{Maturity value} = \$2350\left[1 + 0.10\left(\frac{103}{365}\right)\right] = \$2416.32$$

a. Bank discount proceeds $= S(1 - dt)$

$$= \$2416.32\left[1 - 0.12\left(\frac{65}{365}\right)\right]$$

$$= \$2364.68$$

b. Simple discount proceeds $= \dfrac{S}{1 + rt}$

$$= \dfrac{\$2416.32}{1 + 0.12\left(\frac{65}{365}\right)}$$

$$= \$2365.76$$

For a given discount rate, the simple discount method is always preferred by the seller of the note since the proceeds are greater.

c. We now want to determine the discount rate that makes the simple discount proceeds equal to $2364.68. The dollar amount of the return to the purchaser of the note would be

$$\$2416.32 - \$2364.68 = \$51.64$$

The per annum rate of return on the $2364.68 investment during the 65-day holding period would be

$$r = \dfrac{I}{Pr} = \dfrac{\$51.64}{\$2364.68\left(\frac{65}{365}\right)} = 0.1226 = 12.26\%$$

Therefore, a discount rate of 12.26% used with the simple discount method is equivalent to 12% used with the bank discount method. ∎

*APPENDIX 7B: OTHER DEMAND LOANS

The two most common arrangements for structuring demand loans were discussed in Section 7.5. Two other arrangements are presented in this appendix.

STRAIGHT-LINE LOANS

Loans for a specific purpose, such as the acquisition of a capital asset, will typically require regular payments of principal. A **straight-line loan** requires *equal* monthly payments of principal *in addition to the interest* that has accrued since the last payment. The principal balance will then be reduced by the same amount each month. The loan will be fully repaid on a predetermined date even if the interest rate changes during the term of the loan.

For a repayment schedule, the format presented in Figure 7.5 works best. The main change in completing the schedule for a straight-line loan is that, at the outset, we know the (fixed) principal portion of each payment but not the full amount of each payment. (In a blended-payment case, we initially know the full amount of each fixed payment but not the principal portion of each payment.)

EXAMPLE 7B   *REPAYMENT SCHEDULE: STRAIGHT-LINE LOAN*

Sonia obtained a $10,000 variable-rate (prime plus 2%) demand loan on February 1 (of a leap year) to purchase a new car. She agreed to pay interest plus $900 toward principal on the first day of each month. The prime rate of interest was initially 10.5%, but it dropped to 10% on March 17 and fell another 0.5% on December 9. Construct a repayment schedule showing the first three and the last three payments.

▼ SOLUTION

Since the principal will be reduced by $900 each month, the principal balance will be $100 after the eleventh payment. Therefore, the loan will be fully repaid (or retired) after the twelfth payment, and the principal portion of the twelfth payment will be only $100.

Begin the schedule by entering, in chronological order, the dates of payments and of interest rate changes. Information known about these events can also be entered. At this point, the schedule will have the following entries and the calculations can begin.

Date	Number of days	Interest rate	Interest	Accrued interest	Payment made	Principal portion	Balance
Feb 1	—	12.5%				—	$10,000
March 1		12.5				$900	
March 17		12.5					
April 1		12				900	
May 1		12				900	
.		.				.	
.		.				.	
.		.				.	
Nov 1							
Dec 1		12				900	
Dec 9		12					
Jan 1		11.5				900	
Feb 1		11.5				100	

Proceed row by row to construct the schedule. The circled numbers (①, ②, etc.) within the schedule refer to the sample calculations listed below the schedule.

Date	Number of days	Interest rate	Interest	Accrued interest	Payment made	Principal portion	Balance
Feb 1	—	12.5%	—	—	—	—	$10,000
March 1	29	12.5	$99.32①	$99.32	$999.32②	$900	9100
March 17	16	12.5	49.86③	49.86			
April 1	15	12	44.88④	94.74⑤	994.74⑥	900	8200
May 1	30	12	80.88	80.88	980.88	900	7300
.	.	.	.	.	.	.	.
.	.	.	.	.	.	.	.
Nov 1							1900
Dec 1	30	12	18.74	18.74	918.74	900	1000
Dec 9	8	12	2.63	2.63			
Jan 1	23	11.5	7.25	9.88	909.88	900	100
Feb 1	31	11.5	0.98	0.98	100.98	100	0

① $I = Prt = \$10,000(0.125)\left(\dfrac{29}{365}\right) = \$99.32$

② Payment $= \$900.00 + \$99.32 = \$999.32$

③ $I = \$9100(0.125)\left(\dfrac{16}{365}\right) = \$49.86$

④ $I = \$9100(0.12)\left(\dfrac{15}{365}\right) = \$44.88$

⑤ Accrued interest $= \$49.86 + \$44.88 = \$94.74$

⑥ Payment $= \$900 + \$94.74 = \$994.74$

FIXED-PERCENTAGE-PAYMENT LOANS

The *minimum* monthly payment required on a revolving personal line of credit is sometimes specified as a percentage of the current balance on the loan. Three percent is commonly stated as the fixed percentage. The following example illustrates the calculations required to maintain a loan repayment schedule.

■ EXAMPLE 7C   *REPAYMENT SCHEDULE: FIXED-PERCENTAGE-PAYMENT LOAN*

Fiona and Luc St. Armand obtained a $75,000 line of credit from Canada Trust. Since the line of credit is on a demand basis and is fully secured by a mortgage on the St. Armand's home, they qualify for the best rate of interest available on a line of credit—the prime rate. On the 23rd of each month, the St. Armands must make a minimum payment of 3% of the balance owed on the loan.

On May 8 when the prime rate stood at 8%, the St. Armands took a first draw of $20,000. Effective June 15, the prime rate dropped by 0.25%. On July 3, they obtained a $10,000 draw, but later, on July 30, they applied a $5000 payment against the principal balance. Prepare a loan repayment schedule showing the allocation to interest and principal of the payments required on May 23, June 23, July 23, and August 23. Assume that the St. Armands made the minimum required payment on the 23rd of each month, and that the interest accrual each month is up to but not including the 23rd day.

☑ SOLUTION

Because of the revolving feature of the loan, we need to adapt the format of Figure 7.4 to construct the repayment schedule; accordingly, we change the title of column (6) to "Required payment" (see below), to reflect the fact that the minimum required payment is no longer just the accrued interest. Begin the schedule by entering, in chronological order, the dates of advances, payments, and interest rate changes. Then proceed row by row to construct the schedule. The circled numbers (①, ②, etc.) in the body of the schedule refer to the sample calculations listed below the schedule. The interest portion of each required payment is the amount of accrued interest on the payment date.

Date	Number of days	Interest rate	Interest	Accrued interest	Required payment	Principal repaid (advanced)	Balance
May 8	—	—	—	—	—	($ 20,000.00)	$20,000.00
May 23	15	8.00%	$ 65.75①	$ 65.75	$600.00②	534.25③	19,465.75④
June 15	23	8.00	98.13	98.13			
June 23	8	7.75	33.07	131.20	583.97	452.77	19,012.98
July 3	10	7.75	40.37	40.37		(10,000.00)	29,012.98
July 23	20	7.75	123.21	163.58	870.39	706.81	28,306.17
July 30	7	7.75	42.07	42.07		5000.00	23,306.17
Aug 23	24	7.75	118.77	160.84	699.19	538.35	22,767.82

① $I = Prt = \$20,000(0.08)\left(\frac{15}{365}\right) = \$65.75$
② Required payment = 0.03 (Current balance) = 0.03($20,000) = $600.00
③ Principal repaid = Required payment − Accrued interest = $600.00 − $65.75 = $534.25
④ Balance = $20,000 − $534.25 = $19,465.75

■

REVIEW PROBLEMS

Answers to the odd-numbered review problems are at the end of the book.

1. Calculate the maturity value of a $1500 face value, 4-month note dated December 31, 1997, and bearing interest at 9.5% pa.

2. A 4-month non-interest-bearing note issued on November 30, 1977, for $3300 was discounted at 7.25% on February 1. What were the proceeds of the note?

3. A 6-month note dated June 30 for $7900 bears interest at 7.5%. Determine the proceeds of the note if it is discounted at 9.75% on September 1.

4. An investor is prepared to buy short-term promissory notes at a price that will provide her with a return on investment of 12%. What amount would she pay on August 5 for a 150-day note dated June 18 for $5700 with interest at 8.25% pa?

5. An agreement stipulates payments of $4500, $3000, and $5500 in 4, 8, and 12 months, respectively, from today. What is the highest price an investor will offer today to purchase the agreement if he requires a minimum return of 10.5% pa?

•6. An assignable loan contract executed 3 months ago requires two payments of $3200 with interest at 9% from the date of the contract, to be paid 4 and 8 months after the contract date. The payee is offering to sell the contract to a finance company in order to raise urgently needed cash. If the finance company requires a return of 16% pa, what price will it be prepared to pay today for the contract?

7. Calculate the price of a $50,000, 91-day Province of Nova Scotia Treasury bill on its issue date if the current market rate of return is 6.773% pa.

8. A $100,000, 182-day Province of New Brunswick Treasury bill was issued 66 days ago. What will it sell at today to yield the purchaser 7.48%?

9. A $100,000, 90-day commercial paper certificate issued by Bell Canada was sold on its issue date for $98,450. What annual rate of return (to four significant figures) will it yield to the buyer?

•10. A $100,000, 182-day Government of Canada Treasury bill was purchased on its date of issue to yield 6.5% pa.

    a. What price did the investor pay?

    b. Calculate the market value of the T-bill 85 days later if the annual rate of return then required by the market has:
    (i) Risen to 7%.   (ii) Remained at 6.5%.   (iii) Fallen to 6%.

    c. Calculate the rate of return actually realized by the investor if the T-bill is sold at each of the three prices calculated in part *b*.

11. A chartered bank offers a rate of 5.500% on investments of $25,000 to $59,999 and a rate of 5.750% on investments of $60,000 to $99,999 in 90- to 365-day GICs. How much more will an investor earn from a single $80,000, 180-day GIC than from two $40,000, 180-day GICs?

•12. Suppose that the current rates on 60- and 120-day GICs are 5.50% and 5.75%, respectively. An investor is weighing the alternatives of purchasing a 120-day GIC versus purchasing a 60-day GIC and then reinvesting its maturity value in a second 60-day GIC. What would the interest rate on 60-day GICs have to be 60 days from now for the investor to end up in the same financial position with either alternative?

13. An Investment Savings account offered by a trust company pays a rate of 3.00% on the first $1000 of daily closing balance, 3.75% on the portion of the balance between $1000 and $3000, and 4.25% on any balance in excess of $3000. What interest will be paid for

the month of January if the opening balance was $3678, $2800 was withdrawn on the 14th of the month, and $950 was deposited on the 25th of the month?

•14. George borrowed $4000 on demand from the Royal Bank on January 28 for an RRSP contribution. Because he used the loan proceeds to purchase the Royal Bank's mutual funds for his RRSP, the interest rate on the loan was set at the bank's prime rate. George agreed to make blended monthly payments of $600 (except for a smaller final payment) on the 21st of each month beginning February 21. The prime rate was initially 6.75%, dropped to 6.5% effective May 15, and decreased another 0.25% on July 5. It was not a leap year. Construct a repayment schedule showing the amount of each payment and the allocation of each payment to interest and principal.

•15. Mayfair Fashions has a $90,000 line of credit from the Bank of Montreal. Interest at prime plus 2% is debited from Mayfair's current account on the 24th of each month. Mayfair initially drew down $40,000 on March 8 and another $15,000 on April 2. On June 5, $25,000 of principal was repaid. If the prime rate was 8.25% on March 8 and rose by 0.25% effective May 13, what were the first four interest debits charged to the store's account?

SELF-TEST EXERCISE

Answers to the self-test problems are at the end of the book.

1. A 5-month non-interest-bearing note for $1700 was dated January 31, 1996. On March 1 the payee sold the note to a friend at a discount that provided the friend with a 10% pa rate of return until the due date. What price did the payee receive?

•2. On October 15 Nash Hardware gave Ace Tool Manufacturing a 90-day promissory note for $8500 as additional security on its account with Ace. The note bears interest at 9% pa. By November 10 Nash has enough cash to pay off the debt. What is the least amount that Ace might accept in settlement of the account if Ace has short-term debt on which it pays an interest rate of 12%?

•3. A conditional sale contract requires two payments 3 and 6 months after the date of the contract. Each payment consists of $1900 principal plus interest at 12.5% on $1900 from the date of the contract. One month into the contract, what price would a finance company pay for the contract if it requires an 18% rate of return on its purchases?

•4. A $25,000, 91-day Province of Newfoundland Treasury bill was originally purchased at a price that would yield the investor a 9.438% pa rate of return if the T-bill is held until maturity. Thirty-four days later the investor sold the T-bill through his broker for $24,575.

   a. What price did the original investor pay for the T-bill?

   b. What rate of return will the second investor realize if she holds the T-bill until maturity?

   c. What rate of return did the first investor realize during his holding period?

5. Paul has $20,000 to invest for 6 months. For this amount, his bank pays 6.3% on a 90-day GIC and 6.5% on a 180-day GIC. If the interest rate on a 90-day GIC is the same 3 months from now, how much more interest will Paul earn by purchasing the 180-day GIC than by buying a 90-day GIC and then reinvesting its maturity value in a second 90-day GIC?

•6. Duncan Developments Ltd. obtained a $120,000 line of credit from its bank to subdivide a parcel of land it owned into four residential lots and to install water, sewer, and underground electrical services. Amounts advanced from time to time are payable on demand to its bank. Interest at prime plus 4% on the daily principal balance is charged to the developer's bank account on the 26th of each month. The developer must apply at least $30,000 from the proceeds of the sale of each lot against the loan principal. Duncan drew down $50,000 on June 3, $40,000 on June 30, and $25,000 on July 17. Two lots quickly sold, and Duncan repaid $30,000 on July 31 and $35,000 on August 18. The initial prime rate of 8% changed to 8.25% effective July 5 and 8.5% effective July 26. Prepare a repayment schedule showing loan activity and interest charges up to and including the interest payment on August 26.

 •7. Ms. Wadeson obtained a $15,000 demand loan from the Canadian Imperial Bank of Commerce on May 23 to purchase a car. The interest rate on the loan was prime plus 2%. The loan required blended payments of $700 on the 15th of each month beginning June 15. The prime rate was 7.5% at the outset, dropped to 7.25% on July 26, and then jumped by 0.5% on September 14. Prepare a loan repayment schedule showing the details of the first five payments.

SUMMARY OF NOTATION AND KEY FORMULAS

S = Maturity value of a promissory note

The following symbols were introduced in Appendix 7A.

d = Rate of bank discount
P_b = Proceeds of a promissory note (bank discount method)

Formula (7–1) $\text{Proceeds} = \dfrac{S}{1 + rt}$ Finding the proceeds of a promissory note (simple discount method)

Formula (7–2) $P_b = S(1 - dt)$ Finding the proceeds of a promissory note (bank discount method)

> **Valuation Principle:** The fair market value of an investment is the sum of the present values of the expected cash flows. The discount rate used in the present-value calculations should be the market-based rate of return required for this type of investment.

GLOSSARY OF TERMS

Blended-payment loan   A loan repaid by equal regular payments that include both interest and principal.

Commercial paper   Promissory notes issued by large corporations to borrow funds for the short term.

Demand loan   A type of loan on which the lender is entitled to demand full repayment at any time without notice.

Discount   The difference between a promissory note's maturity value and the amount for which it is sold.

Discounting   The process of calculating the present value of future cash flows.

Discount rate   The interest rate used in calculating the present value of future cash flows.

Face value   The principal amount specified on a private promissory note. The amount paid at maturity of a Treasury bill or a corporation's commercial paper.

Issue date   The date on which a promissory note was written or "made" and the date from which interest, if any, is computed.

Legal due date   The date, three days after expiry of a promissory note's term, beyond which the note is in default.

Loan repayment schedule   A table presenting details of the interest charges, loan payments, and outstanding balances on a loan.

Maker   The party (debtor) promising to pay the promissory note at its maturity.

Payee   The party (creditor) to whom a payment is to be made.

Proceeds   The amount received from the sale of a promissory note.

Promissory note   A written promise by one party to pay a certain sum of money to another party on a specific date, or on demand.

Revolving loan   A loan whose outstanding balance can fluctuate within a maximum credit limit.

Straight-line loan   A loan requiring equal monthly payments of principal in addition to the interest that has accrued to each payment date.

Term   The time period for which a loan is made.

Treasury bills   Promissory notes issued by the federal government and most provincial governments to borrow money for short terms.

8

COMPOUND INTEREST

LEARNING OBJECTIVES

After completing this chapter, you will be able to:

- Convert between nominal and periodic rates of interest
- Calculate maturity value, beginning principal, future value, and present value in compound interest applications, by both the algebraic method and the preprogrammed financial calculator method
- Calculate the maturity value of compound-interest Guaranteed Investment Certificates (GICs)
- Calculate the redemption value of a compound-interest Canada Savings Bond (CSB)
- Adapt the concepts and equations of compound interest to cases of compound growth

- Calculate the economically equivalent payment or value on any date, of a specified payment or stream of payments, given the interest rate that money can earn
- Calculate the price of "stripped" bonds and long-term promissory notes discounted before their maturity dates
- Calculate the unknown loan payment when all but one of the payments is known
- Compare the economic values of two payment streams

INTRODUCTION

The simple-interest method discussed in Chapter 6 is restricted primarily to loans and interest-earning investments having terms of less than 1 year. The compound-interest method is employed in virtually all instances where the term exceeds 1 year, and in a few cases where the duration is less than or equal to 1 year.

In the **compound-interest method,** interest is *periodically* calculated and *added* to the principal balance. Suppose, for example, that a beginning principal of $1000 earns 10% compounded annually. In the first year, the interest earned will be $100. At the end of the first year, this interest will be converted to principal. The principal at the start of the second year will then be $1100. It will earn $1100 × 0.10 = $110 interest in the second year. The extra $10 interest in the second year results from earning the 10% interest rate during the second year on the $100 interest earned in the first year. With simple interest, only the original principal would continue to earn interest.

The basic concepts of maturity value, time value of money, future value, present value, and equivalent payments were developed in a simple-interest context in Chapter 6. They have similar interpretations and significance in a compound-interest environment. However, the algebraic formulas used to calculate these amounts are different. Some of these formulas have been programmed into financial calculators to expedite frequently required calculations.

8.1 BASIC CONCEPTS

The time interval between successive conversions of interest to principal is called the **compounding period** or **conversion period.** The effect of converting interest to principal is that the interest earned in a compounding period will itself earn interest in all subsequent periods. The accelerating growth this produces in the combined principal and interest will be illustrated in Section 8.2.

In many circumstances, interest is compounded more often than once each year. The number of compoundings per year is called the **compounding frequency** or **conversion frequency.** The common frequencies and the corresponding compounding or conversion periods encountered in the financial industry are listed in Table 8.1.

TABLE   8.1

Compounding Frequencies and Periods

Compounding or conversion frequency	Number of compoundings or conversions per year	Compounding or conversion period
Annual	1	1 year
Semiannual	2	6 months
Quarterly	4	3 months
Monthly	12	1 month

The annual interest rate on which a compound interest calculation is based is known as the **nominal**[1] **interest rate.** To fully specify how interest is to be compounded, both the nominal interest rate and the compounding frequency must be

---

[1]The use of "nominal," meaning "in name only," is appropriate because the nominal annual rate of interest is not numerically equal to the actual rate of interest realized over a full year. This distinction is discussed in Chapter 9.

given—for example, 9% compounded semiannually or 10.5% compounded monthly. The **periodic interest rate** is the rate of interest earned in *one* conversion period. It is determined from the nominal (annual) rate as follows:

$$\text{Periodic interest rate} = \frac{\text{Nominal interest rate}}{\text{Number of conversions per year}}$$

Using the notation

j = Nominal interest rate
m = Number of compoundings or conversions per year
i = Periodic interest rate

the connection between the periodic and nominal rates of interest may be expressed algebraically as:

Periodic Interest Rate

$$\boxed{i = \frac{j}{m}}$$

(8–1)

Trap

A common mistake made when calculating the periodic interest rate for quarterly compounding is to divide the nominal interest rate by 3 instead of by 4. The mistake results from thinking of the length of the compounding period (3 months) instead of the frequency of compounding (4 per year).

■ **EXAMPLE 8.1A**   **CALCULATING THE PERIODIC INTEREST RATE**

Calculate the periodic interest rate corresponding to:

a. 10.5% compounded annually.

b. 9.75% compounded semiannually.

c. 9.0% compounded quarterly.

d. 9.5% compounded monthly.

☑ **SOLUTION**

Employing formula (8–1), we obtain:

a. $i = \dfrac{j}{m} = \dfrac{10.5\%}{1} = 10.5\%$ (per year)

b. $i = \dfrac{9.75\%}{2} = 4.875\%$ (per half year)

c. $i = \dfrac{9.0\%}{4} = 2.25\%$ (per quarter)

d. $i = \dfrac{9.5\%}{12} = 0.7916\%$ (per month)   ■

■ **EXAMPLE 8.1B**   **CALCULATING THE COMPOUNDING FREQUENCY**

For a nominal interest rate of 8.4%, what is the compounding frequency if the periodic interest rate is:

a. 4.2%?   *b.* 8.4%?   *c.* 2.1%?   *d.* 0.70%?

☑ SOLUTION

The number of compoundings or conversions in a year is given by the value of m in formula (8–1). Rearranging this formula to solve for m, we obtain

$$m = \frac{j}{i}$$

a. $m = \dfrac{8.4\%}{4.2\%} = 2$ which corresponds to semiannual compounding.

b. $m = \dfrac{8.4\%}{8.4\%} = 1$ which corresponds to annual compounding.

c. $m = \dfrac{8.4\%}{2.1\%} = 4$ which corresponds to quarterly compounding.

d. $m = \dfrac{8.4\%}{0.7\%} = 12$ which corresponds to monthly compounding.   ■

■ EXAMPLE 8.1c   CALCULATING THE NOMINAL INTEREST RATE

Determine the nominal rate of interest if:

a. The periodic rate is 1.75% with quarterly compounding.

b. The periodic rate is 0.8$\overline{3}$% with monthly compounding.

☑ SOLUTION

Rearranging formula (8–1) to solve for j, the nominal interest rate, we obtain

$$j = mi$$

a. $j = 4(1.75\%) = 7\%$

b. $j = 12(0.8\overline{3}\%) = 10.0\%$

The nominal interest rates are 7% compounded quarterly and 10.0% compounded monthly, respectively.   ■

EXERCISE 8.1

Answers to the odd-numbered problems are at the end of the book.
Calculate the missing values in problems 1 through 9.

Problem	Nominal interest rate (%)	Compounding frequency	Periodic interest rate (%)
1.	10.8	Quarterly	?
2.	11.75	Semiannually	?
3.	10.5	Monthly	?
4.	?	Semiannually	4.95
5.	?	Monthly	0.91667
6.	?	Quarterly	2.9375
7.	9.5	?	2.375
8.	8.25	?	4.125
9.	13.5	?	1.125

8.2 MATURITY VALUE OF A LOAN OR INVESTMENT

CALCULATING THE MATURITY VALUE

Maturity value has the same meaning in both simple-interest and compound-interest contexts. The **maturity value** is the total amount due on the expiry or maturity date of a loan or investment. However, a new formula for the maturity value must be derived for cases where compound interest is earned. The symbols P and S are again used to represent the principal amount and maturity value, respectively, of the loan or investment. The general problem is to determine the maturity value at the end of n compounding periods if interest at the rate i is earned each period.

Since interest is added to the principal at the end of each compounding period, the principal will be higher at the beginning of every successive period. Let us work through the accumulation of principal and interest one period at a time. This is indicated by the series of steps on the time line in Figure 8.1. The serial number for each compounding period is located at the end of the respective period.

FIGURE 8.1

Calculating the Maturity Value of a Loan or Investment

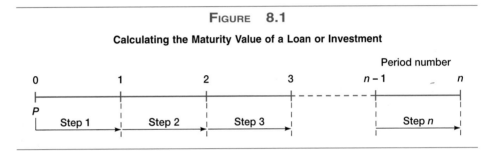

The interest earned on the principal P during the first period will be iP. At the end of the first period,

$$
\begin{aligned}
\text{Total amount} &= \text{Principal} + \text{Interest} \\
&= P + iP \\
&= P(1 + i)
\end{aligned}
$$

Note that the total amount at the end of the period is $(1 + i)$ times as large as the principal at the beginning of the period. After the interest is converted to principal, the beginning principal for the second compounding period will be $P(1 + i)$. The amount at the end of the second period will again be $(1 + i)$ times as large as the principal at the start of the period. Therefore, at the end of the second interval,

$$
\begin{aligned}
\text{Total amount} &= (\text{Beginning principal}) \times (1 + i) \\
&= P(1 + i) \times (1 + i) \\
&= P(1 + i)^2
\end{aligned}
$$

This amount becomes the beginning principal for the third period. It, in turn, will grow to

$$
\begin{aligned}
\text{Total amount} &= (\text{Beginning principal}) \times (1 + i) \\
&= P(1 + i)^2 \times (1 + i) \\
&= P(1 + i)^3
\end{aligned}
$$

at the end of the third period. The pattern is now evident. After all n compounding periods, the maturity value will be:

Maturity Value (Compound interest)

$$S = P(1 + i)^n \qquad \text{(8–2)}$$

With m compoundings per year, the total number of compounding periods, n, in the complete term of the loan or investment can be calculated using

Number of Compounding Periods

$$n = m \times (\text{Number of years in the term}) \qquad \text{(8–3)}$$

If we need to calculate the principal amount that must be invested at the periodic rate i in order to attain a specified maturity value after n compounding periods, we would use formula (8–2) rearranged to solve for P. That is,

$$P = \frac{S}{(1 + i)^n} = S(1 + i)^{-n}$$

Tip

The $P = S(1 + i)^{-n}$ version leads to the more efficient calculation of P. First calculate $(1 + i)^{-n}$. In the procedure for using the calculator's $\boxed{y^x}$ function, press the $\boxed{+/-}$ key immediately after entering the positive exponent n. This will make the exponent negative. Then complete the execution of the $\boxed{y^x}$ function and multiply the result by the value for S.

■ **EXAMPLE 8.2A**   CALCULATING THE MATURITY VALUE OF A LUMP INVESTMENT

What will be the maturity value of $10,000 invested for five years at 9.75% compounded semiannually?

☑ **SOLUTION**

Given: $P = \$10,000$, Term of investment = 5 years, $j = 9.75\%$, $m = 2$
The interest rate per 6-month compounding period is

$$i = \frac{j}{m} = \frac{9.75\%}{2} = 4.875\% \text{ (per half year)}$$
$$n = m \times \text{Term (in years)} = 2(5) = 10$$

The maturity value will be

$$\begin{aligned}
S &= P(1 + i)^n \\
&= \$10,000(1 + 0.04875)^{10} \\
&= \$10,000(1.6096066) \\
&= \$16,096.07
\end{aligned}$$

The investment will grow to $16,096.07 after 5 years.   ■

GRAPHS OF MATURITY VALUE VERSUS TIME

COMPARISON OF MATURITY VALUES AT COMPOUND AND SIMPLE INTEREST   The effect of compound interest is to produce an accelerating growth in an investment's value as time passes. An example is illustrated in Figure 8.2. The curved line is a plot of the maturity value of $100 invested at 10% compounded annually for terms of up to 10 years. For this case,

$$S = P(1 + i)^n = \$100(1 + 0.10)^n = \$100(1.10)^n$$

FIGURE   8.2

Comparison of Maturity Values at Compound and Simple Interest

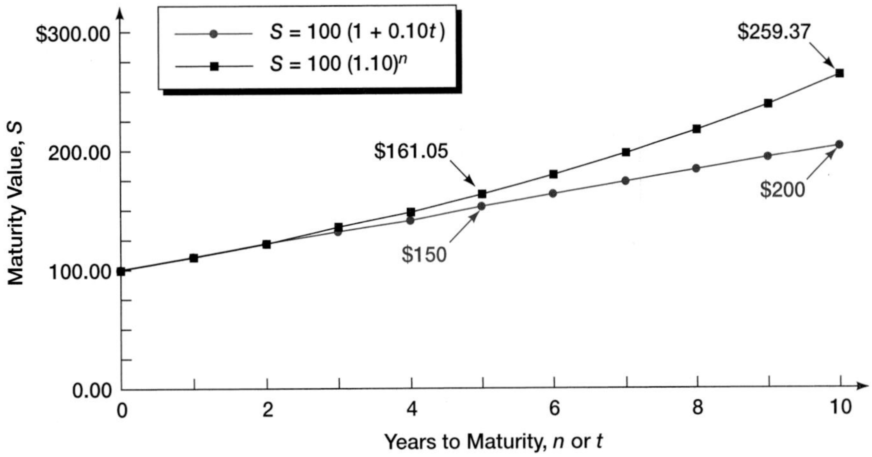

The coloured straight line running from $100 to $200 indicates the combined total of principal plus interest calculated on a simple-interest basis. Ten dollars is earned every year on the original principal but it is not paid or reinvested. In this instance,

$$S = P(1 + rt) = \$100(1 + 0.10t)$$

The compounding of interest causes the maturity value to increase by the *same percentage* (10%) each year. This produces an escalating dollar increase in successive years because the principal used as the base for the 10% increase is larger each year. Consequently, the maturity value curve rises more steeply as time passes. This accelerating growth pattern, known as **exponential growth,** occurs whenever a quantity grows by a fixed percentage in each successive period.

THE DEPENDENCE OF MATURITY VALUE ON THE NOMINAL INTEREST RATE   Figure 8.3 shows the increase in value of $100 invested at four different *annually* compounded rates of interest for 25 years. Note the particularly dramatic increase in maturity values beyond 15 years at the higher interest rates.

The ratio of the total interest earnings after 25 years for the 10% and 12% cases is

$$\frac{\$100(1.12)^{25} - \$100}{\$100(1.10)^{25} - \$100} = \frac{\$1600.01}{\$983.47} = 1.63$$

The ratio of the corresponding compound annual rates of interest is 12% : 10% = 1.2. These two ratios demonstrate that an increase in the compound rate of interest produces a disproportionately larger increase in the interest earnings. For a given pair of compound interest rates, the ratio (of the interest earnings at the higher rate to the

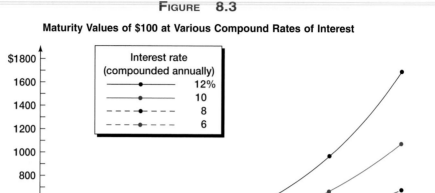

FIGURE   8.3

Maturity Values of $100 at Various Compound Rates of Interest

earnings at the lower rate) is larger at longer maturities. Two implications of these properties of compound interest are:

- An individual should begin an investment plan early in life to realize the dramatic effects of compounding over the long run.
- An investor should try to obtain the best available rate of return (at the investor's acceptable level of risk). An extra 0.5% or 1% in the annual rate of return has a disproportionately greater effect on the maturity value, particularly in the long run.

THE DEPENDENCE OF THE MATURITY VALUE ON THE COMPOUNDING FREQUENCY
Figure 8.4 compares the increase in value over a 25-year period of $100 invested at 12% compounded monthly and at 12% compounded annually. For a given term, monthly compounding produces the greater maturity value. Annual and monthly compounding are, respectively, the lowest and highest compounding frequencies that are ordinarily encountered. Therefore, curves for semiannual and quarterly compounding would, if shown, lie *between* these two curves.

The effect of monthly compounding versus annual compounding results in a surprisingly large difference between the accumulated values in the longer term. After 15 years, the accumulated value with monthly compounding is about 10% larger than with annual compounding. The gap continues to widen in both dollar and percent terms as time passes. After 20 years, it is almost 13% and after 25 years, it is 16.4%!

■ EXAMPLE 8.2B   *THE PRINCIPAL NEEDED TO PRODUCE A SPECIFIED MATURITY VALUE*

What amount must be invested now in a savings account earning 8% compounded monthly to accumulate a total of $10,000 after 3½ years?

FIGURE   8.4

Maturity Values at the Same Nominal Rate but Different Compounding Frequencies

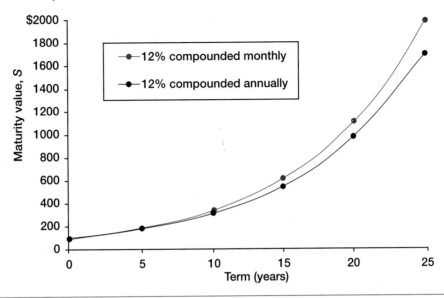

✓ SOLUTION

Given: $j = 8\%$, $m = 12$, $S = \$10,000$, Term $= 3\frac{1}{2}$ years

$$i = \frac{8\%}{12} = 0.\overline{6}\% \text{ (per month)}$$

$$n = m \times \text{Term} = 12(3.5) = 42$$

Rearranging formula (8–2) to solve for P,

$$P = S(1 + i)^{-n} = \$10,000(1 + 0.00\overline{6})^{-42} = \$7564.86$$

A total of $7564.86 must be invested now to accumulate $10,000 after 3½ years. ∎

■ EXAMPLE 8.2c   CALCULATING THE MATURITY VALUE WHEN THE INTEREST RATE CHANGES

George invested $5000 at 9.25% compounded quarterly. After 18 months, the rate changed to 9.75% compounded semiannually. What amount will George have accumulated 3 years after the initial investment?

✓ SOLUTION

The period rate of interest is

$$i = \frac{j}{m} = \frac{9.25\%}{4} = 2.3125\% \text{ (per quarter)}$$

for the first 18 months and

$$i = \frac{9.75\%}{2} = 4.875\% \text{ (per half year)}$$

for the next 18 months. Because of the interest rate change, the solution should be done in two steps, as indicated by the following diagram.

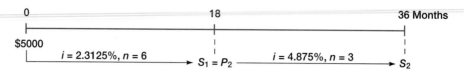

The "maturity value" S_1 after 18 months becomes the beginning "principal" P_2 for the remainder of the 3 years.

Step 1: Calculate the amount S_1 after 18 months.

$$S_1 = P(1 + i)^n = \$5000(1.023125)^6 = \$5735.12$$

Step 2: Calculate the amount S_2 at the end of the 3 years.

$$S_2 = P_2(1 + i)^n = \$5735.12(1.04875)^3 = \$6615.44$$

George will have accumulated $6615.44 after 3 years. ■

■ EXAMPLE 8.2D   COMPARING TWO NOMINAL RATES OF INTEREST

Other things being equal, would an investor prefer an interest rate of 10.5% compounded monthly or 11% compounded annually for a 2-year investment?

☑ SOLUTION

The preferred rate will be the one that results in the higher maturity value. Pick an arbitrary initial investment, say $1000, and calculate the maturity value at each rate.

For $i = \dfrac{10.5\%}{12} = 0.875\%$ and $n = 12(2) = 24,$

$$S = \$1000(1.00875)^{24} = \$1232.55$$

For $i = \dfrac{11\%}{1} = 11\%$ and $n = 1(2) = 2,$

$$S = \$1000(1.11)^2 = \$1232.10$$

The rate of 10.5% compounded monthly is slightly better. The more frequent compounding more than offsets the lower nominal rate. ■

■ EXAMPLE 8.2E   THE BALANCE OWED AFTER PAYMENTS ON A COMPOUND INTEREST LOAN

Fay borrowed $5000 at an interest rate of 11% compounded quarterly. On the first, second, and third anniversaries of the loan, she made payments of $1500. What payment made on the fourth anniversary will extinguish the debt?

☑ SOLUTION

At each anniversary we will first calculate the amount owed (S) and then deduct the payment to obtain the principal balance (P) at the beginning of the next year. The periodic interest rate is

$$i = \frac{j}{m} = \frac{11\%}{4} = 2.75\%$$

The sequence of steps is indicated by the following time diagram.

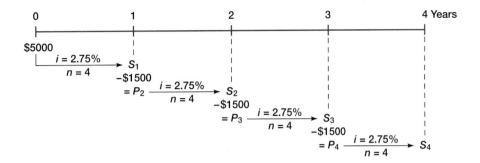

$$S_1 = P(1 + i)^n = \$5000(1.0275)^4 = \$5573.11$$
$$P_2 = S_1 - \$1500 = \$5573.11 - \$1500 = \$4073.11$$
$$S_2 = P_2(1 + i)^n = \$4073.11(1.0275)^4 = \$4539.97$$
$$P_3 = \$4539.97 - \$1500 = \$3039.97$$
$$S_3 = \$3039.97(1.0275)^4 = \$3388.42$$
$$P_3 = \$3388.42 - \$1500 = \$1888.42$$
$$S_4 = \$1888.42(1.0275)^4 = \$2104.87$$

A payment of \$2104.87 on the fourth anniversary will pay off the debt. ∎

Point of Interest

The "Magic" of Compound Interest

*I don't know the names of the Seven Wonders of the World, but I do know the Eighth Wonder: **Compound Interest**.*

Baron Rothschild

Many books and articles on personal financial planning write with similar awe about the "miracle" or "magic" of compound interest. The authors would seem to have the reader believe that mysterious, almost mystical forces are involved. One book states that "one of the greatest gifts that you can give your children is a compound interest table" (which you will be able to construct by the end of this chapter). *The Wealthy Barber,* a Canadian best-seller, laments that "it's a real tragedy that most people don't understand compound interest and its wondrous powers."

The books do have a legitimate point, even if it seems overstated to those who are familiar with the relatively simple mathematics of compound interest. Most people underestimate the long-term growth of compound-interest investments. They also do not take seriously enough the advice to start saving and investing early in life to take advantage of the compounding of investment returns over a 30- to 40-year time frame.

The reason people tend to underestimate the effects of long-term compounding is that they are inclined to think in terms of proportional relationships. Under a strict direct proportion, it we invest an amount for twice as long, we will earn twice as much interest. Or if we realize an annual return of 9% instead of 8%, our investment's earnings will be ⁹⁄₈ times larger. These two statements are accurate in the simple-interest case, and they may be reasonable approximations in the *short run* with compound interest. However, they are likely to be grossly in error in the *longer term* with compound interest. The following table illustrates the character of long-term growth under compound interest.

(continued)

(concluded)

Term (years)	Maturity value ($)
5	1469
10	2159
15	3172
20	4661
25	6848
30	10,063

An initial principal of $1000 is invested at 8% compounded annually. Observe that the *dollar change* in value in each successive 5-year period gets progressively larger. The increase in the maturity value during the last 5 years is almost as large as the increase in the entire first 20 years! However, the *percentage change* in value in each 5-year interval is constant: 46.93%.

If the $1000 earns 9% compounded annually instead of 8%, the maturity value after 30 years will be $13,268. The interest rate has been increased by one-eighth (9% versus 8%) but the dollars of interest *earned* during the 30 years will be increased by over one-third ($12,268 vs. $9063)!

The so-called "miracle" or "magic" of compound interest is just the well-known pattern in mathematics and science called *exponential growth*. A quantity grows exponentially if it increases by the *same percentage* each period. For compound interest, the constant percentage increase each period is, of course, the periodic interest rate.

EXERCISE 8.2

Answers to the odd-numbered problems are at the end of the book.
Note: Those who prefer using financial calculators to solve compound-interest problems should cover Section 8.3 before doing these problems.

Calculate the missing values in problems 1 through 10.

Problem	Principal ($)	Term	Nominal rate (%)	Compounding frequency	Maturity value ($)
1.	5000	7 years	10	Semiannually	?
2.	8500	5.5 years	9.5	Quarterly	?
3.	12,100	3¼ years	7.5	Monthly	?
4.	?	10 years	9.9	Annual	10,000.00
5.	?	27 months	8.5	Quarterly	5437.52
6.	?	42 months	7.5	Semiannually	9704.61
7.	?	18 months	13	Monthly	8000.00
8.	2500	4½ years	10.5	Quarterly	?
9.	?	27 years	6.7	Annual	28,801.12
10.	4400	6¾ years	11	Monthly	?

11. How much more will an investment of $1000 be worth after 25 years if it earns 11% compounded annually instead of 10% compounded annually? Calculate the difference in dollars and as a percentage of the smaller maturity value.

12. How much more will an investment of $1000 be worth after 25 years if it earns 6% compounded annually instead of 5% compounded annually? Calculate the difference in dollars and as a percentage of the smaller maturity value.

13. How much more will an investment of $1000 earning 9% compounded annually be worth after 25 years than after 20 years? Calculate the difference in dollars and as a percentage of the smaller accumulated value.

14. How much more will an investment of $1000 earning 9% compounded annually be worth after 15 years than after 10 years? Calculate the difference in dollars and as a percentage of the smaller accumulated value.

15. A $1000 investment is made today. Calculate its maturity values for the six combinations of terms and annually compounded interest rates in the following table.

Interest	Term		
rate (%)	20 years	25 years	30 years
8	?	?	?
10	?	?	?

16. Suppose that an individual invests $1000 at the beginning of each year for the next 30 years. At the end of the 30 years, how much more will the first investment be worth than the 16th investment if both earn 8.5% compounded annually?

17. To motivate individuals to start savings plans at an early age, financial planners will sometimes present the results of the following type of calculation: How much must a 25-year-old individual invest 5 years from now for the investment to have the same maturity value at age 55 as a current investment of $1000? Assume that both investments earn 8% compounded annually.

18. Calculate the maturity amount of a $1000 RRSP[2] contribution after 25 years if it earns an interest rate of 9% compounded:
    a. Annually.   b. Semiannually.   c. Quarterly.   d. Monthly.

19. Calculate the maturity amount of a $1000 RRSP contribution after 5 years if it earns an interest rate of 9% compounded:
    a. Annually.   b. Semiannually.   c. Quarterly.   d. Monthly.

20. By calculating the maturity value of $100 invested for 1 year at each rate, determine which rate of return an investor would prefer.

    a. 8.0% compounded monthly.

    b. 8.1% compounded quarterly.

    c. 8.2% compounded semiannually.

    d. 8.3% compounded annually.

21. By calculating the maturity value of $100 invested for 1 year at each rate, determine which rate of return an investor would prefer.

    a. 12.0% compounded monthly.

    b. 12.1% compounded quarterly.

    c. 12.2% compounded semiannually.

    d. 12.3% compounded annually.

22. What is the maturity value of a $3000 loan for 18 months at 9.5% compounded semiannually? How much interest is charged on the loan?

23. What total amount of interest will be earned by $5000 invested at 7.5% compounded monthly for 3½ years?

24. What amount must be invested at 7.5% compounded semiannually for 8 years to reach a maturity value of $10,000?

25. Ross has just been notified that the combined principal and interest on an amount that he borrowed 27 months ago at 11% compounded quarterly is now $2297.78. How much of this amount is principal and how much is interest?

•26. Jeff borrowed $3000, $3500, and $4000 from his father on January 1 of 3 successive years at college. Jeff and his father agreed that interest would accumulate on each amount at the low rate of 5% compounded semiannually. Jeff is to start repaying the

---

[2]Some features of Registered Retirement Savings Plans (RRSPs) will be discussed in Section 8.4. At this point, simply view an RRSP contribution as an investment.

loan on the January 1 following graduation. What consolidated amount will he owe at that time?

•27. Mrs. Vanderberg has just put $5000 in each of three trust accounts for her grandchildren. They will have access to the accumulated funds on their 19th birthdays. Their current ages are 12 years, 7 months (Donna); 10 years, 3 months (Tim); and 7 years, 11 months (Gary). If the trust accounts earn 8% compounded monthly, what amount will each grandchild receive at age 19?

•28. Michelle has just received an inheritance from her grandfather's estate. She will be entering college in 3½ years and wants to immediately purchase three compound-interest investment certificates so that one will mature at $4000 at the beginning of her first academic year, the second will mature at $5000 at the start of her second year, and the third will mature at $6000 for her third year. She can obtain rates of 7.75% compounded semiannually for terms of 3 to 5 years and 8% compounded quarterly for terms of 5 to 7 years. What principal amount should she invest in each certificate?

•29. Nelson borrowed $5000 for 4½ years. For the first 2½ years the interest rate on the loan was 13.2% compounded monthly. Then the rate became 10.25% compounded semiannually. What total amount was required to pay off the loan if no payments were made before the expiry of the 4½-year term?

•30. Scott has just invested $60,000 in a 5-year Guaranteed Investment Certificate (GIC) earning 10.5% compounded semiannually. When the GIC matures, he will reinvest its entire maturity value in a new 5-year GIC. What will be the maturity value of the second GIC if it yields:

   a. The same rate as the current GIC?

   b. 1% pa more than the current GIC?

   c. 1% pa less than the current GIC?

•31. A deposit of $2500 earned interest at 7.5% compounded quarterly for 1½ years and then 6.8% compounded monthly for 2 years. How much interest did the deposit earn in the 3½ years?

•32. A debt of $7000 accumulated interest at 13.5% compounded quarterly for 15 months, after which the rate changed to 12.5% compounded semiannually for the next 6 months. What was the total amount owed at the end of the entire 21-month period?

•33. Megan borrowed $1900 3½ years ago at 11% compounded semiannually. Two years ago she made a payment of $1000. What amount is required today to pay off the remaining principal and the accrued interest?

•34. Duane borrowed $3000 from his grandmother 5 years ago. The interest on the loan was to be 5% compounded semiannually for the first 3 years and 9% compounded monthly thereafter. If he made a $1000 payment 2½ years ago, what is the amount now owed on the loan?

•35. A loan of $4000 at 12% compounded monthly requires three payments of $1000 at 6, 12, and 18 months after the date of the loan and a final payment of the full balance after 2 years. What is the amount of the final payment?

••36. If the total interest earned on an investment at 8.2% compounded semiannually for 8½ years was $1175.98, what was the original investment?

••37. Peggy has never made any payments on a 5-year-old loan from her mother at 6% compounded annually. The total interest owed is now $845.56. How much did she borrow from her mother?

••38. Dr. Sawicki obtained a variable-rate loan of $10,000. The lender required payment of at least $2000 each year. After 9 months the doctor paid $2500, and another 9 months later she paid $3000. What amount was owed on the loan after 2 years if the interest rate was 11.25% compounded monthly for the first year and 11.5% compounded quarterly for the second year?

8.3 USING FINANCIAL CALCULATORS

Certain computations involving compound interest are performed so frequently that formulas for them are permanently programmed into calculators designed for business and financial applications.

Ideally, business students should be able to solve compound-interest problems using both an algebraic method and a financial calculator's preprogrammed functions. The algebraic approach strengthens mathematical skills and intuition. It provides greater flexibility for handling nonstandard cases and adapting spreadsheet software to specific applications. Financial calculators, on the other hand, offer time-saving efficiencies and reduce the likelihood of mechanical errors in routine computations.

At some colleges, business students are expected to learn both the algebraic and the financial calculator approaches to solving compound-interest problems. At other colleges, just one method is emphasized. However, even in this second group there is no clear consensus on a preferred approach. Consequently, *both* an algebraic solution and a financial calculator solution will be presented for most example problems involving compound interest.

KEY DEFINITIONS AND CALCULATOR OPERATION

The basic, lowest-price financial calculator produced by any well-known manufacturer may be used in conjunction with this text. There are a few variations from one model to another in the labelling of the keys and in the operating procedures. In the appendix to this chapter, instructions are provided for adapting each of five popular models to the generic calculator instructions used in the text.

All financial calculators have five basic compound interest functions.[3] Each function is associated with a specific function key, and each function key will be represented here by a rectangular box containing the key's label. The generic labels and key definitions we will employ are:

$\boxed{\text{n}}$ = n, the number of compounding periods

$\boxed{\text{i}}$ = i, the periodic interest rate

$\boxed{\text{PV}}$ = P, the principal or present value

$\boxed{\text{FV}}$ = S, the maturity value or future value

$\boxed{\text{PMT}}$ = the periodic annuity payment (not used until Chapter 10)

The appendix to this chapter points out any variations from the preceding generic key labels for the following five calculator models.

---

[3]Some financial calculators have additional specialized function keys. This text does not use these functions for the following reasons:
- Since some calculators do not have the extra functions, instructions or solutions using such functions would no longer apply to all calculators.
- The labelling of keys and the procedures for using the more advanced financial functions differ substantially from one calculator model to another. It would be too cumbersome to deal with the specifics for each calculator.
- Some educators are of the opinion that such functions encourage a "black box" approach to the solution of problems. Students tend to focus on the *mechanical procedure* required to make the "black box" work its wonders rather than on *understanding* the concepts on which the solution is based.

- Sharp EL-733A Business/Financial Calculator.
- Sharp EL-735 Business/Financial Calculator.
- Texas Instruments BA 35 Business Analyst.
- Texas Instruments BA II Plus Advanced Business Analyst.
- Hewlett-Packard HP-10B Business Calculator.

In a couple of instances, the default definition of a key's function may differ from the definition listed above. For these cases, the appendix shows how to adjust the calculator's settings to redefine a key so that the calculator will accept the generic instructions. A few unique operating features of each calculator are also discussed in the appendix.

Each of the five basic function keys has two uses:

1. Saving in memory a numerical value of the variable which the key represents.
2. Computing the value of the variable which the key represents.

Any of the four variables in the formula

$$S = P(1 + i)^n$$

may be computed after saving the numerical values of the other three variables in the appropriate memory locations. As an illustration, suppose we want to calculate the maturity value of $1000 invested at 8% compounded semiannually for 3 years. We must first save the known values for n, i, and P in the $\boxed{\textbf{n}}$, $\boxed{\textbf{i}}$, and $\boxed{\textbf{PV}}$ memories. They may be saved in any sequence. To save $1000 in the $\boxed{\textbf{PV}}$ memory, just enter the digits for 1000 and press $\boxed{\textbf{PV}}$. Even though 1000 remains in the display, it will also be stored in the memory. Then enter values for the other two variables in the same manner.

ENTER:	Then PRESS:	Display shows:
1000	$\boxed{\textbf{PV}}$	1000
4	$\boxed{\textbf{i}}$	4
6	$\boxed{\textbf{n}}$	6

Note that the periodic interest rate must be entered in *percent form* rather than in its decimal equivalent form. For all compound interest problems in Chapters 8 and 9, the value 0 must be stored in the $\boxed{\textbf{PMT}}$ memory. Once entered, it will remain there until a different value is entered.

Now we are ready to compute the maturity value of the $1000 investment. Your calculator will probably have a "Compute" key[4] labelled $\boxed{\textbf{COMP}}$ or $\boxed{\textbf{CPT}}$. If you press this key followed by $\boxed{\textbf{FV}}$, the calculator will compute the maturity value S in formula (8–2) and display the result.

PRESS:	Then PRESS:	Display shows:
$\boxed{\textbf{COMP}}$	$\boxed{\textbf{FV}}$	−1265.32

(If your calculator does not give this numerical result, it is probable that your particular model is not yet set in its "financial mode." Consult the chapter appendix for instructions on setting the calculator's operating mode.) The maturity value of $1000

---

[4]The Hewlett-Packard 10B calculator does not have a "Compute" key. Refer to the appendix to this chapter for specific instructions on this model.

invested at 8% compounded semiannually for 3 years is therefore $1265.32. The significance of the negative sign[5] will be discussed in the next subsection.

Tips

1. After any computation, the values that were saved in the memories still remain. Therefore, if values of any of the five financial variables do not change for the subsequent calculation, they do not need to be reentered.
2. Most calculators will retain the values in their memories if the calculators are turned off and then, even days later, turned back on.

CASH-FLOW SIGN CONVENTION

Cash flow is a term frequently used in the fields of finance and accounting to refer to a cash payment. A cash inflow is the same as a cash receipt; a cash outflow is a cash disbursement.

An appreciation of the usefulness of a cash-flow sign convention can be gained from considering the following two cases.

- With an initial $1000 deposit, you open a bank account that will earn 5% compounded monthly. What will be the balance in the account 1 year from now if you *deposit* $50 at the end of each month?
- With an initial $1000 deposit, you open a bank account that will earn 5% compounded monthly. What will be the balance in the account 1 year from now if you *withdraw* $50 at the end of each month?

A financial calculator that employs a cash-flow sign convention can answer either of these problems in a *single computation.* Note that the magnitudes of the cash flows are the same in both cases. The only difference is that the monthly payment flows *into* the account in the first case and *out of* the account in the second case. Virtually all financial calculators have been programmed to distinguish cash inflows from cash outflows by the use of a **cash-flow sign convention.**

Most financial calculators[6] use the standard sign convention employed in finance.[7]

Cash-Flow Sign Convention:
   Cash inflows (receipts) are positive.
   Cash outflows (disbursements) are negative.

The only difference between the financial calculator solutions for the preceding bank account deposit/withdrawal scenarios would be the sign used with the $50 monthly cash flow.

In any compound-interest problem in Chapters 8 and 9, there are two cash flows, P and S (or ⟨ **PV** ⟩ and ⟨ **FV** ⟩). These flows are always in *opposite* directions. For example, if you are granted a loan, you initially receive the loan principal (positive cash

---

[5]The Texas Instruments BA 35 does not display a negative sign at this point.

[6]The Texas Instruments BA 35 calculator employs a modified version of this sign convention. Users of the BA 35 are referred to the Appendix of this chapter for details of the modification.

[7]Two widely used integrated electronic spreadsheets, Microsoft's Excel and Corel's Quattro Pro, also employ this sign convention in their financial functions.

flow). At the end of the term, you pay back the maturity value (negative cash flow). Consequently, if you enter a *positive* value in the (PV) memory, the calculator interprets it as an initial cash *inflow* (a loan). The calculator will compute a *negative* value for (FV), the maturity value, because you must pay the maturity value as a cash *outflow* on the maturity date in order to repay the loan.

On the other hand, if you make an investment, the principal is initially paid out (negative cash flow). At the end of the term, you receive the maturity value (positive cash flow). Consequently, if you save a *negative* value in the (PV) memory, the calculator views it as an investment problem (initial cash *outflow*). It will calculate a *positive* value for the maturity value because you will receive the maturity value as a cash *inflow* on the maturity date.

Example problems 8.2A, 8.2B, 8.2C, and 8.2E will now be repeated as Examples 8.3A, 8.3B, 8.3C, and 8.3D, respectively, to illustrate the use of a financial calculator.

■ EXAMPLE 8.3A   CALCULATING THE MATURITY VALUE OF A LUMP INVESTMENT

What will be the maturity value of $10,000 invested for 5 years at 9.75% pa compounded semiannually?

☑ SOLUTION

Given: $P = \$10,000$, Term $= 5$ years, j $= 9.75\%$, $m = 2$

$$i = \frac{j}{m} = \frac{9.75\%}{2} = 4.875\%$$
$$n = m \times \text{Term} = 2(5) = 10$$

ENTER:	Then PRESS:	Display shows:
10000	(+/-) (PV)	−10000
4.875	(i)	4.875
10	(n)	10
0	(PMT)	0
	(COMP) (FV)	16,096.07

Notes:

1. The $10,000 investment is entered into (PV) as a negative number because it is an outflow. The calculated maturity value is positive because it will be an inflow to the investor.

2. Zero should be kept in the (PMT) memory for all problems in Chapters 8 and 9. We will assume this to be the case hereafter.   ■

■ EXAMPLE 8.3B   THE PRINCIPAL NEEDED TO PRODUCE A SPECIFIED MATURITY VALUE

What amount must be invested now in a savings account earning 8% compounded monthly to accumulate a total of $10,000 after 3½ years?

☑ SOLUTION

Given: $j = 8\%$, $m = 12$, $S = \$10,000$, Term $= 3½$ years

$$i = \frac{8\%}{12} = 0.\overline{6}\%$$
$$n = m \times \text{Term} = 12(3.5) = 42$$

ENTER:	Then PRESS:	Display shows:
10000	FV	10000
0.6666667	i	0.6666667
42	n	42
	COMP PV	−7564.86

Note: The value $10,000 was entered into FV as a positive number because this amount will be a cash inflow for the investor.

The sum of $7564.86 must be invested now to accumulate a total of $10,000 after 3½ years.   ∎

■ EXAMPLE 8.3c   CALCULATING THE MATURITY VALUE WHEN THE INTEREST RATE CHANGES

George invested $5000 at 9.25% compounded quarterly. After 18 months the rate changed to 9.75% compounded semiannually. What amount will George have accumulated 3 years after the initial investment?

✓ SOLUTION

Time diagrams are as useful in the financial calculator approach as in the algebraic approach.

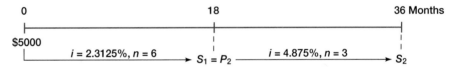

The following format allows a compact presentation of a financial calculator solution. Each computation of a financial function is a separate section in the table. The proper sequence of steps in each section is from top to bottom within a column, starting at the column on the left. Then work from left to right across the columns. For example, in the calculation of S_1, the digits 5000 are entered followed by pressing the +/− key to reverse the sign (since the $5000 is a cash outflow). Then press the PV key to save −5000 as the value of P. Next enter 6 followed by the n key to save 6 as the value of n. Then 2.3125 is saved in i . Finally, pressing COMP and FV in sequence executes the calculation of the value for S_1. The result (5735.12) appears in the calculator's display.

Calculate S_1.					Result
ENTER: 5000		6	2.3125		
PRESS: +/−				COMP	
PV		n	i	FV	5735.12
Calculate S_2.					
ENTER:		3	4.875		
PRESS: +/−				COMP	
PV		n	i	FV	6615.43

George's investment will have grown to $6615.43 after 3 years.

Note: When one of the financial function keys is pressed, the number that is in the display at the time will go into the memory. Therefore, it was not necessary to key in 5735.12 at the start of step 2 since it was in the display from the end of step 1. Its sign was changed to negative because step 2 should be viewed as another investment problem: The cash inflow from step 1 is reinvested (cash outflow) in step 2.   ■

■ **EXAMPLE 8.3D**   **THE BALANCE OWED AFTER PAYMENTS ON A COMPOUND-INTEREST LOAN**

Fay borrowed $5000 at an interest rate of 11% compounded quarterly. On the first, second, and third anniversaries of the loan, she made payments of $1500. What payment made on the fourth anniversary would extinguish the debt?

SOLUTION

As the time diagram indicates, calculate the amount owed on the first anniversary. Then deduct $1500 to get the principal amount at the beginning of the second year. Repeat for successive years.

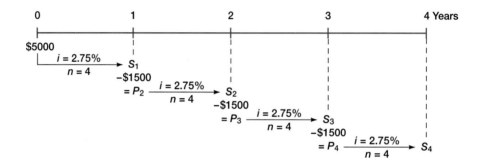

Calculate S_1.						Result
ENTER:	5000	2.75	4			
PRESS:	PV	i	n	COMP	FV	−5573.11
Calculate P_2						
ENTER:			1500			
PRESS:	+/−	−	=			4073.11
Calculate S_2.						
ENTER:		(n and i are				
PRESS:	PV	unchanged)		COMP	FV	−4539.97
Calculate P_3.						
ENTER:			1500			
PRESS:	+/−	−	=			3039.97
Calculate S_3.						
ENTER:						
PRESS:	PV	COMP	FV			−3388.42

```
┌─────────────────────────────────────────────────┬──────────┐
│ Calculate P₄.                                     │          │
│ ENTER:                          1500              │          │
│ PRESS:    ( +/- )   ( - )   ( = )                 │  1888.42 │
├─────────────────────────────────────────────────┼──────────┤
│ Calculate S₄.                                     │          │
│ ENTER:                                            │          │
│ PRESS:    ( PV )  ( COMP )  ( FV )                │ -2104.87 │
└─────────────────────────────────────────────────┴──────────┘
```

The final payment required to extinguish the loan is $2104.87. ∎

EXERCISE 8.3

Answers to the odd-numbered problems are at the end of the book.

Solve the problems in Exercise 8.2 using the preprogrammed functions on a financial calculator.

8.4 OTHER APPLICATIONS OF COMPOUNDING

COMPOUND-INTEREST INVESTMENTS

A "pure" compound-interest investment is one in which the initial principal accumulates compound interest at a *constant rate* for the *entire term* of the investment. The maturity value may then be calculated in a single step using $S = P(1 + i)^n$. Some compound-interest investments change the interest rate during the term of the investment. In such cases, a modified version of formula (8–2) must be used to calculate the maturity value.

Certain compound interest instruments are preferred by many people for holding within Registered Retirement Savings Plans (RRSPs). The automatic reinvestment of periodic interest earnings reduces the time and effort required to manage an RRSP. As a consequence of the income tax exposure of accrued interest,[8] compound interest investments are less commonly owned outside tax-deferred plans such as RRSPs. Note that an RRSP is not a type of investment. It is an investment trust arrangement that is granted certain tax advantages in order to encourage individuals to accumulate savings for retirement. The Income Tax Act sets out strict rules covering such matters as the type of investments that may be held within an RRSP. There are two main advantages of using an RRSP to accumulate savings.

- An eligible contribution to an RRSP is deductible from the contributing individual's taxable income. The individual's income tax payable is thereby reduced.
- The earnings of investments held in the RRSP are not subject to income tax until they are withdrawn from the plan.

---

[8]Individuals are required to "include in taxable income any *accrued* interest that is not paid at least annually." As a consequence, an investor holding a compound interest investment (outside a tax-deferred plan) whose term is more than 1 year must pay income tax on each year's accrued interest before receiving the total accumulated interest on the investment's maturity date. Other sources of cash must be used to pay the tax each year on the accrued interest income. To better match the timing of interest income and the tax payable thereon, investors generally prefer to have the interest income paid out at least once each year. A portion may then be used to pay the tax liability on the interest income. The investor can achieve compounding by reinvesting the interest proceeds as soon as they are received. However, each interest payment will be reinvested at the interest rate prevailing at that time.

GUARANTEED INVESTMENT CERTIFICATES   Guaranteed investment certificates (GICs) with maturities of 1 to 7 years may be purchased at virtually any branch of a bank, trust company, or credit union. Although a GIC may be issued in the name of a mortgage-lending subsidiary of the financial institution, it is fully guaranteed as to principal and interest by the parent institution. The minimum investment is usually $1000. GICs are normally not redeemable prior to maturity. Two versions of GICs are usually offered.

- The *periodic-payment version* has options with the interest being paid monthly, semiannually, or annually. A quarterly payment option is quite rare.
- The *compound-interest version* usually offers annual or semiannual compounding options. The accumulated compound interest is paid on the maturity date. For the reason previously mentioned, this version is purchased primarily for holding in tax-deferred plans.

■ EXAMPLE 8.4A   CALCULATING THE PAYMENT FROM A PERIODIC-PAYMENT GIC

What regular payment will an investor receive from a $9000, 4-year, monthly payment GIC earning a nominal rate of 8.25% compounded monthly?

✓ SOLUTION

The interest rate per payment interval is

$$i = \frac{j}{m} = \frac{8.25\%}{12} = 0.6875\%$$

The monthly payment will be

$$Pi = \$9000 \times 0.006875 = \$61.88$$ ■

■ EXAMPLE 8.4B   COMPARING GICS HAVING DIFFERENT NOMINAL RATES

Suppose a bank quotes nominal annual interest rates of 8.6%, 8.5%, and 8.4% on 5-year GICs with annual, semiannual, and monthly compounding, respectively. Which rate should an investor choose?

✓ SOLUTION

An investor should choose the rate that results in the highest maturity value.

j	m	i	n
8.6%	1	8.6 %	5
8.5	2	4.25	10
8.4	12	0.7	60

Choose an amount to invest, say $1000, and calculate the maturity values for the three alternatives.

ALGEBRAIC SOLUTION

$$
\begin{aligned}
S &= P(1 + i)^n \\
&= \$1000(1.086)^5 &&= \$1510.60 &&\text{for } m = 1 \\
&= \$1000(1.0425)^{10} &&= \$1516.21 &&\text{for } m = 2 \\
&= \$1000(1.007)^{60} &&= \$1519.74 &&\text{for } m = 12
\end{aligned}
$$

The investor should choose the monthly compounded alternative. The highest compounding frequency more than compensates for the lowest nominal rate in this instance.

FINANCIAL CALCULATOR SOLUTION

Find the maturity value with annual compounding.	Result
ENTER: 1000 5 8.6	
PRESS: [+/-] [PV] [n] [i] [COMP] [FV]	1510.60
Find the maturity value with semiannual compounding.	
ENTER: 10 4.25	
PRESS: [n] [i] [COMP] [FV]	1516.21
Find the maturity value with monthly compounding.	
ENTER: 60 0.7	
PRESS: [n] [i] [COMP] [FV]	1519.74

The investor should choose the monthly compounded option since it results in the highest maturity value.   ∎

CANADA SAVINGS BONDS   Every November 1, the Government of Canada sells a new issue (called a Series) of Canada Savings Bonds (CSBs). They are popular among individual Canadians because CSBs are guaranteed by the federal government and because CSBs can be cashed in for their face value plus accrued interest at *any time* at any branch of a bank, trust company, credit union, or caisse populaire. In recent years the bonds have been issued with 12-year maturities. Beginning with the November 1994 issue, minimum interest rates are guaranteed for the first 3 years. Subject to such guarantees, the Government of Canada may subsequently adjust the rates upward or downward from time to time in response to changes in prevailing interest rate levels. The CSBs are issued in two forms:

- *Regular interest "R" bonds*, which pay interest to the owner on November 1 of each year.
- *Compound interest "C" bonds*, which automatically convert accrued interest to principal on November 1 of each year.

Table 8.2 lists the issue and maturity dates of compound interest Series CS42 to CS50.

TABLE   8.2

Issue and Maturity Dates of Canada Savings Bonds

Series	Issue date	Maturity date
CS42	November 1, 1987	November 1, 1997
CS43	November 1, 1988	November 1, 1998
CS44	November 1, 1989	November 1, 2001
CS45	November 1, 1990	November 1, 2002
CS46	November 1, 1991	November 1, 2003
CS47	November 1, 1992	November 1, 2004
CS48	November 1, 1993	November 1, 2005
CS49	November 1, 1994	November 1, 2006
CS50	November 1, 1995	November 1, 2007

Table 8.3 presents the rates of interest earned by Series CS42 to CS50 Canada Savings Bonds for individual years ended November 1, 1988, to November 1, 1997. When the compound rate of interest changes from period to period, formula (8−2) must be modified to reflect the specific rates, i_1, i_2, i_3, . . . , i_n, for each of the n successive compounding periods.

Maturity Value (Variable Periodic Rate of Interest)

$$S = P(1 + i_1)(1 + i_2)(1 + i_3) \cdots (1 + i_n)$$ (8−2a)

TABLE 8.3

Interest Rates on Canada Savings Bonds

Period	Interest rate (%)
Year ended November 1, 1988	9.00
Year ended November 1, 1989	10.1$\overline{6}$
Year ended November 1, 1990	10.91$\overline{6}$
Year ended November 1, 1991	10.75
Year ended November 1, 1992	7.50
Year ended November 1, 1993	6.00
Year ended November 1, 1994	5.125
Year ended November 1, 1995	6.375
Year ended November 1, 1996	6.75①
Year ended November 1, 1997	7.50②

① Guaranteed minimum rate for Series CS42 to CS49. Minimum rate for Series CS50 is 5.25%.
② Guaranteed minimum rate for Series CS42 to CS49. Minimum rate for Series CS50 is 6.00%.

The annual rates in Table 8.3 should be used in conjunction with formula (8−2a) to calculate the redemption value of a compound interest CSB on November 1 of any year. When a CSB is redeemed between anniversary dates, the following rules apply:

- Accrued interest is paid to the first day of the month in which redemption occurs.
- The interest paid for the partial year is calculated on a simple interest basis. That is, obtain the additional interest for the partial year using $I = Prt$ where

    $P =$ the accumulated principal amount as at the preceding November 1
    $r =$ the prescribed annual interest rate on CSBs for the year of redemption
    $t =$ the number of months (from the preceding November 1 to the first day of the month of redemption) divided by 12

Example 8.4C illustrates the calculation of the redemption value of a compound interest CSB on a November 1 anniversary date and on a general date between anniversaries.

■ EXAMPLE 8.4C   CALCULATING THE REDEMPTION VALUE OF A COMPOUND INTEREST CANADA SAVINGS BOND

A $1000 face value Series CS45 compound interest Canada Savings Bond (CSB) was presented to a credit union branch for redemption. What amount did the owner receive if the redemption was requested on:

a. November 1, 1995?   *b.* January 17, 1996?

☑ SOLUTION

a. From Table 8.2 we find that Series CS45 CSBs were issued on November 1, 1990. November 1, 1995, falls on the fifth anniversary of the issue date. The rate of interest earned in each year is obtained from Table 8.3. Substituting these values into formula (8–2a), we have

$$S = P(1 + i_1)(1 + i_2)(1 + i_3)(1 + i_4)(1 + i_5)$$
$$= \$1000(1.1075)(1.075)(1.06)(1.05125)(1.06375)$$
$$= \$1411.25$$

The owner received $1411.25 on November 1, 1995.

b. For a redemption that took place on January 17, 1996, the bond's owner would have been paid extra interest for November 1995 and December 1995. The amount of the extra interest was

$$I = \$1411.25(0.0675)\frac{2}{12} = \$15.88$$

Therefore, the total amount the owner was paid on January 17, 1996, was

$$\$1411.25 + \$15.88 = \$1427.13 \qquad ■$$

VARIABLE-RATE GICs Some financial institutions offer Guaranteed Investment Certificates whose interest rate changes in a prescribed manner during the term of the GIC. Formula (8–2a) may be used to determine the maturity value of the compound-interest version of such GICs.

■ EXAMPLE 8.4D   *MATURITY VALUE OF A VARIABLE-RATE GIC*

A chartered bank offers an investment called an Escalator Guaranteed Investment Certificate. In successive years of its 5-year term, it pays annual interest rates of 5%, 6%, 7%, 8%, and 9%, respectively, *compounded* at the end of each year. The bank also offers regular 5-year GICs paying a fixed rate of 7% compounded annually. Calculate and compare the maturity values of $1000 invested in each type of GIC. (Note that 7% is the average of the five yearly rates paid on the Escalator GIC.)

☑ SOLUTION

Using formula (8–2a), the maturity value of the Escalator GIC is

$$S = \$1000(1.05)(1.06)(1.07)(1.08)(1.09) = \$1401.94$$

Using formula (8–2), the maturity value of the regular GIC is

$$S = \$1000(1.07)^5 = \$1402.55$$

The Escalator GIC will mature at $1401.94, but the regular GIC will mature at $1402.55 ($0.61 more). We can also conclude from this example that compound interest rates that vary from year to year will not have the same effect as the average of the annual rates. ■

COMPOUND GROWTH

It is generally understood that quoted rates of economic growth, sales growth, inflation, population growth, wage increase, and so on are to be compounded in successive periods. For example, it is understood that a forecast population growth rate of 2% per year for the next 5 years means that the population is expected to grow at the rate of 2% compounded annually for the next 5 years. The mathematical formulas developed for compound interest may be adapted to such cases of compound growth.

To adapt $S = P(1 + i)^n$ to compound-growth applications, the following interpretations are placed on the variables:

P = Initial size or quantity
i = Periodic rate of growth
n = Number of periods with growth rate i
S = Final size or quantity

A decline or reduction in a quantity is handled mathematically by treating it as *negative growth.* For example, suppose that a firm's annual sales volume is projected to decline by 5% per year for 4 years, from its current level of 100,000 units. The expected sales volume after 4 years may be obtained using $S = P(1 + i)^n$ where $i = (-5\%) = (-0.05)$. That is,

$$\begin{aligned} \text{Sales (after 4 years)} &= 100,000[1 + (-0.05)]^4 \\ &= 100,000(0.95)^4 \\ &= 81,450 \text{ units} \end{aligned}$$

This represents an overall decline of 18.55% in the annual volume of sales. Note that the overall decline is less than 20%, a result you might incorrectly obtain by simply adding 5% for each of the 4 years.

■ EXAMPLE 8.4E   THE LONG-TERM EFFECT OF INFLATION ON PURCHASING POWER

If the rate of inflation for the next 20 years is 4% per year, what annual income will be needed 20 years from now to have the same purchasing power as a $30,000 annual income today?

☑ SOLUTION

The required income will be $30,000 compounded at 4% per year for 20 years.

Given: $P = \$30,000$, $i = 4\%$, $n = 20$

ALGEBRAIC SOLUTION

$$S = P(1 + i)^n = \$30,000(1.04)^{20} = \$65,733.69$$

FINANCIAL CALCULATOR SOLUTION

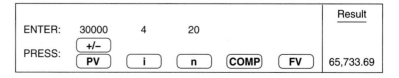

						Result
ENTER:	30000	4	20			
PRESS:	+/− PV	i	n	COMP	FV	65,733.69

After a 4% rate of inflation for 20 years, an annual income of $65,734 will be required to have the same purchasing power as $30,000 today.   ■

▪ EXAMPLE 8.4F   *COMPOUND ANNUAL DECREASE IN POPULATION*

The population of an economically depressed region is expected to fall by 2% per year for the next 10 years. If the region's current population is 100,000, what is the expected population 10 years from now?

☑ SOLUTION

The 2% "negative growth" should be compounded for 10 years.

Given: $P = 100{,}000$, $i = -2\%$, $n = 10$

ALGEBRAIC SOLUTION

$$S = P(1 + i)^n$$
$$= 100{,}000[1 + (-0.02)]^{10}$$
$$= 100{,}000(0.98)^{10}$$
$$= 81{,}707$$

FINANCIAL CALCULATOR SOLUTION

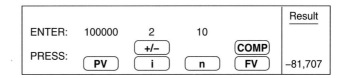

					Result
ENTER: 100000	2		10		
PRESS:	+/-			COMP	
PV	i		n	FV	−81,707

The region's population is expected to drop to about 81,707 during the next 10 years.

▪

EXERCISE 8.4

Answers to the odd-numbered problems are at the end of the book.

1. Krista invested $18,000 in a 3-year GIC earning a nominal interest rate of 7.5%. If interest is paid semiannually, what is each interest payment?

2. Eric invested $22,000 in a 5-year GIC earning a nominal interest rate of 7.25%. If interest is paid monthly, what is each interest payment?

3. Mr. Dickson purchased a 7-year, $30,000 compound-interest GIC with funds in his RRSP. If the interest rate on the GIC is 8.25% compounded semiannually, what will be its maturity value?

4. Mrs. Sandhu placed $11,500 in a 4-year compound-interest GIC earning 6.75% compounded monthly. What is the GIC's maturity value?

5. A trust company offers 3-year compound-interest GICs paying 7.2% compounded monthly or 7.5% compounded semiannually. Which rate should an investor choose?

6. If an investor has the choice between rates of 10% compounded semiannually and 10.25% compounded annually for a 6-year GIC, which rate should be chosen?

•7. For a given term of compound-interest GIC, the nominal interest rate with annual compounding is typically 0.25% higher than the rate with semiannual compounding and 0.5% higher than the rate with monthly compounding. Suppose that the rates for 5-year GICs are 8.75%, 8.5%, and 8.25% for annual, semiannual, and monthly compounding, respectively. How much more will an investor earn over 5 years on a $10,000 GIC at the most favourable rate than at the least favourable rate?

8. The fall 1995 issue of compound-interest Canada Savings Bonds guaranteed minimum annual rates of 5.25%, 6%, and 6.75% in the first 3 years. The fall 1995 issue of compound-interest British Columbia Savings Bonds guaranteed minimum annual rates of 6.75%, 6%, and 6% in the first 3 years. Assuming that the respective governments do not raise the rates above the guaranteed minima, how much more will $10,000 earn in the first 3 years if invested in BC Savings Bonds instead of Canada Savings Bonds?

9. Using the information given in problem 8, calculate the interest earned in the third year from a $10,000 investment in each savings bond.

10. Using the information given in problem 8, how much would have to be initially invested in each type of savings bond to have an accumulated value of $15,000 after 3 years?

11. What amount did the owner of a $5000 face value Series CS42 Canada Savings Bond receive when she redeemed the bond on:

   a. November 1, 1991?　　　b. August 21, 1992?

12. What amount did the owner of a $10,000 face value Series CS44 CSB receive when he redeemed the bond on:

   a. November 1, 1995?　　　b. May 19, 1996?

13. What was the redemption value of a $300 face value series CS43 CSB on March 8, 1996?

14. What was the redemption value of a $500 face value series CS45 CSB on June 12, 1997?

In each of problems 15 through 22, calculate the maturity value of the 5-year compound interest GIC whose interest rate for each year is given. Also calculate the dollar amount of interest earned in the fourth year.

Problem	Amount invested ($)	Year 1(%)	Year 2(%)	Interest rate Year 3(%)	Year 4(%)	Year 5(%)
15.	2000	7.50	7.50	7.50	7.50	7.50
16.	5000	6.75	6.75	6.75	6.75	6.75
17.	3000	7.00	7.00	8.00	8.00	8.00
18.	4500	7.25	7.25	7.25	8.50	8.50
19.	8000	6.00	7.00	8.00	9.00	10.00
20.	2500	6.50	7.00	7.50	8.00	8.50
21.	6300	7.20	7.60	8.00	8.00	8.00
22.	7500	7.00	7.75	8.50	9.25	10.00

23. In November 1995, the Bank of Montreal advertised rates of 5.5%, 6.125%, 6.75%, 7.375%, and 8% in successive years of its 5-year RateRiser GIC. In the compound-interest version of the GIC, interest was compounded at the end of each year. At the same time, the bank was selling fixed-rate 5-year compound-interest GICs yielding 6.75% compounded annually. What total interest would be earned during the 5-year term on a $5000 investment in each type of GIC?

24. On the same date that the Bank of Montreal was advertising rates of 6%, 7%, 8%, 9%, 10%, 11%, and 12% in successive years of its 7-year compound-interest RateRiser GIC, it offered 8% compounded annually on its 7-year fixed-rate GIC. How much more will a $10,000 investment in the preferred alternative be worth at maturity?

25. Using the information given in problem 24, calculate the interest earned in the fourth year from a $10,000 investment in each GIC.

26. Using the information given in problem 24, how much would have to be initially invested in each GIC to have a maturity value of $20,000?

27. How much will you need 20 years from now to have the purchasing power of $100 today if the (compound annual) rate of inflation during the period is:

    a. 3%?   b. 5%?   c. 7%?

28. How much money was needed 15 years ago to have the purchasing power of $1000 today if the average (compound annual) rate of inflation has been:

    a. 2%?   b. 4%?   c. 6%?

29. If the inflation rate for the next 10 years is 3.5% per year, what hourly rate of pay in 10 years will be equivalent to $15/hour today?

30. A city's population stood at 120,000 after 5 years of 3% annual growth. What was the population 5 years previously?

31. Mr. and Mrs. Stephens would like to retire in 15 years at an annual income level that would be equivalent to $35,000 today. What is their retirement income goal if, in the meantime, the annual rate of inflation is:

    a. 3%?   b. 4.5%?   c. 6%?

32. In 1987 the number of workers in the forest industry was forecast to decline by 3% per year, reaching 80,000 in 1997. How many were employed in the industry in 1987?

•33. A pharmaceutical company had sales of $28,600,000 in the year just completed. Sales are expected to decline by 4% per year for the next 3 years until new drugs, now under development, receive regulatory approval. Then sales should grow at 8% per year for the next 4 years. What are the expected sales for the final year of the 7-year period?

•34. A 1989 study predicted that the rural population of the prairie provinces would decline by 2% per year during the next decade. If this occurs, what fraction of the rural population will be lost during the 1990s?

8.5 EQUIVALENT VALUES

FUTURE VALUE AND PRESENT VALUE

Recall in Chapter 6 on simple interest we showed that the maturity-value formula $S = P(1 + rt)$ can also be used to calculate the economically equivalent value of a scheduled payment on another date. S represents the future value at a later date of a scheduled payment P. Alternatively, P represents the present value at an earlier date of a scheduled payment S.

The compound-interest maturity-value formula $S = P(1 + i)^n$ may similarly be used to calculate a scheduled payment's equivalent value n compounding periods later. S is then called the *future value* of scheduled payment P. In the form $P = S(1 + i)^{-n}$, the same formula gives the *present value, n* compounding periods earlier, of a scheduled payment S. In either case, i represents the periodic interest rate that money can earn during the n compounding periods. The applications of formula (8−2) may be summarized as follows:

Maturity Value or Future Value

Present Value

$$S = P(1 + i)^n$$

$$P = \frac{S}{(1+i)^n} = S(1 + i)^{-n} \qquad (8\text{--}2)$$

The factor $(1 + i)^n$ is called the **compounding factor** or **accumulation factor**. If the substitution $P = \$1$ is made in formula (8–2), S will be equal to $\$(1 + i)^n$. The compounding factor may therefore be interpreted as the future value of $\$1$ compounded at the periodic rate i for n periods.

The process of calculating the (smaller) present value of a (larger) scheduled payment is sometimes called "discounting the payment." It is from this context that the name **discount factor** arises for the quantity $1/(1 + i)^n$, or $(1 + i)^{-n}$. If we put $S = \$1$ in formula (8–2), P will be equal to the $\$(1 + i)^{-n}$. Consequently, the discount factor may be interpreted as the present value of $\$1$ discounted at the periodic rate i for n periods.

To obtain the combined equivalent value on a particular focal date of two or more scheduled payments, first calculate the equivalent value of each payment on the focal date. Then add the equivalent values. (See Example 8.5C.)

■ EXAMPLE 8.5A   CALCULATING AN EQUIVALENT PAYMENT

Mr. and Mrs. Espedido's property taxes, amounting to $2450, are due on July 1. What amount should the city accept if the taxes are paid 8 months in advance and the city can earn 6% compounded monthly on surplus funds?

☑ SOLUTION

The city should accept an amount that is equivalent, 8 months earlier, to $2450, allowing for the rate of interest that the city can earn on its surplus cash. This equivalent amount is the present value of $2450, 8 months earlier.

Given: $S = \$2450$, $j = 6\%$ compounded monthly, $m = 12$, $n = 8$

$$i = \frac{j}{m} = \frac{6\%}{12} = 0.5\% \text{ (per month)}$$

ALGEBRAIC SOLUTION

Present value, $P = S(1 + i)^{-n} = \$2450(1.005)^{-8} = \$2354.17$

FINANCIAL CALCULATOR SOLUTION

						Result
ENTER:	2450	0.5	8			
PRESS:	FV	i	n	COMP	PV	−2354.17

The city should be willing to accept $2354.17 on a date 8 months before the scheduled due date.   ■

■ EXAMPLE 8.5B   COMPARING THE ECONOMIC VALUES OF ALTERNATIVE PAYMENT PLANS

Florence can pay the membership dues at her golf club with a single payment of $1500 at the beginning of the year or by playing $770 at the beginning of the year and another $770 on a date 6 months later. Which alternative is to her financial advantage if she can earn 7% compounded quarterly on short-term investments?

☑ SOLUTION

We will take the approach of comparing the equivalent value, at the beginning of the year, of the two-payment alternative to $1500. Florence should choose the alternative with the lower economic value.

To calculate the present value of the second payment, we set $S = \$770$, $i = 1.75\%$, and $n = 2$.

ALGEBRAIC SOLUTION

$$P = S(1 + i)^{-n} = \$770(1.0175)^{-2} = \$743.74$$

The equivalent value, at the beginning of the year, of the two-payment plan is

$$\$770 + \$743.74 = \$1513.74$$

Florence should choose the single-payment alternative. The economic advantage, however, is $13.74, not $40.

FINANCIAL CALCULATOR SOLUTION

						Result
ENTER:	770	1.75	2			
PRESS:	FV	i	n	COMP	PV	−743.74

The equivalent value, at the beginning of the year, of the two-payment plan is

$$\$770 + \$743.74 = \$1513.74$$

Florence should choose the single-payment alternative. The economic advantage, however, is $13.74, not $40.   ■

■ EXAMPLE 8.5c *CALCULATING THE EQUIVALENT VALUE OF TWO PAYMENTS*

Two payments of $10,000 each must be made 1 year and 4 years from now. If money can earn 9% compounded monthly, what single payment 2 years from now would be equivalent to the two scheduled payments?

☑ SOLUTION

When more than one payment is involved in a problem, it is helpful to present the given information in a time diagram. Some of the necessary calculations may be indicated on the diagram. In this case, the calculation of the equivalent values, 2 years from now, of the scheduled payments is indicated by constructing arrows from the scheduled payments to the date of the replacement payment.

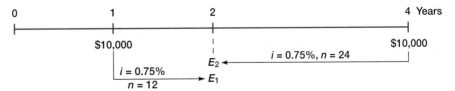

The single equivalent payment will be $E_1 + E_2$.

ALGEBRAIC SOLUTION

$$E_1 = \text{Future value of \$10,000, 12 months later}$$
$$= \$10,000(1.0075)^{12}$$
$$= \$10,938.07$$

$$E_2 = \text{Present value of \$10,000, 24 months earlier}$$
$$= \$10,000(1.0075)^{-24}$$
$$= \$8358.31$$

The equivalent single payment is

$$\$10,938.07 + \$8358.31 = \$19,296.38$$

FINANCIAL CALCULATOR SOLUTION

								Result
Calculate E_1, the future value of \$10,000.								Result
ENTER:	10000		0.75		12			
PRESS:	PV		i		n	COMP	FV	−10,938.07
Calculate E_2, the present value of \$10,000.								
ENTER:	10000				24			
PRESS:	FV				n	COMP	PV	−8358.31

The equivalent single payment is the sum of these two equivalent values, \$19,296.38.

■

■ EXAMPLE 8.5D   *DEMONSTRATING ECONOMIC EQUIVALENCE*

Show why the recipient of the payments in Example 8.5C should be indifferent between receiving the scheduled payments and receiving the replacement payment.

◪ SOLUTION

If the recipient ends up in the same economic position under either alternative, then he should not care which alternative is used.

   We will calculate how much money the recipient will have, under each alternative, at the end of 4 years, assuming that any amounts received are invested at 9% compounded monthly.

   The alternatives are presented in the following two time diagrams.

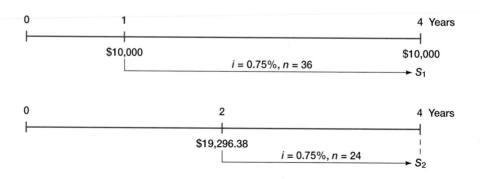

ALGEBRAIC SOLUTION

With the scheduled payments, the total amount that the recipient will have after 4 years is

$$S_1 + \$10{,}000 = \$10{,}000(1.0075)^{36} + \$10{,}000$$
$$= \$13{,}086.45 + \$10{,}000$$
$$= \$23{,}086.45$$

With the single replacement payment, the recipient will have

$$S_2 = \$19{,}296.38(1.0075)^{24} = \$23{,}086.45$$

Under either alternative, the recipient will have $23,086.45 after 4 years.

FINANCIAL CALCULATOR SOLUTION

Calculate S_1, the future value of $10,000						Result
ENTER: 10000 0.75 36						
PRESS: [+/-] [PV] [i] [n] [COMP] [FV]						13,086.45
Calculate S_2, the future value of $19,296.38						
ENTER: 19296.38 24						
PRESS: [+/-] [PV] [n] [COMP] [FV]						23,086.45

With the scheduled payments the recipient will have

$$S_1 + \$10{,}000 = \$23{,}086.45$$

after 4 years. This is the same amount as with the single replacement payment.

Note that the [PV] value is entered as a negative number because we are taking the view that the payments will be invested (cash outflows) as soon as they are received.   ■

■ **EXAMPLE 8.5E**   *CALCULATING THE EQUIVALENT VALUE OF TWO INTEREST-EARNING PAYMENTS*

Two payments of $10,000 each, plus interest accruing at the rate of 10% compounded quarterly from a date 9 months ago, must be made 1 year and 4 years from now. If money can earn 9% compounded monthly, what single payment 2 years from now would be equivalent to the two scheduled payments? (This problem is the same as Example 8.5C, with the change that the scheduled payments accrue interest.)

☑ SOLUTION

In this case, we do not know at the outset the size of the scheduled payments. Therefore, the first step must be to calculate these scheduled payments. The first time diagram below is constructed for this step.

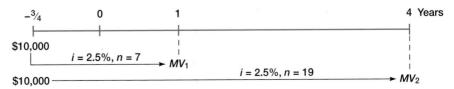

MV_1 and MV_2 represent the maturity values, at the indicated dates, of the two $10,000 principal amounts. Once MV_1 and MV_2 are determined, the remainder of the solution is just like the solution to Example 8.5C. The time diagram becomes:

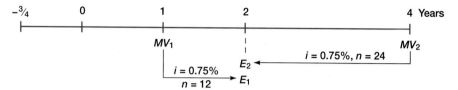

The single equivalent payment will be $E_1 + E_2$.

ALGEBRAIC SOLUTION

$$MV_1 = \$10,000(1.025)^7 = \$11,886.86$$
$$MV_2 = \$10,000(1.025)^{19} = \$15,986.50$$

$$\begin{aligned} E_1 &= \text{Future value of } MV_1, \text{ 12 months later} \\ &= \$11,886.86(1.0075)^{12} \\ &= \$13,001.93 \\ E_2 &= \text{Present value of } MV_2, \text{ 24 months earlier} \\ &= \$15,986.50(1.0075)^{-24} \\ &= \$13,362.02 \end{aligned}$$

The single equivalent payment 2 years from now is

$$E_1 + E_2 = \$13,001.93 + \$13,362.02 = \$26,363.95$$

FINANCIAL CALCULATOR SOLUTION

Calculate MV_1.						Result
ENTER:	10000	2.5	7			
PRESS:	PV	i	n	COMP	FV	−11,886.86
Calculate MV_2.						
ENTER:			19			
PRESS:			n	COMP	FV	−15,986.50
Calculate E_1, the future value of MV_1.						
ENTER:	11886.86	0.75	12			
PRESS:	PV	i	n	COMP	FV	−13,001.93
Calculate E_2, the present value of MV_2.						
ENTER:	15986.50		24			
PRESS:	FV		n	COMP	PV	−13,362.02

The equivalent payment 2 years from now is the sum of E_1 and E_2, that is, $26,363.95.

◼

APPLICATIONS TO VALUATION

STRIPPED BONDS A compound-interest investment that has been popular for holding within RRSPs is the *residue* of a *stripped bond*. Marketable bonds will be covered in considerable detail in Chapter 15. The only information you need at this point is that the **residue** of a stripped (marketable) bond entitles its owner to receive a single payment called the *face value* of the bond on its maturity date. The maturity date could be as much as 30 years in the future.

The pricing of stripped bonds is conceptually similar to the pricing of short-term investments such as T-bills. The residue of a stripped bond is purchased at a discount to its face value. According to the Valuation Principle, the fair market price to pay for a stripped bond is the present value of the bond's face value. However, the discounting is done on a compound-interest basis instead of the simple-interest basis used for T-bills. The discount rate used in the present-value calculation is the prevailing compound rate of return in the financial markets for bonds of similar risk and maturity. If this periodic rate of return is i for the n conversion periods remaining until maturity, we use formula (8–2) to obtain

$$\text{Price} = \frac{\text{Face value}}{(1 + i)^n} = \text{Face value} (1 + i)^{-n}$$

■ EXAMPLE 8.5F CALCULATING THE PRICE OF THE RESIDUE OF A STRIPPED BOND

A $10,000 face value stripped bond has 15½ years remaining until maturity. If the prevailing market rate of return is 8.75% compounded semiannually, what will be the price of the bond's residue?

☑ SOLUTION

Given: S = $10,000, j = 8.75%, m = 2, Term = 15½ years

$$i = \frac{j}{m} = \frac{8.75\%}{2} = 4.375\%, \qquad n = 31$$

Price = Present value of the face value

ALGEBRAIC SOLUTION

$$\text{Price} = S(1 + i)^{-n} = \$10,000(1.04375)^{-31} = \$2651.61$$

FINANCIAL CALCULATOR SOLUTION

						Result
ENTER:	31	4.375	10000			
PRESS:	n	i	FV	COMP	PV	–2651.61

The price of the bond will be $2651.61. ■

LONG-TERM PROMISSORY NOTES A long-term promissory note is a note whose term is longer than 1 year. Unless otherwise indicated, interest-bearing long-term notes accrue interest on their face value on a compound-interest basis. There is no statutory requirement to allow 3 days of grace.

Long-term promissory notes are also negotiable. Consequently they may be sold before maturity. The procedure for finding the selling price, or proceeds, parallels that for short-term notes. The **proceeds** represent the present value, on the date of sale, of the note's maturity value. The discounting is done on a compound-interest basis using $P = S(1 + i)^{-n}$.

■ EXAMPLE 8.5G   CALCULATING THE PROCEEDS OF A LONG-TERM PROMISSORY NOTE

A 5-year promissory note with a face value of $3500, bearing interest at 11% compounded semiannually, was sold 21 months after its issue date to yield the buyer 10% compounded quarterly. What amount was paid for the note?

☑ SOLUTION

We should find the maturity value of the note and then discount the maturity value (at the required yield) to the date of the sale.

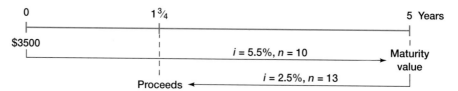

ALGEBRAIC SOLUTION

$$\text{Maturity value} = \$3500(1.055)^{10} = \$5978.51$$

$$\text{Price paid} = \$5978.51(1.025)^{-13} = \$4336.93$$

FINANCIAL CALCULATOR SOLUTION

Calculate the maturity value.						Result
ENTER: 3500	10	5.5				
PRESS: PV	n	i	COMP	FV		−5978.51
Calculate the price or proceeds.						
ENTER:	13	2.5				
PRESS:	n	i	COMP	PV		4336.93

Note: The FV memory already contained −5978.51 at the beginning of step 2.

The amount paid for the note was $4336.93.   ■

APPLICATIONS TO LOANS

In Section 6.7 we demonstrated that the original principal amount of a loan equals the sum of the present values of all of the payments required to pay off the loan. In other words, the original loan is the equivalent value (on the date the loan was advanced) of all the payments. This fundamental property also applies to loans bearing a compound rate of interest. As with simple interest, the interest rate that must be used in the present-value calculations is the rate of interest charged on the loan. The relationship will be used in this and later chapters to calculate the size of one or more loan payments.

■ EXAMPLE 8.5H   CALCULATION OF LOAN PAYMENTS

Fay borrowed $5000 at an interest rate of 11% compounded quarterly. On the first, second, and third anniversaries of the loan, she made loan payments of $1500. What payment was made on the fourth anniversary to extinguish the debt?

☑ SOLUTION

Let the final payment be x. As indicated in the following time diagram, the sum of the present values of the payments on the date of the original loan equals $5000.

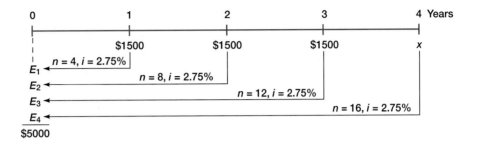

The equation of value is

$$\$5000 = E_1 + E_2 + E_3 + E_4$$

ALGEBRAIC SOLUTION

$$E_1 = \$1500(1.0275)^{-4} = \$1345.75$$
$$E_2 = \$1500(1.0275)^{-8} = \$1207.36$$
$$E_3 = \$1500(1.0275)^{-12} = \$1083.20$$
$$E_4 = x(1.0275)^{-16} = 0.6478742x$$

The equation of value becomes

$$\$5000 = \$1345.75 + \$1207.36 + \$1083.20 + 0.6478742x$$
$$x = \frac{\$5000 - \$3636.31}{0.6478742} = \$2104.87$$

FINANCIAL CALCULATOR SOLUTION

Calculate E_1 E_2, E_3, E_4 in sequence.						Result
ENTER: 1500 2.75 4						
PRESS: FV i n	COMP	PV				−1345.75
ENTER: 8						
PRESS: n	COMP	PV				−1207.36
ENTER: 12						
PRESS: n	COMP	PV				−1083.20
ENTER: 16 1						
PRESS: n FV	COMP	PV				−0.6478742

The equation of value is then solved as in the algebraic solution. A final payment of $2104.87 is needed to extinguish the debt.   ■

EXERCISE 8.5

Answers to the odd-numbered problems are at the end of the book.

In problems 1 through 10, calculate the equivalent values on the indicated dates based on the time value of money given in the fourth column. Assume that payments due in the past have not yet been made.

Problem	Scheduled payments	Date of equivalent value	Interest rate (%)	Compounding frequency
1.	$5000 due 1½ years ago	2½ years from now	8.25	Annually
2.	$7000 due in 8 years	1½ years from now	9.9	Semiannually
3.	$1300 due in 3½ years	9 months from now	10.5	Quarterly
4.	$3000 due in 5 months	3 years from now	7.5	Monthly
5.	$1400 due 3 years ago, $1800 due in 2 years	Today	12	Quarterly
6.	$900 due 15 months ago, $500 due in 7 months	3 months from now	10	Monthly
7.	$1000 due in 3½ years, $2000 due in 5½ years	1 year from now	7.75	Semiannually
8.	$1500 due 9 months ago, $2500 due in 4½ years	2¼ years from now	9	Quarterly
•9.	$2100 due 1½ years ago, $1300 due today, $800 due in 2 years	6 months from now	10.5	Monthly
•10.	$750 today, $1000 due in 2 years, $1250 due in 4 years	18 months from now	9.5	Semiannually

•11. Repeat problem 7 with the change that both payments accrue interest at the rate of 8.5% compounded semiannually from today.

•12. Repeat problem 8 with the change that both payments accrue interest at the rate of 7.5% compounded monthly from a date 2 years ago.

•13. Repeat problem 9 with the change that all payments accrue interest at the rate of 9% compounded monthly from a date 2¼ years ago.

•14. Repeat problem 10 with the change that all payments accrue interest at the rate of 10% compounded quarterly from a date 15 months ago.

15. What amount today is equivalent to $2000 4 years ago if money earned 10.5% compounded semiannually over the last 4 years?

16. What amount today is equivalent to $3500 3½ years from now if money can earn 9% compounded quarterly?

17. What amount 15 months ago is equivalent to $2600 1½ years from now if money earns 9% compounded monthly during the intervening time?

18. What amount in 2 years' time is equivalent to $2300 1½ years ago if money earns 9.25% compounded semiannually during the intervening time?

19. What payment 6 months from now would be equivalent to payments of $500 due (but not paid) 4 months ago and $800 due in 12 months, if money can earn 7.5% compounded monthly?

20. What single payment 1 year from now would be equivalent to $2500 due in 3 months and another $2500 due in 2 years if money is worth 7% compounded quarterly?

21. Gordon can receive a $77 discount if he pays his property taxes now, or he can pay the full amount of $2250 when payment is due in 9 months. Which alternative is to his advantage if he can earn 6% compounded monthly on short-term investments? In current dollars, how much is the advantage?

22. Gwen is considering two offers on a residential building lot that she wishes to sell. Mr. Araki's offer is $58,000 payable immediately. Ms. Jorgensen's offer is for $10,000 down and $51,000 payable in 1 year. Which offer has the greater economic value if Gwen can earn 6.5% compounded semiannually on funds during the next year? In current dollars, how much more is this offer worth?

23. A lottery winner is offered the choice between $20,000 paid now or $12,000 now and another $12,000 in 5 years. Which option should the winner choose if money can now earn 10% compounded semiannually over a 5-year term? How much more is the preferred choice worth in current dollars?

24. Daniel makes annual payments of $2000 to the vendor of a residential lot that he purchased a few years ago. At the time of the fourth from the last payment, Daniel asks the vendor for a "payout" figure that would immediately settle the debt. What amount, not including the regular payment, should the payee be willing to accept if money can earn 8.5% compounded semiannually?

•25. Ingrid can sell her boat for $8500 at the end of September. Alternatively, she can pay $500 in advance for 6 months' insurance and storage charges and then sell the boat at the end of next March for $9300. Which alternative is to her financial advantage if she can earn 6.6% compounded quarterly on short-term investments? How much is the advantage in current dollars?

•26. Commercial Finance Co. buys conditional sale contracts from furniture retailers at discounts that provide a 16.5% compounded monthly rate of return on the purchase price. What total price should Commercial Finance pay for the following three contracts: $950 due in 4 months, $780 due in 6 months, and $1270 due in 5 months?

•27. Teresita has three financial obligations to the same person: $2700 due in 1 year, $1900 due in 1½ years, and $1100 due in 3 years. She wishes to settle the obligations with a single payment in 2¼ years, when her inheritance will be released from her mother's estate. What amount should the creditor accept if money is worth 10.5% compounded quarterly?

••28. Repeat problem 26 with the change that each contract accrues interest from today at the rate of 12% compounded monthly.

••29. Repeat problem 27 with the change that each obligation accrues interest at the rate of 12% compounded monthly from a date 9 months ago when the obligations were incurred.

30. A $1000 face value stripped bond residue has 22 years remaining until maturity. What is its price if the market rate of return on such bond residues is 9.5% compounded semiannually?

31. What price should be paid for a $5000 face value stripped bond residue with 19.5 years remaining to maturity if it is to yield the buyer 8.25% compounded semiannually?

32. If the current discount rate on 15-year stripped bond residues is 10.75% compounded semiannually, how many $1000 face value bond residues can be purchased with $10,000?

33. Mrs. Janzen wishes to purchase 13-year-maturity stripped bond residues with $12,830 cash now in her RRSP. If these stripped bonds are now priced to yield 10.25% compounded semiannually, how many $1000 denomination bond residues can she purchase?

34. A $6800 non-interest-bearing promissory note is discounted at 11.5% compounded quarterly, 3½ years before maturity. What are the proceeds from the sale of the note?

35. A $4900 5-year non-interest-bearing promissory note was sold 2 years before maturity to yield the buyer 13% compounded monthly. What did the buyer pay for the note?

36. A 4-year $8000 promissory note bearing interest at 13.5% compounded monthly was discounted 21 months after issue to yield 12% compounded quarterly. What were the proceeds from the sale of the note?

37. An 8-year note for $3800 with interest at 11% compounded semiannually was sold after 3 years and 3 months to yield the buyer 14% compounded quarterly. What price did the buyer pay?

38. A promissory note called for a payment of $2000 with interest at 9% compounded quarterly 2 years after the issue date, and a second payment of $1500 with interest at 9% compounded quarterly 3 years after the issue date. What would be the appropriate price to pay for the note 6 months after the issue date to yield the buyer 10% compounded semiannually?

•39. A promissory note requires two payments 3 and 5 years from the issue date. Each payment is to include a principal amount of $2500 plus interest at 10% compounded annually on $2500 from the date of issue to the payment date. What will be the proceeds of the note 20 months after the issue date if it is discounted to yield 9% compounded monthly?

•40. A $15,000 loan at 11.5% compounded semiannually is advanced today. Two payments of $4000 are to be made 1 and 3 years from now. The balance is to be paid in 5 years. What will the third payment be?

•41. A $4000 loan at 10% compounded monthly is to be repaid by three equal payments due 5, 10, and 15 months from the date of the loan. What is the size of the payments?

•42. A $10,000 loan at 8% compounded semiannually is to be repaid by three equal payments due 2½, 4, and 7 years after the date of the loan. What is the size of each payment?

•43. A $6000 loan at 9% compounded quarterly is to be settled by two payments. The first payment is due after 9 months and the second payment, half the amount of the first payment, is due after 1½ years. Determine the size of each payment.

•44. A $7500 loan at 9% compounded monthly requires three payments at 5-month intervals after the date of the loan. The second payment is to be twice the size of the first payment and the third payment is to be double the amount of the second payment. Calculate the size of the second payment.

•45. Three equal payments were made 2, 4, and 6 years after the date on which a $9000 loan was granted at 10% compounded quarterly. If the balance immediately after the third payment was $5169.81, what was the amount of each payment?

*8.6 EQUIVALENT PAYMENT STREAMS

In Section 8.5 we learned how to calculate the equivalent value on any date of one or more scheduled payments. We will now turn to the more general problem of determining when two multiple-payment streams are equivalent. This issue arises, for example, in rescheduling the number or timing of payments on a debt.

Suppose payments of $2000 and $1000 were originally scheduled to be paid 1 year and 5 years, respectively, from today. They are to be replaced by two equal payments due 2 and 4 years from today. The size of the two equal payments is to be calculated so that the recipient will be in the same economic position as a result of receiving either the originally scheduled stream or the replacement stream. We will allow for a time value of money of 7% compounded semiannually. In other words, any payment received can be invested to earn 7% compounded semiannually.

Figure 8.5 presents the given information in a time diagram. Each payment stream is shown on its own time line. The equal but unknown replacement payments are each represented by x.

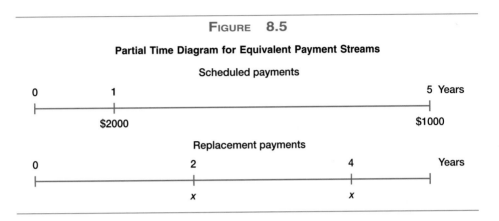

FIGURE   8.5

Partial Time Diagram for Equivalent Payment Streams

We must calculate a value for x so that the two streams satisfy the following Criterion for Equivalence.

> **Criterion for the Equivalence of Two Payment Streams:** Two payment streams are equivalent if the sum of the equivalent values of the payments in one stream equals the sum of the equivalent values of the payments in the other stream, all evaluated at the same focal date.

In Figure 8.6 the date of the first replacement payment 2 years from today has been chosen as the focal date. Consequently, that payment's equivalent value is equal to its nominal value, x. The equivalent value of the other payments on the focal date are indicated by E_1, E_2, and E_3.

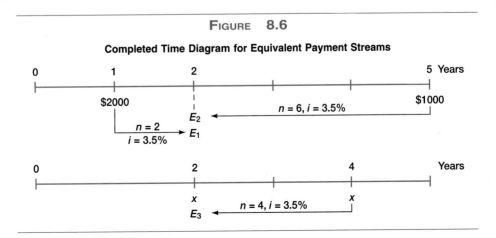

FIGURE   8.6

Completed Time Diagram for Equivalent Payment Streams

The equation of value expressing the Criterion for Equivalence is

$$E_1 + E_2 = x + E_3$$

The equivalent values of the individual payments are calculated in the usual way.

$$
\begin{aligned}
E_1 &= \text{Future value of \$2000 1 year later} \\
&= \$2000(1.035)^2 \\
&= \$2142.45 \\
E_2 &= \text{Present value of \$1000 3 years earlier} \\
&= \$1000(1.035)^{-6} \\
&= \$813.50 \\
E_3 &= \text{Present value of } x \text{ 2 years earlier} \\
&= x(1.035)^{-4} \\
&= 0.871442x
\end{aligned}
$$

Substituting these amounts into the equation of value, we obtain

$$
\begin{aligned}
\$2142.45 + \$813.50 &= x + 0.871442x \\
\$2955.95 &= 1.871442x \\
x &= \$1579.50
\end{aligned}
$$

Equal payments of $1579.50, 2 and 4 years from now, are equivalent to the scheduled payments of $2000 in 1 year and $1000 in 5 years.

Tip

For an equivalent-payment problem in a simple-interest environment, the answers depend slightly on the choice of focal date. In a compound-interest context, the answer is the same regardless of the choice of the focal date.[9] Therefore, problems will generally not specify a particular focal date to be used in the solution. But be careful to use just one focal date within a solution.

   The calculations will usually be simplified if the focal date is set at the date of one of the unknown payments. Then that payment's equivalent value is simply its nominal value.

■ **EXAMPLE 8.6A**   *CALCULATING TWO PAYMENTS IN A THREE-PAYMENT REPLACEMENT STREAM*

A financial obligation was to be settled by a payment of $1500 on a date 1 year ago and a second payment of $2500 on a date 4 years after the first payment. The debtor missed the first payment and now wishes to pay $1000 today and to make two more payments in 1½ and 3 years. The payment due in 3 years is to be twice as large as the payment due in 1½ years. What should these payments be if the creditor can earn 8% compounded semiannually on any payments received?

☑ **SOLUTION**

Let the payment due in 1½ years be x. The scheduled and replacement streams are presented in the following time diagrams. The date of the first unknown payment has been chosen as the focal date, and the symbols for equivalent values on the focal date are indicated.

---

[9]The assumption is, however, that a compounding date will be chosen as the focal date.

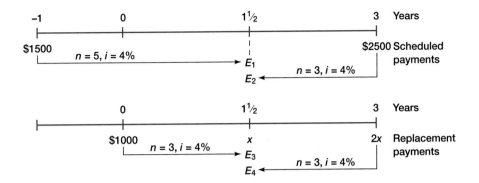

For equivalence of the two payment streams,

$$E_1 + E_2 = x + E_3 + E_4$$

ALGEBRAIC SOLUTION

$$E_1 = \text{Future value of \$1500, 2½ years later}$$
$$= \$1500(1.04)^5$$
$$= \$1824.98$$
$$E_2 = \text{Present value of \$2500, 1½ years earlier}$$
$$= \$2500(1.04)^{-3}$$
$$= \$2222.49$$
$$E_3 = \text{Future value of \$1000, 1½ years later}$$
$$= \$1000(1.04)^3$$
$$= \$1124.86$$
$$E_4 = \text{Present value of } 2x, \text{ 1½ years earlier}$$
$$= 2x(1.04)^{-3}$$
$$= 1.777993x$$

Substituting these values into the equation of value, we obtain

$$\$1824.98 + \$2222.49 = x + \$1124.86 + 1.777993x$$
$$\$4047.47 = 2.777993x + \$1124.86$$
$$x = \frac{\$4047.47 - \$1124.86}{2.777993}$$
$$= \$1052.06$$

The payments should be $1052.06 in 1½ years and $2104.12 in 3 years.

FINANCIAL CALCULATOR SOLUTION

Calculate E_1.						Result
ENTER:	1500	5	4			
PRESS:	PV	n	i	COMP	FV	−1824.98
Calculate E_2.						
ENTER:	2500	3				
PRESS:	FV	n		COMP	PV	−2222.49

Calculate E_3.					
ENTER:	1000				
PRESS:	PV		COMP	FV	−1124.86
Calculate E_4.					
ENTER:	2				
PRESS:	FV		COMP	PV	−1.777993

Now these values are substituted into the equation of value, as illustrated in the preceding algebraic solution. ∎

■ EXAMPLE 8.6B   *REPLACEMENT STREAM WHEN SCHEDULED PAYMENTS ACCRUE INTEREST*

One year ago Greg borrowed $5000 from Cheray and agreed to repay the loan with two payments, 3 and 5 years after the date of the loan. Each payment is to consist of a principal portion of $2500 plus interest on that $2500 at 8% compounded quarterly from the date of the agreement. Greg now wishes to settle the debt by making two equal payments, one in 6 months and the other in 2½ years. What size of payments will put Cheray in an equivalent financial position if money now earns 7% compounded semiannually?

☑ SOLUTION

The scheduled payments—the maturity values of the two $2500 components of the principal—must be calculated first. Then the calculation of the two replacement payments is very similar to the example worked out in the main body of this section.

ALGEBRAIC SOLUTION

Step 1: Calculation of the Scheduled Payments

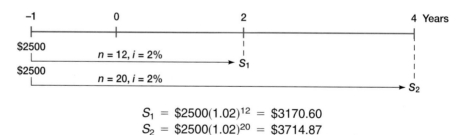

$$S_1 = \$2500(1.02)^{12} = \$3170.60$$
$$S_2 = \$2500(1.02)^{20} = \$3714.87$$

Step 2: Calculation of the Replacement Payments
Let each replacement payment be represented by x, and let the date of the first replacement payment be the focal date. The following time diagrams present the scheduled and replacement streams, and their equivalent value symbols at the focal date.

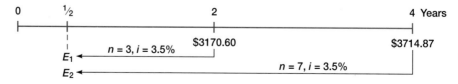

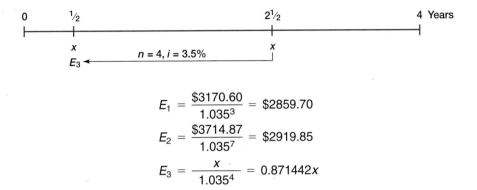

$$E_1 = \frac{\$3170.60}{1.035^3} = \$2859.70$$

$$E_2 = \frac{\$3714.87}{1.035^7} = \$2919.85$$

$$E_3 = \frac{x}{1.035^4} = 0.871442x$$

The equation of value is

$$E_1 + E_2 = x + E_3$$
$$\$2859.70 + \$2919.85 = x + 0.871442x$$
$$\$5779.55 = 1.871442x$$
$$x = \$3088.29$$

Two equal payments of $3088.29, 6 months and 2½ years from now, will put Cheray in an equivalent financial position.

FINANCIAL CALCULATOR SOLUTION

Step 1: Calculation of the Scheduled Payments

Calculate S_1.						Result
ENTER: 2500	12	2				
PRESS: [PV]	[n]	[i]	[COMP]	[FV]		−3170.60
Calculate S_2.						
ENTER:	20					
PRESS:	[n]		[COMP]	[FV]		−3714.87

Step 2: Calculation of the Replacement Payments

Calculate E_1.						Result
ENTER: 3170.60	3	3.5				
PRESS: [FV]	[n]	[i]	[COMP]	[PV]		−2859.70
Calculate E_2.						
ENTER: 3714.87	7					
PRESS: [FV]	[n]		[COMP]	[PV]		−2919.85
Calculate E_3.						
ENTER: 1	4					
PRESS: [FV]	[n]		[COMP]	[PV]		−0.871442

These equivalent values are now substituted in the equation of value, which was solved in the preceding algebraic solution.   ■

EXERCISE 8.6

Answers to the odd-numbered problems are at the end of the book.

In problems 1 through 8, calculate the replacement payment(s) if money can earn the rate of return specified in the last two columns. Assume that payments scheduled for dates now past have not been made.

Problem	Scheduled payments	Replacement payments	Interest rate (%)	Compounding frequency
1.	$3000 15 months ago, $2000 today	$1500 today, and a payment in 9 months	6	Quarterly
2.	$1750 7 months ago, $2900 in 11 months	A payment in 2 months, $3000 in 12 months	9	Monthly
•3.	$1400 in 3 months, $2300 in 21 months	Two equal payments in 9 and 27 months	13	Semiannually
•4.	$850 2 years ago, $1760 6 months ago	Two equal payments in 3 months and in 9 months	11	Quarterly
•5.	$400 8 months ago, $650 3 months ago	A payment in 2 months and another, twice as large, in 7 months	10.5	Monthly
•6.	$2000 in 6 months, $2000 in 2 years	A payment in 1 year and another, half as large, in 3 years	12.5	Semiannually
•7.	$4500 today	Three equal payments today, in 4 months, and in 9 months	7.2	Monthly
•8.	$5000 today, $10,000 in 5 years	Three equal payments in 1, 3, and 5 years	10.75	Annually

•9. Repeat problem 3 with the change that the scheduled payments consist of $1400 and $2300 principal portions *plus interest* on these respective principal amounts at the rate of 10.5% compounded quarterly starting today.

••10. Repeat problem 6 with the change that the scheduled payments consist of $2000 principal portions *plus interest* on these respective principal amounts at the rate of 9% compounded monthly beginning today.

••11. Repeat problem 8 with the change that the scheduled payments consist of $5000 and $10,000 principal portions *plus interest* on these respective principal amounts at the rate of 12% compounded semiannually starting 2 years ago.

••12. Repeat problem 2 with the change that the scheduled payments consist of $1750 and $2900 principal portions *plus interest* on these respective principal amounts at the rate of 10.5% compounded monthly starting 15 months ago.

•13. The owner of a residential building lot has received two purchase offers. Mrs. A is offering a $20,000 down payment plus $40,000 payable in 1 year. Mr. B's offer is $15,000 down plus two $25,000 payments due 1 and 2 years from now. Which offer has the greater economic value if money can earn 9.5% compounded quarterly? How much more is it worth in current dollars?

•14. During its January sale, Furniture City is offering terms of 25% down with no further payments and no interest charges for 6 months when the balance is due. Furniture City sells the conditional sale contracts from these credit sales to a finance company. The finance company discounts the contracts to yield 18% compounded monthly. What cash amount should Furniture City accept on a $1595 item in order to end up in the same financial position as if the item were sold under the terms of the January sale?

•15. Henri has decided to purchase a $25,000 car. He can either liquidate some of his investments and pay cash or accept the dealer's proposal that Henri pay $5000 down and $8000 at the end of each of the next 3 years.

a. Which choice should Henri make if he can earn 7% compounded semiannually on his investments? In current dollars, what is the economic advantage of the preferred alternative?

b. Which choice should Henri make if he can earn 11% compounded semiannually on his investments? In current dollars, what is the economic advantage of the preferred alternative?

(Hint: When choosing among alternative streams of cash inflows, we should select the one with the greatest economic value. When choosing among alternative streams of cash outflows, we should select the one with the least economic value.)

•16. A lottery prize gives the winner a choice between (1) $10,000 now and another $10,000 in 5 years, or (2) four $7000 payments—now and in 5, 10, and 15 years.

a. Which alternative should the winner choose if money can earn 7% compounded annually? In current dollars, what is the economic advantage of the preferred alternative?

b. Which alternative should the winner choose if money can earn 11% compounded annually? In current dollars, what is the economic advantage of the preferred alternative?

•17. CompuSystems was supposed to pay a manufacturer $19,000 on a date 4 months ago and another $14,000 on a date 2 months from now. CompuSystems is proposing to pay $10,000 today and the balance in 5 months, when it will receive payment on a major sale to the provincial government. What will the second payment be if the manufacturer requires 18% compounded monthly on overdue accounts?

•18. Payments of $5000 and $7000 are due 3 and 5 years from today. They are to be replaced by two payments due 1½ and 4 years from today. The first payment is to be half the amount of the second payment. What should the payments be if money can earn 7.5% compounded semiannually?

•19. Two payments of $3000 are due today and 5 years from today. The creditor has agreed to accept three equal payments due 1, 3, and 5 years from now if the payments are based on the recognition that money can earn 7.5% compounded monthly. What payments will the creditor accept?

•20. Payments of $8000 due 15 months ago and $6000 due in 6 months are to be replaced by a payment of $4000 today; a second payment in 9 months; and a third payment, three times as large as the second, in 1½ years. What should the last two payments be if money is worth 11% compounded quarterly?

•21. The principal plus interest at 14% compounded quarterly on a $15,000 loan made 2½ years ago is due in 2 years. The debtor is proposing to settle the debt by a payment of $5000 today and a second payment in 1 year that will place the lender in an equivalent financial position, given that money can now earn only 10% compounded semiannually.

a. What should be the amount of the second payment?

b. Demonstrate that the lender will be in the same financial position 2 years from now with either repayment alternative.

••22. Three years ago, Andrea loaned $2000 to Hether. The principal with interest at 13% compounded semiannually is to be repaid 4 years from the date of the loan. Eighteen months ago, Hether borrowed another $1000 for 3½ years at 11% compounded semian-nually. Hether is now proposing to settle both debts with two equal payments to be made 1 and 3 years from now. What should the payments be if money now earns 10% compounded quarterly?

••23. Repeat problem 18 with the change that the scheduled payments consist of $5000 and $7000 principal portions *plus interest* from today on these respective principal amounts at the rate of 9.6% compounded monthly.

••24. Repeat problem 19 with the change that the scheduled payments consist of $3000 prin-cipal portions *plus interest* on these respective principal amounts at the rate of 12% compounded semiannually starting 2½ years ago when the obligations were contracted.

••25. Repeat problem 20 with the change that the scheduled payments consist of $8000 and $6000 principal portions *plus interest* on these respective principal amounts at the rate of 7½% compounded monthly from a date 27 months ago when the debts were incurred.

APPENDIX: INSTRUCTIONS FOR SPECIFIC MODELS OF FINANCIAL CALCULATORS

This appendix has two goals:

- To point out commonly used features that tend to be unique to each of the models described below.
- To show how to set the calculator so that it will accept the generic instructions provided in the text.

SHARP EL-733A AND EL-735 BUSINESS/FINANCIAL CALCULATORS

KEY LABELS These two calculators have the same financial function key labels as are used in the generic instructions in the text. To accept the generic instructions, the calculators must be in the "financial" mode.

The EL-733A employs three calculation modes—the "normal" mode, the "finan-cial" mode, and the "statistics" mode. Every time the (2nd F) and (MODE) keys are pressed in sequence, the calculator will change its calculation mode. When it is in the financial mode, a small rectangle containing the abbreviation "FIN" appears in the display. When it is in the statistics mode, "STAT" appears in the display. Neither "FIN" nor "STAT" is seen when the calculator is in the normal mode. Repeated pressing of the (2nd F) and (MODE) keys will cycle the calculator through the three modes.

The EL-735 employs two calculation modes—the financial mode and the statistics mode. It will switch between these modes whenever the (2nd F) and (STAT) keys are pressed in sequence. A small rectangle containing the abbreviation "STAT" appears in the display when the calculator is in the statistics mode. When the "STAT" rectangle is absent, the calculator is in the financial mode.

CHECKING FINANCIAL FUNCTION MEMORIES To check the contents of the memory associated with any of the five basic financial function keys of the EL-733A, press (2nd F) and (RCL) followed by the function key. On the EL-735 calculator, simply press (RCL) followed by the function key. In both cases, the current value in the memory will appear in the display (and still remain in the memory).

ANNUITY DUE CALCULATIONS   The calculator must be in the "begin" submode of the financial mode before you can compute a value for an annuity due. On the EL-733A, this submode is activated by pressing the BGN key. "BGN" will then appear in small block letters in the display. To return the calculator to the "end" submode for *ordinary* annuity calculations, press BGN again. "BGN" then disappears from the display.

On the EL-735, this submode is activated by pressing the 2nd F and BGN/END keys in sequence. "BGN" will appear in small block letters in the display. To return the calculator to the "end" submode for *ordinary* annuity calculations, press 2nd F and BGN/END again. "BGN" then disappears from the display.

TEXAS INSTRUMENTS **BA 35** BUSINESS ANALYST

KEY LABELS   The keys labelled %i , N , and CPT correspond to i , n , and COMP, respectively, in the generic instructions. To accept the generic instructions, the calculator must be in the financial mode. The BA 35 is placed in the financial mode by pressing the 2nd and FIN keys in sequence. "FIN" will then appear in small block letters in the display.

CASH-FLOW SIGN CONVENTION   The BA 35 employs the standard cash-flow sign convention for the FV and PMT values but *reverses* the rule[10] for the value of PV ! In other words, *for the* PV *function only, cash inflows are negative and cash outflows are positive.* When following the generic instructions, *BA 35 users must remember to reverse the sign used in the text for the value of* PV .

CHECKING FINANCIAL FUNCTION MEMORIES   The contents of the memory associated with any of the five basic financial function keys may be checked by pressing 2nd and RCL followed by the function key. The current value in the memory will appear in the display (and still remain in the memory).

ANNUITY DUE CALCULATIONS   To compute one of the functions for an annuity *due,* press DUE followed by the function key instead of CPT followed by the function key.

TEXAS INSTRUMENTS **BA II PLUS** ADVANCED BUSINESS ANALYST

KEY LABELS   The keys labelled N and CPT correspond to n and COMP, respectively, in the generic instructions. The I/Y key will behave like the generic i key after the following sequence of steps.

2nd   P/Y

1   ENTER

2nd   QUIT

This setting needs to be made only once. It will not change (even when the calculator is turned off) until it is repeated with a different number used in the middle step.

---

[10]The reason Texas Instruments has chosen to use an *inconsistent sign convention* with the BA 35 is that, for a limited range of basic problems, the user can get away with not using (or even being aware of) the cash-flow sign convention. However, most courses at this level include some applications where, if you do not employ the BA 35's awkward sign convention, you would have to *artificially* make one of the numbers saved in memory negative in order to get the correct answer. In other applications, the calculated result will have the right magnitude but with a negative sign; in the absence of an understanding of the BA 35's sign convention, the negative sign would seem to be an anomalous quirk. To avoid having to invoke seemingly artificial rules for particular applications, rigorously obey the calculator's cash-flow sign convention.

CHECKING FINANCIAL FUNCTION MEMORIES   The contents of the memory associated with any of the five basic financial function keys may be checked by pressing [RCL] followed by the function key. The current value in the memory will appear in the display (and still remain in the memory).

ANNUITY DUE CALCULATIONS   To execute any of the functions for an annuity *due,* first set the BA II PLUS in the "annuity due" or "begin" mode using the following procedure.

[2nd]   [BGN]
[2nd]   [SET]
[2nd]   [QUIT]

"BGN" will appear in small block letters in the upper-right corner of the display when the calculator is in the annuity due mode.

Whenever you change from an annuity due calculation to an ordinary annuity calculation or vice versa, you must switch calculator modes by repeating the steps listed above. BGN is absent from the display in the ordinary annuity mode.

HEWLETT-PACKARD HP-10B BUSINESS CALCULATOR

KEY LABELS   The key labelled [N] corresponds to [n] in the generic instructions. Whereas other calculators use a key labelled [2nd] or [2nd F] as a shift key for accessing the secondary function of any key, the HP-10B employs a solid coloured key to access the secondary "coloured" functions. This key is denoted herein by a solid black rectangle: ■.

The [I/YR] key will behave like the periodic interest rate key, [i], after the following key sequence:

1 ■   [P/YR]

This setting needs to be made only once. It will not change (even when the calculator is turned off) until it is repeated and a number different from 1 is used.

After you enter the known variables in the memories of the basic financial function keys, the remaining unknown variable is calculated by pressing just its key; it is *not* preceded by a [COMP] keystroke. (There is no [COMP] key.)

CHECKING FINANCIAL FUNCTION MEMORIES   The contents of the memory associated with any of the five basic financial function keys may be checked by pressing [RCL] followed by the function key. The current value in the memory will appear in the display (and still remain in the memory).

ANNUITY DUE CALCULATIONS   For annuity *due* calculations, the HP-10B must be placed in the "annuity due" or "begin" mode with the following keystrokes:

■   [BEG/END]

"BEGIN" will appear in small block letters in the display.

Whenever you change from an annuity *due* calculation to an *ordinary* annuity calculation or vice versa, you must switch calculator modes by repeating the ■ [BEG/END] keystrokes. "BEGIN" is absent from the display when the calculator is in *ordinary* annuity mode.

REVIEW PROBLEMS

Answers to the odd-numbered review problems are at the end of the book.

1. At the same time as compound-interest Canada Savings Bonds were being sold with guaranteed minimum annual rates of 5.25%, 6%, and 6.75% in the first 3 years of their 12-year term, a trust company offered 3-year "Bond-Beater" GICs paying 5.75%, 6.5%, and 7.25% compounded annually in the 3 successive years. If the CSBs earn their minimum interest rates, how much more will $4000 earn over the 3 years if invested in the GIC?

2. A trust company offers a "Step-up" GIC that pays an increasing rate of interest in each successive year of its term. The compound-interest version of the GIC with a 4-year term pays 5.25%, 5.75%, 6.25%, and 6.75% compounded annually in years 1 to 4, respectively.

   a. What is the maturity value of $8000 invested in a Step-up GIC?

   b. How much interest will this GIC earn in the third year?

   c. How much more or less interest will it earn over the entire 4-year term than the trust company's standard 4-year GIC paying 6% compounded annually?

3. A credit union's "Move-up" GIC pays rates of 6%, 7%, and 8% compounded semiannually in successive years of a 3-year term.

   a. What will be the maturity value of $12,000 invested in this GIC?

   b. How much interest will be earned in the second year?

4. Use the data in Tables 8.2 and 8.3 to determine the redemption value of a $500 face value Series CS44 Canada Savings Bond on:

   a. November 1, 1995.   *b.* April 15, 1996.

5. Jacques has just been notified that the combined principal and interest on an amount he borrowed 19 months ago at 8.4% compounded monthly is now $2297.78. How much of this amount is principal and how much is interest?

•6. Marilyn borrowed $3000, $3500, and $4000 from her grandmother on December 1 of 3 successive years at college. They agreed that interest would accumulate at the rate of 4% compounded semiannually. Marilyn is to start repaying the loan on June 1 following the third loan. What consolidated amount will she owe at that time?

7. Accurate Accounting obtained a private loan of $25,000 for 5 years. No payments were required, but the loan accrued interest at the rate of 9% compounded monthly for the first 2½ years and then at 8.25% compounded semiannually for the remainder of the term. What total amount was required to pay off the loan?

8. Isaac borrowed $3000 at 10.5% compounded quarterly 3½ years ago. One year ago he made a payment of $1200. What amount will extinguish the loan today?

9. What amount 3 years ago is equivalent to $4800 on a date 1½ years from now if money earns 8% compounded semiannually during the intervening time?

•10. If the total interest earned on an investment at 6.6% compounded monthly for 3½ years was $1683.90, what was the original investment?

•11. Principal payments of $2400, $1200, and $3000, along with interest accruing on the respective principal, were originally scheduled to be paid 1½ years ago, today, and 15 months from today, respectively. Each principal amount accrues interest at 8% compounded quarterly from a date 2 years ago. Using 6% compounded quarterly as the time value of money, what payment 6 months from now would be equivalent to the three scheduled payments?

•12. A furniture store is advertising television sets for 25% down and no interest on the balance, which is payable in a lump amount 6 months after the date of sale. When asked what discount would be given for cash payment on an $1195 set, the salesclerk offered $40. If you can earn 8% compounded monthly on short-term funds:

  a. Should you pay cash and take the discount, or purchase the set on the advertised terms?

  b. What is the economic advantage, in today's dollars, of the preferred alternative?

13. If an investor has the choice between rates of 7.5% compounded semiannually and 7.75% compounded annually for a 6-year GIC, which rate should be chosen?

•14. A 5-year, compound-interest GIC purchased for $1000 earns 6% compounded annually.

  a. How much interest will the GIC earn in the fifth year?

  b. If the rate of inflation during the 5-year term is 4% per year, what will be the percent increase in the purchasing power of the invested funds over the entire 5 years?

•15. A $1000 face value stripped bond residue has 19 years remaining until maturity. What is its price if the market rate of return on such bond residues is 7.9% compounded semiannually? At this market rate of return, what will be the increase in the value of the stripped bond during the fifth year of ownership?

16. A 4-year $7000 promissory note bearing interest at 10.5% compounded monthly was discounted 18 months after issue to yield 9.5% compounded quarterly. What were the proceeds from the sale of the note?

•17. A promissory note called for a payment of $1500 with interest at 8% compounded quarterly 2 years after the issue date, and a second payment of $2500 with interest on the $2500 at 8% compounded quarterly 4 years after the issue date. What would be the appropriate price to pay for the note 18 months after the issue date to yield the buyer 10.5% compounded semiannually?

18. If the inflation rate for the next 10 years is 4.5% per year, what hourly rate of pay in 10 years will be equivalent to $15 per hour today?

19. A 1988 study predicted that employment in base metal mining would decline by 3.5% per year for the next 5 years. What percentage of total base metal mining jobs was expected to be lost during the 5-year period?

•20. Two payments of $5000 were scheduled 18 months ago and 1 year from now. They are to be replaced by a payment of $3000 today, a second payment in 18 months, and a third payment, twice as large as the second, in 3 years. What should the last two payments be if money is worth 9% compounded semiannually?

•21. Three equal payments were made 1, 2, and 3 years after the date on which a $10,000 loan was granted at 10.5% compounded monthly. If the balance immediately after the third payment was $5326.94, what was the amount of each payment?

•22. Carla has decided to purchase a $30,000 car. She can either liquidate some of her investments and pay cash or accept the dealer's terms of $7000 down and successive payments of $10,000, $9000, and $8000 at the end of each of the next 3 years.

  a. Which choice should Carla make if she can earn 7% compounded semiannually on her investments? In current dollars, how much is the economic advantage of the preferred alternative?

  b. Which choice should Carla make if she can earn 10% compounded semiannually on her investments? In current dollars, how much is the economic advantage of the preferred alternative?

••23. Four years ago John borrowed $3000 from Arlette. The principal with interest at 10% compounded semiannually is to be repaid 6 years from the date of the loan. Fifteen months ago John borrowed another $1500 for 3½ years at 9% compounded quarterly. John is now proposing to settle both debts with two equal payments to be made 2 and 3½ years from now. What should the payments be if money now earns 8% compounded quarterly?

••24. Two payments of $3000 plus accrued interest are scheduled to be paid 6 months and 2½ years from today. Interest accrues on each principal amount at the rate of 9% compounded quarterly from the date of the contract 1 year ago. These scheduled payments are to be replaced by an equivalent stream composed of two payments. The first replacement payment is to be made 1 year from today and the second payment, half the size of the first payment, is due 2 years from today. What should the two payments be if money can earn 7% compounded semiannually?

SELF-TEST EXERCISE

Answers to the self-test problems are at the end of the book.

1. On the same date that the Bank of Montreal was advertising rates of 6.5%, 7%, 7.5%, 8%, and 8.5% in successive years of its 5-year compound-interest "RateRiser GIC," it offered 7.5% compounded annually on its 5-year fixed-rate GIC.

   a. What will be the maturity values of $10,000 invested in each GIC?

   b. How much interest will each GIC earn in the third year?

2. For the 30 years ended December 31, 1993, the annually compounded rate of return on the portfolio of stocks represented by the TSE 300 Index was 10.40%. For the same period, the compound annual rate of inflation (as measured by the increase in the consumer price index) was 5.71%.

   a. What was $1000 invested in the TSE 300 stock portfolio on December 31, 1963, worth 30 years later?

   b. What amount of money was needed on December 31, 1993, to have the same purchasing power as $1000 on December 31, 1963?

   c. For an investment in the TSE 300 stock portfolio, what was the percent increase in purchasing power of the original $1000?

3. A $1000 face value Series CS43 Canada Savings Bond was redeemed on March 14, 1996. What amount did the bond's owner receive? (Obtain the issue date and the interest rate paid on the bond from Tables 8.2 and 8.3.)

4. Maynard Appliances is holding a "Fifty-Fifty Sale." Major appliances may be purchased for nothing down and no interest to pay if the customer pays 50% of the purchase price in 6 months and the remaining 50% in 12 months. Maynard then sells the conditional sale contracts at a discount to Consumers Finance Co. What will the finance company pay Maynard for a conditional sale contract in the amount of $1085 if it requires a return of 14% compounded quarterly?

•5. On February 1 of 3 successive years, Roger contributed $3000, $4000, and $3500, respectively, to his RRSP. The funds in his plan earned 9% compounded monthly for the first year, 8.5% compounded quarterly for the second year, and 7.75% compounded semiannually for the third year. What was the value of his RRSP 3 years after the first contribution?

•6. Payments of $1800 and $2400 were made on a $10,000 variable-rate loan 18 and 30 months after the date of the loan. The interest rate was 11.5% compounded semiannually for the first 2 years and 10.74% compounded monthly thereafter. What amount was owed on the loan after 3 years?

7. Donnelly Excavating has received two offers on a used backhoe that Donnelly is advertising for sale. Offer 1 is for $10,000 down, $15,000 in 6 months, and $15,000 in 18 months. Offer 2 is for $8000 down plus two $17,500 payments 1 and 2 years from now. What is the economic value of each offer today if money is worth 10.25% compounded semiannually? Which offer should be accepted?

8. A bank is advertising a Five-Year Escalator GIC. It can be purchased in a compound-interest version paying annually compounded rates of 6%, 6.5%, 7.5%, 8.5%, and 9.5% in successive years. At the same time, the bank's regular 5-year compound-interest GIC yields 7.5% compounded annually for the full term. Which GIC will have the higher maturity value? How much more would be earned on $10,000 invested in the preferred GIC for 5 years?

9. A 3-year $6000 promissory note bears interest at 9% compounded monthly. It was sold 1 year into its term at a price that yields the purchaser 11% compounded semiannually. What was the selling price?

10. To satisfy more stringent restrictions on toxic waste discharge, a pulp mill will have to reduce toxic wastes by 10% from the previous year's level every year for the next 5 years. What fraction of the current discharge level is the target level?

•11. Payments of $2300 due 18 months ago and $3100 due in 3 years are to be replaced by an equivalent stream of payments consisting of $2000 today and two equal payments due 2 and 4 years from now. If money can earn 9.75% compounded semiannually, what should be the amount of each of these two payments?

•12. A $6500 loan at 11.25% compounded monthly is to be repaid by three equal payments due 3, 6, and 12 months after the date of the loan. Calculate the size of each payment.

SUMMARY OF NOTATION AND KEY FORMULAS

j = Nominal annual interest rate
m = Number of compoundings or conversions per year
i = Periodic interest rate
P = Principal amount of the loan or investment; present value
S = Maturity value of the loan or investment; future value
n = Number of compounding or conversion periods

In the context of compound growth,

P = Initial size or quantity
i = Periodic rate of growth
n = Number of periods with growth rate i
S = Final size or quantity

The symbols representing the financial calculator memories and functions are

n	= n, the number of compounding periods
i	= i, the periodic interest rate
PV	= P, the principal or present value
FV	= S, the maturity value or future value
PMT	= the periodic annuity payment (Chapter 10)

Formula (8–1) $i = \dfrac{j}{m}$ Finding the periodic interest rate

Formula (8–2) $S = P(1 + i)^n$ Finding the maturity or future value

Formula (8–2) $P = \dfrac{S}{(1+i)^n} = S(1 + i)^{-n}$ Finding the principal or present value

Formula (8–2a) $S = P(1 + i_1)(1 + i_2)(1 + i_3) \cdots (1 + i_n)$ Finding the maturity value with compounding at a variable interest rate

Formula (8–3) $n = m \times$ (Number of years in the term)   Finding the number of compounding periods

---

Cash-Flow Sign Convention: Cash inflows (receipts) are positive.
Cash outflows (disbursements) are negative.

Criterion for the Equivalence of Two Payment Streams: Two payment streams are equivalent if the sum of the equivalent values of the payments in one stream equals the sum of the equivalent values of the payments in the other stream, all evaluated at the same focal date.

GLOSSARY OF TERMS

Accumulation factor   See *compounding factor.*

Cash flow   Refers to a cash disbursement (cash outflow) or cash receipt (cash inflow).

Cash-flow sign convention   Widely recognized rules for indicating the direction of cash movement by attaching an algebraic sign to the dollar amount of the cash flow. Cash inflows (receipts) are positive, and cash outflows (disbursements) are negative.

Compounding factor   The factor $(1 + i)^n$ in the compound-interest formula. It is numerically equal to the future value of $1.

Compounding frequency   The number of compoundings that take place per year.

Compounding period   The time interval between two successive conversions of interest to principal.

Compound-interest method   The procedure for calculating interest wherein interest is periodically calculated and added to the principal balance.

Conversion frequency   See *compounding frequency.*

Conversion period   See *compounding period.*

Discount factor   The quantity $1/(1 + i)^n$ or $(1 + i)^{-n}$. It is numerically equal to the present value of $1.

Exponential growth   The growth pattern when a quantity grows by the same percentage in each successive period.

Maturity value   The total amount due on the expiry or maturity date of a loan or investment.

Nominal interest rate   The stated annual interest rate on which the compound-interest calculation is based.

Periodic interest rate   The rate of interest earned in one conversion or compounding period.

Proceeds   The selling price of a promissory note. It is the present value, on the date of sale, of the note's maturity value.

Residue   The component of a stripped bond that entitles its owner to receive a single payment, the face value of the bond, on the maturity date of the bond.

Term   The length of time for which a loan or investment is made.

9

COMPOUND INTEREST: FURTHER TOPICS AND APPLICATIONS

LEARNING OBJECTIVES

After completing this chapter, you will be able to:

- Calculate the interest rate and term in compound interest applications, by both the algebraic method and the preprogrammed financial calculator method

- Explain the meaning and significance of an equivalent rate of interest and of the effective rate of interest

- Given a nominal interest rate, calculate the equivalent interest rate at another compounding frequency

- Given a nominal interest rate, calculate the effective interest rate, and vice versa

INTRODUCTION

The problems encountered in Chapter 8 required the calculation of either the present value or the future value. We begin this chapter by learning how to handle compound-interest problems where either the interest rate or the total time interval must be calculated.

It was demonstrated in Chapter 8 that nominal interest rates cannot be directly compared if they have different compounding frequencies. To make the comparison, the nominal rates must be converted to equivalent interest rates that all have the *same* compounding frequency. Sections 9.3 and 9.4 present two approaches for the interest rate comparison.

Total rates of return from various investments cannot be directly compared if the holding periods were of different lengths. In order to make such comparisons, the standard practice is to convert the rate of return for a short holding period to an equivalent annual rate of return. The procedure for doing this is developed in Appendix 9B.

9.1 SOLVING FOR THE PERIODIC INTEREST RATE, *i*

ALGEBRAIC METHOD Solving the basic equation $S = P(1 + i)^n$ for *i* is more difficult than solving for S or P. First divide both sides of the equation by P and then interchange the two sides, giving

$$(1 + i)^n = \frac{S}{P}$$

Now take the *n*th root[1] of both sides of the equation. The left side becomes simply $(1 + i)$ and we have

$$1 + i = \sqrt[n]{\frac{S}{P}}$$

Therefore,

Periodic Rate of Interest

$$\boxed{i = \sqrt[n]{\frac{S}{P}} - 1 = \left(\frac{S}{P}\right)^{1/n} - 1} \qquad (9\text{–}1)$$

FINANCIAL CALCULATOR METHOD The procedure for calculating *i* is similar to the procedure for calculating S or P. That is, the values for the three known variables—S, P, and n in this situation—are entered into the appropriate memories. The computation of *i* is then executed by pressing the (COMP) and (i), or (CPT) and (i), keys in sequence.

Trap

When values are being entered for both (FV) and (PV), it is imperative that your calculator's cash-flow sign convention be employed. If it is ignored or used incorrectly, an error message will appear in the display or an incorrect answer may result.

---

[1] It was shown in the appendix to Chapter 2 that taking the *n*th root of a quantity is equivalent to raising it to the exponent 1/n.

■ EXAMPLE 9.1A CALCULATING THE PERIODIC AND NOMINAL RATES OF INTEREST

The maturity value of a 3-year, $5000, compound-interest Guaranteed Investment Certificate (GIC) was $6193.60. To three significant figures, calculate the nominal rate of interest paid on the GIC if interest was compounded:

a. Annually.   *b.* Quarterly.

☑ SOLUTION

Given: P = $5000, S = $6193.60
In part *a, m* = 1, *n* = 3(1) = 3. In part *b, m* = 4, *n* = 3(4) = 12.

ALGEBRAIC SOLUTION

Formula (9–1) enables us to calculate the interest rate for one compounding period.

a. $i = \left(\dfrac{S}{P}\right)^{1/n} - 1$

$= \left(\dfrac{\$6193.60}{\$5000.00}\right)^{1/3} - 1$

$= (1.23872)^{0.\overline{3}} - 1$

$= 0.073967$

$= 7.397\%$

The nominal rate of interest on the GIC was $j = mi$ = 1(7.40%) = 7.40% compounded annually.

b. $i = \left(\dfrac{S}{P}\right)^{1/n} - 1$

$= \left(\dfrac{\$6193.60}{\$5000.00}\right)^{1/12} - 1$

$= (1.23872)^{0.08\overline{3}} - 1$

$= 0.018000$

$= 1.800\%$

The nominal rate of interest on the GIC was $j = mi$ = 4(1.80%) = 7.20% compounded quarterly.

FINANCIAL CALCULATOR SOLUTION

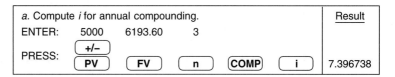

a. Compute *i* for annual compounding.	Result
ENTER: 5000 6193.60 3	
PRESS: +/− PV FV n COMP i	7.396738

The nominal rate of interest on the GIC was $j = mi$ = 1(7.40%) = 7.40% compounded annually.

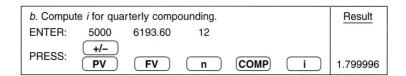

b. Compute *i* for quarterly compounding.	Result
ENTER: 5000 6193.60 12	
PRESS: +/− PV FV n COMP i	1.799996

The nominal rate of interest on the GIC was $j = mi$ = 4(1.80%) = 7.20% compounded quarterly.

■

Trap

The calculation of *i* is usually not the last step in a problem. Typically the nominal interest rate or the effective interest rate (discussed in Section 9.4) is requested rather than the periodic rate of interest. Do not forget to complete the extra step needed to directly answer the question.

■ EXAMPLE 9.1B   *CALCULATING A SEMIANNUALLY COMPOUNDED RATE OF RETURN*

Mr. Dunbar paid $10,000 for a $50,000 face value stripped bond having $19\frac{1}{2}$ years remaining until maturity. What semiannually compounded rate of return will he earn on his investment?

☑ SOLUTION

Given: $P = \$10,000$, $S = \$50,000$, $m = 2$, Term=19.5 years

$$n = 2(19.5) = 39$$

ALGEBRAIC SOLUTION

$$i = \left(\frac{S}{P}\right)^{1/n} - 1$$

$$= \left(\frac{\$50,000}{\$10,000}\right)^{1/39} - 1$$

$$= 5^{0.0256410} - 1$$

$$= 0.04213$$

$$= 4.213\% \text{ (per half year)}$$

$$j = 2i = 8.43\%$$

FINANCIAL CALCULATOR SOLUTION

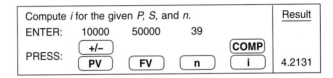

Compute *i* for the given *P*, *S*, and *n*.				Result
ENTER: 10000 50000 39			COMP	
PRESS: +/– PV FV n i				4.2131

$$j = 2i = 8.43\%$$

Mr. Dunbar will earn 8.43% compounded semiannually on his stripped bond investment.

■

■ EXAMPLE 9.1C   *CALCULATING AN EQUIVALENT ANNUALLY COMPOUNDED RATE OF RETURN FROM AN ANNUAL RETURN SERIES*

For the 10 individual years from 1985 to 1994 inclusive, the Industrial Growth Fund posted returns of 28.1%, 7.5%, 11.7%, 17.5%, 12.8%, –15.0%, 2.3%, –4.8%, 46.9%, and –1.4%, respectively. Calculate the fund's equivalent annually compounded rate of return for the 3-year and 10-year periods ended December 31, 1994.

BACKGROUND INFORMATION Long-term performance data for mutual funds are published once each month in most major newspapers. Each fund's *equivalent annually compounded* rate of return is quoted for the most recent 3-, 5-, and 10-year periods. Suppose, for example, the figure quoted for a fund's 5-year annually compounded rate of return is 12.4%. This means that if you had invested $1000 in the mutual fund 5 years ago (and reinvested all cash distributions in additional units of the fund), your holdings would now be worth

$$S = P(1 + i)^n = \$1000(1.124)^5 = \$1794.04$$

The actual year-by-year rates of return can be quite erratic. This example illustrates how the medium- and long-term compound annual rates of return are calculated from the actual rates of return for each year.

☑ SOLUTION

The equivalent annually compounded rate of return for an n-year period cannot be obtained by simply averaging the annual returns for the n individual years. Instead, the required rate of return for the 3-year and 10-year periods may be obtained by using a two-step procedure, as follows:

* Use formula (8–2a) to calculate how much $1000 invested in the fund at the beginning of the period was worth on December 31, 1994.
* Use formula (9–1) to calculate the equivalent annually compounded rate that would produce the same growth over the same number of years.

The value on December 31, 1994, of a $1000 investment made on December 31, 1991, was

$$S = P(1 + i_{1992})(1 + i_{1993})(1 + i_{1994})$$
$$= \$1000(1 - 0.048)(1 + 0.469)(1 - 0.014)$$
$$= \$1378.91$$

Similarly, the value on December 31, 1994, of a $1000 investment made on December 31, 1984, was

$$S = \$1000(1 + i_{1985})(1 + i_{1986})(1 + i_{1987}) \cdots (1 + i_{1994})$$
$$= \$1000(1 + 0.281)(1 + 0.075)(1 + 0.117) \cdots (1 - 0.014)$$
$$= \$2444.49$$

The second step for each period may be done either algebraically or with a calculator's financial functions.

ALGEBRAIC SOLUTION

3-year period	10-year period
$i = \left(\dfrac{S}{P}\right)^{1/n} - 1$	$i = \left(\dfrac{S}{P}\right)^{1/n} - 1$
$= \left(\dfrac{\$1378.91}{\$1000.0}\right)^{1/3} - 1$	$= \left(\dfrac{\$2444.49}{\$1000.0}\right)^{1/3} - 1$
$= 11.30\%$	$= 9.35\%$

The equivalent annually compounded rates of return for the 3- and 10-year periods ended December 31, 1994, are 11.30% and 9.35%, respectively.

FINANCIAL CALCULATOR SOLUTION

Compute the annually compounded rate of return for 1992–1994.	Result
ENTER: 1000 1378.91 3	
PRESS: [+/−] [PV] [FV] [n] [COMP] [i]	11.304
Compute the annually compounded rate of return for 1985–1994.	
ENTER: 2444.49 10	
PRESS: [FV] [n] [COMP] [i]	9.350

Note: For the second computation in the above table, −1000 remains in [PV] from the preceding computation.

The equivalent annually compounded rates of return for the 3- and 10-year periods ended December 31, 1994, are 11.30% and 9.35%, respectively. ∎

■ EXAMPLE 9.1D   CALCULATING AN INFLATION-ADJUSTED (REAL) RATE OF RETURN

The values of the TSE 300 Total Return Index and of the consumer price index (CPI) at the end of 1984 and 1994 are presented in the following table.

Date	TSE 300 Total Return Index	Consumer price index
December 31, 1984	3389.3	93.7
December 31, 1994	8205.7	131.6

For the decade, calculate (to three significant figures) the equivalent annually compounded *real* rate of return on the TSE 300 portfolio.

BACKGROUND INFORMATION   Price inflation causes the growth in the purchasing power represented by an investment's dollar value to be less than the (nominal) rate of return on the investment. This example will demonstrate how to adjust long-term rates of return for inflation in order to obtain an investment's *real* rate of return—the rate of growth in the investment's purchasing power.

The investment we will use to illustrate the inflation adjustment is the Toronto Stock Exchange (TSE) 300 portfolio. This portfolio is commonly used as a benchmark for evaluating the performance of Canadian common stock portfolios. Essentially, it contains common shares of each of the 300 largest companies that trade on the exchange. It represents a "no-brainer" portfolio in the sense that a company is included simply because it has reached a certain size, not because a thorough financial analysis indicates that the company's shares should perform better than others. The TSE 300 Total Return Index has been constructed so that it varies in direct proportion to the market value of the 300-stock portfolio. In other words, if the index rises by 10% over a period of time, then investors know that the value of the benchmark portfolio would also increase by 10% during the same period.

☑ SOLUTION

A $1000 investment in the TSE 300 portfolio on December 31, 1984, would have been worth

$$\$1000 \times \frac{8205.7}{3389.3} = \$2421.06$$

on December 31, 1994. However, the purchasing power of the portfolio in 1984 dollars is only

$$\$2421.06 \times \frac{93.7}{131.6} = \$1723.81$$

In terms of constant (purchasing power) 1984 dollars, the portfolio has grown from $P = \$1000$ to $S = \$1723.81$ in 10 years. The final step—calculating the annually compounded rate that would produce this overall growth in real purchasing power—may be done either algebraically or using a calculator's financial functions.

ALGEBRAIC SOLUTION

$$i = \left(\frac{S}{P}\right)^{1/n} - 1 = \left(\frac{\$1723.81}{\$1000.0}\right)^{1/10} - 1 = 5.60\%$$

FINANCIAL CALCULATOR SOLUTION

Compute the annually compounded real rate of growth.	Result
ENTER: 1000 1723.81 10	
PRESS: [+/−] [PV] [FV] [n] [COMP] [i]	5.596

Hence, the real rate of return on the TSE 300 portfolio was 5.60% compounded annually.[2] ∎

EXERCISE 9.1

Answers to the odd-numbered problems are at the end of the book.

Calculate percentages to the nearest 0.01% or to four significant figures, whichever is less accurate. Calculate the nominal rate of interest in problems 1 through 6.

Problem	Principal($)	Maturity amount ($)	Compounding frequency	Nominal rate (%)	Term
1.	3400	4297.91	Annually	?	3 years
2.	1000	4016.94	Annually	?	20 years
3.	1800	2299.16	Quarterly	?	2 years, 9 months
4.	6100	13,048.66	Semiannually	?	7 years, 6 months
5.	950	1165.79	Monthly	?	2 years, 5 months
6.	4300	10,440.32	Annually	?	8 years, 6 months

7. When he died in 1790, Benjamin Franklin left $4600 to the city of Boston, with the stipulation that the money and its earnings could not be used for 100 years. The bequest grew to $332,000 by 1890. What equivalent compound annual rate of return did the bequest earn?

8. The Templeton Growth Fund, an international equity mutual fund, presented a graph in a December 1995 advertisement showing that a $10,000 investment in the fund at the end of November 1954 would have grown to over $3,540,000 by November 30, 1995. What (equivalent) compound annual rate of return did the fund realize over this period?

9. Anders discovered an old pay statement from 11 years ago. His monthly salary at the time was $2550 versus his current salary of $4475 per month. At what (equivalent) compound annual rate has his salary grown during the period?

10. Aggregate consumer credit in Canada rose from $42.4 billion in July 1984 to $115 billion in July 1995. What was the average compound annual rate of increase in consumer credit during the period?

---

[2]An alternative approach that is not strictly correct is often used in business. The three-step procedure is:
- Determine the annually compounded (nominal) rate of return on the TSE 300 portfolio. It was

$$i = \left(\frac{S}{P}\right)^{1/n} - 1 = \left(\frac{8205.7}{3389.3}\right)^{1/10} - 1 = 0.092447 = 9.24\% \text{ compounded annually}$$

- Determine the annually compounded rate of inflation. It was

$$i = \left(\frac{S}{P}\right)^{1/n} - 1 = \left(\frac{131.6}{93.7}\right)^{1/10} - 1 = 0.03455 = 3.46\% \text{ compounded annually}$$

- View the difference between the two annual rates as the real rate of return. This gives

Real rate of return = 9.24% − 3.46% = 5.78%

versus the strictly correct value of 5.60%. The approximation is good enough for most practical purposes.

11. Mr. and Mrs. Markovich note that the home they purchased 17 years ago for $70,000 is now appraised at $260,000. What was the (equivalent) annual rate of appreciation in the value of their home during the 17-year period?

12. If the population of a city grew from 53,500 at the beginning of 1988 to 64,300 at the end of 1995, what was the city's (equivalent) annual rate of growth during the period?

13. The aggregate market value of mutual fund assets administered by members of the Investment Funds Institute of Canada increased by a factor of 14 from the end of 1984 to the beginning of 1995. What was the (equivalent) compound annual rate of increase in mutual fund assets during the period?

14. The population of the Atlantic provinces grew from 2.030 million at the beginning of 1970 to 2.337 million at the beginning of 1992. During the same period the population of British Columbia increased from 2.107 million to 3.273 million. What was the (equivalent) annual rate of population growth in each region during the period?

15. If the number of workers in steel manufacturing in Canada declined by 30% from the end of 1987 to the beginning of 1994, what was the compound annual rate of attrition in the industry?

16. The Canadian consumer price index (based on a value of 100 in 1971) rose from 97.2 in 1970 to 210.6 in 1980. What was the (equivalent) annual rate of inflation in the decade of the 1970s?

17. The consumer price index (based on a value of 100 in 1986) rose from 67.2 in 1980 to 119.5 in 1990. What was the (equivalent) annual rate of inflation in the decade of the 1980s?

•18. A 4-year promissory note for $3800 plus interest at 9.5% compounded semiannually was sold 18 months before maturity for $4481. What quarterly compounded (annual) rate of return will the buyer realize on her investment?

•19. A $6000, 3-year promissory note bearing interest at 11% compounded semiannually was purchased 15 months into its term for $6854.12. What monthly compounded discount rate was used in pricing the note?

•20. Using the data given in problems 16 and 17, calculate the average rate of inflation for the 1970–1990 period. (*Note:* Simply averaging the two answers to problems 16 and 17 will give only an approximation of the correct result.)

•21. If, at the beginning of 1975, a Canadian had invested (1) $1000 in a portfolio of the TSE 300 Index stocks and (2) $1000 in 3-month Treasury bills (and repeatedly used the proceeds of maturing bills to buy new issues), the two portfolios would have grown to $10,791 and $6964, respectively (before taxes), by the beginning of 1995.

   a. Calculate the equivalent annually compounded return on each portfolio for the period.

   b. Given that the equivalent compound annual rate of inflation during the period was 5.88%, what was the final purchasing power of each portfolio in 1975 dollars?

   c. What was the equivalent annually compounded real rate of return on each portfolio?

•22. If, at the beginning of 1975, an American had invested (1) $1000 in a portfolio of the Standard & Poor's (S&P) 500 Index stocks and (2) $1000 in 3-month Treasury bills (and repeatedly used the proceeds of maturing bills to buy new issues), the two portfolios would have grown to $15,238 and $4304, respectively (before taxes), by the beginning of 1995.

   a. Calculate the equivalent annually compounded return on each portfolio for the period.

   b. Given that the average compounded rate of inflation during the period was 5.4%, what was the final purchasing power of each portfolio in 1975 dollars?

   c. What was the equivalent compound annual real rate of return on each portfolio?

•23. In recent years Canadian stocks as a group have significantly underperformed U.S. stocks. Consider that in mid-August of 1987, the TSE 300 Stock Price Index was at

4100 at the same time as the S&P 500 Stock Price Index in the United States stood at 335. By mid-August 1995, the S&P 500 Stock Price Index had risen to 560 and the TSE Stock Price Index to 4620.

   a. Calculate the compound annual change in the price of each group of stocks during the period.

   b. By what multiple did the overall 8-year percent increase in prices of U.S. stocks (as represented by the S&P 500 stocks) outperform Canadian stocks (as represented by the TSE 300 stocks)?

•24. An investment earned 12% compounded semiannually for 2 years and 10% compounded annually for the next 3 years. What was the equivalent annually compounded rate of return for the entire 5-year period?

•25. A portfolio earned 20%, –20%, 0%, 20%, and –20% in 5 successive years. What was the portfolio's 5-year equivalent annually compounded rate of return?

•26. A portfolio earned 20%, 15%, –10%, 25%, and –5% in 5 successive years. What was the portfolio's 5-year equivalent annually compounded rate of return?

•27. At the end of 1995, the Templeton Growth Fund was the largest mutual fund in Canada. This fund invests primarily in common stocks of foreign companies. The aggregate market value of its holdings at the end of 1995 was close to $4 billion (Canadian). What 3-year, 5-year, and 10-year equivalent annually compounded returns to December 31, 1995, did the fund report if its annual returns in successive years from 1986 to 1995 inclusive were 19.7%, –5.1%, 12.3%, 21.1%, –13.6%, 30.3%, 15.2%, 36.3%, 3.8%, and 14.1%, respectively?

•28. At the end of 1995, the Bullock American Fund had the highest 10-year compound annual return of any mutual fund based in Canada. This fund invests primarily in common stocks of American companies. What 3-year, 5-year, and 10-year equivalent annually compounded returns to December 31, 1995, did the fund report if its annual returns in successive years from 1986 to 1995 inclusive were 29.1%, –2.3%, –5.5%, 44.1%, 10.5%, 81.9%, 4.3%, 20.3%, –9.4% and 30.9%, respectively?

9.2 SOLVING FOR THE NUMBER OF COMPOUNDING PERIODS, *n*

ALGEBRAIC METHOD   Manipulation of $S = P(1 + i)^n$ to isolate *n* requires the use of logarithms. Logarithms are briefly discussed in Appendix 9A. Example 9AB in that appendix derives the following formula for the number of compounding periods.

Number of Compounding Periods

$$n = \frac{\ln\left(\frac{S}{P}\right)}{\ln(1+i)} \qquad (9\text{–}2)$$

FINANCIAL CALCULATOR METHOD   The procedure for calculating *n* is similar to the procedure for *S* or *P*. That is, the values for the three known variables—*S*, *P*, and *i*—are entered in the appropriate memories. Then *n* is computed by pressing the $\boxed{\text{COMP}}$ and $\boxed{n}$, or $\boxed{\text{CPT}}$ and $\boxed{n}$, keys in sequence.

> **Tip**
>
> Remember that formulas (9–1) and (9–2) are merely alternative versions of $S = P(1 + i)^n$ with different variables isolated. Each formula contains the same information as any of the others. Any one of them may be derived from either of the others by strictly algebraic manipulations.

NONINTEGER VALUES FOR n Up to this point, we have encountered only cases in which the number of compounding periods is an integer. It can easily happen that an investment or a loan has a term that is not an exact whole number of compounding periods. When this occurs, n is no longer an integer: it includes the decimal fraction for the last partial compounding period. Otherwise, the procedures are the same as for integer values of n. Formulas (8–2), (9–1), and (9–2) and the preprogrammed financial calculator functions may be used with either integer or noninteger values for n.

■ EXAMPLE 9.2A   CALCULATING THE NUMBER OF COMPOUNDING PERIODS

What is the term of a compound interest GIC if $4000 invested at 7.5% compounded annually will earn interest totalling $1742.52?

☑ SOLUTION

Given: $P = \$4000$, $j = i = 7.5\%$, total interest = $1742.52
   The maturity value of the GIC is

$$S = P + \text{Total interest} = \$4000 + \$1742.52 = \$5742.52$$

ALGEBRAIC SOLUTION

The number of compounding periods required for $4000 to grow to $5742.52 is

$$n = \frac{\ln\left(\frac{S}{P}\right)}{\ln(1 + i)} = \frac{\ln\left(\frac{\$5742.52}{\$4000.00}\right)}{\ln(1.075)} = \frac{\ln(1.43563)}{\ln(1.075)} = \frac{0.3616038}{0.0723207} = 5.000$$

Since each compounding period equals 1 year, the term of the GIC is 5 years.

Tip

The most efficient keystroke sequence for calculating n is:

5742.52 [÷] 4000 [=] [ln] [÷] 1.075 [ln] [=]

If the natural logarithm function is the secondary function of a key on your calculator, you must press the [2nd F] or [2nd] key before the [ln] key in the above sequence.

FINANCIAL CALCULATOR SOLUTION

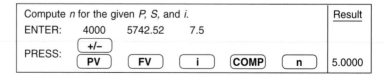

Compute n for the given P, S, and i.						Result
ENTER: 4000 5742.52 7.5						
PRESS: [PV] (+/−) [FV] [i] [COMP] [n]						5.0000

Since each compounding period equals 1 year, the term of the GIC is 5 years.   ■

■ EXAMPLE 9.2B   CALCULATING AND INTERPRETING A NONINTEGER n

Rounded to the nearest month, how long will it take a city's population to grow from 75,000 to 100,000 if the annual growth rate is 2%?

☑ SOLUTION

In effect, we are given: $P = 75,000$, $S = 100,000$, and $j = i = 2\%$/year.

ALGEBRAIC SOLUTION

Using formula (9–2) to calculate the required number of compounding periods, we obtain

$$n = \frac{\ln\left(\dfrac{S}{P}\right)}{\ln(1 + i)} = \frac{\ln\left(\dfrac{100{,}000}{75{,}000}\right)}{\ln(1.02)} = \frac{0.28768}{0.019803} = 14.527$$

The conclusion of the solution follows the Financial Calculator Solution box.

FINANCIAL CALCULATOR SOLUTION

Compute n for the given P, S, and i.					Result
ENTER: 75000 100000 2					
PRESS: [+/–] [PV] [FV] [i] [COMP] [n]					14.527

The mathematics tells us that it requires 14.527 compounding periods for a periodic growth rate of 2% to cause 75,000 to grow to 100,000. The 100,000 figure will be reached slightly more than halfway through the 15th compounding period. Since we have annual compounding in this case, a population of 100,000 is expected to be reached after 0.527 of the 15th year has elapsed. This corresponds to

$$0.527 \times 12 \text{ months} = 6.32 \text{ months into the 15th year}$$

Rounded to the nearest month, it will take 14 years and 6 months for the city's population to reach 100,000. ∎

■ EXAMPLE 9.2c   *CALCULATING AN INVESTMENT'S DOUBLING TIME*

Rounded to the nearest month, how long will it take an investment to double in value if it earns:

a. 6% compounded annually?   *b.* 10% compounded annually?

☑ SOLUTION

We require the maturity value of an investment to be twice the initial investment. Therefore, we can simply set $P = \$1$ and $S = \$2$. In part *a*, $j = i = 6\%$ per year; in part *b*, $j = i = 10\%$ per year.

ALGEBRAIC SOLUTION

Substituting in formula (9–2),

$$a.\ n = \frac{\ln\left(\dfrac{S}{P}\right)}{\ln(1+i)} = \frac{\ln(2)}{\ln(1.06)} = \frac{0.69315}{0.058269} = 11.896$$

The doubling time is 11 years and 0.896×12 months = 10.75 months. An investment earning 6% compounded annually will double in 11 years and 11 months (rounded to the nearest month).

b. $n = \dfrac{\ln(2)}{\ln(1.10)} = 7.2725$

The doubling time is 7 years and 0.2725×12 months $= 3.27$ months. An investment earning 10% compounded annually will double in 7 years and 3 months (rounded to the nearest month).

FINANCIAL CALCULATOR SOLUTION

a. Compute the doubling time at 6% compounded annually.				Result
ENTER: 1 2 6				
PRESS: [+/–] [PV] [FV] [i] [COMP] [n]				11.896

The doubling time is 11 years and 0.896×12 months $= 10.75$ months. An investment earning 6% compounded annually will double in 11 years and 11 months (rounded to the nearest month).

b. Compute the doubling time at 10% compounded annually.				Result
ENTER: 1 2 10				
PRESS: [+/–] [PV] [FV] [i] [COMP] [n]				7.2725

The doubling time is 7 years and 0.2725×12 months $= 3.27$ months. An investment earning 10% compounded annually will double in 7 years and 3 months (rounded to the nearest month).   ∎

RULE OF 72 Investors have a rule of thumb for a quick *estimate* of the number of years it will take an investment to double at a known compound annual rate of return.[3] The rule, known as the **Rule of 72,** is:

$$\text{Doubling time (in years)} \approx \frac{72}{\text{Percent annual rate of return}}$$

For example, an investment earning 9% compounded annually will double in approximately $\frac{72}{9} = 8$ years, whereas an investment at 12% compounded annually will double in about $\frac{72}{12} = 6$ years.

    The answers in Example 9.2C provide an indication of the accuracy of the Rule of 72. At an annually compounded rate of 6%, we calculated a doubling time of 11.90 years. The Rule of 72 provides an estimate of 12.00 years. At 10% compounded annually, we calculated a doubling time of 7.27 years. The Rule of 72 provides an estimate of 7.20 years. In both cases, the estimate is within 1% of the correct value.

■ **EXAMPLE 9.2D**   *SOLVING FOR A NONINTEGER n IN A DISCOUNTING PROBLEM*

A financial contract guaranteed the payment of $4000 plus interest at a fixed rate of 9.6% compounded quarterly 2 years after the contract's date of issue. Sometime before the maturity date, the original owner sold the contract for $4327.70. The sale

---

[3]The approximation is very good for interest rates between 5% and 11%: The value calculated for the doubling time is within 2% of its true value.

price represented the fair market value given the market rate of 8.5% compounded semiannually for similar maturities. How long before the maturity date did the sale take place?

☑ SOLUTION

The fair market value on the date of sale was the present value of the expected payment at the maturity date of the contract. In other words, $4327.70 was the present value, on the date of sale, of the contract's maturity value discounted at the market rate of return. Therefore, the solution requires two steps, which are indicated in the following time diagram. First calculate the maturity value of the debt. Then determine how long it was before the maturity date that $4327.70 was the present value of the maturity value.

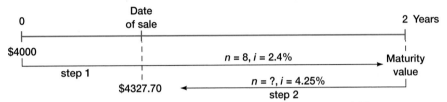

For the maturity value calculation, $n = 2 \times 4 = 8$ and $i = \frac{9.6\%}{4} = 2.4\%$. In the second step, $i = \frac{8.5\%}{2} = 4.25\%$.

ALGEBRAIC SOLUTION

The maturity value of the contract was

$$S = P(1 + i)^n = \$4000(1.024)^8 = \$4835.70$$

The number of compounding periods between the date of sale and the maturity date was

$$n = \frac{\ln\left(\frac{S}{P}\right)}{\ln(1 + i)} = \frac{\ln\left(\frac{\$4835.70}{\$4327.70}\right)}{\ln(1.0425)} = \frac{0.110990}{0.0416217} = 2.6666$$

Each compounding period is 6 months long. Therefore, the date of sale was

$$2.6666 \times 6 \text{ months} = 16.00 \text{ months}$$

before the maturity date.

FINANCIAL CALCULATOR SOLUTION

Calculate the maturity value of the debt.	Result
ENTER: 4000 8 2.4	
PRESS: [+/-] [PV] [n] [i] [COMP] [FV]	4835.70
Compute n between the date of sale and the maturity date.	
ENTER: 4327.70 4.25	
PRESS: [+/-] [PV] [i] [COMP] [n]	2.6666

Since each compounding period is 6 months long, the date of sale was

$$2.6666 \times 6 \text{ months} = 16.00 \text{ months}$$

before the maturity date.   ■

Trap

The calculation of n is usually not the last step in a problem. A problem involving the calculation of n usually expects, as the final answer, the total time in years and months (rather than the number of compounding periods). Do not forget to complete the extra step necessary to directly answer the problem.

■ **EXAMPLE 9.2E**   *CALCULATING THE TIME UNTIL MATURITY OF A BOND RESIDUE*

A stripped bond residue having a $10,000 face value was purchased for $3142.31. At this price, the bond residue provided the investor with a return of 7.938% compounded semiannually until its maturity. How long before the maturity date was the bond purchased? Assume that each half year is exactly 182 days long.

✓ SOLUTION

We learned in Section 8.4 that the purchase price of stripped bond residue equals the present value, on the date of purchase, of the bond's face value discounted at the required rate of return. In this example, $3142.31 was the present value of $10,000 discounted at 7.938% compounded semiannually. In order to determine the length of time from the date of purchase to the maturity date, we must first calculate the number of compounding periods between these dates. We have

$$P = \$3142.31, \; S = \$10,000, \text{ and } i = \frac{7.938\%}{2} = 3.969\%$$

ALGEBRAIC SOLUTION

$$n = \frac{\ln\left(\frac{S}{P}\right)}{\ln(1 + i)} = \frac{\ln\left(\frac{\$10,000}{\$3142.31}\right)}{\ln(1.03969)} = \frac{1.15762690}{0.03892259} = 29.7417731$$

Each compounding period is a half year. The partial period is

$$0.7417731 \times 182 \text{ days} = 135.00 \text{ days long}$$

Hence, the bond was purchased with 14 years, 6 months, and 135 days remaining until its maturity date.

FINANCIAL CALCULATOR SOLUTION

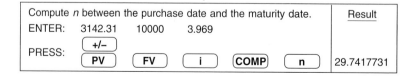

Compute n between the purchase date and the maturity date.	Result
ENTER: 3142.31 10000 3.969	
PRESS: +/− PV FV i COMP n	29.7417731

Each compounding period is a half year. The partial period is

$$0.7417731 \times 182 \text{ days} = 135.00 \text{ days long}$$

Hence, the bond was purchased with 14 years, 6 months, and 135 days remaining until its maturity date.   ■

Exercise 9.2

Answers to the odd-numbered problems are at the end of the book.
Calculate the term of each loan or investment in problems 1 through 6.

Problem	Principal ($)	Maturity amount ($)	Compounding frequency	Nominal rate (%)	Term
1.	1100	4483.92	Annually	6.3	? years, ? months
2.	4625	8481.61	Annually	7.875	? years, ? months
3.	5670	10,365.39	Semiannually	9.5	? years, ? months
4.	2000	3172.42	Annually	8.75	? years, ? months
5.	2870	3837.30	Monthly	10	? years, ? months
6.	3250	4456.90	Quarterly	7.5	? years, ? months

7. How long before a scheduled payment of $3252 will a payment of $2150 be equivalent? Money is worth 12% compounded quarterly.

8. Marilyn was supposed to pay $1450 to Bernice on March 1. Some time later Marilyn paid Bernice an equivalent payment of $1609.90, allowing for a time value of money of 9% compounded monthly. When did Marilyn make the payment?

9. What is the remaining time until the maturity date of a $10,000 stripped bond if it is purchased for $2603.35 to yield 9.5% compounded semiannually until maturity?

10. Rounded to the nearest month, how long will it take a town's population to:

    a. Grow from 32,500 to 40,000 if the annual growth rate is 3%?

    b. Shrink from 40,000 to 32,500 if the annual rate of decline is 3%?

11. Rounded to the nearest month, how long will it take an investment to double if it earns:

    a. 8.4% compounded annually?   b. 10.5% compounded semiannually?

12. Rounded to the nearest month, how long will it take an investment to triple if it earns:

    a. 9% compounded annually?   b. 8% compounded quarterly?

13. Rounded to the nearest quarter year, how long will it take an investment to quadruple if it earns:

    a. 8% compounded annually?   b. 9% compounded semiannually?

14. Rounded to the nearest month, how long will it take money to lose half of its purchasing power if the annual inflation rate is:

    a. 3%   b. 6%

15. Rounded to the nearest month, how long will it take money to lose 90% of its purchasing power if the annual rate of inflation is:

    a. 4%   b. 10%

•16. Simon loaned $3000 to Lauren for a 3-year term at 7.6% compounded quarterly. Before the maturity date, Simon agreed to accept $3383.33 in settlement of the debt. Simon allowed for a time value of money of 8% compounded quarterly in setting the prepayment amount. How far into the 3-year term was the loan settled?

•17. When discounted to yield 10.5% compounded monthly, a $2600, 3-year promissory note bearing interest at 12.25% compounded annually was priced at $3283.57. How long after the issue date did the discounting take place?

•18. The proceeds from the sale of a $4500, 5-year promissory note bearing interest at 9% compounded quarterly were $6055.62. How long before its maturity date was the note sold if it was discounted to yield 10.5% compounded monthly?

•19. If money is worth 7.5% compounded monthly, how long (to the nearest day) after a scheduled payment of $4000 would $5000 be an equivalent payment? For the purpose of determining the number of days in a partial month, assume that a full month has 30 days.

•20. If money is worth 8% compounded quarterly, how long (to the nearest day) before a scheduled payment of $6000 would $5000 be an equivalent payment? For the purpose of determining the number of days in a partial calendar quarter, assume that a full quarter has 91 days.

•21. Wilf paid $416.71 for a $1000 face value stripped bond residue. At this price the investment will yield a return of 7.86% compounded semiannually. How long (to the nearest day) before its maturity date did Wilf purchase the bond? Assume that each half year has exactly 182 days.

•22. A $5000 face value stripped bond residue may be purchased today for $1073.36 yielding the purchaser 7.27% compounded semiannually until the residue matures. How much time (to the nearest day) remains until the maturity date? Assume that each half year has exactly 182 days.

•23. $7500 was borrowed for a 4-year term at 9% compounded quarterly. The terms of the loan allow prepayment of the loan based on discounting the loan's maturity value at 7% compounded quarterly. How long (to the day) before the maturity date was the loan prepaid if the payout amount was $9380.24? For the purpose of determining the number of days in a partial calendar quarter, assume that a full quarter has 91 days.

9.3 Equivalent Interest Rates

Equivalent interest rates are different nominal interest rates that produce the same maturity value of a given principal after 1 year. Hence, the same amount of interest will be earned on a given principal invested for a year at either of two equivalent interest rates. The definition of equivalent interest rates suggests a three-step procedure for calculating a nominal interest rate so that it is equivalent to another nominal rate:

1. Calculate the maturity value of any principal amount invested for 1 year at the given nominal rate.
2. Calculate the new periodic rate, i, that will produce the same maturity value of the same principal after 1 year.
3. Convert this periodic rate to its corresponding nominal (annual) rate.

The following example illustrates the procedure.

■ EXAMPLE 9.3A   CALCULATION OF THREE EQUIVALENT INTEREST RATES

An interest rate of 10% compounded quarterly is equivalent to what nominal rate of interest compounded:

a. Annually?   b. Semiannually?   c. Monthly?

✓ SOLUTION

The given rate is $j = 10\%$ with $m = 4$. Therefore, $i = 2.5\%$ per quarter.

ALGEBRAIC SOLUTION

Step 1: This calculation is the same for parts *a, b,* and *c.* The maturity value of $100 invested for 1 year at 10% compounded quarterly is

$$S = P(1 + i)^n = \$100(1.025)^4 = \$110.38$$

a. The advantage of choosing to invest $P = \$100$ is that we can simply look at the value for S ($110.38) and immediately answer part *a.* That is, the annually compounded rate that will cause a $100 investment to earn $10.38 interest in a year is 10.38%. The choice of some arbitrary value for P would require that steps 2 and 3 be completed to obtain the answer for part *a.*

Step 2: Calculate the periodic rate that, compounded at the new frequency, will also cause $100 to grow to $110.38 after one year. Use formula (9–1) with $P = \$100$ and $S = \$110.38$.

b. With semiannual compounding, there are $n = 2$ compoundings in a year.

$$i = \left(\frac{S}{P}\right)^{1/n} - 1 = \left(\frac{\$110.38}{\$100}\right)^{1/2} - 1 = (1.1038)^{0.5} - 1 = 0.05062 = 5.062\%$$

c. With monthly compounding, there are $n = 12$ compoundings in a year.

$$i = \left(\frac{S}{P}\right)^{1/n} - 1 = \left(\frac{\$110.38}{\$100}\right)^{1/12} - 1 = (1.1038)^{0.08\overline{3}} - 1 = 0.008264 = 0.8264\%$$

Step 3: Convert the periodic rate to its corresponding nominal annual rate.

b. The nominal rate is $j = mi = 2(5.062\%) = 10.12\%$ compounded semiannually.

c. The nominal rate is $j = mi = 12(0.8264\%) = 9.92\%$ compounded monthly.

FINANCIAL CALCULATOR SOLUTION

Step 1: Calculate the maturity value of $100 after 1 year at 10% compounded quarterly.						Result
ENTER:	100	4	2.5			
PRESS:	[+/−] [PV]	[n]	[i]	[COMP]	[FV]	110.381
Step 2: Calculate the new periodic rate that gives the same maturity value in 1 year. *a.* $n = 1$ for annual compounding.						
ENTER		1	110.38			
PRESS:		[n]	[FV]	[COMP]	[i]	10.38
b. $n = 2$ for semiannual compounding.						
ENTER:		2				
PRESS:		[n]		[COMP]	[i]	5.062

c. n = 12 for monthly compounding.

ENTER:	12			
PRESS:	n	COMP	i	0.8264

Note: At the beginning of step 2, the appropriate values (−100 and 110.38) are already in PV and FV.

Step 3: Convert the periodic rate to its corresponding nominal annual rate ($j = mi$).

a. Nominal rate = $1i$ = 10.38% compounded annually.

b. Nominal rate = $2i$ = 2(5.062%) = 10.12% compounded semiannually.

c. Nominal rate is $12i$ = 12(0.8264%) = 9.92% compounded monthly.

EXERCISE 9.3

Answers to the odd-numbered problems are at the end of the book.

Throughout this Exercise, calculate interest rates to the nearest 0.01%. Calculate the equivalent interest rates in problems 1 through 12.

Problem	Given interest rate	Equivalent interest rate
1.	10% compounded annually	?% compounded semiannually
2.	10% compounded annually	?% compounded quarterly
3.	10% compounded annually	?% compounded monthly
4.	10% compounded semiannually	?% compounded annually
5.	10% compounded semiannually	?% compounded quarterly
6.	10% compounded semiannually	?% compounded monthly
7.	10% compounded quarterly	?% compounded annually
8.	10% compounded quarterly	?% compounded semiannually
9.	10% compounded quarterly	?% compounded monthly
10.	10% compounded monthly	?% compounded annually
11.	10% compounded monthly	?% compounded semiannually
12.	10% compounded monthly	?% compounded quarterly

Calculate the equivalent interest rate in problems 13 through 20.

Problem	Given interest rate	Equivalent interest rate
13.	9% compounded semiannually	?% compounded annually
14.	10% compounded quarterly	?% compounded annually
15.	8.25% compounded annually	?% compounded monthly
16.	12% compounded monthly	?% compounded semiannually
17.	7.5% compounded semiannually	?% compounded quarterly
18.	11.5% compounded quarterly	?% compounded monthly
19.	8.5% compounded quarterly	?% compounded semiannually
20.	10.5% compounded monthly	?% compounded quarterly

21. What annually compounded interest rate is equivalent to:

a. 9% compounded semiannually?

b. 9% compounded quarterly?

c. 9% compounded monthly?

22. What monthly compounded interest rate is equivalent to:

    a. 9% compounded annually?

    b. 9% compounded semiannually?

    c. 9% compounded quarterly?

23. For a 3-year GIC investment, what nominal rate compounded monthly would put you in the same financial position as 7.5% compounded semiannually?

24. A trust company pays 7.5% compounded semiannually on its 3-year GICs. Above what nominal rate of interest would you choose an annually compounded GIC of the same maturity?

25. You are offered a loan at a rate of 12% compounded monthly. Below what nominal rate of interest would you choose semiannual compounding instead?

26. Banks usually quote residential mortgage interest rates on the basis of semiannual compounding. An independent mortgage broker is quoting rates with monthly compounding. What rate would the broker have to give to match 9.5% compounded semiannually available from a bank?

27. A credit union pays 8.25% compounded annually on 5-year compound-interest GICs. It wants to set the rates on its semiannually and monthly compounded GICs of the same maturity so that investors will earn the same total interest. What should be the rates on the GICs with the higher compounding frequencies?

28. A bank offers a rate of 7.5% compounded semiannually on its 4-year GICs. What monthly and annually compounded rates should it quote in order to have the same interest costs with all three nominal rates?

9.4 EFFECTIVE INTEREST RATE

Would you prefer to earn an interest rate of 11.8% compounded monthly or 12.0% compounded semiannually? The higher compounding frequency favours the former rate, whereas the higher nominal rate favours the second alternative. How much better is a rate of return of 10% compounded monthly than 10% compounded semiannually? These questions invite a comparison of nominal interest rates. But nominal interest rates may be directly compared *only if* they have the same compounding frequency.

There is a natural preference in business for comparing investment rates of return and interest rates on the basis of annual compounding. An *annually* compounded rate of return also represents the *actual* percentage increase in value in a year. It is logical, then, that the standard practice for comparing nominal interest rates is to convert each rate to its **effective interest rate**—the equivalent annually compounded interest rate. Then a direct comparison may be made.

Since the effective interest rate is the *equivalent* annually compounded rate, it may be calculated using the approach of Section 9.3. That is, to obtain the effective rate, calculate the annually compounded rate that is equivalent to the given nominal rate. The advantage of this method is that it reminds us of the meaning of the effective interest rate.

Alternatively, a formula may be used to calculate the effective interest rate. This formula can be derived by using the approach of Section 9.3 for a general case. Let

f = Effective interest rate = Annually compounded nominal interest rate
m = Number of compoundings per year (as in earlier chapters)

An initial principal P invested at the annually compounded rate f will grow to $P(1 + f)$ after 1 year. The same principal invested at the periodic rate i will amount to $P(1 + i)^m$ after a year. For the two interest rates to be equivalent, the two maturity values must be equal. Therefore,

$$P(1 + f) = P(1 + i)^m$$

Divide both sides by P and move the 1 from the left to the right side to obtain

Effective Interest Rate

$$\boxed{f = (1 + i)^m - 1}$$

(9–3)

Legislation governing lending and the granting of credit usually imposes requirements on the lender to disclose to the borrower the true cost of borrowing. The most common requirement is for the disclosure of the effective interest rate.[4]

Compounding clearly takes place when interest is added to the principal amount of a loan or investment. But *compounding* also *occurs whenever interest is paid, regardless of the use to which the interest is put.* The recipient of the interest may choose to not reinvest the interest; the key point is that the *interest was made available for reinvestment.* For example, most savings accounts pay interest monthly and most demand loans charge interest monthly. Even though the "simple-interest method" is commonly used in these cases to calculate the interest for the exact number of days in each month, the fact that the accrued interest is paid or collected each month makes the nominal rate of interest a monthly compounded rate.

■ EXAMPLE 9.4A   CALCULATING THE EFFECTIVE RATE GIVEN A NOMINAL INTEREST RATE

What is the effective rate of interest corresponding to 10.5% compounded monthly?

☑ SOLUTION

For $j = 10.5\%$ and $m = 12$,

$$i = \frac{10.5\%}{12} = 0.875\% \text{ per month}$$

ALGEBRAIC SOLUTION

$$
\begin{aligned}
f &= (1 + i)^m - 1 \\
&= 1.00875^{12} - 1 \\
&= 1.11020 - 1 \\
&= 0.11020 \\
&= 11.02\%
\end{aligned}
$$

FINANCIAL CALCULATOR SOLUTION

Instead of using formula (9–3), a more intuitive approach is to determine the annually compounded rate of interest that produces the same maturity value of a $100 investment after 1 year as the given nominal rate.

---

[4]There is no consistent terminology in the various federal and provincial statutes for what we call the effective interest rate. Other terms used include "true rate of interest" and "yearly rate of interest."

ENTER:	100	12	0.875			Result
PRESS:	[+/-] [PV]	[n]	[i]	[COMP]	[FV]	111.020

An annually compounded rate of 11.02% would produce the same interest earnings ($11.02). Therefore, the effective rate of interest is 11.02%. ∎

■ EXAMPLE 9.4B   SELECTING THE BEST AMONG ALTERNATIVE NOMINAL INTEREST RATES

Which is the most attractive of the following interest rates:
a. 12% compounded annually?   b. 11.75% compounded semiannually?
c. 11.5% compounded quarterly?   d. 11.25% compounded monthly?

☑ SOLUTION

The preferred rate is the one that has the highest effective rate.

ALGEBRAIC SOLUTION

	j	m	i	f
a.	12%	1	0.12	$f = j$ when $m = 1$, $f = 0.12 = 12.00\%$
b.	11.75%	2	0.05875	$f = (1.05875)^2 - 1 = 0.12095 = 12.10\%$
c.	11.5%	4	0.02875	$f = (1.02875)^4 - 1 = 0.12006 = 12.01\%$
d.	11.25%	12	0.009375	$f = (1.009375)^{12} - 1 = 0.11849 = 11.85\%$

The most attractive rate is 11.75% compounded semiannually, since it has the highest effective rate of 12.10%.

FINANCIAL CALCULATOR SOLUTION

	Result
a. $f = j$ when $m = 1$.	12%

b. Compute the future value of $100 in 1 year.

ENTER:	100	2	5.875		f
PRESS:	[+/-] [PV]	[n]	[i]	[COMP] [FV]	112.095

c. Compute the future value of $100 in 1 year.

ENTER:	4	2.875		f
PRESS:	[n]	[i]	[COMP] [FV]	112.006

d. Compute the future value of $100 in 1 year.

ENTER:	12	0.9375		f
PRESS:	[n]	[i]	[COMP] [FV]	111.849

The preferred rate (giving the largest maturity value and the highest effective rate) is 11.75% compounded semiannually. ∎

■ EXAMPLE 9.4C   FINDING THE EFFECTIVE RATE GIVEN THE PRINCIPAL AND MATURITY VALUE

Calculate the effective rate of interest if $100 grew to $150 in $3\frac{1}{2}$ years with quarterly compounding.

☑ SOLUTION

The problem could be solved by first finding the quarterly compounded nominal rate that produces the given maturity value. Then the corresponding effective rate could be calculated. But this two-step solution is unnecessarily long.

   The essential question (which may be answered in one step) is: At what annually compounded rate will $100 grow to $150 after $3\frac{1}{2}$ years?

ALGEBRAIC SOLUTION

The annually compounded rate can be obtained by substituting $P = \$100$, $S = \$150$, and $n = 3.5$ in formula (9–1).

$$i = \left(\frac{S}{P}\right)^{1/n} - 1 = \left(\frac{\$150}{\$100}\right)^{1/3.5} - 1 = 1.5^{0.28571} - 1 = 0.1228$$

The effective rate is 12.28%.

FINANCIAL CALCULATOR SOLUTION

Compute i needed for $100 to become $150 in $3\frac{1}{2}$ periods.				Result
ENTER:	100	150	3.5	
PRESS:	+/−			COMP
	PV	FV	n	i 12.28

Annual compounding at 12.28% will cause $100 to grow to $150 in $3\frac{1}{2}$ years. The effective rate of interest is therefore 12.28%.   ■

■ EXAMPLE 9.4D   CALCULATING THE EFFECTIVE RATE ON A CHARGE CARD

The monthly statement for a bank charge card quotes an annual interest rate of 18% and a daily interest rate of 0.049315% $\left(= \frac{18\%}{365}\right)$. Calculate the effective interest rate if the interest charges must be paid each month.

☑ SOLUTION

Since the accrued interest is paid each month, we have monthly compounding with

$$i = \frac{18\%}{12} = 1.5\% \quad \text{and} \quad m = 12$$

ALGEBRAIC SOLUTION

$$f = (1 + i)^m - 1 = 1.015^{12} - 1 = 0.19562$$

That is, the effective rate is 19.56%.

FINANCIAL CALCULATOR SOLUTION

Calculate the future value of $100 invested at 18% compounded monthly for 1 year. The interest earned will numerically equal the effective interest rate.

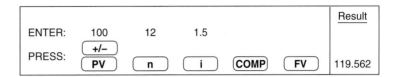

					Result
ENTER:	100	12	1.5		
PRESS:	+/− PV	n	i	COMP FV	119.562

The effective interest rate is therefore 19.56%.   ■

■ **EXAMPLE 9.4E**   *CALCULATING A NOMINAL INTEREST RATE GIVEN THE EFFECTIVE RATE*

What monthly compounded (nominal) rate of interest has an effective rate of 10%?

☑ SOLUTION

Given: $f = 0.10$, $m = 12$

We need to calculate i and then $j = mi$.

ALGEBRAIC SOLUTION

Substitute the known quantities into formula (9−3),

$$f = (1 + i)^m - 1$$

and solve for i:

$$0.10 = (1 - i)^{12} - 1$$
$$1.10 = (1 - i)^{12}$$
$$1.1^{1/12} = 1 + i$$
$$i = 1.1^{0.083333} - 1 = 0.007974$$
$$j = 12i = 0.09569 = 9.57\% \text{ compounded monthly}$$

FINANCIAL CALCULATOR SOLUTION

Since $f = 10\%$, $100 will grow to $110 in 1 year. Find the periodic rate for 1 month that gives the same maturity value.

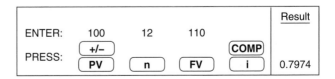

					Result
ENTER:	100	12	110		
PRESS:	+/− PV	n	FV	COMP i	0.7974

$$j = 12i = 12(0.7974\%) = 9.57\% \text{ compounded monthly}$$

Therefore, 9.57% compounded monthly has an effective rate of 10%.   ■

Point of Interest

Redefining "Effective" to Make It More Effective

At the peak of the Registered Retirement Savings Plan (RRSP) season in February 1990, a well-known Canadian trust company placed prominent advertisements in major newspapers purporting to illustrate that an *annually* compounded interest rate on 3- and 5-year GICs resulted in an "effective annual yield" that exceeded the quoted annually compounded rate. The following table was presented in the advertisements.

Term (years)	Annually compounded rate (%)	Effective annual yield (%)
1	11.25	11.25
3	11.00	12.25
5	11.00	13.70

The advertisement claimed that the "true measure of performance" was the "effective annual yield," which it described as "the average annual return over the life of the investment as a result of compounded interest." The calculation of this "effective annual yield" went as follows. A 5-year $1000 GIC invested at 11.0% compounded annually will earn interest totalling $685.06 over the 5-year term. The average amount of interest earned per year is $685.06 ÷ 5 = $137.01, for an "effective annual yield" of 13.70% on the $1000 face value.

How does this trust company's use of "effective annual yield" differ from our definition of effective interest rate? Since effective interest rate means the equivalent annually compounded rate, the actual effective interest rate for each of the GICs is simply the quoted annually compounded rate. What the trust company has done is to calculate the equivalent annual *simple* rate of interest that would produce a single interest payment on the GIC's maturity date equal to the total compound interest earnings over the life of the GIC. Naturally, this simple annual rate is larger than the equivalent annually compounded rate. To call it an "effective annual yield" is, at best, confusing. At worst, it is a deception designed to take advantage of the general public's vague understanding that effective rates of interest provide the proper basis for comparing interest rates.

EXERCISE 9.4

Answers to the odd-numbered problems are at the end of the book.

Calculate the missing interest rates, rounded to the nearest hundredth of a percent, in problems 1 through 20.

Problem	Nominal rate and compounding frequency	Effective rate (%)
1.	15% compounded semiannually	?
2.	15% compounded quarterly	?
3.	15% compounded monthly	?
4.	7.5% compounded semiannually	?
5.	7.5% compounded quarterly	?
6.	7.5% compounded monthly	?
7.	?% compounded semiannually	15
8.	?% compounded quarterly	15
9.	?% compounded monthly	15
10.	?% compounded semiannually	7.5
11.	?% compounded quarterly	7.5
12.	?% compounded monthly	7.5
13.	12% compounded monthly	?

Problem	Nominal rate and compounding frequency	Effective rate (%)
14.	18% compounded monthly	?
15.	11.5% compounded quarterly	?
16.	9.9% compounded semiannually	?
17.	?% compounded semiannually	10.25
18.	?% compounded quarterly	14
19.	?% compounded monthly	10
20.	?% compounded monthly	20

21. The nominal rate of interest charged on most credit and charge cards is usually more than twice the prime rate in the banking system. What is the effective rate of interest on a credit card that calculates interest at the rate of 1.8% per month?

22. During most of the 1980s the major department store chains calculated interest on their charge accounts at the rate of 2.4% per month. What effective rate of interest were they charging?

23. If an invoice indicates that interest at the rate of 2% per month will be charged on over-due amounts, what effective rate of interest will be charged?

24. If the nominal rate of interest paid on a savings account is 4% per annum paid monthly, what is the effective rate of interest?

25. If an interest rate of 8.9% compounded semiannually is charged on a car loan, what effective rate of interest should be disclosed to the borrower?

26. A company reports that its sales have grown 3% per quarter for the last eight fiscal quarters. What annual growth rate has the company been experiencing for the last 2 years?

27. If a $5000 investment grew to $6450 in 30 months of monthly compounding, what effective rate of return was the investment earning?

28. After 27 months of quarterly compounding, a $3000 debt had grown to $3810. What effective rate of interest was being charged on the debt?

29. Lisa is offered a loan from a bank at 12.25% compounded monthly. A credit union offers similar terms but a rate of 12.5% compounded semiannually. Which loan should she accept? Present calculations that support your answer.

30. Craig can buy a 3-year compound-interest GIC paying 7.5% compounded semiannually or 7.4% compounded monthly. Which option should he choose? Present calculations that support your answer.

31. Camille can obtain a residential mortgage loan from a bank at 9.5% compounded semi-annually or from an independent mortgage broker at 9.4% compounded monthly. Which source should she pick if other terms and conditions of the loan are the same? Present calculations that support your answer.

32. ABC Ltd. reports that its sales are growing at the rate of 1.3% per month. DEF Inc. reports sales increasing by 4% each quarter. What is each company's effective annual rate of growth?

33. Columbia Trust wants its annually, semiannually, and monthly compounded 5-year GICs all to have an effective interest rate of 7.75%. What nominal annual rates should it quote for the three compounding options?

34. Belleville Credit Union has established interest rates on its 3-year GICs so that the effective rate of interest is 7% on all three compounding options. What are the monthly, semiannually, and annually compounded rates?

•35. A department store chain currently charges 18% compounded monthly on its credit card. To what amount should it change the monthly compounded rate if it wants to add 2% to the effective interest rate?

•36. An oil company wants to drop the effective rate of interest on its credit card by 3%. If it currently charges 1.7% per month, to what should it reduce the monthly rate?

*APPENDIX 9A: LOGARITHMS

Prior to the advent of sophisticated calculators and computers, logarithms were used extensively in a variety of complex calculations in science, engineering, and finance. Now specialized calculators and software reduce most computations of any significant complexity to entering the numerical values for the variables, and instructing the calculator or computer to execute a function or program. Consequently, the direct use of logarithms is now less common. Much of their utilization is hidden within the application software.

A strictly algebraic approach to the solution of certain compound interest problems involves the use of logarithms. However, if financial calculator functions are employed, logarithms are not needed.

BASIC CONCEPTS OF LOGARITHMS   To develop an understanding of logarithms, consider the problem of finding the value of x so that

$$50 = 10^x$$

We know that:

$$10 = 10^1 \quad \text{and} \quad 100 = 10^2$$

Since 50 is between 10 and 100, we can deduce that x will have a value between 1 and 2. We could try a series of values for x and eventually, through a trial-and-error approach, arrive at a reasonable estimate of the true value of x. If this type of calculation is done frequently (and it is in many fields), it is preferable to have a more precise and more efficient method for obtaining the value of x. This need resulted in the development and use of logarithms.

Instead of saying that "x is the exponent to which the base 10 must be raised in order to give a value of 50," the language used in logarithms is

"x is the logarithm of 50 to the base 10"

The notation used to represent this statement is

$$x = \log_{10} 50$$

Since we use a base 10 number system in most of our mathematics, 10 is a commonly used base for logarithms. The logarithm of a number to the base 10 is called the *common logarithm* or *common log* of the number. In the present example, we can say that

"x is the common log of 50"

When no subscript appears in the mathematical representation of a logarithm, the base 10 or common log is understood. That is,

$$x = \log 50 \quad \text{means} \quad x = \log_{10} 50$$

Some calculators have a key (or a second function of a key) labelled $\boxed{\textbf{log}}$. If you enter 50 and then press $\boxed{\textbf{log}}$, the common logarithm of 50 will be calculated and will appear in the display. We obtain

$$x = \log 50 = 1.69897$$

The value may be verified by showing that

$$10^{1.69897} = 50$$

Many *financial* calculators do not have the $\boxed{\textbf{log}}$ function, but all have a function labelled $\boxed{\textbf{In}}$ or $\boxed{\textbf{In x}}$. This denotes the *natural logarithm,* which is calculated using the base 2.718281828. This is a number that arises in several natural phenomena[5] and is represented by the symbol *e*. Consequently, if

$$50 = 2.718281828^x = e^x$$

then

$$x = \log_e 50 = \ln 50 = 3.912023$$

As a check on this value, we can verify that

$$2.718281828^{3.912023} = 50$$

The logarithm of a negative number is undefined. In other words, no value exists for the logarithm of a negative number. This happens because both 10 and *e* raised to any exponent always give a positive value.

■ **EXAMPLE 9AA**   *CALCULATING THE COMMON AND NATURAL LOGARITHMS OF NUMBERS*

a. $\log 1 = \log 10^0 = 0$

b. $\ln 1 = 0$

c. $\log 10 = \log 10^1 = 1$

d. $\ln 2.718 = 1.000$

e. $\log 100 = \log 10^2 = 2$

f. $\ln 7.389 = 2.000$

g. $\log 1000 = \log 10^3 = 3$

h. $\ln 20.09 = 3.000$

i. $\log 10^n = n$

j. $\ln e^n = n$

k. $\log 0.1 = -1$

l. $\ln 0.3679 = -1.000$

m. $\log 0.01 = -2$

n. $\ln 0.1353 = -2.000$

o. $\log 10^{-n} = -n$

p. $\ln e^{-n} = -n$

q. $\log 1.115 = 0.0472749$

r. $\ln 1.115 = 0.1088544$

s. $\log 1.008\overline{3} = 0.0036041$

t. $\ln 1.008\overline{3} = 0.0082988$ ■

RULES OF LOGARITHMS   The rules of logarithms show how the logarithm of a product, quotient, or power may be expanded in terms of the logarithms of the individual factors. Their derivation is straightforward and can be found in any algebra text that introduces logarithms.

---

[5]On the basis of the brief coverage of logarithms in this section, you should not expect to have any insight into why 2.718281828 should arise "naturally." It is a nonterminating decimal that has been rounded here at the tenth figure.

> **Rules of Logarithms:**
> 1. The Product Rule: $\ln (ab) = \ln a + \ln b$
> 2. The Quotient Rule: $\ln \left(\dfrac{a}{b}\right) = \ln a - \ln b$
> 3. The Power Rule: $\ln (a^k) = k(\ln a)$

These rules apply to both natural and common logarithms.

> **Trap**
> Note the following inequalities in order to avoid some frequently made errors.
>
> $$\ln (a + b) \neq \ln a + \ln b \qquad \ln (ab) \neq (\ln a)(\ln b)$$
> $$\ln (a - b) \neq \ln a - \ln b \qquad \ln \left(\frac{a}{b}\right) \neq \frac{\ln a}{\ln b}$$

■ EXAMPLE 9AB   DERIVATION OF FORMULA (9–2)

Solve $S = P(1 + i)^n$ for n.

☑ SOLUTION

First divide both sides of the equation by P and then interchange the two sides, giving

$$(1 + i)^n = \frac{S}{P}$$

Next take logarithms of both sides and use the Power Rule to expand $\ln(1+i)^n$. We obtain

$$n \times \ln(1 + i) = \ln\left(\frac{S}{P}\right)$$

Finally, division of both sides by $\ln(1 + i)$ yields

$$n \doteq \frac{\ln\left(\dfrac{S}{P}\right)}{\ln(1 + i)}$$

■

*APPENDIX 9B: ANNUALIZED RATES OF RETURN AND GROWTH

Suppose that investment A provided a total return of 3.1% during a 4-month holding period, and investment B's total return over a 7-month period was 5.25%. Which investment generated the "better" rate of return? Although B produced the larger total return, it required a significantly longer holding period to do so. Consequently, we cannot conclude that the larger holding-period return is the "better" rate of return.

In order to compare rates of return that apply to different short-term holding periods, the returns must be restated in terms of the same duration of holding period. One possibility would be to compare the average return per month from each investment. However, there is a preference in business for quoting and comparing rates of return on the basis of a 1-year holding period, even when the actual holding period is much less than 1 year. An **annualized rate of return** is the annual rate of return that will result if a short-term rate of return continues for an entire year. In economics and business, short-term rates of change are also usually quoted as annualized rates.

Two methods are used to annualize short-term rates. They make different assumptions regarding compounding and, as a consequence, do not give the same number for the annualized rate. Unfortunately, the terminology employed in the following paragraphs is not used consistently in business or finance to distinguish between the two types of annualized rate. You can expect to find either one referred to as the "annualized rate." It is up to you to infer the type of the quoted annualized rate from the context or from the prevailing practice.

SIMPLE ANNUALIZED RATE   One approach to annualizing a rate of return is to simply extend the short-term rate, on a proportionate basis, to a full year. For example, a return of 2.5% for a 3-month holding period would be multiplied by 4 to give an annualized rate of 10%. This calculation is the reverse of the procedure used in Chapters 6 and 7 to calculate a short-term interest rate from a *simple* annual rate. Therefore, the annualized rate of return obtained by this approach is a *simple* rate of return: it assumes that the short-term rate *does not compound* when extended to a full year. For the general case, the basic proportion is

$$\frac{\text{Short-term rate}}{\text{Simple annualized rate}} = \frac{\text{Holding period (in years)}}{1 \text{ year}}$$

After rearranging to isolate "Simple annualized rate," we obtain

$$\text{Simple annualized rate} = \frac{1 \text{ year}}{\text{Holding period}} \times \text{Short-term rate}$$

Note that the same time units must be used for the "holding period" as for "1 year." For example, if the holding period is in days, then 365 days must be used for "1 year."

EFFECTIVE ANNUALIZED RATE   By definition, the holding period for a short-term investment is less than 1 year. The proceeds from a short-term investment become available for reinvestment in less than 1 year. Therefore, an investor has the opportunity to benefit from the compounding of the investment's earnings. A rigorous method for annualizing a short-term rate of return should recognize this opportunity for compounding. The standard practice is to use formula (9−3)[6] for the effective interest rate, with the following interpretations placed on i and m:

i = Holding-period return, or percent growth during a partial year

m = Number of such periods or partial years in a full year = $\dfrac{1 \text{ year}}{\text{Holding period}}$

In this context, m will often be a noninteger. For instance, the proceeds from a 60-day investment can, in principle, be reinvested or compounded $\frac{365}{60} = 6.083$ times during a year.

The effect of including compounding is to make the effective annualized rate *larger* than the corresponding simple annualized rate.

---

[6]The assumption implied in the use of formula (9−3) is that the short-term performance of the investment can be repeatedly duplicated for a whole year. Suppose, for example, that an investment produced a return of 10% over a 16-week period. The approach for calculating the *effective* annualized rate of return is to assume that the investment proceeds can be reinvested immediately to earn another 10% in the subsequent 16-week period, and so on for a full year. The effective annualized rate of return will then be the result of compounding a 10% periodic rate for $\frac{52}{16} = 3.25$ compounding periods.

■ EXAMPLE 9BA   *ANNUALIZING A HOLDING-PERIOD RETURN*

A money market mutual fund uses money received from individual investors to purchase a variety of Treasury bills and other short-term debt investments. As these investments mature, the mutual fund reinvests the proceeds in other short-term investments.

Because of the short-term nature of a money market mutual fund's investments, a fund's current rate of return is more relevant to individual investors than is the fund's actual rate of return for the past 1 or 2 years. Consequently, the financial media usually obtain each money market fund's holding-period return for the most recent 7 days and calculate the corresponding annualized rates of return. The simple annualized rate is called the *current yield* and the effective annualized rate is called the *effective yield.* (Normally, the 7-day holding-period return is not quoted.)

Suppose that a money market mutual fund's holding-period return for the most recent 7 days was 0.102%. What current yield and effective yield would be reported for the fund in the financial pages?

☑ SOLUTION

$$
\begin{aligned}
\text{Current yield} &= \text{Simple annualized rate} \\
&= \frac{1 \text{ year}}{\text{Holding period}} \times \text{Short-term rate} \\
&= \frac{365 \text{ days}}{7 \text{ days}} \times 0.00102 \\
&= 0.05319 \\
&= 5.32\%
\end{aligned}
$$

ALGEBRAIC SOLUTION

$$
\begin{aligned}
\text{Effective yield} &= \text{Effective annualized return} \\
&= (1 + i)^m - 1 \\
&= (1.00102)^{365/7} - 1 \\
&= 1.00102^{52.143} - 1 \\
&= 0.5460 \\
&= 5.46\%
\end{aligned}
$$

FINANCIAL CALCULATOR SOLUTION

The financial functions may be used instead of formula (9−3) to calculate the effective annualized rate. The approach is similar to the use of these functions in Section 9.4 to calculate the effective interest rate. Choose an initial investment of $100 and compute the maturity value after 1 year, where a periodic rate of 0.102% ($i = 0.102\%$) is compounded every 7 days ($n = \frac{365 \text{ days}}{7 \text{ days}} = 52.143$).

						Result
ENTER:	100	52.143	0.102			
PRESS:	+/− PV	n	i	COMP	FV	105.460

Since $100 will grow to $105.46 in 1 year, the effective annualized return is 5.46%. The financial pages would report a current yield of 5.32% and an effective yield of 5.46%.   ■

■ EXAMPLE 9BB   CONVERTING A SIMPLE ANNUALIZED RATE TO AN EFFECTIVE ANNUALIZED RATE

A \$10,000 face value Treasury bill, with 42 days remaining to maturity, was purchased to yield 10% per annum simple interest. What effective annualized rate of return was earned on the T-bill?

☑ SOLUTION

We can use the simple annualized rate of return to calculate the 42-day holding-period return. Then formula (9–3) or the functions on a financial calculator may be employed to obtain the effective annualized rate.

$$\text{Holding-period return, } i = \frac{42}{365} \times 10\% = 1.1507\%$$

$$\text{Number of compounding periods in a year, } m = \frac{365}{42} = 8.6905$$

ALGEBRAIC SOLUTION

The effective annualized rate is

$$f = (1 + i)^m - 1 = (1.011507)^{8.6905} - 1 = 0.10454 = 10.45\%$$

FINANCIAL CALCULATOR SOLUTION

Compute the future value of \$100 after 1 year.					Result
ENTER:	100	8.6905	1.1507		
PRESS:	[+/-] [PV]	[n]	[i]	[COMP] [FV]	110.454

Since \$100 will grow to \$110.45 in 1 year, the effective annualized rate of return is 10.45%.   ■

■ EXAMPLE 9BC   CALCULATING ANNUALIZED RATES OF INFLATION

If Statistics Canada reported that the consumer price index (CPI) rose from 136.2 to 136.7 in the previous month, what was:

a. The simple annualized rate of inflation during the month?
b. The effective annualized rate of inflation during the month?

☑ SOLUTION

The percent increase in the CPI during the month was

$$i = \frac{\text{CPI(final)} - \text{CPI(initial)}}{\text{CPI(initial)}} \times 100\% = \frac{136.7 - 136.2}{136.2} \times 100\% = 0.3671\%$$

a. $$\text{Simple annualized rate} = \frac{1 \text{ year}}{\text{Partial year}} \times \text{Short-term rate}$$
$$= \frac{12 \text{ months}}{1 \text{ month}} \times 0.3671\%$$
$$= 4.41\%$$

b. Now calculate the annual rate of inflation on the assumption that the inflation rate for the previous month (0.3671%) will be repeated and compounded each month for a year.

ALGEBRAIC SOLUTION

$$f = (1 + i)^m - 1 = 1.003671^{12} - 1 = 0.0450 = 4.50\%$$

FINANCIAL CALCULATOR SOLUTION

Choose a beginning price level of 100 and compute the price level after 12 months of compound increase at 0.3671% per month.

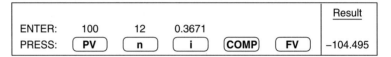

						Result
ENTER:	100	12	0.3671			
PRESS:	PV	n	i	COMP	FV	−104.495

Price levels will be at 104.50 (up from 100) after 1 year at this inflation rate. The effective annualized inflation rate is therefore 4.50%. ∎

■ EXAMPLE 9BD *ANNUALIZING A SHORT-TERM RATE OF ECONOMIC GROWTH*

Canada's gross domestic product (GDP), in constant 1986 dollars, dropped from $561.25 billion in the fourth quarter of 1990 to $553.30 billion in the first quarter of 1991. Between the two successive quarters, what was:

a. The simple annualized rate of decline in the economy as measured by the GDP?

b. The effective annualized rate of decline in the economy as measured by GDP?

Calculate the rates to three significant figures.

☑ SOLUTION

The percent change in the GDP during the month was

$$i = \frac{\text{GDP(final)} - \text{GDP(initial)}}{\text{GDP(initial)}} \times 100\% = \frac{553.30 - 561.25}{561.25} \times 100\% = -1.4165\%$$

a.
$$\begin{aligned}
\text{Simple annualized rate} &= \frac{1 \text{ year}}{\text{Partial year}} \times \text{Short-term rate} \\
&= \frac{12 \text{ months}}{3 \text{ months}} \times (-1.4165\%) \\
&= -5.67\%
\end{aligned}$$

The economy declined at the simple annual rate of 5.67% during the quarter.

b. Now calculate the annual rate of change on the assumption that the rate of GDP decline will be repeated and compounded for four successive quarters.

ALGEBRAIC SOLUTION

$$f = (1 + i)^m - 1 = (1 - 0.014165)^4 - 1 = 0.94453 - 1 = -5.55\%$$

FINANCIAL CALCULATOR SOLUTION

Choose a beginning GDP level of 100 and compute the GDP level after 1 year of compound decline at 1.4165% per quarter.

ENTER:	100	4	1.4165			Result
PRESS:	PV	n	+/- i	COMP	FV	−94.453

The GDP level will be at 94.45 (down from 100) after 1 year at this rate of decline. The effective annualized rate of decline in the GDP during the quarter was 5.55%.

∎

■ EXAMPLE 9BE *CONVERTING A CASH DISCOUNT TO AN ANNUALIZED RATE OF RETURN*

Cash discounts offered on invoices usually represent an opportunity to realise a large effective annualized return on "investment." Consider the case in which the terms of payment are 2/10, net 30 on an invoiced amount of $100. The two natural alternatives[7] facing the purchaser are to pay $98 after 10 days or $100 an additional 20 days later (at the end of the 30-day credit period). The word investment was placed in quotation marks in the first sentence because the choice can be viewed as an investment issue. The purchaser would need to earn more than $2 on an investment of $98 for 20 days to put money to a better use than taking the cash discount.

At what simple and effective annualized rates of return would the purchaser be indifferent between taking the cash discount after 10 days, or paying the full price on the last day of the credit period?

▩ SOLUTION

The purchaser will be indifferent if $98 can earn exactly $2 in 20 days. The holding-period return would have to be

$$i = \frac{\$2}{\$98} \times 100\% = 2.041\%$$

The corresponding simple annualized rate would be

$$\frac{365}{20} \times 2.041\% = 37.25\%$$

and the effective annualized rate would have to be
$$f = (1 + i)^m - 1 = (1.02041)^{365/20} - 1 = 0.4459 = 44.59\%$$

The cash discount represents a simple annualized return on "investment" of 37.25% and an effective annualized return on "investment" of 44.59%.[8]   ∎

■ EXAMPLE 9BF *CONVERTING A VOLUME DISCOUNT TO AN ANNUALIZED RATE OF RETURN*

An accounting firm normally restocks its supplies every month. The vendor of the supplies offers a 3% discount if the firm will order twice as much every 2 months. Viewed as an investment decision, what effective annualized return on investment does the volume discount represent?

---

[7]It is a fundamental tenet of credit management to use "free" credit to its limit. Since the percent discount is the same at any time within the discount period, a purchaser intending to take advantage of the cash discount should pay on the last day of the discount period. Similarly, a purchaser not taking the cash discount should use the full credit period.

[8]Another interpretation is that, if the purchaser does not have the cash on hand to take advantage of the cash discount, it would be to her advantage to borrow $98 for 20 days at any effective interest rate below 44.6% rather than forgo the discount and pay $100 on the last day of the 30-day credit period.

☑ Solution

Suppose the regular monthly order has been for $1000 worth of supplies. (The answer will not depend on the actual dollar amount of the regular order.) The choice is between paying $1000 now and another $1000 in a month versus paying $2000 $(1 - 0.03) = \$1940$ now. By "investing" an extra $940 now, the firm avoids paying $1000 in 1 month's time. In effect, the $940 earns $60 in 1 month. The holding-period return for this "investment" is

$$i = \frac{\$60}{\$940} \times 100\% = 6.383\%$$

The effective annualized return on investment is

$$f = (1 + i)^m - 1 = (1.06383)^{12} - 1 = 1.101 = 110.1\%$$

The volume discount represents an effective annualized return on investment of 110.1%.   ∎

Exercise 9B

Answers to the odd-numbered problems are at the end of the book.

Calculate percentages to the nearest 0.01% or to four significant figures, whichever is less accurate.

1. If the holding-period return on a money market mutual fund for the most recent 7 days is 0.111%, what current (simple) yield and effective annualized yield will be quoted for the fund in the financial press?

2. If the holding-period return on a money market mutual fund for the most recent 7 days is 0.097%, what current (simple) and effective annualized yields will be quoted for the fund in the financial pages?

3. The current (simple annualized) yield on a money market mutual fund, based on the return for the most recent 7 days, is 5.62%. What effective (annualized) yield will be reported for the fund?

4. The current (simple annualized) yield, based on the holding-period return for the most recent 7 days, is reported for a money market mutual fund as 6.17%. What is the fund's corresponding effective (annualized) yield?

5. A bank pays a simple-interest rate of 6.7% pa on 30- to 179-day GICs of at least $100,000. What is the effective annualized rate of return:

   a. On a 40-day GIC?   *b.* On a 160-day GIC?

6. A T-bill with 125 days remaining to maturity is discounted to yield 8.6% pa simple interest. What is the effective annualized rate of return on the T-bill?

7. A non-interest-bearing promissory note for $600 was sold for $550, 83 days before its legal due date. What effective annualized yield did the buyer realise when she collected the face value on the legal due date?

8. Neil's common stock portfolio increased in value over a 2-month period from $78,900 to $84,300. What were the simple and effective annualized rates of total return over the period?

9. The M3 money supply in Canada increased from $331.12 billion in December 1991 to $333.81 billion in January 1992. What were the simple and effective annualized rates of increase in M3 during that month?

10. If the TSE 300 stock price index declined from 3852 to 3748 over a 50-day period, what were the simple and effective annualized rates of decline in the index during the period?

11. Danielle's shares in the Industrial Growth Fund (an equity mutual fund) dropped in price from $12.86 to $12.56 over a 3-month period. What were the simple and effective annualized rates of return during the period?

12. The Calgary Real Estate Board reports that house prices increased by 8% during the first 7 months of the year. If prices continue to rise at the same rate for the subsequent 5 months, what will be the (compound) increase for the entire year?

13. If the consumer price index rose by 1% over a 2-month period, what were the simple and effective annualized rates of inflation during the 2-month period?

14. The consumer price index rose from 131.2 to 132.1 during the second quarter of a year. What was the effective annualized rate of inflation during the quarter?

•15. An income tax preparation service discounts income tax refunds at the statutory maximum amount of 15% on the first $300. For example, a taxpayer eligible for a $200 tax refund can sell the refund to the discounter for immediate payment of $170. What is the discounter's effective annualized rate of return in this example if Revenue Canada takes

   a. 25 days   b. 50 days

   to process the tax return and refund the tax? (*Note:* With Revenue Canada's EFILE electronic tax return filing system, the turnaround time should be less than 3 weeks.)

•16. Jennifer has enough laundry detergent on hand to last another 5 weeks. Her favourite brand is on special this week at $7.49 instead of the regular price of $8.95. What simple and effective annualized "returns on investment" are realised by buying a box now at the special price instead of paying the regular price in 5 weeks? Assume that a year has exactly 52 weeks.

•17. An accountant is planning to register in a professional development workshop dealing with recent changes to the Income Tax Act. Registrations received at least 45 days prior to the workshop date receive an "early bird" discount of $30 from the $295 registration fee. What are the simple and effective annualized "returns on investment" that result from registering 45 days in advance instead of on the date of the workshop?

•18. Melanie and David have decided to have a February holiday in Barbados. Their travel agent has advised them that the airlines will implement a general fare increase of 6% for tickets purchased after November 15. What is their effective annualized "return on investment" if they pay for their tickets on November 15 instead of January 20?

•19. The *Vancouver Sun* newspaper offers an annual subscription for $121 and a 6-month subscription for $65.

   a. If a 6-month renewal 6 months from now still costs $65, calculate the effective annualized rate of return on the extra $56 spent now for a 1-year subscription.

   b. If the 6-month subscription rate is $2 higher 6 months from now, calculate the effective annualized rate of return on the extra $56 spent now for a 1-year subscription.

•20. The annual dues for members in a golf club are $1410 at the beginning of the year or two payments of $739 each, due at the start of the year and 6 months later. What is the effective annualized rate of return on the extra $671 spent "up front" for the full year's dues as opposed to the two installments?

•21. The terms of payment on an invoice are 3/10, n/90. What are the simple and effective annualized rates of return earned by taking the cash discount on the last day of the discount period instead of paying the full price on the last day of the credit period?

•22. The terms of payment on an invoice are $1\frac{1}{2}$/10, EOM. What are the simple and effective annualized rates of return earned by taking the cash discount on the last day of the discount period instead of paying the full price on the last day of the credit period? (Remember that if no credit period is stated, it is understood to extend 20 days beyond the discount period.)

REVIEW PROBLEMS

Answers to the odd-numbered review problems are at the end of the book.

Calculate percentages to the nearest 0.01% or to four significant figures, whichever is less accurate.

1. A sum of $10,000 invested in the Altamira Equity Fund at the end of December 1988 would have grown to $43,679 by the end of December 1995. What compound annual rate of return did the fund realise during this period?

2. Maxine found an old pay statement from 9 years ago. Her hourly wage at the time was $6.75 versus her current wage of $10.40 per hour. At what average (compound) annual rate has her wage grown over the period?

3. If a company's sales grew from $165,000 for the 1988 fiscal year to $485,000 in the 1996 fiscal year, what has been the compound annual rate of growth of sales during the period?

•4. An investor's portfolio increased in value by 53% over a 5-year period, while the consumer price index rose from 121.6 to 135.3. What was the annually compounded real rate of return on the portfolio for the 5 years?

•5. A portfolio earned −13%, 18%, 5%, 24%, and −5% in 5 successive years. What was the portfolio's 5-year compound annual return?

•6. In terms of the total portfolio under management, the Trimark Fund was the fastest growing of the major mutual funds in Canada in 1995. It grew (through new contributions and appreciation of its holdings) by 45% in 1995. The Trimark Fund invests primarily in common stocks of foreign companies. What 3-year, 5-year, and 10-year compound annual returns to December 31, 1995, did the fund report if its annual returns in successive years from 1986 to 1995 inclusive were 10.3%, −2.3%, 22.8%, 15.9%, −9.9%, 28.3%, 29.0%, 31.6%, 14.9%, and 16.7%, respectively?

7. Terry was supposed to pay $800 to Becky on March 1. At a later date, Terry paid Becky an equivalent payment in the amount of $895.67. If they provided for a time value of money of 8% compounded monthly, when did Terry make the payment?

8. What is the time remaining until the maturity date of a $100,000 stripped bond if it has just been purchased for $19,725.75 to yield 8.5% compounded semiannually until maturity?

•9. When discounted to yield 9.5% compounded quarterly, a $4500, 4-year promissory note bearing interest at 11.5% compounded semiannually was priced at $5697.84. How long after the issue date did the discounting take place?

•10. The population of a mining town declined from 17,500 at the end of 1987 to 14,500 at the end of 1992. If the population continues to decrease at the same compound annual rate, how long, to the nearest month, will it take for the population to drop by another 3000?

11. How long, to the nearest day, will it take a $10,000 investment to grow to $12,000 if it earns 8% compounded semiannually? Assume that a half year has 182 days.

12. For a 3-year GIC investment, what nominal rate compounded monthly would put you in the same financial position as 6.5% compounded quarterly?

13. You are offered a loan at a rate of 10.5% compounded monthly. Below what nominal rate of interest would you choose semiannual compounding instead?

14. A bank offers a rate of 7% compounded semiannually on its 4-year GICs. What monthly and annually compounded rates should it quote in order to have the same interest costs with all three nominal rates?

15. If an invoice indicates that interest at the rate of 1.5% per month will be charged on overdue amounts, what effective rate of interest will be charged?

16. If the nominal rate of interest paid on a savings account is 3% per annum paid monthly, what is the effective rate of interest paid?

17. If an interest rate of 6.9% compounded semiannually is charged on a car loan, what effective rate of interest should be disclosed to the borrower?

18. If a $15,000 investment grew to $21,805 in $4\frac{1}{2}$ years of quarterly compounding, what effective rate of return was the investment earning?

19. Camille can obtain a residential mortgage loan from a bank at 8.75% compounded semi-annually or from an independent mortgage broker at 8.6% compounded monthly. Which source should she pick if other terms and conditions of the loan are the same? Present calculations that support your answer.

•20. A department store wants to drop the effective rate of interest on its credit card by 2%. If it currently charges 1.5% per month, to what should it reduce the monthly rate?

SELF-TEST EXERCISE

Answers to the self-test problems are at the end of the book.

Calculate percentages to the nearest 0.01% or to four significant figures, whichever is less accurate.

1. The home that the Bensons purchased 13 years ago for $85,000 is now appraised at $215,000. What has been the annual rate of appreciation of the value of their home during the 13-year period?

2. If the consumer price index rose from 109.6 to 133.8 over an $8\frac{1}{2}$-year period, what was the average compound annual inflation rate during the period?

•3. A company's sales dropped 10% per year for 5 years.

   a. What annual rate of sales growth for the subsequent 5 years would return the sales to the original level?

   b. To the nearest month, how long would it take for sales to return to the original level if they increased at 10% per year?

•4. An investor's portfolio increased in value from $35,645 to $54,230 over a 6-year period. At the same time, the consumer price index rose by 26.5%. What was the portfolio's annually compounded real rate of return?

•5. One of the most erratic mutual funds during the 1986–1995 period was Goldfund Ltd., which invests primarily in gold and gold-mining companies. What 3-year, 5-year, and 10-year compound annual returns to December 31, 1995, did the fund report if its annual returns in successive years from 1986 to 1995 inclusive were 34.0%, 22.6%, −29.7%, 10.1%, −2.7%, −11.3%, −5.9%, 115.4%, −4.1%, and −16.2%, respectively?

6. To the nearest month, how long will it take an investment to increase in value by 150% if it earns 9% compounded quarterly?

•7. Gerald borrowed $5600 for 3 years at 8.4% compounded semiannually. Partway into the term of the loan, the lender agreed to a prepayment of $6569.19 in settlement of the debt. The settlement amount was based on discounting the maturity amount of the debt at 7.5% compounded monthly. How far into the 3-year term was the loan settled?

•8. An investor paid $3658.46 to purchase a $10,000 face value stripped bond for her RRSP. At this price the investment will provide a return of 7.67% compounded semiannually. How long (to the nearest day) after the date of purchase will the bond mature and the RRSP receive $10,000 cash? Assume that each half year is exactly 182 days long.

9. A trust company pays 8.375% compounded annually on its 5-year GICs. Above what nominal interest rate would you choose a semiannually compounded GIC of the same maturity?

10. Janet has approached three lenders for a loan to purchase a new car. The car dealer itself offers financing through General Motors Acceptance Corporation at 11.6% compounded quarterly. Her bank quotes a rate of 11.5% compounded monthly, and a credit union will charge 11.75% compounded semiannually. Which lender should she choose if other terms of the loans are essentially the same?

11. A $6000 investment grew to $7900 after 33 months of semiannual compounding. What effective rate of return was the investment earning?

SUMMARY OF NOTATION AND KEY FORMULAS

f = Effective rate of interest
m = Number of compoundings per year
i = Periodic rate of interest

In the context of annualized rate of return or annualized rate of growth (Appendix 9B),

f = Effective annualized rate of return or rate of growth
i = Holding-period return, or percent growth during a partial year
m = Number of such periods or partial years in a full year = $\dfrac{1 \text{ year}}{\text{Holding period}}$

Formula (9–1) $i = \sqrt[n]{\dfrac{S}{P}} - 1$ Finding the periodic rate of return

$= \left(\dfrac{S}{P}\right)^{1/n} - 1$

Formula (9–2) $n = \dfrac{\ln\left(\dfrac{S}{P}\right)}{\ln(1+i)}$ Finding the number of compounding periods

Formula (9–3) $f = (1 + i)^m - 1$ Finding the effective rate of interest or the effective annualized rate of return

GLOSSARY OF TERMS

Annualized rate of return   The annual rate of return that results if a short-term rate of return continues for an entire year.

Effective interest rate   The equivalent annually compounded rate of interest.

Equivalent interest rates   Different nominal interest rates that produce the same maturity value of a given principal after 1 year.

Rule of 72   A rule of thumb for making a quick estimation of the number of years it will take an investment to double at a known compound annual rate of return.

10 ORDINARY ANNUITIES: FUTURE VALUE AND PRESENT VALUE

LEARNING OBJECTIVES

After completing this chapter, you will be able to:

- Define and distinguish between ordinary simple annuities and ordinary general annuities

- Calculate the interest rate per payment interval given the interest rate per compounding interval

- Calculate the future value of both the "simple" and the "general" types of ordinary annuities

- Calculate the present value of both the "simple" and the "general" types of ordinary annuities

- Calculate the economic value of either type of ordinary annuity at the beginning or end of its term

- Calculate the fair market value of a cash-flow stream that includes an annuity

- Calculate the principal balance owed on a loan immediately after any payment

INTRODUCTION

A large number of personal and business transactions involve a series of equal regular payments. Examples are payments of wages, pensions, rent, personal loans, insurance premiums, mortgages, leases, term loans, bond interest, and preferred share dividends.

An **annuity** is a series of equal payments at regular intervals. Clearly, a significant portion of both personal and business expenditures and receipts take the form of annuities. The widespread occurrence and importance of annuities justify a thorough coverage of the theory and applications of annuities in Chapters 10 to 13.

We begin with the definitions of terms used in the discussion of annuities. Some annuity applications require the determination of a *single* payment, either at the beginning or at the end of an annuity, that is economically equivalent to the annuity. In other words, these applications require the present value or future value of the annuity. After development of techniques for calculating the future value and present value of annuities, several applications are presented.

10.1 TERMINOLOGY

The length of time between successive payments in an annuity is called the **payment interval.** The total time from the beginning of the first payment interval to the end of the last payment interval is the **term of the annuity.** We will use the symbols:

R = Size of each payment in an annuity
n = Number of payments in the term of the annuity

If a loan requires equal monthly payments, the payments are made at the *end* of each 1-month payment interval during the term of the loan. These loan payments are an example of an ordinary annuity. In an **ordinary annuity,** the payments are made at the *end* of each payment interval.

Figure 10.1 shows the time diagram for the general case of an *ordinary* annuity composed of n payments, each of size R. The serial number for each payment interval is placed above the tick mark at the end of the respective interval.

FIGURE 10.1

Time Diagram for an *n*-Payment Ordinary Annuity

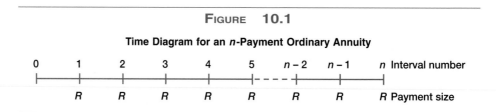

Trap

Do not confuse the "beginning of an annuity" with the "date of the first payment." The *beginning of an annuity* means the "beginning of the annuity's term" or the "beginning of the first payment interval." This occurs one payment interval *before* the first payment in an *ordinary* annuity.

Similarly, the *end of an annuity* refers to the "end of the annuity's term" or the "end of the last payment interval." This does coincide with the last payment of an ordinary annuity.

10.2 FUTURE VALUE OF AN ORDINARY ANNUITY

The **future value of an annuity** is the single amount, at the end of the annuity, that is economically equivalent to the annuity. Additional notation that will be used is

p = Interest rate per payment interval
S_n = Future value of an n-payment ordinary annuity

Tip

Be clear on the distinction between i and p. We have used and will continue to use i to represent the interest rate per *compounding* interval. For annuity calculations, we will also need to use the interest rate, p, that applies to each *payment* interval. In the next section, we will learn how, in general, to calculate a value for p from the value of i.

　　Also note that *lowercase p* is used for the interest per payment interval. In Chapters 6 to 9, *uppercase P* represented the principal amount of a loan or investment.

FUTURE VALUE USING THE ALGEBRAIC METHOD

Figure 10.2 is a time diagram for an ordinary annuity consisting of four $1000 payments. Suppose the payments can earn 8% compounded every *payment* interval ($p = 8\%$). The task is to calculate the total accumulated amount (future value) of the payments and their interest earnings at the end of the annuity. We will first determine this amount by using $S = P(1 + i)^n$ to calculate the future value of each of the four individual payments.

FIGURE　10.2

The Future Value of a Four-Payment Annuity

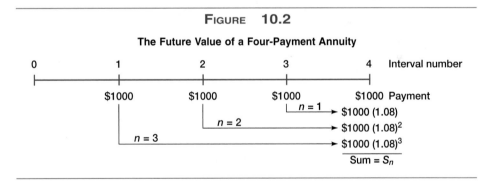

The future value of the annuity is

$$S_n = \$1000 + \$1000(1.08) + \$1000(1.08)^2 + \$1000(1.08)^3$$
$$= \$1000 + \$1080 + \$1166.40 + 1259.71$$
$$= \$4506.11$$

The payments along with earned interest will amount to $4506.11 by the end of the annuity.

　　If an annuity consists of many payments, this "brute force" approach to the calculation of the future value can become very time-consuming and laborious. Fortunately, there is a relatively compact formula for the future value of an ordinary annuity. The derivation of the following formula is presented in Appendix 10A.

Future Value of an Ordinary Annuity

$$S_n = R\left[\frac{(1 + p)^n - 1}{p}\right]$$ (10–1)

The factor

$$\frac{(1 + p)^n - 1}{p}$$

is called the **compounding factor for annuities** or the **accumulation factor for annuities.** When $R = \$1$, S_n equals the compounding factor. Therefore, the compounding factor can be interpreted as the future value of a \$1 annuity.

Let us now use formula (10–1) to obtain the future value of the annuity shown in Figure 10.2. We are given $R = \$1000$, $p = 8\% = 0.08$, and $n = 4$. Substituting these values into formula (10–1), we obtain

$$
\begin{aligned}
S_n &= \$1000\left[\frac{(1 + 0.08)^4 - 1}{0.08}\right] \\
&= \$1000\left(\frac{1.360489 - 1}{0.08}\right) \\
&= \$4506.11
\end{aligned}
$$

This is the same result as previously obtained with the "brute force" approach. As the number of payments in an annuity increases, the time saved by employing formula (10–1) increases proportionately.

FUTURE VALUE USING THE FINANCIAL CALCULATOR FUNCTIONS

The correspondence between the key labels and the algebraic variables in formula (10–1) is:

$\boxed{\text{n}}$ = n, the number of annuity payments

$\boxed{\text{i}}$ = p, the interest rate per payment interval (in percent)

$\boxed{\text{PMT}}$ = R, the size of the annuity payment

$\boxed{\text{FV}}$ = S_n, the future value of the annuity

To calculate the future value of an annuity, enter the known values for n, p, and R into the $\boxed{\text{n}}$, $\boxed{\text{i}}$, and $\boxed{\text{PMT}}$ memories. Remember to obey your calculator's cash-flow sign convention for the number entered into $\boxed{\text{PMT}}$. Zero should be entered into $\boxed{\text{PV}}$. Then the $\boxed{\text{COMP}}$ $\boxed{\text{FV}}$ keystrokes instruct the calculator to compute the future value of the n annuity payments.

Tip

If you do not have zero in the $\boxed{\text{PV}}$ memory, the calculator interprets the amount in $\boxed{\text{PV}}$ as an *additional* single cash flow occurring at the beginning of the annuity. Then at the $\boxed{\text{COMP}}$ $\boxed{\text{FV}}$ command, the calculator will compute the *combined* future value of the annuity and the amount in $\boxed{\text{PV}}$. This feature is useful in cases where, in a single calculation, we wish to obtain the total future value of an annuity and an initial "lump" amount.

APPLICATIONS OF THE FUTURE VALUE OF AN ANNUITY

Most applications of the future-value calculation fall into two categories:

- Determining the total amount of principal plus interest that will be accumulated at the end of a series of equal regular investments earning p per payment interval.
- Determining the single payment at the end of an annuity that is economically equivalent to the annuity. The value that should be used for p in this case is the time value of money. In other words, p is the interest rate (per payment interval) at which money could be invested.

■ EXAMPLE 10.2A   *THE FUTURE VALUE OF AN ORDINARY ANNUITY HAVING $p = i$*

Heinz has been contributing $300 at the end of each month for the past 15 months to a savings plan that earns 6% compounded monthly. What amount will he have 1 year from now if he continues with the plan?

☑ SOLUTION

The total accumulated amount will be the future value of $n = 27$ contributions of $R = \$300$ each. Payments and compounding both occur at 1-month intervals. Therefore, the interest per payment interval equals the interest per compounding interval. That is,

$$p = i = \frac{6\%}{12} = 0.5\% = 0.005$$

ALGEBRAIC SOLUTION

$$S_n = R\left[\frac{(1 + p)^n - 1}{p}\right]$$
$$= \$300\left(\frac{1.005^{27} - 1}{0.005}\right)$$
$$= \$300\left(\frac{1.1441518 - 1}{0.005}\right)$$
$$= \$8649.11$$

FINANCIAL CALCULATOR SOLUTION

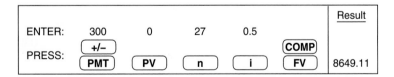

ENTER:	300	0	27	0.5		Result
PRESS:	+/- PMT	PV	n	i	COMP FV	8649.11

One year from now, Heinz will have accumulated $8649.11.   ■

■ EXAMPLE 10.2B   *CALCULATING AN ORDINARY ANNUITY'S FUTURE VALUE WHERE $p = i$ AND THE INTEREST RATE CHANGES DURING THE TERM OF THE ANNUITY*

Calculate the future value of an ordinary annuity with payments of $600 every 6 months for 16 years. The interest rate will be 8% compounded semiannually for the first $5\frac{1}{2}$ years and 9% compounded semiannually for the subsequent $10\frac{1}{2}$ years.

☑ SOLUTION

Because the compounding interval and the payment interval are both 6 months,

$$p = i = \frac{8\%}{2} = 4\% = 0.04 \text{ for the first } 5\tfrac{1}{2} \text{ years}$$

$$p = i = \frac{9\%}{2} = 4.5\% = 0.045 \text{ for the subsequent } 10\tfrac{1}{2} \text{ years}$$

As a consequence of the interest rate change during the term of the annuity, the algebraic solution has three steps, indicated in the following time diagram.

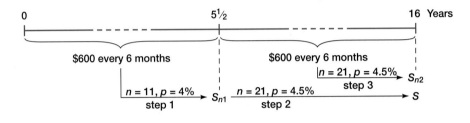

Step 1: Calculate the future value, S_{n1}, of the first 11 payments, after $5\tfrac{1}{2}$ years.

Step 2: Determine the future value, S, of the step 1 result an additional $10\tfrac{1}{2}$ years later.

Step 3: To the value of S from step 2, add the future value, S_{n2}, of the last 21 annuity payments.

ALGEBRAIC SOLUTION

$$S_{n1} = \$600\left(\frac{1.04^{11} - 1}{0.04}\right) = \$600\left(\frac{1.539454 - 1}{0.04}\right) = \$8091.81$$

$$S = \$8091.81(1.045^{21}) = \$8091.81(2.5202412) = \$20{,}393.32$$

$$S_{n2} = \$600\left(\frac{1.045^{21} - 1}{0.045}\right) = \$600\left(\frac{2.5202412 - 1}{0.045}\right) = \$20{,}269.88$$

$$S + S_{n2} = \$40{,}663.20$$

The future value of the annuity is $40,663.20.

FINANCIAL CALCULATOR SOLUTION

The second and third steps may be combined because the calculator can calculate the combined future value of an initial lump amount in (**PV**) and an annuity.

Calculate S_{n1}.						Result
ENTER:	600	4	0	11		
PRESS:	+/- PMT	i	PV	n	COMP FV	8091.81
Calculate $(S + S_{n2})$.						
ENTER:			4.5	21		
PRESS:	+/-	PV	i	n	COMP FV	40,663.20

For step 2 of the financial calculator solution, the $8091.81 already accumulated after the first $5\frac{1}{2}$ years must be treated as a lump investment (cash outflow) at the beginning of the next $10\frac{1}{2}$ years. With $8091.81 still in the display from step 1, the keystrokes (+/−) and (**PV**) change the sign of $8091.81 and store it in the PV memory as an initial lump investment.

The result from the second step is that the future value of the annuity is $40,663.20.   ∎

■ EXAMPLE 10.2C *COMPARING THE ECONOMIC VALUES OF ALTERNATIVE CASH FLOWS*

You have received two offers on a residential building lot that you want to sell. Mr. Walcott has offered $10,000 down and $5000 every 3 months for 4 years. Ms. Bartlett's offer is $10,000 down and $90,000 4 years from now. Compare the economic values of the two offers if money can earn 8% compounded quarterly.

☑ SOLUTION

Since both offers include the *same* down payment, the down payment does not need to be considered further in the comparison. The comparison is then between the annuity paying $5000 every 3 months for 4 years and the $90,000 lump payment in 4 years. To make the comparison, the equivalent values of all monetary amounts must be determined at the *same* focal date. The natural choice for the focal date is 4 years from now because the lump payment occurs on that date and the annuity ends on that date. The economic value of the annuity on the focal date will be its future value, allowing for a time value of money equal to 8% compounded quarterly. For the annuity,

$$R = \$5000 \qquad n = 16 \qquad \text{and} \qquad p = i = \frac{8\%}{4} = 2\% = 0.02$$

ALGEBRAIC SOLUTION

$$S_n = \$5000\left(\frac{1.02^{16} - 1}{0.02}\right) = \$93,196.43$$

FINANCIAL CALCULATOR SOLUTION

						Result
ENTER:	5000	0	2	16		
PRESS:	+/−				COMP	
	PMT	PV	i	n	FV	93,196.43

The economic value of Mr. Walcott's offer is greater by $3196.43 (measured in dollars 4 years hence, not in current dollars).   ∎

■ EXAMPLE 10.2D *CALCULATING THE FUTURE VALUE AFTER AN INTERRUPTION OF PAYMENTS*

Mr. Cloutier, just turned 43, makes monthly contributions of $300 to his Registered Retirement Savings Plan (RRSP). He intends to continue making the same contributions until age 60. He plans to retire then, cease further contributions, and allow the plan to continue to accumulate earnings until he reaches age 65. If the RRSP earns 8% compounded monthly for the next 22 years, and Mr. Cloutier already has $34,500 in his RRSP, what amount will his RRSP contain when he reaches age 65?

☑ Solution

Mr. Cloutier will make 12(17) = 204 more $300 contributions to his RRSP.

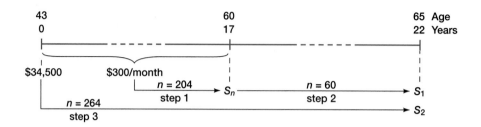

The time diagram indicates the three steps for the algebraic solution. First calculate the future value, S_n, of the contribution annuity at age 60. Then determine the future value, S_1, at age 65 of S_n. Finally, calculate the future value, S_2, at age 65 of the initial $34,500 in the RRSP. The total amount in the RRSP at age 65 will be the sum of S_1 and S_2. In a financial calculator solution, the first two steps may be combined. That is, compute the combined future value at age 60 of both the initial $34,500 and the contribution annuity.

Algebraic Solution

$$S_n = \$300\left(\frac{1.00\overline{6}^{204} - 1}{0.00\overline{6}}\right) = \$300\left(\frac{3.8786483 - 1}{0.00\overline{6}}\right) = \$129{,}539.17$$

$$S_1 = \$129{,}539.17(1.00\overline{6})^{60} = \$129{,}539.17(1.4898457) = \$192{,}993.38$$

$$S_2 = \$34{,}500(1.00\overline{6})^{264} = \$34{,}500(5.7785875) = \$199{,}361.27$$

The total amount in the RRSP when Mr. Cloutier reaches age 65 will be

$$S_1 + S_2 = \$192{,}993.38 + \$199{,}361.27 = \$392{,}354.65$$

Tip

Improving the Precision of Algebraic Solutions

To achieve accuracy to the penny in the preceding algebraic solution, the Significant Figure Rule says we should maintain at least 9 significant figures in intermediate numbers. Consequently, if we enter the value for $p = i$ by "punching in" 0.0066667 (5 significant figures) on an 8-digit display calculator or 0.006666667 (7 significant figures) on a 10-digit display calculator, the answer will be limited to 4- and 6-figure precision, respectively. (If you try to manually enter more digits than the calculator can display, the extra digits will be ignored.) To make matters worse, the calculation of powers having a large exponent can lead to rounding errors *larger* than would normally be expected from the Significant Figure Rule.

Precision will be improved if the value for $p = i$ is obtained by dividing 0.08 by 12. Then the calculator's internal value will have at least two more significant figures than are shown in the display. The value should be saved in the calculator's memory and recalled whenever it is needed.

FINANCIAL CALCULATOR SOLUTION

Find the combined future value of $34,500 and the annuity at age 60.					Result
ENTER: 34500 300 204 0.66666667					
PRESS: [+/-] [+/-] [COMP]					
[PV] [PMT] [n] [i] [FV]					263,352.54

Find the future value of $263,352.54 at age 65					
ENTER: 0 60					
PRESS: [+/-] [COMP]					
[PV] [PMT] [n] [FV]					392,354.65

The total amount in the RRSP when Mr. Cloutier reaches age 65 will be $392,354.65.

■

EXERCISE 10.2

Answers to the odd-numbered problems are at the end of the book.

All annuities in this exercise are ordinary annuities with $p = i$.
Determine the future value of the annuities in problems 1 through 8.

Problem	Periodic payment ($)	Payment interval	Term	Interest rate (%)	Compounding frequency
1.	500	1 year	13 years	11.5	Annually
2.	100	3 months	$5\frac{1}{2}$ years	10	Quarterly
3.	75	1 month	$2\frac{1}{2}$ years	8	Monthly
4.	2000	6 months	$12\frac{1}{2}$ years	7.5	Semiannually
5.	175	1 month	$8\frac{1}{4}$ years	11	Monthly
6.	700	1 quarter	7 years, 9 months	9	Quarterly
7.	3500	6 months	19 years	9.25	Semiannually
8.	435	1 month	6 years, 7 months	8.5	Monthly

9. This problem is designed to demonstrate the dependence of the future value of an annuity on the number of payments. Using $p = 10\%$, calculate the future value of an annuity for which the number of $1000 payments is

   a. 5   *b.* 10   *c.* 15   *d.* 20   *e.* 25   *f.* 30

   Note that the future value increases proportionately more than *n* as *n* is increased.

10. This problem is designed to demonstrate the dependence of the future value of an annuity on the interest rate. If an annuity consists of 20 annual payments of $1000, calculate its future value at an annually compounded interest rate of

    a. 9%   *b.* 10%   *c.* 11%   *d.* 12%

    Note that the future value increases proportionately more than the interest rate.

11. Calculate and rank the economic values 8 years from now of the following cash-flow streams.
    (i) A single payment of $5000 today.
    (ii) An ordinary annuity starting today with eight annual payments of $910.
    (iii) An ordinary annuity starting in 3 years with five annual payments of $1675.

Do the calculations and ranking for each of the following two cases.

a. Money can earn 8% compounded annually for the next 8 years.

b. Money can earn 10% compounded annually for the next 8 years.

12. Josie spends $60 at the end of each month on cigarettes. If she stops smoking and invests the same amount in an investment plan paying 6% compounded monthly, how much will she have after 5 years?

•13. Calculate the future value of an ordinary annuity consisting of quarterly payments of $1200 for 5 years, if the rate of interest was 10% compounded quarterly for the first 2 years and will be 9% compounded quarterly for the last 3 years.

•14. Herb has made contributions of $2000 to his RRSP at the end of every 6 months for the past 8 years. The plan has earned 9.5% compounded semiannually. He has just moved the funds to another plan, paying 8% compounded quarterly. He will now contribute $1500 at the end of every 3 months. What total amount will he have in the plan 7 years from now?

•15. Marika has already accumulated $18,000 in her RRSP. If she contributes $2000 at the end of every 6 months for the next 10 years, and $300 per month for the subsequent 5 years, what amount will she have in her plan at the end of the 15 years? Assume that her plan will earn 9% compounded semiannually for the first 10 years and 9% compounded monthly for the next 5 years.

The strong dependence of an annuity's future value on *n* (as demonstrated in problem 9) means that it is important to start a savings plan as early as possible in order to accumulate a substantial retirement fund. Problems 16 to 19 reinforce this point in different ways.

16. How much more will you have in your RRSP 30 years from now if you start to contribute $1000 per year at the end of this year instead of waiting 5 years to begin contributing $1000 at each year-end? Assume that the funds earn 8% compounded annually in the RRSP.

17. How much more will you have in your RRSP at age 65 if you begin annual $1000 contributions to your plan on your 26th birthday instead of on your 27th birthday? Assume that the RRSP earns 8% compounded annually and that the last contribution is on your 65th birthday.

18. How much more will you have in your RRSP 30 years from now if you make fixed contributions of $3000 at the end of each of the next 30 years, instead of waiting 15 years and making annual contributions that are twice as large for half as many years? Assume that the RRSP earns 8% compounded annually.

•19. Leona contributed $3000 per year to her RRSP on every birthday from age 21 to age 30 inclusive. She stopped employment to raise a family and made no further contributions. Her husband, John, started to make annual contributions of $3000 to his RRSP on his 31st birthday and plans to continue up to and including his 65th birthday. Assuming that both of their plans earn 8% compounded annually over the years, calculate and compare the amounts in their RRSPs at age 65.

10.3 "SIMPLE" AND "GENERAL" TYPES OF ORDINARY ANNUITIES

DISTINCTION BETWEEN SIMPLE AND GENERAL ANNUITIES

An annuity that has its payment interval equal to the compounding interval is called a **simple annuity.** Consequently, $p = i$ for simple annuities. All *ordinary* annuities encountered in the examples and problems in Section 10.2 were also *simple* annuities. Consequently, their complete description is "ordinary simple annuities."

It often happens that the payment and compounding intervals are not of equal length. For example, most mortgage loans are structured with monthly payments based on semiannual compounding. An annuity in which the payment interval and compounding interval are not equal is called a **general annuity.**[1]

In Section 10.2, we learned how to calculate the future value of an ordinary annuity but only encountered cases where $p = i$. Hence, at this point we know how to calculate the future value for only an *ordinary simple* annuity. The next subsection will show how to determine p for a *general* annuity. Substitution of this value for p in formula (10−1) will enable us to calculate the future value of an *ordinary general* annuity.

INTEREST PER PAYMENT INTERVAL FOR A GENERAL ANNUITY

Formula (10−1) assumes that the interest rate p compounds only at the end of each payment interval. For a *simple* annuity, the payment interval equals the compounding interval and consequently, $p = i$. For a *general* annuity, these intervals are not equal. We must calculate a value for p so that p compounded every payment interval *has the same effect* as i compounded every compounding interval.

The calculation of p will be illustrated with a specific example before we develop a general formula. Consider the case of an annuity where payments are made semiannually but interest is earned at the rate of 12% compounded monthly. The annuity is shown in a time diagram in Figure 10.3. No values are specified for R and n because they are not involved in the calculation of p.

FIGURE   10.3

An *n*-Payment Ordinary General Annuity with Semiannual Payments and Interest Compounded Monthly

						1						2	etc.	n	Payment number
0	1	2	3	4	5	6	7	8	9	10	11	12	etc.	6n	Compounding number
						0.5						1	etc.		Years
						R						R	etc.	R	Payment

We *cannot* use 6% (obtained either from $\frac{12\%}{2}$ or from $6i = 6 \times 1\% = 6\%$) as the value for p. Attempting to use 6% for p would ignore the fact that $i = 1\%$ compounds every month. The value for p must be the interest rate that, compounded every 6 months (the payment interval) *has the same effect* as $i = 1\%$ compounded every month (the compounding interval). Therefore, p will be a little larger than 6% due to the compounding of the 1% earned each month for 6 months.

If p compounded every 6 months is to have the same effect as $i = 1\%$ compounded every month, then $100 invested at either rate for 6 months[2] will have the same maturity value. Using formula (8−2) to calculate maturity values,

Maturity value of $100 invested for 6 months at p per half year $= \$100(1 + p)^1$

Maturity value of $100 invested for 6 months at $i = 1\%$ per month $= \$100(1.01)^6$

---

[1] Another name sometimes used instead of general annuity is *complex annuity.*

[2] The term chosen for the investment simulation must include an integer number of compoundings for both alternatives. Any multiple of 6 months can be used in this particular case.

Since the maturity values are to be equal, then

$$\$100(1 + p)^1 = \$100(1.01)^6$$

Division of both sides by $100 gives

$$1 + p = 1.01^6$$
$$p = 1.01^6 - 1 = 0.06152015 = 6.152015\%$$

The decimal equivalent value for p would be used in formula (10–1).

We can obtain the general formula for calculating p by generalizing the elements in

$$p = 1.01^6 - 1$$

Quite clearly, 1.01 comes from $(1 + i)$. The −1 term is already a general element because it did not arise as a particular value for any variable. The exponent 6 results from the fact that there were 6 compoundings within the payment interval. If we define

c = Number of compoundings per payment interval

then $c = 6$ in the preceding example, and the general formula for p is

Interest Rate per Payment Interval

$$\boxed{p = (1 + i)^c - 1}$$

(10–2)[3]

Although c was an integer in the preceding example, c will be a fraction whenever the compounding interval is longer than the payment interval. For example, most mortgage loans are based on semiannual compounding but require monthly payments. For such loans, $c = \frac{1}{6}$ because there is only one-sixth of a compounding interval (6 months) per payment interval (1 month).

> **Tip**
>
> When the payment interval is shorter than the compounding interval, c is less than 1. In this case, the thought process for obtaining c from its definition is tricky and prone to error. Since we tend to think in terms of the payment frequency and the compounding frequency, a safer approach is to use
>
> $$c = \frac{\text{Number of compoundings per year}}{\text{Number of payments per year}}$$
>
> (10–3)

■ **EXAMPLE 10.3A** *CALCULATING THE INTEREST RATE PER PAYMENT INTERVAL*

To five significant figures, calculate the interest rate per payment interval for:

a. Monthly payments and $j = 12\%$ compounded quarterly.

b. Semiannual payments and $j = 12\%$ compounded quarterly.

---

[3]Note that the general formula gives $p = i$ for the case of a simple annuity. Since $c = 1$ for a simple annuity, then $p = (1 + i)^1 - 1 = 1 + i - 1 = i$.

☑ SOLUTION

a.
$$i = \frac{j}{m} = \frac{12\%}{4} = 3\% \text{ per quarter}$$

$$c = \frac{\text{Number of compoundings per year}}{\text{Number of payments per year}}$$

$$= \frac{4}{12}$$

$$= 0.\overline{3} \text{ compoundings per payment interval}$$

Thus,

$$p = (1 + i)^c - 1$$
$$= 1.03^{0.333333} - 1$$
$$= 1.0099016 - 1$$
$$= 0.0099016$$
$$= 0.99016\% \text{ per month}$$

b. $i = 3\%$ again and $c = \dfrac{4}{2} = 2$ compoundings per payment interval

Thus,

$$p = 1.03^2 - 1 = 0.060900 = 6.0900\% \text{ per half year}$$ ∎

FUTURE VALUE OF AN ORDINARY GENERAL ANNUITY

To obtain the future value of an *ordinary general* annuity, the interest rate per payment interval, p, is calculated using formula (10–2). Then this value is substituted in formula (10–1) for an algebraic solution, or saved in the ⬚ i ⬚ memory for a financial calculator solution.

Tip

Improving the Precision of Calculated Results

When $c = \frac{1}{12}$, $\frac{1}{6}$, or $\frac{1}{3}$, the decimal equivalent value is a *repeating* decimal. Some care should be taken to use your calculator so that maximum precision is realized in the value you obtain for p. To calculate $(1 + i)^c$, do not manually enter c by rounding its decimal equivalent value. Instead, first calculate c by dividing 1 by 12, 6, or 3, and save the value in memory. In this way, at least two more digits are retained internally than you see in the display. Then when the exponent is required for the ⬚ y^x ⬚ function, recall the value for c from the memory.

Typically, the value obtained for p will be used in a future-value or present-value computation such as formula (10–1). Again, to maximize precision, p's value should be saved in memory as soon as it is calculated from formula (10–2) in order to retain as many digits as possible. Whenever it is needed in subsequent calculations, it can be recalled from the memory.

■ **EXAMPLE 10.3B**   *CALCULATING THE FUTURE VALUE OF AN ORDINARY GENERAL ANNUITY*

If $1000 is invested at the end of every year at 8% compounded semiannually, what will be the total value of the periodic investments after 25 years?

✓ SOLUTION

The total value of the periodic investments will be their future value. Since the compounding period differs from the payment interval, the value for p must be determined first. Since

$$R = \$1000 \qquad n = 25 \qquad i = \frac{8\%}{2} = 4\% \qquad c = \frac{2}{1} = 2$$

then

$$p = (1 + i)^c - 1 = 1.04^2 - 1 = 0.0816 = 8.16\%$$

ALGEBRAIC SOLUTION

$$S_n = R\left[\frac{(1 + p)^n - 1}{p}\right]$$
$$= \$1000\left(\frac{1.0816^{25} - 1}{0.0816}\right)$$
$$= \$1000(74.836806)$$
$$= \$74,836.81$$

The total value after 25 years will be $74,836.81.

FINANCIAL CALCULATOR SOLUTION

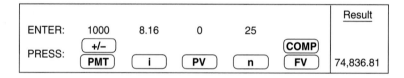

						Result
ENTER:	1000	8.16	0	25		
PRESS:	+/– PMT	i	PV	n	COMP FV	74,836.81

The total value of the investments after 25 years will be $74,836.81. ∎

EXERCISE 10.3

Answers to the odd-numbered problems are at the end of the book.

Calculate to three significant figures the interest rate per payment interval for each of the general annuities in problems 1 through 10.

Problem	Payment frequency	Compounding frequency	Nominal interest rate (%)
1.	Annually	Quarterly	10
2.	Quarterly	Monthly	9
3.	Semiannually	Quarterly	8
4.	Annually	Monthly	7.5
5.	Monthly	Quarterly	11
6.	Monthly	Semiannually	9.5
7.	Quarterly	Annually	7.75
8.	Semiannually	Annually	9.25
9.	Monthly	Annually	10.25
10.	Quarterly	Semiannually	8.5

Determine the future value of the ordinary general annuities in problems 11 to 16.

Problem	Periodic payment ($)	Payment interval	Term (years)	Nominal rate (%)	Compounding frequency
11.	400	3 months	11	11.5	Annually
12.	150	1 month	$6\frac{1}{2}$	10	Quarterly
13.	2750	6 months	$3\frac{1}{2}$	8	Monthly
14.	1500	3 months	$13\frac{1}{2}$	7.5	Semiannually
15.	3500	1 year	17	10.5	Monthly
16.	950	6 months	$8\frac{1}{2}$	9	Quarterly

17. Mr. and Mrs. Krenz are contributing to a Registered Education Savings Plan (RESP) they have set up for their children. What amount will they have in the RESP after 8 years of contributing $500 at the end of every calendar quarter if the plan earns 9% compounded monthly? How much of the total amount is interest?

18. What is the future value 8 years from now of each of the following cash-flow streams if money can earn 9% compounded semiannually?

    a. A single payment of $5000 today.

    b. An ordinary annuity starting today with eight annual payments of $900.

    c. An ordinary annuity starting in 3 years with 20 quarterly payments of $400.

19. An ordinary annuity consists of 25 annual payments of $1000. Calculate its future value if the funds earn:

    a. 9% compounded annually.

    b. 9% compounded quarterly.

    c. 9% compounded monthly.

•20. How much larger will the value of an RRSP be at the end of 25 years if the contributor makes month-end contributions of $300 instead of year-end contributions of $3600? In both cases the RRSP earns 8.5% compounded semiannually.

•21. How much larger will the value of an RRSP be at the end of 25 years if the RRSP earns 9% compounded monthly instead of 9% compounded annually? In both cases a contribution of $1000 is made at the end of every 3 months.

•22. An ordinary annuity consists of 40 semiannual payments of $600. What is its future value if the funds earn 9% compounded quarterly for the first $8\frac{1}{2}$ years and 8% compounded semiannually for the remainder of the term of the annuity?

•23. A savings plan requires end-of-month contributions of $100 for 25 years. What will be the future value of the plan if it earns 7% compounded quarterly for the first half of the annuity's term and 8% compounded semiannually for the last half of the term?

•24. Calculate and compare the economic values 9 years from now of the following cash-flow streams if money can earn 9% compounded semiannually.

    a. A single payment of $10,000 due in 9 years.

    b. An ordinary annuity starting today with nine annual payments of $800.

    c. An ordinary annuity starting in 3 years with 24 quarterly payments of $330.

•25. An investment plan requires year-end contributions of $1000 for 25 years. What will be the future value of the plan if it earns $7\frac{1}{2}$% compounded monthly for the first 10 years and 8% compounded semiannually thereafter?

•26. Monty expects to contribute $300 at the end of every month to his RRSP for the next 5 years. For the subsequent 10 years, he plans to contribute $2000 at the end of each calendar quarter. How much will be in his RRSP at the end of the 15 years if the funds earn 8% compounded semiannually?

•27. Gloria has just made her ninth annual $2000 contribution to her RRSP. She now plans to make semiannual contributions of $2000. The first contribution will be made 6 months from now. How much will she have in her RRSP 15 years from now if the plan has earned and will continue to earn 8% compounded quarterly?

••28. What will be the amount in an RRSP after 25 years if contributions of $3000 are made at each year-end for the first 7 years and month-end contributions of $500 are made for the next 18 years? Assume that the plan earns 8% compounded quarterly for the first 12 years and 7% compounded semiannually for the next 13 years.

10.4 PRESENT VALUE OF AN ORDINARY ANNUITY

The **present value of an annuity** is the single amount, at the beginning of the annuity, that is economically equivalent to the annuity. The additional symbol needed for this section is

A_n = Present value of an n-payment ordinary annuity

PRESENT VALUE USING THE ALGEBRAIC METHOD

An ordinary annuity composed of four payments of $1000 is shown in a time diagram in Figure 10.4. Suppose we want to find the present value of the annuity if money can earn 8% per payment interval. A "brute force" method is indicated in the diagram. In this approach, the present values of the four payments are individually calculated and then added.

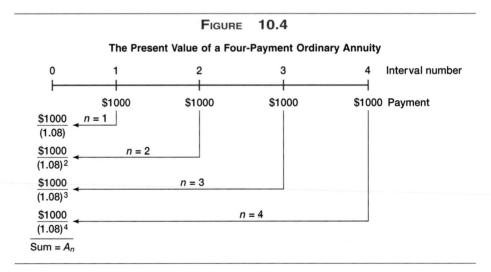

FIGURE 10.4

The Present Value of a Four-Payment Ordinary Annuity

The present value of the annuity is

$$A_n = \frac{\$1000}{1.08} + \frac{\$1000}{1.08^2} + \frac{\$1000}{1.08^3} + \frac{\$1000}{1.08^4}$$
$$= \$925.926 + \$857.339 + \$793.832 + \$735.030$$
$$= \$3312.13$$

As in the case of the future-value calculation, there is a formula that makes the present-value calculation more efficient. Its derivation from formula (10–1) is given in Appendix 10B.

Present Value of an Ordinary Annuity

$$A_n = R\left[\frac{1 - (1 + p)^{-n}}{p}\right] \tag{10–4}$$

The factor

$$\frac{1 - (1 + p)^{-n}}{p}$$

is called the **discount factor for annuities** or the **present-value factor for annuities.** When $R = \$1$, A_n equals the discount factor. Therefore, the discount factor can be interpreted as the present value of a $1 annuity.

Using formula (10–4) to calculate the present value of the preceding four-payment annuity, substitute $R = \$1000$, $n = 4$, and $p = 0.08$, which gives

$$A_n = \$1000\left[\frac{1 - (1 + 0.08)^{-4}}{0.08}\right]$$
$$= \$1000\left(\frac{1 - 0.7350299}{0.08}\right)$$
$$= \$3312.13$$

This is the same result as previously obtained by the "brute force" approach. As the number of payments in an annuity increases, the time saved by employing formula (10–4) increases proportionately.

PRESENT VALUE USING THE FINANCIAL CALCULATOR FUNCTIONS

The correspondence between the key labels and the algebraic variables in formula (10–4) is:

$\boxed{n}$ = n, the number of annuity payments

$\boxed{i}$ = p, the interest rate per payment interval (in percent)

$\boxed{PMT}$ = R, the size of the annuity payment

$\boxed{PV}$ = A_n, the present value of the annuity

To calculate the present value of an annuity, enter the known values for n, p, and R into the $\boxed{n}$, $\boxed{i}$, and $\boxed{PMT}$ memories. Remember to obey your calculator's cash-flow sign convention for the number entered into $\boxed{PMT}$. Zero should be entered into $\boxed{FV}$. Then the $\boxed{COMP}$ $\boxed{PV}$ keystrokes instruct the calculator to compute the future value of the n annuity payments.

Tip

If you do not have zero in the $\boxed{FV}$ memory, the calculator interprets the amount in $\boxed{FV}$ as an *additional* single cash flow occurring at the end of the annuity. Then at the $\boxed{COMP}$ $\boxed{PV}$ command, the calculator will compute the *combined* present value of the annuity and the amount in $\boxed{FV}$. This feature is useful in cases where, in a single calculation, we wish to obtain the combined present value of an annuity and a terminal "lump" payment.

CALCULATION OF p   For a present-value calculation, the interest rate per payment interval is determined in exactly the same manner as for a future-value calculation. That is, $p = i$ if the annuity is a simple annuity. For a general annuity, use formula (10–2) to calculate p.

■ EXAMPLE 10.4A   *THE PRESENT VALUE OF AN ORDINARY SIMPLE ANNUITY*

Determine the present value on December 31 of $500 paid at the end of each subsequent calendar quarter for $6\frac{1}{2}$ years if money is worth 9% compounded quarterly.

☑ SOLUTION

Given: $R = \$500$, Term $= 6\frac{1}{2}$ years, $j = 9\%$, $m = 4$

Therefore,

$$p = i = \frac{9\%}{4} = 2.25\% \quad \text{and} \quad n = 4(6.5) = 26$$

ALGEBRAIC SOLUTION

$$A_n = R\left[\frac{1 - (1 + p)^{-n}}{p}\right]$$
$$= \$500\left(\frac{1 - 1.0225^{-26}}{0.0225}\right)$$
$$= \$500\left(\frac{1 - 0.5607300}{0.0225}\right)$$
$$= \$500(19.52311)$$
$$= \$9761.56$$

FINANCIAL CALCULATOR SOLUTION

						Result
ENTER:	500	2.25	26	0	(COMP)	
PRESS:	(PMT)	(i)	(n)	(FV)	(PV)	−9761.56

The present value of the $500, $6\frac{1}{2}$-year annuity on December 31 is $9761.56.
    Remember that the financial calculator treats all problems as loan or investment applications. Since $500 was entered with a positive sign (cash inflow), the computed present value is the amount that would have to be paid or invested (cash outflow) at the beginning of the annuity's term to purchase the annuity inflows.   ■

■ EXAMPLE 10.4B   *THE PRESENT VALUE OF AN ANNUITY AND A TERMINAL LUMP PAYMENT*

A certain investment pays back $50 at the end of every 6 months for 17 years. At the end of the 17 years, the investment pays back $1000 in addition to the regular $50 payment. What is the present value of all of the payments if money can earn 8.5% compounded semiannually?

☑ SOLUTION

Given: For the annuity,

$$R = \$50 \qquad \text{Term} = 17 \text{ years} \qquad j = 8\tfrac{1}{2}\% \qquad m = 2$$

For the lump payment,

$$S = \$1000 \qquad \text{Term} = 17 \text{ years} \qquad j = 8\tfrac{1}{2}\% \qquad m = 2$$

Therefore,

$$p = i = \frac{8.5\%}{2} = 4.25\% \qquad \text{and} \qquad n = 2(17) = 34$$

ALGEBRAIC SOLUTION

The combined present value is

$$
\begin{aligned}
A_n + P &= R\left[\frac{1 - (1 + p)^{-n}}{p}\right] + \frac{S}{(1 + i)^n} \\
&= \$50\left(\frac{1 - 1.0425^{-34}}{0.0425}\right) + \frac{\$1000}{1.0425^{34}} \\
&= \$50\left(\frac{1 - 0.2428923}{0.0425}\right) + \frac{\$1000}{4.1170503} \\
&= \$890.715 + \$242.892 \\
&= \$1133.61
\end{aligned}
$$

FINANCIAL CALCULATOR SOLUTION

The preprogrammed financial calculator can calculate the combined present value of an annuity and a lump payment occurring at the end of the annuity.

						Result
ENTER:	50	1000	34	4.25		
PRESS:	PMT	FV	n	i	COMP PV	−1133.61

The present value of the payments is $1133.61.   ∎

■ EXAMPLE 10.4c   *THE PRESENT VALUE OF TWO ANNUITIES IN SERIES*

A two-level retirement annuity will pay $2000 per month for the first 10 years and $3000 per month for the next 15 years. What is the present value, 1 month before the first payment, of the entire stream of annuity payments? Money can earn 7.5% compounded monthly.

☑ SOLUTION

We are asked to find the present value 1 month *before* the first payment. The payments viewed from this focal date occur at the *end* of each month. Therefore, the two annuities should be treated as *ordinary* annuities. Since the compounding interval equals the payment interval, both annuities are *simple* annuities. The given information is presented in the following time diagram.

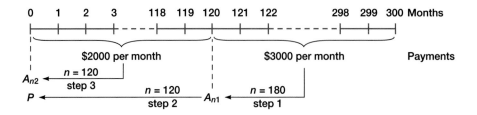

The interest rate per payment interval is

$$p = i = \frac{7.5\%}{12} = 0.625\%$$

The time diagram indicates three steps:

> *Step 1.* Calculate the present value, A_{n1}, of the $3000 annuity at its commencement.
> *Step 2.* Calculate the present value, P, of A_{n1}, at time 0.
> *Step 3.* Calculate the present value, A_{n2}, of the $2000 annuity at time 0.

The combined present value will then be $P + A_{n2}$.

ALGEBRAIC SOLUTION

$$A_{n1} = R\left[\frac{1 - (1 + p)^{-n}}{p}\right]$$

$$= \$3000\left(\frac{1 - 1.00625^{-180}}{0.00625}\right)$$

$$= \$3000\left(\frac{1 - 0.3257911}{0.00625}\right)$$

$$= \$323,620.28$$

Steps 2 and 3 may be combined, as in Example 10.4b, or handled separately.

$$P + A_{n2} = \frac{\$323,620.28}{1.00625^{120}} + \$2000\left(\frac{1 - 1.00625^{-120}}{0.00625}\right)$$

$$= \frac{\$323,620.28}{2.1120646} + \$2000\left(\frac{1 - 0.4734704}{0.00625}\right)$$

$$= \$153,224.61 - \$168,489.49$$

$$= \$321,714.10$$

FINANCIAL CALCULATOR SOLUTION

Step 1						Result
ENTER:	3000	0	0.625	180		
PRESS:	PMT	FV	i	n	COMP PV	−323,620.28

```
┌─────────────────────────────────────────────────────────────┬─────────────┐
│ Steps 2 and 3                                                 ┆             │
│   ENTER:              2000              120                   ┆             │
│            ┌─────┐                         ┌──────┐           ┆             │
│            │ +/− │                         │ COMP │           ┆             │
│   PRESS:   └─────┘                         └──────┘           ┆             │
│            ┌────┐  ┌─────┐         ┌───┐   ┌────┐             ┆             │
│            │ FV │  │ PMT │         │ n │   │ PV │             ┆ −321,714.10 │
│            └────┘  └─────┘         └───┘   └────┘             ┆             │
└─────────────────────────────────────────────────────────────┴─────────────┘
```

The present value of the entire stream of annuity payments is $321,714.10. ∎

EXERCISE 10.4

Answers to the odd-numbered problems are at the end of the book.

Determine the present value of each of the ordinary annuities specified in problems 1 through 14.

Problem	Periodic payment ($)	Payment interval	Term	Discount rate (%)	Compounding frequency
1.	500	1 year	13 years	11.5	Annually
2.	100	3 months	$5\frac{1}{2}$ years	10	Quarterly
3.	75	1 month	$2\frac{1}{2}$ years	8	Monthly
4.	2000	6 months	$12\frac{1}{2}$ years	7.5	Semiannually
5.	175	1 month	$8\frac{1}{4}$ years	11	Monthly
6.	700	1 quarter	7 years, 9 months	9	Quarterly
7.	1240	6 months	$9\frac{1}{2}$ years	9.9	Semiannually
8.	350	1 month	11 years, 5 months	8.75	Monthly
9.	400	3 months	11 years	11.5	Annually
10.	150	1 month	$6\frac{1}{2}$ years	10	Quarterly
11.	2750	6 months	$3\frac{1}{2}$ years	8	Monthly
12.	1500	3 months	$13\frac{1}{2}$ years	7.5	Semiannually
13.	3500	1 year	17 years	10.5	Monthly
14.	950	6 months	$8\frac{1}{2}$ years	9	Quarterly

15. This problem is designed to demonstrate the dependence of the present value of an annuity on the number of payments. Using 10% compounded annually as the time value of money, calculate the present value of an ordinary annuity paying $1000 per year for:

    a. 5 years   *b.* 10 years   *c.* 20 years

    d. 30 years   *e.* 100 years   *f.* 1000 years

    Observe that the present value increases with increasing *n,* but at a diminishing rate. In this case, the 970 payments from year 30 to year 1000 cause the present value to increase by only about 6%.

16. This problem is designed to demonstrate the dependence of the present value of an annuity on the discount rate. For an ordinary annuity consisting of 20 annual payments of $1000, calculate the present value using an annually compounded discount rate of:

    a. 5%   *b.* 10%   *c.* 11%   *d.* 15%

    Observe that the present value decreases as the discount rate is increased. However, the present value decreases proportionately less than the increase in the discount rate.

17. With great fanfare, a provincial minister of public works announces a program of high-way construction in his province "worth $100 million." Details of the program reveal that $5 million will be spent each calendar quarter for the next 5 years. If the first $5 million expenditure takes place 3 months from now, what is the current economic value (to the nearest $1000) of the program if money is worth 8% compounded annually?

18. The Ottawa Senators fired their coach 2 years into his 5-year contract, which paid $30,000 at the end of each month. If the team owners buy out the remaining term of the coach's contract for its economic value at the time of firing, what will be the settlement amount? Use 7.5% compounded monthly as the time value of money.

•19. The Toronto Raptors announce the signing of their top draft pick to a "7-year deal worth $21.6 million." The player will earn $200,000 at the end of each month for the first 3 years, and $300,000 at the end of each month for the subsequent 4 years. How do the Raptors get the $21.6 million figure? To the nearest $1000, what is the current economic value of the deal if money can earn 7% compounded annually?

•20. An annuity contract pays $2000 semiannually for 15 years. What is the present value of the annuity 6 months before the first payment if money can earn 8% compounded semi-annually for the first 6 years and 10% compounded semiannually for the next 9 years?

•21. An annuity contract pays $2000 semiannually for 15 years. What is the present value of the annuity 6 months before the first payment if money can earn 7.5% compounded monthly for the first 5 years and 9% compounded annually for the next 10 years?

•22. An annuity paying $800 at the end of each quarter for the first $4\frac{1}{2}$ years is followed by a second annuity paying $2000 at the end of each half year for the subsequent $4\frac{1}{2}$ years. What is the combined present value of the two annuities at the beginning of the first annuity? Assume that the time value of money is 8% compounded quarterly.

•23. An annuity paying $500 at the end of each month for the first $2\frac{1}{2}$ years is followed by a second annuity paying $2000 at the end of each quarter for the subsequent $3\frac{1}{2}$ years. What is their combined present value at the beginning of the first annuity? Assume the time value of money is 7% compounded semiannually.

10.5 APPLICATIONS OF THE PRESENT VALUE OF AN ANNUITY

More applications require the present-value calculation than the future-value calcula-tion. Fundamentally, all present-value applications involve a *valuation*—placing a price tag on the remaining payments of an annuity. Three categories of applications are discussed in this section. A key issue in each category will be the basis for choosing the discount rate to be used in the present-value calculation.

THE MARKET VALUE OF AN ANNUITY

We look to the Valuation Principle (Section 7.2) for guidance in calculating the fair market value of any series of cash flows. It instructs us to calculate the present value of the cash flows, discounting them at the prevailing *market-determined* rate of return on investments of similar risk and term. Hence,

> Fair market value of an annuity = Present value of the annuity payments (discounted at the *market rate of return*)

Current market rates offered by insurance companies to purchasers of annuities are periodically reported in the major financial papers. Alternatively, market rates on annuities of various terms may be obtained from annuity brokers.

Instances where the fair market value of an annuity needs to be determined are:

- An investor wishes to determine the price to pay for an annuity.
- An individual wishes to calculate the lump amount that must be accumulated in order to purchase a desired annuity at retirement. (The market rate on the retirement date must be estimated in this case.)

The cash flows from some investments include an annuity component. For example, bonds pay a fixed dollar amount of interest every 6 months until the face value of each bond is repaid at maturity. Some preferred shares pay fixed quarterly dividends until the par value of each share is repaid on the redemption date. These two types of investments trade in financial markets. Consequently, valuation at *prevailing market* rates of return is important on a day-by-day (or even hour-by-hour) basis. The value of the investment is the present value of *all* remaining payments. The annuity *component* can be valued separately and added to the present value of the *other* cash flows.

■ EXAMPLE 10.5A *CALCULATING THE PURCHASE PRICE OF AN ANNUITY*

What amount is needed to purchase an annuity paying $1000 at the end of each month for 20 years if the lump purchase price earns 7.2% compounded monthly?

☑ SOLUTION

The annuity is an ordinary simple annuity with

$$R = \$1000 \quad \text{and} \quad n = 20(12) = 240 \text{ payments}$$

The amount required to purchase the annuity is the present value, A_n, of the payments discounted at $p = i = \frac{7.2\%}{12} = 0.6\%$ per month.

ALGEBRAIC SOLUTION

$$A_n = R\left[\frac{1 - (1 + p)^{-n}}{p}\right]$$
$$= \$1000\left[\frac{1 - (1 + 0.006)^{-240}}{0.006}\right]$$
$$= \$127,008.43$$

FINANCIAL CALCULATOR SOLUTION

Compute the present value of all 240 payments.					Result
ENTER: 1000	0	0.6	240		
PRESS: (PMT)	(FV)	(i)	(n)	(COMP) (PV)	−127,008.43

The purchase price of the annuity is $127,008.43.   ■

■ EXAMPLE 10.5B *CALCULATING THE FAIR MARKET VALUE OF A PREFERRED SHARE*

The preferred shares of Dominion Trust Co. will pay a $0.75 per share dividend at the end of every calendar quarter until their redemption $8\frac{1}{2}$ years from now. At that time, a shareholder will also receive the $40 par value of each share. What is the fair market value of a share if preferred shares of similar risk are currently generating a total rate of return of 6.5% compounded semiannually?

☑ SOLUTION

The fair market value of the shares will be the combined present value of the dividends and the $40 payment of the par value. The dividend stream constitutes an *ordinary general* annuity having

$$R = \$0.75 \qquad n = 8.5(4) = 34 \qquad i = \frac{6.5\%}{2} = 3.25\%$$

Then

$$c = \frac{2 \text{ compoundings per year}}{4 \text{ payments per year}} = 0.5$$

and

$$p = (1 + i)^c - 1 = 1.0325^{0.5} - 1 = 0.0161201 = 1.61201\% \text{ per quarter}$$

ALGEBRAIC SOLUTION

Fair market value = Present value of dividends + Present value of par value

Formulas (10–4) and (8–2) are needed to calculate the two present values in the preceding equation. In employing formula (8–2), we can use either

- $S(1 + i)^{-n}$ with $i = 0.0325$ and $n = 17$, the total number of compoundings of i, or

- $S(1 + p)^{-n}$ with $p = 0.0161201$ and $n = 34$, the number of compoundings of p.

They will give the same answer because p compounded every 3 months is equivalent to i compounded every 6 months. We will use $S(1 + p)^{-n}$ since $(1 + p)^{-n}$ must be calculated in any event for formula (10–4).

$$\begin{aligned}
\text{Fair market value} &= R\left[\frac{1 - (1 + p)^{-n}}{p}\right] + S(1 + p)^{-n} \\
&= 0.75 \times \left[\frac{1 - 1.0161201^{-34}}{0.0161201}\right] + \$40(1.0161201)^{-34} \\
&= \$19.513 + \$23.224 \\
&= \$42.74
\end{aligned}$$

FINANCIAL CALCULATOR SOLUTION

Fair market value = Present value of the dividends + Present value of the par value

The combined present value may be obtained in a single computation.

Compute the combined present value of the dividends and par value.					Result
ENTER: 0.75 40 1.61201 34					
PRESS: (PMT) (FV) (i) (n) (COMP)(PV)					$42.737

The fair market value of a preferred share is $42.74.   ■

■ EXAMPLE 10.5c   PRICING AN ANNUITY TO PROVIDE A REQUIRED RATE OF RETURN

Crazy Ed's Furniture Mart held a promotion for purchases exceeding $500. Customers could pay 10% down and then pay the balance in six equal monthly payments with no interest charged. Crazy Ed's sold the conditional sale contracts to a finance company. The finance company purchased the contracts at a discounted price so that the six payments would provide a rate of return on the purchase price of 18% compounded monthly. What did it pay for a $1200 contract (six payments of $200)?

☑ SOLUTION

The six instalment payments form an ordinary simple annuity. The finance company would have determined the price by calculating the present value of this annuity. To build the required rate of return into the purchase price, the payments had to be discounted at the required rate of return. We need to calculate the present value of $n = 6$ payments of $R = \$200$ discounted at $p = i = 1.5\%$ per month.

ALGEBRAIC SOLUTION

$$A_n = \$200\left[\frac{1 - (1 + 0.015)^{-6}}{0.015}\right] = \$1139.44$$

FINANCIAL CALCULATOR SOLUTION

Compute the present value of the six instalment payments					Result
ENTER: 200	0	1.5	6		
PRESS:				(COMP)	
(PMT)	(FV)	(i)	(n)	(PV)	−1139.44

The finance company paid $1139.44 for the contract.   ■

THE ECONOMIC VALUE OF AN ANNUITY

Some examples of this application have already been encountered in Section 10.4. The following discussion develops this valuation concept further. *Economic* value is a somewhat looser notion than *market* value. It is used in contexts where a monetary value needs to be placed on a cash-flow stream that does not necessarily come from an investment. For example, financial settlements in personal injury actions often involve a lump payment to replace the injured's future employment income. In such cases, we cannot refer to a financial market for the appropriate discount rate. There may be laws, established practices, and so forth that provide guidance for setting the discount rate in specific situations. Typically, the rate used is close to the rate of return that can be earned on a low-risk investment. For example, if the cash flows being discounted are spread over the next 10 years, the market rate of return on 10-year annuities would be a suitable choice for the discount rate.

Current economic value of an annuity	= Present value of the annuity payments (discounted at a *rate of return that money can earn on low-risk investments*)

■ EXAMPLE 10.5D   *COMPARING THE ECONOMIC VALUES OF TWO ANNUITIES*

An eligible individual may elect to start collecting the Canada Pension Plan (CPP) monthly retirement benefit at any time between the ages of 60 and 65. The payments are then reduced (from the amount that would otherwise be paid after age 65) by 0.5% for each month before age 65. For example, if the retiree chooses to receive the first pension payment 1 month after turning 60, the CPP payments will be decreased by (60 months) × (0.5%) = 30%. The reduction is permanent, extending to payments after age 65 as well.

The average life expectancy of a woman aged 60 is another 22 years. If a woman aged 60 lives just the expected 22 years, compare the economic values at age 60 of the two alternatives of collecting a 100% pension from age 65 versus a 70% pension from age 60. Assume that money is worth 7.5% compounded monthly.

☑ SOLUTION

The economic value of a stream of pension payments at age 60 will be the present value of the payments discounted at

$$p = i = \frac{7.5\%}{12} = 0.625\% \text{ per month}$$

The alternative retirement annuities are illustrated in the following time diagrams. *R* represents the 100% monthly pension payment commencing at age 65. Therefore, 0.70*R* will be the monthly payment on a 70% pension starting at age 60.

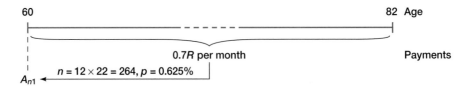

A_{n1} is the present value at age 60 of the reduced pension payments.

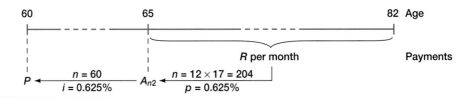

A_{n2} is the present value at age 65 of the full pension payments. *P* is the present value at age 60 of A_{n2}.

ALGEBRAIC SOLUTION

$$A_{n1} = 0.7R\left(\frac{1 - 1.00625^{-264}}{0.00625}\right)$$

$$= 0.7R\left(\frac{1 - 0.1930386}{0.00625}\right)$$

$$= 90.38R$$

$$A_{n2} = R\left(\frac{1 - 1.00625^{-204}}{0.00625}\right)$$

$$= 115.113R$$

$$P = \frac{A_{n2}}{1.00625^{60}} = \frac{115.113R}{1.453294} = 79.21R$$

Therefore, the age 60 option is worth

$$\frac{90.38R - 79.21R}{79.21R} \times 100\% = 14.1\%$$

more than the age 65 option, assuming that money is worth 7.5% compounded monthly and the woman survives to age 82.

FINANCIAL CALCULATOR SOLUTION

Find the present values of the coefficients of R in the two alternative pension streams.

Calculate A_{n1}.						Result
ENTER:	0.7	0	264	0.625		
PRESS:	PMT	FV	n	i	COMP PV	−90.38
Calculate A_{n2}.						
ENTER:	1	204			COMP	
PRESS:	PMT	n			PV	−115.113
Calculate P.						
ENTER:	+/−	0	60		COMP	
PRESS:	FV	PMT	n		PV	−79.21

The age 60 option is worth

$$\frac{90.38R - 79.21R}{79.21R} \times 100\% = 14.1\%$$

more than the age 65 option, assuming that money is worth 7.5% compounded monthly and the woman survives to age 82. ■

LOAN BALANCE AND SELLING PRICE

LOAN BALANCE Most loans require equal payments at the end of each payment interval. In these cases, the loan payments constitute an *ordinary* annuity. In Section 6.7 we established the general principle that

> Original loan = Present value of all the payments (discounted at the *contractual rate of interest on the loan*)

Furthermore, the balance owed on a loan at any point is

> Principal balance = Present value of the remaining payments (discounted at the *contractual rate of interest on the loan*)

Both principles apply whether or not the loan payments form an annuity. Where the payments do form an annuity, formulas (10−4) and (10−2) are used for the present-value calculations.

SELLING PRICE (OR PROCEEDS FROM THE SALE) OF A LOAN CONTRACT Most loan contracts permit the lender to sell and assign the contract to another party at any time during the term of the loan. The purchaser is then entitled to receive the remaining payments from the borrower. In determining the price to pay, the purchaser will expect a rate of return that is competitive with prevailing rates on the date of purchase. Therefore, the *purchaser's required rate of return* is used in the present-value calculation to discount the remaining payments. That is,

> Selling price of a loan (or Proceeds from the sale of a loan) = Present value of the remaining payments (discounted at the *purchaser's required rate of return*)

If loans with similar terms are offered by financial institutions, the industry rates on such loans set a reference point for both the vendor and purchaser in negotiating an appropriate discount rate.

■ EXAMPLE 10.5E   *CALCULATING THE ORIGINAL LOAN AND A SUBSEQUENT BALANCE*

The monthly payment on a 5-year loan with interest at 12% compounded monthly is $255.81.

a. What was the original principal amount of the loan?

b. What is the balance owed just after the 17th payment?

☑ SOLUTION

Customizing two of the principles discussed earlier in this section to the present problem, we have

> Original principal = Present value of all 60 payments
> Balance after 17 payments = Present value of the remaining 43 payments

The loan payments form an ordinary simple annuity with

$$R = \$255.81, \quad \text{and} \quad p = i = \frac{12\%}{12} = 1\% \text{ per month.}$$

ALGEBRAIC SOLUTION

a.
$$\text{Original principal} = \$255.81\left(\frac{1 - 1.01^{-60}}{0.01}\right)$$
$$= \$255.81\left(\frac{1 - 0.5504496}{0.01}\right)$$
$$= \$11,499.95$$

b.
$$\text{Balance} = \$255.81\left(\frac{1 - 1.01^{-43}}{0.01}\right) = \$8904.75$$

FINANCIAL CALCULATOR SOLUTION

a. Calculate original principal.					Result
ENTER: 255.81 60 1 0					
PRESS: PMT n i FV COMP PV					−11,499.95
b. Calculate balance after 17 payments.					
ENTER 43					
PRESS: n COMP PV					−8904.75

The original loan was $11,499.95, and the balance after 17 payments is $8904.75. ∎

■ EXAMPLE 10.5F CALCULATING THE PROCEEDS FROM THE SALE OF A LOAN CONTRACT

What will be the proceeds from the sale of the loan in Example 10.5E just after the seventeenth payment, if the purchaser's required monthly compounded rate of return is:

a. 10.5%?   b. 12%?   c. 13.5%?

☑ SOLUTION

In each case,

$$\text{Proceeds} = \begin{array}{l}\text{Present value of the remaining 43 payments} \\ \text{discounted at the required rate of return}\end{array}$$

ALGEBRAIC SOLUTION

a. For $p = i = 10.5\%/12 = 0.875\%$,

$$\text{Proceeds} = \$255.81\left(\frac{1 - 1.00875^{-43}}{0.00875}\right)$$

$$= \$255.81\left(\frac{1 - 0.687555}{0.00875}\right)$$

$$= \$9134.46$$

b. For $p = i = 12\%/12 = 1\%$,

$$\text{Proceeds} = \$255.81\left(\frac{1 - 1.01^{-43}}{0.01}\right) = \$8904.75$$

which, from Example 10.5E, is also the balance owed on the loan after 17 payments.

c. For $p = i = 13.5\%/12 = 1.125\%$,

$$\text{Proceeds} = \$255.81\left(\frac{1 - 1.01125^{-43}}{0.01125}\right)$$

$$= \$255.81\left(\frac{1 - 0.6181345}{0.01125}\right)$$

$$= \$8683.11$$

Financial Calculator Solution

	Result
a. Calculate the proceeds for $p = i = 10.5\%/12 = 0.875\%$. ENTER: 0.875 255.81 0 43 PRESS: [i] [PMT] [FV] [n] [COMP] [PV]	−9134.46
b. Calculate the proceeds for $p = i = 12\%/12 = 1\%$. ENTER: 1 PRESS: [i] [COMP] [PV]	−8904.75
c. Calculate the proceeds for $p = i = 13.5\%/12 = 1.125\%$. ENTER: 1.125 PRESS: [i] [COMP] [PV]	−8683.11

This example illustrates the following general results:

- The proceeds from the sale of a debt contract *equal* the balance owed on the debt only if the required rate of return *equals* the contractual rate of interest on the debt.
- If the required rate of return is *less* than the contractual rate of interest on the debt, the selling price will be *greater* than the balance.
- If the required rate of return is *greater* than the contractual rate of interest on the debt, the selling price will be *less* than the balance. ∎

Point of Interest

Valuing the Pension Benefits of MPs and MLAs

In the early 1990s, the most controversial financial benefit received by members of Parliament (MPs) and members of (provincial) Legislative Assemblies (MLAs) was their pension plan. The widely held view was that most plans for MPs and MLAs were unduly generous and very costly to taxpayers. The pension plans became popular subjects for editorials and letters to editors of the print media. The electorate has put enough "heat" on politicians in recent years that some provincial governments and the federal government have reduced pension entitlements that will accrue in respect of future years of service. For the most part, benefits for years of service up to the date of the amendments were not reduced. Consequently, the magnitude of the pension entitlements of departing politicians will continue to be a subject for outraged commentary over the remainder of the 1990s.

Virtually all analyses of politicians' pension entitlements are fundamentally flawed because the time value of money is ignored. This Point of Interest will first present a typical example of a faulty analysis. Then a more rigorous determination of the current economic value of future pension benefits will be made.

Just after British Columbia's provincial election in May 1996, the B.C. branch of the Canadian Taxpayers Federation (CTF) issued a news release stating that "... 12 departing MLAs will collect an estimated $10,000,000 in pension benefits." Accounting for one-sixth of the total amount was a 48-year-old former member with 13.1 years of service. Based on his salary and various allowances as an MLA and cabinet minister (for a portion of the period of service), the former member qualified for an immediate pension of $42,770 per year.

The pension plan of the British Columbia MLAs is "fully indexed." This means the annual pension will rise each year by the *(continued)*

(concluded)

same percentage as the increase in the Consumer Price Index. Assuming an annual inflation rate of 3%, the CTF estimated this former member's pension benefits over the 26.4 years remaining until age 75 to be $1,685,000.

Typical of most commentaries on politicians' pension plans, the $1,685,000 was obtained by simply adding the *nominal* dollar amounts of expected pension payments up to age 75. This implies that a dollar received at age 74 has the same economic value in May of 1996 as a dollar received in the very first pension cheque. We know better—the current economic value of the future pension payments is the present value of the payments discounted at the time value of money.

Since this is an exercise in estimation, it is reasonable to make the simplifying assumption that each year's pension is paid in a lump amount at the year-end. Formula (10−4) for the present value of an ordinary annuity requires the periodic payments to be equal. Therefore, the formula cannot be used here with the annual pension payments growing at the 3% rate of inflation. A brute-force approach would be to calculate the present value of each annual payment. Let us instead use the following formula for the present value of a series of n periodic payments which grow at the rate, g, per payment interval.

$$\frac{R}{p - g}\left[1 - \left(\frac{1 + g}{1 + p}\right)^n\right]$$

Note that when the payments do not increase, then $g = 0$ and the formula reduces to formula (10−4).

We still need to choose an appropriate value for p, the time value of money (per payment interval). At the time of the press release, the annual yields on Government of Canada bonds ranged from about 6% for 2-year terms to 8% for 25-year maturities. Therefore, it is reasonable to use 7% compounded annually as an *average* time value of money over the $n = 26.4$ years of annual pension payments to age 75. The economic value in May of 1996 of the future pension payments was

$$\frac{\$42,770}{0.07 - 0.03}\left[1 - \left(\frac{1.03}{1.07}\right)^{26.4}\right] = \$678,000$$

This value is only 40% of the CTF's figure of $1.685 million. Therefore, analyses which ignore the time value of money can produce a gross overstatement of the value of the benefits.

Even though reported figures typically overestimate the economic value of politicians' pension benefits by a wide margin, pension plans such as the one enjoyed by British Columbia MLAs are, nevertheless, very generous. In the vast majority of private- and public-sector plans, the employer and employee make equal contributions to the plan. In contrast, a rigorous analysis including the time value of money reveals the BC taxpayers must, in effect, contribute $5 to the MLA's pension plan for every $1 contributed by the MLA.

EXERCISE 10.5

Answers to the odd-numbered problems are at the end of the book.

1. Mr. and Mrs. Dafoe are doing some estimates of the amount of funds they will need in their RRSP to purchase an annuity paying $3000 at the end of each month for various terms and interest rates. For each combination of term and monthly compounded interest rate in the following table, calculate the initial amount required to purchase the annuity.

Term of	Interest rate	
annuity	8%	9%
20 years	?	?
25 years	?	?

2. The Montreal Canadiens have just announced the signing of Finnish hockey sensation Gunnar Skoroften to a 10-year contract at $1.2 million per year. The media are reporting the deal as being worth $12 million to the young Finn. What current economic value would you place on the contract if Skoroften will be paid $100,000 at the end of each month and money can earn 9% compounded monthly?

3. Ms. Ho is buying a 25% interest in an accounting partnership by end-of-month payments of $537.66, including interest at 8% compounded semiannually, for 12 years.

   a. What valuation was placed on the partnership at the beginning of the payments?

   b. What total amount of interest will she pay over the 12 years?

4. What amount will be required to purchase a 20-year annuity paying $2500 at the end of each month if the annuity provides a return of 8.75% compounded annually?

5. Colin and Marie have received two purchase offers on their boat. One is for $7900 cash, and the other is for $1000 down plus four payments of $2000 at 6-month intervals beginning 6 months from now. Which offer should they accept if money can earn 10% compounded semiannually?

6. You can purchase a residential building lot for $45,000 cash or for $10,000 down and quarterly payments of $2500 for 4 years. The first payment would be due 3 months after the purchase date. If the money you would use for a cash purchase can earn 8% compounded quarterly during the next 4 years, which option should you choose? What is the economic advantage in current dollars of the preferred alternative?

7. You have received two offers on the used car you wish to sell. Mr. Lindberg is offering $8500 cash, and Mrs. Martel's offer is five semiannual payments of $1900 including one on the purchase date. Which offer has the greater economic value if money can earn 10% compounded semiannually? What is the economic advantage in current dollars of the preferred alternative?

8. Osgood Appliance Centre is advertising refrigerators for six monthly payments of $199, including a payment on the date of purchase. What cash price should Osgood accept if it would otherwise sell the conditional sale agreement to a finance company to yield 18% compounded monthly?

9. If money can earn 9.75% compounded monthly, how much more money is required to fund an ordinary annuity paying $200 per month for 30 years than to fund the same monthly payment for 20 years?

10. An Agreement for Sale contract on a house requires payments of $4000 at the end of every 6 months. The contract has 7 years to run. The payee wants to sell her interest in the contract. What will an investor pay in order to realize an annually compounded rate of return on the purchase price of:

    a. 8%?   b. 10%?   c. 12%?

11. A conditional sale contract between Classic Furniture and the purchaser of a dining room set requires month-end payments of $250 for 15 months. Classic Furniture sold the contract to Household Finance Co. at a discount to yield 19.5% compounded monthly. What price did Household pay Classic Furniture?

12. Kent sold his car to Carolyn for $2000 down and monthly payments of $160.70 for $3\frac{1}{2}$ years, including interest at 12% compounded quarterly. What was the selling price of the car?

13. For its "One-Year No-Interest Sale," Flemmings Furniture advertises that, on any purchase over $499, the customer's down payment needs to cover only 10% of the ticketed price plus any sales tax not already included in the ticketed price. The balance of the purchase price is then paid in 12 equal monthly payments with no interest charges.

Money is worth 11.5% compounded monthly to Flemmings because it can use surplus cash to pay down the balance on its operating loan on which interest accrues at 11.5% compounded monthly. What cash amount (not including sales tax) should Flemmings be willing to accept (instead of the no-interest plan) on an item ticketed at $1000?

•14. A conditional sale contract requires the debtor to make six quarterly payments of $569, with the first payment due in 6 months. What amount will a finance company pay to purchase the contract on the date of sale if the finance company requires a rate of return of 20% compounded quarterly?

•15. If money can earn 10% compounded annually for the next 20 years, which of the following annuities has the greater economic value today: $1000 paid at the end of each of the next 10 years, or 10 annual payments of $2500 with the first payment occurring 11 years from today?

•16. A Government of Canada bond will pay $50 at the end of every 6 months for the next 15 years and will pay an additional $1000 lump payment at the end of the 15 years. What is the appropriate price to pay if you require a rate of return of 9% compounded semiannually?

•17. A mortgage broker offers to sell you a mortgage loan contract that will pay $800 at the end of each month for the next $3\frac{1}{2}$ years, at which time the principal balance of $45,572 is due and payable. What is the highest price you should pay for the contract if you require a return of at least 10.5% compounded monthly?

•18. What is the maximum price you should pay for a contract guaranteeing month-end payments of $500 for the next 12 years if you require a rate of return of at least 8% compounded monthly for the first 5 years and at least 9% compounded monthly for the next 7 years?

•19. A lottery offers the winner the choice between a $150,000 cash prize or month-end payments of $1000 for $12\frac{1}{2}$ years, increasing to $1500 per month for the next $12\frac{1}{2}$ years. Which alternative would you choose if money can earn 8.25% compounded monthly over the 25-year period?

20. Manuel purchased a boat for $2000 down with the balance to be paid by 36 blended monthly payments of $224.58 including interest at 10% compounded monthly.

   a. What was the purchase price of the boat?

   b. If the principal balance may be prepaid at any time, what is the payout amount just after the ninth payment?

21. A 20-year loan requires semiannual payments of $1333.28 including interest at 10.75% compounded semiannually.

   a. What was the original amount of the loan?

   b. If the principal balance may be prepaid at any time, what is the payout amount (not including the scheduled payment) $8\frac{1}{2}$ years after the date of the loan?

•22. Bosco class A preferred shares pay quarterly dividends of $1.00. The shares must be redeemed at $50 by Bosco $15\frac{1}{4}$ years from now, when the last dividend is paid. What is the fair market value of the shares if the rate of return required by the market on similar preferred shares is:

   a. 7% compounded quarterly?

   b. 8% compounded quarterly?

   c. 9% compounded quarterly?

••23. An individual qualifying for Canada Pension Plan benefits may elect to start collecting the CPP monthly retirement benefit at any time between the ages of 60 and 70. If the retirement benefit starts after age 65, the pension payments are increased (from the amount that would otherwise be paid at age 65) by 0.5% for each month after age 65. For example, if the retiree chooses to begin receiving the benefit after turning 68, the CPP payments will be increased by (36 months)×(0.5%)=18%.

The average life expectancy of a man aged 65 is another 15 years. If a man aged 65 lives just the expected 15 years, compare the economic values at age 65 of the two alternatives of collecting a 100% pension from age 65 versus a 118% pension from age 68. Assume that money is worth 7.5% compounded monthly.

••24. The British Columbia Teachers' Pension Plan allows a teacher to begin collecting a retirement pension before age 60, but the pension is reduced by 3% for each year the retiring teacher's age is under 60. For example, a teacher retiring at age 56 would receive 88% of the monthly pension that she would receive at age 60 with the same number of years of service. The reduction is permanent, extending to payments beyond age 60.

Suppose that a female teacher will live the average life expectancy of 28 additional years for a woman aged 55. Compare the economic values at age 55 of the two alternatives of collecting an 88% pension from age 55 versus collecting a 100% pension from age 60. Assume that money is worth 7.5% compounded monthly.

*Appendix 10A: Derivation of the Formula for the Future Value of an Ordinary Annuity

The future value of an n-payment ordinary annuity will be the sum of the future values of all of the individual payments comprising the annuity. This approach is taken in Figure 10.5 where formula (8–2), $S = P(1 + i)^n$, is used to obtain the future value of each payment at the end of the annuity. Replace i by p, the interest rate per payment interval.

$$R(1 + p)^1 = \text{Future value of the second-to-last payment}$$
$$R(1 + p)^2 = \text{Future value of the third-to-last payment}$$

$$\cdot$$
$$\cdot$$
$$\cdot$$

$$R(1 + p)^{n-3} = \text{Future value of the third payment}$$
$$R(1 + p)^{n-2} = \text{Future value of the second payment}$$
$$R(1 + p)^{n-1} = \text{Future value of the first payment}$$

The future value S_n of the annuity is

$$S_n = R(1 + p)^{n-1} + R(1 + p)^{n-2} + \cdots + R(1 + p)^2 + R(1 + p) + R$$

If the annuity contains many payments, this procedure of calculating and adding the future values of all of the individual payments becomes very laborious and time-consuming. We would much prefer a more compact and efficient formulation. An algebraic breakthrough[4] can be made if we first multiply both sides of the above equation by $(1 + p)$:

$$(1 + p)S_n = R(1 + p)^n + R(1 + p)^{n-1} + \cdots + R(1 + p)^3 + R(1 + p)^2 + R(1 + p)$$

---

[4]Do not feel that you should have been able to anticipate this step, which appears, at first, to complicate the expression rather than simplify it.

FIGURE 10.5

The Future Value of an Ordinary Annuity

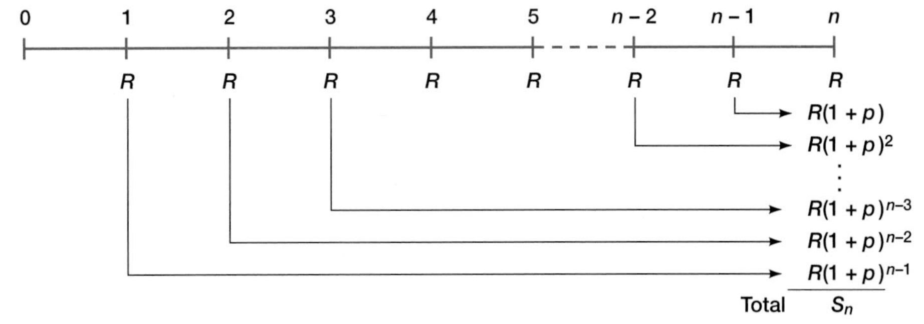

Now if we subtract the equation for S_n from the equation of $S_n(1 + p)$, we achieve a major simplification. This step is presented below, where the terms on the right side of the equation are arranged to make it clear which terms will disappear as a result of the subtraction.

$$(1 + p)S_n - S_n = R(1 + p)^n$$
$$+ R(1 + p)^{n-1} + \cdots + R(1 + p)^3 + R(1 + p)^2 + R(1 + p)$$
$$- R(1 + p)^{n-1} - \cdots - R(1 + p)^3 - R(1 + p)^2 - R(1 + p) - R$$

Expand the left side and complete the subtraction on the right side:

$$S_n + p \times S_n - S_n = R(1 + p)_n - R$$

Simplifying the left side and extracting the common factor R on the right side gives

$$p \times S_n = R[(1 + p)^n - 1]$$

Finally, if both sides are divided by p, we obtain

$$S_n = R\left[\frac{(1 + p)^n - 1}{p}\right] \tag{10-1}$$

*APPENDIX 10B: DERIVATION OF THE FORMULA FOR THE PRESENT VALUE OF AN ORDINARY ANNUITY

The present value A_n of an ordinary annuity will be the sum of the present values, at the beginning of the first payment interval, of all the individual payments in the annuity. We could derive a formula for the present value using an approach similar to that of Appendix 10A for formula (10−1). However, now that we have the formula for an annuity's future value, there is a simpler way. This approach uses the insight that the following cash flows are economically equivalent to one another:

- The scheduled annuity payments.
- A single payment at the end of the annuity's term equal to its future value.
- A single payment at the beginning of an annuity's term equal to its present value.

Hence, the present value A_n of an annuity will also equal the present value, n periods earlier, of a single payment equal to S_n. Using formula (8–2) in the form

$$P = S(1 + i)^{-n}$$

we obtain

$$A_n = S_n(1 + p)^{-n}$$

Now use formula (10–1) to substitute for S_n:

$$
\begin{aligned}
A_n &= R\left[\frac{(1 + p)^n - 1}{p}\right] \times (1 + p)^{-n} \\
&= R\left[\frac{(1 + p)^n(1 + p)^{-n} - 1(1 + p)^{-n}}{p}\right] \\
&= R\left[\frac{(1 + p)^{n-n} - (1 + p)^{-n}}{p}\right] \\
A_n &= R\left[\frac{1 - (1 + p)^{-n}}{p}\right]
\end{aligned}
$$

$$(10\text{--}4)$$

21901.45

REVIEW PROBLEMS

Answers to the odd-numbered review problems are at the end of the book.

1. You can purchase a residential building lot for $60,000 cash or for $10,000 down and month-end payments of $1000 for 5 years. If money has a time value of 7.5% compounded monthly, which option should you choose?

2. A victim of a car accident won a judgement for wages lost over a 2-year period ended 9 months before the date of the judgement. In addition, the court awarded interest at 6% compounded monthly on the lost wages from the date they would have otherwise been received to the date of the judgement. If the monthly salary had been $5500, what was the total amount of the award (on the date of the judgement)?

3. Dr. Wilson is buying a 50% interest in a veterinary practice by end-of-month payments of $714.60, including interest at 7% compounded semiannually for 15 years.

   a. What valuation was placed on the partnership at the beginning of the payments?

   b. What total amount of interest will she pay over the 15 years?

4. What minimum amount of money earning 7% compounded semiannually will sustain withdrawals of $1000 at the end of every month for 12 years?

•5. Calculate the future value of an ordinary annuity consisting of monthly payments of $300 for 5 years if the rate of interest was 9% compounded monthly for the first 2 years and will be 7.5% compounded monthly for the last 3 years.

•6. How much larger will the value of an RRSP be at the end of 20 years if the contributor makes month-end contributions of $500 instead of year-end contributions of $6000? In both cases the RRSP earns 7.5% compounded semiannually.

•7. Charlene has made contributions of $3000 to her RRSP at the end of every half year for the past 7 years. The plan has earned 9% compounded semiannually. She has just moved the funds to another plan paying 7.5% compounded quarterly, and will now contribute $2000 at the end of every 3 months. What total amount will she have in the plan 5 years from now?

•8. What percentage more funds will you have in your RRSP 20 years from now by making fixed contributions of $3000 at the end of every 6 months for the next 20 years, instead of waiting 10 years and making semiannual contributions that are twice as large for half as many years? Assume that the RRSP earns 8% compounded semiannually.

•9. A mortgage broker offers to sell you a mortgage loan contract that will pay $900 per month for the next $2\frac{3}{4}$ years, at which time the principal balance of $37,886 is due and payable. What should you pay for the contract if you require a return of 7.2% compounded monthly?

•10. What is the appropriate price to pay for a contract guaranteeing payments of $1500 at the end of each quarter for the next 12 years if you require a rate of return of 8% compounded quarterly for the first 5 years and 9% compounded quarterly for the next 7 years?

11. A 15-year loan requires monthly payments of $587.33 including interest at 8.4% compounded monthly.

   a. What was the original amount of the loan?

   b. If the principal balance may be prepaid at any time, what is the payout amount (not including the scheduled payment) after $7\frac{1}{2}$ years?

•12. If Evan contributes $2000 to his RRSP at the end of every quarter for the next 15 years and then contributes $1000 at each month's end for the subsequent 10 years, how much will he have in his RRSP at the end of the 25 years? Assume that the RRSP earns 8% compounded semiannually.

SELF-TEST EXERCISE

Answers to the self-test problems are at the end of the book.

1. Calculate the amounts that will be accumulated after 20 years if:

   a. $1000 is invested at the end of every 6 months at 8.5% compounded semiannually.

   b. $2000 is invested at the end of every year at 8.5% compounded annually.

2. Louiselle purchased a recreational vehicle for $9000 down, with the balance to be paid by 60 blended monthly payments of $812.47 including interest at 10.5% compounded monthly.

   a. What was the purchase price of the recreational vehicle?

   b. If the principal balance may be prepaid at any time, what is the payout amount 2 years after the purchase date (not including the scheduled payment on that date)?

3. What price will a finance company pay for a conditional sale contract requiring 15 monthly payments of $180.50 if the company requires a rate of return of 21% compounded semiannually? The first payment is due 1 month from now.

•4. Dr. Krawchuk has made deposits of $2000 to his RRSP at the end of each calendar quarter for 6 years. He then left general practice for specialist training and did not make further contributions for $2\frac{1}{2}$ years. What amount was in his RRSP at the end of this period if the plan earned 10% compounded quarterly over the entire $8\frac{1}{2}$ years?

•5. A Province of Ontario bond has $14\frac{1}{2}$ years remaining until it matures. The bond pays $231.25 interest at the end of every 6 months. At maturity, the bond also repays its $5000 face value. What is the fair market value of the bond if similar provincial bonds are currently providing investors with a return of 7.8% compounded semiannually?

•6. A court-ordered award for family support calls for payments of $800 per month for 5 years, followed by payments of $1000 per month for 10 more years. If money is worth 10.5% compounded monthly, what is the economic value of the award 1 month before the first payment?

•7. Calculate the future value of an annuity consisting of payments of $800 at the end of each calendar quarter for 7 years. The rate of interest earned will be 10% compounded quarterly for the first 30 months and 9% compounded semiannually for the remainder of the annuity's term.

SUMMARY OF NOTATION AND KEY FORMULAS

R = Size of each payment in an annuity
n = Number of payments in the annuity
p = Interest rate per payment interval
i = Interest rate per compounding interval
c = Number of compoundings per payment interval
S_n = Future value of an n-payment ordinary annuity
A_n = Present value of an n-payment ordinary annuity

The financial calculator keys have the following definitions in annuity problems:

$\boxed{\text{n}}$ = n, the number of annuity payments

$\boxed{\text{i}}$ = p, the interest rate per payment interval

$\boxed{\text{PMT}}$ = R, the size of the annuity payment

For calculating the present value of an annuity,

$\boxed{\text{FV}}$ = Lump payment at the end of the annuity

$\boxed{\text{COMP}}$ $\boxed{\text{PV}}$ computes the combined present value of the annuity and the terminal lump payment

For calculating the future value of an annuity,

$\boxed{\text{PV}}$ = Lump payment at the beginning of the annuity

$\boxed{\text{COMP}}$ $\boxed{\text{FV}}$ computes the combined future value of the annuity and the initial lump payment

Formula (10–1) $S_n = R\left[\dfrac{(1 + p)^n - 1}{p}\right]$ Finding the future value of an ordinary annuity

Formula (10–2) $p = (1 + i)^c - 1$ Finding the interest rate per payment interval

Formula (10–3) $c = \dfrac{\text{Number of compoundings per year}}{\text{Number of payments per year}}$ Finding the number of compoundings per payment interval

Formula (10–4) $A_n = R\left[\dfrac{1 - (1 + p)^{-n}}{p}\right]$ Finding the present value of an ordinary annuity

GLOSSARY OF TERMS

Accumulation factor for annuities   See *compounding factor for annuities.*

Annuity   A series of equal payments at regular intervals.

Compounding factor for annuities   The quantity $[(1 + p)^n - 1]/p$. It is numerically equal to the future value of an ordinary annuity with $1 payments.

Discount factor for annuities   The quantity $[1 - (1 + p)^{-n}]/p$. It is numerically equal to the present value of an ordinary annuity with $1 payments.

Future value of an annuity   The single amount, at the end of the annuity, that is economically equivalent to the annuity.

General annuity   An annuity in which the payment interval and the compounding interval are not equal.

Ordinary annuity   An annuity in which the payments are made at the end of each payment interval.

Payment interval   The length of time between successive payments in an annuity.

Present-value factor for annuities   See *discount factor for annuities.*

Present value of an annuity   The single amount, at the beginning of the annuity, that is economically equivalent to the annuity.

Simple annuity   An annuity in which the payment interval equals the compounding interval.

Term of an annuity   The total time from the beginning of the first payment interval to the end of the last payment interval.

11 ANNUITIES DUE: FUTURE VALUE AND PRESENT VALUE

LEARNING OBJECTIVES

After completing this chapter, you will be able to:

- Define and distinguish between ordinary annuities and annuities due
- Calculate the future value of both the "simple" and "general" types of annuities due
- Calculate the present value of both the "simple" and "general" types of annuities due

- Calculate the economic value of either type of annuity due at the beginning or end of its term
- Calculate the book value of a capital lease at any point in the term of the lease

INTRODUCTION

If an equipment lease or a real estate lease requires equal monthly payments, the payments are usually made at the *beginning* of each 1-month payment interval during the term of the lease. These lease payments are an example of an annuity due. In an **annuity due,**[1] the payments are made at the *beginning* of each payment interval.

Figure 11.1 shows the time diagram for the general case of an annuity *due* consisting of *n* payments, each of size *R*. Again, the serial number for each payment interval is placed above the tick mark at the end of the respective interval.

FIGURE   11.1

Time Diagram for an *n*-Payment Annuity Due

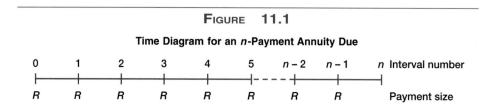

Trap

Do not confuse the "end of an annuity" with the "date of the last payment." The *end of an annuity* means the end of the annuity's term or the end of the last payment interval. This occurs one payment interval *after* the last payment in an annuity *due.*

Similarly, the *beginning of an annuity* refers to the beginning of the annuity's term or the beginning of the first payment interval. This happens to coincide with the first payment of an annuity due.

Most of the concepts and applications of ordinary annuities discussed in Chapter 10 are transferable to annuities due. A small modification must be made to formulas (10−1) and (10−4) to calculate the future value and the present value of an annuity due. A minor procedural change will likewise allow a financial calculator to directly compute the future value or the present value of an annuity due. These changes are developed in the next two sections.

11.1 FUTURE VALUE OF AN ANNUITY DUE

The future value of an annuity is the single amount, at the end of the annuity, that is economically equivalent to the annuity. Since the payments in an annuity *due* occur at the *beginning* of each *payment* interval, the end of the annuity (and its future value focal date) occur one payment interval *after* the last payment. In contrast, the end of an *ordinary* annuity (and its future value focal date) *coincide* with the last payment.

To distinguish the symbol for the future value of an annuity *due* from the symbol for the future value of an *ordinary* annuity, the word "due" is placed in brackets after S_n. That is,

S_n(due) = Future value of an *n*-payment annuity due

The symbols *R, n, i, p,* and *c* retain the same meaning they have for ordinary annuities.

---

[1]Occasionally, an annuity due is called an *annuity in advance.* The corresponding name then used for an *ordinary* annuity is *annuity in arrears.*

FUTURE VALUE USING THE ALGEBRAIC METHOD

The formula for the future value of an annuity *due* may be quickly derived from the formula for the future value of an *ordinary* annuity. The key insight that suggests the connection may be gained from Figure 11.2. In the figure, *n* annuity payments of size *R* are shown on each of two time lines. We usually decide whether to classify an annuity as "ordinary" or "due" based on a focal date for the start or the end of the annuity. Usually, the focal date is either given in the information or implied by the context. In Figure 11.2, no focal date is given or implied. Consequently, we are free to choose whether to treat the annuity as an ordinary annuity or an annuity due.

FIGURE   11.2

The Relationship between S_n(due) and S_n

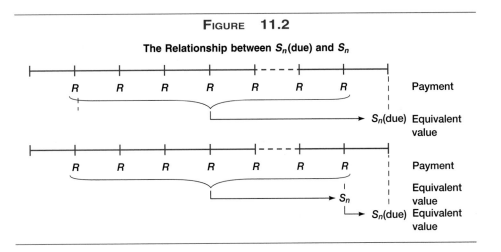

In the upper part of the figure, the payments are viewed as an annuity *due*. The focal date for its future value, S_n(due), is at the end of the annuity (one payment interval after the last payment). In the lower part of the figure, the payments are viewed as an *ordinary* annuity. The focal date for its future value, S_n, is at the end of the annuity (coincident with the last payment).

Each of these future values is the single amount that is economically equivalent, at the respective focal date, to the annuity. The two future values are thus equivalent to each other, allowing for the time interval between them. Consequently, S_n(due) will equal the future value of S_n one payment interval later, and we can write

$$S_n\text{(due)} = S_n \times (1 + p)$$

This relation means that the future value of an annuity *due* is simply the factor $(1 + p)$ larger than the future value of an *ordinary* annuity. Substituting from formula (10−1) for S_n, we obtain

Future Value of an Annuity Due

$$\boxed{\begin{aligned} S_n\text{(due)} &= S_n \times (1 + p) \\ &= R\left[\frac{(1 + p)^n - 1}{p}\right] \times (1 + p) \end{aligned}} \qquad (11\text{--}1)$$

If the payment interval equals the compounding interval, we have a *simple annuity due* and $p = i$. Otherwise, the annuity is a *general annuity due* and p must first be determined using formula (10−2), $p = (1 + i)^c - 1$.

FUTURE VALUE USING THE FINANCIAL CALCULATOR FUNCTIONS

To calculate the future value of an annuity *due* using a preprogrammed financial calculator, the relationship $S_n(\text{due}) = S_n \times (1 + p)$ suggests the following two-step approach. First compute the annuity's future value as though it were an *ordinary* annuity. Then multiply the result by $(1 + p)$. Although the additional step is simple, even this minor complication can be avoided. If the financial calculator is "informed" that the annuity in question is an annuity *due,* it will directly compute $S_n(\text{due})$. Refer to the appendix to Chapter 8 for specific instructions on how to operate your particular calculator model for an annuity due calculation. In the presentation of financial calculator solutions in this text, " $\boxed{\text{BGN}}$ mode" will indicate that the calculator is to be set for an annuity due calculation.

APPLICATIONS OF THE FUTURE VALUE CALCULATION

As for the future value of an ordinary annuity, most applications of the future value of an annuity due fall into two categories:

- Determining the total amount of principal plus interest that will be accumulated at the end of a series of equal regular investments earning p per payment interval.
- Determining the *single* payment at the *end* of an annuity that is economically equivalent to the annuity. The value that should be used for p in this case is the time value of money. In other words, p is the interest rate (per payment interval) at which money could be invested.

The annuity should be treated as an annuity *due* if, relative to the terminal focal date for the future value calculation, the payments are at the *beginning* of each payment interval.

■ EXAMPLE 11.1A   *CALCULATING THE FUTURE VALUE OF A SIMPLE ANNUITY DUE*

How much will Stan accumulate in his Registered Retirement Savings Plan (RRSP) by age 60 if he makes semiannual contributions of $2000 starting on his 27th birthday? Assume that the RRSP earns 8% compounded semiannually and that no contribution is made on Stan's 60th birthday.

☑ SOLUTION

The accumulated amount will be the future value of the contributions on Stan's 60th birthday. From the focal date at his 60th birthday, the RRSP contributions form an annuity *due.* $S_n(\text{due})$ will give the accumulated amount on Stan's 60th birthday. We are given $R = \$2000$, $j = 8\%$, and $m = 2$, and the term of the annuity $= 33$ years.

Since payments and compounding both occur semiannually,

$$p = i = \frac{8\%}{2} = 4\% \quad \text{and} \quad n = 33(2) = 66 \text{ payments}$$

ALGEBRAIC SOLUTION

Substitute the known values into formula (11–1):

$$S_n(\text{due}) = R\left[\frac{(1 + p)^n - 1}{p}\right](1 + p)$$

$$= \$2000\left(\frac{1.04^{66} - 1}{0.04}\right)(1.04)$$

$$= \$2000\left(\frac{13.310685 - 1}{0.04}\right)(1.04)$$

$$= \$640{,}155.60$$

Stan will have $640,155.60 in his RRSP at age 60.

FINANCIAL CALCULATOR SOLUTION

BGN mode						Result
ENTER:	2000	0	4	66		
PRESS:	+/− PMT	PV	i	n	COMP FV	640,155.60

Stan will have $640,155.60 in his RRSP at age 60. ∎

■ EXAMPLE 11.1B   *CALCULATING THE FUTURE VALUE OF A GENERAL ANNUITY DUE*

To the nearest dollar, how much will Stan accumulate in his RRSP by age 60 if he makes semiannual contributions of $2000 beginning on his 27th birthday? Assume that the RRSP earns 8% compounded annually and that no contribution is made on his 60th birthday. (This example is the same as Example 11.1A except for the change that interest is compounded annually instead of semiannually.)

☑ SOLUTION

By treating the contributions as an annuity *due* (as in Example 11.1A), $S_n(\text{due})$ will be the accumulated amount on Stan's 60th birthday. However, the contributions now form a *general* annuity due because the payment interval (6 months) differs from the compounding interval (1 year). Therefore, $p \neq i$ but must be calculated using formula (10–2). We are given $R = \$2000$ and $j = 8\%$ compounded annually, and the annuity's term is 33 years. Then

$$i = \frac{j}{m} = \frac{8\%}{1} = 8\% = 0.08$$

$$n = 2(33) = 66$$

$$c = \frac{1 \text{ compounding per year}}{2 \text{ payments per year}} = 0.5$$

and

$$p = (1 + i)^c - 1 = 1.08^{0.5} - 1 = 0.03923048 = 3.923048\% \text{ per half year}$$

ALGEBRAIC SOLUTION

$$S_n(\text{due}) = \$2000\left[\frac{(1.03923048)^{66} - 1}{0.03923048}\right] \times (1.03923048)$$

$$= \$2000\left[\frac{12.676046 - 1}{0.03923048}\right] \times (1.03923048)$$

$$= \$618{,}606$$

Stan will have $618,606 in his RRSP at age 60.

FINANCIAL CALCULATOR SOLUTION

BGN mode						Result
ENTER:	2000	0	3.923048	66		
PRESS:	+/− PMT	PV	i	n	COMP FV	618,606

Stan will have $618,606 in his RRSP at age 60.   ∎

■ **EXAMPLE 11.1C** *CALCULATING THE FUTURE VALUE OF A SIMPLE ANNUITY DUE WHERE AN INTEREST RATE CHANGE OCCURS DURING THE TERM OF THE ANNUITY*

Stephanie intends to contribute $2500 to her RRSP at the beginning of every 6 months starting today. If the RRSP earns 8% compounded semiannually for the first 7 years and 7% compounded semiannually thereafter, what amount will she have in the plan after 20 years?

☑ SOLUTION

Note: It seems that the question does not make it clear whether the regular contribution Stephanie will make 20 years from today should be included in the amount we are to calculate. The understanding we should take from a question asked in this way is that we are to determine the amount after 20 years of *20 years' contributions.* The regular contribution due 20 years from today will be Stephanie's 41st contribution. It is the first contribution for the 21st year. Therefore it should *not* be included in the amount we are expected to calculate.

The amount in the plan will be the future value of the contributions. The contributions form a simple annuity due when viewed from the focal date at 20 years. However, the future value cannot be calculated in one step because of the interest rate change after 7 years. The given information and the steps required for an algebraic solution are indicated in the following time diagram. Steps 2 and 3 may be combined in a financial calculator solution.

ALGEBRAIC SOLUTION

The future value of the first 14 contributions after 7 years will be

$$S_{n1}(\text{due}) = \$2500\left[\frac{(1.04^{14} - 1)}{0.04}\right] \times (1.04)$$
$$= \$2500(18.291911) \times (1.04)$$
$$= \$47,558.97$$

Now use formula (8−2) to obtain S, the future value of S_{n1} an additional 13 years later.

$$S = \$47,558.97(1.035)^{26} = \$116,327.27$$

The future value, 20 years from now, of the last 26 payments will be

$$S_{n2}(\text{due}) = \$2500\left[\frac{(1.035)^{26} - 1}{0.035}\right] \times (1.035)$$
$$= \$2500(41.3131017) \times (1.035)$$
$$= \$106,897.65$$

The total amount in the RRSP after 20 years will be

$$S + S_{n2}(\text{due}) = \$116,327.27 + \$106,897.65 = \$223,224.92$$

FINANCIAL CALCULATOR SOLUTION

						Result
BGN mode. Step 1: Calculate S_{n1}(due).						
ENTER:	0	2500	4	14		
PRESS:	PV	+/− PMT	i	n	COMP FV	47,558.97
Steps 2, 3, and 4. These steps may be done simultaneously.						
ENTER:			3.5	26		
PRESS:	+/− PV		i	n	COMP FV	223,224.92

Stephanie will have \$223,224.92 in her RRSP after 20 years. ■

Point of Interest

The Ten-Percent Solution (for Achieving Financial Security)

In 1989 *The Wealthy Barber* by David Chilton was published by Stoddart Publishing Co. Ltd. Its engaging style and common-sense approach to personal financial planning made it a Canadian best-seller. In the book, the principles of financial planning and money management are revealed through conversations between an unlikely financial hero, barber shop proprietor Roy Miller, and his patrons.

The following extract is from the chapter entitled "The Ten-Percent Solution." Tom and Dave, now in their late 20s, have arrived for their biweekly haircut accompanied by Dave's sister Cathy. They are all eager to hear the "golden secret" on which Roy has based the promise: "I guarantee you that someday you'll be rich."

To impress the wealth-building potential of compound interest upon Tom, Dave, and Cathy, Roy poses two questions to them.

With your current knowledge of annuities, you should be able to obtain the answers that amaze Tom, Dave, and Cathy. Roy is speaking at the start of the excerpt.

"Wealth beyond your wildest dreams is possible if you learn the golden secret: *Invest ten percent of all you make for long-term growth.* If you follow that one simple guideline, someday you'll be a very rich man."

"That's it?" asked Tom. "I could have gotten that from a Bank of Nova Scotia commercial!"

"Patience, Tom," replied Roy. "I'll tell you things that turn a seemingly simple sentence into an extremely powerful thought.

"Cathy, if you invested \$2400 a year, say \$200 a month, for the next 30 years, and averaged a 15% return a year, how

(continued)

(concluded)

much money do you think you'd end up with?" challenged Roy.

"Well, $2400 times 30 is $72,000 . . . plus growth . . . I don't know . . . I'd say $200,000. Maybe not quite that much," Cathy concluded.

"Wrong. The answer is $1,402,000," Roy declared.

"Get real" was Tom's initial reaction. When he realized that Roy was serious, he paled. "What about inflation? And where am I going to get 15%? For that matter, where am I going to get $200 per month?" he stammered.

"All good questions, Tom, and we'll get to them in due course. Dave, you try one. If you had started putting $30 a month away, the equivalent of a dollar a day, at age 18 and you continued until age 65, averaging a 15% annual return, how much would you end up with?"

"I hate math, Roy, but I'll give it a shot," replied Dave. Thirty dollars a month is $360 a year, times 47 years . . . Anybody have a calculator?"

"It's just under $17,000," injected Roy.

"Plus growth, I'll say about $70,000."

"Close," responded Roy. "The answer is $2,679,000."

"Bull," scoffed Tom.

"No, not bull . . . magic. The magic of compound interest—interest on principal and interest, not just simple interest on principal. The eighth wonder of the world. Thirty dollars a month, a dollar a day, will magically turn into over two and a half million. And do you know what's even more impressive? You know someone who has done it," Roy said proudly.

"Thirty-five years ago, I started my savings with $30 a month, which was approximately 10% of my earnings. I have achieved a 15% average annual return, actually a little higher. In addition, as my income rose, my 10% saving component rose accordingly. Thirty dollars a month became $60, then $100, and eventually hundreds of dollars a month. You three are looking at a very wealthy man!"

"Are you trying to tell us that by saving 10% of every pay cheque, you've turned yourself into a millionaire?" an intense Tom demanded.

"Precisely," was the incredible response.

Roy Miller, a millionaire! Dave sat stunned. Roy was clearly deriving great pleasure from the disbelief on their three faces.

"Compound interest . . . mind-boggling, isn't it!" he went on. "It's a real tragedy that most people don't understand compound interest and its wondrous powers."

Does Roy obtain the $1,402,000 answer to the first question by assuming:

- An annual investment of $2400 earning 15% compounded annually, or a monthly investment of $200 at 15% compounded monthly?

- The periodic investment occurs at the beginning of each compounding interval, or at the end of each interval?

Regarding the answer to the second question, is Roy assuming that the $30 is invested at the beginning or at the end of each month?

Roy's advice is sound enough; however, the assumption of a *long-term* rate of return of 15% compounded monthly is unrealistic. The corresponding effective rate of return is 16.1%. Very few reasonably diversified investments actually provided a 10-year compound annual rate of return of at least 16% through the decade of 1980s. A couple of Canadian mutual funds investing in Japanese stocks achieved this return, but these same funds performed very poorly over the first 6 years of the 1990s. Since it appears that the average rate of inflation during the 1990s will be significantly lower than during the 1980s, the 10-year rates of return on various types of investments are also likely to be lower in the 1990s than in the 1980s.

Roy's calculations and analysis also overlook the impact of income taxes on investment returns. For investments held outside an RRSP, investors in the middle tax bracket will pay tax rates in the range of 30% to 43% on various types of investment income and taxable capital gains. If investment returns are accumulating within an RRSP, income tax will be paid when the funds are withdrawn.

EXERCISE 11.1

Answers to the odd-numbered problems are at the end of the book.

In problems 1 through 14, determine the future value of each annuity due.

Problem	Periodic payment ($)	Payment interval	Term	Nominal rate (%)	Compounding frequency
1.	400	1 year	11 years	11.5	Annually
2.	150	3 months	$6\frac{1}{2}$ years	10	Quarterly
3.	275	1 month	$3\frac{1}{2}$ years	8	Monthly
4.	1500	6 months	$13\frac{1}{2}$ years	7.5	Semiannually
5.	325	1 month	$7\frac{1}{4}$ years	11	Monthly
6.	950	1 quarter	8 years, 9 months	9	Quarterly
7.	329	$\frac{1}{2}$ year	8 years, 6 months	8.75	Semiannually
8.	1000	12 months	25 years	7.25	Annually
9.	500	3 months	12 years	11	Annually
10.	200	1 month	$7\frac{1}{2}$ years	10	Quarterly
11.	3000	6 months	$4\frac{1}{2}$ years	8	Monthly
12.	1700	3 months	$11\frac{1}{2}$ years	7.5	Semiannually
13.	2500	1 year	16 years	10.5	Monthly
14.	750	6 months	$6\frac{1}{2}$ years	9	Quarterly

15. If, on the first day of each month from August 1, 1995, up to and including February 1, 1997, Valerie deposited $200 in an investment savings account paying 6.75% compounded monthly, what was the balance in the account on March 1, 1997? How much of the total was interest?

16. If Hans contributes $1500 to his RRSP on February 1, 1990, and every 6 months thereafter to and including February 1, 2017, what amount will he accumulate in the RRSP by August 1, 2017? Assume that the RRSP will earn 8.5% compounded semiannually. How much of the total will be interest?

17. Many people make their annual RRSP contribution for a taxation year close to the end of the year. Financial advisers encourage clients to contribute as early as possible in the year. How much more will there be in an RRSP at the end of 25 years if annual contributions of $5000 are made at the beginning of each year instead of at the end? Assume that the RRSP will earn:

    a. 8% compounded annually.   *b.* 8% compounded monthly.

18. What will be the value of an RRSP 25 years from now if $2000 is contributed at the beginning of every 6 months and the RRSP earns $8\frac{1}{4}$% compounded annually?

•19. What will be the amount in an RRSP after 25 years if contributions of $2000 are made at the beginning of each year for the first 10 years and contributions of $4000 are made at the beginning of each year for the subsequent 15 years? Assume that the RRSP will earn 8% compounded quarterly.

•20. Fay contributed $3000 per year to her RRSP on every birthday from age 21 to 30 inclusive. She then ceased employment to raise a family and made no further contributions. Her husband Fred contributed $3000 per year to his RRSP on every birthday from age 31 to 64 inclusive. Assuming that both of their plans earn 8% compounded annually over the years, calculate and compare the amounts in their RRSPs at age 65.

11.2 PRESENT VALUE OF AN ANNUITY DUE

The present value of an annuity is the single amount, at the beginning of the annuity, that is economically equivalent to the annuity. Since the payments in an annuity *due* occur at the *beginning* of each *payment* interval, the beginning of the annuity (and the focal date for the present-value calculation) coincides with the first payment.

To distinguish the symbol for the present value of an annuity *due* from the symbol for the present value of an *ordinary* annuity, the word "due" is placed in parentheses after A_n. That is,

$$A_n(\text{due}) = \text{Present value of an } n\text{-payment annuity due}$$

PRESENT VALUE USING THE ALGEBRAIC METHOD

The formula for $A_n(\text{due})$ may be quickly derived from the formula for A_n by a line of reasoning similar to that used to derive the formula for $S_n(\text{due})$ from the formula for S_n. The derivation is presented in the appendix to this chapter. The outcome is a complete parallel to the future value case. That is,

$$A_n(\text{due}) = A_n \times (1 + p) \qquad \text{corresponding to} \qquad S_n(\text{due}) = S_n \times (1 + p)$$

Therefore, we have the simple but general rule that *both the future value and the present value of an annuity due are* $(1 + p)$ *times the respective future and present values of an ordinary annuity.* Substituting from formula (10−4) for A_n, we obtain

Present Value of an Annuity Due

$$\boxed{\begin{aligned} A_n(\text{due}) &= A_n \times (1 + p) \\ &= R\left[\frac{1 - (1 + p)^{-n}}{p}\right] \times (1 + p) \end{aligned}} \qquad (11{-}2)$$

PRESENT VALUE USING THE FINANCIAL CALCULATOR FUNCTIONS

Before giving the keystroke command to compute an annuity's present value, the financial calculator must be "informed" that the annuity in question is an annuity *due*. The appendix to Chapter 8 gives specific instructions on how to set or operate your particular calculator model for an annuity due calculation. The term "$\boxed{\text{BGN}}$ mode" will be used in solutions to example problems to indicate that the calculator is to be set for an annuity due calculation.

ANNUITY CLASSIFICATION FLOWCHART

We now have two bases for classifying an annuity. Based on the *timing* of the payment within the payment interval, an annuity is classified as *either* an *ordinary* annuity *or* an annuity *due*. *Independent* of the ordinary/due classification, an annuity is *either* a *simple* annuity *or* a *general* annuity based on whether or not the payment interval equals the compounding interval. These two classification criteria give four categories of annuities:

- Ordinary simple annuity.
- Ordinary general annuity.
- Simple annuity due.
- General annuity due.

The examples and exercise problems in this chapter concentrate on the two types of annuities due. However, in later chapters problems will not be segregated by annuity category.

Tip

The mathematics for each of the four annuity categories is unique in some minor respect. Therefore, immediately after extracting the raw data from an annuity problem, you should determine and explicitly state the type of annuity at hand. If you intend to use the financial calculator functions, set the calculator in the proper mode (ordinary or **BGN**)) at this time. Failure to intentionally take these small steps at the outset sometimes results in one of them being overlooked later when you become preoccupied with more profound aspects of the solution.

The flowchart in Figure 11−3 presents a procedure for asking the key questions that lead to the correct decisions about the type of annuity. The mathematical consequences of each decision are also indicated in the diagram.

Tip

Information that resolves the ordinary versus due alternatives may lie in subtle wording of the problem. Look for a key word or phrase that provides the clue. Some examples of wording which suggests an annuity *due* are:

- "Payments at the beginning of each. . . ."
- "Payments in advance."
- "First payment made today."
- "Payments starting now."

Table 11.1 summarises the criteria and mathematics that apply to each category of annuity. The relevant formulas for each case may be obtained from the appropriate cell in the table.

TABLE   11.1

Summary of the Formulas Applicable to Each Category of Annuity

	ORDINARY ANNUITIES (payment at the end of each payment interval)	ANNUITIES DUE (payment at the beginning of each payment interval)
SIMPLE ANNUITIES (Compounding interval = Payment interval)	$p = i$ Formulas (10−1), (10−4) for S_n, A_n	$p = i$ Formulas (11−1), (11−2) for S_n(due), A_n(due)
GENERAL ANNUITIES (Compounding interval ≠ Payment interval)	$p = (1 + i)^c − 1$ Formulas (10−1), (10−4) for S_n, A_n	$p = (1 + i)^c − 1$ Formulas (11−1), (11−2) for S_n(due), A_n(due)

FIGURE   11.3

Annuity Classification Flowchart

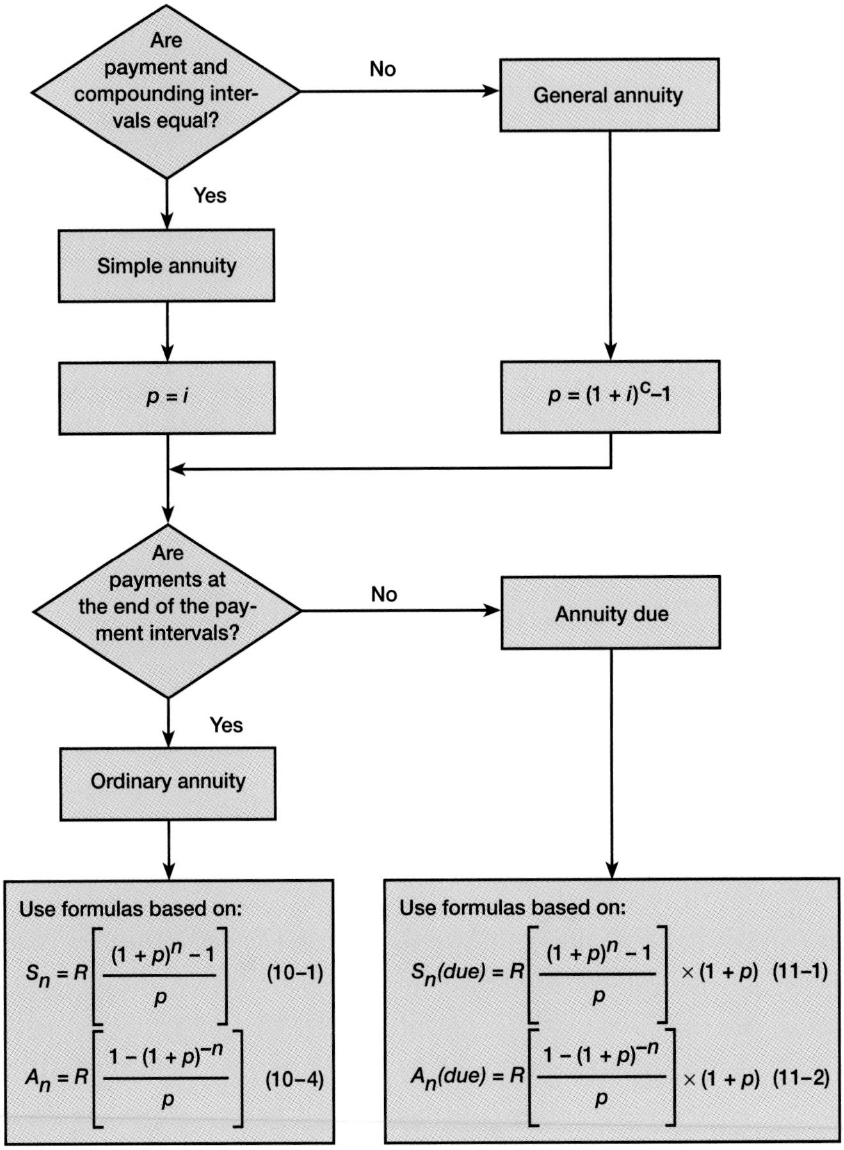

APPLICATIONS OF THE PRESENT-VALUE CALCULATION

Two applications discussed in Section 10.5 (in the context of ordinary annuities) also pertain to annuities due. The key ideas are repeated here for convenient reference.

THE MARKET VALUE OF AN ANNUITY

Fair market value of an annuity	=	Present value of the annuity payments (discounted at the *market rate of return*)

THE ECONOMIC VALUE OF AN ANNUITY

Current economic value of an annuity	$=$ Present value of the annuity payments (discounted at a *rate of return that money can earn on low-risk investments*)

■ EXAMPLE 11.2A   FINDING THE ECONOMIC VALUE OF A SIMPLE ANNUITY DUE

A lottery offers the winner a choice between a $300,000 cash prize or quarterly payments of $7000 beginning immediately and continuing for 20 years. Which alternative should the winner pick if money is worth:

a. 8% compounded annually?   *b.* 7% compounded annually?

☑ SOLUTION

For the quarterly payment annuity, $R = \$7000$, term $= 20$ years, and $n = 4(20) = 80$ payments. In part *a*, $j = 8\%$ compounded annually; in part *b*, $j = 7\%$ compounded annually. Following the flowchart in Figure 11.3, we conclude that the annuity is

- *General* since the answer to the first question is "no."
- *Due* since the answer to the second question is "no" (when the annuity is viewed from "today").

Consequently, formula (10–2) must be used to calculate p. For an algebraic approach, formulas (11–1) and (11–2) are relevant. For a financial calculator solution, the calculator must be in the ⬚ **BGN** ⬚ mode.

The solution "idea" is that the annuity alternative should be chosen if its economic value today exceeds $300,000. In other words, choose the annuity if its present value, using the time value of money as the discount rate, exceeds $300,000.

ALGEBRAIC SOLUTION

a. $i = j = 8\%$ and $c = \dfrac{1 \text{ compounding per year}}{1 \text{ payment per year}} = 0.25$

$$p = (1 + i)^c - 1 = 1.08^{0.25} - 1 = 1.9426547\%$$

$$A_n(\text{due}) = R\left[\frac{1 - (1 + p)^{-n}}{p}\right] \times (1 + p)$$

$$= \$7000\left[\frac{1 - 1.019426547^{-80}}{0.019426547}\right](1.019426547)$$

$$= \$7000\left[\frac{1 - 0.2145482}{0.019426547}\right](1.019426547)$$

$$= \$288,521 \text{ (to the nearest dollar)}$$

The $300,000 lump prize should be chosen because it is worth $11,479 more (in current dollars).

b. $i = j = 7\%$ and $c = 0.25$

$$p = (1 + i)^c - 1 = 1.07^{0.25} - 1 = 1.7058525\%$$

$$A_n(due) = R\left[\frac{1 - (1 + p)^{-n}}{p}\right] \times (1 + p)$$

$$= \$7000\left[\frac{1 - 1.017058525^{-80}}{0.017058525}\right](1.017058525)$$

$$= \$7000\left[\frac{1 - 0.2584190}{0.017058525}\right](1.017058525)$$

$$= \$309,500 \text{ (to the nearest dollar)}$$

The annuity should be chosen because it is worth $9500 more (in current dollars).

FINANCIAL CALCULATOR SOLUTION

See the early parts of the algebraic solutions for the calculation of the values for p.

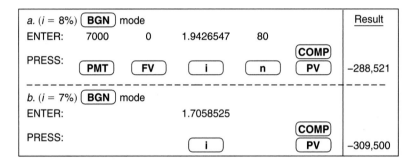

a. The $300,000 lump prize should be chosen because it is worth $11,479 more (in current dollars).

b. The annuity should be chosen because it is worth $9500 more (in current dollars).   ■

■ EXAMPLE 11.2B   VALUING AN OBLIGATION THAT MAY BE VIEWED AS AN ANNUITY DUE

Mayfair Furniture is advertising a chesterfield and reclining chair combination for $131.83 down and 11 monthly payments of $131.83, including interest at 15% compounded annually. What is the ticket or cash price of the set?

✔ SOLUTION

The customer makes a down payment of $131.83 and borrows

$$\text{Cash price} - \text{Down payment}$$

at an interest rate of 15% compounded annually. The loan is repaid by 11 monthly payments of $131.83.

Since the down payment equals the other 11 payments, an equivalent view is that Mayfair lends the full ticket price, which the customer repays by 12 monthly payments starting immediately. In this view, the cash price will equal the present value, $A_n(due)$, of 12 payments forming an annuity due. With $R = \$131.83$, $n = 12$, $i = 15\%$ per year, and $c = \frac{1}{12} = 0.08\overline{3}$, we obtain

$$p = (1 + i)^c - 1 = 1.15^{0.08\overline{3}} - 1 = 1.1714917\% \text{ per month}$$

ALGEBRAIC SOLUTION

$$\text{Cash price} = \$131.83\left[\frac{1 - 1.01171492^{-12}}{0.01171492}\right](1.01171492)$$

$$= \$131.83(11.134076)(1.01171492)$$

$$= \$1485.00$$

FINANCIAL CALCULATOR SOLUTION

BGN mode						Result
ENTER: 131.83		0	1.171492	12		
PRESS:	+/–				COMP	
	PMT	FV	i	n	PV	1485.00

The ticket or cash price of the combination is $1485.00. ■

■ EXAMPLE 11.2c *FINDING THE ECONOMIC VALUE OF A GENERAL ANNUITY DUE WHERE THE DISCOUNT RATE CHANGES*

An annuity will pay $1000 at the end of June 2003 and every 6 months thereafter up to and including a payment at the end of June 2016. To the nearest dollar, what will be the economic value of the annuity on June 30, 2003, if money will be worth 8% compounded quarterly for the first 5 years and 8% compounded semiannually for the remainder of the annuity's term?

☑ SOLUTION

The problem asks for the economic value of the annuity on June 30, 2003—this *coincides* with the date of the first payment. Viewed from this focal date, the payments form an annuity *due*. For the first 5 years, the payments occur semiannually but compounding takes place quarterly. Hence, the first $n = 10$ payments form a *general annuity due* having

$$R = \$1000 \qquad i = \frac{8\%}{4} = 2\% \qquad c = \frac{4}{2} = 2$$

$$p = (1 + i)^c - 1 = 1.02^2 - 1 = 0.404 = 4.04\%$$

The determination of the number of payments requires care. Even though there are 13 years between June 30, 2003, and June 30, 2016, do not conclude that there are 26 payments. Note that the first payment is *on* June 30, 2003, and the last payment is *on* June 30, 2016. Thus, there will be 27 payments in all, with the last 17 being paid while the interest rate is 8% compounded semiannually. Since payments and compounding both occur semiannually for the last $n = 17$ payments, they form a *simple* annuity due with

$$R = \$1000 \qquad i = \frac{8\%}{2} = 4\% \qquad p = i = 4\%$$

The following diagram organises the given information and indicates the three steps required in an algebraic solution. Steps 2 and 3 may be combined in a financial calculator approach.

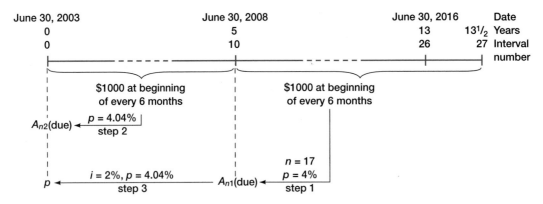

ALGEBRAIC SOLUTION

$$A_{n1}(\text{due}) = R\left[\frac{1 - (1 + p)^{-n}}{p}\right] \times (1 + p)$$

$$= \$1000\left[\frac{1 - 1.04^{-17}}{0.04}\right](1.04)$$

$$= \$12,652.30$$

$$A_{n2}(\text{due}) = \$1000\left[\frac{1 - 1.0404^{-10}}{0.0404}\right](1.0404) = \$8421.80$$

To calculate the present value on June 30, 2003, of the lump amount $A_{n1}(\text{due})$, we can use formula (8–2) with either:

- 5(4) = 20 quarters at $i = 2\%$ compounded each quarter, or
- 5(2) = 10 compoundings at $p = 4.04\%$ each half-year.[2]

Taking the former option,

$$P = \frac{A_{n1}(\text{due})}{1.02^{20}} = \frac{\$12,652.30}{1.02^{20}} = \$8514.64$$

The economic value of the annuity on June 30, 2003, is

$$\$8514.64 + \$8421.80 = \$16,936$$

FINANCIAL CALCULATOR SOLUTION

Compute $A_{n1}(\text{due})$. BGN mode					Result
ENTER: 1000	0	4	17		
PRESS:				COMP	
PMT	FV	i	n	PV	−12,652.30
Compute $A_{n2}(\text{due}) + P$. BGN mode					
ENTER:	12652.30	4.04	10		
PRESS:				COMP	
	FV	i	n	PV	−16,936.43

The economic value of the annuity on June 30, 2003, is $16,936 to the nearest dollar.

■

---

[2]Remember that formula (10–2) makes p compounded every payment interval (6 months) have the same effect as i compounded every compounding interval (3 months).

THE BOOK VALUE OF A LEASE It was mentioned in the chapter introduction that each regular payment on a real estate or equipment lease is made at the beginning of the rental interval to which it applies. Such lease payments constitute an annuity due when viewed from the beginning of the term of the lease.

When a business enters into a long-term, noncancellable lease for machinery or equipment, Generally Accepted Accounting Principles (GAAP) usually require that the lease be recognized in the firm's statement of financial position (balance sheet). The accounting entry for the lease transaction shows the simultaneous acquisition of a capital asset (called a *leasehold*) and a long-term liability for the lease payments.[3] It is logical that the initial economic or monetary value used for both the asset and the liability is the present value of all the lease payments.

The following considerations determine the choice of the discount rate used in the present-value calculation. Firms tend to view a long-term lease of equipment as an alternative to buying the equipment using mostly borrowed funds. Furthermore, a long-term lease obligation has a key characteristic of a term loan: *fixed* payments are required for a specified period. For these reasons, GAAP require a firm to use the interest rate it would pay to finance the purchase of the equipment as the discount rate in the present-value calculation.[4] At any point during the term of the lease, the present value of the remaining lease payments is known as the "book value" of the lease liability.

The lease liability reported on a firm's balance sheet should be the lease's book value as at the date of the balance sheet. As time passes and fewer payments remain, the book value of the liability decreases, and it reaches zero at the end of the term of the lease.[5]

■ **EXAMPLE 11.2D** *THE BOOK VALUE OF A LEASE LIABILITY*

National Engineering Services acquired a computer under a capital lease agreement. National pays the lessor $9600 per year at the beginning of each year for 5 years. If National can obtain 5-year financing at 11.5% compounded annually:

a. What long-term lease liability will National initially report in its financial statements?

b. What liability will be reported at the end of the second year?

✓ **SOLUTION**

The initial liability is the present value of all of the lease payments. At any later time, the liability reported in the financial statements is the present value of the remaining payments. In both cases, the discount rate used should be the interest rate at which the firm could have borrowed at the time of signing the lease. When viewed from the date of the financial statements in either part *a* or part *b,* the lease payments form a *simple* annuity *due* with $R = \$9600$ and $p = i = 11.5\%$. In part *a, n* = 5, while in part *b, n* = 3.

---

[3]A sufficient condition for requiring this capital-lease method is that the present value of the lease payments (discounted at an appropriate market interest rate) exceeds 90% of the fair market value of the leased asset.

[4]As a general principle in accounting, the reported value of *any* long-term liability is the present value of future contractual payments discounted at the firm's borrowing rate on the date the liability was incurred.

[5]On the asset side of the balance sheet, the leasehold asset is also reduced to zero over the term of the lease. However, GAAP allows a leasehold to be amortized on a different basis than the writedown of the lease liability. Consequently, the book values of the leasehold asset and the lease liability differ somewhat during the term of the lease. Amortization of a leasehold asset is discussed in accounting textbooks.

ALGEBRAIC SOLUTION

a.   Initial liability $= \$9600\left(\dfrac{1 - 1.115^{-5}}{0.115}\right)(1.115) = \$39{,}068.29$

b. Two years later, three lease payments remain.

Liability $= \$9600\left(\dfrac{1 - 1.115^{-3}}{0.115}\right)(1.115) = \$25{,}931.72$

FINANCIAL CALCULATOR SOLUTION

a. BGN mode. Calculate the present value of 5 payments.	Result
ENTER: 9600 11.5 5 0	
PRESS: +/- PMT i n FV COMP PV	39,068.29
b. BGN mode. Calculate the present value of 3 payments.	
ENTER: 3	
PRESS: n COMP PV	25,931.72

The initial capital lease liability is $39,068.29, and the liability 2 years later is $25,931.72. ∎

EXERCISE 11.2

Answers to the odd-numbered problems are at the end of the book.

In problems 1 through 14, determine the present value of each annuity due.

Problem	Periodic payment ($)	Payment interval	Term	Nominal rate (%)	Compounding frequency
1.	400	1 year	11 years	11.5	Annually
2.	150	3 months	$6\frac{1}{2}$ years	10	Quarterly
3.	275	1 month	$3\frac{1}{2}$ years	8	Monthly
4.	1500	6 months	$13\frac{1}{2}$ years	7.5	Semiannually
5.	325	1 month	$7\frac{1}{4}$ years	11	Monthly
6.	950	1 quarter	8 years, 9 months	9	Quarterly
7.	329	$\frac{1}{2}$ year	8 years, 6 months	8.75	Semiannually
8.	1000	12 months	25 years	7.25	Annually
9.	500	3 months	12 years	11	Annually
10.	200	1 month	$7\frac{1}{2}$ years	10	Quarterly
11.	3000	6 months	$4\frac{1}{2}$ years	8	Monthly
12.	1700	3 months	$11\frac{1}{2}$ years	7.5	Semiannually
13.	2500	1 year	16 years	10.5	Monthly
14.	750	6 months	$6\frac{1}{2}$ years	9	Quarterly

15. The Associated Press newswire carried the following story on June 6, 1995.

An 8-month-pregnant university student who recently moved back in with her parents to save money is clear on what she intends to do with her Powerball jackpot of nearly $87.6 million: "If I want it, I'll buy it. Today we're all getting new cars for the whole family."

Pam Hiatt, 26, accepted the first $4.38 million cheque from Idaho governor Phil Batt. She will receive the fortune in 20 yearly payments of $4.38 million.

On the date she received the first cheque, what, in fact, was the economic value of the jackpot if the time value of money was:

a. 7% compounded annually?   *b.* 9% compounded annually?

16. Under the headline "Local Theatre Project Receives $1 Million!" a newspaper article explained that the Theatre Project had just received the first of 10 annual grants of $100,000 from the Hinton Foundation. What is the current economic value of all the grants if money is worth 7.5% compounded monthly?

17. You have received two offers on the used car you wish to sell. Mr. Lindberg is offering $8500 cash, and Mrs. Martel's offer is five semiannual payments of $1900, including a payment on the purchase date. Which offer has the greater economic value if money can earn 10% compounded semiannually? What is the economic advantage in current dollars of the preferred alternative?

18. Osgood Appliance Centre is advertising refrigerators for six monthly payments of $199, including a payment on the date of purchase. What cash price should Osgood accept if it would otherwise sell the conditional sale agreement to a finance company to yield 18% compounded monthly?

19. A rental agreement requires the payment of $900 at the beginning of each month.

    a. What single payment at the beginning of the rental year should the landlord accept instead of monthly payments if money is worth 9% compounded monthly?

    b. Show that the landlord will be equally well off at the end of the year under either payment arrangement if rental payments are invested at 9% compounded monthly.

20. What amount of money earning 9% compounded semiannually will sustain withdrawals of $1200 at the beginning of every month for 15 years?

21. The lease contract for a computer workstation requires quarterly payments of $2100 at the beginning of every 3-month period for 5 years. The lessee would otherwise have to pay an interest rate of 13% compounded quarterly to borrow funds to purchase the workstation.

    a. If the lease is treated as a capital lease, what amount will the lessee initially report in its financial statements as the long-term lease liability arising from the transaction?

    b. What will the liability be at the end of the fourth year?

22. Beaudoin Haulage has signed a 5-year lease with GMAC on a new dump truck. Beaudoin intends to capitalise the lease and report it as a long-term liability. Lease payments of $1700 are made at the beginning of each month. To purchase the truck, Beaudoin would have had to borrow funds at 11.25% compounded monthly.

    a. What initial liability should Beaudoin report on its balance sheet?

    b. How much will the liability be reduced during the first year of the lease?

•23. What is the current economic value of an annuity due consisting of 22 quarterly payments of $700 if money is worth 9% compounded quarterly for the first 3 years and 10% compounded quarterly thereafter?

•24. Calculate and rank the economic values of the following cash-flow streams:
    (i) A single payment of $10,000 on a date 8 years from now.
    (ii) An annuity due starting today with eight annual payments of $850.
    (iii) An annuity due starting in 8 years with eight annual payments of $1700.
    Do the calculations and ranking for each of two cases:

    a. Money earns 8% compounded annually for the next 16 years.

    b. Money earns 10% compounded annually for the next 16 years.

••*25.* Two insurance companies gave the following quotations on premiums for essentially the same long-term disability insurance coverage for a 25-year-old. Paul Revere Insurance Co. quoted monthly premiums of $54.83 from ages 26 to 30 inclusive and $78.17 from ages 31 to 64 inclusive. The monthly premiums from Provident Insurance Co. are "flat" at $69.35 from ages 26 to 64 inclusive. All premiums are paid at the beginning of each month. The insurance broker recommended the Provident coverage because the aggregate lifetime premiums up to the client's 65th birthday are $32,455.80 versus $35,183.16 for the Paul Revere policy. Is the choice that simple? (*Hint:* Calculate and compare the economic value on the client's 26th birthday of each policy's stream of premiums assuming a time value of money of 9% compounded monthly.)

*APPENDIX: DERIVATION OF THE FORMULA FOR THE PRESENT VALUE OF AN ANNUITY DUE

The formula for A_n(due) may be quickly derived from the formula for A_n by a line of reasoning similar to that used in Section 11.1 to derive the formula for S_n(due) from the formula for S_n. In Figure 11.4, n annuity payments of size R are shown along each of two time lines. In the upper part of the figure, the payments are viewed as an annuity *due.* The focal date for the annuity's present value, A_n(due), is at the beginning of the annuity (coincident with the first payment). In the lower part of the figure, the payments are viewed as an *ordinary* annuity. The focal date for the annuity's present value, A_n, is at the beginning of the annuity (one payment interval before the first payment).

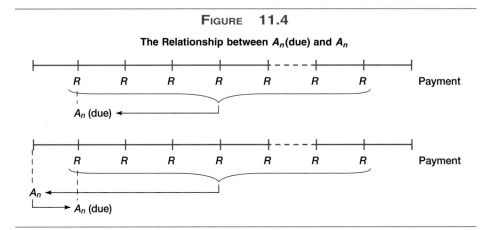

FIGURE   11.4

The Relationship between A_n(due) and A_n

Each of these present values is the single amount that is economically equivalent, at the respective focal date, to the annuity. The two present values are thus equivalent to each other, allowing for the time interval between them. Consequently, A_n(due) will equal the future value of A_n one payment interval later. That is,

$$A_n(\text{due}) = A_n \times (1 + p)$$

This relation means that the present value of an annuity *due* is simply a factor $(1 + p)$ larger than the present value of an *ordinary* annuity. Substituting from formula (10–4) for A_n, we obtain

$$A_n(\text{due}) = R\left[\frac{1 - (1 + p)^{-n}}{p}\right] \times (1 + p) \qquad (11-2)$$

REVIEW PROBLEMS

Answers to the odd-numbered review problems are at the end of the book.

1. Brunswick Trucking has signed a 5-year lease with Ford Credit Canada Ltd. on a new truck. Generally accepted accounting principles require that the lease be capitalized and reported as a long-term liability. Lease payments of $1900 are made at the beginning of each month. To purchase the truck, Brunswick Trucking would have had to borrow funds at 10.5% compounded monthly.

   a. What initial liability should Brunswick report on its balance sheet?

   b. How much will the liability be reduced during the first year of the lease?

2. What minimum amount of money earning 7% compounded semiannually will sustain withdrawals of $1000 at the beginning of every month for 12 years?

•3. What is the economic value at the beginning of an annuity due if it consists of 19 semi-annual payments of $1500? Money is worth 9% compounded semiannually for the first 5 years and 10% compounded semiannually thereafter.

•4. What will be the amount in an RRSP after 30 years if contributions of $4000 are made at the beginning of each year for the first 10 years, and contributions of $6000 are made at the beginning of each year for the subsequent 20 years? Assume that the RRSP will earn 8.25% compounded annually.

•5. A rental agreement requires the payment of $1000 at the beginning of each month.

   a. What single payment at the beginning of the rental year should the landlord accept instead of monthly payments if money is worth 8% compounded monthly?

   b. Show that the landlord will be equally well off at the end of the year under either payment arrangement if rental payments are invested at 8% compounded monthly.

•6. Mick contributed $5000 at the beginning of each year for 25 years to his RRSP. Assume that the RRSP earns 8% compounded annually. What percentage of the RRSP's value 25 years from now will come from contributions made in the first 5 years?

•7. What amount is required to purchase an annuity that pays $4000 at the end of each quarter for the first 5 years and then pays $2500 at the beginning of each month for the subsequent 15 years? Assume that the annuity payments are based on a rate of return on the invested funds of 7.5% compounded quarterly.

SELF-TEST EXERCISE

Answers to the self-test problems are at the end of the book.

1. Calculate the amount that will be accumulated after 20 years if:

   a. $1000 is invested at the beginning of every 6 months at 8.5% compounded semiannually.

   b. $2000 is invested at the beginning of every year at 8.5% compounded annually.

2. A life insurance company quoted an annual premium of $387.50 (payable at the beginning of the year) for a $250,000 term insurance policy on a 35-year-old male non-smoker. Alternatively, the insured can pay $33.71 at beginning of each month by preauthorised cheques. Which payment plan would an applicant choose solely on the basis of money being worth 10% compounded monthly?

3. A 7-year capital lease of an executive jet requires semiannual payments of $200,000 at the beginning of each 6-month period. The company can borrow funds for 5 to 7 years at 10.75% compounded semiannually.

a. What long-term lease liability will the firm set up at the start of the term of the lease?

b. What liability will remain halfway through the term of the lease?

•4. Calculate the future value of an annuity consisting of payments of $800 at the beginning of each calendar quarter for 7 years. Assume that the rate of interest earned will be 10% compounded quarterly for the first 30 months and 9% compounded semiannually for the remainder of the annuity's term.

SUMMARY OF NOTATION AND KEY FORMULAS

$S_n(due)$ = Future value of an n-payment annuity due
$A_n(due)$ = Present value of an n-payment annuity due

Formula (11–1) $S_n(due) = S_n \times (1 + p)$
$$= R\left[\frac{(1 + p)^n - 1}{p}\right] \times (1 + p)$$

Finding the future value of an annuity due

Formula (11–2) $A_n(due) = A_n \times (1 + p)$
$$= R\left[\frac{1 - (1 + p)^{-n}}{p}\right] \times (1 + p)$$

Finding the present value of an annuity due

GLOSSARY OF TERMS

Annuity due   An annuity in which the periodic payments occur at the beginning of each payment interval.

12 ANNUITIES: PAYMENT SIZE, TERM, AND INTEREST RATE

CHAPTER OUTLINE

LEARNING OBJECTIVES

After completing this chapter, you will be able to:

- Calculate the payment size in each of the four types of annuities
- Calculate the number of payments and term in each of the four types of annuities
- Calculate the interest rate per payment interval for each of the four types of annuities

- Calculate the nominal interest rate and effective interest rate for each of the four types of annuities

INTRODUCTION

Chapters 10 and 11 dealt with the calculation and applications of the future value and present value of annuities. We learned that the future value and the present value of an annuity can be calculated if we have numerical values for the three variables:

R = Size of each payment in an annuity
n = Number of payments in the annuity
p = Interest rate per payment interval

There are many circumstances in which either the present value or the future value of an annuity is known but one of the variables, R, n, or p, must be determined. Each of the three sections of this chapter deals with the calculation of one of these variables. The algebraic approach will adapt the formulas already developed in Chapters 10 and 11 for S_n, S_n(due), A_n, and A_n(due). With the experience already gained in the financial calculator approach in Chapters 10 and 11, the adjustments needed to compute R, n, or p are virtually self-evident. In this chapter, there is relatively little of a fundamental or conceptual nature that is new. However, the ability to solve for R, n, or p enables us to deal with many more scenarios involving annuities.

12.1 CALCULATING THE PERIODIC PAYMENT

Some examples of circumstances in which the periodic payment, R, must be calculated are:

- Determining the size of blended payments on a loan.
- Determining the amount that must be saved on a periodic basis to reach a savings goal.
- Determining the periodic payment that will be delivered by an annuity purchased with a lump investment.
- Determining the lease payments required to provide a required rate of return to the lessor.
- Determining the annuity payments that are economically equivalent to a single lump payment.

To calculate R for an annuity, n and p must be given or readily determined from the given information. In addition, we must know the present value or the future value of the annuity. In other words, we must also know the value of *one* of S_n, S_n(due), A_n, or A_n(due).

ALGEBRAIC METHOD

The four formulas for S_n, S_n(due), A_n, and A_n(due) can be easily rearranged to isolate R in each case. Listing them here would add another four complex formulas to our inventory of annuity formulas. To avoid the extra formula "clutter," the following approach is recommended.

1. Substitute the known values in the *existing* formula for whichever of the four quantities, S_n, S_n(due), A_n, or A_n(due), is known.
2. Simplify the numerical coefficient of R.
3. Rearrange the equation to solve for R.

FINANCIAL CALCULATOR METHOD

The values for n and p are entered in the ⬚ n and ⬚ i memories, respectively.

If the future value of the annuity is known, it is entered in ⬚ FV. In the ⬚ PV memory, enter any *initial lump* payment whose future value is included in the amount in ⬚ FV. Otherwise, store "0" in ⬚ PV. Remember to obey the cash-flow sign convention for amounts entered in ⬚ FV and ⬚ PV.

If the present value of the annuity is known, it is entered in ⬚ PV. In the ⬚ FV memory, enter any *final lump* payment whose present value is included in the amount in ⬚ PV. Otherwise, store "0" in ⬚ FV.

If the annuity in question is an annuity *due,* set the calculator for an annuity due calculation at any point before the ⬚ COMP ⬚ PMT command is given.

Trap

Two of the most common errors made when using financial calculators to solve annuity problems are:

- Forgetting to put the calculator in the "annuity due" mode for an annuity due.

- Forgetting to switch *out* of the "annuity due" mode when the next problem involves an ordinary annuity.

■ EXAMPLE 12.1A   CALCULATING THE PERIODIC AMOUNT NEEDED TO BE SAVED TO REACH A TARGET

Markham Auto Body wishes to accumulate a fund of $150,000 during the next 18 months in order to open at a second location. What constant amount should it pay at the end of each month into a money market savings account with an investment dealer, in order to attain its savings objective? The planning assumption is that the account will earn 4.8% compounded monthly.

☑ SOLUTION

The savings target of $150,000 represents the future value of the contributions. The monthly payments form an ordinary simple annuity having

$$S_n = \$150{,}000 \qquad n = 18 \qquad \text{and} \qquad p = i = \frac{4.8\%}{12} = 0.40\%$$

ALGEBRAIC SOLUTION

Substituting the given values in formula (10–1),

$$S_n = R\left[\frac{(1 + p)^n - 1}{p}\right]$$

$$\$150{,}000 = R\left(\frac{1.004^{18} - 1}{0.004}\right)$$

$$= R(18.625254)$$

$$R = \frac{\$150{,}000}{18.625254} = \$8053.58$$

FINANCIAL CALCULATOR SOLUTION

						Result
ENTER:	0	150000	0.4	18	COMP	
PRESS:	PV	FV	i	n	PMT	−8053.58

Markham Auto Body should make monthly contributions of $8053.58 to the account in order to accumulate $150,000 after 18 months.   ∎

◼ EXAMPLE 12.1B   CALCULATING THE SIZE OF LEASE PAYMENTS

A lease that has $2\frac{1}{2}$ years to run is recorded on a company's books as a liability of $27,369. If the company's cost of borrowing was 12% compounded monthly when the lease was signed, what is the lease payment at the beginning of each month?

☑ SOLUTION

The "book value" of the lease liability is the present value of the remaining lease payments, discounted at the interest rate that the company would have paid (when the lease was signed) to borrow funds. The lease payments constitute a simple annuity due with

$$A_n(\text{due}) = \$27,369 \qquad n = 30 \qquad \text{and} \qquad p = i = 1\%$$

ALGEBRAIC SOLUTION

Substituting the given values in formula (11–2),

$$A_n(\text{due}) = R\left[\frac{1 - (1 + p)^{-n}}{p}\right] \times (1 + p)$$

$$\$27,369 = R\left(\frac{1 - 1.01^{-30}}{0.01}\right)(1.01)$$

$$= R(25.807708)(1.01)$$

$$= 26.065785R$$

$$R = \$1050.00$$

FINANCIAL CALCULATOR SOLUTION

BGN mode.						Result
ENTER:	27369	0	30	1	COMP	
PRESS:	PV	FV	n	i	PMT	−1050.00

The monthly lease payment is $1050.00.   ∎

◼ EXAMPLE 12.1C   CALCULATING THE PAYMENT SIZE IN AN ORDINARY GENERAL ANNUITY

An interest-bearing promissory note for $5000 requires payments at the end of each quarter for 4 years. If the interest rate on the note is 13.5% compounded monthly, what is the size of each payment?

☑ SOLUTION

The original principal equals the present value of all payments discounted at the contractual rate of interest on the note. Since payments are made at the *end* of each quarter and interest is compounded monthly, the payments form an ordinary general annuity with

$$A_n = \$5000 \qquad n = 4(4) = 16 \qquad i = \frac{13.5\%}{12} = 1.125\% \qquad \text{and} \qquad c = \frac{12}{4} = 3$$

Then,

$$p = (1 + i)^c - 1 = 1.01125^3 - 1 = 0.0341311 = 3.41311\%$$

ALGEBRAIC SOLUTION

Substituting the preceding values into formula (10−4), we obtain

$$\$5000 = R\left(\frac{1 - 1.0341311^{-16}}{0.0341311}\right)$$
$$= R(12.17334)$$
$$R = \frac{\$5000}{12.17334} = \$410.73$$

FINANCIAL CALCULATOR SOLUTION

						Result
ENTER:	5000	0	3.41311	16		
PRESS:	PV	FV	i	n	COMP PMT	−410.73

The size of the quarterly payments is \$410.73   ■

■ EXAMPLE 12.1D   *CALCULATING R TO ATTAIN A SAVINGS GOAL WHEN SOME SAVINGS ALREADY EXIST*

Mr. Walters has already accumulated \$104,000 in his Registered Retirement Savings Plan (RRSP). His goal is to build it to \$250,000 with equal contributions at the beginning of each 6-month period for the next 7 years. If his RRSP earns 8.5% compounded semiannually, what must be the size of further contributions?

☑ SOLUTION

The \$250,000 target will be the combined future value of the \$104,000 already in the RRSP and the annuity due formed by the next 14 payments. That is,

$$\$250,000 = \text{Future value of } \$104,000 + S_n(\text{due})$$

where $n = 14$ and $p = i = 8.5\%/2 = 4.25\%$.

ALGEBRAIC SOLUTION

Using formulas (8−2) and (11−1), we obtain

$$\$250,000 = \$104,000(1.0425^{14}) + R\left(\frac{1.0425^{14} - 1}{0.0425}\right)(1.0425)$$
$$= \$186,250.84 + R(19.39966)$$

$$R = \frac{\$250,000 - \$186,250.84}{19.39966}$$

$$= \$3286.10$$

Mr. Walters must make semiannual contributions of $3286.10 to reach his goal.

FINANCIAL CALCULATOR SOLUTION

The financial calculator can simultaneously accommodate the initial lump amount (stored in (PV)) and the annuity.

BGN mode					Result
ENTER: 104000	250000	14	4.25		
PRESS: +/-				COMP	
PV	FV	n	i	PMT	-3286.10

Mr. Walters must make semiannual payments of $3286.10 to reach the $250,000 target.   ∎

◼ EXAMPLE 12.1E   CALCULATING THE SIZE OF LOAN PAYMENTS REQUIRED TO REACH A TARGET BALANCE

Mr. and Mrs. Morisseau obtained a $20,000 home improvement loan from their bank at an interest rate of 10.5% compounded monthly.

a. What is the size of the blended monthly payments required to pay off the loan in 10 years?

b. What size of blended monthly payments will reduce the balance to $10,000 after 5 years?

☑ SOLUTION

The key idea that will be used is

$$\text{Original principal} = \text{Present value of all payments}$$

This principle applies whether or not all payments are equal. In part b the $10,000 balance after 5 years can be viewed as the amount which, if paid with the last monthly payment, would pay off the loan.

The monthly payments form an ordinary simple annuity having $p = i = \frac{10.5\%}{12} = 0.875\%$.

In part a,

$$n = 10(12) = 120 \quad \text{and} \quad A_n = \$20,000$$

In part b,

$$n = 5(12) = 60 \quad \text{and} \quad \$20,000 = A_n + \text{Present value of } \$10,000$$

ALGEBRAIC SOLUTION

a. Using formula (10−4),

$$\$20,000 = R\left(\frac{1 - 1.00875^{-120}}{0.00875}\right) = R(74.10976)$$

$$R = \frac{\$20,000}{74.10976} = \$269.87$$

b. Now formulas (10−4) and (8−2) must both be employed.

$$\$20,000 = R\left(\frac{1 - 1.00875^{-60}}{0.00875}\right) + \frac{\$10,000}{1.00875^{60}}$$
$$= R(46.52483) + \$5929.08$$

Solving for *R*,

$$46.52483R = \$20,000 - \$5929.08 = \$14,070.92$$
$$R = \frac{\$14,070.92}{46.52483} = \$302.44$$

FINANCIAL CALCULATOR SOLUTION

a.						Result
ENTER:	20000	0	120	0.875		
PRESS:	PV	FV	n	i	COMP PMT	−269.87
b.						
ENTER:	60	10000				
PRESS:	n	+/− FV			COMP PMT	−302.44

Monthly payments of $269.87 will pay off the loan in 10 years. Payments of $302.44 will reduce the balance to $10,000 after 5 years. ∎

■ EXAMPLE 12.1F   *CALCULATING THE PERIODIC INVESTMENT REQUIRED TO PURCHASE A SPECIFIED ANNUITY ON A FUTURE DATE*

Douglas and Margaret Kuramoto have already accumulated $125,000 in their RRSPs. They are attempting to estimate the annual contributions they must make in order to retire in 15 years, when Doug turns 60. Their goal is to have enough funds in the RRSP to purchase a 25-year annuity that will pay $5000 at the end of each month. The planning assumptions are an 8% annually compounded return on their RRSPs and an 8.1% monthly compounded return on the annuity purchased with their RRSP funds. What combined RRSP contributions should they make at the end of each of the next 15 years?

☑ SOLUTION

The given information and the steps in the solution are presented in the following time diagram.

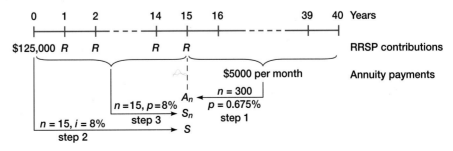

The total amount in the RRSPs 15 years from now will be the future value, S, of the $125,000 already in the RRSPs plus the future value, S_n, of 15 more annual contributions of size R. The amount needed to purchase the annuity paying $5000 per month will be the present value, A_n, of the 300 payments discounted at

$$p = i = \frac{8.1\%}{12} = 0.675\%$$

The central idea for the solution is that the future value of the RRSP, 15 years from now, must equal the present value of the annuity, 15 years from now. That is,

$$S + S_n = A_n$$

ALGEBRAIC SOLUTION

The amount that will be needed to purchase the annuity is

$$A_n = R\left[\frac{1 - (1 + p)^{-n}}{p}\right]$$
$$= \$5000\left(\frac{1 - 1.00675^{-300}}{0.00675}\right)$$
$$= \$5000\left(\frac{1 - 0.1328949}{0.00675}\right)$$
$$= \$642,300.03$$

The future value of the initial $125,000 is

$$S = P(1 + i)^n = \$125,000(1.08)^{15} = \$396,521.14$$

The future value of the 15 annual contributions is

$$S_n = R\left[\frac{(1 + p)^n - 1}{p}\right] = R\left(\frac{1.08^{15} - 1}{0.08}\right) = 27.152114R$$

Substitute these values for A_n, S, and S_n into

$$S + S_n = A_n$$

giving

$$\$396,521.14 + 27.152114R = \$642,300.03$$
$$27.152114R = \$245,778.89$$
$$R = \$9051.92$$

The Kuramotos must make annual contributions of $9051.92.

FINANCIAL CALCULATOR SOLUTION

The present value of the annuity from step 1 also represents the combined future value of both the RRSP contribution annuity and the initial $125,000. The financial calculator can compute the annual RRSP contribution in one operation if the initial $125,000 is entered in $\boxed{\textbf{PV}}$ as an initial lump investment.

Compute A_n.					Result
ENTER: 5000	0	300	0.675		
				COMP	
PRESS: PMT	FV	n	i	PV	−642,300.03

```
┌─────────────────────────────────────────────────┬─────────┐
│  Compute R.                                       │         │
│  ENTER:            125000    15      8            │         │
│                  ┌────┐  ┌────┐              ┌──────┐       │
│                  │+/- │  │+/- │              │ COMP │       │
│  PRESS:          └────┘  └────┘  ┌───┐ ┌───┐ └──────┘       │
│                  ┌────┐  ┌────┐  │ n │ │ i │ ┌──────┐       │
│                  │ FV │  │ PV │  └───┘ └───┘ │ PMT  │  -9051.92│
│                  └────┘  └────┘              └──────┘       │
└─────────────────────────────────────────────────┴─────────┘
```

The Kuramotos must contribute $9051.92 per year to their RRSPs.   ■

Point of Interest

To Lease or Buy a New Car?

The popularity of leasing instead of purchasing a new vehicle has grown rapidly in recent years. In 1994, 20% of new vehicles were leased. The percentage increased to over 30% in 1996. This rapid growth of leasing suggests that there may be an economic advantage to leasing. We will analyse lease versus purchase alternatives to determine if this is the case.

The main elements of a typical lease contract are as follows:

• The lessee makes fixed beginning-of-month payments for the term of the lease. (The most common term is 2 years, although terms from 1 to 5 years are available).
• The lessee is responsible for all vehicle operating costs (including insurance) during the term of the lease. In this respect, leasing does not differ from owning a vehicle.
• At the end of the term, the lessee can return the vehicle to the lessor, or purchase the vehicle at a predetermined price (called the *residual value* in the lease contract.)

No down payment is required at the beginning of a lease. Therefore, the purchase transaction that most closely parallels a lease transaction has:

• No down payment—the entire purchase price would be paid with borrowed funds.
• The term of the loan equal to the term of the lease.

The following data were obtained from the leasing department of a dealer for a major automobile manufacturer. The manufacturer's leasing/financing subsidiary is the lessor in the lease transaction and the lender in the purchase transaction. Both the lease and the loan have 4-year terms.

Lease	
Lease price:	$19,995
Administration fee:	$65
Total lease price:	$20,060
Term of lease:	48 months
Monthly lease payment:	$342.23
Provincial sales tax:	$23.96
GST:	$23.96
Total monthly payment:	$390.15
Interest rate:	10%
Residual value:	$10,800

In this case, the monthly lease payment of $342.23 includes a monthly management fee of $20.06 (which is 0.1% per month of the total lease price). The other component of the $342.23 monthly payment is the basic lease payment of $322.17. It compensates the lessor for the vehicle's expected depreciation (from $20,060 to $10,800 over the term of the lease) and, in addition, provides the lessor with a rate of return of 10% compounded monthly on the lessor's investment in the vehicle. This basic lease payment can be calculated by determining the payment in an equivalent loan problem. Calculate the *beginning-of-month* payment that will reduce the balance owed after 4 years on a $20,060 loan at 10% compounded monthly to $10,800. Both the provincial sales tax and the Goods and Services Tax (GST) are charged on the $342.23 monthly lease payment to give the total monthly payment of $390.15.

(*continued*)

(concluded)

Purchase	
Retail selling price:	$19,995
Administration fee:	$65
Provincial sales tax:	$1404.20
GST:	$1404.20
Total selling price:	$22,868.40
Term of loan:	48 months
Interest rate:	7.9%
Monthly payment:	$557.21

The retail selling price is not the inflated "sticker price" but rather the basic selling price. It is also the amount previously disclosed as the lease price.

Note that the interest rate charged on the loan-to-purchase is 2.1% lower than the interest rate impounded in the lease payments. This means that the lessor *expects* a 2.1% higher rate of return on its investment than the lender requires on the loan. The reason for this "spread" is that the lessor takes on a higher risk than the lender. The lessor faces the possibility that the market price of the vehicle after 4 years will be less than $10,800. Furthermore, the lender has better security than the lessor in the event of default because the vehicle owner's larger monthly payments allow the owner to build equity in the vehicle as the loan is repaid. The lessee does not build equity; the lessee's smaller monthly payments approximately cover only the vehicle's actual depreciation.

For an economic comparison of leasing versus purchasing, we will calculate the present value of each alternative's payment stream. The same time value of money should be used as the discount rate in both cases. In the purchase transaction, the owner/borrower can prepay the loan without penalty at any time and thereby effectively earn the rate of interest on the loan. Hence, we are justified in using 7.9% compounded monthly as the discount rate for both payment streams.

We know that if loan payments are discounted at the interest rate on the loan, the present value is the original loan principal. Therefore, the current economic value of the payments to purchase the vehicle is $22,868.

The present value of the annuity due formed by the 48 lease payments of $390.15 discounted at 7.9% compounded monthly is

$$A_n\,(due) = \$390.15 \left(\frac{1 - 1.00658\overline{3}^{-48}}{0.00658\overline{3}} \right)$$
$$\times\ (1.00658\overline{3}) = \$16,117$$

To be in the same position as the purchaser who owns a vehicle worth $10,800 at the end of the 4 years, the lessee would have to exercise the option after 4 years to purchase the vehicle for $10,800 plus 14% in taxes. Therefore, the appropriate present value of leasing expenditures to compare to the $22,868 figure for the purchase alternative is

$$\$16,117 + 1.14(\$10,800)$$
$$\times\ (1.00658\overline{3})^{-48} = \$25,102$$

In current dollars, leasing costs $25,102 − $22,868 = $2334 more than purchasing. Leasing has a higher economic cost because of (1) the higher interest rate built into the lease rates and (2) the administration fee added to the monthly lease payment.

In spite of its economic disadvantage, leasing has grown in popularity primarily because monthly lease payments are lower than the loan payments required to purchase a car with a relatively small down payment. More people can manage the smaller lease payments on their monthly income than can manage the larger loan payments. However, we have demonstrated that it is the lessee who takes on the greater *economic burden.*

EXERCISE 12.1

Answers to the odd-numbered problems are at the end of the book.

Calculate the periodic payment for each of the annuities in problems 1 through 20.

Problem	Present or future value ($)	Type of annuity	Payment interval	Term	Nominal interest rate (%)	Compounding frequency
1.	FV=76,055	Ordinary	1 year	13 years	10.5	Annually
2.	FV=35,790	Ordinary	3 months	$5\frac{1}{2}$ years	10	Quarterly
3.	FV=4357	Ordinary	1 month	$2\frac{1}{2}$ years	7.5	Monthly
4.	FV=50,000	Ordinary	6 months	$12\frac{1}{2}$ years	8	Semiannually
5.	PV=20,832	Ordinary	1 month	$8\frac{1}{4}$ years	13.5	Monthly
6.	PV=35,531	Ordinary	1 quarter	7 years, 9 months	9.9	Quarterly
7.	PV=20,049	Ordinary	6 months	19 years	9.25	Semiannually
8.	PV=35,104	Ordinary	1 month	6 years, 7 months	8.4	Monthly
9.	PV=25,000	Due	6 months	$8\frac{1}{2}$ years	9.5	Semiannually
10.	PV=50,000	Due	12 months	12 years	8.9	Annually
11.	FV=100,000	Due	3 months	15 years, 3 months	9	Quarterly
12.	FV=30,000	Due	1 month	7 years, 9 months	8.25	Monthly
13.	PV=25,000	Ordinary	3 months	$8\frac{1}{2}$ years	9.5	Semiannually
14.	PV=50,000	Ordinary	1 month	12 years	8.9	Annually
15.	FV=100,000	Ordinary	1 year	15 years	9	Quarterly
16.	FV=30,000	Ordinary	6 months	7 years	8.25	Monthly
17.	PV=30,000	Due	3 months	$10\frac{1}{2}$ years	8.5	Semiannually
18.	PV=45,000	Due	1 month	11 years	9.9	Annually
19.	FV=150,000	Due	1 year	16 years	11	Quarterly
20.	FV=25,000	Due	6 months	$7\frac{1}{2}$ years	8.25	Monthly

21. In order to accumulate $200,000 after 25 years, calculate the amounts that must be invested at the end of each year at:

    a. 8% compounded annually.   b. 10% compounded annually.

22. Calculate the amounts that must be invested at the end of each year at 9% compounded annually in order to accumulate $200,000 after:

    a. 25 years.   b. 30 years.

23. To accumulate $200,000 after 20 years, what amount must be invested each year if the investment earns 9% compounded annually and the contributions are made:

    a. At the beginning of each year?   b. At the end of each year?

24. What maximum annual withdrawals will a $200,000 fund earning 9% compounded annually sustain for 20 years if the withdrawals are made:

    a. At the beginning of each year?   b. At the end of each year?

25. John has $20,000 available to purchase an annuity. What end-of-month payments can he expect if the funds earn 7.5% compounded monthly and the payments run for:

    a. 10 years?   b. 20 years?

26. What payments can be expected at the end of each quarter from a 10-year annuity purchased for $25,000 if the funds earn:

    a. 10% compounded quarterly?   b. 8% compounded quarterly?

27. Heather wants to accumulate $4000 for a trip to Europe 1 or 2 years from now. Her savings account pays 6% compounded monthly. What amount must she deposit at the beginning of each month to reach the target in:

    a. 1 year?   b. 2 years?

28. The interest rate charged on a $20,000 loan is 12% compounded monthly. Calculate the monthly payments and the total interest paid during the life of the loan if the loan is to be paid off over:

    a. 5 years.   b. 10 years.   c. 15 years.

    d. 20 years.   e. 25 years.

29. Karen obtained a $20,000 loan at 10.5% compounded monthly. What semiannual payment will repay the loan in $7\frac{1}{2}$ years?

30. Fletcher's Machine Shop wants to start a fund to accumulate half of the expected $1,000,000 cost of expanding their facilities in 9 years. What amounts must be paid into the fund earning 7.5% compounded semiannually in order to reach the target if the payments are made:

    a. At the beginning of every 6 months?

    b. At the end of every 6 months?

31. Triex Manufacturing wants to accumulate $500,000 as the equity portion of the financing required for an expansion planned to begin in 5 years. If today Triex makes the first of equal quarterly payments into a fund earning 8.25% compounded monthly, what size should these payments be?

32. Brenda and Tom want to save $30,000 over the next 4 years for a down payment on a house. What amount must they regularly save from their month-end pay cheques if their savings can earn 5.5% compounded semiannually?

33. Henry can buy a farm for $350,000 with terms of $50,000 down and the balance payable over 20 years by quarterly payments including interest at 8% compounded annually. What will be the size of the payments?

34. An insurance company wishes to offer customers a monthly instalment alternative to the annual premium plan. All premiums are payable at the beginning of the period of coverage. The monthly payment plan is to include an interest charge of 15% compounded monthly on the unpaid balance of the annual premium. What will be the monthly premium per $100 of annual premium?

35. Advance Leasing calculates the monthly payments on its 3-year leases on the basis of recovering the capital cost of the leased equipment and earning an 18% compounded monthly rate of return on its capital investment. What will be the monthly lease rate on equipment that costs $8500?

36. Seth is supposed to pay $10,000 to Megan today. What payments at the end of each quarter for the next 2 years would be economically equivalent to the scheduled payment if money can earn 7.5% compounded quarterly?

37. Ardith is scheduled to make a lump payment of $25,000, 11 months from now, to complete a real estate transaction. What end-of-month payments for the next 11 months should the vendor be willing to accept instead of the lump payment if he can invest the funds at 5.4% compounded monthly?

38. Shane is about to have his 25th birthday. He has set a goal of retiring at age 55 with $700,000 in an RRSP. For planning purposes he is assuming that his RRSP will earn 8% compounded annually.

    a. What contribution on each birthday from age 25 to 54 inclusive will be required to accumulate the desired amount in his RRSP?

    b. If he waits 5 years before starting his RRSP, what contribution on each birthday from age 30 to 54 inclusive will be required to accumulate the target amount?

39. Wendy will soon turn 33. She wants to accumulate $500,000 in an RRSP by her 60th birthday. How much larger will her annual contributions have to be if they are made at the end of each year (between her 33rd and 60th birthdays) instead of at the beginning of each year? Assume that her RRSP will earn 9% compounded annually.

40. CompuLease leases computers and peripheral equipment to businesses. What lease payments must CompuLease charge at the beginning of each quarter of a 5-year lease if it is to recover the $20,000 capital cost of a system and earn 16% compounded quarterly on its investment?

41. Island Water Taxi has decided to lease another boat for 5 years rather than to finance the purchase of the boat at an interest rate of 13.5% compounded monthly. It is treating the lease as a capital lease and has set up a long-term lease liability of $43,000. What is the lease payment at the beginning of each month?

42. Murray is about to have his 28th birthday. He wants to accumulate $600,000 in an RRSP by age 60. How much larger will his annual contributions have to be if they are made at the end of each year instead of the beginning of each year? Assume that his RRSP will earn 8% compounded semiannually.

•43. Advantage Leasing calculates its 5-year lease rates so that it recovers the capital cost of the equipment plus an 18% compounded quarterly return on investment over the term of the lease. What will be the required lease payments on a machine that cost $25,000 if the lease payments are made:

    a. At the beginning of every month?

    b. At the beginning of each 6-month period?

•44. The interest rate on a $200,000 loan is 11% compounded quarterly.

    a. What payments at the end of every quarter will reduce the balance to $150,000 after $3\frac{1}{2}$ years?

    b. If the same payments continue, what will be the balance 7 years after the date that the loan was received?

•45. Beatty Transport obtained a $50,000 term loan for 5 years at 11% compounded semiannually, for the purchase of another truck.

    a. What are the monthly payments on the loan?

    b. If the outstanding balance may be prepaid at any time, what is the payout amount at the end of the second year?

•46. On the date of his granddaughter's birth, Mr. Parry deposited $5000 in a trust fund earning 8.25% compounded annually. After the granddaughter's 19th birthday, the trust account is to make end-of-month payments to her for 4 years to assist her with the costs of post-secondary education. If the trust account earns 7.5% compounded monthly during these 4 years, what will be the size of the monthly payments?

•47. Elizabeth has been able to transfer a $25,000 retiring allowance into an RRSP. She plans to let the RRSP accumulate earnings at the rate of 8.75% compounded annually for 10 years and then purchase a 15-year annuity making payments at the beginning of each quarter. What size of payment can she expect if the funds in the annuity earn 9% compounded quarterly?

•48. Mr. and Mrs. Friedrich have just opened a Registered Education Savings Plan (RESP) for their daughter. They want the plan to pay $3000 at the beginning of each half year for 4 years, starting 9 years from now when their daughter will enter college or university. What semiannual contributions, including one today, must they make for the next 9 years if the RESP earns 8.25% compounded semiannually?

•49. Four years from now, Tim and Justine plan to take a year's leave of absence from their jobs and travel through Asia, Europe, and Africa. They want to accumulate enough savings during the next 4 years that the savings fund can pay them $3000 at each month-end for the entire year of leave. What amount must they pay into the fund at the end of every calendar quarter for the next 4 years to reach their goal? The planning assumptions are that their savings will earn 6% compounded quarterly for the next 4 years and 4.2% compounded monthly during the fifth year.

•50. Beth and Nelson want to accumulate a combined total of $600,000 in their RRSPs by the time Beth reaches age 60, which will be 30 years from now. They plan to make equal contributions at the end of every 6 months for the next 25 years, and then to make no further contributions for the subsequent 5 years of semiretirement. For planning purposes, assume that their RRSPs will earn 7% compounded semiannually for the next 30 years.

  a. What should be their combined semiannual RRSP contributions?

  b. What combined monthly amount can they expect if they use the $600,000 in their RRSPs 30 years from now to purchase 25-year ordinary annuities? Assume that the funds used to purchase the annuities will earn 7.2% compounded monthly.

•51. Jack Groman's financial plan is designed to accumulate sufficient funds in his RRSP over the next 28 years to purchase an annuity paying $6000 at the end of each month for 25 years. He will be able to contribute $7000 to his RRSP at the end of each year for the next 10 years. What year-end contribution must he make for the subsequent 18 years to achieve his objective? For these projections, assume that Jack's RRSP will earn 7.5% compounded annually and that the annuity payments are based on a return of 7.5% compounded monthly.

•52. Dr. Collins wants the value of her RRSP 30 years from now to have the purchasing power of $500,000 in current dollars.

  a. Assuming an inflation rate of 5% per year, what nominal dollar amount should Dr. Collins have in her RRSP after 30 years?

  b. Assuming her RRSP will earn 8.5% compounded semiannually, what contributions should she make at the end of every 3 months to achieve the goal?

•53. Ambleside Golf Club's board of directors has set next year's membership fee at $1900 payable at the beginning of the year. The board has instructed its accountant to calculate beginning-of-quarter and beginning-of-month payment plans that provide a 15% semiannually compounded rate of return on the unpaid balance of the annual fee. What will be the amounts of the quarterly and monthly payments?

••54. Connie and Rich have just received an inheritance of $225,000. This amount can be invested to earn 5% compounded quarterly after tax. Their first priority is to accumulate enough funds to be able to purchase, 23 years from now, a 25-year annuity paying $4000 at each month's end. What interest earnings can they withdraw at the end of each quarter until the date of purchase of the annuity, and still leave sufficient funds to purchase the annuity? Assume that the annuity earns 6.6% compounded monthly.

•55. Harold, just turned 27, wants to accumulate by age 60 an amount in his RRSP that will have the purchasing power of $300,000 in current dollars. What annual contributions on his 28th through 60th birthdays are required to meet this goal if the RRSP earns 8.5% compounded annually and the rate of inflation is 5% per year?

•56. A Registered Education Savings Plan (RESP) is a government-approved plan developed to help parents and grandparents save money for their children's or grandchildren's post-secondary education. Income earned on contributions to the plan is not taxed while in the plan. As funds are withdrawn to pay for a child's or grandchild's post-secondary education, the earnings are taxed as income of the student (who will usually have a very low tax rate).

Ken and Barbara have two children, aged 3 and 6. At the end of every 6 months for the next $12\frac{1}{2}$ years, they wish to contribute equal amounts sufficient for their RESP to make 12 semiannual payments of $5000, the first occurring 6 months after the last contribution. If the RESP earns 8.5% compounded semiannually, what must be the size of the regular contributions?

••57. Cynthia currently has $31,000 in her RRSP. She plans to contribute $5000 at the end of each year for the next 17 years and then use the accumulated funds to purchase a 20-year annuity making month-end payments.

    a. If her RRSP earns 8.75% compounded annually for the next 17 years, and the fund from which the annuity is paid will earn 8.25% compounded monthly, what monthly payments will she receive?

    b. If the rate of inflation for the next 17 years is 4% pa, what will be the purchasing power (in today's dollars) of the monthly payments at the start of the annuity?

••58. Mr. Parmar wants to retire in 20 years and purchase a 25-year annuity that will make payments, each initially having the purchasing power of $6000 in today's dollars, at the end of every quarter. If he already has $54,000 in his RRSP, what contributions must he make at the end of every half year for the next 20 years to achieve his retirement goal? Assume that the rate of inflation for the next 20 years will be 4.5% pa, the RRSP will earn 8% compounded semiannually, and the rate of return on the fund from which the annuity is paid will be 8% compounded quarterly.

••59. Mr. Ng contributed $500 to an RRSP at the beginning of each calendar quarter for the past 20 years. The plan earned 10% compounded quarterly for the first 10 years and 12% compounded quarterly for the last 10 years. He is converting the RRSP to a Registered Retirement Income Fund (RRIF) and intends to withdraw equal amounts at the beginning of each month for 15 years. If the funds in the RRIF earn 8.25% compounded monthly, what maximum monthly amount can be withdrawn?

12.2 CALCULATING THE NUMBER OF PAYMENTS

Some examples where the number of payments, n, must be calculated are:

- Determining the time required for periodic payments to pay off a loan.
- Determining the time required for a periodic savings plan to reach a savings goal.
- Determining how long an annuity purchased with a lump investment will deliver a specified payment.

To calculate n for an annuity, R and p must be given or readily determined from the given information. In addition, we must know the present value *or* the future value of the annuity. In other words, we must also know the value of *one* of S_n, $S_n(\text{due})$, A_n, or $A_n(\text{due})$.

ALGEBRAIC METHOD

The procedure recommended in Section 12.1 for calculating R was to substitute the known values in the existing formula for S_n, $S_n(\text{due})$, A_n, or $A_n(\text{due})$, and then solve for R. By taking this approach, we avoided the introduction of versions of formulas (10−1), (10−4), (11−1), and (11−2) rearranged to isolate R.

A corresponding procedure may be taken to calculate n. However, the process of solving the resulting equation for n is not as straightforward as solving for R. This is because n appears as an exponent in the formula whereas R appears as a simple literal coefficient. Furthermore, the process of isolating n requires some familiarity with the manipulation of logarithms. Because of these complications, formulas for the direct calculation of n are presented in Table 12.1. Keep in mind that they are *not* new relationships—they are merely rearranged versions of the corresponding formulas (10–1), (10–4), (11–1), and (11–2). The derivation of formula (10–1a) from formula (10–1) is presented in Appendix 12A.

TABLE   12.1

Formulas for Calculating the Number of Payments in an Annuity

Known variables	Formula	
S_n, R, p	$n = \dfrac{\ln\left(1 + \dfrac{pS_n}{R}\right)}{\ln(1 + p)}$	(10–1a)
A_n, R, p	$n = -\dfrac{\ln\left(1 - \dfrac{pA_n}{R}\right)}{\ln(1 + p)}$	(10–4a)
S_n(due), R, p	$n = \dfrac{\ln\left[1 + \dfrac{pS_n(\text{due})}{R(1 + p)}\right]}{\ln(1 + p)}$	(11–1a)
A_n(due), R, p	$n = -\dfrac{\ln\left[1 - \dfrac{pA_n(\text{due})}{R(1 + p)}\right]}{\ln(1 + p)}$	(11–2a)

These two alternative approaches to the algebraic calculation of n are illustrated in Example 12.2A. Part a is solved by substituting known values in the future-value or present-value formula and then isolating n. Part b is solved by using a formula from Table 12.1. In all other examples involving the calculation of n, only the latter approach will be employed.

FINANCIAL CALCULATOR METHOD

The financial calculator method is similar to that for computing R. Enter the known values for (PMT), (i), (FV), and (PV). The keystroke combination (COMP) (n) will execute the computation of the number of payments.

Tip

The value obtained for n will not be an integer in all cases. To illustrate the interpretation of a noninteger value for n, suppose $n = 21.3$ in a particular case. This means that there are 22 payments, but the last payment is smaller than the others. Prevailing business practice is to allow a full payment interval for the final reduced payment. Even though the fractional part of n in this case is 0.3, it is only an approximation to say that the last payment is 30% of the size of the others. The method for calculating the exact size of the final payment will be presented in Chapter 14.

> **Trap**
>
> A problem may ask for the *term* of the annuity rather than the number of payments in the annuity. To obtain the term of the annuity from the number of payments, remember that n (rounded to the next larger integer) will also represent the number of *payment* intervals. Do not make the mistake of thinking that n also represents the number of compounding periods of the periodic rate i. (In Chapters 8 and 9, n did represent the latter quantity in compound interest calculations involving lump payments rather than annuities.)

■ EXAMPLE 12.2A   *CALCULATING THE TIME REQUIRED TO PAY OFF A LOAN*

Roy and Lynn are discussing the terms of a $20,000 home improvement loan with their bank's lending officer. The interest rate on the loan will be 12% compounded monthly.

a. How long will it take to repay the loan if the monthly payments are $220?

b. How long will it take to repay the loan if Roy and Lynn pay an extra $20 per month?

c. Calculate the approximate total of the (nominal) interest savings over the life of the loan as a result of making payments of $240 instead of $220 per month.

✓ SOLUTION

The original loan equals the present value of all the payments. The payments form an ordinary simple annuity with $A_n = \$20,000$ and $p = i = 1\%$. In part *a*, $R = \$220$ while in part *b*, $R = \$240$.

ALGEBRAIC SOLUTION

a. The approach used to calculate n in this part will be to first substitute the known values in formula (10–4). Then the resulting equation will be simplified and rearranged to solve for n.

$$A_n = R\left[\frac{1 - (1 + p)^{-n}}{p}\right] \qquad (10\text{--}4)$$

Substituting the known values gives

$$\$20,000 = \$220\left(\frac{1 - 1.01^{-n}}{0.01}\right)$$

Multiplication of both sides by $\frac{0.01}{\$220}$ yields

$$\frac{\$20,000}{\$220}(0.01) = 1 - 1.01^{-n}$$

Rearranging to isolate 1.01^{-n} on the left-hand side, we have

$$1.01^{-n} = 1 - 0.90\overline{90}$$

Taking logarithms of both sides,

$$-n \ln 1.01 = \ln 0.09\overline{09}$$

Hence,

$$n = -\frac{\ln 0.09\overline{09}}{\ln 1.01} = -\frac{-2.3979}{0.0099503} = 240.99$$

It will take 241 payments, requiring 20 years and 1 month, to pay off the loan. The last payment will be slightly less than $220.

b. The approach used in this part will be to substitute the known values in formula (10−4a).

$$n = -\frac{\ln\left(1 - \dfrac{pA_n}{R}\right)}{\ln(1 + p)}$$

$$= -\frac{\ln\left[1 - \dfrac{0.01(\$20,000)}{\$240}\right]}{\ln(1.01)}$$

$$= -\frac{\ln(0.16667)}{\ln(1.01)}$$

$$= -\frac{-1.79176}{0.0099503}$$

$$= 180.07$$

It will take 181 months (15 years and 1 month) to pay off the loan. The last payment will be *approximately* 0.07($240) = $17.

c. With monthly payments of $220, the total of all payments is approximately

$$241(\$220) = \$53,020$$

of which $33,020 will be interest.

With monthly payments of $240, the total of all payments is approximately

$$180(\$240) = \$43,200$$

of which $23,200 is interest. The savings of interest is approximately

$$\$53,020 - \$43,200 = \$9820.$$

There is a significant result here that has general implications for managing long-term debt. By increasing their monthly payments by less than 10%, Roy and Lynn will have the loan paid off 5 years sooner and will reduce their total interest costs by about 30%. This is one of the main reasons that personal financial planners encourage individuals to push themselves to make even slightly larger payments on long-term debt.

FINANCIAL CALCULATOR SOLUTION

a. Compute n for $A_n = \$20,000$, $R = \$220$, $i = 1\%$.					Result
ENTER: 20000	220	1	0		
PRESS:	+/−			COMP	
PV	PMT	i	FV	n	240.99
b. Compute n again with $R = \$240$.					
ENTER: 240					
PRESS:	+/−	PMT	COMP	n	180.07

It will take 241 payments (requiring 20 years, 1 month) of $220 (except the last payment of slightly less than $220) to pay off the loan. Alternatively, just 181 payments (requiring 15 years, 1 month) of $240 (except the last payment of approximately $17) will repay the loan.

c. See part c of the algebraic solution.   ■

■ EXAMPLE 12.2B   CALCULATING THE TIME REQUIRED TO REACH A SAVINGS GOAL AND THE LENGTH OF TIME A FUND WILL SUSTAIN REGULAR WITHDRAWALS

a. Annual contributions of $5000 will be made at every year-end to an RRSP. To the nearest year, how long will it take for the funds in the RRSP to grow to $500,000 if they earn 7.5% compounded annually?

b. If the $500,000 will be used to purchase an annuity earning 8% compounded quarterly and paying $12,000 at the end of each quarter, how long after the purchase date will the annuity payments continue?

☑ SOLUTION

In part a, $500,000 will be the future value, S_n, of an ordinary simple annuity having $R = \$5000$ and $p = i = 7.5\%$. In part b, the accumulated $500,000 becomes the present value of an ordinary simple annuity having $R = \$12,000$ and $p = i = 2\%$.

ALGEBRAIC SOLUTION

a. Substitute the known values in formula (10–1a).

$$n = \frac{\ln\left(1 + \dfrac{pS_n}{R}\right)}{\ln(1 + p)} = \frac{\ln\left[1 + \dfrac{0.075(\$500,000)}{\$5000}\right]}{\ln(1.075)} = \frac{2.1401}{0.07232} = 29.59135$$

It is not strictly correct to conclude that it will take 29.59 years[1] for the RRSP to grow to $500,000; it will actually take slightly longer. However, the interest earned during the 30th year will allow the RRSP to reach $500,000 before the 30th contribution is made. Rounded to the nearest year, it will take 30 years for the RRSP to accumulate $500,000.

b. Substitute the known values in formula (10–4a).

$$n = -\frac{\ln\left(1 - \dfrac{pA_n}{R}\right)}{\ln(1 + p)} = -\frac{\ln\left[1 - \dfrac{0.02(\$500,000)}{\$12,000}\right]}{\ln(1.02)} = -\frac{-1.7917}{0.019803} = 90.48$$

There will be 91 quarterly payments, with the last payment being roughly half the size of the others. Therefore, the annuity payments will run for

$$\frac{91}{4} = 22.75 \text{ years} = 22 \text{ years, 9 months}$$

---

[1]The value obtained for n is actually telling us that the RRSP will reach $500,000 after 29.59135 years if, at that time, a (30th) payment of (essentially) 0.59135 × $5000 is paid into the plan. In other words, when a savings plan is terminated partway through a payment interval, the mathematics assumes a different behaviour in the final interval from our usual practice of not paying a cent before a full payment interval has passed. To calculate precisely when the RRSP will reach $500,000 (including accrued interest),
• Calculate the amount in the RRSP after 29 contributions (years).
• Use formula (9–2) to calculate the fraction of a period (year) required for the amount from the preceding step to grow to $500,000.

FINANCIAL CALCULATOR SOLUTION

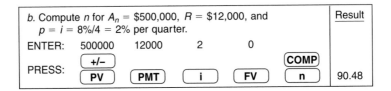

a. Compute *n* for *R* = $5000, *p* = *i* = 7.5%, and S_n = $500,000   Result

ENTER:	5000	7.5	500000	0		
PRESS:	+/− PMT	i	FV	PV	COMP n	29.59

See the discussion in part *a* of the algebraic solution. Rounded to the nearest year, it will take 30 years for the RRSP to accumulate $500,000.

b. Compute *n* for A_n = $500,000, *R* = $12,000, and   Result
   p = *i* = 8%/4 = 2% per quarter.

ENTER:	500000	12000	2	0		
PRESS:	+/− PV	PMT	i	FV	COMP n	90.48

There will be 91 quarterly payments, with the last payment being roughly half the size of the others. Therefore, the annuity payments will run for

$$\frac{91}{4} = 22.75 \text{ years} = 22 \text{ years, 9 months}$$ ∎

■ EXAMPLE 12.2C   CALCULATING *n* GIVEN THE PRESENT VALUE OF A SIMPLE ANNUITY DUE

How long can an account sustain quarterly withdrawals of $2000 beginning today if the account contains $100,000 and earns 6% compounded quarterly?

✓ SOLUTION

The amount currently in the account represents the present value of the future withdrawals. Since the first withdrawal is today, the withdrawals form a simple annuity due with

$$A_n(\text{due}) = \$100,000 \qquad R = \$2000 \qquad \text{and} \qquad p = i = \frac{6\%}{4} = 1.5\%$$

ALGEBRAIC SOLUTION

Substitute the known values in formula (11−2*a*).

$$n = -\frac{\ln\left[1 - \dfrac{pA_n(\text{due})}{R(1 + p)}\right]}{\ln(1 + p)} = -\frac{\ln\left[1 - \dfrac{0.015(\$100,000)}{\$2000(1.015)}\right]}{\ln(1.015)} = -\frac{-1.342914}{0.0148886} = 90.20$$

The 91st withdrawal will exhaust the account. Since withdrawals are made at the beginning of each quarter, the 91st withdrawal will occur 90 calendar quarters, or $22\frac{1}{2}$ years, after the date of the first withdrawal.

FINANCIAL CALCULATOR SOLUTION

BGN mode						Result
ENTER: 100000	2000	0	1.5			
PRESS: +/– PV	PMT	FV	i	COMP		
					n	90.20

See the conclusion at the end of the algebraic solution. ■

■ EXAMPLE 12.2D   CALCULATING *n* GIVEN THE FUTURE VALUE OF AN ORDINARY GENERAL ANNUITY

If, 1 month from now, Maurice makes the first monthly contribution of $250 to an RRSP that earns 8% compounded annually, how long will it take him to accumulate $100,000?

☑ SOLUTION

Since the contributions are made monthly but compounding occurs annually, the payments form a *general* annuity having

$$S_n = \$100{,}000 \qquad R = \$250 \qquad i = 8\% \qquad \text{and} \qquad c = \frac{1}{12} = 0.08\overline{3}$$

Then

$$p = (1 + i)^c - 1 = (1.08)^{0.08\overline{3}} - 1 = 0.0064340 = 0.64340\%$$

ALGEBRAIC SOLUTION

Substitute these values in formula (10–1*a*).

$$n = \frac{\ln\left(1 + \dfrac{pS_n}{R}\right)}{\ln(1 + p)} = \frac{\ln\left[1 + \dfrac{0.0064340(\$100{,}000)}{\$250}\right]}{\ln(1.0064340)} = \frac{1.27357}{0.0064134} = 198.58$$

FINANCIAL CALCULATOR SOLUTION

						Result
ENTER: 250	0	100000	0.64340			
PRESS: +/– PMT	PV	FV	i	COMP		
					n	198.58

Since payments are at the end of each month, it will take 199 months (or 16 years and 7 months) to accumulate $100,000. ■

■ EXAMPLE 12.2E   CALCULATING *n* GIVEN THE PRESENT VALUE OF A GENERAL ANNUITY DUE

What will be the term of an annuity purchased with savings of $210,000 if the payments are $2000 at the beginning of every month and the rate of return is 9% compounded semiannually?

☑ SOLUTION

The purchase amount represents the present value of the future payments. Since the first withdrawal is today and the payment interval differs from the compounding interval, the payments form a *general* annuity *due* with

$$A_n(\text{due}) = \$210{,}000 \qquad R = \$2000 \qquad i = \frac{9\%}{2} = 4.5\% \qquad \text{and} \qquad c = \frac{2}{12} = 0.1\overline{6}$$

Then

$$p = (1 + i)^c - 1 = (1.045)^{0.1666667} - 1 = 0.00736312 = 0.736312\%$$

ALGEBRAIC SOLUTION

Substitute the known values in formula (11−2*a*).

$$n = -\frac{\ln\left[1 - \dfrac{pA_n(\text{due})}{R(1 + p)}\right]}{\ln(1 + p)} = -\frac{\ln\left[1 - \dfrac{0.00736312(\$210{,}000)}{\$2000(1.00736312)}\right]}{\ln(1.00736312)} = -\frac{-1.45876}{0.007336} = 198.8$$

The annuitant will receive 198 payments of $2000 and a final payment smaller than $2000. Although the final payment is received 198 months after the date of the first payment (and the start of the annuity), the annuity's term includes all 199 payment intervals. Therefore, the annuity's term is 199 months, or 16 years and 7 months.

FINANCIAL CALCULATOR SOLUTION

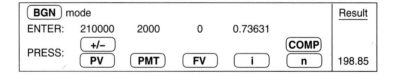

See the concluding paragraph in the algebraic solution. ∎

EXERCISE 12.2

Answers to the odd-numbered problems are at the end of the book.

Calculate the term, expressed in years and months, of each of the annuities in problems 1 through 20.

Problem	Present or future value ($)	Type of annuity	Payment interval	Periodic payment ($)	Nominal interest rate (%)	Compounding frequency
1.	PV = 50,000	Ordinary	6 months	4352.53	9.5	Semiannually
2.	FV = 100,000	Ordinary	1 year	900.46	8.9	Annually
3.	PV = 200,000	Ordinary	3 months	5807.91	9	Quarterly
4.	FV = 30,000	Ordinary	1 month	209.59	8.25	Monthly
5.	PV = 100,000	Ordinary	1 year	10,000.00	8.75	Annually
6.	PV = 100,000	Ordinary	1 month	1000.00	9	Monthly
7.	FV = 100,000	Ordinary	6 months	5000.00	7.5	Semiannually
8.	FV = 100,000	Ordinary	3 months	3000.00	10	Quarterly

Problem	Present or future value ($)	Type of annuity	Payment interval	Periodic payment ($)	Nominal interest rate (%)	Compounding frequency
9.	$FV = 117{,}896$	Due	1 year	3000.00	8.75	Annually
10.	$FV = 22{,}500$	Due	1 month	150.75	9	Monthly
11.	$PV = 13{,}405$	Due	6 months	1000.00	7.5	Semiannually
12.	$PV = 20{,}000$	Due	3 months	858.67	10	Quarterly
13.	$FV = 74{,}385$	Ordinary	3 months	1200.00	8.75	Annually
14.	$FV = 22{,}500$	Ordinary	6 months	1075.68	9	Monthly
15.	$PV = 5825.85$	Ordinary	1 year	1000.00	7.5	Semiannually
16.	$PV = 20{,}000$	Ordinary	1 month	358.87	10	Quarterly
17.	$FV = 58{,}898.50$	Due	3 months	1200.00	10.25	Annually
18.	$FV = 30{,}000$	Due	6 months	636.22	9	Monthly
19.	$PV = 6601.13$	Due	1 year	1000.00	8.5	Semiannually
20.	$PV = 20{,}000$	Due	1 month	236.18	12	Quarterly

21. How long will it take end-of-month deposits of $100 to accumulate $10,000 in a savings account that pays interest of 5.25% compounded monthly?

22. How long will $10,000, in a savings account that earns 5.25% compounded monthly, sustain month-end withdrawals of $100?

23. If $300,000 is used to purchase an annuity earning 7.5% compounded monthly and paying $2500 at the end of each month, what will be the term of the annuity?

24. How much longer will it take year-end RRSP contributions of $1000 to accumulate $100,000 than annual contributions of $1100? Assume that the RRSP earns 8% compounded annually.

25. How much longer will it take to pay off a $100,000 loan with monthly payments of $1000 than with monthly payments of $1100? The interest rate on the loan is 10.5% compounded monthly.

26. How much longer will it take monthly payments of $1000 to pay off a $100,000 loan if the monthly compounded rate of interest on the loan is 10.5% instead of 9.75%?

27. How long will it take annual contributions of $2000 to grow to $200,000 if the savings earn 9% compounded annually and the contributions are made:

    a. At the beginning of each year?   b. At the end of each year?

28. How long will a $200,000 fund earning 9% compounded annually sustain annual withdrawals of $20,000 if the withdrawals are made:

    a. At the beginning of each year?   b. At the end of each year?

29. Kim wants to save half of the $16,000 purchase price of a new car by making monthly deposits of $300, beginning today, into a savings account earning 5.25% compounded monthly. How long will it take him to reach his goal?

30. Central Personnel's accountant set up a long-term lease liability of $11,622.73 to recognize a new contract for the lease of office furniture. She used the firm's 10.5% monthly compounded cost of borrowing as the discount rate. If the lease payments at the beginning of each month are $295, what is the term of the lease?

31. What duration of annuity paying $5000 at the end of every quarter can be purchased with $200,000 if the invested funds earn 8.5% compounded semiannually?

32. Bonnie and Clyde want to take a 6-month leave of absence from their jobs to travel extensively in South America. How long will it take them to save $40,000 for the leave if they make month-end contributions of $700 through their employer's salary deferral plan? The salary deferral plan earns 7.5% compounded semiannually.

33. Finest Furniture will sell a colour television set priced at $1395 for $50 down and blended payments of $50 per month, including interest at 13.5% compounded monthly. How long after the date of purchase will the final payment be made?

34. The payments required on a contractual obligation are $500 per month. The contract was purchased for $13,372 just *before* a regular payment date. The purchaser determined this price based on his required rate of return of 9.75% compounded monthly. How many payments will he receive?

35. How much longer will a $100,000 fund earning 9% compounded monthly sustain beginning-of-month withdrawals of $900 than beginning-of-month withdrawals of $1000?

36. How much less time will it take to accumulate savings of $100,000 with beginning-of-month deposits of $220 than with beginning-of-month deposits of $200? The savings earn 6% compounded monthly.

•37. How many more RRSP contributions of $1000 at the beginning of every 6 months will it take to surpass $150,000 if the funds earn 8% compounded semiannually than if they earn 10% compounded semiannually?

•38. Mrs. McPherson wants to use $10,000 from her late husband's estate to assist her grandson when he enters college in 7 years. If the $10,000 is invested immediately at 8% compounded monthly, how long can the grandson make beginning-of-month withdrawals of $500 (or less if a final withdrawal) once he starts college?

•39. A 65-year-old male can purchase either of the following annuities from a life insurance company for $50,000. A 25-year term annuity will pay $386 at the end of each month. A life annuity will pay $485 at month-end until the death of the annuitant. Beyond what age must the man survive for the life annuity to have the greater economic value? Use 8% compounded monthly as the time value of money.

•40. A 60-year-old woman can purchase either of the following annuities from a life insurance company for $50,000. A 30-year term annuity will pay $367 at the end of each month. A life annuity will pay $405 at month-end until the death of the annuitant. Beyond what age must the woman survive for the life annuity to have the greater economic value? Use 8% compounded monthly as the time value of money.

•41. If you contribute $500 to an RRSP at the beginning of every 3 months for 25 years and then use the accumulated funds to purchase an annuity paying $1500 at the beginning of each month, what will be the term of the annuity? Assume that the RRSP earns 8.5% compounded quarterly and the funds invested in the annuity earn 7.5% compounded monthly.

•42. Quantum Research Ltd. has arranged debt financing from its parent company to complete the development of a new product. Quantum "draws down" $10,000 at the beginning of each month. If interest accumulates on the debt at 12% compounded quarterly, how long will it take to reach the credit limit of $1 million?

•43. *a.* How long will it take monthly payments of $500 to repay a $50,000 loan if the interest rate on the loan is 10.25% compounded semiannually?

   b. How much will the time to repay the loan be reduced if the payments are $50 per month larger?

•44. Jamshid borrowed $350 from his mother at the beginning of every month for $2\frac{1}{2}$ years while he attended Seneca College.

   a. If the interest rate on the accumulating debt was 6% compounded semiannually, what amount did he owe to his mother at the end of the $2\frac{1}{2}$-year period?

   b. If he made the first monthly payment of $175 on the loan at the end of the first month following the $2\frac{1}{2}$-year period, how long after the date he entered college will he have the loan repaid?

••45. Dr. Weisberg has just used the funds in her RRSP to purchase a 20-year annuity earning 8% compounded quarterly and paying $12,865 at the beginning of each 3 months. Dr. Weisberg made her last regular semiannual contribution of $3000 to her RRSP 6 months before purchasing the annuity. How long had she contributed to the RRSP if it earned 8% compounded semiannually?

••46. Harold's RRSP is already worth $56,000. How many contributions of $2000 at the end of every 6 months must he make in order to exceed $250,000? Assume the RRSP earns 9.75% compounded monthly.

••47. As a result of the closure of the mine at which he had been employed, Les Orr received a $27,000 severance settlement on his 53rd birthday. He "rolled" the severance pay into a new RRSP and then, at age 62, used the accumulated funds to purchase an annuity paying $491.31 at the beginning of each month. If the RRSP and the annuity earn 8.5% compounded annually, what is the term of the annuity?

••48. Mr. van der Linden has just used the funds in his RRSP to purchase a 25-year annuity earning 8% compounded semiannually and paying $3509 at the beginning of each month. Mr. van der Linden made his last regular semiannual contribution of $2500 to his RRSP 6 months before purchasing the annuity. How long did he contribute to the RRSP if it earned 8% compounded annually?

12.3 CALCULATING THE INTEREST RATE

Some examples of circumstances in which the interest rate must be calculated are:

- Determining the rate of return required for a periodic savings plan to reach a savings goal in a specified length of time.
- Determining the implied interest rate earned by a lump investment used to purchase a specified annuity.
- Determining the interest rate implied by specified loan payments.
- Determining the implied interest rate charged when a periodic payment plan is offered as an alternative to a lump payment.
- Determining the interest rate implied by the specified payments in a capital lease of equipment.

The interest rate that may be obtained most readily is p, the interest rate per payment interval. To calculate p for an annuity, we must know the values of R and n, and the value of *one* of S_n, S_n(due), A_n, or A_n(due).

ALGEBRAIC METHOD

Problems requiring the calculation of p pose some special difficulties for an algebraic approach. The formulas for S_n, S_n(due), A_n, or A_n(due) cannot be rearranged through algebraic manipulations to isolate p. Consequently, no formulas can be given for p corresponding to those for n in Table 12.1.

In Appendix 12B, an approximation technique called "the trial-and-error method" is presented. It is a rather inefficient procedure for improving an *estimate* of the solution to an equation. With each repetition or *iteration* of the procedure, the approximation gets closer to the correct solution. The solutions presented for example problems in this section will use only the financial calculator method. The trial-and-error method is illustrated in Appendix 12B by employing it to solve Example 12.3A a second time.

FINANCIAL CALCULATOR METHOD

The financial calculator approach to computing p presents no complications. Enter the known values for ⌈**PMT**⌉, ⌈**n**⌉, ⌈**FV**⌉, and ⌈**PV**⌉. The keystroke combination ⌈**COMP**⌉ ⌈**i**⌉ will execute the computation[2] of p, the interest rate per payment interval.

CALCULATION OF NOMINAL AND EFFECTIVE INTEREST RATES

Most annuity problems requiring the calculation of an interest rate will want the *nominal* rate of interest, j, or the *effective* interest rate, f. The interest rate directly obtained from both the algebraic and financial calculator methods is p, the interest rate per payment interval. Two existing formulas may be adapted for the conversion of p to j or f. Recall that

$$j = mi \quad (8\text{--}1) \qquad \text{and} \qquad f = (1 + i)^m - 1 \quad (9\text{--}3)$$

where m is the number of times that the *periodic* rate, i, compounds in a year. By changing the interpretation placed on m, these formulas may be used to obtain j or f from p. That is,

$$j = mp \quad (8\text{--}1a) \qquad \text{and} \qquad f = (1 + p)^m - 1 \quad (9\text{--}3a)$$

where m is interpreted as the number of times that p compounds in a year. (This also makes m the number of annuity payments in a year.) Unless instructed otherwise, calculate interest rates accurate to the nearest 0.01%.

■ **EXAMPLE 12.3A** *FINDING THE RATE OF RETURN ON FUNDS USED TO PURCHASE AN ANNUITY*

A life insurance company advertises that $50,000 will purchase a 20-year annuity paying $420 at the end of each month. What (monthly compounded) nominal rate of return and effective rate of return is the annuity investment earning? (Calculate interest rates accurate to 0.01%.)

✓ **SOLUTION**

The payments constitute an ordinary annuity having

$$A_n = \$50{,}000 \qquad R = \$420 \qquad \text{and} \qquad n = 20(12) = 240$$

					Result
ENTER: 50000	420	0	240	⌈COMP⌉	
PRESS: ⌈+/−⌉ ⌈PV⌉	⌈PMT⌉	⌈FV⌉	⌈n⌉	⌈i⌉	0.67143

The nominal interest rate is

$$j = mp = 12(0.67143\%) = 8.06\% \text{ compounded monthly}$$

and the effective interest rate is

$$f = (1 + p)^m - 1 = 1.0067143^{12} - 1 = 0.0836 = 8.36\% \qquad ■$$

---

[2]The calculator takes longer to execute the computation because it too uses an iterative procedure requiring a few seconds to calculate p.

■ EXAMPLE 12.3B   CALCULATING THE RATE OF RETURN REQUIRED TO REACH A SAVINGS GOAL IN A SPECIFIED PERIOD

What semiannually compounded rate of return must Rachel earn in her RRSP if contributions of $3000 at the beginning of each 6-month period are to accumulate to $600,000 after 25 years?

☑ SOLUTION

The payments form an annuity due whose future value after 25 years is to be $600,000. That is,

$$S_n(\text{due}) = \$600{,}000 \qquad R = \$3000 \qquad \text{and} \qquad n = 25(2) = 50$$

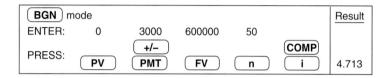

Rachel's RRSP must earn

$$j = mp = 2(4.713\%) = 9.43\% \text{ compounded semiannually} \qquad ■$$

■ EXAMPLE 12.3C   CALCULATING THE IMPLIED DISCOUNT RATE IN A CAPITALIZED LEASE

Camco Manufacturing has recorded a new 5-year lease as a long-term liability of $47,341. If the lease payments are $3000 at the beginning of each quarter, what quarterly compounded discount rate was used in valuing the lease?

☑ SOLUTION

Generally Accepted Accounting Principles (GAAP) require the initial liability for a capital lease to be recorded as the present value of all the lease payments discounted at the firm's cost of borrowing. The lease payments form an annuity due with

$$A_n(\text{due}) = \$47{,}341 \qquad R = \$3000 \qquad \text{and} \qquad n = 5(4) = 20$$

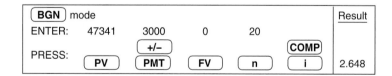

The discount rate used in valuing the lease was

$$j = mp = 4(2.648\%) = 10.59\% \text{ compounded quarterly} \qquad ■$$

■ EXAMPLE 12.3D   CALCULATING THE IMPLIED INTEREST RATE FOR AN INSTALMENT PAYMENT OPTION

Rolling Meadows Golf and Country Club allows members to pay annual dues in a single payment of $1714 at the beginning of the year or in payments of $160.50 at the beginning of each month. What is the effective rate of interest being paid by members who choose the monthly payment plan?

✓ SOLUTION

In effect, the golf club lends the $1714 annual membership fee to members who choose the monthly payment option. These members then repay the "loan" by 12 beginning-of-month payments of $160.50. As an aside, the total "interest" effectively charged is

$$12(\$160.50) - \$1714.00 = \$212.00$$

The solution idea invokes the fundamental principle that the original "loan" equals the present value of all the payments. We need to calculate the discount rate that makes $1714 the present value of the 12 payments. The payments constitute an annuity due having

$$A_n(\text{due}) = \$1714 \qquad R = \$160.50 \qquad \text{and} \qquad n = 12$$

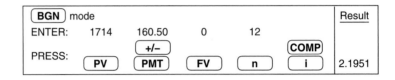

The effective interest rate used to discount the payments was

$$f = (1 + p)^m - 1 = 1.021951^{12} - 1 = 0.2977 = 29.77\%$$

The effect of the dues structure is that monthly dues members are being charged an effective interest rate[3] of 29.77% on the unpaid balance of their dues.   ■

■EXAMPLE 12.3E   CALCULATING THE IMPLIED RETURN ON INVESTMENT EARNED BY BULK PURCHASES INSTEAD OF SMALL PERIODIC PURCHASES

Darla and Matthew buy $60 worth of canned goods at the beginning of each month. When they arrive at the grocery store for the current month's shopping, a case lot sale featuring 20% off the regular prices is in progress. Calculate their effective return on investment if they "invest" in a year's supply of canned goods instead of paying the regular price for 1 month's supply at the beginning of every month.

✓ SOLUTION

The alternatives being considered are

- Paying $60 at the beginning of each month.
- Buying a year's supply at a total cost of $12(\$60)(1 - 0.2) = \$576$

The rate of return on investment[4] will be the discount rate that makes the present value of the twelve $60 "payments" equal to $576. These payments form an annuity *due* having

$$A_n(\text{due}) = \$576 \qquad R = \$60 \qquad \text{and} \qquad n = 12$$

---

[3] The effective rate of interest being charged is substantially more than

$$\frac{\text{Total "interest" charged}}{\text{Initial amount of the "loan"}} \times 100\% = \frac{\$212}{\$1714} \times 100\% = 12.4\%$$

because (*a*) the "borrower" does not have use of the entire $1714 for the whole year and (*b*) most interest is paid before the end of the year. Since the average principal balance during the year will be only about $800, the first factor alone will roughly double the conceptually flawed estimate of 12.4%.

[4] The total "savings" are $12(\$60) - \$576 = \$144$

BGN mode					Result
ENTER:	576	60	0	12	
PRESS:	+/− PV	PMT	FV	n	COMP i	4.3444

The effective rate of return on investment is

$$f = (1 + p)^m - 1 = 1.043444^{12} - 1 = 0.6658 = 66.58\%$$ ■

■ EXAMPLE 12.3F CALCULATING THE INTEREST RATE EQUIVALENT OF A CASH REBATE

When car sales are sluggish, it is common for automobile manufacturers to offer new car purchasers the choice of a cash rebate or interest rates that are significantly lower than may be obtained from financial institutions. For example, a manufacturer's advertisement might boldly announce, "3.9% factory financing over 48 months or $1500 cash back." If a car buyer finances $15,000 of a car's purchase price at the low interest rate instead of paying cash and qualifying for the $1500 rebate, what is the buyer's effective rate of interest?

✓ SOLUTION

To determine the true cost of the 3.9% financing, we should compare the following alternatives available to the car buyer.

- Borrowing $15,000 at 3.9% from the car manufacturer.
- Borrowing $13,500 elsewhere at prevailing rates and paying cash for the car, thereby qualifying for the $1500 rebate.

A front-end cost of the "cheap" 3.9% financing is the forgone $1500 rebate. If the monthly payments on a $13,500 loan over 48 months at the prevailing market interest rate are lower than the payments on the $15,000 loan at 3.9%, the customer will be further ahead borrowing the lesser amount at the higher rate.

We will solve the problem by calculating the interest rate on a 4-year $13,500 loan that will make the monthly payments exactly the same as those on a 4-year $15,000 loan at 3.9%. Although it is generally not made clear in the advertisements, the manufacturer's quoted rates are monthly compounded rates.

The payments on the 4-year $15,000 loan form an ordinary annuity having

$$A_n = \$15,000 \quad n = 48 \quad \text{and} \quad p = i = \frac{3.9\%}{12} = 0.325\%$$

Compute the payments on the $15,000 loan.					Result
ENTER:	15000	0	0.325	48	
PRESS:	PV	FV	i	n	COMP PMT	−338.02

The rate of return on the initial "investment" of $576 will be more than double the amount:

$$\frac{\text{Total savings}}{\text{Total expenditure}} \times 100\% = \frac{\$144}{\$576} \times 100\% = 25\%$$

because (a) the average "investment" throughout the year will be only about half of the initial expenditure of $576, and (b) Darla and Matthew do not have to wait a full year for the "investment returns"—some savings are realised every month.

Next determine the interest rate on a 4-year, $13,500 loan that would have the same monthly payment.

Compute p on a $13,500 4-year loan if $R = \$338.02$.	Result
ENTER: 13500 338.02 0 48	
PRESS: PV +/− PMT FV n COMP i	0.7769

The buyer's effective rate of interest on the 3.9% financing option is

$$f = (1 + p)^m - 1 = 1.00776912 - 1 = 0.0973 = 9.73\%$$

If the car buyer can obtain financing from another source at an effective rate below 9.73%, it would be better to borrow $13,500 from that source rather than $15,000 at 3.9% (compounded monthly) through the car dealer.

Consumer credit legislation requires lenders offering the cash-back/reduced-interest rate alternatives to include the cash rebate in disclosures of the cost of borrowing and the true interest rate. However, industry practices and terminology are inconsistent. In some cases the quoted "effective interest rate" really is the effective rate as we have defined it, but in other instances it is what we have been calling the nominal annual rate. ∎

EXERCISE 12.3

Answers to the odd-numbered problems are at the end of the book.

Calculate all interest rates accurate to the nearest 0.01%.

Calculate the nominal and effective rates of interest for each of the annuities in problems 1 through 16. Find the nominal rate whose compounding frequency equals the payment frequency.

Problem	Present or future value ($)	Type of annuity	Payment interval	Periodic payment ($)	Term of annuity
1.	$PV = 27{,}207.34$	Ordinary	1 year	4000.00	10 years
2.	$PV = 100{,}000$	Ordinary	6 months	6918.51	$12\frac{1}{2}$ years
3.	$PV = 50{,}000$	Ordinary	3 months	2377.16	7 years, 9 months
4.	$PV = 35{,}820$	Ordinary	1 month	500.00	$8\frac{3}{4}$ years
5.	$FV = 500{,}000$	Ordinary	6 months	3030.02	25 years
6.	$FV = 291{,}955$	Ordinary	3 months	2500.00	$13\frac{1}{4}$ years
7.	$FV = 100{,}000$	Ordinary	1 month	251.33	15 years, 5 months
8.	$FV = 138{,}809$	Ordinary	1 month	775.00	$9\frac{1}{4}$ years
9.	$FV = 75{,}000$	Due	6 months	1557.78	11 years, 6 months
10.	$PV = 18{,}143$	Due	1 year	2000.00	18 years
11.	$FV = 37{,}670$	Due	3 months	500.00	$9\frac{1}{2}$ years
12.	$PV = 45{,}000$	Due	1 month	533.42	13 years, 8 months
13.	$FV = 75{,}000$	Ordinary	1 month	318.07	11 years
14.	$PV = 48{,}215$	Ordinary	1 year	5000.00	20 years
15.	$FV = 75{,}000$	Due	1 month	357.29	10 years
16.	$PV = 39{,}936$	Due	1 year	5000.00	25 years

17. If $100,000 will purchase a 20-year annuity paying $830 at the end of each month, what monthly compounded nominal (annual) rate and effective rate of interest will the funds invested in the annuity earn?

18. If regular month-end deposits of $200 in a savings account amounted to $7727.62 after 3 years, what monthly compounded nominal (annual) rate and effective rate of interest were paid on the account?

19. After $10\frac{1}{2}$ years of contributions of $2000 at the end of every 6 months to an RRSP, the accumulated amount stood at $65,727.82. What semiannually compounded nominal rate and effective annual rate of return were earned by the funds in the RRSP?

20. What quarterly compounded nominal rate and effective rate of interest are being charged on a $5000 loan if quarterly payments of $302.07 will repay the loan in $5\frac{1}{2}$ years?

21. A $9000, 4-year term loan requires monthly payments of $234.36. What are the monthly compounded nominal rate and the effective rate of interest on the loan?

22. A finance company paid a furniture retailer $1050 for a conditional sale contract requiring 12 end-of-month payments of $100. What effective rate of return will the finance company realize on the purchase?

23. If a furniture retailer offers a financing plan on a $1500 purchase requiring four equal quarterly payments of $400 including the first payment on the purchase date, what effective rate of interest is being charged on the unpaid balance?

24. An RRSP is now worth $223,000 after contributions of $2500 at the beginning of every 6 months for 14 years. What effective rate of return has the plan realised?

25. Pembroke Golf Club's initiation fee is $5500. It offers an instalment payment alternative of $1000 down and $1000 at the end of each year for 5 years. What effective rate of interest is being charged on the instalment plan?

26. For $150,000, Continental Life Insurance Co. will sell a 20-year annuity paying $1200 at the end of each month. What effective rate of return does the annuitant earn?

27. In an insurance settlement for bodily injury, a court awarded Mr. Goodman $103,600 for 2 years' loss of wages of $4000 per month plus interest on the lost wages to the end of the 2 years. What effective rate of interest has the court allowed on the lost wages?

28. If contributions of $1500 at the beginning of every 3 months resulted in an RRSP worth $434,960 after 20 years, what quarterly compounded nominal rate and effective rate of interest did the RRSP earn?

29. As of the date of Victory Machine Shop's most recent financial statements, 3 years remained in the term of a capital lease reported as a long-term liability of $13,824. If the beginning-of-month lease payments are $450, what monthly compounded nominal (annual) discount rate was used in valuing the lease?

30. If a furniture store offers to sell a refrigerator priced at $1195 on a conditional sale contract requiring 12 monthly payments of $110 (including a payment on the date of sale), what effective rate of interest is being charged to the customer?

31. For the past 13 years, Ms. Perrault has contributed $2000 at the beginning of every 6 months to a mutual fund. If the mutual fund statement at the end of the 13 years reports that her fund units are worth a total of $131,483, what has been the semiannually compounded nominal rate and the effective rate of return on her investments over the 13 years?

•32. The annual membership dues in the Rolling Meadows Golf and Country Club can be paid by four payments of $449.40 at the beginning of each calendar quarter instead of by a single payment of $1714 at the beginning of the year. What effective rate of interest is the club charging the quarterly instalment payers on the unpaid balance of their annual dues?

•33. The Stapleton family consumes one 5-kg bag of powdered milk each month. The price is currently $29.50 per bag, but the milk marketing board has just approved general price increases in dairy products that will result in 10% price increases at the retail level within 2 weeks. If the Stapletons "invest" in 12 bags of the powdered milk at the current price and thereby avoid paying the increased price at the end of each of the next 12 months, what will be their effective rate of "return on investment"?

•34. The Lifestyle Fitness and Exercise Centre charges annual membership fees of $300 (in advance) or six "easy" payments of $60 at the beginning of every 2 months. What effective interest rate is a bimonthly member paying on the unpaid balance of the annual dues, assuming that he continues to renew the membership for a full year?

•35. A major daily newspaper charges $120 for an annual subscription paid in advance or $13 per month payable at the end of each month to the carrier. What is the effective interest rate being charged to the monthly payment subscribers?

•36. A magazine offers a 1-year subscription rate of $15.95 and a 3-year subscription rate of $39.95, both payable at the start of the subscription period. Assuming that you intend to continue to subscribe for 3 years and that the 1-year rate does not increase for the next 2 years, what rate of "return on investment" will be earned by paying for a 3-year subscription now instead of three consecutive 1-year subscriptions?

•37. Continental Life Insurance Company of Canada offered $250,000 of term life insurance to a 40-year-old female nonsmoker for an annual premium of $447.50 (in advance) or for monthly premium payments (in advance) of $38.82 by preauthorized cheques. What effective rate of interest is charged to those who pay monthly?

•38. A provincially owned insurance company allows people to purchase automobile insurance coverage for a 1-year or a 3-month term. Individuals purchasing 3-month coverage pay one-fourth of the annual premium plus an added charge of 3% of the annual premium. The same charge must be paid at every 3-month renewal. Given the alternatives of buying a full year's coverage versus four consecutive 3-month policies, what effective interest rate is the insurance company charging the purchasers of 3-month policies?

•39. The same disability insurance policy offers four alternative premium payment plans: an annual premium of $666.96, semiannual premiums of $341.32, quarterly premiums of $172.62, and monthly premiums of $58.85. In every case, the premiums are payable in advance. What effective rate of interest is the insurance company charging clients who pay their premiums:

   a. Semiannually?   *b.* Quarterly?   *c.* Monthly?

•40. A $500,000 life insurance policy for a 26-year-old offers four alternative premium payment plans: an annual premium of $470.00, semiannual premiums of $244.40, quarterly premiums of $123.37, and monthly premiums of $42.30. In every case, the premiums are payable in advance. What effective rate of interest is the insurance company charging if the premium is paid:

   a. Semiannually?   *b.* Quarterly?   *c.* Monthly?

••41. An advertisement for General Motors trucks offered "2.9% 12-month financing or $1000 cash back." A truck buyer financed $17,000 at the low interest rate instead of paying $16,000 cash (after the $1000 rebate). What was the effective rate of interest on the loan if the forgone cash rebate was treated as part of the cost of financing? (The 2.9% interest rate was a monthly compounded nominal annual rate.)

••42. A Chrysler advertisement offered "$1250 cash back or 4.9% factory financing over 48 months" to purchasers of a Dodge Shadow or Plymouth Sundance. A customer financed $10,000 at the low interest rate instead of paying $8750 cash (after the $1250 rebate). What was the effective rate of interest on the loan if the forgone cash rebate was treated as part of the cost of financing? (The 4.9% interest rate was a monthly compounded nominal annual rate.)

*APPENDIX 12A: DERIVATION OF A FORMULA FOR n FROM THE FORMULA FOR S_n

The formula for the future value of an ordinary annuity is

$$S_n = R\left[\frac{(1 + p)^n - 1}{p}\right] \qquad (10\text{--}1)$$

Multiplication of both sides of the equation by $\frac{p}{R}$ gives

$$\frac{pS_n}{R} = (1 + p)^n - 1$$

Rearranging this equation to isolate $(1 + p)^n$ on the left-hand side, we obtain

$$(1 + p)^n = 1 + \frac{pS_n}{R}$$

Now take (natural) logarithms of both sides and use the rule that $\ln(a^k) = k(\ln a)$.

$$n\ln(1 + p) = \ln\left(1 + \frac{pS_n}{R}\right)$$

Therefore,

$$n = \frac{\ln\left(1 + \dfrac{pS_n}{R}\right)}{\ln(1 + p)} \qquad (10\text{--}1a)$$

*APPENDIX 12B: THE TRIAL-AND-ERROR METHOD FOR CALCULATING THE INTEREST RATE PER PAYMENT INTERVAL

The trial-and-error method is a procedure for taking an *estimate* of the solution to an equation and improving upon the estimate. The procedure may be repeated as often as needed to obtain the desired degree of accuracy in the solution. Each repetition of the procedure is called an *iteration*.

To describe the procedure in general terms, let us contemplate a situation where S_n, R, and n are known, and we need to calculate the value for p. Since S_n is known, the appropriate formula to work with is:

$$S_n = R\left[\frac{(1 + p)^n - 1}{p}\right] \qquad (10\text{--}1)$$

The steps in the procedure are listed in the following table.

Step	Comment
1. Divide both sides of the formula by R. Evaluate the left-hand side (LHS).	The steps are the same in any of the other cases where we start with a formula for A_n, S_n(due), or A_n(due).
2. Substitute the most recent estimate for p and evaluate the right-hand side (RHS).	For the very first estimate, make an educated guess at a reasonable value. For example, try $p = 3\%$ for a 3-month payment interval, or $p = 1\%$ for a 1-month payment interval.
3. Compare the values obtained from steps 1 and 2.	Is the RHS side larger or smaller than the LHS?

Step	Comment
4. Choose a new value for p that will make the RHS's value closer to the LHS's value.	Use some intuition here. A higher p makes future values larger but present values smaller. Therefore, a higher p makes compounding factors larger but discount factors smaller.
5. Repeat steps 2, 3, and 4 until p is obtained to the desired accuracy.	As a final optional step to exit the "loop," the *interpolation* procedure described in Appendix 12C may be employed. It uses the last two estimates of p that cause the RHS to be too high in one instance and too low in the other.

Example 12.3a, previously solved using the financial calculator method, will now be repeated as Example 12b to illustrate the trial-and-error method including interpolation.

■ **EXAMPLE 12B** *FINDING THE RATE OF RETURN ON FUNDS USED TO PURCHASE AN ANNUITY*

A life insurance company advertises that $50,000 will purchase a 20-year annuity paying $420 at the end of each month. What nominal and effective rates of return is the annuity investment earning? (Calculate interest rates accurate to 0.02%.)

☑ **SOLUTION**

The payments constitute an ordinary annuity having

$$A_n = \$50,000 \qquad R = \$420 \qquad \text{and} \qquad n = 20(12) = 240$$

Substitute these values in formula (10−4) and divide both sides by $R = \$420$.

$$\frac{\$50,000}{\$420} = 199.05 = \left[\frac{1 - (1 + p)^{-240}}{p}\right]$$

The general trial-and-error procedure suggested an initial guess at p of 1% for each month in the payment interval. The payment interval here is just 1 month. In this instance, we can make our initial guess somewhat more "educated" than simply $p = 1\%$ with the following observation. If each monthly annuity payment of $420 were entirely interest, the interest rate per payment interval would be $\frac{\$420}{\$50,000} \times 100\% = 0.84\%$. Since part of the payment is, in fact, a return of principal, p must be less than 0.84%. Therefore, choose $p = 0.75\%$ as the initial guess.

The results of successive iterations should be tabulated.

Iteration number	Estimate of p	$(1 + p)^{-240}$	RHS
1	0.0075	0.16641	111.14
2	0.0070	0.18747	116.08*
3	0.0067	0.20136	119.20
	p = solution		119.05
4	0.00672	0.20040	118.99

*At this point it can be observed that a 0.0005 decrease in p caused the RHS to increase by about 5. Therefore, a 0.0001 decrease in p will cause the RHS to increase by about 1. Since we still need the RHS to be another 3 units larger, p should be reduced by another 0.0003.

The iterations have continued to the point where iterations 3 and 4 closely "bracket" the solution. In other words, estimate 3 for p gives a value for the RHS that is a little too large, while estimate 4 gives a value for the RHS that is a little too small. This condition is ideal for using interpolation (Appendix 12C) instead of further iterations to improve the estimate. Using the interpolation proportion from Appendix 12C, we obtain

$$\frac{p - 0.0067}{0.00672 - 0.0067} \approx \frac{119.05 - 119.20}{118.99 - 119.20}$$

$$\frac{p - 0.0067}{0.00002} \approx \frac{-0.15}{-0.21}$$

$$p - 0.0067 \approx 0.00002(0.714)$$

$$p \approx 0.0067 + 0.000014$$

$$\approx 0.006714$$

$$\approx 0.6714\%$$

The nominal interest rate is

$$j = mp = 12(0.6714\%) = 8.06\% \text{ compound monthly}$$

and the effective interest rate is

$$f = (1 + p)^m - 1 = 1.006714^{12} - 1 = 0.0836 = 8.36\%$$ ∎

*APPENDIX 12C: INTERPOLATION

Interpolation is a technique used to estimate a value that is not included in a table of values. The ideas and the procedure involved are best illustrated with a numerical example.

x	y
0.0	–2.0
0.5	–1.75
1.0	–1.0
1.5	0.25
2.0	2.0

The table presents a few pairs of values of an independent variable x and the dependent variable y. Suppose that we wish to *estimate* the value for x at which y will equal zero. An inspection of the table reveals that y passes through zero for a value of x somewhere between 1.0 and 1.5. To interpolate means to find the *intermediate* value within an interval.

The values of x and y that bracket the interval containing $y = 0$ are extracted and presented in the x and y columns in Table 12.2. The symbol x_i represents the intermediate value of x at which y equals zero.

TABLE 12.2

Subdividing an Interval for Interpolation

$$1.5 - 1.0 \left\{ \begin{matrix} 1.0 \\ x_i \\ 1.5 \end{matrix} \right\} \; x_i - 1.0 \qquad 0.25 - (-1.0) \left\{ \begin{matrix} -1.0 \\ 0.0 \\ 0.25 \end{matrix} \right\} \; 0 - (-1.0)$$

Interpolation is an application of ratios and proportions. It assumes that x_i splits the interval between $x = 1.0$ and $x = 1.5$ in the same proportional parts as $y = 0$ splits the interval between $y = -1.0$ and $y = 0.25$. Consequently,

$$\frac{\text{Subinterval between } x = 1.0 \text{ and } x_i}{\text{Interval between } x = 1.0 \text{ and } x = 1.5} = \frac{\text{Subinterval between } y = -1.0 \text{ and } y = 0}{\text{Interval between } y = -1.0 \text{ and } y = 0.25}$$

The subintervals and intervals referred to in this proportion are indicated by the braces in Table 12.2. Substituting the sizes of the subintervals and intervals, we have

$$\frac{x_i - 1.0}{1.5 - 1.0} = \frac{0 - (-1.0)}{0.25 - (-1.0)}$$

Solving the proportion for x_i gives $x_i = 1.4$.

You may have already arrived at this result by reasoning that $y = 0$ is four-fifths of the distance through the interval from $y = -1.0$ to $y = 0.25$. Therefore, x_i should be four-fifths of the distance from $x = 1.0$ to $x = 1.5$, that is, at $x = 1.4$. This is good intuition, but a systematic approach is needed for cases where the numbers are not so "nice."

Moving from this particular case to the general case, suppose that (x_i, y_i) is some intermediate point between (x_1, y_1) and (x_2, y_2). Table 12.3 is the general version of Table 12.2.

TABLE   12.3

Interpolation: The General Case

$$x_2 - x_1 \left\{ \begin{array}{c} \overline{x_1} \\ x_i \\ x_2 \end{array} \right\} \; x_i - x_1 \qquad y_2 - y_1 \left\{ \begin{array}{c} \overline{y_1} \\ y_i \\ y_2 \end{array} \right\} \; y_i - y_1$$

In general, the proportion for subdividing two intervals in the same ratio is

**Interpolating
between (x_1, y_1)
and (x_2, y_2)**

$$\boxed{\frac{x_i - x_1}{x_2 - x_1} = \frac{y_i - y_1}{y_2 - y_1}}$$

If either x_i or y_i is known, the *approximate* value of the other may be calculated by solving the proportion for the unknown.

> **Tip**
>
> When substituting numerical values for x_1, y_1, x_2, and y_2, maintain the same order of subscripts on both sides of the proportion.

It was previously stated that the interpolation method *assumes* that the two corresponding intervals are subdivided in the same ratio, and that the resulting answer is usually only an *estimate* or *approximation*. The answer will be strictly correct only in cases where the actual mathematical relation between the variables is linear.[5] The pairs of (x,y) values used earlier in this section were obtained from the nonlinear equation $y = x^2 - 2$. The actual value of x that makes $y = 0$ is $x = 1.414$ (to four-figure accuracy). The smaller the intervals that are used in the interpolation, the closer the interpolated value will be to the correct result.

---

[5]The interpolation method described here is technically known as *linear interpolation* because it assumes that the mathematical relationship between the two variables is linear (at least within the interval under consideration).

Interpolation is most commonly used to estimate values that fall within the intervals in tables of values. The trial-and-error method for solving nonlinear equations can use interpolation as a final step to improve the accuracy of the solution.

■ EXAMPLE 12C   *INTERPOLATING IN A TABLE OF VALUES*

Table 12.4 is extracted from an extensive set of monthly mortgage tables. These tables enable the user to look up the monthly payment per $1000 of the initial mortgage loan for various lengths of the repayment period, and for various (semiannually compounded) rates of interest on the loan. If the actual value of the interest rate or of the loan duration in a particular case is not provided in the table, interpolation may be used, as demonstrated below, to estimate the monthly payment per $1000 of the loan.

TABLE   12.4

Monthly Payment to Repay a $1000 Mortgage Loan

Loan duration (years)	Interest rate		
	9.5%	10.5%	11.5%
3	$31.95	$32.40	$32.85
4	25.04	25.50	25.96
5	20.91	21.38	21.86
7	16.25	16.74	17.25
10	12.84	13.37	13.91
12	11.56	12.11	12.67
15	10.33	10.92	11.51
20	9.20	9.83	10.48
25	8.61	9.28	9.97

a. Determine the monthly payment required on a $75,000 mortgage loan at an interest rate of 10.5% to be repaid over 18 years.

b. Determine the monthly payment required on a $95,000 mortgage loan at an interest rate of 9.9% to be repaid over 5 years.

☑ SOLUTION

a. First use interpolation to determine the monthly payment on a $1000 mortgage at 10.5% for 18 years. Then multiply that payment by 75 to obtain the monthly payment on a $75,000 mortgage with the same terms.

Construct a table that shows the durations and monthly payments (from the 10.5% column in Table 12.4) that bracket the target values.

Loan duration	Monthly payment
$\left\{\begin{array}{c}15\\18\\20\end{array}\right.$	$\left\{\begin{array}{c}\$10.92\\m_i\\9.83\end{array}\right.$

$$\frac{18 - 15}{20 - 15} = \frac{m_i - \$10.92}{\$9.83 - \$10.92}$$
Equate the ratios for subinterval : full interval

$$\frac{3}{5} = \frac{m_i - \$10.92}{-\$1.09}$$
Simplify

$$m_i - \$10.92 = -\$1.09 \times \frac{3}{5}$$
Solve for m_i

$$m_i = -\$0.654 + \$10.92 = \$10.266$$
$$\text{Monthly payment} = 75 \times \$10.266 = \$769.95$$

The correct figure for the monthly payment is actually $763.32. The interpolation approximation used with the values in Table 12.4 has resulted in an error of $6.63. Relative to the size of the payment, the error is less than 1%. The error would be smaller if monthly payments were known for durations closer to 18 years.

b. Construct a table showing the interest rates and monthly payments (from the "5 years" row in Table 12.4) that bracket the target values.

Interest rate	Monthly payment
9.5%	$20.91
9.9	m_i
10.5	21.38

$$\frac{9.9 - 9.5}{10.5 - 9.5} = \frac{m_i - \$20.91}{\$21.38 - \$20.91} \qquad \text{Equate ratios}$$

$$\frac{0.4}{1.0} = \frac{m_i - \$20.91}{\$0.47} \qquad \text{Simplify}$$

$$m_i = (0.4 \times \$0.47) + \$20.91 \qquad \text{Solve}$$
$$= \$21.098$$

$$\text{Monthly payment} = 95 \times \$21.098 = \$2004.31$$

The exact answer is $2004.56. The approximation in this case is very good. ∎

EXERCISE 12C

Answers to the odd-numbered problems are at the end of the book.

1. From the following table of values for x and y, estimate by interpolation:

   a. The value for x at which $y = 0$.

   b. The value for x at which $y = -0.55$.

   c. The value for y when $x = 3.15$.

x	y
1.0	−1.500
1.5	−1.375
2.0	−1.000
2.5	−0.375
3.0	0.500
3.5	1.625

2. Using Table 12.4 estimate the monthly payment required on a mortgage loan of $64,500 at an interest rate of 10.7% to be repaid over 15 years.

3. Using Table 12.4, estimate the monthly payment required on a mortgage loan of $77,400 at an interest rate of 9.5% to be repaid over 6 years and 6 months.

4. Using Table 12.4, estimate the monthly payment required on a mortgage loan of $59,800 at an interest rate of 11.5% to be repaid over 4 years and 3 months.

REVIEW PROBLEMS

Answers to the odd-numbered problems are at the end of the book.

Interest rates should be calculated accurate to the nearest 0.01%.

1. Calculate the amounts that must be invested at the end of every 6 months at 7.75% compounded semiannually in order to accumulate $500,000 after:

    a. 20 years.   *b.* 30 years.

2. What month-end payments discounted at 8.25% compounded monthly will have a present value of $50,000 if the payments run for:

    a. 15 years?   *b.* 30 years?

3. What maximum annual withdrawals will a $300,000 fund earning 7.75% compounded annually sustain for 25 years if the withdrawals are made:

    a. At the beginning of each year?   *b.* At the end of each year?

4. How many more deposits of $1000 at the beginning of each quarter will it take to accumulate savings of $100,000 than it will take deposits of $1100 at the beginning of each quarter, if the savings earn 6% compounded quarterly?

5. For $100,000, Royal Life Insurance Co. will sell a 20-year annuity paying $802.76 at the end of each month. What monthly compounded nominal rate and effective rate of return does the annuitant earn on the invested funds?

6. If $400,000 accumulated in an RRSP is used to purchase an annuity earning 7.2% compounded monthly and paying $4500 at the end of each month, what will be the term of the annuity?

7. After contributing $2000 at the end of each quarter for $13\frac{3}{4}$ years, Foster has accumulated $205,064 in his RRSP. What effective annual rate of return was earned by the RRSP over the entire period?

8. What semiannually compounded nominal rate and effective rate of interest are being charged on a $12,000 loan if semiannual payments of $1204.55 will repay the loan in 7 years?

9. An RRSP is now worth $316,000 after contributions of $3500 at the beginning of every 6 months for 17 years. What effective rate of return has the plan realised?

10. How much longer will it take to pay off a $100,000 loan with monthly payments of $1000 than with monthly payments of $1050, if the interest rate on the loan is 9% compounded monthly?

11. If $100,000 will purchase a 20-year annuity paying $739 per month, what monthly compounded nominal rate and effective rate of interest do the funds invested in the annuity earn?

12. Suppose that $5000 is contributed at the beginning of each year to an RRSP that earns 8% compounded annually.

    a. How many contributions will it take to accumulate the first $500,000?

    b. How many more contributions will it take for the RRSP to accumulate the second $500,000?

13. An annuity purchased for $175,000 pays $4000 at the end of every quarter. How long will the payments continue if the funds earn 7% compounded semiannually?

14. A finance company paid a furniture retailer $1934 for a conditional sale contract requiring 12 end-of-month payments of $175. What effective rate of return does the finance company earn on the purchase?

15. The membership dues at Shoreline Golf and Country Club are $1410 payable at the beginning of the year, or four payments of $368.28 payable at the beginning of each quarter. What effective rate of interest is the club charging members who pay their dues quarterly?

16. Apex Fabricating wants to accumulate $800,000 as the equity portion of the financing required for an expansion expected to begin in 4 years. If today Apex makes the first of equal quarterly payments into a fund earning 6.75% compounded monthly, what should the size of these payments be?

17. How many more RRSP contributions of $300 at the beginning of every month are required to surpass $200,000 if the funds earn 8% compounded monthly than if they earn 10% compounded monthly?

18. As of the date of Colony Farm's most recent financial statements, $3\frac{1}{2}$ years remained in the term of a capital lease reported as a long-term liability of $26,244. If the beginning-of-month lease payments are $750, what monthly compounded nominal (annual) discount rate was used in valuing the lease?

19. If a furniture store offers to sell a washer-dryer combination priced at $1395 on a conditional sale contract requiring 12 monthly payments of $125 (including a payment on the date of sale), what effective rate of interest is being charged?

20. A magazine offers a 1-year subscription rate of $23.95 and a 3-year subscription rate of $59.95, both payable at the beginning of the subscription period. Assuming that you intend to continue to subscribe for 3 years and that the 1-year subscription rate does not increase for the next 2 years, what effective rate of return on "investment" will be earned by paying for a 3-year subscription now instead of three consecutive 1-year subscriptions?

21. Sovereign Life Insurance Company of Canada offers $250,000 of term life insurance to a 45-year-old male for an annual premium of $716 (in advance) or for monthly premium payments (in advance) of $62.50 by preauthorized cheques. What effective rate of interest is charged to those who pay monthly?

22. Howardson Electric obtained a $90,000 loan at 9.75% compounded monthly. What size of semiannual payments will repay the loan in 10 years?

23. Fred is about to have his 27th birthday. He has set a goal of retiring at age 58 with $1,000,000 in his RRSP. For planning purposes, he is assuming that his RRSP will earn 8% compounded annually.

    a. What contributions on each birthday from age 27 to 57 inclusive will be required to accumulate the desired amount in his RRSP?

    b. If he waits 5 years before starting his RRSP, what contributions on each birthday from age 32 to 57 inclusive will be required to reach the target?

•24. The interest rate on a $100,000 loan is 9.5% compounded quarterly.

    a. What quarterly payments will reduce the balance to $75,000 after 5 years?

    b. If the same payments continue, what will be the balance 10 years after the date that the loan was received?

•25. Mr. Braun wants the value of his RRSP 25 years from now to have the purchasing power of $400,000 in current dollars.

    a. Assuming an inflation rate of 4% per year, what nominal dollar amount should Mr. Braun have in his RRSP after 25 years?

    b. What contributions should he make at the end of every 3 months to achieve the goal if his RRSP earns 7.5% compounded semiannually?

•26. *a.* How long will it take monthly payments of $600 to repay a $65,000 loan if the interest rate on the loan is 9.5% compounded semiannually?

   b. How much will the time to repay the loan be reduced if the payments are $50 per month larger?

•27. A 70-year-old male can purchase the annuities described below from a life insurance company for the same lump amount. A 20-year-term annuity will pay $394 at each month-end. A life annuity will pay $440 at the end of each month until the death of the annuitant. Beyond what age must the man survive for the life annuity to have the greater economic value? Use 7.2% compounded monthly as the time value of money.

•28. Angelo borrowed $250 per month from his mother at the beginning of every month for $3\frac{1}{2}$ years while he attended university.

   a. If the interest rate on the accumulating debt was 5% compounded semiannually, what amount did he owe his mother at the end of the $3\frac{1}{2}$-year period?

   b. He made the first monthly payment of $200 on the loan at the end of the first month following the $3\frac{1}{2}$-year period. How long after the end of the $3\frac{1}{2}$-year period will it take him to repay the loan?

•29. The Ciminelli family uses one economy-size box of laundry detergent every 3 months. The price is normally $12.50 per box, but the detergent is currently on "special" for $10.75 per box. If Mrs. Ciminelli "invests" in four extra boxes at the sale price today instead of buying the detergent at the regular price when needed 3, 6, 9, and 12 months from now, what will be her effective rate of "return on investment"?

•30. Suppose that $5000 is contributed at the beginning of each year for 25 years to an RRSP that earns 10% compounded annually. By what percentage would annual contributions have to be increased in order to have the same future value after 25 years if the plan earns only 8% compounded annually?

•31. Suppose you contribute $2000 to an RRSP at the beginning of every 6 months for 25 years, and then use the accumulated funds to purchase an annuity paying $2500 at the beginning of each month. How long after the start of the annuity will the last payment be made? Assume that the RRSP earns 8% compounded semiannually and the funds invested in the annuity earn 7.5% compounded monthly.

•32. Capital Leasing calculates its 5-year lease rates so that it recovers the capital cost of the equipment plus a rate of return on investment of 16% compounded semiannually over the term of the lease. What will be the required lease payments on a machine that cost $35,000 if the lease payments are made:

   a. At the beginning of every month?

   b. At the beginning of each 6-month period?

•33. Noreen's RRSP is currently worth $125,000. She plans to contribute for 10 more years and then let the plan continue to grow through internal earnings for an additional 5 years. If the RRSP earns 8% compounded annually, how much must she contribute at the end of every 6 months for the next 10 years to have $500,000 in the RRSP 15 years from now?

••34. Yvette Pronovost's financial plan is designed to accumulate enough funds in her RRSP over the next 30 years that she can then purchase an annuity paying $7000 at the end of each month for 25 years. She will be able to contribute $5000 to her RRSP at the end of each year for the next 10 years. What year-end contributions must she make for the subsequent 20 years to achieve her objective? For these projections, assume that Yvette's RRSP will earn 8% compounded annually and that the annuity payments are based on a return of 7.5% compounded monthly.

396 521.14

••35. By the time he turns 60, Justin (just turned age 31) wants to accumulate an amount in his RRSP that will have the purchasing power of $250,000 in current dollars. What annual contributions on his 32nd through 60th birthdays inclusive are required to meet this goal if the RRSP earns 8% compounded annually and the rate of inflation is 4% per year?

SELF-TEST EXERCISE

Answers to the self-test problems are at the end of the book.

1. The interest rate on a $30,000 loan is 11.25% compounded monthly.

   a. What monthly payments are required to pay off the loan in 8 years?

   b. What monthly payments would be required to reduce the balance to $10,000 after 5 years?

2. How much sooner will a $65,000 loan at 10.5% compounded monthly be paid off if the monthly payments are $625 instead of $600? What will be the approximate saving in total (nominal) interest costs over the life of the loan?

3. Excel Leasing calculates the payments on long-term equipment leases so that it earns a 15% compounded quarterly rate of return on its capital investment in the equipment. What beginning-of-month payments will Excel charge on a 4-year lease of a photocopier costing $7650?

4. If $2000 is contributed to an RRSP at the end of every 6 months for 20 years, what effective rate of return must the funds in the plan earn if it is to be worth $250,000 at the end of the 20 years?

5. What payments must be made at the end of each quarter to an RRSP earning 7.5% compounded annually so that its value $8\frac{1}{2}$ years from now will be $15,000?

6. A promissory note requiring quarterly payments of $500 was sold for $7147.52 just after a scheduled payment. The note was discounted to yield the buyer 15% compounded monthly. How long did the note have to run after the date of sale?

7. The McGowans are arranging a $90,000 mortgage loan from their bank. The interest rate on the loan will be 7.9% compounded semiannually.

   a. What will the monthly payments be if the loan has a 20-year term?

   b. If the McGowans choose to pay $800 per month, how long will it take to pay off the loan?

•8. Ms. Bowers wants to be able to purchase a 20-year annuity at age 62 that will pay her $3500 at the beginning of each month. If she starts making quarterly contributions to an RRSP on her 35th birthday and continues them up to but not including her 62nd birthday, what should be the size of each contribution? Assume that her RRSP will earn 8% compounded quarterly and that the annuity fund will earn 7.5% compounded monthly.

•9. Mr. and Mrs. Zolob contributed $50 on the first of each month to an RESP they set up for their grandson Jeff. By the time he entered Mohawk College, 14 years and 5 months of contributions had accumulated. The grandparents' contributions stopped, and Jeff started beginning-of-month withdrawals of $500. How long will these payments last if the RESP has earned and will continue to earn 8.25% compounded monthly?

•10. A series of $500 contributions were made at 3-month intervals to a fund earning 7.5% compounded quarterly. The accumulated amount continued to earn 7.5% compounded quarterly for 3 years after the last contribution, ending the period at $13,232.56. How many $500 contributions were made?

•11. New Look Fitness Centre offers a 1-year membership for $250 in advance or a 3-month membership for $80 in advance. What effective rate of interest is an individual paying if she buys four consecutive 3-month memberships instead of a 1-year membership?

•12. A life insurance company is calculating the monthly premium that it will offer clients as an alternative to paying the full annual premium. With both alternatives, premiums are payable at the beginning of the period of coverage. If the monthly payment by preauthorized cheque is calculated to yield the insurance company 16% compounded semiannually on the unpaid balance of the annual premium, what should be the monthly premium per $100 of annual premium?

••13. An advertisement for Ford trucks offered "5.9% financing (for 48 months) or $2000 cash back." A truck buyer financed $20,000 at the low interest rate instead of paying $18,000 cash (after the $2000 rebate). What was the effective rate of interest on the loan if the forgone cash rebate is treated as part of the cost of financing? (The 5.9% interest rate is a monthly compounded nominal annual rate.)

SUMMARY OF NOTATION AND KEY FORMULAS

In the context of formulas (8–1a) and (9–3a) below,

m = the number of annuity payment intervals in a year

Formula (10–1a) $\quad n = \dfrac{\ln\left(1 + \dfrac{pS_n}{R}\right)}{\ln(1 + p)}$ $\qquad$ Finding the number of annuity payments given S_n, R, and p

Formula (10–4a) $\quad n = -\dfrac{\ln\left(1 - \dfrac{pA_n}{R}\right)}{\ln(1 + p)}$ $\qquad$ Finding the number of annuity payments given A_n, R, and p

Formula (11–1a) $\quad n = \dfrac{\ln\left[1 + \dfrac{pS_n(\text{due})}{R(1 + p)}\right]}{\ln(1 + p)}$ $\qquad$ Finding the number of annuity payments given $S_n(\text{due})$, R, and p

Formula (11–2a) $\quad n = -\dfrac{\ln\left[1 - \dfrac{pA_n(\text{due})}{R(1 + p)}\right]}{\ln(1 + p)}$ $\qquad$ Finding the number of annuity payments given $A_n(\text{due})$, R, and p

Formula (8–1a) $\quad j = mp$ $\qquad$ Finding the nominal interest rate corresponding to p

Formula (9–3a) $\quad f = (1 + p)^m - 1$ $\qquad$ Finding the effective interest rate corresponding to p

13

OTHER ANNUITIES

CHAPTER OUTLINE

13.1 Perpetuities

13.2 Deferred Annuities

13.3 Integrated Applications

LEARNING OBJECTIVES

After completing this chapter, you will be able to:

- For a perpetuity, calculate either present value, payment size, or periodic interest rate, given values of the other two quantities

- For a deferred annuity, calculate either present value, future value, payment size, number of payments, or period of deferral, given values of the other

four quantities and the periodic interest rate

- Analyse scenarios involving combinations of lump payments and annuities, and requiring the integration of two or more topics covered in Chapters 8 through 13

INTRODUCTION

Two special cases of annuities are examined in this chapter. The first is *perpetuities*—annuities with payments that continue forever. The mathematics of perpetuities turns out to be surprisingly simple. The second special case is *deferred* annuities, in which the start of the payments is delayed. For example, a retiring employee might use a lump-sum retirement allowance to purchase from a life insurance company a 20-year annuity with monthly payments that would start after a 3-year period of deferral. To conclude our study of annuities, we consider some comprehensive problems involving elements from various topics covered in Chapters 8 through 13.

13.1 PERPETUITIES

A **perpetuity** is an annuity with payments that continue forever. An individual might, for example, donate or bequeath a substantial amount of money to a college to establish a scholarship fund that is to pay out a fixed dollar amount of scholarship awards each year forever. The initial amount used to establish a perpetuity is sometimes called an *endowment.* The endowment is invested, and the perpetuity payments are made from the investment earnings. Suppose, for example, that a $100,000 bequest is made to Humber College to endow a perpetual bursary fund. If the college invests the funds to earn an effective annual rate of 7%, $7000 can be paid out in bursaries on each anniversary of the bequest. The principal amount will neither grow nor diminish in subsequent years.

PRESENT VALUE OF AN ORDINARY PERPETUITY

Figure 13.1 presents a time diagram for an *ordinary* perpetuity with payments of size R at the *end* of each payment interval.

FIGURE   13.1

Time Diagram for the Payments of an Ordinary Perpetuity

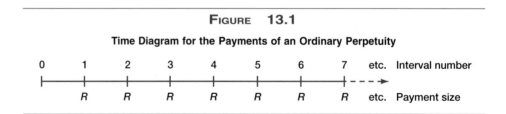

The formula for the relationship between the payment size and the initial amount required to sustain the payments in perpetuity is easily derived. Let

A = Initial endowment or principal amount funding an *ordinary* perpetuity

Suppose the endowment is invested to earn an interest rate p per payment interval. The dollar amount of interest earned in the first payment interval will be Ap. If this interest is paid out instead of being added to the original principal, the principal at the beginning of the second payment interval will remain at A. It will again earn interest Ap during the second payment interval. Therefore, we see that Ap can be paid out at the end of every payment interval and the principal will remain at A. In summary, an amount A earning p per payment interval can sustain periodic payments of

$$R = Ap$$

forever.

Since a lump amount A can be invested to generate a perpetuity with payments Ap, then A can also be interpreted as the single amount at the *beginning* of a perpetuity that is economically equivalent to the perpetuity (when money can earn p per payment interval). In Chapter 10, we defined the present value of an annuity as its economically equivalent amount at the beginning of the annuity. Accordingly, a third interpretation of A is that it represents the present value of the perpetuity.

Present Value of an Ordinary Perpetuity

$$A = \frac{R}{p} \qquad (13\text{--}1)$$

If the payment interval equals the compounding interval, then $p = i$ and the perpetuity is an ordinary *simple* perpetuity. Otherwise, we have an ordinary *general* perpetuity and p must be calculated using formula (10–2), that is, $p = (1 + i)^c - 1$.

The future value of any perpetuity is an undefined or *indeterminate* quantity. Conceptually, it represents the accumulated amount from an infinite number of payments plus interest thereon for an infinite length of time.

■ EXAMPLE 13.1A   CALCULATING THE ENDOWMENT AND THE REQUIRED RATE OF RETURN TO SUSTAIN AN ORDINARY PERPETUITY

A chartered bank is considering the establishment in perpetuity of the Visiting Professor Chair in Public Policy at a university. The cost would be $7500 at the end of each month.

a. If money can earn 6% compounded monthly in perpetuity, what endowment would be required to fund the position?

b. What monthly compounded nominal rate would an endowment of $1.25 million have to earn to fully fund the position?

☑ SOLUTION

a. The payments form an ordinary simple perpetuity having

$$R = \$7500 \qquad \text{and} \qquad p = i = 0.5\% \text{ per month.}$$

The required endowment is

$$A = \frac{R}{p} = \frac{\$7500}{0.005} = \$1,500,000$$

b. With $A = \$1,250,000$ and $R = \$7500$ per month, the required interest rate per payment interval is

$$p = \frac{R}{A} = \frac{\$7500}{\$1,250,000} = 0.006 = 0.6\% \text{ per month}$$

The required nominal rate of return is

$$j = mp = 12(0.6\%) = 7.2\% \text{ compounded monthly} \qquad ■$$

■ EXAMPLE 13.1B   CALCULATING THE PRICE OF A PERPETUAL PREFERRED SHARE

Some preferred shares promise a fixed periodic dividend in perpetuity.

a. What is the fair market value of a perpetual preferred share just after payment of its quarterly $0.50 dividend if the market requires a return of 7.5% compounded quarterly on preferred share issues of similar risk?

b. What will be an investor's quarterly compounded nominal rate of return if she is able to purchase these shares at $25.00 each?

☑ SOLUTION

Invoking the Valuation Principle, the fair market value of a share is the present value of the expected dividend payments discounted at the rate of return required in the financial market. Viewed from the purchase date, the dividend payments form an ordinary simple perpetuity.

a. We want the present value, *A*, when payments of *R* = $0.50 are discounted at

$$p = i = \frac{7.5\%}{4} = 1.875\% \text{ per payment interval. Then}$$

$$A = \frac{R}{p} = \frac{\$0.50}{0.01875} = \$26.67$$

Thus, the fair market value of a share is $26.67.

b. If the investor can purchase the shares at a lower price than the fair market value in *a*, her rate of return will be greater than 7.5% compounded quarterly because she will receive the same dividends from a smaller investment. The return per payment interval will be

$$p = \frac{R}{A} = \frac{\$0.50}{\$25.00} = 0.02 = 2\%$$

The nominal rate of return will be

$$j = mp = 4(2\%) = 8\% \text{ compounded quarterly} \qquad \blacksquare$$

PRESENT VALUE OF A PERPETUITY DUE

The payments in a perpetuity *due* are made at the *beginning* of each payment interval and continue forever. Comparing Figure 13.2 with Figure 13.1, it can be seen that a perpetuity *due* is equivalent to an immediate payment *R* followed by an *ordinary* perpetuity. Therefore, the present value of a perpetuity due, *A*(due), is *R* plus the present value of an ordinary perpetuity. That is,

$$A(\text{due}) = R + A = Ap + A = A(1 + p)$$

FIGURE 13.2

Time Diagram for a Perpetuity Due

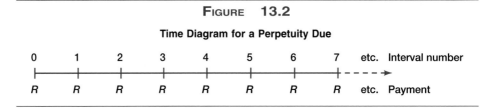

This result could also have been anticipated from our knowledge that the present value of an annuity *due* is (1 + *p*) times the present value of an *ordinary* annuity.

**Present Value of a
Perpetuity Due**

$$\boxed{\begin{aligned} A(\text{due}) &= A(1 + p) \\ &= \frac{R}{p}(1 + p) \end{aligned}}$$

(13–2)

As in the case of an ordinary perpetuity, $A(\text{due})$ has three interpretations:

- The initial endowment required to fund a perpetuity due.
- The lump amount at the *beginning* of a perpetuity due that is economically equivalent to the perpetuity (if money can earn p per payment interval).
- The present value of a perpetuity due.

■ EXAMPLE 13.1c   *A PERPETUITY BEGINNING AFTER A PERIOD OF DEFERRAL*

Mrs. Paquette set up a trust fund with an initial contribution of $150,000. The funds are to be immediately invested, and the first semiannual payment of a perpetuity is to be made in 5 years. The payments are to be used for the care of her disabled son for the rest of his life and then paid to the Canadian Diabetes Society. If the funds in trust earn 7% compounded semiannually, what are the maximum payments that the trust can make in perpetuity?

☑ SOLUTION

The solution idea is shown in the time diagram below. The future value of the $150,000 contribution after 5 years will be the amount funding the perpetuity.

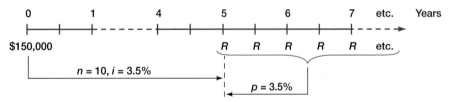

Viewed from the focal date 5 years from now, the payments form a perpetuity *due* with $p = i = 3.5\%$. The word equation for the solution idea is

Future value of $150,000 = Present value of perpetuity due

Using formulas (8–2) and (13–2),

$$P(1 + i)^n = \frac{R}{p}(1 + p)$$

$$\$150,000(1.035)^{10} = \frac{R}{0.035}(1.035)$$

$$\$211,589.81 = R(29.571429)$$

$$R = \$7155.21$$

The trust can make semiannual payments of $7155.21 in perpetuity.   ■

■ EXAMPLE 13.1d   *CALCULATING THE INITIAL ENDOWMENT FOR A GENERAL PERPETUITY*

What amount must be placed today in a perpetual fund earning 8% compounded semiannually if monthly payments of $500 in perpetuity are to start

a. Today?

b. 1 month from today?

c. 1 year from today?

☑ SOLUTION

In every case, the required initial amount is the present value *today* of the payments. Since payments are made monthly but compounding takes place semiannually, the payments in each part form a *general* perpetuity having

$$R = \$500 \qquad i = \frac{8\%}{2} = 4\% \qquad c = \frac{2}{12} = 0.1\overline{6} \qquad \text{and}$$

$$p = (1 + i)^c - 1 = 1.04^{0.1\overline{6}} - 1 = 0.006558197$$

a. The payments constitute a general perpetuity *due.* Using formula (13–2), we obtain

$$A(\text{due}) = \frac{\$500}{0.006558197}(1.006558197) = \$76,740.47$$

The initial endowment required is $76,740.47.

b. With today as the focal date, the payments form an *ordinary* general perpetuity. Formula (13–1) can be used to calculate the required initial endowment. Since we already have the present value of the perpetuity *due* in part *a,* we can instead use the observation from earlier in the section that $A(\text{due}) = A + R$. Then

$$A = A(\text{due}) - R = \$76,740.47 - \$500 = \$76,240.47$$

The initial amount required to fund the perpetuity is $76,240.47.

c. Viewed from a focal date 1 year from now, the payments constitute a general annuity *due.* Therefore, 1 year from now the fund must hold the $76,740.47 amount calculated in part *a* in order to sustain the perpetuity. The amount that must be placed in the fund today is the present value of $76,740.47 on a date 1 year earlier. Using formula (8–2), this present value is

$$P = \frac{S}{(1 + i)^n} = \frac{\$76,740.47}{1.04^2} = \$70,950.88$$

The initial amount that must be placed in the perpetual fund is $70,950.88. ■

EXERCISE 13.1

Answers to the odd-numbered problems are at the end of the book.

1. Mrs. O'Reilly made a bequest of $125,000 to Medicine Hat College for perpetual scholarships for women in business studies. The funds were received in August and the college decided to immediately award the first scholarships. What amount can be awarded every August if the scholarship fund earns 7.5% compounded annually?

2. What amount is required to fund a perpetuity that immediately begins quarterly payments of $2000 if the funds can be invested to earn 8% compounded quarterly?

3. How much more is required to fund a perpetuity due than an ordinary perpetuity, if both are to make semiannual payments of $10,000 and the funds sustaining the annuities earn:

   a. 7% compounded semiannually?

   b. 8% compounded semiannually?

   (*Hint:* Before you rush into any calculations, think about the basic difference between the two types of perpetuity.)

4. Mrs. Fitzgerald wishes to set up a trust paying $500 at each month-end in perpetuity to the foreign missions operated by her church. What initial amount must she place in the trust if it can earn 7.5% compounded monthly on long-term investments?

5. A company's preferred shares pay a $2 dividend every 6 months in perpetuity. What is the fair market value of the shares just after payment of a dividend if the rate of return required by the market on shares of similar risk is

   a. 9% compounded semiannually?

   b. 10% compounded semiannually?

6. A company's perpetual preferred shares pay a semiannual dividend of $3.00. The next dividend will be paid very soon.

   a. At what price would the shares provide an investor with a 9% semiannually compounded rate of return?

   b. If the shares are trading at $78, what nominal rate of return will they provide to a purchaser?

7. The Real Estate Foundation of Manitoba has agreed to endow a perpetual scholarship and bursary fund for business students at Red River College. The provincial government will match the grant under its Matching Dollars Program. The fund is to pay out $5000 per year in scholarships and bursaries commencing 1 year after the fund is endowed. If the college can earn 7% annually on its perpetual investments, what grant is required from the Real Estate Foundation?

8. The alumni association of a university is initiating a 1-year drive to raise money for a perpetual scholarship endowment fund. The goal is to offer 10 scholarships per year, each worth $2000.

   a. How large a fund is required to begin awarding the scholarships 1 year after the funds are in place if the funds can be invested to earn 7.25% compounded annually in perpetuity?

   b. Suppose that, during its fund-raising year, the alumni association finds an insurance company that will pay 7.6% in perpetuity. How much less money does the association need to raise?

   c. What dollar amount in scholarships can be awarded annually if the alumni association raises only $200,000? Use the interest rate from part b.

9. An old agreement requires a town to pay $500 per year in perpetuity to the owner of a parcel of land for a water well dug on the property in the 1920s. The well is no longer used, and the town wants to buy out the contract, which is now an administrative nuisance. What amount (including the regular scheduled payment) should the landowner be willing to accept on the date of the next scheduled payment if long-term low-risk investments now earn 9% compounded annually?

10. How much more money is required to fund a perpetuity due than a 30-year annuity due if the funds can earn 7% compounded quarterly and both pay $1000 quarterly?

11. What amount is required to fund a perpetuity that begins annual payments of $2000 immediately, if the funds can be invested to earn 8% compounded quarterly?

12. The alumni of the Northern Alberta Institute of Technology (NAIT) donated a total of $37,500 during a special drive to raise money for the institution's scholarship and bursary fund. If the fund earns 9% compounded semiannually, what additional amount of annual awards can NAIT grant starting 1 year from now?

13. Mr. O'Connor set up a trust account paying $500 per month in perpetuity to the local SPCA. These payments consume all the interest earned monthly by the trust. Between what amounts does the balance in the trust account fluctuate if it earns 8% compounded annually?

14. A provincial power utility reached an agreement several decades ago to pay the owner of a parcel of land adjacent to a dam $400 every 6 months in perpetuity for a right-of-way across the property. Both the current landowner and the utility are now agreeable to replacing the regular payments by a single amount (including the scheduled payment) at the next payment due date. If long-term money now earns 9% compounded annually, what is a fair settlement for both parties?

15. A city sells plots in its cemetery for $500 plus an amount calculated to provide for the cost of maintaining the grounds in perpetuity. This cost is figured at $15 per plot due at the beginning of each quarter. If the city can invest the funds to earn 6.5% compounded annually in perpetuity, what is the price of a plot?

•16. Donations to a memorial fund for a recently deceased politician are to be used to endow a $2000 annual scholarship in her name at the college from which she graduated. Funds totalling $20,856 were donated. How long before the first scholarship can be awarded must the funds be invested at 7.8% compounded annually in order to build the fund to a sustainable level?

•17. Mr. Chan has donated $1 million to a college to set up a perpetuity for the purchase of books and journals for a new library to be built and named in his honour. The donation will be invested and earnings will compound for 3 years, at which time the first of the quarterly perpetuity payments will be made. If the funds earn 8% compounded quarterly, what will be the size of the payments?

•18. How much would have to be dedicated today to a fund earning 8.5% compounded semi-annually if semiannual payments of $5000 are to start

  a. Today?

  b. 1 year from now?

  c. 5 years from now?

•19. What sum of money, invested today in a perpetual fund earning 7.5% compounded semiannually, will sustain quarterly perpetuity payments of $1000 starting

  a. Today?

  b. 3 months from today?

  c. 1 year from today?

•20. A wealthy benefactor has donated $1,000,000 to establish a perpetuity that will be used to support the operating costs of a local heritage museum scheduled to open in 3 years' time. If the funds earn 7.2% compounded monthly, what monthly payments, starting 3 years from now, can the museum expect?

•21. A number of major forest companies have pledged to contribute a combined total of $34,650 at the end of every 3 months for 4 years to a fund that will be used to endow the Forest Resource Policy Chair at a major university. If the funds earn 9% compounded quarterly for the next 4 years and then earn 7.5% compounded monthly when the chair is endowed in perpetuity, what monthly payments starting 4 years from now can be sustained?

•22. How much more money is required to fund a perpetuity due than a 30-year annuity due if the funds can earn 8% compounded quarterly and both pay $500 monthly?

•23. A legal dispute delayed for 18 months the disbursement of a $500,000 bequest designated to provide quarterly payments in perpetuity to a children's hospice. While under the jurisdiction of the court, the funds earned interest at the rate of 5% compounded semiannually. The hospice has just invested the $500,000 along with its earnings in a perpetual fund earning 7.8% compounded semiannually. What payments will the hospice receive beginning 3 months from now?

13.2 Deferred Annuities

In a **deferred annuity,** the start of the periodic payments is delayed by more than one payment interval. Figure 13.3 presents a time diagram for a deferred annuity. The time interval until the beginning of the first payment *interval* is called the **period of deferral.** It is always possible to choose the period of deferral so that the payments, when viewed from the end of the period of deferral, constitute an ordinary annuity.[1]

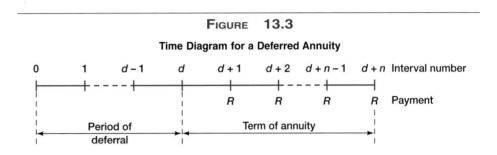

Figure 13.3

Time Diagram for a Deferred Annuity

You already know enough from the preceding chapters to handle deferred annuities. In fact, deferred annuity scenarios occasionally appeared in the more challenging problems in Chapters 10, 11, and 12 without mention of the term "deferred annuity." These problems required at least two steps to deal with the disguised deferred annuity. There are two reasons for devoting a section to deferred annuities. The first is that deferred annuities are widely available investment instruments designed to generate a future income stream. The second is that we can develop an algebraic formulation for deferred annuities that, in most instances, combines two steps into one. Whether you choose, in an algebraic approach, to use the new formulation or to stay with the earlier two-step method is a matter of preference.

Algebraic Method

Three additional variables are needed for a discussion of deferred annuities.

d = Number of compounding intervals for p in the period of deferral
$A_n(\text{def})$ = Present value of a deferred annuity
$S_n(\text{def})$ = Future value of a deferred annuity

We will consider only cases where d is an integer.

The focal date for the present value of a deferred annuity, $A_n(\text{def})$, is at the *beginning* of the period of deferral. A formula for $A_n(\text{def})$ can be derived using the two-step procedure indicated in Figure 13.4. First, the present value of the annuity payments at the *end* of the period of deferral is just the present value, A_n, of an *ordinary* annuity calculated from formula (10−4). That is,

$$A_n = R\left[\frac{1 - (1 + p)^{-n}}{p}\right]$$

[1] The same deferred annuity can equivalently be viewed in terms of a deferral period that is one payment interval longer, followed by an annuity *due.* We will take the *ordinary* annuity view in our exposition and example problems.

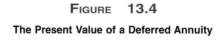

Figure 13.4

The Present Value of a Deferred Annuity

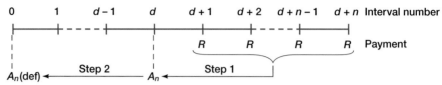

Then formula (8−2) is employed in the second step to obtain the present value, A_n(def), at the *beginning* of the period of deferral (d compounding intervals earlier) of the lump amount, A_n. That is,

$$A_n(\text{def}) = \frac{A_n}{(1 + p)^d}$$

Substitution of the expression for A_n gives

Present Value of a Deferred Annuity

$$A_n(\text{def}) = R\left[\frac{1 - (1 + p)^{-n}}{p(1 + p)^d}\right] \qquad (13\text{-}3)$$

If the compounding interval equals the payment interval, we have a deferred *simple* annuity and $p = i$. Otherwise, it is a deferred *general* annuity and formula (10−2) must be used to calculate p.

In some applications of deferred annuities, A_n(def) is known but *one* of R, n, d, or p is the unknown quantity. In cases where R or n or d is the unknown variable, formula (13−3) can be rearranged to isolate the desired variable. The rearrangement to isolate R is best done *after* the known values are substituted in formula (13−3) and the expression inside the square brackets is simplified.

The algebraic manipulations required to isolate n and d from the general formula (13−3) are not so straightforward. The following *versions* of formula (13−3) are stated without derivation. Remember that they assume the period of deferral is chosen such that the annuity payments form an *ordinary* annuity when viewed from the end of the period of deferral.

Known variables		Formula	
A_n(def), R, d, p	$n =$	$-\dfrac{\ln\left[1 - \dfrac{p(1 + p)^d A_n(\text{def})}{R}\right]}{\ln(1 + p)}$	$(13\text{-}3a)$
A_n(def), R, n, p	$d =$	$\dfrac{\ln\left\{\dfrac{R[1-(1 + p)^{-n}]}{pA_n(\text{def})}\right\}}{\ln(1 + p)}$	$(13\text{-}3b)$

If p is the unknown quantity, an algebraic solution requires the trial-and-error method explained in Appendix 12B.

The focal date for the future value, S_n(def), of a deferred annuity is at the time of the *last* payment. Viewed from this focal date, the deferred annuity is no different from an *n*-payment *ordinary* annuity ending on this date. Therefore, S_n(def) will equal the future value, S_n, of an ordinary annuity, as given by formula (10–1). The future value is not affected by the length of the deferral period.

Future Value of a Deferred Annuity

$$\boxed{S_n(\text{def}) = S_n}$$

(13–4)

FINANCIAL CALCULATOR METHOD

Formulas such as (13–3), (13–3*a*), and (13–3*b*) are not preprogrammed in most financial calculators. Consequently, a financial calculator solution to a deferred annuity problem must handle the period of deferral and the associated (ordinary) annuity separately. With the focal date located at the *end* of the period of deferral, the annuity payments form an *ordinary* annuity with a present value (at this focal date) of A_n. As previously indicated in Figure 13.4, A_n(def) is the present value *d* periods earlier of A_n. Alternatively, A_n may be viewed as the future value *d* periods later of A_n(def).

■ EXAMPLE 13.2A   CALCULATING THE PRESENT VALUE OF A DEFERRED ANNUITY

Mr. and Mrs. Templeton are setting up a fund to help finance their granddaughter's college education. They want her to be able to withdraw $1000 at the beginning of every 3 months for 3 years starting in $5\frac{1}{2}$ years. If the fund can earn 7.2% compounded quarterly, what single amount contributed today will provide for the payments?

☑ SOLUTION

The required contribution is the present value of the deferred annuity. In order to have an ordinary annuity following the period of deferral, the period of deferral must end, and the term of the annuity must begin, one payment interval (3 months) before the first payment. This makes the period of deferral $5\frac{1}{4}$ years.

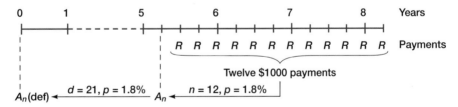

Since payments and compounding both occur quarterly, this is a deferred simple annuity with

$$R = \$1000 \quad n = 3(4) = 12 \quad d = 5.25(4) = 21 \quad \text{and} \quad p = i = \frac{7.2\%}{4} = 1.8\%$$

ALGEBRAIC SOLUTION

Substituting the values of the variables in formula (13–3), we obtain

$$A_n(\text{def}) = R\left[\frac{1 - (1 + p)^{-n}}{p(1 + p)^d}\right] = \$1000\left[\frac{1 - (1.018)^{-12}}{0.018(1.018)^{21}}\right] = \$7361.06$$

FINANCIAL CALCULATOR SOLUTION

The solution must be obtained by the two steps indicated in the time diagram.

Compute the present value of the annuity at $5\frac{1}{4}$ years.					Result
ENTER: 1000 0 12 1.8					
PRESS: PMT FV n i COMP PV					−10,706.41
Compute the present value of the above result at today's date.					
ENTER: 0 21					
PRESS: +/− FV PMT n COMP PV					−7361.06

The Templetons can provide the desired financial support to their granddaughter by putting $7361.06 into the fund.   ∎

■ EXAMPLE 13.2B   *CALCULATING THE PAYMENT SIZE IN A DEFERRED ANNUITY*

Budget Appliances is planning a promotion on a washer-dryer combination with a total price of $1750. Buyers will pay "no money down and no payments for 6 months." The first of 12 equal monthly payments is required 6 months from the purchase date. What should the monthly payments be if the store is to earn 15% compounded monthly on its account receivable during both the deferral period and the repayment period?

✓ SOLUTION

In effect, Budget Appliances makes a $1750 loan to the customer on the date of the sale. As for all loans, the initial loan equals the present value of all the payments. Viewed from the date of the sale, the payments form a deferred annuity—a 12-payment ordinary annuity following a 5-month period of deferral.

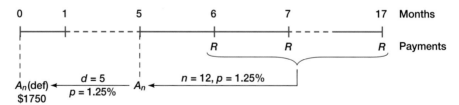

The payments form a deferred simple annuity having

$$A_n(\text{def}) = \$1750 \qquad n = 12 \qquad d = 5 \qquad \text{and} \qquad p = i = \frac{15\%}{12} = 1.25\%$$

Substitution in formula (13–3) gives

$$\$1750 = R\left[\frac{1 - (1.0125)^{-12}}{0.0125(1.0125)^5}\right]$$
$$= R(10.41208)$$

Hence,

$$R = \frac{\$1750}{10.41208} = \$168.07$$

Monthly payments of $168.07 will provide the merchant with a return of 15% compounded monthly on the account receivable.

FINANCIAL CALCULATOR SOLUTION

If A_n were known, then the payment size R could be readily calculated using the preprogrammed financial functions. Motivated by the need to know A_n in order to calculate R, another view of the problem, one more suited to a financial calculator solution, is illustrated in the following time diagram.

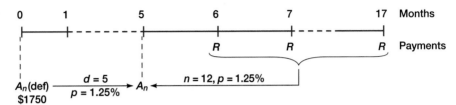

Whereas the focal date in the first time diagram was the date of the transaction, the focal date in the second diagram is at the end of the deferral period. In words, the equation of value is

$$\begin{array}{c}\text{Future value of the purchase price} \\ \text{at the end of month 5}\end{array} = \begin{array}{c}\text{Present value of the payments} \\ \text{at the end of month 5}\end{array}$$

The left-hand side (LHS) of the equation represents the original price plus 5 months' worth of accrued interest. This is the new principal that the 12 payments must repay along with further interest at 15% compounded monthly.

The LHS can be directly calculated. This will give us A_n and R may then be computed.

Compute the future value of $1750 on a date 5 months later.	Result
ENTER: 1750 0 5 1.25	
PRESS: [+/-] [PV] [PMT] [n] [i] [COMP] [FV]	1862.14
Compute R, knowing A_n = $1862.14.	
ENTER: 0 12	
PRESS: [+/-] [PV] [FV] [n] [COMP] [PMT]	168.07

The monthly payments should be $168.07.   ∎

■ EXAMPLE 13.2c CALCULATING THE LENGTH OF THE DEFERRAL PERIOD

Mrs. Sevard purchased a deferred annuity from an insurance company for $9697. Based on earnings at the rate of 8% compounded quarterly, the annuity will make quarterly payments of $1000 for 4 years. If the first payment is to be received on October 1, 1998, when did Mrs. Sevard purchase the deferred annuity?

☑ SOLUTION

If we calculate the length of the period of deferral, we can go back from the date of the first payment to determine the date of purchase.

The key idea on which we base the solution is that $9697 is the present value of the annuity payments on the date of purchase.

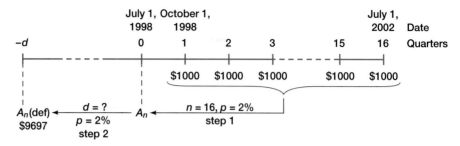

The payments form a deferred simple annuity with

$$A_n(\text{def}) = \$9697 \qquad R = \$1000 \qquad n = 16 \qquad \text{and} \qquad p = i = 2\%$$

For the payments to be treated as an *ordinary* annuity, the annuity's *term* must start on July 1, 1998 (one payment interval before the first payment). It follows that the period of deferral ends on July 1, 1998. The two steps for a financial calculator solution are indicated in the time diagram. For an algebraic solution, the two steps are already combined in formula (13–3*b*).

Algebraic Solution

Substituting in formula (13–3*b*), we obtain

$$d = \frac{\ln\left\{\dfrac{R[1 - (1 + p)^{-n}]}{pA_n(\text{def})}\right\}}{\ln(1 + p)} = \frac{\ln\left[\dfrac{\$1000(1 - 1.02^{-16})}{0.02 \times \$9697}\right]}{\ln 1.02} = \frac{\ln 1.400197}{\ln 1.02} = 17.00$$

The period of deferral is therefore 17.00 calendar quarters (4 years, 3 months) before July 1, 1998. That places the date of purchase of the deferred annuity at April 1, 1994.

Financial Calculator Solution

Compute the present value of the annuity on July 1, 1998.					Result
ENTER: 1000	0	16	2		
PRESS: (PMT)	(FV)	(n)	(i)	(COMP) (PV)	−13,577.71
Compute the number of compounding periods needed for $9697 to be the present value of $13,577.71					
ENTER:		0	9697		
PRESS: (+/−) (FV)	(PMT)	(+/−) (PV)		(COMP) (n)	17.00

The period of deferral is therefore 17.00 calendar quarters (4 years, 3 months) before July 1, 1998. That places the date of purchase of the deferred annuity at April 1, 1994.

■

■ EXAMPLE 13.2D   CALCULATING THE NUMBER OF PAYMENTS IN A DEFERRED ANNUITY

$10,000 is invested in a fund earning 9.25% compounded semiannually. Five years later the first semiannual withdrawal of $1000 is taken from the fund. After how many withdrawals will the fund be depleted? (The final payment that extinguishes the fund will be smaller than $1000. Include it in the count.)

☑ SOLUTION

In order to treat the payments as an *ordinary* annuity, the annuity's *term* must start 6 months (one payment interval) before the first payment. The period of deferral is, therefore, $4\frac{1}{2}$ years long. The payments constitute a deferred simple annuity having

$$A_n(\text{def}) = \$10,000 \qquad R = \$1000 \qquad d = 9 \qquad \text{and} \qquad p = i = \frac{9.25\%}{2} = 4.625\%$$

ALGEBRAIC SOLUTION

The present value of the withdrawals, discounted at 9.25% compounded semiannually back to the date of the initial investment, is $10,000. Substitution of the preceding values in formula (13–3a) gives

$$
\begin{aligned}
n &= -\frac{\ln\left[1 - \dfrac{p(1 + p)^d A_n(\text{def})}{R}\right]}{\ln(1 + p)} \\[2mm]
&= -\frac{\ln\left[1 - \dfrac{0.04625(1.04625)^9 \$10,000}{\$1000}\right]}{\ln(1.04625)} \\[2mm]
&= -\frac{\ln[0.305246]}{\ln(1.04625)} \\[2mm]
&= -\frac{-1.1866}{0.045212} \\[2mm]
&= 26.25
\end{aligned}
$$

The fund will be depleted after 27 withdrawals. (The last withdrawal will be about $250.)

FINANCIAL CALCULATOR SOLUTION

The solution idea best suited to a financial calculator approach is indicated in the following time diagram and expressed by the word equation

$$\begin{matrix}\text{Future value of \$10,000} \\ \text{at the end of the deferral period}\end{matrix} = \begin{matrix}\text{Present value of the payments} \\ \text{at the end of the deferral period}\end{matrix}$$

First calculate the left-hand side and then, knowing A_n, compute n.

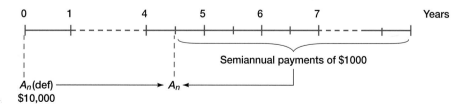

Compute the future value of $10,000 after $4\frac{1}{2}$ years.	Result
ENTER: 10000 0 9 4.625 PRESS: [+/-] [PV] [PMT] [n] [i] [COMP][FV]	15,021.71
Compute n knowing A_n is the result from the previous step. ENTER: 1000 0 PRESS: [+/-] [PV] [PMT] [FV] [COMP][n]	26.25

The fund will be depleted after 27 withdrawals. (The last withdrawal will be about $250.) ■

■ EXAMPLE 13.2E   CALCULATING THE PRESENT VALUE OF A DEFERRED GENERAL ANNUITY

Maureen has just had her 55th birthday and plans to retire from teaching at age 60. While reviewing Maureen's personal financial statement, her financial adviser points out that she has omitted a significant asset: the current economic value of earned pension entitlements. They estimate that the 25 years of service that she has already accumulated entitle her to an average monthly pension of $3500 (including inflation indexing) after age 60. Based on a 22-year life expectancy from age 60 and a time value of money equal to 8% compounded semiannually, estimate the current economic value of Maureen's earned pension entitlements.

☑ SOLUTION

The current economic value of the pension entitlements can be estimated by calculating the present value of the expected pension payments discounted at the time value of money. The expected payments form a deferred annuity with a 5-year period of deferral.

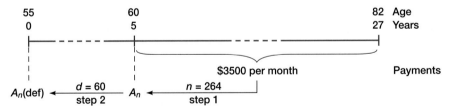

The diagram indicates the two steps in the financial calculator solution. Since the pension payments will be received monthly but the discount rate is compounded semiannually, the payments form a deferred *general* annuity having

$$R = \$3500 \qquad n = 22(12) = 264 \qquad d = 5(12) = 60 \qquad i = \frac{8\%}{2} = 4\%$$

$$\text{and} \qquad c = \frac{2}{12} = 0.1\overline{6}$$

Then

$$p = (1 + i)^c - 1 = 1.04^{0.1\overline{6}} - 1 = 0.006558197 = 0.6558197\%$$

ALGEBRAIC SOLUTION

Substitution of the preceding values in formula (13–3) gives

$$A_n(\text{def}) = \$3500\left[\frac{1 - (1.006558197)^{-264}}{0.006558197(1.006558197)^{60}}\right] = \$296,345$$

FINANCIAL CALCULATOR SOLUTION

Compute the present value at the end of the deferral period.					Result
ENTER: 3500	0	264	0.6558195		
PRESS: PMT	FV	n	i	COMP PV	−438,662.91
Compute the present value at the start of the deferral period.					
ENTER:	0	60			
PRESS: +/− FV	PMT	n		COMP PV	−296,344.95

The current economic value of the earned pension entitlements is $296,345. In other words, if Maureen did not belong to the pension plan, she would need current savings of $296,345 in a personal RRSP earning 8% compounded semiannually in order to duplicate the future pension benefits to age 82. ∎

■ EXAMPLE 13.2F   CALCULATING THE TERM OF A DEFERRED GENERAL ANNUITY

Morris is retiring at age 61 with $177,000 in his RRSP. If he uses the funds in his RRSP at age 65 to purchase an annuity paying $6000 at the end of each quarter, what will be the term of the annuity? Assume that no further contributions are made to the RRSP between ages 61 and 65. Also assume that funds invested in the RRSP and in the annuity earn 8% compounded annually.

☑ SOLUTION

Viewed from age 61, the payments form a deferred *general* annuity with

$$A_n(\text{def}) = \$177,000 \quad R = \$6000 \quad d = 4(4) = 16 \quad i = 8\% \quad c = \frac{1}{4} = 0.25$$

$$\text{and} \quad p = (1 + i)^c - 1 = 1.08^{0.25} - 1 = 0.01942655 = 1.942655\%$$

The following time diagram indicates the solution ideas for the algebraic and financial calculator solutions.

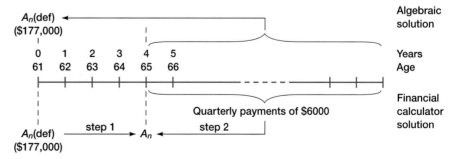

ALGEBRAIC SOLUTION

Formula (13–3a) will allow us to directly calculate the number of payments in the deferred annuity.

$$n = -\frac{\ln\left[1 - \dfrac{p(1 + p)^d A_n(\text{def})}{R}\right]}{\ln(1 + p)}$$

$$= -\frac{\ln\left[1 - \dfrac{0.01942655(1.01942655)^{16}\$177{,}000}{\$6000}\right]}{\ln(1.01942655)}$$

$$= -\frac{\ln(0.22033)}{\ln(1.01942655)}$$

$$= -\frac{-1.5126}{0.019240}$$

$$= 78.62$$

The term of the annuity will be 79 quarters, or 19 years and 9 months.

FINANCIAL CALCULATOR SOLUTION

Compute the future value of $177,000 on a date 4 years later.					Result
ENTER: 177000	0	16	1.942655		
PRESS: +/− PV	PMT	n	i	COMP FV	240,806.56
Compute n for an annuity having this present value.					
ENTER: 6000	0				
PRESS: +/− PV	PMT	FV		COMP n	78.619

The term of the annuity will be 79 quarters, or 19 years and 9 months.   ■

Point of Interest

The Value of a College Education

The 1991 Canadian Census* reported an average employment income of $22,100 for individuals whose highest level of education was high-school graduation. In contrast, the average employment income of those possessing a college certificate or diploma was $27,300. Each figure represents an average across all ages and years of experience of working individuals in the respective group. To make our analysis more pertinent to the late 1990s, we will increase both 1991 income figures by 15%. The adjusted average annual incomes are $31,400 for college graduates and $25,400 for high-school graduates.

To estimate the economic value added by a college education, the following factors must be taken into consideration.

- The difference in annual income while working.
- A college grad's lost years of employment while in college.
- A college grad's additional "up-front" costs while attending college.
- The effect of inflation on future earnings.
- The time value of money.

*Data from the 1996 census were not available at the time of publication.

(*continued*)

(*continued*)

We must choose a focal date at which to calculate the economic value of the differences in employment income and in costs faced by high-school grads and college grads over their careers. Let us select the date of high-school completion as the focal date. This is also the date on which the future college graduate began his or her first summer job before entering college.

Consider Pat who is about to graduate from high school on his or her 18th birthday. Pat is evaluating two alternative scenarios:

1. Immediately entering the work force and working until age 60 at an annual salary of $25,400 (in constant dollars as of the focal date).
2. Going to college for 3 years and then working until age 60 at an annual salary of $31,400 (in constant dollars as of the focal date). A college student incurs costs not faced by a working high-school graduate. Let us assume that the annual amount of these *incremental* costs of attending college are $7000. (For the purpose of this analysis, costs of food, clothing, accommodation, transportation, and so on, are *not* included if they would be incurred regardless of whether Pat works full time or goes to college.) Also assume that summer and part-time employment income while in college is $4000 per year. Under these assumptions, the incremental costs exceed a college student's income by $3000 per year.

Inflation can be handled by either of two approaches. One approach is to use current forecasts of the future rate of inflation. Each successive year's income and incremental costs would then be increased by the forecast rate of inflation. The time value of money should be the average rate of return on low-risk (government) bonds. This was the general approach employed in the Point of Interest in Chapter 10.

The alternative approach is based on the observation that, over the last few decades, the nominal rate of return on low-risk bonds has tended to rise and fall with the rate of inflation. This happened because the *real* rate of return (the difference between the nominal rate of return and the rate of inflation) expected by investors is quite stable over time. For the last 20 years, the "spread" between the nominal rate of return on low-risk bonds and the rate of inflation has averaged about 3.5%. In other words, the *real* rate of return on these bonds has tended to remain in the neighbourhood of 3.5%. Given this tendency, the second approach for handling inflation is to assume a zero rate of inflation and use 3.5% for the (real) time value of money. Two advantages result from taking this approach for the valuation exercise at hand.

1. The future cash flows are expressed in current dollars.
2. The cash flows form constant-payment annuities enabling us to use the mathematics we have learned for annuities.

Taking the zero-inflation approach, the relevant annual net cash flows for the two alternatives are summarized in the following table. Cash outflows are enclosed in parentheses.

Years	Relevant Annual Net Cash Flow		Net advantage for college grad
	High school only	College grad	
1 to 3	$25,400	($ 3000)	($28,400)
4 to 42	$25,400	$31,400	$ 6000

The economic value (on the date of high-school graduation) of a college diploma is the present value of the cash-flow differences in the last column. For the purpose of this estimation, it is reasonable to assume that the cash flows occur at the year-end.

(*continued*)

(concluded)

The $6000 annual advantage in years 4 to 42 inclusive forms a deferred annuity whose present value is

$$A_n(def) = R\left[\frac{1 - (1 + p)^{-n}}{p(1 + p)^d}\right]$$

$$= \$6000\left[\frac{1 - (1.035)^{-39}}{0.035(1.035)^3}\right]$$

$$= \$114,199$$

The present value of the three annual net cash *outflows* of $28,400 is $79,566. The net present value of all the relevant cash flows is

$$\$114,199 - \$79,566 = \$34,633$$

Hence, the average economic value of a college education (under the stated assumptions) is $34,633. Given the approximations and assumptions involved, let us round the number to $35,000.

Be careful how you interpret this estimate. Even though it is evaluated with the focal date at high-school graduation/college entry, do not deduct from it any forgone earnings while in college or any costs of going to college. They have already been included in the analysis. In effect, *the $35,000 figure is the economic value added on the day you graduate from high school if you decide to go to (and ultimately graduate from) college* instead of directly entering the work force. In the years ahead, you will convert this intangible asset to cash inflows

in the form of increased income. Also, do not view the $35,000 amount as the simple sum of the increase in earnings in future years. Rather, it is the value in *current dollars* of the increase in future earnings *adjusted for inflation* and *adjusted for the time value of money*. The sum of the nominal dollar amounts of increased earnings in the years ahead is a much larger (but not particularly meaningful) number.

There are two additional factors which make the $35,000 figure an underestimate of the average current economic value of a college certificate or diploma. The first is that many college programs are only 2 years in length. One year less in college (and one year more in full-time employment) would add over $30,000 to the estimate of the economic value. The second factor is that the unemployment rate is significantly higher among high-school grads than among college grads.[†] The income figures used in this analysis are averages for employed individuals. The economic value figure for a college certificate or diploma will be larger if adjustments are made for the average duration of unemployment in each group.

[†]This state of affairs is likely to become more pronounced in the years ahead. From 1990 to 1994, the total number of jobs in Canada filled by high school grads *declined* by 158,000 while the number filled by college grads *increased* by 646,000!

EXERCISE 13.2

Answers to the odd-numbered problems are at the end of the book.

Determine the unknown value for each of the deferred annuities in problems 1 through 24. In every case, the annuity is understood to be an ordinary annuity after the period of deferral.

Problem	Deferral period	Periodic payment ($)	Interest rate (%)	Compounding and payment frequency	Term (years)	Present value ($)
1.	5 years	2000.00	7	Semiannually	10	?
2.	$3\frac{1}{2}$ years	750.00	8	Quarterly	5	?
3.	$2\frac{3}{4}$ years	500.00	9	Monthly	$3\frac{1}{2}$	?
4.	4 years	?	7.75	Annually	10	20,000.00
5.	6 years	?	9.5	Semiannually	$7\frac{1}{2}$	25,000.00
6.	27 months	?	10	Quarterly	20	50,000.00

Problem	Deferral period	Periodic payment ($)	Interest rate (%)	Compounding and payment frequency	Term (years)	Present value ($)
7.	?	1500.00	7.9	Annually	8	6383.65
8.	?	1076.71	7	Quarterly	$12\frac{1}{2}$	30,000.00
9.	?	400.00	9.75	Monthly	15	33,173.03
10.	7 years	9427.11	8.7	Annually	?	40,000.00
11.	$4\frac{1}{2}$ years	2500.00	8.5	Semiannually	?	25,550.39
12.	$5\frac{1}{2}$ years	253.89	6.75	Monthly	?	15,000.00

Problem	Deferral period	Periodic payment ($)	Payment interval (months)	Interest rate (%)	Compounding frequency	Term (years)	Present value ($)
13.	5 years	2000.00	6	7	Quarterly	10	?
14.	$3\frac{1}{2}$ years	750.00	3	8.25	Monthly	5	?
15.	$2\frac{3}{4}$ years	500.00	1	9	Quarterly	$3\frac{1}{2}$	?
•16.	4 years	?	6	7.5	Monthly	10	20,000.00
•17.	6 years	?	1	9.5	Semiannually	$7\frac{1}{2}$	25,000.00
•18.	27 months	?	1	10	Quarterly	20	50,000.00
•19.	?	1500.00	3	7.9	Annually	8	28,355.14
•20.	?	356.83	1	7	Quarterly	$12\frac{1}{2}$	30,000.00
•21.	?	400.00	6	9.75	Monthly	15	4608.07
••22.	7 years	3764.77	6	8.7	Annually	?	40,000.00
••23.	$4\frac{1}{2}$ years	2500.00	3	8.5	Semiannually	?	37,958.58
••24.	$5\frac{1}{2}$ years	752.43	3	6.75	Monthly	?	15,000.00

25. Marion's grandfather's will established a trust that will pay her $1500 every 3 months for 11 years. The first payment will be made 6 years from now, when she turns 19. If money is worth 9% compounded quarterly, what is the economic value today of the bequest?

26. What amount of money invested now will provide monthly payments of $200 for 5 years, if the ordinary annuity is deferred for $3\frac{1}{2}$ years and the money earns 7.5% compounded monthly?

27. Sam wants to purchase, using an inheritance he recently received, a deferred annuity that will pay $5000 every 3 months between age 60 (when he plans to retire) and age 65 (when his permanent pension will begin). The first payment is to be 3 months after he reaches 60, and the last is to be on his 65th birthday. If Sam's current age is 50 years and 6 months, and the invested funds will earn 6% compounded quarterly, what amount must he invest in the deferred annuity?

28. What price will a finance company pay to a merchant for a conditional sale contract that requires 15 monthly payments of $231 beginning in 6 months? The finance company requires a rate of return of 18% compounded monthly.

•29. What amount must be invested today to allow for quarterly payments of $2500 at the end of every quarter for 15 years after a 6-year deferral period? Assume that the funds will earn 9% compounded semiannually.

•30. What is the current economic value of an inheritance that will pay $2000 to the beneficiary at the beginning of every 3 months for 20 years, starting when the beneficiary reaches 20 years of age, $4\frac{1}{2}$ years from now? Assume that money is worth 9% compounded monthly.

•31. To sell a farm that it had acquired in a foreclosure action, the Royal Bank agreed to monthly payments of $2700 for 20 years, with the first payment due 15 months from the date of sale. If the purchaser paid 15% down and the interest rate on the balance is 9% compounded annually, what was the purchase price?

32. As of Brice's 54th birthday, he has accumulated $154,000 in his Registered Retirement Savings Plan (RRSP). What size of end-of-month payments in a 20-year annuity will these funds purchase at age 65 if he makes no further contributions? Assume that his RRSP and the investment in the annuity will earn 8.25% compounded monthly.

33. Leslie received a $40,000 settlement when her employer declared her job redundant. Under special provisions of the Income Tax Act, she was eligible to place $22,000 of the amount in an RRSP. Fifteen years from now, she plans to transfer the amount then in the RRSP to a Registered Retirement Income Fund (RRIF) and make equal withdrawals at the end of every 3 months for 20 years. If both the RRSP and the RRIF earn 8.5% compounded quarterly, what will be the amount of each withdrawal?

34. A firm obtained a $3 million low-interest loan from a government agency to build a factory in an economically depressed region. The loan is to be repaid in semiannual payments over 15 years, and the first payment is due 3 years from today, when the firm's operations are expected to be well established.

   a. What will the payments be if the interest rate on the loan is 6% compounded semiannually?

   b. What is the nominal amount of interest that will be paid over the lifetime of the loan?

•35. During a 1-week promotion, Al's Appliance Warehouse is planning to offer terms of "nothing down and nothing to pay for 4 months" on major appliances priced above $500. Four months after the date of sale, the first of eight equal monthly payments is due.

   a. If the customer is to pay interest at the rate of 12% compounded monthly on the outstanding balance from the date of sale, what will be the monthly payments on an automatic dishwasher priced at $995?

   b. Appliances will be sold on these terms under a conditional sale contract. Al's Appliance Warehouse has made arrangements to immediately sell such contracts to Consumer Finance Co. at a price that will yield the finance company 15.6% compounded monthly. What amount will Al's Appliance Warehouse receive from Consumer Finance Co. for the dishwasher contract?

•36. a. What is the payment size on a conditional sale contract written for a $1700 transaction that requires a 15% down payment and the balance to be paid in 12 equal monthly payments? The first payment is due 6 months after the date of the purchase. The retailer charges an interest rate of 14% compounded semiannually on the unpaid balance.

   b. If a finance company discounts the conditional sale contract to yield 16% compounded annually, what price will it pay to the retailer?

•37. Mr. Donatelli moved from Toronto to Winnipeg to take a job promotion. After selling their Toronto home and buying a home in Winnipeg, the Donatellis have $85,000 in cash on hand. If the funds are used to purchase a deferred annuity from a life insurance company providing a rate of return of 8.25% compounded annually, what payments will they receive at the end of every 6 months for 20 years after a 9-year deferral period?

••38. A property development company obtained a $2.5 million loan to construct a commercial building. The interest rate on the loan is 12% compounded semiannually. The lender granted a period of deferral until rental revenues become established.

    a. What quarterly payments, the first required 18 months from the date of the loan, are required to pay off the loan over a 20-year period?

    b. If the payments are set 10% larger in part *a,* how many fewer payments will be required to pay off the loan?

•39. $10,000 was invested in a fund earning 7.5% compounded monthly. How many monthly withdrawals of $300 beginning $3\frac{1}{2}$ years after the date of the initial investment can be taken? Count the final smaller withdrawal.

•40. Nancy borrowed $8000 from her grandfather to buy a car when she started college. The interest rate being charged is only 4.5% compounded monthly. Nancy is to make the first $200 monthly payment on the loan 3 years after the date of the loan. Measured from the date of the first payment, how long will it take her to pay off the loan?

•41. Twelve years ago, Mr. Lawton rolled a $17,000 retiring allowance into an RRSP that subsequently earned 10% compounded semiannually. Three years ago he transferred the funds to an RRIF and, on the same date, took the first of a series of quarterly withdrawals of $1000. If the RRIF earns 8% compounded quarterly, how long after the first withdrawal will the RRIF be fully depleted?

•42. Novell Electronics recently bought a patent that will allow it to bring a new product to market in $2\frac{1}{2}$ years. Sales forecasts indicate that the product will increase the quarterly profits by $28,000. If the patent cost $150,000, how long after the date of the patent purchase will it take for the additional profits to repay the original investment along with a return on investment of 15% compounded quarterly? Assume that the additional profits are received at the end of each quarter.

•43. Helen and Morley borrowed $20,000 from Helen's father to make a down payment on a house. The interest rate on the loan is 8% compounded annually, but no payments are required for 2 years. The first monthly payment of $300 is due on the second anniversary of the loan. How long after the date the $20,000 was borrowed will the last loan payment be made?

•44. Bernice is about to retire with $139,000 in her RRSP. She will make no further contributions to the plan, but will allow it to accumulate earnings for another 6 years and then purchase an annuity providing payments of $5000 at the end of each quarter. Assume that the RRSP will earn 8.5% compounded annually and the funds invested in the annuity will earn 7.5% compounded monthly. How long after the purchase of the annuity will its payments continue?

•45. To the nearest month, how long (before the first withdrawal) must a $10,000 deposit earning 8.5% compounded semiannually be allowed to grow before it can provide 40 semiannual withdrawals of $1000?

•46. How long (before the first withdrawal) must a $19,665 deposit earning 9.5% compounded semiannually be allowed to grow before it can provide 60 quarterly withdrawals of $1000?

•47. A $35,000 loan bearing interest at 10% compounded quarterly was repaid, after a period of deferral, by quarterly payments of $1573.83 over 12 years. What was the time interval between the date of the loan and the first payment?

•48. A finance company paid a merchant $3975 for a conditional sale contract after discounting it to yield 18% compounded monthly. If the contract is for 20 monthly payments of $256.96 following a payment-free period, what is the time interval between the date of sale and the first payment?

•49. Mrs. Corriveau has just retired at age 58 with $160,360 in her RRSP. She plans to live off other savings for a few years and allow her RRSP to continue to grow on a tax-deferred basis until there is a sufficient amount to purchase a 25-year annuity paying $2000 at the end of each month. If her RRSP and the annuity each earns 7.5% compounded monthly, how much longer must she let her RRSP grow (before she buys the annuity)?

•50. Duncan retired recently and plans to utilize other savings for a few years while his RRSP continues to grow on a tax-deferred basis. The RRSP is currently worth $142,470. How long will it be until the amount in the RRSP is large enough to purchase a 25-year annuity paying $1700 at the end of each month? Assume that the RRSP and the annuity will earn 8.75% compounded semiannually.

•51. Fred asked two life insurance companies to give quotes on a 20-year deferred annuity (with a 5-year deferral period) that can be purchased for $100,000. Northwest Mutual quoted payments of $1205 payable at the end of each month. Liberty Standard stated that all their annuity options provide a rate of return equal to 8% compounded annually. Which company offers the better rate of return?

••52. The lease on the premises occupied by the accounting firm of Heath and Company will soon expire. The current landlord is offering to renew the lease for 7 years at $2100 per month. The developers of a new building, a block away from Heath's present offices, are offering the first year of a 7-year lease rentfree. For the subsequent 6 years the rent would be $2500 per month. All rents are paid at the beginning of each month. Other things being equal, which lease should Heath accept, if money is worth 10.5% compounded monthly?

13.3 INTEGRATED APPLICATIONS

The example problems and exercises in each section of the text have been chosen primarily to illustrate the concepts and techniques introduced in that section. Since a problem is likely to be an application of the narrow scope of the section under study, step 3 of the problem-solving procedure (suggested in Section 2.4) becomes virtually self-evident. (Step 3 is, "Identify the principle, concept, or idea that can be used to construct a word equation.") However, when problems arise in business, the solution concept or idea is not usually implied so clearly.

The purpose of this section is to present some interesting, comprehensive, and challenging problems that may involve any type of annuity as well as lump payments. The solution for a problem may call upon any of the content of Chapters 8 through 13.

Trap

When writing an equation involving the future and/or present values of two or more payments, *all* equivalent values included in the equation must be evaluated at the *same focal date*. If you do not shift all the payments (in a particular step of the solution) to a single focal date on the time line, you will be violating some aspect of the time value of money. Although the focal date can be changed *between* successive steps, there can be only *one* focal date *within* any step.

■ **EXAMPLE 13.3A**   *REDUCING A LOAN'S TERM BY MORE FREQUENT, SMALLER PAYMENTS*

Claire obtained an $18,000 loan from a trust company at an interest rate of 12% compounded annually. Once the total annual payment is agreed upon, the trust company will allow the borrower the choice of making the payments quarterly, monthly, semimonthly, or weekly. In Claire's case the total payments are to be $2400 per year, but she can choose to pay $600 quarterly, $200 monthly, or $100 semimonthly. Calculate how long it will take to pay off the loan in each case. Explain why the time required to repay the loan shortens as smaller payments are made more frequently.

✓ SOLUTION

For each alternative, we need to calculate the number of payments, n, that makes

$$A_n = \$18{,}000$$

Since the compounding interval differs from the payment interval in every instance, the three payment streams form ordinary *general* annuities. The value for p in each case is calculated in the following table.

Payment frequency	R	c	$p = (1 + i)^c - 1$
Quarterly	$600	$\frac{1}{4} = 0.25$	$1.12^{0.25} - 1 = 0.028737$
Monthly	200	$\frac{1}{12} = 0.08\overline{3}$	$1.12^{0.08\overline{3}} - 1 = 0.0094888$
Semimonthly	100	$\frac{1}{24} = 0.041\overline{6}$	$1.12^{0.041\overline{6}} - 1 = 0.0047332$

ALGEBRAIC SOLUTION

The calculation of n will be presented for the case of quarterly payments. Formula (10−4a) may be similarly employed for the other two payment frequencies.

$$n = -\frac{\ln\left(1 - \dfrac{pA_n}{R}\right)}{\ln(1 + p)} = -\frac{\ln\left(1 - \dfrac{0.028737 \times \$18{,}000}{\$600}\right)}{\ln(1.028737)} = 69.93$$

The results from calculating n are summarized below.

Payment frequency	R	Number of payments, n	Term of the loan	
Quarterly	$600	69.93	70 quarters	= 17 years, 6 months
Monthly	200	203.7	204 months	= 17 years, 0 months
Semimonthly	100	404.6	405 half months	= 16 years, $10\frac{1}{2}$ months

It is apparent that the loan's term shortens as a given total annual amount is allocated to smaller, more frequent payments. This happens because the more frequent the payments, the earlier the principal balance is reduced. As a consequence, subsequent interest charges are lower. Consider, for example, the cases of quarterly and monthly payments. The first $200 monthly payment will reduce the principal somewhat. The interest charged in the second month will be less than in the first month because it is calculated on the reduced principal. In contrast, the first quarterly payment must pay the interest on the *full* $18,000 for each of the first 3 months. Therefore, the *interest* component of the first quarterly $600 payment will be *greater* than the sum of the interest components of the first three $200 monthly payments. Consequently, the *principal* component of the $600 payment will be *smaller* than the sum of the principal components of the first three $200 monthly payments. This same effect will repeat and compound every quarter. Therefore, monthly payments will reduce the principal balance faster and pay off the loan sooner than quarterly payments.

FINANCIAL CALCULATOR SOLUTION

						Result
Case 1: R = $600 quarterly						
ENTER:	18000	0	600	2.87373		
			+/-		COMP	
PRESS:	PV	FV	PMT	i	n	69.93
Case 2: R = $200 monthly						
ENTER:			200	0.94888		
			+/-		COMP	
PRESS:			PMT	i	n	203.7
Case 3: R = $100 semimonthly						
ENTER:			100	0.47332		
			+/-		COMP	
PRESS:			PMT	i	n	404.6

Refer to the table and explanation in the algebraic solution for the completion of the solution. ∎

■ EXAMPLE 13.3B   *A MULTIPLE-STEP PROBLEM IN PERSONAL FINANCIAL PLANNING*

Victor and his financial adviser are investigating Victor's ability to achieve his goals for retirement income. He wishes to retire in 30 years at age 60. His plan is to use some of the funds in his RRSP at that time to purchase a 10-year annuity paying $5000 at the end of each month. Then, at age 70, he would use the balance of the funds in his RRSP to purchase a 20-year annuity paying at least $7000 at each month's end.

Victor anticipates that he can contribute $5000 to his RRSP at the beginning of each of the next 15 years and $10,000 at the beginning of each of the subsequent 15 years. Can Victor achieve the desired retirement income if the RRSP earns 8% compounded semiannually and the funds used to purchase the annuities earn 7.5% compounded monthly?

✓ SOLUTION

The key test to determine whether Victor can achieve his goal is whether there will be sufficient funds in his RRSP at age 70 to purchase a 20-year annuity paying $7000 at the end of each month. The general strategy for the solution will be to

- Calculate the expected amount in the RRSP at age 60.
- Deduct the amount required to purchase the 10-year annuity.
- Calculate the expected amount in the RRSP at age 70.
- Compare the latter amount to the amount required to purchase the 20-year annuity.

A more detailed listing of the steps and the time diagrams follow.

Step 1:   Calculate the future value at age 45 of the $5000 per year RRSP contributions.
Step 2:   Calculate the future value at age 60 of the step 1 result.
Step 3:   Calculate the future value at age 60 of the $10,000 per year RRSP contributions.
Step 4:   Add the step 2 and step 3 results.

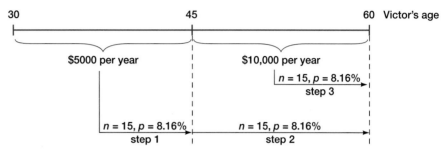

Step 5:   Calculate the amount required (present value) to purchase the 10-year, $5000 per month annuity.
Step 6:   Subtract the step 5 result from the step 4 result.
Step 7:   Calculate the future value of the step 6 result (the RRSP balance) at age 70.
Step 8:   Calculate the amount required (present value) to purchase the 20-year, $7000 per month annuity.
Step 9:   Compare the step 7 and step 8 results.

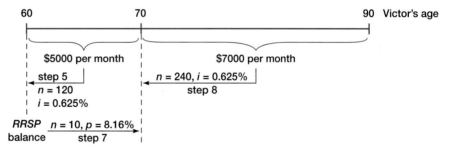

The two RRSP contribution streams are general annuities due having

$$i = \frac{8\%}{2} = 4\% \qquad c = \frac{2}{1} = 2 \qquad \text{and} \qquad p = 1.04^2 - 1 = 0.0816 = 8.16\%$$

The income annuities are ordinary simple annuities with $p = i = \frac{7.5\%}{12} = 0.625\%$

ALGEBRAIC SOLUTION

Step 1:

$$S_n(\text{due}) = \$5000\left(\frac{1.0816^{15} - 1}{0.0816}\right)(1.0816) = \$148,680.07$$

Step 2:

$$S = \$148,680.07(1.0816^{15}) = \$482,228.57$$

Step 3:

$$S_n(due) = \$10,000\left(\frac{1.0816^{15} - 1}{0.0816}\right)(1.0816) = \$297,360.14$$

Step 4:

$$\$482,228.57 + \$297,360.14 = \$779,588.71$$

Step 5:

$$A_n = \$5000\left(\frac{1 - 1.00625^{-120}}{0.00625}\right) = \$421,223.71$$

Step 6:

$$\$779,588.71 - \$421,223.71 = \$358,365.00$$

Step 7:

$$S = \$358,365(1.0816^{10}) = \$785,221.84$$

Step 8:

$$A_n = \$7000\left(\frac{1 - 1.00625^{-240}}{0.00625}\right) = \$868,924.92$$

Therefore, when Victor reaches age 70, the RRSP will fall short by

$$\$868,925 - \$785,222 = \$83,703$$

of having enough to purchase the 20-year annuity.

FINANCIAL CALCULATOR SOLUTION

Step 1: **BGN** mode						Result
ENTER:	5000	8.16	15	0		
PRESS:	+/-				COMP	
	PMT	i	n	PV	FV	148,680.07
Steps 2, 3, and 4: **BGN** mode						
ENTER:		10000				
PRESS:	+/-	+/-			COMP	
	PV	PMT			FV	779,588.71
Step 5:						
ENTER:	5000	0.625	120	0		
PRESS:					COMP	
	PMT	i	n	FV	PV	−421,223.71
Step 6:						
ENTER:		779,588.71				
PRESS:	+				=	358,365.00
Step 7:						
ENTER:		10	8.16			
PRESS:	+/-				COMP	
	PV	n	i	PMT	FV	785,221.84

```
---------------------------------------------+--------
Step 8:
ENTER:     7000      0.625      240        0
                                                (COMP)
PRESS:    ( PMT )    ( i )     ( n )    ( FV )   ( PV )    -868,924.92
-------------------------------------------------------
```

Step 9:   More is required—$83,703 more—to purchase the 20-year annuity than Victor will have in the RRSP at age 70. Therefore, he will not be able to receive $7000 per month from age 70 to age 90 based on the planned RRSP contributions.   ■

EXERCISE 13.3

Answers to the odd-numbered problems are at the end of the book.

•1. Monthly payments were originally calculated to repay a $20,000 loan at 12.75% compounded monthly over a 10-year period. After 1 year the debtor took advantage of an option in the loan contract to increase the loan payments by 15%. How much sooner will the loan be paid off?

•2. On May 23, 1992, a woman won a US$9,346,862 jackpot on a $1 slot machine at Harrah's in Reno, Nevada. The payoff was not made as a single payment, but in 20 equal annual instalments, with the first instalment paid on the date of the win.

   a. What was the economic value of this jackpot on May 23, 1992, if money was worth 7% compounded semiannually?

   b. When will the prize have an economic value equal to the reported nominal value of US$9,346,862? (Name the month and year.)

•3. Sheila already has $67,000 in her RRSP. How much longer must she contribute $4000 at the end of every 6 months to accumulate a total of $500,000 if the RRSP earns 9% compounded quarterly? (*Note:* An algebraic solution will require a trial-and-error approach analogous to that in Appendix 12B for calculating *p*.)

•4. What amount is required to purchase an annuity that pays $5000 at the end of each quarter for the first 10 years and then pays $2500 at the beginning of each month for the subsequent 10 years? The rate of return on the invested funds is 8.5% compounded quarterly.

•5. Natalie's RRSP is currently worth $133,000. She plans to contribute for another 7 years and then let the plan continue to grow through internal earnings for another 3 years. If the RRSP earns 8.25% compounded annually, how much must she contribute at the end of every 6 months for the next 7 years in order to have $350,000 in the RRSP 10 years from now?

•6. Capital Leasing calculates its 5-year lease rates to recover 90% of its capital investment and to earn a 16% semiannually compounded return on this 90% portion of the capital investment from the date of purchase to the end of the lease period. (It usually recovers the remaining 10% of the capital investment and a suitable return on this portion of the investment through sale of the used equipment to the lessee or another party at the end of the lease.) On average, equipment is purchased 3 months before it is leased, to allow for an inventory holding period and instalation at the lessee's premises. What will the monthly lease payment be on a $40,000 piece of machinery?

•7. Interprovincial Distributors Ltd. is planning to open a distribution centre in Calgary in 5 years. It can purchase a suitable piece of land for the distribution warehouse now for $450,000. Annual taxes on the vacant land, payable at the end of each year, would be close to $9000. What price would the property have to exceed 5 years from now to make it financially advantageous to purchase the property now instead of 5 years from now? Assume that Interprovincial can otherwise earn 12% compounded semiannually on its capital.

•8. Canadian Pacific class B preferred shares have just paid their quarterly $1.00 dividend and are trading on the Toronto Stock Exchange (TSE) at $37.50. What will the price of the shares have to be 3 years from now for a current buyer of the shares to earn 13% compounded annually on the investment?

•9. If Gayle contributes $1000 to her RRSP at the end of every quarter for the next 10 years and then contributes $1000 at each month's end for the subsequent 15 years, how much will she have in her RRSP at the end of the 25 years? Assume that the RRSP earns 8.5% compounded semiannually.

•10. It will cost A-1 Courier $1300 to convert a van from gasoline to natural gas fuel. The remaining useful life of the van is estimated at 5 years. To financially justify the conversion, what must be the reduction in the monthly cost of fuel to repay the original investment along with a return on investment of 13% compounded semiannually? Assume that the fuel will be purchased at the beginning of each month.

••11. Conrad has two loans outstanding, which he can repay at any time. He has just made the 11th monthly payment on an $8500 loan at 13.5% compounded monthly for a 3-year term. The 22nd monthly payment of $338.70 was also made today on the second loan, which has a 5-year term and an interest rate of 13% compounded semiannually. Conrad is finding the total monthly payments too high, and interest rates on similar loans are now down to 11.25% compounded monthly. He wishes to reduce his monthly cash outflow by obtaining a debt consolidation loan just sufficient to pay off the balances on the two loans. What would his monthly payment be on a 5-year term loan at the new rate?

••12. The monthly payments on a $10,000 loan at 11.25% compounded monthly were calculated to repay the loan over a 6-year period. After 11 payments, the borrower was temporarily unemployed and, with the approval of the lender, missed the next 3 payments.

   a. What amount paid along with the scheduled 15th payment will put the loan repayment back on the original schedule?

   b. If the size of the loan payments, beginning with the 15th payment, is recalculated to make up for the missed payments over the remainder of the scheduled term of the loan, what will the new payments be?

••13. The average annual costs of supporting a child born today are estimated as follows:

Years 1–6	$8400
Years 7–12	5400
Years 13–17	7200
Years 18–19	9600

The costs in the early years include child-care expenses or forgone earnings of the care-giving parent.

   a. What is the aggregate total cost (ignoring the time value of money) of raising a child to age 19?

   b. What is the total economic value, at the date of birth of a child, of these future expenditures, allowing for a time value of money of 6% compounded monthly? Assume that the annual costs are paid in equal end-of-month amounts.

   c. What will be the economic value at age 19 of the past expenditures, allowing for a time value of money of 6% compounded monthly?

••14. To compensate for the effects of inflation during their retirement years, the Pelyks intend to purchase a combination of annuities that will provide the following pattern of month-end income:

Calendar years, inclusive	Income
2005–2009	$ 5000
2010–2014	6000
2015–2019	7500
2020–2030	10,000

How much will they need in their RRSPs when they retire at the beginning of 2005 to purchase the annuities, if the annuity payments are based on a rate of return of 8% compounded semiannually?

••15. For its "Tenth Anniversary Salebration," Pioneer Furniture is offering terms of 10% down, no interest, and no payments for 6 months. The balance must then be paid in six equal payments, with the first payment due 6 months after the purchase date. The conditional sale contract calculates the monthly payments to include interest at the rate of 15% compounded monthly after the end of the interest-free period. Immediately after the sale of the furniture, Pioneer sells the contract to Afco Finance at a discount to yield Afco 18% compounded semiannually from the date of the sale. What cash payment will Pioneer receive from Afco on a piece of furniture sold for $2000?

••16. Patrick contributes $1000 at the beginning of every quarter to his RRSP. In addition, he contributes another $2000 to the RRSP each year from his year-end bonus. If the RRSP earns 9.5% compounded semiannually, what will be the value of his RRSP after 23 years?

••17. Reg is developing a financial plan that would enable him to retire 30 years from now at age 60. Upon reaching age 60, he would use some of the funds in the plan to purchase a 10-year annuity that pays $5000 at the end of each month. Then, at age 70, he will use the remaining funds in the RRSP to purchase a 20-year annuity paying $6000 at each month's end. What contributions must he make to an RRSP at the beginning of each quarter for 30 years to achieve his retirement goal if the RRSP earns 8.5% compounded semiannually, and the annuities earn 7.5% compounded monthly?

•18. Cynthia currently has $31,000 in her RRSP. She plans to contribute $5000 at the end of each year for the next 17 years and then use the accumulated funds to purchase a 20-year annuity making end-of-month payments.

   a. If her RRSP earns 8.75% compounded annually for the next 17 years, and the fund from which the annuity is paid will earn 8.25% compounded monthly, what monthly payments will she receive?

   b. If the average annual rate of inflation for the next 17 years is 4%, what will be the purchasing power in today's dollars of the monthly payments 17 years from now?

••19. A major car manufacturer is developing a promotion offering new car buyers the choice between "below-market" 4-year financing at 6.9% compounded monthly or a cash rebate. On the purchase of a $20,000 car, what cash rebate would make a car buyer indifferent between the following alternatives?
   • Financing through the car dealer at the reduced interest rate.
   • Taking the cash rebate and obtaining bank financing at 10.5% compounded monthly for the net "cash" price.

•20. Mr. Parmar wants to retire in 20 years and purchase a 25-year annuity that will make end-of-quarter payments, each having the purchasing power at the start of the annuity of $6000 in today's dollars. If he already has $54,000 in his RRSP, what semiannual contributions must he make for the next 20 years to achieve his retirement goal? Assume that the annual rate of inflation for the next 20 years will be 4.5%, the RRSP will earn 8% compounded semiannually, and the rate of return on the fund from which the annuity is paid will be 8% compounded quarterly.

REVIEW PROBLEMS

Answers to the odd-numbered review problems are at the end of the book.

1. If money can earn 8% compounded annually, what percentage more money is required to fund an ordinary perpetuity paying $1000 at the end of every year than to fund an ordinary annuity paying $1000 per year for 25 years?

2. A company's preferred shares pay a $1.25 dividend every 3 months in perpetuity. What is the fair market value of the shares just after payment of a dividend if the rate of return required by the market on shares of similar risk is:

   a. 8% compounded quarterly?

   b. 9% compounded quarterly?

3. What amount of money invested now will provide payments of $500 at the end of every month for 5 years following a 4-year period of deferral? The money will earn 7.2% compounded monthly.

4. What price will a finance company pay to a merchant for a conditional sale contract that requires 12 monthly payments of $249, with the first payment due 6 months from now? The finance company requires a return of 16.5% compounded monthly.

•5. How much will have to be dedicated today to a fund earning 8% compounded quarterly if beginning-of-quarter payments in perpetuity of $2000 are to start:

   a. Today?

   b. 1 year from now?

   c. 5 years from now?

•6. The common shares of Bancorp Ltd. are forecast to pay annual dividends of $3 at the end of each of the next 5 years, followed by dividends of $2 per year in perpetuity. What is the fair market value of the shares if the market requires a 14% annually compounded rate of return on shares having a similar degree of risk?

•7. Donations to a memorial fund for a recently deceased professor are to be used to endow a $3000 annual scholarship in his name at the university. Funds totalling $27,830 were donated. How long must the funds be invested at 7.8% compounded monthly before the first of the perpetual scholarships can be paid out?

•8. As of Betty's 56th birthday, she has accumulated $195,000 in her RRSP. What end-of-month payments in a 20-year annuity will these funds purchase at age 65 if she makes no further contributions but continues to earn 8.4% compounded monthly on her RRSP? Assume that the funds in the annuity will earn 7.2% compounded monthly.

•9. If $30,000 is placed in a fund today earning 7% compounded quarterly, how many quarterly withdrawals of $2000 can be made if the first withdrawal occurs 3 years from today? Count the final withdrawal, which will be less than $2000.

•10. A $30,000 loan bearing interest at 9% compounded monthly was repaid, after a period of deferral, by monthly payments of $425.10 for 10 years. What was the time interval between the date of the loan and the first payment?

•11. How much more money is required to fund a perpetuity due than a 25-year annuity due if the funds can earn 7% compounded quarterly and both pay $500 monthly?

•12. What is the current economic value of an inheritance that will pay $2500 to the beneficiary at the beginning of every 3 months for 20 years starting when the beneficiary reaches 21 years of age, $5\frac{1}{4}$ years from now? Assume that money can earn 6% compounded monthly.

•13. What will be the payment size on a conditional sale contract written for a $1450 transaction that required a 10% down payment with the balance to be paid by 12 equal monthly payments? The first payment is due 6 months after the date of the purchase. The retailer charges an interest rate of 13% compounded semiannually on the unpaid balance.

•14. After selling their Vancouver home and buying another in Saskatoon, the Martels have $120,000 cash on hand. If the funds are used to purchase a deferred annuity providing a rate of return of 7.25% compounded annually, what payments will they receive at the end of every 6 months for a 25-year term starting 8 years from now?

•15. Georgina is about to retire with $188,000 in her RRSP. She will make no further contributions to the plan, but will allow it to accumulate earnings for another 5 years and then purchase an annuity providing payments of $6000 at the end of each quarter. What will be the annuity's term if the RRSP earns 8% compounded annually and the funds invested in the annuity earn 7.5% compounded monthly?

••16. The monthly payments on a $30,000 loan at 10.5% compounded monthly were calculated to repay the loan over a 10-year period. After 32 payments were made, the borrower became unemployed and, with the approval of the lender, missed the next 3 payments.

   a. What amount paid along with the scheduled 36th payment will put the loan repayment back on the original schedule?

   b. If the size of the loan payments, beginning with the 36th payment, are recalculated to make up for the missed payments over the remainder of the scheduled term of the loan, what will the new payments be?

SELF-TEST EXERCISE

Answers to the self-test problems are at the end of the book.

1. Dr. Pollard donated $50,000 to the Canadian National Institute for the Blind. The money is to be used to make semiannual payments in perpetuity (after a period of deferral) to finance the recording of books on tape for the blind. The first perpetuity payment is to be made 5 years from the date of the donation. If the funds are invested at 7.5% compounded semiannually, what will be the size of the payments?

2. Mrs. McTavish wants to establish an annual $5000 scholarship in memory of her husband. The first scholarship is to be awarded 2 years from now. If the funds can earn 8.25% compounded annually, what amount must Mrs. McTavish pay now to fund the scholarship in perpetuity?

3. Mr. Larsen's will directed that $200,000 be invested to establish a perpetuity making payments at the beginning of each month to his wife for as long as she lives and subsequently to the Canadian Heart Foundation. What will the payments be if the funds can be invested to earn 7.5% compounded semiannually?

•4. Jeanette wishes to retire in 30 years at age 55 with retirement savings that have the purchasing power of $300,000 in today's dollars.

   a. If the rate of inflation for the next 30 years is 4% per year, how much must she accumulate in her RRSP?

   b. If she contributes $3000 at the end of each year for the next 5 years, how much must she contribute annually for the subsequent 25 years to reach her goal? Assume that her RRSP will earn 8% compounded annually.

   c. The amount in part a will be used to purchase a 30-year annuity. What will the month-end payments be if the funds earn 8.25% compounded monthly?

•5. What percentage more money is required to fund a perpetuity due than to fund a 30-year annuity due if the funds can earn 7% compounded semiannually? The perpetuity and the annuity each pays $1000 semiannually.

•6. C&D Stereo sold a stereo system on a plan that required no down payment and nothing to pay until January 1 (4 months away). Then the first of 12 monthly payments of $226.51 must be made. The payments were calculated to provide a return on the account receivable of 16.5% compounded monthly. What was the selling price of the stereo system?

•7. Weston Holdings Ltd. loaned $3.5 million to a subsidiary to build a plant in Winnipeg. No payments are required for 2 years, to allow the operations of the plant to become well established. The first monthly payment of $40,000 is due 2 years after the date the loan was received. If the interest rate charged on the intercompany loan is 9% compounded monthly, how long (measured from the date of the first payment) will it take the subsidiary to pay off the loan?

•8. Mr. Sandstrom's will directed that $20,000 be placed in each of two investment trusts for his grandchildren, Lena and Axel. On each grandchild's 18th birthday, he or she is to receive the first of a series of equal quarterly payments running for 15 years. Lena has just turned 13, and Axel's age is 8 years, 6 months. If the funds earn 9.25% compounded semiannually, what size of payment will each grandchild receive?

••9. Martha's RRSP is currently worth $97,000. She plans to contribute $5000 at the beginning of every 6 months until she reaches age 60, 12 years from now. Then she intends to use half of the funds in the RRSP to purchase a 20-year annuity making month-end payments. Five years later she will use half of the funds then in her RRSP to purchase another 20-year annuity making month-end payments. Finally, at age 70, she will use all the funds remaining in her RRSP to purchase a third 20-year annuity also making end-of-month payments. What will be her monthly income at age 67 and at age 72 if her RRSP earns 8% compounded annually and the funds invested in the annuities earn 7.5% compounded monthly?

Summary of Notation and Key Formulas

A = Present value of an *ordinary* perpetuity

$A(\text{due})$ = Present value of a perpetuity *due*

d = Number of compounding intervals for p in the period of deferral

$A_n(\text{def})$ = Present value of a deferred annuity

$S_n(\text{def})$ = Future value of a deferred annuity

Formula (13–1) $A = \dfrac{R}{p}$

Finding the present value of an ordinary perpetuity

Formula (13–2) $A(\text{due}) = A(1 + p) = \dfrac{R}{p}(1 + p)$

Finding the present value of a perpetuity due

Formula (13–3) $A_n(\text{def}) = R\left[\dfrac{1 - (1 + p)^{-n}}{p(1 + p)^d}\right]$

Finding the present value of a deferred annuity

Formula (13–3a) $n = -\dfrac{\ln\left[1 - \dfrac{p(1 + p)^d A_n(\text{def})}{R}\right]}{\ln(1 + p)}$

Finding the number of payments in a deferred annuity

$$\text{Formula } (13\text{-}3b) \quad d = -\frac{\ln\left\{\dfrac{R[1-(1 + p)^{-n}]}{pA_n(\text{def})}\right\}}{\ln(1 + p)}$$

Finding the number of compounding intervals for p in the period of deferral

$$\text{Formula } (13\text{-}4) \quad S_n(\text{def})=S_n$$

Finding the future value of a deferred annuity

GLOSSARY OF TERMS

Deferred annuity   An annuity in which the start of the periodic payments is delayed by more than one payment interval.

Period of deferral   The time interval until the beginning of the first payment *interval* in a deferred annuity.

Perpetuity   An annuity in which the payments continue forever.

14

AMORTIZATION OF LOANS

LEARNING OBJECTIVES

After completing this chapter, you will be able to:

- Calculate the payment size, initial loan, or amortization period of blended-payment loans, given values of the other two quantities and the interest rate on the loan

- Calculate the principal balance after any payment

- Calculate the principal and interest components of any blended payment

- Calculate the final payment on a loan when it differs from the others

- Construct an amortization schedule for a blended-payment loan

- Adjust mortgage loan balances and amortization periods to reflect prepayments of principal

- Calculate the effective cost of borrowing when a brokerage fee is charged on a mortgage loan

- Calculate the market value (or cash equivalent value) of mortgage loans and of real estate transactions involving a vendor take-back mortgage

- Calculate the principal balance and property owner's equity at any point in a reverse mortgage loan

INTRODUCTION

One of the most common and most important applications of annuities is the **amortization of a loan**—the repayment of a loan by periodic payments that, with the possible exception of the final payment, are equal in size. These payments are often described as blended payments of principal and interest. In **blended payments,** part of each regular payment is the interest that has accrued on the outstanding principal during the previous payment interval. The remainder of the payment is applied to reduce the outstanding principal.

When we used the *simple*-interest method in Section 7.5 to determine the interest portion of blended payments, we calculated the interest for the exact number of days in each payment interval. For blended payments on *compound*-interest loans, the interest portion is based on a *constant* interest rate per payment interval, regardless of small variations in the actual interval length. For example, a compound interest loan requiring monthly payments uses a constant value for *p,* the interest rate per payment interval, regardless of whether the month has 28, 30, or 31 days. Mortgage loans, most personal term loans, and many fixed-rate term loans to businesses employ this approach.

The first two sections of this chapter develop the techniques for calculating the payment size, the outstanding balance on any payment date, and the interest and principal components of any payment.

Mortgage loans play a prominent role in the financial affairs of both businesses and individuals. Therefore, some of the issues and calculations involved in mortgage financing are discussed in considerable detail in the last two sections of the chapter.

14.1 LOANS HAVING ALL PAYMENTS EQUAL

The length of time over which a loan is scheduled to be fully repaid is called the **amortization period.** After the lender and borrower agree on the amount of a loan, the rate of interest, and the payment frequency, there are two alternative approaches to determining the payment size and the amortization period:

- The amortization period is selected first, and then the payment size is calculated so that the loan will be fully repaid (or amortized) during the chosen amortization period.
- The amount of each payment is specified first, and then the number of payments required to fully repay the loan is calculated. This number of required payments establishes the amortization period.

The second approach is often used when the borrower has a preferred payment size, arising perhaps from budgetary restrictions. When the payment size is chosen in this way, the final required payment is almost certain to differ from the others. This poses some mathematical complications which are discussed in Section 14.2. This section deals only with cases in which all the payments are equal.

CALCULATING THE PAYMENT SIZE

The calculation of loan payments has already been discussed in Section 12.1. The procedure is reviewed here for consolidation with related topics that are to follow. The fundamental principle on which the calculation of the loan payment is based is

> Original loan = Present value of all of the payments (discounted at the contractual rate of interest on the loan)

Hence, when the payments form an *ordinary* annuity,[1] the payment size is the value of R that satisfies

$$A_n = R\left[\frac{1 - (1 + p)^{-n}}{p}\right] \tag{10–4}$$

where, in the context of blended-payment loans,

A_n = Original loan
p = Interest rate per payment interval
n = Total number of payments needed to repay the loan

SIZE OF PAYMENT REQUIRED TO REACH A PARTICULAR BALANCE AFTER A SPECIFIED TERM   The task in this scenario is to calculate the size of the periodic payment that will reduce the original loan to a predetermined balance after a specified period of time. We need to keep in mind that the target balance also represents the extra terminal "lump" payment that would pay off the loan at the end of the term. Since the original loan equals the present value of all loan payments, then

$$\text{Original loan} = \begin{array}{c}\text{Present value} \\ \text{of any number} \\ \text{of payments}\end{array} + \begin{array}{c}\text{Present value} \\ \text{of the balance} \\ \text{after these payments}\end{array}$$

$$= R\left[\frac{1 - (1 + p)^{-n}}{p}\right] + \frac{\text{Target balance}}{(1 + p)^n}$$

where n now represents the number of payments of size R required to reach the target balance. The algebraic approach to determining R is to:

- Substitute the known values for the original loan, n, p, and the target balance in the preceding equation.
- Simplify the coefficient of R.
- Rearrange the equation to solve for R.

The following diagram presents the procedure for the financial calculator approach. The target balance is saved as a cash outflow in FV because the original loan saved in PV is the *combined* present value of the n periodic payments and a terminal payment equal to the target balance.

Computing the required payment size to reach a target balance.					Result
ENTER: Original loan	Target balance	p	Number of payments		
PRESS: PV	+/− FV	i	n	COMP PMT	−Payment

---

[1] A loan in which the payments form an annuity *due* is primarily an academic fiction. Suppose a borrower were to receive a loan and then be required to make the first payment on the same day that the loan was advanced. The payment would be applied entirely against the principal since no interest would have yet accrued. The first payment is, therefore, a pointless money shuffle. Such a loan would much more logically be structured with a smaller amount initially advanced and the payments forming an *ordinary* annuity.

■ EXAMPLE 14.1A   CALCULATING THE SIZE OF LOAN PAYMENTS REQUIRED TO REACH A TARGET BALANCE

Mr. and Mrs. Blencoe obtained a $25,000 home improvement loan from their bank at an interest rate of 10.5% compounded monthly. What size of blended monthly payments will reduce the balance to $15,000 after 5 years?

▨ SOLUTION

The monthly payments form an ordinary simple annuity having

$$p = i = \frac{10.5\%}{12} = 0.875\% \qquad n = 5(12) = 60 \qquad \text{and}$$

$$\$25{,}000 = A_n + \text{Present value of } \$15{,}000$$

ALGEBRAIC SOLUTION

$$\$25{,}000 = R\left(\frac{1 - 1.00875^{-60}}{0.00875}\right) + \$15{,}000(1.00875^{-60})$$

$$= R(46.52483) + \$8893.616$$

Solving for R,

$$46.52483R = \$25{,}000 - \$8893.616 = \$16{,}106.384$$

$$R = \frac{\$16{,}106.384}{46.52483} = \$346.19$$

FINANCIAL CALCULATOR SOLUTION

Computing the payment size required for a $15,000 balance after 5 years.					Result
ENTER: 25000	15000	0.875	60		
	+/−			COMP	
PRESS: PV	FV	i	n	PMT	−346.19

Monthly payments of $346.19 will reduce the balance to $15,000 after 5 years.   ■

Trap

Since the loan balance in the preceding scenario is to be reduced by $10,000 over a 5-year period, you may be tempted to think that the monthly payment is the same as that required to pay off a $10,000 loan at the same interest rate over a 5-year period. However, this reasoning ignores the fact that the borrower must also carry and pay interest on the other $15,000 throughout the entire 5 years.[2]

---

[2]An alternative solution idea is suggested by the view that the $25,000 loan consists of a $10,000 component that is paid off in 5 years, and a $15,000 component on which interest only is paid. The monthly payment will be the sum of:
• The monthly payment required to pay off the $10,000 component in 5 years ($214.94).
• One month's interest on the other $15,000 (that is, 0.00875 × $15,000 = $131.25).

CALCULATING THE PRINCIPAL BALANCE

The principal balance owed partway through the amortization period must be determined if the borrower wishes to pay off the entire balance of the loan or to prepay some principal with an extra "balloon" payment. A **balloon payment** is any payment of principal over and above the regular periodic payments.

PROSPECTIVE METHOD   This method was used in Section 11.2 to obtain the balance owed on a loan. (At that point it was not called the Prospective Method because there was no alternative method from which it needed to be distinguished.) The reason for now introducing a second method is that the Prospective Method has a minor limitation which can lead to a small error in the calculated balance. The error will be demonstrated in Example 14.1*b* and its cause explained in the subsequent discussion. For now, we will just restate the familiar concept with its new name.

 The Prospective Method is based on the insight that the principal balance is related to the *remaining* payments in the same way that the original loan is related to *all* the payments. That is,

Principal Balance (Prospective Method)

| Principal balance = Present value of the *remaining* payments (discounted at the interest rate on the loan) | (14–1) |

RETROSPECTIVE METHOD   As the word "retrospect" suggests, this method for calculating the balance owed on a loan is based on the payments *already made.* (In contrast, the Prospective Method obtains the balance from payments yet to be made—the "prospective" payments.) To understand the basis for it, consider Figure 14.1, which shows the original loan, the payments that have already been made, and the balance after the most recent payment.

FIGURE   **14.1**

A Loan Is Equivalent to a Series of Payments and the Principal Balance at the End of the Payments

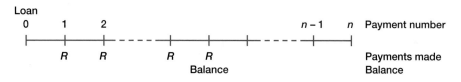

 The original loan is economically equivalent to the combination of the payments already made and the outstanding principal balance at the time of the last of these payments. In other words, the economic value of the initial loan at *any* focal date will equal the combined economic value of the payments already made and the balance, all taken to the *same* focal date. Figure 14.2 shows the loan and the payments shifted to a focal date coinciding with the last payment and the balance. The word equation expressing the economic equivalence at this focal date is

$$\begin{array}{ccc} \text{Future value} & & \text{Future value} & & \text{Principal balance} \\ \text{of the} & = & \text{of the payments} & + & \text{after the most} \\ \text{original loan} & & \text{already made} & & \text{recent payment} \end{array}$$

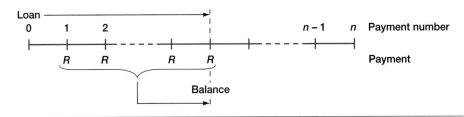

FIGURE   14.2

Payments Taken to the Most Recent Payment Date as a Focal Date

---

Rearranging this word equation to isolate the principal balance on the left side, we obtain

Principal Balance (Retrospective Method)

$$\begin{array}{|c|}\hline \text{Principal balance} \\ \text{after any payment} \end{array} = \begin{array}{c} \text{Future value} \\ \text{of the loan} \end{array} - \begin{array}{c} \text{Future value} \\ \text{of payments} \\ \text{already made} \end{array} \qquad (14\text{--}2)$$

■ **EXAMPLE 14.1B**   *CALCULATING THE PRINCIPAL BALANCE AND THE NEW PAYMENT SIZE ON THE DATE OF A CHANGE IN THE INTEREST RATE ON A LOAN*

Foothills Fabricating obtained a $75,000 loan from the Federal Business Development Bank to purchase some machinery. The monthly payments are based on an interest rate of 10.2% compounded monthly and a 10-year amortization period. However, the interest is fixed for only a 5-year term. The payments will then be recalculated so that, at the new market-based interest rate, the balance will be paid off over the remaining 5 years.

a. Calculate the balance owed on the loan after 2 years by both the Prospective Method and the Retrospective Method.

b. What will the payments be for the last 5 years if the interest rate becomes 9% compounded monthly?

☑ **SOLUTION**

The monthly payments must be determined before the balance can be calculated by either the Prospective Method or the Retrospective Method. The payments are initially calculated as though the interest rate of 10.2% compounded monthly would continue for the entire 10 years. Hence, determine R for part *a*, given

$$A_n = \$75,000 \qquad n = 10(12) = 120 \qquad \text{and} \qquad p = i = \frac{10.2\%}{12} = 0.85\%$$

For the last 5 years in part *b*, calculate the new R such that

$$A_n = \text{Balance after the first 5 years} \quad n = 5(12) = 60 \quad \text{and } p = i = \frac{9\%}{12} = 0.75\%$$

ALGEBRAIC SOLUTION

a. Substituting the known values in formula (10−4), we obtain

$$\$75,000 = R\left[\frac{1 - (1.0085)^{-120}}{0.0085}\right]$$

Then

$$R = \frac{\$75{,}000}{75.040862} = \$999.4555 = \$999.46$$

Using the Prospective Method, the balance after 2 years will be the present value of the remaining $8(12) = 96$ payments. That is,

$$\text{Balance} = \$999.46\left[\frac{1 - (1.0085)^{-96}}{0.0085}\right] = \$999.46(65.444183) = \$65{,}408.84$$

Using the Retrospective Method,

$$\text{Balance} = \begin{array}{c}\text{Future value of } \$75{,}000 \\ \text{two years later}\end{array} - \begin{array}{c}\text{Future value of the} \\ \text{first 24 payments}\end{array}$$

$$= \$75{,}000(1.0085)^{24} - \$999.46\left(\frac{1.0085^{24} - 1}{0.0085}\right)$$

$$= \$91{,}893.105 - \$26{,}484.678$$

$$= \$65{,}408.43$$

The balance after 2 years is $65,408.84 (Prospective Method) or $65,408.43 (Retrospective Method). An explanation for the $0.41 difference follows this example. It is evident from this example that the Retrospective Method entails significantly more calculations than the Prospective Method when the algebraic approach is used.

b. First obtain the balance owed after the first 5 years and then calculate the monthly payment required to pay off this balance over the remaining 5 years at the new interest rate.
Using the Retrospective Method,

$$\begin{array}{c}\text{Principal balance} \\ \text{after five years}\end{array} = \begin{array}{c}\text{Future value of } \$75{,}000 \\ \text{five years later}\end{array} - \begin{array}{c}\text{Future value of the} \\ \text{first 60 payments}\end{array}$$

$$= \$75{,}000(1.0085)^{60} - \$999.46\left(\frac{1.0085^{60} - 1}{0.0085}\right)$$

$$= \$124{,}627.940 - \$77{,}805.711$$

$$= \$46{,}822.23$$

This balance is also the present value of the remaining 60 payments. Now use formula (10−4) to obtain R.

$$\$46{,}822.23 = R\left[\frac{1 - (1.0075)^{-60}}{0.0075}\right]$$

$$R = \frac{\$46{,}822.23}{48.173374} = \$971.9525 = \$971.95$$

The payments for the last 5 years will be $971.95 per month.

FINANCIAL CALCULATOR SOLUTION

a.

Compute the size of the loan payments.					Result
ENTER: 75000	0	0.85	120		
PRESS:				COMP	
PV	FV	i	n	PMT	−999.4554

Compute the balance after 24 payments by the Prospective Method.

ENTER:	96	999.46		
PRESS:	n	+/– PMT		COMP PV	65,408.84

Compute the balance after 24 payments by the Retrospective Method.

ENTER:	24	999.46	75000	
PRESS:	n	+/– PMT	PV	COMP FV	–65,408.43

Understand why this last procedure accomplishes the Retrospective Method. It computes the future value of the original loan (stored in $\boxed{\text{PV}}$) less (because of the $\boxed{\text{+/–}}$ sign change) the future value of the 24 payments ($\boxed{\text{n}}$) of $999.46 ($\boxed{\text{PMT}}$).

The balance after 2 years is $65,408.84 (Prospective Method) or $65,408.43 (Retrospective Method). An explanation for the $0.41 difference follows this example. It is evident from this example that the Retrospective Method requires no more steps than the Prospective Method when the financial calculator approach is used.

b.

Compute the balance after 60 payments by the Retrospective Method. | Result

ENTER:	60	999.46	75000	
PRESS:	n	+/– PMT	PV	COMP FV	–46,822.23

Compute the new size of the loan payments with $p = 0.75\%$.

ENTER:		0	0.75	60	
PRESS:	+/– PV	FV	i	n	COMP PMT	–971.95

The payments for the last 5 years will be $971.95 per month. ∎

RECONCILIATION OF THE RESULTS OF THE PROSPECTIVE AND RETROSPECTIVE METHODS There is normally a small discrepancy between the principal balances obtained from the two methods. Its origin is the prevailing practice in business of rounding the *calculated* loan payment to the nearest cent. For example, the calculated payment of $999.4555 was rounded to $999.46 in the preceding example. As a consequence, each payment in that example was $0.0045 larger than needed to precisely pay off the loan with 120 monthly payments. If 120 payments of $999.46 are actually made, the cumulative overpayment will be about

$$120(\$0.0045) = \$0.54$$

The last payment can, therefore, be reduced by about $0.54 and still pay off the loan.[3]

We can now understand why the two methods gave us slightly different balances. The Prospective Method used information that, 2 years into the amortization period, 96 payments of $999.46 are still *required* to pay off the loan. In fact, each payment

---

[3]In general, the maximum error will occur when R is rounded up or down by almost half a cent. This upper limit on the error is about $(0.5¢) \times$ (total number of payments). Although the discrepancy is not a material amount, the software used by many financial institutions will make the appropriate adjustment to the final payment.

could be about half a cent smaller and still settle the loan. On the other hand, the Retrospective Method calculated the balance based on *payments that had actually been made.* It properly credited the borrower for the small overpayment on each of the 24 payments already made.

In summary, the Retrospective Method *always* gives the *strictly correct* balance. The balance obtained by the Prospective Method is usually in error by a small amount.[4]

Prospective Method or Retrospective Method?   Solutions to example problems in this chapter will use the Prospective Method for the *algebraic* approach. For most practical purposes, the error in the calculated balance is too small and immaterial to warrant the extra computational complexity of the Retrospective Method.

On the other hand, the Retrospective Method poses no additional complications or calculations for a financial calculator approach. Therefore, the Retrospective Method will be used for financial calculator solutions to example problems in order to gain the full accuracy available with this method. Answers at the end of the book were obtained with the Retrospective Method.

CALCULATING THE INTEREST AND PRINCIPAL COMPONENTS OF A PAYMENT

Proper accounting procedures require a business to allocate a loan payment to principal and interest. Only the interest portion of a payment is a business expense; only the interest portion of a payment received is revenue. Individual investors must also determine the interest and principal components of loan payments for reporting interest income and interest expense in their tax returns.

In the preceding subsection we learned how to directly determine the balance owed on a loan after any payment. We will now use appropriately chosen loan balances to calculate the interest and principal components of any payment. The interest portion of a blended payment is the interest that has accrued on the outstanding balance during the preceding payment interval. Since the interest rate for a payment interval is *p,* then

Interest Component of a Blended Payment

$$\boxed{\text{Interest component} = p \times \text{Balance after the previous payment}} \qquad (14\text{–}3)$$

where the balance after the previous payment is determined by either the Prospective Method or (preferably) the Retrospective Method. If the payment interval equals the compounding interval, the loan payments form a simple annuity and $p = i$. Otherwise, the payments form a general annuity and p must be calculated using formula (10–2), $p = (1 + i)^c - 1$.

The principal portion of a blended payment reduces the loan balance from the value it had after the previous payment to a new, lower balance. In other words, the principal component of a payment is just the difference between the previous balance and the new balance after the current payment.

---

[4]Note that there is no inherent *conceptual* flaw in the Prospective Method. Both methods would give the same balance if the loan payment were not rounded to the nearest cent. Alternatively, both methods will give the same balance based on the rounded payment if the strictly correct value is used for the *final* payment. It is when the Prospective Method is given incorrect information about the final payment that it yields a slightly incorrect result.

**Principal
Component of a
Blended Payment**

$$\boxed{\text{Principal component} = \begin{array}{c}\text{Balance after the}\\\text{previous payment}\end{array} - \begin{array}{c}\text{Balance after the}\\\text{current payment}\end{array}} \quad (14\text{–}4)$$

> **Tip**
> Once either the principal portion or the interest portion of any payment has been calculated, the easiest way to obtain the other component is to subtract the known component from the payment since
>
> $$R = \text{Principal component} + \text{Interest component}$$

INTEREST AND PRINCIPAL COMPONENTS OF AN INVESTMENT-ANNUITY PAYMENT
The breakdown of investment-annuity payments into interest and principal components uses the same concepts and techniques as for loan payments. This becomes more apparent when you realize that a lender, by granting a loan requiring equal periodic payments, is in effect purchasing an annuity from the borrower. The price the lender "pays" for the annuity (or the amount "invested" in the annuity) is the principal amount of the loan. Similarly, when we buy or invest in an annuity, we are in a sense lending the funds to the annuity issuer, who subsequently repays the "loan" with interest. The rate of return on our annuity investment may be viewed as the rate of interest we charge on the "loan."

■ EXAMPLE 14.1c   CALCULATING THE INTEREST AND THE PRINCIPAL COMPONENTS OF A PAYMENT AND OF A GROUP OF CONSECUTIVE PAYMENTS

A $9500 personal loan at 10.5% compounded monthly is to be repaid over a 4-year term by equal monthly payments.

a. Calculate the interest and principal components of the 29th payment.

b. How much interest will be paid in the second year of the loan?

☑ SOLUTION

The loan payments form an ordinary simple annuity with

$$A_n = \$9500 \qquad n = 4(12) = 48 \qquad \text{and} \qquad p = i = \frac{10.5\%}{12} = 0.875\%$$

In part *a*, the size of the loan payments must be obtained before any balances can be calculated. A "brute force" approach to part *b* would be to calculate and add the interest components of each of payments 13 to 24 inclusive. A much less laborious procedure uses the idea that the total interest in payments 13 to 24 inclusive equals the difference between total amount paid and the overall reduction in principal. That is,

$$\begin{aligned}\text{Interest paid in year 2} &= 12R - \text{Principal paid in year 2}\\ &= 12R - \left(\begin{array}{c}\text{Balance after}\\12\text{ payments}\end{array} - \begin{array}{c}\text{Balance after}\\24\text{ payments}\end{array}\right)\end{aligned}$$

ALGEBRAIC SOLUTION

a. Calculate the size of the payments by solving for *R* in

$$\$9500 = R\left[\frac{1 - (1.00875)^{-48}}{0.00875}\right] = R(39.05734)$$

$$R = \frac{\$9500}{39.05734} = \$243.23$$

Then

$$\frac{\text{Interest component}}{\text{of the 29th payment}} = p \times \left(\frac{\text{Balance after}}{\text{the 28th payment}}\right)$$

where

$$\frac{\text{Balance after}}{\text{the 28th payment}} = \frac{\text{Present value of the}}{\text{remaining 20 payments}}$$

$$= \$243.23\left(\frac{1 - 1.00875^{-20}}{0.00875}\right)$$

$$= \$4444.96$$

Hence,

$$\frac{\text{Interest component}}{\text{of the 29th payment}} = 0.00875 \times (\$4444.96) = \$39.89$$

and

$$\text{Principal component} = R - \text{Interest component}$$
$$= \$243.23 - \$38.89$$
$$= \$204.34$$

•

b.

$$\frac{\text{Balance after}}{12 \text{ payments}} = \frac{\text{Present value of the}}{\text{remaining 36 payments}}$$

$$= \$243.23\left(\frac{1 - 1.00875^{-36}}{0.00875}\right)$$

$$= \$7483.44$$

Similarly,

$$\frac{\text{Balance after}}{24 \text{ payments}} = \frac{\text{Present value of the}}{\text{remaining 24 payments}} = \$5244.73$$

Using the equation developed near the beginning of the solution,

$$\text{Interest paid in year 2} = 12(\$243.23) - (\$7483.44 - \$5244.73)$$
$$= \$680.05$$

FINANCIAL CALCULATOR SOLUTION

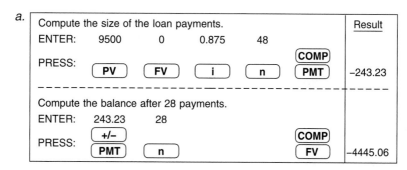

$$\text{Interest component of payment 29} = p \times \text{(Balance after 28 payments)}$$
$$= 0.00875(\$4445.06)$$
$$= \$38.89$$

$$\text{Principal component of payment 29} = R - \text{Interest component}$$
$$= \$243.23 - \$38.89$$
$$= \$204.34$$

b.

Compute the balance after 12 payments.	Result
ENTER:　　　　12	
PRESS:　　n　　COMP FV	−7483.53
Compute the balance after 24 payments.	
ENTER:　　　　24	
PRESS:　　n　　COMP FV	−5244.84

Using the equation developed near the beginning of the solution,

$$\text{Total interest in year 2} = 12(\$243.23) - (\$7483.53 - \$5244.84)$$
$$= \$680.07$$ ■

■ EXAMPLE 14.1D　CALCULATING THE INTEREST AND PRINCIPAL COMPONENTS OF ANNUITY PAYMENTS

Joanna purchased a 20-year annuity with $100,000 accumulated in her RRSP. The payments are received at the end of every 3 months and represent a rate of return of 7.5% compounded semiannually.

a. Calculate the interest and principal components of the 15th payment.

b. How much of the payments received in the second year represents the recovery of principal from her initial investment of $100,000?

☑ SOLUTION

The payments form an ordinary *general* annuity having

$$A_n = \$100,000 \qquad n = 20(4) = 80 \qquad i = \frac{7.5\%}{2} = 3.75\% \qquad \text{and} \qquad c = \frac{2}{4} = 0.5$$

Then

$$p = (1 + i)^c - 1 = 1.0375^{0.5} - 1 = 0.018577438 = 1.8577438\%$$

The size of the quarterly payments must first be determined from the requirement that

$$A_n = \text{Present value of all the payments}$$

ALGEBRAIC SOLUTION

a.
$$\$100,000 = R\left[\frac{1 - (1 + 1.018577438)^{-80}}{0.018577438}\right]$$
$$= R(41.483766)$$
$$R = \$2410.58$$

Interest portion of payment 15 = p × Balance after 14 payments
= p × Present value of the last 66 payments
$$= 0.018577438(\$2410.58)\left(\frac{1 - 1.018577438^{-66}}{0.018577438}\right)$$
= \$1695.24

Principal portion of payment 15 = R − Interest portion
= \$2410.58 − \$1695.24
= \$715.34

1675.42

b. Payments 5 to 8 inclusive were received in the second year.

$$\frac{\text{Total principal in}}{\text{payments 5 to 8}} = \frac{\text{Balance after}}{\text{payment 4}} - \frac{\text{Balance after}}{\text{payment 8}}$$
= \$97,726.26 − \$95,278.79
= \$2447.47

FINANCIAL CALCULATOR SOLUTION

a.

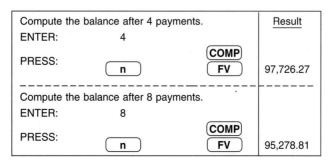

Interest component of payment 15 = p × Balance after payment 14
= 0.018577438 × \$91,252.56
= \$1695.24

Principal component = R − Interest component = \$715.34

b. Payments 5 to 8 inclusive were received in the second year.

$$\frac{\text{Total principal in}}{\text{payments 5 to 8}} = \frac{\text{Balance after}}{\text{payment 4}} - \frac{\text{Balance after}}{\text{payment 8}}$$

Compute the balance after 4 payments. ENTER: 4	Result
PRESS: n COMP FV	97,726.27
Compute the balance after 8 payments. ENTER: 8	
PRESS: n COMP FV	95,278.81

Principal recovered in year 2 = \$97,726.27 − \$95,278.81 = \$2447.46   ■

AMORTIZATION SCHEDULE

An amortization schedule is a table that:

- Breaks down each payment into its interest and principal components.
- Gives the principal balance outstanding after each payment.

Typical headings for the columns of an amortization schedule are presented in Table 14.1.

TABLE   14.1

Column Headings for an Amortization Schedule

Payment number	Payment	Interest portion	Principal portion	Principal balance
				Loan
0	—	—	—	
1	R			
etc.	etc.			

The schedule is developed by completing a row for each successive payment. The procedure for each payment is:

- Calculate the interest portion of the payment using

$$\text{Interest portion} = p \times \text{Balance after the previous payment}$$

- Calculate the principal portion of the payment from

$$\text{Principal portion} = R - \text{Interest portion}$$

- Calculate the new principal balance from

$$\text{New balance} = \text{Previous balance} - \text{Principal portion}$$

As explained in the discussion of the Retrospective Method, a consequence of rounding the calculated payment, R, to the nearest cent is that the last payment may be a few cents more or less than the other payments. The three-step procedure for completing a row in the amortization schedule must be altered for the final payment because its precise amount is not known at the outset. For the *final payment,*

- Calculate the interest portion of the payment using

$$\text{Interest portion} = p \times \text{Balance after the previous payment}$$

- The principal portion of the payment will simply be the previous principal balance (making the new balance zero).
- Calculate the final payment using

$$\text{Final payment} = \text{Interest portion} + \text{Principal portion}$$

PARTIAL AMORTIZATION SCHEDULE   A particular circumstance may require only a portion of a loan's amortization schedule. Suppose, for example, details are needed for only the monthly payments made in the fourth year of a 5-year loan. The partial schedule must, therefore, present details of payments 37 to 48 inclusive. The key figure needed to "get the ball rolling" is the principal balance after the 36th payment. After this amount is obtained (by either the Prospective Method or, preferably, the Retrospective Method), the three-step routine for each successive payment can begin.

■ EXAMPLE 14.1E CONSTRUCTING A FULL AMORTIZATION SCHEDULE

Marpole Carpet Cleaning borrowed $7000 from Richmond Credit Union at 12.5% compounded quarterly. The loan is to be repaid in equal quarterly payments over a 2-year term. Construct an amortization schedule for the loan. Calculate the total interest paid.

☑ SOLUTION

The loan payments form an ordinary simple annuity having

$$A_n = \$7000 \quad n = 8 \quad \text{and} \quad p = i = \frac{12.5\%}{4} = 3.125\%$$

The size of the payments must be calculated before beginning the amortization schedule.

ALGEBRAIC SOLUTION

$$\$7000 = R\left(\frac{1 - 1.03125^{-8}}{0.03125}\right)$$
$$R = \frac{\$7000(0.03125)}{1 - 0.7817867}$$
$$= \$1002.46$$

FINANCIAL CALCULATOR SOLUTION

						Result
ENTER:	7000	3.125	8	0		
PRESS:					COMP	
	PV	i	n	FV	PMT	−1002.46

Payment number	Payment	Interest portion	Principal portion	Principal balance
0	—	—	—	$7000.00
1	$1002.46	$ 218.75①	$ 783.71②	6216.29③
2	1002.46	194.26	808.20	5408.09
3	1002.46	169.00	833.46	4574.63
4	1002.46	142.96	859.50	3715.13
5	1002.46	116.10	886.36	2828.77
6	1002.46	88.40	914.06	1914.71
7	1002.46	59.83	942.63	972.08
8	1002.46	30.38	972.08	0.00
Total	$8019.68	$1019.68	$7000.00	

① Interest portion   = p × Previous balance
                                          = 0.03125($7000) = $218.75
② Principal portion   = R − Interest portion
                                          = $1002.46 − $218.75 = $783.71
③ Balance after payment = Previous balance − Principal portion
                                          = $7000 − $783.71 = $6216.29

The accuracy of the calculations can be checked by adding the figures in the "principal portion" column. Their total should equal the amount of the original loan.

The total interest paid may be determined by adding the entries in the "interest portion" column or by calculating the difference between the total of the payments and the original amount of the loan. That is,

$$\text{Interest paid} = 8(\$1002.46) - \$7000 = \$1019.68 \qquad \blacksquare$$

■ EXAMPLE 14.1F CONSTRUCTING A PARTIAL LOAN AMORTIZATION SCHEDULE

Martin obtained a 5-year term loan for $11,000 from his bank to purchase a new car. The blended monthly payments include interest at 11.25% compounded monthly. Construct a partial amortization schedule showing details of the first two payments, payments 32 and 33, and the last two payments. Calculate the total interest charges over the life of the loan.

☑ SOLUTION

The detailed calculations for the algebraic and financial calculator methods should now be familiar and will be omitted here to make the solution more compact.

The loan payments form an ordinary simple annuity in which

$$A_n = \$11,000 \qquad n = 60 \qquad p = i = 11.25\%/12 = 0.9375\%$$

Solving

$$\$11,000 = \text{Present value of 60 payments}$$

for R gives

$$R = \$240.54$$

Payment number	Payment	Interest portion	Principal portion	Principal balance
0	—	—	—	$11,000.00
1	$ 240.54	$ 103.13①	$ 137.41②	10,862.59③
2	240.54	101.84	138.70	10,723.89
.	.	.	.	.
31				6083.05④
32	240.54	57.03	183.51	5899.54
33	240.54	55.31	185.23	5714.31
.	.	.	.	.
58				474.43⑤
59	240.54	4.45	236.09	238.34
60	240.57	2.23	238.34	0.00
Total	$14,432.43	$3432.43⑥	$11,000.00	

① Interest portion of first payment = $p \times$ Previous balance
   = 0.009375($11,000)
   = $101.13
② Principal portion of the first payment = R − Interest portion
   = $240.54 − $103.13
   = $137.41
③ Balance after the first payment = Previous balance − Principal portion
   = $11,000 − $137.41
   = $10,862.59
④ Balance after 31 payments = Future value of $11,000 − Future value of 31 payments
   = $6083.05
⑤ Balance after 58 payments = Future value of $11,000 − Future value of 58 payments
   = $474.43
⑥ Total interest = 59($240.54) + $240.57 − $11,000
   = $3432.43

■ EXAMPLE 14.1G *CONSTRUCTING A FULL AMORTIZATION SCHEDULE WHERE THE PAYMENTS FORM A GENERAL ANNUITY*

Healey Fishing obtained a $40,000 loan for a major refit of a troller. The loan contract requires seven equal annual payments including interest at 11.5% compounded semiannually. Construct the full amortization schedule for the loan. Calculate the total interest paid over the life of the loan.

☑ SOLUTION

The loan payments form an ordinary *general* annuity in which

$$A_n = \$40,000 \quad n = 7 \quad i = \frac{11.5\%}{2} = 5.75\% \quad c = \frac{2}{1} = 2 \quad \text{and}$$

$$p = 1.0575^2 - 1 = 0.11830625 = 11.830625\%$$

The payment size is the value of R that makes

$$\$40,000 = \text{Present value of 7 payments}$$

ALGEBRAIC SOLUTION

$$\$40,000 = R\left(\frac{1 - 1.11830625^{-7}}{0.11830625}\right)$$

$$R = \frac{\$40,000(0.11830625)}{1 - 0.4571669}$$

$$= \$8717.69$$

FINANCIAL CALCULATOR SOLUTION

						Result
ENTER:	40000	0	7	11.830625		
PRESS:	PV	FV	n	i	COMP PMT	–8717.69

Payment number	Payment	Interest portion	Principal portion	Principal balance
0	—	—	—	$40,000.00
1	$8717.69	$ 4732.25	$ 3985.44	36,014.56
2	8717.69	4260.75	4456.94	31,557.62
3	8717.69	3733.46①	4984.23②	26,573.39③
4	8717.69	3143.80	5573.89	20,999.50
5	8717.69	2484.37	6233.32	14,766.18
6	8717.69	1746.93	6970.76	7795.42
7	8717.67④	922.25	7795.42	0.00
Total		$21,023.81	$40,000.00	

① Interest portion = 0.11830625($31,557.62) = $3733.46
② Principal portion = $8717.69 − $3733.46 = $4984.23
③ Balance after payment = $31,557.62 − $4984.23 = $26,573.39
④ The last payment may differ by a few cents from the calculated "equal" payment. This is the cumulative result of rounding the calculated payment ($8717.688) and each interest portion to the nearest cent. To adjust for these rounding errors, the last payment is determined by adding the interest portion ($922.25) of the last payment to the balance ($7795.42) after the second-to-last payment.

$$\text{Total interest paid} = 6(\$8717.69) + \$8717.67 - \$40,000$$
$$= \$21,023.81$$

EXERCISE 14.1

Answers to the odd-numbered problems are at the end of the book.

Each of the loans in problems 1 through 6 requires equal blended payments at the end of each payment interval. The compounding period equals the payment interval. Calculate the principal portion of the payment having the serial number listed in the second-to-last column, and the interest portion of the payment having the serial number listed in the last column.

Problem	Original principal ($)	Amortization period (years)	Payment interval (months)	Nominal rate (%)	Principal portion of payment	Interest portion of payment
1.	12,000	3	3	10.5	5	9
2.	40,000	8	1	11	75	43
3.	14,000	6	6	12.5	8	10
4.	25,000	5	3	11	15	6
5.	45,000	15	1	9.75	117	149
6.	30,000	10	1	12	99	41

Each of the loans in problems 7 through 14 requires equal blended payments at the end of each payment interval. The loan payments in these problems form ordinary general annuities. Calculate the principal portion of the payment having the serial number listed in the second-to-last column, and the interest portion of the payment having the serial number listed in the last column.

Problem	Original principal ($)	Amortization period (years)	Payment interval	Nominal rate (%)	Compounding period (months)	Principal portion of payment	Interest portion of payment
7.	7000	10	1 year	10	6	7	4
8.	9000	8	1 year	11	1	4	7
9.	10,000	7	6 months	9.5	12	6	10
10.	25,000	5	1 month	10.25	12	38	4
11.	70,000	12	3 months	10.75	6	11	30
12.	4000	2	1 month	13	3	21	13
13.	45,000	15	1 month	10.5	6	117	149
14.	30,000	10	6 months	12	3	19	9

Each of the loans in problems 15 through 22 requires equal blended payments at the end of each payment interval. Calculate the total principal paid in the year listed in the second-to-last column and the total interest paid in the year listed in the last column.

Problem	Original principal ($)	Amortization period (years)	Payment interval (months)	Nominal rate (%)	Compounding period (months)	Principal paid in year	Interest paid in year
•15.	14,000	6	6	12.5	6	2	5
•16.	25,000	5	3	11	3	4	2
•17.	45,000	15	1	9.75	1	11	6
•18.	30,000	10	1	12	1	3	8
•19.	25,000	5	1	10.25	12	2	4
•20.	70,000	12	3	10.75	6	9	4
•21.	4000	7	1	13	3	6	3
•22.	45,000	15	1	10.5	6	5	10

23. A $37,000 loan at 10.8% compounded semiannually is to be repaid by equal semiannual payments over 10 years.

   a. What amount of principal is to be repaid by the 6th payment?

   b. What will be the interest portion of the 16th payment?

   c. How much will the principal be reduced by payments 6 to 15 inclusive?

   d. How much interest will be paid in the third year?

24. A 10-year annuity providing a rate of return of 8% compounded quarterly was purchased for $25,000. The annuity makes payments at the end of each quarter.

   a. How much of the 25th payment will be interest?

   b. What will be the principal portion of the 13th payment?

   c. How much interest will be paid by payments 11 to 20 inclusive?

   d. How much principal will be repaid in the second year?

•25. Guy borrowed $6000 at 12.75% compounded monthly and agreed to repay the loan in equal quarterly payments over 4 years.

   a. How much of the 5th payment will be interest?

   b. What will be the principal repaid by the 11th payment?

   c. How much interest will be paid by payments 5 to 12 inclusive?

   d. How much will the principal be reduced in the second year?

•26. A 25-year annuity was purchased with $225,000 that had accumulated in a Registered Retirement Savings Plan (RRSP). The annuity provides a semiannually compounded rate of return of 9.5% and makes equal month-end payments.

   a. What amount of principal will be included in the 206th payment?

   b. What will be the interest portion of the 187th payment?

   c. How much will the principal be reduced by payments 50 to 100 inclusive?

   d. How much interest will be paid in the 14th year?

•27. Monica bought a $1250 stereo system for 20% down, with the balance to be paid with interest at 15% compounded monthly in six equal monthly payments. Construct the full amortization schedule for the debt. Calculate the total interest paid.

•28. Dr. Alvano borrowed $8000 at 10% compounded quarterly to purchase a new X-ray machine for his clinic. The agreement requires quarterly payments during a 2-year amortization period. Prepare the full amortization schedule for the loan. Calculate the total interest charges.

•29. Golden Dragon Restaurant obtained a $9000 loan at 12.75% compounded annually to replace some kitchen equipment. Prepare a complete amortization schedule if the loan is to be repaid by semiannual payments over a 3-year term.

•30. Valley Produce received $50,000 in vendor financing at 11.5% compounded semiannually for the purchase of harvesting machinery. The contract requires equal annual payments for 7 years to repay the debt. Construct the amortization schedule for the debt. How much interest will be paid over the 7-year term?

•31. Suppose that the loan in problem 28 permits an additional prepayment of principal on any scheduled payment date. Prepare another amortization schedule that reflects a prepayment of $1500 with the third scheduled payment.

•32. Suppose that the loan in problem 30 permits an additional prepayment of principal on any scheduled payment date. Prepare another amortization schedule that reflects a prepayment of $10,000 with the second scheduled payment. How much interest is saved as a result of the prepayment?

•33. Cloverdale Nurseries obtained a $60,000 loan at 10.5% compounded monthly to build an additional greenhouse. Monthly payments were calculated to amortize the loan over 6 years. Construct a partial amortization schedule showing details of the first two payments, payments 43 and 44, and the last two payments.

•34. Jean and Walter Pereira financed the addition of a swimming pool using a $24,000 home improvement loan from their bank. Monthly payments were based on an interest rate of 11% compounded semiannually and a 5-year amortization. Construct a partial amortization schedule showing details of the first two payments, payments 30 and 31, and the last two payments. What total interest will they pay over the life of the loan?

•35. Elkford Logging's bank will fix the interest rate on a $60,000 loan at 10.5% compounded monthly for the first 4-year term of an 8-year amortization period. Monthly payments are required on the loan.

   a. If the prevailing interest rate on 4-year loans at the beginning of the second term is 9% compounded monthly, what will be the monthly payments for the last 4 years?

   b. What will be the interest portion of the 23rd payment?

   c. Calculate the principal portion of the 53rd payment.

••36. Christina has just borrowed $12,000 at 11% compounded semiannually. Since she expects to receive a $10,000 inheritance in 2 years when she turns 25, she has arranged with her credit union to make monthly payments that will reduce the principal balance to exactly $10,000 in 2 years.

   a. What monthly payments will she make?

   b. What will be the interest portion of the 9th payment?

   c. Determine the principal portion of the 16th payment.

14.2 LOANS HAVING A DIFFERENT FINAL PAYMENT

CALCULATING THE NUMBER OF PAYMENTS

The size of the payments on a loan is sometimes chosen to fit the borrower's budget, or chosen to be a "round" number that both the borrower and the lender can easily remember. Then the number of payments required to amortize the loan must be obtained using the methods presented in Section 12.2. In the algebraic approach, the number of payments of size, R, required to repay a loan, A_n, is

$$n = -\frac{\ln\left(1 - \frac{pA_n}{R}\right)}{\ln(1 + p)} \qquad (10\text{--}4a)$$

where p is the interest rate per payment interval.

When the payment size is somewhat arbitrarily chosen, the value obtained for n will rarely be an integer. As mentioned in Section 12.2, the fractional part of n means that the last payment will be smaller than the others. The calculation of the size of the last payment will be addressed later in this section.

CALCULATING THE PRINCIPAL BALANCE

Neither the Prospective Method nor the Retrospective Method for determining the principal balance is altered in any way when n is not an integer. The Retrospective

Method has two advantages when the payment size is known but the number of payments is not given.

The first advantage is that the Retrospective Method does not require the total number of payments to be determined before a balance can be calculated. The method is based on the number of payments made up to and including the focal date for the balance. The Prospective Method, on the other hand, requires that the total number of payments be calculated first in order to determine how many payments remain.

The second advantage is that the Retrospective Method involves a "nicer" number for n than the Prospective Method. The number of payments *already made* is *always* an integer. In contrast, the Prospective Method uses the number of *remaining* payments, which is not an integer when the last payment differs from the others. Furthermore, seven or eight significant figures may need to be retained in the value for *n* in order to achieve the desired accuracy in the calculated balance.

■ EXAMPLE 14.2A   CALCULATING THE NUMBER OF PAYMENTS AND THE LOAN'S BALANCE

Meditech Laboratories borrowed $28,000 at 10% compounded quarterly to purchase new testing equipment. Payments of $1500 are to be made every 3 months.

a. How long will it take to pay off the loan?

b. Calculate the balance after the 10th payment using the Prospective Method.

c. Calculate the balance after the 10th payment using the Retrospective Method.

☑ SOLUTION

The loan payments form an ordinary simple annuity in which

$$A_n = \$28,000 \qquad R = \$1500 \text{ except for the last payment} \qquad \text{and} \qquad p = i = 2.5\%$$

The number of payments required to pay off the loan is the value of *n* satisfying

$$\$28,000 = \text{Present value of } n \text{ payments of } \$1500$$

ALGEBRAIC SOLUTION

a.
$$n = -\frac{\ln\left(1 - \dfrac{pA_n}{R}\right)}{\ln(1 + p)} = -\frac{\ln\left(1 - \dfrac{0.025 \times \$28,000}{\$1500}\right)}{\ln 1.025} = 25.457357$$

Therefore, 26 payments, taking $\frac{26}{4} = 6.5$ years = 6 years and 6 months, are required to fully repay the loan.

b. After 10 payments,

$$\text{Balance} = \text{Present value of the remaining } 15.457357 \text{ payments}$$
$$= \$1500\left[\frac{1 - (1 + p)^{-n}}{p}\right]$$
$$= \$1500\left(\frac{1 - 1.025^{-15.457357}}{0.025}\right)$$
$$= \$19,037.29$$

c. After 10 payments (requiring $2\frac{1}{2}$ years),

$$\text{Balance} = \begin{array}{c}\text{Future value of}\\ \$28{,}000 \text{ after } 2.5 \text{ years}\end{array} - \begin{array}{c}\text{Future value of}\\ \text{first 10 payments}\end{array}$$

$$= P(1 + i)^n - R\left[\frac{(1 + p)^n - 1}{p}\right]$$

$$= \$28{,}000(1.025)^{10} - \$1500\left(\frac{1.025^{10} - 1}{0.025}\right)$$

$$= \$35{,}842.367 - \$16{,}805.073$$

$$= \$19{,}037.29$$

FINANCIAL CALCULATOR SOLUTION

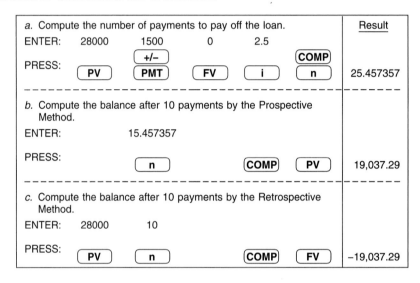

a. Compute the number of payments to pay off the loan.	Result
ENTER: 28000 1500 0 2.5	
PRESS: [PV] [+/−][PMT] [FV] [i] [COMP][n]	25.457357
b. Compute the balance after 10 payments by the Prospective Method.	
ENTER: 15.457357	
PRESS: [n] [COMP][PV]	19,037.29
c. Compute the balance after 10 payments by the Retrospective Method.	
ENTER: 28000 10	
PRESS: [PV] [n] [COMP][FV]	−19,037.29

a. Therefore, 26 payments, taking $\frac{26}{4} = 6.5$ years $= 6$ years and 6 months, are required to fully repay the loan.

b., c. After 10 payments, the balance will be $19,037.29.

Note: The Retrospective Method now gives exactly the same balance as the Prospective Method. This happens because there is no rounding of the payment size and the noninteger value used for *n* recognizes that the final payment differs from the others. For loans encountered in Section 14.1, the Retrospective Method assumed all payments were equal when, in fact, the final payment should have been a few cents different due to rounding of the calculated loan payment to the nearest cent. ■

CALCULATING THE FINAL PAYMENT

The final payment must cover the principal balance remaining after the second-to-last payment plus the interest for one payment interval on that balance. That is,

$$\begin{array}{c}\text{Final}\\ \text{payment}\end{array} = \left(\begin{array}{c}\text{Balance after the}\\ \text{second-to-last payment}\end{array}\right) + p \times \left(\begin{array}{c}\text{Balance after the}\\ \text{second-to-last payment}\end{array}\right)$$

Hence

Size of Final Payment

$$\text{Final payment} = (1 + p) \times \left(\begin{array}{c}\text{Balance after the}\\ \text{second-to-last payment}\end{array}\right) \qquad (14\text{--}5)$$

■ EXAMPLE 14.2B *CALCULATING THE SIZE OF THE FINAL PAYMENT*

Calculate the final payment in Example 14.2A, where we determined that $n = 25.457357$ quarterly payments of $1500 are needed to pay off a $28,000 loan at an interest rate of 10% compounded quarterly.

☑ SOLUTION

The final payment is the balance after the 25th payment plus 3 months' interest on that balance. That is,

$$\text{Final payment} = (1 + p) \times \text{Balance after 25 payments}$$

ALGEBRAIC SOLUTION

Using the Prospective Method, the balance after the 25th payment is the present value of the remaining $25.457357 - 25 = 0.457357$ payments. That is,

$$\text{Balance after 25 payments} = \$1500\left(\frac{1 - 1.025^{-0.457357}}{0.025}\right) = \$673.79$$

Therefore,

$$\begin{aligned}\text{Final payment} &= (1 + p) \times \text{Balance after 25 payments}\\ &= 1.025 \times \$673.79\\ &= \$690.63\end{aligned}$$

FINANCIAL CALCULATOR SOLUTION

Using the Retrospective Method, the balance after the 25th payment is the future value of the initial $28,000 loan after $6\frac{1}{4}$ years minus the future value of the first 25 payments.

Compute the balance after 25 payments.					Result
ENTER: 1500	28000	2.5	25		
PRESS: +/- PMT	PV	i	n	COMP FV	-673.79

Hence,

$$\begin{aligned}\text{Final payment} &= (1 + p) \times \text{Balance after 25 payments}\\ &= 1.025 \times \$673.79\\ &= \$690.63\end{aligned}$$

> **Trap**
>
> When the number of payments, *n,* required to amortize a loan is not an integer, it is tempting but incorrect to calculate the size of the last payment simply by multiplying *R* by the fractional part of *n.* This calculation will give only an approximate value for the size of the last payment. In the preceding example, the actual final payment was $690.63, whereas
>
> $$(\text{Fractional part of } n) \times \text{Payment} = 0.457357 \times \$1500 = \$686.03$$

CALCULATING THE INTEREST AND THE PRINCIPAL COMPONENTS OF A PAYMENT

The techniques developed in Section 14.1 for calculating the interest and principal components of any payment may also be used for loans in which the last payment is smaller than the others.

■ **EXAMPLE 14.2c   CONSTRUCTING A PARTIAL LOAN AMORTIZATION SCHEDULE WHERE THE FINAL PAYMENT IS SMALLER THAN THE OTHERS**

Martha obtained a loan from her bank for $11,000 at 10.5% compounded monthly to purchase a new car. The blended monthly payments were set at $250. Construct a partial amortization schedule showing details of the first two payments, payments 27 and 28, and the last two payments. Calculate the total interest charges.

☑ SOLUTION

The loan payments constitute an ordinary simple annuity in which

$$A_n = \$11,000 \qquad p = i = 10.5\%/12 = 0.875\% \qquad \text{and} \qquad R = \$250$$

except for the final payment. Obtain *n* by solving

$$\$11,000 = \text{Present value of } n \text{ payments of } \$250$$
$$n = 55.800772$$

There will be 56 payments in all, with the last payment being *approximately* 0.8($250) = $200.

Payment number	Payment	Interest portion	Principal portion	Principal balance
0	—	—	—	$11,000.00
1	$ 250	$ 96.25①	$ 153.75②	10,846.25③
2	250	94.90	155.10	10,691.15
.	.	.	.	.
.	.	.	.	.
26				6533.07④
27	250	57.16	192.84	6340.23
28	250	55.48	194.52	6145.71
.	.	.	.	.
.	.	.	.	.
54				444.74⑤
55	250	3.89	246.11	198.63
56	200.37⑥	1.74	198.63	0.00
Total	$13,950.37	$2950.37⑦	$11,000.00	

(1) Interest portion = $p \times$ Previous balance
$\qquad$ = 0.00875($11,000)
$\qquad$ = $96.25
(2) Principal portion = R − Interest portion
$\qquad$ = $250 − $96.25
$\qquad$ = $153.75
(3) New balance = Former balance − Principal portion
$\qquad$ = $11,000 − $153.75
$\qquad$ = $10,846.25
(4) Balance = Present value of the remaining 29.800772 payments
$\qquad$ = $6533.07
(5) Balance = Present value of the remaining 1.800772 payments
$\qquad$ = $444.74
(6) Final payment = Balance after 55 payments $\times$ (1 + p)
$\qquad$ = $198.63(1.00875)
$\qquad$ = $200.37
(7) Total interest = Total of payments − Initial loan
$\qquad$ = 55($250) + $200.37 − $11,000
$\qquad$ = $2950.37

■ EXAMPLE 14.2D   *INTEREST AND PRINCIPAL COMPONENTS OF LOAN PAYMENTS FORMING A GENERAL ANNUITY WITH THE FINAL PAYMENT SMALLER THAN THE OTHERS*

Monthly payments of $300 are made on a $10,000 loan at 9% compounded semiannually.

a. What is the interest component of the 10th payment?

b. What is the principal component of the 20th payment?

☑ SOLUTION

The loan payments form a general annuity having

$$A_n = \$10,000 \qquad R = \$300 \text{ except for the final payment}$$
$$i = 4.5\% \qquad \text{and} \qquad c = \frac{2}{12} = 0.1\overline{6}$$

Then

$$p = (1 + i)^c - 1 = 1.045^{0.1\overline{6}} - 1 = 0.007363123 = 0.7363123\%$$

ALGEBRAIC SOLUTION

In order to use the Prospective Method for calculating loan balances, we must first determine the total number of payments required to pay off the loan.

$$n = -\frac{\ln\left(1 - \dfrac{pA_n}{R}\right)}{\ln(1 + p)} = -\frac{\ln\left(1 - \dfrac{0.007363123 \times \$10,000}{\$300}\right)}{\ln(1.007363123)} = 38.38760$$

a.   Interest component of the 10th payment $= p \times$ Balance after 9 payments

$\qquad\qquad\qquad\qquad = p \times$ Present value of remaining 29.38760 payments

$$= 0.007363123(\$300)\left(\frac{1 - 1.007363123^{-29.38760}}{0.007363123}\right)$$

$\qquad\qquad\qquad\qquad = \$58.18$

b. Principal component $=$ $\begin{pmatrix}\text{Balance after} \\ \text{19 payments}\end{pmatrix}$ $-$ $\begin{pmatrix}\text{Balance after} \\ \text{20 payments}\end{pmatrix}$

$\qquad\qquad$ of the 20th payment

$$= \begin{pmatrix}\text{Present value of remaining} \\ \text{19.38760 payments}\end{pmatrix} - \begin{pmatrix}\text{Present value of remaining} \\ \text{18.38760 payments}\end{pmatrix}$$

$$= \$5401.72 - \$5141.50$$

$$= \$260.22$$

FINANCIAL CALCULATOR SOLUTION

If the Retrospective Method is used to calculate principal balances, the total number of payments required to pay off the loan is not needed.

a. $\qquad$ Interest portion of payment 10 $= p \times$ Balance after payment 9

Compute the balance after nine payments by the Retrospective Method.					Result
ENTER:	10000	300	9	0.7363123	
		+/−			COMP
PRESS:	PV	PMT	n	i	FV	−7901.63

Interest portion of payment 10 $= 0.007363123 \times \$7901.63 = \$58.18$

b. $\qquad$ Principal component $=$ Balance after $-$ Balance after

$\qquad\qquad$ of the 20th payment $\quad$ 19 payments $\quad$ 20 payments

Compute the balance after 19 payments using the Retrospective Method.				Result
ENTER:	19			
PRESS:	n	COMP	FV	−5401.72
Compute the balance after 20 payments using the Retrospective Method.				
ENTER:	20			
PRESS:	n	COMP	FV	−5141.50

Principal component of payment 20 $= \$5401.72 - \$5141.50 = \$260.22$ ■

EXERCISE 14.2

Answers to the odd-numbered problems are at the end of the book.

The final payment on each of the loans in problems 1 through 8 will differ from the indicated value of all the other payments. All payments are made at the end of the payment interval. Calculate the principal portion of the payment having the serial number listed in the second-to-last column, and the interest portion of the payment having the serial number listed in the last column. Also determine the amount of the final payment for each loan.

Problem	Original principal ($)	Payment ($)	Payment interval (months)	Nominal rate (%)	Compounding period (months)	Principal portion of payment	Interest portion of payment
1.	12,000	1000	3	10.5	3	9	5
2.	40,000	600	1	11	1	43	77

Problem	Original principal ($)	Payment ($)	Payment interval (months)	Nominal rate (%)	Compounding period (months)	Principal portion of payment	Interest portion of payment
3.	14,000	1200	6	12.5	6	7	12
4.	25,000	500	1	10.25	12	11	41
5.	70,000	2500	3	10.75	6	30	11
6.	4000	150	1	13	3	14	22
7.	45,000	500	1	10.5	6	149	117
8.	30,000	2500	6	12	3	9	19

Most of the following problems are variations of problems in Section 14.1, with the size of the periodic payments given instead of the duration of the loan or investment annuity.

9. A $37,000 loan at 10.8% compounded semiannually is to be repaid by semiannual payments of $3000 (except for a smaller final payment).

   a. What amount of principal will be repaid by the 16th payment?

   b. What will be the interest portion of the 6th payment?

   c. How much will the principal be reduced by payments 8 to 14 inclusive?

   d. How much interest will be paid in the fifth year?

10. An annuity providing a rate of return of 8% compounded quarterly was purchased for $27,000. The annuity pays $1000 at the end of each quarter (except for a smaller final payment).

    a. How much of the 16th payment will be interest?

    b. What will be the principal portion of the 33rd payment?

    c. How much interest will be paid by payments 20 to 25 inclusive?

    d. How much principal will be repaid in the sixth year?

•11. Guy borrowed $6000 at 12.75% compounded monthly and agreed to make quarterly payments of $500 (except for a smaller final payment).

    a. How much of the 11th payment will be interest?

    b. What will be the principal repaid by the 6th payment?

    c. How much interest will be paid by payments 3 to 9 inclusive?

    d. How much will the principal be reduced in the third year?

•12. An annuity paying $2000 at the end of each month (except for a smaller final payment) was purchased with $225,000 that had accumulated in an RRSP. The annuity provides a semiannually compounded rate of return of 9.5%.

    a. What amount of principal will be included in the 137th payment?

    b. What will be the interest portion of the 204th payment?

    c. How much will the principal be reduced by payments 145 to 156 inclusive?

    d. How much interest will be paid in the 20th year?

•13. Monica bought a $1250 stereo system for 20% down and payments of $200 per month (except for a smaller final payment) including interest at 15% compounded monthly. Construct the full amortization schedule for the debt. Calculate the total interest paid.

•14. Dr. Alvano borrowed $7500 at 10% compounded quarterly to purchase a new X-ray machine for his clinic. The agreement requires quarterly payments of $1000 (except for a smaller final payment). Prepare the full amortization schedule for the loan. Calculate the total interest charges.

•15. Golden Dragon Restaurant obtained a $9000 loan at 12.75% compounded annually to replace some kitchen equipment. Prepare a complete amortization schedule if payments of $2000 (except for a smaller final payment) are to be made semiannually.

•16. Valley Produce received $50,000 in vendor financing at 11.5% compounded semiannually for the purchase of harvesting machinery. The contract requires annual blended payments of $12,000 (except for a smaller final payment). Construct the complete amortization schedule for the debt. How much interest will be paid over the entire life of the loan?

•17. Suppose that the loan in problem 14 permits an additional prepayment of principal on any scheduled payment date. Prepare another amortization schedule that reflects a prepayment of $1000 with the third scheduled payment.

•18. Suppose that the loan in problem 16 permits an additional prepayment of principal on any scheduled payment date. Prepare another amortization schedule that reflects a prepayment of $10,000 with the second scheduled payment. How much interest is saved as a result of the prepayment?

•19. Cloverdale Nurseries obtained a $60,000 loan at 10.5% compounded monthly to build an additional greenhouse. Construct a partial amortization schedule for payments of $1000 per month (except for a smaller final payment) showing details of the first two payments, payments 56 and 57, and the last two payments.

•20. Jean and Walter Pereira financed the addition of a swimming pool using a $24,000 home improvement loan from their bank. Monthly payments of $500 (except for a smaller final payment) include interest at 11% compounded semiannually. Construct a partial amortization schedule showing details of the first two payments, payments 28 and 29, and the last two payments. What total interest will the Pereiras pay over the life of the loan?

••21. Elkford Logging's bank will fix the interest rate on a $60,000 loan at 10.5% compounded monthly for the first 4 years. After 4 years, the interest rate will be fixed at the prevailing 3-year rate. Monthly payments of $1000 (except for a smaller final payment) are required on the loan.

    a. If the interest rate after 4 years is 9% compounded monthly, when will the loan be paid off?

    b. What will be the amount of the final payment?

    c. What is the interest portion of the 32nd payment?

    d. Calculate the principal portion of the 58th payment.

14.3 MORTGAGE LOANS—FUNDAMENTALS

The largest single loan that most of us will ever obtain is likely to be a mortgage loan to finance the purchase of a home. Residential mortgage credit constitutes about 70% of the total household credit in Canada. Mortgage financing is also very common in the commercial sector. In fact, a higher proportion of commercial properties and residential rental properties is encumbered by mortgages than is the case for owner-occupied dwellings.

BASIC CONCEPTS AND DEFINITIONS

A mortgage loan is a loan secured by some *physical* property. The **face value** of the mortgage is the original principal amount that the borrower promises to repay. Often the borrowed money constitutes a portion of the funds used to purchase the property. If the property securing the loan is something other than real estate, it is called a *chattel* mortgage. This section will deal only with mortgage loans secured by real property.

The borrower is usually the owner of the property. The borrower/owner is referred to as the **mortgagor** and the lender as the **mortgagee.** The mortgage contract states the lender's rights and remedies in the event that the borrower defaults on the repayment of the loan. It is registered against the title of the property at the provincial government's land titles office.

Even though a homeowner may already have a mortgage loan, the remaining equity in the home can sometimes be used as security for another mortgage loan. This second lender's claim, in the event of default on the loan, will rank behind the claim of the existing mortgagee. Because of this ranking of the claims against the property in the event of default, the existing mortgage is referred to as the *first mortgage* and the additional mortgage as the *second mortgage.* Loans advertised by financial institutions as "home equity loans" or "home improvement loans" will usually be secured by a second mortgage.

The most common amortization periods over which mortgages are scheduled to be repaid are 20 and 25 years. Usually a lender will commit to a fixed interest rate for only a shorter period or term. The **term** of a mortgage loan is the length of time from the date on which the loan is advanced until the date on which the remaining principal balance is due and payable. Most institutional lenders offer terms of 6 months to 5 years. In recent years, lenders have begun to offer longer terms as they have become increasingly convinced that future rates of inflation will be low and stable. At the expiry of the term of a mortgage loan, the lender will normally renew the loan for another term, but at the prevailing market rate of interest on the date of renewal. The payments are adjusted so that the borrower continues with the original amortization period but at the new interest rate.

CALCULATING THE PAYMENT AND THE BALANCE

The federal Interest Act requires that the mortgage contract "contains a statement showing . . . the rate of interest chargeable, calculated yearly or half-yearly, not in advance." In the terminology of this text, the interest rate must be disclosed as the equivalent semiannually compounded (nominal) rate or the equivalent annually compounded rate.[5] The semiannually compounded rate has become the industry standard both for public advertising and for disclosure in the mortgage contract. The majority of mortgages require monthly payments. With interest compounded semiannually, monthly payments form an ordinary *general* annuity with $c = \frac{1}{6}$.

Some mortgage loans are based on a monthly compounded nominal rate of interest. Monthly compounding of interest is rare in first mortgages but more common in second mortgages. Monthly payments constitute an ordinary *simple* annuity if interest is compounded monthly.

Most people receive their wages semimonthly, biweekly, or weekly. Budgeting and cash-flow planning are simplified if a constant loan payment is made in each pay

---

[5]The Interest Act makes the lender liable for a very severe penalty for failing to disclose the rate of interest as required by the act. In that event, the Interest Act states that "no interest whatever shall be chargeable, payable, or recoverable, on any part of the principal money advanced." The borrower would be entitled to a refund of any interest already paid and consequently would have the loan on an interest-free basis.

period. In addition, there will be significant interest savings over the life of a mortgage if the total amount of mortgage payments in a year is paid with more frequent, smaller payments than with less frequent, larger payments. Mortgage lenders are becoming increasingly flexible in structuring mortgages for weekly, biweekly, or semimonthly payments.

Usually the borrower chooses a standard amortization period of 15, 20, or 25 years. The payments for the initial term are then calculated *as though* the interest rate is fixed for the *entire* amortization period. As has been demonstrated several times for other loans in Sections 12.1 and 14.1, the payment size is calculated such that:

$$\text{Original loan} = \frac{\text{Present value of all of the payments}}{\text{(discounted at the interest rate on the loan)}}$$

Lenders will sometimes round the calculated payment up to the next $1 or the next $10. This will shorten the amortization period slightly. The revised *n* and the final payment may be determined as explained in Section 14.2.[6] Example 14.3B provides an illustration of this case.

Occasionally, a preferred payment size is chosen by the borrower. As long as the resulting amortization period is no more than 25 years, most mortgage lenders will agree to this approach.

The principal balance on the mortgage loan after any payment may be calculated using either the Prospective Method or (preferably) the Retrospective Method. The balance at the end of a mortgage's term becomes, in effect, the beginning loan amount for the purpose of calculating the new payment size upon renewal of the mortgage loan for another term at a new interest rate. Part *b* of Example 14.3A demonstrates this procedure.

The principal and interest components of any mortgage payment may be calculated as described in Section 14.1 for blended-payment loans. Particularly when the amortization period is 20 or 25 years, the blended payments in the first few years are primarily interest. Consider a mortgage loan at 8.5% compounded semiannually with a 25-year amortization period. Figure 14.3 shows how the interest and principal components of the monthly payments change over the lifetime of the loan. At any point in the 25-year amortization, the interest portion of a payment is the vertical distance *below* the curve. The principal portion of the payment is the remainder of the 100%, that is, the vertical distance *above* the curve. For example, the payment at the end of year 14 is about 60% interest and 40% principal. During the first 5 years, more than 80% of every payment is interest. Consequently, the principal balance declines very slowly during the early years.

Figure 14.4 illustrates how the balance owed on a $100,000 mortgage loan at 8.5% compounded semiannually declines during its 25-year amortization period. As expected from the discussion in the preceding paragraph, the balance decreases slowly in the early years. It takes about one-quarter of the entire amortization period to pay off just the first $10,000 (10% of the original loan). More than 18 years are required to reduce the balance to one-half of the original principal. The rate at which the principal is reduced accelerates in later years as an ever-increasing portion of each payment is applied to the principal.

---

[6]There is, however, little point in doing these calculations in an early term since *n* and the final payment will change each time the interest rate and the payment size are altered upon renewal of the mortgage.

FIGURE   14.3

The Composition of Mortgage Payments during a 25-Year Amortization

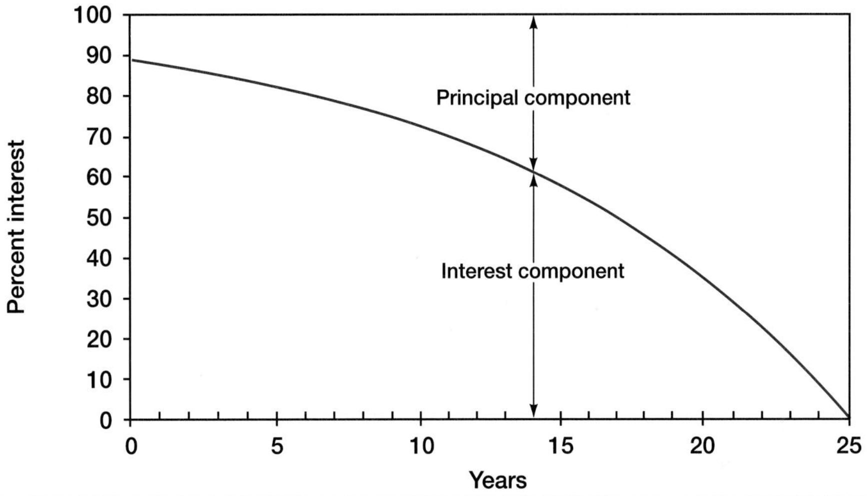

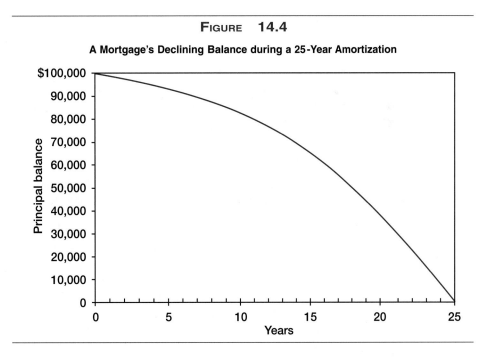

FIGURE   14.4

A Mortgage's Declining Balance during a 25-Year Amortization

■ EXAMPLE 14.3A   CALCULATING THE PAYMENTS ON A MORTGAGE LOAN AT ITS BEGINNING AND AT RENEWAL

A $50,000 mortgage loan is written with a 20-year amortization period, a 3-year term, and an interest rate of 9.5% compounded semiannually. Payments are made monthly. Calculate:

a. The balance at the end of the 3-year term.

b. The size of the payments upon renewal for 5 years at 10.5% compounded semiannually (with the loan maintaining its original 20-year amortization).

✓ SOLUTION

The mortgage payments constitute an ordinary general annuity having

$$A_n = \$50,000 \quad n = 20(12) = 240 \quad i = \frac{9.5\%}{2} = 4.75\% \quad \text{and} \quad c = \frac{2}{12} = 0.1\overline{6}$$

Then

$$p = (1 + i)^c - 1 = 1.0475^{0.1\overline{6}} - 1 = 0.00776438317$$

The monthly payment must be determined in part *a* before the balance can be obtained. The term of the mortgage is irrelevant for the payment calculation; find the payments that will pay off the loan in 20 years if the interest rate remains at 9.5% compounded semiannually.

Part *b* is handled in the same way as a new mortgage having an original principal equal to the balance from part *a* but with a 17-year amortization period and an interest rate of 10.5% compounded semiannually. In part *b*,

$$p = (1 + i)^c - 1 = 1.0525^{0.1\overline{6}} - 1 = 0.00856451515$$

ALGEBRAIC SOLUTION

a. Solving

$$\$50,000 = R\left[\frac{1 - 1.007764383^{-240}}{0.007764383}\right]$$

for *R* gives *R* = $460.12. Using the Prospective Method, the balance after 3 years (36 payments) will be the present value of the remaining 204 payments. That is,

$$A_n = \$460.12\left[\frac{1 - 1.00776438317^{-204}}{0.00776438317}\right] = \$47,027.51$$

b. The monthly payment upon renewal is the value of *R* such that the present value of 17 years' payments (*n* = 204) discounted at the new interest rate (*p* = 0.008564515) equals the balance obtained in part *a*. That is,

$$\$47,027.51 = R\left[\frac{1 - 1.008564515^{-204}}{0.008564515}\right]$$

The solution is *R* = $488.54.

The balance after the initial 3-year term will be $47,027.51, and the payments upon renewal of the mortgage at 10.5% compounded semiannually will rise to $488.54 per month.

FINANCIAL CALCULATOR SOLUTION

a. Compute the size of the loan payments.						Result
ENTER: 50000	0	0.776438317	240			
					COMP	
PRESS: PV	FV	i		n	PMT	-460.115
Compute the balance after 36 payments by the Retrospective Method.						
ENTER: 36	460.12					
	+/-				COMP	
PRESS: n	PMT				FV	-47,026.83

The balance after 3 years will be $47,026.83. Note that the calculated payment ($460.115) was rounded to the penny and reentered in the second step. The balance differs from that obtained by the Prospective Method in the algebraic solution. The cause of differing balances from the two methods was explained in Section 14.1. The technically correct answer is the one obtained using the Retrospective Method.

b. Compute the payment size at renewal.						Result
ENTER: 47026.83	0	0.8564515	204			
					COMP	
PRESS: PV	FV	i		n	PMT	-488.533

The payments upon renewal will be $488.53. ∎

■ EXAMPLE 14.3B   CALCULATIONS IN WHICH THE MORTGAGE PAYMENT IS ROUNDED TO THE NEXT HIGHER $10

The monthly payments for the first 5-year term of a $20,000 mortgage loan were based on a 10-year amortization and an interest rate of 9.9% compounded semiannually. The payments were rounded up to the next higher $10.

a. Calculate the size of the monthly payments.

b. What is the principal balance at the end of the 5-year term?

c. If the interest rate at renewal is 9% compounded semiannually for a 5-year term, calculate the new monthly payments, also rounded to the next higher $10.

d. Calculate the size of the last payment.

☑ SOLUTION

The calculations in parts a, b, and c run parallel to those in parts a and b of Example 14.3A. Therefore, only the financial calculator approach will be presented for this variation of the same type of problem.

a. The payments form an ordinary general annuity with

$$A_n = \$20{,}000 \quad n = 10(12) = 120 \quad i = \frac{9.9\%}{2} = 4.95\% \quad \text{and} \quad c = \frac{2}{12} = 0.1\overline{6}$$

Then

$$p = (1 + i)^c - 1 = 1.0495^{0.1\overline{6}} - 1 = 0.0080848171$$

Compute the size of the loan payments.					Result
ENTER: 20000	0	0.80848171	120		
PRESS: PV	FV	i	n	COMP PMT	−261.01

The monthly payment rounded to the next higher $10 is $270.

b.

Compute the balance after 5 years ($n = 60$) by the Retrospective Method.			Result
ENTER: 60	270		
PRESS: n	+/− PMT	COMP FV	−11,679.06

c. At the new nominal rate of 9% compounded semiannually,

$$p = (1 + i)^c - 1 = 1.045^{0.1\overline{6}} - 1 = 0.007363123$$

Compute the new payment size.					Result
ENTER:	0	0.7363123	60		
PRESS: +/− PV	FV	i	n	COMP PMT	−241.51

The monthly payment on renewal, rounded to the next higher $10, will be $250.

d. Since the payment size was rounded up, fewer than 60 payments may be required to extinguish the debt and the last payment will be less than $250.

Compute the number of $250 payments required to pay off the loan.		Result
ENTER:	250	
PRESS:	+/− PMT	COMP n	57.4634124

Therefore, only 58 payments will be required, with the final payment being the balance after 57 payments plus 1 month's interest. That is,

$$\text{Last payment} = \text{Balance after 57 payments} \times (1 + p)$$

Compute the balance after 57 payments.		Result
ENTER: 57		
PRESS: n	COMP FV	−115.23

Hence,

$$\text{Last payment} = \$115.23 \times (1.007363123) = \$116.08$$

QUALIFYING FOR A MORTGAGE LOAN

Mortgage lenders set eligibility criteria which quantify three key lending principles.

*   The loan should not exceed a certain fraction of the value of the property securing the loan.
*   The payments associated with home ownership should not exceed a certain percentage of the borrower's regular gross income.
*   The payments associated with home ownership *and* all other debt should not exceed a certain percentage of the borrower's regular gross income.

The first principle is intended to ensure that the lender has adequate security should the borrower default on the mortgage loan. The second and third are intended to ensure that the borrower has adequate income to comfortably make payments on both mortgage debt and other personal debt.

The three key mortgage eligibility criteria are normally expressed as ratios that are defined in the following table. Typical upper limits for what are termed *conventional first mortgages* are listed in the second column.

	Definition of ratio	Typical maximum (%)
Loan-to-value ratio $=$	$\dfrac{\text{Initial mortgage principal}}{\text{Appraised value of the property}}$	75
Gross debt service (GDS) ratio $=$	$\dfrac{\text{Average total payment per month on mortgage loan, property taxes, and heat}}{\text{Gross monthly income}}$	30–33
Total debt service (TDS) ratio $=$	$\dfrac{\text{Average total payment per month on all debt, property taxes, and heat}}{\text{Gross monthly income}}$	37–42

The ranges given for the GDS and TDS ratios reflect variations among lenders. Any particular lender usually has a single limit for each ratio. A borrower must qualify on *all* three ratios. If a prospective homeowner is eligible[7] for Canada Mortgage and Housing Corporation's First Home Loan Insurance, the upper limits are 95% for the loan-to-value ratio, 35% for the GDS ratio, and 42% for the TDS ratio.

■ EXAMPLE 14.3c   *DETERMINING THE MAXIMUM MORTGAGE LOAN FOR WHICH A BORROWER QUALIFIES*

The Schusters have saved $35,000 for the down payment on a home. Their gross monthly income is $3200. They want to determine the maximum conventional mortgage loan for which they can qualify in order to know the highest price they can pay for a home. They have 18 months remaining of $300-per-month payments on their car loan. Their bank has upper limits of 32% for the GDS ratio and 40% for the TDS ratio.

a. Allowing for property taxes of $150 per month and heating costs of $100 per month, what maximum monthly mortgage payment do the GDS and TDS ratios permit?

---

[7]To qualify under this program, the home must become the purchaser's principal residence. Furthermore, at least one of the buyers must not have owned a home as a principal residence during the preceding 5 years.

b. Based on the result in part *a,* what is the maximum mortgage loan for which the Schusters would qualify? Use a 25-year amortization and an interest rate of 8% compounded semiannually for a 5-year term. Round the answer to the nearest $100.

c. Based on a $35,000 down payment and the maximum loan from part *b,* what is the highest price they can pay for a home? Round the answer to the nearest $100.

☑ SOLUTION

a. The GDS ratio allows

$$\frac{\text{Maximum mortgage payment} + \text{Property taxes} + \text{Heating costs}}{\text{Gross income}} = 0.32$$

Hence,

Maximum mortgage payment + $150 + $100 = 0.32($3200)
Maximum mortgage payment = 0.32($3200) − $250 = $774

The TDS ratio allows

$$\frac{\text{Maximum payments on all debt} + \text{Property taxes} + \text{Heating costs}}{\text{Gross income}} = 0.40$$

Hence,

Maximum mortgage payment + $150 + $100 + $300 = 0.40($3200)
Maximum mortgage payment = 0.40($3200) − $550 = $730

For the Schuster's situation, the TDS ratio is the more restrictive ratio. It limits the maximum mortgage payment to $730 per month.

b. The TDS ratio restricts the Schusters to a maximum mortgage payment of $730 per month. For a loan at 8% compounded semiannually with a 25-year amortization,

$$n = 25(12) = 300 \qquad i = 4\% \qquad c = 0.1\overline{6} \qquad \text{and} \qquad p = 1.04^{0.1\overline{6}} - 1 = 0.006558197$$

The maximum loan permitted by the TDS ratio is

$$\begin{aligned} A_n &= \text{Present value of 300 payments of \$730} \\ &= \$730\left(\frac{1 - 1.006558197^{-300}}{0.006558197}\right) \\ &= \$95{,}600 \text{ rounded to the nearest \$100} \end{aligned}$$

c. The maximum loan-to-value ratio for a conventional first mortgage loan is 75%. Therefore, if the Schusters borrow the maximum amount ($95,600) permitted by the TDS ratio,

$$\frac{\$95{,}600}{\text{Minimum house value}} = 0.75$$

Hence,

$$\text{Minimum house value} = \frac{\$95{,}600}{0.75} = \$127{,}500$$

At this price, the minimum down payment required is

$$\$127,500 - \$95,600 = \$31,900$$

Since the Schusters have \$35,000 for a down payment, they satisfy the loan-to-value criterion with \$3100 to spare. Therefore, the maximum price[8] they can pay for a home is

$$\$127,500 + \$3100 = \$130,600$$ ∎

Common Prepayment Privileges and Penalties

Any payments beyond the regular contractual payments on a mortgage loan are called **prepayments.** Unless they include a penalty, prepayments are applied entirely to the reduction of principal, since the regular payments already cover interest charges. Mortgages that place no restrictions or penalties on extra payments by the borrower are called **fully open mortgages.** At the other extreme are **closed mortgages,** which do not allow any prepayment without a penalty. A borrower must pay a higher interest rate on an open mortgage than on a closed mortgage with the same term—typically an extra 0.5% for a 6-month-term open mortgage or an extra 1% to 1.25% for a 1-year-term open mortgage.

Between the extremes of the two categories just described are **partially open mortgages,** which grant limited penalty-free prepayment privileges. Prepayments beyond those specifically permitted usually incur significant penalties. The more common prepayments allowed on partially open mortgage loans are:

- *Annual lump payment.* Once each year on a regular payment date, the borrower can prepay without penalty up to 10% of the original amount of the mortgage loan. A few lenders permit a lump payment of up to 15%.

- *Annual increase in the regular payment.* Once each year, the borrower can increase the size of the regular payments by up to 10% for the remainder of the mortgage's term. A few lenders allow an annual increase of as much as 15%.

- *"Double-up."* On any payment date, the borrower can pay twice the regular monthly payment. Taken to the extreme, the borrower could double *every* payment.

When the mortgage contract offers more than one of these options, the borrower can take advantage of two or more simultaneously.

The implementation of these prepayment privileges varies among lending institutions. For example, the annual lump payment may be permitted only in a particular month. "Each year" might mean a calendar year or it might refer to a year between mortgage anniversary dates. Prepayment privileges may be allowed only after an initial "closed period." Examples of typical closed periods are: the first year of a 2-year term mortgage, the first 2 years of a 3-year term mortgage, and the first 3 years of a 4- or 5-year term mortgage.

It is not unusual for homeowners to sell their house partway through the term of a closed or a partially open mortgage. If a mortgage has a *portability* clause, it may be

---

[8]Mortgage lenders usually base the loan-to-value ratio on the *lesser* of the purchase price or the value placed on the property by an independent appraiser. In this example, the appraised value would have to be \$127,500 or more for the Schusters to qualify for a \$95,600 mortgage loan.

The Schusters also need to keep in mind that they will have significant legal, appraisal, survey, and registration costs in connection with the purchase transaction. If they have not otherwise provided for these costs, the \$3100 "surplus" down payment would more wisely be viewed as a reserve to cover the transaction costs.

transferred to the next property purchased by the borrower. A small proportion of mortgages are *assumable*. An assumable mortgage loan may be transferred to the new owner of the property if the new owner satisfies the lender's GDS and TDS ratios. The most typical scenario, however, is for the vendor to "pay out" the balance owed on the mortgage. Such a payout is usually treated as a prepayment. The mortgage contract usually provides for a financial penalty on any prepayment not specifically permitted by the contract. The most common prepayment penalty is the *greater* of:

- Three months' interest on the amount prepaid.
- The lender's reduction in interest revenue on the amount prepaid over the remainder of the mortgage's term.[9]

The former is usually interpreted to mean[10] "three times 1 month's interest on the amount prepaid." The latter is usually interpreted to mean the *current economic value* of the reduction in interest revenue when the prevailing market interest rate for "relending" the prepaid funds is lower than the rate on the existing mortgage. Example 14.3F illustrates the calculation of the 3 months of interest penalty. The second option for the penalty involves the calculation of the fair market value of the mortgage's payment stream. This is a more advanced topic that will be treated in Section 14.4.

Another increasingly common feature of mortgages is a "skip-a-payment" provision. This allows the borrower to miss one monthly payment each year. Whereas making a prepayment will shorten the time required to ultimately pay off a mortgage, skipping a payment will lengthen the time.

■ EXAMPLE 14.3D   *THE CONSEQUENCES OF A 10% LUMP PREPAYMENT*

The interest rate for the first 5-year term of an $80,000 mortgage loan amortized by monthly payments over 25 years is 10.5% compounded semiannually. The mortgage contract gives the borrower the privilege of prepaying up to 10% of the original mortgage loan, once each year, without interest penalty. Suppose that, at the end of the second year of the mortgage, the mortgagor makes a prepayment of $8000.

a. How much will the amortization period be shortened?

b. What will be the principal balance at the end of the 5-year term?

☑ SOLUTION

a. The $8000 prepayment at the time of the 24th regular monthly payment will be applied entirely to reducing the principal. To answer the question, we must take the following steps:

Step 1. Calculate the payments based on a 25-year amortization.
Step 2. Calculate the balance after 24 payments.
Step 3. Reduce this balance by $8000.
Step 4. Calculate the number of monthly payments needed to pay off this new balance.
Step 5. Calculate the reduction in the original 25-year amortization period.

---

[9]The following is an extract from a mortgage contract stating this option. "The amount, if any, by which interest at the rate on this mortgage exceeds interest at the current reinvestment interest rate, calculated on the amount prepaid by you, for the remaining term of the mortgage. The 'current reinvestment interest rate' at the time of prepayment means the rate at which we would lend to you on the security of a similar mortgage of your property for a term commencing on the date of prepayment and expiring on the balance due date of the mortgage."

[10]The ambiguity that exists is whether or not *p,* the interest per payment interval (one month), should be compounded when calculating the 3 months' interest. The usual interpretation is to not compound the interest.

Only the financial calculator method for the solution will be presented.

Step 1: Solve for R so that

$$\$80{,}000 = \text{Present value of 300 payments}$$

where the discount rate per payment interval is

$$p = (1 + i)^c - 1 = 1.0525^{0.1\overline{6}} - 1 = 0.008564515$$

Compute the monthly mortgage payment.					Result
ENTER: 80000 0 0.8564515 300					
PRESS: [PV] [FV] [i] [n] [COMP] [PMT]					−742.664

The size of the monthly payment is $742.66.

Step 2: Calculate the balance after 24 payments.

Compute the balance using the Retrospective Method.			Result
ENTER: 742.66			
PRESS: [+/−] [PMT] 24 [n] [COMP] [FV]			−78,475.18

Step 3: The balance after the $8000 prepayment is $70,475.18.

Step 4: Calculate the number of payments of $742.66 required to have a present value of $70,475.18.

Compute the number of payments to pay off the new balance.			Result
ENTER: 70475.18 0			
PRESS: [PV] [FV] [COMP] [n]			196.44

After the $8000 prepayment, 197 more payments will pay off the loan.

Step 5: Without the prepayment, $300 - 24 = 276$ payments remain after the 24th payment. Therefore, the $8000 prepayment reduces the amortization period by

$$276 - 197 = 79 \text{ months} = 6 \text{ years, 7 months}$$

b. Beginning with the balance of $70,475.18 after the $8000 prepayment, calculate the new balance after another 36 payments are made.

Compute the balance using the Retrospective Method.		Result
ENTER: 36		
PRESS: [n] [COMP] [FV]		−64,639.83

The balance at the end of the 5-year term will be $64,639.83

■ EXAMPLE 14.3E   *THE CONSEQUENCES OF A 10% INCREASE IN THE PAYMENT SIZE*

Two and one-half years ago the Simpsons borrowed $90,000 secured by a mortgage against the home they purchased at the time. The monthly payments, based on an interest rate of 11% compounded semiannually for a 5-year term, would amortize the debt over 25 years. The mortgage has a prepayment clause that allows the Simpsons to increase the monthly payments up to 10% once in each year after a 2-year closed period. Any increase is to be a permanent increase. If the Simpsons increase future payments by 10% starting with the 31st payment:

a. How much will the amortization period be shortened?

b. What will be the principal balance at the end of the first 5-year term?

☑ SOLUTION

Only the financial calculator method will be presented for the solution.

a. The following steps are required to answer the question.
  Step 1: Calculate the original size of the payments.
  Step 2: Calculate the balance after $2\frac{1}{2}$ years (30 payments).
  Step 3: Calculate the size of the payments after a 10% increase.
  Step 4: Calculate the number of the new, larger payments needed to amortize the balance from step 2.
  Step 5: Calculate the reduction from the original 25-year amortization period.

  Step 1: The interest rate per payment interval is

$$p = (1 + i)^c - 1 = 1.055^{0.1\overline{6}} - 1 = 0.0089633939$$

The Simpsons have been making monthly payments of $866.28.

  Step 2:

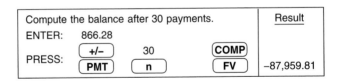

  Step 3: The increased monthly payment will be

$$1.1(\$866.28) = \$952.91$$

  Step 4: Now solve for the number of payments of $952.91 required to pay off the $87,959.81 balance.

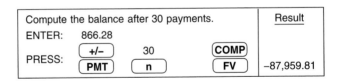

Only 197 of the larger payments are needed to pay off the loan.

Step 5: The total time to amortize the loan will be 30 + 197 = 227 months instead of the original 300 months. The amortization period will be shortened by 73 months, or 6 years, 1 month. (Note that the 10% increase in the size of the payments after $2\frac{1}{2}$ years will reduce the time required to pay off the loan by about 25%!)

b. By the end of the 5-year term, another 30 payments of $952.91 will have been made.

Compute the balance using the Retrospective Method.	Result
ENTER: 30	
PRESS: [n] [COMP] [FV]	−82,326.64

The balance at the end of the initial 5-year term will be $82,326.64.

■ EXAMPLE 14.3F *CALCULATING THE 3 MONTHS' INTEREST PENALTY ON A PREPAYMENT*

Robert and Joanne have sold their house and wish to pay out the $45,557 balance owed on their mortgage loan. The mortgage contract permits prepayment of any part of the principal at any time, but with a penalty of 3 months' interest on the amount prepaid. If the interest rate on their mortgage is 10% compounded semiannually, what interest penalty must they pay?

☑ SOLUTION

The interest rate per 1-month payment interval is

$$p = (1 + i)^c - 1 = 1.05^{0.1\overline{6}} - 1 = 0.008164844$$

One month's interest on the current balance is

$$p \times \text{Balance} = 0.008164844(\$45,557) = \$371.97$$

Therefore, the 3 months' interest prepayment penalty is

$$3(\$371.97) = \$1115.91$$

Point of Interest

An Analysis of the "Savings" Derived from Choosing a Shorter Mortgage Amortization Period

High on the list of priorities that financial advisers recommend for developing a personal financial plan is the accelerated repayment of mortgage debt. Although it is generally sound advice, the analysis commonly given to illustrate the financial benefits from the early repayment of loans is fundamentally flawed.

We will first present the calculations typically used to show the "savings" resulting from amortizing a mortgage loan over 20 years instead of 25 years. Try to use your understanding of the time value of money and the mathematics of finance to identify

the flaw in the line of reasoning before we reveal it. Then we will critically discuss the nature of the "savings" and why early repayment of your mortgage should still be a high-priority goal.

Consider a $100,000 mortgage loan at 9.75% compounded monthly. (We are using monthly compounding instead of the more usual semiannual compounding merely to simplify the calculations without sacrificing the generality of the outcome.) You can confirm that monthly payments of $891.14 are *(continued)*

(*continued*)

required for a 25-year amortization, whereas monthly payments of $948.52 would pay off the loan in 20 years. This means that a 6.4% increase in the size of the monthly payment results in a 20% reduction in the time required to pay off the loan.

At this point, the conventional financial wisdom points out that the total of the payments over the life of the 25-year mortgage is

$$12 \times 25 \times \$891.14 = \$267,342$$

whereas the total of the payments over the life of the 20-year mortgage is

$$12 \times 20 \times \$948.52 = \$227,645$$

rounded to the nearest dollar. Therefore, the shorter amortization period results in a "savings" of

$$\$267,342 - \$227,645 = \$39,697$$

This is indeed impressive. Even though we must make monthly payments on the 20-year mortgage that are 6.4% larger, the extra amounts are more than offset by the fact that we make the payments for 5 fewer years. It seems clear that the borrower should do everything possible to find the extra

$$\$948.52 - \$891.14 = \$57.38$$

each month in order to "save" almost $40,000! (This is your last chance to identify the flaw in this analysis.)

The line of reasoning that arrives at the "savings" figure of $39,697 ignores the time value of money. The comparison of the total *nominal* dollar amounts of payments made over the lifetimes of the two mortgages implies that $1 paid today has the same economic value as $1 paid 5, 10, 15, 20, or 25 years from now. (Recall from Section 6.4 that payments occurring on different dates should be compared only after calculating their economically equivalent values at the *same* focal date.) With the 20-year amortization, the borrower is paying an extra $57.38 every month for the first 20 years to "save" less valuable dollars during the subsequent 5 years. Therefore, we should expect that an analysis recognizing the time value of money will substantially reduce the true *economic* value of the "savings" below the nominal $39,697.

To gain further insight into the economic benefit of choosing the 20-year amortization instead of the 25-year amortization, let us consider Jack and Jill, who each obtain a $100,000 mortgage loan at 9.75% compounded monthly. Both Jack and Jill are able to make the monthly payments of $948.52 on a 20-year amortization. Jack decides to take the 20-year amortization. Jill chooses the 25-year amortization and plans to invest the $57.38 difference between her monthly payment of $891.14 and the $948.52 she would pay on a 20-year amortization.

Let us compare the economic positions, 20 years from now, of Jack and Jill with respect to the $948.52 that each of them has paid every month for the previous 20 years. Through a mathematical time warp, we join Jack and his friends at his mortgage-burning party in celebration of the final payment on his mortgage. Still vengeful over a nasty childhood incident in which Jill tripped him as he went up the hill to fetch a pail of water, Jack invites Jill to the party, knowing full well that she has 5 years remaining on her mortgage loan with a balance equal to:

$$\begin{pmatrix} \text{Present value of} \\ \text{last 60 payments} \end{pmatrix} = \$42,186$$

As Jack smugly raises a match to his mortgage contract, he asks Jill when she will be inviting everyone over for her mortgage burning.

"Pick a date," replies Jill.

"How so?" asks Jack in surprise.

"Well . . . you see," explains Jill, "when we originally obtained the mortgage loans 20 years ago, I began to faithfully invest the $57.38 difference between my monthly payment on a 25-year amortization and your larger monthly payment on the 20-year amortization. As it turns out, I have been able to earn the same 9.75% monthly compounded rate of return on the invested funds as we have been paying on our mortgage loans. Consequently, my investments are now worth

$$\begin{pmatrix} \text{Future value of 240} \\ \text{payments of \$57.38} \end{pmatrix} = \$42,186$$

(*continued*)

(*concluded*)

This is exactly equal to the current balance on my mortgage loan. I could use these funds to pay off the mortgage, so, in effect, I am mortgage-free . . . just like you."

The example of Jack and Jill demonstrates that there is no economic advantage of one amortization period over the other if the time value of money equals the interest rate on the loan. The economic values of the two loan payment streams are then equal on any (focal) date.

If the time value of money is less than the interest rate on the loan, the loan with the shorter amortization period has the lower economic value and should be preferred by the borrower. (For alternative cash-outflow streams, you should choose the stream with the smaller economic value.) If the time value of money is greater than the interest rate on the loan, the loan with the longer amortization period has the smaller economic value and should be preferred by the borrower.

There are still very good reasons for accelerating the repayment of mortgage loans (and any other personal debt). However, the economic benefits are not as great as suggested by an analysis that ignores the time value of money. The good reasons are:

- Most people are not able to earn as large a rate of return on investments (of similar low risk) as they pay on their debt. This is particularly true after adjusting for income tax. The imputed rate of return realised on funds "invested" to reduce personal debt is the rate of interest paid on the debt. This imputed interest income is not taxable. If an individual's marginal tax rate is 40%, she would have to earn a 13.75% rate of interest on a taxable investment to attain the same *after-tax* rate of return as effectively earned by paying down the principal on her mortgage bearing interest at 8.25%.

- Most people are more readily motivated to invest in the reduction of personal debt than to put money in other investments.

Exercise 14.3

Answers to the odd-numbered problems are at the end of the book.

1. A $100,000 mortgage loan at 8.2% compounded semiannually has a 25-year amortization. Assuming that the interest rate does not change for the entire 25 years, calculate to the nearest dollar the principal reduction in each successive 5-year interval in the amortization period.

2. The interest rate on a $100,000 mortgage loan is 9% compounded semiannually.

   a. Calculate the monthly payment for each of 15-, 20-, and 25-year amortizations.

   b. By what percentage must the monthly payment be increased for a 20-year amortization instead of a 25-year amortization?

   c. By what percentage must the monthly payment be increased for a 15-year amortization instead of a 25-year amortization?

   d. Calculate the total interest paid over each of the three amortization periods (assuming that the interest rate is fixed for the entire amortization period).

3. A $100,000 mortgage loan has a 25-year amortization.

   a. Calculate the monthly payment at interest rates of 8%, 9%, and 10% compounded semiannually.

   b. By what percentage does the monthly payment on the 10% mortgage exceed the monthly payment on the 9% mortgage?

   c. Calculate the total interest paid over the entire 25-year amortization period at each of the three interest rates.

4. The Graftons can afford a maximum mortgage payment of $1000 per month. The current interest rate is 8.25% compounded semiannually. What is the maximum mortgage loan they can afford if the amortization period is:

   a. 15 years?   *b.* 20 years?   *c.* 25 years?

5. The Tarkanians can afford a maximum mortgage payment of $1000 per month. What is the maximum mortgage loan they can afford if the amortization period is 25 years and the interest rate is:

   a. 8% compounded semiannually?   *b.* 9% compounded semiannually?

6. Calculate the monthly payment on a $100,000 mortgage loan:

   a. At 8.5% compounded semiannually with a 20-year amortization.

   b. At 9.5% compounded semiannually with a 25-year amortization.

   (Other things being the same, mortgage payments are larger for higher interest rates and smaller for longer amortization periods. Note in part *b* that the 1% higher interest rate more than offsets the effect of the 5-year increase in the amortization period.)

•7. The Switzers are nearing the end of the first 5-year term of a $100,000 mortgage loan with a 25-year amortization. The interest rate has been 8.5% compounded semiannually for the initial term. How much will their monthly payments increase if the interest rate upon renewal is 9.5% compounded semiannually?

•8. The Melnyks are nearing the end of the first 3-year term of a $100,000 mortgage loan with a 20-year amortization. The interest rate has been 9% compounded semiannually for the initial term. How much will their monthly payments decrease if the interest rate upon renewal is 8% compounded semiannually?

•9. The interest rate for the first 3 years of an $80,000 mortgage loan is 10.5% compounded semiannually. Monthly payments are calculated using a 25-year amortization.

   a. What will be the principal balance at the end of the 3-year term?

   b. What will the monthly payments be if the loan is renewed at 9.5% compounded semiannually (and the original amortization period is continued)?

•10. Five years ago, Ms. Halliday received a mortgage loan from the Bank of Nova Scotia for $60,000 at 11.25% compounded semiannually for a 5-year term. Monthly payments were based on a 25-year amortization. The bank is agreeable to renewing the loan for another 5-year term at 10% compounded semiannually. Calculate the principal reduction that will occur in the second 5-year term if:

   a. The payments are recalculated based on the new interest rate and a continuation of the original 25-year amortization.

   b. Ms. Halliday continues to make the same payments as she made for the first 5 years (resulting in a reduction of the amortization period).

•11. A $40,000 mortgage loan charges interest at 9.75% compounded *monthly* for a 4-year term. Monthly payments were calculated for a 15-year amortization and then rounded up to the next higher $10.

   a. What will be the principal balance at the end of the first term?

   b. What will the monthly payments be on renewal for a 3-year term if it is calculated for an interest rate of 9% compounded monthly and an 11-year amortization period, but again rounded to the next higher $10?

•12. A $95,000 mortgage written at 10.75% compounded semiannually is to be repaid by quarterly payments calculated for a 20-year amortization and then rounded to the next higher $100. Determine the number of payments that must be made and the size of the final payment if the interest rate does not change over the life of the mortgage.

•13. The interest rate for the first 5 years of a $27,000 mortgage loan was 11.25% compounded semiannually. The monthly payments computed for a 10-year amortization were rounded to the next higher $10.

    a. Calculate the principal balance at the end of the first term.

    b. Upon renewal at 10.5% compounded semiannually, monthly payments were calculated for a 5-year amortization and again rounded up to the next $10. What will be the amount of the last payment?

•14. The Delgados have a gross monthly income of $6000. Monthly payments on personal loans total $500. Their bank limits the gross debt service ratio at 33% and the total debt service ratio at 42%.

    a. Rounded to the nearest $100, what is the maximum 25-year mortgage loan for which they can qualify on the basis of their income? Assume monthly heating costs of $120 and property taxes of $200 per month. Current mortgage rates are 8.6% compounded semiannually.

    b. Rounded to the nearest $100, what minimum down payment must they have to qualify for the maximum conventional mortgage on a new home?

•15. The Archibalds are eligible for Canada Mortgage and Housing Corporation's First Home Loan Insurance. Consequently, their limits are 95% for the loan-to-value ratio, 35% for the GDS ratio, and 42% for the TDS ratio.

    a. Rounded to the nearest $100, what is the maximum 25-year mortgage loan for which they can qualify if their gross monthly income is $5000 and their payments on personal debt amount to $600 per month? Assume monthly heating costs of $100 and property taxes of $175 per month. Current mortgage rates are 8.25% compounded semiannually.

    b. If they make the minimum down payment, what is the maximum price (rounded to the nearest $100) they can pay for a home? (Assume the purchase price equals the appraised value.)

•16. A mortgage loan requires monthly payments of $683.52 for the initial 5-year term of a 25-year amortization. If the loan was for $75,000, calculate the semiannually compounded nominal rate of interest on the loan.

•17. The interest rate on a $100,000 mortgage loan is 8.75% compounded semiannually.

    a. What are the monthly payments for a 25-year amortization?

    b. Suppose that the borrower instead makes weekly payments equal to one-fourth of the monthly payment calculated in part *a.* When will the loan be paid off if the interest rate does not change? Assume there are exactly 52 weeks in a year.

•18. A $100,000 mortgage at 8.2% compounded semiannually with a 25-year amortization requires monthly payments. The mortgage allows the mortgagor to prepay up to 10% of the original principal once each year. How much will the amortization period be shortened if, on the first anniversary of the mortgage, the mortgagor makes (in addition to the regular payment) a prepayment of:

    a. $5000?   *b.* $10,000?

•19. A $100,000 mortgage at 8.2% compounded semiannually with a 20-year amortization requires monthly payments. The mortgage allows the mortgagor to prepay up to 10% of the original principal once each year. How much will the amortization period be shortened if, on the first anniversary of the mortgage, the mortgagor makes (in addition to the regular payment) a prepayment of:

    a. $5000?   *b.* $10,000?

•20. A $100,000 mortgage at 8% compounded semiannually with a 25-year amortization requires monthly payments. The mortgage entitles the mortgagor to increase the regular payment by up to 10% once each year. How much will the amortization period be shortened if, after the 12th payment, the payments are increased by:

   a. 5%?   b. 10%?

•21. A $100,000 mortgage at 8% compounded semiannually with a 20-year amortization requires monthly payments. The mortgage allows the mortgagor to increase the regular payment by up to 10% once each year. How much will the amortization period be shortened if, after the 12th payment, the payments are increased by:

   a. 5%?   b. 10%?

•22. A $100,000 mortgage at 8.5% compounded semiannually with a 25-year amortization requires monthly payments. The mortgage allows the mortgagor to "double up" on a payment once each year. How much will the amortization period be shortened if the mortgagor doubles the tenth payment?

•23. A $100,000 mortgage at 8.8% compounded semiannually with a 20-year amortization requires monthly payments. The mortgage allows the mortgagor to "double up" on a payment once each year. How much will the amortization period be shortened if the mortgagor doubles the eighth payment?

•24. A $100,000 mortgage at 8.75% compounded semiannually with a 20-year amortization requires monthly payments. The mortgage allows the mortgagor to miss a payment once each year. How much will the amortization period be lengthened if the mortgagor misses the 9th payment? (The interest that accrues during the 9th month is converted to principal at the end of the 9th month.)

•25. A $100,000 mortgage at 8.25% compounded semiannually with a 25-year amortization requires monthly payments. The mortgage allows the mortgagor to miss a payment once each year. How much will the amortization period be lengthened if the mortgagor misses the 12th payment? (The interest that accrues during the 12th month is converted to principal at the end of the 12th month.)

•26. A $100,000 mortgage at 9.1% compounded semiannually with a 20-year amortization requires monthly payments. How much will the amortization period be shortened if a $10,000 lump payment is made along with the 12th payment and payments are increased by 10% starting in the third year?

•27. A $100,000 mortgage at 8.8% compounded semiannually with a 25-year amortization requires monthly payments. How much will the amortization period be shortened if payments are increased by 10% starting in the second year and a $10,000 lump payment is made along with the 24th payment?

•28. Monthly payments on a $70,000 mortgage are based on an interest rate of 11.5% compounded semiannually and a 20-year amortization. If a $5000 prepayment is made along with the 32nd payment,

   a. How much will the amortization period be shortened?

   b. What will be the principal balance after 4 years?

•29. The interest rate for the first 5 years of a $120,000 mortgage is 9.9% compounded semiannually. Monthly payments are based on a 25-year amortization. If a $5000 prepayment is made at the end of the second year,

   a. How much will the amortization period be shortened?

   b. What will be the principal balance at the end of the 5-year term?

•30. A $100,000 mortgage loan at 9% compounded *monthly* has a 25-year amortization.

  a. What prepayment at the end of the first year will reduce the time required to pay off the loan by 1 year?

  b. Instead of the prepayment in part a, what prepayment at the end of the 10th year will reduce the time required to pay off the loan by 1 year?

•31. After 3 years of the first 5-year term at 10.25% compounded semiannually, Dean and Cindy decide to take advantage of the privilege of increasing the payments on their $100,000 mortgage loan by 10%. The monthly payments were originally calculated for a 20-year amortization.

  a. How much will the amortization period be shortened?

  b. What will be the principal balance at the end of the 5-year term?

•32. The MacLellans originally chose to make payments of $800 per month on a $69,000 mortgage written at 10.5% compounded semiannually for the first 5 years. After 3 years they exercised the right under the mortgage contract to increase the payments by 10%.

  a. If the interest rate does not change, when will they extinguish the mortgage debt?

  b. What will be the principal balance at the end of the 5-year term?

••33. The monthly payments on the Wolskis' $83,000 mortgage were originally based on a 25-year amortization and an interest rate of 9.9% compounded semiannually for a 5-year term. After 2 years, they elected to increase their monthly payments by $50, and at the end of the fourth year they made a $5000 prepayment.

  a. How much have they shortened the amortization period?

  b. What was the principal balance at the end of the 5-year term?

•34. In the 3 years since Mr. and Mrs. Rosano obtained their $66,000 mortgage loan, the interest rate for a 5-year term mortgage has fallen from 12% to 10%, both compounded semiannually. The mortgage contract allows the mortgagor to prepay any principal amount after the third anniversary of the mortgage upon payment of an additional 3 months' interest on the principal amount prepaid. If the Rosanos were to refinance the current balance on their mortgage to take advantage of the current low rates, what would be the amount of the 3 months of interest penalty? The original mortgage loan requires monthly payments based on a 20-year amortization.

•35. Twenty-seven months ago Mr. and Mrs. Currie obtained a $90,000 mortgage loan at 11% compounded semiannually for a 5-year term. Their monthly payments are based on a 20-year amortization. Their property has been expropriated for a new highway. What amount is required to settle the mortgage debt if there is a penalty of 3 months' interest on any prepayment in excess of 10% of the original principal?

*14.4 MORTGAGE LOANS—ADDITIONAL TOPICS

A mortgage loan sometimes imposes costs on the borrower in addition to interest charges. The effective cost of borrowing, discussed in the first subsection, is a way of expressing the combined amount of interest charges and other costs as an equivalent rate of interest.

A mortgage loan represents an investment of funds by the lender. Most mortgage contracts can be sold by the lender to another investor at any time during the term of the mortgage. The second topic of this section addresses the matter of determining the fair market value of a mortgage contract.

The last subsection discusses reverse mortgages, a type of mortgage loan the availability and popularity of which have grown rapidly in Canada since 1990.

THE EFFECTIVE COST OF BORROWING

Some mortgage lenders, particularly individual investors, use the services of a mortgage broker. The broker finds a borrower who needs mortgage financing, determines the financial condition and creditworthiness of the borrower, and conducts negotiations with the borrower. All or a substantial portion of the broker's remuneration for these services is taken out of the principal amount of any loan that is advanced. Consequently, the borrower receives less than the face value of the loan but must repay the entire face value over the amortization period. The amount retained to compensate the broker is variously called the brokerage fee, the bonus, the placement fee, the commission, the finder's fee, or the discount. A mortgage loan in which such an amount, by whatever name, is retained by the broker or lender is called a *bonused mortgage*.[11]

A brokerage fee or bonus represents a cost of borrowing in addition to the interest charges. It is desirable, particularly from a borrower's point of view, to have a means of combining the interest and the brokerage fee in order to obtain some measure of the overall "true" cost of borrowing.[12] Borrowers can then use this cost to compare mortgage loan alternatives offered by various lenders.

Most provinces in Canada have passed legislation requiring disclosure of the impact of brokerage fees on the cost of borrowing. The most common requirement is for the disclosure of an effective annual interest rate that impounds the brokerage fee. We can gain an insight into how to obtain this effective interest rate by taking the following view. Since the borrower initially receives net or "useful" loan proceeds of only

Face value of the mortgage loan − Brokerage fee

then the payments made over the term of the loan effectively reduce the loan balance by only

(Face value of the mortgage loan − Brokerage fee) − (End-of-term balance)

The effective interest rate we want is the rate implied by the mortgage payments reducing the loan balance from just the initial *net* loan proceeds to the end-of-term balance.

> **Effective Cost of Borrowing:** The effective or "true" cost of borrowing for a bonused mortgage loan is the annually compounded discount rate that makes the combined present value of the payments during the term of the mortgage and the balance at the end of the term equal to the net loan proceeds.

This definition of the effective cost of borrowing suggests a two-step procedure for calculating it.

---

[11]The choice of this name clearly originates with the mortgage brokers, not with the borrowers!

[12]Mortgage lenders routinely require an official land survey, an official appraisal of the property's market value, and a title search of the property that is to secure the mortgage loan. Most mortgages make provision for the lender to directly pay the survey and appraisal costs, legal fees, and other disbursements, and to deduct them from the loan proceeds advanced to the borrower. These are not considered a cost of borrowing in the same sense as interest and brokerage fees. A prudent purchaser of real estate will incur most of these expenses even if a mortgage loan is not required. Therefore, these other charges are not deducted from the face value of the loan for the purpose of calculating the "true" cost of borrowing.

1. Solve for p, the interest rate per payment interval, that satisfies

$$\begin{pmatrix} \text{Face value of} \\ \text{the mortgage} \end{pmatrix} - \begin{pmatrix} \text{Brokerage} \\ \text{fee} \end{pmatrix}$$
$$= \begin{pmatrix} \text{Present value of} \\ \text{the mortgage payments} \\ \text{during the term} \end{pmatrix} + \begin{pmatrix} \text{Present value of} \\ \text{the balance at} \\ \text{the end of the term} \end{pmatrix}$$

2. Calculate the effective annual interest rate corresponding to p using

$$f = (1 + p)^m - 1 \qquad\qquad (9\text{--}3a)$$

where m in this context represents the number of payment intervals in a year.

■ EXAMPLE 14.4A   *Calculating the "True" or Effective Cost of Borrowing*

A mortgage broker arranged a $50,000 face value mortgage loan at 10.75% compounded semiannually. The loan has a 5-year term and requires monthly payments that would repay the face value in 20 years. A brokerage fee of $3767.45 was deducted from the face value. What is the borrower's effective annual cost of borrowing (over the 5-year term)?

☑ SOLUTION

The borrower receives only

$$\$50,000 - \$3767.45 = \$46,232.55$$

but must make payments that would amortize $50,000 over 20 years. The brokerage fee of $3767.45 is viewed, for the purpose of this calculation, as a "front-end" interest charge. The steps in the solution are

Step 1:   Calculate p corresponding to 10.75% compounded semiannually.
Step 2:   Calculate the payment size.
Step 3:   Calculate the balance at the end of the term.
Step 4:   Calculate the value for p that makes the funds actually received ($46,232.55) equal to the combined present value of the 60 payments and the balance owed (from step 3) at the end of the 5-year term.
Step 5:   Convert the periodic rate from step 4 to the effective annual rate.

Step 1:

$$p = (1 + 0.05375)^{0.1\overline{6}} - 1 = 0.008764053$$

Step 2: Compute the mortgage payment.					Result
ENTER: 50000 0 0.8764053 240					
PRESS: [PV] [FV] [i] [n] [COMP] [PMT]					−499.756
Step 3: Compute the balance at the end of the term.					
ENTER: 499.76 60					
PRESS: [+/−] [PMT] [n] [COMP] [FV]					−45,167.50
Step 4: Compute the interest rate per payment interval.					
ENTER: 46232.55					
PRESS: [PV] [COMP] [i]					1.05324

Step 5: The corresponding effective annual rate is

$$f = (1 + p)^m - 1$$
$$= 1.0105324^{12} - 1$$
$$= 0.13397$$
$$= 13.40\%$$

The impact of the brokerage fee is to make the effective annual rate for the overall cost of borrowing 13.40% (compared to

$$f = 1.05375^2 - 1 = 0.11039 = 11.04\%$$

for the quoted interest rate of 10.75% compounded semiannually).   ∎

■ EXAMPLE 14.4B   *DETERMINING WHICH MORTGAGE LOAN HAS THE LOWER "TRUE" COST OF BORROWING*

Maurice intends to raise $50,000 for his business by obtaining a mortgage loan secured by his home. He is considering two alternatives. A mortgage broker will approve a $52,000 face value loan at 10.5% compounded semiannually but will retain a $2000 commission. A credit union will grant a $50,000 loan at 11.5% compounded semiannually with no other fees. Either loan would have a 5-year term and would require monthly payments based upon a 15-year amortization. Which loan is a better deal for Maurice?

☑ SOLUTION

The choice is not as simple as selecting the loan with the lower payments, because when the loans are renewed after 5 years, their balances will not be equal. The best decision criterion is to choose the loan with the lower effective rate of interest (including any brokerage fee).

For the credit union loan, the cost of borrowing is just the interest cost. The effective annual interest rate is

$$f = (1 + i)^m - 1 = 1.0575^2 - 1 = 0.118306 = 11.83\%$$

For the loan from the broker, the commission or brokerage fee is also a cost of borrowing. The $2000 front-end commission cost must be combined with the actual interest costs and expressed as an effective rate of interest for the 5-year term. To determine this rate, we will:

Step 1: Calculate *p* corresponding to 10.5% compounded semiannually.
Step 2: Calculate the payments on the brokered loan.
Step 3: Calculate the balance on the brokered loan at the end of the 5-year term.
Step 4: Calculate the periodic rate that is implied if the payments in step 1 and the balance in step 3 were for a $50,000 loan instead of a $52,000 loan.
Step 5: Convert the periodic rate to an effective annual rate.

Step 1:

$$p = (1 + 0.0525)^{0.1\overline{6}} - 1 = 0.0085645151$$

Step 2: Compute the mortgage payment.					Result
ENTER: 52000	0	0.85645151	180		
PRESS: [PV]	[FV]	[i]	[n]	[COMP] [PMT]	−567.653

Step 3: Compute the balance at the end of the term.

ENTER: 567.65   60

PRESS: [+/-]   [COMP]
           [PMT]   [n]   [FV]   −42,460.06

Step 4: Compute the equivalent rate per payment interval.

ENTER: 50000

PRESS: [COMP]
           [PV]   [i]   0.9475206

Step 5:   The corresponding effective annual rate is

$$f = (1 + p)^m - 1$$
$$= 1.0009475206^{12} - 1$$
$$= 0.11982$$
$$= 11.98\%$$

The credit union loan has a slightly (0.15%) lower effective annual cost of borrowing, making it the better choice.   ∎

VALUATION OF MORTGAGES

A mortgage loan represents an investment by the lender in the form of a loan to the borrower. The mortgage contract specifies the stream of future payments to which the lender is entitled. If the payments are received as scheduled, the lender's rate of return on the principal outstanding from time to time is the rate of interest charged on the loan.

The original lender can sell his legal interest in the mortgage contract to another investor without the consent of the borrower. This might be done, for example, if the lender needs to raise a substantial amount of cash before the expiry of the current term of the mortgage. The central question for both the original lender and the new investor is: What price should be paid for the right to receive the remaining payments?

Suppose there are 2 years remaining in the 5-year term of a mortgage loan. Also suppose that interest rates in general have *risen* over the past 3 years. If the new investor were to pay an amount equal to the current principal balance, her rate of return on investment would equal the contractual interest rate on the mortgage loan. Since prevailing interest rates are now higher than that contractual rate, she will prefer the alternative of investing her funds by making a new loan. Consequently, the owner of the mortgage must expect to receive a price lower than the outstanding balance on the mortgage. The price must be low enough that the remaining scheduled payments provide a rate of return to the purchaser equal to the *prevailing* rate on new 2-year-term mortgages. Then investors will be indifferent between the alternatives of buying the existing mortgage or making a new loan.

We again turn to the Valuation Principle (discussed in Section 7.2) for guidance. The fair market value is the present value of the expected payments discounted at the *prevailing market-based* rate of return. Adapting the Valuation Principle to the specific case of mortgage valuation,

Fair market value of a mortgage	=	Present value of the payments remaining in the current term	+	Present value of the principal balance at the end of the term

---

Tip

Remember that it is the *contractual* rate of interest on the mortgage loan that is used as the discount rate in the original calculation of the mortgage payments, and in the calculation of the balance owed on the loan at any point. It is the *prevailing market* rate that is used to discount both the payments and the end-of-term balance to determine the mortgage's fair market value at any later date.

■ EXAMPLE 14.4c   CALCULATING THE FAIR MARKET VALUE OF A MORTGAGE PARTWAY THROUGH ITS TERM

A $65,000 mortgage loan was made 3 years ago at 11% compounded semiannually. The monthly payments for the first 5-year term were based on a 20-year amortization. What price can the lender expect to receive by selling the mortgage if the current rate on new mortgage loans for a 2-year term is:

a. 12% compounded semiannually?

b. 11% compounded semiannually?

c. 10% compounded semiannually?

☑ SOLUTION

The fair market value of the mortgage will be the present value of the 24 payments remaining in the 5-year term plus the present value of the principal balance due at the end of the term. The discount rate used should be the prevailing rate of return required on similar investments in the capital markets. From the point of view of an investor, the existing mortgage has 2 years to go until the end of its term, and it must offer a rate of return that is competitive with the rate on new 2-year term mortgage loans.

The three steps in the solution are:

Step 1: Calculate the size of the monthly payment.

Step 2: Calculate the principal balance after 5 years.

Step 3: Calculate the combined present value of the remaining 24 payments and the balance from step 2. The discount rate should be the current market rate on new 2-year term mortgages.

Step 1: The interest rate per payment interval for the existing mortgage is

$$p = 1.055^{0.1\overline{6}} - 1 = 0.0089633939$$

Compute the mortgage payment.					Result
ENTER: 65000 0 0.89633939 240					
PRESS: PV FV i n (COMP) PMT					−660.166
Step 2: Compute the balance at the end of the term.					
ENTER: 660.17 60					
PRESS: (+/−) PMT n (COMP) FV					−58,873.28

Step 3: Calculate *p* for each of the three current market rates.

a. $\qquad p = 1.06^{0.1\overline{6}} - 1 = 0.0097587942$

b. $\qquad p = 1.055^{0.1\overline{6}} - 1 = 0.0089633939$

c. $\qquad p = 1.05^{0.1\overline{6}} - 1 = 0.0081648461$

Using each of these discount rates, calculate the combined present value of the remaining 24 payments and the balance from step 2.

a.				Result
ENTER: 0.97587942		24		
PRESS: [i]		[n]	[COMP] [PV]	60,697.75
b.				
ENTER: 0.89633939				
PRESS: [i]			[COMP] [PV]	61,722.33
c.				
ENTER: 0.81648461				
PRESS: [i]			[COMP] [PV]	62,770.61

The price that the lender can expect to receive for the mortgage is:

a. $60,697.75   *b.* $61,722.33   *c.* $62,770.61

Notes: The outstanding balance on the mortgage at the time of sale (after 36 payments) is $61,722.33. The market prices calculated above provide specific examples of the following three general results.

1. When the required return in the market *equals* the contractual rate on the mortgage, the fair market value is the *actual* principal balance currently owed on the mortgage (part *b*).
2. When the market requires a rate of return *greater* than the contractual rate, investors pay *less* than the principal balance in order to obtain the higher rate of return (part *a*).
3. When the market will accept a rate of return *less* than the contractual rate, investors will pay *more* than the principal balance owed and still earn the competitive rate of return (part *c*). ■

In addition to transactions involving the sale of mortgages, the calculation of the fair market value of a mortgage may also arise in a circumstance involving a vendor take-back mortgage or a mortgage prepayment penalty.

VENDOR TAKE-BACK MORTGAGE   A prospective purchaser may propose to buy a property with a cash down payment and with the balance of the purchase price set up as a loan payable by the purchaser to the vendor. The loan would normally be secured by a mortgage contract between the purchaser and the vendor. A mortgage arising in this context is called a **vendor take-back mortgage.**

It is common with a vendor take-back mortgage for the purchaser to try to negotiate an interest rate that is below the current market rate. This would confer a financial benefit to the buyer at the expense of the vendor. (If the vendor were instead to receive the full purchase price in cash, the funds could be invested in another mortgage loan at the higher current market rate.) The value of the financial benefit to the purchaser of the property is the difference between the *face* value and the *fair market* value of the vendor take-back mortgage. Example 14.4D presents a scenario in which the economic value of this benefit is determined.

MORTGAGE PREPAYMENT PENALTY   In Section 14.3 it was pointed out that the most common penalty on a prepayment not specifically permitted in the mortgage contract is the *greater* of:

*   Three months' interest on the amount prepaid.
*   The lender's reduction in interest revenue on the amount prepaid over the remainder of the mortgage's term.[13]

The second alternative is relevant only in cases where the prevailing interest rates on mortgage loans have had a net decline between the date of issue of a mortgage and the date of prepayment. Suppose, for example, a mortgage loan written at 10% compounded semiannually is prepaid when 2 years remain in its term. If the prevailing market rate on a new mortgage loan for a 2-year term is 8% compounded semiannually, then the lender will suffer a reduction in interest revenue because of the 2% interest rate differential. However, to simply add the *nominal* differences between corresponding interest components of the 24 payments would overstate the *current* economic value of the reduced interest revenue. This is because $1 of lost interest revenue from the 24th payment is not worth as much *today* as $1 lost from the first payment.

The current economic value of the lender's loss is best determined by an approach that does not attempt to directly calculate the reductions in interest revenue. Assuming that the remaining 24 payments will be paid as provided by the mortgage contract, the market value of the mortgage *exceeds* the principal balance because the prevailing market interest rate (8%) is *less* than the contractual rate (10%) on the mortgage. The lender could sell the mortgage for its market value. Therefore, the borrower should reasonably expect to pay this market value rather than the principal balance in order that the lender not suffer any economic loss. In effect, the prepayment penalty the borrower pays under the second alternative is the difference between the fair market value of the mortgage and the principal balance. That is,

$$\begin{array}{c} \text{Penalty to prepay} \\ \text{the mortgage balance} \end{array} = \begin{array}{c} \text{Fair market value} \\ \text{of the mortgage} \end{array} - \text{Principal balance}$$

Example 14.4E provides an illustration of this calculation.

■ **EXAMPLE 14.4D**   *CALCULATING THE EQUIVALENT CASH PRICE ON A PROPERTY SALE THAT INCLUDES A VENDOR TAKE-BACK MORTGAGE AT A BELOW-MARKET INTEREST RATE*

A house is listed for $125,000. A potential purchaser makes a "full-price" offer of $125,000 subject to the vendor's taking back a $75,000 mortgage at 8% compounded semiannually. Monthly payments would be based on a 25-year amortization. The

---

[13]The rationale for the second option is that the lender should be placed in the same economic position as if the borrower had fulfilled his obligations under the mortgage contract. Under basic contract law, if one party breaches a contract, the other party is normally entitled to be put in the same position as if the breach had not occurred.

current market rate for mortgages with terms of 5 years and longer is 10% compounded semiannually. To the nearest dollar, calculate the equivalent cash value of the offer if the term of the vendor take-back mortgage is:

a. 25 years.   *b.* 5 years.

☑ SOLUTION

The cash equivalent value of the offer is the cash price that would put the vendor in the same economic position as the actual offer. Since the vendor could sell the proposed mortgage for its fair market value, the cash equivalent value of the offer is the down payment of $50,000 plus the fair market value of the vendor take-back mortgage. The steps for obtaining the mortgage's fair market value are:

Step 1: Calculate the payments on the vendor take-back mortgage.
Step 2: Calculate the balance owed at the end of the mortgage's term.
Step 3: Calculate the combined present value of the mortgage payments during the term and the balance at the end of the term. Use the current market rate as the discount rate.

Step 1: The interest rate per payment interval on the take-back mortgage is

$$p = 1.04^{0.1\overline{6}} - 1 = 0.0065581969$$

Compute the mortgage payment.					Result
ENTER: 75000	0	0.65581969	300		
PRESS: PV	FV	i	n	COMP PMT	−572.410

a. Step 2: If the term equals the full amortization period, the balance at the end of the term will be $0.
Step 3: The market interest rate per payment interval is

$$p = 1.05^{0.1\overline{6}} - 1 = 0.0081648461$$

Discount all 300 payments at the market rate.			Result
ENTER: 0.81648461	572.41		
PRESS: i	+/− PMT	COMP PV	63,993.09

The cash equivalent value of the offer is $50,000 + $63,993 = $113,993.

b.

Step 2: Compute the balance at the end of the 5-year term.			Result
ENTER: 75000	0.65581969	60	
PRESS: PV	i	n	COMP FV	−69,101.83
Step 3: Discount 60 payments and the balance.			
ENTER:	0.81648461		
PRESS:	i	COMP PV	69,489.78

The cash value of the offer is $50,000 + $69,490 = $119,490.   ∎

■ EXAMPLE 14.4E   CALCULATING THE PENALTY ON PREPAYMENT OF A MORTGAGE'S BALANCE

Robert and Joanne have sold their house and wish to pay out the $45,557 balance owed on their mortgage loan with 2 years remaining in its term. The mortgage contract permits prepayment of the balance at any time, but with a penalty equal to the *greater* of:

- Three months' interest on the balance.
- The difference between the fair market value of the mortgage and the balance.

The interest rate on the mortgage is 10% compounded semiannually, and the monthly payments are $500. The market rate for new 2-year mortgages is 8.5% compounded semiannually. What will be the penalty for prepaying the balance?

☑ SOLUTION

The contractual interest rate per 1-month payment interval is

$$p = (1 + i)^c - 1 = 1.05^{0.1\overline{6}} - 1 = 0.0081648460$$

One month's interest on the current balance is

$$p \times \text{Balance} = 0.008164846(\$45,557) = \$371.97$$

Therefore, 3 months' interest is 3($371.97) = $1115.91.

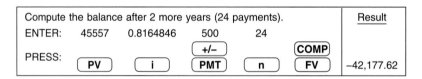

Compute the balance after 2 more years (24 payments).					Result
ENTER: 45557	0.8164846	500	24		
		+/−		COMP	
PRESS: PV	i	PMT	n	FV	−42,177.62

The fair market value of the mortgage is the combined present value of 24 payments of $500 and the $42,177.62 balance (2 years from now), discounted at the current market rate per payment interval. This rate is

$$p = (1 + i)^c - 1 = 1.0425^{0.1\overline{6}} - 1 = 0.0069610621$$

Compute the mortgage's market value.		Result
ENTER: 0.69610621		
	COMP	
PRESS: i	PV	46,724.99

The penalty under the second alternative would be

$$\$46,724.99 - \$45,557 = \$1167.99$$

Since this amount is larger than 3 months' interest, the prepayment penalty is $1167.99.   ■

REVERSE MORTGAGE LOANS

In a standard mortgage loan, the homeowner makes regular payments to the lender. Each payment includes the interest accrued since the previous payment plus a principal portion that reduces the balance owed on the loan. The homeowner's equity is the difference between the market value of the property and the balance owed on the mortgage loan. As the mortgage payments continue, the owner's equity increases until it reaches 100% of the market value when the mortgage loan is paid off.

The reverse mortgage loan is a relatively recent development on the Canadian scene. Its name derives from the fact that the principal amount owed on a **reverse mortgage** loan *increases* as time passes. This characteristic is opposite to the pattern of a declining principal balance on a standard mortgage. Also in contrast with a standard mortgage, a reverse mortgage loan is usually repaid by a single lump payment. In both cases, the loan is secured by a mortgage charge registered on the title of the property.

There are two categories of arrangements for reverse mortgage loans. The first is aimed at enabling homeowners to supplement their incomes for a protracted period. The second can provide funds to a homeowner for a single major expenditure. Both are described below and illustrated by examples.

The Lender Makes Equal Periodic Advances of Principal   In the purest form of reverse mortgage loan, the lender makes regular payments to the homeowner. The payments represent periodic advances of principal to the borrower. Interest is charged each payment interval on the principal balance outstanding after the previous advance. At the end of each compounding period, the accrued interest is converted to principal. Consequently, the principal balance increases at an accelerating rate because of the compounding of interest on an ever-increasing balance. One of or the earliest of the following events can trigger repayment of the loan.

• The expiry of the term of the loan (specified in the mortgage contract).
• The accumulating debt reaching a predetermined maximum dollar amount.
• The accumulating debt reaching a predetermined percentage (usually in the 60% to 70% range) of the property's market value.

This kind of arrangement would tend to attract only homeowners who have the intention from the beginning of selling the home to pay off the loan before or when the loan must be repaid.

Excluding appreciation in the market value of the property as time passes, the owner's equity will diminish as the debt against the property rises. With appreciation, the dollar amount of the owner's equity will decrease more slowly. If the periodic advances on the loan are relatively small, it is possible that the increase in market value of the property could exceed the growth in the debt. In this circumstance, the owner's equity would continue to rise.

■ **EXAMPLE 14.4F**   *Calculating the Duration of a Reverse Mortgage Loan Based on an Estimated Rate of Appreciation of the Property*

The Jorgensens have entered into a reverse mortgage agreement with a trust company. Their home, currently appraised at $130,000, secures the mortgage. They will receive $600 at the end of each month and will be charged an interest rate of 10.75% compounded semiannually on the principal balance. The mortgage may be paid off at any time, but in no event later than 90 days after the date on which the principal plus accrued interest equals 70% of the value of their home.

a. How much will the balance owed increase in the fifth year? How much of this increase is interest charges?

b. If the home appreciates in value by 5% per year, how long will it take for the amount owed on the mortgage to reach 70% of the market value of the home?

☑ SOLUTION

a. The amount owed on the loan at any date is the future value of all payments received from the lender. The interest rate per payment interval accruing on the payments received is

$$p = 1.05375^{0.1\overline{6}} - 1 = 0.00876405$$

Compute the future value after 4 years.					Result
ENTER: 600 0 0.87640531 48				COMP	
PRESS: PMT PV i n FV					−35,613.65
Compute the future value after 5 years.					
ENTER: 60				COMP	
PRESS: n FV					−47,102.41

The balance will increase in the fifth year by

$$\$47,102.41 - \$35,613.65 = \$11,488.76$$

Of this increase, 12($600) = $7200 will be advances of principal and the remainder, $4288.76, will be interest charges converted to principal.

b. Let n represent the number of months until the debt equals 70% of the home's market value. The amount of the debt at that point will be

$$S_n = \$600\left(\frac{1.0087640531^n - 1}{0.0087640531}\right)$$

The market value of the home will be

$$S = \$130,000(1 + p)^n$$

where

$$p = 1.05^{0.08\overline{3}} - 1 = 0.00407412$$

To determine n, we need to solve

$$S_n = 0.7\,S$$
$$\$600\left(\frac{1.00876405^n - 1}{0.00876405}\right) = 0.7(\$130,000)1.00407412^n$$
$$1.00876405^n - 1 = 1.329214(1.00407412^n)$$

We will use the trial-and-error method to solve the equation. Collect all terms and factors involving n on the left-hand side (LHS) of the equation, so that only one side's value changes as we try new estimates of n.

$$\frac{1.00876405^n - 1}{1.00407412^n} = 1.329214$$

Trial number	Estimated n	LHS
1	200	2.096
2	175	1.769
3	150	1.468
4	140 ⌐	1.3542 ⌐
	$\begin{bmatrix} n \\ 135 \end{bmatrix}$	$\begin{bmatrix} 1.3292 \\ 1.2983 \end{bmatrix}$
5		

Interpolating for a better estimate of n, we obtain

$$\frac{n - 135}{140 - 135} = \frac{1.3292 - 1.2983}{1.3542 - 1.2983}$$

$$\frac{n - 135}{5} = \frac{0.0309}{0.0559}$$

$$n = 5(0.553) + 135$$

$$= 137.7 \text{ months}$$

It will take 138 months, or $11\frac{1}{2}$ years, for the debt to reach 70% of the value of the home, assuming a 5% annual rate of price increase. ∎

THE LENDER MAKES A SINGLE LUMP-SUM ADVANCE TO THE HOMEOWNER   In the case of a lump-sum loan advance, interest is again calculated and converted to principal at the end of each compounding interval. Repayment of the loan may be triggered by the same criteria as listed previously for the periodic-advance reverse mortgage loan.

Reverse mortgages are primarily of interest to retired people who own a debt-free home and wish to use that equity to supplement their income, while continuing to occupy their home. But they are usually reluctant to enter into either of the reverse mortgage arrangements described so far. Should they live long enough, they face the prospect of *both* selling their home to repay the loan and also losing the income stream generated by the loan. Consequently, neither of these two types of reverse mortgage has achieved any degree of popularity in its basic form.

Some institutional lenders, working in cooperation with life insurance companies, have developed creative variations of the second type of reverse mortgage. These provide a loan repayment option with which many retirees are prepared to live (and die). Under a **life annuity reverse mortgage,** the lender grants a lump-sum loan for the *lifetime* of an individual or of the last survivor of a couple. The loan is secured by a mortgage against the home of the borrower or borrowers. The borrower is *guaranteed* the use of the home for the rest of his or her life, or for the lifetime of the last surviving spouse in the case of the joint life annuity reverse mortgage. No periodic payments are made on the mortgage. After the death of the homeowner, his or her estate is obligated to repay the loan. If, however, the total amount owed exceeds the selling price of the property, the lenders under the plan absorb the shortfall.

The loan is used to purchase a life annuity for a single homeowner or a joint life annuity for a couple.[14] The payments in a life annuity continue until the death of the annuitant; in a joint life annuity, payments continue until the death of the last surviving

---

[14]By law, only life insurance companies are permitted to sell life annuities. Most of the plans will permit the borrower to use some portion (typically 35%) of the loan amount for purposes other than purchasing the life annuity.

annuitant. Consequently, the life annuity reverse mortgage is an attractive arrangement for retired homeowners, enabling them to convert equity in their home to a permanent income stream. They continue to own and live in the home for as long as they wish. They continue to benefit from any appreciation in the value of the property. They do not face the prospect of being forced to sell the property to repay the loan, nor is there the danger that the income stream[15] will end during their lifetimes.

Under life annuity reverse mortgage contracts, the lenders must structure the loans so that, in the vast majority of cases, the market value of the home will exceed the balance owed on the loan upon the death of the homeowner or the last surviving spouse. Consequently, life annuity reverse mortgage loans are available only to homeowners over the age of 60. Furthermore, the initial lump loan is limited to a rather low percentage of the property's market value. For single women it is about 15% of market value at age 65, 25% at age 70, and 30% at age 75. For single men the limits are 7 or 8 percentage points higher at each age, because of men's significantly lower life expectancies. (See Table 14.2.) To arrive at these initial loan-to-value ratios, the lenders have also built in a *conservative* estimate of the rate of appreciation of residential real estate values in future years. For the last 20 years, the actual rate has averaged about 7% per year in major Canadian cities. Nevertheless, in the small proportion of cases in which the mortgagors live far beyond the normal life expectancy, the loan balance may ultimately exceed the property's market value. To provide for such losses, reverse mortgage lenders typically charge an interest rate that is 1% higher than the prevailing rate on conventional 5-year-term mortgages.

TABLE   14.2

Life Expectancies (years)

Age	Male	Female
65	15.2	19.0
70	12.0	15.4
75	9.4	12.0

The balance owed on the loan at any point will be the *future* value of the initial lump loan compounded at the rate of interest charged on the loan. The *expected* market value of the home at a future date is the *future* value of the current market value compounded at the *expected* rate of appreciation of property values. The expected owner's equity at any point is the difference between these two future values. That is,

$$\text{Expected owner's equity at a future date} = \text{Expected market value of the home} - \text{Balance owed on the mortgage}$$

where

$$\text{Balance owed on a reverse mortgage} = \text{Future value of the initial loan advanced}$$

and

$$\text{Expected market value of the property} = \text{Future value of the current market value}$$

---

[15]A further attraction is that the interest component of the life annuity payments is not subject to income tax.

Figure 14.5 illustrates a scenario in which a $50,000 reverse mortgage loan at 10% compounded semiannually is secured by a mortgage on a home with a current market value of $150,000. The two curves on the graph show the accumulating amount owed on the mortgage loan over a 25-year period and the value of the home assuming a 5% annually compounded rate of appreciation. The owner's equity on any date is the vertical separation of the two curves on that date. Whenever the rate of interest charged on the mortgage exceeds the rate of appreciation of the home's market value, the owner's equity will decline as a percentage of the market value. In this case, the owner's equity will be entirely consumed after 23 years by the more rapidly growing debt. Should the borrower or borrowers live longer than 23 years, the lender will suffer a loss equal to the vertical separation of the two curves on the ultimate date of sale.

FIGURE   14.5

Mortgage Balance and Property Value versus Time

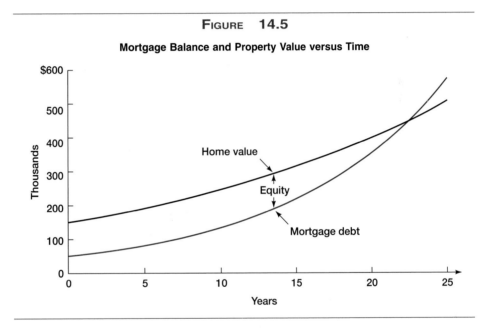

EXAMPLE 14.4G   *A REVERSE MORTGAGE IN WHICH ONLY AN INITIAL LUMP-SUM ADVANCE OF PRINCIPAL IS MADE*

Commonwealth Life Insurance Company will lend lump sums under lifetime reverse mortgage arrangements. The insurance company must calculate the maximum loan-to-value ratio that it will offer to each age of borrower. This ratio is the fraction of the home's appraised value that the company will lend as a lump sum. The ratio is calculated so that the future value of the mortgage loan reaches the expected future value of the property on a date that is well beyond the life expectancy of the borrower. In these future-value calculations, the initial lump-sum loan is compounded at its fixed contractual rate, and the property's current appraised value is compounded at the expected rate of appreciation of residential properties in the neighbourhood.

Calculate the maximum initial loan-to-value ratio for a reverse mortgage loan at 10.5% compounded semiannually on a property owned by a 65-year-old man if the balance on the loan is allowed to reach the anticipated market value of the property 7 years beyond the 15-year life expectancy of men aged 65. Assume a 5% annual rate of appreciation in the value of residential properties.

☑ SOLUTION

Let V represent the property's current appraised value, and let x represent the maximum fraction of V that Commonwealth will initially lend.

The maximum amount that can be loaned is xV. The amount owed on the loan after 22 years (life expectancy + 7 years) will be

$$S = P(1 + i)^n = xV(1.0525)^{44} = 9.5011xV$$

The expected value of the home in 22 years is

$$S = V(1.05)^{22} = 2.9253V$$

Now solve for the value of x that makes these two amounts equal.

$$9.5011xV = 2.9253V$$
$$x = \frac{2.9253}{9.5011}$$
$$= 0.308$$
$$= 30.8\%$$

The maximum initial loan-to-value ratio for lump-sum loans to 65-year-old men is 30.8%. ∎

■ EXAMPLE 14.4H   *A REVERSE MORTGAGE IN WHICH THE LUMP-SUM PRINCIPAL AMOUNT ADVANCED IS USED TO PURCHASE A LIFE ANNUITY*

An insurance company will make a $40,000 lump-sum lifetime loan at 10.5% compounded semiannually to a 65-year-old woman under a reverse mortgage agreement. The loan proceeds will be used to purchase a life annuity. If the life annuity payments are based on an interest rate 2% below the mortgage rate, and also on the average 19-year life expectancy for a woman aged 65, what end-of-month annuity payments can the woman expect?

☑ SOLUTION

We have seen in earlier chapters that the purchase price of an investment annuity is the present value of the annuity payments discounted at the rate of return on the annuity. In this example,

$$A_n = \$40,000 \qquad n = 19(12) = 228 \qquad i = 4.25\% \qquad c = \frac{1}{6}$$

$$p = 1.0425^{1/6} - 1 = 0.00696106$$

The size of the annuity payments is the value of R in

$$\$40,000 = R\left(\frac{1 - 1.00696106^{-228}}{0.00696106}\right)$$

The solution is $R = \$350.52$. The woman can expect monthly annuity payments of $350.52. ∎

EXERCISE 14.4

Answers to the odd-numbered problems are at the end of the book.

Problems 1 through 6 concern the effective cost of borrowing when a mortgage loan involves brokerage fees.

•1. The Gills have arranged a second mortgage loan with a face value of $21,500 at an interest rate of 13.5% compounded monthly. The face value is to be fully amortized by equal monthly payments over a 5-year period. The Gills received only $20,000 of the face value, the difference being a bonus retained by the lender. What is the actual cost of borrowing, including the bonus, expressed as an effective annual rate?

•2. A mortgage loan having a face value of $63,000 is arranged by a mortgage broker. From this face value, the broker deducted her fee of $3000. The mortgage is written at a contract rate of 8% compounded semiannually for a 5-year term. Monthly payments are calculated on a 25-year amortization. What is the annual cost of borrowing including the brokerage fee, expressed as an effective annual rate?

•3. A borrower has arranged a $105,000 face value, bonused mortgage loan with a broker at an interest rate of 10.8% compounded semiannually. Monthly payments are based on a 15-year amortization. A $5000 placement fee will be retained by the broker. What is the effective annual cost of the funds actually advanced to the borrower if the contractual interest rate is for:

  a. A 5-year term?

  b. A 10-year term?

  c. The entire 15-year amortization period?

•4. A local mortgage broker has arranged a mortgage loan with a face value of $77,500, which included a finder's fee of $2500. The loan is to be amortized by monthly payments over 20 years at 12% compounded semiannually. What is the actual cost of borrowing, expressed as an effective annual rate, if the contractual interest rate is for:

  a. A 3-year term?

  b. A 7-year term?

  c. The entire 20-year amortization period?

•5. A borrower has the choice between two mortgage loans. Both are to be amortized by monthly payments over 10 years. A mortgage broker will charge a fee of $2200 for an $82,200 face value loan at 10.25% compounded semiannually. A trust company will grant an $80,000 loan (with no other fees) at 10.75% compounded semiannually. Determine which loan has the lower effective annual cost of borrowing if the contractual interest rates are for:

  a. A 5-year term.

  b. The entire 10-year amortization period.

•6. Calculate the effective annual cost of borrowing for each of the following three financing alternatives. All interest rates are for a 7-year term and all mortgages use a 20-year amortization to calculate the monthly payments. Bank B will lend $90,000 at 10.75% compounded semiannually. Credit union C will lend $90,000 at 10.5% compounded monthly. Mortgage broker M will lend $93,000 at 10.25% compounded semiannually but will retain $3000 as a brokerage fee.

Problems 7 through 16 require the calculation of the fair market value of mortgage loans.

•7. The vendor of a residential property accepted a $40,000 take-back mortgage to facilitate the sale. The agreement calls for quarterly payments to amortize the loan over 10 years at an interest rate of 7% compounded semiannually. What was the cash value (or fair market value) of the mortgage at the time of the sale if the market interest rate on 10-year term mortgages was:

  a. 10.5% compounded semiannually?

  b. 9% compounded semiannually?

•8. The vendor of a property agrees to take back a $55,000 mortgage at a rate of 7.5% compounded semiannually with monthly payments of $500 for a 2-year term. Calculate the market value of the mortgage if financial institutions are charging 9.5% compounded semiannually on 2-year term mortgages.

•9. A mortgagee wishes to sell his interest in a closed mortgage contract that was written 21 months ago. The original loan was for $60,000 at 12% compounded semiannually for a 5-year term. Monthly payments are being made on a 20-year amortization schedule. What price can the mortgagee reasonably expect to receive if the current semiannually compounded interest rate on 3- and 4-year term mortgages is:

    a. 11%?   *b.* 12%?   *c.* 13%?

•10. An investor is considering the purchase of an existing closed mortgage that was written 20 months ago to secure a $45,000 loan at 10% compounded semiannually paying $500 per month for a 4-year term. What price should the investor pay for the mortgage if she requires a semiannually compounded rate of return on investment of:

    a. 11%?   *b.* 10%?   *c.* 9%?

•11. A property is listed for $175,000. A potential purchaser makes an offer of $170,000, consisting of $75,000 cash and a $95,000 mortgage back to the vendor bearing interest at 8% compounded semiannually with monthly payments for a 10-year term and a 10-year amortization. Calculate the equivalent cash value of the offer if 10-year mortgage rates in the market are at 10.25% compounded semiannually.

•12. What is the equivalent cash value of the offer in problem 11 if the vendor financing arrangement is for the same 10-year amortization but with:

    a. A 5-year term?   *b.* A 1-year term?

•13. The owner of a property listed at $145,000 is considering two offers. Offer C is for $140,000 cash. Offer M is for $50,000 cash and a mortgage back to the vendor for $100,000 at a rate of 8% compounded semiannually and payments of $750 per month for the 5-year term. If current 5-year rates are 10.25% compounded semiannually, what is the cash equivalent value of M's offer?

•14. You are interested in purchasing a house listed for $180,000. The owner seems quite determined to stay at the asking price, but you think that the true market value is $165,000. It may be that the owner would accept an offer whose nominal value is the psychologically important $180,000 figure but whose cash value is close to your $165,000 figure. What would be the cash value of the following offer if long-term mortgage rates were 10.5% compounded semiannually? The offer is for the "full" price of $180,000, consisting of $60,000 down and the balance by a $120,000 mortgage in favour of the vendor. Monthly payments for a 20-year term are to be based on a 20-year amortization and an interest rate of 8.5% compounded semiannually.

•15. The Phams are 2 years into the first 5-year term of a 25-year $80,000 mortgage loan at 10.5% compounded semiannually. Interest rates on 3-year term mortgage loans are now 9% compounded semiannually. A job transfer necessitates the sale of the Phams' home. To prepay the closed mortgage, the mortgage contract requires that the Phams pay a penalty equal to the greater of:

    a. 3 months' interest on the balance.

    b. The difference between the fair market value of the mortgage and the balance.

    What would be the amount of the penalty if they paid out the balance after 2 years of monthly payments?

•16. A $75,000 mortgage loan at 9% compounded semiannually has a 5-year term and a 25-year amortization. Prepayment of the loan at any time within the first 5 years leads to a penalty equal to the greater of:

    a. 3 months' interest on the balance.

    b. The difference between the fair market value of the mortgage and the balance.

    What would be the amount of the penalty if the balance were paid out just after the 19th monthly payment and the prevailing rate on 3- and 4-year-term mortgages were 8% compounded semiannually?

Problems 17 through 26 involve reverse mortgages.

•17. What size of month-end reverse mortgage payments can be received so that the amount owed on the mortgage just equals 70% of the market value of the property securing the mortgage after 15 years? The interest rate on the mortgage is 11% compounded semiannually. The property, currently appraised at $150,000, is expected to appreciate at 6% per annum.

••18. Mrs. Simmons receives payments of $700 at the end of every month on a reverse mortgage. Her home was appraised at $160,000 at the time the mortgage contract was signed. If the interest rate on the principal balance is 10.5% compounded semiannually and the value of her home increases 6% per year, what is the debt-to-market value ratio after:

    a. 5 years?   *b.* 10 years?   *c.* 15 years?

•19. Repeat part *b* of Example 14.4F for a 7% pa increase in home prices. A comparison of the two results provides an indication of the sensitivity of the number of reverse mortgage payments to the assumed rate of appreciation of property values.

•20. Mr. and Mrs. Ewasiuk obtained a $45,000 lump-sum loan under a lifetime reverse mortgage agreement to purchase a joint life annuity. The loan represented an initial loan-to-market value ratio of 30% of their home's appraised value. If the interest rate on the loan is 11.25% compounded semiannually and property prices increase at 6% per year, what will be the equity in their home, expressed both in dollars and as a percentage of market value, after:

    a. 5 years?   *b.* 10 years?   *c.* 15 years?   *d.* 20 years?

•21. Mrs. Yokoyama obtained a $50,000 lump-sum loan under a lifetime reverse mortgage agreement to purchase a life annuity. The loan represented an initial loan-to-market value ratio of 30% of her home's appraised value. The interest rate on the loan is 10.5% compounded semiannually. After 10 years, what will be the equity in her home, expressed both in dollars and as a percentage of market value, if property prices increase at:

    a. 4% per year?   *b.* 6% per year?   *c.* 8% per year?

•22. Calculate the maximum initial loan-to-value ratio that a lender will approve for a lifetime reverse mortgage loan at 10.5% compounded semiannually on a property owned by a 65-year-old woman, if the balance on the loan is projected to reach the market value of the property 7 years beyond the 19-year life expectancy for women aged 65. Assume a 5% annual rate of appreciation in the value of residential properties.

•23. Repeat problem 22 for a 7% annual rate of appreciation in the value of residential properties. A comparison with the answer to problem 22 will provide an indication of the sensitivity of the maximum initial loan-to-value ratio to the assumed rate of appreciation of property values.

•24. Referring to problem 20:

    a. What will be the lender's loss (balance owed on the mortgage less the property's market value) if the last surviving spouse dies after 24 years?

    b. What will be the lender's loss if the last surviving spouse dies after 20 years but the average annual rate of property appreciation is 5% instead of 6%?

••25. For the 6% appreciation rate scenario in problem 21, how long would Mrs. Yokoyama have to live before the mortgage lender would start to lose money (in the sense that the full amount owed on the mortgage exceeds the market value of the property)?

•26. An insurance company will make a $35,000 lump-sum loan at 10.75% compounded semiannually to a 65-year-old man under a lifetime reverse mortgage agreement. The loan proceeds will be used to purchase a life annuity. If the life annuity payments are based on an interest rate 1.5% below the mortgage rate and on a 15-year life expectancy for a man aged 65, what end-of-month annuity payments can the man expect?

REVIEW PROBLEMS

Answers to the odd-numbered review problems are at the end of the book.

1. Jessica bought a $1150 television set for 25% down and the balance to be paid with interest at 11.25% compounded monthly in six equal blended monthly payments. Construct the full amortization schedule for the debt. Calculate the total interest paid.

•2. Givens, Hong, and Partners obtained a $7000 term loan at 10.75% compounded annually for new boardroom furniture. Prepare a complete amortization schedule in which the loan is repaid by equal semiannual payments over 3 years.

3. A $28,000 loan at 10.5% compounded quarterly is to be repaid by equal quarterly payments over a 7-year term.

   a. What amount of principal will be repaid by the 6th payment?

   b. What will be the interest portion of the 22nd payment?

   c. How much will the principal be reduced by payments 10 to 15 inclusive?

   d. How much interest will be paid in the second year?

•4. A 20-year annuity was purchased with $180,000 that had accumulated in an RRSP. The annuity provides a semiannually compounded rate of return of 7.5% and makes equal month-end payments.

   a. What amount of principal will be included in the 134th payment?

   b. What will be the interest portion of the 210th payment?

   c. How much will the principal be reduced by payments 75 to 100 inclusive?

   d. How much interest will be paid in the sixth year?

5. Metro Construction received $60,000 in vendor financing at 10.5% compounded semiannually for the purchase of a loader. The contract requires blended semiannual payments of $10,000 until the debt is paid off. Construct the complete amortization schedule for the debt. How much total interest will be paid over the life of the loan?

6. Suppose that the loan in problem 5 permits an additional prepayment of principal on any scheduled payment date. Prepare another amortization schedule that reflects a prepayment of $5000 with the third scheduled payment. How much interest is saved as a result of the prepayment?

7. An annuity providing a rate of return of 7.5% compounded monthly was purchased for $45,000. The annuity pays $500 at the end of each month.

   a. How much of the 37th payment will be interest?

   b. What will be the principal portion of the 92nd payment?

   c. How much interest will be paid by payments 85 to 96 inclusive?

   d. How much principal will be repaid in the fifth year?

•8. Niagara Haulage obtained an $80,000 loan at 9.75% compounded monthly to build a storage shed. Construct a partial amortization schedule for payments of $1200 per month showing details of the first two payments, payments 41 and 42, and the last two payments.

•9. The interest rate for the first 5 years of a $90,000 mortgage loan is 9.25% compounded semiannually. Monthly payments are calculated using a 20-year amortization.

   a. What will be the principal balance at the end of the 5-year term?

   b. What will be the new payments if the loan is renewed at 10.5% compounded semiannually (and the original amortization period is continued)?

•10. A mortgage calls for monthly payments of $802.23 for 25 years. If the loan was for $95,000, calculate the semiannually compounded nominal rate of interest on the loan.

•11. A $25,000 home improvement (mortgage) loan charges interest at 9.75% compounded monthly for a 3-year term. Monthly payments are based on a 10-year amortization and rounded up to the next $10. What will be the principal balance at the end of the first term?

•12. The interest rate for the first 5 years of a $95,000 mortgage is 9.5% compounded semi-annually. Monthly payments are based on a 25-year amortization. If a $3000 prepayment is made at the end of the third year:

a. How much will the amortization period be shortened?

b. What will be the principal balance at the end of the 5-year term?

•13. After 2 years of the first 5-year term at 10.25% compounded semiannually, Dean and Cindy decide to take advantage of the privilege of increasing the payments on their $110,000 mortgage loan by 10%. The monthly payments were originally calculated for a 25-year amortization.

a. How much will the amortization period be shortened?

b. What will be the principal balance at the end of the 5-year term?

•14. Thirty-one months ago Mr. and Mrs. Chapelle obtained a $72,000 mortgage loan at 10% compounded semiannually for a 5-year term. Their monthly payments are based on a 20-year amortization. They have had to sell the house because of a job change. What amount is required to pay off the mortgage if there is a penalty of 3 months' interest on any prepayment in excess of 10% of the original principal?

•15. A mortgage broker has arranged a mortgage loan with a face value of $46,500, which includes a finder's fee of $1500. The loan is to be amortized by monthly payments over a 15-year period at 10.25% compounded semiannually. What is the actual cost of borrowing, expressed as an effective annual rate, if the contractual interest rate is for:

a. A 3-year term?   b. A 5-year term?

•16. Ms. Finch wishes to sell a closed mortgage contract just after receiving the 29th payment. The original loan was for $60,000 at 11% compounded semiannually for a 5-year term. Monthly payments are being made on a 25-year amortization schedule. What price can she reasonably expect to receive if the current semiannually compounded interest rate on 2- and 3-year term mortgages is:

a. 10%?   b. 12%?

•17. The owner of a property listed at $195,000 is considering two offers. Mr. and Mrs. Sharpe are offering $191,000 cash. The Conlins' "full-price" offer consists of $65,000 cash and a mortgage back to the vendor for $130,000 at a rate of 7.5% compounded semiannually with payments of $1000 per month for a 5-year term. If current 5-year rates are 8.5% compounded semiannually, what is the cash equivalent value of the Conlins' offer? Which offer should be accepted?

•18. Mr. and Mrs. Eubank obtained a $51,000 lump-sum loan under a lifetime reverse mortgage agreement to purchase a joint life annuity. The loan represented an initial loan-to-market value ratio of 30% of their home's appraised value. If the interest rate on the loan is 10.75% compounded semiannually and property prices increase at 5% per year, what will be the equity in their home, expressed both in dollars and as a percentage of market value, after:

a. 10 years?   b. 20 years?

c. What will be the lender's loss if the last surviving spouse dies after 25 years?

580   Chapter 14

•19. Calculate the maximum initial loan-to-value ratio that a lender will approve for a lifetime reverse mortgage loan at 9.75% compounded semiannually on a property owned by a 70-year-old woman, if the balance on the loan is projected to reach the market value of the property 5 years beyond the $15\frac{1}{2}$-year life expectancy for women aged 70. Assume a 5% annual rate of appreciation in the value of residential properties.

SELF-TEST EXERCISE

Answers to the self-test problems are at the end of the book.

1. A $16,000 loan is to be amortized by blended monthly payments over a 5-year period. The interest rate on the loan is 10.8% compounded monthly.

   a. What is the interest portion of the 29th payment?

   b. Determine the principal portion of the 46th payment.

   c. How much will the principal be reduced in the second year?

   d. How much interest will be paid in the third year?

•2. The interest rate on a $6400 loan is 10% compounded semiannually. If the loan is to be repaid by monthly payments over a 4-year term, prepare a partial amortization schedule showing details of the first two payments, payments 34 and 35, and the last two payments.

••3. A $255,000 amount from an RRSP is used to purchase an annuity paying $7500 at the end of each quarter. The annuity provides an annually compounded rate of return of 10%.

   a. What will be the amount of the final payment?

   b. What will be the interest portion of the 27th payment?

   c. What will be the principal portion of the 53rd payment?

   d. How much will the principal balance be reduced by payments 14 to 20 inclusive?

   e. How much interest will be paid by the payments received in the 6th year?

•4. A mortgage contract for $45,000 written 10 years ago is just at the end of its second 5-year term. The interest rates were 13% compounded semiannually for the first term and 11.75% compounded semiannually for the second term. If monthly payments throughout have been based on a 25-year amortization, calculate the principal balance at the end of the second term.

•5. The interest rate for the first 3 years of an $87,000 mortgage is 9.5% compounded semiannually. Monthly payments are based on a 20-year amortization. If a $4000 prepayment is made at the end of the 16th month:

   a. How much will the amortization period be shortened?

   b. What will be the principal balance at the end of the 3-year term?

•6. Calculate the annual cost of borrowing, expressed as an effective interest rate, if a mortgage broker retains $3300 from a $110,000 face value mortgage loan written at 11% compounded semiannually for a 5-year term. The required monthly payments would amortize the face value in 25 years.

•7. There are two offers on a property listed at $185,000. Mr. Smith is offering $183,000 cash. Ms. Jones's offer consists of $100,000 cash and a mortgage back to the vendor for $90,000 at a rate of 7.5% compounded semiannually and payments of $700 per month for a 3-year term. If current 3-year rates are 9.5% compounded semiannually, what is the equivalent cash value of Ms. Jones's offer?

•8. Mr. Lamelin borrowed $30,000 at 11% compounded semiannually under a lifetime reverse mortgage agreement to purchase a life annuity. The loan represented an initial loan-to-market value ratio of 27% of his home's appraised value. If he dies $12\frac{1}{2}$ years later and the house is sold at its market value, what proceeds of the sale will pass to his estate after payout of the mortgage? Assume that property values will rise at 7% per annum.

•9. Calculate the maximum initial loan-to-value ratio that a lender will approve for a lifetime reverse mortgage loan at 11% compounded semiannually on a property owned by a 70-year-old man. The lender is prepared to allow the balance on the loan to reach the projected market value of the property 6 years beyond the 12-year life expectancy for men aged 70. Assume a 6% annual rate of appreciation in the value of residential properties.

SUMMARY OF NOTATION AND KEY FORMULAS

The following relationships were developed for loans with blended payments. The interest rate used in every case is the contractual rate of interest (per payment interval) on the loan.

$$\text{Original loan} = \begin{array}{c}\text{Present value} \\ \text{of any number} \\ \text{of payments}\end{array} + \begin{array}{c}\text{Present value} \\ \text{of the balance} \\ \text{after these payments}\end{array}$$

$$\begin{array}{c}\text{Principal balance} \\ \text{after any payment} \\ \text{(Prospective Method)}\end{array} = \begin{array}{c}\text{Present value of the} \\ \textit{remaining} \text{ payments}\end{array} \qquad (14\text{--}1)$$

$$\begin{array}{c}\text{Principal balance} \\ \text{after any payment} \\ \text{(Retrospective Method)}\end{array} = \begin{array}{c}\text{Future value} \\ \text{of the loan}\end{array} - \begin{array}{c}\text{Future value} \\ \text{of payments} \\ \text{already made}\end{array} \qquad (14\text{--}2)$$

$$\begin{array}{c}\text{Interest component} \\ \text{of a loan payment}\end{array} = p \times \begin{array}{c}\text{Balance after the} \\ \text{previous payment}\end{array} \qquad (14\text{--}3)$$

$$\begin{array}{c}\text{Principal component} \\ \text{of a loan payment}\end{array} = \begin{array}{c}\text{Balance after the} \\ \text{previous payment}\end{array} - \begin{array}{c}\text{Balance after the} \\ \text{current payment}\end{array} \qquad (14\text{--}4)$$

$$\begin{array}{c}\text{Final payment} \\ \text{on a loan}\end{array} = (1 + p) \times \left(\begin{array}{c}\text{Balance after the} \\ \text{second-to-last payment}\end{array}\right) \qquad (14\text{--}5)$$

The following formulas from Chapters 8 and 10 are needed for the preceding calculations.

Formula (8–2) $S = P(1 + i)^n$ or $P = S(1 + i)^{-n}$ Finding the future value or present value of a lump amount

Formula (10–1) $S_n = R\left[\dfrac{(1 + p)^n - 1}{p}\right]$ Finding the future value of an ordinary annuity

Formula (10–2) $p = (1 + i)^c - 1$ Finding the interest rate per payment interval

Formula (10–4) $A_n = R\left[\dfrac{1 - (1 + p)^{-n}}{p}\right]$ Finding the present value of an ordinary annuity

Formula (10–4a) $n = -\dfrac{\ln\left(1 - \dfrac{pA_n}{R}\right)}{\ln(1 + p)}$ Finding the number of annuity payments given A_n, R, and p

The following ratios are used by mortgage lenders to determine whether an applicant qualifies for a mortgage loan.

$$\text{Loan-to-value ratio} = \frac{\text{Initial mortgage principal}}{\text{Appraised value of the property}}$$

$$\begin{matrix}\text{Gross debt service}\\\text{(GDS) ratio}\end{matrix} = \frac{\begin{matrix}\text{Average total payment per month on}\\\text{mortgage loan, property taxes, and heat}\end{matrix}}{\text{Gross monthly income}}$$

$$\begin{matrix}\text{Total debt service}\\\text{(TDS) ratio}\end{matrix} = \frac{\begin{matrix}\text{Average total payment per month on}\\\text{all debt, property taxes, and heat}\end{matrix}}{\text{Gross monthly income}}$$

Note: When using the following relationship to obtain the fair market value of a mortgage contract, the discount rate used is the prevailing market rate of interest on new mortgages whose term equals the *remainder* of the existing mortgage's term.

$$\begin{matrix}\text{Fair market value}\\\text{of a mortgage}\end{matrix} = \begin{matrix}\text{Present value of the}\\\text{payments remaining}\\\text{in the current term}\end{matrix} + \begin{matrix}\text{Present value of the}\\\text{principal balance}\\\text{at the end of the term}\end{matrix}$$

$$\begin{matrix}\text{Penalty to prepay mortgage}\\\text{loan balance (based on}\\\text{lender's economic loss)}\end{matrix} = \begin{matrix}\text{Fair market value}\\\text{of the mortgage}\end{matrix} - \text{Principal balance}$$

GLOSSARY OF TERMS

Amortization of a loan   The repayment of a loan by periodic payments that, with the possible exception of the last payment, are equal in size.

Amortization period   The total length of time to repay a blended-payment loan.

Balloon payment   Any payment of principal over and above the regular periodic payments.

Blended payments   Equal periodic payments combining principal with the interest that has accrued on the outstanding principal since the previous payment.

Closed mortgage   A mortgage that does not allow any prepayments.

Face value (of a mortgage)   The principal amount that a borrower promises to repay.

Fully open mortgage   A mortgage that places no restrictions or penalties on extra payments by the borrower.

Life annuity reverse mortgage   A reverse mortgage in which the lump sum advanced on the mortgage loan is used to purchase a life annuity, and the borrower is entitled to occupy the mortgaged home for the rest of his or her life.

Mortgagee   The party lending money on the security of a mortgage.

Mortgagor   The party borrowing money and giving a mortgage as security on a loan.

Open mortgage   See *fully open mortgage* and *partially open mortgage.*

Partially open mortgage   A mortgage that grants limited penalty-free prepayment privileges.

Prepayment   Any loan payment beyond the regular contractual payments.

Reverse mortgage   A mortgage in which the principal amount owed on the mortgage loan increases as time passes.

Term   The length of time from the date on which a loan is advanced until the date on which the principal balance outstanding is due and payable.

Vendor take-back mortgage   A mortgage securing a loan granted by the vendor to the purchaser as part of the purchase price in the sale of real property.

CHAPTER

15 BONDS AND SINKING FUNDS

CHAPTER OUTLINE

LEARNING OBJECTIVES

After completing this chapter, you will be able to:

- Calculate the market value of a bond on any date
- Calculate the yield to maturity of a bond on an interest payment date
- Calculate the premium or discount on a bond
- Prepare a schedule for amortizing a bond's premium or discount
- Calculate the payment for a sinking fund
- Prepare a sinking fund schedule

Introduction

A *bond* is a certificate representing a debt obligation of the bond issuer (borrower) to the bond holder (lender). Bonds are issued by the federal government, by the 10 provinces, by government agencies, and by many corporations whose shares trade on a stock exchange.

The sale of bonds to investors is the primary means by which the three levels of government and their agencies finance their considerable debts. At the end of 1996, bonds of the sort described in this chapter accounted for $270 billion of the $590 billion gross federal government debt. Another $325 billion in bonds issued or guaranteed by provincial governments was also outstanding. Municipal bonds represented an additional $37 billion, while Canadian corporations had bond financing totalling $152 billion.

It is clear that bonds play a prominent role in financing the debt of our governments and corporations. Since every debt represents an investment by the lender, bonds are also a significant component of many investment portfolios. Pension funds, insurance companies, mutual funds, and chartered banks are the largest investors in bonds. At some point most of us will have investments in bonds, if only indirectly through one of these institutional investors. There is an active, efficient market for the sale and purchase of bonds after their initial issue. Thus, a bond purchaser is not locked in for the entire lifetime of the bond. The bond can be readily sold in the "bond market" at a price that reflects prevailing rates of return.

The chapter begins with a discussion of the terminology and features of bonds. Then the concepts and mathematics needed to calculate bond prices and rates of return on bond investments are developed.

Many bond issues require that the borrower provide for the future repayment of the principal amount of the loan by making regular payments to what is called a *sinking fund.* The last section of this chapter deals with the calculations required to determine the size of sinking fund payments and the balance in a sinking fund at any date.

15.1 Basic Concepts and Definitions

We will adopt the widespread practice of using the term "bond" loosely, to refer to both true bonds and debentures. The technical distinction between a true bond and a debenture is that a **bond** is secured by specific assets of the issuer, whereas a **debenture** is backed only by the general credit of the issuer. Therefore, Government of Canada "bonds" are, in fact, debentures since no particular assets secure them. The distinction is not important for the mathematics of bonds.

Unlike blended-payment loans, in which each payment includes a principal portion that reduces the debt, bonds require the issuer (borrower) to make only periodic interest payments. Then, on the **maturity date** of the bond, the full principal amount is repaid along with the last interest payment.

The bond certificate sets out the main features of the loan contract. The following data are needed in the calculation of a bond's market price.

- The **issue date** is the date on which the loan was made and on which interest starts to be earned.

- The **face value** (or *denomination*) is the principal amount that the issuer is required to pay the owner of the bond on its maturity date. The face value is usually the principal amount loaned when the bond was issued. The most common face values are $1000, $5000, and $25,000, although larger denominations are often issued to institutional investors. No principal is repaid on individual bonds before the maturity date.

- The **coupon rate**[1] is the *nominal* annual rate of interest paid on the face value of the bond. The vast majority of bonds pay interest at 6-month intervals measured from the issue date. Therefore, the coupon rate is a *semiannually compounded* rate of interest.

Canada Savings Bonds (described in Section 8.4) and various provincial "*savings* bonds" should be distinguished from the *marketable* bonds discussed in this chapter. The owner of a *savings* bond can cash it in before its scheduled maturity date and receive the full face value plus accrued interest. This is done simply by presenting the savings bond to a bank, a trust company, or an investment dealer for early redemption. Government of Canada and provincial government *marketable* bonds do not have this open-redemption privilege. If the owner of such bonds wants to liquidate them, the bonds can be sold through investment dealers participating in the "bond market."[2] We will now address the question of how the prices of bonds are established in the bond market.

15.2 BOND PRICE ON AN INTEREST PAYMENT DATE

Most bonds pay interest semiannually, offer no early redemption privileges, and are redeemed for their face value at maturity. The expression used for the last feature is "redeemable *at par.*" In this section we will be primarily concerned with pricing bonds having these typical features. But before we begin the mathematics of bond pricing, we should understand why bond prices change in the bond market.

DEPENDENCE OF BOND PRICES ON PREVAILING INTEREST RATES

When a bond is originally issued, its coupon rate has to be a competitive rate so that the issuer (borrower) can sell the bond for its face value. For example, an issuer cannot expect a prudent investor to pay $1000 for a 9% coupon bond if other issuers are offering otherwise similar bonds with a 10% coupon rate.

After the issue date, prevailing interest rates in the financial markets are likely to change, and the coupon rate offered on *subsequent new* bond issues must change accordingly. However, the coupon rate on a previously issued bond is *contractually fixed* for the life of that issue. If the coupon rate on a bond exceeds the current competitive rate of return, investors will be willing to pay more than the face value for that bond. If the coupon rate on a bond is less than the current competitive rate of return, investors will buy the bond only at some appropriate discount from the bond's face value.

To make the discussion more specific, consider the four hypothetical Government of Canada bonds listed in Table 15.1. The issue dates and initial terms have been chosen so that, as of today's date, every bond has 5 years remaining until maturity.

---

[1]This term originated many years ago when it was customary for the bond certificate to have interest coupons attached to its margin. At each interest payment date, the bond holder would clip off the matured coupon and present it to a bank to receive payment in cash. Most bonds are now registered in the owner's name, and interest payments are made by cheques sent through the mail.

[2]For the most part, bonds are not bought and sold at a particular physical location corresponding to the stock exchanges for common shares. The "bond market" consists of the network of investment dealers who act as intermediaries between bond buyers and sellers.

Consequently, the four bonds represent identical investments except for different coupon rates. Since the newly issued bond A has a coupon rate of 10%, we can conclude that the bond market currently requires a 10% semiannually compounded rate of return on 5-year maturity bonds.

TABLE   15.1

Relative Prices of $1000 Face Value Bonds

Bond	Issue date	Initial term (years)	Coupon rate (%)	Bond price
A	Today	5	10	$1000
B	5 years ago	10	12	More than $1000
C	10 years ago	15	10	$1000
D	15 years ago	20	8	Less than $1000

We will now develop the line of reasoning for the relative bond prices in the last column of Table 15.1. Bonds C and A both carry a 10% coupon and have 5 years remaining until maturity. Therefore, bond C is identical to bond A from this point onward. Its market value will always be the same as the market value of bond A. Today that value is $1000. When a bond trades at its face value, it is said to trade "at par." Any bond will trade at par if its coupon rate equals the prevailing rate of return required in the bond market for bonds of a similar maturity and degree of risk.

Bond B carries a coupon rate that is 2% above the current competitive rate for 5-year Government of Canada bonds. It will pay $60 in interest every 6 months, whereas bond A will pay only $50 every 6 months. If investors could buy bond B for $1000, they would receive a 12% rate of return on their investment. Investors will preferentially buy bond B and bid its price above $1000. As the purchase price rises, the rate of return on investment (purchase price) declines since the future interest payments to the bond owner remain fixed, regardless of the amount paid for the bond.

Trap

You cannot conclude that B's price will rise to $1200 on the reasoning that the $120 annual interest from an investment of $1200 provides the market's required return of 10%. This reasoning overlooks the $200 capital loss resulting from paying a purchase price of $1200 but receiving only the $1000 face value at maturity. The capital loss prorated to each of the 5 years until maturity is $40, which is 3.3% of the $1200 investment. Hence, the average annual rate of *total* return on a $1200 investment would be only *approximately* 10% − 3.3% = 6.7%. When investors pay *more* than the face value to buy a bond, they must factor in the effect of the overall *capital loss*. In the present example, the market value of the bond will be above $1000 but well below $1200 in order to provide a 10% semiannually compounded rate of *total* return *on the purchase price*.

The price of bond B will rise to a level at which the $60 semiannual interest payments, combined with the *capital loss* when the $1000 face value is received at maturity, provide a 10% semiannually compounded rate of *total* return *on the purchase price*.

Bond D makes interest payments of only $40 every 6 months. Investors will not buy bond D until its price falls to some point below $1000. It will settle at a price at which the $40 semiannual interest payments, combined with the capital *gain* when the $1000 face value is received at maturity, provide a 10% semiannually compounded rate of *total* return *on the purchase* price.

SUMMARY   The following general relationships among bond price, coupon rate, and market rate may be inferred from the preceding discussion.

1. If the coupon rate *exceeds* the required market rate of return, the bond price will *exceed* the face value. If the coupon rate is *less* than the market rate, the bond price will be *less* than the face value.
2. Bond prices move in a direction *opposite* to the *change* in the market rate.
   - If prevailing interest rates *decline,* bond prices *rise.*
   - If prevailing interest rates *rise,* bond prices *fall.*

CALCULATING A BOND'S PRICE ON AN INTEREST PAYMENT DATE

The pricing or valuation of bonds is yet another example of use of the Valuation Principle to establish a fair market value for an expected stream of future cash payments. To apply the Valuation Principle, we need to:

- Determine the amount and timing of the future payments.
- Determine the rate of return currently required in the bond market on similar bonds.
- Calculate the present value of the future payments using this rate of return as the discount rate.

The following notation will be used to develop the mathematics of bond valuation:

F = Face value of the bond
b = Coupon rate per interest payment interval (normally 6 months)
p = The bond market's required rate of return per interest payment interval
n = Number of interest payments remaining until the maturity date

The regular semiannual interest payment from the bond will be:

$$\text{Face value} \times \text{Coupon rate per payment interval} = Fb$$

In this section we consider the case in which a bond is to be sold immediately after the seller has received an interest payment. Figure 15.1 illustrates the future payments that a prospective purchaser/investor can expect to receive. The purchaser expects n periodic interest payments of size Fb and, coincident with the final interest payment, the face value F. According to the Valuation Principle, the fair market value of the bond is the present value of these future payments discounted at the *prevailing rate of return* required on similar bonds in the bond market. That is,

$$\begin{array}{c} \text{Fair market} \\ \text{value of a bond} \end{array} = \begin{array}{c} \text{Present value of the} \\ \text{interest payments} \end{array} + \begin{array}{c} \text{Present value of} \\ \text{the face value} \end{array}$$

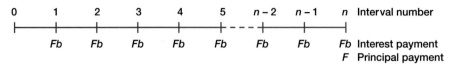

FIGURE   15.1

Expected Payments from a Bond

Since the interest payments form an ordinary annuity, we can use formula (10−4) to obtain the present value of the interest payments. The present value of the face value is calculated using formula (8−2). Hence,

Bond Price (on an Interest Payment Date)

$$\text{Bond price} = Fb\left[\frac{1 - (1 + p)^{-n}}{p}\right] + F(1 + p)^{-n} \qquad (15-1)$$

> **Tip**
>
> The bond's coupon rate is used only to determine the size of the periodic interest payments. The prevailing market rate of return is used to discount the future payments when calculating the bond's price.

■ **EXAMPLE 15.2A**   *CALCULATING THE PRICE OF A BOND ON AN INTEREST PAYMENT DATE*

Calculate the prices of bonds B, C, and D in Table 15.1.

☑ **SOLUTION**

Since the new issue of 5-year bonds carries a 10% coupon rate, the current return required by the market on 5-year bonds is 10% compounded semiannually. Therefore, we will use $p = 5\%$ for valuing all three bonds.

For bond B	$F = \$1000$	$n = 10$	$b = 6\%$	$Fb = \$60$
For bond C	$F = \$1000$	$n = 10$	$b = 5\%$	$Fb = \$50$
For bond D	$F = \$1000$	$n = 10$	$b = 4\%$	$Fb = \$40$

ALGEBRAIC SOLUTION

$$\text{Price of bond B} = \$60\left(\frac{1 - 1.05^{-10}}{0.05}\right) - \$1000(1.05^{-10})$$
$$= \$463.304 + \$613.913$$
$$= \$1077.22$$

$$\text{Price of bond C} = \$50\left(\frac{1 - 1.05^{-10}}{0.05}\right) - \$1000(1.05^{-10})$$
$$= \$386.087 + \$613.913$$
$$= \$1000.00$$

$$\text{Price of bond D} = \$40\left(\frac{1 - 1.05^{-10}}{0.05}\right) - \$1000(1.05^{-10})$$
$$= \$308.869 + \$613.913$$
$$= \$922.78$$

FINANCIAL CALCULATOR SOLUTION

Compute the price of bond B.						Result
ENTER:	60	1000	5	10		
PRESS:	[PMT]	[FV]	[i]	[n]	[COMP] [PV]	−1077.22
Compute the price of bond C.						
ENTER:	50					
PRESS:	[PMT]				[COMP] [PV]	−1000.00
Compute the price of bond D.						
ENTER:	40					
PRESS:	[PMT]				[COMP] [PV]	−922.78

The prices of bonds B, C, and D are $1077.22, $1000, and $922.78, respectively. These prices confirm the relative prices deduced in the last column of Table 15.1. ∎

■ EXAMPLE 15.2B   CALCULATING A BOND'S PRICE CHANGE RESULTING FROM A CHANGE IN THE PREVAILING INTEREST RATE

A $5000 face value bond has a coupon rate of 11% and a maturity date of March 1, 2008. Interest is paid semiannually. On September 1, 1992, the prevailing interest rate on long-term bonds abruptly rose from 8% to 8.25% compounded semiannually. What were the bond's prices before and after the interest rate change?

☑ SOLUTION

Given: F = $5000, b = 5.5%.
September 1, 1992, was an interest payment date, after which $15\frac{1}{2}$ years remain until maturity of the bond (n = 31). The semiannual interest paid on the bond is

$$Fb = \$5000(0.055) = \$275$$

On September 1, 1992, the prevailing market rate rose from

$$p = \frac{8\%}{2} = 4\% \quad \text{to} \quad p = \frac{8.25\%}{2} = 4.125\%$$

ALGEBRAIC SOLUTION

$$\text{Bond price before rate increase} = \$275\left(\frac{1 - 1.04^{-31}}{0.04}\right) - \$5000(1.04^{-31})$$
$$= \$4836.836 + \$1482.301$$
$$= \$6319.14$$
$$\text{Bond price after rate increase} = \$275\left(\frac{1 - 1.04125^{-31}}{0.04125}\right) - \$5000(1.04125^{-31})$$
$$= \$4762.507 + \$1428.120$$
$$= \$6190.63$$

Although the bond's price remained above the face value (since $b > p$), the bond price decreased by $128.51 as a result of the interest rate increase.

FINANCIAL CALCULATOR SOLUTION

Compute the bond's price before the interest rate change.	Result
ENTER: 275 1000 4 31	
PRESS: (PMT) (FV) (i) (n) (COMP)(PV)	−6319.14
Compute the bond's price after the interest rate change.	
ENTER: 4.125	
PRESS: (i) (COMP)(PV)	−6190.63

The bond's price dropped from $6319.14 to $6190.63 as a result of the interest rate increase. ∎

■ EXAMPLE 15.2c   CALCULATING THE CAPITAL GAIN FROM AN INVESTMENT IN BONDS

David Healey purchased 10 bonds, each with a face value of $1000 and paying an 8% coupon rate, on a date when the bonds still had $9\frac{1}{2}$ years remaining until maturity and the market interest rate for bonds of this maturity was 10% compounded semiannually. Two and one-half years later, when the interest rate had declined to 8.5% compounded semiannually, he sold the bonds. What was the capital gain (or loss) on the bond investment?

☑ SOLUTION

$$\text{Capital gain} = \text{Selling price} - \text{Purchase price}$$

For calculating the purchase price of each bond,

$$F = \$1000 \quad b = 4\% \quad Fb = \$40 \quad n = 19 \quad \text{and} \quad p = 5\%$$

For calculating the selling price of each bond,

$$Fb = \$40 \quad \text{again, but} \quad n = 14 \quad \text{and} \quad p = 4.25\%$$

ALGEBRAIC SOLUTION

$$
\begin{aligned}
\text{Purchase price} &= \$40\left(\frac{1 - 1.05^{-19}}{0.05}\right) - \$1000(1.05^{-19}) \\
&= \$483.413 + \$395.734 \\
&= \$879.15 \\
\text{Selling price} &= \$40\left(\frac{1 - 1.0425^{-14}}{0.0425}\right) - \$1000(1.0425^{-14}) \\
&= \$415.636 + \$558.387 \\
&= \$974.02 \\
\text{Capital gain} &= 10(\$974.02 - \$879.15) \\
&= \$948.70
\end{aligned}
$$

FINANCIAL CALCULATOR SOLUTION

Compute the purchase price of each bond.	Result
ENTER: 40 1000 5 19	
PRESS: PMT FV i n COMP PV	−879.15
Compute the selling price of each bond.	
ENTER: 4.25 14	
PRESS: i n COMP PV	−974.02

Capital gain = 10($974.02 − $879.15) = $948.70 ∎

BOND PREMIUM AND BOND DISCOUNT Figure 15.2 shows graphs of bond price versus the prevailing market interest rate for two 10% coupon, $1000 face value bonds. One bond has 5 years remaining until maturity, and the other has 10 years.

FIGURE   **15.2**

Bond Price versus Market Interest Rate for Two Maturities of 10% Coupon Bonds

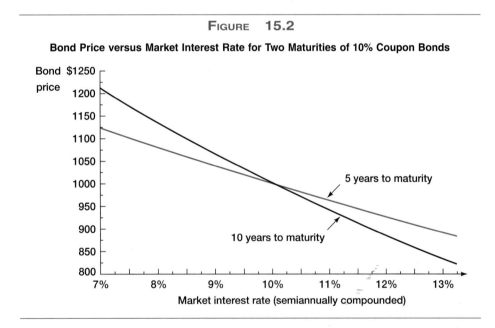

Most of the following points have been discussed earlier in this section. The graph expresses them in a pictorial form.

• *Criterion for trading at par.* When the coupon rate equals the market rate ($b = p$), a bond's price equals its face value, F. This happens because the regular interest payments by themselves will provide precisely the market's required rate of return on the purchase price.

- *Criterion for trading at a premium.* When the coupon rate exceeds the market rate ($b > p$), the bond's price will exceed its face value by an amount known as the **bond premium.** That is,

  Bond premium = Bond price − Face value   when $b > p$

- *Criterion for trading at a discount.* When the coupon rate is less than the prevailing market rate ($b < p$), the bond's price will be below its face value by an amount known as the **bond discount.** That is,

  Bond discount = Face value − Bond price   when $b < p$

- *Size of the premium or discount.* For a given time until maturity, a larger difference between b and p results in a bigger premium or discount. For a given spread between b and p, a longer-maturity bond will have a larger premium or discount.

EXERCISE 15.2

Answers to the odd-numbered problems are at the end of the book.

Note: **Unless otherwise indicated, assume that:**

- **The face value of a bond is $1000.**
- **Bond interest is paid semiannually.**
- **The bond was originally issued at its face value.**
- **Bonds are redeemed at their face value at maturity.**
- **Market rates of return and yields to maturity are compounded semiannually.**

Calculate the purchase price of each of the $1000 face value bonds in problems 1 through 8.

Problem	Issue date	Maturity date	Purchase date	Coupon rate (%)	Market rate (%)
1.	June 1, 1983	June 1, 2003	June 1, 1986	12.25	9.75
2.	March 15, 1982	March 15, 2007	Sept 15, 1989	16.0	10.0
3.	Jan 1, 1987	Jan 1, 2002	July 1, 1987	9.3	10.6
4.	Sept 20, 1986	Sept 20, 2006	Sept 20, 1987	9.75	11.5
5.	Aug 1, 1986	Aug 1, 2006	Aug 1, 1990	9.5	11.5
6.	July 1, 1989	July 1, 2009	Jan 1, 1990	9.7	11.9
7.	June 1, 1984	June 1, 2009	June 1, 1992	14.25	9.0
8.	April 1, 1985	April 1, 2005	Oct 1, 1991	12.0	9.1

9. Bonds A, B, C, and D all have a face value of $1000 and carry a 10% coupon. The time remaining until maturity is 5, 10, 15, and 25 years for A, B, C, and D, respectively. Calculate their market prices if the rate of return required by the market on these bonds is 8% compounded semiannually. Summarize the observed pattern or trend in a brief statement.

10. Bonds E, F, G, and H all have a face value of $1000 and carry a 10% coupon. The time remaining until maturity is 5, 10, 15, and 25 years for E, F, G, and H, respectively. Calculate their market prices if the rate of return required by the market on these bonds is 12% compounded semiannually. Summarize the observed pattern or trend in a brief statement.

11. Bonds J, K, and L all have a face value of $1000 and all have 20 years remaining until maturity. Their respective coupon rates are 10%, 11%, and 12% compounded semiannu-

ally. Calculate their market prices if the rate of return required by the market on these bonds is 9% compounded semiannually. Summarize the observed pattern or trend in a brief statement.

12. Bonds M, N, and Q all have a face value of $1000 and all have 20 years remaining until maturity. Their respective coupon rates are 8%, 7%, and 6% compounded semiannually. Calculate their market prices if the rate of return required by the market on these bonds is 9% compounded semiannually. Summarize the observed pattern or trend in a brief statement.

13. Bonds E and F both have a face value of $1000 and 12 years remaining until maturity. Their coupon rates are 8% and 12%, respectively. Calculate the price of both bonds if the required rate of return is 10% compounded semiannually.

•14. A $1000, 10% coupon bond has 15 years remaining until maturity. The rate of return required by the market on these bonds has recently been 10% (compounded semiannually). Calculate the price change if the required return abruptly:

   a. Rises to 11%.

   b. Rises to 12%.

   c. Falls to 9%.

   d. Falls to 8%.

   Then answer the following questions.

   e. Is the price change caused by a 2% interest rate increase twice the price change caused by a 1% interest rate increase?

   f. Is the price change caused by a 1% interest rate increase equal in magnitude to the price change caused by a 1% interest rate decrease?

•15. This problem investigates the sensitivity of the prices of bonds with different maturities to interest rate changes. Bonds G, H, and J all have a face value of $1000 and carry a 10% coupon. The time remaining until maturity is 5, 10, and 25 years for G, H, and J, respectively. Calculate the price change of each bond if the prevailing market rate increases from 10% to 11% compounded semiannually. Briefly describe the observed trend.

•16. This problem investigates the sensitivity of the prices of bonds having differing coupon rates to interest rate changes. Bonds K and L both have a face value of $1000 and 15 years remaining until maturity. Their coupon rates are 8% and 12%, respectively. If the prevailing market rate decreases from 10% to 9% compounded semiannually, calculate the price change of each bond:

   a. In dollars.

   b. As a percentage of the initial price.

   c. Are high-coupon or low-coupon bonds more sensitive to a given interest rate change? Justify your response using the results from part b.

17. A $1000, 9.5% coupon bond has $13\frac{1}{2}$ years remaining until maturity. Calculate the bond premium if the required return in the bond market is 8.2% compounded semiannually.

18. A $1000, 11.25% coupon bond has $8\frac{1}{2}$ years remaining until maturity. Calculate the bond premium if the required return in the bond market is 8.5% compounded semiannually.

19. A $1000, 9% coupon bond has 16 years remaining until maturity. Calculate the bond discount if the required return in the bond market is 10.2% compounded semiannually.

20. A $1000, 8.25% coupon bond has $21\frac{1}{2}$ years remaining until maturity. Calculate the bond discount if the required return in the bond market is 9.7% compounded semiannually.

•21. Three years after the issue of a $10,000, 8.75% coupon, 25-year bond, the rate of return required in the bond market on long-term bonds is 8.1% compounded semiannually.

    a. At what price would the bond then sell?

    b. What capital gain or loss (expressed as a percentage of the original investment) would the owner realize by selling the bond at that price?

•22. Four and one-half years ago Gavin purchased 20 $1000 bonds in a new Province of Ontario issue with a 20-year maturity and an 8.5% coupon. If the prevailing market rate is now 9.6% compounded semiannually:

    a. What would be the proceeds from the sale of Gavin's bonds?

    b. What would be the capital gain or loss (expressed as a percentage of the original investment)?

•23. Three years ago Quebec Hydro sold an issue of 20-year, 10.5% coupon bonds. Calculate an investor's percent capital gain for the entire 3-year holding period if the current semiannually compounded return required in the bond market is:

    a. 9%.   *b.* 10.5%.   *c.* 12%.

•24. Two and one-half years ago the Province of Saskatchewan sold an issue of 25-year, 11% coupon bonds. Calculate an investor's percent capital gain for the entire $2\frac{1}{2}$-year holding period if the current rate of return required in the bond market is:

    a. 12%.   *b.* 11%.   *c.* 10%.

••25. During periods of declining interest rates, long-term bonds can provide investors with impressive capital gains. The best example in recent times occurred in the early 1980s. In September 1981 the bond market was pricing long-term bonds to provide a rate of return of over 18.5% compounded semiannually. Suppose you had purchased 10% coupon bonds in September 1981 with 20 years remaining until maturity, priced to yield 18.5%. Four and one-half years later (in March 1986) the bonds could have been sold at a prevailing market rate of 9.7% compounded semiannually. What would have been your semiannually compounded rate of total return on the bonds during the $4\frac{1}{2}$-year period?

••26. The downside of the long-term bond investment story occurs during periods of rising long-term interest rates, when bond prices fall. During the 2 years preceding September 1981, long-term bond yields rose from 11% to 18.5%. Suppose you had purchased 10% coupon bonds with 22 years remaining until maturity in September 1979 and sold them in September 1981. What would have been your semiannually compounded rate of total return on the bonds during the 2-year period?

15.3 YIELD TO MATURITY ON AN INTEREST PAYMENT DATE

If a bond is purchased at the price given by formula (15–1) and *held until it matures,* the purchaser will realize a semiannually compounded rate of return of 2*p* on the purchase price. This rate of return is called the *yield to maturity*[3] (YTM) of the bond. The **yield to maturity** of a bond is *defined* as the discount rate that makes the present value, on the purchase date, of the bond's remaining cash flows equal to its purchase price. Although this definition suggests how a bond's yield to maturity may be calculated, it is not particularly helpful in understanding the significance to an investor of a bond's yield to maturity. A useful *interpretation* of yield to maturity is that it

---

[3]The yield to maturity is sometimes called the "yield" or the "bond yield." For instance, quotations of bond prices and yields to maturity in the financial pages use just "yield" or "bond yield" to mean yield to maturity. In other situations, however, "yield" is sometimes used to refer to a bond's "current yield" (defined as the annual coupon interest expressed as a percentage of the bond's market price). Use of the simple term "yield" should be discouraged, because of this ambiguity.

represents the rate of return a bondholder will realize if the bond is held from the purchase date until maturity. A bond's yield to maturity is established by the price at which it is purchased: the higher the purchase price, the lower the bond's yield to maturity. It is standard practice to calculate and quote a yield to maturity as a semiannually compounded nominal annual rate.

In the previous section, we were, in essence, answering the question: Given the market-determined yield to maturity, what should be the price of a bond in order for it to provide this yield to maturity? The other question that a bond investor commonly faces is: What yield to maturity will a bond provide if it is purchased at a particular offered price?

To answer the second question, the mathematical task is to solve formula (15−1) for *p* given the bond price. The (semiannually compounded) yield to maturity is then 2*p*. The algebraic approach requires the trial-and-error method (Appendix 12B) of substituting estimates for *p* into the right side of the formula. Interpolation (Appendix 12C) may be used to reduce the number of trial-and-error iterations. Because the financial calculator method for calculating the yield to maturity is so much more efficient than the algebraic method, the algebraic method is illustrated in only one of the following examples.

■ EXAMPLE 15.3A   CALCULATING THE YIELD TO MATURITY OF A BOND

A $1000 face value Province of Manitoba bond, bearing interest at 9.75% payable semiannually, has 11 years remaining until maturity. What is the bond's yield to maturity at its current market price of $1021?

☑ SOLUTION

Given: *F* = $1000, *b* = 4.875%, *Fb* = $48.75, *n* = 22, and bond price = $1021. This bond's yield to maturity is the (semiannually compounded) discount rate that gives a combined present value of $1021 for

*   22 interest payments of $48.75
*   The $1000 face value payable at maturity.

That is, the YTM is the value of 2*p*, where *p* is the solution to

$$\$1021 = \underbrace{\$48.75\left[\frac{1 - (1 + p)^{-22}}{p}\right]}_{\text{Term } ①} + \underbrace{\$1000(1 + p)^{-22}}_{\text{Term } ②}$$

ALGEBRAIC SOLUTION

Use the trial-and-error method to find values of *p* that produce values of the right-hand side (RHS) that bracket $1021 within 1% or 2%. We can deduce that *p* will be a little less than *b* = 4.875% since the bond price is a little more than $1000.

Trial number	Estimated *p*	Term ①	Term ②	RHS
1	0.0475 ⌐	656.58	360.26	1016.84 ⌐
	[*p*			⌐1021.00
2	⌐0.047 ⌐	659.62	364.06	1023.68 ⌐

Interpolating to improve the estimated value of p:

$$\frac{p - 0.047}{0.0475 - 0.047} \doteq \frac{1021.00 - 1023.68}{1016.84 - 1023.68}$$

$$\frac{p - 0.047}{0.0005} \doteq \frac{-2.68}{-6.84}$$

$$p - 0.047 \doteq 0.0005(0.392)$$

$$p \doteq 0.047 + 0.0002$$

$$\doteq 0.0472$$

$$\doteq 4.72\%$$

The bond's YTM is $2p = 9.44\%$ compounded semiannually.

FINANCIAL CALCULATOR SOLUTION

						Result
ENTER	48.75	22	1000	1021		
				+/−	COMP	
PRESS:	PMT	n	FV	PV	i	4.7195

The bond's semiannually compounded YTM is

$$2p = 2(4.7195\%) = 9.44\% \qquad \blacksquare$$

■ EXAMPLE 15.3B   CALCULATING THE YIELD TO MATURITY OF A HIGH-RISK OR "DEEP-DISCOUNT" BOND

A corporation's financial condition may deteriorate to the point that there is some uncertainty about its ability to make future interest payments on its bonds or to redeem the bonds at maturity. Investors will be unwilling to buy the bonds at prices that reflect market yields to maturity on bonds of healthy corporations. The prices of bonds of the financially distressed corporation will fall to a level determined primarily by the degree of perceived risk rather than the prevailing market rate of return. It is still useful to calculate the YTM on such "deep-discount" bonds. The YTM represents the rate of return the bond purchaser will realise if (a) the corporation does manage to meet all the scheduled payments on time and (b) the bond is held through to the maturity date.

Calculate the YTM on the $1000, 12% coupon bonds of Beaucamp Corp., which are trading at $500. The bonds have $7\frac{1}{2}$ years remaining until maturity.

✓ SOLUTION

Given: $F = \$1000$, $b = 6\%$, $Fb = \$60$, $n = 15$, and bond price $= \$500$. The YTM is $2p$, where p is the solution to

$$\$500 = \$60\left[\frac{1 - (1 + p)^{-15}}{p}\right] + \$1000(1 + p)^{-15}$$

FINANCIAL CALCULATOR SOLUTION

						Result
ENTER:	60	1000	500	15		
			+/−		COMP	
PRESS:	PMT	FV	PV	n	i	14.237

The bond's YTM is $2p = 2(14.237) = 28.47\%$ compounded semiannually.   ■

Exercise 15.3

Answers to the odd-numbered problems are at the end of the book.

Note: **Unless otherwise indicated, assume that:**

- **The face value of a bond is $1000.**
- **Bond interest is paid semiannually.**
- **The bond was originally issued at its face value.**
- **Bonds are redeemed at their face value at maturity.**
- **Market rates of return and yields to maturity are compounded semiannually.**

1. A bond with a face value of $1000 and 15 years remaining until maturity pays a coupon rate of 10%. Calculate its yield to maturity if it is priced at $900.

2. A bond with a face value of $1000 and 15 years remaining until maturity pays a coupon rate of 10%. Calculate its yield to maturity if it is priced at $1100.

3. Bonds A and C both have a face value of $1000 and pay a coupon rate of 9%. They have 5 and 20 years, respectively, remaining until maturity. Calculate the yield to maturity of each bond if it is purchased for $950.

4. Bonds D and E both have a face value of $1000 and pay a coupon rate of 9%. They have 5 and 20 years, respectively, remaining until maturity. Calculate the yield to maturity of each bond if it is purchased for $1050.

•5. A $1000 Government of Canada bond carrying a 10% coupon is currently priced to yield 10% compounded semiannually until maturity. If the bond price abruptly rises $20, what is the change in the yield to maturity if the bond has:

   a. 3 years remaining to maturity?

   b. 15 years remaining to maturity?

•6. A $1000 Nova Corporation bond carrying an 11% coupon is currently priced to yield 10% compounded semiannually until maturity. If the bond price abruptly falls $25, what is the change in the yield to maturity if the bond has:

   a. 2 years remaining to maturity?

   b. 12 years remaining to maturity?

•7. In the spring of 1992 it became apparent that Olympia & York (O&Y) would have serious difficulty in servicing its debt. Because of this risk, investors were heavily discounting O&Y's bond issues. On April 30, 1992, an Olympia & York bond issue paying an 11.25% coupon rate and maturing on October 31, 1998, traded at $761.50 (per $1000 of face value). (This was at a time when Government of Canada bonds with a similar coupon and maturity date were trading at a premium of about 10% above par.) If O&Y had managed to make the contractual payments on these bonds, what yield to maturity would investors who purchased those bonds on April 30, 1992, have realised? (P.S.: They didn't!)

15.4 Bond Price on Any Date

The previous section dealt with the calculation of a bond's price on an interest payment date. This limits us to valuing a particular bond on just the 2 days in a year when the interest payments are made.[4] But bonds trade in the financial markets *every* business day. We need to develop the further steps required to calculate a bond's price on any date, given the yield to maturity required in the market.

---

[4]There are two special circumstances in which rules are needed to remove ambiguities.
1. If a bond's maturity date is the last day of a month, both semiannual coupons are paid on the *last* day of the month. This means, for example, that a bond maturing on September 30 pays its March coupon on March 31 (rather than on March 30). A bond maturing on October 31 pays an April coupon on April 30.
2. If a bond's maturity date is August 29 or 30, it pays a February coupon on February 28 (or February 29 in a leap year).

Calculating a Bond's Price on Any Date

Consistent with the Valuation Principle, a bond's market price will still be the present value on the purchase date of the future payments of interest and face value. At first it appears that each payment must be discounted over a nonintegral number of intervals to get its present value on a general purchase date. We can, however, use our understanding of equivalent values to develop an equivalent but simpler procedure. The present value of the future payments may be obtained in two-steps.

Step 1: Determine the present value of the future payments on the interest payment date *preceding* the purchase date. (This is the calculation that was presented in Section 15.2).

Step 2: Calculate the equivalent (future) value of the step 1 result on the purchase date. The industry practice is to calculate this future value on a *compound-interest* basis[5] using formula (8–2), $S = P(1 + i)^n$. In this context, $i = p$, the market rate per interest payment interval, and n is the fraction of the payment interval that has elapsed since the most recent interest payment. That is,

$$n = \frac{\text{Number of days since the most recent interest payment}}{\text{Total number of days in the full payment interval}}$$

This procedure is equivalent to (but mathematically easier than) the direct discounting of the future payments to the purchase date.

Price of a Bond (between interest payment dates):   The bond price is the future value, on the purchase date, of the remaining payments' present value at the preceding interest payment date.

■ Example 15.4a   *Pricing a Bond between Interest Payment Dates*

A $1000, 20-year, 11% coupon bond was issued on August 15, 1994. It was sold on November 3, 1996, to yield the purchaser 8.8% compounded semiannually until maturity. At what price did the bond sell?

☑ Solution

Given: $F = \$1000$, $b = 5.5\%$, $Fb = \$55$, $p = 4.4\%$, and $n = 36$ coupon payments remaining.

Step 1: Calculate the present value of the remaining payments at the most recent interest payment date (August 15, 1996) using formula (15–1).

Step 2: Calculate the future value on the date of sale (November 3, 1996) of the amount from step 1. The interval from August 15 to November 3, 1996, was $308 - 228 = 80$ days. The total length of the interest payment interval from August 15, 1996, to February 15, 1997, was

$$46 + (366 - 228) = 184 \text{ days}$$

---
[5]Many textbooks do this second step on a *simple*-interest basis. In our notation, they use $S = P(1 + rt)$ with $r = p$ and t equal to the same fraction as we calculate for n in this context. This is not the method used in the bond market. The resulting value for the price is too large by a small fraction of 1%. Presumably the reason the texts use a simple-interest approximation is that the notion of compounding interest for *less than one* compounding period is a more difficult concept than the familiar idea of calculating simple interest for an interval of up to 183 days.

The fraction of the payment interval that had elapsed when the bond was sold was

$$n = \frac{80}{184} = 0.4347826$$

ALGEBRAIC SOLUTION

Step 1:

$$\text{Present value (August 15)} = \$55\left(\frac{1 - 1.044^{-36}}{0.044}\right) + \$1000(1.044^{-36})$$
$$= \$984.728 + \$212.218$$
$$= \$1196.95$$

Step 2:   Price (November 3) $= \$1196.95(1.044^{0.4347826}) = \$1219.57$

The bond sold for \$1219.57 on November 3, 1996.

FINANCIAL CALCULATOR SOLUTION

Step 1: Calculate the payments' present value on August 15, 1996.					Result
ENTER: 55 1000 4.4 36					
PRESS: PMT FV i n COMP PV					−1196.95
Step 2: Calculate the future value on Nov. 3, 1996, of the step 1 result.					
ENTER: 0 0.4347826					
PRESS: PMT n COMP FV					1219.57

The bond sold for \$1219.57 on November 3, 1996. (It traded at a premium because the coupon rate exceeded the market's required rate of return.) ∎

■ EXAMPLE 15.4B   *PRICING A BOND BETWEEN INTEREST PAYMENT DATES*

On January 15, 1992, Westcoast Transmission issued 20-year bonds having a 7.6% coupon rate. At what price did \$1000 face value bonds trade on April 10, 1996, if the required return was 8.2% compounded semiannually?

☑ SOLUTION

Given: $F = \$1000$, $b = 3.8\%$, $Fb = \$38$, $p = 4.1\%$, and $n = 32$ coupon payments remaining.

Step 1:   Calculate the present value of the remaining payments at the most recent interest payment date (January 15, 1996).

Step 2:   Calculate the future value on the date of sale (April 10, 1996) of the amount from step 1. The interval from January 15 to April 10, 1996 (a leap year), was $101 - 15 = 86$ days long. The total length of the interest payment interval from January 15, 1996, to July 15, 1996, was

$$197 - 15 = 182 \text{ days}$$

The fraction of the payment interval that had elapsed when the bond was sold was

$$n = \frac{86}{182} = 0.4725275$$

ALGEBRAIC SOLUTION

Step 1: With $p = 4.1\%$, the bond price on January 15, 1996, would have been

$$\text{Present value (January 15)} = \$38\left(\frac{1 - 1.041^{-32}}{0.041}\right) + \$1000(1.041^{-32})$$

$$= \$670.631 + \$276.425$$

$$= \$947.065$$

Step 2:   Price (April 10) $= \$947.06(1.041^{0.4725275}) = \$965.21$

The bonds sold for \$965.21 on April 10, 1996.

FINANCIAL CALCULATOR SOLUTION

Step 1: Calculate the payments' present value on January 15, 1996.					Result
ENTER: 38 1000 4.1 32					
PRESS: PMT FV i n COMP PV					−947.06
Step 2: Calculate the future value on April 10, 1996, of the step 1 result.					
ENTER: 0 0.4725275					
PRESS: PMT n COMP FV					965.21

The bonds sold for \$965.21 on April 10, 1996. (They traded at a discount because the coupon rate was less than the market's required rate of return.) ■

QUOTATION OF BOND PRICES

Even if prevailing interest rates do not change, the price of a bond obtained by the procedure of the preceding subsection will change as time passes, for two reasons. First, the price changes with the accrual and periodic payment of coupon interest. The accrual of interest causes a bond's price to rise steadily after an interest payment. Then the price will abruptly fall by the amount Fb on the day when the interest payment is made. The result of this cycle's repeating itself every 6 months is a "sawtooth" pattern of price change as time passes. Figure 15.3 illustrates the pattern for the case of a bond selling at a premium. Figure 15.4 presents the corresponding graph for a bond selling at a discount. The graphs show how the market price of a \$1000 face value bond changes over the last six interest payment intervals before the bond's maturity date (assuming that prevailing market interest rates do not change). Note that much of the bond price axis between \$0 and \$1000 has been omitted to show the details of the bond price changes on a larger scale. As an indication of the scale in the neighbourhood of the \$1000 face value, keep in mind that Fb will be in the \$35 to \$60 range for coupon rates in the 7% to 12% range.

The second reason the price will change as time passes is that the premium or discount will diminish. The size of the premium on any date in Figure 15.3 is the amount by which the downward-sloping dashed line exceeds \$1000 on that date. The size of the discount on any date in Figure 15.4 is the amount by which \$1000 exceeds the upward-sloping dashed line on that date. By the time a bond reaches its maturity date, any bond premium or discount will be eliminated.

FIGURE   15.3

Price Change Over Time for a Bond Trading at a Premium

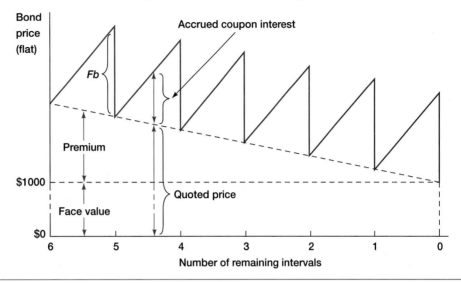

FIGURE   15.4

Price Change Over Time for a Bond Trading at a Discount

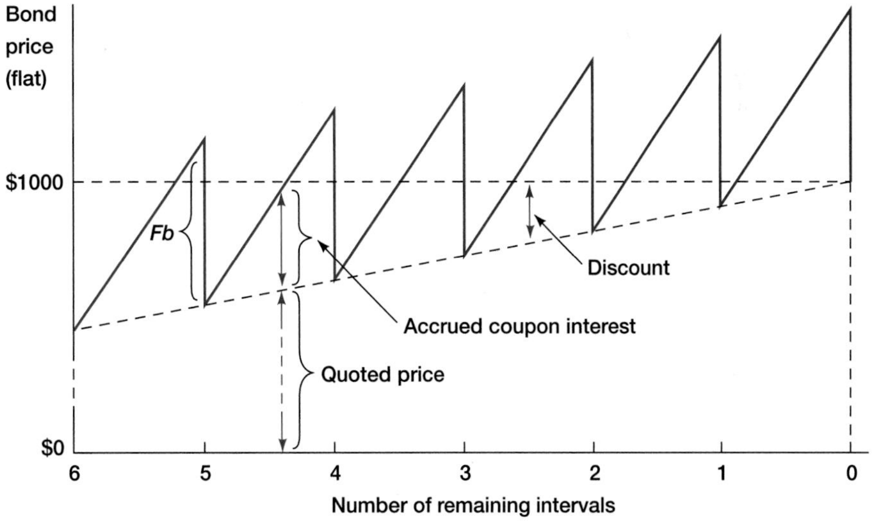

FLAT PRICE VERSUS QUOTED PRICE   The bond price that we have been calculating and that was plotted to give the sawtooth graphs in Figures 15.3 and 15.4 is called the **flat price** in bond transactions. It is the *actual* amount paid by the purchaser and received by the seller (ignoring brokerage charges).

Consider the consequences if the financial pages were to list the flat prices for various bonds each day. Before an investor can make meaningful comparisons among bond prices, the prices must be adjusted for their differing amounts of accrued coupon interest. As an extreme example, the flat prices of two otherwise identical bonds would differ by almost Fb if one bond paid coupon interest yesterday and the other bond will pay interest tomorrow. To permit the direct comparison of bond prices, the general practice is to deduct the accrued coupon interest from the flat price to obtain what is called the **quoted price.** That is,

$$\text{Quoted price} = \text{Flat price} - \text{Accrued coupon interest}$$

It is the quoted price that is reported in the financial pages and quoted by brokers to their clients. In Figures 15.3 and 15.4, the flat price on one particular date is broken down into its "accrued-interest" and "quoted-price" components. The quoted price includes the premium or discount but does not reflect the accrued coupon interest. When they purchase bonds, investors are aware that accrued coupon interest will be added to the quoted price.

Table 15.2 lists some bond quotations taken from the *Financial Post* on October 5, 1995. Since there can be several face value denominations in any bond issue, bond prices are quoted as a *percentage* of face value. The dollar price of any denomination may then be readily calculated. For example, the price of a $5000 face value bond quoted at 102.25(%) would be

$$\$5000 \times 1.0225 = \$5112.50$$

Even though the bond yield (meaning yield to maturity) can be calculated from the other information in the table, it is nevertheless quoted since many bond investors are unable to perform this calculation.

TABLE   15.2

Bond Price Quotations (October 6, 1995)

Issuer	Coupon rate (%)	Maturity date	Quoted price (%)	Bond yield (%)
Government of Canada	6.50	June 1, 2004	93.15	7.592
Government of Canada	10.50	March 15, 2021	126.53	8.035
Province of Nova Scotia	9.60	Jan 30, 2022	111.20	8.524
Province of New Brunswick	8.25	March 22, 2000	103.40	7.341
Ontario Hydro	10.00	Oct 17, 2014	116.87	8.230
Bell Canada	10.35	Dec 15, 2009	116.25	8.369
Bombardier	11.10	May 15, 2001	114.75	7.799
Trans Canada Pipeline	9.45	March 20, 2018	108.00	8.637

CALCULATING THE ACCRUED COUPON INTEREST   The prevailing practice is to calculate the accrued coupon interest on a *simple-interest* basis. Formula (6–1) can be adapted to this application. That is,

$$I = Prt = Fbt$$

where t is the fraction of the payment interval (containing the valuation date) that has elapsed since the most recent interest payment. That is,

$$t = \frac{\text{Number of days since the most recent interest payment}}{\text{Total number of days in the full payment interval}}$$

■ **EXAMPLE 15.4c** *CALCULATING THE ACCRUED COUPON INTEREST AND THE QUOTED PRICE, GIVEN THE FLAT PRICE*

In Example 15.4b, we calculated the (flat) price on April 10, 1996, of a $1000 face value, 7.6% coupon Westcoast Transmission bond maturing January 15, 2012. The calculated price, based on an 8.2% yield to maturity, was $965.21.

a. How much of that price was interest that had accrued in favour of the previous owner since the most recent interest payment date?

b. What price would the financial press and securities brokers have quoted for these bonds on April 10, 1996?

■ **SOLUTION**

a. The number of days from the interest payment on January 15, 1996, to the April 10, 1996, valuation date was

$$101 - 15 = 86$$

The number of days in the full payment interval (from January 15 to July 15) was

$$197 - 15 = 182$$

The coupon interest that accrued over these 86 days was

$$I = Prt = Fbt = \$1000(0.038)\frac{86}{182} = \$17.96$$

Hence, $17.96 of the $965.21 flat price was accrued interest.

b. Brokers and financial media report the quoted price.

$$\begin{aligned}
\text{Quoted price} &= \text{Flat price} - \text{Accrued interest} \\
&= \$965.21 - \$17.96 \\
&= \$947.25
\end{aligned}$$

Bond investors understand that they must pay the accrued interest of $17.96 in addition to the quoted price.   ■

■ **EXAMPLE 15.4d** *CALCULATING THE ACCRUED COUPON INTEREST AND THE QUOTED PRICE, GIVEN THE YIELD TO MATURITY*

For the Bombardier bond listed in Table 15.2, show how the quoted price may be calculated from the other information provided in the table. What additional accrued interest did the purchaser of a $10,000 face value bond on October 6, 1995, have to pay?

■ **SOLUTION**

From the table, we see that the Bombardier bond issue maturing May 15, 2001, pays a coupon rate of 11.10%. The bond market was pricing the bonds on October 6, 1995, to yield 7.799% (compounded semiannually) until maturity. We will base our calculations on a $1000 face value bond. Thus,

$$F = \$1000 \qquad b = 5.55\% \qquad Fb = \$55.50 \qquad p = \frac{7.799\%}{2} = 3.8995\%$$

$$\text{and} \qquad n = 12 \text{ payments remaining}$$

The determination of the quoted price between interest payment dates first requires the two-step calculation of the flat price. Then the accrued coupon interest must be calculated and deducted from the flat price to obtain the quoted price.

In both the algebraic solution and the financial calculator solution, we need the fraction of the payment interval that has elapsed up to October 6, 1996. That fraction is

$$\frac{280 - 136}{320 - 136} = \frac{144}{184} = 0.7826087$$

ALGEBRAIC SOLUTION

Step 1: Calculate the present value on the previous interest payment date (May 15, 1996) of the remaining payments.

$$\text{Present value (May 15)} = \$55.50\left(\frac{1 - 1.038995^{-12}}{0.038995}\right) + \$1000(1.038995^{-12})$$
$$= \$523.922 + \$631.886$$
$$= \$1155.81$$

Step 2: Calculate the flat price on October 6, 1996, by calculating the future value of the step 1 result with compound interest at 7.799% compounded semiannually.

$$\text{Flat price (October 6)} = \$1155.81(1.038995)^{0.7826087} = \$1190.94$$

Step 3: Calculate and deduct the accrued coupon interest.

$$\text{Accrued coupon interest} = Fbt$$
$$= \$1000(0.0555)0.7826087$$
$$= \$43.43$$
$$\text{Quoted price} = \text{Flat price} - \text{Accrued interest}$$
$$= \$1190.94 - \$43.43$$
$$= \$1147.51$$

This price is 114.75% of the $1000 face value and verifies the price quoted in Table 15.2. The purchaser of a $10,000 face value bond had to pay 10 times the accrued interest calculated above for a $1000 face value bond. That is, the purchaser paid the quoted price of $11,475.10 plus an additional 10($43.43) = $434.30 for accrued coupon interest. ∎

EXERCISE 15.4

Answers to the odd-numbered problems are at the end of the book.

Note: Unless otherwise indicated, assume that:

• The face value of a bond is $1000.
• Bond interest is paid semiannually.
• The bond was originally issued at its face value.
• Bonds will be redeemed at their face value at maturity.
• Market rates of return and yields to maturity are compounded semiannually.

Calculate the purchase price of each of the $1000 face value bonds in problems 1 through 8.

Problem	Issue date	Maturity date	Purchase date	Coupon rate (%)	Market rate (%)
1.	June 1, 1983	June 1, 2003	June 15, 1992	12.25	9.75
2.	March 15, 1982	March 15, 2007	Oct 5, 1988	16.0	10.0
3.	Jan 1, 1987	Jan 1, 2002	April 15, 1987	9.3	10.6
4.	Sept 20, 1986	Sept 20, 2006	June 1, 1989	9.75	11.5
5.	Aug 1, 1986	Aug 1, 2006	Dec 15, 1990	9.5	11.5
6.	July 1, 1989	July 1, 2009	April 9, 1990	9.7	11.9
7.	June 1, 1984	June 1, 2009	June 25, 1992	14.25	9.0
8.	April 1, 1985	April 1, 2005	Dec 20, 1991	12.0	9.1

Problems 9 through 16 require the calculation of bond prices between interest payment dates.

•9. A $1000, 11% coupon bond issued by Bell Canada matures on October 15, 2011. What was its price on June 11, 1992, if its yield to maturity was 9.9% compounded semiannually?

•10. A $1000, 8.5% coupon, 25-year Government of Canada bond was issued on June 1, 1986. At what price did it sell on April 27, 1990, if the market's required return was 11.2% compounded semiannually?

•11. A $1000, 9.25% coupon bond issued by Ontario Hydro on January 6, 1979, matures on January 6, 2004. What was its market price on August 8, 1981, when the required yield to maturity was 17% compounded semiannually?

•12. A $1000, 15.5% coupon, 25-year Government of Canada bond was issued on March 15, 1982. At what price did it trade on June 4, 1986, when the market's required return was 9.2% compounded semiannually?

•13. A $1000, 9% coupon, 20-year Province of Ontario bond was issued on March 15, 1992. Calculate its price on March 15, April 15, May 15, June 15, July 15, August 15, and September 15, 1993, if the yield to maturity on every date was 10% compounded semiannually.

•14. A $1000, 11% coupon, 15-year Province of Quebec bond was issued on November 20, 1991. Calculate its price on May 20, June 20, July 20, August 20, September 20, October 20, and November 20, 1993, if the yield to maturity on every date was 9.6% compounded semiannually.

••15. A $5000, 9% coupon, 20-year bond issued on August 1, 1986, was purchased on April 25, 1990, to yield 11.5% to maturity, and then sold on December 27, 1991, to yield 8.8% to maturity. What was the investor's capital gain or loss:

   a. In dollars?

   b. As a percentage of her original investment?

••16. A $10,000, 14% coupon, 25-year bond issued on June 15, 1984, was purchased on March 20, 1987, to yield 9% to maturity, and then sold on April 20, 1990, to yield 11.5% to maturity. What was the investor's capital gain or loss:

   a. In dollars?

   b. As a percentage of his original investment?

Problems 17 through 22 require the calculation of quoted bond prices and accrued interest.

•17. A $1000 face value, 11% coupon bond pays interest on May 15 and November 15. If its flat price on August 1 was $1065.50, at what price (expressed as a percentage of face value) would the issue have been reported in the financial pages?

•18. A $5000 bond was sold for $4860 on September 17. If the bond pays $200 interest on June 1 and December 1 of each year until maturity, what price (expressed as a percentage of face value) would have been quoted for bonds of this issue on September 17?

•19. If a broker quotes a price of 108.50 for a bond on October 23, what amount will a client pay per $1000 face value? The 10.5% coupon rate is payable on March 1 and September 1 of each year. The subsequent February has 28 days.

•20. Calculate the quoted price on April 15, 1987, of the bond described in problem 3.

•21. Calculate the quoted price on June 1, 1989, of the bond described in problem 4.

••22. Using the given bond yields, verify the October 6, 1995, quoted prices in Table 15.2 for the following bonds:

  a. Government of Canada 6.5% coupon, maturing June 1, 2004.

  b. Government of Canada 10.5% coupon, maturing March 15, 2021.

  c. Province of Nova Scotia 9.6% coupon, maturing January 30, 2022.

  d. Province of New Brunswick 8.25% coupon, maturing March 22, 2000.

  e. Ontario Hydro 10% coupon, maturing October 17, 2014.

  f. Bell Canada 10.35% coupon, maturing December 15, 2009.

  g. Trans Canada Pipeline 9.45% coupon, maturing March 20, 2018.

*15.5 AMORTIZATION OF BOND PREMIUM AND DISCOUNT

The origin and calculation of bond premiums and discounts were discussed in Section 15.2. We will now look at the premiums and discounts from an accountant's perspective. The point of view and the schedules developed here provide the basis for the accounting treatment of bond premiums, discounts, and interest payments.

AMORTIZATION OF A BOND PREMIUM

Bonds are priced at a premium when the coupon rate *exceeds* the yield to maturity required in the market. Suppose that a bond paying a 10% coupon rate is purchased 3 years before maturity to yield 8%. The purchase price that provides this yield to maturity is $1052.42. The interest payment after 6 months that would, by itself, provide the required rate of return of 8% compounded semiannually on the amount invested is

$$0.04 \times \$1052.42 = \$42.10$$

Consequently, the actual first coupon payment of $50 pays $50 − $42.10 = $7.90 more than is necessary to provide the required rate of return for the first 6 months.[6]

The accounting view is that the appropriate amount to treat as interest *earned* in a period is the amount that gives the required rate of return on the investment. For the bond described above, this would be $42.10. The remaining $7.90 of the coupon payment is regarded as a refund or repayment of a portion of the original premium, leaving a net investment (called the bond's *book value*) of

$$\$1052.42 - \$7.90 = \$1044.52$$

---

[6]Individual bond investors view the "excess" interest each period as a partial offset for the $52.42 capital *loss* that they will incur when the bond is redeemed for its $1000 face value at maturity. Revenue Canada also takes this view in the sense that individual investors report the full coupon payments as interest income year by year but are allowed to claim the full $52.42 capital loss in the year the bond matures.

The same reasoning and treatment are applied in subsequent periods to future coupon payments.

> **Tip**
>
> Earned interest is always calculated on the *book value* of the bond *after the previous coupon payment,* using an interest rate equal to the *original yield to maturity* set on the bond's date of purchase.

The effect of this treatment is to periodically *reduce* the book value of the bond (and the book value of the premium). After the final coupon payment, this procedure will result in the bond's book value becoming the $1000 face value that is received along with the last interest coupon. The process of reducing the premium in this way is referred to as the **amortization of the bond premium.** The details of the decomposition of each coupon payment and the reduction of the bond premium are often tabulated in a bond premium amortization schedule. A full amortization schedule for the bond just described is developed in the following example.

■ EXAMPLE 15.5A CONSTRUCTION OF A BOND PREMIUM AMORTIZATION SCHEDULE

Prepare a complete bond premium amortization schedule for the 10% coupon bond described in the preceding discussion. It was purchased for $1052.42 on a date 3 years before maturity to yield 8% to maturity. How much of the $300 received in coupon payments over the 3 years would accountants treat as interest income?

☑ SOLUTION

Coupon number	Coupon payment	Interest on book value	Premium amortized	Book value of bond	Unamortized premium
0	—	—	—	$1052.42	$52.42
1	$ 50	$ 42.10①	$ 7.90②	1044.52③	44.52④
2	50	41.78	8.22	1036.30	36.30
3	50	41.45	8.55	1027.75	27.75
4	50	41.11	8.89	1018.86	18.86
5	50	40.75	9.25	1009.61	9.61
6	50	40.39	9.61	1000.0	0.00
	$300	$247.58	$52.42		

① Interest on book value = 0.5 × Yield rate × Book value after previous coupon payment
  = 0.04 × $1052.42 = $42.10
② Premium amortized = Coupon payment − Interest on book value
  = $50 − $42.10 = $7.90
③ New book value = Previous book value − Premium amortized
  = $1052.42 − $7.90 = $1044.52
④ Unamortized premium = Current book value − Face value
  = $1044.52 − $1000 = $44.52

Of the $300 received in coupon interest payments, accountants would treat $247.58 as interest income for the 3 years. The remaining $52.42 would be treated as a refund of a portion (the bond premium) of the principal amount of the original investment. ■

AMORTIZATION OF A BOND DISCOUNT

Bonds are priced at a discount when the coupon rate is *less* than the yield to maturity required in the market. Suppose that a bond paying a 10% coupon rate is purchased 3 years before maturity to yield 12%. The purchase price that provides this yield to maturity is $950.83. The interest payment after 6 months that would, by itself, provide the required rate of return of 8% compounded semiannually on the amount invested is

$$0.04 \times \$950.83 = \$57.05$$

Consequently, the actual first coupon payment of $50 pays $7.05 *less* than needed to provide the required rate of return for the first 6 months.[7]

The accounting view is that the appropriate amount to record as the interest *earned* in a period is the amount that gives the required rate of return on the investment. For the bond described above, this would be $57.05. The $7.05 deficiency in the coupon interest payment is converted to principal, giving an increased investment or *book value* of

$$\$950.83 + \$7.05 = \$957.88$$

The same reasoning and treatment are applied in subsequent periods to future coupon payments.

The effect of this treatment is to periodically *increase* the book value of the bond and to simultaneously *reduce* the book value of the discount. After the final coupon payment, the bond's book value will reach the $1000 face value that is received along with the last interest coupon. The process of reducing the discount in this way is referred to as the **amortization of the bond discount.** The details of the decomposition of each coupon payment and the reduction of the bond discount are often tabulated in a bond discount amortization schedule. A full amortization schedule for the bond just described is developed in the following example.

■ EXAMPLE 15.5B   *CONSTRUCTION OF A BOND DISCOUNT AMORTIZATION SCHEDULE*

Prepare the complete bond discount amortization schedule for the 10% coupon bond described in the preceding discussion. It was purchased for $950.83 on a date 3 years before maturity to yield 12% to maturity. Even though $300 is received in coupon payments over the 3 years, what total interest income would accountants recognize for the 3 years?

☑ SOLUTION

Coupon number	Coupon payment	Interest on book value	Discount amortized	Book value of bond	Unamortized discount
0	—	—	—	$950.83	$49.17
1	$50	$57.05	$ 7.05	957.88	42.12
2	50	57.47①	7.47②	965.35③	34.65④
3	50	57.92	7.92	973.27	26.73
4	50	58.40	8.40	981.67	18.33

[7]Individual bond investors recognize that the interest "deficiency" each period will ultimately be offset by the $49.17 capital *gain* they will realize when the bond is redeemed for its $1000 face value at maturity.

Coupon number	Coupon payment	Interest on book value	Discount amortized	Book value of bond	Unamortized discount
5	50	58.90	8.90	990.57	9.43
6	50	59.43	9.43	1000.00	0.00
Total:	$300	$349.17	$49.17		

① Interest on book value = 0.5 × Yield rate × Book value after previous coupon payment
  = 0.06 × $957.88 = $57.47
② Discount amortized = Interest on book value − Coupon payment
  = $57.47 − $50 = $7.47
③ New book value = Previous book value + Discount amortized
  = $957.88 + $7.47 = $965.35
④ Unamortized discount = Face value − Current book value
  = $1000 − $965.35 = $34.65

Accountants will treat both the $300 from coupon payments and an amount equal to the original discount as interest income during the 3 years. The total interest income reported in the financial statements over the 3 years will, therefore, be $349.17. (In contrast, individual investors will record, for tax reporting purposes, $100 of interest income each year and a $49.17 capital gain when the face value is received at maturity.) ∎

Tip

The *book value* of a bond after any coupon payment may be obtained *directly* (without working through a bond premium or discount amortization schedule). The book value equals the present value of the *remaining* interest and principal payments from the bond, discounted at the bond's yield to maturity. This approach is used to obtain an intermediate book value in the construction of a *partial* amortization schedule for a bond premium or discount.

EXERCISE 15.5

Answers to the odd-numbered problems are at the end of the book.

Note: Unless otherwise indicated, assume that:

- Bond interest is paid semiannually.
- Bonds will be redeemed at their face value at maturity.
- Market rates of return and yields to maturity are compounded semiannually.

Calculate the purchase price and construct a bond premium amortization schedule for each of the bonds described in problems 1 through 4. Determine the total interest that will be recorded for accounting purposes from the purchase date until maturity.

••1. A $1000 face value, 9% coupon, 5-year bond is purchased 3 years before maturity to yield 8% compounded semiannually until maturity.

••2. A $5000 face value bond with an 11% coupon is purchased $3\frac{1}{2}$ years before maturity to yield 9.5% to maturity.

••3. The yield to maturity on a $1000 face value, 10% coupon, 20-year bond purchased with 12 years remaining until maturity is 8.8%. Show details of the first three and the last three coupon interest payments in a partial amortization schedule.

••4. A $10,000 face value, 13% coupon bond is purchased $16\frac{1}{2}$ years before maturity at a price that will yield 10% until maturity. Show details of the first three and the last three coupon payments in a partial amortization schedule.

Calculate the purchase price and construct a bond discount amortization schedule for
each of the bonds described in problems 5 through 8. Determine the total interest that
will be recorded for accounting purposes from the purchase date until maturity.

••5. A $1000 face value, 8% coupon bond is purchased 3 years before maturity to yield 9.5%
compounded semiannually until maturity.

••6. A $5000 face value, 9% coupon, 10-year bond is purchased $2\frac{1}{2}$ years before the matu-
rity date at a price that will yield 11% until maturity.

••7. The yield to maturity on a $1000 face value, 8.5% coupon bond purchased with 11
years remaining until maturity is 10.4%. Show details of the first three and the last three
coupon interest payments in a partial amortization schedule.

••8. A $10,000 face value, 8.6% coupon, 25-year bond is purchased $14\frac{1}{2}$ years before matu-
rity at a price that will yield 10% until maturity. Show details of the first three and the last
three coupon payments in a partial amortization schedule.

*15.6 SINKING FUNDS

A **sinking fund** is an interest-earning account into which periodic payments are made
to accumulate a specific amount of money by a certain date. The accumulated funds
are typically used to acquire an asset requiring a substantial capital expenditure, or to
retire the principal amount of a debt.

SINKING FUND FOR A CAPITAL EXPENDITURE

A sinking fund can be established by a business or other organization to accumulate
funds for a future project, to replace equipment, to expand production facilities, or to
make an acquisition.

The simplest sinking fund arrangement requires *equal periodic* contributions. The
amount of each contribution is determined so that the required amount of money will
be accumulated by the target date, assuming a conservative compound rate of return
on the money in the sinking fund. The sinking fund is usually set up with the interval
between contributions equal to the compounding interval. The payments then constitute a *simple* annuity and $p = i$. (Only simple-annuity cases will be encountered in this
discussion.) The payment size is calculated so that the *future value* of the payments
on the target date equals the amount needed on that date. If the sinking fund
payments are made at the *end* of each payment interval, their size is obtained by
solving for R in formula (10−1) for an *ordinary* annuity:

$$S_n = R\left[\frac{(1 + p)^n - 1}{p}\right]$$

(10–1)

where the following interpretations are placed on the variables:

S_n = Amount of funds needed on the target date
p = Interest rate earned by the sinking fund per contribution interval
n = Number of sinking fund contributions

If the sinking fund payments are made at the *beginning* of each payment interval,
they form an annuity *due*. To calculate the required periodic sinking fund contributions,
we must solve for R in formula (11−1):

$$S_n(\text{due}) = R\left[\frac{(1 + p)^n - 1}{p}\right] \times (1 + p)$$

(11–1)

A table presenting details of the interest earned in each period and the accumulated amount in the sinking fund at the end of each payment interval is called a *sinking fund schedule.* The accumulated amount or balance in the sinking fund at the *end* of any interval will be the future value of the sinking fund payments already made. The following relationships are used in constructing a sinking fund schedule.

$$\begin{array}{c} \text{Balance at the end of} \\ \text{any payment interval} \end{array} = \begin{array}{c} \text{Future value of the} \\ \text{payments already made} \end{array}$$

$$\begin{array}{c} \text{Interest earned in} \\ \text{any payment interval} \end{array} = p \times \begin{array}{c} \text{Amount in the sinking fund} \\ \text{at the beginning of the interval} \end{array}$$

> **Trap**
>
> The amount in a sinking fund at the beginning of a payment interval is not necessarily equal to the amount in the fund at the end of the preceding interval. Suppose contributions to the fund are made at the *beginning* of each interval (thereby forming an annuity due). Then the amount in the sinking fund at the beginning of an interval will be the balance from the end of the preceding interval *plus* the payment size, R.

$$\begin{array}{c} \text{Increase in the sinking fund's balance} \\ \text{during any payment interval} \end{array} = R + \begin{array}{c} \text{Interest earned} \\ \text{during the interval} \end{array}$$

This increase can be added to the balance from the end of the preceding interval to obtain the new balance at the end of the current interval.

NOTATION FOR THE COMPOUNDING FACTOR FOR ANNUITIES By this point, the mechanics of calculating the future value of an ordinary annuity or an annuity due should be "second nature" to you. Details of the mechanics, whether in the algebraic method or the financial calculator method, should no longer need to be shown in solutions to example problems. Instead of fully writing out the compounding factor for annuities, we will use the following notation for it.[8]

$$s_{\overline{n}|p} = \frac{(1 + p)^n - 1}{p}$$

In terms of this notation, the compact representations of the future value of an ordinary annuity and an annuity due are

$$S_n = R s_{\overline{n}|p} \qquad \text{and} \qquad S_n(due) = R s_{\overline{n}|p} (1 + p)$$

respectively. Suppose, for example, we want to write instructions to calculate the future value of an ordinary annuity having $n = 20$ payments of size $R = \$300$ earning interest at the rate of $p = 5\%$ per payment interval. The symbol "⌐" is used only to separate the values for n and p. In terms of the new notation, we can simply write

$$\$300 s_{\overline{20}|5\%}$$

---

[8]The notation is widely used in actuarial science and is more commonly used in the mathematics of finance than any other notation.

The expression is read as "$300 *s* angle 20 at 5%." This representation informs the reader that:

- The annuity's future value is to be calculated. (This is indicated by the appearance of the lowercase *s*.)
- The type of annuity is an ordinary annuity since no $(1 + p)$ factor appears.
- The values to be used for the variables are $R = \$300$, $n = 20$, and $p = 5\%$.

The reader can then choose to obtain the annuity's future value by using either the algebraic formula or a financial calculator's functions.

■ EXAMPLE 15.6A   *PREPARATION OF A COMPLETE SINKING FUND SCHEDULE IN WHICH THE PAYMENTS FORM AN ORDINARY ANNUITY*

Babuin Engineering plans to undertake a $900,000 expansion 6 years from now. By that time, Babuin wants to accumulate half of the cost of the expansion by making payments into a sinking fund at the end of each of the next 6 years. It is anticipated that the money in the sinking fund will earn 7% compounded annually.

a. What should be the size of the annual payments?

b. How much of the money in the sinking fund at the end of the 6 years will be interest earnings?

c. Prepare a sinking fund schedule. Verify the answer to part *b* by summing the "interest earned" column.

✓ SOLUTION

a. The future value of the six sinking fund payments, invested at 7% compounded annually, must be $450,000. We must solve for the value of *R* in

$$S_n = \$450,000 = Rs_{\overline{6}|7\%}$$

ALGEBRAIC SOLUTION

$$\$450,000 = R\left(\frac{1.07^6 - 1}{0.07}\right)$$
$$= R(7.1532907)$$
$$R = \frac{\$450,000}{7.1532907}$$
$$= \$62,908.11$$

The annual sinking fund payment should be $62,908.11.

FINANCIAL CALCULATOR SOLUTION

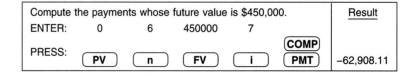

Compute the payments whose future value is $450,000.					Result
ENTER: 0 6 450000 7				**COMP**	
PRESS: [PV] [n] [FV] [i] [PMT]					−62,908.11

The annual sinking fund payment should be $62,908.11.

b. The total of the payments into the sinking fund will be

$$6 \times \$62,908.11 = \$377,448.66$$

The remainder of the $450,000 will be interest earned. That is,

$$\text{Interest earned} = \$450,000 - \$377,448.66 = \$72,551.34$$

c.

Payment interval number	Payment (at end)	Interest earned	Increase in the fund	Balance in fund (end of interval)
0	—	—	—	0
1	$ 62,908.11	0	$ 62,908.11	$ 62,908.11
2	62,908.11	$ 4403.57 ①	67,311.68 ②	130,210.79 ③
3	62,908.11	9115.39	72,023.50	202,243.29
4	62,908.11	14,157.03	77,065.14	279,308.43
5	62,908.11	19,551.59	82,459.70	361,768.13
6	62,908.11	25,323.77	88,231.88	450,000.01
	$377,448.66	$72,551.35 ④	$450,000.01 ⑤	

① Interest earned = 0.07(Amount at the beginning of the interval)
$\quad\quad\quad\quad = 0.07(\$62,908.11)$
$\quad\quad\quad\quad = \$4403.57$
② Increase in the fund = Interest earned + Payment
$\quad\quad\quad\quad = \$4403.57 + \$62,908.11$
$\quad\quad\quad\quad = \$67,311.68$
③ Balance = Previous balance + Increase in the fund
$\quad\quad\quad\quad = \$62,908.11 + \$67,311.68$
$\quad\quad\quad\quad = \$130,210.79$
④ Column total = $72,551.35
$\quad\quad\quad\quad$ = Total interest earned (confirming the answer in part b)
⑤ The total of the increases to the fund should equal the final total in the sinking fund.   ∎

■ EXAMPLE 15.6B   *PREPARATION OF A COMPLETE SINKING FUND SCHEDULE IN WHICH THE PAYMENTS FORM AN ANNUITY DUE*

Repeat Example 15.6A, with the change that the sinking fund payments are made at the *beginning* of each year.

✓ SOLUTION

a. Now we obtain the payment size by solving for R in

$$S_n(\text{due}) = \$450,000 = Rs_{\overline{6}|7\%}(1.07)$$

ALGEBRAIC SOLUTION

$$\$450,000 = R\left(\frac{1.07^6 - 1}{0.07}\right)(1.07)$$
$$= R(7.6540211)$$
$$R = \$58,792.63$$

FINANCIAL CALCULATOR SOLUTION

BGN mode						Result
ENTER:	0	6	450000	7		
PRESS:	PV	n	FV	i	COMP PMT	−58,792.63

b. Interest earned = $450,000 − Total of payments
$\quad\quad\quad\quad = \$450,000 - (6 \times \$58,792.63)$
$\quad\quad\quad\quad = \$97,244.22$

c.

Payment interval number	Payment (at start)	Interest earned	Increase in the fund	Balance in fund (end of interval)
0	—	—	—	0
1	$ 58,792.63	$ 4115.48	$ 62,908.11	$ 62,908.11
2	58,792.63	8519.05①	67,311.68②	130,219.79③
3	58,792.63	13,230.87	72,023.50	202,243.29
4	58,792.63	18,272.51	77,065.14	279,308.43
5	58,792.63	23,667.07	82,459.70	361,768.13
6	58,792.63	29,439.25	88,231.88	450,000.01
	$352,755.78	$97,244.23	$450,000.01	

① Interest earned = 0.07(Amount at the beginning of the interval)
$\qquad$ = 0.07(Balance at end of previous interval + R)
$\qquad$ = 0.07($62,908.11 + $58,792.63)
$\qquad$ = $8519.05
② Increase in the fund = Interest earned + Payment
$\qquad$ = $8519.05 + $58,792.63
$\qquad$ = $67,311.68
③ Balance = Previous balance + Increase in the fund
$\qquad$ = $62,908.11 + $67,311.68
$\qquad$ = $130,219.79

■ EXAMPLE 15.6C *PREPARATION OF A PARTIAL SINKING FUND SCHEDULE*

The board of directors of Babuin Engineering (see Example 15.6A) decide that the firm's cash flow can be managed better if the sinking fund payments are made quarterly instead of annually. The goal is still to accumulate $450,000 after 6 years, but now with end-of-quarter payments. The sinking fund will earn 6.8% compounded quarterly. Construct a partial sinking fund schedule showing details of payments 1, 2, 15, 16, 23, and 24.

☑ SOLUTION

The first step is to calculate the size of the payments so that their future value is $450,000. The payments will form an ordinary simple annuity with $n = 24$ and $p = i = 1.7\%$. Solve for R in

$$S_n = \$450,000 = Rs_{\overline{24}|\,1.7\%}$$

Following the same procedure as in Example 15.6A gives

$$R = \$15,341.14$$

Payment interval number	Payment (at end)	Interest earned	Increase in the fund	Balance in fund (end of interval)
0	—	—	—	0
1	$15,341.14	0	$15,341.14	$ 15,341.14
2	15,341.14	$260.80①	15,601.94②	30,943.08③
.	.	.	.	.
.	.	.	.	.
.	.	.	.	.
14				240,200.61④

Payment interval number	Payment (at end)	Interest earned	Increase in the fund	Balance in fund (end of interval)
15	15,341.14	4083.41	19,424.55	259,625.16
16	15,341.14	4413.63	19,754.77	279,379.93
.	.	.	.	.
.	.	.	.	.
.	.	.	.	.
22				405,164.24 ⑤
23	15,341.14	6887.79	22,228.93	427,393.17
24	15,341.14	7265.68	22,606.82	449,999.99
	$368,187.36	$81,812.63	$449,999.99	

① $0.017 \times \$15,341.14 = \$260.80$
② $\$260.80 + \$15,341.14 = \$15,601.94$
③ $\$15,601.94 + \$15,341.14 = \$30,943.08$
④ Future value after 14 payments $= \$15,341.14 s_{\overline{14}|1.7\%} = \$240,200.61$
⑤ Future value after 22 payments $= \$15,341.14 s_{\overline{22}|1.7\%} = \$405,164.24$

SINKING FUND FOR DEBT RETIREMENT

Recall from the discussion of bonds earlier in this chapter that no principal is repaid to the bond owner before the maturity of the bond. In some circumstances, bond investors may have concerns about the ability of the borrower to repay the full principal amount at a maturity date several years in the future. To ease this concern, many corporate, regional government, and municipal government bonds carry a sinking fund provision.[9] The purpose of the sinking fund is to provide for the repayment of all or a substantial portion of the principal amount of the bond issue.

A trust company is usually appointed as the trustee to administer the sinking fund. The bond issuer does not have access to the money in the sinking fund; the funds are accumulated for the express purpose of repaying the principal amount of the debt. There are two ways to set up a sinking fund for a bond issue:

- The borrower makes periodic payments to the trustee. The trustee invests the funds in low-risk securities (such as federal government bonds and Treasury bills). On the maturity date of the bond issue, the accumulated funds are used to repay all or a substantial portion of the principal amount of the debt.
- The trustee uses the periodic payments received from the bond issuer to retire a portion of the bond issue each year. To do this in any particular year, the trustee chooses the cheaper of the following two alternatives: (*a*) A specified percentage of the issue may be called and redeemed at a predetermined redemption price per bond. (*b*) If, however, the bonds can be purchased in the bond market for less than the redemption price, the trustee will buy enough bonds for the year's prescribed debt retirement.

The second sinking fund arrangement is more common. However, the first involves the more interesting mathematics, which we will discuss in the remainder of this section.

---

[9]Sinking funds are primarily associated with debentures rather than with true bonds, because debentures are not secured by specific fixed assets of the borrower. A debt issue that has a sinking fund provision usually includes the words *sinking fund* in its full title.

The simplest contribution arrangement requires *equal* regular payments to the sinking fund after the initial issue[10] of the bonds. The payment size is calculated so that

$$\text{Future value of the} \atop \text{sinking fund payments} = {\text{Principal amount of} \atop \text{the debt to be retired}}$$

A conservative compound rate of return is assumed for the sinking fund. We will consider only cases in which contributions are made at the end of every 6 months and compounding occurs semiannually. In these cases, the sinking fund contributions form an ordinary simple annuity.

The sinking fund schedule for a debt retirement usually includes an additional column for the **book value of the debt,** defined as:

$$\text{Book value} \atop \text{of the debt} = {\text{Principal amount} \atop \text{of the debt}} - {\text{Balance in the} \atop \text{sinking fund}}$$

The book value of a debt can be interpreted as the balance that would still be owed on the debt if the money in the sinking fund were immediately applied to reduce the debt.

Keep in mind that, under a sinking fund arrangement, the borrower is making *two* series of payments, each one constituting an annuity. One is the sinking fund payments to the fund's trustee. The other is the semiannual interest payments to the lenders or bondholders. The combined total of the annual interest payments and the annual sinking fund payments is sometimes called the **annual cost of the debt.** It represents the total annual cash outflow arising from the debt obligation.

Tip

Distinguish the roles of the two interest rates that are involved in sinking fund debt. The contractual rate of interest on the debt determines the regular interest *expense* paid by the borrower to the lender. The interest rate earned by the sinking fund determines the interest *revenue* earned by the sinking fund. Although the lender does not directly receive the earnings of the sinking fund, the lender still benefits from the interest earnings: they will eventually be used to repay the principal amount of the debt.

■ **EXAMPLE 15.6D**   *CALCULATING THE SINKING FUND PAYMENT SIZE, ANNUAL COST OF DEBT, AND BOOK VALUE OF DEBT*

Abacus Corp. raised $20 million from an issue of sinking fund bonds. The bonds have a 12-year term and a 9% coupon rate. The bond indenture requires Abacus to make equal semiannual contributions to a sinking fund to provide for the retirement of the full principal amount of the bond issue at its maturity.

a. If the sinking fund earns 6.5% compounded semiannually, what is the size of the semiannual sinking fund payments?

b. What is the annual cost of the debt?

c. What is the book value of the debt after 6 years?

---

[10]In cases where the sinking fund is structured to retire only a portion of the debt, there may be an initial 5- or 10-year "contribution holiday" during which the issuer makes no sinking fund payments.

✓ SOLUTION

a. The future value of the sinking fund payments invested at 6.5% compounded semiannually for 12 years is to be $20 million. Therefore, the payment size will be the value of *R* that satisfies

$$\$20,000,000 = Rs_{\overline{24}|\,3.25\%}$$
$$= R(35.525359)$$
$$R = \frac{\$20,000,000}{35.525359}$$
$$= \$562,978.13$$

b. The annual cost of the debt is the total of the bond interest and sinking fund payments made in a year. The semiannual interest paid on the debt is

$$\frac{0.09}{2} \times \$20,000,000 = \$900,000$$

Hence,

$$\text{Annual cost of the debt} = 2(\$562,978.13 + \$900,000)$$
$$= \$2,925,956.26$$

c. The book value of the debt after 6 years will be the principal amount of the debt ($20,000,000) less the amount in the sinking fund. Hence,

$$\text{Book value} = \$20,000,000 - \$562,978.13s_{\overline{12}|\,3.25\%}$$
$$= \$20,000,000 - \$8,104,230.85$$
$$= \$11,895,769.15$$

■ EXAMPLE 15.6E   *CONSTRUCTION OF A PARTIAL SINKING FUND SCHEDULE*

The town of Port Barlow has received approval to borrow $12 million through the provincial government's Municipal Finance Authority (MFA) to install a secondary sewage treatment system. The MFA is the central borrowing agency for financing the capital requirements of member municipalities and regional governments. It enters the capital markets to borrow the funds needed by its members. It also manages the collection of funds from the borrowers for both the payment of interest and the accumulation of sinking funds to retire the principal portion of each debt issue.

Bond coupon interest at the rate of 10% compounded semiannually is payable every 6 months. In addition, Port Barlow must make payments at the end of every 6 months into a sinking fund that will accumulate the full principal amount of the debt after 15 years. The sinking fund earns 8% compounded semiannually. Round sinking fund payments and interest earnings to the nearest dollar.

a. Calculate the combined interest and sinking fund payment that Port Barlow must send to the MFA every 6 months.

b. What will be the balance in the sinking fund halfway through the term of the debt?

c. How much will the balance in the sinking fund increase during the 10th year?

d. How much interest will the sinking fund earn in the first half of the 7th year?

e. Construct a partial sinking fund schedule showing details on the first three and the last three payments.

◪ SOLUTION

a. Every 6 months the town of Port Barlow must pay the semiannual interest of

$$\$12,000,000(0.05) = \$600,000$$

plus the sinking fund payment. The size of the sinking fund payments is determined from the requirement that their future value after 15 years at 8% compounded semiannually be $12,000,000. We want the value of R in

$$S_n = \$12,000,000 = Rs_{\overline{30}|4\%}$$

ALGEBRAIC SOLUTION

$$\$12,000,000 = R\left(\frac{1.04^{30} - 1}{0.04}\right)$$
$$= R(56.084938)$$
$$R = \$213,961$$

The total semiannual payment is $813,961.

FINANCIAL CALCULATOR SOLUTION

Compute the payments whose future value is $12 million.					Result
ENTER: 0 30 12000000 4				COMP	
PRESS: PV n FV i PMT					−213,961

The total semiannual payment is therefore $813,961.

b. The amount in the sinking fund at any point will be the future value of the payments already contributed. Halfway through the 15-year term, the 15th sinking fund payment of $213,961 will have just been made.

$$S_n = \$213,961 s_{\overline{15}|4\%}$$
$$= \$4,284,267$$

After $7\frac{1}{2}$ years, there will be $4,284,267 in the sinking fund.

c. Increase in the balance during the 10th year

$$= \text{Balance after 10 years} - \text{Balance after 9 years}$$
$$= \$213,961 s_{\overline{20}|4\%} - \$213,961 s_{\overline{18}|4\%}$$
$$= \$6,371,347.4 - \$5,487,118.2$$
$$= \$884,229$$

d. Interest earned in the first half of year 7

$$= 0.04(\text{Amount in the fund at the end of year 6})$$
$$= 0.04(\$213,961 s_{\overline{12}|4\%})$$
$$= 0.04(\$3,214,936.3)$$
$$= \$128,597$$

e. Partial sinking fund schedule:

Payment interval number	Payment	Interest earned	Increase in the fund	Balance in fund (end of interval)	Book value of the debt
0	—	—	—	0	$12,000,000
1	$ 213,961	0	$ 213,961	$ 213,961	11,786,039
2	213,961	$8558 ①	222,519 ②	436,480 ③	11,563,520 ④
3	213,961	17,459	231,420	667,900	11,332,100
.	.	.	.	.	
.	.	.	.	.	
.	.	.	.	.	
27				10,074,186 ⑤	1,925,814
28	213,961	402,967	616,928	10,691,114	1,308,886
29	213,961	427,645	641,606	11,332,720	667,280
30	213,961	453,309	667,270	11,999,990	10
	$6,418,830	$5,581,160	$11,999,990		

① Interest earned = 0.04(Amount at the beginning of the interval)
    = 0.04($213,961)
    = $8558

② Increase in fund = Interest earned + Payment
    = $8558 + $213,961
    = $222,519

③ Balance = Previous balance + Increase in the fund
    = $213,961 + $222,519
    = $436,480

④ Book value = Debt principal − Sinking fund balance
    = $12,000,000 − $436,480
    = $11,563,520

⑤ Balance in sinking fund at any point = Future value of payments up to that point
    = $213,961s$_{\overline{27}|4\%}$
    = $10,074,186

Point of Interest

A Sinking Fund Arrangement for a Debenture Issue

The Municipal Finance Authority (MFA) of British Columbia is the agency through which municipalities and regional districts in the province finance their long-term capital requirements. On December 6, 1979, the MFA sold a $54,100,000, 12.25% sinking fund debenture issue due December 6, 1999. The debentures were issued in denominations of $1000, $5000, and $25,000. Most of the debentures ($46.9 million) were fully *registered*. The semiannual interest payments are mailed directly to the owners of registered debentures. The remainder of the debentures ($7.2 million) were issued as *bearer debentures;* the owner's name does not appear on the face of such debentures. A bearer debenture is like cash in that whoever has possession is presumed to own it. For receipt of interest payments, coupons attached to a bearer debenture must be removed as they come due, and must be presented at a bank for payment.

The debenture issue's sinking fund provision required that a specified principal amount of the issue be redeemed on every anniversary of the issue date. The amount to be redeemed on successive anniversaries increased steadily from $800,000 on the first anniversary to $6.3 million on the 20th anniversary (and maturity date). A few weeks before each anniversary, the Municipal Finance Authority's computer randomly selects the serial numbers of a sufficient number of debentures to satisfy the sinking fund redemption requirement. The owners of selected
(*continued*)

(*concluded*)

registered debentures are notified through the mail. The holders of selected bearer debentures are advised by notices placed in widely read newspapers. The following notice appeared about one month before the sinking fund redemption due on December 6, 1992. The circled numbers in the margin refer to the following explanatory notes.

① The eight-character codes are serial numbers of individual bearer debentures. The letters AM, AV, and AX in the serial numbers signify $1000, $5000, and $25,000 face value debentures, respectively. The larger-denomination debentures that are listed were called for partial redemption: $1000 per $5000 face value debenture and $2000 per $25,000 face value debenture.

② Only the bearer debentures have attached interest coupons; interest earned by registered debentures is automatically mailed every 6 months to the address of the registered owner.

③ When debentures selected for partial redemption are submitted to the MFA, the MFA will reissue debentures having the same coupon rate and maturity date, but with face values equal to the unredeemed portion of the original face values.

④ The serial numbers of registered debentures drawn by lot for redemption are not listed in this notice because the registered owners are notified directly by mail. If, as with most sinking fund debenture issues, this issue were composed entirely of registered debentures, no public notice would have been published.

MUNICIPAL FINANCE AUTHORITY OF BRITISH COLUMBIA
NOTICE OF PARTIAL REDEMPTION FOR SINKING FUND PURPOSES

To the holders of Municipal Finance Authority of British Columbia
Twenty Year $12\frac{1}{4}$% Sinking Fund Debentures due December 6, 1999

NOTICE IS HEREBY GIVEN THAT pursuant to the terms of the Municipal Finance Authority of British Columbia, Twenty Year $12\frac{1}{4}$% Sinking Fund Debentures due December 6, 1999, the underlisted coupon Debentures have been drawn by lot for redemption (in whole or in part to the extent indicated) for sinking fund purposes and will be redeemed on December 6, 1992 (the "redemption date").

Coupon Debentures in denomination of $1000 called in full:

| 25AM0587 | 25AM0599 | 25AM0609 | 25AM0624 | 25AM0639 |

① Coupon Debentures in denominations of $5,000 and $25,000 called in part:

| $1000 of 25AV0089 | $1000 of 25AV0109 | $1000 of 25AV0111 | $1000 of 25AV0153 |
| $1000 of 25AV0222 | $1000 of 25AV0224 | $1000 of 25AV0225 | $2000 of 25AX0805 |

The redemption price of each Twenty Year $12\frac{1}{4}$% Sinking Fund Debenture so drawn will be paid in the case of unregistered Debentures, to the bearer thereof and, in the case of Debentures registered as to principal, to the registered holder thereof upon presentation and surrender of the Debenture, together with all unmatured coupons

② appertaining thereto, to the Authority at the address below.

With respect to coupon Debentures of which a part only of the principal amount is being redeemed, the Authority, upon presentation and surrender of the Debenture together with all unmatured coupons appertaining thereto, will issue to such holder,

③ without charge, a Twenty Year $12\frac{1}{4}$% Sinking Fund Debenture or Debentures due December 6, 1999 of aggregate principal amount equal to the unredeemed part of the principal amount of the Debenture so surrendered.

④ Certain other registered Debentures have also been drawn by lot for redemption and a Notice of Partial Redemption is being mailed to the registered holders thereof.

Dated: October 22, 1992
MUNICIPAL FINANCE AUTHORITY OF BRITISH COLUMBIA
200-880 DOUGLAS STREET, VICTORIA, B.C. V8W 2B7

EXERCISE 15.6

Answers to the odd-numbered problems are at the end of the book.

For each of the sinking funds in problems 1 through 8, calculate (rounded to the nearest dollar):

a. The size of the periodic sinking fund payment.
b. The balance in the sinking fund at the time indicated in the last column. (Round the sinking fund payment to the nearest dollar *before* calculating the balance.)

Problem	End-of-term amount of sinking fund ($ millions)	Term (years)	Sinking fund rate of return (%)	Payment and compounding interval	Payment at beginning or end of interval?	Balance at the end of interval:
1.	12	10	7	6 months	End	12
2.	7	5	6	3 months	End	6
3.	15	15	6.5	1 year	End	11
4.	8	10	7.5	1 month	End	65
5.	6	5	5.25	1 month	Beginning	27
6.	10	10	6.5	3 months	Beginning	28
7.	18	15	6.75	6 months	Beginning	19
8.	5	10	5.75	1 year	Beginning	8

Each of the bond issues in problems 9 through 16 has a sinking fund requirement for retiring the entire principal amount of the issue on its maturity date. In each case calculate (to the nearest dollar):

a. The size of the sinking fund payment at the end of every 6 months.
b. The annual cost of the debt.
c. The book value of the debt at the end of the indicated interval. (Round the sinking fund payment to the nearest dollar before calculating the book value.)

The coupon rates and rates of return on the sinking fund investments are compounded semiannually.

Problem	Principal amount of bond issue ($ millions)	Term (years)	Sinking fund rate of return (%)	Coupon rate (%)	Book value at the end of interval
•9.	10	10	7	10	12
•10.	8	5	6	8.5	6
•11.	15	15	6.5	9	21
•12.	12	10	7.5	10.5	15
•13.	7	5	5.75	8	7
•14.	9	10	6.5	9.25	18
•15.	11	15	7.5	10.25	19
•16.	10	10	7	9.75	11

For problems 17 through 20, construct the complete sinking fund schedule. Calculate the total interest earned by adding up the "interest earned" column and by calculating the difference between the final balance in the fund and the total of the contributed payments. Round the sinking fund payments and periodic interest earnings to the nearest dollar.

Problem	End-of-term amount of sinking fund ($)	Term (years)	Sinking fund rate of return (%)	Payment and compounding interval	Payment at beginning or end of interval?
•17.	800,000	3	7	6 months	End
•18.	675,000	6	6	1 year	End
•19.	1,000,000	5	6.75	1 year	Beginning
•20.	550,000	4	5.75	6 months	Beginning

•21. For the sinking fund described in problem 2, prepare a partial sinking fund schedule showing details of payments 1, 2, 11, 12, 19, and 20. Round the sinking fund payments and periodic interest earnings to the nearest dollar.

•22. For the sinking fund described in problem 5, prepare a partial sinking fund schedule showing details of payments 1, 2, 39, 40, 59, and 60. Round the sinking fund payments and periodic interest earnings to the nearest dollar.

•23. For the bond sinking fund described in problem 9, prepare a partial sinking fund schedule (including the book value of the debt) showing details of the first three and the last three payments. Round the sinking fund payments and periodic interest earnings to the nearest dollar.

•24. For the bond sinking fund described in problem 10, prepare a partial sinking fund schedule (including the book value of the debt) showing details of the first three and the last three payments. Round the sinking fund payments and periodic interest earnings to the nearest dollar.

•25. To provide for the automation of a production process in 5 years, Dominion Chemicals is starting a sinking fund to accumulate $600,000 by the end of the 5 years. Round the sinking fund payments and the periodic interest earnings to the nearest dollar.

    a. If the sinking fund earns 7.5% compounded monthly, what monthly payments starting today should be made to the fund?

    b. How much interest will be earned in the fourth year?

    c. In what month will the fund pass the halfway point?

    d. How much interest will be earned in the 35th month?

•26. Repeat problem 25, with the change that the sinking fund payments are to be made at the end of every month.

••27. Thermo-Tech Systems recently sold a $20 million bond issue with a 20-year maturity and a coupon rate of 11% compounded semiannually. The bond indenture contract requires Thermo-Tech to make equal payments at the end of every 6 months into a sinking fund administered by National Trust. The sinking fund should accumulate the full $20 million required to redeem the bonds at their maturity. Round the sinking fund payments and periodic interest earnings to the nearest dollar.

    a. What must the size of the sinking fund payments be if the fund earns 8.5% compounded semiannually?

    b. How much interest will the fund earn in the sixth year?

    c. How much will the fund increase in the 27th payment interval?

    d. Construct a partial sinking fund schedule showing details of the first two and the last two payments, and the total of the interest earned.

••28. The town of Mount Hope is financing a $4.5 million upgrade to its water system through the province's Municipal Finance Authority. The MFA obtained financing via a bond issue with interest at 9.5% per annum payable semiannually. Also, at the end of every 6 months, the town is to make equal payments into a sinking fund administered by the MFA so that the necessary funds are available to repay the $4.5 million debt when it matures in 17 years. The sinking fund earns 7.5% compounded semiannually. Round the sinking fund payments and periodic interest earnings to the nearest dollar.

a. Calculate the size of the sinking fund payments.

b. How much will the fund increase in the 18th payment interval?

c. How much interest will the fund earn in the 10th year?

d. Construct a partial sinking fund schedule showing details of the 9th, 10th, and last two payments, and the total of the interest earned.

••29. A sinking fund is to be set up to provide for the repayment of 80% of the principal amount of a $1 million debt in 10 years. Equal payments are to be made at the beginning of each quarter. The sinking fund will earn 7% compounded quarterly. Round the sinking fund payments and periodic interest earnings to the nearest dollar.

a. Calculate the size of the sinking fund payments.

b. Construct a partial sinking fund schedule showing details of the first two and the last two payments, and the total of the interest earned.

••30. Repeat problem 29, with the change that the sinking fund payments are to be made at the end of every quarter.

REVIEW PROBLEMS

Answers to the odd-numbered review problems are at the end of the book.

1. A $1000, 7.5% coupon bond has $19\frac{1}{2}$ years remaining until maturity. Calculate the bond discount if the required return in the bond market is 8.6% compounded semiannually.

2. Four years after the issue of a $10,000, 9.5% coupon, 20-year bond, the rate of return required in the bond market on long-term bonds was 7.8% compounded semiannually.

   a. At what price did the bond then sell?

   b. What capital gain or loss (expressed in dollars) would the original owner have realised by selling the bond at that price?

3. Four and one-half years ago Glenda purchased fifteen $1000 bonds in a Province of New Brunswick issue carrying an 8.5% coupon and priced to yield 9.8% (compounded semiannually). The bonds then had 18 years remaining until maturity. The bond market now requires a yield to maturity on the bonds of 8.0% compounded semiannually. If Glenda sells the bonds today, what will be the dollar amount of her capital gain or loss?

•4. A $1000, 9.5% coupon Government of Canada bond has 10 years remaining until its maturity. It is currently priced at 108.25 (percent of face value).

   a. What is the bond's yield to maturity?

   b. If the bond price abruptly rises $25, what is the change in its yield to maturity?

•5. A $1000, 12.25% coupon, 20-year Government of Canada bond was issued on June 15, 1985. At what price did it trade on December 10, 1989, when the market's required return was 10.2% compounded semiannually?

•6. If a broker quotes a price of 111.25 for a bond on September 10, what amount will a client pay per $1000 face value? The 11.25% coupon rate is payable on May 15 and November 15 of each year.

 ••7. The yield to maturity on a $1000 face value, 10.5% coupon, 15-year bond purchased with 11 years remaining until maturity is 8.8%. Show details of the first three and the last three coupon interest payments in a partial schedule for the amortization of the bond premium or discount.

 ••8. The yield to maturity on a $1000 face value, 8.25% coupon bond purchased with 7 years remaining until maturity is 9.4%. Show details of the first three and the last three coupon interest payments in a partial schedule for the amortization of the bond premium or discount.

 •9. Laurentian Airways is preparing for the replacement of one of its passenger jets in 3 years by making payments to a sinking fund at the beginning of every 6 months for the next 3 years. The fund can earn 6% compounded semiannually, and the capital required in 3 years is $750,000. Prepare a complete sinking fund schedule. Round the sinking fund payments and periodic interest earnings to the nearest dollar.

 •10. The municipality of Duncan has financed a sewage treatment plant by issuing $18 million worth of sinking fund debentures. The debentures have a 15-year term and pay a coupon rate of 9% compounded semiannually. Rounding the sinking fund payments, interest payments, and periodic interest earnings to the nearest dollar,

   a. What equal payments at the end of every 6 months will be necessary to accumulate $18 million after 15 years if the sinking fund can earn 6.25% compounded semiannually?

   b. What is the annual cost of the debt to Duncan taxpayers?

   c. Construct a partial sinking fund schedule (including the book value of the debt) showing details of the first three and the last three payments.

SELF-TEST EXERCISE

Answers to the self-test problems are at the end of the book.

1. A $1000 face value, 9.8% coupon, Province of Alberta bond with 18 years to run until maturity is currently priced to yield investors 9.5% compounded semiannually until maturity. How much lower would the bond's price have to be to make the yield to maturity 10% compounded semiannually?

2. Two and one-half years ago Nova Scotia Power sold an issue of 25-year, 12.5% coupon bonds. If the current semiannually compounded return required in the bond market is 10%, calculate the percent capital gain or loss on the bonds over the entire $2\frac{1}{2}$-year holding period.

3. Calculate the yield to maturity on a bond purchased for $1034.50 if it carries an 11.5% coupon and has $8\frac{1}{2}$ years remaining until maturity.

•4. A New Brunswick Electric bond issue carrying a 13.25% coupon matures on November 1, 2004. At what price did $1000 face value bonds trade on June 10, 1992, if the yield to maturity required by the bond market on that date was 9.3% compounded semiannually?

5. Calculate the quoted price on June 10, 1992, of the bond in problem 4.

••6. A $5000 face value, 9% coupon bond is purchased $2\frac{1}{2}$ years before maturity to yield 10.5% compounded semiannually until maturity. Construct a bond discount amortization schedule. What total interest will be recorded for accounting purposes from the purchase date until the maturity date?

•7. The Cowichan Regional District borrowed $500,000 through the Provincial Finance Authority to purchase firefighting equipment. At the end of every 6 months, the regional district must make a sinking fund payment of a size calculated to accumulate $500,000 after 7 years to repay the principal amount of the debt. The sinking fund earns 7% compounded semiannually. Construct a partial sinking fund schedule showing details of the first two and the last two payments. Round the sinking fund payments and periodic interest earnings to the nearest dollar.

SUMMARY OF NOTATION AND KEY FORMULAS

In the context of bond pricing,

F = Face value of the bond
b = Coupon rate per interest payment interval (normally 6 months)
p = The bond market's required rate of return per payment interval
n = Number of interest payments remaining until the maturity date

In the context of sinking funds,

S_n = Amount of funds needed on the target date
p = Interest rate earned by the sinking fund per payment interval
n = Number of sinking fund contributions

Formula (15–1) $\text{Bond price} = Fb\left[\dfrac{1 - (1 + p)^{-n}}{p}\right] + F(1 + p)^{-n}$ Finding the price of a bond on a coupon interest payment date

Formula (10–1) $S_n = R\left[\dfrac{(1 + p)^n - 1}{p}\right]$ Finding the amount in a sink-ing fund after n contributions of size R at the end of each contribution interval

Formula (11–1) $S_n(\text{due}) = R\left[\dfrac{(1 + p)^n - 1}{p}\right] \times (1 + p)$ Finding the amount in a sinking fund after n contributions of size R at the beginning of each contribution interval

> **Price of a Bond (between interest payment dates):**   The bond price is the future value, on the purchase date, of the remaining payments' present value at the preceding interest payment date.

The connection between a bond's quoted price and its flat price is:

$$\text{Quoted price} = \text{Flat price} - \text{Accrued coupon interest}$$

The following relationships were developed for sinking funds.

$$\text{Balance at the end of any payment interval} = \text{Future value of the payments already made}$$

$$\text{Interest earned in any payment interval} = p \times \text{Amount in the sinking fund at the beginning of the interval}$$

$$\text{Increase in the sinking fund's balance during any payment interval} = R + \text{Interest earned during the interval}$$

$$\text{Book value of the debt} = \text{Principal amount of the debt} - \text{Balance in the sinking fund}$$

GLOSSARY OF TERMS

Amortization of the bond discount   The process of increasing a bond's book value over the time remaining until maturity, by periodically reducing the bond's discount.

Amortization of the bond premium   The process of reducing a bond's book value over the time remaining until maturity, by periodically reducing the bond's premium.

Annual cost of a debt   The combined total of the annual interest payments on the debt and the annual payments into a sinking fund for retirement of the principal amount of the debt.

Bond   A debt instrument secured by specific assets. The bond issuer (borrower) promises to pay the accrued interest periodically and to repay the full principal amount of the debt on its maturity date. The term "bond" is sometimes used in a generic sense to refer to both true bonds and debentures.

Bond discount   The amount by which a bond's face value exceeds its (quoted) price.

Bond premium   The amount by which a bond's quoted price exceeds its face value.

Book value of a debt   The amount by which the principal balance owed on the debt exceeds the funds accumulated in a sinking fund for retiring the debt.

Coupon rate   The nominal annual rate of interest paid on the face value of a bond.

Debenture   A debt instrument having most of the characteristics of a bond except that no *specific* assets secure the debt.

Face value   The principal amount that the issuer will pay to the owner of a marketable bond on its scheduled maturity date.

Flat price   The actual or full amount paid by a bond purchaser and received by the bond seller.

Issue date   The date on which (*a*) the bond loan was originally made and (*b*) interest starts to be earned.

Maturity date (of a bond)   The date on which the full principal amount is repaid along with the last interest payment.

Quoted price   The full purchase price (flat price) less any accrued coupon interest.

Sinking fund   An interest-earning account into which periodic payments are made for the purpose of accumulating a desired amount of money by a certain date.

Yield to maturity   The discount rate that makes the present value of the bond's remaining cash flows equal to its purchase price.

*16 BUSINESS INVESTMENT DECISIONS

LEARNING OBJECTIVES

After completing this chapter, you will be able to:

- Calculate the net present value of a capital investment opportunity and decide whether the investment should be made

- Choose the best combination of investments from a group of acceptable capital investment opportunities under conditions of capital rationing

- Select the best investment from two or more mutually exclusive investments

- Calculate the internal rate of return of a capital investment opportunity, and decide whether the investment should be made

- Calculate the payback period of a capital investment opportunity

INTRODUCTION

This chapter will introduce analytical techniques used by managers to assist them in making decisions on capital investments. Most capital expenditures fall into two categories: replacement and expansion. Existing plant or equipment may be replaced because it is worn out, defective, obsolete, or inefficient. Production capacity may be expanded to produce more of existing lines of products or to introduce new products.

Three criteria for guiding business investment decisions will be presented. Two of them rest on a solid economic foundation but the third is flawed in some respects. Given the long-term nature of capital investments, any rigorous analysis must recognize the time value of money. Most of the concepts and mathematical techniques needed for the evaluation of business investment projects have already been presented in previous chapters. What remains is to learn the terminology and procedures for using this knowledge to analyse potential capital investments.

16.1 COMPARISON OF BUSINESS AND PERSONAL INVESTMENT DECISIONS

The fundamental principles that should guide both personal and business investment decisions are the same. The Valuation Principle, introduced in Section 7.2 and subsequently applied to many types of investments available to individuals, is relevant to business investments as well. Using the Valuation Principle to determine the fair market value of an investment requires three steps:

Step 1: Identify or estimate the cash flows expected from the investment.
Step 2: Determine the rate of return appropriate for the type of investment.
Step 3: Calculate the sum of the present values of the cash flows estimated in step 1, discounted at the rate of return determined in step 2.

If cash flows are actually received as forecast in step 1, an investor will realise the step 2 rate of return on the price calculated in step 3. A *higher* purchase price will result in a rate of return that is *smaller* than the discount rate; a *lower* price will yield a rate of return *greater* than the discount rate.

Personal and business investment analyses differ more in form than in substance because the nature of the investments tends to differ. Personal investments fall primarily into a limited number of categories, such as Treasury bills, Guaranteed Investment Certificates (GICs), bonds, and stocks. There is often a considerable degree of similarity among investments within each category. In addition, the individual investor can usually depend on competitive bidding in the financial markets to set fair prices for widely traded securities. In these cases, the individual investor may not explicitly use the Valuation Principle in selecting investments.

For business investments in plant and equipment, the way in which the asset will be used and the resulting pattern of cash flows tend to make each investment situation unique. There are likely to be ongoing cash outflows as well as cash inflows associated with a business investment. These factors argue for a comprehensive and rigorous approach in business, to handle the great variety of investment possibilities.

Personal and business investment decision makers take different perspectives in determining the discount rate used with the Valuation Principle. The individual investor looks to the capital markets for guidance in determining the current competitive rate of return from a category of investments. The business manager takes the view that capital projects must be financed by borrowing funds and/or by raising equity capital from the owners. Therefore, *a business investment project must provide a rate of return at least equal to the return required by the providers of the capital.* The average rate of return required by a firm's sources of debt and equity financing is called the firm's **cost of capital.**[1] *The cost of capital becomes the firm's discount rate in applying the Valuation Principle to the analysis of capital investment opportunities.*

There are three possible outcomes of a comparison between the initial capital investment required and the present value of future cash flows calculated according to the Valuation Principle.

- The required initial investment *equals* the present value of the future cash flows discounted at the firm's cost of capital. The cash flows will then provide a rate of return on the initial investment exactly *equal* to the discount rate—the firm's cost of capital. The investment will earn just enough to provide the sources of financing with their required rate of return. This is, therefore, the *minimum condition* for acceptance of a capital investment project.

- The required initial investment is *greater than* the present value of the future cash flows discounted at the firm's cost of capital. This investment will not earn enough to provide the sources of financing with their required rate of return. In this case, the investment opportunity should be *rejected.*

- The required initial investment is *less* than the present value of the future cash flows discounted at the firm's cost of capital. The investment will earn more than the discount rate—more than is needed to give the suppliers of capital their required return. The extra economic profit belongs to the firm's owners (the providers of equity capital). The prospective investment should be *accepted.*

The preceding discussion leads to the following decision criterion for investments:

> **Investment Acceptance Criterion:** Undertake a business investment opportunity if the required initial investment is less than or equal to the present value of the investment's subsequent cash flows, discounted at the firm's cost of capital.

The following example considers an investment opportunity with features that are typical of business investment opportunities. Cash flows are unequal and include a cash outflow subsequent to the initial investment. The investment, if undertaken, must be financed with borrowed funds.

Note: Forecasts of future cash flows involve varying degrees of uncertainty; they are merely best estimates based on the information available to the analyst. Therefore, all calculations in this chapter will be rounded to the nearest dollar. Even quoting numerical results to the nearest dollar suggests a degree of precision that does not really exist in these types of analyses. However, it does permit you to verify the accuracy of your calculations.

---

[1] Strictly speaking, the firm's cost of capital should be a *weighted* average of the rates of return required by the debt investors (lenders) and the equity investors (owners).

■ EXAMPLE 16.1A   *EVALUATING A BUSINESS INVESTMENT OPPORTUNITY*

A low-risk, 4-year investment promises to pay $3000, $6000, and $5000 at the end of the first, second, and fourth years, respectively. A cash injection of $1000 is required at the end of the third year. The investment may be purchased for $10,000, which would have to be borrowed at an interest rate of 10%. Use the Valuation Principle to determine whether the investment should be undertaken.

☑ SOLUTION

The purchase price at which a 10% rate of return would be realised on the amount invested is the present value of the cash flows discounted at 10%.

$$\begin{aligned} \text{Price for a 10%} \atop \text{rate of return} &= \frac{\$3000}{1.10} + \frac{\$6000}{1.10^2} + \frac{(-\$1000)}{1.10^3} + \frac{\$5000}{1.10^4} \\ &= \$2727 + \$4959 - \$751 + \$3415 \\ &= \$10,350 \end{aligned}$$

The $10,000 offering price should be accepted. By paying a price that is *below* $10,350, the purchaser will realise a rate of return on investment *greater* than the 10% cost of capital to finance the investment.

   Interpretation: The $10,350 figure for the present value of the investment's cash flows represents the amount today that is *equivalent* to the cash-flow stream from the investment. By paying $10,000 today for a payment stream that is worth $10,350 today, the firm's value is immediately increased by $350 (in current dollars).   ■

THE ECONOMIC VALUE THAT AN INVESTMENT ADDS TO A FIRM   The preceding example illustrates the following general statement concerning the value added to a firm by an investment that satisfies the investment acceptance criterion.

$$\begin{array}{ccc} \text{Value added} & \text{Present value of the} & \text{Required} \\ \text{to the firm} & = \text{future net cash flows} & - \text{initial investment} \end{array}$$

■ EXAMPLE 16.1B   *EVALUATING A BUSINESS INVESTMENT OPPORTUNITY*

Repeat the problem in Example 16.1A, with the change that the interest rate on the loan to finance the investment is 12% instead of 10%.

☑ SOLUTION

The purchase price at which a 12% rate of return would be realised on the amount invested is the present value of the cash flows discounted at 12%.

$$\begin{aligned} \text{Price for a 12%} \atop \text{rate of return} &= \frac{\$3000}{1.12} + \frac{\$6000}{1.12^2} + \frac{(-\$1000)}{1.12^3} + \frac{\$5000}{1.12^4} \\ &= \$2679 + \$4783 - \$712 + \$3178 \\ &= \$9928 \end{aligned}$$

The $10,000 offering price should be rejected. Paying a price that is *above* $9928 would result in a rate of return on investment that is *less* than the 12% cost of capital to finance the investment.

Interpretation: The $9928 figure for the present value of the investment's cash flows represents the amount today that is *equivalent* to the cash-flow stream from the investment. If $10,000 is invested today for a payment stream that is worth $9928 today, the firm's value will immediately be decreased by $72 (in current dollars). ■

COST MINIMIZATION Consider a situation in which the replacement of a piece of machinery is essential to the operation of an entire production line. Suppose either machine A or machine B will do the job equally well. Then the imputed cash inflows and other benefits will be the same whether we obtain machine A or machine B. In such a case, the scope of the financial analysis can be narrowed to finding the lowest-cost alternative. This involves a comparison of the *current* economic values of the future cash *outflows* for each alternative. The best choice is the one having the *lowest* present value of cash outflows.[2]

■ EXAMPLE 16.1C   *EVALUATING LEASE VERSUS PURCHASE ALTERNATIVES*

Laven and Co., Certified General Accountants, are considering whether to buy or lease a photocopy machine. A 5-year lease requires payments of $550 at the beginning of every 3 months. The same machine can be purchased for $9000 and would have a trade-in value of $1500 after 5 years. If the accounting firm can borrow funds at 11% compounded quarterly, should it buy or lease a photocopy machine?

☑ SOLUTION

The preferred alternative is the one having the lower present value of expenditures (net of any amounts recovered from resale, salvage, or trade-in).

As mentioned previously in Section 11.2, leasing is usually regarded as an alternative to borrowing the funds to purchase the asset. Therefore, the appropriate discount rate to use in the present-value calculation is the firm's cost of borrowing. For the present-value calculation, the lease payments form a simple annuity due with

$$R = \$550 \qquad n = 5(4) = 20 \qquad \text{and} \qquad p = i = \frac{11\%}{4} = 2.75\%$$

If the photocopy machine is purchased, there is an initial expenditure of $9000 and a $1500 recovery from trading it in 5 years later.

ALGEBRAIC SOLUTION

$$PV(\text{lease}) = A_n(\text{due})$$
$$= \$550\left(\frac{1 - 1.0275^{-20}}{0.0275}\right)(1.0275)$$
$$= \$8605$$
$$PV(\text{purchase}) = \$9000 - \$1500(1.0275^{-20})$$
$$= \$9000 - \$872$$
$$= \$8128$$

Hence, purchasing the photocopying machine is the lower-cost alternative. The current economic value of the differences in net costs over the 5-year lifetime is $477.

---

[2]If the alternatives do not have equal lifetimes, the analysis must go beyond a simple comparison of the present values of cash outflows over the respective lifetimes. The additional analysis needed will be presented in Section 16.3.

FINANCIAL CALCULATOR SOLUTION

BGN mode. Compute the present value of the lease payments.				Result
ENTER:	550	0	2.75	20	
PRESS:	+/− PMT	FV	i	n	COMP PV	8605

Compute the present value of the trade-in value.

ENTER:	0	1500		
PRESS:	PMT	FV		COMP PV	−872

The present value of the purchase expenditures is

$$\$9000 - \$872 = \$8128$$

compared to the $8605 present value of the lease payments. In current dollars, the purchase alternative costs $477 less than the lease alternative. Therefore, the accounting firm should purchase the photocopy machine.   ■

EXERCISE 16.1

Answers to the odd-numbered problems are at the end of the book.

Unless otherwise indicated in the following exercises, assume that the initial capital investment occurs at the beginning of the first year and subsequent cash flows occur at the end of each year.

•1. Vencap Enterprises is evaluating an investment opportunity that can be purchased for $30,000. Further product development will require contributions of $30,000 in year 1 and $10,000 in year 2. Then returns of $20,000, $60,000, and $40,000 are expected in the 3 following years.

a. Use the Valuation Principle to determine whether Vencap should make the investment if its cost of capital is 15%.

b. By what amount will the current economic value of Vencap be increased or decreased if it proceeds with purchasing the investment for $30,000?

•2. Repeat problem 1 with the change that Vencap's cost of capital is 18%.

•3. What price should Vencap offer for the investment opportunity described in problem 1 if it requires a 20% return on investment?

•4. The timber rights to a tract of forest can be purchased for $90,000. The harvesting agreement would allow 25% of the timber to be cut in each of the first, second, fourth, and fifth years. The purchaser of the timber rights would be required to replant, at its expense, the logged areas in years 3 and 6. Arrowsmith Lumber calculates that its profit in each of the 4 cutting years would be $50,000 and that the cost of replanting the harvested areas in each of years 3 and 6 would be $20,000.

a. Should Arrowsmith Lumber buy the timber rights if its cost of capital is 14%?

b. By what amount would the economic value of Arrowsmith Lumber be increased or decreased if it proceeded with purchasing the timber rights for $90,000?

•5. Repeat problem 4 with the change that Arrowsmith Lumber's cost of capital is 18%.

•6. At what price would Arrowsmith Lumber be willing to purchase the timber rights described in problem 4 if it requires a return on investment of 20%?

•7. A machine can be leased for 4 years at $1000 per month payable at the beginning of each month. Alternatively, it can be purchased for $43,000 and sold for $5000 after 4 years. Should the machine be purchased or leased if the firm's cost of borrowing is:

    a. 12% compounded monthly?   *b.* 9% compounded monthly?

•8. A real estate salesperson can lease an automobile for 5 years at $500 per month payable at the beginning of each month, or purchase it for $28,000. She can obtain a loan at 9.75% compounded monthly to purchase the car. Should she lease or buy the car if:

    a. The trade-in value after 5 years is $5000?

    b. The trade-in value after 5 years is $8000?

•9. A college can purchase a telephone system for $30,000 or lease a system for 5 years for a front-end charge of $3000 and regular payments of $1500 at the beginning of every quarter (including the first quarter). The system can be purchased at the end of the lease period for $3000.

    a. Should the college lease or buy the system if it can borrow funds at 10% compounded quarterly?

    b. What is the current economic value of the savings with the lower-cost option?

•10. Rocky Mountain Bus Tours needs an additional bus for 3 years. It can lease a bus for $2100 payable at the beginning of each month, or it can buy a similar bus for $110,000, using financing at the rate of 12% compounded monthly. The bus's resale value after 3 years is expected to be $60,000.

    a. On strictly financial considerations, should the company lease or buy the bus?

    b. What is the financial advantage in current dollars of the preferred choice?

••11. Ralph Harder has been transferred to Regina for 5 years. He has found an attractive house that he can buy for $120,000 or rent for $900 per month, payable at the beginning of each month. He estimates that the resale value of the house in 5 years will be $145,000 net of the selling commission. If he buys the house, the average (month-end) costs for repairs, maintenance, and property taxes will be $250. Should Mr. Harder rent or buy the house if mortgage rates are:

    a. 10.5% compounded monthly?   *b.* 9% compounded monthly?

16.2 THE NET PRESENT VALUE OF AN INVESTMENT

The example problems in Section 16.1 demonstrated that an investment should be undertaken only if the present value of the future cash flows equals or exceeds the initial capital expenditure. That is, an investment should be accepted if

$$\text{Present value of future cash flows } - \text{ Initial outlay } \geq 0$$

The cash flows projected for a business's capital investment are usually more complicated than the simple examples considered in the previous section. Usually there will be both cash inflows and cash outflows each year from the operation of the capital project.[3] There may also be further cash flows of a capital nature if, for example, the plant or equipment is refurbished or sold. However, the basic concepts and framework for the analysis of more general cases are the same. The present value of future cash inflows *less* the present value of future cash outflows must *exceed*

---

[3]A rigorous analysis of capital investments requires the calculation of cash flows before interest charges and after income tax (including the tax savings from any capital cost allowance on a depreciable asset). You will learn how to make these adjustments if you take a course in managerial finance. In this chapter we will use *profit* or *operating profit* to mean the net, before interest, after-tax cash flow from the investment during an accounting period.

the initial expenditure. Then the investment will produce a net economic benefit to the firm *after providing the required rate of return to the sources of the invested capital.*

If the initial capital expenditure is included among the cash outflows, the investment decision criterion may be restated in terms of the cash inflows and cash outflows over the lifetime of the investment.

Accept an investment if:

$$\text{Present value of cash inflows} - \text{Present value of cash outflows} \geq 0$$

The left side of this inequality is called the **net present value** (NPV) of the investment's cash flows.

Net Present Value

$$\text{NPV} = \frac{\text{Present value}}{\text{of cash inflows}} - \frac{\text{Present value}}{\text{of cash outflows}}$$

Then the investment decision criterion may be stated as follows:

> **NPV Investment Criterion:**
> Accept the investment if NPV $\geq$ 0.
> Reject the investment if NPV $<$ 0.

For business investments, the firm's cost of capital for financing an investment is used as the discount rate in the NPV calculation. To simplify the calculations of present values, the assumption is usually made that the cash inflows and outflows within each year are concentrated at the *end* of the year.[4] Then the total cash outflow in any particular year can be deducted from the total cash inflow for the same year to obtain a single *net cash flow* for the year. The initial capital investment outlay is assumed to occur at the *beginning* of the first year.

If an investment has a positive NPV, it means that there will be money left over *after:*

- Payment (to the investors providing the financing) of a rate of return equal to the discount rate in the NPV calculation.

- Repayment of the principal amount of the financing.

Therefore, the NPV of an investment project is the economic value, measured in today's dollars, that the project will add to the firm. This added value belongs to the owners of the business and serves to increase the market value of the owners' equity.

> **Significance of the NPV of a Capital Investment:**   The net present value of an investment represents the value that the investment adds to the firm on the date that the investment is made.

A negative NPV does not necessarily mean that the investment will cause the firm to suffer an accounting loss. It does mean, however, that the project's cash flows are not sufficient to provide the sources of financing with their full required return.

---

[4]The errors introduced by ignoring the time value of money *within* each year are small for projects extending over many years. Generally speaking, these errors are smaller than the uncertainties in forecasting the magnitude and timing of the cash flows.

■ EXAMPLE 16.2A   USING THE NPV CRITERION TO EVALUATE A CAPITAL INVESTMENT

A firm is contemplating the purchase of a $10,000 machine that would reduce labour costs by $4000 in each of years 1 and 2, and by $3000 in each of years 3 and 4. The machine's salvage value at the end of year 4 is $1000. Should the machine be purchased if the firm's cost of capital is 15% compounded annually?

☑ SOLUTION

Profits would rise by $4000 in years 1 and 2 and by $3000 in years 3 and 4 as a result of purchasing the machine. These profit increases plus the salvage value in year 4 are the net cash flows that the investment will generate.

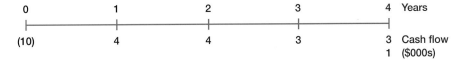

$$\text{NPV} = \$4000(1.15^{-1}) + \$4000(1.15^{-2}) + \$3000(1.15^{-3}) + \$4000(1.15^{-4}) - \$10,000$$
$$= \$3478 + \$3025 + \$1973 + \$2287 - \$10,000$$
$$= \$763$$

Since the NPV > 0, the machine should be purchased. The savings will add $783 to the value of the firm in addition to repaying the financing for the purchase.   ■

NOTATION FOR THE DISCOUNT FACTOR FOR ANNUITIES   In Section 15.6 the notation $s_{\overline{n}|p}$ was introduced to represent the compounding factor for annuities. The corresponding notation symbolizing the discount factor for annuities is

$$a_{\overline{n}|p} = \frac{1 - (1 + p)^{-n}}{p}$$

In terms of this notation, the compact expressions for the present value of an ordinary annuity and an annuity due are

$$A_n = Ra_{\overline{n}|p} \quad \text{and} \quad A_n(due) = Ra_{\overline{n}|p}(1 + p)$$

respectively. Suppose, for example, we want to write instructions for calculating the present value of an ordinary annuity having $n = 20$ payments of size $R = \$300$ and earning interest at the rate of $p = 5\%$ per payment interval. In terms of the new notation, we can simply write

$$\$300a_{\overline{20}|5\%}$$

The expression is read as "$300 a angle 20 at 5%." This representation informs the reader that:

- The annuity's present value is to be calculated. (This is indicated by the appearance of the lowercase a.)
- The type of annuity is an ordinary annuity since no $(1 + p)$ factor appears.
- The values to be used for the variables are $R = \$300$, $n = 20$, and $p = 5\%$.

The reader can then choose to obtain the annuity's present value by using either the algebraic formula or a financial calculator's functions.

■ EXAMPLE 16.2B *USING THE NPV CRITERION WHEN CASH FLOWS FORM ANNUITIES*

Digitel Electronics' engineering and marketing departments have prepared forecasts for the development costs and operating profits of the next generation of their digital electrical meters. Development costs for each of the next 3 years will be $50,000. Manufacturing equipment costing $100,000 will be purchased near the end of year 3. Annual profits for the normal 5-year product life (years 4 to 8 inclusive) are projected to be $80,000. The salvage value of the manufacturing equipment at the end of year 8 is $20,000. Should Digitel proceed with the product development if its annually compounded cost of capital is:

a. 14%?   *b.* 15.5%?   *c.* 17%?

☑ SOLUTION

The cash flows are presented on a time line below. Our convention is to assume cash flows occur at the year's end unless otherwise indicated. Cash outflows (negative) are placed in parentheses. Digitel should proceed with the product development if the net present value of the cash flows, discounted at the cost of capital, is greater than or equal to zero.

0	1	2	3	4	5	6	7	8	Years
	(50)	(50)	(50) (100)	80	80	80	80	80 20	Cash flow ($000s)

NPV = Present value of cash inflows − Present value of cash outflows

To reduce the number of calculations, do not break up annuities. In this problem there is an ordinary simple annuity with three $50,000 payments and a deferred (3 years) ordinary simple annuity with five $80,000 payments.

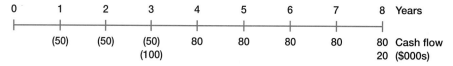

$$\text{NPV} = \frac{\$80,000a_{\overline{5}|p}}{(1 + p)^3} + \frac{\$20,000}{(1 + p)^8} - \$50,000a_{\overline{3}|p} - \frac{\$100,000}{(1 + p)^3}$$

a. For $p = i = 14\%$,

$$\text{NPV} = \$185,379 + \$7011 - \$116,082 - \$67,497 = \$8811$$

Since NPV > 0, Digitel should proceed with the project. The interpretation of the NPV is that the current economic value of the funds remaining after repaying the sources of financing is $8811. This is also the increase in the firm's current value as a result of investing in the product development project.

b. For $p = i = 15.5\%$,

$$\text{NPV} = \$172,007 + \$6315 - \$113,221 - \$64,901 = \$200$$

Given the sizes of the cash flows in the forecast, this is basically a zero-NPV investment. This does not imply that there is no profit. Rather, it means that the estimated profits will just be sufficient to repay the project's financing along with a 15.5% rate of return on the funds while they are invested in the project. This is acceptable but represents the threshold for acceptability.

c. For $p = i = 17\%$, we obtain NPV=−$7414. In this case the project will fall short (by $7414 in terms of current dollars) of repaying the financing along with the required 17% rate of return on investment. Digitel should not proceed in this case. ■

EXERCISE 16.2

Answers to the odd-numbered problems are at the end of the book.

Use the NPV investment criterion to answer the following problems. Unless otherwise indicated, assume that the initial capital investment occurs at the beginning of the first year and that subsequent cash flows occur at the end of the year. Show calculations that justify your decision.

•1. St. Lawrence Bus Lines is offered a contract for busing schoolchildren that will produce an annual profit of $36,000 for 7 years. To fulfill the contract, St. Lawrence would have to buy three buses at a total cost of $165,000. At the end of the contract the resale value of the buses is estimated to be $40,000. Should St. Lawrence Bus Lines sign the contract if its cost of capital is:

    a. 12%?   *b.* 15%?   *c.* 18%?

•2. An automotive parts plant is scheduled to be closed in 10 years. Nevertheless, its engineering department thinks that some investments in computer-controlled equipment can be justified by savings in labour and energy costs within that time frame. The engineering department is proposing a four-phase program that would require the expenditure of $100,000 at the beginning of each of the next 4 years. Each successive phase would produce additional annual savings of $30,000, $27,000, $22,000, and $22,000. The savings from any phase are in addition to annual savings already realised from previous phases. There will be no significant residual value. The firm's cost of capital is 14%. As the plant's financial analyst, what phases, if any, of the proposal would you accept?

•3. The pro forma projections for growing a 20-hectare ginseng crop require the expenditure of $150,000 in the summer that the crop is planted and an additional $50,000 in each of the next two summers to cultivate and fertilize the growing crop. After payment of the costs of harvesting the crop, the profit should be $200,000 in the third summer after planting, and $300,000 in the fourth summer. Allowing for a cost of capital of 15% compounded annually, what is the economic value of the project at the time of planting? (*Hint:* The project's economic value is its NPV.)

•4. A proposed strip mine would require the investment of $1 million at the beginning of the first year and a further investment of $1.5 million at the end of the first year. Mining operations are expected to yield annual profits of $500,000 beginning in year 2. The ore body will sustain 10 years of mining operations. At the beginning of the 12th year, the mining company would have to spend $500,000 on environmental restoration. Would the project provide the mining company with a rate of return exceeding its 18% cost of capital? (*Hint:* The project will provide a rate of return exceeding the cost of capital if it has a positive NPV.)

•5. The development of a new product will require the expenditure of $150,000 at the beginning of each of the next 3 years. When the product reaches the market in year 4, it is expected to increase the firm's annual profit by $90,000 for 7 years. Then the product will be replaced by a new model, and $100,000 of the original expenditures should be recoverable. If the firm's cost of capital is 14%, should it proceed with the project?

•6. The introduction of a new product will require an initial investment of $45,000. The annual profit expected from the new product is forecast to be $9000 for years 1 to 3, $6000 for years 4 to 6, and $4000 for years 7 to 12. Should the firm proceed with the investment if its required compound annual return is 15%?

••7. Jasper Ski Corp. is studying the feasibility of installing a new chair lift to expand the capacity of its downhill-skiing operation. Site preparation would require the expenditure of $400,000 at the beginning of the first year. Construction would take place early in the second year at a cost of $1.8 million. The lift would have a useful life of 12 years and a residual value of $400,000. The increased capacity should generate increased annual profits of $300,000 at the end of years 2 to 5 inclusive and $500,000 in years 6 to 13 inclusive. Should Jasper proceed with the project if it requires a return on investment of 16%?

••8. A capital project would require an immediate investment of $150,000 and a further investment of $40,000 on a date 4 years from now. On the operating side, the project is expected to lose $30,000 in the first year and $10,000 in the second, to break even in the third year, and to turn annual profits of $60,000 in years 4 to 7 and $30,000 in years 8 to 10. The estimated residual value at the end of the 10th year is $50,000. Is the project acceptable if a return on investment of 17% is required?

••9. To manufacture a new product, a company must immediately invest $275,000 in new equipment. At the end of years 3 and 5, there will have to be a major overhaul of the equipment at a cost of $40,000 on each occasion. The new product is expected to increase annual operating profits by $75,000 in each of the first 4 years and by $55,000 in each of the next 3 years. The equipment will then be salvaged to recover about $30,000. Should the product be manufactured if the company's cost of capital is 14% compounded annually?

••10. A new machine that will lead to savings in labour costs of $16,000 per year can be purchased for $52,000. However, it will cost $1500 per year for the first 4 years and $2500 per year for the next 4 years to service and maintain it. In addition, its annual electrical power consumption will cost $1000. After a service life of 8 years, the salvage value of the machine is expected to be $5000. Should the machine be acquired if the company requires a minimum return on investment of 15%?

16.3 COMPARING INVESTMENT PROJECTS

Normally a firm should accept every investment project that has a positive net present value. Any positive NPV project produces a net economic benefit to the firm after the sources of financing have received their required returns. The NPV gives the magnitude of the economic benefit on the date of the initial capital expenditure.

There are two circumstances in which a business will not necessarily proceed with all the positive-NPV investments available to it. In these situations, choosing one of the projects may exclude the selection of other positive NPV projects. Some refinements to our selection criterion are needed to rank or select from projects that, in some sense, are competing alternatives.

CAPITAL RATIONING

Capital rationing is the circumstance in which there is a limit on the total amount of capital funds that a firm may invest during a period. In this situation, the firm should *choose the group of projects that have the highest combined NPV* subject to the limitation on the total capital budget. By this choice, the increase in the firm's value is maximized.

■ EXAMPLE 16.3A　SELECTING CAPITAL PROJECTS SUBJECT TO A CAPITAL RATIONING CONSTRAINT

The strategic planning group at Hardy Toy Co. has identified the following positive-NPV projects, ranked in order of their NPV. All projects are independent—selection of any project neither requires nor precludes the selection of any other project.

Capital investment project	Initial capital investment	Project NPV
Expand production facilities	$270,000	$195,000
Open western distribution centre	250,000	155,000
Introduce toy A	90,000	130,000
Buy out regional wooden toy maker	155,000	120,000
Introduce game B	60,000	80,000
Purchase plastic moulding machine	54,000	70,000
Introduce toy C	110,000	65,000
Introduce plastic recycling process	56,000	63,000
Replace old packaging machine	62,000	40,000
Introduce new doll	60,000	31,000

The board of directors has imposed a $600,000 capital expenditure limit for the next year. What projects should the company undertake within the capital budget restriction?

✓ Solution

The company will want to choose the group of projects with the largest combined NPV, subject to the requirement that the total initial capital investment must not exceed $600,000. To obtain the "biggest bang per invested buck," it is helpful to calculate each project's NPV per dollar of initial investment. In the following table, the projects are ranked on the basis of this ratio (presented in the third column).

Project number	Capital investment project	NPV per invested dollar	Initial capital investment	Cumulative capital investment
1	Introduce toy A	$1.44	$ 90,000	$ 90,000
2	Introduce game B	1.33	60,000	150,000
3	Purchase plastic moulding machine	1.30	54,000	204,000
4	Introduce plastic recycling process	1.13	56,000	260,000
5	Buy out regional wooden toy maker	0.77	155,000	
6	Expand production facilities	0.72	270,000	
7	Replace old packaging machine	0.65	62,000	
8	Open western distribution centre	0.62	250,000	
9	Introduce toy C	0.59	110,000	
10	Introduce new doll	0.52	60,000	

Until the capital budget constraint becomes a consideration, the projects with the highest NPV per invested dollar are automatically selected. The first four projects require a total investment of $260,000, leaving $340,000 available for others. If project 5 is chosen next, project 6 cannot be undertaken, because it would take the total investment beyond the $600,000 limit. But projects 7 and 9 can still be included, along with 5, while remaining within the $600,000 limit. Therefore, one group of projects that must be considered is projects 1, 2, 3, 4, 5, 7, and 9, for which

Required total capital investment = $587,000
Total net present value = $225,000

If we do not include project 5, we can proceed with project 6 and still have enough funds remaining in the $600,000 global budget to undertake project 7 as well. This second combination (projects 1, 2, 3, 4, 6, and 7) has

$$\text{Required total capital investment} = \$592,000$$
$$\text{Total net present value} = \$235,000$$

The second group should be selected since it adds $10,000 more economic value to Hardy Toy Co.   ∎

MUTUALLY EXCLUSIVE PROJECTS

Alternative capital investments, any one of which will substantially satisfy the same need or purpose, are called **mutually exclusive projects.** For example, three different machines that fabricate the same product are mutually exclusive projects if any one of them will satisfy the firm's requirements. Only one will be selected even if each one has a positive NPV.

If the mutually exclusive projects all have the *same* lifetime, a direct comparison may be made among the NPVs of the projects. The one with the largest positive NPV should be chosen because it provides the greatest economic benefit to the firm.

If projects have *unequal* lifetimes, it is *not* a simple matter of selecting the project with the largest lifetime NPV. A fair comparison requires a common time frame that might involve replacements for one or more of the short-lived alternatives. However, we cannot arbitrarily pick the duration of the common time period because net cash flows are generally spread unevenly over each project's lifetime. Either of two methods—the *replacement chain method* or the *equivalent annual cash flow method*—may be used to properly account for unequal investment lifetimes and uneven cash flows.

REPLACEMENT CHAIN METHOD The replacement chain approach repeats the replacement cycle of one or more of the mutually exclusive alternatives until *all* terminate on the *same* date. Then the NPVs of all cash flows within this common time horizon are calculated for each project. The one with the highest positive NPV should be selected.

■ EXAMPLE 16.3B   *REPLACEMENT CHAIN METHOD WITH MUTUALLY EXCLUSIVE PROJECTS*

A machine shop is trying to decide which of two types of metal lathe to purchase. The more versatile Japanese lathe costs $32,000 and will generate an annual profit of $16,000 for 3 years. Its trade-in value after 3 years will be about $10,000. The more durable German lathe costs $42,000 and will increase profits by $12,000 per year for 6 years. Its trade-in value at that point is estimated at $15,000. Based on an NPV calculation at a 10% cost of capital, which lathe should be purchased?

✓ SOLUTION

We will first determine the lifetime NPV of a capital investment in each lathe.

Time diagram for the Japanese lathe

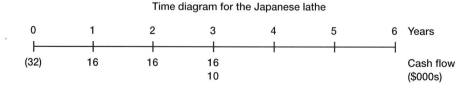

Time diagram for the German lathe

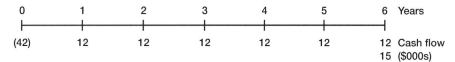

The NPV for the acquisition of the Japanese lathe is

$$NPV_J = \$16,000a_{\overline{3}|\,10\%} + \$10,000(1.10)^{-3} - \$32,000$$
$$= \$39,790 + \$7513 - \$32,000$$
$$= \$15,303$$

The NPV for the purchase of the German lathe is

$$NPV_G = \$12,000a_{\overline{6}|\,10\%} + \$15,000(1.10)^{-6} - \$42,000$$
$$= \$18,730$$

A comparison of the NPVs at this point would not necessarily lead to a valid conclusion (to purchase the higher-NPV German lathe). For a fair comparison, an adjustment must be made for the unequal service lives of the two lathes.

Since the machine shop is prepared to commit to the German lathe for 6 years, it is logical to infer that it is also prepared to have a Japanese lathe for 6 years. By including one replacement cycle of the Japanese lathe in the analysis, we obtain a common time frame of 6 years for both alternatives.

To reconsider the Japanese option, it is not necessary to begin again with each year's cash flows. Remember the significance of the present value of a number of cash flows—it is the single amount that is equivalent, at the focal date, to all the cash flows. Therefore, an investment's NPV is equivalent to all the cash flows included in its calculation. The actual cash flows for 6 years with the Japanese lathe may be replaced by inflows of $15,303 at the beginning of each 3-year service life. The following equivalent time diagram may be used for 6 years of operation with the Japanese lathe.

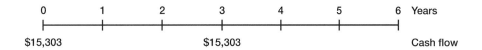

The NPV for 6 years with the Japanese lathe is

$$NPV_J = \$15,303 + \$15,303(1.10)^{-3} = \$26,800$$

With the alternative investments transformed to a common time horizon, the Japanese lathe gives the higher NPV. Therefore, it should be selected.   ∎

The replacement chain method works well when the service life of one alternative is an integer multiple of the service life of a second alternative (as in Example 16.3B). But what if the service lives of two competing alternatives were 5 years and 7 years? We would have to consider five cycles of the 7-year lifetime and seven cycles of the 5-year lifetime to have a common time frame containing a whole number of replacement cycles of both alternatives. If there are more than two alternatives, the replacement chain approach becomes more unwieldy. In these cases the equivalent annual cash-flow method is simpler.

EQUIVALENT ANNUAL CASH-FLOW METHOD In this approach, we calculate the *constant annual* cash flow during each project's lifetime that has the same NPV as the *actual* cash flows. Since the equivalent annual flows also apply to any number of replacement cycles, we can directly compare the equivalent annual cash flows of competing projects. *The project with the largest positive equivalent annual cash flow should be selected.*

■ **EXAMPLE 16.3c** *EQUIVALENT ANNUAL CASH-FLOW METHOD WITH MUTUALLY EXCLUSIVE PROJECTS*

Repeat the problem in Example 16.3B using the equivalent annual cash-flow method.

☑ **SOLUTION**

Recall that the NPV for one 3-year investment cycle in the Japanese lathe was

$$NPV_J = \$15,303$$

and that the NPV for one 6-year investment cycle in the German lathe was

$$NPV_G = \$18,730$$

For the Japanese lathe, the equivalent annual cash flow is the value of R_J satisfying

$$\$15,303 = R_J a_{\overline{3}|\,10\%}$$

The solution is $R_J = \$6154$.

For the German lathe, the equivalent annual cash flow is the solution to

$$\$18,730 = R_G a_{\overline{6}|\,10\%}$$

The value for R_G is $4301.

Since the Japanese lathe has the larger equivalent annual cash flow, it should be selected.

Note: The ratio of the two equivalent annual cash flows in this solution is

$$\frac{R_J}{R_G} = \frac{\$6154}{\$4301} = 1.431$$

The ratio of the NPVs of investments in the two lathes calculated in Example 16.3B for a common 6-year time horizon is:

$$\frac{NPV_J \text{ for 6 years}}{NPV_G \text{ for 6 years}} = \frac{\$26,800}{\$18,730} = 1.431$$

The equality of the two ratios demonstrates the equivalence of the two methods.   ■

Tip

Remember that unequal lives do not have to be taken into account when *independent* projects are being selected under conditions of capital rationing. Unequal lives are a consideration only for *mutually exclusive* projects.

COST MINIMIZATION When mutually exclusive alternatives generate the same benefits or services or cash inflows, it is sufficient to focus on the cash outflows. We should select the lowest-cost alternative, recognizing the time value of money. When the time horizons of the competing alternatives are the same, the present values of the lifetime cash outflows may be directly compared. However, when the time horizons differ, calculate the *equivalent annual cash outflow* for each alternative. Select the one with the *smallest* equivalent annual cash outflow.

EXERCISE 16.3

Answers to the odd-numbered problems are at the end of the book.

Problems 1, 2, and 3 require the selection of independent capital investments subject to a capital budget limitation.

•1. A firm has identified the following four investment opportunities and calculated their net present values. If the firm's capital budget for this period is limited to $300,000, which projects should be selected?

Project	Initial investment	NPV
A	$100,000	$ 25,000
B	60,000	40,000
C	130,000	60,000
D	200,000	110,000

•2. The investment committee of a company has identified the following seven projects with positive NPVs. If the board of directors has approved a $3 million capital budget for the current period, which projects should be selected?

Project	Initial investment	NPV
1	$1,000,000	$600,000
2	1,800,000	324,000
3	750,000	285,000
4	600,000	270,000
5	450,000	113,000
6	150,000	21,000
7	250,000	20,000

•3. Mohawk Enterprises is considering the following investment opportunities.

Project	Initial investment	Year 1	Year 2	Year 3	Year 4
			Profit for year		
A	$30,000	$12,000	$ 9000	$ 8000	$20,000
B	36,000	6000	23,000	10,000	14,000
C	18,000	10,000	0	0	20,000
D	22,000	0	18,000	2500	11,000
E	28,000	26,000	0	0	17,000
F	20,000	6000	7000	10,000	11,000

If Mohawk's cost of capital is 15% per annum and its capital budget is limited to $90,000, what projects should it choose?

Exercises 4 through 11 require the selection of the best investment from two or more mutually exclusive alternatives.

•4. A small regional airline has narrowed down the possible choices for its next passenger plane purchase to two alternatives. The Eagle model costs $250,000 and would have an estimated resale value of $50,000 after 7 years. The Albatross model has a $325,000 price and would have an estimated resale value of $150,000 after 7 years. The annual operating profit from the Eagle would be $75,000. Because of its greater fuel efficiency and slightly larger seating capacity, the Albatross's annual profit would be $95,000. Which plane should the airline purchase if its cost of capital is 15%? In current dollars, what is the economic advantage of selecting the preferred alternative over the other?

•5. Carl Williams does custom wheat combining in southern Alberta. He will purchase either a new Massey or a new Deere combine to replace his old machine. The Massey combine costs $95,000, and the Deere combine costs $78,000. Their trade-in values after 6 years would be about $25,000 and $20,000, respectively. Because the Massey cuts an 18-foot swath versus the Deere's 15-foot swath, Carl estimates that his annual profit with the Massey will be 10% higher than the $35,000 he could make with the Deere. The Massey equipment dealer will provide 100% financing at 11% per annum, and the Deere dealer will approve 100% financing at 10% per annum. Which combine should Carl purchase? How much more, in current dollars, is the better alternative worth?

••6. A business is evaluating two mutually exclusive projects. Project A requires an immediate investment of $6000 plus another $8000 in 3 years. It would produce a profit of $6000 in the second year, $18,000 in the fourth year, and $12,000 in the seventh year. Project B requires an immediate investment of $5000, another $8000 in 2 years, and a further $5000 in 4 years. It would produce an annual profit of $5200 for 7 years. Neither project would have any residual value after 7 years. Which project should be selected if the required rate of return is 16%? What is the economic advantage, in current dollars, of the preferred project over the other?

••7. A company must choose between two investments. Investment C requires an immediate outlay of $50,000 and then, in 2 years, another investment of $30,000. Investment D requires annual investments of $25,000 at the beginning of each of the first 4 years. C would return annual profits of $16,000 for 10 years beginning with the first year. D's profits would not start until year 4 but would be $35,000 in years 4 to 10 inclusive. The residual values after 10 years are estimated to be $30,000 for C and $20,000 for D. Which investment should the company choose if its cost of capital is 15%? How much more is the preferred project worth today?

•8. Machine A costs $40,000 and is forecast to generate an annual profit of $15,000 for 4 years. Machine B, priced at $60,000, will produce the same annual profits for 8 years. The trade-in value of A after 4 years is expected to be $10,000, and the resale value of B after 8 years is also estimated to be $10,000. If either machine satisfies the firm's requirements, which one should be selected? Use a required return of 14%.

•9. A sawmill requires a new saw for cutting small-dimension logs. Model H, with a 3-year service life, costs $100,000 and will generate an annual profit of $55,000. Model J, with a 4-year service life, costs $140,000 and will return an annual profit of $58,000. Neither saw will have significant salvage value. If the mill's cost of capital is 16%, which model should be purchased?

••10. A landscaping business will buy one of three rototillers. The initial cost, expected service life, and trade-in value (at the end of the service life) of each model are presented in the following table. The annual profit from rototilling services is $700.

Model	Cost	Service life (years)	Trade-in value
A	$1000	2	$200
AA	1400	3	450
AAA	2100	6	700

Which model should be purchased if the required return on investment is 20%?

••11. A freelance trucker is trying to decide whether to buy a 15-ton or a 25-ton truck. A 15-ton vehicle would cost $75,000; it would have a service life of 7 years and a trade-in value of about $15,000 at 7 years of age. A 25-ton truck would cost $100,000, and would have a service life of 6 years and a trade-in value of about $20,000 at 6 years of age. The estimated annual profit (after provision for a normal salary for the driver-owner) would be $24,000 for the smaller truck and $32,000 for the larger truck. Which truck should be purchased if the cost of financing a truck is 12.5% compounded annually? What is the average annual economic benefit of making the right decision?

Problems 12 through 15 require the selection of the lowest-cost alternative.

•12. *Consumer Digest* recently reported that car batteries X, Y, and Z have average service lives of 3, 4, and 6 years, respectively. Grace found that the best retail prices for these batteries in her town are $60, $75, and $105. If money is worth 10% compounded annually, which battery has the lowest equivalent annual cost?

•13. The provincial government's Ministry of Forest Resources requires a spotter plane for its fire service. The price of a Hawk is $120,000, and its annual operating costs will be $30,000. Given the heavy use it will receive, it will be sold for about $30,000 after 5 years and replaced. A more durable but less efficient Falcon, priced at $100,000, will cost $40,000 per year to operate, will last 7 years, and will have a resale value of $40,000. If the provincial government pays an interest rate of 9% compounded annually on its mid-term debt, which plane has the lower equivalent annual cost?

••14. Neil always trades in his car when it reaches 5 years of age because of the large amount of driving he does in his job. He is investigating whether there would be a financial advantage in buying a 2-year-old car every 3 years instead of buying a new car every 5 years. His research indicates that, for the make of car he prefers, he could buy a 2-year-old car for $12,000, whereas a new car of the same model sells for $20,000. In either case, the resale value of the 5-year-old car would be $4000. Repairs and maintenance average $300 per year for the first 2 years of the car's life and $1000 per year for the next 3. Which alternative has the lower equivalent annual cost if money is worth 11% compounded annually?

••15. A construction company has identified two machines that will accomplish the same job. The Caterpillar model costs $80,000 and has a service life of 8 years if it receives a $15,000 overhaul every 2 years. The International model costs $105,000 and should last 12 years with a $10,000 overhaul every 3 years. In either case, the overhaul scheduled for the year of disposition would not be performed, and the machine would be sold for about $10,000. If the company's cost of capital is 15%, which machine should be purchased?

16.4 INTERNAL RATE OF RETURN

Business managers often prefer to discuss and compare investment opportunities in terms of an annual rate of return on investment. The net present value calculation does not provide the rate of return on the invested funds.

Recall that the net cash flows from an investment project having an NPV of zero will be just sufficient to repay the project's financing, including a rate of return *equal* to the discount rate. Therefore, the rate of return on investment for a zero-NPV project equals the discount rate (cost of capital) used in the NPV calculation. This special case suggests a technique for determining the rate of return on investment from any project. If we can find a discount rate that makes the NPV of the project's net cash flows equal to zero, then that discount rate is the project's rate of return on investment. In the context of business capital investments, this rate of return is often called the **internal rate of return** (IRR).

> **Internal Rate of Return (IRR):**   An investment's IRR is the discount rate that makes the net present value of the investment equal to zero.

When the periodic cash flows from a capital investment form an annuity, a financial calculator may be used to compute p. Otherwise, the trial-and-error approach (Appendix 12B) followed by interpolation (Appendix 12C) must be used to solve for the IRR.[5] The basic procedure is:

1. Make a reasonable estimate of the investment's IRR. Start with an estimate larger than the cost of capital if the project has a positive NPV.
2. Calculate the investment's NPV using the estimated IRR as the discount rate.
3. Make a better estimate of the IRR. If the NPV in step 2 was positive, choose a larger value for the estimated IRR. If the NPV was negative, choose a smaller value for the IRR. Repeat steps 2 and 3 until positive and negative NPVs have been obtained for two IRR estimates whose difference is less than 1%.
4. Interpolate between these two IRR estimates to calculate the IRR at which the investment's NPV is zero. This interpolation step should give the IRR accurate to within ±0.1%.

A positive-NPV investment has an IRR greater than the cost of capital, whereas a negative-NPV investment has an IRR less than the cost of capital. The NPV investment decision criterion developed in Section 16.2 may now be expressed in terms of the investment's IRR.

> **IRR Investment Criterion:**
> Accept the investment if IRR ≥ Cost of capital.
> Reject the investment if IRR < Cost of capital.

The internal rate of return is the rate of return earned on the *unrecovered portion of an investment.* As net cash flows are received from a project, the invested funds are gradually recovered. The IRR continues to be earned only on the unrecovered portion

---

[5]Advanced models of financial calculators have preprogrammed functions that permit the calculation of the NPV and IRR for a nonuniform series of cash flows.

of the original investment. The recovered funds will subsequently earn the rate of return for the next project in which they are reinvested.[6]

■ EXAMPLE 16.4A   CALCULATION OF AN INVESTMENT'S IRR BY TRIAL AND ERROR

A project requires an immediate investment of $20,000 and an additional investment of $10,000 in 1 year. It will generate an annual profit of $8000 in years 2 to 8 and have a residual value of $5000 at the end of the eighth year. Calculate the project's internal rate of return. Should the project be undertaken if the firm's cost of capital is 14%?

☑ SOLUTION

The cash flows are presented in the time diagram below.

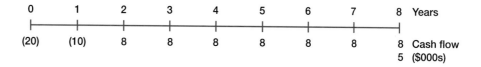

The project's net present value at the discount rate p is

$$\text{NPV} = -\$20{,}000 - \underbrace{\frac{\$10{,}000}{1+p}}_{\text{Term } ①} + \underbrace{\frac{\$8000 \; a_{\overline{7}|p}}{1+p}}_{\text{Term } ②} + \underbrace{\frac{\$5000}{(1+p)^8}}_{\text{Term } ③}$$

The project's internal rate of return is the value for p that makes the NPV zero. We begin a trial-and-error process to find values for p that will make the sum of the terms in the NPV expression a few hundred dollars above and a few hundred dollars below zero. Then interpolation can be used to improve the estimate for the IRR. A natural choice for the first trial in this case is $p = 14\%$ (the cost of capital).

Trial number	Estimated p	Term ①	Term ②	Term ③	NPV
1	0.14	-$8772	$30,093	$1753	$3074
2	0.15	-8695	28,941	1635	1881
3	0.16	-8621	27,852	1575	756
4	⌈ 0.165 ⌉ IRR	-8584	27,329	1474	⌈ 219 ⌉ 0
5	0.168 ⌋	-8562	27,022	1444	-96 ⌋

---

[6]An alternative definition of the IRR is that it is the discount rate that makes the present value of the future cash flows equal to the initial capital outlay. From this version of the definition, it is clearer that the IRR is a new name for a familiar concept. The returns on investment that we calculated for various investment instruments in previous chapters are the internal rates of return for those investments. For example, the yield to maturity on a bond (Section 15.3) could also be called the bond's IRR. It is merely prevailing business practice that dictates which term is used for the same quantity in different contexts.

Interpolating,

$$\frac{IRR - 0.165}{0.168 - 0.165} \doteq \frac{0 - \$219}{-\$96 - \$219} = \frac{\$219}{\$315} = 0.695$$
$$IRR - 0.165 \doteq 0.003(0.695)$$
$$IRR \doteq 0.165 + 0.0021$$
$$\doteq 0.167$$
$$\doteq 16.7\%$$

The project's IRR is 16.7%. Since the IRR is greater than the cost of capital, the project should be accepted. (This conclusion is consistent with the outcome of the first trial, where the project had a positive NPV when the cost of capital was used as the discount rate.)

EXERCISE 16.4

Answers to the odd-numbered problems are at the end of the book.

Determine the IRR in the following problems to the nearest 0.1%.

1. A 10-year license to distribute a product should increase the distributor's profit by $10,000 per year. If the license can be acquired for $50,000, what is the investment's IRR?

2. Burger Master bought the food concession for a baseball stadium for 5 years at a price of $1.2 million. If the operating profit is $400,000 per year, what IRR will Burger Master realise on its investment?

•3. Calculate the IRR of each of the four stages of the cost reduction proposal in problem 2 of Exercise 16.2. Based on the IRR investment criterion, which stages should be approved at a 14% cost of capital?

•4. A project requires an initial investment of $60,000. It will generate an annual profit of $12,000 for 8 years and have a terminal value of $10,000. Calculate the project's IRR. Should it be accepted if the cost of capital is 15%?

•5. An investment of $100,000 will yield annual profits of $20,000 for 10 years. The proceeds on disposition at the end of the 10 years are estimated at $25,000. On the basis of its IRR and a 16% cost of capital, should the investment be made?

•6. Determine the IRR on the school bus contract in problem 1 of Exercise 16.2. At which of the three costs of capital would the contract be financially acceptable?

••7. A $100,000 capital investment will produce annual profits of $25,000 for the first 5 years and $15,000 for the next 5 years. It will have no residual value. What is its IRR? Should it be undertaken if the cost of capital is 15%?

••8. A natural resource development and extraction project would require an investment of $1 million now and $1 million at the end of each of the next 4 years. Then it would generate annual profits of $2 million in each of the following 5 years. There would be no residual value. What would be the IRR of the project? Would it be acceptable to a company requiring a 16% return on investment?

••9. The introduction of a new product would require an initial investment of $120,000. The forecast profits in successive years of the anticipated 4-year product life are $25,000, $60,000, $50,000, and $35,000. Determine the IRR of the investment. Should the product be introduced if the firm's cost of capital is 15%?

••10. A venture requiring an immediate investment of $500,000 and an additional investment of $200,000 in 3 years' time will generate annual profits of $150,000 for 7 years starting next year. There will be no significant terminal value. Calculate the IRR of the investment. Should the investment be undertaken at a 13% cost of capital?

••11. Determine the IRR on the strip-mine proposal in problem 4 of Exercise 16.2. Should the mine be developed, given the mining company's 18% cost of capital?

16.5 COMPARISON OF NPV AND IRR METHODS

For independent projects, the NPV and IRR investment decision criteria lead to the same "accept" or "reject" conclusion.[7] If the NPV criterion is satisfied, the IRR criterion will also be met.

The NPV approach has the advantage that it also quantifies the magnitude of the economic benefit to the firm of undertaking a capital investment. The primary objective of the managers of a firm is to maximize the value of the firm. The NPV analysis relates directly to this objective since it gives the amount that each potential investment will add to the firm's value. Nevertheless, studies of actual business practice reveal that more managers prefer to base business investment decisions on the IRR than on the NPV. This seems to reflect a traditional bias toward measures of profitability stated as percentage rates of return. Managers are also inclined to think in terms of the spread between the cost of capital and the (internal) rate of return on an investment.

A flawed investment decision can result if the IRR is used to rank projects that are mutually exclusive, or to rank projects that are competing for a limited capital budget. In these cases, it can happen that the project with the larger IRR has the smaller NPV. The ranking should be based strictly on the projects' NPVs. Then the project that adds the most value to the firm will be selected.

In summary, the NPV approach to evaluating and ranking capital investment opportunities *always* works. It also gives the amount by which the investment will increase the value of the firm. There are some situations, particularly the ranking of mutually exclusive investments, in which the IRR method can lead to a suboptimal decision.[8]

■ EXAMPLE 16.5A   *RANKING PROJECTS WITH UNEVEN CASH FLOWS*

The initial investment and subsequent profits for two mutually exclusive, 3-year projects are forecast as follows:

	Project S	Project T
Initial investment	$100,000	$100,000
Year 1 profit	100,000	25,000
Year 2 profit	20,000	25,000
Year 3 profit	20,000	110,000

a. Rank the projects on the basis of their IRRs.

b. Rank the projects on the basis of their NPVs if the firm's cost of capital is 15%.

[7]An exception sometimes occurs in situations in which there is more than one sign reversal among the periodic net cash flows. In such cases there can be more than one discount rate that makes the project's NPV equal to zero, and the IRR investment criterion will not necessarily apply. These cases will not be encountered in this text; they are considered in texts on managerial finance.

[8]The fundamental reason for this limitation can be traced to a subtle point. Any valuation of cash flows based on a present-value calculation implicitly assumes that cash flows from the investment may be reinvested at the discount rate used in the present-value calculation. An NPV ranking of projects therefore assumes the same reinvestment rate (the cost of capital) for all projects. An IRR ranking of projects assumes a different reinvestment rate for each project—namely, each project's own internal rate of return. It is not a fair comparison to rank projects on the basis of a criterion that does not use the same reinvestment rate for all projects being compared. Therefore, an IRR ranking of projects may differ from an NPV ranking, and the latter should take precedence.

c. Rank the projects on the basis of their NPVs if the firm's cost of capital is 12%.

d. Which project should be selected if the cost of capital is 12%?

☑ SOLUTION

a. The IRR of project S is the value of *p* in

$$0 = \frac{\$100{,}000}{1 + p} + \frac{\$20{,}000}{(1 + p)^2} + \frac{\$20{,}000}{(1 + p)^3} - \$100{,}000$$

$$\underbrace{\qquad}_{\text{Term } ①} \quad \underbrace{\qquad}_{\text{Term } ②} \quad \underbrace{\qquad}_{\text{Term } ③}$$

Estimate *p* by the trial-and-error method.

Trial number	Estimated *p*	Term ①	Term ②	Term ③	RHS
1	0.15	$86,957	$15,123	$13,150	$15,230
2	0.20	83,333	13,889	11,574	8796
3	0.25	80,000	12,800	10,240	3040
4	0.28 ⎤	78,125	12,207	9537	−131 ⎤
	⎡ IRR				⎡ 0
5	⎣ 0.278 ⎦	78,247	12,245	9582	⎣ 74 ⎦

Interpolating,

$$\frac{IRR - 0.278}{0.28 - 0.278} \doteq \frac{0 - \$74}{-\$131 - \$74} = \frac{\$74}{\$205} = 0.361$$

$$IRR - 0.278 \doteq 0.002(0.361)$$

$$IRR \doteq 0.278 + 0.0007$$

$$\doteq 0.2787$$

$$\doteq 27.87\% \text{ for project S}$$

The IRR for project T may be similarly shown to be 20.91%. Therefore, project S has the greater IRR and, on that basis, would rank ahead of project T.

b. At a cost of capital of 15%, the NPV of project S is

$$NPV_S = \frac{\$100{,}000}{1.15} + \frac{\$20{,}000}{1.15^2} + \frac{\$20{,}000}{1.15^3} - \$100{,}000$$

$$= \$86{,}957 + \$15{,}123 + \$13{,}150 - \$100{,}000$$

$$= \$15{,}230$$

The NPV of project T may be calculated in a similar manner to give

$$NPV_T = \$12{,}970$$

Therefore, project S has the greater NPV and ranks ahead of project T. This is the same as the IRR ranking in part *a*.

c. At a cost of capital of 12%, the NPVs of the two projects can be calculated again using the same method as in part *b*. The values are

$$NPV_S = \$19{,}465 \qquad NPV_T = \$20{,}547$$

In this case, T has the larger NPV and ranks ahead of S. We note from parts *b* and *c* that the NPV ranking can depend on the cost of capital.

d. A project's IRR is not affected by the cost of capital. On the basis of the IRR, project S would always be selected over project T.

   At a 12% cost of capital, the IRR and NPV rankings do not agree. We should let the NPV ranking take precedence and select the project that adds the greater value to the firm. Therefore, project T should be chosen. ∎

▪ EXAMPLE 16.5B   RANKING PROJECTS WITH UNIFORM CASH FLOWS

A company is considering two mutually exclusive projects. The initial investment required and the expected profits are presented in the following table. Neither project will have any residual value.

	Project A	Project B
Initial investment	$50,000	$100,000
Year 1 profit	28,000	50,000
Year 2 profit	28,000	50,000
Year 3 profit	28,000	50,000

a. Rank the projects on the basis of their IRRs.

b. What project should be chosen if the company's cost of capital is 17%?

c. What project should be chosen if the cost of capital is 14%?

☑ SOLUTION

a. Each project's yearly profit forms a simple annuity. The IRR of project A is the value of p in

$$0 = \$28{,}000a_{\overline{3}|p} - \$50{,}000$$

Similarly, the IRR of project B is the solution to

$$0 = \$50{,}000a_{\overline{3}|p} - \$100{,}000$$

An algebraic solution to these equations requires a trial-and-error approach.

FINANCIAL CALCULATOR SOLUTION

When the periodic cash flows form an annuity, we can use the calculator's basic financial functions to solve for p.

a.
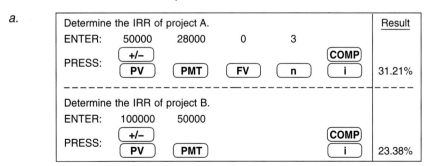

On the basis of their IRRs, project A would be selected over project B.

b. At a cost of capital of 17%,

$$NPV_A = \$28,000a_{\overline{3}|17\%} - \$50,000 = \$11,868$$
$$NPV_B = \$50,000a_{\overline{3}|17\%} - \$100,000 = \$10,479$$

Since $NPV_A > NPV_B$, project A should be selected.

c. At a cost of capital of 14%,

$$NPV_A = \$28,000a_{\overline{3}|14\%} - \$50,000 = \$15,006$$
$$NPV_B = \$50,000a_{\overline{3}|14\%} - \$100,000 = \$16,082$$

Since $NPV_B > NPV_A$, project B should be selected (even though $IRR_A > IRR_B$). ∎

EXERCISE 16.5

Answers to the odd-numbered problems are at the end of the book.

Calculate internal rates of return to the nearest 0.1%.

•1. Two mutually exclusive investments are available to a firm. Project C, requiring a capital investment of $150,000, will generate an annual profit of $43,000 for 6 years. Project D is expected to yield an annual profit of $30,000 for 6 years on an initial investment of $100,000.

   a. Calculate the internal rate of return on each project. Based upon their IRRs, which project should be selected?

   b. Which project should be selected if the firm's cost of capital is 15%?

   c. Which project should be selected if the firm's cost of capital is 12%?

•2. Academic Publishing is trying to decide which of two books to publish. The larger book will cost $100,000 to publish and print. Sales are expected to produce an annual profit of $32,000 for 5 years. The smaller book will cost $60,000 to publish and print, and should generate an annual profit of $20,000 for 5 years.

   a. Calculate the internal rate of return on each book. On the basis of their IRRs, which book should be published?

   b. Which book should be published if the firm's cost of capital is 17%?

   c. Which book should be published if the firm's cost of capital is 14%?

••3. Due to a restricted capital budget, a company can undertake only one of the following 3-year projects. Both require an initial investment of $650,000 and will have no significant terminal value. Project XXX is anticipated to have annual profits of $400,000, $300,000, and $200,000 in successive years, whereas Project YYY's only profit, $1.05 million, comes at the end of year 3.

   a. Calculate the IRR of each project. On the basis of their IRRs, which project should be selected?

   b. Which project should be selected if the firm's cost of capital is 14%?

   c. Which project should be selected if the firm's cost of capital is 11%?

••4. Two mutually exclusive projects each requires an initial investment of $50,000 and should have a residual value of $10,000 after 3 years. The following table presents their forecast annual profits.

Year	Project 1	Project 2
1	$10,000	$50,000
2	15,000	10,000
3	50,000	5000

a. Calculate the IRR of each project. On the basis of their IRRs, which project should be selected?

b. Which project should be selected if the firm's cost of capital is 14%?

c. Which project should be selected if the firm's cost of capital is 12%?

••5. A company is examining two mutually exclusive projects. Project X requires an immediate investment of $100,000 and produces no profit until year 3. Then the annual profit is $60,000 for years 3 to 5 inclusive. Project Y requires an investment of $50,000 now and another $50,000 in 1 year. It is expected to give annual profit of $40,000 in years 2 to 5.

a. Calculate the IRR of each project. On the basis of their IRRs, which project is preferred?

b. Which project should be selected if the firm's cost of capital is 15%?

c. Which project should be selected if the firm's cost of capital is 12%?

••6. A company is evaluating two mutually exclusive projects. Both require an initial investment of $240,000 and have no appreciable disposal value. Their expected profits over their 5-year lifetimes are as follows:

Year	Project Alpha	Project Beta
1	$140,000	$ 20,000
2	80,000	40,000
3	60,000	60,000
4	20,000	100,000
5	20,000	180,000

The company's cost of capital is 12%. Calculate the NPV and IRR for each project. Which project should be chosen? Why?

16.6 THE PAYBACK PERIOD

Many smaller firms still use the payback period as a measure of the attractiveness of a capital investment. The **payback period** is the number of years it takes to recover an initial investment outlay from the investment's future operating profits. For example, if an initial capital investment of $450,000 generates an annual profit of $100,000 for 10 years, it has a $4\frac{1}{2}$-year payback. A firm that uses this approach establishes a maximum payback period for an acceptable investment. Investment opportunities that have a payback period shorter than or equal to the maximum should be accepted.

The payback approach to investment selection has three serious shortcomings. The first is that the payback calculation ignores the time value of money—there is no discounting of the future cash flows. In the example above, $1 in year 5 is treated as having the same value as $1 of the initial investment. A second flaw is that the payback calculation ignores the profits and residual value that would be received beyond the maximum payback period. The third weakness is that the maximum acceptable payback period is set by the firm in a rather arbitrary manner without rigorous economic justification. The payback method is included in our coverage of investment decision criteria not because it has any great merit, but only because it is still widely used.

■ **EXAMPLE 16.6**   **CALCULATION OF THE PAYBACK PERIOD; COMPARISON OF DECISIONS BASED ON PAYBACK VERSUS NPV**

A firm is considering three independent projects. They all require the same initial investment of $90,000 and have no residual value after 8 years. All three generate the same aggregate total of profits ($160,000), but the profits are distributed differently over the 8-year period, as presented in the following table.

	Annual profit		
Year	Project A	Project B	Project C
1	$25,000	$20,000	$ 0
2	25,000	20,000	0
3	25,000	20,000	45,000
4	25,000	20,000	45,000
5	15,000	20,000	15,000
6	15,000	20,000	15,000
7	15,000	20,000	20,000
8	15,000	20,000	20,000

a. Which projects should be accepted if the firm has a 4-year payback requirement?

b. Which projects would be accepted on the NPV criterion if the firm's cost of capital is 14%?

☑ **SOLUTION**

a. To be accepted on the payback criterion, a project must have cumulative profits after 4 years that equal or exceed the original capital investment ($90,000). The following table presents the cumulative profits from the three projects at the end of each year.

	Cumulative profits		
Year	Project A	Project B	Project C
1	$ 25,000	$ 20,000	$ 0
2	50,000	40,000	0
3	75,000	60,000	45,000
4	100,000	80,000	90,000
5	115,000	100,000	105,000
6	130,000	120,000	120,000
7	145,000	140,000	140,000
8	160,000	160,000	160,000

Assuming that the profits accumulate uniformly within each year, the payback periods are:

$$\text{Project A:} \quad 3 + \frac{\$15,000}{\$25,000} = 3.6 \text{ years}$$

$$\text{Project B:} \quad 4 + \frac{\$10,000}{\$20,000} = 4.5 \text{ years}$$

$$\text{Project C:} \quad 4.0 \text{ years}$$

Projects A and C will be accepted because they recover the original investment within the 4-year payback period. Project B will be rejected on the same criterion.

b. The net present value of project A is

$$\begin{aligned} NPV_A &= \$25,000a_{\overline{4}|\,14\%} + \$15,000a_{\overline{4}|\,14\%}(1.14)^{-4} - \$90,000 \\ &= \$72,843 + \$25,877 - \$90,000 \\ &= \$8720 \end{aligned}$$

The net present value of project B is

$$NPV_B = \$20,000a_{\overline{8}|\,14\%} - \$90,000 = \$2777$$

The net present value of project C is

$$\begin{aligned} NPV_C &= \frac{\$45,000}{1.14^3} + \frac{\$45,000}{1.14^4} + \frac{15,000}{1.14^5} + \frac{\$15,000}{1.14^6} \\ &\quad + \frac{\$20,000}{1.14^7} + \frac{\$20,000}{1.14^8} - \$90,000 \\ &= \$30,374 + \$26,644 + \$7790 + \$6834 \\ &\quad + \$7993 + \$7011 - \$90,000 \\ &= -\$3354 \end{aligned}$$

Since projects A and B each has a positive NPV, they should be accepted. Project C, with a negative NPV, should be rejected.

Note: Since there is no fundamental economic rationale behind the payback period, we should not expect a high degree of consistency between investment decisions based on a payback period and decisions based on the NPV criterion. In this example project B was accepted based on its NPV but was rejected because its payback period exceeded 4 years. Conversely, project C failed to satisfy the NPV criterion but met the payback requirement. A general statement that can be made is that the shorter a project's payback period, the more likely it is to have a positive NPV.

Point of Interest

The Actual Use of Investment Criteria by Businesses

Discounted-cash-flow techniques—primarily the net present value (NPV) and internal rate of return (IRR) methods—started to be used by large corporations in the early 1950s. An early study concluded that, in 1955, only 9% of large American firms used some form of discounted-cash-flow analysis in making capital investment decisions.[9] A 1965 survey of 105 Canadian companies revealed that 30% of them employed a discounted-cash-flow method as their primary investment selection *(continued)*

[9]Alexander A. Robichek and James G. MacDonald, *Financial Management in Transition, Long-Range Planning Service,* Report no. 268 (Menlo Park, Calif.: Stanford Research Institute, 1966).

(*continued*)

criterion. Most of the others used the pay-back method or some other rule of thumb.[10]

The shift to increased usage of NPV and IRR techniques continued as more and more accounting and business school graduates were educated in discounted-cash-flow techniques. A 1976 survey of 99 Canadian corporations indicated that a small majority of large corporations were employing a discounted-cash-flow method as the primary standard for selecting capital investments.[11]

In 1985 Blazouske, Carlin, and Kim surveyed the chief financial officers of all the corporations listed in the *Financial Post* 500 industrials to determine the techniques used by large companies for choosing capital investments.[12] The corporations were asked, among other things, to indicate the primary and secondary methods they used in 1980 and in 1985 for evaluating investment projects. The responses received from 208 of the 500 Canadian companies are summarized in the following table.

Technique	Primary method 1980	Primary method 1985	Secondary method 1980	Secondary method 1985
IRR	38%	40%	7%	13%
NPV	22	25	10	11
Payback	25	19	41	44
Other method	12	13	11	12
No method used	3	3	31	20

The data indicate that the trend of the previous 3 decades to more widespread use of discounted-cash-flow methods continued between 1980 and 1985. The percentage of firms employing IRR or NPV as the primary selection criterion increased from 60% in 1980 to 65% in 1985. The proportion using payback or another method as the primary

basis dropped from 37% in 1980 to 32% in 1985.

It is noteworthy that, in 1985, 80% of the firms used more than one project evaluation technique and 63% used payback as either their primary or their secondary approach. These statistics raise two related questions: Why are multiple techniques used, since an investment's NPV seems to directly give what the firm needs to know? Why is the obviously flawed payback method still so widely used?

The answers lie partly in the uncertainty involved in forecasting the revenues and expenses associated with an investment. Particularly for new ventures, marketing and sales personnel tend to make overly optimistic sales projections. Therefore, investment decision makers commonly employ additional approaches to obtain confirmation of the results of the primary method. For example, a project with a small positive NPV is more likely to be undertaken if it has a 3-year payback period than if it has a 5-year payback. If two mutually exclusive investments have similar NPVs, the one with the shorter payback period will normally be preferred because the invested capital will be recovered more quickly. The faster-payback project is usually viewed as less risky because revenue and expenditure forecasts tend to be more reliable for earlier years than for later years.

Studies indicate that small firms use discounted-cash-flow techniques less extensively than large firms. L. R. Runyon conducted a study in the early 1980s of 214 firms whose owners' equity was in the $0.5 million to $1 million range.[13] He found that only 14% of them used a discounted-cash-flow approach. Almost 70% of these small companies relied on the payback method or some other seriously flawed technique. An-

(*continued*)

[10]J. T. Nicholson and J. D. Ffolliott, "Investment Evaluation Criteria of Canadian Companies," *Business Quarterly* (Summer 1966).

[11]Helen Baumgartner and V. Bruce Irvine, "A Survey of Capital Budgeting Techniques Used in Canadian Companies," *Cost and Management* (January–February 1977), pp. 51–55.

[12]J. D. Blazouske, I. Carlin, and S. H. Kim, "Current Capital Budgeting Practices in Canada," *CMA Magazine* (March 1988), pp. 51–54.

[13]L. R. Runyon, "Capital Expenditure Decision Making in Small Firms," *Journal of Business Research* (September 1983), pp. 389–97.

(*concluded*)

other 9% did not use any formal capital investment analysis at all!

Several factors contribute to the relatively low usage of discounted-cash-flow techniques by small firms for the analysis of investment projects. Three important ones are:

- Small firms are less likely to have individuals with the necessary financial skills to carry out an NPV or IRR analysis.

- For benefits beyond those already provided by a simple approach such as the payback method, the cost of a rigorous discounted-cash-flow analysis may not be justifiable for small capital investments.

- Since small projects and small firms typically face greater uncertainty in their cash flows, a greater emphasis on short-term cash flows and the payback period is often justified.

Differences exist across countries in the relative importance placed on the various capital investment criteria. For example, the payback method is more widely used in Japan than in Canada and the United States. A 1988 survey[14] of Japanese companies revealed that 47% still used a payback period as the primary investment criterion. Only 30% used either the NPV or the IRR criterion as the primary basis for investment decisions. Nevertheless, the trend in Japan is toward increased usage of discounted-cash-flow methods.

Where the payback method is used, comparative studies report that Japanese companies use a longer payback period as the cut-off point than American companies do. For example, a 1988 study[15] of firms in advanced manufacturing technologies found that 50% of Japanese companies used a maximum payback period of at least 4 years. Eighty-eight percent of U.S. companies used a shorter cutoff for payback.

EXERCISE 16.6

Answers to the odd-numbered problems are at the end of the book.

1. The expected profits from a $52,000 investment are $8000 in year 1, $12,000 in each of years 2 to 5, and $6000 in each of years 6 and 7.

    a. What is the investment's payback period?

    b. If the firm's required payback period is 4 years, will it make the investment?

2. A firm is considering the purchase of a $30,000 machine that would save labour costs of $5000 per year in the first 3 years and $6000 per year for the next 4 years. Will the firm purchase the machine if the payback requirement is:

    a. 5 years?   *b.* 6 years?

•3. Projects X and Y both require an initial investment of $100,000. Project X will generate an annual operating profit of $25,000 per year for 6 years. Project Y produces no profit in the first year but will yield an annual profit of $25,000 for the 7 subsequent years. Rank the projects based on their payback periods and on their NPVs (at a 10% cost of capital).

•4. A capital investment requiring a single initial cash outflow is forecast to have an operating profit of $50,000 per year for 5 years. There is no salvage value at the end of the 5 years. If the investment has an IRR of 17%, calculate its payback period.

---

[14]N. B. Gultekin and T. Taga, "Financial Management in Japanese Corporations," Working Paper, University of Pennsylvania, 1989.

[15]NAA Tokyo Affiliate, "Management Accounting in the Advanced Manufacturing Surrounding: Comparative Study on Survey in Japan and U.S.A.," 1988.

••5. Investment proposals A and B require initial investments of $45,000 and $35,000, respectively. Both have an economic life of 4 years with no residual value. Their expected profits are as follows:

Year	Proposal A	Proposal B
1	$16,250	$12,500
2	17,500	12,500
3	17,500	15,000
4	17,500	15,000

If the firm's cost of capital is 14%, rank the proposals based on their:

a. NPVs.   *b.* IRRs.   *c.* Payback periods.

REVIEW PROBLEMS

Answers to the odd-numbered review problems are at the end of the book.

•1. A manufacturer's sales rep can lease an automobile for 5 years at $385 per month payable at the beginning of each month, or purchase it for $22,500. He can obtain a loan at 9% compounded monthly to purchase the car. Should he lease or buy the car if:

 a. The trade-in value after 5 years is $5000?

 b. The trade-in value after 5 years is $7000?

••2. Jurgen Wiebe has been transferred to Winnipeg for 5 years. He has found an attractive house that he can buy for $150,000 or rent for $1150 per month, payable at the beginning of each month. He estimates that the resale value of the house in 5 years will be $175,000 net of the selling commission. If he buys the house, the average (end-of-month) costs for repairs, maintenance, and property taxes will be $300. Should Mr. Wiebe rent or buy the house if the interest rate on 5-year mortgage loans is 8.25% compounded monthly?

•3. A proposed open-pit mine would require the investment of $2 million at the beginning of the first year and a further investment of $1 million at the end of the first year. Mining operations are expected to yield annual profits of $750,000, beginning in year 2. The ore body will sustain 8 years of ore extraction. At the beginning of the 10th year, the mining company must spend $1 million on cleanup and environmental restoration. Will the project provide the mining company with a rate of return exceeding its 16% cost of capital?

•4. The development of a new product will require the expenditure of $125,000 at the beginning of each of the next 2 years. When the product reaches the market in year 3, it is expected to increase the firm's annual profit by $50,000 for 8 years. (Assume that the profit is received at the end of each year.) Then $75,000 of the original expenditures should be recoverable. If the firm's cost of capital is 14%, should it proceed with the project?

••5. A new machine that will lead to savings in labour costs of $20,000 per year can be purchased for $60,000. However, it will cost $2000 per year for the first 4 years and $3000 per year for the next 4 years to service and maintain the machine. In addition, its annual fuel consumption will cost $1500. After a service life of 8 years, the salvage value of the machine is expected to be $10,000. Should the machine be acquired if the company requires a minimum annual rate of return on investment of 15%?

•6. The investment committee of a company has identified the following seven projects with positive NPVs. If the board of directors has approved a $4.5 million capital budget for the current period, which projects should be selected?

Project	Initial investment	NPV
1	$1,125,000	$428,000
2	2,700,000	486,000
3	675,000	170,000
4	375,000	30,000
5	1,500,000	900,000
6	225,000	32,000
7	900,000	405,000

•7. Machine X costs $50,000 and is forecast to generate an annual profit of $16,000 for 5 years. Machine Y, priced at $72,000, will produce the same annual profits for 10 years.

The trade-in value of X after 5 years is expected to be $10,000, and the resale value of Y after 10 years is also thought to be $10,000. If either machine satisfies the firm's requirements, which one should be selected? Use a required return of 14%.

•8. A U-Print store requires a new photocopier. A Sonapanic copier with a 4-year service life costs $35,000 and will generate an annual profit of $14,000. A higher-speed Xorex copier with a 5-year service life costs $43,500 and will return an annual profit of $17,000. Neither copier will have significant salvage value. If U-Print's cost of capital is 16%, which model should be purchased?

•9. The provincial government's Ministry of Fisheries requires a new patrol boat. The price of a Songster is $45,000, and its annual operating costs will be $5000. It will be sold for about $10,000 after 5 years, and replaced. A more durable and more efficient Boston Wailer, priced at $55,000, would cost $4000 per year to operate, last 7 years, and have a resale value of $20,000. If the provincial government pays an interest rate of 8% compounded annually on its midterm debt, which boat has the lower equivalent annual cost?

10. A 7-year license to distribute a product should increase the distributor's profit by $18,000 per year. If the license can be acquired for $70,000, what is the investment's IRR?

•11. An investment of $300,000 will yield annual profits of $55,000 for 8 years. The proceeds on disposition of the investment at the end of the 8 years are estimated at $125,000. On the basis of its IRR and a 15% cost of capital, should the investment be made?

••12. A $500,000 capital investment will produce annual profits of $100,000 for the first 4 years and $150,000 for the next 4 years. It will have no residual value. What is its IRR? Should it be undertaken if the cost of capital is 15%?

••13. A company is examining two mutually exclusive projects. Project P requires an immediate investment of $225,000 and produces no profit until the fourth year. Then the expected annual profit is $120,000 for years 4 to 7 inclusive. Project Q requires an investment of $225,000 now and is expected to generate an annual profit of $55,000 in years 1 to 7. Neither project has any residual value after 7 years.

   a. Calculate the IRR of each project. On the basis of their IRRs, which project is preferred?

   b. Which project should be selected if the firm's cost of capital is 16%?

   c. Which project should be selected if the firm's cost of capital is 13%?

14. The expected profits from an $80,000 investment are $15,000 in year 1 and $20,000 in each of years 2 to 7.

   a. What is the investment's payback period?

   b. If a firm's required payback period is 4 years, will it make the investment?

   c. If the firm's cost of capital is 14%, will it make the investment?

SELF-TEST EXERCISE

Answers to the self-test problems are at the end of the book.

•1. Rainbow Aviation needs an additional plane for 5 years. It could buy the plane for $180,000, using funds borrowed at 11.25% compounded monthly and then sell the plane for an estimated $70,000 after 5 years. Alternatively, it could lease the plane for $2800, payable at the beginning of each month. Which alternative should Rainbow Aviation choose? What is the economic value of the financial advantage on the initial date of the preferred alternative?

•2. Huron Charters can purchase a sailboat for $50,000 down and a $30,000 payment due in 1 year. The boat would generate additional annual operating profits of $12,000 for the first 5 years and $15,000 for the next 5 years. New sails costing $8000 would be required after 5 years. After 10 years the boat would be replaced; its resale value would be about $30,000. Should Huron purchase the sailboat if its cost of capital is 15% compounded annually?

•3. A company's board of directors has imposed an $800,000 limit on capital spending for the current year. Management has identified the following five projects as all providing a return on investment greater than the cost of capital. Which projects should be chosen?

Project	Initial investment	NPV
A	$200,000	$ 63,000
B	400,000	100,000
C	350,000	90,000
D	250,000	75,000
E	100,000	20,000

•4. A company is considering two mutually exclusive investment projects. Each requires an initial investment of $25,000. Project A will generate an annual profit of $6000 for 8 years and have a residual value of $5000. Project B's profits are more irregular: $15,000 in the first year, $19,000 in the fifth year, and $24,000 (including the residual value) in the eighth year. Which project should be chosen if the required return on investment is 18% compounded annually?

••5. A firm can manufacture the same product with either of two machines. Machine C requires an initial investment of $55,000 and would earn a profit of $30,000 per year for 3 years. It would then be replaced, because repairs would be required too frequently after 3 years. Its trade-in value would be $10,000. Machine D costs $100,000 and would have a service life of 5 years. The annual profit would be $5000 higher than machine C's profit because of its lower repair and maintenance costs. Its recoverable value after 5 years would be about $20,000. Which machine should be purchased if the firm's cost of capital is 16%? What is the average annual economic advantage of the preferred choice?

•6. A potato farmer needs to buy a new harvester. Two types have performed satisfactorily in field trials. The SpudFinder costs $70,000 and should last for 5 years. The simpler TaterTaker costs only $40,000 but requires an extra operator at $10,000 per season. This machine has a service life of 7 years. The disposal value of either machine is insignificant. If the farmer requires a 13% return on investment, which harvester should she buy?

•7. A capital investment requiring one initial cash outflow is forecast to have the operating profits listed below. The investment has an NPV of $20,850, based on a required rate of return of 12%. Calculate the payback period of the investment.

Year	Operating profit
1	$74,000
2	84,000
3	96,000
4	70,000

••8. The introduction of a new product will require a $400,000 investment in demonstration models, promotion, and staff training. The new product will increase annual profits by $100,000 for the first 4 years and $50,000 for the next 4 years. There will be no significant recoverable amounts at the end of the 8 years. The firm's cost of capital is 13%. Calculate the expected IRR on the proposed investment in the new product. Should the new product be introduced? Why?

•9. The initial investment and expected profits from two mutually exclusive capital investments being considered by a firm are as follows:

	Investment A	Investment B
Initial investment	$70,000	$65,000
Year 1 profit	30,000	50,000
Year 2 profit	80,000	50,000

a. Calculate the internal rate of return for each investment. Which one would be selected based on an IRR ranking?

b. Which investment should be chosen if the firm's cost of capital is 14%?

c. Which investment should be chosen if the firm's cost of capital is 17%?

SUMMARY OF NOTATION AND KEY FORMULAS

NPV = Net present value (of an investment)
IRR = Internal rate of return (of an investment)

The following relationships and criteria were developed in the chapter.

$$\text{Value added to the firm} = \text{Present value of the future net cash flows} - \text{Required initial investment}$$

$$\text{NPV} = \text{Present value of cash inflows} - \text{Present value of cash outflows}$$

NPV Investment Criterion:

Accept the investment if NPV $\geq$ 0.
Reject the investment if NPV $<$ 0.

IRR Investment Criterion:

Accept the investment if IRR $\geq$ Cost of capital.
Reject the investment if IRR $<$ Cost of capital.

GLOSSARY OF TERMS

Capital rationing   The circumstance in which there is a limit on the total amount of capital funds that a firm may invest during a period.

Cost of capital   The average of the rates of return required by a firm's various sources of financing.

Internal rate of return   The discount rate that makes the net present value of all an investment's cash flows equal to zero.

Mutually exclusive projects   Alternative capital investments, any one of which will substantially satisfy the same need or purpose.

Net present value   The present value of cash inflows minus the present value of cash outflows.

Payback period   The number of years it will take to recover an initial investment outlay from the investment's future operating profits.

*17 DEPRECIATION AND DEPLETION

LEARNING OBJECTIVES

After completing this chapter, you will be able to:

- Prepare asset depreciation schedules based on the:
  Straight-line method
  Units-of-production method
  Service-hours method
  Double-declining-balance method
  Capital-cost-allowance method
  Complex declining-balance method
  Sum-of-the-years'-digits method

- Calculate the depreciation expense and year-end book value for any year of a declining-balance method without working through the depreciation schedule

- Prepare a depletion schedule for a natural resource–based asset

INTRODUCTION

The market value of most machinery, vehicles, equipment, and physical plant declines with use and with the passage of time. It is important in business to recognize this decline in the value of physical assets for two reasons. The first is to present realistic values of the assets in the firm's financial statements. The second is to convert the reduction in the value of an asset during an accounting period to an operating expense of that period. **Depreciation** is an accounting procedure by which the recorded or book value of an asset is reduced during its projected lifetime in a systematic and rational manner.

Companies that own and extract natural resources consume their resource bases over time. **Depletion** is an accounting procedure by which the recorded value of a resource-based asset is reduced during its projected lifetime in a systematic and rational manner.

Depreciation and depletion procedures involve both computing the depreciation and depletion amounts, and making the appropriate accounting entries. This chapter considers only the mathematics of depreciation and depletion.

17.1 DEPRECIATION CONCEPTS AND DEFINITIONS

The **service life** or **useful life** of an asset is the expected length of time that the asset will be used in the operations of the business. The amount that is expected to be recovered upon the sale or disposal of the asset at the end of its service life is called the **salvage value** or **residual value.** The difference between the cost of acquiring the asset and its salvage value should be reported as part of the business's operating expenses during the asset's service life.

The key issue in depreciation is establishing the basis for allocating an asset's total depreciation to the accounting periods during its service life. Later sections in this chapter discuss a few methods that are approved under Generally Accepted Accounting Principles (GAAP). These methods are classified in Figure 17.1 according to the basis used to allocate the depreciation to successive accounting periods. In principle, the method chosen for any particular asset should be the one that best reflects the actual pattern of decline in the market value of the asset.

Depreciation methods may first be classified according to whether the decline in value of an asset tends to be proportional to the amount of use, or to result primarily from the passage of time. Machinery for which wear and tear on moving parts is the main cause of deterioration would fall in the first category. Equipment for which obsolescence is the prime cause of diminishing value would be in the second group.

For assets whose value depends primarily on age, two patterns are recognized for the reduction in value over time. If there is a *steady* decline in value, *straight-line depreciation* is used. But many assets lose a disproportionate amount of their value early in their service life. Automobiles are a prime example of an asset that exhibits such *accelerated depreciation.* In these cases, a systematic method is needed for allocating diminishing dollar amounts of depreciation to successive accounting periods.

A table presenting details of the depreciation expense allocated to each accounting period, and the asset's diminishing value at the end of successive periods, is called a **depreciation schedule.** Typical headings for a depreciation schedule are presented in Figure 17.2.

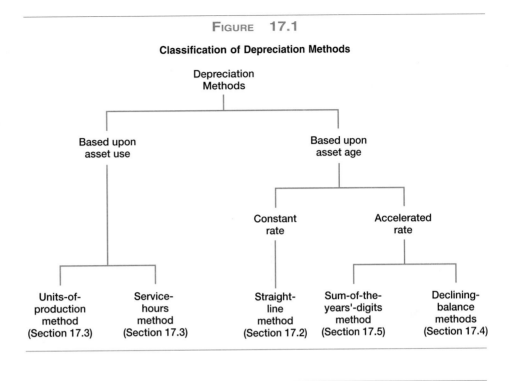

FIGURE   17.1

Classification of Depreciation Methods

FIGURE   17.2

Column Headings for a Depreciation Schedule

Period or year	Depreciation expense	Accumulated depreciation	Book value

The **depreciation expense** is the reduction in the value of the asset during the period. The depreciation expense will appear on the firm's income statement for the current period as one of the operating expenses. The **accumulated depreciation** is the cumulative total of all past and current depreciation expenses reported for the asset. An asset's **book value** at any point in its service life is its original cost minus the accumulated depreciation. That is,

$$\text{Book value} = \text{Acquisition cost} - \text{Accumulated depreciation}$$

The book value at the end of any accounting period will also equal the asset's book value at the end of the previous period less the current period's depreciation expense. That is,

$$\text{Book value} = \text{Previous book value} - \text{Current depreciation expense}$$

17.2 STRAIGHT-LINE DEPRECIATION

The *straight-line depreciation method* assumes that the asset's value declines by the *same dollar amount* in every period of its service life. Therefore, an equal portion of the asset's total lifetime depreciation is allocated to each accounting period.

Straight-Line Depreciation

$$\frac{\text{Depreciation}}{\text{per period}} = \frac{\text{Acquisition cost} - \text{Residual value}}{\text{Total number of periods in the service life}} \qquad (17-1)$$

■ **EXAMPLE 17.2** *PREPARATION OF A DEPRECIATION SCHEDULE USING STRAIGHT-LINE DEPRECIATION*

A manufacturing business bought a new machine for $35,000. The machine's market value is expected to decline steadily until it is sold for about $4000 after 5 years. Using the straight-line depreciation method:

a. Calculate the annual depreciation expense.

b. Prepare the depreciation schedule.

☑ **SOLUTION**

a. $\text{Annual depreciation expense} = \dfrac{\text{Acquisition cost} - \text{Residual value}}{\text{Service life}}$

$$= \frac{\$35,000 - \$4000}{5}$$

$$= \$6200$$

b. Straight-line depreciation schedule:

Year	Depreciation expense	Accumulated depreciation	Book value
0	—	—	$35,000
1	$ 6200	$ 6200	28,800
2	6200	12,400 ①	22,600 ②
3	6200	18,600	16,400
4	6200	24,800	10,200
5	6200	31,000	4000
	$31,000		

① Accumulated depreciation = Accumulated depreciation at end of previous year
  + Current year's depreciation expense
  = $6200 + $6200
  = $12,400

② Book value = Acquisition cost − Accumulated depreciation
  = $35,000 − $12,400
  = $22,600

or

  Book value = Book value at end of previous year
    − Current year's depreciation expense
  = $28,800 − $6200
  = $22,600

■

EXERCISE 17.2

Answers to the odd-numbered problems are at the end of the book.

In all problems, round the periodic depreciation expense to the nearest dollar.

•1. Equipment costing $48,000 is expected to have a scrap value of $2000 after 7 years of use. Use straight-line depreciation to:

a. Calculate the annual depreciation expense rounded to the nearest dollar.

b. Construct a depreciation schedule.

•2. Office furniture acquired at a cost of $19,700 is expected to be replaced in 6 years, at which time its residual value will be about $2000. Based on straight-line depreciation:

    a. Calculate the semiannual depreciation expense.

    b. Construct a partial depreciation schedule showing the last four semiannual periods.

3. Even though a new machine acquired at a cost of $95,000 is physically capable of being used for 10 years, it is expected to be replaced by more efficient machinery after 6 years. The resale value in 6 years is estimated to be $17,000. Using the straight-line depreciation method:

    a. Calculate the depreciation expense that will be claimed in the fourth year.

    b. Calculate the book value of the machine at the end of the fourth year.

•4. A brewery installed four new fermentation tanks at a total capital cost of $386,000. The tanks have an expected service life of 20 years, after which their salvage value will be approximately $25,000. If the straight-line method is used to depreciate the tanks:

    a. What depreciation expense will be reported on the tanks in the quarterly financial statements?

    b. What will be the book value of the tanks after 12 years?

    c. In what quarter will the book value first drop below $100,000?

17.3 UNITS-OF-PRODUCTION AND SERVICE-HOURS METHODS

Suppose the decline in value of an asset is roughly proportional to its use in the operations of the business. It is then logical to allocate the lifetime depreciation based on the fraction of the expected lifetime units of use[1] "consumed" in each accounting period. The unit of use for manufacturing equipment might be a unit of output or an hour of operation. For a vehicle, the unit of use might be 1 hour of operation or 100 km travelled.

Depreciation per Unit of Use

$$\text{Depreciation per unit of use} = \frac{\text{Acquisition cost} - \text{Residual value}}{\text{Total lifetime units of use}} \qquad (17\text{--}2)$$

The depreciation expense allocated to a particular accounting period will be the depreciation per unit multiplied by the number of units of use consumed during the period. That is,

$$\text{Depreciation expense} = \frac{\text{Depreciation}}{\text{per unit}} \times \frac{\text{Number of units of use}}{\text{during the period}}$$

If the unit of use is a unit of output, the method is called the *units-of-production method.* If the unit of use is an hour of operation, the procedure is often called the *service-hours method.*

These methods will result in depreciation amounts that are close to those obtained by the straight-line method if the asset is used a similar amount in each period. Because of its simplicity, the straight-line method tends to be employed in such cases unless the use of the asset varies substantially from one accounting period to the next.

---

[1]The total lifetime units of use will be an estimate based, for example, on previous experience, or on specifications supplied by the asset's manufacturer.

■ EXAMPLE 17.3A *A DEPRECIATION SCHEDULE BASED ON THE UNITS-OF-PRODUCTION METHOD*

Smith Transport Ltd. purchased a new truck for $170,000. Smith Transport usually replaces trucks after they have accumulated 250,000 km. The estimated resale value of this truck with 250,000 km on it is $30,000.

a. Calculate the depreciation per 100 km travelled.

b. Construct a depreciation schedule for the first 4 years if the distance driven in successive years is 47,500 km, 56,800 km, 67,100 km, and 43,300 km.

☑ SOLUTION

a. A unit of use is 100 km travelled. The useful service life is 250,000 km, which represents

$$\frac{250,000 \text{ km}}{100 \text{ km per unit}} = 2500 \text{ lifetime units}$$

$$\begin{aligned} \text{Depreciation per unit of use} &= \frac{\text{Acquisition cost} - \text{Residual value}}{\text{Total lifetime units of use}} \\ &= \frac{\$170,000 - \$30,000}{2500} \\ &= \$56 \text{ per 100 km travelled} \end{aligned}$$

b. Depreciation schedule:

Year	Units of use	Depreciation expense	Accumulated depreciation	Book value
0	—	—	—	$170,000
1	475	$26,600①	$ 26,600	143,400
2	568	31,808②	58,408③	111,592④
3	671	37,576	95,984	74,016
4	433	24,248	120,232	49,768
		$120,232		

① Depreciation expense = Number of units of use × Depreciation per unit of use
= 475($56)
= $26,600
② Depreciation expense = 568($56) = $31,808
③ Accumulated depreciation = Accumulated depreciation at end of previous period
+ Current year's depreciation expense
= $26,600 + $31,808
= $58,408
④ Book value = Acquisition cost − Accumulated depreciation
= $170,000 − $58,408
= $111,592   ■

■ EXAMPLE 17.3B *A DEPRECIATION SCHEDULE BASED ON THE SERVICE-HOURS METHOD*

Suppose that, in Example 17.3A, the service life of the truck is based on the hours of operation instead of the distance travelled. (This might be more appropriate if the truck is driven on difficult roads as well as on open highways.) If the useful service life of the truck is 3500 operating hours:

a. Calculate the depreciation per hour of operation.

b. Construct a depreciation schedule for the first 4 years if the hours of operation in successive years are 595, 710, 839, and 614.

☑ SOLUTION

a. The unit of use is an hour of truck operation. For a service life of 3500 hours, the depreciation expense per unit of use is:

$$\frac{\$170,000 - \$30,000}{3500} = \$40 \text{ per hour}$$

b. Depreciation schedule:

Year	Units of use	Depreciation expense	Accumulated depreciation	Book value
0	—	—	—	$170,000
1	595	$ 23,800①	$ 23,800	146,200
2	710	28,400②	52,200③	117,800④
3	839	33,560	85,760	84,240
4	614	24,560	110,320	59,680
		$110,320		

① Depreciation expense = 595($40) = $23,800
② Depreciation expense = 710($40) = $28,400
③ Accumulated depreciation = $23,800 + $28,400 = $52,200
④ Book value = $170,000 − $52,200 = $117,800   ∎

EXERCISE 17.3

Answers to the odd-numbered problems are at the end of the book.

In all problems, round each period's depreciation expense to the nearest dollar.

•1. An airline purchased a new passenger jet for $1,350,000. The airline will fly the jet for about 2 million air-miles and then sell it for an estimated $250,000.

a. Calculate the depreciation per 1000 air-miles.

b. Prepare a depreciation schedule for the first 4 years if the distance flown in successive years is 385,000, 463,000, 342,000, and 417,000 air-miles.

•2. Suppose that, in problem 1, the service life of the jet is based on the number of logged air-hours instead of the distance travelled. If the useful service life of the jet is 5000 air-hours,

a. Calculate the depreciation per air-hour.

b. Construct a depreciation schedule for the first 4 years if the air-hours logged in successive years are 962, 1134, 855, and 1083.

•3. When Precision Manufacturing purchased a milling machine for $73,000, Precision's chief engineer estimated that the machine would process 3500 units during its useful life and then have a resale value of about $10,000. The actual output in the first 4 years of operation was, in order, 637, 572, 749, and 802 units. Prepare a depreciation schedule for the first 4 years.

•4. Suppose that, in problem 3, the service life of the milling machine is based on the number of hours in operation instead of the number of units processed. Construct a depreciation schedule for the first 4 years if the useful service life is 7500 operating hours and the number of hours in use in successive years was 1265, 1046, 1621, and 1728.

17.4 DECLINING-BALANCE METHODS

An accelerated-depreciation method is commonly used when an asset's value is expected to diminish by larger dollar amounts in the earlier years than in the later years. The three declining-balance methods described in this section all produce accelerated depreciation. Section 17.5 presents a fourth accelerated-depreciation procedure.

With declining-balance methods of depreciation, each year's depreciation is a *fixed percentage* of the asset's book value at the end of the preceding year. This causes the dollar amount of depreciation to steadily diminish year after year as the same percentage depreciation rate is applied to the declining book value. The three methods described in this section differ in how the appropriate percentage depreciation rate is determined.

DOUBLE-DECLINING-BALANCE METHOD

In the double-declining-balance method, the (decimal equivalent of the) depreciation rate is calculated as follows:

Double-Declining-Balance Depreciation Rate

$$\begin{array}{c}\text{Depreciation rate} \\ \text{(per year)}\end{array} = 2 \times \frac{1}{\text{Service life of the asset (in years)}} \qquad (17\text{--}3)$$

The second factor may be viewed as the asset's straight-line depreciation rate if its salvage value is zero. The "double" in the name for this method comes from using a declining-balance depreciation rate that is twice the straight-line rate.

Figure 17.3 presents a comparison of the annual depreciation amounts and book values calculated by the straight-line and double-declining-balance methods. In both cases, the asset has an acquisition cost of $1000 and a service life of 5 years. The annual straight-line depreciation expense, assuming no salvage value, would be 20% of the acquisition cost. Under double-declining-balance depreciation, the amount of depreciation expense in any year is $(2 \times 20\%) = 40\%$ of the book value at the end of the previous year.

FIGURE   17.3

Comparison of Straight-Line and Double-Declining-Balance Methods of Depreciation

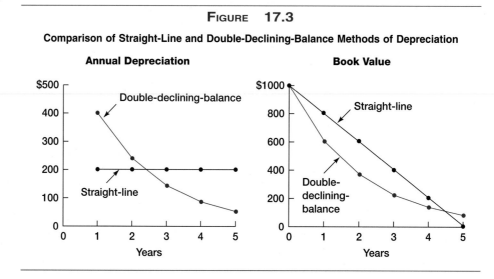

Compared to the straight-line method, the double-declining-balance method results in higher depreciation expense in the early years, but smaller depreciation expense in later years. Consequently, the book value declines more rapidly in the early years but less rapidly in later years under double-declining-balance depreciation. Similar conclusions would be reached from a comparison of this section's other two accelerated-depreciation methods to straight-line depreciation.

■ **EXAMPLE 17.4A** *A PARTIAL DEPRECIATION SCHEDULE BASED ON THE DOUBLE-DECLINING-BALANCE METHOD*

A company expects a machine that it purchased for $36,000 to be used for 10 years. Using the double-declining-balance method of depreciation:

a. Calculate the rate of depreciation.

b. Prepare a partial depreciation schedule showing details for the first 5 years. Round each year's depreciation expense to the nearest dollar.

☑ SOLUTION

a. For a 10-year service life,

$$\text{Depreciation rate} = 2 \times \frac{100\%}{10} = 20\%$$

b. Depreciation schedule:

Year	Depreciation expense	Accumulated depreciation	Book value
0	—	—	$36,000
1	$ 7200	$ 7200	28,800
2	5760①	12,960②	23,040③
3	4608	17,568	18,432
4	3686	21,254	14,746
5	2949	24,203	11,797
	24,203		

① Depreciation expense = Depreciation rate × Book value at end of previous year
= 0.20($28,800) = $5760
② Accumulated depreciation = $7200 + $5760 = $12,960
③ Book value = $28,800 − $5760 = $23,040 ■

CAPITAL-COST-ALLOWANCE METHOD

In calculating its taxable income for a fiscal year, a company can deduct from its revenues various business expenses allowed by Revenue Canada. Revenue Canada will not necessarily permit the deduction of the same depreciation expense that would be acceptable under GAAP in the business's financial statements.

Revenue Canada identifies about 40 classes of depreciable assets. For each class it specifies the *maximum* depreciation rate that may be used to calculate the annual depreciation expense deductible for income tax purposes. **Capital cost allowance** (CCA) is the term used for depreciation expense claimed for tax purposes. For the vast majority of asset classes, the capital cost allowance is calculated on a declining-balance basis. The prescribed CCA rate is applied to the undepreciated capital cost (book value) from the end of the previous period.

Table 17.1 lists the maximum CCA rates for six common asset classes.[2] Generally speaking, higher CCA rates are prescribed for assets that depreciate more rapidly. In the year of acquisition of the asset, only half of the prescribed rate may be used. This is known as the *half-rate rule* or *half-year rule.*

TABLE   17.1

Rates of Capital Cost Allowance

CCA class	Partial description	CCA rate (%)
3	Concrete, stone, and brick buildings	5
6	Frame, log, and corrugated iron buildings	10
7	Boats	15
8	Some types of machinery and equipment	20
10	Automobiles, trucks, buses, and computers	30
12	Most books and applications software	100

Sometimes an asset does not, in fact, depreciate as rapidly as the maximum prescribed CCA rate. In such cases, businesses commonly use the maximum CCA rate to maximize their tax-deductible expenses and minimize the income on which tax must be paid. The financial statements prepared for shareholders usually reflect a more realistic rate of depreciation.[3]

■ EXAMPLE 17.4B   *PREPARATION OF A PARTIAL CAPITAL-COST-ALLOWANCE SCHEDULE*

Reliable Plumbing purchased a new van for $20,000. The van is in CCA asset class 10 with a maximum CCA rate of 30%. Prepare a partial capital-cost-allowance schedule showing details for the first 4 years with the maximum CCAs taken.

☑ SOLUTION

Year	Capital cost allowance	Accumulated CCA	Undepreciated capital cost (book value)
0	—	—	$20,000
1	$ 3000①	$ 3000	17,000
2	5100②	8100③	11,900④
3	3570	11,670	8330
4	2499	14,169	5831
	$14,169		

---

① CCA in first year = (CCA rate/2)(Acquisition cost)
     = (0.30/2)($20,000) = $3000

② CCA in any subsequent year = CCA rate × Undepreciated capital cost
     at the end of the previous year
     = 0.30($17,000) = $5100

③ Accumulated CCA = Accumulated CCA at end of previous year
     + Current year's CCA
     = $3000 + $5100 = $8100

④ Undepreciated capital cost (book value) = Undepreciated capital cost at end of
     previous year − Current year's CCA
     = $17,000 − $5100 = $11,900

■

---

[2] A business may use any CCA rate up to the prescribed maximum.

[3] If the CCA rate is realistic for a particular asset, accountants will often use the CCA rate as the depreciation rate in the financial statements as well as in the calculation of taxable income.

COMPLEX DECLINING-BALANCE METHOD

The double-declining-balance depreciation rate and the CCA rate, presented in the preceding subsections, are determined without reference to an asset's residual or salvage value. A method that has more theoretical appeal is to determine the *compound* annual rate of *decrease* in value that will give the expected residual value at the end of the service life. This is an application of the compound growth ideas presented in Section 8.4.

We will use the symbols:

d = Annually compounded rate of depreciation
n = Number of years in the service life

The compound-interest formula $S = P(1 + i)^n$ may be used if we place the following interpretations on the variables.

P = Acquisition cost of the asset
$i = -d$ (since we have compound decline instead of compound growth)
S = Residual value of the asset after n years

Making these substitutions, we have

$$\text{Residual value} = \text{Acquisition cost} \times (1 - d)^n$$

Solving for d, we obtain

$$\frac{\text{Residual value}}{\text{Acquisition cost}} = (1 - d)^n$$

$$1 - d = \sqrt[n]{\frac{\text{Residual value}}{\text{Acquisition cost}}}$$

**Complex
Declining-Balance
Rate of
Depreciation**

$$\boxed{d = 1 - \sqrt[n]{\frac{\text{Residual value}}{\text{Acquisition cost}}}} \qquad (17\text{--}4)$$

Complex declining-balance depreciation is rarely used in actual practice. This is partly because of its seeming mathematical complexity, and partly because it gives very high—often unrealistically high—rates of depreciation when the residual value is a small fraction of the acquisition cost.

■ **EXAMPLE 17.4c**   *A DEPRECIATION SCHEDULE BASED ON THE COMPLEX DECLINING-BALANCE METHOD OF DEPRECIATION*

Custom Excavating purchased a new loader for $37,000. The firm expects to sell the loader for $10,000 in 4 years. Using the complex declining-balance method of depreciation:

a. Calculate the rate of depreciation.

b. Prepare the 4-year depreciation schedule.

✔ SOLUTION

a. Using formula (17−4),

$$\text{Depreciation rate, } d = 1 - \sqrt[n]{\frac{\text{Residual value}}{\text{Acquisition cost}}}$$

$$= 1 - \sqrt[4]{\frac{\$10{,}000}{\$37{,}000}}$$

$$= 1 - 0.2702703^{0.25}$$

$$= 1 - 0.7210237$$

$$= 0.2789763$$

$$= 27.89763\%$$

b. Depreciation schedule:

Year	Depreciation expense	Accumulated depreciation	Book value
0	—	—	$37,000.00
1	$10,322.12	$10,322.12	26,677.88
2	7442.50①	17,764.62②	19,235.38③
3	5366.21	23,130.83	13,869.17
4	3869.17	27,000.00	10,000.00
	$27,000.00		

① Depreciation expense = Depreciation rate × Book value at end of previous year
= 0.2789763 ($26,677.88)
= $7442.50
② Accumulated depreciation = $10,322.12 + $7442.50 = $17,764.62
③ Book value = $26,677.88 − $7442.50 = $19,235.38   ∎

DIRECT CALCULATION OF DEPRECIATION AND BOOK VALUE IN ANY YEAR

Suppose we wish to calculate the amount of depreciation expense for a particular year, or the book value at the end of the year. One approach would be to construct a depreciation schedule and complete the calculations through to the year of interest. This is a lengthy, tedious procedure, and an unnecessary one if we do not need the depreciation information for the prior years. We can instead develop formulas that permit the direct calculation of the depreciation expense and the book value. We will use the notation:

C = Acquisition cost of the asset
d = Rate of depreciation on the declining balance

The compound interest formula (8−2) may be used to calculate the asset's book value after t years of depreciation at the compound annual rate d.

$$\text{Book value} = C(1 - d)^t$$

The depreciation expense claimed in year t will be the book value at the end of year $(t - 1)$ multiplied by the depreciation rate, d. That is,

$$\text{Depreciation expense} = C(1 - d)^{t-1} \times d$$

In summary,

**Double-Declining-
Balance and
Complex
Declining-Balance
Methods**

> Book value at the end of year $t = C(1 - d)^t$
> Depreciation expense in year $t = dC(1 - d)^{t-1}$

(17–5)

where d is obtained using formula (17–3) for the double-declining-balance method or formula (17–4) for the complex declining-balance method.

Because of the half-rate rule in the capital-cost-allowance method, the depreciation rate in the first year is $d/2$ instead of d. Therefore, the first $(1 - d)$ factor in each of the formulas above must be changed to $(1 - d/2)$. That is,

**Capital Cost
Allowance Method**

> Book value at the end of year $t = C\left(1 - \dfrac{d}{2}\right)(1 - d)^{t-1}$
>
> Capital cost allowance in year $t = \left(\dfrac{d}{2}\right)C$ for $t = 1$
>
> $\qquad\qquad = dC\left(1 - \dfrac{d}{2}\right)(1 - d)^{t-2}$ for $t \geq 2$

(17–6)

■ **EXAMPLE 17.4D** *DIRECT CALCULATION OF THE DEPRECIATION EXPENSE AND BOOK VALUE IN ANY YEAR UNDER EACH OF THE THREE DECLINING-BALANCE METHODS*

A company purchased a machine for $120,000 and expects to use it for 10 years. The resale value after 10 years is estimated to be $15,000. The machine falls into CCA asset class 8.

a. Determine the rate of depreciation for each of the three declining-balance methods discussed in this section.

b. Prepare a table presenting the depreciation expense and the year-end book value for the first 3 years and the last 2 years, using formulas (17–5) and (17–6) for the three declining-balance methods discussed in this section. Round each year's depreciation expense or CCA and the book value to the nearest dollar.

✓ **SOLUTION**

a. Using formula (17–3) for the double-declining-balance method,

$$d = 2 \times \frac{1}{10 \text{ years}} = 0.2$$

For the CCA method, Table 17.1 gives a CCA rate of $d = 0.20\%$ for asset class 8. Using formula (17–4) for the complex declining-balance method,

$$d = 1 - \sqrt[10]{\frac{\$15,000}{\$120,000}}$$
$$= 1 - 0.125^{0.1}$$
$$= 1 - 0.8122524$$
$$= 0.1877476$$

This problem is designed so that the depreciation rates for the three methods are similar. Normally they would not be this close.

b. The following table provides a comparison of depreciation expenses and book values for the three declining-balance methods.

Year	Double-declining-balance method		Capital cost allowance method		Complex declining-balance method	
	Depreciation expense	Book value	CCA	Book value	Depreciation expense	Book value
0	—	$120,000	—	$120,000	—	$120,000
1	$ 24,000	96,000	$ 12,000④	108,000⑤	$ 22,530	97,470
2	19,200	76,800	21,600⑥	86,400⑦	18,300	79,170
3	15,360①	61,440②	17,280	69,120	14,864	64,306
.	.	.	.	.	.	.
.	.	.	.	.	.	.
.	.	.	.	.	.	.
9	4027	16,106	4530	18,119	4269⑧	18,467⑨
10	3221	12,885	3624	14,496	3467	15,000
	107,115③		105,504		105,000	

① Depreciation in year 3 $= dC(1 - d)^{3-1}$ Formula (17–5)
$$= 0.20(\$120,000)(1 - 0.20)^2$$
$$= \$15,360$$

② Book value, end of year 3 $= C(1 - d)^3$ Formula (17–5)
$$= \$120,000(1 - 0.20)^3$$
$$= \$61,440$$

③ Accumulated depreciation $= C -$ Book value
$$= \$120,000 - \$12,885$$
$$= \$107,115$$

④ CCA in year 1 $= \left(\dfrac{d}{2}\right)C$ Formula (17–6)
$$= \left(\dfrac{0.20}{2}\right)\$120,000$$
$$= \$12,000$$

⑤ Book value, end of year 1 $= C\left(1 - \dfrac{d}{2}\right)(1 - d)^{1-1}$ Formula (17–6)
$$= C\left(1 - \dfrac{d}{2}\right) \times 1$$
$$= \$120,000\left(1 - \dfrac{0.20}{2}\right)$$
$$= \$108,000$$

⑥ CCA in year 2 $= dC\left(1 - \dfrac{d}{2}\right)(1 - d)^{2-2}$
$$= 0.20(\$120,000)\left(1 - \dfrac{0.20}{2}\right) \times 1$$
$$= \$21,600$$

⑦ Book value, end of year 2 $= C\left(1 - \dfrac{d}{2}\right)(1 - d)^{2-1}$
$$= \$120,000(1 - 0.10)(1 - 0.20)$$
$$= \$86,400$$

⑧ Depreciation in year 9 $= dC(1 - d)^{9-1}$ Formula (17–5)
$$= 0.1877476(\$120,000)(1 - 0.1877476)^8$$
$$= \$4269$$

⑨ Book value, end of year 9 $= C(1 - d)^9$ Formula (17–5)
$$= \$120,000(1 - 0.2)^9$$
$$= \$18,467$$

Note: Where formulas (17–5) and (17–6) are used repeatedly to calculate depreciation and book value for a few years, time may be saved and the risk of computational error reduced by using the functions on a financial calculator, as demonstrated in the following table.

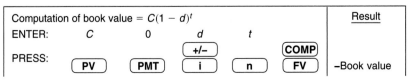

Computation of book value $= C(1 - d)^t$					Result
ENTER: C	0	d	t		
PRESS: PV	PMT	+/– i	n	COMP	–Book value

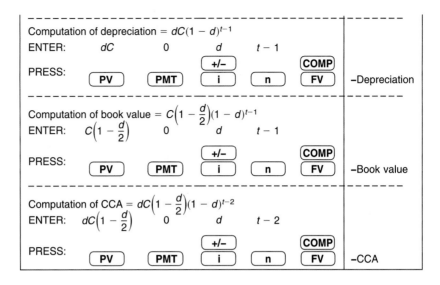

EXERCISE 17.4

Answers to the odd-numbered problems are at the end of the book.

In all problems below, round depreciation expense and book value to the nearest dollar.

••1. An accounting firm bought a computer workstation for $12,400. The firm expects that the station will be obsolete after 4 years, with a resale value of only $1500. The workstation is in CCA class 10, which has a CCA rate of 30% applied to the declining balance. Construct a depreciation schedule covering the 4 years and based on:

   a. The double-declining-balance method.

   b. The capital-cost-allowance method.

   c. The complex declining-balance method.

••2. A sawmill bought a $160,000 turbine for the generation of electrical power from wood waste. It is estimated that $15,000 will be recovered upon disposition of the turbine after a useful lifetime of 15 years. Electrical generating equipment is included in CCA class 2, with a declining-balance CCA rate of 6%. Calculate the depreciation expense and year-end book value for years 1, 8, and 15 based on:

   a. The double-declining-balance method.

   b. The capital-cost-allowance method.

   c. The complex declining-balance method.

••3. Trans-Continental Movers built a concrete block warehouse and truck repair centre in Winnipeg for $370,000. The building is likely to satisfy Trans-Continental's needs for the next 20 years, after which the resale value of the building is estimated to be $150,000. Concrete buildings belong in CCA class 3, which has a CCA rate of 5%. Calculate the amount of depreciation expense that will be claimed in each of the four successive 5-year periods if the depreciation method used is:

   a. The double-declining-balance method.

   b. The capital-cost-allowance method.

   c. The complex declining-balance method.

••4. For the concrete block building in problem 3, calculate the depreciation expense for the 10th year and the 20th year if the depreciation method used is:

a. The double-declining-balance method.

b. The capital-cost-allowance method.

c. The complex declining-balance method.

••5. Comeau Construction bought a trailer home to use as an office on its construction sites. Comeau paid $27,000 for the trailer and estimates that its residual value after a 12-year service life will be $5000. The trailer falls in CCA class 6, with a declining-balance CCA rate of 10%. Prepare a partial depreciation schedule showing details for years 1, 2, 3, 7, and 12 if the depreciation is based on:

a. The double-declining-balance method.

b. The capital-cost-allowance method.

c. The complex declining-balance method.

17.5 SUM-OF-THE-YEARS'-DIGITS METHOD

As with the declining-balance methods in Section 17.4, each year's depreciation expense based on the sum-of-the-years'-digits method is less than the previous year's depreciation. The pattern of diminishing depreciation expense results from the application of a *declining depreciation rate* to a *fixed cost base*. (In declining-balance methods, the pattern results from applying a *fixed depreciation rate* to a *declining cost base*.) With n again representing the service life in years, the formula for computing the percentage of the fixed cost base to be depreciated in year t is:

Sum-of-the-Years'-Digits Method

$$\text{Depreciation rate for year } t = \frac{n - t + 1}{n(n + 1)/2} \qquad (17\text{–}7)$$

The *fixed* cost base is:

$$\text{Cost base} = \text{Acquisition cost} - \text{Residual value}$$

The depreciation schedule for an asset with a 5-year service life, acquisition cost C, and no residual value is presented in the following table.

Year	Depreciation expense	Accumulated depreciation	Year-end book value
1	$\frac{5}{15}C$	$\frac{5}{15}C$	$\frac{10}{15}C$
2	$\frac{4}{15}C$	$\frac{9}{15}C$	$\frac{6}{15}C$
3	$\frac{3}{15}C$	$\frac{12}{15}C$	$\frac{3}{15}C$
4	$\frac{2}{15}C$	$\frac{14}{15}C$	$\frac{1}{15}C$
5	$\frac{1}{15}C$	$\frac{15}{15}C$	0

Notice that the denominator of formula (17–7) gives the sum of the serial numbers of the years in the service life. That is,

$$\frac{5(5 + 1)}{2} = 15 = 1 + 2 + 3 + 4 + 5$$

This is the reason for the name "sum-of-the-years'-digits method." Also note that the numerators given by formula (17−7) are the individual years' serial numbers in reverse order.

This method results in an accelerated depreciation. Remember that each year's depreciation is based on the difference between the acquisition cost and the residual value, not on the declining book value. Although the method is accepted under GAAP, it is seldom used in practice.

■ EXAMPLE 17.5   *A DEPRECIATION SCHEDULE USING THE SUM-OF-THE-YEARS'-DIGITS METHOD*

A company bought a machine for $120,000 and expects to use it for 10 years. The resale value after 10 years is estimated to be $15,000. Using the sum-of-the-years'-digits method of depreciation, prepare the depreciation schedule. Include a column for the depreciation rate used each year. (The schedule can be compared with the table in Example 17.4D, where the same machine was depreciated by the three declining-balance methods.)

☑ SOLUTION

The depreciation rate for year t is

$$\frac{n - t + 1}{n(n + 1)/2} = \frac{10 - t + 1}{10(11)/2} = \frac{11 - t}{55}$$

The fixed cost base is

$$\$120,000 - \$15,000 = \$105,000$$

The depreciation schedule is shown below.

Year	Depreciation rate	Depreciation expense	Accumulated depreciation	Book value
0	—	—	—	$120,000
1	10/55	$ 19,091	$ 19,091	100,909
2	9/55①	17,182②	36,273③	83,727④
3	8/55	15,273	51,546	68,454
4	7/55	13,364	64,910	55,090
5	6/55	11,455	76,365	43,635
6	5/55	9545	85,910	34,090
7	4/55	7636	93,546	26,454
8	3/55	5727	99,273	20,727
9	2/55	3818	103,091	16,909
10	1/55	1909	105,000	15,000
	55/55	$105,000		

① Depreciation rate $(t = 2) = \dfrac{11 - 2}{55} = \dfrac{9}{55}$

② Depreciation expense = Depreciation rate × Cost base

$\qquad = \dfrac{9}{55} \times \$105,000$

$\qquad = \$17,182$

③ Accumulated depreciation = $19,091 + $17,182 = $36,273

④ Book value = Previous book value − Depreciation expense

$\qquad = \$100,909 - \$17,182$

$\qquad = \$83,727$

■

EXERCISE 17.5

Answers to the odd-numbered problems are at the end of the book.

In all problems, round depreciation expense and book value to the nearest dollar.

•1. Equipment costing $48,000 is expected to have negligible scrap value after 7 years of use. Use the sum-of-the-years'-digits method of depreciation to construct a depreciation schedule.

•2. Office furniture acquired at a cost of $19,700 is expected to be replaced in 6 years, when its resale value will be about $2000. Based on sum-of-the-years'-digits depreciation, construct a depreciation schedule for the furniture.

•3. Do problem 1 of Exercise 17.4 using the sum-of-the-years'-digits method of depreciation.

•4. For the turbine described in problem 2 of Exercise 17.4, prepare a partial depreciation schedule for the first 4 years, based on the sum-of-the-years'-digits method.

17.6 DEPLETION

Most of the expenditures made by a firm in the exploration and development of a resource property are not treated as business expenses of the period when incurred. Instead, they are accumulated and reported as part of the value of a resource-based asset on the firm's balance sheet. Later, as the resource is extracted, the asset value is systematically reduced. The reduction in asset value calculated for an accounting period becomes an operating expense (called the *depletion expense*) in the period.

The depletion method most commonly used is the *units-of-production method.* It is a similar idea to the units-of-production method of depreciating a fixed asset. To obtain the depletion charge per extracted unit of the resource, the original total of the exploration and development costs, less any residual value when extraction is completed, is divided by the total estimated reserves.

Depletion Charge per Unit Produced

$$\text{Depletion per unit} = \frac{\text{Total original costs} - \text{Residual value}}{\text{Total estimated units of reserves}} \quad (17\text{–}8)$$

Then the depletion charge for an accounting period is the number of units produced during the period multiplied by the unit depletion charge. That is,

$$\text{Depletion charge} = \frac{\text{Depletion charge}}{\text{per unit}} \times \frac{\text{Number of}}{\text{units produced}}$$

The effect of this procedure is to prorate the original exploration and development costs to the portion of the total reserves extracted in an accounting period.

■ EXAMPLE 17.6   *A DEPLETION SCHEDULE BASED ON THE UNITS-OF-PRODUCTION METHOD*

North Star Resources Ltd. spent $1.3 million to explore and prove a 480,000-tonne gold-bearing ore body. Then it spent $4.9 million to develop a mine and mill at the site. When the reserves are depleted, North Star should be able to recover about $800,000 from the sale of the mine and mill equipment. Prepare a depletion schedule for the first 4 years of operation if the tonnage of extracted ore in successive years was 22,300, 31,500, 36,100, and 34,800 tonnes.

☑ SOLUTION

$$\text{Total exploration and development costs} = \$1.3 \text{ million} + \$4.9 \text{ million}$$
$$= \$6.2 \text{ million}$$
$$\text{Depletion charge per tonne of ore mined} = \frac{\$6,200,000 - \$800,000}{480,000}$$
$$= \$11.25$$

The depletion schedule is shown below.

Year	Units produced	Depletion expense	Accumulated depletion	Book value
0	—	—	—	$6,200,000
1	22,300	$ 250,875	$ 250,875	5,949,125
2	31,500	354,375①	605,250②	5,594,750③
3	36,100	406,125	1,011,375	5,188,625
4	34,800	391,500	1,402,875	4,797,125
		$1,402,875		

① Depletion expense = Depletion charge per tonne × Year's output tonnage
= $11.25(31,500)
= $354,375
② Accumulated depletion
= Current depletion expense + Accumulated depletion at end of previous year
= $354,375 + $250,875
= $605,250
③ Book value = Book value at end of previous year − Current depletion expense
= $5,949,125 − $354,375
= $5,594,750

■

Exercise 17.6

Answers to the odd-numbered problems are at the end of the book.

•1. Gibraltar Mines purchased a proven 3.5-million-tonne copper ore body from Nu-West Resources for $24,000,000. Gibraltar then built a mine and smelter on the site at a cost of $18 million. The salvage value of the mine and refinery will only be sufficient to restore the site to required environmental standards when the ore body is exhausted. Construct a depletion schedule for the first 4 years of operation if the amount of ore processed in successive years was 55,300, 63,200, 68,100, and 59,500 tonnes.

•2. MacMillan Forest Products purchased the timber harvesting rights to a tract of crown land for $4,000,000. A survey showed that the amount of recoverable wood was 250,000 cubic metres. To haul out the logs, the company had to build logging roads costing $1,750,000. There is no residual value in the project. Prepare the depletion schedule for the first 4 years of logging if the volume harvested in successive years was 26,800, 38,900, 54,100, and 61,600 cubic metres.

•3. It cost Canoco Oil $400,000 to buy the oil exploration rights in an area, $775,000 to explore and prove oil reserves of 250,000 barrels, and $1,800,000 to drill and bring two wells into production. When the reserves are exhausted, the residual value of the equipment is expected to be $200,000. Prepare a depletion schedule for the first 4 years of operation if the oil production in successive years was 9550, 14,420, 13,780, and 15,130 barrels.

•4. Dominion Coal Co. paid $500,000 for the mineral rights on a property, $1,200,000 for geological survey and exploration work, and $4.2 million to build a mine on the site. The coal reserves were originally estimated at 1,250,000 tonnes. Dominion expects to recover $400,000 from the disposal of mine equipment when the coal is depleted. Construct a depletion schedule for the first 4 years of operation if the amount of coal mined in successive years was 31,400, 45,600, 42,900, and 39,500 tonnes.

REVIEW PROBLEMS

Answers to the odd-numbered problems are at the end of the book.

In all problems, round depreciation or depletion expense and book value to the nearest dollar.

•1. Although a new assembly machine acquired at a cost of $135,000 is physically capable of being used for 7 years, it is expected to be replaced by a more efficient machine after 5 years. The resale value in 5 years is estimated to be $30,000. Using the straight-line depreciation method,

   a. Calculate the depreciation expense that will be claimed in the fourth year.

   b. Calculate the book value of the machine at the end of the fourth year.

•2. When Trident Manufacturing bought a grinding machine for $43,000, Trident's chief engineer estimated that the machine would process 5000 units during its useful life and then have a resale value of about $5000. The actual throughput in the first 4 years of operation was, in order, 850, 610, 725, and 685 units. Prepare a depreciation schedule for the first 4 years.

••3. A dairy farmer installed new milking parlour and refrigeration equipment for $80,000. It is estimated that $10,000 can be recovered upon disposition of the equipment after a useful lifetime of 10 years. Dairy equipment falls in CCA class 8, with a declining-balance CCA rate of 20%. Calculate the depreciation expense and year-end book value for years 1, 5, and 10 based on:

   a. The double-declining-balance method.

   b. The capital-cost-allowance method.

   c. The complex declining-balance method.

•4. Equipment costing $60,000 is expected to have negligible scrap value after 5 years of use. Use the sum-of-the-years'-digits method of depreciation to construct a depreciation schedule.

••5. Four years ago Dofasco purchased an electric furnace for $800,000. The furnace's manufacturer stated that the furnace should have a service life of 2000 batches or 6000 hours of operation. In any event, Dofasco expected to replace the furnace after 4 years for a salvage value of about $50,000. The furnace's CCA class has a declining-balance CCA rate of 25%. The numbers of batches of steel processed in the 4 successive years were 438, 527, 489, and 390. The hours of use in those years were 1210, 1545, 1440, and 1160, respectively. Prepare a depreciation schedule for the 4 years based on:

   a. The straight-line method.

   b. The units-of-production method.

   c. The service-hours method.

   d. The double-declining-balance method.

   e. The capital-cost-allowance method.

   f. The complex declining-balance method.

   g. The sum-of-the-years'-digits method.

•6. Dominion Paving purchased a gravel pit, including the necessary extraction and crushing equipment, for $850,000. It is estimated that 100,000 tonnes of gravel can be recovered from the pit. The pit and equipment are not expected to have any significant resale value when the gravel is depleted. Prepare a depletion schedule for the first 4 years of operation if the amount of gravel removed in successive years was 10,400, 14,300, 16,900, and 11,200 tonnes.

SELF-TEST EXERCISE

Answers to the self-test problems are at the end of the book.

In all problems, round depreciation or depletion expense and book value to the nearest dollar.

••1. Four years ago General Motors of Canada bought a welding robot for an automobile assembly line for $90,000. The robot's manufacturer stated that the robot should have a service life of 10,000 cars or 5000 hours of operation. In any event, GM expected to replace the robot after 4 years for an estimated trade-in value of about $15,000. The robot's CCA class has a declining-balance CCA rate of 30%. The number of cars welded in the 4 successive years were 2153, 2439, 2645, and 2380. The hours of use in those years were 1113, 1278, 1309, and 1247, respectively. Prepare a depreciation schedule for the 4 years based on:

   a. The straight-line method.

   b. The units-of-production method.

   c. The service-hours method.

   d. The double-declining-balance method.

   e. The capital-cost-allowance method.

   f. The complex declining-balance method.

   g. The sum-of-the-years'-digits method.

•2. Maritime Shipping purchased a new tugboat for $330,000. Its estimated service life is 15 years, after which its salvage value will be roughly $30,000. Tugs are in CCA asset class 7, with a declining-balance CCA rate of 15%. Calculate the depreciation expense claimed for the first and seventh years of ownership, and the book value at the end of the ninth year, based on:

   a. The straight-line method.

   b. The double-declining-balance method.

   c. The capital-cost-allowance method.

   d. The complex declining-balance method.

•3. Webster Oil purchased an undeveloped oil field estimated to contain 2.4 million barrels of oil for $20 million. The company spent another $8 million to bring six wells into production and $2 million on pipelines from the wells to the collector station and tanks at the collector station. Prepare the depletion schedule for the first 4 years of operation if the oil production in successive years was 76,500, 135,200, 158,700, and 150,900 barrels. The wells, tanks, and pipelines are not expected to have any significant salvage value when the field is depleted.

SUMMARY OF NOTATION AND KEY FORMULAS

d = Rate of depreciation (on the declining balance)
n = Number of years in the service life
C = Acquisition cost of the asset

Formula (17–1) $$\frac{\text{Depreciation}}{\text{per period}} = \frac{\text{Acquisition cost} - \text{Residual value}}{\text{Total no. of periods in service life}}$$ Finding the amount of straight-line depreciation per period.

Formula (17–2) $\quad \dfrac{\text{Depreciation per}}{\text{unit of use}} = \dfrac{\text{Acquisition cost} - \text{Residual value}}{\text{Total lifetime of units of use}}$

Finding the amount of depreciation per unit of use.

Formula (17–3) $\quad \dfrac{\text{Depreciation}}{\text{rate per year}} = 2 \times \dfrac{1}{\text{Service life of the asset in years}}$

Finding the double-declining-balance rate of depreciation

Formula (17–4) $\quad d = 1 - \sqrt[n]{\dfrac{\text{Residual value}}{\text{Acquisition cost}}}$

Finding the complex declining-balance rate of depreciation

Formula (17–5) $\quad$ Book value at the end of year $t = C(1 - d)^t$
Depreciation in year $t = dC(1 - d)^{t-1}$

Finding the book value at the end of year t and the amount of depreciation for year t in the double-declining-balance and the complex declining-balance methods of depreciation

Formula (17–6) $\quad$ Book value at the end of year t

$$= C\left(1 - \dfrac{d}{2}\right)(1 - d)^{t-1}$$

Capital cost allowance in year t

$$= \left(\dfrac{d}{2}\right)C \qquad\qquad \text{for } t = 1$$

$$= dC\left(1 - \dfrac{d}{2}\right)(1 - d)^{t-2} \qquad \text{for } t \geq 2$$

Finding the book value at the end of year t and the amount of capital-cost-allowance for year t in the capital- cost-allowance method of depreciation

Formula (17–7) $\quad \dfrac{\text{Depreciation}}{\text{rate for year } t} = \dfrac{n - t + 1}{\dfrac{n(n + 1)}{2}} \times 100\%$

Finding the sum-of-the-years'-digits rate of depreciation for year t

Formula (17–8) $\quad \dfrac{\text{Depletion}}{\text{per unit}} = \dfrac{\text{Total original costs} - \text{Residual value}}{\text{Total estimated units of reserves}}$

Finding the depletion charge per unit of production

GLOSSARY OF TERMS

Accumulated depreciation   The cumulative total of all past and current depreciation expenses reported for an asset.

Book value   The acquisition cost of a depreciable asset minus the accumulated depreciation.

Capital cost allowance   Depreciation expense that may be deducted from revenues for the purpose of calculating taxable income.

Depletion   An accounting procedure by which the recorded value of a resource-based asset is reduced during its projected lifetime in a systematic and rational manner.

Depreciation   An accounting procedure by which the recorded or book value of an asset is reduced during its projected lifetime in a systematic and rational manner.

Depreciation expense The reduction in the book value of an asset determined for the current period.

Depreciation schedule A table presenting the details of the depreciation expense allocated to each accounting period and the asset's book value at the end of each period.

Residual value See *salvage value.*

Salvage value The amount that is expected to be recovered upon the sale or disposal of the asset at the end of its service life.

Service life The length of time that an asset is expected to be used in the operations of the business.

Useful life See *service life.*

*18

CONSUMER CREDIT

LEARNING OBJECTIVES

After completing this chapter, you will be able to:

- Explain the operation of and calculate the interest charges on department store charge accounts
- Explain the operation of and calculate the interest charges on bank charge accounts

- Construct a repayment schedule for a student loan

INTRODUCTION

By the end of 1995, total household debt in Canada had reached $462 billion. This represented an average debt of over $15,000 for each of nearly 30 million Canadians. On every measure, Canadian households were more indebted than ever before. Of particular note, household debt had reached 88% of annual disposable income, up from 56% only 10 years earlier. Residential mortgage loans accounted for 74% of the aggregate household debt. The other 26% is referred to as **consumer credit**—debt incurred by individuals for personal consumption expenditures and personal financing needs.

Consumer credit has grown much more rapidly than measures of personal income or the national economy in recent years. The $120 billion of consumer debt at the end of 1995 represented a 22.5% increase during the preceding 3 years! Consumer credit includes credit card debt, term loans for the purchase of vehicles and boats, agreements under conditional sale contracts for the purchase of furniture and appliances, student loans, and personal loans for any other nonbusiness purpose. Chartered banks supply over two-thirds of total consumer credit. Other sources, in descending order of importance, are caisses populaires and credit unions, sales finance and consumer loan companies, trust companies, department stores, and life insurance companies.

The mathematics of term loans and debt under conditional sale contracts does not depend on whether the debt is incurred for personal or business purposes. These areas were covered in Chapters 10, 12, and 14. With minor variations among lending institutions, personal lines of credit are handled in the same manner as revolving demand loans (Section 7.5). Personal lines of credit commonly require the borrower to make minimum monthly payments. The stipulated minimum is usually something like "the greater of 3% of the outstanding balance or $50."

Two forms of consumer credit are given special attention in this chapter. Credit card accounts have some complicated rules for calculating interest charges. Student loans are discussed because they are particularly relevant to students, and have a few unique "wrinkles" affecting interest calculations and loan amortization.

18.1 CHARGE ACCOUNTS

Charge accounts are associated with credit cards issued by major financial institutions, department stores, retailing chains, and oil companies. By the end of 1995, there were over 59 million credit cards in circulation—2.6 credit cards for every Canadian over the age of 18. Between them, MasterCard and Visa accounted for 28.5 million cards with a total outstanding balance of $17.7 billion. This was the most rapidly growing component of consumer debt, increasing by 54% during the preceding 3 years.

Charge accounts are a form of *variable* or *revolving credit.* The cardholder can charge purchases up to the credit limit approved by the card issuer. A monthly statement provides details of the transactions during the 1-month billing period ending on the *statement date* or *billing date.* It gives each of the following amounts needed to calculate the new balance.

$$\text{New balance} = \text{Previous balance} + \text{Current purchases} + \text{Interest charges} - \text{Payments} - \text{Returns and credits}$$

Bank charge accounts add any "cash advances" to the right side of this equation. The format of a bank charge account's monthly statement is presented in Figure 18.1.

FIGURE   18.1

A Sample Bank Credit Card Monthly Statement

$ ¢			Bank of Credit	**Last statement** 07 Mar 97	**Card number** 1234 2345 3456 4567	**This statement** 07 Apr 97	**Payment due by** 28 Apr 97

Trans. date M D	Posting date M D	Ref no.	Description	Amount		
					Previous balance	109.07
					Purchases	16.32
03/23	03/26	1	Shoppers Drug Mart Nanaimo BC	16.32	Cash advances	
					Interest	
					Other	
					Payments	109.07 CR
03/27	03/27	2	Payment Received-Thank you	109.07 CR		
					Credit adjustments	0.00 CR
					New balance $	16.32
					Amount past due	0.00
					Minimum payment	0.00
					Credit limit	7000.00
					Credit available	7000.00
					Paid $	0.00

Interest charges for current and past transactions:

	Current statement	Last month's statement	Previous statements	Total interest charge	Interest rate Annual %	Daily
Cash advances	0.00	0.00	0.00	0.00	16.75000	0.04589
Purchases and other	0.00	0.00	0.00	0.00	16.75000	0.04589

The cardholder may pay any amount between a specified minimum (typically 5% to 10% of the new balance) and the entire balance. The payment must be received by the credit card issuer on or before a specified *due date,* which is typically about 3 weeks after the statement date. The interval between the statement date and the due date is called the *grace period.* If the account is paid in full during the grace period, no interest charges will appear on the next statement.[1]

Visa and MasterCard calculate interest charges differently from the method used by most major retail chains and department stores. The procedure used to calculate interest charges on any particular charge account is found in the contract issued with the credit card. In addition, the procedure is usually summarized on the reverse side of the monthly statement.

INTEREST CHARGES ON RETAIL CHAIN AND DEPARTMENT STORE CHARGE ACCOUNTS   The rules for these accounts are quite straightforward.

- One month's interest is charged on the *previous* month's balance (except in the circumstance described in the second rule). The interest calculation uses

---

[1]An exception occurs with bank credit cards in a particular situation. Example 18.1A at the end of this section will illustrate the exception.

one-twelfth of the nominal annual rate regardless of the number of days in the 1-month interval between statement dates. The current interest rate for 1 month and the corresponding nominal annual rate are quoted somewhere on the statement, typically on the back side.

- If a partial payment of at least 50% of the previous month's balance was made *before* its due date, *most* major department store charge accounts deduct the partial payment *before* calculating the interest charge on the current statement.

INTEREST CHARGES ON BANK CHARGE ACCOUNTS   The rules for these accounts are rather complicated in their application.

- No interest is charged for *purchases* on the statement on which they *first* appear.
- On *cash advances,* interest is charged on the first statement from (and including) the date on which cash was advanced.
- If the balance is not paid *in full* by the specified due date, interest will be charged on the next statement on *all* of the previous period's purchases *retroactively* to (and including) the dates on which the various purchases were posted to the account. For example, suppose a bank credit card's billing date is the 7th of each month and the due date is the 28th of the month. Further suppose that a cardholder with zero previous balance charged a single $200 purchase to the account on October 10. The November 7 statement will show a $200 balance payable. If a $200 payment is received by the bank on or before November 28, there will be no interest charges on the December 7 statement. If instead, the cardholder pays only $100 on, say, November 20, the December 7 statement will include interest charges on $200 from October 10 to November 19 inclusive, and interest charges on the unpaid $100 from November 20 to December 7 inclusive.
- Interest is calculated on a simple-interest basis for the exact number of days in the relevant period.
- A payment is applied first to interest charges, then to the previous balance, then to current cash advances, and finally to current purchases.[2]

The calculations of interest charges for these two broad categories of charge accounts are illustrated in the following example.

■ EXAMPLE 18.1A   *COMPARISON OF CREDIT CARD INTEREST CALCULATION METHODS*

Mrs. Winkelaar made a $200 purchase on October 10 and a $300 purchase on October 20 using her charge account, which previously had a zero balance. Assume that purchases are posted to the charge account on the date of purchase. Her monthly statements are dated on the 7th of each month and the payment due date is the 28th of the month. Interest is charged at the nominal rate of 24% per annum. Mrs. Winkelaar makes no further purchases on the account, pays $300 on November 28,

---

[2]Although bank credit cards typically charge a *lower* nominal *rate* of interest than retail store credit cards, the *dollar* amount of bank interest charges on purchases can work out to be *higher* for two reasons. The bank interest charges can go all the way back to the date of posting of the transaction instead of just to the first statement date following the purchase. Also, the bank credit cards do not deduct partial payments of 50% or more of the outstanding balance before calculating the interest charges on the next month's statement.

and pays the December 7 balance on December 28. Calculate the interest charges on her November 7, December 7, and January 7 statements for three cases:

a. The account is with department store A. Store A's policy is to deduct partial payments (if received before the due date) of at least 50% of the previous balance before calculating the current statement's interest charge.

b. The account is with department store B. Store B's policy is to charge 1 month's interest on the previous month's balance unless that balance was paid *in full* before the due date.

c. The account is a bank charge account.

☑ SOLUTION

a. In the first two of the following tables, the term "qualifying payments" refers to any payments or credits that are deducted from the *previous* period's ending balance before calculating the interest charge. For store A, these are payments received during the grace period (from the 8th to the 28th inclusive) totalling at least 50% of the ending balance on the previous statement. The "adjusted previous balance" is the balance on which the *current* period's interest charge is based. It is the *previous* period's "ending balance" minus the *current* period's "qualifying payments."

Billing period	Purchases	Qualifying payments	Other payments	Adjusted previous balance	Interest	Ending balance
Oct 8–Nov 7	$500	$ 0	$0	$ 0	$0	$500
Nov 8–Dec 7	0	300	0	200	4①	204
Dec 8–Jan 7	0	204	0	0	0	0

① Interest $= \dfrac{0.24}{12} \times \$200 = 0.02 \times \$200 = \$4.00$

Mrs. Winkelaar's only interest charge is $4.00 on her December 7 statement.

b. For store B, only payment of the previous statement's *entire* balance within the grace period qualifies for interest forgiveness.

Billing period	Purchases	Qualifying payments	Other payments	Adjusted previous balance	Interest	Ending balance
Oct 8–Nov 7	$500	$ 0	$ 0	$ 0	$ 0	$500
Nov 8–Dec 7	0	0	300	500	10①	210
Dec 8–Jan 7	0	210	0	0	0	0

① Interest $= 0.02 \times \$500 = \$10.00$

Mrs. Winkelaar's only interest charge is $10.00 on her December 7 statement.

c. A different tabular format is needed for a bank charge account because interest charges depend on the varying balance *during* a billing period, not just on the balance at the end of the billing period.

Date	Transaction	Amount	Balance earning interest: In the current billing period	Balance earning interest: In the next billing period	Period of interest accrual (inclusive dates)
Oct 10	Purchase	$ 200.00①		$200.00②	Oct 10–Oct 19④
Oct 20	Purchase	300.00①		500.00②	Oct 20–Nov 7③ ④
Nov 7	Interest charges	0①	$500.00②	0	Nov 8–Nov 27④
Nov 28	Payment	(300.00)	200.00	0	Nov 28–Dec 7③ ④
Dec 7	Interest charges	15.45⑤	200.00	0⑥	Dec 8–Dec 27⑦
Dec 28	Payment	(215.45)⑥	0	0	
Jan 7	Interest charges	2.63⑦			

① No interest is charged for *purchases* on the statement where they *first* appear.

② Since the $500 balance was not received in full on or before the November 28 due date, interest is charged in the December 7 statement retroactive to the posting dates of the purchases in October. On the statement date, the previous "balance earning interest in the next billing period" is transferred to the "balance earning interest in the current billing period."

③ The interest calculation *includes* the statement date in the current billing period.

④ The day on which a purchase or payment is made is counted with the subsequent days at the new balance.

⑤ Interest charges $= \left(\$200 \times 0.24 \times \dfrac{10}{365}\right) + \left(\$500 \times 0.24 \times \dfrac{19+20}{365}\right) + \left(\$200 \times 0.24 \times \dfrac{10}{365}\right)$

$\qquad\qquad\qquad = \$1.315 + \$12.82 + \$1.315$

$\qquad\qquad\qquad = \$15.45$

⑥ Payments are applied first to interest. Since a payment exceeding the December 7 interest charge was received on or before the due date, the $15.45 interest charge is not included in either of the interest-earning balances.

⑦ Interest charges $= \left(\$200 \times 0.24 \times \dfrac{20}{365}\right) = \$2.63$

This circumstance is the exception (mentioned in footnote 1 earlier in this section) to the general rule that no interest will be charged if the balance is paid in full during the grace period. Because the balance on the December 7 statement included charges which *first* appeared on previous statements, the account holder must still pay interest on the "old" charges for the time period *between* the statement date (December 7) and the payment date (December 28).

Mrs. Winkelaar's interest charges are $0, $15.45, and $2.63 on the three successive statements. ∎

■ EXAMPLE 18.1B   TREATMENT OF CASH ADVANCES ON BANK CREDIT CARDS

Repeat Example 18.1A for the bank credit card case where, in addition to the two purchase transactions in October, Mrs. Winkelaar also took a $100 cash advance on October 15.

☑ SOLUTION

Date	Transaction	Amount	Balance earning interest: In the current billing period	Balance earning interest: In the next billing period	Period of interest accrual (inclusive dates)
Oct 10	Purchase	$ 200.00		$200.00	Oct 10–Oct 14
Oct 15	Cash advance	100.00	$100.00①	200.00	Oct 15–Oct 19①
Oct 20	Purchase	300.00	100.00	500.00	Oct 20–Nov 7
Nov 7	Interest charges	1.58①	600.00	0	Nov 8–Nov 27
Nov 28	Payment	(300.00)	301.58	0	Nov 28–Dec 7
Dec 7	Interest charges	17.44②	301.58	0	Dec 8–Dec 27
Dec 28	Payment	(319.02)	0	0	
Jan 7	Interest charges	3.97③			

① Interest is charged on a cash advance on the statement where it first appears. The day on which the money was advanced is counted with the subsequent days at the new balance.

$$\text{Interest charges} = \left(\$100 \times 0.24 \times \frac{5+19}{365}\right) = \$1.58$$

$$② \text{Interest charges} = \left(\$200 \times 0.24 \times \frac{10}{365}\right) + \left(\$500 \times 0.24 \times \frac{19}{365}\right)$$
$$+ \left(\$600 \times 0.24 \times \frac{20}{365}\right) + \left(\$301.58 \times 0.24 \times \frac{10}{365}\right)$$
$$= \$1.315 + \$6.247 + \$7.890 + \$1.983$$
$$= \$17.44$$

$$③ \text{Interest charges} = \left(\$301.58 \times 0.24 \times \frac{20}{365}\right) = \$3.97$$

Mrs. Winkelaar's interest charges are $1.58, $17.44, and $3.97 on the three successive statements. ∎

EXERCISE 18.1

Answers to the odd-numbered problems are at the end of the book.

•1. Rhonda's September 14 statement from Eaton's contains the following information: previous balance, $543.68; purchases, $217.98; purchase returns, $48.33; payment received, $150.00. The payment due date is October 5. Calculate:

a. The credit service charge (interest charge) on the current statement based on a nominal rate of 18% pa.

b. The new balance.

c. The service charge that will appear on the October 14 statement if Rhonda makes a payment of $200 on October 1.

•2. Donovan's Zellers statement dated March 3 contains the following information: previous balance, $832.79; purchases, $113.62; purchase returns, $56.98; payment received, $250.00. The payment due date is March 28. Calculate:

a. The credit service charge (interest charge) on the current statement based on a nominal rate of 28.8% pa.

b. The new balance.

c. The credit charge that will appear on the April 3 statement if Donovan makes a payment of $400 on March 21. Zellers policy is that if a payment of 50% or more of the previous balance is received on or before the payment due date, the payment will be deducted from the balance before the credit charge is calculated.

••3. Laurie opened a charge account on August 1. She made purchases of $75 on August 5, $110 on August 18, $145 on September 14, and $65 on October 5. Assume that purchases are posted to the charge account on the date of purchase. Her monthly statements are dated on the 20th of the month, and the payment due date is on the 10th of the subsequent month. Interest charges are based on a nominal rate of 18%. Laurie made payments of $50 on September 5 and $100 on October 3. Calculate the interest charges and balance on her August 20, September 20, and October 20 statements for two cases:

a. The account is with a national retail department store.

b. The account is a bank charge account.

••4. Reg made a $500 purchase on April 10 and a $200 purchase on April 20, using his charge account, which previously had a zero balance. Assume that purchases are posted to the charge account on the date of purchase. His monthly statements are dated on the 5th of each month and the payment due date is the 26th of the month. Interest is charged at the nominal rate of 21%. Reg made no further purchases on the account, paid $400 on May 26, and paid the June 5 balance on June 26. Calculate the interest charges on his May 5, June 5, and July 5 statements for three cases:

a. The account is with department store C. Store C's policy is to deduct partial payments (if received on or before the due date) of at least 50% of the previous balance before calculating the current statement's interest charge.

b. The account is with department store D. Store D's policy is to charge 1 month's interest on the previous month's balance unless that balance was paid *in full* before the due date.

c. The account is a bank charge account.

••5. Repeat problem 4 for the bank credit card case where, in addition to the two purchase transactions in April, Reg took a $200 cash advance on April 16.

18.2 STUDENT LOANS

The first significant debt incurred by many who pursue post-secondary education is a student loan. All provincial governments and the federal government offer student loan programs. As long as a student is eligible for interest-free status,[3] the respective governments pay the interest charges on student loans from banks, trust companies, and other approved lenders. Six months after completing a program or otherwise ceasing to qualify for interest exemption, the student must begin to repay the loans. For example, if final examinations end on May 17 and the student does not return to college the following September, the 6-month grace period will run from June 1 to November 30. Before December 1, the student must arrange with the lender to consolidate all Canada Student Loans (CSLs) into a single loan. Provincial student loans must be consolidated separately. The terms of repayment are usually negotiated at the time of consolidation. The first payment on a consolidated loan is due 1 month after the end of the grace period. In the current example, the first payment is due December 31.[4]

On Canada Student Loans, the borrower is responsible for interest accruing at the floating rate of prime + 2.5% during the 6-month grace period. The borrower may pay the accrued interest at the end of the grace period or *capitalize* it (that is, convert the accrued interest to principal). As of the summer of 1996, all provinces except Prince Edward Island continue to exempt students from interest charges on the respective province's student loans during the 6-month grace period.

Depending on the amount of the student loan, fixed monthly payments may be spread over as many as 114 months. On Canada Student Loans, the borrower can choose either a *floating* interest rate of prime + 2.5% or a *fixed* rate of prime + 5%. In the latter case, the prime rate used is the lender's prime rate at the time repayment is negotiated. The borrower cannot subsequently switch from fixed to floating or floating to fixed during the term of the loan.

The interest rate for the repayment of provincial student loans in Ontario, Manitoba, and British Columbia is *fixed* at prime + 1%. The other provinces offer the same fixed or floating rate alternatives as are available for CSLs. On all student loans, the interest portion of each monthly payment is calculated using the simple-interest method and the exact number of days since the previous payment. In determining the

---

[3] One of the key requirements is that the student carry and pass at least 60% of a full program course load in every semester.

[4] Most lenders schedule end-of-month payments but a few arrange beginning-of-month payments.

length of the time interval for the interest calculation, lenders count the payment date with the days preceding the payment. A loan repayment schedule can be constructed with the same format as used in Section 7.5 for blended-payment demand loans.

Student loans may be prepaid in part or in full at any time without penalty.

■ EXAMPLE 18.2A   CONSTRUCTING A REPAYMENT SCHEDULE FOR A CANADA STUDENT LOAN

Heidi had Canada Student Loans totalling $5300 when she graduated from college. Her 6-month grace period ended on November 30, and she chose to have the grace period's accrued interest converted to principal. Heidi chose the floating interest rate option (prime + 2.5%) when the prime rate was at 7.5%. Monthly payments beginning December 31 were set at $76, which, subject to subsequent changes in the prime rate, would spread the loan payments over the maximum 114 months.

Prepare a loan repayment schedule up to and including the payment on the following March 31. The intervening February had 29 days. The prime rate increased from 7.25% to 7.5% per annum on the preceding August 3 and rose another 0.5% effective January 14.

✓ SOLUTION

The period from June 1 to August 3 has $215 - 152 = 63$ days, and the period from August 3 to (and including) November 30 has $335 - 215 = 120$ days. The accrued interest at the end of the grace period was

$$I = Pr_1t_1 + Pr_2t_2$$
$$= \$5300(0.0975)\frac{63}{365} + \$5300(0.10)\frac{120}{365}$$
$$= \$89.19 + \$174.25$$
$$= \$263.44$$

The consolidated loan balance at the end of November was $5300.00 + $263.44 = $5563.44.

Date	Number of days①	Interest rate	Interest	Accrued interest	Payment made	Principal portion	Balance
Nov 30	—	—	—	—	—	—	$5563.44
Dec 31	31	10.0%	$47.25②	$47.25	$76	$28.75	5534.69
Jan 13	13③	10.0	19.71	19.71			
Jan 31	18	10.5	28.66	48.37	76	27.63	5507.06
Feb 29	29	10.5	45.94	45.94	76	30.06	5477.00
March 31	31	10.5	48.84	48.84	76	27.16	5449.84

① Since lenders usually include the payment date when calculating the interest charge for the current period, each interval here is the number of days from (but not including) the preceding date to (and including) the date in the first column.
② Interest $= Prt = \$5563.44(0.10)\frac{31}{365} = \$47.25$
③ Since the new prime rate is effective January 14, January 13 is the last day counted at the 10% rate.   ■

■ EXAMPLE 18.2B   REPAYMENT SCHEDULE FOR AN ONTARIO, A BC, OR A MANITOBA STUDENT LOAN

Matthew finished his college program in April. By that time the combined total of his Ontario Student Loans had reached $4900. Three weeks before the expiry of his grace period, he met with a representative of the Canadian Imperial Bank of

Commerce to negotiate the terms of repayment. Matthew agreed to end-of-month payments of $100, beginning 1 month after the end of the grace period. The prime rate of interest was 7% per annum at the time the payments were set. Construct a repayment schedule showing details of the first four payments. The relevant February has 28 days. The prime rate dropped by 0.25% on December 7.

☑ Solution

The following points are based on information in the general discussion of student loans at the beginning of this section.

- Matthew's grace period runs from May 1 to October 31 inclusive. Therefore, the first payment is due on November 30.
- Matthew is not responsible for the accrued interest during the grace period.
- The interest rate is *fixed* at prime + 1% (that is, at 8%) for the life of the loan. Any *subsequent* change in the prime rate (such as the 0.25% drop on December 7) does not affect the interest rate on the loan.

Date	Number of days	Interest rate	Interest	Accrued interest	Payment made	Principal portion	Balance
Oct 31	—	—	—	—	—	—	$4900.00
Nov 30	30	8.0%	$32.22	na	$100	$67.78	4832.22
Dec 31	31	8.0	32.83	na	100	67.17	4765.05
Jan 31	31	8.0	32.38	na	100	67.62	4697.43
Feb 28	28	8.0	28.83	na	100	71.17	4626.26

■

EXERCISE 18.2

Answers to the odd-numbered problems are at the end of the book.

•1. Sarah's Canada Student Loans totalled $9400 by the time she graduated from college in May. She arranged to capitalize the interest on November 30 and to begin monthly payments of $135 on December 31. Sarah elected the floating rate interest option (prime + 2.5%). The prime rate stood at 6.75% on June 1, dropped to 6.5% effective September 3, and then increased by 0.25% on January 17. Prepare a repayment schedule presenting details of the first three payments. February has 28 days.

•2. Harjap completed his college program in December and on June 30 paid all the interest that had accrued (at prime + 2.5%) on his $5800 Canada Student Loan during the 6-month grace period. He selected the fixed rate option (prime + 5%) and agreed to make end-of-month payments of $95 beginning July 31. The prime rate began the grace period at 8% and rose by 0.5% effective March 29. On August 13, the prime rate rose another 0.5%. The relevant February had 28 days.

   a. What amount of interest accrued during the grace period?

   b. Calculate the total interest paid in the first three regular payments and the balance owed after the third payment.

•3. Monica finished college on June 3 with Canada Student Loans totalling $6800. She decided to capitalize the interest that accrued (at prime + 2.5%) during the grace period. In addition to regular end-of-month payments of $200, she made an extra $500 lump payment on March 25. This prepayment was applied first to accrued interest and then against the principal. The prime rate dropped from 9% to 8.75% effective September 22 and declined another 0.5% effective March 2. Calculate the balance owed on the floating rate option after the regular March 31 payment. The relevant February had 28 days.

•4. Drew's grace period for his $4200 Ontario Student Loan ended October 31. The interest rate on Ontario Student Loans is fixed at prime + 1%. When he agreed to payments of $100 per month starting November 30, the prime rate was at 7.75%. Calculate the total interest paid in the first three payments and the balance after the third payment. The prime rate rose to 8% effective January 10.

•5. Ruth made an initial lump payment of $500 on her $6000 BC Student Loan on November 30, the last day of the grace period. She arranged with the Royal Bank to make end-of-month payments of $150, beginning December 31. The rate was fixed at 10% (representing prime + 1%). Prepare a repayment schedule presenting details of the initial lump payment and the first three regular payments. The prime rate dropped by 0.25% on December 10. The relevant February has 29 days.

•6. Kari had Nova Scotia Student Loans totalling $3800 when she completed her program in December. She made arrangements with her credit union to start end-of-month payments of $60 after the expiry of the grace period. Kari chose the floating interest rate option (at prime + $2\frac{1}{2}$%) when the prime rate was at 7%. Prepare a loan repayment schedule up to and including the September 30 payment. The prime rate had two 0.25% increases, the first effective August 1, and the second effective September 28.

•7. Seth had accumulated Alberta Student Loans totalling $5200 by the time he graduated from Mount Royal College in May. He arranged with the Bank of Nova Scotia to choose the floating-rate option (at prime + $2\frac{1}{2}$%) and to begin monthly payments of $110 on December 31. Prepare a loan repayment schedule up to and including the February 28 payment. The prime rate was initially at 7.25%. It dropped by 0.25% effective January 31. Seth made an additional lump payment of $300 on February 14. Prepayments are applied first to accrued interest and then to principal.

Point of Interest

Revelations of Interest—Cost of Credit Disclosure Legislation

All provinces and the federal government have enacted legislation requiring lenders in the consumer credit market to disclose information about the cost of credit to their customers. The main goal of disclosure legislation is to ensure that consumers receive fair, accurate, and standardised information before making a borrowing decision. Consumers then have a good basis for comparing alternative sources of credit.

Federal legislators have tended to deal with cost of credit disclosure through acts governing financial institutions such as the Bank Act, the Trust and Loan Companies Act, and the Co-operative Credit Associations Act. Provinces have addressed cost of credit disclosure primarily within consumer protection legislation. Since no great effort has been made to coordinate lawmaking, it is not surprising that inconsistency or confusion frequently arises about what, when, and how disclosure should be made.

At its 1990 annual meeting, the Uniform Law Conference of Canada adopted a resolution calling for "the incorporation into relevant federal and provincial legislation . . . of *uniform* statutory provisions regarding the disclosure of the cost of credit in consumer credit transactions."

In June 1994, the federal and provincial governments signed the Agreement on Internal Trade. Among other things, they agreed to "complete negotiations on the harmonization of cost of credit disclosure no later than January 1, 1996," and to "adopt such harmonized legislation no later than January 1, 1997." As of the summer of 1996, the negotiations are still not completed and it is highly unlikely that the second deadline will be met. However, the parties remain committed to the goal of harmonization.

While everyone can support the principle that cost of credit disclosure laws *(continued)*

(*concluded*)

should be uniform across the country, the specifics of some proposals are contentious. Most notable among them is what interest rate should be disclosed. The case has been made throughout this text that only *effective* (annual) *rates:*

- Truly reflect the effects of compounding and the time value of money.

- Have numerical values that may be directly compared.

For *mortgage* loans secured by real property, the harmonization proposals align with the current provisions of the Interest Act. The lender may disclose *either* the effective annual rate *or* the semiannually compounded nominal rate. Of much greater concern is the "*annual percentage rate* (APR)" to be disclosed for most other loans. In a July 1995 proposal, the APR is defined by the formula

$$APR = \frac{C}{T \times P}$$

where

C = the total interest and noninterest charges over the term of the loan

P = the average principal outstanding at the end of each of a series of equal interest calculation periods

T = the term of the loan in years

Noninterest charges are charges paid by the borrower as a condition of obtaining a loan. Examples include a loan arrangement fee, a brokerage fee, or a loan administration fee. For the APR to make any sense,[5] the definition for P must be interpreted to mean the outstanding principal *before deduction of the principal component of a payment* received at the end of the "interest calculation period." But this is contrary to the meaning in the mathematics of finance of the expression "principal outstanding at the end of a period."

If there are no noninterest charges, the APR formula gives the *equivalent nominal* annual rate that has the same compounding frequency as the payment frequency.[6]

Even though the APR is not the conceptually preferred effective rate of interest, at least its formula appears to have the advantage of simplicity. However, the facade of simplicity crumbles when thoughts turn to determining a number for P, even for as common a case as a blended-payment loan. The calculation of P for a multi-payment loan would require many steps affording numerous opportunities for making an error.

Yet another problem is that the formula contemplates only cases in which payments are made at *equal* intervals. While this is by far the most common repayment arrangement, deferred payment loans and "miss-a-payment" loans are not uncommon. The 1995 harmonization proposal did not address such messy cases. Also note that a given dollar amount of noninterest charges enters the APR calculation in the same way regardless of *when* the charges are paid during the term of the loan. In other words, the APR formula ignores the time value of money (with respect to these charges).

By this point you are getting the picture that the federal/provincial working group who drafted the proposals had a tough time getting even the simple stuff right. Difficult issues surrounding open credit and leasing still remained. Although we will be better off with harmonized cost of credit legislation, it appears there will still be ample room for confusion and we will still have flawed measures of the cost of credit. The outcome may be that Canadians will be more uniformly confused about more uniformly flawed measures!

---

[5]Consider the calculation of the APR in the trivial case of a $1000 loan at 10% compounded annually and repaid by a single payment after one year.

[6]You can confirm this by calculating the APR for easy cases such as a $1000 loan at 10% compounded quarterly and repaid by two semiannual payments of $538.28.

*APPENDIX: RULE OF 78/SUM-OF-THE-DIGITS METHOD

Rule of 78 and *sum-of-the-digits method* are two names for a particular procedure used to calculate the amount required to prepay some blended-payment loans.

For a loan that is subject to the Rule of 78, the payment size is the same as for a blended-payment loan. The total interest paid over the full term of a loan is also the same in both cases. Normally, the interest component of any payment in a blended-payment loan is the interest that has accrued on the outstanding balance since the previous payment. If the loan is subject to the Rule of 78, the total interest is allocated among the payments in a different way. The nature of the reallocation is to shift some interest from later payments to earlier payments. (Corresponding shifts of principal are made in the opposite direction to keep the payments equal.) Consequently, the payment size and the total interest over the life of the loan are left unchanged. However, a borrower who *prepays* a loan under the sum-of-the-digits method is charged more interest and credited with less principal reduction than under the standard method presented in Chapter 14 for blended-payment loans.

The redistribution of principal and interest caused by the application of the Rule of 78 is clearly to the benefit of the lender at the expense of the borrower. The true cost of borrowing can be substantially higher than the effective rate of interest calculated using formula (9–3). Consumer groups and legislators view the Rule of 78 as taking unfair advantage of retail borrowers. The consumer protection acts in most provinces now include provisions that preclude the use of the Rule of 78 in the *consumer credit* area.

The use of the Rule of 78 with *commercial loans* is still permitted in some provinces. The implication is that business borrowers should have enough financial knowledge to be able to look out for themselves. Because the Rule of 78 may survive for some time in a few areas of commercial lending, its mechanics will be described in this appendix.

If a borrower wishes to prepay a loan subject to the Rule of 78, the payout amount is not simply the principal balance plus any accrued interest. Instead, the payout amount is based on the following idea:

$$\text{Amount required to prepay a loan} = \text{Nominal dollar amount of the remaining payments} - \text{Interest rebate}$$

It is in the calculation of the interest rebate that the lender effectively shifts a disproportionate amount of the interest charges to the early payments. The procedure is best illustrated by using a specific example.

Consider a $5000 loan at 9% compounded monthly that is to be repaid over 5 years by monthly payments of $100. Using formula (10–4) or the financial calculator approach, we obtain $103.79 as the monthly payment. The total interest cost over the life of the loan is determined in the usual way.

$$\text{Total interest} = 60(\$103.79) - \$5000 = \$1227.40$$

If the borrower wishes to prepay the loan after 6 months, the fraction of the $1227.40 that will be refunded is

$$\frac{\text{Sum of the digits of the remaining payments}}{\text{Sum of the digits of all of the payments}}$$

The term "sum of the digits" is used in this context to mean the sum of the counting numbers of the payments. With 60 payments in total and 54 remaining to be paid, the ratio in this case is

$$\frac{1 + 2 + 3 + \cdots + 52 + 53 + 54}{1 + 2 + 3 + \cdots + 58 + 59 + 60}$$

There is a simple formula for the sum of the first n integers:

$$\text{Sum of the first } n \text{ integers} = \frac{n(n + 1)}{2}$$

Using this formula, the ratio of the two sums of digits for the loan under discussion is

$$\frac{(54 \times 55)/2}{(60 \times 61)/2} = \frac{54 \times 55}{60 \times 60} = 0.8114754$$

Therefore, the rebate of unearned interest charges is

$$0.8114754 \times \$1227.40 = \$996.00$$

and the amount required to pay off the loan under the Rule of 78 is

$$54(\$103.79) - \$996.00 = \$4608.66$$

In general,

$$\text{Interest rebate} = \frac{\text{Sum of the digits of the remaining payments}}{\text{Sum of the digits of all the payments}} \times \text{Interest charges for the full term}$$

The name "Rule of 78" originates from the frequent occurrence of 1-year loans on which the sum of the digits for 12 payments ($n = 12$) is 78.

    The reallocation of interest charges from later to earlier payments increases the effective interest rate during the actual time interval for which the funds were borrowed. In the case being considered, the effective rate is obtained from the discount rate that makes the combined present value of the six payments and the payout amount equal to the $5000 borrowed. Using a financial calculator to obtain the discount rate per payment interval,

					Result
ENTER: 5000	4608.66	6	103.79		
	+/−		+/−	COMP	
PRESS: PV	FV	n	PMT	i	0.79709

The actual effective rate during the 6 months was

$$f = (1 + p)^m - 1 = (1.0079709)^{12} - 1 = 0.1000 = 10.00\%$$

rather than

$$f = (1 + i)^m - 1 = (1.0075)^{12} - 1 = 0.0938 = 9.38\%$$

    The longer the term of a loan and the earlier the loan balance is prepaid, the larger will be the effective rate. The increase can be very significant when a borrower prepays the balance on a long-term loan within the first year. It can even happen that the amount required to prepay the loan after a few payments is greater than the original loan! Example 18AB will demonstrate such an extreme case.

■ EXAMPLE 18AA   *FINDING THE AMOUNT TO PAY OFF A LOAN SUBJECT TO THE RULE OF 78*

Bruno's Upholstery purchased a new van and financed $10,000 of the purchase price through General Motors Acceptance Corporation. The loan was to be repaid by 36 monthly payments of $332.14.

a. Determine the total interest charges over the full term of the loan.

b. After a profitable year, Bruno has enough cash to pay off the loan. Use the sum-of-the-digits method to calculate the payout amount just after the 12th regular payment.

☑ SOLUTION

a.

$$\text{Total interest charges} = \text{Total payments} - \$10,000$$
$$= 36(\$332.14) - \$10,000$$
$$= \$1957.04$$

b.

$$\frac{\text{Interest}}{\text{rebate}} = \frac{\text{Sum of the digits of the last 24 payments}}{\text{Sum of the digits of all 36 payments}} \times \$1957.04$$

$$= \frac{24(25)/2}{36(37)/2} \times \$1957.04$$

$$= 0.4504505(\$1957.04)$$

$$= \$881.55$$

$$\text{Payout amount} = 24(\$332.14) - \$881.55 = \$7089.81$$

Note: The principal balance after 12 payments on a declining-balance schedule is only $7055.88.   ■

■ EXAMPLE 18AB   *A CASE IN WHICH THE LOAN PAYOUT AMOUNT EXCEEDS THE ORIGINAL LOAN*

Cliff's Bungee Jump obtained a $12,000 10-year loan at 18% compounded monthly to purchase a portable building to use as an on-site office. The monthly payments are $216.22. After operating for 6 months, business is going so well that Cliff can pay off the loan using retained earnings and funds from a loan at a significantly lower rate of interest.

a. What is the payout amount on the loan just after the sixth monthly payment if the lender uses the sum-of-the-digits method?

b. If Cliff goes ahead with the payout, what effective rate of interest will he have paid on the loan during the 6-month period?

☑ SOLUTION

a.

Compute the size of the loan payments.					Result
ENTER: 12000 0 1.5 120					
PRESS: PV FV i n (COMP) PMT					−216.22

$$\text{Total interest charges} = 120(\$216.22) - \$12,000 = \$13,946.40$$

$$\text{Interest rebate} = \frac{\text{Sum of digits of last 114 payments}}{\text{Sum of digits of all 120 payments}} \times \$13,946.40$$

$$= \frac{114(115)/2}{120(121)/2} \times \$13,946.40$$

$$= \$12,592.10$$

$$\text{Payout amount} = \text{Total of remaining payments} - \text{Interest rebate}$$

$$= 114(\$216.22) - \$12,592.10$$

$$= \$12,056.98$$

Note that the payout amount after 6 months is *greater* than the original loan! This example has three features that increase the likelihood of this outcome: the loan term is long, the interest rate is high, and the prepayment occurs early in the term of the loan. (The payout amount calculated on a declining-balance method is only $11,774.35.)

b. The effective rate of interest on the loan for the 6 months until payout is the discount rate that makes the combined present value of the six payments and the payout amount equal to the $12,000 borrowed.

Compute the interest rate per payment interval.					Result
ENTER: 12000	12056.98	6	216.22		
	+/−		+/−	COMP	
PRESS: PV	FV	n	PMT	i	1.87734

The actual effective rate during the 6 months was

$$f = (1 + p)^m - 1 = (1.0187734)^{12} - 1 = 0.2501 = 25.01\% \qquad \blacksquare$$

EXERCISE 18A

Answers to the odd-numbered problems are at the end of the book.

Use the Rule of 78/sum-of-the-digits method to calculate the loan payout amounts in the following problems.

1. A 12-month loan of $2000 is to be repaid by monthly payments of $180.52. What is the payout amount:

   a. After 2 months?   *b.* After 6 months?

2. A 3-year loan of $6000 is to be repaid by monthly payments of $208. What is the payout figure:

   a. After 2 months?   *b.* After 18 months?

3. A 10-year loan of $15,000 is to be repaid by monthly payments of $242. What amount is required to pay off the loan:

   a. After 2 months?   *b.* After 5 years?

4. A 5-year loan of $10,000 at 12% compounded quarterly is to be repaid by quarterly payments.

   a. What amount is required to pay off the loan after 6 months?

   b. If the loan is paid out after 6 months, what effective rate of interest will the borrower have paid?

5. Weston Veterinary Clinic purchased a truck for $18,000, paying $3000 down and financing the remainder through a 4-year loan from Ford Credit Canada Limited at 12% compounded monthly.

    a. If the loan were to be prepaid just after the first payment, calculate the first month's interest:
        (i) Based on the Rule of 78.
        (ii) Based on the rate of 1% per month on the declining balance.

    b. A year and a half after the purchase date, the clinic requested a payout figure on the loan. Also, for tax purposes, the clinic requested the total amount of interest charged for the 18 months based on the payout figure. Calculate these two amounts based on the Rule of 78.

6. Pizza Palace financed $9000 of the $11,500 purchase price of a new car through Chrysler Credit Canada Limited. The loan at 10.5% compounded monthly is to be repaid by monthly payments over 3 years.

    a. If the loan were to be prepaid just after the first payment, calculate the first month's interest:
        (i) Based on the Rule of 78.
        (ii) Based on the rate of 0.875% per month on the declining balance.

    b. Just after the 13th payment, Pizza Palace requested a payout figure. Calculate the payout amount and the amount of interest actually charged for the 13 months based on the Rule of 78.

SELF-TEST EXERCISE

Answers to the self-test problems are at the end of the book.

1. Charlotte's Sears statement, dated January 5, contains the following information: previous balance, $834.65; purchases, $345.79; purchase returns, $76.88; payment received, $300.00. The payment due date is January 28. Calculate:

   a. The credit charge on the current statement based on a nominal rate of 20.4% pa.

   b. The new balance.

   c. The interest charge that will appear on the February 5 statement if Charlotte makes a payment of $300 on January 25.

2. Roxanne's Canada Student Loans totalled $7200 by the time she finished college in April. The accrued interest at prime + 2.5% for the grace period was converted to principal on October 31. She chose the floating interest rate option and began monthly payments of $120 on November 30. The prime rate of interest was 8% on May 1, 7.75% effective July 9, and 7.5% effective December 13. Prepare a repayment schedule presenting details of the first three payments.

SUMMARY OF NOTATION AND KEY FORMULAS

To calculate the balance owed on a revolving credit account:

$$\text{New balance} = \text{Previous balance} + \text{Current purchases} + \text{Interest charges} - \text{Payments} - \text{Returns and credits}$$

GLOSSARY OF TERMS

Consumer credit Loans acquired by individuals for personal consumption expenditures and personal financing needs.

Answers to Odd-Numbered Problems

Exercise 1.1

1. 4
3. 24
5. 20
7. 49
9. 0.5
11. 6
13. 255
15. 9

Exercise 1.2

1. $0.875 = 87.5\%$
3. $2.35 = 235\%$
5. $-1.4 = -140\%$
7. $0.025 = 2.5\%$
9. $2.02 = 202\%$
11. $0.75 = 75\%$
13. $0.8\overline{3} = 83.\overline{3}\%$
15. $7.\overline{7} = 777.\overline{7}\%$
17. $1.\overline{1} = 111.\overline{1}\%$
19. $-0.0\overline{259} = -2.\overline{592}\%$
21. 11.38
23. 0.5545
25. 1.002
27. 40.10
29. $0.16667 = 16.667\%$
31. $0.016667 = 1.6667\%$
33. $0.68493 = 68.493\%$
35. $0.0091667 = 0.91667\%$
37. $94.68
39. $410.99
41. $3384.52
43. $720.04
45. $14,435.88
47. $6648.46
49. $7159.48
51. $1830.07

Exercise 1.3

1. $6.13
3. 13.0%
5. $75.00
7. $174.98
9. 200%
11. $90.00
13. $19.47
15. 62.1%
17. $105.26
19. 1.00%
21. $0.05
23. $150.00
25. $593.78
27. $125.00
29. $2000.00
31. 1.50% of sales
    17.7% of salary
33. 80
35. $154,000
37. $84,000
39. $75,000
41. 2.60%

Exercise 1.4

1. *a.* $24.231 per hour
   b. $23.774 per hour
3. *a.* $20.423 per hour
   b. $1751.29
5. $796.50
7. $328.75
9. *a.* $465.96
   b. $4090.91 per week
11. *a.* $3988.00
    b. 7.2668%
13. 3.50%
15. $110,833.33

EXERCISE 1.5

1. 1.53
3. 3.50
5. 8.9783%
7. 7.53
9. 43.74 days
11. *a.* $10.674
    b. $10.664
    c. $2548.70
13. 52.2%
15. 25.50

EXERCISE 1A

1.

Quarter	GST remittance (Refund)
1	$ 10,875.55
2	(23,821.35)
3	28,605.36
4	11,537.26

3. *a.* $23,433
   b. $25,185
   c. $25,307.64
5. *a.* $5337.27
   b. $6345.42
7. $3827.88
9. $4317.15
11. *a.* 7.4837
    b. 7.1273

REVIEW PROBLEMS

1. *a.* 23
   b. −40
   c. $205.39
   d. $2275.40
   e. $343.08
   f. $619.94
   g. $457.60
   h. $1549.56
3. $125.00
5. $8.\overline{3}$%
7. *a.* $29.026 per hour
   b. $2372.85
9. 4.50%
11. 26.1

SELF-TEST EXERCISE

1. *a.* 164
   b. 29
   c. $1295.88
   d. $208.62
   e. $3735.16
2. $59.70
3. $84,000
4. $3894.61
5. $2667
6. 2.10%
7. $81,308.33

CHAPTER 2   REVIEW OF ALGEBRA

EXERCISE 2.1

1. 0
3. $6x^2y$
5. $7x^2 + 7xy - 4y^2$
7. $8x + 3y$
9. $25x - 16$
11. $-0.7x + 3.45$
13. $18.8x - 8.5$
15. $3.0509P$
17. $2.9307k$

19. $12a^2b - 20a^2 + 24ab$
21. $-10x^3y + 5x^2y^2 + 15xy^3$
23. $20r^2 - 7rt - 6t^2$
25. $2a^2 + 34a + 99$
27. $6x$
29. $x - y$
31. $\dfrac{x^2 - 2x + 3}{4}$
33. $2ab - 3a^2$
35. 23.75

37. -44.8

39. $315.11

41. $346.22

43. $2430.38

45. $1378.42

47. $1794.22

49. $1071.77

Exercise 2.2

1. a^5

3. b^4

5. $(1 + i)^{13}$

7. x^{28}

9. t^2

11. x^2

13. $4(1 + i)^2$

15. $\dfrac{t^3}{2r}$

17. $\dfrac{81a^{12}b^8}{(a - b)^4}$

19. $-\dfrac{y}{2x^4}$

21. 16

23. 18.5203

25. 1,000,000

27. 1.07006

29. 1.00990

31. -4

33. -0.197531

35. 20.1569

37. 15.9637

39. 1.00908

Exercise 2.3

1. 2

3. 43

5. 200

7. 0.5

9. 9

11. 30

13. $286.661

15. $699.472

17. $391.011

Exercise 2.4

1. 125.44

3. $2.61

5. $13.00

7. 2 24-exposure rolls
   22 36-exposure rolls

9. Joan will invest $20,000
   Sue will invest $14,000

11. 42 units of product Y

13. $73,451.62 per child
    $24,483.87 per grandchild

15. $12,040

17. 18 minutes for cutting
    11 minutes for assembly
    6 minutes for painting

Exercise 2.5

1. 5.26%

3. 286%

5. 18.2%

7. $118.26

9. 105.2 cm

11. $25.00

13. 11.1%

15. $80.00

17. $42.86

19. 0.619% less

21. $131.25

23. $125.00

25. $658.80

27. $99.96

29. 200%

31. $10,075

33. $230.00

35. $375.00

37. $129.00

39. *a.* -15.3%
    b. 2.65%
    c. -13.0%

41. 565

43. -20% in 1995
    -25% in 1996

45. $665,000

47. 7.14% reduction

49. $1.43

51. $80,000

EXERCISE 2.6

Prob.	%Y	%G	%ROI
1.	10%	10%	20%
3.	11.11%	−4.44%	6.67%
5.	10.31%	−16.53%	−6.22%
7.	8.00%	−100%	−92.00%

9. $Y = \$100.00$
    $\%G = 10.00\%$
    $\%ROI = 15.00\%$

11. $\%Y = 6.70\%$
    $\%G = -1.70\%$
    $V_f = \$3666.50$

13. $\%Y = 10.00\%$
    $V_i = \$3000.00$
    $Y = \$300.00$

15. $Y = \$128.00$
    $\%G = -8.00\%$
    $V_f = \$1472.00$

17. a. 9.50%
    b. 3.40%
    c. $1290.00
    d. 12.90%

19. 24.07%

21. a. 28.28%
    b. 20.94%

23. $1.50

25. $1073.34

27. $1533.33

EXERCISE 2.7

1. $16.385 per hour

3. $15.158 per hour

5. 56.25%

7. −33.33%

9. 100%

11. 7.44%

13. 207.13%

15. a. $192 million
    b. $288 million

17. a. 159.37%

b. 148.83%
   The constant 10% increases produce a
   10.54% higher cumulative increase.

19. a. 15,075
    b. 1194

21. 8.07% decrease

23. a. $12.82
    b. $3.00

25. 7.06% increase
    17.45% underperformance

27. 17.07% increase
    7.44% underperformance

29.

End of year	$100 in Campbell shares	$100 in TSE 300
1990	$ 47.80	$ 85.20
1991	$ 51.72	$ 95.42
1992	$ 41.12	$ 94.08
1993	$132.86	$124.75
1994	$117.18	$124.50

REVIEW PROBLEMS

1. a. $0.7y + 2.2\overline{6}$
   b. $2.996843P$

3. a. $252.59
   b. $1468.56

5. a. 589.020
   b. 0.00826484

7. a. $34.58
   b. $500.00
   c. $117.65
   d. $199.50
   e. $562.00
   f. $350.00
   g. $210.00

9. a. 238.24%
   b. $7.48

11. a. 8.00%
    b. −2.00%
    c. $900.00
    d. 6.00%

13. a. $25.26
    b. $5.13

15. $4400 in ABC Ltd.
    $3400 in XYZ Inc.

Self-Test Exercise

1. *a.* $-60y^2 + 45y - 51$
   b. $2.925b - 21$
   c. $3.05587x$
   d. $\dfrac{4m - 3nm}{2n}$

2. $4505.14

3. *a.* $-\dfrac{9}{x}$
   b. $-\dfrac{8b^3}{a^9}$

4. *a.* 1.19641
   b. 0.00816485

c. 41.1527
d. 9.11858

5. *a.* $280.97
   b. $436.96

6. *a.* 79.27%
   b. -79.27%

7. 18.40%

8. 36.75%

9. *a.* -57.54%
   b. $7.51

10. $46,350 to Hugh
    $52,080 to Ken

Chapter 3   Ratios and Proportions

Exercise 3.1

1. 3 : 16
3. 3 : 1 : 2
5. 2 : 3
7. 3 : 5 : 7
9. 8 : 13 : 5
11. 1 : 6
13. 7 : 10
15. 3 : 4
17. 15 : 8
19. 2 : 6 : 3
21. $2.5\overline{3} : 1$
23. 1 : 4.58
25. 1 : 2.61
27. 3.35 : 1 : 1.78
29. 1 : 1.54 : 2.29
31. 1 : 2.47 : 1.37
33. 5 : 7 : 8
35. 3.36 : 1 : 2.18
37. 8 : 7 : 5

Exercise 3.2

1. 42
3. 232.9
5. 28.70
7. 0.0155

9. ⅓
11. $n = 90$; $m = 75$
13. $g = 5$; $f = 375$
15. $r = 11.21$; $s = 19.01$
17. $2658.86
19. 11.06 hours
21. $18,888.75
23. $459 million in U.S. stocks
    $323 million in Japanese stocks
    $187 million in British stocks
25. 4.5 litres of fruit juice
    1.8 litres of ginger ale
27. Wholesale cost = $2.955 million
    Overhead expenses = $1.553 million
29. $1.23 million budget reduction
    11 staff reduction
31. $4.345 million
33. *a.* $14,889
    b. $19,852

Exercise 3.3

See the answers to Exercise 2.5.

Exercise 3.4

1. $75.85
3. $406.85

5. *a.* $1592.00
   b. $1722.49

7. *a.* $168,750 to A
       $450,000 to B
       $281,250 to C
   b. $7,237,500 to A
       $19,300,000 to B
       $12,062,500 to C

9. *a.* $389,838 to Industrial Products
       $265,799 to Fine Paper
       $183,363 to Containers & Packaging
   b. $480,724 to Industrial Products
       $189,342 to Fine Paper
       $168,934 to Containers & Packaging

11. *a.* $542,500
    b. W will own 443 shares
        Y will own 517 shares
        Z will own 590 shares
    c. $50,050 from W
        $58,450 from Y
        $66,500 from Z

EXERCISE 3.5

1. C$ 2517.57
3. ¥ 1,160,870
5. C$ 2932.34
7. C$ 9442.44
9. £ 45,933.35
11. DM 55,322.63
13. *a.* 0.26574
    b. 0.011641
    c. 0.53842
    d. 0.93195
15. C$ 64.13
17. C$ 713.53
19. C$ 0.28 per pound
21. C$ has appreciated by 4.52%
23. E(US$: C$) = 0.746067
    E(C$: US$) = 1.34036
25. E(US$: C$) = 0.73543
27. E(C$: DM) = 0.919397
29. C$ 142.08 increase
31. C$ 9.45 per oz. increase
33. £ 1690.55 either way
35. US$ 0.40 more expensive in the U.S.

EXERCISE 3.6

1. 151.3
3. $9000.74
5. 9.374
7. $3645.75
9. 122.2
11. $1021.31
13. *a.* $1311.98
    b. $1491.60
    c. 17.96%
15. 20.80% more
17. *a.* $161.16
    b. 8.90% for 1978
        9.60% for 1979
        11.95% for 1980
        11.42% for 1981
        8.25% for 1982

EXERCISE 3A

1. 0.5223

REVIEW PROBLEMS

1. *a.* 6 : 20 : 15
   b. 3 : 2 : 4
   c. 3 : 6 : 2
   d. 5 : 4 : 3
3. Mark:Ben:Tanya = 5 : 3 : 7
5. 194 nurses; 97 aides
7. $111,111
9. $3774.06 to A
   $11,382.08 to B
   $4642.69 to C
   $8776.18 to D
11. $25,546 to Huey
    $28,859 to Dewey
    $30,375 to Louie
13. E(C2 : C1) = 0.05530
    E(C1 : C2) = 18.08
15. *a.* (i) 5.6% (ii) 1.5%
    b. $122.70

SELF-TEST EXERCISE

1. *a.* 18.06
   b. a = 332.8; b = 205.4
2. 11 : 14 : 6

3. 95,025 units
4. $3.39 billion for health care
   $2.30 billion for social services
5. $1.52
6. Ms. L received $4000
   Mr. M received $2666.67
   Mr. P received $1333.33

7. $148,798 to Wife
   $106,284 to Son
   $75,918 to Stepson
8. 1,574,638 lira
9. $25.88 per hour
10. Decrease of C$ 845.58
11. Alberta coal is C$ 0.41 cheaper per metric tonne

CHAPTER 4   MATHEMATICS OF MERCHANDISING

EXERCISE 4.1

1. $83.00, $166.00
3. $21.33, 16⅔%
5. $1750.00, $1137.50
7. $27.40, 45.0%
9. $3256.00, $407.00
11. $83.70
13. $185.95
15. 22.0%
17. 26.55%
19. $169,900
21. *a.* $5087.50
    b. $495
23. 46.9 points
25. 107.5 hours

EXERCISE 4.2

1. 41.67%, $57.75
3. 37.56%, $149.00
5. 36.00%, $187.88
7. 12.00%, $1380.08
9. 38.80%, 10.00%
11. $4350.00 from retailers
    $3915.00 from wholesalers
    $3621.38 from distributors
13. *a.* $286.23
    b. 38.26%
15. *a.* $285.36
    b. $15.02
    c. $320.00
    d. 35.87%
17. 3.00%
19. 2.78%

EXERCISE 4.3

1. $2317.70
3. $799.18
5. $3765.25
7. $1450.61
9. $1337.70, $1000.00
11. $510.20, $305.29
13. $1722.97, $1700.00
15. $507.61, 1.50%
17. *a.* May 15
    b. June 4
    c. $788.00
    d. $1066.32
    e. $262.33
19. $1557.66
21. *a.* $8163.27
    b. $6608.73
23. $2303.07
25. $15,828.35
27. $2600.00

EXERCISE 4.4

1. *a.* $20.00
   b. $12.00
   c. $8.00
   d. 66.67%
   e. 40.00%
3. *a.* $23.85
   b. $23.85
   c. $0
   d. 42.86%
   e. 30.00%

5. *a.* $23.10

   b. $26.95

   c. −$3.85

   d. 42.86%

   e. 30.00%

7. OE = $32.10

   SP = $199.95

   %M = 31.11% of C

   %M = 23.73% of SP

9. OP = $127.00

   C = $1555.00

   %M = 27.97% of C

   %M = 21.86% of SP

11. M = $15.00

    SP = $39.47

    C = $24.47

    %M = 61.29% of C

13. SP = $11.00

    M = $4.40

    OP = $1.25

    %M = 66.67% of C

15. *a.* SP = $363.60

    b. %M = 32.89% of C

    c. %M = 24.75% of SP

    d. $330.60

17. *a.* $37.90

    b. 31.03%

19. 150%

21. *a.* $30.47

    b. 45.95%

23. *a.* $21.00

    b. 69.10%

    c. $1091.07

25. $17.60

Exercise 4.5

1. SP = $277.50

   %M = 33.33% of SP

   %D = 21.62%

   RSP = $217.50

3. C = $24.99

   %M = 100.0% of C

   D = $24.99

   RSP = $24.99

5. SP = $29.62

   %M = 53.87% of C

D = $7.41

RSP = $22.21

7. C = $225.71

   %M = 42.86% of SP

   D = $158.00

   RSP = $237.00

9. *a.* 59.95%

   b. 37.48%

   c. 37.48%

11. $114.40

13. *a.* 25.72%

    b. 13.84%

Exercise 4.6

1. SP = $178.00

   RSP = $133.50

   ROP = −$17.80

3. D = $17.88

   %OE = 20.00% of C

   %M = 60.00% of C

5. SP = $167.70

   C = $83.85

   ROP = −$13.98

7. *a.* $285.12

   b. 32.00% of C

9. *a.* 15%

   b. $19.76 loss per unit

11. 23.61%

13. *a.* 25.00%

    b. −$6.12

    c. 25.00%

15. *a.* $950.00

    b. $1187.50

17. *a.* $2975.00

    b. $39.67 loss

Review Problems

1. $352.08

3. 27.5%

5. *a.* $825.80

   b. $33,852

7. $5.00

9. 12.50%

11. *a.* 10,657

b. 341 in 1980–84
   536 in 1985–89
   460 in 1990–94

13. *a.* $6.94

   b. $2.50

15. $1886.18

17. $8532.56

19. 122.2%

21. $287.00

23. *a.* $59.63

   b. 26.83%

25. *a.* $2187.50

   b. $2734.38

Self-Test Exercise

1. Source B is $1.80 cheaper
2. $1160.95
3. $169,300
4. *a.* $780.48
   b. $720.00

c. 34.69%

d. $34.38

5. *a.* 4.80%

   b. 4.00%

6. $1075.25 million and $695.98 million

7. $3089.25

8. 1.75%

9. *a.* $67.30

   b. $61.24

10. *a.* $20.65

   b. 76.50%

   c. $18.59

11. *a.* 153.3%

   b. 6.52%

12. *a.* 25.00%

   b. $25.20 loss per pair

   c. 25.00%

13. *a.* $1728.00

   b. 47.50%

Chapter 5   Applications of Linear Equations

Exercise 5.1

1. $(x,y) = (4,2)$
3. $(a,b) = (3,5)$
5. $(x,y) = (7,14)$
7. $(c,d) = (500,1000)$
9. $(v,w) = (\frac{3}{2}, -\frac{1}{3})$
11. $(x,y) = (17.0, 6.24)$
13. $(e,f) = (250,125)$
15. 238 student members
    345 regular members
17. $1.21 per litre, $1.98 per dozen
19. Maurice: $39,000, Marcel: $44,000
21. $1.50
23. 23 six-packs, 87 single cans
25. 9 production workers, 9 assembly workers

Exercise 5.2

1. *a.* $8.00

   b. 150 units per week

   c. (i) Loss of $240 per week
      (ii) Profit of $800 per week

   d. 200 units per week

3. *a.* $27

   b. 2000 borgels per month

   c. $13,500 per month

   d. $10,800 loss per month

   e. 84.4% of capacity

   f. Decreases by 71 borgels per month

5. *a.* 8000 units; $240,000

   b. $100,000; $27,500

   c. $210,000; $30.00

7. *a.* 28 participants

   b. $200 profit

   c. 20 participants

9. *a.* 311 tickets at $23
      205 tickets at $28

   b. $780 at $23 per ticket
      $1260 at $28 per ticket

11. *a.* $40.97

   b. $40.58

13. *a.* 12.72 tonnes per hectare

   b. 1.03 tonnes per hectare

   c. (i) $130 per hectare
      (ii) $155 per hectare

EXERCISE 5.3

1.

x:	-3	0	6
y:	-6	0	12

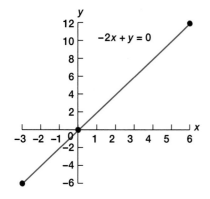

$-2x + y = 0$

7.

x:	0	3000	6000
y:	5000	18500	32000

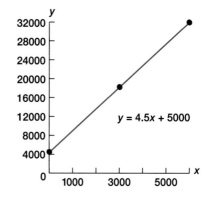

$y = 4.5x + 5000$

3.

x:	-3	0	6
y:	10	4	-8

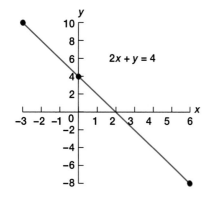

$2x + y = 4$

Graphical solution to problem 1, Exercise 5.2

$TR = \$20X$
$TC = \$1200 + \$12X$

X:	0	250
TR:	$ 0	$5000
TC:	$1200	$4200

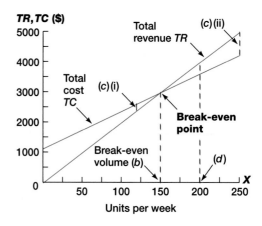

b. 150 units per week

c. (i) Loss of $240 per week
   (ii) profit of $800 per week

d. 200 units per week

5.

x:	-8	0	12
y:	-3	3	12

$3x - 4y + 12 = 0$

Graphical solution to problem 7, Exercise 5.2

$TR = \$135X$
$TC = \$700 + \$110X$

X:	15	36
TR:	$2025	$4860
TC:	$2350	$4860

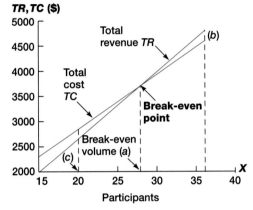

TR, TC ($)

a. 28 participants

b. $200 profit

c. 20 participants

REVIEW PROBLEMS

1. a. $(a,b) = (5, -2)$
   b. $(x,y) = (11.4, -6.32)$

3. $3.55 per kg for ling cod
   $4.10 per kg for red snapper

5. a. SP = $12.00
      NI = $80,000

b. NI = $100,000
   VC = $20.00

c. Unit sales = 20,000
   FC = $108,000

7. a. $6000
   b. $60 million per year
   c. $12 million

9. a. $4.0 million
   b. $3,770,778
   c. $4,666,667
   d. 50%
   e. NI will increase to $533,334

SELF-TEST EXERCISE

1. $(x,y) = (7, -2)$

2. 456

3. $7.80 in the "reds"
   $10.92 in the "blues"

4. a. 2500, 2500
   b. (i) $3000, $2000
      (ii) $1800 loss, $1200 loss
   c. The 30% commission rate will result in a higher profit if attendance surpasses the break-even point. However, if attendance falls short of breakeven, the 30% commission will produce the larger loss.

5. a. 36.2%
   b. (i) $1480 per month
      (ii) $2390 loss per month
   c. Reduce the price to $47

CHAPTER 6   SIMPLE INTEREST

EXERCISE 6.1

1. $83.13
3. 8 months
5. $567.23
7. 7 months
9. $114.58
11. $6500.00
13. 8.10%
15. 13 months
17. $195.00, $198.80

EXERCISE 6.2

1. $118.63
3. $4149.86
5. $1171.28
7. 8.5%
9. March 9, 1997
11. January 29, 1997
13. $22.09
15. 5.50%
17. 41 days

19. March 18
21. $196.03
23. $3112.28

EXERCISE 6.3
1. $3182.31
3. $780.00
5. $14,100.00
7. 10.70%
9. 18.50%
11. 182 days
13. 8 months
15. $5169.38
17. $19,324.57
19. 16.00%
21. 7.82%
23. January 8
25. $5604.26
27. $23,542.33

EXERCISE 6.5
1. $535.99
3. $5460.62
5. 7.25%
7. 90 days
9. 251 days
11. *a.* The later payment
    b. 10.86%
13. *a.* The later payment
    b. 1.03% per month
15. $974.58
17. $457.49
19. $1146.65
21. $2902.06 today
    $2933.99 in 2 months
    $2966.63 in 4 months
    $3000.00 in 6 months
    $3033.75 in 8 months
    $3067.50 in 10 months
    $3101.25 in 12 months
23. Jody's scholarship
25. 8.11%

EXERCISE 6.6
1. $816.79
3. $1958.60
5. $4442.98
7. $2028.97
9. *a.* $3722.94
   b. $3904.76
   c. The equivalent value of a given payment
      stream will be higher at a later date
      because of the time value of money.
11. $2364.29, $2350.80
    The $900 and $1400 payments have a $13.49
    greater economic value (in today's dollars).
13. $1856.32
15. $18,260.36

EXERCISE 6.7
1. $1083.45
3. $876.21
5. $505.54
7. $859.48
9. $1321.52
11. $2719.68
13. $1419.61
15. $2165.97

EXERCISE 6.8
1. $707.36
3. $3530.83
5. $2067.76
7. $1305.20 in 2 months
   $2610.40 in 5 months
9. $1218.65
11. $2719.68
13. $1710.55
15. $2359.60
17. $3468.84

REVIEW PROBLEMS
1. 4.75%
3. $70.96
5. $43,426.53

7. $1028.14
9. $8459.14
11. $2173.14
13. $3106.16
15. $3423.59

SELF-TEST EXERCISE

1. 11.90%
2. September 8
3. $9736.45

4. 109.32%
5. $59,430.77
6. *a.* The early-booking price saves $25.51
   b. 11.30%
7. $3762.76
8. The second payment is $2710.93
   The third payment is $5421.86
9. *a.* $9571.35
   b. $9663.06

CHAPTER 7   APPLICATIONS OF SIMPLE INTEREST

EXERCISE 7.1

1. September 19
3. 100 days
5. October 25
7. March 3
9. $1032.53
11. $2600.00
13. 9.0%
15. 45 days
17. $988.09
19. $2760.61
21. 7.5%
23. *a.* March 3, 1998
    b. March 1, 1998
25. $1036.23
27. $3257.12
29. $763.17
31. $3000.91

EXERCISE 7.2

1. *a.* $967.47
   b. $974.54
   c. The closer the purchase date to the payments, the smaller the discount will be for a given time value of money.
3. *a.* $1944.27

b. $1935.26
c. The payments from B are received one month later. This makes their value today less than the value of the payments from A.
5. $10,974.71
7. $7854.11

EXERCISE 7.3

1. $24,530.79
3. $988,083.44
5. $99,347 for the 30-day maturity
   $98,702 for the 60-day maturity
   $98,066 for the 90-day maturity
7. 7.245%
9. *a.* 8.269%
   b. 7.043%
   c. 10.515%

EXERCISE 7.4

1. *a.* $15,258.90
   b. $15,437.62
3. $166.44
5. $15.48
7. $5.65 more
9. $9.22
11. $52.28

720   Answers to Odd-Numbered Problems

Exercise 7.5

1.

Date	Number of days	Interest rate	Interest	Accrued interest	Interest charged to account	Principal repaid (advanced)	Balance
5-Feb						($15,000)	$15,000
29-Feb	24	8.50%	$83.84	$83.84	$83.84		15,000
15-Mar	15	8.50%	52.40	52.40		10,000	5,000
31-Mar	16	8.50%	18.63	71.03	71.03		5,000
30-Apr	30	8.50%	34.93	34.93	34.93		5,000
1-May	1	8.50%	1.16	1.16		(7,000)	12,000
31-May	30	8.50%	83.84	85.00	85.00		12,000

The interest charged to Dr. Robillard's account was $83.84 on February 29, $71.03 on March 31, $34.93 on April 30, and $85.00 on May 31.

3.

Date	Number of days	Interest rate	Interest	Accrued interest	Interest charged to account	Principal repaid (advanced)	Balance
3-Jul						($ 25,000)	$25,000
20-Jul	17	10.00%	$116.44	$116.44	$116.44		25,000
29-Jul	9	10.00%	61.64	61.64		(30,000)	55,000
5-Aug	7	10.00%	105.48	167.12			55,000
20-Aug	15	9.75%	220.38	387.50	387.50		55,000

The amounts of interest charged on July 20 and August 20 were $116.44 and $387.50, respectively.

5.

Date	Number of days	Interest rate	Interest	Accrued interest	Interest charged to account	Principal repaid (advanced)	Balance
7-Oct						($30,000)	$30,000
15-Oct	8	11.75%	$ 77.26	$ 77.26	$ 77.26		30,000
15-Nov	31	11.75%	299.38	299.38	299.38		30,000
24-Nov	9	11.75%	86.92	86.92		(15,000)	45,000
15-Dec	21	11.75%	304.21	391.13	391.13		45,000
17-Dec	2	11.75%	28.97	28.97			45,000
23-Dec	6	11.50%	85.07	114.04		(20,000)	65,000
15-Jan	23	11.50%	471.03	585.07	585.07		65,000

7.

Date	Number of days	Interest rate	Interest	Accrued interest	Interest charged to account	Principal repaid (advanced)	Balance
31-Mar						($30,000)	$30,000
18-Apr	18	10.75%	$159.04	$159.04	$159.04		30,000
28-Apr	10	10.75%	88.36	88.36		(10,000)	40,000
14-May	16	10.75%	188.49	276.85			40,000
18-May	4	11.00%	48.22	325.07	325.07		40,000
1-Jun	14	11.00%	168.77	168.77		(15,000)	55,000
18-Jun	17	11.00%	281.78	450.55	450.55	5,000	50,000
3-Jul	15	11.00%	226.03	226.03		10,000	40,000
18-Jul	15	11.00%	180.82	406.85	406.85		40,000

9.

Date	Number of days	Interest rate	Interest	Accrued interest	Payment made	Principal portion	Balance
1-Apr							$6,000.00
1-May	30	11.25%	$55.48	$55.48	$1,000.00	$944.52	5,055.48
1-Jun	31	11.25%	48.30	48.30	1,000.00	951.70	4,103.78
7-Jun	6	11.25%	7.59	7.59			4,103.78
1-Jul	24	11.00%	29.68	37.27	1,000.00	962.73	3,141.05
1-Aug	31	11.00%	29.35	29.35	1,000.00	970.65	2,170.40
27-Aug	26	11.00%	17.01	17.01			2,170.40
1-Sep	5	11.25%	3.34	20.35	1,000.00	979.65	1,190.75
1-Oct	30	11.25%	11.01	11.01	1,000.00	988.99	201.76
1-Nov	31	11.25%	1.93	1.93	203.69	201.76	0.00

Total of the interest charges = $203.69

11.

Date	Number of days	Interest rate	Interest	Accrued interest	Payment made	Principal portion	Balance
23-Feb							$2,500.00
15-Apr	51	9.00%	$31.44	$31.44	$500.00	$468.56	2,031.44
15-May	30	9.00%	15.03	15.03	500.00	484.97	1,546.47
15-Jun	31	9.00%	11.82	11.82	500.00	488.18	1,058.29
15-Jul	30	9.50%	8.26	8.26	500.00	491.74	566.55
31-Jul	16	9.50%	2.36	2.36			566.55
15-Aug	15	9.75%	2.27	4.63	500.00	495.37	71.18
15-Sep	31	9.75%	0.59	0.59	71.77	71.18	0.00

Review Problems

1. $1548.02
3. $7941.02
5. $12,128.95
7. $49,169.71
9. 6.385%
11. $98.63
13. $6.73

15.

Date	Number of days	Interest rate	Interest	Accrued interest	Interest charged to account	Principal repaid (advanced)	Balance
8-Mar						($40,000)	$40,000
24-Mar	16	10.25%	$179.73	$179.73	$179.73		40,000
2-Apr	9	10.25%	101.10	101.10		(15,000)	55,000
24-Apr	22	10.25%	339.79	440.89	440.89		55,000
13-May	19	10.25%	293.46	293.46			55,000
24-May	11	10.50%	174.04	467.50	467.50		55,000
5-Jun	12	10.50%	189.86	189.86		25,000	30,000
24-Jun	19	10.50%	163.97	353.83	353.83		30,000

The first four interest debits were, in order, $179.73, $440.89, $467.50, and $353.93.

Self-Test Exercise

1. $1644.14
2. $8507.52
3. $3780.22
4. *a.* $24,425.26
   b. 11.074%
   c. 6.581%
5. $14.90

7.

Date	Number of days	Interest rate	Interest	Accrued interest	Payment made	Principal portion	Balance
23-May							$15,000.00
15-Jun	23	9.50%	$ 89.79	$ ~~89.79~~	$700.00	$610.21	14,389.79
15-Jul	30	9.50%	112.36	~~112.36~~	700.00	587.64	13,802.15
26-Jul	11	9.50%	39.52	39.52			13,802.15
15-Aug	20	9.25%	69.96	~~109.48~~	700.00	590.52	13,211.63
14-Sep	30	9.25%	100.44	100.44			13,211.63
15-Sep	1	9.75%	3.53	~~103.97~~	700.00	596.03	12,615.60
15-Oct	30	9.75%	101.10	~~101.10~~	700.00	598.90	12,016.70

CHAPTER 8   COMPOUND INTEREST

EXERCISE 8.1

1. 2.7% per quarter
3. 0.875% per month
5. 11.0% compounded monthly
7. Quarterly compounding
9. Monthly compounding

EXERCISE 8.2

1. $9899.66
3. $15,428.20
5. $4500.00
7. $6589.58
9. $5000.00
11. $2750.75; 25.39%
13. $3018.67; 53.86%
15. Interest

rate	20 years	25 years	30 years
8%	$4660.96	$ 6848.48	$10,062.66
10%	$6727.50	$10,834.71	$17,449.40

17. $1469.33
19. a. $1538.62
    b. $1552.97
    c. $1560.51
    d. $1565.68
21. 12.0% compounded monthly
23. $1495.57
25. Principal = $1800.00
    Interest = $497.78
27. Donna will receive $8340.04
    Tim will receive $10,045.40
    Gary will receive $12,099.47
29. $8478.69

31. $700.69
33. $1525.07
35. $1694.44
37. $2499.99

EXERCISE 8.4

1. $675.00
3. $52,831.32
5. 7.5% compounded semiannually
7. $126.01
9. $678.93 from the B.C Bonds
   $753.06 from the Canada Savings Bonds
11. a. $7375.43
    b. $7790.30
13. $528.98
15. $2871.26; $186.34
17. $4326.73; $296.76
19. $11,749.59; $881.95
21. $9154.17; $627.86
23. $1930.03 on the RateRiser GIC
    $1931.22 on the fixed-rate GIC
25. $1102.44 from the RateRiser GIC
    $1007.77 from the fixed-rate GIC
27. a. $180.61
    b. $265.33
    c. $386.97
29. $21.16 per hour
31. a. $54,529
    b. $67,735
    c. $83,880
33. $34,425,064

EXERCISE 8.5

1. $6865.65
3. $977.59
5. $3417.01
7. $2247.35
9. $4642.01
11. $3351.83
13. $5445.47
15. $3011.67
17. $2031.83
19. $1302.79
21. $21.76 advantage (in current dollars) to paying taxes when due
23. The $20,000 payment is worth $633.04 more in current dollars.
25. There is no significant difference between the alternatives.
27. $6144.79
29. $8066.80
31. $1033.53
33. 47 bond residues can be purchased.
35. $3783.44
37. $4655.39
39. $5938.63
41. $1447.87
43. $4370.19; $2185.09
45. $3000.00

EXERCISE 8.6

1. $3902.32
3. $1925.11
5. $382.66; $765.32
7. $1539.02
9. $2167.15
11. $8878.74
13. Mr. B's offer is worth $2064 more in current dollars.
15. a. The cash price has a $947.64 advantage in current dollars.
    b. The instalment purchase has a $552.68 advantage in current dollars.
17. $25,591.07
19. Three payments of $2096.90

21. $19,759.46
23. $5515.00; $11,030.00
25. $3703.02; $11,109.06

REVIEW PROBLEMS

1. $67.73
3. a. $14,750.38
   b. $906.75
5. Principal = $2012.56
   Interest = $285.22
7. $38,288.36
9. $3372.42
11. $7972.59
13. 7.75% compounded annually
15. Current price = $229.44
    Increase in value = $25.20
17. $4327.07
19. 16.32%
21. $2500.00
23. $3917.24

SELF-TEST EXERCISE

1. a. $14,354.74 for the RateRiser GIC
      $14,356.29 for the fixed-rate GIC
   b. $854.66 from the RateRiser GIC
      $866.72 from the fixed-rate GIC
2. a. $19,456.84
   b. $5290.32
   c. 267.8%
3. $1763.25
4. $979.19
5. $12,322.58
6. $9267.27
7. Offer 1 is worth $37,180.13
   Offer 2 is worth $38,164.23
   Offer 2 should be accepted
8. $61.80 more will be earned from the Escalator GIC.
9. $6338.16
10. 59.05%
11. $1975.49
12. $2311.51

CHAPTER 9   COMPOUND INTEREST: FURTHER TOPICS AND APPLICATIONS

EXERCISE 9.1

1. 8.125% compounded annually
3. 9.00% compounded quarterly
5. 8.50% compounded monthly
7. 4.37% compounded annually
9. 5.25% compounded annually
11. 8.02% compounded annually
13. 30.20% compounded annually
15. 5.77% per year
17. 5.93%
19. 10.80% compounded monthly
21. *a.* TSE 300 portfolio: 12.63%
    T-bill portfolio: 10.19%
    b. TSE 300 portfolio: $3441.78
    T-bill portfolio: $2221.16
    c. TSE 300 portfolio: 6.37%
    T-bill portfolio: 4.07%
23. *a.* TSE 300 stocks: 1.50%
    S&P 500 stocks: 6.63%
    b. 5.30
25. −1.62%
27. 3-year return = 17.31%
    5-year return = 19.36%
    10-year return = 12.45%

EXERCISE 9.2

1. 23 years
3. 6 years and 6 months
5. 2 years and 11 months
7. 3.5 years
9. 14.5 years
11. *a.* 8 years and 7 months
    b. 6 years and 9 months
13. *a.* 18 years
    b. 15¾ years
15. *a.* 56 years and 5 months
    b. 21 years and 10 months
17. 23 months
19. 2 years, 11 months, and 24 days
21. 11 years and 129 days
23. 1 year, 9 months, and 57 days

EXERCISE 9.3

1. 9.76% compounded semiannually
3. 9.57% compounded monthly
5. 9.88% compounded quarterly
7. 10.38% compounded annually
9. 9.92% compounded monthly
11. 10.21% compounded semiannually
13. 9.20% compounded annually
15. 7.95% compounded monthly
17. 7.43% compounded quarterly
19. 8.59% compounded semiannually
21. *a.* 9.20% compounded annually
    b. 9.31% compounded annually
    c. 9.38% compounded annually
23. 7.39% compounded monthly
25. 12.30% compounded semiannually
27. 7.95% compounded monthly
    8.09% compounded semiannually

EXERCISE 9.4

1. 15.56%
3. 16.08%
5. 7.71%
7. 14.48% compounded semiannually
9. 14.06% compounded monthly
11. 7.30% compounded quarterly
13. 12.68%
15. 12.01%
17. 10.00% compounded semiannually
19. 9.57% compounded monthly
21. 23.87%
23. 26.82%
25. 9.10%
27. 10.72%
29. Accept the credit union loan
31. Choose the bank mortgage loan
33. 7.75% compounded annually
    7.61% compounded semiannually
    7.49% compounded monthly
35. 19.68% compounded monthly

Exercise 9B

1. Current yield = 5.79%
   Effective yield = 5.96%
3. 5.78%
5. a. 6.90%
   b. 6.83%
7. 46.62%
9. Simple rate = 9.75%
   Effective rate = 10.20%
11. Simple rate = −9.33%
    Effective rate = −9.01%
13. Simple rate = 6.00%
    Effective rate = 6.15%
15. a. 972.7%
    b. 227.5%
17. Simple rate = 91.83%
    Effective rate = 138.7%
19. a. 34.72%
    b. 43.14%
21. Simple rate = 14.11%
    Effective rate = 14.91%

Review Problems

1. 23.44% compounded annually
3. 14.43% compounded annually

5. 4.89%
7. August 1 of the following year
9. 1.75 years
11. 2 years and 118 days
13. 10.73% compounded semiannually
15. 19.56%
17. 7.02%
19. Choose the bank mortgage

Self-Test Exercise

1. 7.40% compounded annually
2. 2.37%
3. a. 11.11%
   b. 5 years and 6 months
4. 3.12% compounded annually
5. 3-year return = 20.07%
   5-year return = 7.64%
   10-year return = 5.98%
6. 10 years and 4 months
7. 22 months
8. 13 years and 131 days
9. 8.21% compounded semiannually
10. Choose the credit union loan
11. 10.52%

CHAPTER 10   ORDINARY ANNUITIES: FUTURE VALUE AND PRESENT VALUE

Exercise 10.2

1. $13,551.86
3. $2481.66
5. $28,023.46
7. $346,122.02
9. a. $6105.10
   b. $15,937.42
   c. $31,772.48
   d. $57,275.00
   e. $98,347.06
   f. $164,494.02
11. a. (i) $9254.65
    (ii) $9679.33
    (iii) $9826.56

b. (i) $10,717.94
   (ii) $10,406.66
   (iii) $10,226.04
13. $30,014.43
15. $188,830.07
17. $20,115.29
19. Leona will have $125,616 more than John

Exercise 10.3

1. 10.381%
3. 4.040%
5. 0.908%
7. 1.884%
9. 0.816%

11. $33,515.32

13. $21,764.70

15. $156,049.64

17. $23,135.41; $7135.41

19. a. $84,700.90

   b. $88,673.74

   c. $89,635.35

21. $20,885.53 larger

23. $88,869.62

25. $73,953.35

27. $195,703.18

EXERCISE 10.4

1. $3291.74

3. $2033.16

5. $11,355.21

7. $15,047.05

9. $10,120.92

11. $16,464.70

13. $26,388.76

15. a. $3790.79

   b. $6144.57

   c. $8513.56

   d. $9426.91

   e. $9999.27

   f. $10,000.00

17. $82,211,000

19. $16,767,320

21. $34,429.70

23. $34,513.13

EXERCISE 10.5

1.

	8%	9%
20 years	$358,662.88	$333,434.86
25 years	$388,693.57	357,484.87

3. a. $200,000

b. $27,423.04

5. The multiple-payment offer is worth $191.90 more

7. Mrs. Martel's offer is worth $137.31 more

9. $2193.15

11. $3304.30

13. $946.36

15. The $1000 annuity has the greater economic value

17. $59,623.78

19. Choose the $150,000 cash prize

21. a. $21,750.01

   b. $17,365.12

23. The pension-at-age-65 option has a 20.7% higher economic value

REVIEW PROBLEMS

1. Choose the 5-year-payment option

3. a. $160,000

   b. $48,628

5. $21,901.45

7. $130,346.18

9. $57,970.62

11. a. $59,999.80

   b. $39,119.37

SELF-TEST EXERCISE

1. a. $100,822.83

   b. $96,754.03

2. a. $46,800.03

   b. $24,997.20

3. $2376.15

4. $82,819.01

5. $5623.01

6. $81,160.11

7. $30,795.12

CHAPTER 11   ANNUITIES DUE: FUTURE VALUE AND PRESENT VALUE

EXERCISE 11.1

1. $8964.56

3. $13,366.94

5. $43,362.43

7. $8404.79

9. $48,508.71

11. $33,130.87

13. $108,964.03

15. Balance = $4021.14
    Interest = $221.14

17. *a.* $29,242.38

    b. $31,700.88

19. $223,904.52

Exercise 11.2

1. $2707.11

3. $10,111.90

5. $19,603.86

7. $4058.70

9. $13,865.77

11. $23,142.25

13. $20,457.00

15. *a.* $49.65 million

    b. $43.58 million

17. Mrs. Martel's offer is worth $137.31 more

19. *a.* $10,368.61

21. *a.* $31,524.95

b. $8011.65

23. $12,262.47

25. The present value on the client's 26th birthday of each premium stream is $9049.96 for Paul Revere and $9033.82 for Provident. There is a $16.13 advantage with Provident.

Review Problems

1. *a.* $89,170.65

   b. $14,312.37

3. $19,611.84

5. *a.* $11,572.42

7. $253,885.59

Self-Test Exercise

1. *a.* $105,107.80

   b. $104,978.12

2. The monthly payment plan is slightly better

3. *a.* $2,037,008

   b. $1,203,077

4. $31,516.97

Chapter 12 Annuities: Payment Size, Term, and Interest Rate

Exercise 12.1

1. $3000.00

3. $132.50

5. $349.99

7. $1130.00

9. $2077.58

11. $762.57

13. $1075.51

15. $3324.24

17. $1060.28

19. $3298.84

21. *a.* $2735.76

    b. $2033.61

23. *a.* $3586.51

    b. $3909.30

25. *a.* $237.40

    b. $161.12

27. *a.* $322.65

    b. $156.50

29. $1974.83

31. $20,006.16

33. $7419.89

35. $302.75

37. $2222.05

39. $401.90

41. $978.42

43. *a.* $622.06

    b. $3599.09

45. *a.* $1081.05

    b. $33,137.29

47. $1727.32

49. $1962.61

51. $12,554.29

53. $501.07 quarterly
    $169.04 monthly
55. $9269.72
57. *a.* $2638.88
    b. $1354.73
59. $1459.87

EXERCISE 12.2

1. 8 years and 6 months
3. 16 years and 9 months
5. 25 years
7. 8 years
9. 17 years
11. 9 years
13. 10 years
15. 8 years
17. 8 years
19. 9 years
21. 7 years
23. 18 years and 7 months
25. 4 years and 8 months
27. *a.* 26 years
    b. 27 years
29. 25 months from today (26th deposit)
31. 22 years and 3 months
33. 2 years and 9 months
35. 4 years and 4 months
37. 6 more contributions
39. Beyond age 79 years and 7 months
41. 16 years and 10 months
43. *a.* 18 years and 2 months
    b. 3 years and 10 months
45. 26 years
47. 18 years and 4 months

EXERCISE 12.3

1. 7.70% compounded annually
   7.70%
3. 10.50% compounded quarterly
   10.92%
5. 8.50% compounded semiannually
   8.68%
7. 9.00% compounded monthly
   9.38%

9. 11.50% compounded semiannually
   11.83%
11. 13.00% compounded quarterly
    13.65%
13. 9.80% compounded monthly
    10.25%
15. 10.28% compounded monthly
    10.78%
17. 7.90% compounded monthly
    8.19%
19. 8.50% compounded semiannually
    8.68%
21. 11.40% compounded monthly
    12.01%
23. 19.16%
25. 3.62%
27. 8.16%
29. 11.25% compounded monthly
31. 12.60% compounded semiannually
    13.00%
33. 19.53%
35. 65.48%
37. 9.24%
39. *a.* 9.86%
    b. 9.78%
    c. 13.45%
41. 15.30%

EXERCISE 12C

1. *a.* 2.714
   b. 2.357
   c. 0.8375
3. $1347.92

REVIEW PROBLEMS

1. *a.* $5418.78
   b. $2204.89
3. *a.* $25,527.54
   b. $27,505.93
5. 7.45% compounded monthly
   7.71%
7. 8.775%
9. 10.36%
11. 6.39% compounded monthly
    6.58%

13. 20 years and 9 months

15. 12.55%

17. 29

19. 17.43%

21. 10.76%

23. *a.* $7506.74

    b. $11,580.67

25. *a.* $1,066,335

    b. $3737.03

27. 86 years

29. 27.77%

31. 20 years and 10 months

33. $2383.97

35. $7499.21

SELF-TEST EXERCISE

1. *a.* $475.31

   b. $531.10

2. 5 years and 3 months

   $30,760

3. $209.61

4. 10.54%

5. $322.29

6. 5 years and 3 months

7. *a.* $740.13

   b. 16 years and 11 months

8. $1144.74

9. 3 years and 2 months

10. 18

11. 103.54%

12. $8.93

13. 12.02%

CHAPTER 13   OTHER ANNUITIES

EXERCISE 13.1

1. $8720.93

3. *a.* $10,000

   b. $10,000

5. *a.* $44.44

   b. $40.00

7. $35,714.29

9. $6055.56

11. $26,262.38

13. $77,711.79 and $78,211.79

15. $1460.28

17. $24,867.49

19. *a.* $54,828.73

   b. $53,828.73

   c. $50,936.84

21. $4090.29

23. $10,399.26

EXERCISE 13.2

1. $20,150.88

3. $14,032.77

5. $4132.71

7. 4 years

9. 1 year and 4 months

11. 12 years

13. $20,035.79

15. $14,074.16

17. $675.54

19. 3 years

21. 3 years

23. 7 years and 6 months

25. $24,949.52

27. $48,752.43

29. $48,559.18

31. $327,454.29

33. $2027.98

35. *a.* $133.98

   b. $973.31

37. $8821.74

39. 51

41. 20 years and 3 months

43. 10 years and 11 months

45. 8 years and 3 months

47. 2 years and 6 months

49. 7 years

51. Northwest Mutual

EXERCISE **13.3**

1. 1 year and 11 months
3. 15 years
5. $2412.64
7. $863,467
9. $572,376.63
11. $367.67
13. *a.* $138,000
    b. $82,857.57
    c. $258,342
15. $1643.51
17. $1429.49
19. $1330.69

REVIEW PROBLEMS

1. 17.10%
3. $18,858.53
5. *a.* $102,000
   b. $94,232.23
   c. $68,643.08

7. 4 years and 9 months
9. 23 (with the 23rd withdrawal being about $60)
11. $15,298.16
13. $122.62
15. 27 years and 3 months

SELF-TEST EXERCISE

1. $2611.53
2. $55,987.12
3. $1223.38
4. *a.* $973,019.25
   b. $11,660.99
   c. $7309.97
5. 14.54%
6. $2390.05
7. 16 years and 10 months
8. Lena: $946.39
   Axel: $1421.64
9. $3111.71 per month at age 67
   $5048.10 per month at age 72

CHAPTER **14**   AMORTIZATION OF LOANS

EXERCISE **14.1**

	Principal portion	Interest portion
1.	$ 958.05	$ 116.05
3.	1250.18	281.51
5.	284.00	108.76
7.	779.37	569.91
9.	656.25	200.41
11.	959.81	1017.07
13.	284.62	117.32
	Total principal	Total interest
15.	$1904.23	$ 646.03
17.	3681.81	3454.84
19.	4492.22	883.95
21.	714.50	382.87

23. *a.* $1395.08
    b. $709.99
    c. $17,878.32
    d. $3422.31

25. *a.* $153.74
    b. $401.63
    c. $910.28
    d. $1393.78

27.
Payment number	Payment	Interest portion	Principal portion	Principal balance
0				$1000.00
1	$174.03	$12.50	$161.53	838.47
2	174.03	10.48	163.55	674.92
3	174.03	8.44	165.59	509.33
4	174.03	6.37	167.66	341.67
5	174.03	4.27	169.76	171.91
6	174.06	2.15	171.91	0.00
		$44.21		

29.
Payment number	Payment	Interest portion	Principal portion	Principal balance
0				$9000.00
1	$1840.85	$556.54	$1284.31	7715.69
2	1840.85	477.12	1363.73	6351.96
3	1840.85	392.79	1448.06	4903.90
4	1840.85	303.25	1537.60	3366.30
5	1840.85	208.17	1632.68	1733.62
6	1840.82	107.20	1733.62	0.00

31.

Payment number	Payment	Interest portion	Principal portion	Principal balance
0				$8000.00
1	$1115.74	$200.00	$ 915.74	7084.26
2	1115.74	177.11	938.63	6145.63
3	2615.74	153.64	2462.10	3683.53
4	1115.74	92.09	1023.65	2659.88
5	1115.74	66.50	1049.24	1610.64
6	1115.74	40.27	1075.47	535.17
7	548.55	13.38	535.17	0.00
		$742.99		

33.

Payment number	Payment	Interest portion	Principal portion	Principal balance
0				$60,000.00
1	$1126.74	$525.00	$ 601.74	59,398.26
2	1126.74	519.73	607.01	58,791.25
.	.	.	.	.
.	.	.	.	.
.	.	.	.	.
42				29,616.38
43	1126.74	259.14	867.60	28,748.78
44	1126.74	251.55	875.19	27,873.59
.	.	.	.	.
.	.	.	.	.
.	.	.	.	.
70				2224.07
71	1126.74	19.46	1107.28	1116.79
72	1126.56	9.77	1116.79	0.00

35. *a.* $900.41

b. $440.20

c. $648.12

EXERCISE 14.2

	Principal portion	Interest portion	Last payment
1.	$ 842.78	$ 240.19	$ 604.28
3.	467.58	566.86	664.87
5.	1374.54	1644.11	2130.46
7.	404.87	191.82	373.51

9. *a.* $2205.35

b. $1696.62

c. $11,933.60

d. $2865.32

11. *a.* $78.86

b. $359.40

c. $979.13

d. $1659.12

13.

Payment number	Payment	Interest portion	Principal portion	Principal balance
0				$1000.00
1	$200.00	$12.50	$187.50	812.50
2	200.00	10.16	189.84	622.66
3	200.00	7.78	192.22	430.44
4	200.00	5.38	194.62	235.82
5	200.00	2.95	197.05	38.77
6	39.25	0.48	38.77	0.00
		$39.25		

15.

Payment number	Payment	Interest portion	Principal portion	Principal balance
0				$9000.00
1	$2000.00	$556.54	$1443.46	7556.54
2	2000.00	467.28	1532.72	6023.82
3	2000.00	372.50	1627.50	4396.32
4	2000.00	271.86	1728.14	2668.18
5	2000.00	164.99	1835.01	833.17
6	884.69	51.52	833.17	0.00

17.

Payment number	Payment	Interest portion	Principal portion	Principal balance
0				$7500.00
1	$1000.00	$187.50	$ 812.50	6687.50
2	1000.00	167.19	832.81	5854.69
3	2000.00	146.37	1853.63	4001.06
4	1000.00	100.03	899.97	3101.09
5	1000.00	77.53	922.47	2178.62
6	1000.00	54.47	945.53	1233.09
7	1000.00	30.83	969.17	263.92
8	270.52	6.60	263.92	0.00
		$770.52		

19.

Payment number	Payment	Interest portion	Principal portion	Principal balance
0				$60,000.00
1	$1000.00	$525.00	$475.00	59,525.00
2	1000.00	520.84	479.16	59,045.84
.	.	.	.	.
.	.	.	.	.
.	.	.	.	.
55				26,629.91
56	1000.00	233.01	766.99	25,862.92
57	1000.00	226.30	773.70	25,089.22
.	.	.	.	.
.	.	.	.	.
.	.	.	.	.
84				1435.19
85	1000.00	12.56	987.44	447.75
86	451.67	3.92	447.75	0.00

21. *a.* 7 years and 1 month after date of loan.

b. $486.42

c. $377.72

d. $814.34

EXERCISE 14.3

1. $7660 in first 5 years
   $11,448 in 2nd 5 years
   $17,109 in 3rd 5 years
   $25,571 in 4th 5 years
   $38,212 in last 5 years

3. *a.* $763.21 at a rate of 8%
      $827.98 at a rate of 9%
      $894.49 at a rate of 10%
   b. 8.03%
   c. $128,963 at 8%
      $148,394 at 9%
      $168,347 at 10%

5. *a.* $131,025
   b. $120,776

7. $57.14

9. *a.* $77,587.44
   b. $692.26

11. *a.* $33,866.00
    b. $410.00

13. *a.* $16,456.38
    b. $90.45

15. *a.* $157,200
    b. $165,500

17. *a.* $811.61
    b. 19 years and 28 weeks

19. *a.* 2 years and 1 month
    b. 3 years and 10 months

21. *a.* 1 year and 11 months
    b. 3 years and 5 months

23. 5 months

25. 8 months

27. 9 years and 2 months

29. *a.* 3 years and 1 month
    b. $106,008.91

31. *a.* 3 years and 4 months
    b. $87,282.67

33. *a.* 6 years and 8 months
    b. $70,357.69

35. $88,826.77

EXERCISE 14.4

1. 18.135%

3. *a.* 12.607%
   b. 12.144%
   c. 12.068%

5. *a.* The trust company's loan has an effective rate that is 0.38% lower.
   b. The trust company's loan has an effective rate that is 0.19% lower.

7. *a.* $34,488.28
   b. $36,699.09

9. *a.* $60,024.46
   b. $58,538.34
   c. $57,100.64

11. $161,588.89

13. $141,749.57

15. $2922.73

17. $566.16

19. 14 years and 5 months

21. *a.* $107,580; 43.61%
    b. $159,348; 53.39%
    c. $220,694; 61.33%

23. 40.59%

25. 27 years and 4 months

REVIEW PROBLEMS

1.

Payment number	Payment	Interest portion	Principal portion	Principal balance
0				$862.50
1	$148.50	$ 8.09	$140.41	722.09
2	148.50	6.77	141.73	580.36
3	148.50	5.44	143.06	437.30
4	148.50	4.10	144.40	292.90
5	148.50	2.75	145.75	147.15
6	148.53	1.38	147.15	0.00
		$28.53		

3. *a.* $785.01
   b. $236.32
   c. $5579.53
   d. $2516.16

5.

No.	Payment	Interest portion	Principal portion	Principal balance
0				$60,000.00
1	$10,000.00	$ 3150.00	$6850.00	53,150.00
2	10,000.00	2790.38	7209.62	45,940.38
3	10,000.00	2411.87	7588.13	38,352.25
4	10,000.00	2013.49	7986.51	30,365.74
5	10,000.00	1594.20	8405.80	21,959.94
6	10,000.00	1152.90	8847.10	13,112.84
7	10,000.00	688.42	9311.58	3801.26
8	4,000.83	199.57	3801.26	0.00
		$14,000.83		

7. *a.* $226.25

 b. $385.64

 c. $1414.28

 d. $3664.33

9. *a.* $79,914.89

 b. $872.38

11. $19,719.03

13. *a.* 5 years and 11 months

 b. $99,423.78

15. *a.* 11.98%

 b. 11.51%

17. $190,115. Accept the Sharpe offer.

19. 38.62%

SELF-TEST EXERCISE

1. *a.* $86.32

 b. $302.74

 c. $2840.92

 d. $992.09

2.

Payment number	Payment	Interest portion	Principal portion	Principal balance
0				$6400.00
1	$161.70	$52.26	$109.44	6290.56
2	161.70	51.36	110.34	6180.22
.	.	.	.	.
.	.	.	.	.
33				2274.13
34	161.70	18.57	143.13	2131.00
35	161.70	17.40	144.30	1986.70
.	.	.	.	.
.	.	.	.	.
46				319.47
47	161.70	2.61	159.09	160.38
48	161.69	1.31	160.38	0.00

3. *a.* $7023.10

 b. $4989.79

 c. $4664.05

 d. $13,861.82

 e. $20,976.85

4. $39,453.90

5. *a.* 2 years and 1 month

 b. $77,157.87

6. 12.20%

7. $185,596

8. $144,452

9. 41.54%

CHAPTER 15 BONDS AND SINKING FUNDS

EXERCISE 15.2

1. $1205.58

3. $904.79

5. $855.15

7. $1452.73

9. Bond A: $1081.11
 Bond B: $1135.90
 Bond C: $1172.92
 Bond D: $1214.82
 The longer a bond's maturity, the greater the premium for a given difference: "Coupon rate – Market rate."

11. Bond J: $1092.01
 Bond K: $1184.02
 Bond L: $1276.02
 The greater the difference, "Coupon rate – Market rate," the greater the price premium.

13. Bond E: $862.01
 Bond F: $1137.99

15. Bond G: −$37.69
 Bond H: −$59.75
 Bond J: −$84.66
 The longer a bond's maturity, the more sensitive the bond's price is to market interest rate changes.

17. $104.96

19. $93.70

21. *a.* $10,662.58

    b. 6.62%

23. *a.* 12.94%

    b. 0%

    c. −10.78%

25. 28.49% compounded semiannually

EXERCISE 15.3

1. 11.41% compounded semiannually

3. Bond A: 10.30% csa
   Bond C: 9.57% csa

5.   *a.* 0.78% decrease
    b. 0.26% decrease

7. 17.54% compounded semiannually

EXERCISE 15.4

1. $1170.68

3. $930.62

5. $891.23

7. $1461.14

9. $1110.82

11. $563.91

13. March 15: $915.66
    April 15: $923.22
    May 15: $930.59
    June 15: $938.27
    July 15: $945.77
    August 15: $953.57
    September 15: $916.44

15. *a.* $1070.62
    b. 25.55%

17. 104.22%

19. $1100.08

21. $869.49

EXERCISE 15.5

1. Price: $1026.21; total interest: $243.79.

Coupon number	Coupon payment	Interest on book value	Premium amortized	Book value of bond	Unamortized premium
0	—	—	—	$1026.21	$26.21
1	$ 45.00	$ 41.05	$ 3.95	1022.26	22.26
2	45.00	40.89	4.11	1018.15	18.15
3	45.00	40.73	4.27	1013.87	13.87
4	45.00	40.55	4.45	1009.43	9.43
5	45.00	40.38	4.62	1004.81	4.81
6	45.00	40.19	4.81	1000.00	0.00
	$270.00	**$243.79**	$26.21		

3. Price: $1087.85; total interest: $1112.15.

Coupon number	Coupon payment	Interest on book value	Premium amortized	Book value of bond	Unamortized premium
0	—	—	—	$1087.85	$87.85
1	$ 50.00	$ 47.87	$ 2.13	1085.71	85.71
2	50.00	47.77	2.23	1083.48	83.48
3	50.00	47.67	2.33	1081.16	81.16
.	.	.	.	.	.
.	.	.	.	.	.
.	.	.	.	.	.
21				1016.52	16.52
22	50.00	44.73	5.27	1011.25	11.25
23	50.00	44.50	5.50	1005.75	5.75
24	50.00	44.25	5.75	1000.00	0.00
	$1200.00	**$1112.15**	$87.85		

5. Price: $961.63; total interest: $278.37.

Coupon number	Coupon payment	Interest on book value	Discount amortized	Book value of bond	Unamortized discount
0	—	—	—	$ 961.63	$38.37
1	$ 40.00	$ 45.68	$ 5.68	967.30	32.70
2	40.00	45.95	5.95	973.25	26.75
3	40.00	46.23	6.23	979.48	20.52
4	40.00	46.53	6.53	986.00	14.00
5	40.00	46.84	6.84	992.84	7.16
6	40.00	47.16	7.16	1000.00	0.00
	$240.00	**$278.37**	$38.37		

7. Price: $877.20; total interest: $1057.80.

Coupon number	Coupon payment	Interest on book value	Discount amortized	Book value of bond	Unamortized discount
0	—	—	—	$ 877.20	$122.80
1	$ 42.50	$ 45.61	$ 3.11	880.31	119.69
2	42.50	45.78	3.28	883.59	116.41
3	42.50	45.95	3.45	887.04	112.96
.	.	.	.	.	.
.	.	.	.	.	.
.	.	.	.	.	.
19				974.23	25.77
20	42.50	50.66	8.16	982.39	17.61
21	42.50	51.08	8.58	990.97	9.03
22	42.50	51.53	9.03	1000.00	0.00
	$935.00	$1057.80	$122.80		

EXERCISE 15.6

	Payment	Balance
1.	$424,333	$6,196,094
3.	$620,292	$9,534,856
5.	$ 87,284	$2,506,640
7.	$344,297	$9,268,208

	Payment	Annual cost of debt	Book value
9.	$353,611	$1,707,222	$4,836,586
11.	$302,726	$1,955,452	$6,081,667
13.	$614,137	$1,788,274	$2,311,969
15.	$204,464	$1,536,428	$5,478,509

17.

Payment interval number	Payment (at end)	Interest earned	Increase in the fund	Balance in fund (end of interval)
0	—	—	—	$ 0
1	$122,135	$ 0	$122,135	122,135
2	122,135	4275	126,410	248,545
3	122,135	8699	130,834	379,379
4	122,135	13,278	135,413	514,792
5	122,135	18,018	140,153	654,945
6	122,135	22,923	145,058	800,003
		$67,193	$800,003	

19.

Payment interval number	Payment (at start)	Interest earned	Increase in the fund	Balance in fund (end of interval)
0	—	—	—	$ 0
1	$163,710	$ 11,050	$ 174,760	174,760
2	163,710	22,847	186,557	361,317
3	163,710	35,439	199,149	560,466
4	163,710	48,882	212,592	773,058
5	163,710	63,232	226,942	1,000,000
		$181,450	**$1,000,000**	

21.

Payment interval number	Payment (at end)	Interest earned	Increase in the fund	Balance in fund (end of interval)
0	—	—	—	$ 0
1	$302,720	$ 0	$302,720	302,720
2	302,720	4541	307,261	609,981
3	302,720	9150	311,870	921,851
.	.	.	.	.
.	.	.	.	.
.	.	.	.	.
10				3,239,928
11	302,720	48,599	351,319	3,591,247
12	302,720	53,869	356,589	3,947,836
.	.	.	.	.
.	.	.	.	.
.	.	.	.	.
17				5,812,634
18	302,720	87,190	389,910	6,202,544
19	302,720	93,038	395,758	6,598,302
20	302,720	98,975	401,695	6,999,997

23.

Payment interval number	Payment	Interest earned	Increase in the fund	Balance in fund (end of interval)	Book value of the debt
0	—	—	—	$ 0	$10,000,00
1	$353,611	$ 0	$353,611	353,611	9,646,389
2	353,611	12,376	365,987	719,598	9,280,402
3	353,611	25,186	378,797	1,098,395	8,901,605
.	.	.	.	.	.
.	.	.	.	.	.
.	.	.	.	.	.
17				8,028,743	1,971,257
18	353,611	281,006	634,617	8,663,360	1,336,640
19	353,611	303,218	656,829	9,320,189	679,811
20	353,611	326,207	679,818	10,000,007	(7)

25. *a.* $8221

    b. $29,938

    c. The 33rd month

    d. $2003

27. *a.* $198,368

    b. $217,583

    c. $585,395

d.

Payment interval number	Payment	Interest earned	Increase in the fund	Balance in fund (end of interval)	Book value of the debt
0	—	—	—	$ 0	$20,000,000
1	$198,368	$ 0	$ 198,368	198,368	19,801,632
2	198,368	8431	206,799	405,167	19,594,833
3	198,368	17,220	215,588	620,755	19,379,245
.	.	.	.	.	.
.	.	.	.	.	.
.	.	.	.	.	.
37				17,104,453	2,895,547
38	198,368	726,939	925,307	18,029,760	1,970,240
39	198,368	766,265	964,633	18,994,393	1,005,607
40	198,368	807,262	1,005,630	20,000,023	(23)
		$12,065,303			

29. *a.* $13,737

b.

Payment interval number	Payment	Interest earned	Increase in the fund	Balance in fund (end of interval)	Book value of the debt
0	—	—	—	$ 0	$800,000
1	$13,737	$ 240	$13,977	13,977	786,023
2	13,737	485	14,222	28,199	771,801
3	13,737	734	14,471	42,670	757,330
.	.	.	.	.	.
.	.	.	.	.	.
.	.	.	.	.	.
37				718,907	81,093
38	13,737	12,821	26,558	745,465	54,535
39	13,737	13,286	27,023	772,488	27,512
40	13,737	13,759	27,496	799,984	16
		$250,504			

REVIEW PROBLEMS

1. $103.14

3. $2246.55

5. $1217.57

7.

Coupon number	Coupon payment	Interest on book value	Premium amortized	Book value of bond	Unamortized premium
0	—	—	—	$1118.27	$118.27
1	$ 52.50	$ 49.20	$ 3.30	1114.97	114.97
2	52.50	49.06	3.44	1111.53	111.53
3	52.50	48.91	3.59	1107.94	107.94
.	.	.	.	.	.
.	.	.	.	.	.
.	.	.	.	.	.
19				1023.41	23.41
20	52.50	45.03	7.47	1015.94	15.94
21	52.50	44.70	7.80	1008.14	8.14
22	52.50	44.36	8.14	1000.00	0.00
	$1155.00	$1036.73	$118.27		

9.

Payment interval number	Payment (at start)	Interest earned	Increase in the fund	Balance in fund (end of interval)
0	—	—	—	$ 0
1	$112,571	$ 3377	$115,948	115,948
2	112,571	6856	119,427	235,375
3	112,571	10,438	123,009	358,384
4	112,571	14,129	126,700	485,084
5	112,571	17,930	130,501	615,585
6	112,571	21,845	134,416	750,001
		$74,575	$750,001	

SELF-TEST EXERCISE

1. $42.19

2. 22.22%

3. 10.87% compounded semiannually

4. $1301.18

5. $1286.78

6.

Coupon number	Coupon payment	Interest on book value	Discount amortized	Book value of bond	Unamortized discount
0	—	—	—	$4838.76	$161.24
1	$ 225.00	$ 254.03	$ 29.03	4867.80	132.20
2	225.00	255.56	30.56	4898.35	101.65
3	225.00	257.16	32.16	4930.52	69.48
4	225.00	258.85	33.85	4964.37	35.63
5	225.00	260.63	35.63	5000.00	0.00
	$1125.00	$1286.24	$161.24		

Total interest: $1286.24

7.

Payment interval number	Payment	Interest earned	Increase in the fund	Balance in fund (end of interval)	Book value of the debt
0	—	—	—	$ 0	$500,000
1	$28,285	$ 0	$28,285	28,285	471,715
2	28,285	990	29,275	57,560	442,440
3	28,285	2015	30,300	87,860	412,140
.	.	.	.	.	.
.	.	.	.	.	.
.	.	.	.	.	.
11				371,721	128,279
12	28,285	13,010	41,295	413,016	86,984
13	28,285	14,456	42,741	455,757	44,243
14	28,285	15,951	44,236	499,993	7

CHAPTER 16 BUSINESS INVESTMENT DECISIONS

EXERCISE 16.1

1. *a.* Vencap should make the investment since the present value ($33,694) exceeds the required investment.

   b. $3694

3. $24,640

5. $16,346

7. *a.* Leasing saves $1545 in current dollars.

   b. Purchasing saves $979 in current dollars.

9. *a.* Lease.

   b. $1201

11. *a.* $3421 advantage to renting.

   b. $4249 advantage to buying.

EXERCISE 16.2

1. *a.* Yes (NPV = $17,389).

   b. No (NPV = −$187).

   c. No (NPV = −$15,228).

3. $71,744

5. No (NPV = −$109,521).

7. No (NPV = −$135,946).

9. No (NPV = −$16,653).

EXERCISE 16.3

1. Select B and D.

3. Select F, E, and A (having a combined NPV of $11,639).

5. The Deere's NPV is $4482 larger.

7. Project D is worth $3575 more today.

9. Model H has a $2507 higher equivalent annual cash flow.

11. The 25-ton truck has a $997 higher equivalent annual cash flow.

13. The Falcon has a $317 lower equivalent annual cost.

15. The International has a $1422 lower equivalent annual cost.

EXERCISE 16.4

1. 15.1%

3. Approve phase 1 (IRR = 27.3%).
   Approve phase 2 (IRR = 22.7%).
   Approve phase 3 (IRR = 14.6%).
   Reject phase 4 (IRR = 12.1%).

5. Yes (since IRR = 16.6% > 16.0%).

7. Yes since the IRR of 17.6% exceeds the cost of capital.

9. Yes. The IRR of 15% equals the cost of capital.

11. The IRR of 12.4% is less than the cost of capital. The mine should not be developed.

EXERCISE 16.5

1. *a.* Select D since its IRR (19.91%) is larger than C's IRR (18.10%).

   b. Select D—it has the larger NPV.

   c. Select C—it has the larger NPV.

3. *a.* Select XXX since its IRR (20.82%) is larger than YYY's IRR (17.33%).

   b. Select XXX—it has the larger NPV.

   c. Select YYY—it has the larger NPV.

5. *a.* Select Y since its IRR (17.46%) is larger than X's IRR (16.04%).

   b. Select Y—it has the larger NPV.

   c. Select X—it has the larger NPV.

EXERCISE 16.6

1. *a.* 4.67 years.

   b. No.

3.
Project	NPV	Payback
X	$ 8882	4 years
Y	$10,646	5 years

Prefer X on payback; prefer Y on NPV.

5.
Project	NPV	IRR	Payback
A	$4893	19.14%	2.64 years
B	$4589	20.02%	2.67 years

Project rankings:

Project	NPV	IRR	Payback
A	1	2	1
B	2	1	2

REVIEW PROBLEMS

1. *a.* Leasing produces a $621 savings.

   b. Buying produces a $657 savings.

3. No (NPV = −$316,666 at a 16% cost of capital).

5. Yes (NPV = $15,677).

7. Machine X has a $235 higher equivalent annual cash flow.

9. The Boston Wailer has a $2243 lower equivalent annual cost.

11. No. IRR = 13.91%, below the cost of capital.

13. *a.* Project P IRR = 15.03%.
    Project Q IRR = 15.56%.
    Q is preferred on the basis of the IRR.

   b. Reject both P and Q. Both have a negative NPV and an IRR < 16%.

   c. Select P. P's NPV ($22,375) is larger than Q's NPV ($18,244).

SELF-TEST EXERCISE

1. $10,766 advantage to leasing.

2. No. The investment's NPV = −$7424.

3. Select A, D, and C.

4. Project B has a $1606 higher NPV.

5. C has an annual economic advantage of $996.

6. The TaterTaker produces an equivalent annual cost savings of $858.

7. 2.7 years.

8. IRR = 12.02%. Do not introduce the product since the IRR is less than the cost of capital.

9. *a.* A: IRR = 30.46%
   B: IRR = 34.23%
   B is preferred on the basis of the IRR.

   b. A has a $540 larger NPV.

   c. B has a $179 larger NPV.

CHAPTER 17   DEPRECIATION AND DEPLETION

EXERCISE 17.2

1. *a.* $6571

b.

Year	Depreciation expense	Accumulated depreciation	Book value
0	—	—	$48,000
1	$6571	$ 6571	41,429
2	6571	13,142	34,858
3	6571	19,713	28,287
4	6571	26,284	21,716
5	6571	32,855	15,145
6	6571	39,426	8574
7	6571	45,997	2003

3. *a.* $13,000

   b. $43,000

EXERCISE 17.3

1. *a.* $550

b.

Year	Depreciation expense	Accumulated depreciation	Book value
0	—	—	$1,350,000
1	$211,750	$211,750	1,138,250
2	254,650	466,400	883,600
3	188,100	654,500	695,500
4	229,350	883,850	466,150

3.

Year	Depreciation expense	Accumulated depreciation	Book value
0	—	—	$73,000
1	$11,466	$11,466	61,534
2	10,296	21,762	51,238
3	13,482	35,244	37,756
4	14,436	49,680	23,320

EXERCISE 17.4

1. *a.*

Year	Depreciation expense	Accumulated depreciation	Book value
0	—	—	$12,400
1	$6200	$ 6200	6200
2	3100	9300	3100
3	1550	10,850	1550
4	775	11,625	775

b.

Year	Depreciation expense	Accumulated depreciation	Book value
0	—	—	$12,400
1	$1860	$1860	10,540
2	3162	5022	7378
3	2213	7235	5165
4	1549	8785	3615

c.

Year	Depreciation expense	Accumulated depreciation	Book value
0	—	—	$12,400
1	$5087	$ 5087	7313
2	3000	8087	4313
3	1769	9857	2543
4	1043	10,900	1500

3.

Depreciation method		Total depreciation expense			
		Years 1–5	Years 6–10	Years 11–15	Years 16–20
a.	DDB	$151,519	$89,470	$52,831	$31,196
b.	CCA	76,167	66,471	51,434	39,798
c.	CDB	74,761	59,655	47,601	37,983

5. ***a.***

Year	Depreciation expense	Accumulated depreciation	Book value
0	—	—	$27,000
1	$4500	$ 4500	22,500
2	3750	8250	18,750
3	3125	11,375	15,625
.	.	.	.
.	.	.	.
.	.	.	.
6			9042
7	1507	19,465	7535
.	.	.	.
.	.	.	.
.	.	.	.
11			3634
12	606	23,972	3028

c.

Year	Depreciation expense	Accumulated depreciation	Book value
0	—	—	$27,000
1	$3540	$ 3540	23,460
2	3076	6616	20,384
3	2672	9288	17,712
.	.	.	.
.	.	.	.
.	.	.	.
6			11,619
7	1523	16,904	10,096
.	.	.	.
.	.	.	.
.	.	.	.
11			5754
12	754	22,000	5000

b.

Year	Depreciation expense	Accumulated depreciation	Book value
0	—	—	$27,000
1	$1350	$ 1350	25,650
2	2565	3915	23,085
3	2309	6224	20,777
.	.	.	.
.	.	.	.
.	.	.	.
6			15,146
7	1515	13,369	13,631
.	.	.	.
.	.	.	.
.	.	.	.
11			8944
12	894	18,950	8050

EXERCISE 17.5

1.

Year	Depreciation rate	Depreciation expense	Accumulated depreciation	Book value
0	—	—	—	$48,000
1	25.00%	$12,000	$12,000	36,000
2	21.43	10,286	22,286	25,714
3	17.86	8571	30,857	17,143
4	14.29	6857	37,714	10,286
5	10.71	5143	42,857	5143
6	7.14	3429	46,286	1714
7	3.57	1714	48,000	0

3.

Year	Depreciation rate	Depreciation expense	Accumulated depreciation	Book value
0	—	—	—	$12,400
1	40%	$4360	$ 4360	8040
2	30	3270	7630	4770
3	20	2180	9810	2590
4	10	1090	10,900	1500

EXERCISE 17.6

1.

Year	Depletion expense	Accumulated depletion	Book value
0	—	—	$42,000,000
1	$663,600	$ 663,600	41,336,400
2	758,400	1,422,000	40,578,000
3	817,200	2,239,200	39,760,800
4	714,000	2,953,200	39,046,800

3.

Year	Depletion expense	Accumulated depletion	Book value
0	—	—	$2,975,000
1	$106,005	$106,005	2,868,995
2	160,062	266,067	2,708,933
3	152,958	419,025	2,555,975
4	167,943	586,968	2,388,032

REVIEW PROBLEMS

1. *a.* $21,000
   b. $51,000

3.

Depreciation method	Depreciation expense Year 1	Year 5	Year 10	Year-end book value Year 1	Year 5	Year 10
a. DDB	$16,000	$6554	$2147	$64,000	$26,214	$ 8590
b. CCA	8000	7373	2416	72,000	29,491	9664
c. CDB	15,020	6538	2311	64,980	28,284	10,000

5. *a.*

Year	Depreciation expense	Accumulated depreciation	Book value
0	—	—	$800,000
1	$187,500	$187,500	612,500
2	187,500	375,000	425,000
3	187,500	562,500	237,500
4	187,500	750,000	50,000

b.

Year	Depreciation expense	Accumulated depreciation	Book value
0	—	—	$800,000
1	$164,250	$164,250	635,750
2	197,625	361,875	438,125
3	183,375	545,250	254,750
4	146,250	691,500	108,500

c.

Year	Depreciation expense	Accumulated depreciation	Book value
0	—	—	$800,000
1	$151,250	$151,250	648,750
2	193,125	344,375	455,625
3	180,000	524,375	275,625
4	145,000	669,375	130,625

d.

Year	Depreciation expense	Accumulated depreciation	Book value
0	—	—	$800,000
1	$400,000	$400,000	400,000
2	200,000	600,000	200,000
3	100,000	700,000	100,000
4	50,000	750,000	50,000

e.

Year	Depreciation expense	Accumulated depreciation	Book value
0	—	—	$800,000
1	$100,000	$100,000	700,000
2	175,000	275,000	525,000
3	131,250	406,250	393,750
4	98,438	504,688	295,313

f.

Year	Depreciation expense	Accumulated depreciation	Book value
0	—	—	$800,000
1	$400,000	$400,000	400,000
2	200,000	600,000	200,000
3	100,000	700,000	100,000
4	50,000	750,000	50,000

g.

Year	Depreciation rate	Depreciation expense	Accumulated depreciation	Book value
0	—	—	—	$800,000
1	40.00%	$300,000	$300,000	500,000
2	30.00	225,000	525,000	275,000
3	20.00	150,000	675,000	125,000
4	10.00	75,000	750,000	50,000

SELF-TEST EXERCISE

1. **a.**

Year	Depreciation expense	Accumulated depreciation	Book value
0	—	—	$90,000
1	$18,750	$18,750	71,250
2	18,750	37,500	52,500
3	18,750	56,250	33,750
4	18,750	75,000	15,000

b.

Year	Depreciation expense	Accumulated depreciation	Book value
0	—	—	$90,000
1	$16,148	$16,148	73,852
2	18,293	34,441	55,559
3	19,838	54,279	35,721
4	17,850	72,129	17,871

c.

Year	Depreciation expense	Accumulated depreciation	Book value
0	—	—	$90,000
1	$16,695	$16,695	73,305
2	19,170	35,865	54,135
3	19,635	55,500	34,500
4	18,705	74,205	15,795

d.

Year	Depreciation expense	Accumulated depreciation	Book value
0	—	—	$90,000
1	$45,000	$45,000	45,000
2	22,500	67,500	22,500
3	11,250	78,750	11,250
4	5625	84,375	5625

e.

Year	Depreciation expense	Accumulated depreciation	Book value
0	—	—	$90,000
1	$13,500	$13,500	76,500
2	22,950	36,450	53,550
3	16,065	52,515	37,485
4	11,246	63,761	26,240

f.

Year	Depreciation expense	Accumulated depreciation	Book value
0	—	—	$90,000
1	$32,495	$32,495	57,505
2	20,763	53,258	36,742
3	13,266	66,524	23,476
4	8476	75,000	15,000

g.

Year	Depreciation rate	Depreciation expense	Accumulated depreciation	Book value
0	—	—	—	$90,000
1	40.00%	$30,000	$30,000	60,000
2	30.00	22,500	52,500	37,500
3	20.00	15,000	67,500	22,500
4	10.00	7500	75,000	15,000

2.

Depreciation method	Depreciation expense Year 1	Depreciation expense Year 7	Book value (end of year 9)
a. SL	$20,000	$20,000	$150,000
b. DDB	44,000	18,645	91,030
c. CCA	24,750	20,316	83,178
d. CDB	48,753	18,683	78,285

3.

Year	Depletion expense	Accumulated depletion	Book value
0	—	—	$30,000,000
1	$ 956,250	$ 956,250	29,043,750
2	1,690,000	2,646,250	27,353,750
3	1,983,750	4,630,000	25,370,000
4	1,886,250	6,516,250	23,483,750

CHAPTER 18 CONSUMER CREDIT

EXERCISE 18.1

1. **a.** $8.16

b. $571.49

c. $8.57

3.

	Statement date	Interest charge	Balance
a.	Aug 20	$0.00	$185.00
	Sept 20	2.78	282.78
	Oct 20	4.24	252.02

	Statement date	Interest charge	Balance
b.	Aug 20	$0.00	$185.00
	Sept 20	3.19	283.19
	Oct 20	3.78	251.97

5.

Statement date	Interest charge
May 5	$ 2.30
June 5	22.86
July 5	5.78

Exercise 18.2

1. Grace period interest = $430.21

Date	Number of days	Interest rate	Interest	Accrued interest	Payment made	Principal portion	Balance
30-Nov	—	—	—	—	—	—	$9830.21
31-Dec	31	9.00%	$75.14	~~$75.14~~	$135.00	$59.86	9770.35
16-Jan	16	9.00%	38.55	38.55			9770.35
31-Jan	15	9.25%	37.14	~~75.69~~	135.00	59.31	9711.04
28-Feb	28	9.25%	68.91	~~68.91~~	135.00	66.09	9644.95

3. Grace period interest = $389.50
Balance after Mar 31 payment = $6281.57

5.

Date	Number of days	Interest rate	Interest	Accrued interest	Payment made	Principal portion	Balance
30-Nov	—	—	—	—	—	—	$5500.00
31-Dec	31	10.00%	$ 46.71	~~$46.71~~	$150.00	$103.29	5396.71
31-Jan	31	10.00%	45.84	~~45.84~~	150.00	104.16	5292.55
29-Feb	29	10.00%	42.05	~~42.05~~	150.00	107.95	**5184.60**
			$134.60				

7.

Date	Number of days	Interest rate	Interest	Accrued interest	Payment made	Principal portion	Balance
30-Nov	—	—	—	—	—	—	$5200.00
31-Dec	31	9.75%	$43.06	~~$43.06~~	$110.00	$ 66.94	5133.06
30-Jan	30	9.75%	41.13	41.13			5133.06
31-Jan	1	9.50%	1.34	~~42.47~~	110.00	67.53	5065.53
14-Feb	14	9.50%	18.46	~~18.46~~	300.00	281.54	4783.99
28-Feb	14	9.50%	17.43	~~17.43~~	110.00	92.57	4691.42

Exercise 18A

1. a. $1687.98
   b. $354.65
3. a. $14,978.20
   b. $14,813.64
5. a. (i) $161.65
      (ii) $150.00
   b. Payout amount: $10,284.29
      Total interest: $2394.47

Self-Test Exercise

1. a. $14.19
   b. $817.75
   c. $13.90
2. Grace period interest = $375.44.

Date	Number of days	Interest rate	Interest	Accrued interest	Payment made	Principal portion	Balance
31-Oct	—	—	—	—	—	—	$7575.44
30-Nov	30	10.25%	$63.82	~~$63.82~~	$120.00	$56.18	7519.26
12-Dec	12	10.25%	25.34	25.34			7519.26
31-Dec	19	10.00%	39.14	~~64.48~~	120.00	55.52	7463.74
31-Jan	31	10.00%	63.39	~~63.39~~	120.00	56.61	7407.13

Accumulated depreciation   The cumulative total of all past and current depreciation expenses reported for an asset.

Accumulation factor   See *compounding factor.*

Accumulation factor for annuities   See *compounding factor for annuities.*

Algebraic expression   A statement of the mathematical operations to be carried out on a combination of numbers and variables.

Amortization of a loan   The repayment of a loan by periodic payments that, with the possible exception of the last payment, are equal in size.

Amortization of the bond discount   The process of increasing a bond's book value over the time remaining until maturity, by periodically reducing the bond's discount.

Amortization of the bond premium   The process of reducing a bond's book value over the time remaining until maturity, by periodically reducing the bond's premium.

Amortization period   The total length of time to repay a blended payment loan.

Annual cost of a debt   The combined total in a year of the interest payments on the debt and the sinking fund payments for retirement of the principal amount of the debt.

Annualized rate of return   The annual rate of return that results if a short-term rate of return continues for an entire year.

Annuity   A series of equal payments at regular intervals.

Annuity due   An annuity in which the periodic payments occur at the beginning of each payment interval.

Balloon payment   Any payment of principal over and above the regular periodic payments.

Base   (1) The quantity that is repeatedly multiplied by itself in a power.
(2) The initial amount to which a percent change is applied.

Binomial   An expression containing two terms.

Blended-payment loan   A loan repaid by equal regular payments that include both interest and principal.

Blended payments   Equal periodic payments combining principal with the interest that has accrued on the outstanding principal since the previous payment.

Bond   A debt instrument secured by specific assets. The bond issuer (borrower) promises to periodically pay accrued interest, and to repay the full principal amount of the debt on its maturity date. The term "bond" is sometimes used in a generic sense to refer to both true bonds and debentures.

Bond discount   The amount by which a bond's face value exceeds its quoted price.

Bond premium   The amount by which a bond's quoted price exceeds its face value.

Book value   The acquisition cost of a depreciable asset minus the accumulated depreciation.

Book value of a debt   The amount by which the principal balance owed on the debt exceeds the funds accumulated in a sinking fund for retiring the debt.

Break-even analysis   A procedure for determining the level of sales at which a firm's net income is zero.

Break-even chart   A graph presenting both total costs and total revenue as a function of sales volume so that the break-even point may be determined.

Break-even point   The sales volume at which net income is zero; the intersection of the total cost and total revenue lines on a break-even chart.

Capital cost allowance   Depreciation expense that may be deducted from revenues for the purpose of calculating taxable income.

Capital gain   The amount by which the end-of-period value of an investment exceeds its beginning-of-period value.

Capital loss   The amount by which the beginning-of-period value of an investment exceeds its end-of-period value.

Capital rationing   The circumstance in which there is a limit on the total amount of capital funds that a firm may invest during a period.

Cash discount   A discount allowed for a payment within the discount period.

Cash flow   Refers to a cash disbursement (cash outflow) or cash receipt (cash inflow).

Cash-flow sign convention   Widely recognized rules for indicating the direction of cash movement by attaching an algebraic sign to the dollar amount of the cash flow. Cash *inflows* (receipts) are positive, and cash *outflows* (disbursements) are negative.

Closed mortgage   A mortgage that does not allow any prepayments.

Commercial paper   Promissory notes issued by large corporations to borrow funds for a short term.

Common logarithm (of a number)   The exponent to which the base 10 must be raised in order to equal the number.

Complex fraction   A fraction containing one or more other fractions in its numerator or denominator.

Compound interest method   The procedure for calculating interest wherein interest is *periodically* calculated and *added* to the principal balance.

Compounding   Applying each successive percent change to the cumulative amount after the preceding percent change.

Compounding factor   The factor $(1 + i)^n$ in the compound-interest formula. It is numerically equal to the future value of $1.

Compounding factor for annuities   The quantity $\dfrac{(1 + p)^n - 1}{p}$, which is numerically equal to the future value of an ordinary annuity with $1 payments.

Compounding frequency   The number of compoundings that take place per year.

Compounding period   The time interval between two successive conversions of interest to principal.

Consumer credit   Loans acquired by individuals for personal consumption expenditures and personal financing needs.

Continued ratio   A ratio containing three or more terms.

Contribution margin   The amount by which the unit selling price exceeds the unit variable cost.

Contribution rate   The contribution margin expressed as a percentage of the unit selling price.

Conversion frequency   See *compounding frequency.*

Conversion period   See *compounding period.*

Cost of capital   The average of the rates of return required by a firm's various sources of financing.

Cost-volume-profit analysis   A procedure for estimating a firm's *operating profit* (or net income before taxes) at any sales *volume* given the firm's *cost* structure.

Coupon rate   The nominal annual rate of interest paid on the face value of a bond.

Credit period   The time period given to a customer to pay an invoice.

Debenture   A debt instrument having most of the characteristics of a bond except that no *specific* assets secure the debt.

Declining-balance method   The method of applying loan payments wherein a payment is first applied to paying all accrued interest and then any remainder is used to reduce the principal.

Deferred annuity   An annuity in which the start of the periodic payments is delayed by more than one payment interval.

Demand loan   A loan on which the lender is entitled to demand full repayment at any time without notice.

Depletion   An accounting procedure by which the recorded value of a resource-based asset is reduced during its projected lifetime in a systematic and rational manner.

Depreciation   An accounting procedure by which the recorded or book value of an asset is reduced during its projected lifetime in a systematic and rational manner.

Depreciation expense   The reduction in the book value of an asset determined for the current period.

Depreciation schedule   A table presenting the details of the depreciation expense allocated to each accounting period, and the asset's book value at the end of each period.

Discount   The difference between a promissory note's maturity value and the amount for which it is sold.

Discount factor   The quantity $1/(1 + i)^n$ or $(1 + i)^{-n}$. It is numerically equal to the present value of $1.

Discount factor for annuities   The quantity $\dfrac{1 - (1 + p)^{-n}}{p}$, which is numerically equal to the present value of an ordinary annuity with $1 payments.

Discount period   The time period within which a payment qualifies for a cash discount.

Discount rate   The interest rate used in calculating the present value of future cash flows.

Discount series   Two or more discount rates that are successively applied to the list price.

Economically equivalent payments   Alternative payments that will ultimately put the recipient in the same financial position.

Effective rate of interest   The equivalent annually compounded rate of interest.

End-of-month (EOM) dating   Terms of payment in which the credit and discount periods start at the end of the month in the date of the invoice.

Equation   A statement of the equality of two algebraic expressions.

Equation of value   An equation expressing the economic equivalence of two payment streams at a particular focal date.

Equivalent discount rate   The single discount rate that would produce the same effect as a given discount series.

Equivalent fractions   Fractions that have the same value.

Equivalent interest rates   Different nominal interest rates that produce the same maturity value of a given principal after one year.

Equivalent ratio   A ratio obtained from another ratio by multiplying or dividing each term by the same number.

Equivalent value   An alternative amount on a different date that would place the recipient in the same financial position as the scheduled payment or stream of payments.

Exchange rate   The ratio of equivalent amounts of two currencies.

Exponent   The number of times that the base is multiplied by itself in a power.

Exponential growth   The growth pattern when a quantity grows by the same percentage in each successive period.

Face value   (1) The principal amount specified on a promissory note.
(2) The amount paid at maturity of a Treasury bill or commercial paper.
(3) The principal amount that the issuer will pay to the owner of a marketable bond on its scheduled maturity date.
(4) The initial principal amount of a mortgage.

Factors   The components of a term that are separated by multiplication or division signs; the components of a product or quotient.

Fixed cost   A cost that does not change with the volume of sales.

Flat price   The actual or full amount paid by a bond purchaser and received by the seller. It is the quoted price plus the accrued coupon interest.

Focal date   The date selected for the calculation of the equivalent values.

Fully open mortgage   A mortgage that places no restrictions on extra payments by the borrower.

Future value   A payment's equivalent value at a *subsequent* date, allowing for the time value of money.

Future value of an annuity   The single amount, at the end of the annuity, that is economically equivalent to the annuity.

General annuity   An annuity in which the payment interval does not equal the compounding interval.

General annuity due   An annuity in which the payment interval does *not* equal the compounding interval, and payments occur at the *beginning* of each payment interval.

General perpetuity   A perpetuity in which the compounding period differs from the payment interval.

Improper fraction   A fraction whose numerator is larger than or equal to the denominator.

Income   Revenue earned from an investment without selling any portion of the investment.

Income yield   An investment's income (during a holding period) expressed as a percentage of the amount invested at the beginning of the period.

Interest   The fee or rent that lenders charge to borrowers for the temporary use of the borrowed money.

Internal rate of return   The discount rate that makes the net present value of all an investment's cash flows equal to zero.

Interpolation   A technique used to estimate a value that is not included in a table of values.

Issue date   (1) The date (*a*) on which a promissory note was written or "made" and (*b*) from which interest, if any, accrues.
(2) The date on which (*a*) a loan represented by a bond or Treasury bill was originally made and (*b*) interest starts to be earned.

Legal due date   The date, 3 days after expiry of a promissory note's term, beyond which the note is in default if not paid in full.

Life annuity reverse mortgage   A reverse mortgage in which the lump sum advanced on the mortgage loan is used to purchase a life annuity, and the borrower is entitled to occupy the mortgaged home for the rest of his or her life.

Like terms   Terms having the same literal coefficient.

Linear equation   An equation in which the variable is raised only to the first power.

List price   The price quoted by a supplier of a product before any trade discounts.

Literal coefficient The nonnumerical factor in a term.

Loan repayment schedule A table presenting details of periodic interest charges, payments, and outstanding balances on a loan.

Maker The party (debtor) promising to pay the debt represented by a promissory note at its maturity.

Margin See *markup*.

Markdown (amount) The amount that the price of an item is reduced.

Markdown rate The markdown expressed as a percentage of the regular price.

Markup (amount) The difference between the selling price and the cost of an item of merchandise.

Markup rate The markup expressed as a percentage of either the selling price or the cost of the merchandise.

Maturity date (1) The date on which the principal and accrued interest on an investment will be received. (2) The date on which the principal balance and accrued interest on a debt must be paid.

Maturity value The total of principal plus the interest due on the expiry or maturity date of a loan or investment.

Mill rate The amount of property tax per $1000 of taxable value.

Mixed number A number consisting of a whole number plus a fraction.

Monomial An expression containing only one term.

Mortgagee The party lending money on the security of a mortgage.

Mortgagor The party borrowing money and giving a mortgage as security on the loan.

Mutually exclusive projects Alternative capital investments, any one of which will substantially satisfy the same need or purpose.

Natural logarithm (of a number) The exponent to which the base $e = 2.718281828$ must be raised in order to equal the number.

Net present value The present value of cash inflows minus the present value of cash outflows.

Net price The price paid after the deduction of trade discounts.

Nominal interest rate The stated *annual* interest rate on which the compound-interest calculation is based.

Nonlinear equation An equation in which the variable appears with an exponent other than 1, or appears as part of a mathematical function.

Numerical coefficient The numerical factor in a term.

Open mortgage See *fully open mortgage* and *partially open mortgage.*

Ordinary annuity An annuity in which the payments are made at the *end* of each payment interval.

Ordinary dating Terms of payment in which the credit and discount periods start on the date of the invoice.

Ordinary general annuity An annuity in which the payment interval does *not* equal the compounding interval, and payments are made at the *end* of each payment interval.

Ordinary simple annuity An annuity in which the payment interval *equals* the compounding interval, and payments are made at the *end* of each payment interval.

Partial payment Any payment that is smaller than the initial amount required to fully settle an invoice.

Partially open mortgage A mortgage that grants limited penalty-free prepayment privileges.

Payback period The number of years it will take to recover an initial investment outlay from the investment's future operating profits.

Payee The party (creditor) to whom a payment is to be made.

Payment interval The length of time between successive payments in an annuity.

Payment stream A series of two or more payments required by a single transaction or contract.

Percent capital gain An investment's capital gain (during a holding period) expressed as a percentage of the amount invested at the beginning of the period.

Period of deferral The time interval until the beginning of the first payment *interval* in a deferred annuity.

Periodic interest rate The rate of interest earned in one compounding or conversion period.

Perpetuity An annuity in which the payments continue forever.

Perpetuity due An annuity in which the payments are made at the beginning of each payment interval and continue forever.

Polynomial An expression containing more than one term.

Power A mathematical operation indicating the multiplication of a quantity (the base) by itself a certain number (the exponent) of times.

Prepayment Any loan payment made sooner than required by the loan agreement.

Present value A payment's equivalent value at a *prior* date, allowing for the time value of money.

Present-value factor for annuities See *discount factor for annuities.*

Present value of an annuity The single amount, at the beginning of the annuity, that is economically equivalent to the annuity.

Principal The original amount borrowed or invested.

Proceeds The selling price of a promissory note. It is the present value, on the date of sale, of the note's maturity value.

Promissory note A written promise by one party to pay a certain sum of money to another party on a specific date, or on demand.

Proper fraction A fraction whose numerator is less than the denominator.

Proportion A statement of the equality of two ratios.

Proration A procedure in which an amount is subdivided and allocated on a proportionate basis.

Quoted price The full purchase price (flat price) of a bond less any accrued coupon interest.

Rate of interest The percentage of the principal that will be charged for a specified period of time, normally 1 year.

Rate of return on an investment The investment's combined income and capital gain during a holding period, expressed as a percentage of the amount invested.

Ratio A comparison, by division, of the relative size of two or more quantities.

Receipt-of-goods (ROG) dating Terms of payment in which the credit and discount periods start on the date that the goods are received.

Residual value See *salvage value.*

Residue The component of a stripped bond that entitles its owner to receive a single payment, the face value of the bond, on the maturity date.

Reverse mortgage A mortgage in which the principal amount owed on the mortgage loan *increases* as time passes.

Revolving loan A loan whose outstanding balance can fluctuate within a maximum credit limit.

Root (of an equation) A particular numerical value for the variable that makes the two sides of the equation equal.

Rule of 72 A rule of thumb for a quick estimation of the number of years it will take an investment to double at a known compound annual rate of return.

Salvage value The amount that is expected to be recovered upon the sale or disposal of the asset at the end of its service life.

Service life The length of time that an asset is expected to be used in the operations of the business.

Significant figures All the digits except zeros serving only to position the decimal point.

Simple annuity An annuity in which the payment interval equals the compounding interval.

Simple annuity due An annuity in which the payment interval *equals* the compounding interval, and payments occur at the *beginning* of each payment interval.

Simple interest Interest calculated using the formula $I = Prt$, and paid only when the principal is repaid.

Sinking fund An interest-earning account into which periodic payments are made for the purpose of accumulating a desired amount of money by a certain date.

Straight-line loan A loan requiring equal monthly payments of principal in addition to the interest that has accrued on each payment date.

Substitution Assigning a numerical value to each of the algebraic symbols for the variables in an expression.

Tax rate The fraction of a price or taxable amount that is payable as tax.

Term (1) The time period for which a loan or investment is made.
(2) The length of time from the date on which a loan is advanced until the date on which the principal balance outstanding is due and payable.

Term of an annuity The total time from the beginning of the first payment interval to the end of the last payment interval.

Terms The components of an algebraic expression that are separated by addition or subtraction signs.

Terms of a ratio The numbers being compared in the ratio.

Terms of payment The specifications on an invoice of the length of the credit period, any cash discount offered and the corresponding discount period, and the date on which the credit and discount periods start.

Time value of money The property that a given *nominal* amount of money on a specified date has a different economic value at every other point in time.

Total return The sum of the income and capital gain from an investment during a holding period.

Trade discount A discount granted by the supplier to a purchaser of goods for resale.

Treasury bills   Promissory notes issued (at a discount to face value) by the federal government and most provincial governments to borrow money for short terms.

Trinomial   An expression containing three terms.

Useful life   See *service life*.

Variable costs   Costs that grow in direct proportion to the volume of output or sales.

Vendor take-back mortgage   A mortgage securing a loan granted by the vendor to the purchaser as part of the purchase price in the sale of real property.

Yield to maturity   The discount rate that makes the present value of the bond's remaining cash flows equal to its purchase price.